W9-CUE-628

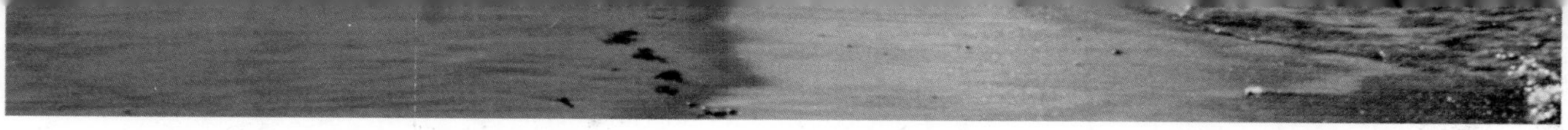

Psychology

Fourth Edition

About the Cover . . .

Psychology has many meanings and the cover touches on some of them. The beach scene depicts us in the environment, and psychology speaks of the ways in which we adapt to the environment and select or fashion environments to suit ourselves. Psychology addresses the ways in which the sounds of waves and the visual rhythms of the sands translate into neural activity in the brain, and how neural activity gives rise to movement of the large muscles of the legs. Psychology addresses the ways in which we commit experiences to memory and sift through memories to ponder one against the other. Psychology speaks of how we summon words to immortalize our passage and how we invoke intelligence to tie the tides to the travels of the Moon. Psychology speaks of our motives for ambling along the shore with others or by ourselves, and of our reasons for musing on the waxing of the waters. Psychology deals with the child's idea that someone made the ocean and with the adolescent's grasp of natural processes. Psychology suggests why some will see the cover image as the dawn of a new day while others will discern the day's descent to night. Psychology even speaks of why it is healthful to stroll on the beach when "the world is too much with us."

In short, the cover touches on the world of psychology and on us. That world encompasses the universe, within and without. It is now but it relates to the past and to the future. It is concrete yet also symbolic. It is all these things, as we are.

The Author

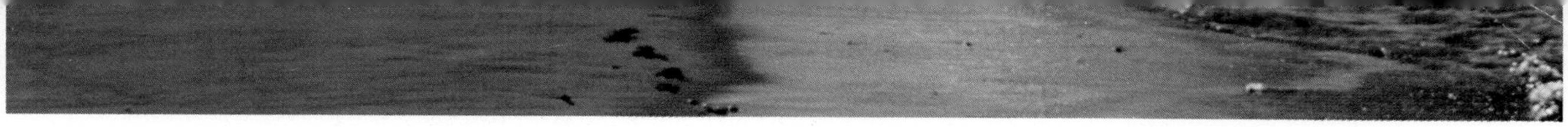

Psychology

Fourth Edition

Spencer A. Rathus

St. John's University

Holt, Rinehart and Winston

Fort Worth Chicago San Francisco
Philadelphia Montreal Toronto
London Sydney Tokyo

Acquisitions Editor: Eve Howard
Developmental Editor: Carol Einhorn
Project Editor: Cathy Crow
Production Manager: Barb Bahnsen
Text and Cover Designer: Alan Wendt
Photo Research: Laurel Anderson/Photosynthesis
Anatomical Art: D. L. Cramer
Copy Editor: Judy Lary
Permissions Editor: Herb Kirk
Indexer: Sheila Ary
Compositor: Waldman Graphics, Inc.
Text Type: 10/12 ITC Garamond Light

Library of Congress Cataloging-in-Publication Data
Rathus, Spencer A.
Psychology.

Bibliography: p.
Includes index.
1. Psychology. I. Title.
BF121.R34 1990 150 89-7472
ISBN 0-03-030214-5

Printed in the United States of America
1-032-9876543

Copyright © 1990, 1987, 1984, 1981 by Holt, Rinehart and Winston, Inc.

All rights reserved. No part of this publication may be reproduced or transmitted in any form or by any means, electronic or mechanical, including photocopy, recording, or any information storage and retrieval system, without permission in writing from the publisher.

Requests for permissions to make copies of any part of the work should be mailed to: Permissions, Holt, Rinehart and Winston, Inc., Orlando, FL 32887.

Address orders:
Holt, Rinehart and Winston, Inc.
Orlando, FL 32887

Address editorial correspondence:
Holt, Rinehart and Winston, Inc.
Suite 3700
301 Commerce Street
Fort Worth, TX 76102

Holt, Rinehart and Winston
The Dryden Press
Saunders College Publishing

Cover photograph: Copyright © 1988 Moore and Moore Publishing

To the memory of my mother,
Sophie Rathus,
the little girl in the pink dress
in the antique portrait on page 220.

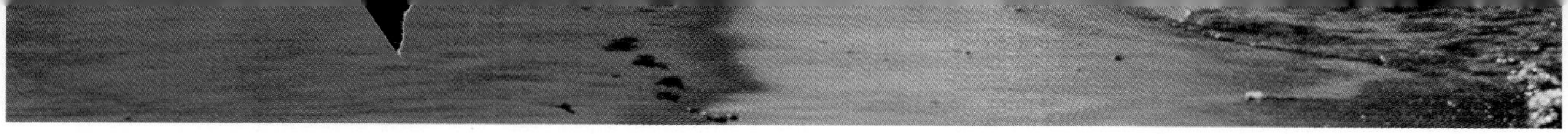

Preface

Writing a textbook can engulf you. Family and friends have a way of asking you to play the basic role of citizen by attending dinner, going to an occasional film, taking a turn at mowing the lawn, and remembering to close the refrigerator door. Under normal circumstances, requests like these are reasonable enough. But composing a book like *Psychology* demands that you lock yourself in your study, spend evenings at the library, and develop a hearing deficit that allows you to ignore most household events, except for the occasional emergency.

Preparing the fourth edition of *Psychology* turned out to be as demanding as the writing of previous editions, for several reasons. First, psychology is a dynamic, evolving field, and keeping abreast of the literature is a full-time job, as any instructor of introductory psychology will attest. Second, it was decided that we would add two chapters (we separated Learning and Memory into two chapters in this edition and added a chapter on Applied Psychology). Third, I have now had the benefit of feedback from colleagues who have used the third edition. Although colleagues agreed that the third edition was superior to earlier editions, they let me know of the ways in which the third edition fell short of perfection. Thus I have integrated the comments and suggestions of dozens of colleagues who used the third edition in the classroom and who reviewed early drafts of the fourth.

Although the fourth edition is quite different from the third, changes were not made simply for the sake of change. Many qualities of *Psychology* contributed to the success of earlier editions, particularly those concerning the coverage, style, and learning aids. My goal in the fourth edition, therefore, was to accurately chronicle the dynamic, changing nature of psychological theory and research while retaining the basic features that have facilitated learning in previous editions. To this end, you will find the following balance of substance and style in *Psychology*, fourth edition.

THE SUBSTANCE: COMPREHENSIVE AND BALANCED COVERAGE

The fourth edition of *Psychology* communicates the true scientific nature and relevance of psychology. The text provides students with a straightforward introduction to the primary research areas in psychology, such as biological psychology; sensation and perception; learning and memory; language, thought, and intelligence; motivation and emotion; development; personality; and social psychology. With that knowledge as a base, the text also illuminates psychology's evolving applications in areas like states of consciousness, health, methods of therapy, human sexuality, industry, the environment, the criminal-justice system, sports, and education. The applied areas of psychology, like the basic areas, are treated with academic rigor. Methods of research and recent findings are emphasized in every field.

Chapter-by-chapter coverage is as follows:

Chapter 1 ("What Is Psychology?") introduces psychology as a science. The history, schools, and specialties of psychology are outlined. Research methods are described. The fourth edition contains a new section on the scientific method. The Psychology and Modern Life section addresses "The Psychology of Studying Psychology."

Chapter 2 ("Biology and Behavior") covers the nervous system, the endocrine system, and heredity. The fourth edition is updated generally and contains a new section, "How Psychologists Study the Functions of the Brain." The Psychology and Modern Life section is entitled "Reproduction, Biology, and Behavior" and addresses chromosomal and genetic abnormalities, genetic counseling and prenatal testing, and genetic engineering.

Chapter 3 ("Sensation and Perception") covers vision and visual perception, hearing, and the other senses. The fourth edition has new sections on "Basic Concepts in Sensation and Perception" and on deafness. The Psychology and Modern Life section focuses on methods of "Pain Management."

Chapter 4 ("States of Consciousness") covers sleep and dreams, the effects of drugs, meditation, biofeedback, and hypnosis. The fourth edition contains updated information on the functions of sleep and the effects of drugs, particularly of cocaine. The Psychology and Modern Life section addresses "Coping with Insomnia" and "Quitting and Cutting Down on Smoking."

Chapter 5 ("Learning") covers classical and operant conditioning, insight learning, latent learning, observational learning, and concept learning. The fourth edition offers greatly expanded coverage of learning (memory has become a separate chapter, Chapter 6). There is new coverage of taste aversion; contingency theory; flooding, systematic desensitization, and counterconditioning; the token economy; and concept learning. The Psychology and Modern Life section focuses on "The Effects of Media Violence."

Chapter 6 ("Memory") is a new chapter. Coverage includes kinds of memory (episodic, semantic, and procedural), processes of memory (encoding, storage, and retrieval), the stage model of memory, the levels-of-processing model of memory, the biology of memory, and high-interest topics such as flashbulb memory and childhood amnesia. The biology of memory is thoroughly updated, and the Psychology and Modern Life section considers "Methods for Improving Memory."

Chapter 7 ("Language, Thought, and Intelligence") covers language and language development, thought and problem solving, and the nature and determinants of intelligence. The fourth edition contains a completely revised section on theories of language development, which includes the learning, nativist, and cognitive views. Theories of intelligence now include Guilford's model and Sternberg's triarchic theory. There is a new section on social-class, racial, and ethnic differences in intelligence. Research on the determinants of intelligence has been updated. The Psychology and Modern Life section focuses on "Teaching Language to Apes."

Chapter 8 ("Motivation and Emotion") covers physiological, stimulus, and social motives and the development and expression of emotions. The fourth edition contains new sections on emotional development and styles of love. There is updated information on hunger and thirst, the expression of emotions, and the facial-feedback hypothesis. The Psychology and Modern Life section addresses "Obesity and Weight Control."

Chapter 9 ("Developmental Psychology") covers development from conception through death. The fourth edition contains new sections on controversies in developmental psychology, states of attachment (Ainsworth's research), dimensions of child-rearing, information-processing approaches to cognitive development, and theories of adult development. Evaluation of the theories of Piaget and Kohlberg is revised. The Psychology and Modern Life section addresses issues in "Day Care" and "Child Abuse."

Chapter 10 ("Personality: Theories and Measurement") covers psychodynamic, trait, learning, and phenomenological theories of personality as well as methods of personality measurement. The fourth edition includes a new section on George Kelly's psychology of personal constructs. Coverage of social-learning theory has been extensively updated and revised. Discussion of each major theoretical approach now concludes with an evaluation that addresses its strengths and weaknesses. The Psychology and Modern Life section discusses "Cognitive versus Psychodynamic Views of Religious Conversion" and "Applying the Barnum Effect to Enhance Self-Efficacy Expectations."

Chapter 11 ("Health Psychology") covers sources of stress, psychological moderators of stress, physiological responses to stress, the immune system, psychological factors and physical illness, and the psychology of being sick. Research on the effects of Type A behavior on health—particularly heart disease—is thoroughly revised. The new section on psychological moderators of the impact of stress includes the effects of self-efficacy expectations, psychological hardiness, a sense of humor, predictability of stressors, and social support. The sections on the immune system and on the psychology of being sick are new. The Psychology and Modern Life section addresses "Ways of Coping with Stress," including "Controlling Irrational Thoughts," "Lowering Arousal," "Coping with Test Anxiety," "Modifying the Type A Behavior Pattern," and "Exercise."

Chapter 12 ("Abnormal Behavior") covers the major disorders found in the DSM–III–R. The fourth edition has extended coverage of the learning and cognitive models. There are new sections on the organization of the DSM–III–R, on post-traumatic stress disorder, and on the eating disorders of anorexia nervosa and bulimia nervosa. The chapter's research base has been thoroughly updated. The Psychology and Modern Life section focuses on "Coping with Depression" and "Suicide Prevention."

Chapter 13 ("Methods of Therapy") covers methods of psychotherapy, behavior therapy, and biological therapy. The fourth edition has new coverage of Margaret Mahler's object-relations approach to therapy and Aaron Beck's cognitive therapy. A new section on evaluation of methods of psychotherapy and behavior therapy describes problems in evaluating therapies as well as reporting results of comparative-outcome studies. The Psychology and Modern Life section considers "Ways of Getting Help," including "Finding a Qualified Therapist" and "Coping with Self-Help Books."

Chapter 14 ("Human Sexuality") covers sex roles and sex differences, sex typing, sexual motivation, the sexual response cycle, and sexual dysfunctions. The fourth edition has a new section on the costs of sex-role stereotyping. Data on sex differences is expanded and updated. Theories of sex typing have been expanded to include biological, psychodynamic, social-learning, and two cognitive approaches: cognitive-developmental theory and gender-schema theory. Coverage of homosexuality, pornography, and sexual dysfunctions has been updated. Given the current concern over AIDS and the mushrooming incidence of other sexually transmitted diseases, the Psychology and Modern Life section addresses "Sexually Transmitted Diseases," including methods of "Safe(r) Sex in the Age of AIDS."

Chapter 15 ("Social Psychology") covers attitudes, social perception, interpersonal attraction, social influence and group behavior. The fourth edition includes new sections on the A–B problem, social decision schemes, and groupthink. Coverage of possible explanations for obedience to authority figures is expanded. The Psychology and Modern Life section considers ways of "Enhancing Social Interactions" by "Handling Low-Balling," "Coping with Prejudice and Discrimination," "Making a Positive First Impression," and using attribution theory to help resolve social conflicts.

Chapter 16 ("Applied Psychology") is new to the fourth edition. It covers industrial/organizational psychology, human-factors psychology, consumer psychology, environmental psychology, community psychology, forensic psychology, sports psychology, and educational psychology. The Psychology and Modern Life section focuses on applying psychological knowledge in "Career Selection."

THE WRITING STYLE

Through its style, the fourth edition of *Psychology* communicates the excitement of psychology. Style has been an important factor in the success of each edition of *Psychology.* The fourth edition of *Psychology,* like previous editions, was deliberately written to meet the needs of students. The text uses humor and personal anecdotes to motivate students and help them understand the subject matter. The personalized approach is exemplified in the way the text "walks a student through" the Milgram studies on obedience to authority in Chapter 15. The student vicariously experiences Milgram's methods, and, as a result, motivation, comprehension, and retention are intensified.

The fourth edition has had the advantage of feedback from hundreds of instructors and thousands of students who have used previous editions. Their input has helped me to retain the engaging and motivating qualities of previous editions and to avoid frivolity and condescension. Colleagues and students have helped me enormously in my continuous quest to craft the sentence structure and the vocabulary so that psychological concepts are accessible to students. I believe that there is a logic to building concepts and vocabulary and that even the most abstract concepts can be presented in energetic prose that includes concrete examples.

Psychology was also written explicitly for the instructor—the instructor who wants to teach from a textbook that is:

comprehensive and balanced

accurate and up-to-date

applied as well as theoretical

clearly written

interest-arousing

easily understood

well-illustrated

LEARNING AIDS

The central task of a textbook is to provide students with information in a format that promotes learning. *Psychology* contains several elements designed to meet this goal.

Chapter Outlines Each chapter begins with an outline that helps organize the subject matter for the student. Care was taken to present the chapter's headings in a succinct, clear manner.

The Psychology and Modern Life section in Chapter 1 highlights the PQ4R study method, in which students are encouraged to preview the subject matter, phrase questions about it, and read to answer them. The chapter outlines are intended to offer one kind of "preview," and students are encouraged to turn them into questions about the subject matter in the chapter. Then they will engage in more active learning.

"Truth-or-Fiction?" Sections These sections come after the chapter outline. "Truth-or-Fiction?" items stimulate student interest by highlighting some of the fascinating research findings in psychology and by challenging common knowledge and folklore.

Many students consider themselves psychologists. Psychology involves the study of human behavior, and even by the age at which students first attend college, they have observed people for many years. The "Truth-or-Fiction?" items prod them to reflect upon the accuracy of their observations and to reconsider conclusions they may have drawn about human nature.

The "Truth-or-Fiction?" items also encourage students to read in order to answer questions—that is, to take a more active approach to learning.

"Truth-or-Fiction Revisited" Sections "Truth-or-Fiction Revisited" inserts are spaced throughout the chapters, occurring at the point at which subjects referred to in the "Truth-or-Fiction?" items are discussed in the text. They provide students with feedback as to whether their assumptions about psychology were accurate.

Glossary Items Defined in the Margins Key terms are defined in the margins, at the points at which they occur in the text. Research shows that many students do not make use of a glossary at the back of a book. Moreover, ready access to glossary items permits students to maintain their concentration on the flow of material in the chapter. Students need not flip back and forth between different sections of the book to decode the vocabulary.

Many glossary terms are written phonetically to help students pronounce them. Students will not have to "unlearn" mispronunciations through embarrassing classroom errors. In many cases, word origins are also provided. Etymology always helped me decode the meanings of new words, and I wanted to share this benefit with students.

Definitions of key terms may be repeated in several chapters, wherever they are brought up in the text. Such repetition reinforces learning and gives the instructor flexibility in the sequencing of reading assignments.

All key terms are boldfaced in the text the first time they appear in the chapter so that students will be immediately aware of whether or not definitions of them are available.

End-of-Book Glossary *Psychology* now has an end-of-book glossary. This glossary is intended for reference when students are not directly involved in reading the chapters. The end-of-book glossary specifies the theory or area of psychology within which the term has a given meaning. For example, the term *displacement* has different meanings within psychodynamic theory and within the study of memory. So, in defining displacement, the end-of-book glossary states "In psychodynamic theory, . . . " and, in another sentence, "In memory theory, . . . " In other words, the end-of-book glossary does not simply repeat the definitions placed in the margins of the chapters; these are complementary but not redundant learning aids.

Illustrations A generous supply of full-color photographs, figures, and drawings illustrates the themes and research findings presented in the text. Most figures have been created or revised for the fourth revision. The illustrations, like the text itself, have undergone a painstaking developmental process to assure their accuracy and their pedagogical effectiveness.

Many figure captions are extensive to reinforce the explanatory power of the illustrations. Also, I wanted the illustrations along with their captions to "stand alone" whenever possible so that students could learn a great deal by reviewing them.

It may seem a small matter, but I usually tried to select photographs with which students could "identify." I believed that students would develop more of a sense that the text is "for them" if they felt familiar with the people in the photographs.

Chapter Summaries Chapter summaries are numbered and now are presented in a question-and-answer format. Thus active learning—that is, reading to answer questions—is promoted even in the summaries.

FEATURES

Psychology also has a number of features that are designed to highlight certain material in the text and to underscore the relevance of psychology to students' lives. In these ways, the features spur motivation and also serve as additional learning aids.

Features in the fourth edition include the following.

Questionnaires Questionnaires throughout the text further stimulate students' interest by helping them satisfy their curiosities about their motives, attitudes, and personality traits. For example, readers can gain insight into why they drink or find out how assertive they are as compared to a national sample of college students. Moreover, the presence of questionnaires actually used by psychologists provides students additional insight into how psychologists conceptualize research variables and collect data.

"A Closer Look" Sections "A Closer Look" sections are found throughout the text. Some of them reinforce the subject matter by focusing on high-interest features, as in the case of Chapter 6's challenge to think of a certain "word" on New Year's Eve in the year 2000. Others offer in-depth discussion of important theoretical issues (consider Chapter 1's insert on ways in which psychologists of different schools conceptualize violence) or of research methods (for example, Chapter 2's discussion of ways in which psychologists study the brain).

"A Closer Look" sections are placed so that they do *not* interrupt the flow of the text. They are fully integrated into the text: The subject matter leads into them, and the sections logically lead into the subject matter that follows.

"Psychology Goes to Work" Inserts These new inserts show how people in various occupations make use of psychological theory and research. For example, a "Psychology Goes to Work" section in Chapter 2 explains the lure of steroids to professional athletes. A section in Chapter 3 shows how optometrists and ophthalmologists make use of principles of visual perception. A section in Chapter 5 shows how business people make use of principles of operant conditioning, as in the case of frequent-flyer programs. Other examples are distributed throughout the text.

"Psychology and Modern Life" Sections To highlight the relevance of psychology to contemporary issues and problems, each chapter now ends with a section on "Psychology and Modern Life." For example, the Psychology and Modern Life section that completes Chapter 1 is about "The Psychology of Studying Psychology," and it provides students with information that can help them do well in all of their courses, not just psychology. The section that completes the chapter on learning (Chapter 5) is about the effects of media violence. A section on sexually transmitted diseases (and what to do about them) completes the chapter on human sexuality (Chapter 14). The chapter on social psychology (Chapter 15) is completed by a section that addresses several issues, including handling the annoying sales practice of low-balling, coping with prejudice and discrimination, making a positive first impression, and using attribution theory to help resolve social conflicts. Other topics include:

genetic counseling and prenatal testing

pain management

coping with insomnia

cutting down on and quitting smoking

weight control

selecting a day-care center

child abuse

coping with stress

coping with depression

suicide prevention

finding a qualified therapist

THE ANCILLARIES

The needs of today's instructors and students demand a full and broad array of ancillary materials to make teaching and learning more effective. *Psychology* is accompanied by a complete, convenient, and carefully conceived package.

Self-Scoring Student Study Guide I wrote the *Student Study Guide* myself to assure that its quality would equal the quality of the text. Its format will be equally useful in traditional or individualized (PSI) settings. The guide features an opening part on study methods ("How to Succeed in College"), coping with text anxiety, and aiming toward a career in psychology. Each chapter includes an overview, learning objectives, a pretest, key terms, exercises, a programmed chapter review that is organized according to learning objectives and major text headings, and a posttest. The third part of the *Study Guide* is a glossary designed to aid students in mastering the vocabulary of psychology.

Annotated Instructor's Edition For the first time, a special edition of the text, containing marginal annotations for the instructor, is being published. These annotations refer the instructor to various items in the Instructor's Manual, including lecture suggestions; activity and demonstration suggestions; connections, which link text material to related concepts in other chapters; and audio-visual suggestions, which cross-reference the text material with Holt, Rinehart and Winston's broad assortment of videos and overhead transparencies for teaching introductory psychology.

Instructor's Manual A separate manual, written by John Haig of Philadelphia College of Textiles and Science, is also available to aid both the novice and the experienced instructor in organizing and teaching the course with *Psychology*. Each chapter of the Instructor's Manual includes teaching objectives and teaching strategies such as lecture suggestions, connections, activity and demonstration suggestions, references and suggestions for further reading, and annotated film recommendations.

Whole Psychology Catalogue Also available to the instructor is this potpourri of handouts, demonstrations, experiments, articles, lecture outlines, and transparency masters.

Test Bank Jim Hail, of McLennan Community College, has written 150 to 200 multiple choice questions for every chapter of *Psychology*. In response to instructors' requests, test items are arranged by learning objectives, and each question is referenced to the corresponding text page.

The text bank is also available on disk for use on the IBM, Apple, or Macintosh computers. The computerized test bank allows the instructor to modify or add questions and to create, scramble, and print tests and answer keys.

This ancillary package is further enhanced by Holt, Rinehart and Winston's extensive selection of audio-visual materials for introductory psychology.

ACKNOWLEDGMENTS

The discipline of psychology owes its progress and its scientific standing to experts who conduct research in many different areas. Similarly, the textbook *Psychology* and its ancillaries owe a great deal of their substance and form to my colleagues who provided expert suggestions and insights at various stages in their development. My sincere thanks to the following individuals, who contributed to the development of the fourth edition:

Barbara Basden, California State University; Jack Brennecke, Mount San Antonio College; Garvin Chastain, Boise State University; John Childers, East Carolina University; Marian Gibney, Phoenix College; Gloria Griffith, Tennesee Technological University; Richard Griggs, University of Florida; Jim Hail, McLennan Community College; Timothy Johnston, University of North Carolina at Greensboro; Karen Jones, University of the Ozarks; Kenneth Kallio, State University of New York, Geneseo; Dan Kimble, University of Oregon; Mike Knight, Central State University; Wolanyo Kpo, Chicago State University; Velton Lacefield, Prairie State College; William Levy, Manchester Community College; Robert G. Lowder, Bradley University; John Malone, University of Tennessee; Marc Marshark, University of North Carolina at Greensboro; George Martin, Mount San Antonio College; Christopher F. Monte, Manhattanville College; Jeffrey S. Nevid, St. John's University; Fred Patrizi, East Central University; Gregory Pezzetti, Rancho Santiago College; Valda Robinson, Hillsborough Community College; Laurie Rotando, Westchester Community College; Larry J. Siegel, University of Lowell; Paul Silverstein, Los Angeles Pierce College; William Sproull, Texas Christian University-South; Sherrill Tabing, Los Angeles Harbor College; Linda Truesdale, Midland

Technical College; Frank J. Vattano, Colorado State University; Glen Weaver, Calvin College; Kenneth Wildman, Ohio Northern University.

Let me also extend my thanks to those who provided critical feedback on earlier editions of the text: Mark H. Ashcraft, Cleveland State University; Gladys J. Baez-Dickreiter, St. Philip's College; Patricia Barker, Schenectady County Community College; Thomas L. Bennett, Colorado State University; Otto Berliner, SUNY—Alfred; Richard A. Block, Montana State University; C. Robert Borresen, Wichita State University; Theodore N. Bosack, Providence College; Betty Bowers, North Central Technical Institute; Peter J. Brady, Clark Technical College; Richard Day, Manchester Community College; Donald L. Daoust, Southern Oregon State College; Carl L. Denti, Dutchess County Community College; Carol Doolin, Henderson County Jr. College; Wendy L. Dunn, Coe College; John Foust, Parkland College; Morton P. Friedman, University of California at Los Angeles; Marvin Goldstein, Rider College; Bernard Gorman, Nassau Community College; Sandra L. Groeltz, DeVry Institute of Technology at Chicago; Arthur Gutman, Florida Institute of Technology; Jim Hail, McLennan Community College; Robert W. Hayes, Boston University; George Herrick, SUNY—Alfred; Sidney Hochman, Nassau Community College; Morton Hoffman, Metropolitan State College; Betsy Howton, Western Kentucky University; John H. Hummel, University of Houston; Sam L. Hutchinson, Radford University; Jarvel Jackson McLennan Community College; Robert L. Johnson, Umpqua Community College; Eve Jones, Los Angeles City College; Charles Karis, Northwestern University; Mary-Louise Kean, University of California—Irvine; Richard Kellogg, SUNY—Alfred; Richard A. King, University of North Carolina—Chapel Hill; Alan Lanning, College of DuPage; Patsy Lawson, Volunteer State Community College; John D. Lawry, Marymount College; Charles Levinthal, Hofstra University; Robert MacAleese, Spring Hill College; Daniel Madsen, University of Minnesota—Duluth; S. R. Mathews, Converse College; Juan Mercado, McLennan Community College; Richard McCarbery, Lorain College; Derrill McGuigan, Rider College; Leroy Metze, Western Kentucky University; Richard E. Miller, Navarro College; Thomas Minor, SUNY at Stony Brook; Thomas Moeschl, Broward Community College; Joel Morgovsky, Brookdale Community College; Walena C. Morse, West Chester University; Basil Najjar, College of DuPage; Jeffrey Nevid, St. John's University; John W. Nichols, Tulsa Junior College; Joseph Palladino, Indiana State University—Evansville; John Pennachio, Adirondack Community College; Terry Pettijohn, Ohio State University—Marion; Gregory Pezzeti, Santa Ana College; Walter Pieper, Georgia State University; Donis Price, Mesa Community College; Louis Primavera, St. John's University; Richard A. Rare, University of Maine; Valda Robinson, Hillsborough Community College; Rene A. Ruiz, New Mexico State University; Patrick J. Ryan, Tompkins-Cortland Community College; H. R. Schiffman, Rutgers University; Jacob Steinberg, Fairleigh Dickinson University; Ann Swint, North Harris County College; Robert S. Tacker, East Carolina University; Francis Terrell, North Texas State University; Harry A. Tiemann, Jr., Mesa College; Douglas Wallen, Mankato State University; Charles Weichert, San Antonio College; Paul Wellman, Texas A&M; Richard Whinery, Ohio University—Chillicothe; Robert Williams, William Jewel College; Keith A. Wollen, Washington State University; Walter Zimmerman, New Hampshire College.

The publishing professionals at Holt, Rinehart and Winston are a particularly able group of individuals, and it is a continuing privilege to work with them. This edition was truly a national effort. I first met Eve Howard, psychology editor, by pure chance in El Paso, Texas. Since then we have worked together in New York and, to bring things full circle, in Texas again. Her outpouring of energy into the fourth edition has been a wonder to behold. Carol Einhorn, developmental editor, organized the suggestions of reviewers from her desk in New York. Jane Perkins, director of editing, design, and production, efficiently supervised the production of the book from her office in suburban Chicago. Cathy Crow, the project editor—also in Chicago—coordinated all the activities necessary to turning a manuscript into a bound book. Alan Wendt, the design director in Chicago, created the beautiful and functional design of the book you now hold in your hands. Laurel Anderson collected the dynamic photographs for the fourth edition in her office on the Atlantic in Gloucester, Massachusetts. Judy Lary, in Madison, Wisconsin, added her fine touch to the manuscript as copyeditor. And Lee Sutherlin, marketing manager for the behavioral and social sciences, developed the marketing campaign for the book in Fort Worth, Texas.

Let me conclude by noting that 1990 is a banner year for the discipline of psychology as well as for my textbook, *Psychology*. This is the centennial of the appearance of William James' two-volume *Principles of Psychology*—the first modern psychology textbook. In this unique year, I am humbled that my own textbook will have disseminated information about psychology to hundreds of thousands of students over its own "four generations." In 1990, that is, *Psychology* appears in its fourth edition. Although *Psychology* cannot expect to have the impact on the discipline of its academic forebear, my muse ever reminds me that both books have the same publisher: James' Henry Holt and Company is the corporate ancestor of today's Holt, Rinehart and Winston.

So let me take this opportunity to express my gratitude to the professors from all corners of the earth who have allowed my book to represent psychology to their students since its first appearance in 1981. We have appeared in English and in foreign tongues. We can say, with pride, that the sun never sets on the classrooms where we try our best to carry on the tradition begun by William James.

Spencer A. Rathus
August 1989

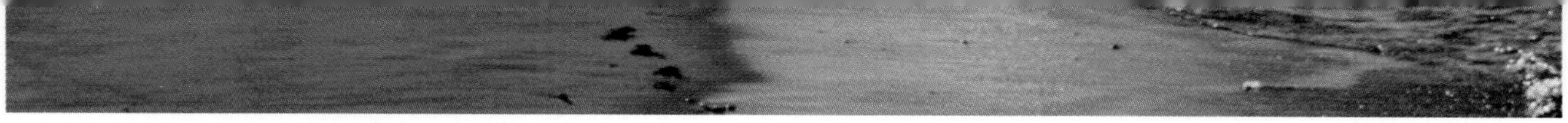

Contents in Brief

Contents

Chapter 2

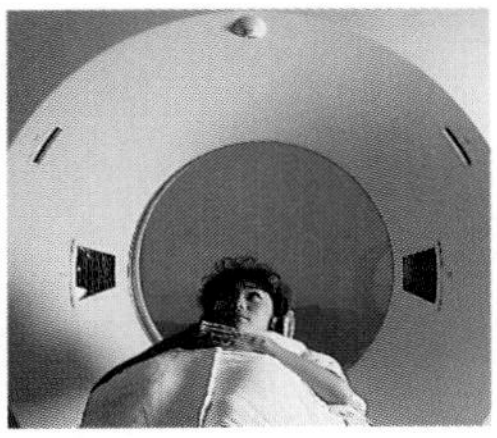

Chapter 3

Chapter 5

Chapter 6

Chapter 8

Motivation and Emotion 301

Chapter 9

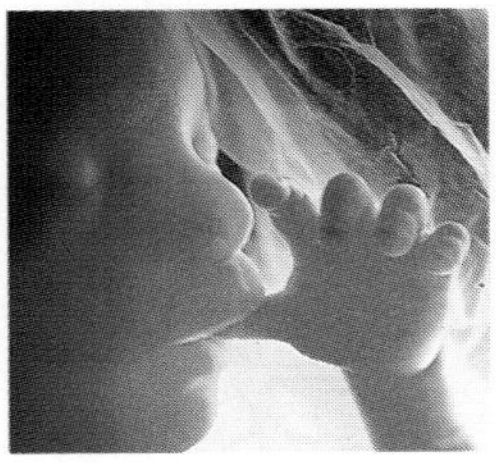

Developmental Psychology 343

Chapter 11

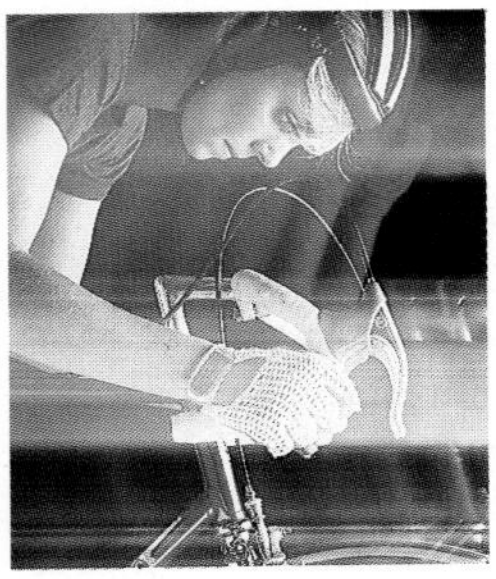

Chapter 12

Chapter 15

Chapter 16

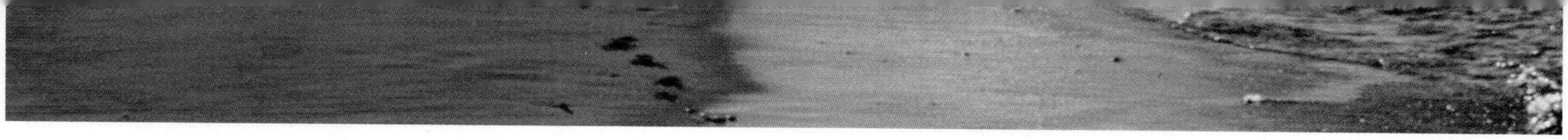

Features

A Closer Look

Psychology Goes to Work

Questionnaire

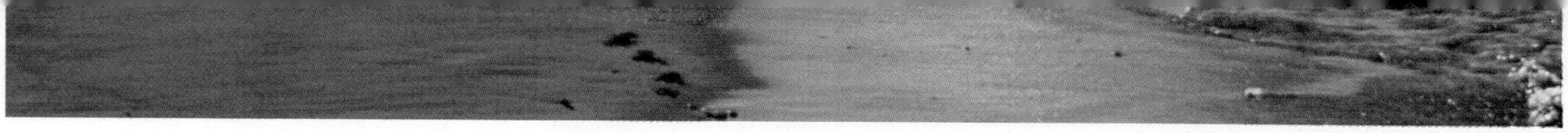

Psychology

Fourth Edition

Outline

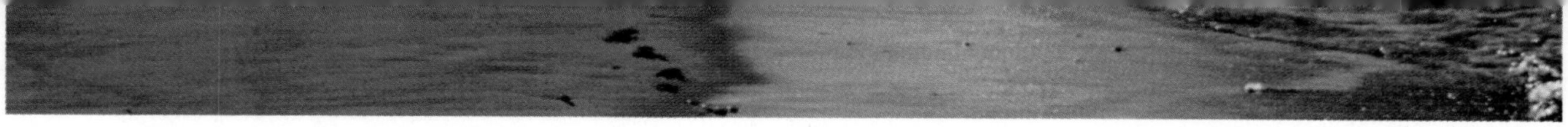

1 What is Psychology?

Truth or Fiction?

- □ Psychologists attempt to control behavior.
- □ Some psychologists measure the effectiveness of television commercials.
- □ Other psychologists serve as expert witnesses in court.
- □ Still other psychologists guide people into eating more healthful diets.
- □ A book on psychology, whose contents are similar to those of the book you are now holding in your hands, was written by Aristotle more than 2,000 years ago.
- □ The ancient Greek philosopher Socrates suggested a research method that is still used in psychology today.
- □ Some psychologists look upon our strategies for solving problems as "mental programs" that are operated by our very "personal computers"—our brains.
- □ Only people use tools.
- □ Alcohol causes aggression.
- □ You could survey 20 million Americans and still not predict accurately the outcome of a presidential election.
- □ Psychologists would not be able to carry out certain research studies without deceiving participants as to the purposes and methods of the studies.

"What a piece of work is man!" wrote William Shakespeare. "How noble in reason! how infinite in faculty! in form, in moving, how express and admirable! in action how like an angel! in apprehension how like a god! the beauty of the world! the paragon of animals!"

You probably had no trouble recognizing yourself in Shakespeare's description—"noble in reason," "admirable," godlike in understanding, head and shoulders above all other animals. That's you to a "t," isn't it? But human behavior is greatly varied, and much of it is not so admirable. A good deal of human behavior, even familiar behavior, is rather puzzling. Consider these examples:

Most adults on crowded city streets will not stop to help a person lying on the sidewalk or to help a lost child. Why?

While most of us watch television, ride a bicycle, jog, or go for a swim, some people seek excitement by driving motorcycles at breakneck speed, skydiving, or taking "uppers." Why?

Most adults who overeat or smoke cigarettes know that they are jeopardizing their health. Yet they continue in their hazardous habits. Why?

Some children seem capable of learning more in school than other children. Their teachers scan their records and find that the more capable children usually have received higher scores on intelligence tests. But what is intelligence? How is intelligence measured? Why do some people have, or seem to have, more of "it" than others?

A rapist or murderer claims to have committed his crime because another "personality" dwelling in him took over, or because a dog prompted him with mental messages. What is wrong with such people? Should they be found guilty of their crimes or be judged not guilty by reason of insanity? Should they go to prison or to a psychiatric facility?

"What a Piece of Work Is Man!" "What a piece of work is man!" wrote William Shakespeare. Psychologists agree. Psychologists use the scientific method to study the observable behavior and mental processes of this most complex and subtle of creatures. Michelangelo's *David,* pictured here, captures the awesome beauty and power of human beings.

Human behavior has always fascinated other human beings. Sometimes we are even "surprised at ourselves," because we experience thoughts or impulses that seem to be out of character or we can't recall something that is on the tip of the tongue. Psychologists, like other people, are intrigued by the mysteries of behavior and make an effort to answer questions such as those we have posed. But whereas most people try to satisfy their curiosities about behavior in their spare time by asking a friend for an opinion or by means of casual observations, psychologists make the scientific study of behavior their life's work.

Psychology is the scientific study of behavior and mental processes. Topics of interest to psychologists have included the nervous system, sensation and perception, learning and memory, language, thought, intelligence, growth and development, personality, stress, abnormal behavior, ways of treating abnormal behavior, sexual behavior, and the behavior of people in social settings, such as groups and organizations.

Not all psychologists would be satisfied by our definition of psychology as the science of behavior and mental processes. Many psychologists, especially **behaviorists,** prefer to limit the scope of psychology to *overt,* or observable, behavior—to activities such as pressing a lever; turning left or right; eating and mating; or even involuntary body functions such as heart rate, dilation of the pupils of the eyes, blood pressure, or emission of brain waves. All these behaviors are public in that they can be measured by simple observation or by laboratory instruments. Even the emission of brain waves is made public by scientific instruments, as we shall see in Chapters 2 and 4, and diverse observers would readily agree about their existence and characteristics. Other psychologists, some of whom are **cognitive** psychologists, focus on the mental representations we form of the world, our memories, our strategies for solving problems, even our biases and prejudices.

Behaviorists are concerned that mental processes are private, not public, events that cannot be verified by observation or use of laboratory instruments. Sometimes mental processes are accepted as being present on the basis of the **self-report** of the person experiencing them. Other times, however, mental processes can be indirectly verified by laboratory instruments, as in the case of dreams. Psychologists have learned that dreams are most likely to occur when particular brain waves are being emitted (see Chapter 4), so a report of dreaming in the absence of these brain waves might be viewed with suspicion.

As a science, psychology brings carefully designed methods of observation, such as the survey and the experiment, to bear on its subject matter.

Psychology The science that studies behavior and mental processes.

Behaviorist A psychologist who believes that psychology should address observable behavior and the relationships between stimuli and responses.

Cognitive Having to do with mental processes such as sensation and perception, memory, intelligence, language, thought, and problem solving.

Self-report A subject's testimony about his or her own thoughts, feelings, or behaviors.

Although most psychologists are interested primarily in human behavior, many others focus on the behavior of animals ranging from sea snails and pigeons to rats and gorillas. Some psychologists believe that research findings with lower animals can be applied, or **generalized,** to humans. Other psychologists argue that people are so distinct that we can only learn about people by studying people.

PSYCHOLOGY AS A SCIENCE

Psychology, like other sciences, seeks to describe, explain, predict, and control the events it studies. Thus, psychology seeks to describe, explain, predict, and control the processes involved in areas such as perception, learning, memory, motivation, emotion, intelligence, personality, and the formation of attitudes.

When possible, descriptive terms and concepts are interwoven into **theories,** which are related sets of statements about events. Theories are based on certain assumptions, and they allow us to derive explanations and predictions. Many psychological theories combine statements about psychological concepts (such as learning and motivation), behavior (such as eating or problem solving), and anatomical structures or biological processes. For instance, our responses to drugs such as alcohol and marijuana reflect the biochemical actions of these drugs and our psychological expectations or beliefs about their effects.

In psychology, many theories have been found to be incapable of explaining or predicting new observations. As a result, they have been revised extensively. For example, the theory that hunger results from stomach contractions may be partially correct for normal-weight individuals, but it is inadequate as an explanation for feelings of hunger among the overweight. In Chapter 8 we shall see that stomach contractions are only one of many factors, or **variables,** involved in hunger. Contemporary theories also focus on biological variables, such as the body's muscle-to-fat ratio, and situational variables, such as the presence of other people who are eating and the time of day.

The notion of controlling behavior and mental processes is highly controversial. Some people erroneously think that psychologists seek ways to make people do their bidding—like puppets dangling on strings. This could not be farther from the truth. Psychologists are generally committed to belief in the dignity of human beings, and human dignity demands that people be free to make their own decisions and choose their own behavior. Psychologists are learning more all the time about the various influences on human behavior, but they implement this knowledge only upon request and in ways they believe will be helpful to an individual or an organization.

Truth or Fiction Revisited

It is true that psychologists attempt to control behavior. However, in practice, this means helping clients engage in behavior that will help them meet their own goals.

WHAT PSYCHOLOGISTS DO

Psychologists share a keen interest in behavior, but in other ways they may differ markedly. Some psychologists engage primarily in basic research, or **pure research.** Pure research has no immediate application to personal or

---

Generalize To go from the particular to the general; to extend.

Theory A formulation of relationships underlying observed events.

Variable A condition that is measured or controlled in a scientific study. A variable can vary in a measurable manner.

Pure research Research conducted without concern for immediate applications.

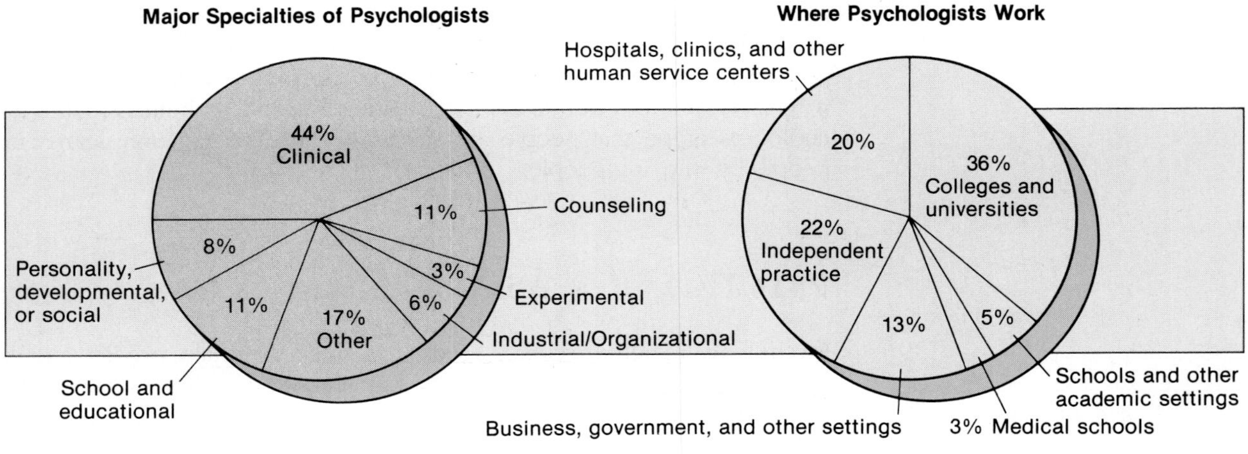

Figure 1.1
Specialties and Work Settings of Psychologists.

A recent survey of doctoral-level psychologists by the American Psychological Association (Stapp, Tucker & VandenBos, 1985) showed that 44 percent identified themselves as clinical psychologists (see chart at left). The single largest group of psychologists works in colleges and universities, while large numbers of psychologists also work in independent practice and in hospitals, clinics, and other human-service settings (see chart at right).

social problems and has thus been characterized as research for its own sake. Other psychologists engage in **applied research,** which is designed to find solutions to specific personal or social problems. Although pure research is spurred onward by curiosity and the desire to know and understand, today's pure research frequently enhances tomorrow's way of life. For example, pure research into learning and motivation with lower animals early in the century has found widespread applications in today's school systems. Pure research into the workings of the nervous system has enhanced knowledge of disorders such as epilepsy, Parkinson's disease, and Alzheimer's disease.

Many psychologists do not engage in research at all. Instead, they apply psychological knowledge to help people change their behavior so that they can meet their own goals more effectively. Numerous psychologists engage primarily in teaching. They disseminate psychological knowledge in classrooms, seminars, and workshops. Figure 1.1 shows that a large percentage of psychologists are employed by colleges and universities, but some of these psychologists counsel students rather than teach.

Let us now explore some of the specialties of psychologists. Although psychologists tend to wear more than one hat, most of them carry out their functions in the following fields.

Applied research Research conducted in an effort to find solutions to particular problems.

Psychotherapy The systematic application of psychological knowledge to the treatment of problem behavior.

Behavior therapy Application of principles of learning to the direct modification of problem behavior.

Clinical and Counseling Psychologists

Clinical psychologists specialize in helping people with psychological problems adjust to the demands of life. Clients' problems may range from anxiety and depression to sexual dysfunctions to loss of goals. Clinical psychologists are trained to evaluate problems through structured interviews and psychological tests. They help their clients resolve their problems and change maladaptive behavior through techniques of **psychotherapy** and **behavior therapy.** Clinical psychologists may work in institutions for the mentally ill or mentally retarded, in outpatient clinics, in college and university clinics, or in private practices.

As you can see in Figure 1.1, clinical psychologists compose the largest subgroup of psychologists, and most lay people think of clinical psychologists when they hear the term *psychologist.* Many clinical psychologists divide their time among clinical practice, teaching, and research.

Counseling psychologists, like clinical psychologists, use interviews and tests to define their clients' problems. Clients of counseling psychologists typically have adjustment problems but do not behave in seriously abnormal ways. Clients may encounter difficulty in making academic or vocational decisions or difficulty in making friends in college. They may experience marital or family conflicts, have physical handicaps, or have adjustment problems, such as those encountered by a convict who is returning to the community.

School and Educational Psychologists

School psychologists are employed by school systems to help identify and assist students who encounter problems that interfere with learning. These range from social and family problems to emotional disturbances and learning disabilities such as **dyslexia.** School psychologists define students' problems through interviews with teachers, parents, and students themselves; through psychological tests such as intelligence and achievement tests; and through direct observation of behavior in the classroom. They consult with teachers, school officials, parents, and other professionals to help students overcome obstacles to learning. They also help make decisions about placement of students in special education and remediation programs.

Educational psychologists, like school psychologists, are concerned with optimizing classroom conditions to facilitate learning. They usually focus, however, on improvement of course planning and instructional methods for a school system rather than on identification of, and assistance to, children with learning problems.

Educational psychologists are usually more concerned than school psychologists about theoretical issues relating to learning, measurement, and child development. They are more likely to do research and to hold faculty posts in colleges and universities. Their research interests include the ways in which variables such as motivation, personality, intelligence, rewards and punishments, and teacher characteristics influence learning. Some educational psychologists specialize in preparing standardized tests, such as the Scholastic Aptitude Tests (SATs).

Developmental Psychologists

Developmental psychologists study the changes—physical, emotional, cognitive, and social—that occur throughout the life span. They attempt to sort out the relative influences of heredity (nature) and the environment (nurture) on specific types of growth and to discover the origins of developmental abnormalities.

We find developmental psychologists conducting research on a wide variety of issues. These include the effects of maternal use of aspirin or heroin on an unborn child, the outcomes of various patterns of child rearing, children's concepts of space and time, adolescent conflicts, and factors that contribute to adjustment among the elderly.

Dyslexia Severely impaired reading ability.

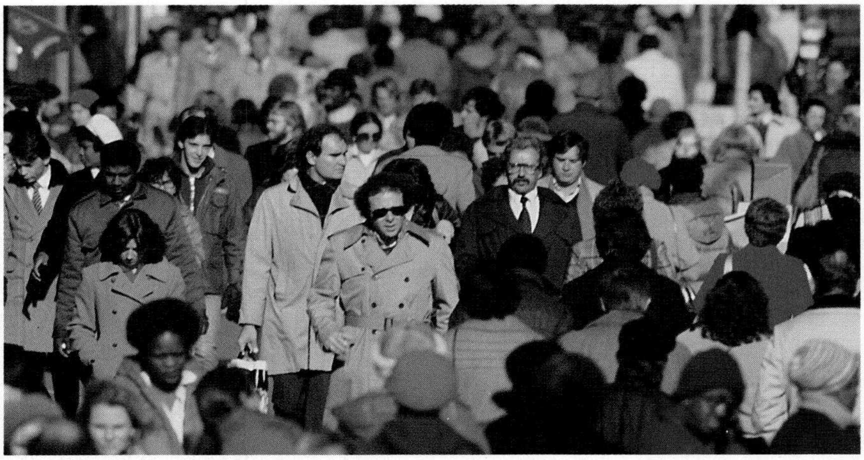

Environmental Psychology. Environmental psychologists focus on the ways in which we influence and are influenced by the physical environment. Among the concerns of environmental psychologists are the effects of crowding and "stimulus overload" on city dwellers.

Personality, Social, and Environmental Psychologists

Personality psychologists attempt to define human traits; to determine influences on human thought processes, feelings, and behavior; and to explain both normal and abnormal patterns of behavior. They are particularly concerned with human issues such as anxiety, aggression, the assumption of sex roles, and learning by observing others. Other topics of interest to personality psychologists include **repression** as a way in which we defend ourselves from feelings of anxiety and guilt, and the effects of television violence.

Social psychologists are primarily concerned with the nature and causes of individuals' thoughts, feelings, and overt behavior in social situations. Whereas personality psychologists tend to look within the person for explanations of behavior, social psychologists tend to focus on social or external influences. The fact of the matter, of course, is that behavior is influenced from within and from without. Both avenues of research are valid.

Social psychologists have historically focused on topics such as attitude formation and attitude change, interpersonal attraction and liking, the nature of sex roles and **stereotypes,** obedience to authority, conformity to group norms, and group decision-making processes. Social psychologists, like personality psychologists, study the problem of human aggression.

Environmental psychologists focus on the ways in which behavior influences and is influenced by the physical environment. Like social psychologists, environmental psychologists are concerned with the effects of crowding on the behavior of city dwellers. Environmental psychologists study ways in which buildings and cities can be designed to better serve human needs. They also investigate the effects of extremes of temperature, noise, and air pollution on people and lower animals.

Experimental Psychologists

Psychologists in all specialties may conduct experimental research. However, those called experimental psychologists conduct research into fundamental processes relevant to more applied specialties. These basic processes include the functions of the nervous system, sensation and perception, learning and

Repression In psychodynamic theory, the automatic ejection of anxiety-evoking ideas from awareness.

Stereotype A fixed, conventional idea about a group.

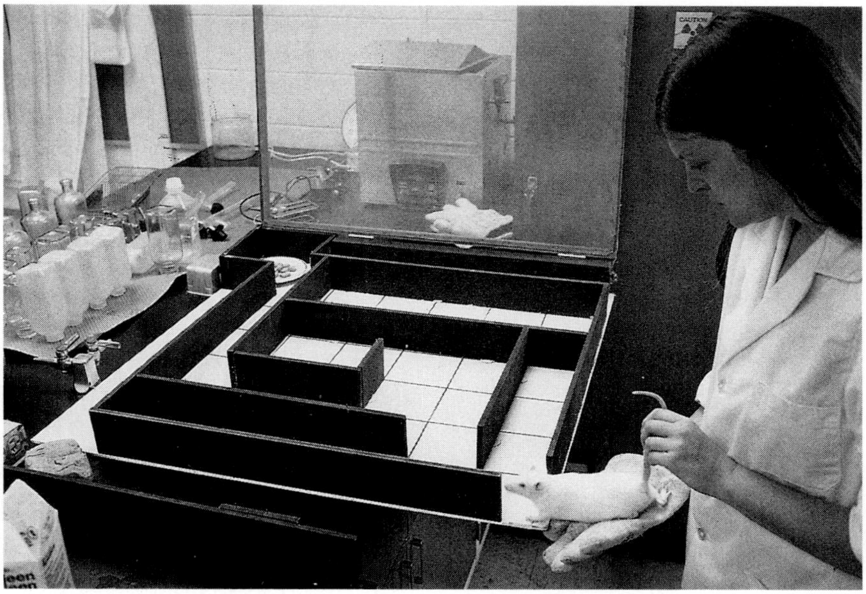

Experimental Psychology. Experimental psychologists conduct research into fundamental psychological processes, such as the functions of the nervous system, sensation and perception, learning and memory, thinking, language, motivation, and emotion. Some of their research is carried out with lower animals, such as laboratory rats, but they also engage in research with humans.

memory, thought, motivation, and emotion, to name but a few. Experimental psychologists who focus on the biological foundations of behavior and seek to understand the relationships between biological changes and psychological events are called biological psychologists.

Experimental psychologists are more likely than other psychologists to engage in basic or pure research. Their findings are often applied by other specialists in practice. Pure research in motivation, for example, has helped clinical and counseling psychologists devise strategies for helping people control weight problems.

Psychologists in Industry

Industrial and organizational psychology are closely related fields. Industrial psychologists focus on the relationships between people and work, whereas organizational psychologists study the behavior of people in organizations, such as business organizations. However, many psychologists are trained in both areas. Industrial and organizational psychologists are employed by business firms to improve working conditions, enhance productivity, and—if they have counseling skills—work with employees who encounter problems on the job. They assist in the processes of hiring, training, and promotion. They devise psychological tests to ascertain whether job applicants have the abilities, interests, and traits that predict successful performance of various jobs.

Consumer psychologists study the behavior of shoppers in an effort to predict and influence their behavior. They advise store managers about how to lay out the aisles of a supermarket to boost impulse buying and how to arrange window displays to attract customers. They devise strategies for enhancing the persuasiveness of newspaper ads and television commercials.

Truth or Fiction Revisited

Some psychologists do measure the effectiveness of television commercials. They are consumer psychologists.

Emerging Fields

There are many other fields and subfields in psychology. Forensic psychologists apply psychological expertise within the criminal justice system. They may serve as expert witnesses in the courtroom, testifying about the competence of defendants to stand trial or describing mental disorders and how they may affect criminal behavior. Psychologists are employed by police departments to assist in the selection of stable applicants; to counsel officers on how to cope with stress; and to train police in the handling of suicide threats, hostage crises, family disputes, and other human problems.

Truth or Fiction Revisited

Other psychologists do serve as expert witnesses in court. They are forensic psychologists.

Health psychologists examine the ways in which behavior and mental processes, such as attitudes, are related to physical health. They study how stress contributes to and influences the courses of diseases ranging from high blood pressure and heart problems to diabetes and cancer. Health psychologists also investigate the factors that contribute to patient compliance with medical advice. In addition, health psychologists guide clients in undertaking more healthful behavior patterns, such as starting to exercise, quitting smoking, and eating a more healthful diet.

Truth or Fiction Revisited

Still other psychologists guide people into eating more healthful diets. Health psychologists do so, along with clinical and counseling psychologists.

Psychologists are continually finding new areas in which to apply their knowledge and skills. Table 1.1 provides more insight into the diverse interests of psychologists.

WHERE PSYCHOLOGY COMES FROM: A BRIEF HISTORY

Psychology is as old as history and as modern as today. Although theoretical developments and research seem to change the face of contemporary psychology every few years, the outline for this textbook could have been written by the Greek philosopher Aristotle (ca. 384–322 B.C.). One of Aristotle's works was called *Peri Psyches,* which translates as "About the Psyche." *Peri Psyches,* like this book, began with a history of psychological thought and historical perspectives on the nature of the mind and behavior. Given his scientific approach, Aristotle made the case that human behavior was subject to rules and laws, just as are the movements of the stars and seas. Then Aristotle delved into his subject matter topic by topic: personality, sensation and perception, thought, intelligence, needs and motives, feelings and emotion, and memory. This book reorganizes these topics somewhat, but each is here.

Truth or Fiction Revisited

It is true that a book on psychology, whose contents are similar to this one, was written by Aristotle more than 2,000 years ago. Its name is *Peri Psyches.*

Table 1.1
Divisions of the American Psychological Association

General Psychology	History of Psychology
Teaching of Psychology	Community Psychology
Experimental Psychology	Psychopharmacology
Evaluation and Measurement	Psychotherapy
Physiological and Comparative Psychology	Psychological Hypnosis
Developmental Psychology	State Psychological Association Affairs
Society of Personality and Social Psychology	Humanistic Psychology
Society for the Psychological Study of Social Issues	Mental Retardation
Psychology and the Arts	Population and Environmental Psychology
Clinical Psychology	Psychology of Women
Consulting Psychology	Psychologists Interested in Religious Issues
Society for Industrial and Organizational Psychology, Inc.	Child, Youth, and Family Services
Educational Psychology	Health Psychology
School Psychology	Psychoanalysis
Counseling Psychology	Clinical Neuropsychology
Psychologists in Public Service	Psychology-Law Society
Military Psychology	Psychologists in Independent Practice
Adult Development and Aging	Family Psychology
Division of Applied Experimental & Engineering Psychologists	Society for the Psychological Study of Lesbian and Gay Issues
Rehabilitation Psychology	Society for the Psychological Study of Ethnic Minority Issues
Consumer Psychology	Media Psychology
Theoretical and Philosophical Psychology	Exercise and Sport Psychology
Experimental Analysis of Behavior	

This constantly evolving list reflects the diversity of interests found among psychologists, as well as areas of social concern and individual specialties. Many psychologists are active in several divisions.

Aristotle also declared that we are basically motivated to seek pleasure and avoid pain, a view that has been employed in modern psychodynamic and learning theories.

There have been many other contributors from ancient Greece. Democritus, for instance, suggested around 400 B.C. that we could think of behavior in terms of a body and a mind. (Contemporary psychologists still talk about the interaction of biological and cognitive processes.) Democritus also pointed out that our behavior was influenced by external stimulation, and he was one of the first to raise the issue of whether or not there is such a thing as free will or choice.

Plato (ca. 427–347 B.C.), the disciple of Socrates, recorded Socrates' advice "Know thyself," which has remained one of the mottos of psychological thought ever since. Socrates claimed that we could not attain reliable self-knowledge through our senses because the senses do not exactly mirror reality. We are even prone to illusions, as we shall see in Chapter 3. Because the senses provide imperfect knowledge, Socrates suggested that we should rely on processes such as rational thought and **introspection** to achieve self-knowledge.

Truth or Fiction Revisited

Socrates did suggest a research method that is still used in psychology today—introspection.

Today we still differentiate between the stimuli that impact upon our sensory receptors and our frequently distorted perceptions and memories. Socrates

Introspection An objective approach to describing one's mental content.

Wilhelm Wundt

also stressed the importance of social psychology. He pointed out that people are social creatures who influence one another profoundly.

If we had room enough and time, we could trace psychology's roots to thinkers more distant than the ancient Greeks, and we could trace its development through the great thinkers of the Renaissance.

As it is, we must move to the development of psychology as a laboratory science during the second half of the nineteenth century. There are so many controversies in psychology that it seems excessive to debate when modern psychology had its debut as an experimental science. But we should note that some historians set the marker date at 1860, when Gustav Theodor Fechner (1801–1887) published his *Elements of Psychophysics.* Fechner's book showed how physical events (such as lights and sounds) were related to psychological sensation and perception, and he showed how we could scientifically measure the effect of these events. Most historians, however, set the birth of psychology as a science in the year 1879, when Wilhelm Wundt (1832–1920) established the first psychological laboratory in Leipzig, Germany.

Structuralism

Wilhelm Wundt, like Aristotle, claimed that the mind was a natural event and could be studied scientifically, just like light, heat, and the flow of blood. Wundt used the method of introspection, recommended by Socrates, to try to discover the basic elements of experience. When presented with various sights and sounds, he and his colleagues tried to look inward as objectively as possible to describe their sensations and feelings.

Wundt and his students—among them Edward Bradford Titchener, who brought Wundt's methodology to Cornell University—founded the school of psychology known as **structuralism.** Structuralism attempted to define the makeup of conscious experience, breaking it down into **objective** sensations, such as sight or taste, and **subjective** feelings, such as emotional responses, will, and mental images (for example, memories or dreams). Structuralists believed that the mind functioned by creatively combining the elements of experience.

Another of Wundt's American students was G. Stanley Hall (1844–1924), whose main interests included the psychological developments of childhood, adolescence, and old age. Hall is usually credited with originating the discipline of child psychology, and he founded the American Psychological Association. The development of child psychology served to alter the widespread belief that children were simply miniature adults.

Functionalism

Toward the end of the nineteenth century, William James (1842–1910), brother of the novelist Henry James, adopted a broader view of psychology that focused on the relation between conscious experience and behavior. James was a major figure in the development of psychology in the United States. He received an MD degree from Harvard University but never practiced medicine. He made his career in academia, teaching at Harvard—first in physiology, then in philosophy, and finally in psychology. He described his views in the first modern psychology textbook, *The Principles of Psychology,* published in 1890 by Henry Holt and Company, the corporate ancestor of Holt, Rinehart and Winston, publisher of the book you now hold in your hands. Though it is a century old, James's book is still considered by

Structuralism The school of psychology that argues that the mind consists of three basic elements—sensations, feelings, and images—which combine to form experience.

Objective Of known or perceived objects rather than existing only in the mind; real.

Subjective Of the mind; personal; determined by thoughts and feelings rather than by external objects.

William James

some to be the "single greatest work in American psychology" (Adelson, 1982, p. 52). In *Principles,* which became known to students as the "Jimmy," James argued that the stream of consciousness is fluid and continuous. His experiences with introspection assured him that experience cannot be broken down into basic units as readily as the structuralists maintained.

James was also one of the founders of the school of **functionalism,** which dealt with overt behavior as well as consciousness. The American philosopher and educator John Dewey (1842–1910) also contributed to functionalist thought. Functionalism addressed the ways in which experience permits us to function more adaptively in our environments, and it used behavioral observation in the laboratory to supplement introspection. The structuralists tended to ask, "What are the parts of psychological processes?" The functionalists tended to ask, "What are the purposes (functions) of overt behavior and mental processes? What difference do they make?"

Dewey and James were influenced by the English naturalist Charles Darwin's (1809–1882) theory of evolution. Earlier in the nineteenth century, Darwin had argued that organisms with adaptive features survive and reproduce, whereas those without such features are doomed to extinction. This doctrine is known as the "survival of the fittest." It suggests that as the generations pass, organisms whose behavior and physical traits (weight, speed, coloring, size, etc.) are best suited to their environments are most likely to survive until maturity and to transmit these traits to future generations.

Functionalism The school of psychology that emphasizes the uses or functions of the mind rather than the elements of experience.

Habit A response to a stimulus that becomes automatic with repetition.

Behaviorism The school of psychology that defines psychology as the study of observable behavior and studies relationships between stimuli and responses.

Functionalists adapted Darwin's view to behavior and proposed that more adaptive behavior patterns are learned and maintained, whereas less adaptive behavior patterns tend to drop out, or to be discontinued. The "fittest" behavior patterns survive. Adaptive actions tend to be repeated and become **habits**. In *Principles'* chapter on habit, James wrote that "habit is the enormous flywheel of society." Habit, in other words, supplies the momentum that maintains civilization from day to day.

The formation of habits is seen in acts such as lifting forks to our mouths and turning doorknobs. At first these acts require full attention. If you are in doubt, stand by with paper towels and watch a baby's first efforts at self-feeding. Through repetition, the acts that make up self-feeding become automatic, or habitual. The multiple acts involved in learning to drive a car also become routine through repetition. We can then perform them without much attention, freeing ourselves to focus on other matters, such as our clever conversation and the cultured sounds issuing from the radio. The idea of learning by repetition is also basic to the behavioral tradition.

Behaviorism

Think of placing a hungry rat in a maze. It meanders down a pathway that comes to an end. It can then turn left or right. If you consistently reward the rat with food for turning right at this choice-point, it will learn to turn right when it arrives there, at least when it is hungry. But what does the rat *think* when it is learning to turn right? "Hmm, last time I was in this situation and turned to the right, I was given some food. Think I'll try that again"?

John B. Watson

Does it seem absurd to try to place yourself in the "mind" of a rat? So it seemed to John Broadus Watson (1878–1958), the founder of American **behaviorism.** But Watson was asked to consider just such a question as one of the requirements for his doctoral degree, which he received from the University of Chicago in 1903. Functionalism was abroad in the land and dominant at the University of Chicago, and functionalists were concerned with the stream of consciousness as well as observable behavior. Watson bridled at the introspective struggles of the functionalists to study conscious-

Figure 1.2
A Couple of Examples of the Power of Reinforcement.

In the photo on the left, we see how our feathered gift to city life has earned its keep in many behavioral experiments on the effects of reinforcement. Here the pigeon pecks the blue button because pecking this button has been followed (reinforced) by the dropping of a food pellet into the cage. In the photo on the right, Magic Raccoon shoots a basket. Behaviorists teach animals complex behaviors, such as shooting baskets, by first reinforcing approximations to the goal (or target behavior). As time progresses, closer approximations are demanded before reinforcement is given.

ness, especially the consciousness of lower animals. He asserted that if psychology was to be a natural science, like physics or chemistry, it must limit itself to observable, measurable events—that is, to behavior.

Response A movement or other observable reaction to a stimulus.

Stimuli Plural of *stimulus.* (1) A feature in the environment that is detected by an organism or leads to a change in behavior (a response). (2) A form of physical energy, such as light or sound, that impinges on the sensory receptors.

Watson agreed with the functionalist focus on the importance of learning, however, and suggested that psychology address the learning of measurable **responses** to environmental **stimuli.** He pointed to the laboratory experiments being conducted by Ivan Pavlov in Russia as a model. Pavlov had found that dogs will learn to salivate when a bell is rung, if ringing the bell has been repeatedly associated with feeding. Pavlov explained the salivation in terms of the laboratory conditions, or **conditioning,** that led to it, not in terms of the imagined mental processes of the dogs. Moreover, the response that Pavlov chose to study, salivation, was a public event that could be measured by laboratory instruments. It was absurd to try to determine what a dog, or person, was thinking.

Watson went to Johns Hopkins University in 1908, where behaviorism took root and soon became firmly planted in American psychology. In 1920 Watson got a divorce so that he could marry a former student, and the scandal forced him to leave academic life. For a while Watson sold coffee and worked as a clerk in a department store. Then he undertook a second productive career in advertising, and he eventually became vice-president of a New York agency.

B. F. Skinner

Harvard University psychologist B. F. Skinner took up the behaviorist call and introduced the concept of **reinforcement** to behaviorism. Organisms, Skinner maintained, learn to behave in certain ways because they have been reinforced for doing so. He demonstrated that laboratory animals will carry out various simple and complex behaviors because of reinforcement. They will peck buttons (Figure 1.2) or turn in circles, then climb ladders and push toys across the floor (see Barnabus the Rat in Chapter 5). Many psychologists adopted the view that, in principle, one could explain intricate human behavior as the summation of instances of learning through

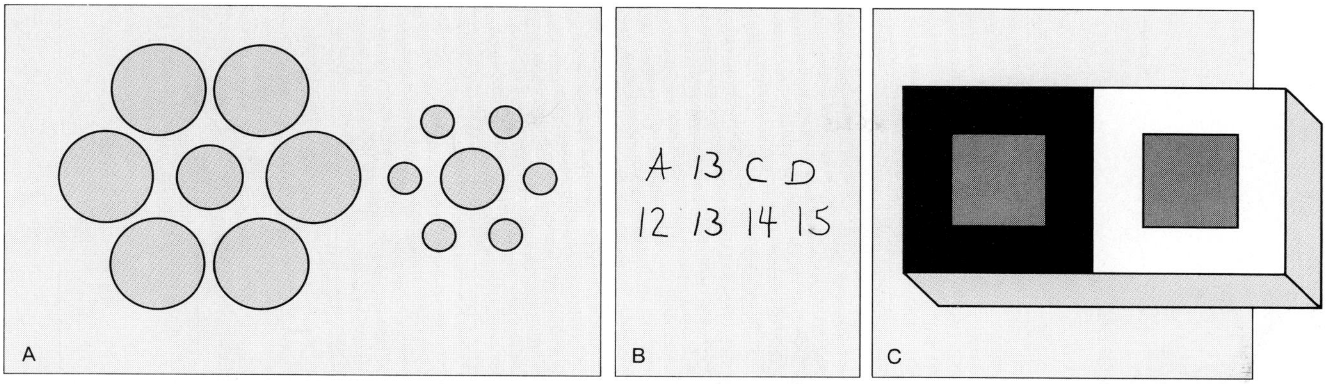

Figure 1.3
The Importance of Context. (A) Are the dots in the center of the configuration the same size? Why not take a ruler and measure their diameters? (B) Is the second symbol in each line the letter B or the number 13? (C) Which of the gray squares is brighter?

Gestalt psychologists have shown that our perceptions depend not only on our sensory impressions but also on the context of our impressions. They argue that human perception cannot be explained in terms of basic units, because we tend to interpret our perceptions of things as wholes, in terms of the contexts in which they occur. You will interpret a man's running toward you very differently depending on whether you are on a deserted street at night or at a track in the morning.

reinforcement. Nevertheless, as a practical matter, they recognized that trying to account for all of a person's behaviors by enumerating his or her complete history of reinforcement would be a hopeless task.

Conditioning A simple form of learning in which stimuli come to signal other stimuli by means of association.

Reinforcement A stimulus that follows a response and increases the frequency of the response.

Gestalt psychology The school of psychology that emphasizes the tendency to organize perceptions into wholes and to integrate separate stimuli into meaningful patterns.

Max Wertheimer

Gestalt Psychology

In the 1920s, another school of psychology—**Gestalt psychology**—was quite prominent in Germany. In the 1930s, the three founders of the school, Max Wertheimer (1880–1943), Kurt Koffka (1886–1941), and Wolfgang Köhler (1887–1967), left Europe to escape the Nazi threat. They carried on their work in the United States, giving further impetus to American ascendance in psychology.

Wertheimer and his colleagues focused on perception and on how perception influences thinking and problem solving. In contrast to the behaviorists, Gestalt psychologists argued that one cannot hope to understand human nature by focusing on clusters of overt behavior alone. In contrast to the structuralists, they claimed that one cannot explain human perceptions, emotions, or thought processes in terms of basic units. Perceptions were *more* than the sums of their parts: Gestalt psychologists saw our perceptions as wholes that give meaning to parts.

Gestalt psychologists illustrated how we tend to perceive separate pieces of information as integrated wholes, including the contexts in which they occur. Consider Figure 1.3. The dots in the centers of the configurations at the left are the same size, yet we may perceive them as being of different sizes because of the contexts in which they appear. The inner squares in the center figure are equally bright, but they may look different because of their contrasting backgrounds. The second symbol in each line at the right is identical, but in the top row we may perceive it as a B and in the bottom row as the number 13. The symbol has not changed, only the context in which it appears. In *The Prince and the Pauper,* Mark Twain dressed a peasant

Figure 1.4
Some Insight into the Role of Insight.

At first the chimpanzee cannot reach the bananas hanging from the ceiling. After some time has passed, it suddenly piles the boxes on top of one another to reach the fruit, behavior suggestive of a "flash of insight." Gestalt psychologists argue that behavior is often too complex to be explained in terms of learning mechanical responses to environmental stimulation.

boy as a prince, and the kingdom bowed to him. Do clothes sometimes make the man or woman?

Gestalt psychologists believed that learning could be active and purposeful, not merely responsive and mechanical, as in Pavlov's experiments. Wolfgang Köhler and the others demonstrated that much learning, especially in learning to solve problems, is accomplished by **insight,** not by mechanical repetition. Köhler was marooned by World War I on one of the Canary Islands, where the Prussian Academy of Science kept a colony of apes, and his research on the island lent him, well, insight into the process of learning by insight.

Consider the chimpanzee in Figure 1.4. At first the ape is unsuccessful in reaching for bananas suspended from the ceiling. Then it suddenly piles the boxes atop one another and climbs them to reach the bananas. It seems that the chimp has experienced a sudden reorganization of the mental elements that represent the problem—that is, it has had a "flash of insight." Köhler's findings suggest that we often manipulate the mentally represented elements of problems until we group them in such a way that we believe we will be able to reach a goal. The manipulations may take quite some time as mental trial and error proceeds. Once the proper grouping has been found, however, we seem to perceive it all at once.

Insight In Gestalt psychology, the sudden reorganization of perceptions, allowing the sudden solution of a problem.

Psychoanalysis The school of psychology that emphasizes the importance of unconscious motives and conflicts as determinants of human behavior.

Psychoanalysis

Psychoanalysis, the school of psychology founded by Sigmund Freud, is very different from the other schools in its background and approach. Freud's theory, more than the others, has invaded the popular culture, and you may

Sigmund Freud

already be familiar with a number of its concepts. For example, an emotionally unstable person is likely to go on a killing spree on at least one television crime show each season. At the show's conclusion, a psychiatrist typically explains that the killer was "unconsciously" doing away with his own mother or father. Or perhaps a friend has tried to "interpret" a slip of the tongue you made or has asked you what you thought might be the symbolic meaning of a dream.

The notions that people are driven by deeply hidden impulses and that verbal slips and dreams represent unconscious wishes largely reflect the influence of Sigmund Freud (1856–1939), a Viennese physician who fled to England in the 1930s to escape the Nazi tyranny. In contrast to the academic psychologists, who conducted research mainly in the laboratory, Freud gained his understanding of human thoughts, emotions, and behavior through clinical interviews with patients. He was astounded at how little insight his patients seemed to have into their motives.

Freud came to believe that unconscious processes, especially primitive sexual and aggressive impulses, were more influential than conscious thought in determining human behavior. Freud thought that most of the mind was unconscious, consisting of a seething cauldron of conflicting impulses, urges, and wishes. People were motivated to gratify these impulses, ugly as some of them were, but at the same time people were motivated to judge themselves as being decent. Thus, they would often delude themselves about their real motives. Because of the assumed motion of underlying forces in personality, Freud's theory is referred to as **psychodynamic.**

Freud devised a method of psychotherapy called psychoanalysis. Psychoanalysis aims to help patients gain insight into many of their deep-seated conflicts and find socially acceptable ways of expressing wishes and gratifying needs.

Today we no longer find psychologists who describe themselves as structuralists or functionalists. Although the school of Gestalt psychology gave birth to current research approaches in perception and problem solving, few would consider themselves Gestalt psychologists. So, too, have the numbers of orthodox behaviorists and psychoanalysts been declining. As we shall see in the following section, many contemporary psychologists in the behaviorist tradition look on themselves as social-learning theorists, and most psychoanalysts consider themselves to be neoanalysts as opposed to traditional Freudians.

HOW TODAY'S PSYCHOLOGISTS VIEW BEHAVIOR

The history of psychological thought has taken many turns, and contemporary psychologists also differ in their approaches. Today there are five broad, influential perspectives in psychology: the biological, cognitive, humanistic, psychoanalytic, and learning-theory perspectives. Each perspective emphasizes different topics of investigation, and each tends to approach its topics in its own ways.

Psychodynamic Referring to Freud's theory, which proposes that the motion of underlying forces of personality determines our thoughts, feelings, and behavior. (From the Greek *dynamis,* meaning "power.")

The Biological Perspective

Psychologists assume that our thoughts, fantasies, dreams, and mental images are made possible by the nervous system and especially by that pivotal part of the nervous system, the brain. Biologically oriented psychologists seek the links between events in the brain—such as the activity of brain cells—and mental processes. As we shall see in Chapter 2, they use techniques such as CAT scans, PET scans, and electrical stimulation of sites in the brain to show that these sites are involved in intellectual activity and emotional and behavioral responses. Through biological psychology we have discovered parts of the brain that are highly active when we listen to music, solve math problems, or suffer from certain mental disorders. We have learned how the production of chemical substances in certain parts of the brain is essential to the storage of information—that is, the formation of memories. Among some lower animals, electrical stimulation of parts of the brain prompts the expression of innate, or built-in, sexual and aggressive behaviors.

Biological psychologists are also concerned about the influences of hormones and genes. For instance, in humans, the **hormone** prolactin stimulates production of milk; but in rats, prolactin also sparks maternal behavior. In lower animals and people, sex hormones stimulate development of the sex organs. In some lower animals, they also determine whether mating behavior will follow stereotypical masculine or feminine behavior patterns.

Genes are the basic units of heredity. Psychologists are vitally interested in the extent of genetic influences on human traits such as intelligence, abnormal behaviors, criminal behaviors, and even the tendency to become addicted to substances such as alcohol and narcotics.

The Cognitive Perspective

Psychologists with a cognitive perspective focus on our mental processes. They investigate the ways in which we perceive and mentally represent the world, how we go about solving problems, how we dream and daydream. Cognitive psychologists, in short, attempt to study all those things we refer to as the *mind.*

Cognitive-Developmental Theory Today the cognitive perspective has many faces. One is the cognitive-developmental theory advanced by the Swiss biologist Jean Piaget (1896–1980). Piaget's innovative study of the intellectual or cognitive development of children has inspired thousands of research projects by developmental and educational psychologists. The focus of this research is to learn how children and adults mentally represent and reason about the world.

According to Piaget and his intellectual descendants, the child's conception of the world grows more sophisticated as the child matures (see Chapter 9). Although experience is essential to children, their perception and understanding of the world unfolds as if guided by an inner clock.

Information Processing Another face of the cognitive perspective is information processing. Psychological thought has been influenced by the status of the physical sciences of the day. For example, Freud's psychodynamic theory was related to the development of thermodynamics in the last century. Many of today's cognitive psychologists have been influenced by concepts of computer science. Computers process information to solve problems. Information is first fed into the computer (encoded so that it can be accepted by the computer as input). Then it is placed in *memory*—or working memory—while it is manipulated. You can also store the information more permanently in *storage* on a floppy disk, a hard disk, or another device. In Chapter 6 we shall see that many psychologists also speak of people as having working memories (short-term memories) and storage (long-term memories).

Hormone A chemical substance that promotes development of body structures and regulates various body functions.

Genes The basic building blocks of heredity.

Thus, many cognitive psychologists focus on information processing in people—the processes by which information is encoded (input), stored (in long-term memory), retrieved (placed in working memory), and manipulated to solve problems (output). Our strategies for solving problems are sometimes referred to as our "mental programs" or "software." In this computer metaphor, our brains are translated into the "hardware" that runs our mental programs. Our brains, that is, become *very* personal computers.

Truth or Fiction Revisited

It is true that some psychologists see our strategies for solving problems as "mental programs" that are operated by our "personal computers," or brains. They are cognitive psychologists, who investigate the ways in which we process information.

Psychologists in the behaviorist tradition argue that cognitions are not directly observable and that cognitive psychologists do not place adequate emphasis on the situational determinants of behavior. Cognitive psychologists counter that human behavior cannot be understood without reference to cognition.

The Humanistic Perspective

Humanistic psychology is a recent school strongly related to Gestalt psychology and cognitive in flavor. Humanism stresses the human capacity for self-fulfillment and the central roles of human consciousness, self-awareness, and the capacity to make choices. Consciousness is seen as the force that unifies our personalities.

Because of its focus on consciousness and self-awareness, humanistic psychology is also labeled **phenomenological.** The word *phenomenon* is derived from the same Greek root as the word *fantasy.* However, *fantasy* implies that one's perceptions are inaccurate and unreal, whereas a *phenomenon* is an event as perceived by a person, and it may be quite realistic. Humanistic psychology considers the person's experience, as perceived by that person, to be the most important event in psychology. Humanists believe that self-awareness, experience, and choice permit us to a large extent to "invent ourselves"—to fashion our growth and our ways of relating to the world—as we progress through life.

I have mentioned that there is an ongoing debate in psychology about whether we are free to choose or whether our behavior is determined by external factors. John Watson's behaviorism was a deterministic stance that assumed that our behavior reflected the summation of the effects of the stimuli impinging upon us. The humanistic approach of American psychologists such as Carl Rogers (1902–1987), Rollo May (born 1909), and Abraham Maslow (1916–1972) asserts that we are basically free to determine our own behavior. To humanists, freedom is a source of both pride and great responsibility. Humanistic psychologists suggest that we are engaged in quests to discover our personal identities and the meanings of our lives.

The goals of humanistic psychology have been more applied than academic. Humanistic psychologists have been involved in devising ways to help people "get in touch" with their feelings and realize their potentials.

Critics, including those in the behaviorist tradition, insist that psychology must be a natural science and address itself to observable events. They argue that our experiences are subjective events that are poorly suited to objective observation and measurement. Humanists such as Carl Rogers (1985) may agree that the observation methods of humanists have sometimes been less

---

Humanistic psychology The school of psychology that assumes the existence of the self and emphasizes the importance of consciousness and self-awareness.

Phenomenological Having to do with the experience of perceiving the world.

than scientific, but they argue that subjective human experience remains vital to the understanding of human nature.

The Psychodynamic Perspective

In the 1940s and 1950s, psychodynamic theory dominated the practice of psychotherapy and was also widely influential in scientific psychology and the arts. Most psychotherapists were psychodynamically oriented, and many renowned artists and writers sought ways to liberate the expression of their unconscious ideas. "Automatic painting" and "automatic writing" were major movements in the humanities.

Today the influence of psychoanalytic thought continues to be felt, although it no longer dominates psychology and its influence has apparently subsided in the humanities as well. Psychologists who follow Freud today are likely to consider themselves to be **neoanalysts.** Neoanalysts such as Karen Horney, Erich Fromm, and Erik Erikson tend to focus less on the roles of unconscious sexual and aggressive impulses in human behavior and more on deliberate choice and self-direction.

Many Freudian ideas are retained in a sort of watered-down form by the population at large. Sometimes we have ideas or inclinations that seem foreign to us. We may say, in the vernacular, that it seems as if something is trying to get the better of us. In the Middle Ages, such thoughts and impulses were usually magically attributed to the Devil or an agent of his. Dreams, likewise, were thought to enter us magically from the spirit world beyond. Today—largely because of Sigmund Freud—many people ascribe uncharacteristic or "improper" ideas and dreams to "unconscious processes" that are assumed to reside deep within. Although people may still consider the wellsprings of the ideas and dreams to be inaccessible, at least their existence and expression is not so likely to be viewed as magical.

Learning-Theory Perspectives

Many psychologists today study the effects of experience on behavior. Learning, to them, is the essential factor in describing, explaining, predicting, and controlling behavior. However, the term *learning* has different meanings for psychologists of different persuasions. Some students of learning find roles for consciousness and insight, whereas others do not. This distinction is found among those who adhere to the behavioral and the social-learning perspectives.

The Behavioral Perspective For John B. Watson, behaviorism was an approach to life as well as a broad guideline for psychological research. Not only did Watson despair of measuring consciousness and mental processes in the laboratory; he also applied behavioral analysis to virtually all situations in his daily life. He viewed people as doing things because of their learning histories, situational influences, and the rewards involved rather than because of conscious choice.

Learning, for Watson and his followers, is exemplified by experiments in conditioning. The results of conditioning are explained in terms of external laboratory procedures and not in terms of changes that have occurred within the organism. Behaviorists do not attempt to find out what an organism has come to "know" through learning. Cognitive psychologists, in con-

Neoanalysts Contemporary followers of Freud who focus less on the roles of unconscious impulses and more on conscious choice and self-direction.

Social-learning theory A school of psychology in the behaviorist tradition that includes cognitive factors in the explanation and prediction of behavior.

trast, view conditioning as a process that alters the organism's mental representation of the environment—one that may encourage but does not compel changes in behavior (Rescorla, 1988).

Albert Bandura

The Social-Learning Perspective Since the early 1960s, **social-learning theorists** have become quite influential in the areas of personality development, abnormal behavior, and methods of therapy. Social-learning theorists such as Albert Bandura, Julian Rotter, and Walter Mischel see themselves as being within the behaviorist tradition because of their strong focus on the role of learning in human behavior. However, they also return to their functionalist roots in the sense that they behold a major role for cognition. Behaviorists emphasize the importance of environmental influences and focus on the learning of habits through repetition and reinforcement. Social-learning theorists, in contrast, suggest that people are capable of modifying or creating their environments, and they emphasize the importance of intentional learning by observing others. It is theorized that through observational learning, we acquire a storehouse of possible responses to life's situations. Social-learning theorists are also humanistic in that they believe that our expectations and values play a role in determining whether we shall *choose* to do the things we have learned how to do.

The following A Closer Look section concerns ways in which psychologists who hold diverse perspectives tend to explain aggression.

A CLOSER LOOK

How Psychologists of Various Perspectives View Aggression

To further comprehension of the ways in which psychologists of various perspectives look at the subject matter of psychology, let us consider the problem of aggression.

Aggression in the Wild. From the sociobiological perspective, aggression is a natural outcome of the process of natural selection. Sociobiologists believe that the underlying purpose of animal behavior is to contribute as many genes as possible to the next generation. More aggressive individuals are more likely to mature and have offspring.

The Biological Perspective Numerous biological structures appear to be involved in aggression. One is the brain structure called the *hypothalamus.* In response to certain environmental stimuli termed "releasers," many lower animals show apparently inborn, or instinctive, aggressive reactions. The hypothalamus appears to be involved in this inborn reaction pattern: Electrical stimulation of part of the hypothalamus triggers stereotypical aggressive behaviors in a number of lower animals. People, whose brains are more complex, appear to have other brain structures that act to inhibit, or moderate, possible inborn response patterns.

An offshoot of the biological perspective called *sociobiology* became popular in the 1970s, and sociobiology suggests that aggression is natural and even desirable for the species. Sociobiology views the gene as the "ultimate unit of life," or the "hereditary units . . . which either fail or prosper as a result of [natural] selection" (Leak & Christopher, 1982, pp. 313–314). Sociobiology argues that the underlying purpose of animal behavior is to contribute as many genes as possible to the next generation. More aggressive individuals are usually more likely to survive to maturity and propagate. Therefore, whatever genes are linked to aggressive behavior are more likely to be transmitted to the following generation. This view is thought to apply to people as well as to lower animals, although our intelligence—our capacity to outwit other species—is the dominant factor in human survival.

Sociobiology has been attacked on numerous grounds. Many scientists argue that it is absurd to suggest that genes can harbor anything akin to an "intent" to be transmitted. Sociobiology also seems to suggest that aggressiveness is natural and desirable. Thus, efforts to control aggression can be seen as being doomed to failure and even morally questionable because they interfere with the natural order of things.

Do not confuse sociobiology with the biological perspective in general. Although the role of sociobiology remains controversial, the biological perspective makes frequent contributions to psychology and human welfare, as we shall see in later chapters.

The Cognitive Perspective Cognitive psychologists assert that our behavior is influenced by our values, by the ways in which we interpret our situations, and by choice. For example, people who believe that aggression is necessary and justified, as during wartime, are likely to act aggressively. People who believe that a particular war or act of aggression is unjust, or who universally oppose aggression, are less likely to behave aggressively.

Jean Piaget and Lawrence Kohlberg have focused on the ways in which we process information to arrive at judgments of guilt or innocence as we mature. For instance, 5-year-old children might consider an act of aggression to be wrong simply because they have been told that aggression is bad. However, an 8-year-old child would also be likely to consider the motives of the aggressor.

Cognitively oriented psychologists also focus on the ways in which our thoughts and beliefs influence our behavior. For example, aggressive adolescents are frequently biased in their processing of social information: They perceive other people to be more aggressive than they actually are (Lochman, 1987), and they assume that other people intend them ill when they do not (Dodge & Frame, 1982; Jurkovic, 1980). Similarly, some rapists, particularly men who rape their dates, tend to misread women's expressed wishes (e.g., Lipton et al., 1987).

Cognitively oriented psychotherapists note that we are more likely to respond aggressively to a provocation when our thoughts intensify the insult or otherwise stir feelings of anger. In Chapter 13 you will see how cognitive therapists teach explosive people to control their aggressive impulses by viewing social provocations as problems demanding solutions, rather than as insults requiring retaliation.

The Humanistic Perspective Humanistic psychologists are generally optimistic about human nature. They do not see aggression as an inevitable state of affairs but rather as a defensive reaction to frustrations imposed on us by people who, for their own reasons, do not want us to develop into what we are capable of being. Humanistic psychotherapists have sought to help clients get in touch with their true motives and potentials and have encouraged them to express their genuine feelings. The faith is that when people are truly free to choose their own directions in life and express their feelings, they do not choose violence.

The Psychodynamic Perspective Whereas many neoanalysts are humanistic in their approach, Sigmund Freud's view of aggression and human nature was quite different from that of the humanists. Freud believed that aggressive impulses were an inevitable result of the frustrations of daily life, even if others tried to give us the freedom to develop as we wished. Children (and adults) would normally desire to vent aggressive impulses on other people, including parents, because even the most attentive parents could not gratify all their children's demands immediately. Yet children, also fearing their parents' retribution and loss of love, would come to tamp down, or

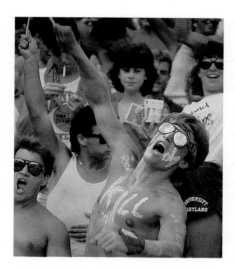

A "Wild" Example of Aggression. According to psychodynamic theory, encouraging aggression on a small scale might help prevent aggression on a large scale. Cheering on one's football team (as in this photo) or personal participation in athletic contests might vent some of the aggressive "steam" that theoretically builds up in the unconscious.

repress, most aggressive impulses. The Freudian perspective, in a sense, sees us as "steam engines." By holding in rather than venting "steam," we set ourselves up for future explosions. And so, built-up aggressive impulses seek outlets. They might be expressed toward parents in other ways, or they might be expressed toward strangers later in life.

In his later years, Freud became so despondent about the mass slaughter in World War I and other human tragedies that he also proposed the existence of a death instinct, Thanatos. Thanatos was the ultimate expression of what Freud saw as the unconscious human wish to return to the stress-free days prior to birth—not a very pretty picture of human nature.

According to psychodynamic theory, the best ways to prevent aggression on a large scale might be to encourage aggression on a small scale. In the steam-engine analogy, verbal aggression (such as by means of wit, sarcasm, or expression of negative feelings) might vent some of the aggressive steam in the unconscious. So might cheering on one's football team or attending prize fights. The venting of part of one's aggressive impulses is referred to by psychoanalysts as catharsis, or purging. Catharsis is theorized to function as a sort of safety valve. But research findings on the usefulness of catharsis are mixed. Some studies suggest that catharsis leads to pleasant reductions in tension and a lowered likelihood of future aggression (e.g., Doob & Wood, 1972). Other studies, however, suggest that letting some steam escape actually encourages more aggression later on (e.g., Geen et al., 1975).

Learning-Theory Perspectives From the behavioral perspective, learning is acquired through principles of reinforcement. Organisms that are reinforced for aggressive behavior are more likely to behave aggressively in similar situations. Environmental consequences make it more likely that strong organisms will be reinforced for aggressive behavior.

From the social-learning perspective, aggressive skills are acquired predominantly by observing others. Social-learning theorists, however, find roles for consciousness and choice. They believe that we are not likely to act aggressively unless we also believe that aggression is appropriate for us under the circumstances.

Consider the roles of media violence. In Chapter 5 we shall see that televised violence can contribute to aggressive behavior in four ways: (1) by increasing viewers' general level of activity and bodily arousal, (2) by encouraging the expression of impulses that we usually constrain, (3) by showing viewers *how* to behave aggressively, and (4) by creating the sense that aggression is a normal part of life. Concerning the latter avenue of fomenting aggression, children who regularly watch violent shows may become less condemnatory of violence and place less value on self-restraint. However, social-learning theorists (Eron, 1987; Huesmann et al., 1983) have found that parents and teachers can mitigate the impact of media violence by informing children that the violent behavior they observe in the media does *not* represent the behavior of most people and that most people do not use aggression to resolve conflicts.

Historic traditions and theoretical perspectives encourage psychologists to focus on various psychological questions and issues in their research. Their research findings are also made meaningful by integrating them with existing perspectives or, when existing perspectives fall short, by creating new perspectives that will encompass them. In the next section, we survey the methods that today's psychologists use in their investigation of behavior. Just as there are many traditions in psychology, there are also many ways of conducting research.

HOW PSYCHOLOGISTS STUDY BEHAVIOR

Do only people use tools? Does alcohol cause aggression? What are the effects of aspirin and narcotics on the fetus? What are the effects of exercise on anxiety and depression? Does pornography trigger crimes of violence?

Many of us have expressed opinions on questions such as these at one time or another, and different psychological theories suggest a number of possible answers. But psychology is an **empirical** science. Within an empirical science, assumptions about the behavior of cosmic rays, chemical compounds, cells, or people must be supported by evidence. Strong arguments, reference to authority figures, even tightly knit theories are not considered to be adequate as scientific evidence. Scientific evidence is obtained by means of the **scientific method.**

The Scientific Method

There are four basic steps to the scientific method:

Step 1: Formulating a Research Question The first step is formulation of a research question. Our daily experiences, psychological theory, even folklore help to generate questions for research. Daily experience in using day-care centers may motivate us to conduct research into whether day care influences development of social skills or the bonds of attachment between children and their mothers. Social-learning principles of observational learning may prompt research into the effects of televised violence.

Step 2: Developing a Hypothesis The second step is the development of a **hypothesis.** A hypothesis is a specific statement about behavior that is tested through research.

One hypothesis about day care might be that preschoolers placed in day care will acquire greater social skills in relating to peers than preschoolers who are cared for in the home. A hypothesis about TV violence might be that elementary school boys who watch more violent TV shows tend to behave more aggressively toward their peers.

Step 3: Testing the Hypothesis The third step is testing the hypothesis. Psychologists test the hypothesis through carefully controlled methods of observation, such as the naturalistic-observation method and the experiment.

For example, we could introduce day-care and non-day-care children to a new child in a college child-research center and observe how each group fares with the new acquaintance. Concerning the effects of TV violence, we could have parents help us tally which TV shows their children watch and rate the shows for violent content. Each boy could receive a total "exposure-to-TV-violence score." We could also gather teacher reports on how aggressively the boys act toward their peers. Then we could determine whether more aggressive boys also watch more violence on television.

Step 4: Drawing Conclusions about the Hypothesis The fourth step is drawing conclusions. Psychologists draw conclusions about the accuracy of their hypotheses on the basis of their research findings. When findings do not bear out their hypotheses, the researchers may modify the theories from which the hypotheses were derived. Research findings often suggest new hypotheses and, consequently, new studies.

In our research on day care, we would probably find that day-care children show somewhat greater social skills than children cared for in the home

Empirical Emphasizing or based on observation and experiment.

Scientific method A four-step method for obtaining scientific evidence in which a hypothesis is formed and tested.

Hypothesis An assumption about behavior that is tested through research.

(see Chapter 9). We would probably also find that more aggressive children spend more time watching television violence (see Chapter 5). But we shall see in the following section that it might be wrong to conclude *from the evidence described* that TV violence *causes* aggressive behavior.

Let us now consider the major research methods used by psychologists: the naturalistic-observation method, the correlational method, the experimental method, the survey method, the testing method, and the case-study method.

The Naturalistic-Observation Method

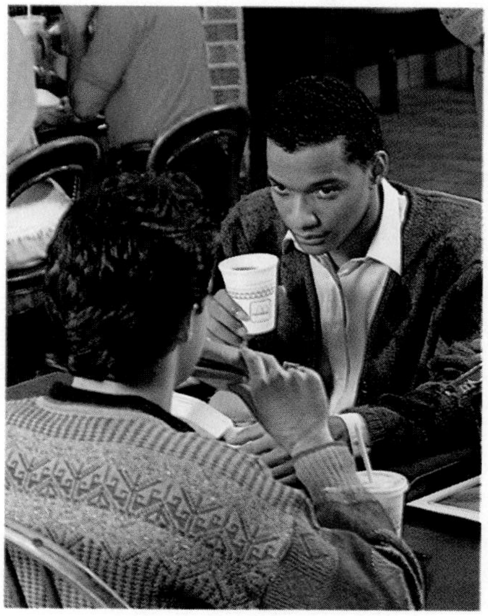

The Naturalistic-Observation Method. In the naturalistic-observation method, psychologists study behavior in the field, "where it happens." For example, psychologists have recorded eating behavior in fast-food restaurants to learn whether or not obese people eat more rapidly or take larger bites than other people.

The next time you go to McDonald's or Burger King for lunch, look around. Pick out slender people and overweight people and observe whether they eat their burgers and fries differently. Do the overweight eat more rapidly? Chew less frequently? Leave less food on their plates? This is precisely the type of research psychologists have recently used to study the eating habits of normal-weight and overweight people. In fact, if you notice some mysterious people at McDonald's peering out over sunglasses and occasionally tapping the head of a partly concealed microphone, perhaps they are recording their observations of other people's eating habits, even as you watch.

This method of scientific investigation is called **naturalistic observation.** Psychologists and other scientists use it to observe behavior in the field, or "where it happens." They try to avoid interfering with the behaviors they are observing by using **unobtrusive** measures. Jane Goodall has observed the behavior of chimpanzees in their natural environment to learn about their social behavior, sexual behavior, use of tools, and other facts of chimp life. As we see in Figure 1.5, her observations have shown us that (1) we were incorrect to think that only people use tools; and (2) kissing, as a greeting, is used by chimpanzees as well as people.

Truth or Fiction Revisited

The naturalistic-observation method has, in fact, taught us that not only people use tools.

But don't conclude that using tools or kissing are inborn, or **instinctive,** behaviors among primates. Chimps, like people, can learn from experience. It may be that they learned how to use tools and to kiss. The naturalistic-observation method provides descriptive information but is not the best method for determining the causes of behavior.

Samples and Populations In naturalistic observation and other methods, the individuals, or subjects, who are observed are referred to as a **sample.** A sample is a segment of a **population,** and we also need to make every effort to ensure that the subjects we observe *represent* our target population, such as Americans, and not subgroups such as southern California Yuppies or Caucasian members of the middle class.

Naturalistic observation A scientific method in which organisms are observed in their natural environments.

Unobtrusive Not interfering.

Instinctive Inborn, natural, unlearned.

Sample Part of a population.

Population A complete group of organisms or events.

The Correlational Method

Are people with higher intelligence more likely to do well in school? Are people with a stronger need for achievement likely to climb higher up the corporate ladder? What is the relationship between stress and health?

Figure 1.5
The Naturalistic-Observation Method.

Jane van Lawick Goodall has used the naturalistic-observation method with chimpanzees, quietly observing them for many years in their natural environments. In using this method, scientists try to avoid interfering with the animals or people they observe, even though this sometimes means allowing an animal to be mistreated by other animals or to die from a curable illness. We learn from Goodall that tools are used by primates other than human beings. The chimp in the left-hand photo is using a stick as a tool to poke around in a termite hill for food. Goodall's observations have also taught us that not only humans use kissing as a social greeting (see right-hand photo). Male chimps have even been observed greeting females by kissing their hands. Very European?

In **correlational research,** psychologists investigate whether one kind of behavior or a trait is related to, or correlated with, another. Consider the variables of intelligence and academic performance. Numerous studies report **positive correlations** between intelligence and achievement. This means that by and large the higher people score on intelligence tests, the better their academic performance is likely to be. In these studies, the variables of intelligence and academic performance are assigned numbers, such as intelligence test scores and academic averages. These numbers are mathematically related and expressed as a **correlation coefficient.** A correlation coefficient is a number that varies between +1.00 and −1.00.* The scores attained on intelligence tests are positively correlated (about +0.60 to +0.70) with overall academic achievement.

There is a **negative correlation** between stress and health. As the amount of stress affecting us increases, the functioning of our immune systems decreases (see Chapter 11). Under high levels of stress, many people have poorer health.

Correlational research may suggest but does not show cause and effect. For instance, it may seem logical to assume that high intelligence makes it possible for children to profit from education. Research has also shown, however, that education contributes to higher scores on intelligence tests.

Thus, correlational research does not allow us to place clear "cause" and "effect" labels on variables. Nevertheless, correlational research can point the way to profitable experimental research. That is, if there were no

Correlational research A scientific method that studies the relationships between variables.

Positive correlation A relationship between variables in which one variable increases as the other also increases.

Correlation coefficient A number between +1.00 to −1.00 that expresses the strength and direction (positive or negative) of the relationship between two variables.

Negative correlation A relationship between two variables in which one variable increases as the other decreases.

*The mathematics of the correlation coefficient are discussed further in Appendix A.

correlation between intelligence and achievement, there would be little purpose in running experiments to determine causal relationships. If there were no relationship between the need for achievement and success, it would be pointless to ask whether the need for achievement contributes to success.

The Experimental Method

Most psychologists would agree that the preferred method for answering questions concerning cause and effect is the experimental method. In an **experiment,** a group of participants receives a **treatment,** such as a dose of alcohol. The participants, also called **subjects,** are then observed carefully to determine whether the treatment makes a difference in their behavior. Does alcohol affect their ability to take tests, for example? In another example, environmental psychologists have varied room temperatures and the background levels of noise to see whether these treatments have an effect on subjects' behavior.

A psychologist may theorize that alcohol leads to aggression because it reduces fear of consequences or because it generally energizes the activity levels of drinkers. He or she may then hypothesize that the treatment of a specified dosage of alcohol will lead to increases in aggression. Let us follow the example of the effects of alcohol on aggression to further our understanding of the experimental method.

Independent and Dependent Variables In an experiment to determine whether or not alcohol causes aggression, experimental subjects would be given a quantity of alcohol and its effects would be measured. Alcohol would be considered an **independent variable.** The presence of an independent variable is manipulated by the experimenters so that its effects may be determined. The independent variable of alcohol may be administered at different levels, or doses, from none or very little to enough to cause intoxication, or drunkenness.

The measured results or outcomes in an experiment are called **dependent variables.** The presence of dependent variables presumably depends on the independent variables. In an experiment to determine whether alcohol influences aggression, aggressive behavior would be a dependent variable. Other dependent variables of interest in an experiment on the effects of alcohol might include sexual arousal, visual-motor coordination, and performance on intellectual tasks such as defining words or doing numerical computations.

Experiments can be quite complex, with several independent and dependent variables. Psychologists often use complex experimental designs and sophisticated statistical techniques to determine the effect of each independent variable, as that variable acts alone and in combination with others, on each dependent variable.

Experimental and Control Groups Ideal experiments use experimental and control subjects or groups. **Experimental subjects** receive the treatment, whereas **control subjects** do not. Every effort is made to ensure that all other conditions are held constant for both experimental and control subjects. In this way, researchers can have confidence that the experimental outcomes reflect the treatments and not chance factors or chance fluctuations in behavior.

In an experiment concerning the effects of alcohol on aggression, experimental subjects would be given alcohol and control subjects would not.

Experiment A scientific method that seeks to discover cause-and-effect relationships by introducing independent variables and observing their effects on dependent variables.

Treatment In experiments, a condition received by participants so that its effects may be observed.

Subjects Participants in a scientific study.

Independent variable A condition in a scientific study that is manipulated so that its effects may be observed.

Dependent variable A measure of an assumed effect of an independent variable.

Experimental subjects Subjects receiving a treatment in an experiment.

Control subjects Experimental participants who do not receive the experimental treatment but for whom all other conditions are comparable to those of experimental subjects.

What Are the Effects of Alcohol? Psychologists have undertaken research to determine alcohol's effects on behavior. Questions have been raised about the soundness of research in which subjects *know* they have drunk alcohol. Why?

In a complex experiment, different experimental groups might receive (1) different dosages of alcohol and (2) different types of social provocations.

Blinds and Double Blinds One experiment on the effects of alcohol on aggression (Boyatzis, 1974) reported that men at parties where beer and liquor were served acted more aggressively than control subjects at parties where only soft drinks were served. But we must be cautious in interpreting these findings, because the experimental subjects *knew* that they had drunk alcohol and the control subjects *knew* that they had not. Aggression that appeared to result from alcohol might not have reflected drinking per se; instead, it might have reflected subjects' expectations about the effects of alcohol. There is reason to be suspicious, because many experiments have shown that people "act in stereotyped ways" when they believe that they have been drinking alcohol (Marlatt & Rohsenow, 1981). For instance, men will become less anxious in social situations, more aggressive, and more sexually aroused—even though they have drunk only a **placebo** such as tonic water.

Well-designed experiments control for the possible effects of expectations by creating conditions under which the subjects are unaware of, or **blind** to, the treatment they have received. Yet researchers may also have expectations. They may, in effect, be "rooting for" a certain treatment. For instance, tobacco-company executives may wish to show that cigarette smoking is harmless. For this reason it is useful if the people measuring the experimental outcomes are also unaware of who has received the treatment. Studies in which both subjects and experimenters are unaware of who has received the treatment are called **double-blind studies.**

Double-blind studies are used in medicine as the standard method of determining the usefulness of new drugs. The drug and the placebo are made up to look and taste the same. Subjects are assigned to the new drug or to the placebo at random, and the key for determining who has taken what is "locked away" until the study is completed. Neither the subjects who take the drugs, the people who hand them out, nor the people who measure the subjects' progress know who has received the drug and who has received the placebo. Only after the final measurements of progress are made is the key unlocked. Then an impartial panel can determine whether the outcomes differed for people who took the drug and people who took the placebo.

In one carefully controlled study on the effects of alcohol, Alan Lang of the University of Wisconsin and his colleagues (1975) pretested a highball of vodka and tonic water to determine that it could not be discriminated by taste from tonic water alone. They recruited as subjects college men who

---

Placebo (pluh-SEE-bow). A bogus treatment that has the appearance of being genuine.

Blind In experimental terminology, unaware of whether or not one has received a treatment.

Double-blind study A study in which neither the subjects nor the persons measuring results know who has received the treatment.

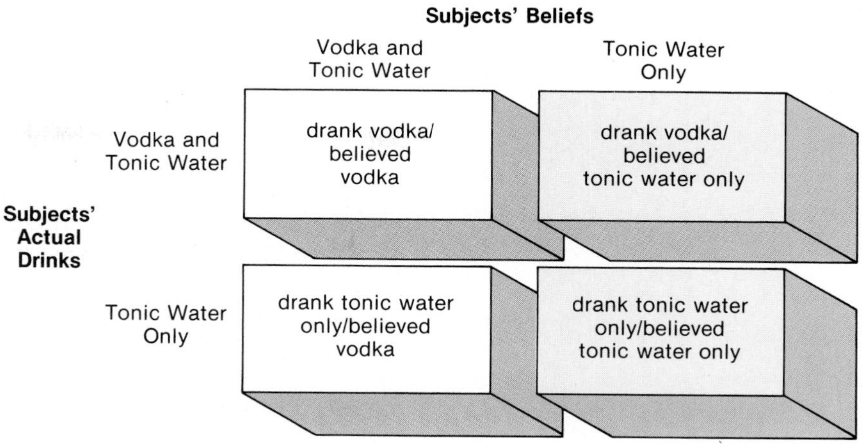

Figure 1.6
The Experimental Conditions in the Lang Study. The taste of vodka cannot be discerned when vodka is mixed with tonic water. For this reason, it was possible for subjects in the Lang study on the effects of alcohol to be kept "blind" as to whether or not they had actually drunk alcohol. Blind studies allow psychologists to control for the effects of subject expectations.

described themselves as social drinkers. Some subjects received vodka and tonic water, whereas others received tonic water only. Of subjects who received vodka, half were misled into believing that they had drunk tonic water only (Figure 1.6). Of subjects receiving tonic water only, half were misled into believing that their drink contained vodka. Thus half the subjects were blind to the treatment they received. Experimenters who measured aggressive responses were also blind concerning which subjects had received vodka.

The research team found that men who believed that they had drunk vodka responded more aggressively to a provocation than men who believed that they had drunk tonic water only. The actual content of the drink was immaterial. That is, men who had actually drunk alcohol acted no more aggressively than men who had drunk tonic water only. The results of the Lang study differ dramatically from those reported by Boyatzis, perhaps because the Boyatzis study did not control for the effects of expectations or beliefs about alcohol.

Is it possible that alcohol does not cause aggression, that centuries of folklore have been in error? Yes, quite possible. Other studies that control for the effects of expectations have shown that alcohol can even decrease aggressive behavior (Marlatt & Rohsenow, 1981).

Truth or Fiction Revisited

Although alcohol is frequently linked to aggression, there is *no* scientific evidence that alcohol causes aggression.

Psychology is an empirical science. Centuries of folklore may stimulate research into certain topics, but folklore is not acceptable evidence within science.

So, what do we make of these findings? Why does belief that one has drunk alcohol increase aggression, whereas alcohol itself may not? Perhaps alcohol gives one a certain social role to play in our culture—the role of the uninhibited social mover. Perhaps alcohol also provides an excuse for aggressive or other antisocial behavior. After all, the drinker can always claim, "It wasn't me; it was the alcohol." What will you think the next time someone says, "It was the alcohol"?

Generalizing from Experimental Results Many factors must be considered in interpreting the results of experiments. In the Lang study, the subjects represented a sample of male college students who were social drinkers—that is, they tended to drink at social gatherings at which alcohol was available. In the discussion of the naturalistic-observation method, it was noted that we need to be certain that the sample under study represents the target population. Whom do male college students represent, other than themselves? To whom can we extend, or generalize, the results?

For one thing, the results may not extend to women, not even to college women. College men also tend to fall within a certain age range (about 18 to 22) and are more intelligent than the general population. We cannot be certain that the findings extend to older men of average intelligence, although it seems reasonable to **infer** that they do. The social drinkers in the Lang study may also differ biologically and psychologically from alcoholics, who have difficulty controlling their drinking. Nor can we be certain that college social drinkers represent people who do not drink at all.

There is a quip in psychology that experiments tend to be run with "rats, sophomores, and soldiers." Why? Because these subjects have been readily available. Still, science is a conservative enterprise, and scientists are cautious about generalizing experimental results to populations other than those from which their samples were drawn.

The Survey Method

In the good old days, when being "sound as a dollar" was a sign of good health, one had to wait until the wee hours of the morning to learn the results of local and national elections. Throughout the evening and early morning hours, suspense would build as ballots from distant neighborhoods and states were tallied. Nowadays one is barely settled with an after-dinner cup of coffee on election night when the news-show computer cheerfully announces (computers do not, of course, have emotions or make "cheerful" announcements, but they certainly seem rather smug at times) that it has examined the ballots of a "scientifically selected sample" and then predicts the next president of the United States. All this may occur with less than 1 percent of the vote tallied. Polls taken before elections also do their share of eroding wonderment and doubt—so much so that supporters of projected winners must sometimes be encouraged to actually vote on Election Day so that predictions will be borne out.

Just as computers and pollsters predict election results and report national opinion on the basis of scientifically selected samples, psychologists conduct **surveys** to learn about behavior that cannot be observed in the natural setting or studied experimentally. Psychologists making surveys may employ questionnaires and interviews or examine public records. By distributing questionnaires and analyzing answers with a computer, psychologists can survey many thousands of people at a time.

In the late 1940s and early 1950s, Alfred Kinsey of Indiana University and his colleagues published two surveys of sexual behavior, based on interviews, that shocked the nation: These were *Sexual Behavior in the Human Male* (1948) and *Sexual Behavior in the Human Female* (1953). Kinsey reported that masturbation was virtually universal in his sample of men at a time when masturbation was still widely thought to impair physical or mental health. He also reported that about one woman in three still single at age 25 had engaged in premarital intercourse.

The survey was the appropriate method for attaining these data, since Kinsey wished to learn what was happening in the United States rather than to study the causes of sexual behavior in depth. If Kinsey had tried to use the naturalistic-observation method, he and his colleagues might have been tossed into jail as Peeping Toms.

Infer Draw a conclusion.

Survey A scientific method in which large samples of people are questioned.

"Would you say Attila is doing an excellent job, a good job, a fair job, or a poor job?"

In addition to compiling self-reports of behavior, surveys are also used to learn about people's opinions, attitudes, and values. For example, more recent surveys concerning sex have found that during the 1970s people were less likely to condemn masturbation and premarital intercourse than were people in Kinsey's era (Hunt, 1974).

Interviews and questionnaires are not foolproof, of course. People may inaccurately recall their behavior or purposefully misrepresent it. Some people try to ingratiate themselves with their interviewers by answering in what they perceive to be the socially desirable direction. The Kinsey studies all relied on male interviewers, for example, and it has been speculated that women interviewees might have been more open and honest with women interviewers. Similar problems may occur when interviewers and those surveyed are from different racial or socioeconomic backgrounds. Other people may falsify attitudes and exaggerate problems to draw attention to themselves or just to try to foul up the results.

The Testing Method

Psychologists also use psychological tests, such as intelligence, aptitude, and personality tests, to measure various traits and characteristics among a population. There is a wide range of psychological tests, and they measure traits ranging from verbal ability and achievement to anxiety, depression, the need for social dominance, musical aptitude, and vocational interests.

Psychological test results, like the results of surveys, can be distorted by respondents who answer in a socially desirable direction or attempt to exaggerate problems. For these reasons, some commonly used psychological tests have items built into them called **validity scales.** Validity scales are sensitive to misrepresentations and alert the psychologist when test results may be deceptive.

Because of validity problems, many psychologists prefer to observe behavior directly when possible.

Validity scales Groups of test items that suggest whether or not the test results are valid (measure what they are supposed to measure).

QUESTIONNAIRE

The Social-Desirability Scale

Do you say what you think, or do you tend to misrepresent your beliefs to earn the approval of others? Do you answer questions honestly, or do you say what you think other people want to hear?

Telling others what we think they want to hear is making the socially desirable response. Falling prey to social desirability may cause us to distort our beliefs and experiences in interviews or on psychological tests. You can complete the following test devised by Crowne and Marlowe (1960) to gain insight into whether you have a tendency to produce socially desirable responses. Read each item and decide whether it is true (T) or false (F) for you. Try to work rapidly and answer each question by circling the T or the F. Then turn to the scoring key in Appendix B to interpret your answers.

T F 1. Before voting I thoroughly investigate the qualifications of all the candidates.

T F 2. I never hesitate to go out of my way to help someone in trouble.

T F 3. It is sometimes hard for me to go on with my work if I am not encouraged.

T F 4. I have never intensely disliked anyone.

T F 5. On occasions I have had doubts about my ability to succeed in life.

T F 6. I sometimes feel resentful when I don't get my way.

T F 7. I am always careful about my manner of dress.

T F 8. My table manners at home are as good as when I eat out in a restaurant.

T F 9. If I could get into a movie without paying and be sure I was not seen I would probably do it.

T F 10. On a few occasions, I have given up something because I thought too little of my ability.

T F 11. I like to gossip at times.

T F 12. There have been times when I felt like rebelling against people in authority even though I knew they were right.

T F 13. No matter who I'm talking to, I'm always a good listener.

T F 14. I can remember "playing sick" to get out of something.

T F 15. There have been occasions when I have taken advantage of someone.

T F 16. I'm always willing to admit it when I make a mistake.

T F 17. I always try to practice what I preach.

T F 18. I don't find it particularly difficult to get along with loudmouthed, obnoxious people.

T F 19. I sometimes try to get even rather than forgive and forget.

T F 20. When I don't know something I don't mind at all admitting it.

T F 21. I am always courteous, even to people who are disagreeable.

T F 22. At times I have really insisted on having things my own way.

T F 23. There have been occasions when I felt like smashing things.

T F 24. I would never think of letting someone else be punished for my wrong-doings.

T F 25. I never resent being asked to return a favor.

T F 26. I have never been irked when people expressed ideas very different from my own.

T F 27. I never make a long trip without checking the safety of my car.

T F 28. There have been times when I was quite jealous of the good fortune of others.

T F 29. I have almost never felt the urge to tell someone off.

T F 30. I am sometimes irritated by people who ask favors of me.

T F 31. I have never felt that I was punished without cause.

T F 32. I sometimes think when people have a misfortune they only got what they deserved.

T F 33. I have never deliberately said something that hurt someone's feelings.

Source: D. P. Crowne and D. A. Marlowe, A new scale of social desirability independent of pathology, *Journal of Consulting Psychology*, 1960, *24*, p. 351, Table 1. Copyright 1960 by the American Psychological Association. Reprinted by permission.

The Case-Study Method

Sigmund Freud developed psychoanalytic theory largely on the basis of **case studies,** or carefully drawn biographies of the lives of individuals. In the case study, as opposed to most other research methods, the psychologist studies one or a handful of individuals in great depth, seeking out the factors that seem to contribute to notable patterns of behavior. Freud studied some patients over a period of several years, meeting with them several times a week.

Case study A carefully drawn biography that may be obtained through interviews, questionnaires, and psychological tests.

Of course, there are bound to be gaps in memory when people are interviewed. People may also distort their pasts because of social desirability and other factors. Interviewers may also have certain expectations and subtly encourage their subjects to fill in gaps in ways that are consistent with their theoretical perspectives.

When doing a case study, of course, it is useful to have regular access to the person being studied, as Freud did with his patients. But case studies of prominent historical figures have also been carried out. These figures include powerful political leaders such as Napoleon and Hitler, great artists such as Michelangelo and Vincent van Gogh, and ingenious scientists such as Leonardo da Vinci and Madame Curie. The goal of such studies is usually to discover the factors that led to the dominant traits of these figures. In these cases, the task is to reconstruct traits and motives on the basis of the figure's writings, public and private records, and, if possible, interviews with people who have known the figure.

The case study is also used in psychological consultation. Psychologists learn whatever they can about individuals, agencies, and business firms so that they can suggest ways in which these clients can more effectively meet their challenges. Psychologists base their suggestions on laboratory research whenever possible, but psychological practice is also sometimes an art in which psychologist and client agree that a suggestion or a treatment has been helpful on the basis of the client's self-report.

A CLOSER LOOK

Becoming a Sophisticated Consumer of Research

Magazines, newspapers, and television shows regularly report the results of psychological, medical, and other kinds of research. We frequently hear about the effects of new drugs on illnesses, the effectiveness (or futility) of ways of handling aggression or drug abuse, and factors that contribute to physical health and psychological well-being. Most laypeople have little basis for judging the accuracy and validity of these reports. However, the knowledge of research methods that you gain from this first chapter can make you a refined consumer of research. First consider the value of random sampling.

The Importance of Random Sampling If the *Literary Digest* had been correct, the Republican candidate Alf Landon would have defeated the incumbent president, Franklin D. Roosevelt, in 1936. Roosevelt actually routed Landon in a landslide of 11 million votes. Even so, the *Digest,* a popular magazine of the day, had predicted a Landon victory. How was so great a discrepancy possible?

The *Digest,* you see, had phoned the voters it surveyed. Today telephone sampling is a widely practiced and reasonably legitimate technique. But the *Digest* poll was taken during the Great Depression, when Americans who had telephones were much wealthier than those who did not. Americans at higher income levels are also more likely to vote Republican. No surprise, then, that the overwhelming majority of those sampled said that they would vote for Landon.

The principle involved here is that survey samples must accurately *represent* the population they are intended to reflect.

Truth or Fiction Revisited

You could, in fact, survey 20 million Americans and still not predict accurately the outcome of a presidential election. The

point is that samples must accurately represent the populations from which they are drawn if we are to be able to extend our findings from the sample to the population.

One way to achieve a representative sample is by means of random sampling. In a random sample, each member of a population has an equal chance of being selected to participate. Researchers can also use a stratified sample, which is drawn so that identified subgroups in the population are represented proportionately in the sample. For instance, 12 percent of the American population is black. Thus, a racially stratified sample would be 12 percent black. As a practical matter, a large randomly selected sample will show reasonably accurate stratification. A random sample of 1,500 people will represent the general American population reasonably well. A haphazardly drawn sample of 20 million, however, might not.

The Kinsey studies on sexual behavior did not adequately represent blacks, poor people, the elderly, and other groups. Large-scale magazine surveys of sexual behavior run by *Redbook* (Tavris & Sadd, 1977) and *Cosmopolitan* (Wolfe, 1981) asked readers to fill out and return questionnaires. Although many thousands of readers responded, did they represent the general American population? Probably not. They may have represented only a subgroup of readers of those magazines who were willing to fill out candid questionnaires about their sexual behavior. For each of her three popular reports on sexual behavior and male–female relationships, Shere Hite (1976, 1981, 1987) distributed about 100,000 survey questionnaires, but her returns numbered only 3,000 (1976), 7,000 (1981), and 4,500 (1987). Do the people who returned her questionnaires represent the general population? Do they even represent the people who received them? What do you think?

Recognizing Operational Definitions Our ability to generalize experimental results also relates to the operational definitions of the independent and dependent variables. The *operational definition* of a variable is limited to the methods used to create or measure that variable. For example, sexual arousal may be operationally defined as subjects' self-reports (based on introspection) that they feel sexually aroused. This would also be considered a subjective definition of arousal since it depends on subjects' private feelings. Unfortunately, self-reports can fall prey to the accidental or purposeful sources of inaccuracy noted in this chapter. For this reason, psychologists prefer to use objective measures whenever possible. Many recent studies define sexual arousal in the male as size of erection and in the female as vaginal blood pressure. Both can be measured directly by objective laboratory instruments.

In the Lang study on alcohol and aggression, alcohol was operationally defined as a certain dose of vodka. Other types of drinks and other dosages of vodka might have had different effects. Aggression was operationally defined as selecting a certain amount of electric shock and administering it to another student participating in a psychological experiment. College men might behave differently when they drink in other situations—for example, when they are insulted by a supporter of an opposing football team or are threatened outside a bar. Still, some psychologists argue that subjects in a laboratory may assign a meaning to the laboratory setting and their actions that makes them comparable to the real-life situation (e.g., Berkowitz & Donnerstein, 1982).

Recognizing the Difference between Correlation and Cause and Effect The popular media frequently fail to distinguish between correlational relationships and cause and effect, even when the scientists who carried out the research were careful to do so. Consider some examples.

In 1988 the results of a Swedish cohabitation study were reported in the media. It turned out that Swedes who lived together prior to marriage (that is, who cohabited) were *more* likely to get divorced later than those who did not. On the surface this finding seems to counter the conventional wisdom—moral issues aside—that cohabitation allows people to find out whether they are compatible before marriage and might ultimately lower the prospects of divorce. Actually, the Swedish study neither confirms nor denies any "conventional wisdom." Cohabiters in the United States and Sweden tend to be more liberal or nontraditional than people who wait until the knot is tied to set up housekeeping. Nontraditional people are also more likely to seek the remedy of divorce when conflicts arise. Thus, the Swedish report just provides information about nontraditional people; it offers nothing about the effects of cohabitation per se.

Next, contemplate research reports that have appeared during the past two decades (e.g., Paffenbarger et al., 1978, 1984, 1986) showing that Harvard alumni who burn up to 2,000 calories a week in exercise have fewer heart attacks than couch potatoes. On the surface it may sound like a prescription to buy some sneakers and do some jogging, but again we have a correlational report, not an experiment. Perhaps people who are healthier *to begin with* are also more likely to exercise.

There is an adage that you can't believe everything you read in the newspapers. It often holds true in the area of research reports, not necessarily because journalists are attempting to deceive us, but because they do not understand the fine points of research.

To properly study behavior, psychologists must not only be skilled in the uses and limitations of various kinds of research methods. They must also adhere to ethical guidelines that govern the treatment of human and animal participants in research, as we shall see in the following section.

ETHICS IN PSYCHOLOGICAL RESEARCH AND PRACTICE

Psychologists adhere to a number of **ethical** standards in research and practice. These are basically intended to assure that psychologists do not undertake research methods or treatments that they believe are harmful to subjects or clients (American Psychological Association, 1981). However, some exceptions may be necessary, as we shall see.

Research with Human Subjects

Human subjects must provide **informed consent** before they participate in research programs. Having a general overview of the research and the opportunity to choose not to participate apparently gives subjects a sense of control and decreases the stress of participating (Dill et al., 1982).

Psychologists treat the records of research subjects and clients as being **confidential.** They do not divulge the names of participants in research and in therapy unless participants specifically request that they do so.

Ethical standards tend to limit the types of research that psychologists may conduct. For example, how can we determine whether early separation

Ethical Moral; referring to one's system of deriving standards for determining what is moral.

Informed consent The term used by psychologists to indicate that a person has agreed to participate in research after receiving information about the purposes of the study and the nature of the treatments.

Confidential Secret; not to be disclosed.

from one's mother impairs social development? One research direction is to observe the development of children who have been separated from their mothers from an early age. It is difficult to draw conclusions from such research, however, because the same factors that led to the separation, such as family tragedy or irresponsible parents, instead of the separation itself, may have led to the observed outcomes. Scientifically, it would be more sound to run experiments in which children were purposefully separated from their mothers at an early age and compared with children who were not. Psychologists would not seriously consider such research because of ethical standards. However, experiments in which infants are purposefully separated from mothers have been run with lower animals, as we shall see below.

The Use of Deception

A number of psychological experiments could not be run without deceiving their human subjects. However, the use of deception raises ethical issues. Before we explore these issues, let us first return briefly to the Lang (Lang et al., 1975) study on alcohol and aggression. In that study, the researchers had to (1) misinform subjects about the beverage they had drunk and (2) mislead subjects into believing that they were giving other participants electric shock when they were actually only pressing switches on a dead control board. (Pressing these switches was the operational definition of aggression in the study.) In the Lang study, students who believed they had drunk vodka were more aggressive than students who believed they had not. The actual content of the beverages was immaterial. This study could not have been run without deceiving the subjects. Foiling their expectations or beliefs was crucial to the experiment, and the potential benefits of the research may well outweigh the possible harmful effects of the deceptions. Certainly it seems preferable that subjects only thought they were shocking other people. After all, would we prefer them actually to deliver painful electric shock?

It should be noted, however, that some psychologists are opposed to the use of deception under any circumstances. Diana Baumrind (1985) argues, for example, that deception-based research is unacceptable because it can harm not only research subjects but also the reputation of the profession of psychology and society at large. In a study that supports Baumrind's views, one group of students participated in experiments in which they were deceived. Afterward they regarded psychologists as being less trustworthy than did students who were not deceived (Smith & Richardson, 1983). Baumrind argues that such deception might eventually cause the public to lose trust in expert authorities.

In any event, many research endeavors continue to rely on the use of deception (Adair et al., 1985). The code of ethics of the American Psychological Association requires that research participants who are deceived be **debriefed** afterward to help eliminate any harmful effects, and the incidence of debriefing has increased in recent years (Adair et al., 1985). Sieber (1983) argues that debriefing must be carried out honestly, skillfully, and sympathetically. After the Lang study was over, the subjects were informed of the deceptions and of the rationale for them. Students who had actually drunk alcohol were given coffee and a **breathalyzer** test so that the researchers could be sure they were not leaving the laboratory in an intoxicated state.

Debrief To receive information about a just-completed procedure.

Breathalyzer A device that measures the quantity of alcohol in the body by analyzing the breath.

Truth or Fiction Revisited

It is true that psychologists cannot carry out certain research studies without deceiving participants as to their purposes and

methods. However, subjects are debriefed after such studies are completed.

Psychologists use deception in research only when the research could not be run without it. As with other ethical dilemmas, deception is used when the psychologist believes that its benefits will outweigh its potential harm.

The Ethics of Animal Research. Now and then, psychologists and other scientists harm animals to answer research questions that may yield important benefits for people. Justifying such harm poses a major ethical dilemma.

Research with Animal Subjects

Psychologists and other scientists frequently turn to animal subjects to conduct research that cannot be carried out with humans. For example, experiments on the effects of early separation from the mother have been done with monkeys and other animals. As you will see in Chapter 9, such research has helped psychologists investigate the formation of parent-child bonds of attachment.

Experiments with infant monkeys highlight some of the dilemmas faced by psychologists and other scientists when they contemplate research with people or animals that has or may have harmful effects. Psychologists and biologists who study the workings of the brain have destroyed sections of the brains of laboratory animals to learn how these areas influence behavior. For instance, as you will learn in Chapter 8, a **lesion** in one part of a brain structure will cause a rat to overeat. A lesion elsewhere will cause the rat to go on a crash diet. Psychologists generalize to people from experiments such as these in the hope that we may find solutions to persistent human problems, such as obesity. Supporters of the use of animals in research argue that many of the major advances in medicine and psychology over the past century could not have taken place without laboratory animals (Bales, 1988; Gallup & Suarez, 1985).

Psychologists must still face the ethical dilemma of subjecting animals to harm. By and large, psychologists follow the principle that they should do so only when they believe that the eventual benefits to people of their research justify the harm done to animals (Rollin, 1985). Still, tradition and law suggest that "there is a limit to the amount of pain an animal should endure in the name of science" (Larson, 1982).

Psychologists are human, of course, and capable of making errors. Occasionally human and animal research participants may be exposed to more harm than anticipated. Generally speaking, however, psychologists make every effort to minimize the possible harmful effects of their research.

Lesion An injury that results in impaired behavior or loss of a function.

SUMMARY

1. **What is psychology?** Psychology is the scientific study of behavior and mental processes.

2. **What are the goals of psychology?** Psychology seeks to describe, explain, predict, and control behavior and mental processes. Psychologists do not attempt to control the behavior of other people against their wills. Instead, they help clients modify their behavior for their own benefit.

3. **What is the role of psychological theory?** Behavior and mental processes are explained through psychological theories, which are sets of statements that involve assumptions about behavior. Explanations and predictions are derived from theories. Theories are revised, as needed, to accommodate new observations. If necessary, they are discarded.

4. **What is the difference between pure and applied research?** Basic or pure research has no immediate applications. Applied research seeks solutions to specific problems.

5. **What do clinical and counseling psychologists do?** Clinical psychologists help people who are behaving abnormally adjust to the demands of life. Counseling psychologists work with individuals who have adjustment problems but do not show abnormal behavior.

6. **What do school and educational psychologists do?** School psychologists assist students with problems that interfere with learning, whereas educational psychologists are more concerned with theoretical issues concerning human learning.

7. **What do developmental psychologists do?** Developmental psychologists study the changes that occur throughout the life span.

8. **What do personality and social psychologists do?** Personality psychologists study influences on our thought processes, feelings, and behavior, whereas social psychologists focus on the nature and causes of behavior in social situations.

9. **What do experimental psychologists do?** Experimental psychologists conduct research into basic psychological processes, such as sensation and perception, learning and memory, and motivation and emotion.

10. **What do industrial and organizational psychologists do?** Industrial psychologists focus on the relationships between people and work, whereas organizational psychologists study the behavior of people in organizations.

11. **What contributions did the ancient Greek philosophers make to psychological thought?** The Greek philosopher Aristotle was among the first to argue that human behavior is subject to rules and laws. Socrates proclaimed "Know thyself" and suggested the use of introspection to gain self-knowledge.

12. **Where did psychology begin as a laboratory science?** Wilhelm Wundt established the first psychological laboratory in Leipzig, Germany in 1879.

13. **What is structuralism?** Structuralism is the school of psychology founded by Wundt that used introspection to study the objective and subjective elements of experience.

14. **What is functionalism?** Functionalism is the school of psychology founded by William James that dealt with observable behavior as well as conscious experience and focused on the importance of habit.

15. **What is behaviorism?** Behaviorism is the school of psychology founded by John B. Watson that argues that psychology must limit itself to observable behavior and forgo excursions into subjective consciousness. Behaviorism focused on learning by conditioning, and B. F. Skinner introduced the concept of reinforcement as an explanation of how learning occurs.

16. **What is Gestalt psychology?** Gestalt psychology is the school of psychology founded by Wertheimer, Koffka, and Köhler that focused on perception and argued that psychologists must focus on the wholeness of human experience.

17. **What is psychoanalysis?** Sigmund Freud founded the school of psychoanalysis, which asserts that people are driven by hidden impulses and that they distort reality to protect themselves from anxiety.

18. **What are the major contemporary perspectives in psychology?** They are the biological, cognitive, humanistic, psychoanalytic, and learning-theory perspectives. Biologically oriented psychologists study the links between behavior and biological events, such as brain activity and the release of hormones. Cognitive psychologists study the ways in which we mentally represent the world and process information. Humanistic psychologists stress the importance of subjective experience and assert that people have the freedom to make choices.

19. **What is the scientific method?** The scientific method is a systematic means of advancing knowledge that consists of four steps: formulating a research question, developing a hypothesis, testing the hypothesis, and drawing conclusions.

20. **What is the naturalistic-observation method?** This method observes behavior carefully and unobtrusively where it happens—in the "field."

21. **What is correlational research?** Correlational research reveals relationships between variables, but it does not determine cause and effect. In a positive correlation, variables increase simultaneously. In a negative correlation, one variable increases while the other decreases.

22. **What is the experimental method?** Experiments are used to seek cause and effect—that is, the effects of independent variables on dependent variables. Experimental subjects are given a treatment, while control subjects are not. Blinds and double blinds may be used to control for the effects of the expectations of the subjects and the researchers themselves.

23. **What is the survey method?** With the survey method, psychologists use interviews or questionnaires or examine public records to learn about behavior that cannot be observed directly.

24. **What is the testing method?** Psychologists use psychological tests, like intelligence, aptitude, and personality tests, to measure various traits and characteristics among a population.

25. **What is the case-study method?** Case studies are carefully drawn biographies of the lives of individuals. The case-study approach is also widely used in psychological consultation and clinical practice.

26. **What are the ethical standards of psychologists?** Ethical standards are intended to prevent mistreatment of human and animal subjects. Limits are set on the discomfort that may be imposed on animals. Records of human behavior are kept confidential. Human subjects are required to give informed consent prior to participating in research.

PSYCHOLOGY AND MODERN LIFE

One of the wonderful things about psychology is that it is relevant to so many aspects of contemporary life. The *Psychology and Modern Life* sections provide examples of how this is so.

Psychology and Modern Life sections are usually related to the subject matter in the chapter. However, the first such section—the psychology of studying psychology—is an exception. The psychology of studying psychology might have been more appropriate following Chapters 5 and 6, on Learning and Memory. It seemed to make more sense, however, to place this section "up front" so that you could apply it at the beginning of the term and not a couple of weeks before final examinations. If you review the section after you have read Chapters 5 and 6, the rationales behind the suggestions will be reinforced.

The Psychology of Studying Psychology

When I first went off to college, I had little idea of what to expect. New faces, a new locale, responsibility for doing my own laundry, new courses—it added up to an overwhelming assortment of changes. Perhaps the most stunning change of all was the new-found freedom. Nobody told me what to read or when to study. It was up to me to plan ahead to do my coursework but somehow manage to leave time for socializing and playing bridge.

Another surprise was that it was no longer enough to enroll in a course and sit in class. I learned that I was not a sponge and would not passively soak up the knowledge. Active measures were required to take in the subject matter.

The problems of soaking up knowledge from this and other textbooks are not entirely dissimilar. Psychological theory and research have taught us that an active approach to learning results in better grades than a passive approach. It is better to look ahead and seek the answers to specific questions than to read the subject matter page by page "like a good student." We tend to remember material better when we attend to it and when it is meaningful. Reading in order to answer questions boosts our attention to it and renders it meaningful. It is also helpful not to try to do it all in one sitting, as in cramming before tests. *Learning takes time.*

Plan Ahead Modern college life makes conflicting demands on students' time. Classes, studying, writing papers, extracurricular activities, athletic meets, and the desire to socialize all compete for the precious hours you devote to your coursework. Therefore, it is helpful to begin your active approach to studying by assessing the amount of material you must master during the term and relating it to your rate of learning. How long does it take you to learn the material in a chapter or in a book? How many hours do you spend studying each day? How much material is there? Does it add up right? Will you make it? It may be that you will not be able to determine the answers until you have gotten into the book for a week or two.

Once you have determined the amount of study time you will need, try to space it out fairly evenly. For most of us, spaced or distributed learning is more efficient than massed learning or cramming. So outline a study schedule that will provide nearly equal time periods each weekday. Leave weekends relatively open so that you can have some time for yourself and your friends as well as some extra hours to digest topics or assignments that are not going down so smoothly.

The following suggestions are derived from psychologists Tim Walter and Al Siebert (1987, pp. 47–48, 77). They will help you with scheduling and with tests for all of your courses, not just psychology:

1. Determine where and when the next test will be and what material will be covered.

2. Ask your instructor what will be most important for you to know, and check with students who have already taken the course to determine the sources of test questions—chapters in the text, lecture notes, student study guides, old exams, and so on.

3. Determine the number of chapters to be read between now and the test.

4. Plan to read a specific number of chapters each week and try to "psych out" your instructor by generating possible test questions from the chapters.

5. In generating possible test questions, keep in mind that good questions often start with phrases such as the following:

   Give several examples of . . .
   Which of the following is an example of . . .
   Describe the functions of . . .
   What is most important about . . .
   List the major . . .
   Compare and contrast . . .
   Describe the structure of . . .

Explain how psychologists have determined that . . .

Why do psychologists advise clients to . . .

Identify the parts of . . .

6. Plan specific study periods each week during which you will generate questions from lecture notes, old exams, the student study guide, and so on.
7. Plan for weekly study periods during which you will compose and take practice tests.
8. Take the practice quizzes in the student study guide. Many instructors reinforce use of the study guide by occasionally taking some exam questions directly from them.
9. Keep a diary or log in which you record your progress, including when, where, and how long you study and how well you perform on practice tests. This sort of diary motivates you to perform more consistently and helps point out your weak spots.

Study a Variety of Subjects Each Day Variety is the spice of life: We are more responsive to novel stimulation. Don't study psychology all day Monday, physics all day Tuesday, and literature all day Wednesday. Study each for a little while each day so that you won't feel bored or dulled by too lengthy an immersion in one subject.*

"Accept Your Humanness" Concerning Your Concentration Span If at first you can't push yourself into studying enough each day, start at a more comfortable level and build toward the amount of study time you'll need by adding a few minutes every day. In behavior modification this is called the method of successive approximations. As noted by Walter and Siebert (1987), "accept your humanness." See what your concentration span is like for each subject—how long you can persist in focusing on coursework without your attention slipping away and perhaps lapsing into daydreaming. Plan brief study breaks before you reach your limit. Get up and stretch. Get a sip of water.

Cope with Distractions Find a study place that is comfortable and free from distractions. Environmental stimuli compete for our attention. A quiet place will help you screen out the background "noise." To better understand how distractions work, consider the case of Benita:

Benita is like most students. She has created a comfy nest for herself in her study area. As she closes the door to the den, the wonderful family pictures covering one wall draw her attention. Benita takes several minutes to gaze nostalgically at the photos of herself and Bill at the ocean. The next thing she knows, she's ready to pull out the slides and not bother with studying. Walking to her desk, she spots a pile of magazines she hasn't had a chance to read. There's the television in the corner. Why not turn it on and catch the last half of the special she wanted to watch? "I can read and watch TV at the same time," she thinks to herself. Everything in the room has a pull for Benita. She feels as though magnetic forces are drawing her to every item in the room.

And that's the trouble. Before she knows it, 20 minutes have slipped away. She glances at the clock and suddenly thinks, "Why have I wasted so much time? Okay, I'll get to work. That's the last time I'll be distracted." That's what she thinks (Walter & Siebert, 1987, p. 68).

Avoid Benita's pitfalls by letting your spot for studying (your room, a study lounge, a place in the library) come to mean studying to you. Do nothing but study there—

Where Do You Study? It is useful to find a place that is comfortable and free from distractions. The library or a study lounge is ideal for many students.

*Here, of course, I am referring to those other subjects. Obviously, you could study this book for several hours every day without becoming bored.

no leafing through magazines, no socializing, no snacking. After you have met a goal, such as finishing half of your studying, you may want to reward yourself with a break and do something like people watching in a busier section of the library.

Use Self-Reward Use rewards for meeting daily study goals. Rewards inspire repetition of desired behavior. Don't be a martyr and try to postpone all pleasures till the end of the term. Some students can do this, but it isn't necessary. And, if you have never spent much time in nonstop studying, you may be demanding too much of yourself. In fact, when you meet your daily study goals, you may want to select one or two of the activities from the Pleasant Events Schedule described in the Psychology and Modern Life section of Chapter 12 (pp. 000–000) to reward yourself the following day or on the weekend. Note these examples from Beverly's reward list (Walter & Siebert, 1987, p. 52). Whenever she successfully completed an important task, such as meeting her daily study goal, Beverly would choose from the following:

1. Listen to record
2. Take nap
3. Eat snack
4. Jog
5. Watch "The People's Court"
6. Play video game
7. Watch music video
8. Call boyfriend
9. Ride bike
10. Go to movie
11. Lunch date
12. Read favorite magazine

PQ4R: Preview, Question, Read, Reflect, Recite, and Review Don't question some of your instructors' assignments. Question all of them. By so doing, you can follow the active **PQ4R** study technique originated by educational psychologist Francis P. Robinson (1970). In PQ4R, you phrase questions about your assignments and then you seek to answer them. PQ4R has helped many students raise their grades (Adams et al., 1982; Anderson, 1985; Benecke & Harris, 1972). There are six steps to PQ4R: previewing, questioning, reading, reflecting, reciting, and reviewing.

Preview Skipping through the pages of a "whodunit" to identify the killer is a sure-fire way to destroy the impact of a mystery novel, but previewing can help you learn textbook material. In fact, many textbooks are written with devices that stimulate you to survey the material before reading it. This book has chapter outlines, "Truth-or-Fiction?" sections, major and minor section heads throughout each chapter, and chapter summaries. If drama and suspense are your goals, begin with the outlines and then read the chapters page by page. But if learning the facts is more important, it may be more effective first to examine the chapter outlines, skim the minor heads not covered in the outlines, and read the summaries—before you get to the meat of the chapters.

Question Generating questions about textbook material has been shown to promote retention (Doctorow et al., 1978; Hamilton, 1985). Phrase questions for each head in the chapter. Write them down in a notebook. Some questions can also be based on material within sections. For courses in which the textbooks do not have helpful major and minor heads, get into the material page by page, and phrase questions as you proceed. You will develop questioning skills with practice, and your questions will help you perceive the underlying structure of each chapter. The following questions are recastings of some of the major and minor heads in Chapter 11.

A. What is the immune system?
- **B.** What are the functions of the immune system?
- **B.** What are the effects of stress on the immune system?

A. What are the relationships between psychological factors and illness?
- **B.** How are psychological factors related to headaches?
  - **C.** What are muscle-tension headaches?
  - **C.** What are migraine headaches?
- **B.** How are psychological factors related to hypertension?

The questions you would have phrased from these heads might have been different, but they might have been as useful as these, or more useful. As you study, you will learn what works for you.

Read Once you have phrased questions, read the subject matter with the purpose of answering them. This sense of purpose will help you focus on the essential points of the material. As you answer each question, write down a few key words in your notebook that will telegraph that answer to you when you recite and review later on. Many students find it helpful to keep two columns in their notebooks: questions in the column to the left, and key words (to the answer) in the column to the right.

If the material you are reading happens to be fine literature, you may wish to read it once just to appreciate its poetic features. When you reread it, however, use PQ4R in order to tease out the essential information it contains.

Reflect As you are reading, think of examples or create mental images of the subject matter. Trying to relate the material to things you already know about makes it meaningful and easier to remember.

Recite Once you have read a section and jotted down the key words to the answer, recite each answer aloud if possible. (Doing so may depend on where you are, who's around, and your level of concern over how you think they'll react to you.) Reciting answers aloud helps us to remember them and provides an immediate check on the accuracy of the key words.

Review Review the material according to a reasonably regular schedule, such as once weekly. Relearning material regularly is much easier than initial learning. Moreover, by reviewing material regularly, we foster retention.

Cover the answer column and read the questions as though they were a quiz. Recite your answers and then check them against the key response words. Reread the subject matter when you forget an answer. Forgetting too many answers may mean that you haven't phrased the questions efficiently for your own use or that you haven't reviewed the material frequently enough. (Maybe you didn't learn it well enough in the first place.) By taking a more active approach to studying, you may find that you are earning higher grades and gaining more pleasure from the learning process.

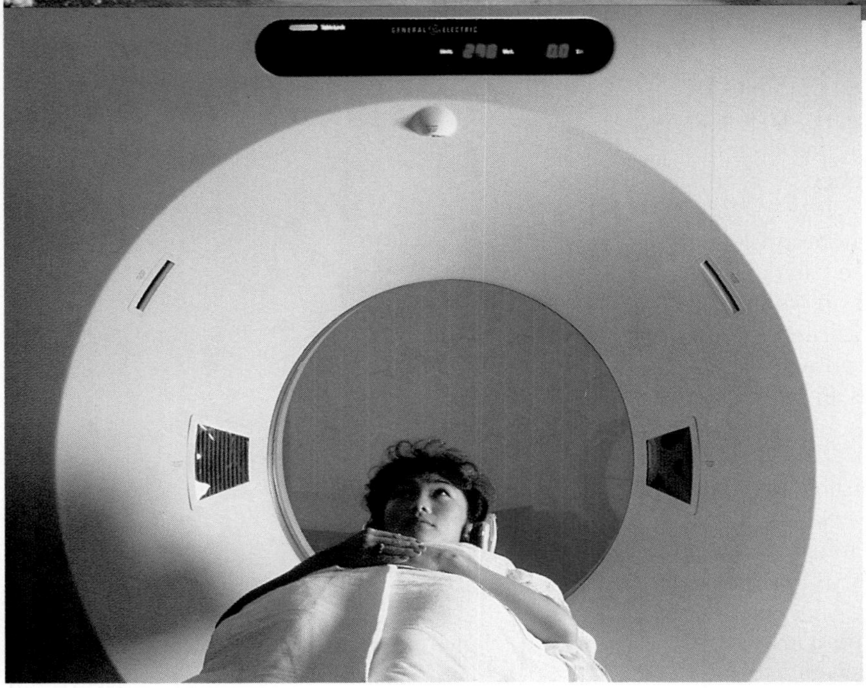

Outline

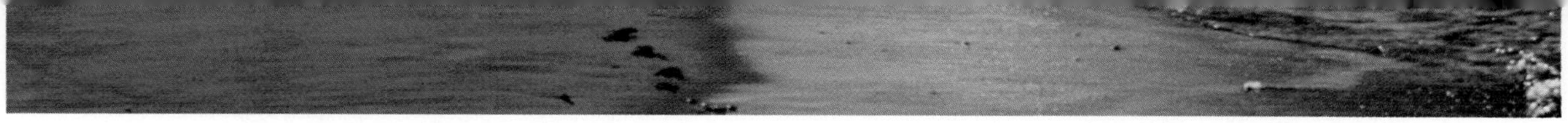

2 Biology and Behavior

Truth or Fiction?

- □ Some cells in your body stretch all the way down your back to your big toe.
- □ Messages travel in the brain by means of electricity.
- □ Our bodies produce natural pain killers that are more powerful than morphine.
- □ The human brain is larger than that of any other animal.
- □ Many men who are paralyzed below the waist can still achieve erection and ejaculate.
- □ Fear can give you indigestion.
- □ If a surgeon were to stimulate a certain part of your brain electrically, you might swear in court that someone had stroked your leg.
- □ Rats will learn to do things that result in a "reward" of a burst of electricity in the brain.
- □ With so many billions of people in the world, you are bound to have a double somewhere, even if you are not an identical twin.
- □ A child can have blue eyes even when both parents have brown eyes.

According to the big-bang theory, our universe began with an enormous explosion that sent countless particles hurtling into every corner of space. For billions of years, these particles have been congregating into immense gas clouds. Galaxies and solar systems have been condensing from the clouds, sparkling for some eons, then winking out. Human beings have only recently evolved on an unremarkable rock circling an average star in a typical spiral-shaped galaxy.

Since the beginning of time, the universe has been in flux. Change has brought life and death and countless challenges. Some creatures have adapted successfully to these challenges and continued to evolve. Others have not met the challenges and have become extinct, falling back into the distant mists of time. Some have left fossil records. Others have disappeared without a trace.

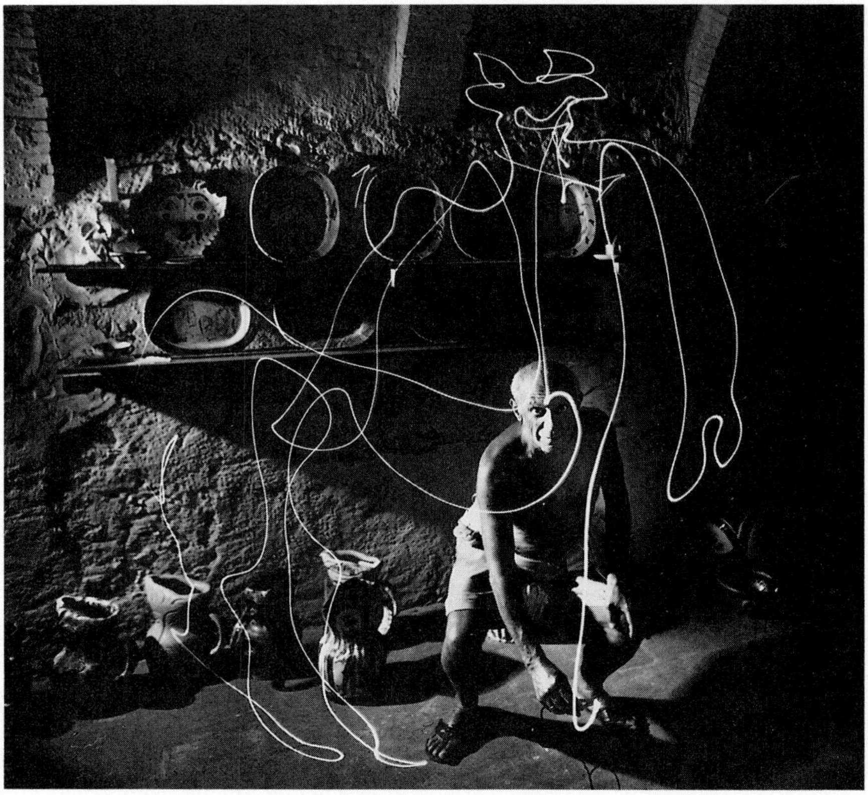

Pablo Picasso at Work. The great artist's nervous system was composed of neurons like those of other people. Physiological psychologists are investigating just how our mental processes and behavior are linked to the functioning of the nervous system and other physiological processes.

At first, human survival on planet Earth required a greater struggle than it does today. We fought predators like the leopard. We foraged across parched lands for food. We might have warred with creatures very much like ourselves—creatures who have since become extinct. We prevailed. The human species has survived and continues to pass on its unique characteristics from generation to generation through genetic material whose complex chemical codes are only now being cracked.

Yet what is passed on from generation to generation? The answer is biological, or **physiological,** structures. There is no evidence that we can inherit thoughts or ideas or images or plans. We do inherit physiological structures, however, that serve as the material base for our observable behaviors, our emotions, and our cognitions (our thoughts, images, and plans).

Just how our mental processes and observable behaviors are linked to physiological structures is the fascinating question being answered piece by piece by a group of psychologists referred to as either **physiological psychologists** or **biological psychologists.** Through systematic probing of the brain and other structures, biological psychologists in recent years seem to be on the threshold of exciting discoveries. Biological psychologists today are unlocking the mysteries of:

1. *Neurons.* Neurons are the building blocks of the nervous system. There are billions of neurons in the body, all transmitting messages of one kind or another.
2. *The nervous system.* Neurons combine to form the various structures of the nervous system. The nervous system has subdivisions that are responsible for muscle movement, perception, automatic functions such as breathing and the secretion of hormones, and psychological phenomena such as thoughts and feelings.

Physiological Having to do with the biological functions and vital processes of organisms.

Physiological psychologists Same as biological psychologists.

Biological psychologists Psychologists who study the relationships between life processes and behavior.

Neuron A nerve cell.

Neurotransmitters Chemical substances involved in the transmission of neural impulses from one neuron to another.

Glial cells Cells that nourish and insulate neurons, direct their growth, and remove waste products from the nervous system.

Soma A cell body.

3. *The cerebral cortex.* The cerebral cortex is the large, wrinkled mass inside your head that you think of as your brain. Actually, it is only one part of the brain—the part that is the most characteristically human.
4. *The endocrine system.* Through secretion of hormones, the endocrine system controls functions ranging from growth in children to production of milk in nursing women.
5. *Heredity.* Within every cell of your body there are about 100,000 genes. These complex chemical substances determine just what type of creature you are, from the color of your hair to your body temperature to the fact that you have arms and legs rather than wings or fins.

NEURONS

Let us begin our journey in a fabulous forest of nerve cells, or **neurons,** that can be visualized as having branches, trunks, and roots, something like trees. As in other forests, many nerve cells lie alongside one another, like a thicket of trees. Neurons can also lie end to end, however, with their "roots" intertwined with the "branches" of neurons that lie below. Trees receive water and nutrients from the soil. Neurons receive "messages" from a number of sources, such as other neurons, pressure on the skin, and light, and they can pass these messages along.

Neurons communicate by means of chemical substances called **neurotransmitters.** Neurons release neurotransmitters that are taken up by other neurons, muscles, and glands. Neurotransmitters cause chemical changes in the receiving neuron so that the message can travel along its "trunk," be translated back into neurotransmitters in its "branches," and then travel through the small spaces between neurons to be received by the "roots" of yet other neurons.

Each neuron transmits and coordinates messages in the form of neural impulses. We are born with about 12 billion neurons, most of which are found in the brain. This is all that we shall ever have. The nervous system also contains billions of **glial cells,** which outnumber the neurons by about a ratio of ten to one (Arms & Camp, 1987). Glial cells nourish and insulate neurons, direct their growth, and remove waste products from the nervous system. But neurons occupy center stage in the nervous system. The messages transmitted by neurons somehow account for phenomena ranging from perception of an itch from a mosquito bite and the coordination of a skier's vision and muscles to the composition of a concerto and the solution of an algebraic equation.

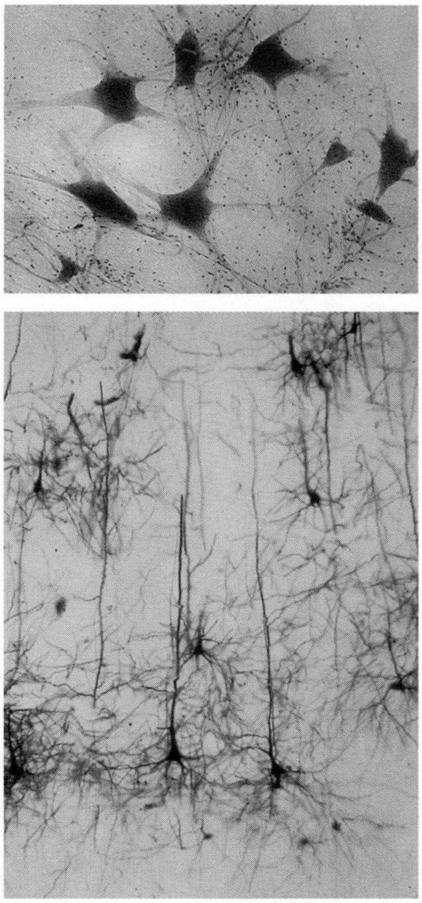

Figure 2.1
Neurons. Neurons take different forms in different parts of the nervous system. The top photo shows spinal neurons and the bottom shows the short neurons of the cerebral cortex.

The Makeup of Neurons

Neurons vary according to their functions and their location (see Figure 2.1). Some in the brain are only a fraction of an inch in length, whereas others in the legs are several feet long.

Truth or Fiction Revisited

It is true that some cells in your body—neurons—stretch all the way down your back to your big toe.

Every neuron is a single nerve cell with a number of common features: a cell body, or **soma,** dendrites, and an axon (see Figure 2.2). The cell body

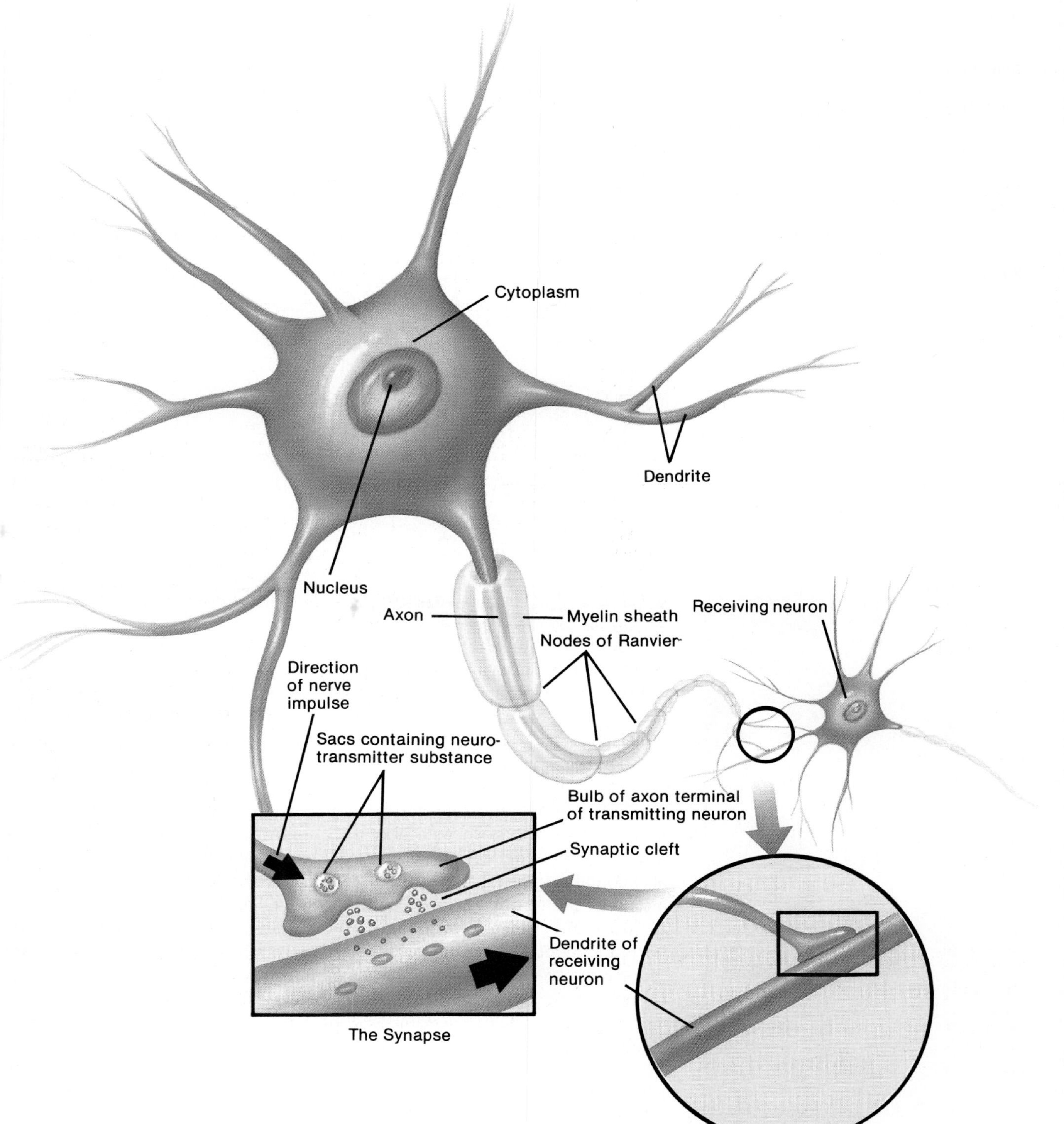

Figure 2.2
The Anatomy of a Neuron.

"Messages" enter neurons through dendrites, are transmitted along the trunklike axon, and then are sent through axon terminals to muscles, glands, and other neurons. A neuron relays its message to another neuron across a junction called a synapse, which consists of an axon terminal from the transmitting neuron, a dendrite of the receiving neuron, and a small gap between the neurons referred to as the synaptic cleft. Axon terminals contain sacs of chemicals called neurotransmitters. Neurotransmitters are released by the transmitting neuron into the synaptic cleft, and many of them are taken up by receptor sites on the dendrites of the receiving neuron. Some neurotransmitters (called "excitatory") influence receiving neurons in the direction of firing; others (called "inhibitory") influence them in the direction of *not* firing. To date, a few dozen possible neurotransmitters have been identified.

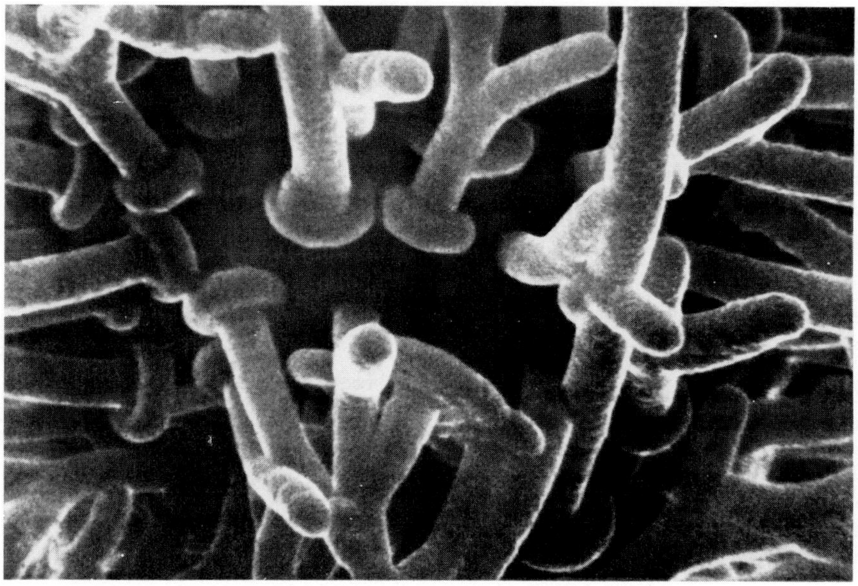

Figure 2.3
Axon Terminals. A much-enlarged photograph of axon terminals.

is enclosed by the cell membrane and contains the nucleus of the cell. The cell body uses oxygen and nutrients to generate energy to carry out the work of the cell. Anywhere from a few to several hundred short fibers, or **dendrites,** extend rootlike from the cell body to receive incoming messages from up to 1,000 adjoining neurons. Each neuron has one **axon** that extends trunklike from the cell body. Axons are very thin, but they can extend for several feet if they are carrying messages from the toes to the spinal cord. Like tree trunks, axons too may branch and extend in different directions. Axons end in smaller branching structures called **terminals** (Figure 2.3). At the tips of the axon terminals are swellings called **knobs.** Neurons carry messages in one direction only, from the dendrites or cell body through the axon to the axon terminals. The messages are then transmitted from the axon terminals to other neurons.

As a child matures, the axons of neurons grow in length and the dendrites and axon terminals proliferate, creating vast interconnected networks for the transmission of complex messages. The number of glial cells also increases as the nervous system develops, contributing to the dense appearance of the structures of the nervous system.

Dendrites Rootlike structures attached to the soma of a neuron that receive impulses from other neurons.

Axon A long, thin part of a neuron that transmits impulses to other neurons from branching structures called terminals.

Terminals Small structures at the tips of axons.

Knobs Swellings at the ends of terminals. Also referred to as *bulbs* or *buttons.*

Myelin sheath A fatty substance that encases and insulates axons, facilitating transmission of neural impulses.

Schwann cell A type of glial cell that wraps around the axons of neurons to form myelin.

Node of Ranvier A noninsulated segment of a myelinated axon.

Myelin Many neurons are wrapped tightly with white, fatty **myelin sheaths.** Myelin actually consists of the membranes of the type of glial cell called the **Schwann cell.** The membranes of Schwann cells expand and wrap repeatedly around the axons of neurons. The high fat content of the Schwann cells insulates the axon from electrically charged atoms, or ions, found in the fluids that encase the nervous system. In this way, leakage of the electric current being carried along the axon is minimized, and messages are conducted more efficiently. Myelin does not uniformly coat the surface of an axon. It is missing at points called **nodes of Ranvier,** where the axon is exposed. Because of the insulation provided by myelin, neural messages, or impulses, travel rapidly from node to node.

Afferent and Efferent Neurons If someone steps on your big toe, the sensation is registered by receptors or sensory neurons near the surface of your skin. Then it is transmitted to the spinal cord and brain through **affer-**

Afferent neurons Neurons that transmit messages from sensory receptors to the spinal cord and brain. Also called sensory neurons.

Efferent neurons Neurons that transmit messages from the brain or spinal cord to muscles and glands. Also called motor neurons.

Mnemonic Aiding memory, usually by linking chunks of new information to well-known schemes.

Neural impulse The electrochemical discharge of a nerve cell, or neuron.

Polarize To ready a neuron for firing by creating an internal negative charge in relation to the body fluid outside the cell membrane.

Resting potential The electrical potential across the neural membrane when it is not responding to other neurons.

Permeability The degree to which a membrane allows a substance to pass through it.

Depolarize To reduce the resting potential of a cell membrane from about −70 millivolts toward zero.

ent neurons, which are perhaps two to three feet long. In the brain, subsequent messages might be buffeted about by associative neurons that are only a few thousandths of an inch long. You experience the pain through this process and perhaps entertain some rather nasty thoughts about the perpetrator, who is now apologizing and begging for understanding. Long before you arrive at any logical conclusions, however, motor neurons, or **efferent neurons,** will have sent messages back to your toe and foot so that you have withdrawn them and begun an impressive hopping routine. Other efferent neurons may have stimulated glands, so that by now your heart is beating more rapidly, you are sweating, and the hairs on the backs of your arms may have even become erect! Being a sport, you might say, "Oh, it's nothing." But considering all the neurons involved, it really was something, wasn't it?

In case you think that afferent and efferent neurons will be hard to distinguish because they sound pretty much the SAME to you, simply remember that they are the "SAME." That is, Sensory = Afferent, and Motor = Efferent. But don't tell your professor I let you in on this **mnemonic** device.

The Neural Impulse

In the late 1700s, Italian physiologist Luigi Galvani engaged in a shocking experiment in a rainstorm. While his neighbors had the sense to remain indoors, Galvani and his wife were out on the porch connecting lightning rods to the heads of dissected frogs whose legs were connected by wire to a well of water. When lightning blazed above, the frogs' muscles contracted repeatedly and violently. This is not a recommended way to prepare frogs' legs; Galvani was demonstrating that the messages (**neural impulses**) that travel along neurons are electrochemical in nature.

Neural impulses travel somewhere between 2 (in nonmyelinated neurons) and 225 miles an hour (in myelinated neurons). This speed is not impressive when compared with that of an electric current in a toaster oven or a lamp, which can travel at the speed of light—over 186,000 miles per second. Distances in the body are short, however, and a message will travel from a toe to the brain in perhaps one-fiftieth of a second.

An Electrochemical Process The process by which neural impulses travel is electrochemical. Chemical changes take place within neurons that cause an electric charge to be transmitted along their lengths. In a resting state, when a neuron is not being stimulated by its neighbors, there are relatively greater numbers of positively charged sodium ions ($Na+$) and negatively charged chloride ($Cl-$) ions in the body fluid outside the neuron than in the fluid within the neuron. Positively charged potassium ($K+$) ions are more plentiful inside, but there are many other negative ions inside that are not balanced by negative ions on the outside, lending the inside an overall negative charge in relation to the outside. The difference in electrical charge **polarizes** the neuron with a negative **resting potential** of about −70 millivolts in relation to the body fluid outside the cell membrane.

When an area on the surface of the resting neuron is adequately stimulated by other neurons, the cell membrane in the area changes its **permeability** to allow sodium ions to enter. As a consequence, the area of entry becomes positively charged, or **depolarized** with respect to the outside (Figure 2.4). The permeability of the cell membrane changes again, allowing no more sodium ions to enter.

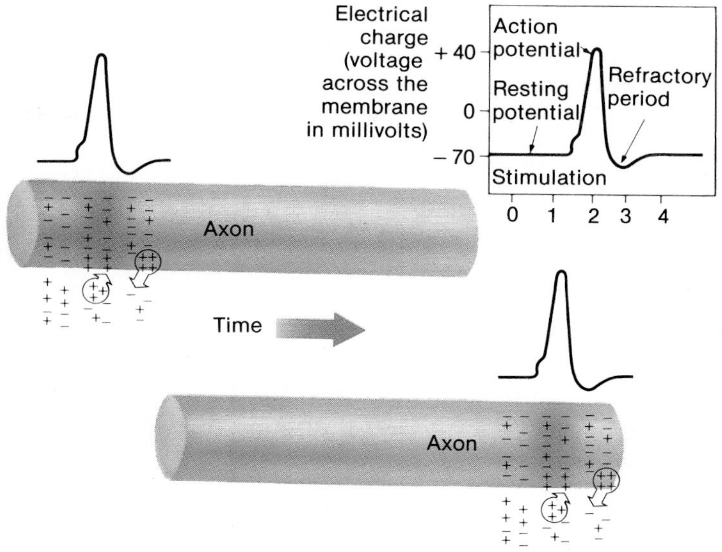

Figure 2.4
The Neural Impulse. When a section of a neuron is stimulated by other neurons, the cell membrane becomes permeable to sodium ions so that an action potential of about +40 millivolts is induced. This action potential is transmitted along the axon. Eventually the neuron fires (or fails to fire) according to the all-or-none principle.

The inside of the cell at the disturbed area has an **action potential** of 110 millivolts. This action potential, added to the −70 millivolts that characterize the resting potential, brings the membrane voltage to a positive charge of +40 millivolts. This inner change causes the next section of the cell to become permeable to sodium ions. At the same time, potassium ions are being pumped out of the area of the cell that was previously affected, which then returns to its resting potential. In this way the neural impulse is transmitted continuously along an axon that is not myelinated. Because the impulse is created anew as it progresses, its strength does not change. As noted earlier, neural impulses are conducted more rapidly along myelinated axons because they jump from node to node.

Truth or Fiction Revisited

It is true that messages travel in the brain by means of electricity. They also travel from neurons to other neurons, muscles, or glands by means of neurotransmitters.

The conduction of the neural impulse along the length of a neuron is what is meant by "firing." Some neurons fire in less than 1/1,000th of a second. In firing, neurons "attempt" to transmit the message to other neurons, muscles, or glands. However, other neurons will not fire unless the incoming messages combine to reach an adequate **threshold.** A weak message may cause a temporary shift in electrical charge at some point along a neuron's cell membrane, but this charge will dissipate if the neuron is not stimulated to threshold.

A neuron may transmit several hundred such messages in a second. Yet, in accord with the **all-or-none principle,** each time a neuron fires it transmits an impulse of the same strength. Neurons fire more frequently when they have been stimulated by larger numbers of other neurons; stronger stimuli result in firing with greater frequency.

For a thousandth of a second or so after firing, a neuron enters an **absolute refractory period,** during which it will not fire in response to stimulation from other neurons. Then, for another few thousandths of a second, the neuron is said to be in a **relative refractory period,** during which it will fire but only in response to messages that are stronger than

Action potential The electrical impulse that provides the basis for the conduction of a neural impulse along an axon of a neuron.

Threshold The point at which a stimulus is just strong enough to produce a response.

All-or-none principle The fact that a neuron fires an impulse of the same strength whenever its action potential is triggered.

Absolute refractory period A phase following firing during which a neuron's action potential cannot be triggered.

Relative refractory period A phase following the absolute refractory period during which a neuron will fire in response to stronger-than-usual messages.

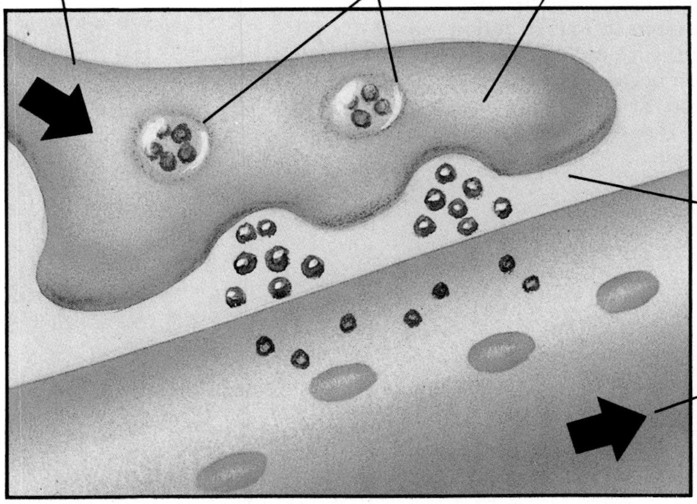

Figure 2.5
The Synapse. Neurons relay their messages to other neurons across junctions called synapses. A synapse consists of an axon terminal from the transmitting neuron, a dendrite of the receiving neuron, and a small gap between the two which is referred to as the synaptic cleft. Molecules of neurotransmitters are released into the synaptic cleft from vesicles within the axon terminal. Many molecules are taken up by receptor sites on the dendrite. Others are broken down or taken up again by the transmitting neuron.

usual. The refractory period is a time of recovery, during which sodium is prevented from passing through the neuronal membrane. When we realize that such periods of recovery might take place hundreds of times per second, it seems a rapid recovery and a short rest indeed.

The Synapse

A neuron relays its message to another neuron across a junction called a **synapse.** A synapse consists of a "branch," or axon terminal from the transmitting neuron; a "root," or dendrite of a receiving neuron; and a small fluid-filled gap between the neurons that is called the synaptic cleft (see Figure 2.5). Although the neural impulse is electrical, it does not just jump the synaptic cleft like a spark. Instead, when a nerve impulse reaches a synapse, axon terminals release chemicals into the synaptic cleft like myriad ships being cast off into the sea.

Neurotransmitters

In the axon terminals are sacs, or synaptic vesicles, that contain chemicals called neurotransmitters. When a neural impulse reaches the axon terminal, the vesicles release varying amounts of these neurotransmitters into the synaptic cleft. From there they influence the receiving neuron. If adequate quantities of neurotransmitters are released by transmitting cells, the receiving neuron will also fire.

As of today, some three dozen different possible neurotransmitters have been identified, and it has been estimated that there may be hundreds of them (Snyder, 1980). Each neurotransmitter has its own chemical structure, and each can fit into a specifically tailored harbor, or **receptor site,** on the dendrite of the receiving neuron. The analogy of a key fitting into a lock has also been used. Once released, not all molecules of a neurotransmitter find their ways into receptor sites of other neurons. "Loose" neurotransmitters

Synapse A junction between the axon terminals of one neuron and the dendrites or soma of another neuron.

Receptor site A location on a dendrite of a receiving neuron tailored to receive a neurotransmitter.

are usually either broken down or reabsorbed by the axon terminal (a process called re-uptake).

Some neurotransmitters act to excite other neurons—that is, to influence receiving neurons in the direction of firing. The synapses between axon terminals with excitatory neurotransmitters and receiving neurons are called **excitatory synapses.** Other neurotransmitters inhibit receiving neurons; that is, they influence them in the direction of not firing. The synapses between axon terminals with inhibitory neurotransmitters and receiving neurons are called **inhibitory synapses.** Neurons may be influenced by neurotransmitters that have been released by up to 1,000 other neurons. The additive stimulation received from all these cells determines whether a particular neuron will also fire and which neurotransmitters will be released in the process.

Neurotransmitters are involved in processes ranging from muscle contraction to emotional response. Excesses or deficiencies of neurotransmitters have been linked to diseases and abnormal behavior.

Acetylcholine **Acetylcholine** (ACh) is a neurotransmitter that controls muscle contractions. ACh is excitatory at synapses between nerves and muscles that involve voluntary movement but inhibitory at the heart and some other locations.

The effects of curare highlight the functioning of ACh. Curare is a poison extracted from plants by South American Indians and used in hunting. If an arrow tipped with curare pierces the skin and the poison enters the body, it prevents ACh from lodging within receptor sites in neurons, resulting in paralysis. The victim is prevented from contracting the muscles used in breathing and dies from suffocation. Botulism, a disease that stems from food poisoning, prevents the release of ACh and has the same effect as curare.

ACh is also normally prevalent in a part of the brain called the **hippocampus,** a structure involved in the formation of memories. When the ACh available to the brain decreases, memory formation is impaired. **Alzheimer's disease** is associated with progressive deterioration of neurons that produce ACh. It is characterized by gradual impairment of memory and other cognitive functions, such as the capacity for abstract thought.

Dopamine **Dopamine** is primarily an inhibitory neurotransmitter. Dopamine is involved in voluntary movements, learning and memory, and emotional arousal. Deficiencies of dopamine are linked to Parkinson's disease, a disorder in which patients progressively lose control over their muscles. They develop muscle tremors and jerky, uncoordinated movements. The drug L-dopa, a substance that the brain converts to dopamine, helps slow the progress of Parkinson's disease.

The mental disorder schizophrenia (see Chapter 12) has also been linked to dopamine. Schizophrenic individuals may have more receptor sites for dopamine in an area of the brain that is involved in emotional responding. For this reason, they may *overutilize* the dopamine that is available in the brain, which leads to hallucinations and disturbances of thought and emotion. The phenothiazines, a group of drugs used in the treatment of schizophrenia, are thought to block the action of dopamine by locking some dopamine out of these receptor sites (Snyder, 1984).

Norepinephrine **Norepinephrine** is produced largely by neurons in the brain stem. Norepinephrine acts both as a neurotransmitter and a hormone. It speeds up the heartbeat and other body processes and is involved in general arousal, learning and memory, and eating. Excesses and deficiencies of norepinephrine have been linked to mood disorders (see Chapter 12).

Excitatory synapse A synapse that influences receiving neurons in the direction of firing by increasing depolarization of their cell membranes.

Inhibitory synapse A synapse that influences receiving neurons in the direction of not firing by encouraging changes in their membrane permeability in the direction of the resting potential.

Acetylcholine A neurotransmitter that controls muscle contractions. Abbreviated *ACh.*

Hippocampus A part of the *limbic system* of the brain that is involved in memory formation.

Alzheimer's disease A progressive disorder characterized by loss of memory and other cognitive functions.

Dopamine A neurotransmitter that is involved in Parkinson's disease and that appears to play a role in schizophrenia.

Norepinephrine A neurotransmitter whose action is similar to that of the hormone *epinephrine,* and that may play a role in depression.

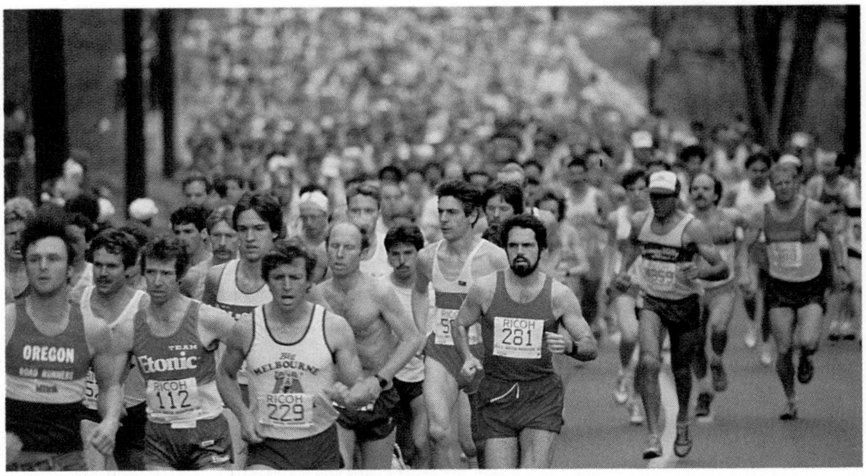

A View of the Boston Marathon. Why have thousands of people taken up long-distance running? Running, of course, promotes cardiovascular conditioning, firms the muscles, and helps us to control weight. But long-distance runners also report experiencing a "runner's high," which may be connected with the release of endorphins. Endorphins are naturally occurring substances similar in function to the narcotic morphine.

The stimulants cocaine and amphetamines ("speed") facilitate the release of dopamine and norepinephrine and also impede their reabsorption by the releasing synaptic vesicles—that is, their re-uptake. As a result, there are excesses of these neurotransmitters in the nervous system, vastly increasing the firing of neurons and leading to a persistent state of high arousal.

Serotonin Also primarily an inhibitory transmitter, **serotonin** is involved in emotional arousal and sleep. Deficiencies of serotonin have been linked to anxiety, mood disorders, and insomnia. The drug LSD (see Chapter 9) decreases the action of serotonin and may also influence the utilization of dopamine. With LSD, "two no's make a yes." By inhibiting an inhibitor, brain activity increases, in this case frequently leading to hallucinations.

Neuropeptides

Neuropeptides are chains of amino acids that act as neurotransmitters (Krieger, 1983). Endorphins and enkephalins are important neuropeptides.

Endorphins The word *endorphin* is the contraction of *endogenous morphine. Endogenous* means "developing from within." **Endorphins,** then, are similar to the narcotic morphine in their functions and effects (Bolles & Faneslow, 1982) and are produced by our own bodies. They occur naturally in the brain and in the bloodstream.

Endorphins are inhibitory neurotransmitters. They lock into receptor sites for chemicals that transmit pain messages to the brain. Once the endorphin "key" is in the "lock," pain-causing chemicals cannot transmit their (frequently unwelcome) messages. There are a number of endorphins. Beta-endorphin has been found to be many times more powerful than morphine, molecule for molecule, whether injected into the bloodstream or directly into the brain (Snyder, 1977).

Truth or Fiction Revisited

It is true that our bodies produce natural pain killers that are more powerful than morphine. They are called endorphins.

In addition to relieving pain, endorphins play a role in regulating respiration, hunger, memory, sexual behavior, blood pressure, mood, and body temper-

---

Serotonin A neurotransmitter, deficiencies of which have been linked to affective disorders, anxiety, and insomnia.

Neuropeptides A group of compounds formed from amino acids (peptides) that function as neurotransmitters.

Endorphins Neurotransmitters that are composed of amino acids and that are functionally similar to morphine.

ature. Endorphins may also increase our sense of self-competence and may be connected with the "runner's high" reported by many long-distance runners.

Enkephalins **Enkephalins** are one specific type of endorphins and, as such, also occur naturally in the brain. The word *enkephalin* derives from roots meaning "in" and the Greek *kephale,* meaning "head." Enkephalins share the pain-relieving effects of endorphins but may be somewhat weaker and shorter-acting.

There you have it—a fabulous forest of neurons in which billions upon billions of vesicles are pouring neurotransmitters into synaptic clefts at any given time: when you are involved in strenuous activity, now as you are reading this page, even as you are passively watching television. This microscopic picture is repeated several hundred times every second. The combined activity of all these neurotransmitters determines which messages will be transmitted and which will not. Your experience of sensations, your thoughts, and your psychological sense of control over your body are very different from the electrochemical processes we have described. Yet somehow, these many electrochemical events are responsible for your psychological sense of yourself and of the world.

THE NERVOUS SYSTEM

There was a time during my childhood when it seemed to me that it was not a very good thing to have a "nervous" system. For instance, if your system were not so nervous, you might be less likely to jump at strange noises.

At some point I learned that a nervous system was not a system that was nervous but a system of nerves that were involved in thought processes, heartbeat, visual-motor coordination, and so on. I also learned that the human nervous system was more complex than that of any other animal and that our brains were larger than those of any other animal. Now this last piece of business is not exactly true. A human brain weighs about three pounds, but elephant and whale brains may be four times as heavy. Still, our brains compose a greater part of our body weight than do those of elephants or whales. Our brains weigh about 1/60th of our body weight. Elephant brains weigh about 1/1,000th of their total weight and whale brains a paltry 1/10,000th of their weight. So, if we wish, we can still find figures to make us proud.

Truth or Fiction Revisited

The human brain is *not* larger than that of any other animal. Elephants and whales have larger brains.

The brain is only one part of the nervous system. A **nerve** is a bundle of axons. The cell bodies of these neurons are not considered to be part of the nerve. The cell bodies are gathered into clumps called **nuclei** in the brain and spinal cord and **ganglia** elsewhere.

The nervous system consists of the brain, the spinal cord, and nerves linking them to receptors in the sensory organs and effectors in the muscles and glands. As shown in Figure 2.6, the brain and spinal cord make up what we refer to as the **central nervous system.** The sensory (afferent) neurons, which receive and transmit messages to the brain and spinal cord, and the motor (efferent) neurons, which transmit messages from the brain or spinal cord to the muscles and glands, make up the **peripheral nervous system.**

Enkephalins Types of endorphins that are weaker and shorter-acting than beta-endorphin.

Nerve A bundle of axons from many neurons.

Nuclei Plural of *nucleus.* A group of neural cell bodies found in the brain or spinal cord.

Ganglia Plural of *ganglion.* A group of neural cell bodies found elsewhere in the body other than the brain or spinal cord.

Central nervous system The brain and spinal cord.

Peripheral nervous system The part of the nervous system consisting of the somatic nervous system and the autonomic nervous system.

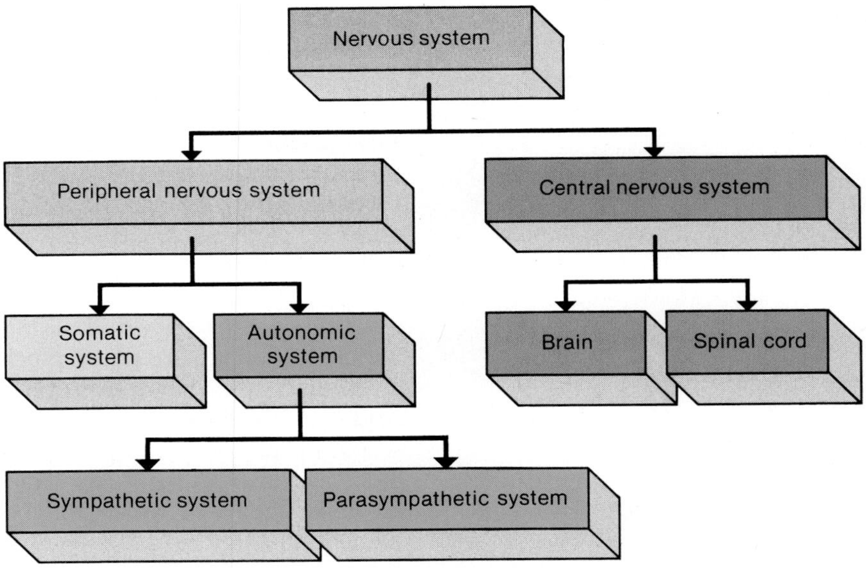

Figure 2.6
The Divisions of the Nervous System. The nervous system contains two main divisions: the central nervous system and the peripheral nervous system. The central nervous system consists of the brain and spinal cord. The peripheral nervous system contains the somatic and autonomic systems. In turn, the autonomic nervous system is composed of sympathetic and parasympathetic divisions.

There is no deep, complex reason for labeling the two major divisions of the nervous system in this way. It is just geography. The peripheral nervous system extends more into the edges, or periphery, of the body.

Let us now examine the nature and functions of the central and peripheral nervous systems.

The Central Nervous System

The central nervous system consists of the spinal cord and the brain.

The Spinal Cord The **spinal cord** is a column of nerves about as thick as a thumb. It transmits messages from receptors to the brain and from the brain to muscles and glands throughout the body (Figure 2.7). The spinal cord is also capable of some "local government" of responses to external stimulation through **spinal reflexes.** A spinal reflex is an unlearned response to a stimulus that may involve only two neurons—a sensory (afferent) neuron and a motor (efferent) neuron (Figure 2.8). In some reflexes, a third neuron, called an **interneuron,** transmits the neural impulse from the sensory neuron through the spinal cord to the motor neuron.

The spinal cord (and the brain) consist of gray matter and white matter. The **gray matter** is composed of nonmyelinated neurons. Some of these nonmyelinated neurons are involved in spinal reflexes, whereas others send axons to the brain. The **white matter** is composed of bundles of longer, myelinated (and thus whitish) axons that carry messages back and forth to and from the brain. As you can see in Figure 2.8, a cross section of the spinal cord shows the gray matter, which includes cell bodies, to be distributed in something of a butterfly-shaped pattern.*

We engage in many reflexes. We blink in response to a puff of air. We swallow when food accumulates in the mouth. A physician may tap the leg below the knee to see if we will show the knee-jerk reflex, a sign that the

*If you turn to the Rorschach inkblot shown on page 423, you can see why many biology and nursing students report that it reminds them of the spinal cord.

Spinal cord A column of nerves within the spine that transmits messages from sensory receptors to the brain and from the brain to muscles and glands throughout the body.

Spinal reflex A simple unlearned response to a stimulus that may involve only two neurons.

Interneuron A neuron that transmits a neural impulse from a sensory neuron to a motor neuron.

Gray matter In the spinal cord, the grayish neurons and neural segments that are involved in spinal reflexes.

White matter In the spinal cord, axon bundles that carry messages back and forth from and to the brain.

Figure 2.7
The Location of Parts of the Nervous System. Note that the spinal cord is protected by a column of bones called vertebrae. The brain is protected by the skull.

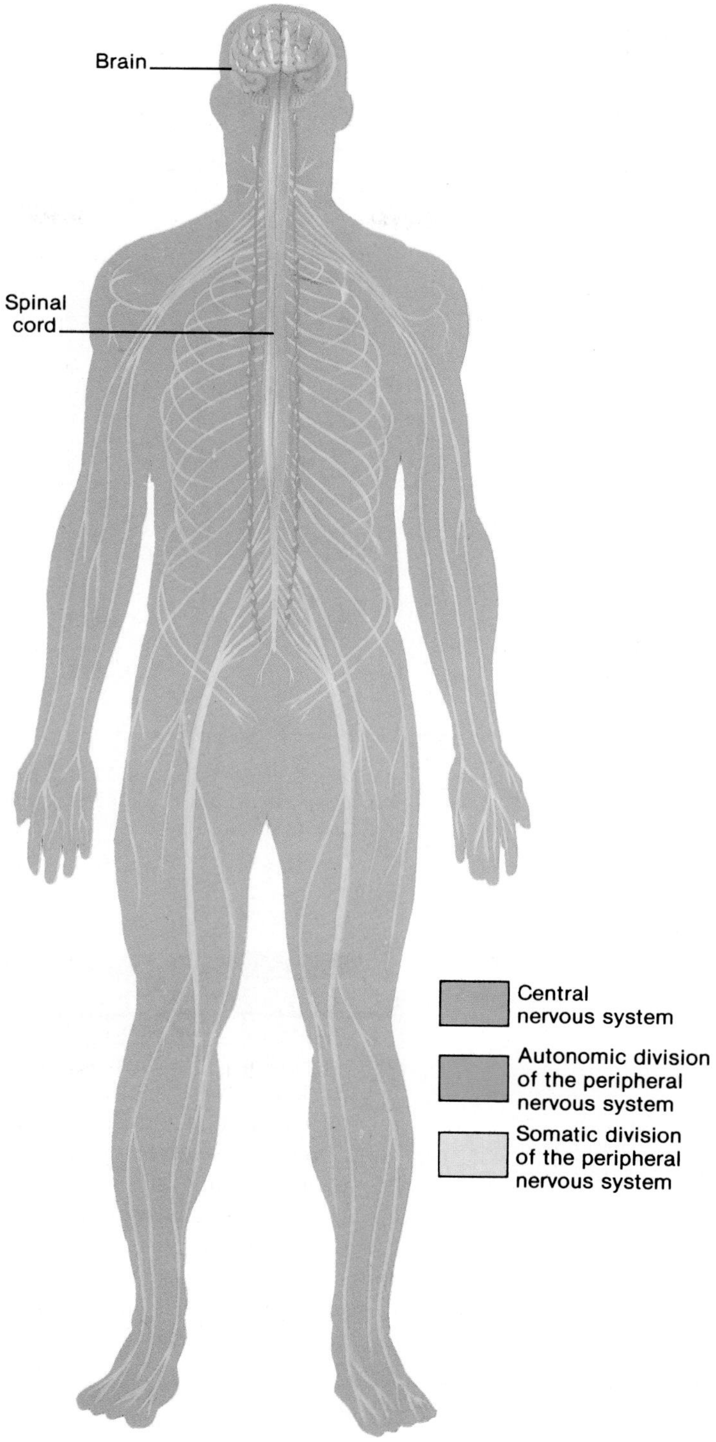

nervous system is operating adequately. Urinating and defecating are reflexes that occur in response to pressure in the bladder and the rectum. Parents typically spend a number of weeks or months toilet training infants, or teaching them to involve their brains in the process of elimination. Learning to inhibit these reflexes makes civilized interaction possible.

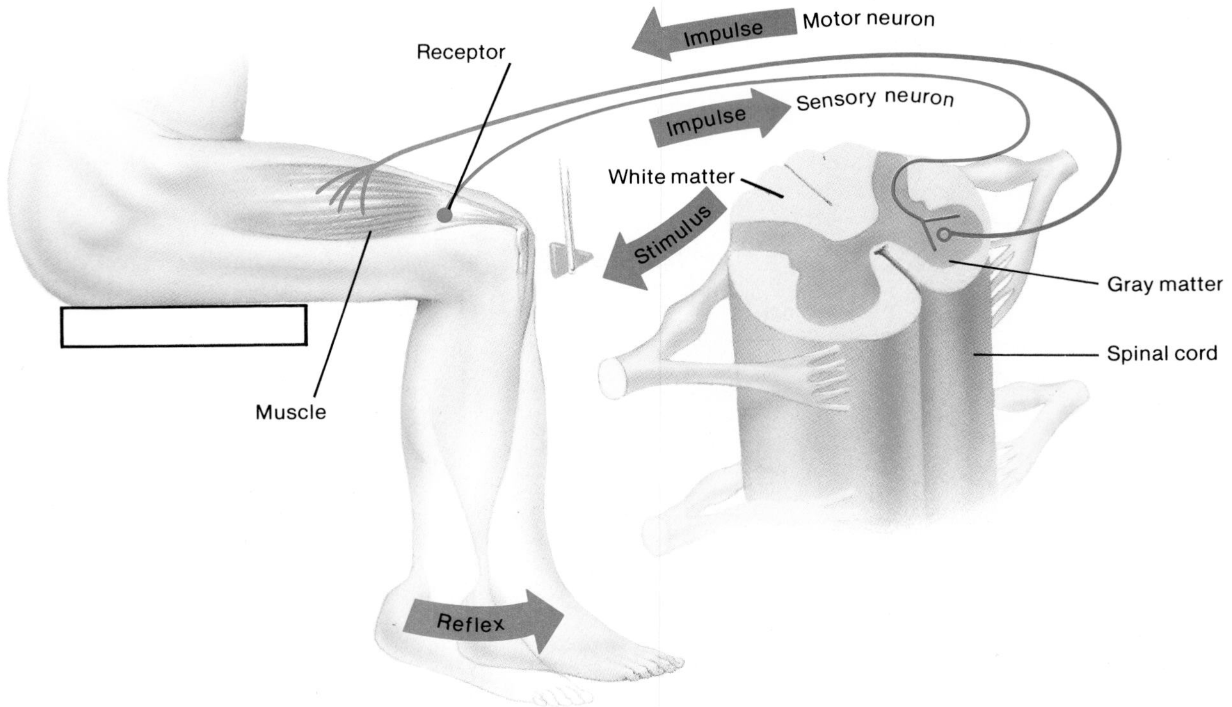

Figure 2.8
The Reflex Arc.

A cross-section of the spinal cord, showing a sensory neuron and a motor neuron, which are involved in the knee-jerk reflex. In some reflexes, interneurons link sensory and motor neurons.

Sexual response also involves many reflexes. Adequate stimulation of the genital organs will lead to erection in the male, vaginal lubrication in the female (both are reflexes that make sexual intercourse possible), and the involuntary muscle contractions of orgasm. As reflexes, these processes need not involve the brain, but most often they do. Feelings of passion, memories of an enjoyable sexual encounter, and sexual fantasies usually contribute to sexual response by transmitting messages from the brain to the genitals through the spinal cord (Rathus, 1983).

Although sexual response in humans is rarely fully mechanical, we can, as noted, respond purely on a reflexive level. Some men and women have spinal cord injuries that prevent genital sensations from reaching the brain. However, genital stimulation in many instances can still lead to the reflexes of sexual arousal and the muscle contractions of orgasm (Comarr, 1970; Money, 1960).

Truth or Fiction Revisited

It is true that many men who are paralyzed below the waist can still achieve erection and ejaculate. These sexual responses are reflexive.

The Brain Every show has a star, and the brain is the undisputed star of the human nervous system. The size and shape of your brain are responsible for your large, delightfully rounded head. In all the animal kingdom, you (and about 5 billion other human beings) are unique because of the capacities for learning and thought made possible by the human brain.

In a moment we shall begin to unveil our knowledge of the workings of the brain, but first let us consider a number of the ways in which researchers have learned about the brain.

A CLOSER LOOK

How Psychologists Study the Functions of the Brain

Just where is that elusive piece of business you think of as your "mind"? Thousands of years ago, it was not generally thought that the mind had a place to hang its hat within the body. It was common to assume that the body was inhabited by demons or souls that could not be explained in terms of substance. After all, if you look inside a human being, the biological structures you find do not look all that different in quality from those of many lower animals. Thus, it seemed to make sense that those qualities that made us distinctly human—thinking, planning, talking, dreaming, composing—were unrelated to substances that you could actually see, feel, and weigh on a scale.

Some ancient Egyptians attributed control of the human being to a little person, or **homunculus,** who dwelled within the skull and regulated our behavior. The Greek philosopher Aristotle thought that the soul had set up living quarters in the heart. After all, serious injury to the heart could be said to cause the soul to take flight from the body. As noted by B. F. Skinner (1987), to be undecided about something in ancient Greece was to have "a divided heart." Skinner goes on to note that phrases such as the following show that modern English is still influenced by the view of the heart as the seat of will, thought, hunger, and joy: "deep in one's heart," "to know something by heart," "to look into someone's heart," and "to have a change of heart."

Through a variety of accidents and research projects, we have come to recognize that mind, or consciousness, dwells essentially within the brain.

Accidents Let us first consider the accidents. From injuries to the brain—some of them minimal, some horrendous—we have learned that injuries to the head can lead to impairments of consciousness and awareness, such as loss of vision and hearing, general confusion, or loss of memory. We have learned that the loss of large portions of the brain may result in little loss of function, but the loss of smaller portions, more sensitively located, can result in language deficits, memory deficits, or death.

Electrical Stimulation of the Brain Experiments in electrical stimulation of areas in animal and human brains have shown that portions of the surface of the brain are associated with specific types of sensations (such as sensation of light or of a touch on the torso) or motor activities (such as movement of a leg); that a tiny group of structures near the center of the brain (the hypothalamus) is involved in sexual and aggressive behavior patterns; and that a rectangular structure that rises from the back part of the brain into the forebrain (the reticular activating system) is involved in wakefulness and sleep.

Lesions Whereas accidents have shown us how destruction of certain parts of the brain is related to behavioral changes in humans, intentional **lesions** in the brains of laboratory animals have led to more specific knowledge. For example, intentional destruction of one part of the limbic system causes rats

Homunculus Latin for "little man." A homunculus within the brain was once thought to govern human behavior.

Lesion An injury that results in impaired behavior or loss of a function.

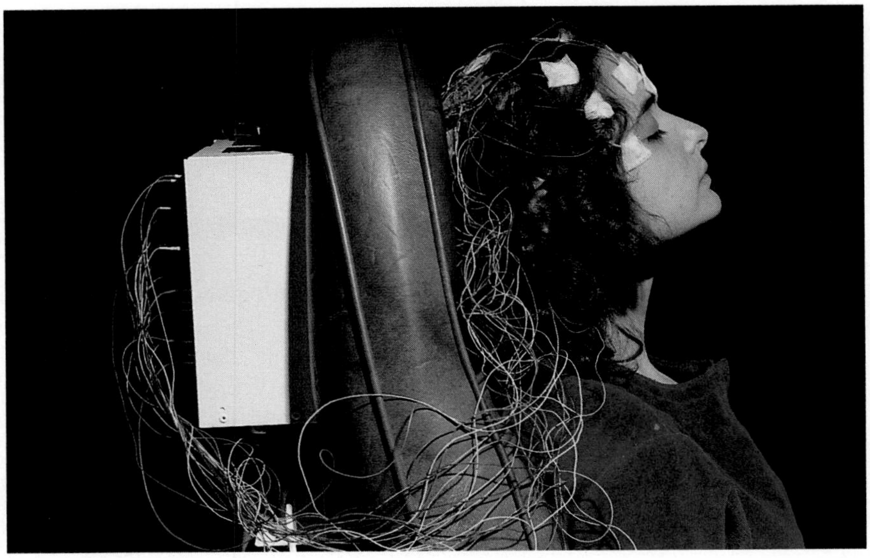

Figure 2.9
The Electroencephalograph. In this method of research, brain waves are detected by placing electrodes on the scalp and measuring the current that passes between them.

Electroencephalograph (ell-eck-tro-en-SEFF-uh-low-graph). An instrument that measures electrical activity of the brain. Abbreviated *EEG.* ("Cephalo-" derives from the Greek ***kephale,*** meaning "head.")

Computerized axial tomography Formation of a computer-generated image of the anatomical details of the brain by passing a narrow X-ray beam through the head and measuring from different angles the amount of radiation that passes through. Abbreviated *CAT scan.*

Positron emission tomography Formation of a computer-generated image of the neural activity of parts of the brain by tracing the amount of glucose used by the various parts. Abbreviated *PET scan.*

and monkeys to show relatively docile behavior. Destruction of another part of the limbic system leads monkeys to show rage responses at the slightest provocation. Destruction of yet another area of the limbic system prevents animals from forming new memories.

The Electroencephalograph Researchers use the **electroencephalograph** (EEG) to record the electrical activity of the brain. When I was an undergraduate psychology student, I first heard that psychologists studied sleep by "connecting" people to the EEG. I had a gruesome image of people somehow being plugged in. Not so. As suggested in Figure 2.9, electrodes are simply attached to the scalp with tape or paste. Later, once the brain activity under study has been duly recorded, the electrodes are simply removed. A bit of soap and water, and you're as good as new.

The EEG can detect minute amounts of electrical activity—called brain waves—that pass between the electrodes. In Chapter 4 we shall see that certain kinds of brain waves have been associated with feelings of relaxation and with the various stages of sleep. Researchers and physicians use the EEG to locate the areas of the brain that respond to certain kinds of stimuli, such as lights or sounds, and to diagnose a number of kinds of abnormal behavior. The EEG is also used in locating tumors.

Contemporary Imaging Techniques In recent years the computer's capacity to generate images of the parts of the brain from various sources of radiation has sparked the development of various imaging techniques that have been useful to researchers and physicians.

In one technique, **computerized axial tomography** (the CAT scan), a narrow X-ray beam is passed through the head and the amount of radiation that passes through is measured simultaneously from multiple angles (see Figure 2.10). The power of the computer enables us to integrate these measurements into a coherent, three-dimensional view of the brain. As a result, many kinds of brain damage and other abnormalities that years ago could be detected only by surgery can now be displayed on a monitor.

A second method, **positron emission tomography** (the PET scan), forms a computer-generated image of the neural activity of parts of the brain by tracing the amount of glucose used (or metabolized) by these parts. More

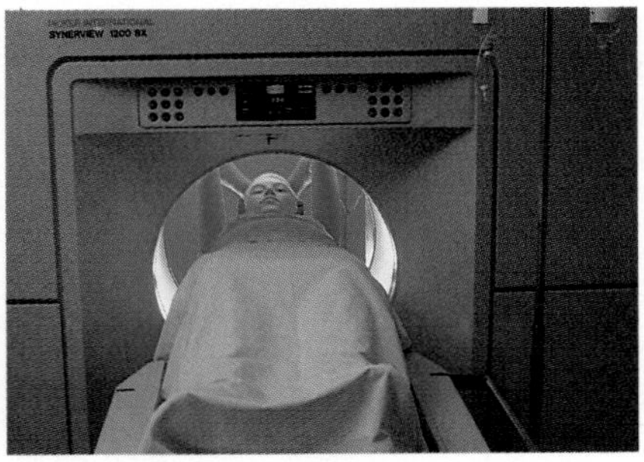

Figure 2.10
The Computerized Axial Tomograph Scan. In the CAT scan, a narrow X-ray beam is passed through the head and the amount of radiation that passes through is measured simultaneously from various angles. The computer enables us to integrate these measurements into a view of the brain.

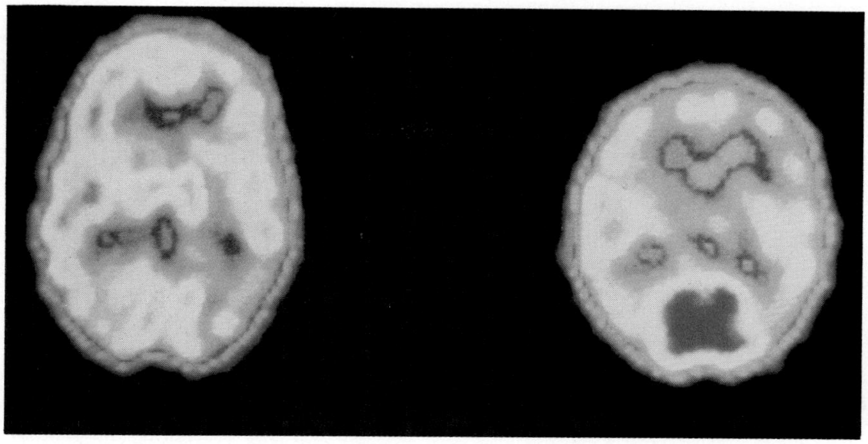

Figure 2.11
The Positron Emission Tomograph Scan. In the PET scan, a computer-generated image of the neural activity of parts of the brain is formed by tracing the amount of glucose metabolized by these parts. Parts of the brain with greater neural activity metabolize more glucose. The image on the left is the PET scan of a normal brain. The image on the right is the brain of a schizophrenic individual.

glucose is metabolized in the parts of the brain in which neural activity is greater. To trace the metabolism of glucose, a harmless amount of a radioactive compound, called a tracer, is mixed with glucose and injected into the bloodstream. When this glucose reaches the brain, the patterns of neural activity are revealed by measurement of the positrons—positively charged particles—that are given off by the tracer. The PET scan has been used by researchers to see which parts of the brain are most active when we are, for example, listening to music, working out a math problem, or using language (Petersen et al., 1988). As shown in Figure 2.11, patterns of neural activity also appear to differ in the brains of normal and schizophrenic individuals. Researchers are exploring the meanings and potential applications of these differences.

A third imaging technique is **nuclear magnetic resonance.** In this method, the person lies in a donut-shaped tunnel that generates a powerful magnetic field. The person is then also exposed to radio waves of certain frequencies. As a result, the parts of the brain emit signals that are measured from multiple angles and, as with the CAT scan, integrated into an image of the brain's anatomy.

All these methods have made it quite clear that the mind is a manifestation of the brain. Without the brain, in other words, there is no mind. Within the brain lies the potential for self-awareness and purposeful activity. Somehow the brain gives rise to mind. Today it is generally agreed that for every **phenomenological** event, such as a thought or a feeling, there are accompanying, underlying neurological events.

Nuclear magnetic resonance Formation of a computer-generated image of the anatomical details of the brain by measuring the signals that they emit when the head is placed in a strong magnetic field.

Phenomenological Having to do with subjective, conscious experience.

Now that we have explored some of the methods of physiological psychologists, let us look at the brain, as shown in Figure 2.12. We shall begin with the back of the head, where the spinal cord rises to meet the brain, and work our way forward. The lower part of the brain, referred to as the hindbrain, consists of three major structures: the medulla, the pons, and the cerebellum.

Many nerves that connect the spinal cord to higher levels of the brain pass through the **medulla.** The medulla regulates vital functions such as heart rate, blood pressure, and respiration. It also plays a role in sleep, sneezing, and coughing. The **pons** is a bulge in the hindbrain that lies

Medulla An oblong-shaped area of the hindbrain involved in regulation of heartbeat and respiration.

Pons A structure of the hindbrain involved in respiration.

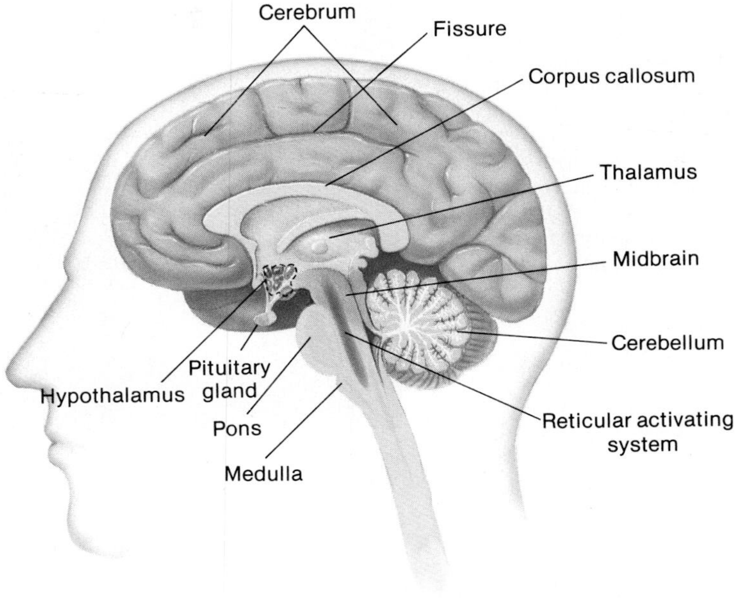

Figure 2.12
The Parts of the Human Brain. This view of the brain, also split top to bottom, labels some of the most important structures.

forward of the medulla. *Pons* is the Latin word for "bridge," and the pons is so named because of the bundles of nerves that pass through it. The pons transmits information about body movement and is also involved in functions related to attention, sleep and alertness, and respiration.

Behind the pons lies the **cerebellum,** which means "little brain" in Latin. The two hemispheres of the cerebellum are involved in maintaining balance and in controlling motor (muscle) behavior. Injury to the cerebellum may lead to lack of motor coordination, stumbling, and loss of muscle tone.

The **reticular activating system** (RAS) begins in the hindbrain and ascends through the region of the midbrain into the lower part of the forebrain. The RAS is vital in the functions of attention, sleep, and arousal. Injury to the RAS may leave an animal **comatose.** Stimulation of the RAS causes it to send messages to the cortex, making us more alert to sensory information. Electrical stimulation of the RAS awakens sleeping animals, and certain drugs called central-nervous-system depressants, such as alcohol, are thought to work, in part, by lowering RAS activity.

Sudden loud noises will stimulate the RAS and awaken a sleeping animal or person. But the RAS may become selective, or acquire the capacity to play a filtering role, through learning. It may allow some messages to filter through to higher brain levels and awareness while screening others out. For example, the parent who has primary responsibility for child care may be awakened by the stirring sounds of an infant, whereas louder sounds of traffic or street noise are filtered out. The other parent, in contrast, may usually sleep through even loud cries. If the first parent must be away for several days, however, the second parent's RAS may quickly acquire sensitivity to noises produced by the child. This sensitivity may rapidly fade again when the first parent returns.

Also located in the midbrain are areas involved in vision and hearing. These include the area that controls eye reflexes such as dilation of the pupils and eye movements.

Five major areas of the front-most part of the brain, or forebrain, are the thalamus, the hypothalamus, the limbic system, the basal ganglia, and the cerebrum.

Cerebellum A part of the hindbrain involved in muscle coordination and balance.

Reticular activating system A part of the brain involved in attention, sleep, and arousal.

Comatose In a coma, a state resembling sleep from which it is difficult to be aroused.

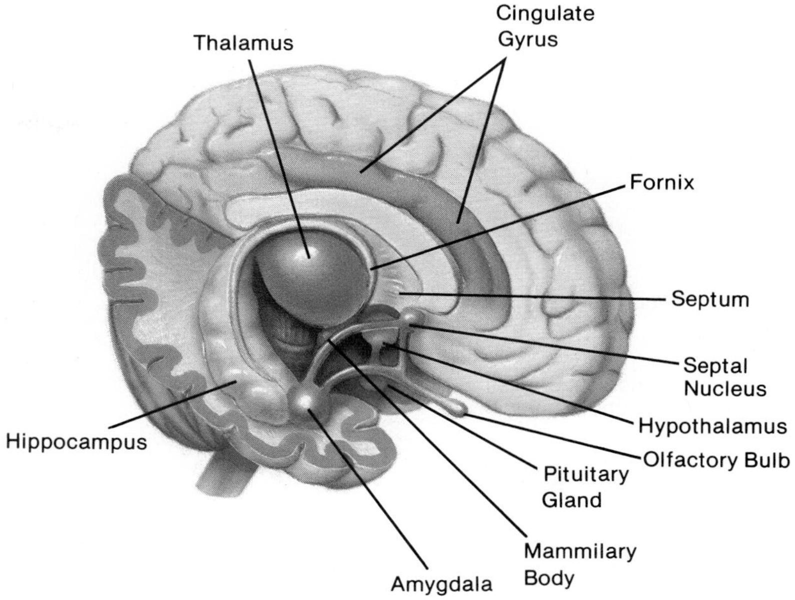

Figure 2.13
The Limbic System. The limbic system consists of the amygdala, hippocampus, septum and septal nuclei, fornix, cingulate gyrus, and parts of the hypothalamus.

The **thalamus** is located near the center of the brain. It consists of two joined lobes that are egg- or football-shaped. The thalamus serves as a relay station for sensory stimulation. Nerve fibers from our sensory systems enter from below; the information carried by them is then transmitted to the cerebral cortex by way of fibers that exit from above. For instance, the thalamus relays sensory input from the eyes to the visual areas of the cerebral cortex. The thalamus is also involved in controlling sleep and attention in coordination with other brain structures, including the RAS.

The **hypothalamus** is a tiny collection of nuclei located beneath the thalamus and above the pituitary gland. The hypothalamus weighs only four grams, yet it is vital in the control of body temperature, the concentration of fluids, the storage of nutrients, and various aspects of motivation and emotion. Experimenters learn many of the functions of the hypothalamus by implanting electrodes in various parts of it and observing the behavioral effects when a current is switched on. In this way it has been found that the hypothalamus is involved in hunger, thirst, sexual behavior, caring for offspring, and aggression.

The hypothalamus, along with parts of the thalamus and other structures, make up the **limbic system** (Figure 2.13). The limbic system lies along the inner edge of the cerebrum and is fully evolved in mammals only. It is involved in memory and in the drives of hunger, sex, and aggression. A part of the limbic system is sometimes removed in an effort to control **epilepsy,** or seizures that stem from sudden neural discharges. People in whom operations have damaged the hippocampus can retrieve old memories but cannot permanently store new information. As a result, they may reread the same newspaper day in and day out, without recalling that they have read it before, or have to be perpetually reintroduced to people they have met just hours earlier (Squire, 1986). As suggested earlier, destruction of an area of the limbic system called the **amygdala** leads monkeys and other mammals to show docile behavior (Carlson, 1986). Destruction of another area of the limbic system—the **septum**—leads some mammals to respond aggressively, even with slight provocation.

Thalamus An area near the center of the brain involved in the relay of sensory information to the cortex and in the functions of sleep and attention.

Hypothalamus A bundle of nuclei below the thalamus involved in body temperature, motivation, and emotion.

Limbic system A group of structures involved in memory and motivation that forms a fringe along the inner edge of the cerebrum.

Epilepsy Temporary disturbances of brain functions that involve sudden neural discharges.

Amygdala A part of the limbic system that apparently facilitates stereotypical aggressive responses.

Septum A part of the limbic system that apparently restrains stereotypical aggressive responses.

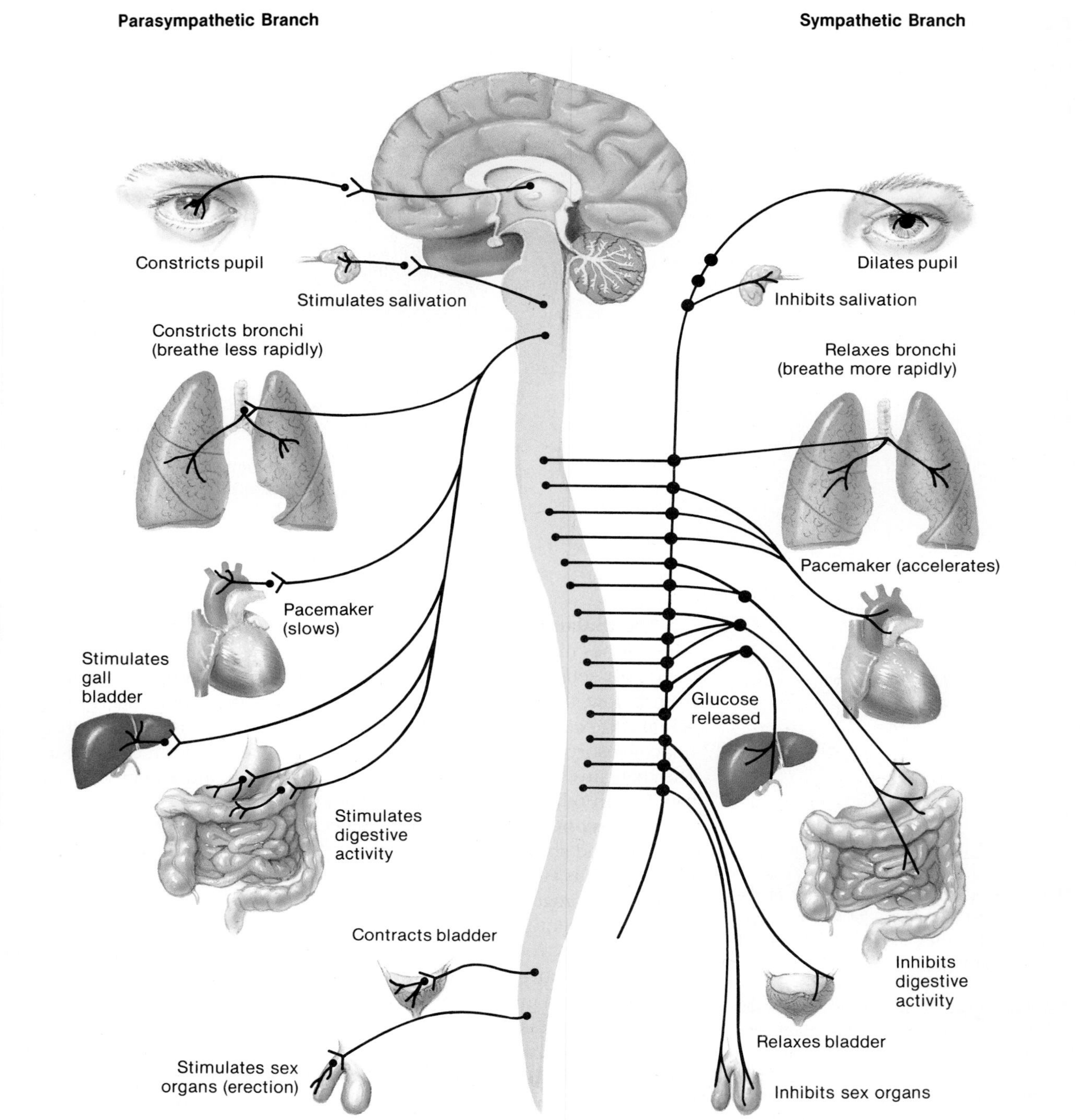

Figure 2.14
The Activities of the Two Branches of the Autonomic Nervous System (ANS).

The parasympathetic branch of the ANS generally acts to replenish stores of energy in the body. It is connected to organs by nerves that originate near the top and bottom of the spinal cord. The sympathetic branch is most active during activities that expend energy. Its neurons collect in clusters or chains of ganglia along the central portion of the spinal cord. The two branches of the ANS frequently have antagonistic effects on the organs they service.

Thus, it appears that the hypothalamus and other parts of the limbic system provide something of a system of "checks and balances." For example, the amygdala and the septum appear to allow us to inhibit some of the

Basal ganglia Ganglia located between the thalamus and cerebrum that are involved in motor coordination.

Cerebrum The large mass of the forebrain, which consists of two hemispheres.

Cerebral cortex The wrinkled surface area (gray matter) of the cerebrum.

Fissures. Valleys.

Corpus callosum A thick fiber bundle that connects the hemispheres of the cortex.

Somatic nervous system The division of the peripheral nervous system that connects the central nervous system with sensory receptors, muscles, and the surface of the body.

Autonomic nervous system The division of the peripheral nervous system that regulates glands and involuntary activities like heartbeat, respiration, digestion, and dilation of the pupils. Abbreviated *ANS.*

Involuntary Automatic, not consciously controlled.

Sympathetic The branch of the ANS that is most active during emotional responses that spend the body's reserves of energy, such as fear and anxiety.

Parasympathetic The branch of the ANS that is most active during processes that restore the body's reserves of energy, like digestion.

---

stereotypical patterns of behavior that are prompted by the hypothalamus. As a result, we have the opportunity to profit from experience and thought and are less likely to flee or attack automatically in the presence of a threat.

The **basal ganglia** are buried beneath the cortex in front of the thalamus. The basal ganglia are involved in the control of postural movements and the coordination of the limbs. Most of the brain's dopamine is produced by neurons in the basal ganglia, and the degeneration of these neurons has been linked to Parkinson's disease. In novel approaches to the treatment of Parkinson's disease tried out in Sweden and Mexico, cells from the adrenal medulla, which produce small amounts of dopamine, have been transplanted to patients' basal ganglia, but results of these operations have been mixed (Kimble, 1988; Kolata, 1988). However, the transplanting of fetal dopamine-producing cells into the brains of rats with Parkinson-like symptoms has apparently improved control over movement (Bjorklund & Stenevi, 1984).

The **cerebrum** is the crowning glory of the brain. Only in human beings does the cerebrum compose such a large proportion of the brain (Figure 2.12). The surface of the cerebrum is wrinkled, or convoluted, with ridges and valleys. This surface is the **cerebral cortex.** The convolutions allow a great deal of surface area to be packed into the brain. We shall explore the cerebral cortex in depth in a later section of this chapter.

Valleys in the cortex are called **fissures.** A most important fissure almost divides the cerebrum in half. The hemispheres of the cerebral cortex are connected by the **corpus callosum** (Latin for "thick body" or "hard body"), a thick fiber bundle. Later we shall see that severing the corpus callosum is not life threatening and leads to some interesting behavior.

The Peripheral Nervous System

The peripheral nervous system consists of sensory and motor neurons that transmit messages to and from the central nervous system. Without the peripheral nervous system, our brains would be isolated from the world: They would not be able to perceive it, and they would not be able to act on it. The two main divisions of the peripheral nervous system are the somatic nervous system and the autonomic nervous system.

The Somatic Nervous System The **somatic nervous system** consists of our sensory (afferent) and motor (efferent) neurons. It transmits messages about sights, sounds, smells, temperature, body positions, and so on to the central nervous system. As a result, we can experience the beauties and the horrors of the world, its physical ecstasies and agonies. Messages from the brain and spinal cord to the somatic nervous system control purposeful body movements, such as raising a hand, winking, or running; breathing; and movements that we hardly attend to—movements that maintain our posture and balance.

The Autonomic Nervous System *Autonomic* means "automatic." The **autonomic nervous system** (ANS) regulates the glands and **involuntary** activities such as heartbeat, digestion, and dilation of the pupils of the eyes even as we sleep.

The ANS has two branches or divisions, the **sympathetic** and the **parasympathetic.** These branches have largely opposing effects; when they work at the same time, their effects can be something of an averaging out of their influences. Many organs and glands are stimulated by both branches of the ANS (Figure 2.14). In general, the sympathetic division is most active during processes that involve the spending of body energy from stored reserves,

Frontal lobe The lobe of the cerebral cortex that lies to the front of the central fissure.

Parietal lobe The lobe that lies just behind the central fissure.

Temporal lobe The lobe that lies below the lateral fissure, near the temples of the head.

Occipital lobe The lobe that lies behind and below the parietal lobe and behind the temporal lobe.

Sensory cortex The section of cortex in which sensory stimulation is projected. It lies just behind the central fissure in the parietal lobe.

such as in a fight-or-flight response to a predator or when you find out that your mortgage payment is going to be increased. The parasympathetic division is most active during processes that replenish reserves of energy, such as during eating (Kimble, 1988). For instance, when we are afraid, the sympathetic division of the ANS accelerates the heart rate. But when we relax, it is the parasympathetic division that decelerates the heart rate. The parasympathetic division stimulates digestive processes, but the sympathetic branch inhibits digestive activity. Since the sympathetic division predominates when we feel fear or anxiety, fear or anxiety can lead to indigestion.

Truth or Fiction Revisited

It is true that fear can give you indigestion. Fear predominantly involves sympathetic activity, and digestion involves counteracting parasympathetic activity.

The autonomic nervous system is of particular interest to psychologists because its activities are linked to various emotions, such as anxiety and love.

THE CEREBRAL CORTEX

We have seen that sensation and muscle activity involve many parts of the nervous system. The essential human activities of thought and language, however, involve the hemispheres of the cerebral cortex.

The Geography of the Cerebral Cortex

Each of the two hemispheres of the cerebral cortex is divided into four parts, or lobes, as shown in Figure 2.15. The **frontal lobe** lies in front of the central fissure, and the **parietal lobe** lies behind it. The **temporal lobe** lies below the side, or lateral, fissure, across from the frontal and parietal lobes. The **occipital lobe** lies behind the temporal lobe and behind and below the parietal lobe.

When light strikes the retinas of the eyes, neurons in the occipital lobe fire, and we "see." Direct artificial stimulation of the occipital lobe also produces visual sensations. You would "see" flashes of light if neurons in the occipital region of the cortex were stimulated with electricity, even if it were pitch black or your eyes were covered. The hearing or auditory area of the cortex lies in the temporal lobe along the lateral fissure. As we shall learn in Chapter 3, sounds cause structures in the ear to vibrate. Messages are relayed to the auditory area of the cortex, and when you hear a noise, neurons in this area are firing.

Just behind the central fissure in the parietal lobe lies an area of **sensory cortex,** in which the messages received from skin senses all over the body are projected. These sensations include warmth and cold, touch, pain, and movement. Neurons in different parts of the sensory cortex fire, depending on whether you wiggle your finger or raise your leg. If a brain surgeon were to stimulate the proper area of your sensory cortex with a small probe known as a pencil electrode, it might seem as if someone were touching your arm or leg.

Truth or Fiction Revisited

It is true that it might seem as though someone had stroked your leg if a surgeon were to stimulate a certain part of your brain with an electrode.

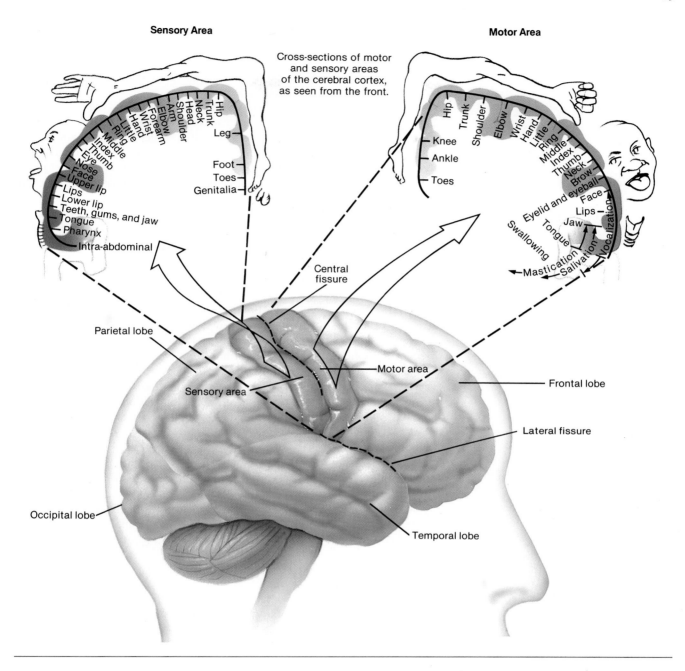

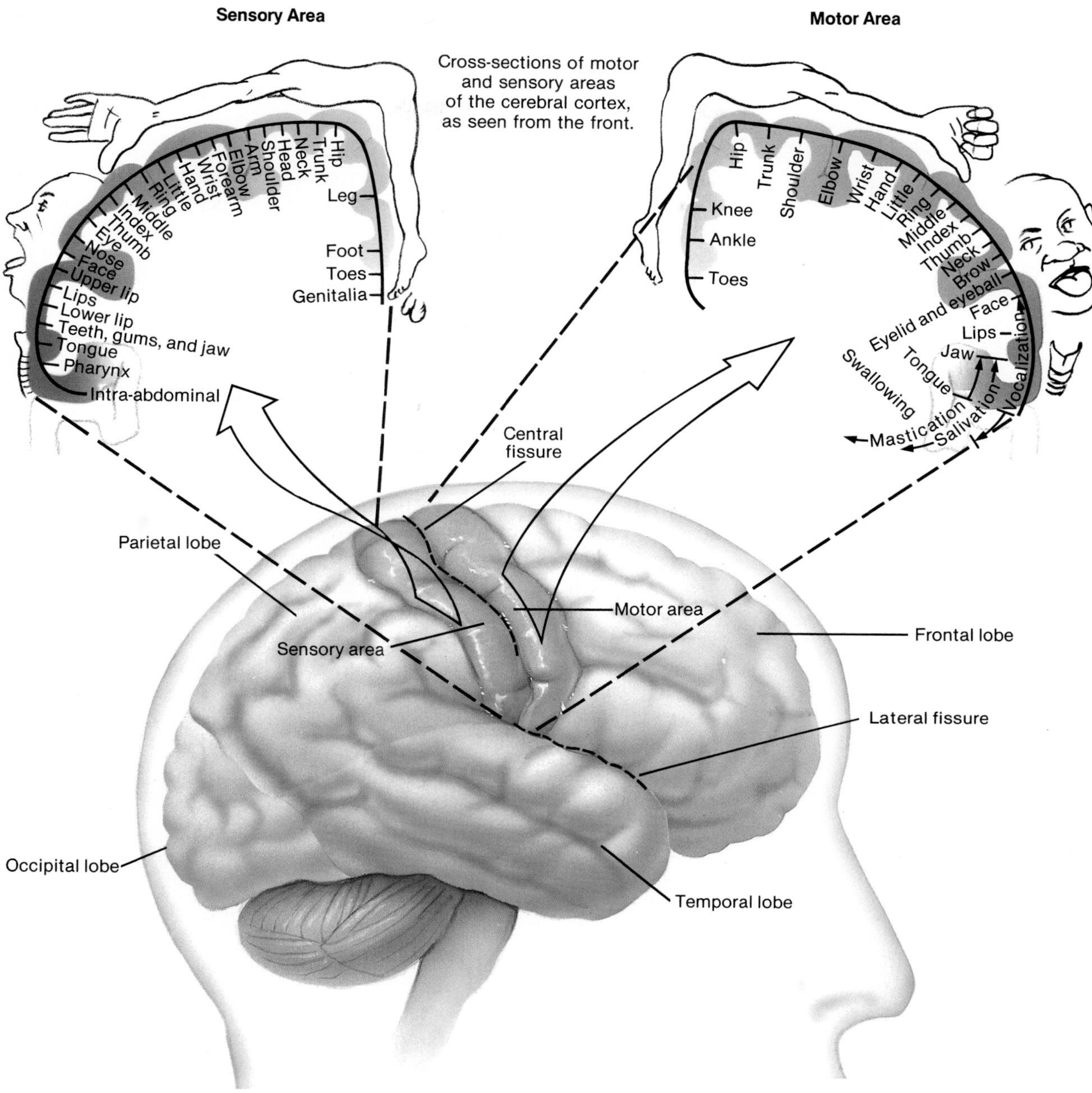

Figure 2.15
The Geography of the Cerebral Cortex.

The cortex is divided into four lobes: frontal, parietal, temporal, and occipital. The visual area of the cortex is located in the occipital lobe. The hearing or auditory cortex lies in the temporal lobe. The sensory and motor areas face each other across the central fissure. What happens when a surgeon stimulates areas of the sensory or motor cortex during an operation?

Figure 2.15 suggests how our faces and heads are overrepresented on this cortex as compared with, say, our trunks and legs. This overrepresentation is one of the reasons that our faces and heads are more sensitive to touch than other parts of the body.

Many years ago it was discovered that patients with injuries to one hemisphere of the brain would show sensory or motor deficits on the opposite side of the body below the head. Experimentation since that time has made it clear that sensory and motor nerves cross in the brain and elsewhere. The left hemisphere controls functions on, and receives inputs from, the right side of the body. The right hemisphere controls functions on, and receives inputs from, the left side of the body.

The **motor cortex** lies in the frontal lobe, just across the valley of the central fissure from the sensory cortex. Neurons in the motor cortex fire when we move certain parts of our body. If a surgeon were to stimulate a certain area of the right hemisphere of the motor cortex with a pencil electrode, you would raise your left leg. Raising the leg would be sensed in the sensory cortex, and you might have a devil of a time trying to figure out whether you had "intended" to raise that leg!

Thought, Language, and the Cortex

Areas of the cerebral cortex that are not primarily involved in sensation or motor activity are called **association areas.** They make possible the breadth and depth of human learning, thought, memory, and language. Association areas, for example, involve memory functions required for simple problem solving. Monkeys with lesions in certain association areas have difficulty remembering which of a pair of cups holds food when the cups have been screened off from them for a few seconds (Bauer & Fuster, 1976; French & Harlow, 1962). Stimulation of many association areas with pencil electrodes during surgery leads some people to report visual/auditory experiences that seem like memories, and sometimes they seem to be attended by appropriate emotions (Penfield, 1969).

Some association areas are involved in the integration of sensory information. Certain neurons in the visual area of the occipital lobe fire in response to the visual presentation of vertical lines. Others fire in response to presentation of horizontal lines. Although one group of cells may respond to one aspect of the visual field and another group of cells may respond to another, association areas "put it all together." As a result, you see a box or an automobile or a road map and not a confusing array of verticals and horizontals.

Language Functions In many ways the left and right hemispheres of the brain tend to duplicate each other's functions, but they are not entirely equal. For 96 percent of those people who are right-handed, the left hemisphere contains language functions and dominates (Rasmussen & Milner, 1975). For 70 percent of left-handed people, the left hemisphere also contains language functions and is dominant. The right hemisphere contains language functions for about 15 percent of left-handed individuals, and the remaining 15 percent of the left-handed contain language functions in both hemispheres.

Within the dominant (usually left) hemisphere of the cortex, the two areas most involved in speech are Broca's area and Wernicke's area (see Figure 2.16). Damage to either area is likely to cause an **aphasia**—that is, a disruption of the ability to understand or produce language.

Broca's area is located in the frontal lobe, near the section of the motor cortex that controls the muscles of the tongue and throat and of other areas of the face that are used when speaking. When Broca's area is damaged, people speak slowly and laboriously, with simple sentences—a pattern termed **Broca's aphasia.** In more severe cases, comprehension and use of syntax may be seriously impaired (Schwartz et al., 1980).

Wernicke's area lies in the temporal lobe near the auditory cortex. This area appears to be involved in the integration of auditory and visual information. Broca's area and Wernicke's area are connected by nerve fibers.

Motor cortex The section of cortex that lies in the frontal lobe, just across the central fissure from the sensory cortex. Neural impulses in the motor cortex are linked to muscular responses throughout the body.

Association areas Areas of the cortex involved in learning, thought, memory, and language.

Aphasia Impaired ability to comprehend or express oneself through speech.

Broca's aphasia A language disorder characterized by slow, laborious speech.

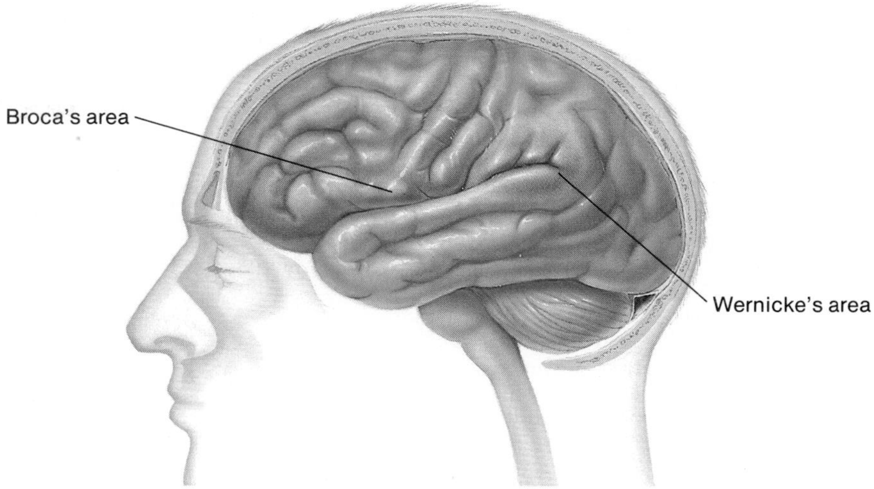

Figure 2.16
Broca's and Wernicke's Areas of the Cerebral Cortex. The two areas of the dominant cortex most involved in speech are Broca's area and Wernicke's area. Damage to either area can produce a characteristic aphasia—that is, a predictable disruption of the ability to understand or produce language.

People with damage to Wernicke's area may show **Wernicke's aphasia,** in which they usually speak freely and with proper syntax. However, their abilities to comprehend other people's speech and to think of the proper words to express their own thoughts are impaired (Gardner, 1978). Thus, Wernicke's area seems to be essential to understanding the relationships between words and their meanings.

Wernicke's aphasia A language disorder characterized by difficulty comprehending the meaning of spoken language.

A CLOSER LOOK

Left Brain, Right Brain?

In recent years, it has become popular to speak of people as being "left brained" or "right brained." The notion is that the hemispheres of the brain are involved in very different kinds of intellectual and emotional functions and responses, along the lines suggested in Figure 2.17. According to this view, people whose left brains are dominant would be basically logical and intellectual. People whose right brains are dominant would be intuitive, creative, and emotional. Those of us fortunate enough to have our "brains" in balance would presumably have the best of it—the capacity for logic combined with emotional richness.

Like so many other popular ideas, the left brain–right brain notion is at best exaggerated. Research does suggest that the dominant (usually the left) hemisphere is somewhat more involved in intellectual undertakings that require logic and problem solving, understanding syntax, associating written words with their sounds, the general comprehension and production of speech, and mathematical computation (Levy, 1985). The nondominant (usually right) hemisphere is relatively more concerned with decoding visual information, aesthetic and emotional responses, imagination, understanding metaphors, and creative mathematical reasoning.

Despite these differences, however, it would be erroneous to think that the hemispheres of the brain act independently or that some people are left-brained and others are right-brained. The functions of the left and right hemispheres overlap to some degree, and the hemispheres tend to respond simultaneously as we focus our attention on one thing or another.

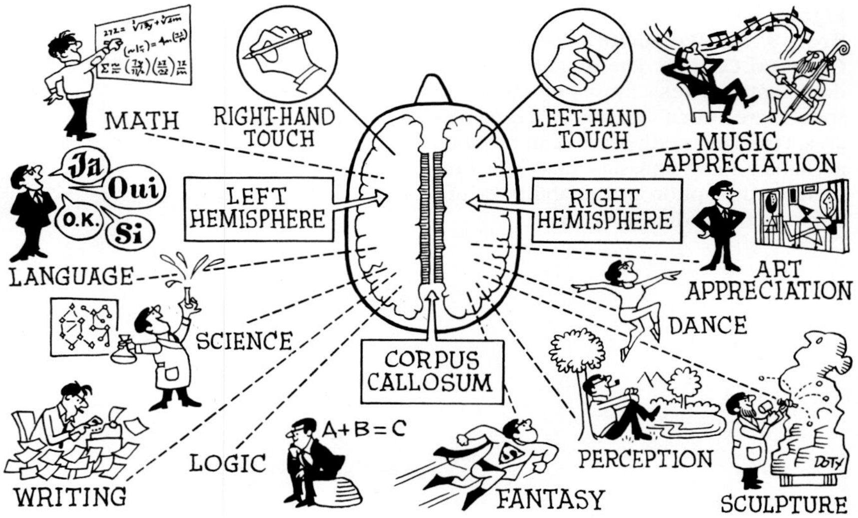

Figure 2.17
Some of the Specializations of the Left and Right Hemispheres of the Cerebral Cortex. This cartoon, which appeared in a popular magazine, exaggerates the "left brain–right brain" notion. It seems to be true that the dominant (usually left) hemisphere is somewhat more involved in intellectual undertakings that require logic and problem solving, while the nondominant (usually right) hemisphere is relatively more concerned with decoding visual information, aesthetic and emotional responses, and imagination. However, each hemisphere has some involvement with logic and with creativity and intuition.

Biological psychologist Jerre Levy (1985) summarizes left-brain and right-brain similarities and differences as follows:

1. The hemispheres are similar enough that each can function quite well independently, but not as well as they function in normal combined usage.
2. The left hemisphere does seem to play a special role in understanding and producing language whereas the right hemisphere does seem to play a special role in emotional response.
3. Both hemispheres are involved in logic.
4. Creativity and intuition are not confined to the right hemisphere.
5. Both hemispheres are educated at the same time, even when instruction is intended to "appeal" to the right hemisphere (as in music) or the left (in a logic class).

Divided-Brain Experiments: When Two Hemispheres Stop Talking to One Another

A number of patients suffering from severe cases of epilepsy have undergone **split-brain operations,** in which the corpus callosum is severed. The purpose of the operation is to try to confine epilepsy to one hemisphere of the cerebral cortex, rather than allow one hemisphere to agitate the other by transmitting a "violent storm of neural impulses" (Carlson, 1988). These operations do seem to help epilepsy patients. People who have undergone them can be thought of as winding up with two brains, yet under most circumstances their behavior remains perfectly normal. However, some of the effects of two hemispheres that have stopped talking to one another can be rather intriguing.

Split-brain operation An operation in which the corpus callosum is severed, usually in an effort to control epileptic seizures.

Gazzaniga (1972, 1983, 1985) has shown that split-brain patients whose eyes are closed may be able to verbally describe an object, such as a key, that they hold in one hand, but they cannot do so when they hold the object

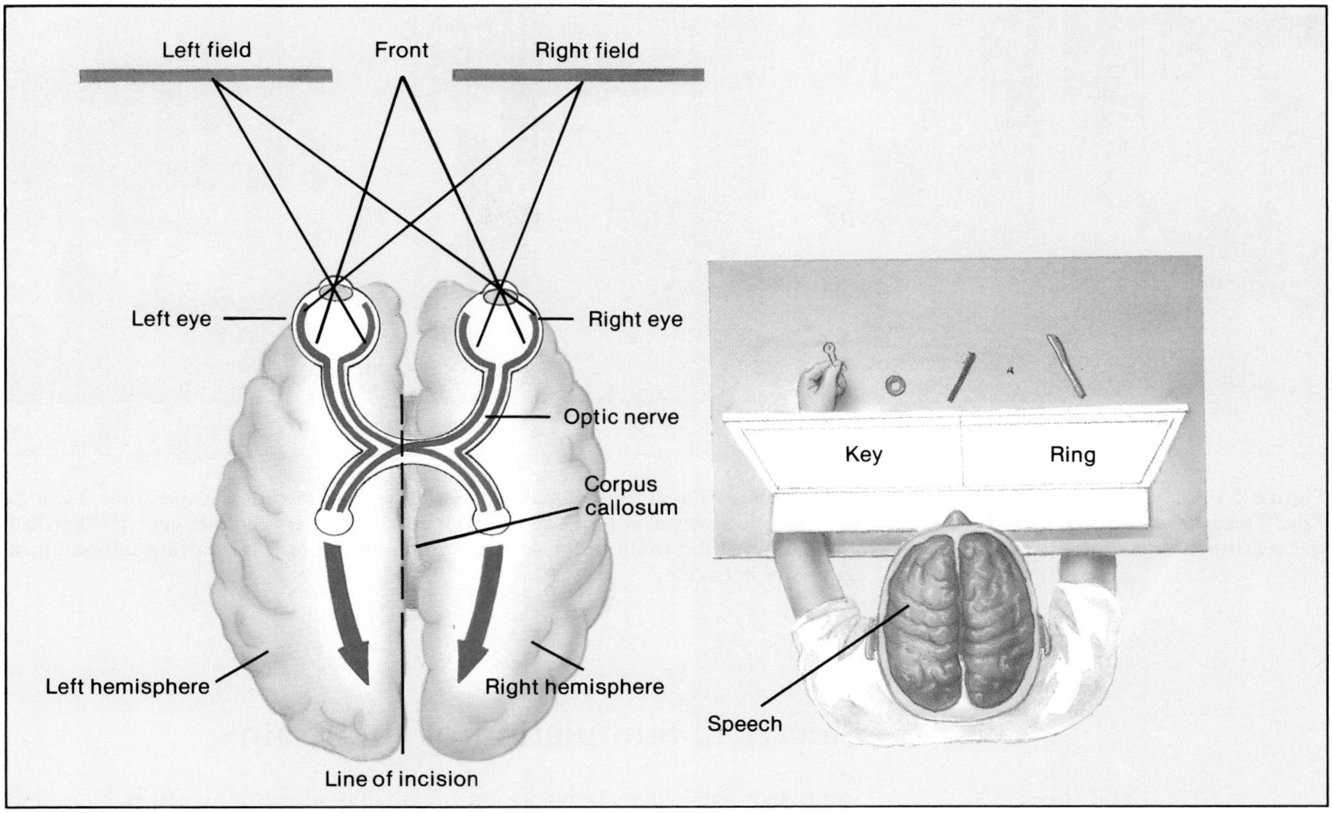

Figure 2.18
A Divided-Brain Experiment.

In the drawing on the left, we see that visual sensations in the left visual field are projected in the occipital cortex of the right hemisphere. Visual sensations from the right visual field are projected in the occipital cortex in the left hemisphere. In the divided-brain experiment diagrammed on the right, a subject with a severed corpus callosum handles a key with his left hand and perceives the written word *key* with his left eye. The word "key" is projected in the right hemisphere. Speech, however, is usually a function of the left (dominant) hemisphere. The written word "ring," perceived by the right eye, is projected in the left hemisphere. So, when asked what he is handling, the divided-brain subject reports "ring," not "key."

in the other hand. As shown in Figure 2.18, if a split-brain patient handles a key with his left hand behind a screen, **tactile** impressions of the key are projected into the right hemisphere, which has little or no language ability. Thus he will not be able to describe the key. If he holds it in his right hand, he will have no trouble describing it because sensory impressions are projected into the left hemisphere of the cortex, which contains language functions. To further confound matters, if the word *ring* is projected into the dominant (left) hemisphere while the patient is asked what he is handling, he will say "ring," not "key."

However, this discrepancy between what is felt and what is said occurs only in split-brain patients. As noted earlier, most of the time the hemispheres work together, even when we are playing the piano or are involved in scientific thought.

In case you have ever wondered whether other people could make us play the piano or engage in scientific thinking by "pressing the right buttons," let us consider some of the effects of electrical stimulation of the brain.

Tactile Of the sense of touch.

Figure 2.19
The "Taming" of a Brave Bull by Electrical Stimulation of the Brain. Brave bulls are dangerous animals that will attack an intruder in the arena. Even in full charge, however, a bull can be stopped abruptly by radio-triggered electrical stimulation of the brain. After several stimulations, there is a lasting inhibition of aggressive behavior.

Electrical Stimulation of the Brain

Some years ago, José Delgado astounded the scientific world by stepping into a bullring armed only with a radio transmitter, a cape, and, perhaps, crossed fingers (Figure 2.19). Describing his experiment in *Physical Control of the Mind* (1969), Delgado explained that he had implanted a radio-controlled electrode in the limbic system of a "brave bull"—a variety bred to respond with a raging charge when it sees any human being. When Delgado pressed a button on the transmitter, sending a signal to a battery-powered receiver attached to the bull's horns, an electrical impulse went into the bull's brain and the animal ceased his charge. After several repetitions, the bull no longer attempted to charge Delgado.

Another effect of electrical stimulation of the brain was discovered accidentally (how many important discoveries are made by accident!) during the 1950s by James Olds and Peter Milner (Olds, 1969). Olds and Milner found that electrical stimulation of an area of the hypothalamus of a rat induced the animal to increase the frequency of whatever it was doing at the time (Figure 2.20). Rats also rapidly learned to engage in behavior, such as pressing a lever, that resulted in more stimulation. Rats, in fact, will stimulate themselves in this area repeatedly, up to 100 times a minute and over 1,900 times an hour. For this reason, Olds and Milner labeled this area of the hypothalamus the rat's "pleasure center."

Figure 2.20
The "Pleasure Center" of the Brain. A rat with an electrode implanted in a section of the hypothalamus that has been termed the "pleasure center" of the brain learns to press a lever in order to receive electrical stimulation.

Truth or Fiction Revisited

It is true that rats will learn to do things that result in a "reward" of a burst of electricity in the pleasure center of the brain.

An experiment with a monkey produced even more astonishing results. Electrical stimulation (ESB) of one part of the monkey's brain caused her to (1) stop whatever she was doing, (2) alter expression, (3) turn her head, (4) stand on two feet and circle, (5) climb up and down a pole, (6) growl, and then (7) attack another monkey (Delgado, 1969).

Since these early days, ESB has been used with people to address a number of problems. For example, Robert Heath of Tulane University claims that ESB has helped some severely disturbed schizophrenia patients (Valenstein, 1978). Cancer or trauma patients suffering unrelenting pain have used ESB to block pain messages in the spinal cord before they reach the brain (Restak, 1975).

However, psychologist Elliot Valenstein (1978) is not quite so impressed by the potential of ESB. He notes, for example, that the bull in the Delgado demonstration did not actually have its aggressive tendencies eliminated by ESB. Instead, the electrical impulses caused the bull to circle to the right. The bull might have become confused, not pacified.

Also, ESB-provoked behavior does not perfectly mimic natural behavior. Behavior brought about by ESB is stereotypical and compulsive. For example, an animal whose "hunger" has been prodded by ESB may eat one type of food only.

The sites for producing pleasant or unpleasant sensations in people may vary from person to person and from day to day. As Valenstein notes, "The impression that brain stimulation in humans can repeatedly evoke the same emotional state, the same memory, or the same behavior is simply a myth. The brain is not organized into neat compartments that correspond to the . . . labels we assign to behavior" (1978, p. 31). I find that thought more than a little comforting.

In our discussion of the nervous system, we have described naturally occurring chemical substances that facilitate or inhibit the transmission of neural messages—neurotransmitters. Let us now turn our attention to other naturally occurring chemical substances that influence behavior—hormones. We shall see that some hormones also function as neurotransmitters.

THE ENDOCRINE SYSTEM

Here are some things you may have heard about hormones and behavior. Are they truth or fiction?

- Some overweight people actually eat very little, and their excess weight is caused by "glands."
- A boy whose growth was "stunted" began to catch up with his agemates after receiving injections of "growth hormone."
- A woman who becomes anxious and depressed just before menstruating is suffering from "raging hormones."
- Women who "pump iron" frequently use hormones to achieve the muscle definition that is needed to win body-building contests.
- People who receive injections of adrenaline often report that they feel as if they are about to experience some emotion, but they're not sure which one.

Let us consider each of these items. Some overweight people do eat relatively little but are "sabotaged" in their weight-loss efforts by hormonal changes that lower the rates at which they metabolize food (Brownell, 1988). Growth hormone, a secretion of the **pituitary gland,** can promote growth. Women may become somewhat more anxious or depressed at the time of menstruation, but the effects of hormones have been exaggerated, and women's response to menstruation reflects their attitudes as well as biological changes. Many top women (and men) bodybuilders do use steroids (hormones that are produced by the **adrenal cortex**) along with human growth hormone to achieve the muscle mass and definition sought by judges in competition (Leerhsen & Abramson, 1985). Steroids and growth hormone promote resistance to stress and muscle growth in both men and women.

Pituitary gland The gland that secretes growth hormone, prolactin, antidiuretic hormone, and others.

Adrenal cortex The outer part of the adrenal glands located above the kidneys. It produces steroids.

Table 2.1
An Overview of Some Major Glands of the Endocrine System

Gland	Hormone	Major Effects
Hypothalamus	Growth-hormone releasing factor	Causes pituitary gland to secrete growth hormone
	Corticotrophin-releasing hormone	Causes pituitary gland to secrete adrenocorticotrophic hormone
	Thyrotropin-releasing hormone	Causes pituitary gland to secrete thyrotropin
	Gonadotrophin-releasing hormone	Causes pituitary gland to secrete follicle-stimulating hormone and luteinizing hormone
	Prolactin-releasing hormone	Causes pituitary gland to secrete prolactin
Pituitary		
Anterior lobe	Growth hormone	Causes growth of muscles, bones, and glands
	Adrenocorticotrophic hormone (ACTH)	Regulates adrenal cortex
	Thyrotrophin	Causes thyroid gland to secrete thyroxin
	Follicle-stimulating hormone	Causes formation of sperm and egg cells
	Luteinizing hormone	Causes ovulation, maturation of sperm and egg cells
	Prolactin	Stimulates production of milk
Posterior lobe	Antidiuretic hormone (ADH)	Inhibits production of urine
	Oxytocin	Stimulates uterine contractions during delivery and ejection of milk during nursing
Pancreas	Insulin	Enables body to metabolize sugar, regulates storage of fats
	Glucagon	Increases levels of sugar and fats in blood
	Somatostatin	Regulates secretion of insulin and glucagon
Thyroid	Thyroxin	Increases metabolic rate
Adrenal		
Cortex	Steroids (e.g., cortisol)	Increase resistance to stress; regulate carbohydrate metabolism
Medulla	Adrenaline (epinephrine)	Increases metabolic activity (heart and respiration rates, blood sugar level, etc.)
	Noradrenaline (norepinephrine)	Raises blood pressure; acts as neurotransmitter
Testes	Testosterone	Promotes growth of male sex characteristics
Ovaries	Estrogen	Regulates menstrual cycle
	Progesterone	Promotes growth of female reproductive tissues; maintains pregnancy
Uterus	(Several)	Maintain pregnancy

Finally, adrenaline, a hormone produced by the **adrenal medulla,** does generally arouse people and thereby heighten general emotional responsiveness. In Chapter 8 you will see that the specific emotion to which this arousal is attributed depends in part on the person's situation.

Ductless Glands The body contains two types of glands: glands with **ducts** and glands without ducts. A duct is a passageway that carries substances to specific locations. Saliva, sweat, and tears (the name of a new rock group?) all reach their destinations by means of ducts. Psychologists are more likely to show interest in the substances secreted by ductless glands because of their behavioral effects (see the summary in Table 2.1). The ductless glands constitute the **endocrine system** of the body, and they secrete substances called **hormones** (from the Greek *horman,* meaning "to stimulate" or "to excite").

Hormones are released directly into the bloodstream. As is the case with neurotransmitters,* hormones have specific receptor sites. Thus, although they are poured into the bloodstream and circulate throughout the body, they act only on hormone receptors in certain locations. For example, certain

*Recall that some hormones, such as norepinephrine, also function as neurotransmitters.

Adrenal medulla The inner part of the adrenal glands that produces adrenaline.

Duct Passageway.

Endocrine system Ductless glands that secrete hormones and release them directly into the bloodstream.

Hormone A substance secreted by an endocrine gland that regulates various body functions.

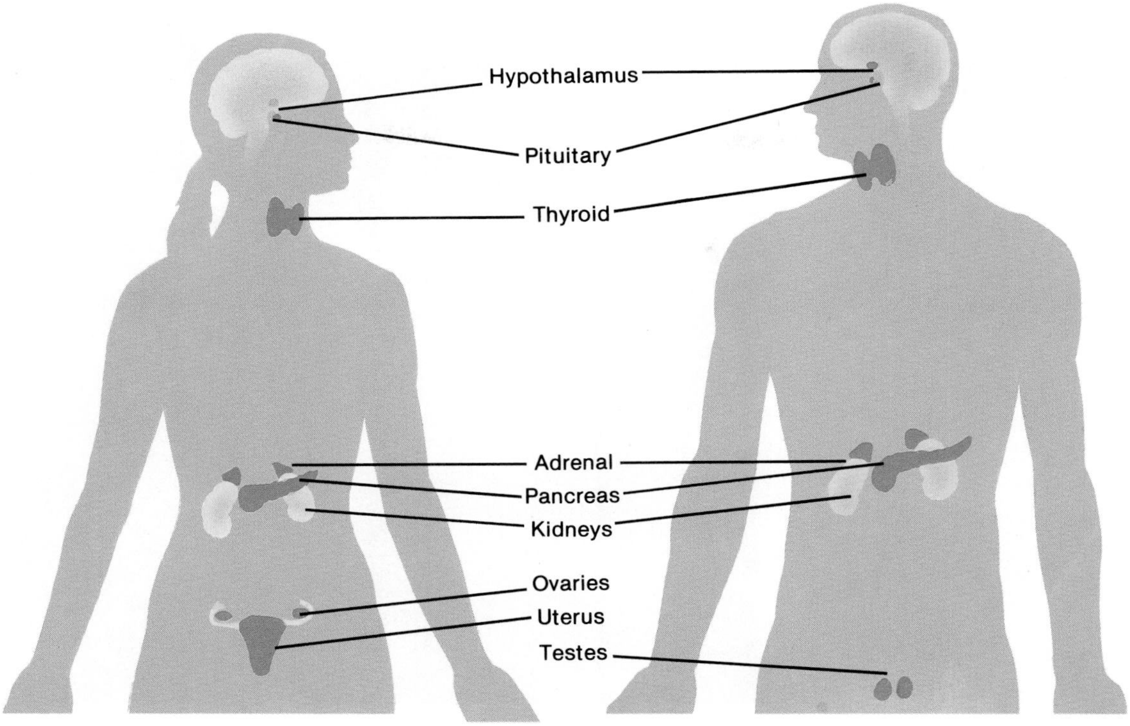

Figure 2.21
Location of Major Glands of the Endocrine System.

hormones released by the hypothalamus influence only the pituitary gland. Some hormones released by the pituitary influence the adrenal cortex, others influence the testes and ovaries, and so on.

Let us now examine the functions of several glands of the endocrine system.

The Hypothalamus

The hypothalamus secretes a number of releasing hormones, or factors, that influence the anterior (front) lobe of the pituitary gland to secrete corresponding hormones. A dense network of blood vessels between the hypothalamus and the pituitary gland provide a direct route of influence (Kimble, 1988).

The Pituitary Gland

The pituitary gland lies just below the hypothalamus (see Figure 2.21). It is about the size of a pea, but it is so central to the body's functioning that it has been referred to as the "master gland." Despite this designation, today we know that the hypothalamus regulates a good deal of pituitary activity.

Much hormonal action helps the body maintain steady states, as in fluid levels, blood sugar levels, and so on. These steady states are achieved by

André the Giant in a scene from the film *The Princess Bride.* Professional wrestler André Rousimoff suffered from acromegaly as a child. Acromegaly is caused by excessive growth hormone and characterized by a protruding forehead, "lantern" jaw, and broad nose.

mechanisms that measure current levels and signal glands to release appropriate regulatory chemicals when these levels deviate from optimal. The maintenance of steady states requires a system in which information is fed back to glands as needed. This type of system is referred to as a **negative feedback** loop. That is, when the required level of a hormone has been secreted, the gland is signaled to stop. With a negative feedback system in effect, even the master gland must serve a master—the hypothalamus. In turn, the hypothalamus, as we shall see in Chapter 8, is responsive to information received from many sources throughout the body.

The anterior and posterior (back) lobes of the pituitary gland produce or secrete many hormones, some of which are listed in Table 2.1. **Growth hormone** regulates the growth of muscles, bones, and glands. An excess of growth hormone can lead to *acromegaly,* a condition in which people may grow two to three feet taller than they normally would. Wrestler "André the Giant," who is over seven feet tall and weighs in at nearly 500 pounds, secreted extremely high levels of growth hormone as a child. In recent years, professional athletes have injected growth hormone as adults to increase their muscle mass, combining it with anabolic steroids, to be discussed later.

Children whose growth patterns seem abnormally slow often catch up to their agemates when growth hormone is administered by a physician. A recently discovered substance, growth-hormone releasing factor (or hGRF), is produced by the hypothalamus and causes the pituitary to produce growth hormone (Kimble, 1988).

Prolactin largely regulates maternal behavior in lower mammals, such as rats, and stimulates production of milk in women. Transfusion of blood from a new mother rat to another female rat will cause the recipient to display typical mothering behaviors.

When the fluid level of the body is low, the hypothalamus stimulates the pituitary gland to secrete **antidiuretic hormone,** which is abbreviated *ADH* and is also referred to as *vasopressin.* ADH increases the reabsorption of urine in order to conserve fluid.

Negative feedback Descriptive of a system in which information that a quantity (e.g., of a hormone) has reached a set point suspends action of the agency (e.g., a gland) that gives rise to that quantity.

Growth hormone A pituitary hormone that regulates growth.

Prolactin A pituitary hormone that regulates production of milk and, in lower animals, maternal behavior.

Antidiuretic hormone A pituitary hormone that inhibits the production of urine. Abbreviated *ADH.*

Oxytocin A pituitary hormone that stimulates labor and lactation.

Neuroendocrine reflex A reflex that involves the nervous system and the endocrine system, such as the ejection of milk.

Oxytocin stimulates labor in pregnant women. Obstetricians may induce labor or increase the strength of uterine contractions during labor by injecting pregnant women with oxytocin. During nursing, stimulation of nerve endings in and around the nipple sends messages to the brain that cause oxytocin to be secreted. Oxytocin then causes contractile cells in the breast to eject milk. Ejection of milk is referred to as a **neuroendocrine reflex.** Prolactin and oxytocin are also secreted in males, but their functions in males—if any—are unknown.

Adrenocorticotrophic hormone (ACTH) is released by the pituitary in response to corticotrophin-releasing hormone (CRH), which is produced by the hypothalamus. ACTH acts on the adrenal cortex, causing it to release a number of hormones, including **cortisol,** which helps the body respond to stress by fighting inflammation and allergic reactions.

Adrenocorticotrophic hormone A pituitary hormone that regulates the adrenal cortex. Abbreviated *ACTH.*

Cortisol A hormone (steroid) produced by the adrenal cortex that helps the body cope with stress by counteracting inflammation and allergic reactions.

Pancreas A gland behind the stomach whose secretions influence the blood sugar level.

Insulin A pancreatic hormone that stimulates the metabolism of sugar.

Glucagon A pancreatic hormone that increases the levels of sugar and fat in the blood.

Hyperglycemia A disorder caused by excess sugar in the blood.

Hypoglycemia A disorder caused by too little sugar in the blood.

Syndrome A cluster of symptoms characteristic of a disorder.

Thyroxin The thyroid hormone that increases metabolic rate.

Metabolism In organisms, a continuous process that converts food into energy.

Hypothyroidism A condition caused by a deficiency of thyroxin and characterized by sluggish behavior and a low metabolic rate.

Cretinism A condition caused by thyroid deficiency in childhood and characterized by mental retardation and stunted growth.

Hyperthyroidism A condition caused by excess thyroxin and characterized by excitability, weight loss, and insomnia.

Corticosteroids Steroids produced by the adrenal cortex that regulate carbohydrate metabolism and increase resistance to stress by fighting inflammation and allergic reactions. Also called *cortical steroids.*

Steroids A family of hormones including testosterone, estrogen, progesterone, and corticosteroids.

The Pancreas

The **pancreas** is influential in controlling the level of sugar in the blood and the urine through the hormones **insulin** and **glucagon.** One form of diabetes (diabetes mellitus) is characterized by excess sugar in the blood—**hyperglycemia**—and in the urine, a condition that can lead to coma and death. Diabetes stems from inadequate secretion or utilization of insulin. People who do not secrete enough insulin of their own may need to inject this hormone daily in order to control diabetes.

The condition **hypoglycemia** is characterized by too little sugar in the blood. Symptoms of hypoglycemia include shakiness, dizziness, and lack of energy, a **syndrome** that is easily confused with anxiety. Many people have sought help for anxiety and learned through a series of blood tests that they are actually suffering from hypoglycemia. This disorder is generally controlled through dietary restrictions.

The Thyroid Gland

Thyroxin is produced by the thyroid gland. Thyroxin affects the body's **metabolism,** or rate of using oxygen and producing energy. Some people who are overweight are suffering from a condition known as **hypothyroidism,** which results from abnormally low secretions of thyroxin. Deficiency of thyroxin can lead to **cretinism** in children, a disorder characterized by stunted growth and mental retardation. Adults who secrete too little thyroxin may feel tired and sluggish and may put on weight. People who produce excess amounts of thyroxin may develop **hyperthyroidism,** a disorder characterized by excitability, insomnia, and weight loss.

The Adrenal Glands

The adrenal glands, located above the kidneys, have an outer layer, or cortex, and an inner core, or medulla. The adrenal cortex is regulated by the pituitary hormone ACTH. The cortex secretes as many as 20 different hormones known as **corticosteroids,** or cortical **steroids.** Cortical steroids (cortisol is one) increase resistance to stress; promote muscle development; and cause the liver to release stored sugar, making energy available for emergencies.

PSYCHOLOGY GOES TO WORK

Steroids and Professional Athletics

Anabolic steroids (synthetic versions of the male sex hormone testosterone) have been used, frequently along with growth hormone, to enhance athletic prowess. Steroids stoke the muscle mass, heighten resistance to stress, and increase the body's energy supply by signaling the liver to release sugar into the bloodstream. Steroids also spur the sex drive. On a psychological level, they boost self-esteem (Taylor, 1985). Steroids are generally outlawed in amateur and professional sports, although they can be prescribed by any physician. When an athlete's physician is uncooperative, steroids are readily available through illicit sources known to many team members.

The lure of steroids is understandable. Sometimes the difference between an acceptable athletic performance and a great one is rather small. Thousands of athletes try to make it in the big leagues, and the "edge" offered by steroids—even if minor—can spell the difference between a fumbling attempt and success. New York Jets rookie lineman Dave Cadigan explained why he chose to use steroids after he "flunked" a urine test in 1987: "I played against a lot of guys that I know for a fact were using steroids. [In college] I played them one year, the next year they come [sic] back 15 pounds heavier, stronger and they looked different. They played better and they hit harder" (Rhoden, 1988). In other words, many athletes fear that the opposition will use steroids, so if they abstain, they will be at a disadvantage. Being at a disadvantage can mean being out of a job.

If steroids help, why the fuss? Some of it is related to the ethics of competition—the notion that all athletes should "play fair." Part of it is related to the fact that steroid use is linked to liver damage and other medical problems. In addition, a number of athletes who have used growth hormone in combination with steroids, like nine-time world-champion weight lifter Larry Pacifico, have developed cardiovascular disorders such as blocked arteries. Steroids may also cause sleep disturbances and, when discontinued, depression and apathy. Moreover, the effects of long-term usage remain unknown.

Bodybuilders. Many women in recent years have taken up bodybuilding, a sport previously reserved for men. Many bodybuilders—male and female—take anabolic steroids, which are synthetic versions of the male hormone testosterone. Anabolic steroids stoke development of the muscle mass.

The **catecholamines** adrenaline and noradrenaline are secreted by the adrenal medulla. **Adrenaline,** also known as epinephrine, is manufactured exclusively by the adrenal glands, but noradrenaline (norepinephrine) is also produced at other sites in the body. The sympathetic branch of the autonomic nervous system causes the adrenal medulla to release a mixture of adrenaline and norepinephrine that helps arouse the body in preparation for coping with threats and stress. Adrenaline is of particular interest to psychologists because of its emotional as well as physiological effects. Adrenaline may intensify most emotions and is particularly important when one is experiencing fear and anxiety. Norepinephrine raises the blood pressure and, in the nervous system, it acts as a neurotransmitter.

Catecholamines A number of chemical substances produced from an amino acid that are important as neurotransmitters (dopamine and norepinephrine) and as hormones (adrenaline and norepinephrine).

Adrenaline A hormone produced by the adrenal medulla that stimulates sympathetic ANS activity. Also called *epinephrine.*

Testosterone A male sex hormone produced by the testes that promotes growth of male sexual characteristics and sperm.

Primary sex characteristics Physical traits that distinguish the sexes and are directly involved in reproduction.

The Testes and the Ovaries

Did you know that if it were not for the secretion of the male sex hormone **testosterone** about six weeks after conception, we would all develop into females? Testosterone is produced by the testes and, in smaller amounts, by the ovaries and adrenal glands (Kimble, 1988). A few weeks following fertilization of an ovum, testosterone stimulates prenatal differentiation of male sex organs. (The quantities produced by the ovaries and adrenal glands are normally insufficient to foster development of male sex organs.)

During puberty, testosterone promotes the growth of muscle and bone and the development of primary and secondary sex characteristics. **Primary sex characteristics** are directly involved in reproduction, such as the growth of the penis and the sperm-producing ability of the testes. **Secondary sex characteristics,** such as growth of the beard and deepening of the voice, differentiate the sexes but are not directly involved in reproduction.

Testosterone levels vary slightly with stress, time of the day or month, and other factors but are maintained at fairly even levels by the hypothalamus, pituitary gland, and testes. Low blood levels of testosterone signal the hypothalamus to produce gonadotropin-releasing hormone (GnRH). GnRH, in turn, signals the pituitary to secrete luteinizing hormone (LH), which stimulates the testes to secrete testosterone, and follicle-stimulating hormone (FSH), which causes sperm cells to develop. The negative feedback loop is completed as follows: High blood levels of testosterone signal the hypothalamus not to secrete GnRH so that production of LH, FSH, and testosterone are suspended.

The ovaries produce **estrogen** and **progesterone.** (Estrogen is also produced in smaller amounts by the testes [Kimble, 1988].) Estrogen is a generic name for several female sex hormones that lead to development of female reproductive capacity and secondary sex characteristics, such as accumulation of fat in the breasts and hips. Progesterone also has multiple functions. It stimulates growth of the female reproductive organs and maintains pregnancy. As with testosterone, estrogen and progesterone levels influence and are also influenced by GnRH, LH, and FSH. In women, FSH causes ova (egg cells) within follicles in the ovaries to ripen.

Secondary sex characteristics Physical traits that differentiate the sexes but are not directly involved in reproduction.

Estrogen A generic term for several female sex hormones that promote growth of female sexual characteristics and regulate the menstrual cycle.

Progesterone A female sex hormone that promotes growth of the sexual organs and helps maintain pregnancy.

Hormonal Regulation of the Menstrual Cycle Whereas testosterone levels remain fairly stable, estrogen and progesterone levels vary markedly and regulate the menstrual cycle. Following menstruation—the monthly sloughing off of the inner lining of the uterus—estrogen levels increase, leading to the development of an ovum (egg cell) and growth of the inner lining of the uterus. The ovum is released by the ovary when estrogens reach peak blood levels. Then the inner lining of the uterus thickens in response to secretion of progesterone, gaining the capacity to support an embryo if fertilization should occur. If the ovum is not fertilized, estrogen and progesterone levels drop suddenly, triggering menstruation once more. Now let us consider a problem that afflicts many women at a certain time in their cycles.

A CLOSER LOOK

Women and PMS: Does Premenstrual Syndrome Doom Women to Misery?

Menstruation has been a source of concern for many women both because of stereotypes about menstruating women and because of physical discomfort suffered by numerous women. For several days prior to and during menstruation, the stereotype has been that "raging hormones" doom women to irritability and poor judgment—two facets of premenstrual syndrome (PMS). This view, as noted by Karen Paige (1973), has cost women many opportunities to assume responsible positions in society:

> *Women, the old argument goes, are eternally subject to the whims and wherefores of their biological clocks. Their raging hormonal cycles make them emotionally unstable and intellectually unreliable. If women have second-class status, we are told, it is because they cannot control the implacable demands of that bouncing estrogen (p. 41).*

Let us first consider whether women show behavioral and emotional deficits prior to and during menstruation. It turns out that the evidence is mixed. Women's moods and performance on verbal and motor tasks tend to be most positive halfway through their menstrual cycles, around time of ovulation (Bardwick, 1971; Ivey & Bardwick, 1968; Kimura, 1988). However, some women show significant levels of anxiety, depression, and fatigue for two to three days before menstruating (Money, 1980).

There is evidence showing a link between hormone levels and mood in women. Paige (1971) studied women whose hormone levels were kept rather even by birth-control pills and others whose hormone levels varied naturally throughout the cycle. She found that women whose hormone levels fluctuated appeared to show somewhat greater anxiety and hostility prior to and during menstruation. However, they did not commit crimes or wind up in mental wards. Other studies suggest that even among women who report premenstrual syndrome, the symptoms are most often mild, although a small percentage of women may have symptoms that are strong enough to interfere with their functioning (Keye, 1983).

Some hormonal changes at the time of menstruation, however, can cause very real and painful problems. For instance, prostaglandins cause uterine contractions. Most contractions go unnoticed, but strong, unrelieved contractions are uncomfortable in themselves and may temporarily deprive the uterus of oxygen, another source of pain (American College of Obstetricians and Gynecologists, 1985). In such cases prostaglandin-inhibiting drugs such as ibuprofen and indomethacin help a number of women (Owen, 1984). Other women report being helped by regular exercise and proper nutrition, including low-fat diets and dietary supplements, particularly B vitamins and minerals such as calcium and magnesium. Stress-management techniques such as relaxation training and social support are also sometimes helpful.

HEREDITY

Spend a moment or two reflecting on some facts of life:

- People cannot breathe underwater (without special equipment).
- People cannot fly (again, without some rather special equipment).
- Fish cannot learn to speak French or do an Irish jig even if you raise them in enriched environments and send them to finishing school (which is why we look for tuna that tastes good, not for tuna with good taste).
- Chimpanzees and gorillas can use sign language but cannot speak.

People cannot breathe underwater or fly (without oxygen tanks, airplanes, or other devices) because of the structures they have inherited. Fish are similarly limited by their **heredity,** or the biological transmission of traits and characteristics from one generation to another. Because of their heredity, fish cannot speak French or do a jig. Chimpanzees and gorillas are capable of understanding and expressing some concepts through American sign language and other nonverbal symbol systems. However, these apes have shown no ability to speak, even though they can make sounds and have voice boxes in their throats somewhat similar to ours. They have probably failed to inherit the humanlike speech areas of the cerebral cortex.

Heredity The transmission of traits from one generation to another through genes.

Genes The basic building blocks of heredity, which consist of deoxyribonucleic acid.

Polygenic Determined by several genes.

Chromosomes Rodlike structures consisting of genes that are found in the nuclei of the body's cells.

Genetics The branch of biology that studies heredity.

Behavior genetics The study of the genetic transmission of structures and traits that give rise to behavior.

Extraversion A trait in which a person directs his or her interest to persons and things outside the self. Sociability.

Neuroticism A trait in which a person is given to anxiety, tension, and emotional instability.

Genes and Chromosomes

Genes are the basic building blocks of heredity. They are the biochemical materials that regulate the development of traits. Some traits, such as blood type, are transmitted by a single pair of genes—one of which is derived from each parent. Other traits, referred to as **polygenic,** are determined by complex combinations of genes.

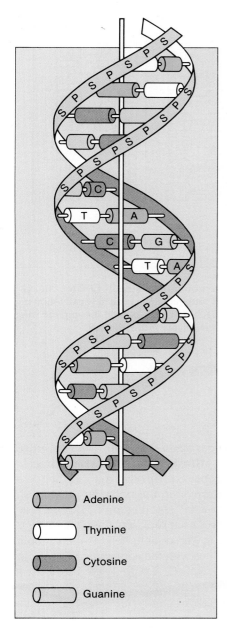

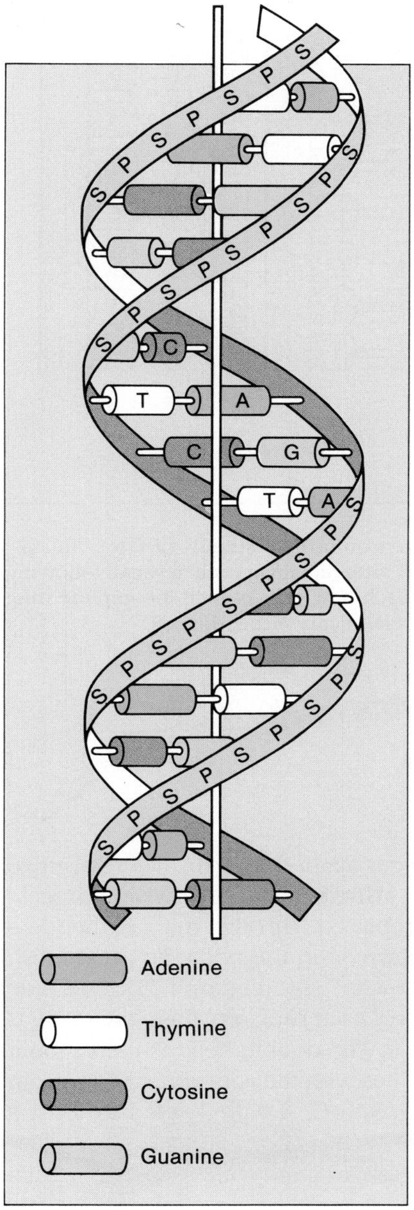

Figure 2.22
The Double Helix of DNA.

Genotype The sum total of our traits as inherited from our parents.

Phenotype The sum total of our traits at a given time, as inherited from our parents and influenced by environmental factors.

Nature In behavior genetics, heredity.

Nurture In behavior genetics, environmental influences on behavior, such as nutrition, culture, socioeconomic status, and learning.

Chromosomes, the genetic structures found in the nuclei of the body's cells, each consist of more than 1,000 genes. A normal human cell contains 46 chromosomes, which are organized into 23 pairs.

We may have about 100,000 genes in every cell in our bodies. Genes occupy various segments along the length of chromosomes. Chromosomes consist of large, complex molecules of deoxyribonucleic acid, which has several chemical components. You can breathe a sigh of relief, for behavior geneticists refer to this acid simply as DNA. The structure of DNA was first demonstrated in the 1950s by the team of James Watson and Francis Crick (1958). As you can see in Figure 2.22, DNA takes the form of a double helix, similar in appearance to a twisting ladder. In all living things, from one-celled animals to fish to people, the sides of the ladder consist of alternating segments of phosphate (P) and a simple sugar (S). The "rungs" of the ladder are attached to the sugars and consist of one of two pairs of bases, either *adenine* with *thymine* (A with T) or *cytosine* with *guanine* (C with G). The sequence of the rungs is the genetic code that will cause the unfolding organism to grow arms or wings, skin or scales.

Genetics and Behavior Genetics

Heredity, or the biological transmission of traits from one generation to another, plays an important role in the determination of traits we consider human and nonhuman. The biological structures we inherit at the same time make our behaviors possible and place limits on them. The field within the science of biology that studies heredity is called **genetics. Behavior genetics** is a specialty that bridges the sciences of psychology and biology. It is concerned with the transmission of structures and traits that give rise to patterns of behavior.

Research suggests that genetic influences are factors not only in physical traits such as height, race, and eye color but also in personality traits such as **extraversion** (Loehlin et al., 1982), **neuroticism** (Scarr et al., 1981), fearfulness and shyness (Daniels & Plomin, 1985; Kagan, 1984; Plomin, 1982), dominance and aggressiveness (Goldsmith, 1983), and antisocial behavior (Mednick, 1985).

The sets of traits specified by our genetic codes are referred to as our **genotypes.** But none of us, as we appear, is the result of heredity, or genotype, alone. We are also influenced by environmental factors such as nutrition, learning, exercise, and (unfortunately) accident and illness. Our actual traits at a given time are our **phenotypes.** That is, our traits, as expressed, represent the interaction of genetic and environmental influences. Thus, a genetic predisposition toward, say, shyness might be enhanced or possibly even reversed by powerful social influences.

Behavior geneticists are attempting to sort out the relative importance of **nature** (heredity) and **nurture** (environmental influences) in the development of various behavior patterns. Psychologists are especially interested in the roles of nature and nurture in intelligence (Plomin & DeFries, 1980), abnormal behavior patterns such as schizophrenia, and social problems such as sociopathy and aggression.

In a general sense, it can be argued that all behavior reflects the influences of both nature and nurture. All organisms inherit a range of structures that set the stage for certain behaviors. Yet environmental influences such as nutrition and learning also help decide whether genetically possible behaviors will be displayed. A potential Shakespeare who is reared in an impoverished neighborhood and never taught to read or write is unlikely to create a *Hamlet.*

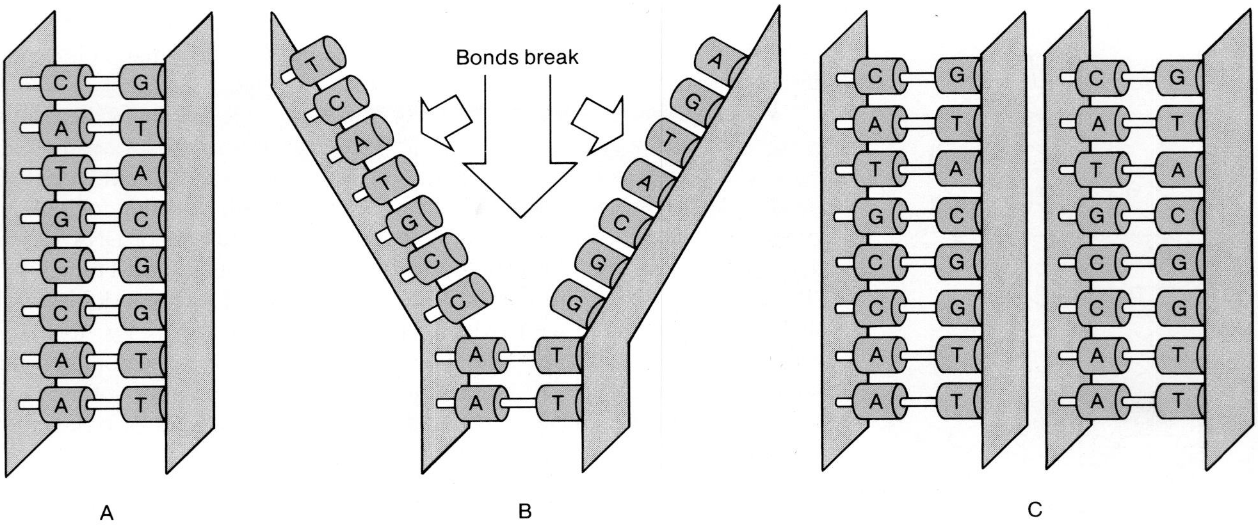

Figure 2.23
The Unzipping of DNA.

During the cell-division process of mitosis, chromosomal strands of DNA "unzip." One side of the ladder and one element of each rung remain in each new cell following division. The double helix is then rebuilt in each new cell, as each incomplete rung combines with the appropriate base from the chemicals within the cell.

Mitosis and Meiosis

We all begin life as a single cell that divides again and again. There are two types of cell division: *mitosis* and *meiosis.* **Mitosis** is the cell-division process by which growth occurs and tissues are replaced. Through mitosis, the identical genetic code is carried into each new cell in the body. To accomplish this, the chromosomal strands of DNA "unzip" (see Figure 2.23). One side of the ladder and one of the two elements of each rung remain in the nucleus of each new cell after division takes place. The double helix is then rebuilt in each cell: Each incomplete rung combines with the appropriate base from the chemicals within the cell (that is, G with C, A with T, etc.) to form a complete ladder. As a consequence, the genetic code is identical in every cell unless **mutations** occur through radiation or other environmental influences.

Sperm and ova are produced through **meiosis,** or reduction division. In meiosis, the 46 chromosomes within the nucleus first divide into 23 pairs. When the cell divides, one member of each pair goes to each newly formed cell. As a consequence, each new cell contains only 23 chromosomes, not 46. Thus, a cell that results from meiosis has half the genetic material of one that results from mitosis.

Through meiosis, we receive 23 chromosomes from our fathers' sperm cells and 23 chromosomes from our mothers' ova. When a sperm cell fertilizes an ovum, the chromosomes form 23 pairs (Figure 2.24). Twenty-two of the pairs contain **autosomes,** which are chromosomes that look alike and possess information about the same set of traits. The 23rd pair consists of **sex chromosomes,** which determine our sex and, in the case of males, look different. We all receive an X sex chromosome (so called because of the "X" shape) from our mothers. If we also receive an X sex chromosome from our fathers, we develop into females. If we receive a Y sex chromosome (named after the "Y" shape) from our fathers, we develop into males.

Mitosis The process of cell division by which the identical genetic code is carried into new cells in the body.

Mutation Sudden variations in the genetic code that usually occur as a result of environmental influences.

Meiosis A process of reduction division in which sperm and ova are formed that each contain 23 chromosomes instead of 46.

Autosomes Chromosomes that look alike and possess information about the same sets of traits. One autosome is received from the father and the corresponding autosome is received from the mother.

Sex chromosomes The twenty-third pair of chromosomes that determine sex and, in the case of males, do not look alike.

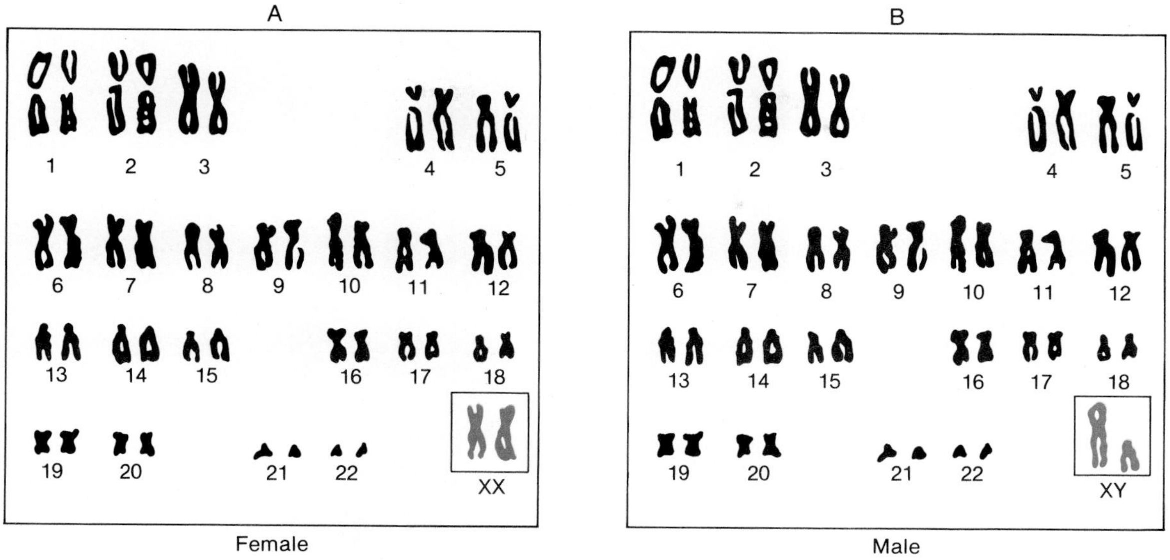

Figure 2.24
The 23 Pairs of Human Chromosomes.

People normally have 23 pairs of chromosomes. Sex is determined by the 23rd pair of chromosomes. Females have two X sex chromosomes (part A), whereas males have an X and a Y sex chromosome (part B).

Identical and Fraternal Twins

The fertilized ovum that carries genetic messages from both parents is called a **zygote.** Now and then a zygote divides into two cells that separate so that each develops into an individual with the same genetic makeup. Such persons are known as identical twins, or **monozygotic (MZ) twins.**

If the woman releases two ova in the same month, and they are both fertilized, they develop into fraternal twins, or **dizygotic (DZ) twins,** and are related as other brothers and sisters are. Identical, or MZ, twins are important in the study of the relative influences of heredity and environment because differences between MZ twins are the result of environmental influences (of nurture, not nature).

MZ twins look alike and are closer in height than DZ twins. Classic research shows that MZ twin sisters begin to menstruate one to two months apart, whereas DZ twins begin to menstruate about a year apart (Petri, 1934). MZ twins resemble one another more strongly than DZ twins on traits such as general irritability and sociability, persistence in performing cognitive tasks, verbal and spatial skills, and perceptual speed (DeFries et al., 1987; Floderus-Myrhed et al., 1980; Matheny, 1983; Scarr & Kidd, 1983).

The possible combinations of traits that can result from the coming together of so many thousands of genes is, practically speaking, unlimited. The chances that two people will show completely identical traits, with the exception of MZ twins (or triplets, quadruplets, etc.), are essentially nil. With the exception of MZ twins or triplets, the odds are against our having "doubles," even though there are billions of people in the world.

Truth or Fiction Revisited

Unless you are a monozygotic twin, you are very unlikely to have a "double" somewhere in the world.

Zygote A fertilized egg cell.

Monozygotic twins Identical, or MZ, twins. Twins who develop from a single zygote, thus carrying the same genetic instructions.

Dizygotic twins Fraternal, or DZ, twins. Twins who develop from separate zygotes.

Monozygotic (Identical) Twins. Identical, or MZ, twins are important in the study of the relative influences of heredity and environment, because differences between MZ twins are the result of environmental influences (of nurture, not nature).

Dominant and Recessive Traits

Traits are determined by pairs of genes. Each member of a pair of genes is called an **allele.** When both alleles for a trait, such as hair color, are the same, the person is said to be **homozygous** for that trait. When the alleles for a trait differ, the person is **heterozygous** for that trait.

Gregor Mendel (1822–1884), an Austrian monk, established a number of laws of heredity through his work with plants. Mid-nineteenth-century science did not permit Mendel to discover the true biochemical nature of the gene in his lifetime. Still, Mendel realized that some traits may result from an "averaging" of the genetic instructions carried by the parents.

Mendel also discovered the "law of dominance." For example, the offspring from the crossing of purebred tall peas and purebred dwarf peas were tall, suggesting that tallness is dominant over dwarfism. We now know that many genes carry **dominant traits** and that many others carry **recessive traits.** When a dominant allele is paired with a recessive allele, the dominant allele appears in the offspring.

Brown hair, for instance, is dominant over blond hair. Therefore, if one parent carries genes for only brown hair and the other for only blond hair, the children will have brown hair.* Brown-haired parents may also carry recessive genes for blond hair, as shown in Figure 2.25. Similarly, the offspring of Mendel's crossing of purebred tall and dwarf peas were impure. They carried recessive genes for dwarfism.

If the recessive gene from one parent combines with the recessive gene from the other, the recessive trait will be shown. In the example given in Figure 2.25, the child will have blond hair. Brown eyes are similarly dominant over blue eyes, and brown-eyed persons may carry recessive genes for blue eyes. Approximately 25 percent of the offspring of parents who each carry a gene for brown and blue eye color will have blue eyes. Mendel had found that 25 percent of the offspring of tall parent peas that carried recessive dwarfism would be dwarfs.

Allele Each member of a pair of genes.

Homozygous Having two identical alleles.

Heterozygous Having two different alleles.

Dominant trait In genetics, a trait that is expressed.

Recessive trait In genetics, a trait that is not expressed when the genes involved are paired with dominant genes, but they are transmitted to future generations and expressed if paired with other recessive genes.

*An exception would occur if the children also inherit a gene for albinism, in which case their hair and eyes would be colorless.

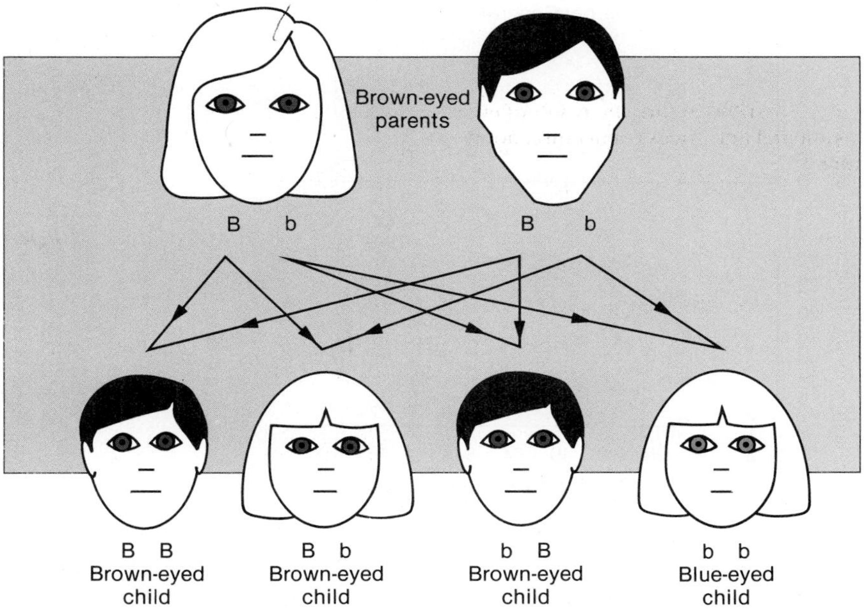

Figure 2.25
Transmission of Dominant and Recessive Traits. Two brown-eyed parents each carry a recessive gene for blue eyes. Their children have an equal opportunity of receiving genes for brown eyes and blue eyes. In such cases, 25 percent of the children show the recessive trait—blue eyes. The other 75 percent show the dominant trait—brown eyes. But two of three who show brown eyes carry the recessive trait for transmittal to future generations.

Truth or Fiction Revisited

It is true that brown-eyed parents can have a child with blue eyes—as long as the parents have recessive genes for blue eyes.

This discussion of eye color has been somewhat simplified. The percentages are not always so perfect because **modifier genes** may alter the expression of the genes for brown and blue eyes, producing hazel or greenish eyes (Scarr & Kidd, 1983). Some genes also function to "switch" other genes "on" or "off" at various times during development. For example, we normally reach reproductive capacity in the teens and not earlier, and men who go bald usually do so during adulthood. Similarly, the heart and the limbs develop at different times in the embryo, again because of the switching on of certain genes by other genes.

Experiments in Selective Breeding

You need not be a psychologist to know that animals can be selectively bred to enhance desired traits over the generations. Simply compare wild African dogs with their descendants—varieties as diverse as the Great Dane; the tiny, nervous Chihuahua; and the pug-nosed, white-trimmed Boston terrier. We breed our cattle and chickens to be bigger and fatter, so that they provide the most food calories for the minimum amount of feed. It also seems that we can selectively breed animals to enhance the presence of traits that are of more interest to psychologists, such as intelligence (although "intelligence" in lower animals does not correspond directly to human intelligence), aggressiveness, and even preference for alcohol over water (Eriksson, 1972).

There is an extensive discussion in Chapter 7 of the roles of heredity (nature) and the environment (nurture) in human intelligence. Here let us illustrate the concept of selective breeding with rats, which have been bred selectively for maze-learning ability (Rosenzweig, 1969; Tryon, 1940) and many other traits.

Modifier genes Genes that alter the action of the phenotypical expression of other genes.

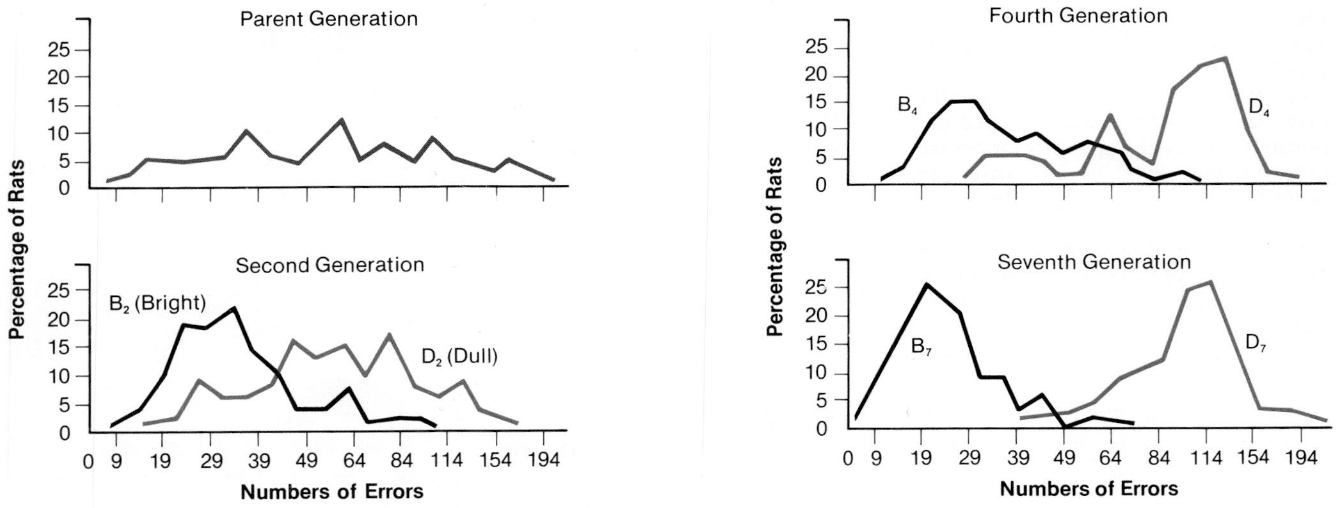

Figure 2.26
Selective Breeding for Maze-Learning Ability.

In the Tryon study, the offspring of maze-bright rats were inbred for six generations. So were the offspring of maze-dull rats. As the generations became further removed, there was progressively less overlap in the maze-learning ability of the offspring of the two groups, even though environmental influences were held as constant as possible for all offspring. Is maze-learning ability in rats similar to intelligence in human beings?

In such studies, an initial group of rats was tested for maze-learning ability by measuring the number of mistakes the rats made in repeated trials as they learned to find a food goal. Rats making the fewest mistakes were labeled B_1, signifying the first generation of "maze-bright" rats. "Maze-dull" rats were labeled D_1. The total distribution of errors, or blind-alley entrances, made by the first (parent) generation is shown in Figure 2.26. These errors were made over a series of 19 runs in the Tryon study.

Maze-bright rats from the first generation were then bred with other maze-bright rats, and maze-dull rats were similarly interbred. The second graph in Figure 2.26 shows how the offspring (B_2) of the maze-bright parents compared with the offspring (D_2) of the maze-dull parents in numbers of errors (blind-alley entrances). The offspring of the maze-bright rats, as a group, clearly made fewer errors than the offspring of the maze-dull, although there was considerable overlap between groups. The brightest offspring of the maze-bright were then interbred, as were the dullest of the maze-dull, for six consecutive generations.

After six generations there was little overlap in maze-learning performance between maze-bright and maze-dull rats. The (spatial relations) superiority of the maze-bright rats did not generalize to all types of learning tasks. We also cannot emphasize too strongly that maze-learning ability in rats is not comparable to the complex groupings of behavior that define human intelligence. Still, experiments such as these suggest that it would be foolhardy to completely overlook possible genetic influences on human intelligence.

Some breeds of dogs, such as Doberman pinschers and German shepherds, have been bred to be more aggressive than other varieties. Within breeds, however, dogs have been selectively bred to show high or low activity levels. Chickens have also been selectively bred for aggressiveness (consider the "sport" of cockfighting) and for level of sexual activity (McClearn & DeFries, 1973; Scott & Fuller, 1965).

In the Psychology and Modern Life section, we explore possible futures for the related technology of genetic engineering.

SUMMARY

1. **What are the parts of the nervous system?** The nervous system consists of neurons, which transmit information through neural impulses, and glial cells, which serve support functions. Neurons have a cell body (soma), dendrites, which receive transmissions, and axons. Chemicals called neurotransmitters travel across synapses to transmit messages to other neurons.

2. **What is myelin?** Many neurons have sheaths of myelin, a fatty substance produced by Schwann cells, that insulate axons and are missing at the nodes of Ranvier. Neural impulses can jump from node to node.

3. **What are afferent and efferent neurons?** Afferent neurons are neurons that transmit sensory messages to the central nervous system. Efferent neurons are neurons that conduct messages from the central nervous system that stimulate glands or cause muscles to contract.

4. **How are neural impulses transmitted?** Neural transmission is electrochemical. An electric charge is conducted along an axon through a process that allows sodium ions into the cell and then pumps them out. The neuron has a resting potential of -70 millivolts and an action potential of $+30$ to $+40$ millivolts.

5. **How do neurons fire?** Excitatory synapses stimulate neurons to fire; inhibitory neurons influence them not to. Neurons fire according to an all-or-none principle. Neurons may fire hundred of times per second, and absolute and relative refractory (insensitive) periods follow each firing.

6. **What are some important neurotransmitters?** These include acetylcholine, which is involved in muscle contractions; dopamine, imbalances of which have been linked to Parkinson's disease and schizophrenia; and norepinephrine, which accelerates the heartbeat and other body processes. A number of neuropeptides, such as beta-endorphin, serve as naturally occurring pain-killers.

7. **What is the central nervous system?** The brain and spinal cord compose the central nervous system. Reflexes involve the spinal cord but not the brain. The somatic and autonomic systems compose the peripheral nervous system.

8. **What are the parts of the brain?** The hindbrain includes the medulla, pons, and cerebellum. The reticular activating system begins in the hindbrain and continues through the midbrain into the forebrain. Important structures of the forebrain include the thalamus, hypothalamus, limbic system, basal ganglia, and cerebrum. The hypothalamus is involved in controlling body temperature and regulating motivation and emotion.

9. **What are the other parts of the nervous system?** The somatic nervous system transmits sensory information about muscles, skin, and joints to the central nervous system; it also controls muscular activity from the central nervous system. The autonomic nervous system (ANS) regulates the glands and involuntary activities like heartbeat, digestion, and dilation of the pupils. The sympathetic division of the ANS dominates in activities that expend the body's resources, such as fleeing from a predator, and the parasympathetic division dominates during processes that build the body's reserves, such as eating.

10. **What are the parts of the cerebral cortex?** The cerebral cortex is divided into the frontal, parietal, temporal, and occipital lobes. The visual cortex is in the occipital lobe, and the auditory cortex is in the temporal lobe. The sensory cortex lies behind the central fissure in the parietal lobe, and the motor cortex lies in the frontal lobe, across the central fissure from the sensory cortex.

11. **What parts of the brain are involved in thought and language?** Association areas of the cortex are involved in thought and language. The language areas of the cortex lie near the intersection of the frontal, temporal, and parietal lobes in the dominant hemisphere. For right-handed people, the left hemisphere of the cortex is usually dominant.

12. **How do split-brain patients behave?** For the most part, their behavior is perfectly normal. However, although they may be able to verbally describe a screened-off object like a pencil that is held in the hand connected to the dominant hemisphere, they cannot do so when the object is held in the other hand.

13. **What makes up the endocrine system?** The endocrine system consists of ductless glands that secrete hormones.

14. **What are some of the pituitary hormones?** The pituitary gland secretes growth hormone; prolactin, which regulates maternal behavior in lower animals and stimulates production of milk in women; ADH, which inhibits the production of urine; and oxytocin, which stimulates labor in pregnant women.

15. **What is the function of insulin?** The pancreas secretes insulin, which enables the body to metabolize sugar. Diabetes, hyperglycemia, and hypoglycemia are all linked to imbalances in insulin.

16. **What hormones are produced by the adrenal glands?** The adrenal cortex produces steroids, which promote development of muscle mass and increase activity level. The adrenal medulla secretes adrenaline (epinephrine), which increases the metabolic rate and is involved in general emotional arousal.

17. **What hormones are secreted by the testes and ovaries?** These are sex hormones such as testosterone, progesterone, and estrogen. Sex hormones are responsible for prenatal sexual differentiation, and female sex hormones regulate the menstrual cycle.

18. **What are genes and chromosomes?** Genes are the basic building blocks of heredity and consist of DNA. A thousand or more genes make up each chromosome. People normally have 46 chromosomes. They receive 23 from the father and 23 from the mother.

19. **What is genetics?** Genetics is the branch of biology concerned with transmission of traits from generation to generation.

20. **What are genotypes and phenotypes?** Our genotypes are the sets of traits we inherit from our parents, whereas our phenotypes—the characteristics that we show at any point in time—are also influenced by environmental factors.

21. **What are mitosis and meiosis?** Through the cell-division process of mitosis, the identical genetic code is carried to each new cell in the body. Chromosomal strands of DNA "unzip" and are rebuilt in each new cell. Sperm and ova are produced through reduction division, or meiosis, in which each new cell contains only 23 chromosomes.

22. **What are monozygotic and dizygotic twins?** Identical twins are monozygotic; that is, they develop from a single zygote, or fertilized egg cell. Fraternal twins are dizygotic. Monozygotic twins are important in the study of the relative influences of nature and nurture.

23. **What are dominant and recessive traits?** Dominant traits are traits that are expressed, whereas recessive traits are those shown only if a recessive gene from one parent combines with a recessive gene from the other. People with recessive genes for illnesses are said to be carriers of those illnesses.

24. **Can animals be bred selectively in order to heighten the influence of desired traits?** Yes. For example, we can breed dogs selectively to heighten physical traits, such as size and strength, and psychological traits, such as aggressiveness. Rats can be selectively bred for maze-learning ability.

PSYCHOLOGY AND MODERN LIFE

In many ways, modern science has revolutionized the process of reproduction. In this section we first see how knowledge of the endocrine system has led to innovations in the prediction of ovulation, innovations that have helped many childless couples conceive. In the chapter we learned about the ways in which genes and chromosomes transmit our genetic heritages to new generations. Here we explore some of the chromosomal and genetic errors that occur and discuss how we have learned to detect them. Finally we consider genetic engineering and see that in the future, it may be possible to correct some of these errors before children are born.

Reproduction, Biology, and Behavior

We begin by discussing a new way in which childless couples can optimize the timing of intercourse in order to become pregnant.

Ovulation-Detecting Kits Some women have difficulty conceiving because of variable menstrual cycles. Although ovulation occurs about 14 days prior to the end of each cycle, women with variable cycles have difficulty predicting ovulation. Newly released ova are capable of being fertilized for about 48 hours, and sperm cannot survive within the female reproductive tract for more than 72 hours. Thus, it is to the couple's advantage to time intercourse to coincide as nearly as possible with ovulation.

Women can now use over-the-counter ovulation-detecting kits to determine the days when they are most fertile. These kits are based on the finding that a day or so before the releasing of an ovum (ovulation), there is a surge of luteinizing hormone (LH) from the pituitary gland. LH is found in the urine as well as in the bloodstream, and several ovulation-predicting kits rely on measurement of changing LH levels.

Chromosomal and Genetic Abnormalities What kinds of things happen when we do not have the normal complement of 46 chromosomes, or when genes are "defective"? There are a number of diseases that reflect chromosomal or genetic abnormalities.

Chromosomal Abnormalities When we do not have the normal complement of 46 chromosomes, physical and behavioral abnormalities may result. The risk of these abnormalities rises with the age of the parents (Hook, 1981).

In Down syndrome (formerly referred to as Down's syndrome), the 21st pair of chromosomes has an extra, or third, chromosome. Down syndrome is thought to be caused by faulty division of the 21st pair of chromosomes during meiosis, an abnormality that becomes increasingly likely among older parents. Although this abnormality is usually attributed to the mother, it should be noted that fathers are responsible for Down syndrome in about 25 percent of cases. Persons with Down syndrome show a downward-sloping fold of skin at the inner corners of the eyes, creating a superficial resemblance to Asians. Hence the old term *mongolism,* which is now recognized to be racist and no longer used.

Down-syndrome children also show a characteristic round face; protruding tongue; and broad, flat nose. They are mentally retarded and may suffer from respiratory problems and malformations of the heart. Most Down-syndrome persons die by middle age. By this time they are also prone to memory loss and childish emotions that stem from a form of senility (Kolata, 1985).

An extra Y sex chromosome is associated with heightening of male secondary sex characteristics in men labeled "supermales." XYY males are somewhat taller than average and develop heavier beards. They are often mildly retarded, especially in language development. At one point it was speculated that XYY syndrome was linked to aggressive criminal behavior, but in Chapter 12 you will see that evidence for this assertion is sketchy at best.

Other sex chromosomal abnormalities include Klinefelter's syndrome, Turner's syndrome, and the XXX "superfemale" syndrome. About one male in 500 has Klinefelter's syndrome, which is caused by an extra X sex chromosome (XXY). XXY males produce less testosterone than normal males, and they are infertile. Nor do male secondary sex characteristics develop. XXY males usually have enlarged breasts and poor muscular development. In terms of cognitive functioning and personality, they are usually mildly mentally retarded and more passive than most males.

About one girl in 10,000 has a single X sex chromosome and, as a result, develops Turner's syndrome. The external genitals of such girls are normal because we all develop as females in the absence of a Y sex chromosome. But these girls' ovaries are poorly developed, and they produce reduced amounts of estrogen. Females with Turner's syndrome are shorter than average and infertile. Psychologically, they are mildly retarded, especially in math and science-related skills.

About one girl in 1,000 has XXX sex chromosomal structure, giving rise to superfemale syndrome. Superfemales are normal in appearance. However, they tend to show lower-than-average language skills and poorer memory for recent events, suggestive of mild mental retardation (Rovet & Netley, 1983).

Genetic Abnormalities Other disorders have been attributed to genes. The enzyme disorder phenylketonuria (PKU) is transmitted by a recessive gene and affects about one child in 14,000. When both parents are carriers of the recessive gene, PKU is transmitted to about one child in four (as shown in Figure 2.25). (Carriers of a disease have a recessive gene for the disease and may transmit the disease to future generations, but they do not have the disease themselves.) One child in four will not carry the recessive gene. The other two, like their parents, will be carriers.

Children with PKU cannot metabolize the protein *phenylalanine*. As a consequence, it builds up in their bodies as phenylpyruvic acid and damages the central nervous system. The psychological results are mental retardation and emotional disturbance. We have no cure for PKU, but PKU can be detected in newborn children by blood or urine analysis. Children with PKU who are placed on diets low in phenylalanine within three to six weeks after birth develop normally. The children also receive protein supplements that compensate for the nutritional loss.

Huntington's chorea, the disease that afflicted folksinger Woodie Guthrie, is a fatal progressive degenerative disorder and a dominant trait. Physical symptoms include uncontrollable muscle movements. Psychological symptoms include personality change and loss of intellectual functioning. Because its onset is delayed until middle adulthood, many with the defect have borne children only to discover, years later, that they and their offspring will inevitably develop it.

Sickle-cell anemia and Tay-Sachs disease are caused by recessive genes. Sickle-cell anemia is most common among blacks and Hispanic Americans. Nearly one black in 10 and one Hispanic American in 20 is a carrier. In sickle-cell anemia, red blood cells take on a sickle shape and clump together, obstructing small blood vessels and decreasing the oxygen supply. Results can include jaundice, painful and swollen joints, and such possibly fatal problems as pneumonia and heart and kidney failure.

Tay-Sachs disease is a fatal degenerative disease of the central nervous system that mainly afflicts Jews of East European origin. About one in 25 American Jews carries the recessive gene for the defect, so the chance that both members of a Jewish couple will carry the gene is about one in 625. Victims of Tay-Sachs disease gradually lose muscle control. They become blind and deaf, retarded and paralyzed, and die by the age of 5.

Some genetic defects, such as hemophilia, are carried on only the X sex chromosome. For this reason, they are called sex-linked genetic abnormalities. They also involve recessive genes. Females, each of whom has two X sex chromosomes, are less likely than males to show sex-linked disorders because the disorders would have to be present in both of their sex chromosomes to be expressed. Sex-linked disorders are shown by the sons of female carriers, however, because the genetic instructions carried in the sons' (single) X sex chromosomes are not canceled by opposing genetic instructions on their Y sex chromosomes. Queen Victoria was a carrier of hemophilia and transmitted the disorder to many of her children, who in turn carried it into a number of the ruling houses of Europe. For this reason, hemophilia has been referred to as the "royal disease."

Genetic Counseling. In genetic counseling, information about a couple's genetic backgrounds is examined to determine the possibility that the couple's children may be genetically defective.

Genetic Counseling and Prenatal Testing In an effort to help parents avert predictable tragedies, genetic counseling is becoming widely used. In this procedure, information about a couple's ages and genetic backgrounds is compiled to determine whether their union may result in children with chromosomal or genetic problems. Some couples whose natural children would be at high risk elect to adopt.

Amniocentesis and CVS Pregnant women may also confirm the presence of certain chromosomal and genetic abnormalities through amniocentesis or chorionic villus sampling (CVS). Amniocentesis is carried out about 14 to 15 weeks after conception, and CVS can be done at 9 to 12 weeks. In amniocentesis, fluid is withdrawn from the amniotic sac (also called the bag of waters) containing the fetus. Sloughed-off fetal cells are then separated from amniotic fluid, grown in a culture, and examined microscopically. In CVS, a small tube is inserted through the vagina and into the uterus, and pieces of material are snipped off from the outer membrane that envelops the amniotic sac and fetus.

These tests are commonly carried out with women who become pregnant past the age of 35 because the chances of Down syndrome increase dramatically as women and their partners approach or pass the age of 40. The tests can also detect the presence of sickle-cell anemia, Tay-Sachs disease, spina bifida, muscular dystrophy, and Rh incompatibility in the fetus.

The tests also permit parents to learn the sex of their unborn child through examination of the 23rd pair of chromosomes. However, amniocentesis carries some risks, and it would be unwise to have the procedure done solely for this purpose. If you were having an amniocentesis, would you want to know the sex of your unborn child, or would you prefer to wait?

Ultrasound Another modern method of prenatal testing uses ultrasound to form a picture of the fetus. Ultrasound is too high in pitch to be detected by the human ear, but it can be "bounced off" the unborn child in the same way that radar is bounced off objects to form "pictures" of them.

Blood Tests The potential for a variety of disorders can be determined by testing the blood of the parents. For instance, recessive genes for sickle-cell anemia and Tay-Sachs disease can be found. A maternal blood test for alpha-fetoprotein can suggest whether the fetus might have neural-tube defects.

Genetic Engineering Someday genetic engineering may provide couples with genetically abnormal embryos the possibility of correcting the problem before the child is born. In genetic engineering, the genetic structures of organisms are changed by direct manipulation of their reproductive cells. In fact, even as you read these words, patents are pending on new life forms—mostly microscopic—that biologists and corporations hope will be marketable.

Research suggests that genetic engineering may lead to some exciting discoveries in the not-too-distant future. These include the following:

- New vaccines for diseases like hepatitis and herpes
- Ways of detecting predispositions for disorders such as cancer, heart disease, and emphysema by studying a newborn's (or fetus's) genetic code
- Prenatal screening for fatal hereditary diseases such as Huntington's chorea and cystic fibrosis*
- Understanding of how "spelling errors" in the genetic code (for example, ATTC rather than ATGC in a given segment of DNA) may cause inherited diseases such as sickle-cell anemia
- Modification of the genetic codes of unborn children to prevent disease
- Creation of new wonder drugs from the materials that compose DNA

I began this section by noting that science has in many ways revolutionized the process of reproduction. In many other ways, thankfully, the process remains more art than science.

*In amniocentesis the general chromosomal structure, rather than the intricate and elusive genetic code, is examined.

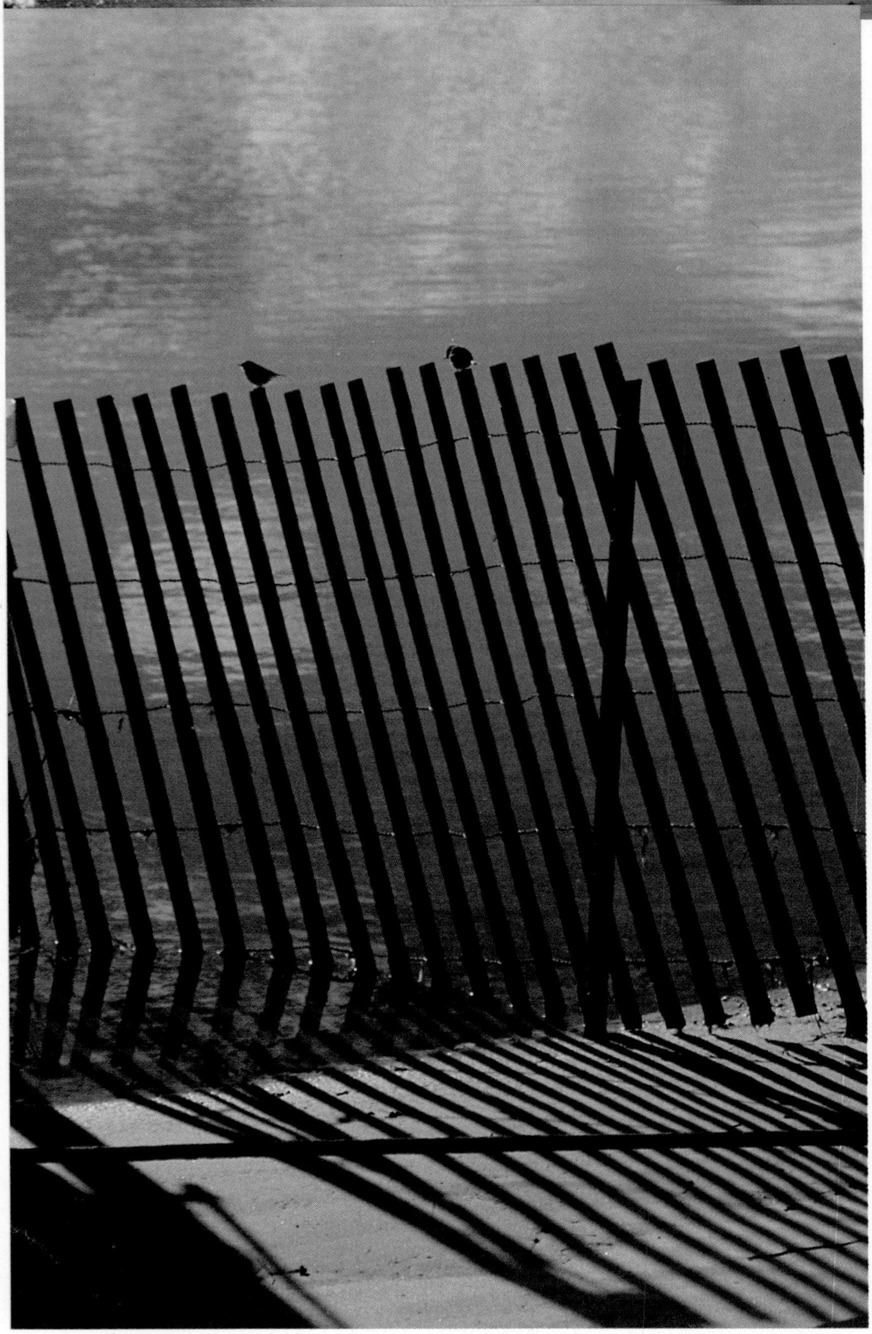

Outline

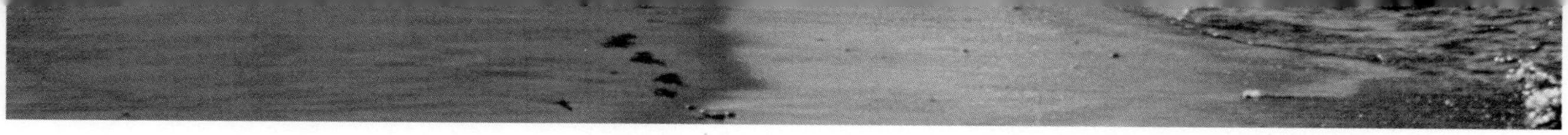

3 Sensation and Perception

Truth or Fiction?

- □ On a clear, dark night you could probably see the light from a candle burning 30 miles away.
- □ If we could see lights of slightly longer wavelengths, warmblooded animals would glow in the dark.
- □ Sometimes we fail to hear things because we don't want to hear them.
- □ White sunlight is actually composed of all the colors of the rainbow.
- □ When we mix blue light and yellow light, we attain green light.
- □ A $500 machine-made violin will produce the same musical notes as a $200,000 Stradivarius.
- □ Onions and apples have the same taste.
- □ Rubbing or scratching a sore toe is often an effective way of relieving pain.
- □ Some people have the ability to read other people's minds.

Five thousand years ago in China, give or take a day or two, an arrow was shot into the air. Where did it land? Ancient records tell us precisely where: in the hand of a fierce warrior and master of the martial arts. As the story was told to me, the warrior had grown so fierce because of a chronic toothache. Incessant pain had ruined his disposition.

On one fateful day our hero watched as invading hordes assembled on surrounding hills. His troops were trembling, and he raised his arms in wild gestures in an effort to boost their morale in the face of the invaders' superior numbers. A slender wooden shaft lifted into the air from a nearby rise, arced, and then descended—right into the warrior's palm. His troops cringed and muttered among themselves, but our hero said nothing. Although he saw the arrow through his palm, he did not scream. He did not run. He did not even complain.

He was astounded. His toothache had vanished. His entire jaw was numb.

Meanwhile the invaders looked on—horrified. They, too, muttered among themselves. What sort of warrior could look upon an arrow through his hand with such indifference? Even with a growing smile? If this was the caliber of warrior in this village, they'd be better off traveling west and looking for a brawl in ancient Sumer or in Egypt. They sounded the retreat and withdrew.

Our warrior received a hero's welcome back in town. A physician offered to remove the arrow without a fee—a tribute to bravery. But the warrior would have none of it. The arrow had done wonders for his toothache, and he would permit no meddling. He already had discovered that if the pain threatened to return, he need only twirl the arrow and it would recede once more.

Things were not so rosy on the home front, however. Although his wife was thrilled to find him jovial once more, the arrow put a crimp in romance. When he put his arm around her, she was in danger of being stabbed. Finally she gave him an ultimatum: it was she or the arrow.

Placed in deep conflict, our warrior consulted a psychologist, who then huddled with the physician and the village elders. After much to-do, they asked the warrior to participate in an experiment. They would remove the arrow and replace it with a pin that the warrior could twirl as needed. If the pin didn't do the trick, they could always fall back on the arrow, so to speak.

To the warrior's wife's relief, the pin worked. And here, in ancient China, lay the origins of the art of **acupuncture**—the use of needles to relieve pain and treat a variety of ills ranging from **hypertension** to some forms of blindness.

I confess that this tale is not entirely accurate. To my knowledge, there were no psychologists in ancient China. (Their loss.) Moreover, the part about the warrior's wife is fictitious. It is claimed, however, that acupuncture as a means for dealing with pain originated in ancient China when a soldier was, in fact, wounded in a hand by an arrow and discovered that a chronic toothache had disappeared. The Chinese, historians say, then set out to map the body by sticking pins here and there to learn how they influenced the perception of pain.

Control of pain is just one of the many issues that interest psychologists who study the closely related concepts of sensation and perception. **Sensation** is the stimulation of sensory receptors and the transmission of sensory information to the central nervous system (the spinal cord or brain). Sensory receptors are located in sensory organs such as the eyes and ears and, as we shall see, in the skin and elsewhere in the body. The stimulation of the senses is mechanical; it results from sources of energy like light and sound or from the presence of chemicals, as in smell and taste.

Perception is not mechanical. Perception is the process by which sensations are organized and interpreted, forming an inner representation of the world. Perception involves much more than sensation. It reflects learning and expectations and the ways in which we organize incoming information about the world. Perception is an active process through which we make sense of sensory stimulation. A human shape and a 12-inch ruler may stimulate paths of equal length among the sensory receptors in our eyes. Whether we interpret the human shape to be a foot-long doll or a full-grown person 15 to 20 feet away is a matter of perception.

In this chapter you will see that your personal map of reality—your ticket of admission to a world of changing sights, sounds, and other sources of sensory input—depends largely on the five senses of vision, hearing, smell, taste, and touch. We shall see, however, that touch is just one of several "skin senses," which also include pressure, warmth, cold, and pain. There are also other senses that alert you to your own body position without your literally having to watch every step you take. As we explore the nature of each of these senses, we shall find that highly similar sensations may lead to quite different perceptions in different people—or within the same person in different situations.

Acupuncture The ancient Chinese practice of piercing parts of the body with needles to deaden pain and treat illness.

Hypertension High blood pressure.

Sensation The stimulation of sensory receptors and the transmission of sensory information to the central nervous system.

Perception The process by which sensations are organized into an inner representation of the world.

First let us explore some of the ways in which psychologists gather information about the processes of sensation and perception.

BASIC CONCEPTS IN SENSATION AND PERCEPTION

Before we begin our journey through the senses, let us consider a number of concepts that apply to all the senses: absolute threshold, difference threshold, signal-detection theory, and sensory adaptation. In doing so we shall learn why we might be able to dim the lights gradually to near darkness without people becoming aware of our mischief. We shall also learn why we might grow unaware of the most savory aromas of delightful dinners.

Absolute Threshold

The weakest amount of a stimulus that can be told apart from no stimulus at all is called the **absolute threshold** for that stimulus. For example, the amount of physical energy required to activate the visual sensory system is the absolute threshold for light. Beneath this threshold, detection of light is impossible (Haber & Hershenson, 1980).

Psychophysicists experiment to determine the absolute thresholds of the senses by presenting stimuli of progressively greater intensity. In the **method of constant stimuli,** researchers use sets of stimuli with magnitudes close to the expected threshold. The order of the stimuli is randomized. Subjects are asked to say yes if they detect a stimulus and no if they do not. The stimuli are then repeatedly presented to the subjects. A subject's absolute threshold for the stimulus is the lowest magnitude of the stimulus that he or she reports detecting 50 percent of the time. Weaker stimuli may be detected, but less than 50 percent of the time. Stronger stimuli, of course, will be detected more than 50 percent of the time.

The relationship between the intensity of a stimulus (a physical event) and its perception (a psychological event) is considered to be **psychophysical.** That is, it bridges psychological and physical events.

As you can see in Table 3.1, absolute thresholds have been determined for the senses of vision, hearing, taste, smell, and touch. Naturally, there are individual differences in absolute thresholds. Some people, that is, are more sensitive to sensory stimuli than others. The same person may also differ somewhat in sensitivity to sensory stimuli from day to day or from occasion to occasion. In the section on signal-detection theory, we shall see that sensitivity reflects psychological as well as physical and biological variables.

If the absolute thresholds for the human senses differed significantly, our daily experiences would be unrecognizable. Our ears are particularly sensitive, especially to sounds low in **pitch.** If they were any more sensitive, we might hear the collisions among molecules of air. If our eyes were sensitive to lights of slightly longer wavelengths, we would perceive infrared light waves. As a result, animals who are warmblooded and thus give off heat—including our mates—would literally glow in the dark.

Truth or Fiction Revisited

It is true that on a clear, dark night you could probably see the light from a candle burning 30 miles away. This figure is in keeping with the absolute threshold for light.

Absolute threshold The minimal amount of energy that can produce a sensation.

Psychophysicist A person who studies the relationships between physical stimuli (like light or sound) and their perception.

Method of constant stimuli A psychophysical method for determining thresholds in which the researcher presents stimuli of various magnitudes and asks the subject to report detection.

Psychophysical Bridging the gap between the physical and psychological worlds.

Pitch The highness or lowness of a sound, as determined by the frequency of the sound waves.

Table 3.1
Absolute Detection Thresholds and Other Characteristics of Human Sensory Systems

Sense	Stimulus	Receptors	Threshold
Vision	Electromagnetic energy	Rods and cones in the retina	A candle flame viewed from a distance of about 30 miles on a clear, dark night
Hearing	Sound pressure waves	Hair cells on the basilar membrane of the inner ear	The ticking of a watch from about 20 feet away in a quiet room
Taste	Chemical substances dissolved in saliva	Taste buds on the tongue in the mouth	About one teaspoon of sugar dissolved in two gallons of water
Smell	Chemical substances in the air	Receptor cells in the upper part of the nasal cavity (the nose)	About one drop of perfume diffused throughout a small house (1 part in 500 million)
Touch	Mechanical displacement or pressure on the skin	Nerve endings located in the skin	The wing of a fly falling on a cheek from a distance of about 0.4 inch

Source: Adapted from Galanter (1962).

Truth or Fiction Revisited

It is true that if we could see lights of slightly longer wavelengths, warmblooded animals would glow in the dark.

Difference Threshold

How much of a difference in intensity between two lights is required before you will detect one as being brighter than the other? The minimum difference in the magnitude of two stimuli required to tell them apart is their **difference threshold.** As is the case with the absolute threshold, psychologists have agreed to the criterion of a difference in magnitudes that can be detected 50 percent of the time.

Psychophysicist Ernst Weber discovered through laboratory research that the difference threshold for perceiving differences in the intensity of light is about 2 percent (actually closer to 1/60th) of their intensity. This fraction, 1/60th, is known as **Weber's constant** for light. A closely related concept is the **just noticeable difference** (jnd), or the minimal amount by which a source of energy must be increased or decreased so that a difference in intensity will be perceived. In the case of light, people can perceive a difference in intensity 50 percent of the time when the brightness of a light is increased or decreased by 1/60th. Weber's constant for light holds whether we are comparing two quite bright or rather dull lights. However, it becomes inaccurate when we compare extremely bright or extremely dull lights.

As you can see in Table 3.2, Weber's research in psychophysics touched on many senses. He derived difference thresholds for different types of sensory stimulation.

Difference threshold The minimal difference in intensity required between two sources of energy so that they will be perceived as being different.

Weber's constant The fraction of the intensity by which a source of physical energy must be increased or decreased so that a difference in intensity will be perceived.

Just noticeable difference The minimal amount by which a source of energy must be increased or decreased so that a difference in intensity will be perceived.

Table 3.2
Weber's Constant for Various Sensory Discriminations

Sense	Type of Discrimination	Weber's Constant
Vision	Brightness of a light	1/60
Hearing	Pitch (frequency) of a tone	1/333
	Loudness of a tone	1/10
Taste	Difference in saltiness	1/5
Smell	Amount of rubber smell	1/10
Touch	Pressure on the skin surface	1/7
	Deep pressure	1/77
	Difference in lifted weights	1/53

A little math will show you the practical importance of these jnd's. Consider weightlifting. Weber's constant for noticing differences in lifted weight is 1/53rd. (Round it off to 1/50th.) That means that one would probably have to increase the weight on a 100-pound barbell by about two pounds before the lifter would notice the difference. Now think of the one-pound dumbbells used by many runners. Increasing the weight of each dumbbell by two pounds would be readily apparent to almost anyone because the increase would be threefold, not a small fraction. Yet the increase is still "only" two pounds. Return to our power lifter. When he is pressing 400 pounds, a two-pound difference is less likely to be noticeable than when he is pressing 100 pounds. This is because our constant two pounds has become a difference of only 1/200th.

Signal-Detection Theory

Our discussion so far has been rather "inhuman." We have written about perception of sensory stimuli as if people are simply switched on by certain amounts of external stimulation. This is not fully accurate. Although people are sensory instruments, they are influenced by complex patterns of psychological stimulation as well as external changes. **Signal-detection theory** has arisen to take into consideration the human elements in sensation and perception.

According to signal-detection theory, several factors determine whether people will perceive sensory stimuli (signals) or a difference between two signals. The intensity of the signal itself is just one factor. Another is the degree to which it can be distinguished from background **noise.** In other words, it is easier to hear a speech in a quiet room than in one where people are clinking silverware and glasses and engaging in competing conversations. The quality of a person's biological sensory system is still another factor. Here we are concerned with the sharpness or acuteness of the individual's sensory system. We consider whether sensory capacity is fully developed or diminished because of illness or advanced years.

Signal-detection theory also considers the roles of psychological factors such as motivation, expectations, and learning. For example, the place in which you are reading this book may be abuzz with signals. If you are outside, perhaps there is a breeze against your face. Perhaps the shadows of passing clouds darken the scene now and then. If you are inside, perhaps there are the occasional clanks and hums of a heating system. Perhaps the odors of dinner are hanging in the air, or the voices from a TV set suggest a crowd

Signal-detection theory The view that the perception of sensory stimuli involves the interaction of physical, biological, and psychological factors.

Noise (1) In signal-detection theory, any unwanted signal that interferes with perception of the desired signal. (2) More generally, a combination of dissonant sounds.

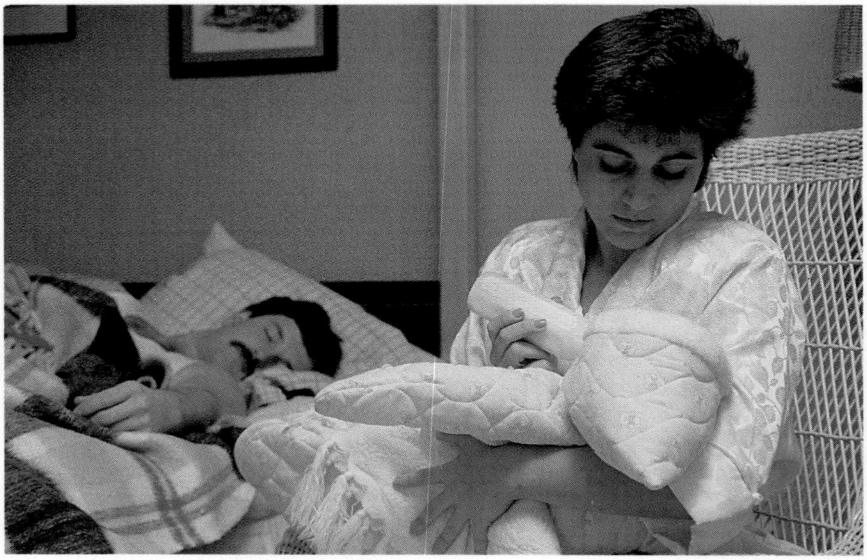

Signal Detection. He sleeps while she is awakened by the baby's crying. Detection of signals, such as a baby's crying, is determined not only by the physical characteristics of the signals but also by psychological factors, such as motivation and attention.

in another room. Yet you are focusing your attention on this page (I hope), so the other signals recede into the backdrop of your consciousness. Thus, one psychological factor in signal detection is the focusing or narrowing of attention to signals the person deems important.

Consider some examples. One parent may sleep through a baby's crying, whereas the other parent is awakened. This is not necessarily because one parent is innately more sensitive to the sounds of crying (although some men may conveniently assume that mothers are). Instead, it may be because one parent has been assigned the task of caring for the baby through the night and is thus more highly motivated to attend to the sounds. Because of training, an artist might notice the use of line or subtle colors that would go undetected by a lay person looking at the same painting.

Truth or Fiction Revisited

It is true that we sometimes fail to hear things because we don't want to hear them. Psychological factors as well as stimulus characteristics influence perception.

Sensory Adaptation

There is a saying that the only thing that remains constant is change. It happens that our sensory systems are admirably suited to a changing environment. **Sensory adaptation** refers to the processes by which we become more sensitive to stimuli of low magnitude and less sensitive to stimuli of relatively constant magnitude.

Sensory adaptation The processes by which organisms become more sensitive to stimuli that are low in magnitude and less sensitive to stimuli that are constant or ongoing in magnitude.

Sensitization The type of sensory adaptation in which we become more sensitive to stimuli that are low in magnitude. Also called *positive adaptation.*

Most of us are familiar with the process by which the visual sense adapts to lower intensities of light. When we first walk into a darkened movie theater, we see little but the images on the screen. As time elapses, however, we become increasingly sensitive to the faces of those around us and the inner features of the theater. The process of becoming more sensitive to stimulation is referred to as **sensitization,** or positive adaptation.

On the other hand, we become less sensitive to ongoing stimulation. Sources of light appear to grow dimmer as we adapt to them. In fact, if you could keep an image completely stable on the retinas of your eyes—which is virtually impossible to accomplish without a still image and stabilizing equipment—the image would fade within a few seconds and be very difficult to see. Similarly, at the beach we soon become less aware of the lapping of the waves. When we live in the city, we become desensitized to traffic sounds except for the occasional backfire or accident. As you may have noticed from experiences with freshly painted rooms, disagreeable odors fade quite rapidly. The process of becoming less sensitive to stimulation is referred to as **desensitization,** or negative adaptation.

Let us now examine how each of the human sensory systems perceives signals from the outer (and inner) environments.

VISION

Our eyes are our "windows on the world." We consider information from vision to be more essential than that from hearing, smell, taste, and touch. Consider the findings of one study in **visual capture:** When we look at a square object through lenses that distort it into a rectangle, we usually perceive it as a rectangle, even though we can feel it with our hands (Rock & Victor, 1964). Because vision is our dominant sense, we consider blindness our most debilitating sensory loss. An understanding of vision requires discussion of the nature of light and of the master of the sensory organs, the eye.

Light

In almost all cultures, light is a symbol of goodness and knowledge. We describe capable people as being "bright" or "brilliant." If we are not being complimentary, we label them as "dull." People who aren't in the know are said to be "in the dark." Just what is this stuff called light?

Visible light is the stuff that triggers visual sensations. It is just one small part of a spectrum of electromagnetic energy (see Figure 3.1) that is described in terms of wavelengths. These wavelengths vary from those of cosmic rays, which are only a few trillionths of an inch long, to some radio waves, which extend for many miles. Radar, microwaves, and X-rays are also forms of electromagnetic energy.

You have probably seen rainbows or light broken down into several colors as it filtered through your windows. Sir Isaac Newton, the British scientist, discovered that sunlight could be broken down into different colors by means of a triangular solid of glass called a **prism** (Figure 3.1). When I took introductory psychology, I was taught that I could remember the colors of the spectrum, from longest to shortest wavelengths, by using the mnemonic device *Roy G. Biv* (red, orange, yellow, green, blue, indigo, violet). I must have been a backward student because I found it easier to recall them in reverse order, using the meaningless acronym *vibgyor.*

Truth or Fiction Revisited

It is true that white sunlight is composed of all the colors of the rainbow.

The wavelength of visible light determines its color, or **hue.** The wavelength for red is longer than that for orange, and so on through the spectrum.

Desensitization The type of sensory adaptation in which we become less sensitive to constant stimuli. Also called *negative adaptation.*

Visual capture The tendency of vision to dominate the other senses.

Visible light The part of the electromagnetic spectrum that stimulates the eye and produces visual sensations.

Prism A transparent triangular solid that breaks down visible light into the colors of the spectrum.

Hue The color of light, as determined by its wavelength.

Figure 3.1
The Visible Spectrum. By passing a source of white light, such as sunlight, through a prism, we break it down into the colors of the visible spectrum. The visible spectrum is just one part—and a narrow part indeed—of the electromagnetic spectrum. The electromagnetic spectrum also includes radio waves, microwaves, X-rays, cosmic rays, and many others. Different forms of electromagnetic energy have different wavelengths, which vary from a few trillionths of a meter to thousands of miles. Visible light varies in wavelength from about 400 to 700 nanometers. What is a nanometer? One *billionth* of a meter. (A meter = 39.37 inches.)

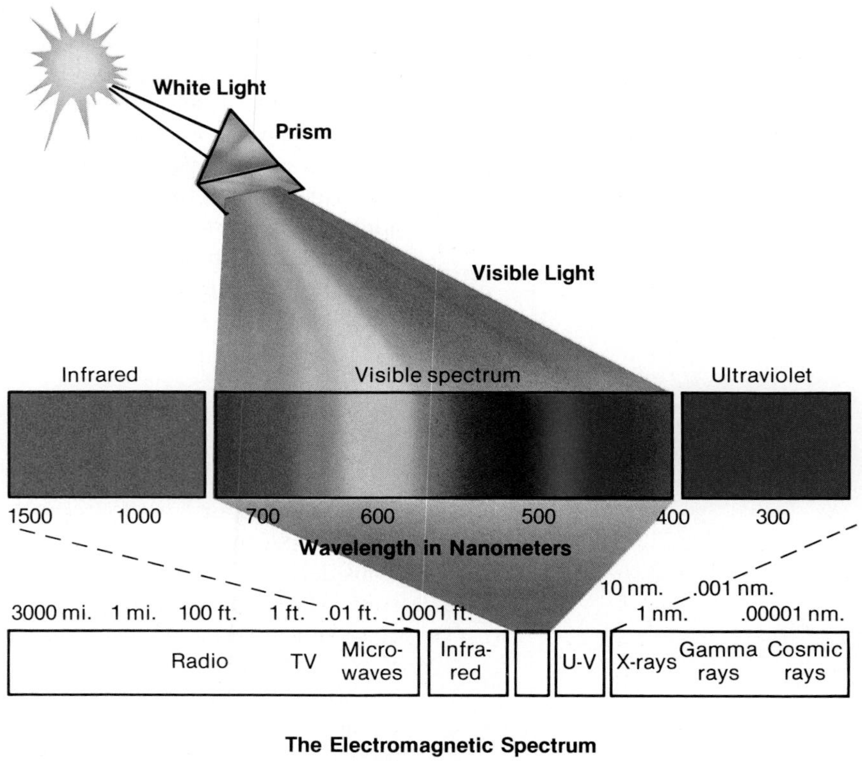

The Eye: Our Living Camera

Consider for a moment that magnificent invention called the camera, which records visual experiences. In the camera, light enters an opening and is focused onto a sensitive surface, or film. Chemical reactions then take place on this surface that create a lasting impression of the image that entered the camera.

The eye—our living camera—is no less remarkable. Consider the major parts of the eye (Figure 3.2). As with a film or television camera, light enters through a narrow opening and is projected onto a sensitive surface. Light first passes through the transparent **cornea,** which covers the front of the eye's surface. (The so-called white of the eye is composed of a hard protective tissue and is called the *sclera*.) The amount of light that passes through the cornea is determined by the size of the opening of the muscle called the **iris,** which is also the colored part of the eye. The opening in the iris is called the **pupil.** Pupil size adjusts automatically to the amount of light; you do not have to try purposefully to open the eye farther to see better under conditions of low lighting. The more intense the light, the smaller the opening. In a similar fashion, we adjust the amount of light allowed into a camera according to its brightness.

Once light passes through the iris, it encounters the **lens.** The lens adjusts or accommodates to the image by changing its thickness. Changes in thickness permit projection of a clear image of the object onto the retina; that is, these changes focus the light according to the object's distance. If you hold a finger at arm's length, then slowly bring it toward your nose, you will feel tension in the eye as the thickness of the lens accommodates to keep

Cornea Transparent tissue forming the outer surface of the eyeball.

Iris A muscular membrane whose dilation regulates the amount of light that enters the eye.

Pupil The apparently black opening in the center of the iris, through which light enters the eye.

Lens A transparent body behind the iris that focuses an image on the retina.

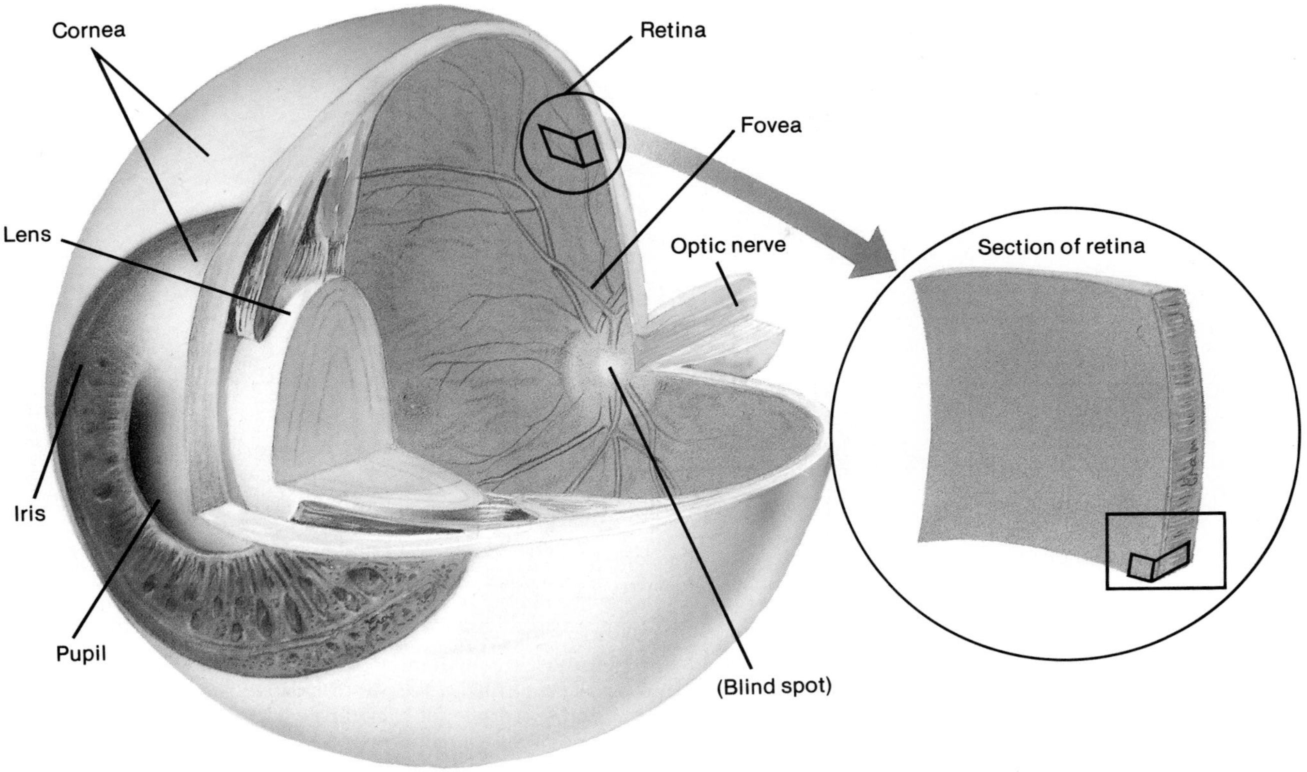

Figure 3.2
The Human Eye.

In both the eye and a camera, light enters through a narrow opening and is projected onto a sensitive surface. In the eye, the photosensitive surface is called the retina, and information concerning the changing images on the retina is transmitted to the brain. In a camera, the photosensitive surface is usually film, which captures a single image. (Highlighted detail of the retina is shown in Figure 3.3.)

Retina The area of the inner surface of the eye that contains rods and cones.

Photoreceptors Cells that respond to light.

Bipolar cells Neurons that conduct neural impulses from rods and cones to ganglion cells.

Ganglion cells Neurons whose axons form the optic nerve.

Optic nerve The nerve that transmits sensory information from the eye to the brain.

Fovea An area near the center of the retina that is dense with cones and where vision is consequently most acute.

Blind spot The area of the retina where axons from ganglion cells meet to form the optic nerve.

the retinal image in focus (Haber & Hershenson, 1980). When people squint to bring an object into focus, they are adjusting the thickness of the lens.

The **retina** is like the film or image surface of the camera. Instead of being composed of film that is sensitive to light (photosensitive), however, the retina consists of photosensitive cells, or **photoreceptors,** called *rods* and *cones.* The retina (Figure 3.3) contains several layers of cells: the rods and cones, **bipolar cells,** and **ganglion cells.** All of these cells are neurons. Light travels past the ganglion cells and bipolar cells and stimulates the rods and cones. The rods and cones then send neural messages through the bipolar cells to the ganglion cells. The axons of the 1 million or so ganglion cells in our retinae form the **optic nerve.** The optic nerve conducts sensory input to the brain, where it is relayed to the visual area of the occipital lobe. Other neurons in the retina—amacrine cells and horizontal cells—make sideways connections at a level near the receptor cells and at another level near the ganglion cells. As a result of these lateral connections, many rods and cones funnel visual information into one bipolar cell, and many bipolar cells funnel information to one ganglion cell. Receptors outnumber ganglion cells by more than 100 to one.

The **fovea** is the most sensitive area of the retina (see Figure 3.2). Receptors there are more densely packed. The **blind spot,** in contrast, is in-

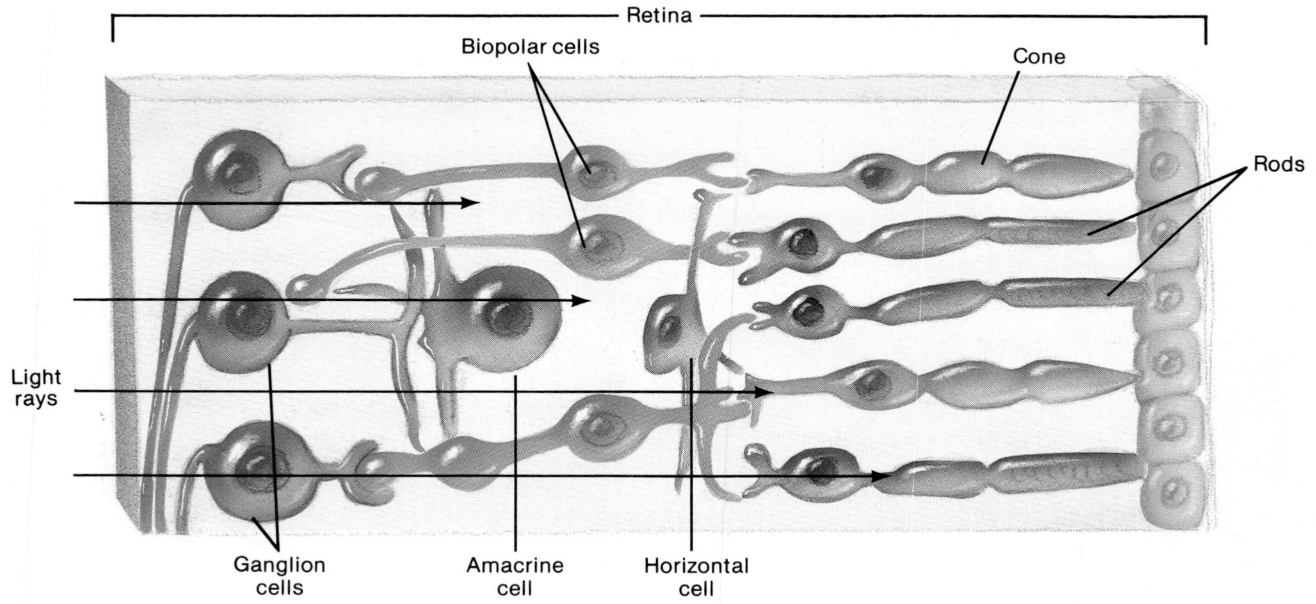

Figure 3.3
The Retina.

After light travels through the vitreous humor of the eye, it finds its way through ganglion neurons and bipolar neurons to the photosensitive rods and cones. These photoreceptors then transmit sensory input back through the bipolar neurons to the ganglion neurons. The axons of the ganglion neurons form the optic nerve, which transmits sensory stimulation through the brain to the visual cortex of the occipital lobe. Amacrine cells and horizontal cells make connections within layers that allow photoreceptors to funnel their information into the ganglion cells.

sensitive to visual stimulation. It is the part of the retina where the axons of the ganglion cells congregate to form the optic nerve (Figure 3.4).

Rods and Cones **Rods** and **cones** are the photoreceptors in the retina (Figure 3.5). About 100 million rods and 5 million cones are distributed across the retina. The fovea is composed almost exclusively of cones. Cones then become more sparsely distributed as you work forward from the fovea toward the lens. Rods, in contrast, are nearly absent at the fovea but are distributed more densely as you approach the lens.

Rods are sensitive only to the intensity of light. They allow us to see in black and white. Cones provide color vision. If you are a camera buff, you know that under conditions of extreme low lighting, it is possible to photograph a clearer image with black-and-white film than with color film. Similarly, rods are more sensitive to light than cones. Therefore, as the illumination grows dim, as during the evening and nighttime hours, objects appear to lose their color well before their outlines fade from view.

Rods Rod-shaped photoreceptors that are sensitive only to the intensity of light.

Cones Cone-shaped photoreceptors that transmit sensations of color.

Dark adaptation The process of adjusting to conditions of lower lighting by increasing the sensitivity of rods and cones.

Light Adaptation As noted earlier, a movie theater may at first seem too dark to allow us to find seats readily. But as time goes on, we come to see the seats and other people clearly. Adjusting to lower lighting is called **dark adaptation.**

Figure 3.6 shows the amount of light needed for detection as a function of the amount of time spent in the dark. The cones and rods adapt at different rates. The cones, which permit perception of color, reach their maximum adaptation to darkness in about ten minutes. The rods, which allow percep-

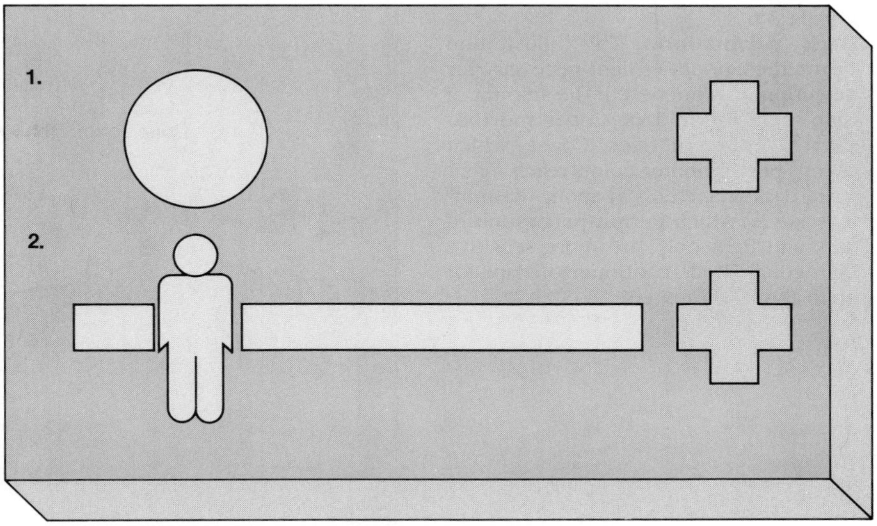

Figure 3.4
Locating the Blind Spots in Your Eyes. To try a "disappearing act," first look at Drawing 1. Close your right eye. Then move the book back and forth about one foot from your left eye while you stare at the plus sign. You will notice the circle disappear. When the circle disappears it is being projected onto the blind spot of your retina, the point at which the axons of ganglion neurons collect to form the optic nerve. Then close your left eye. Stare at the circle with your right eye, and move the book back and forth. When the plus sign disappears, it is being projected onto the blind spot of your right eye. Now look at Drawing 2. You can make this figure disappear and "see" the black line continue through the spot where it was by closing your right eye and staring at the plus sign with your left. When this figure is projected onto your blind spot, your brain "fills in" the line, which is one reason that you're not usually aware that you have blind spots.

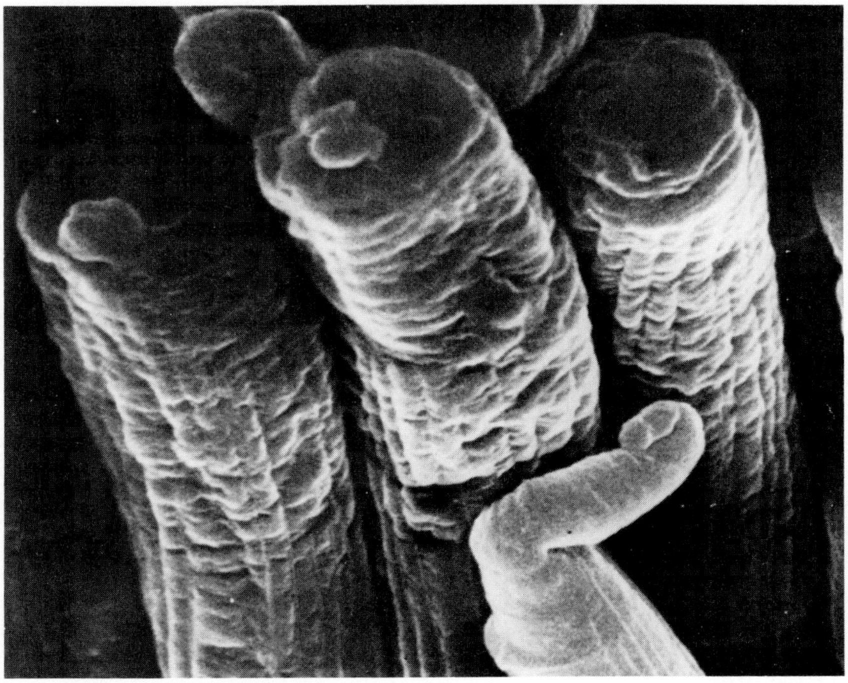

Figure 3.5
A Much (Much!) Enlarged Photograph of Several Rods and a Cone. Cones are usually upright fellows. However, the cone at the bottom right of this photo has been bent by the photographic process. You have about 100 million rods and 5 million cones distributed across the retina of each eye. Only cones provide sensations of color. The fovea of the eye is almost exclusively populated by cones, which are then distributed more sparsely as you work forward toward the lens. Rods, in contrast, are nearly absent at the fovea and become more densely packed as you work forward.

tion of light and dark only, are more sensitive and continue to adapt to darkness for up to about 45 minutes.

Adaptation to brighter lighting conditions takes place much more rapidly. When you emerge from the theater into the brilliance of the afternoon, you may at first be painfully surprised by the featureless blaze around you. The visual experience is not unlike turning the brightness of the TV set to maximum, in which case the edges of objects dissolve into light. Within a

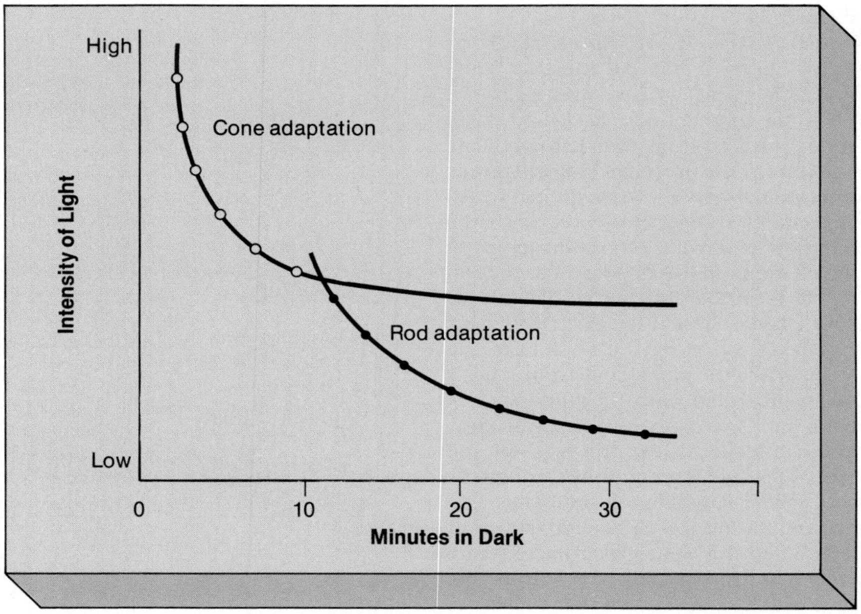

Figure 3.6
Dark Adaptation. This illustration shows the amount of light necessary for detection as a function of the amount of time spent in the dark. Cones and rods adapt at different rates. Cones, which permit perception of color, reach maximum dark adaptation in about ten minutes. Rods, which permit perception of dark and light only, are more sensitive than cones. Rods continue to adapt for up to about 45 minutes.

minute or so of entering the street, however, the brightness of the scene will have dimmed and objects will have regained their edges.

Color Vision

For most of us, the world is a place of brilliant colors—the blue-greens of the ocean, the red-oranges of the lowering sun, the deepened greens of June, the glories of rhododendron and hibiscus. Color is an emotional and aesthetic part of our everyday lives. In this section we explore psychological dimensions of color and then examine theories that concern how we manage to convert different wavelengths of light into perceptions of color.

Psychological Dimensions of Color: Hue, Brightness, and Saturation

As noted earlier, the wavelength of light determines its color, or hue. The brightness of a color is its degree of lightness or darkness. The brighter the color, the lighter it is.

If we bend the colors of the spectrum into a circle, we create a color wheel, as shown in Figure 3.7. Yellow is the lightest color on the color wheel. As we work our way around from yellow to violet-blue, we encounter progressively darker colors.

Warm and Cool Colors Psychologically, the colors on the green-blue side of the color wheel are considered to be cool in temperature, and the colors on the yellow-orange-red side are considered to be warm. Perhaps greens and blues suggest the coolness of the ocean and the sky, whereas things tend to burn red or orange. A room decorated in green or blue may seem more

Figure 3.7
The Color Wheel. A color wheel can be formed by bending the colors of the spectrum into a circle and placing complementary colors across from one another. (A few colors between violet and red that are not found on the spectrum must be added to complete the circle.) When lights of complementary colors, such as yellow and violet-blue, are mixed, they dissolve into neutral gray. The afterimage of a color is also the color's complement.

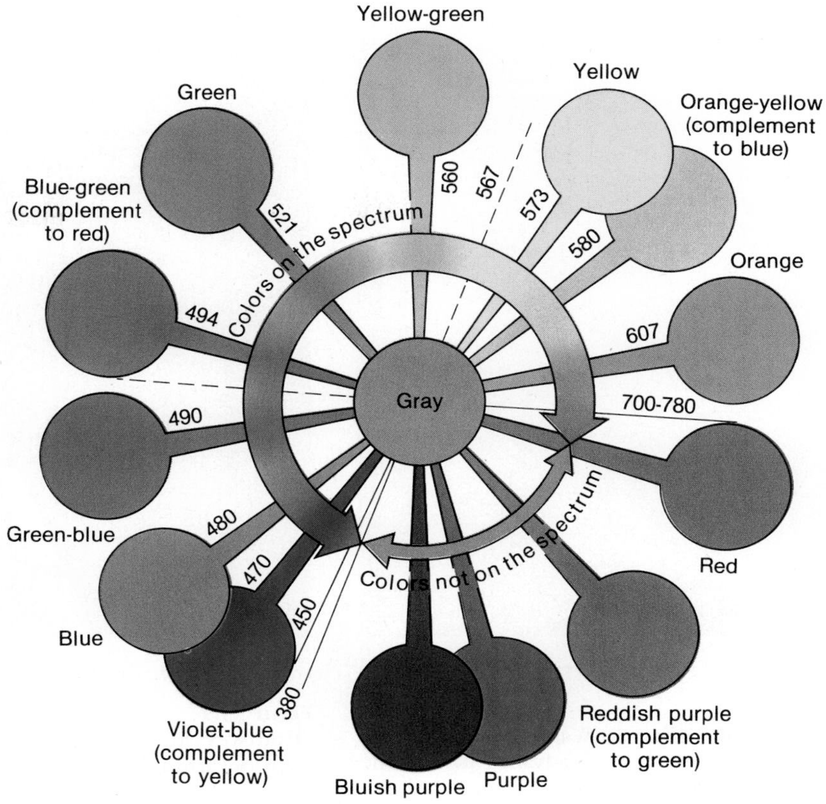

appealing on a hot day in July than a room decorated in red or orange.

When we look at a painting, warm colors seem to advance toward the viewer, which explains, in part, why the oranges and yellows of Mark Rothko's "Orange and Yellow" (Figure 3.8) seem to pulsate toward the observer. Cool colors seem to recede. Notice how the warm Sunoco sign in Allan d'Arcangelo's "Highway No. 2" (Figure 3.9) leaps out toward the viewer. In contrast, the cool blue sky seems to recede into the distance.

The **saturation** of a color is its pureness. Pure hues have the greatest intensity, or brightness. The saturation, and thus the brightness, decreases when another hue or black, gray, or white is added. Artists produce shades of a given hue by adding black and produce tints by adding white.

Complementary versus Analogous Colors

Complementary Colors The colors across from one another on the color wheel are labeled **complementary.** Red-green and blue-yellow are the major complementary pairs. If we mix complementary colors together, they dissolve into gray.

But wait! you say: Blue and yellow cannot be complementary because by mixing pigments of blue and yellow we create green, not gray. True enough, but we have been talking about mixing *lights,* not *pigments.* Light is the source of all color. Pigments reflect and absorb different wavelengths of light selectively. The mixture of lights is an *additive* process, whereas the mixture of pigments is *subtractive* (see Figure 3.10).

Saturation The degree of purity of a color.

Complementary Descriptive of colors of the spectrum that, when combined, produce white or nearly white light.

Figure 3.8
"Orange and Yellow." Warm colors such as orange and yellow seem to advance toward the viewer, while cool colors such as blue and green seem to recede. The oranges and yellows of Rothko's painting seem to pulsate toward the observer.

Figure 3.9
"Highway No. 2." The "warm" Sunoco sign in d'Arcangelo's painting leaps out toward the viewer, while the "cool" blue sky recedes into the distance.

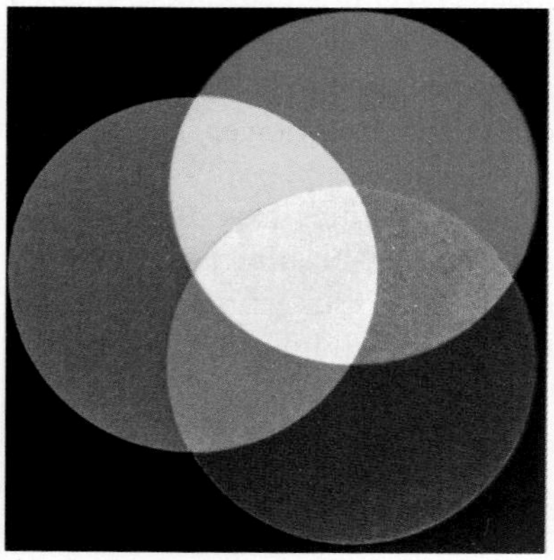

Figure 3.10
Additive Color Mixtures Produced by Lights of Three Colors: Red, Green, and Violet-Blue. In the early 1800s, British scientist Thomas Young discovered that white light and all the colors of the spectrum could be produced by adding various combinations of lights of three colors and varying their intensities.

Truth or Fiction Revisited

It is *not* true that we attain green light when we mix blue light and yellow light. We attain green when we mix *pigments* of blue and yellow.

Pigments attain their colors by absorbing light from certain segments of the spectrum and reflecting the rest. For example, we see most plant life as green because the pigment in chlorophyll absorbs most of the red, blue, and violet wavelengths of light. The remaining green is reflected. A red pigment absorbs most of the spectrum but reflects red. White pigments reflect all colors equally. Black pigments reflect very little light.

In works of art, complementary colors placed next to one another clash, and they seem to pulsate where they meet. Note Richard Anuszkiewicz's painting "Entrance to Green" (Figure 3.11). If you look at the picture from a foot or so away and allow your eyes to relax, you are likely to perceive vibrations in the areas where the lines separate the reddish and greenish colors.

Primary, Secondary, and Tertiary Colors The pigments of red, blue, and yellow are the **primary colors**—those that cannot be produced by mixing pigments of other hues. **Secondary colors** are created by mixing pigments of the primary colors. The three secondary colors are orange (derived from mixing red and yellow), green (blue and yellow), and purple

Figure 3.11
"Entrance to Green." In works of art, there seems to be a pulsating effect where complementary colors come together. If you look at Anuszkiewicz's painting for a while from a foot or so away, you are likely to perceive vibrations where the red and green meet. So-called Op Art works rely on vibrations and other visual responses for their effects.

(red and blue). **Tertiary colors** are created by mixing pigments of primary and adjoining secondary colors, as in yellow-green and bluish-purple.

In his "Sunday Afternoon on the Island of La Grande Jatte" (Figure 3.12), French painter Georges Seurat molded his figures and forms from dabs of pure and complementary colors. Instead of mixing his pigments, he placed points of pure color next to one another. The sensations are of pure color when the painting is viewed from very close (see detail, Figure 3.12). But from a distance, the juxtaposition of pure colors creates the impression of mixtures of color.

Afterimages Before reading on, why don't you try a brief experiment? Look at the strangely colored American flag in Figure 3.13 for at least half a minute. Then look at a sheet of white or gray paper. What has happened to the flag? If your color vision is working properly, and if you looked at the miscolored flag long enough, you should see a flag composed of the familiar red, white, and blue. The flag you perceive on the white sheet of paper is an **afterimage** of the first. (If you didn't look at the green, black, and yellow flag long enough the first time, you may wish to try it again. It will work any number of times.)

In afterimages, persistent sensations of color are followed by perception of the complementary color when the first color is removed. The same holds

Primary colors Colors that cannot be produced by mixing pigments of other hues.

Secondary colors Colors derived by mixing primary colors.

Tertiary colors Colors derived by mixing primary and adjoining secondary colors.

Afterimage The lingering visual impression made by a stimulus that has been removed.

Detail of "Sunday Afternoon on the Island of La Grande Jatte."

Figure 3.12
"Sunday Afternoon on the Island of La Grande Jatte."

The French painter Seurat molded his figures and forms from dabs of pure and complementary colors. Up close, the dabs of pure color are visible. From afar, they create the impression of color mixtures.

Figure 3.13
Three Cheers for the . . . Green, Black, and Yellow? Don't be concerned. We can readily restore Old Glory to its familiar hues. Place a sheet of white paper beneath the book, and stare at the center of the flag for 30 seconds. Then remove the book. You will see a more familiar image on the paper beneath. This is an afterimage. Afterimages such as this led Ewald Hering to doubt the trichromatic theory of color vision and to propose the opponent-process theory in its place. Both theories have received some empirical support.

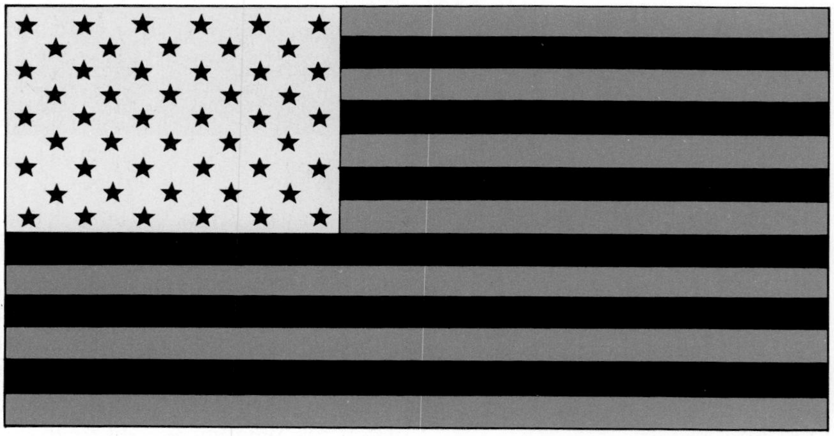

true for black and white; staring at one will create an afterimage of the others. Stare at d'Arcangelo's "Highway 1, No. 2" (Figure 3.9) for 30 seconds. Then look at a sheet of white paper. You are likely to perceive a black stripe down a white highway, along with a blue Sunoco sign and a yellow sky. The phenomenon of afterimages has contributed to one of the theories of color vision, as we shall see later in the section.

Analogous Colors **Analogous** hues lie next to one another on the color wheel, forming families of colors like yellow and orange, orange and red, and green and blue. As we work our way around the wheel, the families intermarry, as blue with violet and violet with red. Works of art that use closely related families of color seem harmonious. For example, Rothko's

Analogous Similar or comparable colors.

"Orange and Yellow" draws on the color family containing analogous oranges and yellows. The title of a Barnett Newman painting, "Who's Afraid of Red, Yellow, and Blue?" suggests the jarring effect that can be achieved by placing colors that are so far apart on the color wheel next to one another.

Theories of Color Vision

Adults with normal color vision can discriminate up to 150 color differences across the visible spectrum (Bornstein & Marks, 1982). Different colors have different wavelengths. Although we can vary the physical wavelengths of light in a continuous manner from shorter to longer, changes in color seem to be discontinuous so that our perception of a color may shift suddenly from blue to green, even though the change in wavelength is smaller than that between two blues.

Our ability to perceive color depends on the eye's transmission of different messages to the brain when lights of different wavelengths stimulate the cones in the retina. In this section we shall explore and evaluate two theories of how lights of different wavelengths are perceived as being of different colors: *trichromatic theory* and *opponent-process theory.* Then we shall discuss the problems of some individuals who are blind to some or all of the colors of the visible spectrum.

Trichromatic Theory *Tri* is a word root meaning "three" (a tricycle has three wheels), and *chromatic* derives from the Greek *chroma,* meaning "color." **Trichromatic theory** is based on an experiment that was run by British scientist Thomas Young in the early 1800s. As in Figure 3.10, Young projected three lights of different colors onto a screen so that they partly overlapped. He found that he could create any color from the visible spectrum by simply varying the intensities of the lights. When all three lights fell on the same spot, they created white light, or the appearance of no color at all. The three lights manipulated by Young were red, green, and blue-violet.

German physiologist Hermann von Helmholtz saw in Young's discovery an explanation of color vision. Von Helmholtz suggested that the eye must have three different types of photoreceptors or cones. Some must be sensitive to red light, some to green, and some to blue. We see other colors when two different types of color receptors are stimulated. The perception of yellow, for example, would result from the simultaneous stimulation of receptors for red and green. Trichromatic theory is also known as the Young-Helmholtz theory, after Thomas Young and Hermann von Helmholtz.

Opponent-Process Theory In 1870, Ewald Hering proposed the **opponent-process theory** of color vision. Opponent-process theory also holds that there are three types of color receptors, but they are not theorized to be red, green, and blue. Hering suggested that afterimages (such as of the American flag shown in Figure 3.13) are made possible by three types of color receptors: red-green, blue-yellow, and a type that perceives differences in brightness from light to dark. A red-green cone could not transmit messages for red and green at the same time. Hering would perhaps have said that when you are staring at the green, black, and yellow flag for 30 seconds, you are disturbing the balance of neural activity. The afterimage of red, white, and blue would then represent the eye's attempt to reestablish a balance.

Evaluation Both theories of color vision may be partially correct (Hurvich, 1981). Research with **microspectrophotometry** supports trichromatic theory. It shows that some cones are sensitive to blue, some to green, and some

Trichromatic theory The theory that color vision is made possible by three types of cones, some of which respond to red light, some to green, and some to blue.

Opponent-process theory The theory that color vision is made possible by three types of cones, some of which respond to red or green light, some to blue or yellow, and some only to the intensity of light.

Microspectrophotometry A method for analyzing the sensitivity of single cones to lights of different wavelengths.

to yellow-red parts of the spectrum—consistent with trichromatic theory.

However, studies of the bipolar and ganglion neurons suggest that messages from the cones are transmitted to the brain and relayed by the thalamus to the occipital lobe in an opponent-process fashion (DeValois & Jacobs, 1984). Some neurons that transmit messages to the visual centers in the brain, for example, are excited or "turned on" by green light but inhibited or "turned off" by red light. Others can be excited by red light but are inhibited by green light. It may be that there is a "neural rebound effect" that would help explain afterimages. With such an effect, a green-sensitive ganglion that had been excited by green light for half a minute or so might switch briefly to inhibitory activity when the light is shut off. The effect would be to perceive red, even though no red light was being shone (Haber & Hershenson, 1980).

These theoretical updates allow for the afterimage effects with the green, black, and yellow flag and are also consistent with Young's experiments in mixing lights of different colors.

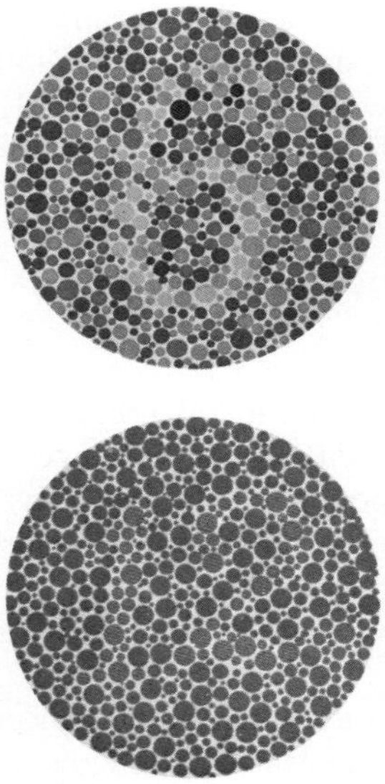

Figure 3.14
Plates from a Test for Color Blindness. Can you see the numbers in these plates from a test for color blindness? A person with red-green color blindness would not be able to see the 6, and a person with blue-yellow color blindness would probably not discern the 12. (Caution: These reproductions cannot be used for actual testing of color blindness.)

Color Blindness

If you can discriminate the colors of the visible spectrum, you have normal color vision and are labeled a **trichromat.** This means that you are sensitive to red-green, blue-yellow, and light-dark. People who are totally color-blind are called **monochromats** and are sensitive to light-dark only. Total color blindness is quite rare. The fully color-blind see the world as trichromats would on a black-and-white television set or in a black-and-white movie.

Partial color blindness is more common than total color blindness. Partial color blindness is a sex-linked trait that strikes mostly males. The recessive genes for the disorder are found on the X sex chromosome, and thus in males they are unopposed by dominant genes on a second X sex chromosome (Nathans et al., 1986). The partially color-blind are called **dichromats.** Dichromats can discriminate only two colors—red and green, or blue and yellow—and the colors that are derived from mixing these colors. Figure 3.14 shows the types of tests that are used to diagnose color blindness. Also see Figure 3.15.

A dichromat might put on one red sock and one green sock but would not mix red and blue socks. Monochromats might put on socks of any color. They would not notice a difference as long as the socks' color did not differ in intensity, or brightness.

When we selectively breed cats and dogs, we are interested in producing coats of certain colors. But if cats and dogs bred human beings, they would be less concerned about our color because their color vision is less well developed (Rosenzweig & Leiman, 1982). Cats, for example, can distinguish fewer colors and only on large surfaces.

Trichromat A person with normal color vision.

Monochromat A person who is sensitive to black and white only and hence color-blind.

Dichromat A person who is sensitive to black-white and either red-green or blue-yellow and hence partially color-blind.

Closure The tendency to perceive a broken figure as being complete or whole.

VISUAL PERCEPTION

Perception, as noted, is the process by which we organize or make sense of our sensory impressions. Although visual sensations are caused by electromagnetic energy, visual perception also relies on our knowledge, expectations, and motivations. Whereas sensation may be thought of as a mechanical process, perception is an active process by which we interpret the world around us.

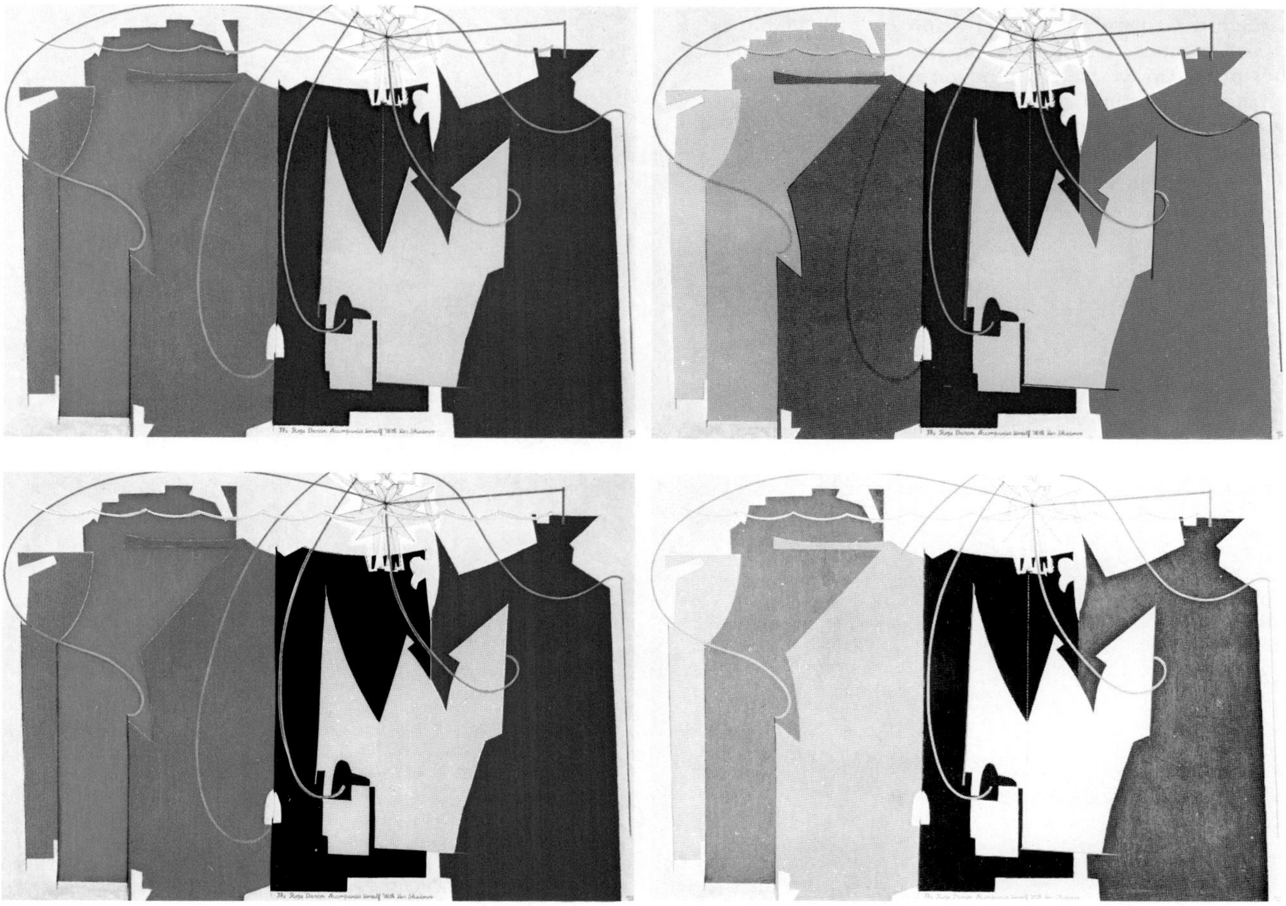

Figure 3.15
Color Blindness.

The painting in the upper left-hand panel—Man Ray's "The Rope Dancer Accompanies Herself with Her Shadows"—appears as it would to a person with normal color vision. If you suffered from red–green color blindness, the picture would appear as it does in the upper right-hand panel. The lower left-hand and lower right-hand panels show how the picture would look to viewers with yellow–blue or total color blindness, respectively.

(Museum of Modern Art, New York. Gift of G. David Thompson.)

Figure 3.16
Closure. Meaningless splotches of ink or a horse and rider? This figure illustrates the Gestalt principle of closure.

For example, just what do you see in Figure 3.16? Do you see random splotches of ink or a rider on horseback? If you perceive a horse and rider, it is not just because of the visual sensations provided by the drawing. Each of the blobs is meaningless in and of itself, and the pattern they form is also less than clear. Despite the lack of clarity, however, you may still perceive a horse and rider. Why? The answer has something to do with your general knowledge and your desire to fit incoming bits and pieces of information into familiar patterns.

In the case of the "horse and rider," your integration of disconnected shards of information into a meaningful whole also reflects what Gestalt psychologists refer to as the principle of **closure,** or the tendency to perceive a complete or whole figure, even when there are gaps in the sensory input.

Figure 3.17
Figure and Ground. How many animals and demons can you find in this Escher print? Do we have white figures on a black background, or black figures on a white background? Figure-ground perception is the tendency to perceive geometric forms against a background.

Perceptual Organization

Earlier in the century, Gestalt psychologists noted consistencies in our integration of bits and pieces of sensory stimulation into meaningful wholes and attempted to formulate rules that governed these processes. Max Wertheimer, in particular, discovered many such rules. As a group, these rules are referred to as the laws of **perceptual organization.** Let us examine a number of these rules, beginning with those concerning figure-ground perception.

Figure-Ground Perception If you look out your window, you may see people, buildings, cars, and streets, or perhaps grass, trees, birds, and clouds. In any event, the objects about you tend to be perceived as figures against backgrounds. Cars against the background of the street are easier to pick out than cars piled on each other in a junkyard. Birds against the sky are more likely to be perceived than, as the saying goes, birds in the bush. Figures are closer to us than their grounds.

When figure-ground relationships are **ambiguous,** or capable of being interpreted in different ways, our perceptions tend to be unstable, to shift back and forth. As an example, take a look at Figure 3.17—a nice leisurely look. How many people, objects, and animals can you find in this Escher print? If your eye is drawn back and forth, so that sometimes you are perceiving light figures on a dark background and then dark figures on a light background, you are experiencing figure-ground reversals. In other words, a shift is occurring in your perception of what is figure and what is ground, or backdrop. Escher was able to have some fun with us because of our tendency to try to isolate geometric patterns or figures from a background. However, in this case the "background" is as meaningful and detailed as the "figure." Therefore, our perceptions shift back and forth.

Perceptual organization The tendency to integrate perceptual elements into meaningful patterns.

Ambiguous Having two or more possible meanings.

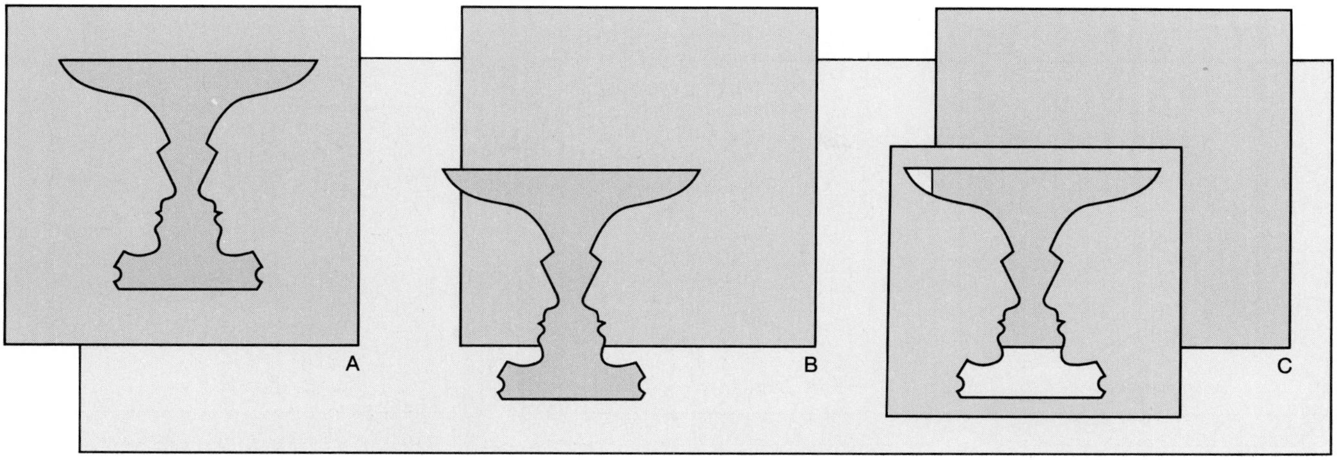

Figure 3.18
The Rubin Vase.

A favorite drawing used by psychologists to demonstrate figure-ground perception. Part A is ambiguous, with neither the vase nor the profiles clearly the figure or the ground. In part B the vase is the figure, and in part C the profiles are.

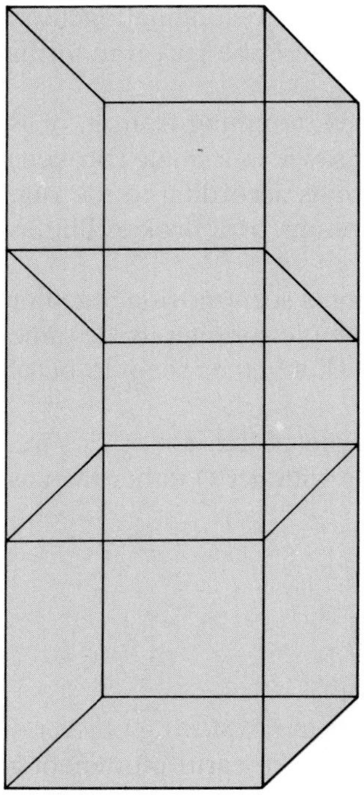

Figure 3.19
A Stack of Necker Cubes. Ambiguity in the drawing of the cubes makes perceptual shifts possible.

Proximity Nearness. The perceptual tendency to group together objects that are near one another.

The Rubin Vase In Figure 3.18 we see a Rubin vase, one of psychologists' favorite illustrations of figure-ground relationships. Note that the figure-ground relationship in part A of the figure is ambiguous. There are no cues that suggest which area must be the figure. For this reason, our perception may shift from seeing the vase as the figure and then seeing two profiles as the figure.

There is no such problem in part B. Since it seems that a blue vase has been brought forward against a colored ground, we are more likely to perceive the vase than the profiles. In part C we are more likely to perceive the profiles than the vase, because the profiles are whole and the vase is broken against the background.

The Necker Cube The Necker cube (Figure 3.19) provides another example of how an ambiguous drawing can lead to perceptual shifts.

Hold this page at arm's length and stare at the center of the figure for 30 seconds or so. Try to allow your eye muscles to relax. (The feeling is of your eyes "glazing over.") After a while you will notice a dramatic shift in your perception of these "stacked boxes," so that what was once a front edge is now a back edge, and vice versa. Again, the dramatic perceptual shift is made possible by the fact that the outline of the drawing permits two interpretations.

Some Other Gestalt Rules for Organization In addition to the law of closure, Gestalt psychologists have noted that our perceptions are guided by rules or laws of *proximity, similarity, continuity,* and *common fate.*

Verbally describe part A of Figure 3.20 without reading further. Did you say that part A consisted of six lines or of three groups of two parallel lines? If you said three sets of lines, you were influenced by the **proximity,** or nearness, of some of the lines. There is no other reason for perceiving them in pairs or subgroups: All lines are parallel and of equal length.

Now describe part B of the figure. Did you perceive the figure as a six-by-six grid, or as three columns of *x*'s and three columns of *o*'s? According

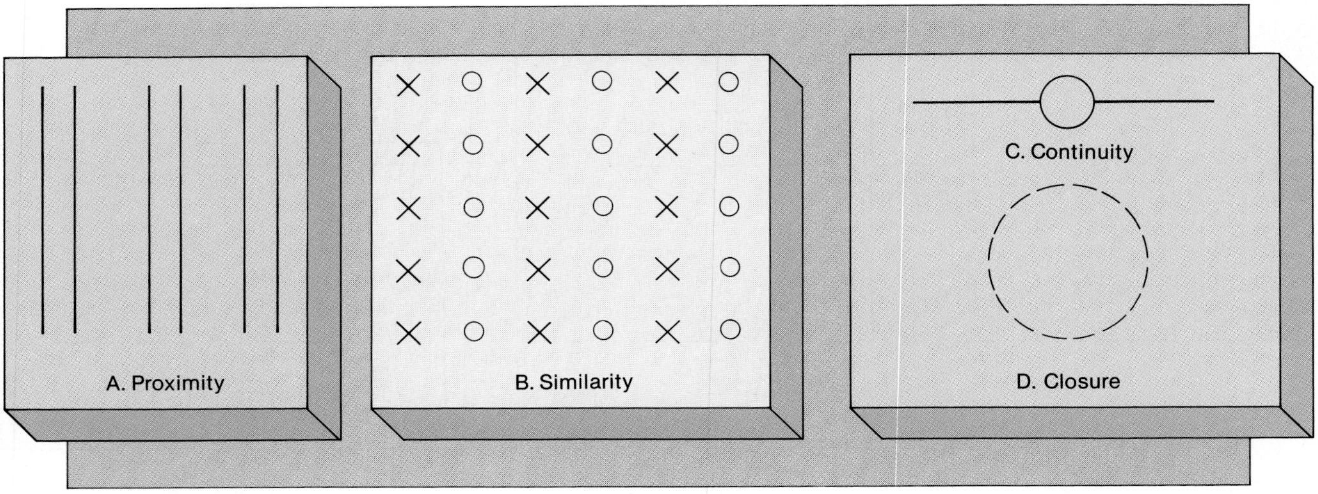

Figure 3.20
Some Gestalt Laws of Perceptual Organization.
These drawings illustrate the Gestalt laws of proximity, similarity, continuity, and closure.

to the law of **similarity,** we perceive similar objects as belonging together. For this reason, you may have been more likely to describe part B in terms of columns than rows or a grid.

What about part C? Is it a circle with two lines stemming from it, or is it a (broken) line that goes through a circle? If you saw it as a single (broken) line, you were probably organizing your perceptions according to the rule of **continuity.** That is, we perceive a series of points or a broken line as having unity.

According to the law of **common fate,** elements seen moving together are perceived as belonging together. A group of people running in the same direction appear unified in purpose. Birds that flock together seem to be of a feather. (Did I get that right?)

Part D of Figure 3.20 provides another example of the law of closure. The arcs tend to be perceived as a circle (or circle with gaps) rather than as just a series of arcs.

Perception of Movement

Consider the importance of the perception of movement. Moving objects—whether they be other people, animals, cars, or tons of earth plummeting down a hillside—harbor the potential for powerful rewards and punishments. As noted in Chapter 9, moving objects capture the attention of even newborn infants.

To understand how we perceive movement, recall what it is like to be on a train that has begun to pull out of the station while the train on the adjacent track remains stationary. If your own train does not lurch as it accelerates, you might think at first that the other train is moving. Or you might not be certain whether your train is moving forward or the other train is moving backward.

The visual perception of movement is based on change of position relative to other objects. To early scientists, whose only instrument for visual

Similarity The perceptual tendency to group together objects that are similar in appearance.

Continuity The tendency to perceive a series of points or lines as having unity.

Common fate The tendency to perceive elements that move together as belonging together.

Figure 3.21
Stroboscopic Motion.

In a motion picture, viewing a series of stationary images at the rate of about 16 to 22 frames per second provides the illusion of movement. This form of apparent movement is termed stroboscopic motion.

observation was the naked eye, it seemed logical that the sun circled the earth. You have to be able to imagine the movement of the earth around the sun as seen from a theoretical point in outer space—you cannot observe it directly.

So, how do you determine which train is moving when your train is pulling out of the station (or that other train is pulling in)? One way is to look for objects you know are stable, like station platform columns, houses, signs, or trees. If you are stationary in relation to them, your train is not moving. Observing people walking on the station platform may not provide the answer, however, because they are also changing their position relative to stationary objects. You might also try to sense the motion of the train in your body. You know from experience how to do these things quite well, although it may be difficult to phrase explanations for them.

We have been considering the perception of real movement. Psychologists have also studied several types of apparent movement, or **illusions** of movement. These include the *autokinetic effect, stroboscopic motion,* and the *phi phenomenon.*

The Autokinetic Effect If you were to sit quietly in a dark room and stare at a point of light projected onto the far wall, after a while it might appear that the light had begun to move, even if it remained quite still. The tendency to perceive a stationary point of light as moving in a dark room is called the **autokinetic effect.**

Over the years, psychologists have run interesting experiments in which they have asked subjects, for example, what the light is "spelling out." The light has spelled out nothing, of course, and the words perceived by subjects have reflected their own cognitive processes, not external sensations. In one study, subjects were asked to judge how far the (stationary) point of light moved (Block & Block, 1951). They provided estimates over a series of trials. Prejudiced subjects arrived at their final judgments more rapidly than nonprejudiced subjects. They were quicker than nonprejudiced subjects to jump to their (erroneous) conclusion.

Stroboscopic Motion Stroboscopic motion makes motion pictures possible. In **stroboscopic motion,** the illusion of movement is provided by the presentation of a rapid progression of images of stationary objects (Beck et al., 1977). So-called motion pictures do not really consist of images that move. Rather, the audience is shown 16 to 22 pictures, or frames, per second, like those in Figure 3.21. Each frame differs slightly from that preceding it. Showing the frames in rapid succession then provides the illusion of movement.

At the rate of at least 16 frames per second, the "motion" in a film seems smooth and natural. With fewer than 16 or so frames per second, the movement looks jumpy and unnatural. That is why slow motion is achieved

Illusions Sensations that give rise to misperceptions.

Autokinetic effect The tendency to perceive a stationary point of light in a dark room as moving.

Stroboscopic motion A visual illusion in which the perception of motion is generated by a series of stationary images that are presented in rapid succession.

through filming perhaps 100 or more frames per second. When they are played back at about 22 frames per second, movement seems slowed down, yet smooth and natural.

The Phi Phenomenon. The phi phenomenon is an illusion of movement that is produced by lights blinking on and off in sequence, as with this New York Stock Exchange electronic "ticker."

The Phi Phenomenon Have you seen news headlines spelled out in lights that rapidly wrap around a building? Have you seen an electronic scoreboard in a baseball or football stadium? When the hometeam scores, some scoreboards suggest the explosions of fireworks. What actually happens is that a row of lights is switched on, then off. As the first row is switched off, the second row is switched on, and so on for dozens, perhaps hundreds of rows. When the switching occurs rapidly, the **phi phenomenon** occurs: the on-off process is perceived as movement.

Like stroboscopic motion, the phi phenomenon is an example of apparent motion. Both stroboscopic motion and the phi phenomenon appear to occur because of the law of continuity. We tend to perceive a series of points as having unity, so the series of lights (points) is perceived as moving lines.

Depth Perception

Think of the problems you might have if you could not judge depth or distance. You might bump into other people, thinking them to be farther away than they are. An outfielder might not be able to judge whether to run toward the infield or the fence to catch a fly ball. You might give your front bumper a workout in stop-and-go traffic. Fortunately, both *monocular and binocular cues* help us perceive the depth of objects. Let us examine a number of them.

Copyright © 1974 by PLAYBOY Magazine.

"Excuse me for shouting, I thought you were further away."

Monocular Cues Now that you have considered how difficult it would be to navigate through life without depth perception, ponder the problems of the artist who attempts to portray three-dimensional objects on a two-dimensional surface. Artists use **monocular cues,** or cues that can be perceived by one eye, to create an illusion of depth. These cues—including perspective, clearness, interposition, shadows, and texture gradient—cause certain objects to appear to be more distant from the viewer than others.

Distant objects stimulate smaller areas on the retina than nearby objects. The amount of sensory input from them is smaller, even though they may be the same size. The distances between far-off objects also appear to be smaller than equivalent distances between nearby objects. For this reason, the phenomonen known as **perspective** occurs; that is, we tend to perceive parallel lines as coming closer, or converging, as they recede from us. However, as we shall see when we discuss *size constancy,* experience teaches us that distant objects that look small will be larger when they are close. In this way, their relative size also becomes a cue to their distance from us.

The two engravings in Figure 3.22 represent impossible scenes in which the artists use principles of perspective to fool the viewer. In the engraving to the left, "Waterfall," note that the water appears to be flowing away from the viewer in a zigzag because the stream becomes gradually narrower (that is, lines that we assume to be parallel are shown to be converging) and the stone sides of the aqueduct appear to be stepping down. However, given that the water arrives at the top of the fall, it must actually somehow be flowing upward. However, the spot from which it falls is no farther from the viewer than the collection point from which it appears to (but does not) begin its flow backward.

Again, distant objects look smaller than nearby objects of the same size. The paradoxes in the engraving to the right, "False Perspective," are made

Phi phenomenon The perception of movement as a result of sequential presentation of visual stimuli.

Monocular cues Stimuli suggestive of depth that can be perceived with only one eye.

Perspective A monocular cue for depth based on the convergence (coming together) of parallel lines as they recede into the distance.

Figure 3.22
What Is Wrong with These Pictures?

In "Waterfall," to the left, how does Dutch artist M. C. Escher suggest that fallen water flows back upward, only to fall again? In "False Perspective," to the right, how does English artist William Hogarth use monocular cues for depth perception to deceive the viewer?

"I'll explain it to you, Stevie. It's called perspective."

Figure 3.23
"Chezt-Yord." How does Op Artist Victor Vasarely use monocular cues for depth perception to lend this picture a three-dimensional quality?

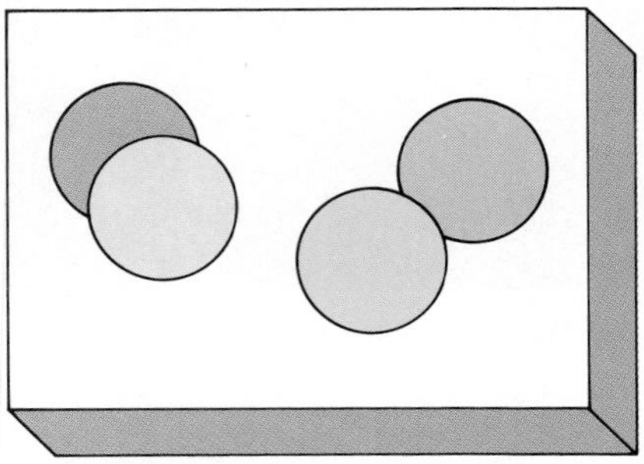

Figure 3.24
The Effects of Interposition. The four circles are all the same size. Which circles appear to be closer—the complete circles or the circles with chunks bitten out of them?

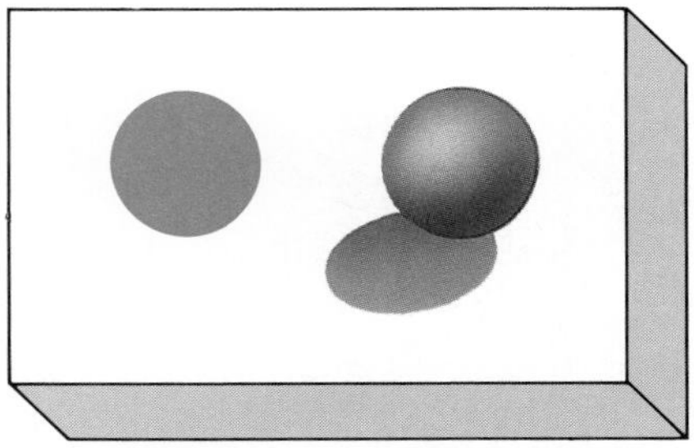

Figure 3.25
Shadowing as a Cue in the Perception of Depth. Shadowing lends the circle on the right a sense of three-dimensionality.

Interposition A monocular cue for depth based on the fact that a nearby object obscures a more distant object behind it.

Shadowing A monocular cue for depth based on the fact that opaque objects block light and produce shadows.

possible by the fact that more distant objects are not necessarily depicted as being smaller than nearby objects. Thus, what at first seems to be background suddenly becomes foreground, and vice versa.

The clearness of an object also suggests its distance from us. Experience shows us that we sense more details of nearby objects. For this reason, artists can suggest that certain objects are closer to the viewer by depicting them in greater detail. Note that the "distant" hill in the Hogarth engraving (Figure 3.22) is given less detail than the nearby plants at the bottom of the picture. Our perceptions are mocked when a man "on" that distant hill in the background is shown conversing with a woman leaning out a window in the middle ground. Note, too, how Vasarley uses clearness (crispness of line) to help provide a three-dimensional effect in "Chezt-Yord" (Figure 3.23).

We also learn that nearby objects can block our views of more distant objects. Overlapping, or **interposition,** is the apparent placing of one object in front of another. Experience encourages us to perceive the partly covered objects as being farther away than the objects that hide parts of them from view (Figure 3.24). In the Hogarth engraving (Figure 3.22), which looks closer: the trees in the background (background?) or the moon sign hanging from the building (or is it buildings?) to the right? How does the artist use interposition to confound the viewer?

Additional information about depth is provided by **shadowing** and is based on the fact that opaque objects block light and produce shadows. Shadows and highlights give us information about objects' three-dimensional shapes and about their relationships to the source of light. The left part of Figure 3.25 is perceived as a two-dimensional circle, but the right part tends to be perceived as a three-dimensional sphere because of the highlight on its surface and the shadow underneath. In the "sphere," the highlighted central area is perceived as being closest to us, with the surface then receding to the edges.

Another monocular cue is **texture gradient.** A gradient is a progressive change, and closer objects are perceived as having progressively rougher textures. In the Hogarth engraving (Figure 3.22), the building just behind the large fisherman's head has a rougher texture and thus seems to be closer than the building with the window from which the woman is leaning. Our surprise is thus heightened when the moon sign is seen as hanging from both buildings.

Motion Cues If you have ever driven in the country, you have probably noticed that distant objects, such as mountains and stars, appear to move

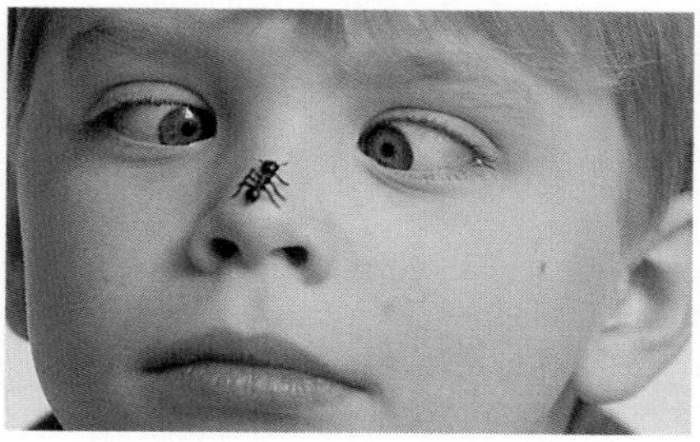

Figure 3.26
Retinal Disparity and Convergence as Cues for Depth. As an object nears your eyes, you begin to see two images of it because of retinal disparity. If you maintain perception of a single image, your eyes must converge on the object.

along with you. Objects at an intermediate distance seem to be stationary, but nearby objects, such as roadside markers, rocks, and trees, seem to go by quite rapidly. The tendency of objects to seem to move backward or forward as a function of their distance is known as **motion parallax.** We learn to perceive objects that appear to move with us as being at greater distances.

Earlier we noted that nearby objects cause the lens of the eye to accommodate or bend more to bring them into focus. The sensations of tension in the eye muscles also provide a monocular cue to depth, especially when we are within about four feet of the objects.

Binocular Cues **Binocular cues,** or cues that involve both eyes, also help us perceive depth. Two binocular cues are *retinal disparity* and *convergence.*

Try a simple experiment. Hold your index finger at arm's length. Now gradually bring it closer, until it almost touches your nose. If you keep your eyes relaxed as you do so, you will see two fingers. An image of the finger will be projected onto the retina of each eye, and each image will be slightly different because the finger will be seen at different angles. The difference between the projected images is referred to as **retinal disparity** and serves as a binocular cue for depth perception (see Figure 3.26). Note that the closer your finger comes, the farther apart the "two fingers" appear to be. Closer objects have greater retinal disparity.

If we try to maintain a single image of the approaching finger, our eyes must turn inward, or converge on it, giving us a cross-eyed look. **Convergence** is associated with feelings of tension in the eye muscles and provides another binocular cue for depth. The binocular cues of retinal disparity and convergence are strongest at near distances.

Texture gradient A monocular cue for depth based on the perception that closer objects appear to have rougher (more detailed) surfaces.

Motion parallax A monocular cue for depth based on the perception that nearby objects appear to move more rapidly in relation to our own motion.

Binocular cues Stimuli suggestive of depth that involve simultaneous perception by both eyes.

Retinal disparity A binocular cue for depth based on the difference in the image cast by an object on the retinas of the eyes as the object moves closer or farther away.

Convergence A binocular cue for depth based on the inward movement of the eyes as they attempt to focus on an object that is drawing nearer.

Size constancy The tendency to perceive an object as being the same size even as the size of its retinal image changes according to its distance.

Perceptual Constancies

The world is a constantly shifting display of visual sensations. What confusion would reign if we did not perceive a doorway to be the same doorway when seen from six feet as when seen from four feet. As we neared it, we might think that it was larger than the door we were seeking and become lost. Or consider the problems of the pet owner who recognizes his dog from the side but not from above, when the shapes differ. Fortunately, these problems tend not to occur—at least with familiar objects—because of perceptual constancies.

The image of a dog seen from 20 feet occupies about the same amount of space on your retina as an inch-long insect crawling in the palm of your hand. Yet you do not perceive the dog to be as small as the insect. Through your experiences you have acquired **size constancy,** or the tendency to perceive the same object as being the same size, even though the size of its image on the retina varies as a function of its distance. Experience teaches us about perspective, that the same object seen at a great distance will appear to be much smaller than when it is nearby. We may joke that people or cars look like ants from airplanes, but we know that they remain people and cars. For this reason, we can say that we *perceive* them to be the same size from great distances, even though the sensory input stimulates many fewer neurons on the retina.

A case study emphasizes the role of experience in the development of size constancy. Anthropologist Colin Turnbull (1961) found that an African Pygmy, Kenge, thought that buffalo perceived across an open field were some form of insect. Turnbull had to drive Kenge down to where the animals were

PSYCHOLOGY GOES TO WORK

Visual Perception, Optometry, and Ophthalmology

Optometry is the profession of examining the eyes and prescribing glasses or other kinds of lenses to correct defects in vision. Ophthalmology is the branch of medicine that deals with disorders of the eye.

Visual acuity One of the concerns of both professions is **visual acuity,** or sharpness of vision, as defined by ability to discriminate visual details. A familiar means of measuring visual acuity is the Snellen Chart (Figure 3.27). If you were to stand 20 feet from the Snellen Chart and could only discriminate the E, we would say that your vision is 20/200. This means that you can see from a distance of 20 feet what a person with normal vision can discriminate from a distance of 200 feet. In such a case you would be quite **nearsighted.** You would have to be unusually close to an object to discriminate its details. A person who could read the smallest line on the chart from 20 feet would have 20/15 vision and be somewhat **farsighted.** Nearsightedness and farsightedness usually stem from problems in focusing on objects at various distances.

You may have noticed that elderly people often hold newspapers or books at a distance. As you reach middle age, the lenses of the eyes become relatively brittle, making it more difficult to accommodate to, or focus on, objects. This condition is called **presbyopia,** from the Greek for "old man," although presbyopia usually begins at about the ages of 38 to 46. The lens structure of people with presbyopia differs from that of farsighted young people. Still, the effect of presbyopia is to make it difficult to perceive nearby visual stimuli. People who had normal visual acuity in their youth often require corrective lenses to read in old age. And people who were initially farsighted often suffer from headaches linked to eyestrain during the later years.

Strabismus In **strabismus,** the eye muscles do not work together, so people appear wall-eyed and seem to be looking at an object with one eye only. Strabismus is found in about 50,000 American children each year and is correctable by surgery. Binocular depth perception requires early experience in viewing objects simultaneously with both eyes. This early experience is essential to the development of binocular cells in the visual cortex, and these cells make possible the perception of binocular cues for depth. Thus, if strabismus is not surgically corrected by about the age of 5, children will never show adequate binocular depth perception.

Astigmatism **Astigmatism** is a visual disorder in which vertical and horizontal contours cannot be focused on simultaneously. If astigmatism is not corrected early in childhood, the child will develop poor acuity for one of these types of contours. As with strabismus, there is a critical period early in life during which the ability to perceive these contours develops. If children are not to suffer permanent visual deficits because of astigmatism, the disorder must be surgically corrected by about the age of 8 (Aslin & Banks, 1978).

Visual acuity Sharpness of vision.

Nearsighted Capable of seeing nearby objects with greater acuity than distant objects.

Farsighted Capable of seeing distant objects with greater acuity than nearby objects.

Presbyopia A condition characterized by brittleness of the lens.

Strabismus A visual disorder in which both eyes cannot focus on the same point at the same time.

Astigmatism A visual disorder caused by abnormal curvature of the lens, so that images are indistinct or distorted.

Color constancy The tendency to perceive an object as being the same color even though lighting conditions change its appearance.

Brightness constancy The tendency to perceive an object as being just as bright even though lighting conditions change its intensity.

grazing to convince him that they were not insects. During the drive, as the buffalo gradually grew in size, Kenge muttered to himself and moved closer to Turnbull in fear. Even after Kenge saw that these animals were, indeed, familiar buffalo, he still wondered how they could grow large so quickly. Kenge, you see, lived in a thick forest and normally did not view large animals from great distances. For this reason, he had not developed size constancy for distant objects. However, Kenge had no difficulty displaying size constancy with objects placed at various distances in his home.

We also have **color constancy,** or the tendency to perceive objects as retaining their color even though lighting conditions may alter their appearance. Your bright orange car may edge toward yellow-gray as the hours wend their way through twilight to nighttime. But when you finally locate it in the parking lot, you will still think of it as being orange. You expect an orange car and still judge it to be "more orange" than the (faded) blue and green cars to either side. However, it would be fiercely difficult to find it in a parking lot filled with yellow and red cars similar in size and shape.

Consider Figure 3.28. The orange squares within the blue squares are the same hue. However, the orange within the dark blue square is perceived as being purer. Why? Again, experience teaches us that the pureness of colors fades as the background grows darker. Since the orange squares are equally pure, we assume that the one in the dark background must be more saturated. We would stand ready to perceive the orange squares as being equal in purity if the square within the darker blue field actually had a bit of black mixed in with it.

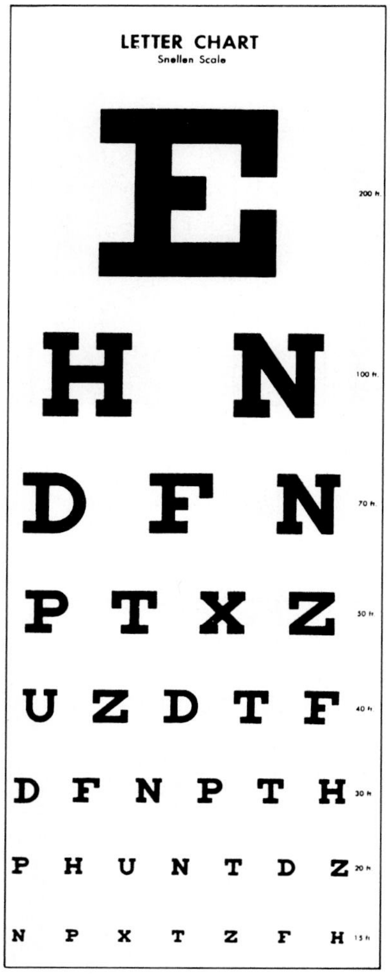

Figure 3.27
The Snellen Chart. The Snellen Chart and others like it are used to assess visual acuity.

Similar to color constancy is **brightness constancy.** As noted in Chapter 1, the same gray square is perceived as being brighter when placed within a black background than when placed within a white background (see Figure 1.3 on p. 13). Again, consider the role of experience. If it were nighttime, we would expect gray to fade to near blackness. The fact that the gray within the black square stimulates the eye with equal intensity suggests that it must be very much brighter than the gray within the white square.

We also perceive objects as maintaining their shapes, even if we perceive them from different angles so that the shape of the retinal image changes dramatically. This tendency is called **shape constancy.** You perceive the top of a coffee cup or a glass to be a circle, even though it is a circle only when seen from above. When seen from an angle, it is an ellipse. When seen on edge, the retinal image of the cup or glass is the same as that of a straight line. So why do you still describe the rim of the cup or glass as being a circle? Perhaps for two reasons: One is that experience has taught you that the cup will look circular when seen from above. The second is that you may have labeled the cup circular or round. Experience and labels make the world a stable place. Can you imagine the chaos that would prevail if we described objects as they stimulated our sensory organs with each changing moment, rather than according to stable conditions?

In another example, a door is a rectangle only when viewed straight on (Figure 3.29). When we move to the side or open it, the left or right edge comes closer and appears to be larger, changing the retinal image to a trapezoid. Yet we continue to think of doors as being rectangles.

The principles of perceptual organization make possible some fascinating illusions, as described in the next section.

Visual Illusions

The principles of perceptual organization make it possible for "our eyes to play tricks on us." Psychologists, like magicians, enjoy pulling a rabbit out of the hat now and then, and I am pleased to be able to demonstrate how the perceptual constancies trick the eye through so-called visual illusions.

The Hering-Helmholtz and Müller-Lyer illusions (Figure 3.30, part A) are named after the people who originated them. In the Hering-Helmholtz illusion, the horizontal lines are straight and parallel. However, the radiating lines cause them to appear to be bent outward near the center. The two lines in the Müller-Lyer illusion are the same length, but the line on the left, with its reversed arrowheads, looks longer.

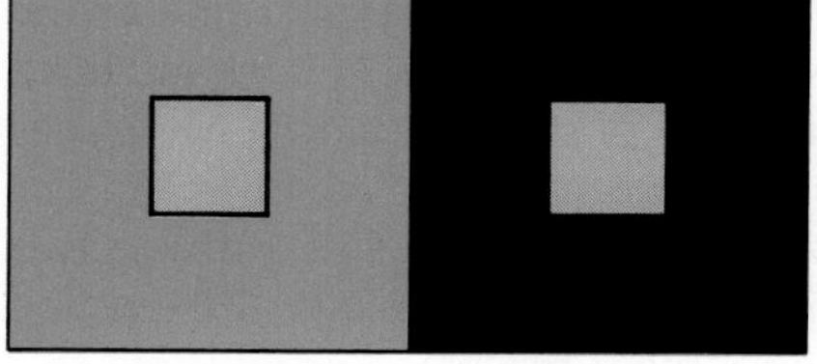

Figure 3.28
Color Constancy. The orange squares within the blue squares are the same hue, yet the orange within the dark blue square is perceived as being purer. Why?

Let us try to explain these illusions. Because of experience and lifelong use of perceptual cues, we tend to perceive the Hering-Helmholtz drawing as being three-dimensional. Because of the tendency to perceive bits of sensory information as figures against grounds, we perceive the white area in the center as being a circle in front of a series of radiating lines, all of which lies in front of a white ground. Next, because of our experience with perspective, we perceive the radiating lines as being parallel. We perceive the two horizontal lines as intersecting the "receding" lines, and we know that they would have to appear bent out at the center if they were to be equidistant at all points from the center of the circle.

Experience probably compels us to perceive the vertical lines in the Müller-Lyer illusion as being the corners of a room as seen from inside a house, at left, and outside a house, at right (see Figure 3.30, part B). In such an example, the reverse arrowheads to the left are lines where the walls meet the ceiling and the floor. We perceive such lines as extending toward

Shape constancy The tendency to perceive an object as being the same shape although the retinal image varies in shape as it rotates.

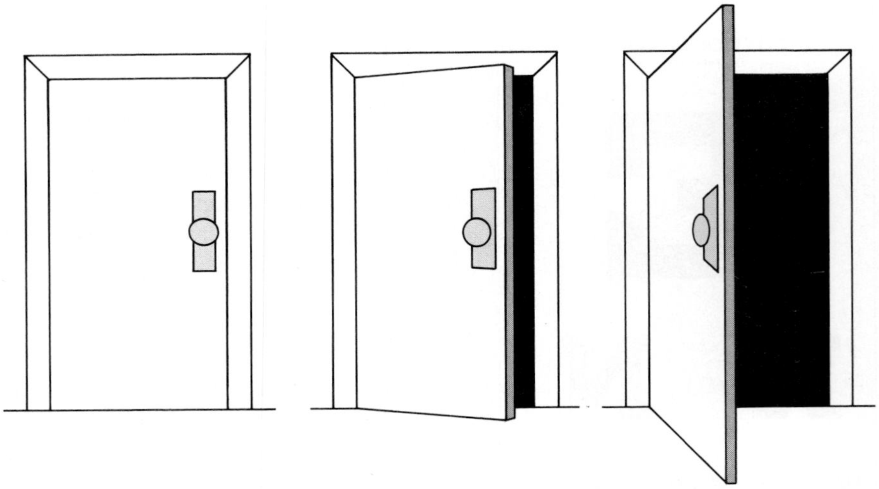

Figure 3.29
Shape Constancy. When closed, this door is a rectangle. When open, the retinal image is trapezoidal. But because of shape constancy, we still perceive the door as being rectangular.

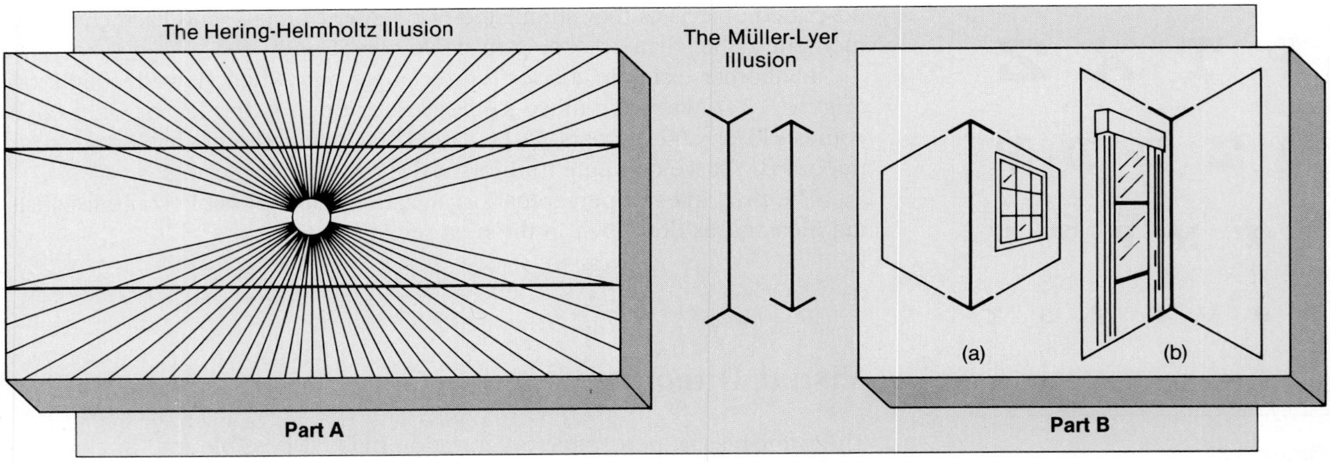

Figure 3.30
The Hering-Helmholtz and Müller-Lyer Illusions.

In the Hering-Helmholtz illusion, are the horizontal lines straight or curved? In the Müller-Lyer illusion, are the vertical lines equal in length?

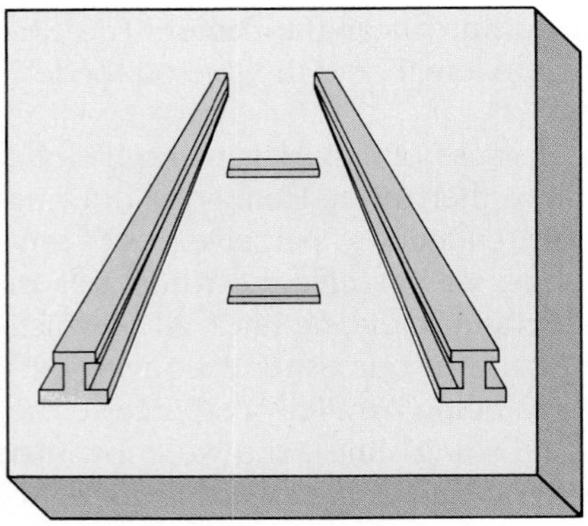

Figure 3.31
The Ponzo Illusion. The two horizontal lines in this drawing are equal in length, but the top line is perceived as being longer. Can you use the principle of size constancy to explain why?

us; they push the corner away from us. The arrowheads to the right are lines where exterior walls meet the roof and foundation. We perceive them as receding from us; they push the corner toward us. The vertical line to the left is thus perceived as being farther away. Since both vertical lines stimulate equal expanses across the retina, the principle of size constancy encourages us to perceive the line to the left as being longer.

Figure 3.31 is known as the Ponzo illusion. In this illusion, the two horizontal lines are the same length. However, do you perceive the top line as being longer? The rule of size constancy may also afford insight into this illusion. Perhaps the converging lines again strike us as being parallel lines receding into the distance, like the train tracks in the drawing on page 115. If so, we assume from experience that the horizontal line at the top is farther down the track—farther away from us. And again, the rule of size constancy tells us that if two objects appear to be the same size and one is farther away, the farther object must be larger. So we perceive the top line as being larger.

Now that you are an expert on these visual illusions, look at Figure 3.32. First take some bets from friends about whether the three cylinders are equal

A CLOSER LOOK

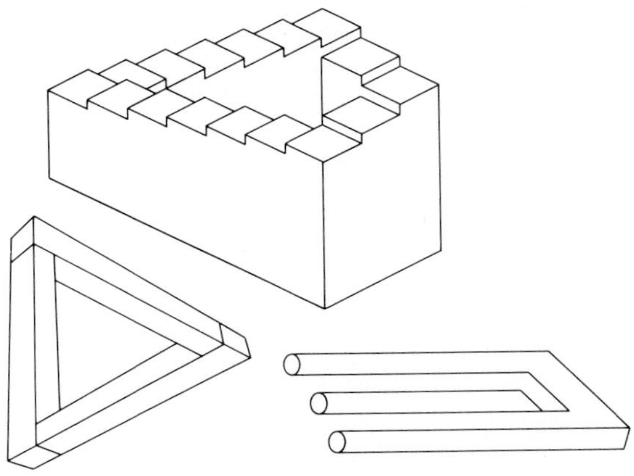

To Perceive the Impossible Drawing

What's wrong with each of these drawings? Each has firm lines. Each has interesting shapes. In fact, if you look at any one corner of a drawing, it makes perfect sense. But take a critical view of the endless staircase in M. C. Escher's "Relativity." What would happen if you were walk up this staircase? Would you ever reach the top? Or what would happen if a ball rolled down and managed to turn all the corners? Would it ever reach bottom?

In each of these drawings, the artist, working in two dimensions, has used perceptual cues in such a way as to encourage us to perceive a three-dimensional figure. Any one segment of each of these drawings makes perfect sense. It's just when you put it all together that you realize that . . . well, you can't put it all together, can you? That would be impossible.

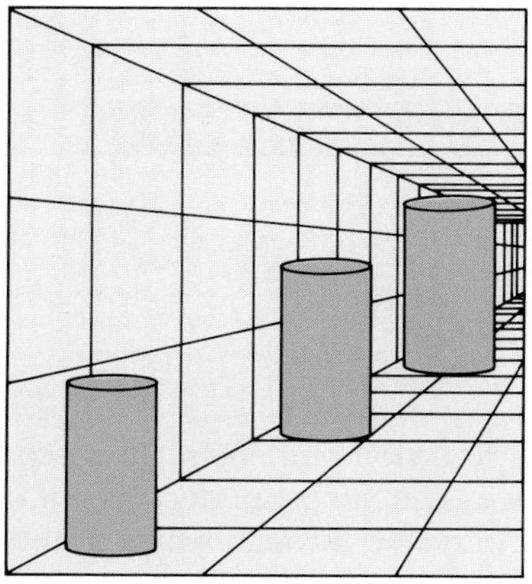

Figure 3.32
An Illusion Created by the Principle of Size Constancy. In this drawing, the three cylinders are the same size, yet they appear to grow larger toward the top of the picture. Can you use the principle of size constancy to explain why?

in height and width. Then get a ruler. Once you have made some money, however, try to explain why the cylinders to the right look progressively larger.

Now let us consider an illusion of movement. Figure 3.33, "Current" is an "optical art" picture by Bridget Riley. When you fix your gaze on any point in the picture, the surrounding areas seem to be in motion. "Current," like many other works of optical art, uses pictorial features to create the illusion of motion. In this case, the pictorial feature is a moiré pattern, in which nearly identical wavy lines are placed next to each other. It is nearly impossible to perceive the continuity of any one line in the picture. Instead, our gaze tends to hop back and forth from line to line. The hopping back and forth leads to the perception of vibrations in the lines, and hence movement.

Speaking of vibrations, the time has come to discuss a way in which we can sense vibrations in the air: hearing.

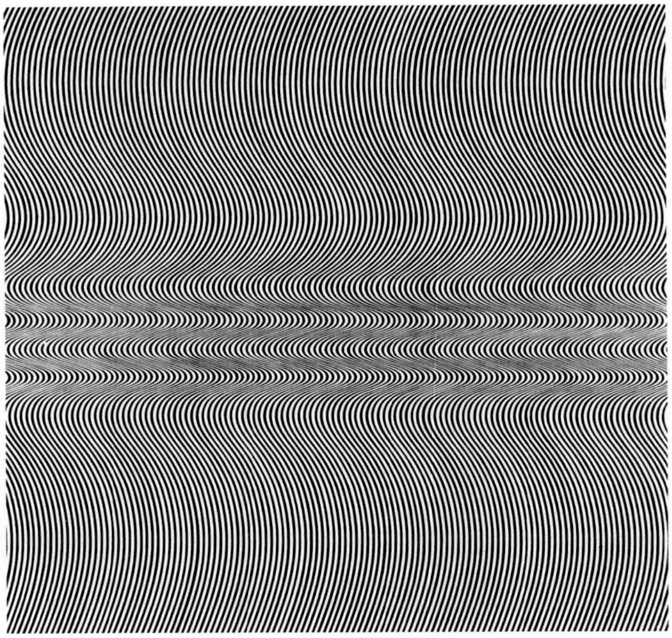

Figure 3.33
"Current." In this Op Art picture by Bridget Riley, the illusion of movement is created with a moiré pattern, in which nearly identical wavy lines are placed next to one another, inducing the perception of movement.

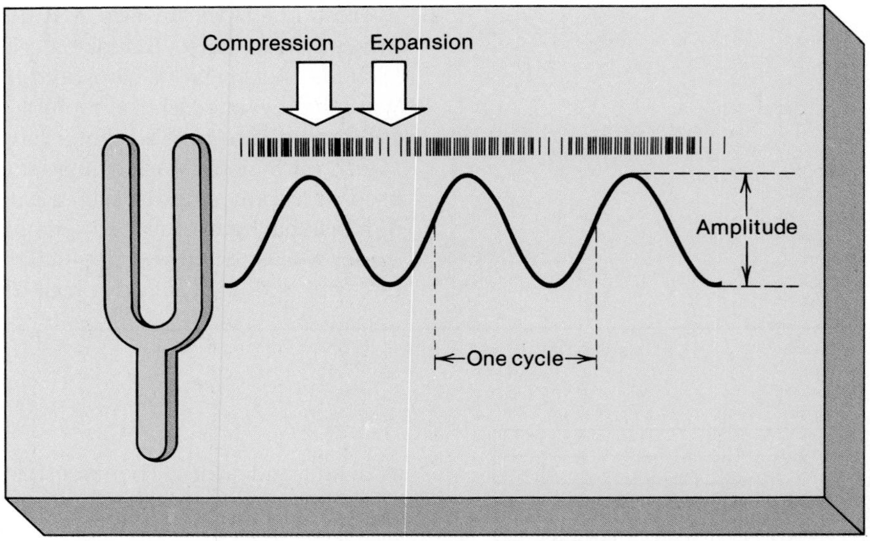

Figure 3.34
Creation of Sound Waves. The vibration of the prongs of a tuning fork alternately compresses and expands air molecules, sending forth waves of sound.

HEARING

Consider the advertising slogan for the science fiction film *Alien:* "In space, no one can hear you scream." It's true. Space is an almost perfect vacuum, and hearing requires a medium, such as air or water, through which sound can travel.

Sound, or **auditory** stimulation, travels through the air like waves. Sound is caused by changes in air pressure that result from vibrations. These vibrations, in turn, can be created by a tuning fork, your vocal cords, guitar strings, or the clap of a book thrown down on a desk.

Figure 3.34 suggests the way in which a tuning fork creates sound waves. During a vibration back and forth, the right prong of the tuning fork moves

Auditory Having to do with hearing.

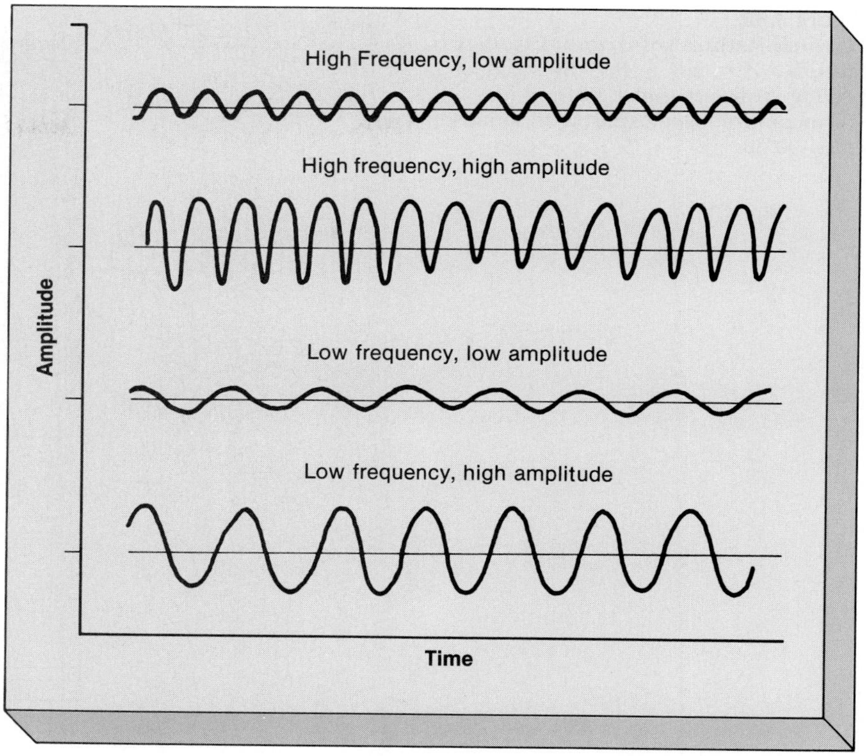

Figure 3.35
Sound Waves of Various Frequencies and Amplitudes. Which sounds have the highest pitch? Which are loudest?

to the right. In so doing, it pushes together, or compresses, the molecules of air immediately to the right. Then the prong moves back to the left, and the air molecules to the right expand. By vibrating back and forth, the tuning fork actually sends air waves in many directions. A cycle of compression and expansion is considered to be one wave of sound. Sound waves can occur many times in one second. The human ear is sensitive to sound waves that vary from frequencies of 20 to 20,000 cycles per second.

Pitch and Loudness

Pitch and loudness are two psychological dimensions of sound.

Pitch The pitch of a sound is determined by its frequency, or the number of cycles per second as expressed in the unit **Hertz** (Hz). One cycle per second is one Hz. The greater the number of cycles per second (Hz), the higher the pitch of the sound. The pitch of women's voices is usually higher than those of men because women's vocal cords are usually shorter and thus vibrate at a greater frequency. The strings of a violin are shorter than those of a viola or bass viol. They vibrate at greater frequencies, and we perceive them to be higher in pitch.

Loudness The loudness of a sound is determined by the height, or **amplitude,** of sound waves. The higher the amplitude of the wave, the louder the sound. Figure 3.35 shows records of sound waves that vary in frequency and amplitude. Frequency and amplitude are independent dimensions. Sounds both high and low in pitch can be either high or low in loudness.

Hertz A unit expressing the frequency of sound waves. One Hertz, or *1 Hz,* equals one cycle per second.

Amplitude Height.

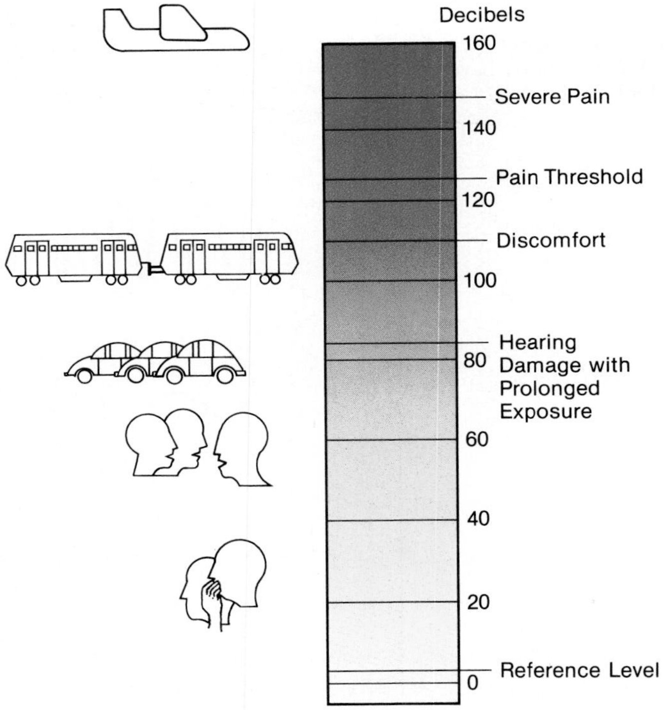

Figure 3.36
Decibel Ratings of Some Familiar Sounds. Zero dB is the threshold of hearing. You may suffer hearing loss if you incur prolonged exposure to sounds of 85–90 dB.

The loudness of a sound is usually expressed in the unit **decibel,** abbreviated *dB,* which is named after the inventor of the telephone, Alexander Graham Bell. Zero dB is equivalent to the threshold of hearing. How loud is that? It's about as loud as the ticking of a watch 20 feet away in a very quiet room (see Table 3.1).

The decibel equivalents of many familiar sounds are shown in Figure 3.36. Twenty dB is equivalent in loudness to a whisper at five feet. Thirty dB is roughly the limit of loudness at which your librarian would like to keep your college library. You may suffer hearing damage if exposed protractedly to sounds of 85 to 90 dB.

When musical sounds (also called tones) of different frequency are played together, we also perceive a third tone that results from the difference in their frequencies. If the combination of tones is pleasant, we say that they are in harmony, or **consonant** (from Latin roots meaning "together" and "sound"). Unpleasant combinations of tones are labeled **dissonant** ("the opposite of" and "sound"). The expression that something "strikes a dissonant chord" means that we find it disagreeable.

Overtones and Timbre In addition to producing the specified musical note, an instrument like the violin also produces a number of tones that are greater in frequency. These more highly pitched sounds are called **overtones.** Overtones result from vibrations elsewhere in the instrument and contribute to the quality or richness—the **timbre**—of a sound.

Truth or Fiction Revisited

It is true that a $500 machine-made violin will produce the same musical notes as a $200,000 Stradivarius. However, the Stradivarius has richer overtones, which lend the instrument its greater value.

Professional musicians require more expensive instruments because of the richness of their overtones—their timbre.

Decibel A unit expressing the loudness of a sound. Abbreviated *dB.*

Consonant In harmony.

Dissonant Incompatible, not harmonious, discordant.

Overtones Tones of a higher frequency than those played that result from vibrations throughout a musical instrument.

Timbre The quality or richness of a sound.

Noise In terms of the sense of hearing, noise is a combination of dissonant sounds.* When you place a spiral shell to your ear, you do not hear the roar of the ocean. Rather, you hear the reflected noise in your vicinity. **White noise** consists of many different frequencies of sound. Yet this mixture can lull us to sleep if the loudness is not too great.

Now let us turn our attention to the marvelous instrument that senses all these different "vibes": the human ear.

The Ear

The human ear is good for lots of things—catching dust, combing your hair around, hanging jewelry from, and nibbling. It is also admirably suited for sensing auditory stimulation, or hearing. It is shaped and structured to capture sound waves, to vibrate in sympathy with them, and to transmit all this business to centers in the brain. In this way, you not only hear something, you can also figure out what it is. You have an outer ear, a middle ear, and an inner ear (see Figure 3.37).

The Outer Ear The outer ear is shaped to funnel sound waves to the **eardrum,** a thin membrane that vibrates in response to sound waves and thereby transmits them to the middle and inner ears.

The Middle Ear The middle ear contains the eardrum and three small bones—the hammer, the anvil, and the stirrup—which also transmit sound by vibrating. These bones were given their names (actually the Latin *malleus, incus,* and *stapes,* which translate as hammer, anvil, and stirrup) because of their shapes. The middle ear functions as an amplifier: It increases the magnitude of the air pressure.

The stirrup is attached to another vibrating membrane, the **oval window.** The round window shown in Figure 3.37 pushes out when the oval window pushes in, and it is pulled in when the oval window vibrates outward, thus balancing the pressure in the inner ear.

The Inner Ear The oval window transmits vibrations into the inner ear, the bony tube called the **cochlea** (from the Greek for "snail"). The cochlea, which has the shape of a snail shell, contains two longitudinal membranes that divide it into three fluid-filled chambers. One of the membranes that lies coiled within the cochlea is called the **basilar membrane.** Vibrations in the fluids within the chambers of the inner ear press against the basilar membrane.

The **organ of Corti,** sometimes referred to as the "command post" of hearing, is attached to the basilar membrane. Thousands of hair cells (receptor cells that project like hair from the organ of Corti) bend in response to the vibrations of the basilar membrane. The bending of these receptor cells generates a neural impulse that is transmitted by the 31,000 neurons that form the **auditory nerve** to the brain (Yost & Nielson, 1985). Within the brain, auditory input is projected onto the hearing areas of the temporal lobes of the cerebral cortex.

White noise Discordant sounds of many frequencies, often producing a lulling effect.

Eardrum A thin membrane that vibrates in response to sound waves, transmitting the waves to the middle and inner ears.

Oval window A membrane that transmits vibrations from the stirrup of the middle ear to the cochlea within the inner ear.

Cochlea The inner ear; the bony tube that contains the basilar membrane and the organ of Corti.

Basilar membrane A membrane that lies coiled within the cochlea.

Organ of Corti The receptor for hearing that lies on the basilar membrane in the cochlea.

Auditory nerve The axon bundle that transmits neural impulses from the organ of Corti to the brain.

*Within the broader context of signal-detection theory, *noise* has a different meaning, discussed earlier in the chapter.

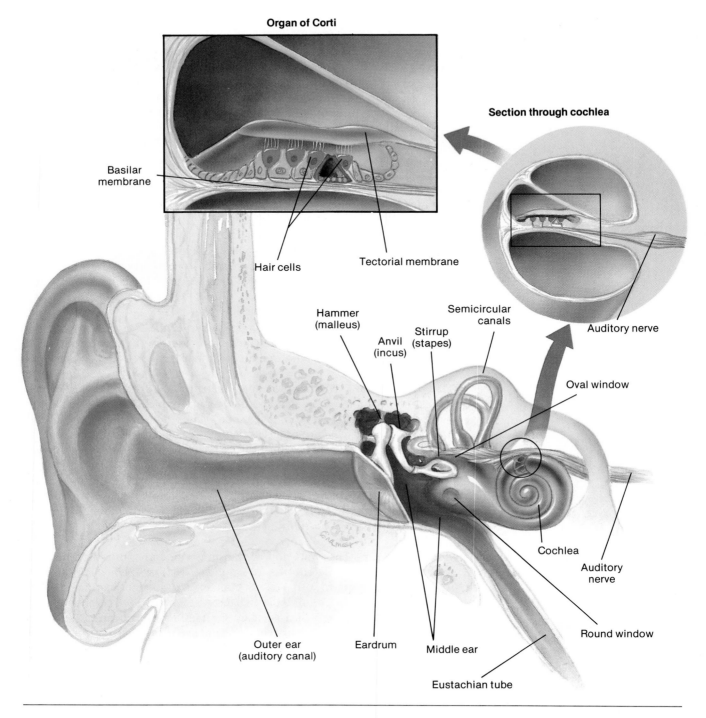

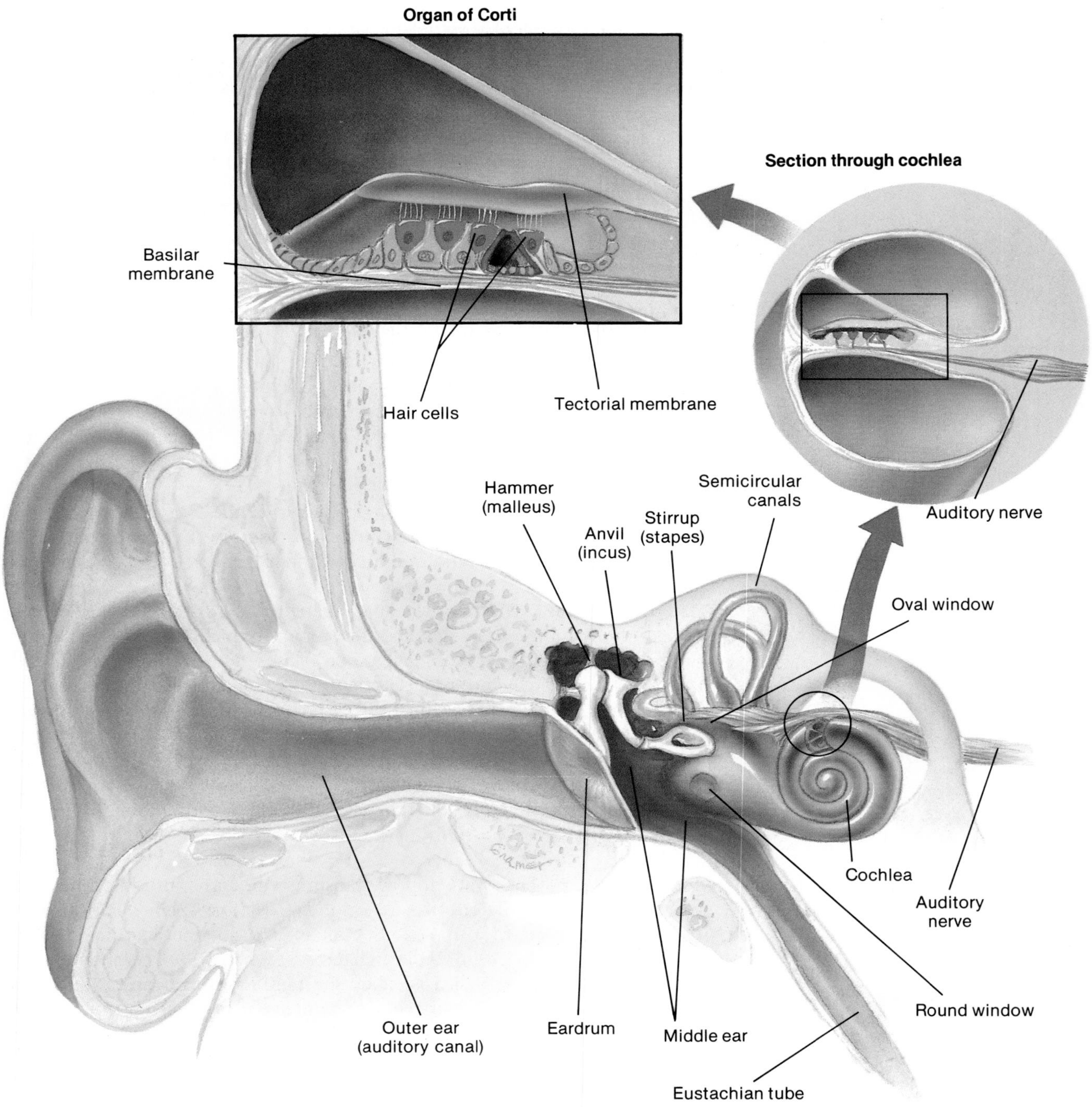

Figure 3.37
The Human Ear.

The outer ear funnels sound to the eardrum. Inside the eardrum, vibrations of the hammer, anvil, and stirrup transmit sound to the inner ear. Vibrations in the cochlea transmit the sound to the auditory nerve by way of the basilar membrane and the organ of Corti.

Locating Sounds

How do you balance the loudness of a stereo set? You sit between the speakers and adjust the volume until the sound seems to be equally loud in each ear. If the sound to the right is louder, the musical instruments will be perceived as being toward the right rather than straight ahead.

There is a resemblance between balacing a stereo set and locating sounds. A sound that is louder in the right ear is perceived as coming from the right. A sound from the right side also reaches the right ear first. Loudness and sequence of stimulating the ears both provide directional cues.

But it may not be easy to locate a sound that is directly in front, in back, or overhead. Such sounds are equally loud in and distant from each ear. So what do we do? Simple—usually we turn our heads slightly to determine in which ear the sound increases. If you turn your head a few degrees to the right and the loudness increases in your left ear, the sound must be in front of you. Of course we also use vision and general knowledge in locating the source of sounds. If you hear the roar of jet engines, most of the time you will make money by betting that the airplane is overhead.

Perception of Loudness and Pitch

We know that sounds are heard because they cause vibration in parts of the ear and information about these vibrations is transmitted to the brain. But what determines the loudness and pitch of our perceptions of these sounds?

The loudness and pitch of sounds appear to be related to the number of receptor neurons on the organ of Corti that fire and how often they fire. Psychologists generally agree that sounds are perceived as being louder when more of these sensory neurons fire. They are not so certain about the perception of pitch. Two of the theories that have been advanced to explain pitch discrimination are *place theory* and *frequency theory*.

Place Theory According to **place theory,** the pitch of a sound is determined by the place along the basilar membrane that vibrates in response to it. In his research with guinea pigs and cadavers, von Békésy (1957) found that receptors at different sites along the membrane fire in response to tones of differing frequencies. By and large, the higher the pitch of a sound, the closer the responsive neurons lie to the oval window. However, the entire membrane appears to be responsive to tones that are low in frequency.

Frequency Theory Place theory does not explain all the phenomena of hearing. For example, it has been found that impulses in the auditory nerve follow the pattern of the sound waves being detected. **Frequency theory** has been developed to account for such occurrences. In general, frequency theory proposes that pitch perception depends on the stimulation of neural impulses that match the frequency of the sound waves. However, frequency theory breaks down for perception of pitches higher than 1,000 Hz, because neural impulses are not able to follow the forms of the sound waves at those levels.

So-called **duplicity theory** advances the view that pitch perception depends both on the place and frequency of neural response. A more comprehensive theory of pitch perception will have to explain (1) why neurons at different sites on the basilar membrane fire in response to different pitches, (2) why impulses in the auditory nerve follow the patterns of sound waves at many frequencies, and (3) how we perceive pitches at above 1,000 Hz.

Unfortunately, not everyone perceives sound, and many of us do not perceive sounds of certain frequencies. Let us consider a number of kinds of hearing problems, or deafness.

Place theory The theory that the pitch of a sound is determined by the section of the basilar membrane that vibrates in response to the sound.

Frequency theory The theory that the pitch of a sound is reflected in the frequency of the neural impulses that are generated in response to the sound.

Duplicity theory A combination of the place and frequency theories of pitch discrimination.

A CLOSER LOOK

Deafness

Do we really "make ourselves deaf" by listening to high-volume rock and roll concerts or tapes? Do constructions workers risk deafness when they fail to protect themselves from the sounds of pneumatic drills? Apparently these risks are very real, but they account for only one kind of deafness—stimulation deafness. Actually, there are three major types of hearing problems or deafness, and each results from a different kind of problem in the ear.

Conduction Deafness **Conduction deafness** occurs because of damage to the structures of the middle ear—either to the eardrum or to the three bones that conduct (and amplify) sound waves from the outer ear to the inner ear. People with conduction hearing loss have high absolute thresholds for detection of sounds at all frequencies. They frequently profit from hearing aids, which provide the amplification that the middle ear does not.

Sensory-Neural Deafness **Sensory-neural deafness** usually stems from damage to the structures of the inner ear, most often the loss of hair cells, which will not regenerate. Sensory-neural deafness can also stem from damage to the auditory nerve. In this form of deafness, people tend to be more sensitive to sounds of some pitches than others. Experimental cochlear implants bypass damaged hair cells to stimulate the auditory nerve directly, and they have helped many patients with this form of deafness (Schmeck, 1988).

Stimulation Deafness **Stimulation deafness** stems from exposure to very loud sounds. As with sensory-neural deafness, some kinds of stimulation deafness, such as Hunter's notch, are limited to particular frequencies—in this case, the frequencies of the sound waves generated by a gun firing. Prolonged exposure to 85 dB can cause stimulation loss. People who attend high-volume rock concerts risk damaging their ears, as do workers who run pneumatic drills or drive high-volume transportation vehicles. The so-called ringing sensation that often follows exposure to loud sounds probably means that hair cells have been damaged (McFadden & Wightman, 1983). If you find yourself suddenly exposed to loud sounds, remember that your fingertips serve as good emergency ear protectors.

Conduction deafness The forms of deafness in which there is loss of conduction of sound through the middle ear.

Sensory-neural deafness The forms of deafness that result from damage to hair cells or the auditory nerve.

Stimulation deafness The forms of deafness that result from exposure to sounds that are excessively loud.

SMELL

Smell and taste are the chemical senses. In the cases of vision and hearing, physical energy impacts on our sensory receptors. With smell and taste, we sample molecules of the substances being sensed.

You could say that we are underprivileged when it comes to the sense of smell. Dogs, for instance, devote about seven times as much area of the cerebral cortex to the sense of smell. Male dogs sniff to determine where the territories of other dogs leave off and to determine whether female dogs are sexually receptive. Dogs even make a living sniffing out marijuana in closed packages and suitcases.

Still, smell has an important role in human behavior. If you did not have a sense of smell, an onion and an apple would taste the same to you! As lacking as our senses of smell may be when we compare them to those of a dog, we can detect the odor of one one-millionth of a milligram of vanilla in a liter of air.

Truth or Fiction Revisited

It is true that onions and apples have the same taste. However, their *flavors* are very different.

An **odor** is a sample of the actual substance being sensed. Odors are detected by sites on receptor neurons in the **olfactory** membrane high in each nostril. Receptor neurons fire when a few molecules of the substance in gaseous form come into contact with them. Firing transmits information about odors to the brain via the **olfactory nerve.** That is how the substance is smelled.

According to various theories, there are several basic odors: flowery, minty, musky, camphoraceous, ethereal, pungent, and putrid. Other odors can then be broken down into combinations of basic odors. According to one theory, we smell substances whose molecules fit the shapes of receptor sites (Amoore, 1970). This theory receives some support from the fact that we can develop an **anosmia,** or "smell blindness," for a particular odor—suggesting that one kind of receptor has been damaged or degenerated. However, we are not certain how many different types of receptors for odor there are. Too, each of our receptors seems to be responsive to two or more odorous substances.

The sense of smell tends to adapt rather rapidly to odors, even obnoxious ones. This might be fortunate if you are using a locker room or an outhouse. But it might not be so fortunate if you are being exposed to fumes from paints or other chemicals, since you may lose awareness of them even though they remain harmful. One odor may also be masked by another, which is how air fresheners work.

Some Recent Studies in Olfaction: "The Nose Knows"

Let us now turn our attention to some recent research concerning the sense of smell. We shall discuss menstrual synchrony as well as olfactory messengers known as pheromones.

Menstrual Synchrony The menstrual cycle is regulated by hormones (see Chapter 2). In 1971, psychologist Martha McClintock reported the phenomenon of **menstrual synchrony.** She monitored the menstrual cycles of 135 women and found that the cycles of friends and roommates converged from an average of 8.5 days apart to within 5 days during one school year.

In a study with laboratory rats, McClintock (1979) caused the reproductive cycles of female rats to converge by circulating air between their cages. The sense of smell was the only source of contact between the animals.

Pheromones: Has Science Found a Magic Potion? For centuries, people have searched for a love potion—a magical formula that could make others fall in love with you or be strongly attracted to you. Some scientists suggest that such potions may exist. They are called **pheromones.**

Many organisms, from insects through mammals, are sexually aroused by these chemical secretions. Pheromones are produced by other members of the species and are detected through the sense of smell. In addition to sexual functions, animals use pheromones to organize food gathering, mark

---

Odor The characteristic of a substance that makes it perceptible to the sense of smell.

Olfactory Having to do with the sense of smell.

Olfactory nerve The nerve that transmits information concerning odors from olfactory receptors to the brain.

Anosmia Lack of sensitivity to a specific odor.

Menstrual synchrony The convergence of the menstrual cycles of women who spend time in close quarters.

Pheromones Chemical secretions detected by the sense of smell that stimulate stereotypical behaviors in other members of the species.

PSYCHOLOGY GOES TO WORK

Winning a Job by a Nose?

So, you're off to that big job interview. You're all spruced up—freshly washed, neat as a button, and about to dab on some perfume or splash on some cologne. After all, it seems, uh, sensible to appeal to your interviewer's sense of smell as well as to his or her business judgment and sense of vision, right? Not necessarily, according to research by psychologist Robert A. Baron of Rensselaer Polytechnic Institute.

Baron (1983) found that women interviewers rate applicants who wear perfume or cologne more positively than those who abstain. Male interviewers, however, consider fragrant cheeks cheeky. That is, they rate redolent applicants—male and female alike—more negatively. For male interviewers, apparently, the smell of success is not so sweet. Male interviewers are most harsh in their ratings of women applicants who wear perfume and also employ "forward" body language, such as leaning toward the interviewer or repeatedly seeking eye contact.

Why this sex difference? Perhaps male interviewers are more rigid than women interviewers, more susceptible to stereotypes that able things do not come in fragrant packages. Male interviewers may think that applicants should limit their presentations to their skills and motivation and not try to nose out the competition.

In any event, perhaps you should find out the gender of your interviewer if you are tempted to render yourself aromatic. Using perfume with the wrong person could be rank frivolity.

territories, sound alarms, and maintain pecking orders. Pheromones induce mating behavior mechanically in insects (Robinson & Robinson, 1979), but—perhaps to the chagrin of romantics—their role in sexual behavior becomes less vital as we rise through the ranks of the animal kingdom.

Mammals secrete pheromones in the vagina. When urine from female mice, containing pheromones, is smeared on the backs of male mice, other male mice attempt to mate with them (Connor, 1972). Male mice (Cooper, 1978) and male guinea pigs (Beauchamp, 1981) show less sexual arousal when their sense of smell is blocked. Vaginal secretions also arouse male monkeys (Michael et al., 1971), but monkeys seek sexual activity even when nose drops have blocked their sense of smell (Goldfoot et al., 1978).

Some people also apparently respond to pheromones, but like monkeys, they do not need them. People can become sexually excited by a glimpse of a loved one, an erotic photo, a whiff of perfume or cologne that stirs a memory, or a lover's voice (Rathus, 1983). However, consider the case of **exaltolide,** a musky substance that is highly concentrated in the urine of adult men. Its odor is more detectable by and appealing to adult women than to children or men (Hassett, 1978). Moreover, women are most sensitive to exaltolide when they are ovulating (and thus capable of conceiving).

Morris and Udry (1978) ran an experiment with married couples in which women dabbed various perfumes on their breasts at bedtime. One perfume contained suspected pheromones. The couples tracked their sexual activity. One couple in five showed significantly more frequent sexual activity when using the pheromone-laced perfume, although the couples did not know when the substance was being used.

We now highlight a study in olfaction that made quite a stink.

Exaltolide A musky substance that is suspected to be a sexual pheromone.

A CLOSER LOOK

On Odors, Stereotypes, and Mate Selection

Now, who would pay you $10 to wear a T-shirt for 48 hours, extracting a promise that you would jog around or do pushups for at least an hour during this period? Psychologists, of course, trying to learn how sensitive we are to one form of "air pollution"—body odor.

Following these two-day exercises, subjects peeled the shirts off and returned them to the experimenters (McBurney et al., 1977) in tightly sealed plastic bags. In a procedure that demonstrates unparalleled commitment to the advancement of psychology, students then smelled the shirts and rated them for relative offensiveness.

There was general agreement about which shirts smelled worse. Anonymous owners of the most putrid were rated as being dirtier, less intelligent, less healthy, fatter, and less appealing to the opposite sex. Yet they were also rated as being stronger, more industrious, and more athletic. Apparently they were seen as tough and hard-working but mindless and dirty drones. Subjects also rated their own shirts as being least offensive.

Schleidt and Hold (1981) found that married couples in West Germany, Italy, and Japan could identify T-shirts worn to bed for a week by their mates—even when blindfolded. Apparently the nose knows its mate. In these studies, both men and women generally considered male odors to be more obnoxious than female odors, although they also generally rated their mates' odor as being less offensive than their own.

There was one exception. The Japanese women considered their husbands' body odors to be more obnoxious than their own. Why? The researchers speculate that the reason is linked to the fact that in Japan marriages are still frequently arranged by families. That is, the Japanese don't always get to sniff out a mate for themselves.

In case you believe that our discussion of these experiments was lacking in taste, we shall devote the next section entirely to matters of taste.

TASTE

Your cocker spaniel may jump at the chance to finish off your ice cream cone, but your Siamese cat may turn up her nose at this golden opportunity. Why? Dogs can perceive the taste quality of sweetness, as can pigs, but cats cannot (Dethier, 1978).

There are four primary taste qualities: sweet, sour, salty, and bitter. The *flavor* of a food involves its taste but is more complex. As noted earlier, apples and onions have the same taste—or the same mix of taste qualities—but their flavor is vastly different. After all, you wouldn't chomp into a nice cold onion on a warm day, would you? The flavor of a food depends on its odor, texture, and temperature as well as its taste. If it were not for odor, heated tenderized shoe leather just might pass for your favorite steak.

Taste is sensed through **taste cells,** or receptor neurons that are located on **taste buds.** You have about 10,000 taste buds, most of which are located near the edges and back of your tongue. As noted in Figure 3.38, taste buds tend to specialize a bit. Some, for example, are more responsive to sweetness, whereas others react to several tastes. Receptors for sweetness lie at the tip of the tongue, and receptors for bitterness lie toward the back of the tongue. Sourness is sensed along the sides of the tongue, and saltiness overlaps the areas sensitive to sweetness and sourness (Figure 3.38). This is why people perceive a sour dish to "get them" at the sides of the tongue.

By eating hot foods and scraping your tongue, you regularly kill off many taste cells. But you need not be alarmed at this unintentional display of oral aggression. Taste cells are the rabbits of the sense receptors, reproducing at the rate of complete renewal every week or so.

Taste cells Receptor cells that are sensitive to taste.

Taste buds The sensory organs for taste. They contain taste cells and are located on the tongue.

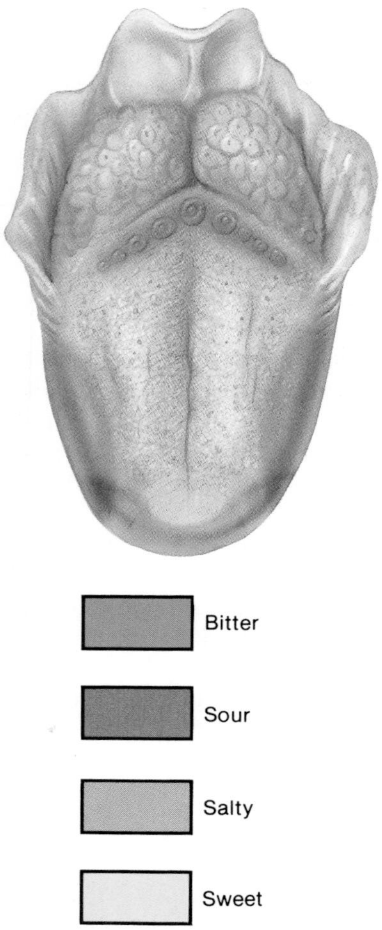

Figure 3.38
Location of Various Taste Buds on the Tongue. Taste buds on different areas of the tongue are sensitive to different primary taste qualities.

A Taste of . . . Well, Certainly Not Honey. The flavors of foods are determined not only by taste but also by their odor, texture, and temperature.

The number of taste cells declines with age. However, Bartoshuk also found that strong taste intensities can be elicited from very small parts of the tongue (Turkington, 1985). It is more likely, according to Bartoshuk, that the "taste" loss associated with the elderly is actually due to a decline in the sense of smell.

THE SKIN SENSES

Earlier it was noted that vision is usually the most dominant of the senses, but 6-month-old infants are sometimes so engrossed with the feel of objects that they may better remember changes in temperature than changes in color (Bushnell et al., 1985). Of course, on a hot, humid July day, we may all pay more attention to a cold breeze than to a change in the color of a neighbor's beach umbrella.

Changes in temperature are just one type of event we sense by means of nerve endings in the skin. We know that the skin discriminates among many kinds of sensations—touch, pressure, warmth, cold, and pain—but how it does so is not so clear. It now seems that we have distinct sensory receptors for pressure, temperature, and pain (Brown & Deffenbacher, 1979). It might also be that some nerve endings receive more than one type of sensory input.

Touch and Pressure

Sensory receptors located around the roots of hair cells appear to fire in response to touching the surface of the skin. You may have noticed that if you are trying to "get the feel of" a fabric or the texture of a friend's hair, you must move your hand over it (Loomis & Lederman, 1986). Otherwise, the sensations quickly fade. If you pass your hand over the skin and then hold it still, again sensations of touching will fade. This sort of "active touching" involves reception of information that concerns not only touch per se but also pressure, temperature, and feedback from the muscles that are involved in movements of our hands.

Other structures beneath the skin are apparently sensitive to pressure. All in all, there are about half a million receptors for touch and pressure spaced throughout the body. Different parts of the body are more sensitive to touch and pressure than others. Psychophysicists use methods such as the **two-point threshold** to assess sensitivity to pressure. This method determines the smallest distance by which two rods touching the skin must be separated before the (blindfolded) subject will report that there are two rods, not one. As revealed by this method, our fingertips, lips, noses, and cheeks are much more sensitive than our shoulders, thighs, and calves. That is, the rods can be closer together when they touch the lips than the shoulders and still be perceived as distinct. Differential sensitivity occurs for at least two reasons: First, nerve endings are more densely packed in the fingertips and face than in other locations. Second, a greater amount of sensory cortex is devoted to the perception of sensations in the fingertips and face.

The sense of pressure, like the sense of touch, undergoes rather rapid adaptation. You may have undertaken several minutes of strategic movements to wind up with your hand on the arm or leg of your date, only to discover that adaptation to this delightful source of pressure saps the sensation.

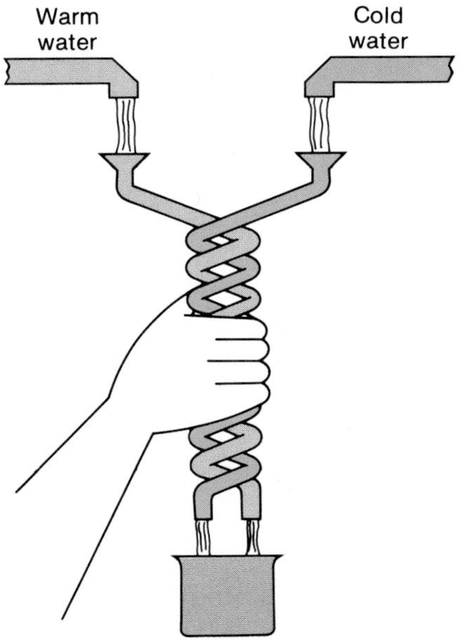

Figure 3.39
Paradoxical Hotness. The perception of hotness usually relies on the simultaneous firing of receptors for cold and pain. However, we also perceive hotness when receptors for warmth and coldness are stimulated simultaneously. Would you be able to hold on to the coils if you perceived intense heat, even if you knew that one coil was filled with warm water and the other with cold water?

Temperature

The receptors for temperature are neurons just beneath the skin. When skin temperature increases, receptors for warmth fire. Decreases in skin temperature cause receptors for cold to fire.

Sensations of temperature are relative. When we are at normal body temperature, we might perceive another person's skin as being warm. When we are feverish, though, the other person's skin might seem cool to the touch. We also adapt to differences in temperature. When we walk out of an air-conditioned house into the desert sun, we at first feel intense heat. Then the sensations of heat tend to fade (although we still may be made terribly uncomfortable by high humidity). Similarly, when we first enter a swimming pool, the water may seem cool or cold because it is below body temperature. Yet after a few moments, an 85-degree-Fahrenheit pool may seem quite warm. In fact, we may chide the tentative newcomer for being overly sensitive.

Note that we have receptors that are sensitive to warmth and to coldness. Sensations of hotness, however, are *not* transmitted by rapid firing of warmth receptors, nor by firing of whole platoons of warmth receptors. Instead, in one of nature's unexpected twists, it turns out that so-called cold receptors fire not only when they are stimulated by objects below skin temperature but also when they are stimulated by objects above 45 degrees centigrade. Warmth receptors also fire in response to hot stimulation, so sensations of hotness rely on the simultaneous firing of receptors for cold and warmth.

A classic experiment showed that simultaneous firing of receptors for warmth and coldness are linked to sensations of hotness, regardless of the nature of the stimulus that is causing the cold receptors to fire. As shown in Figure 3.39, two coils were intertwined. Warm water was run through one of them and cold water through the other. Yet people who grasped the coils simultaneously perceived heat so intense that they had to let go at once.

Pain

Headaches, backaches, toothaches—these are only a few of the types of pain that most of us encounter from time to time. Some of us also suffer indescribable bouts of pain from arthritis, digestive disorders, cancer, and wounds.

Pain is a signal that something is wrong in the body. Pain is adaptive in the sense that it motivates us to do something about it. For some of us, however, chronic pain—pain that even lasts once injuries or illnesses have cleared up—saps our vitality and the pleasures of everyday life.

As shown in Figure 3.40, pain originates at the point of contact, as with a stubbed toe. The pain message to the brain is initiated by the release of various chemicals, including prostaglandins, bradykinin (perhaps the most painful known substance), and the mysterious chemical called P (yes, *P* stands for "pain"). Prostaglandins not only facilitate transmission of the pain message to the brain; they also heighten circulation to the injured area, causing the redness and swelling we call inflammation. Inflammation attracts infection-fighting blood cells to the area to protect against invading bacteria. **Analgesic** drugs such as aspirin and ibuprofen (Motrin, Medipren, Advil, etc.) work by inhibiting prostaglandin production.

The pain message is relayed from the spinal cord to the thalamus and then projected to the cerebral cortex, where the location and intensity of the damage become apparent.

Two-point threshold The least distance by which two rods touching the skin must be separated before the subject will report that there are two rods, not one, on 50 percent of occasions.

Analgesic Giving rise to a state of not feeling pain, though fully conscious.

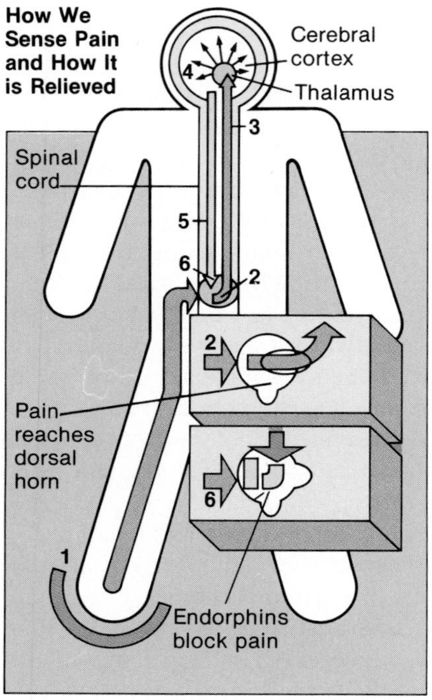

Figure 3.40
Perception of Pain. Pain originates at the point of contact, and the pain message to the brain is initiated by the release of prostaglandins, bradykinin, and substance *P*.

Gate Theory Simple remedies like rubbing and scratching the injured toe frequently help. Why? One possible answer lies in the so-called gate theory of pain, originated by Melzack (1980). From this perspective, only a limited amount of stimulation can be processed by the nervous system at a time. Rubbing or scratching the toe transmits sensations to the brain that, in a sense, compete for neurons. And so, numerous nerves are prevented from transmitting pain messages to the brain. The mechanism is analogous to shutting down a "gate" in the spinal cord. It is something like too many calls flooding a switchboard at once. Such flooding prevents any calls from getting through.

Truth or Fiction Revisited

It is true that rubbing or scratching a sore toe can be an effective way of relieving pain. Rubbing or scratching may flood the gate with messages so that news of the pain does not get through.

Endorphins In response to pain, the brain triggers the release of endorphins (see Chapter 2). Some people who have severe pain that cannot be relieved by available medical treatments have been found to have lower-than-normal concentrations of endorphins in their cerebrospinal fluid (Akil, 1978).

Acupuncture Thousands of years ago, the Chinese began mapping the body to learn where pins might be placed to deaden pain elsewhere. Much of the Chinese practice of acupuncture was unknown in the West, even though Western powers occupied much of China during the 1800s. But early in the 1970s, *New York Times* columnist James Reston underwent an appendectomy in China, with acupuncture as the only anesthetic. He reported no discomfort.

Reston's evidence is anecdotal, of course. The question of whether or not acupuncture can be scientifically demonstrated to provide relief from pain has been controversial. For example, in 1975 the National Institutes of Health reported that acupuncture was no more effective than sugar pills, or **placebos.** Since then, however, a number of studies have suggested that acupuncture can relieve pain in humans, such as chronic back pain (Price et al., 1984). There is also experimental evidence that acupuncture reduces perception of pain in cats and mice (Levitt, 1981).

Some of the effects of acupuncture may be due to the release of endorphins (Kimble, 1988). There is supportive evidence. The drug *naloxone* is known to block the pain-killing effects of morphine. The analgesic effects of acupuncture are also blocked by naloxone. Therefore, it may well be that the analgesic effects of acupuncture can be linked to the morphinelike endorphins.

The Placebo Effect Interestingly, some scientists have also attributed the so-called placebo effect—that is, the way in which expectation of relief sometimes leads to relief from pain and other problems—to release of endorphins (e.g., Levine et al., 1979). In future years we may well find ways of controlling pain without drugs, acupuncture, or other external means. We may learn how to regulate our bodies' own pain-killing systems.

The Psychology and Modern Life section describes a number of ways in which psychologists help people manage pain today.

Placebo A bogus treatment that controls for the effect of expectations.

Kinesthesis The sense that informs us about the positions and motion of parts of our bodies.

KINESTHESIS

Kinesthesis. The dancer receives information about the position and movement of parts of her body through the sense of kinesthesis. Kinesthesis feeds sensory information to her brain from sensory organs in the joints, tendons, and muscles. She can follow her own movements intimately, without visual self-observation.

Try a brief experiment. Close your eyes. Then touch your nose with your index finger. If you weren't right on target, I'm sure you came close. But how? You didn't see your hand moving, and you (probably) didn't hear your arm swishing through the air.

You were able to bring your finger to your nose through your kinesthetic sense, called **kinesthesis** after the Greek words for "motion" *(kinesis)* and "perception" *(aisthesis)*. When you "make a muscle" in your arm, the sensations of tightness and hardness in the arm are also made possible by kinesthesis. Kinesthesis is the sense that informs you about the position and motion of parts of your body. In kinesthesis, sensory information is fed back to the brain from sensory organs in the joints, tendons, and muscles.

Imagine going for a walk without kinesthesis. You would have to watch the forward motion of each leg to be certain that you had raised it high enough to clear the curb. And if you had tried our brief experiment without the kinesthetic sense, you would have had no sensory feedback until you felt the pressure of your finger against your nose (or cheek, or eye, or forehead), and you probably would have missed dozens of times.

Are you in the mood for another experiment? Close your eyes, again. Then "make a muscle" in your right arm. Could you sense the muscle without looking at it or feeling it with your left hand? Of course you could. Kinesthesis also provides information about muscle contractions.

Now let us consider ways in which psychologists are applying knowledge of kinesthesis to help injured people.

A CLOSER LOOK

Behavioral Medicine and Kinesthesis

Behavioral Medicine. Psychologist Bernard Brucker of the University of Miami Medical School uses biofeedback to help a young patient.

Behavioral medicine The application of psychological knowledge in the prevention, detection, treatment, and cure of physical illness.

In 1895, British Nobel laureate Sir Charles S. Sherwood demonstrated the importance of kinesthetic information by cutting the sensory nerves in a primate's arm. The animal did not use the arm again, even though the nerve pathways that carried motor impulses to it were still intact.

Psychologist Neal E. Miller (1985) notes that a major use of biofeedback is to provide heightened information to the brain about what is happening in various areas of the body. In such ways, **behavioral medicine** has led to many apparent miracles. For example, psychologist Bernard Brucker of the University of Miami Medical School taught a spinal-injured man to walk by providing electronic kinesthetic feedback about the working of the leg muscles. The man's injury had deprived him of sensory information from the legs but had not destroyed his motor ability. If the injury had prevented motor impulses from reaching the legs, this treatment would not have worked.

On the other hand, many injured patients have an unsuspected capacity for recovery. In the late 1960s, psychologist Edward Taub demonstrated that a monkey whose sensory pathways had been damaged could regain much of the use of the injured limb if use of the "good" arm was restrained. The restraints apparently motivated the monkey to attend more carefully to any kinesthetic information that was still available from the damaged arm and to learn, by trial and error, to make maximum use of it. In more recent years, Steven Wolf of the Emory University School of Medicine tried the Taub technique by restraining the movements of the "good arms" of patients who were paralyzed on one side. The restraint encouraged many patients to significantly improve their control over the damaged limbs—much more so than physical therapy alone accomplished.

THE VESTIBULAR SENSE

Your **vestibular sense** tells you whether you are upright (physically, not morally). Sensory organs located in the **semicircular canals** (Figure 3.37) and elsewhere in the ears monitor your body's motion and position in relation to gravity. They tell you whether you are falling and provide cues to whether your body is changing speeds, such as when you are in an accelerating airplane or automobile.

Until this point we have discussed perceptions that involve sensation. However, a number of individuals believe that it is possible for certains kinds of information to be perceived directly by the brain—including information about the future. They even believe that some people have the power to move objects around just by thinking about it. Although I do not endorse this kind of extrasensory perception, let me make you aware of the kind of research that has been done on this topic.

Vestibular sense The sense of equilibrium that informs us about our bodies' positions relative to gravity.

Semicircular canals Structures of the inner ear that monitor body movement and position.

Precognition Ability to foresee the future. (From the Latin *prae-,* meaning "before," and *cognitio,* meaning "knowledge.")

Psychokinesis Ability to manipulate objects by thought processes.

Extrasensory perception Perception of objects and events in the absence of stimulation. (*Not* to be confused with hallucination, which is characteristic of certain patterns of abnormal behavior and is defined as confusion of fantasies and reality.)

Telepathy Direct transference of thought from one person to another.

Clairvoyance Ability to perceive things in the absence of sensory stimulation. (A French word meaning "clear-sightedness.")

EXTRASENSORY PERCEPTION

Imagine the wealth you could amass if you had **precognition,** that is, if you were able to perceive future events. Perhaps you would check next month's stock market reports and know in advance what stocks to buy or sell. Or you could make Superbowl and World Series bets with perfect safety.

Or think of the power you would have if you were capable of **psychokinesis,** that is, of manipulating or moving objects from a distance. You may have gotten a glimpse of the types of things that could happen with psychokinesis from films like *The Power, Carrie,* and *The Fury.*

Precognition and psychokinesis are two concepts associated with **extrasensory perception** (ESP)—the perception of objects or events through means other than sensory organs. Two other concepts are **telepathy,** or the direct transmission of thoughts or ideas from person to person, and **clairvoyance,** or the perception of objects that do not stimulate the sensory organs. An example of clairvoyance is "knowing" what card is to be dealt next, although it is still in the deck and unknown to the dealer.

ESP, in short, is extremely controversial. Most psychologists do not believe that it is an appropriate area for scientific inquiry. Scientists study natural events, and ESP smacks of the supernatural, perhaps even of the occult.

Perhaps the best known of the respected ESP researchers was the late Joseph Banks Rhine of Duke University (1971), who studied ESP for several decades, beginning in the late 1920s. In a typical experiment in clairvoyance, Rhine would use a pack of 25 Zener cards, which contained five sets of the

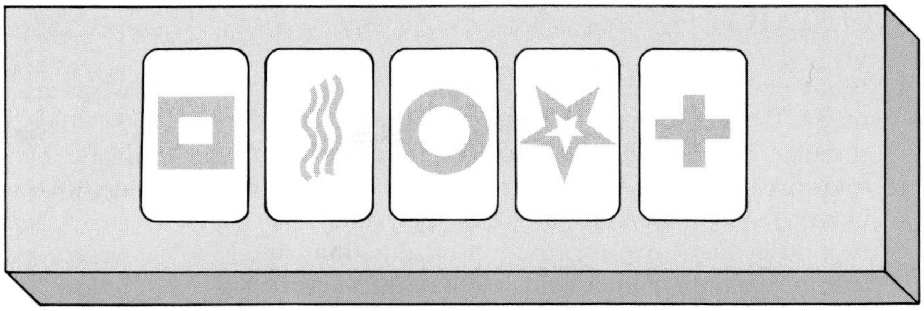

Figure 3.41
Zener Cards. Zener cards have been used in research on clairvoyance. Subjects are asked to predict which card will be turned up.

five cards shown in Figure 3.41. A subject guessing which of the five patterns was about to be turned up would be correct 20 percent of the time (one time in five) by chance alone. Rhine found that some people guessed correctly significantly more often than the 20 percent chance rate and concluded that they may have had some degree of ESP.

More recent studies have been done in clairvoyance with automated equipment, like random-number generators. Other studies have been done in psychokinesis. As of today, there are some studies that claim that individuals have performed tasks requiring ESP at above-chance levels of success. However, these studies have not been accepted by an appreciable segment of the scientific community.

There are many reasons for this skepticism, as noted by Hansel (1980). For one, negative results are rarely reported by ESP researchers. Therefore, we would expect *some* unusual findings (like an individual with a high success rate at ESP tasks over a period of several days) to surface in the literature. In other words, if you flip a coin indefinitely, eventually you will flip ten heads in a row. The odds against this are high, but if you report your eventual success, and do not report the weeks of failure, you give the impression that you have unique coin-flipping ability.

Second, it has not been easy to replicate ESP experiments. Subjects who have "shown" ESP with one researcher have failed to do so with another, or have refused to participate in a study with another. Third, some researchers, including a colleague of Rhine's, have been found tampering with data or equipment. (Rhine himself was never accused of fraud.)

For these and other reasons, ESP research has not received much credibility. To be fair, science has shown, again and again, that "there are more things in heaven and earth" than there were once thought to be. But science has not yet found that ESP is one of those things. For the time being, the great majority of psychologists prefer to study perception that involves sensation. What is life without some sensation?

Truth or Fiction Revisited

It is *not* true that some people have the ability to read other people's minds. It may be that they can make educated guesses about the feelings of people they know or that they can interpret smiles and frowns reasonably well, but they cannot directly read other people's minds.

SUMMARY

1. **What are sensation and perception?** Sensation refers to mechanical processes that involve the stimulation of sensory receptors (neurons) and the transmission of sensory information to the central nervous system. Perception is not mechanical. Perception is the active organization of sensations into a representation of the world, and it reflects learning and expectations.

2. **What are absolute and difference thresholds?** The absolute threshold for a stimulus, like light, is the lowest intensity at which it can be detected. The minimum difference in intensity that can be discriminated is the difference threshold. Difference thresholds are expressed in Weber's constants.

3. **What is signal-detection theory?** Signal-detection theory explains the ways in which stimulus characteristics and psychological factors—for example, motivation, familiarity with a stimulus, and attention—interact to influence whether or not a stimulus will be detected.

4. **What is light?** Light is one part of the spectrum of electromagnetic energy.

5. **How does the eye detect light and transmit it to the brain?** The eye senses and transmits visual stimulation to the occipital lobe of the cerebral cortex. After light passes through the cornea, pupil size determines the amount of light that can pass through the lens. The lens focuses light as it projects onto the retina, which is composed of photoreceptors called rods and cones.

6. **What are rods and cones?** Cones are neurons in the retina that permit perception of color. Rods transmit sensations of light and dark only. Rods are more sensitive than cones to lowered lighting and continue to adapt to darkness once cones have reached peak adaptation.

7. **What are the psychological dimensions of color?** These are hue, brightness, and saturation. The wavelength of light determines its color, or hue. Yellows, oranges, and reds are considered warm colors, whereas blues and greens are considered cool. The saturation of a color is its pureness. When we mix lights of complementary colors, they dissolve into gray. When mixing pigments, the primary colors of red, blue, and yellow are not produced by mixing other hues. Secondary and tertiary colors are produced by mixing other colors.

8. **What are the theories of color vision?** There are two theories of color vision. According to trichromatic theory, there are three types of cones—some sensitive to red, others to blue, and still others to green light. Opponent-process theory proposes three types of color receptors: red-green, blue-yellow, and light-dark. Opponent-process theory better accounts for afterimages, but both theories seem to have some validity.

9. **What are the rules of perceptual organization?** Gestalt rules of perceptual organization influence our grouping of bits of sensory stimulation. These rules concern figure-ground relationships, proximity, similarity, continuity, common fate, and closure.

10. **How do we perceive movement?** We perceive real movement by sensing it across the retina and movement of objects in relation to one another. Distant objects appear to move more slowly than nearby objects, and middle-ground objects may give the illusion of moving backward.

11. **How do we perceive depth?** Depth perception involves monocular and binocular cues. Monocular cues include perspective, clearness, interposition, shadows, texture gradient, motion parallax, and accommodation. Binocular cues include retinal disparity and convergence.

12. **What are the perceptual constancies?** Through experience we develop a number of perceptual constancies. For example, we learn to assume that objects retain their size, shape, brightness, and color despite their distance, their position, or changes in lighting conditions.

13. **What is sound?** Sound is auditory stimulation, or sound waves. It requires a medium such as air or water to be transmitted. Sound waves alternately compress and expand molecules of the medium, creating vibrations.

14. **What is the range of sounds that can be sensed by the human ear?** The human ear can hear sounds varying in frequency from 20 to 20,000 cycles per second. The greater the frequency, the higher the sound's pitch.

15. **What is the loudness of a sound?** The loudness of a sound corresponds to the amplitude of sound waves as measured in decibels (dB). We can suffer hearing loss if exposed to protracted sounds of

85–90 dB or more. Noise is a combination of dissonant sounds.

16. **How does the ear detect sound and transmit it to the brain?** The eardrum, vibrating in sympathy to sound, transmits auditory stimulation through the bones of the middle ear to the cochlea of the inner ear. The basilar membrane of the cochlea transmits stimulation to the organ of Corti, and from there sound travels to the brain by the auditory nerve. Sounds seem louder when more neurons of the organ of Corti fire. Two competing theories account for the perception of pitch: place theory and frequency theory.

17. **How do we detect odors?** We detect them through the sense of smell. Odors are detected by the olfactory membrane in each nostril. An odor is a sample of the substance being smelled. The sense of smell adapts rapidly to odors, even unpleasant ones.

18. **How do we detect tastes?** There are four primary taste qualities: sweet, sour, salty, and bitter. Flavor involves the odor, texture, and temperature of food, as well as its taste. Taste is sensed through taste cells, which are located in taste buds on the tongue.

19. **What are the skin senses?** There are five skin senses: touch, pressure, warmth, cold, and pain. Perception of hotness is caused by simultaneous stimulation of receptors for cold and pain or of receptors for warmth and cold.

20. **How do we detect pain?** Pain originates at the point of contact and is transmitted to the brain by various chemicals, including prostaglandins, bradykinin, and substance *P*.

21. **What is kinesthesis?** Kinesthesis is the sensing of body position and movement, and it relies on sensory organs in the joints, tendons, and muscles. The vestibular sense is housed primarily in the semicircular canals of the ears and tells us whether we are in an upright position.

22. **Does extrasensory perception really exist?** There has been speculation about whether or not extrasensory perception (perception without sensation) is possible. Evidence for extrasensory perception has fallen into disrepute because of underreporting of experimental failures, failure to replicate research with positive results, and cases of outright fraud.

PSYCHOLOGY AND MODERN LIFE

Pain Management

In recent years, psychology has dramatically expanded our arsenal against an age-old enemy: pain. Pain management has traditionally been a medical issue, with the primary treatment being chemical, as in the use of analgesic drugs. Drugs are not always effective, however. In addition, patients can develop tolerance for many analgesic drugs, such as the narcotics morphine and Demerol. When a person acquires tolerance, increased doses are required to achieve the same effects. Because of such problems with the chemical management of pain, health professionals have become more interested in exploring psychological methods for managing pain.

Accurate Information An irony of pain management is that one of the most effective psychological methods is the provision of accurate and thorough information. Most people try *not* to think about their symptoms (and their implications!) during the early phases of an illness (Suls & Fletcher, 1985). Medical doctors, too, tend to neglect the "human" aspects of relating to their patients. That is, they try to do a competent job of diagnosing and treating the causes of pain, but often they fail to discuss with their patients the meaning of their pain or exactly what they can expect.

Yet when it comes to administering painful or discomforting treatments, such as chemotherapy for cancer, knowledge of the details of the treatment, including how long it will last and how much pain will be entailed, often helps patients cope—particularly patients who prefer to receive high levels of information in an effort to maintain control over their situations (Martelli et al., 1987). It has been shown that accurate information helps even small children cope with painful procedures (Jay et al., 1983). Knowledge may permit us to brace ourselves and realize that feelings of pain will come to an end—at least most of the time.

Distraction and Fantasy Although it appears to be generally helpful for patients to have accurate and detailed explanations of painful procedures, psychologists have also been studying ways of minimizing discomfort once these procedures are under way. A number of methods involve the use of distraction or fantasy. For example, imagine that you've injured your leg and you're waiting to see the doctor in an emergency room. You can distract yourself from pain by focusing on environmental details, such as by counting ceiling tiles or the hairs on the back of a finger or by describing the clothing of medical personnel or passers-by (Kanfer & Goldfoot, 1966; McCaul & Haugvedt, 1982). People are also less sensitive to pain when they try to recall lists of meaningless words (Farthing et al., 1984; Spanos et al., 1984). Studies with children ranging in age from 9 into their teens have found that playing video games diminishes the pain and discomfort of the side effects of chemotherapy (Kolko & Rickard-Figueroa, 1985; Redd et al., 1987). While the children are receiving injections of nausea-producing chemicals, they are focusing on battling monsters on the video screen.

Hypnosis In 1842 London physician W. S. Ward amputated a man's leg after using a rather strange anesthetic: hypnosis. According to reports, the patient experienced no discomfort. Several years later, operations were being performed routinely under hypnosis at the infirmary in London. Today hypnosis is used by thousands of professionals as an anesthetic in dentistry, childbirth, and even some forms of surgery. Hundreds of case studies and experiments attest that hypnosis often, though not always, significantly reduces pain (see reviews by Barber, 1982; Turk et al., 1983; Turner & Chapman, 1982b).

Historically, it had been assumed that hypnotism induced a special "trance" state, but contemporary psychologists downplay this concept. Ernest Hilgard (1978), for example, a leading researcher in the study of hypnosis, attributes the pain-reducing effects of hypnosis to relaxation, narrowed attention, and heightened suggestibility.

Relaxation Training If hypnosis does not involve a special trance state, might it be possible to achieve similar benefits by intentionally inducing some of the body effects brought about by hypnosis? It appears so. Relaxation training refers to a number of psychological techniques that relax muscles and lower sympathetic activity. Some relaxation methods focus on relaxing muscle groups. Some involve breathing exercises. Some focus on guided imagery, which distract the pain sufferer as well as deepen feelings of relaxation. Psychologists fostering relaxation may also use suggestions that limbs are becoming warmer and heavier. However, none of these methods are claimed to induce a trance, and their benefits are explained by theories that link behavior to human physiology. These methods appear to be as effective as hypnosis in managing pain (Moore & Chaney, 1985; Turner & Chapman, 1982a).

Coping with Irrational Beliefs Irrational beliefs about pain have been shown to heighten pain. For example, telling oneself that the pain is unbearable and that it will never cease increases discomfort, as found in a study relating knee pain and beliefs about pain (Keefe et al., 1987). Thus, cognitive methods aimed at modifying irrational patient belief systems (see Chapter 13) would also seem to be of promise. One irrational belief noted by psychologist Albert Ellis (1977) is that some people feel obligated to focus their attention on the things that distress them. People who share this belief may be unwilling to allow themselves to be distracted from pain and discomfort.

Other Methods Pain is a source of stress, and psychologists have uncovered many factors that seem to moderate the effects of stress (see Chapter 11). One is a sense of commitment. For example, if we are undergoing a painful medical procedure aimed at diagnosing or treating an illness, it might help for us to see ourselves as *choosing* to participate in the procedure in order to get better, instead of seeing ourselves as helpless victims. A sense of humor also helps. There are often ironies and sillinesses in the most somber situations, and allowing ourselves to perceive them and even to laugh may be beneficial. Supportive social networks also help us cope with stress. And so, having friends visit us—or our visiting ill friends—and encouraging a return to health is as consistent with psychological findings as it is with folklore (Rook & Dooley, 1985).

And don't forget gate theory. When there's pain in the toe, squeeze all your toes. When there's pain in the calf, rub the thighs. People around you may wonder, but you're entitled to experiment with "flooding the switchboard" so that some of the pain messages don't get through. Experimenting to find what you should rub and squeeze may also distract you a bit.

Outline

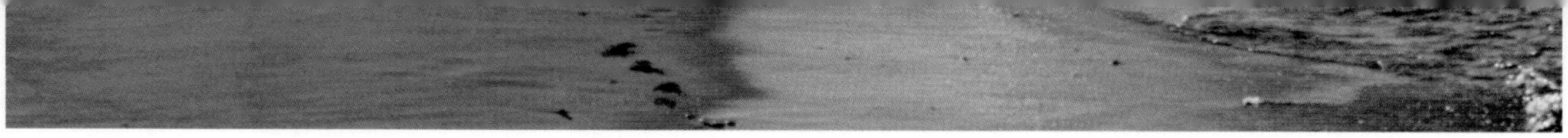

4

States of Consciousness

Truth or Fiction?

- □ People who sleep nine hours or more a night tend to be lazy and happy-go-lucky.
- □ We tend to act out our forbidden fantasies in our dreams.
- □ Many people have insomnia because they try too hard to get to sleep at night.
- □ It is dangerous to awaken a sleepwalker.
- □ Some people drink because alcohol provides them with an excuse for failure.
- □ Heroin was once used as a cure for addiction to morphine.
- □ Coca-Cola once "added life" through a powerful but now illegal stimulant.
- □ Cigarette smokers tend to smoke more when they are under stress.
- □ People have managed to bring high blood pressure under control through meditation.
- □ You can learn to increase or decrease your heart rate just by thinking about it.
- □ People who are easily hypnotized have positive attitudes toward hypnosis.

It is a well-known fact of life that the few individuals who have gained insight into the mysteries of the universe wear flowing robes, have long beards streaked with white, and set up shop on some distant mountaintop. These sages are hard to meet. You've got to wait for the end of the monsoon season, or for a thaw, to make the journey. Then you must enlist one of the last guides who recalls the route. Such guides would typically prefer to watch their donkeys graze in the backyard than make any darn fool trip. But they can be persuaded. (If they couldn't, I'd have to find another tale.)

So it is not surprising that psychologist Robert Ornstein's (1972) account of the experiences of a group of American travelers who were seeking just such a wise old man describes them as scrambling and stumbling through the Himalaya Mountains. As you would expect, the trip was long and arduous. Many would have turned back. But these hardy travelers were searching for the scoop on heightened consciousness, for the key to inner peace and harmony.

Finally, the travelers found themselves at the feet of the venerable guru. They told him of the perils and pitfalls of their journey, of the singular importance they attached to this audience. They implored the guru to share his wisdom, to help them open their inner pathways.

The guru said, "Sit, facing the wall, and count your breaths."

This was it? The secret that had been preserved through the centuries? The wisdom of several lifetimes? The prize for which our seekers had risked life and limb and bank account?

Yes, in a sense this was. Counting your breaths is one method of **meditation**—one way of narrowing your *consciousness* so that the stresses of the outside world can fade away.

In this chapter we shall explore meditation and other states of consciousness. Some of them, like sleep, are quite familiar to you. Others, like meditation, biofeedback, and hypnosis, may seem more exotic. It is also in this chapter that we deal with "consciousness-altering" drugs. First, though, we shall tackle the $64,000 question: What *is* consciousness? This is a dangerous undertaking for at least two reasons. First, some psychologists believe that the science of psychology should not deal with the question of consciousness at all. Second, the meanings of the word are quite varied.

THE $64,000 QUESTION: WHAT *IS* CONSCIOUSNESS?

In 1904, William James wrote an intriguing article entitled "Does Consciousness Exist?" Think about that. *Does consciousness exist?* Do you believe that *you* have consciousness? That you are conscious or aware of yourself? Of the world around you? Would you bear witness to being conscious of, or experiencing, thoughts and feelings? I would bet that you would. And, to be sure, so would William James. Yet James did not think that consciousness was a proper area of study for psychologists, because no scientific method could be devised to directly observe or measure another person's consciousness.

John Watson, the "father of modern behaviorism," also insisted that only observable, measurable behavior was the proper province of psychology. In "Psychology as the Behaviorist Views It," published in 1913, Watson declared, "The time seems to have come when psychology must discard all references to consciousness" (p. 163). The following year Watson was elected president of the American Psychological Association, which further cemented these ideas in the minds of many psychologists.

Despite such objections, and despite the problems involved in defining (much less measuring) consciousness, we will attempt to explore the meanings and varieties of this most intriguing concept.

The Meanings of Consciousness

The word *consciousness* has several meanings. Let's have a look at a few of them.

Consciousness as Sensory Awareness One meaning of consciousness is **sensory awareness** of the environment. The sense of vision permits us to be conscious of, or to see, the sun gleaming in the snow on the rooftops. The sense of hearing allows us to be conscious of, or to hear, a concert.

Meditation As a method for coping with stress, a systematic narrowing of attention that slows the metabolism and helps produce feelings of relaxation.

Sensory awareness Knowledge of the environment through perception of sensory stimulation—one definition of consciousness.

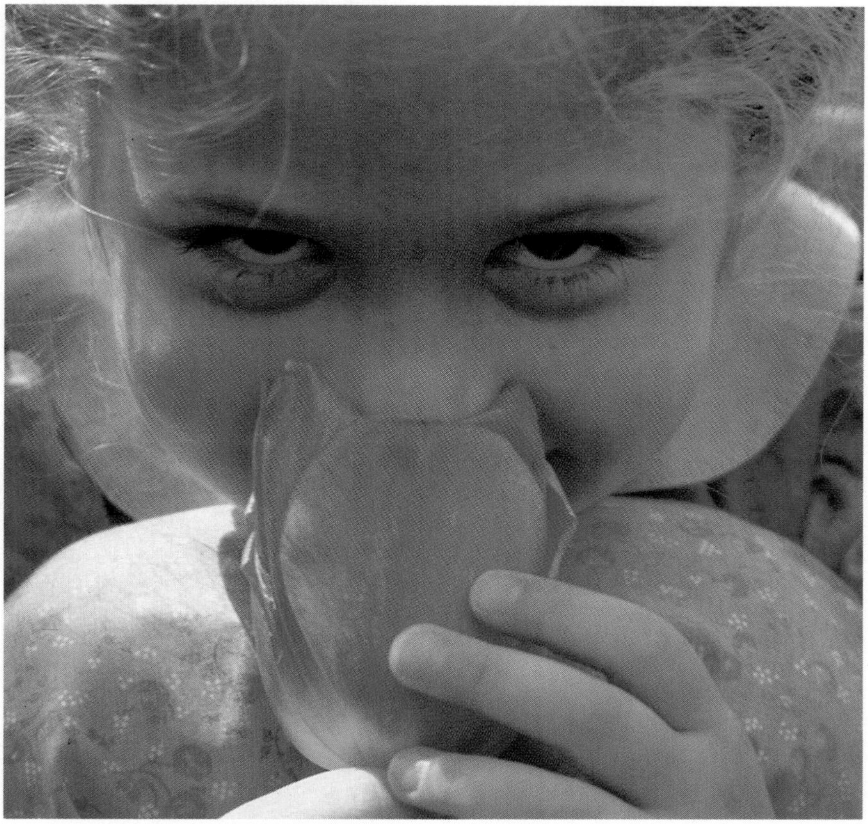

Sensory Awareness. One of the definitions of consciousness is sensory awareness of the world around us.

We are more conscious of, or have greater awareness of, those things to which we pay attention. Many things are going on nearby and in the world at large, yet you are conscious of, or focusing on, the words on this page (perhaps).

Consciousness as Direct Inner Awareness Close your eyes. Imagine spilling a can of bright red paint across a black tabletop. Watch it spread across the black, shiny surface, then spill onto the floor. Although this image may be vivid, you did not "see" it literally. Neither your eyes nor any other sensory organs were involved. You were conscious of the image through **direct inner awareness.**

We are conscious of, or have direct inner awareness of, thoughts, images, emotions, and memories. We are conscious of, or know of, the presence of these cognitive processes without using our senses.

Sigmund Freud, the founder of psychoanalysis, differentiated between thoughts and feelings of which we are conscious, or aware, and those which are preconscious and unconscious (see Figure 4.1). **Preconscious** material is not currently in awareness but is readily available. As you answer the following questions, you will summon up "preconscious" information: What did you eat for dinner yesterday? About what time did you wake up this morning? What's happening outside the window or down the hall right now?

According to Freud, still other mental events are **unconscious,** or unavailable to awareness under most circumstances. Freud believed that certain memories were painful and certain impulses (primarily sexual and aggressive impulses) were unacceptable. Therefore, people would place them out of awareness, or **repress** them, to escape feelings of anxiety, guilt, and shame.

Direct inner awareness Knowledge of one's own thoughts, feelings, and memories without use of sensory organs—another definition of consciousness.

Preconscious In psychodynamic theory, descriptive of material that is not in awareness but can be brought into awareness by focusing one's attention. (The Latin root *prae-* means "before.")

Unconscious In psychodynamic theory, descriptive of ideas and feelings that are not available to awareness.

Repress In psychodynamic theory, to eject anxiety-provoking ideas, impulses, or images from awareness, without knowing that one is doing so.

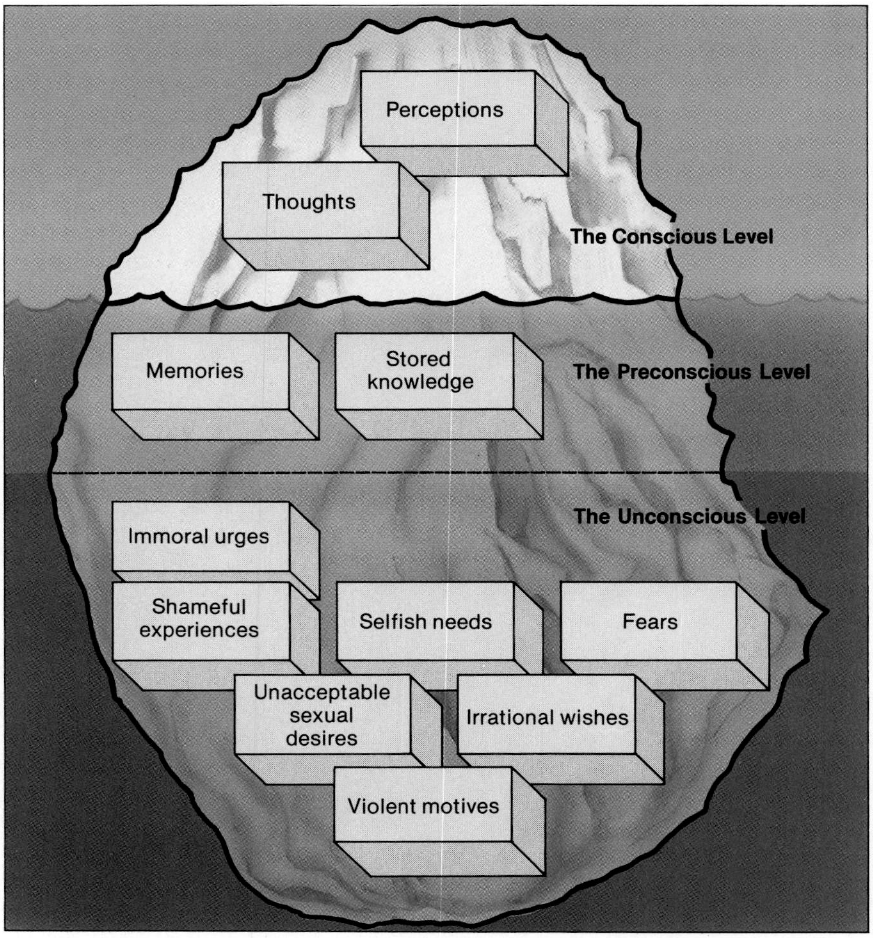

Figure 4.1
Levels of Consciousness, According to Sigmund Freud. According to Freud, many memories, impulses, and feelings exist below the level of conscious awareness. We could note that any film that draws an audience seems to derive its plot from items that populate the unconscious.

Freud theorized that the very process of repression is unconscious, or automatic. After all, you can't choose to stop thinking about an unacceptable impulse and, at the same time, be unaware that it ever existed.

Still, people do sometimes choose to stop thinking about distracting or unacceptable ideas. This conscious method of putting unwanted mental events out of awareness is termed **suppression.** We may suppress thoughts of a date when we need to study for a test. (We may also try to suppress thoughts of an unpleasant test when we are on a date so that the evening will not be ruined.)

Some bodily processes are **nonconscious**—incapable of being experienced either through sensory awareness or direct inner awareness. The growing of hair and the carrying of oxygen in the blood are nonconscious.

Consciousness as Personal Unity: The Sense of Self To the newborn, this world must seem to be a confusing disarray of sensory inputs. But gradually the child begins to sort things out and to better organize his or her perceptions. As we develop, we also learn to differentiate us from that which is not us. We develop a sense of being persons, individuals. There is a totality to our impressions, thoughts, and feelings that makes up our conscious existence—our continuing sense of **self** in a changing world.

In this usage of the word, consciousness *is* self. Cognitive psychologists view a person's consciousness as an important determinant of the person's

---

Suppression The deliberate, or conscious, placing of certain ideas, impulses, or images out of awareness.

Nonconscious Descriptive of bodily processes, such as the growing of hair, of which we cannot become conscious.

Self The totality of impressions, thoughts, and feelings. The sense of self is another definition of consciousness. See Chapter 9.

behavior. Humanistic psychologists (see Chapters 1 and 10) view consciousness—self-awareness and the sense of being a person—as the essence of what it means to be human.

Consciousness as the Waking State The least controversial meaning of the word *consciousness* describes the normal waking state as opposed, for example, to sleep. From this perspective, sleep, meditation, the hypnotic "trance," and the disordered perceptions that can accompany use of consciousness-altering drugs are considered **altered states of consciousness.**

For the remainder of this chapter we shall explore various states of consciousness and the agents that bring them about.

SLEEP AND DREAMS

Sleep has always been a fascinating topic. After all, we spend about one-third of our adult lives sleeping. Most of us complain when we do not sleep at least six hours or so, yet some people sleep for an hour or less a day and lead otherwise healthy and normal lives.

Why do we sleep? Why do we dream? Why do some of us have trouble getting to sleep, and what can we do about it?

The Stages of Sleep

The **electroencephalograph,** or EEG, is one of the major tools of sleep researchers. As described in Chapter 2, the EEG measures the electrical activity of the brain, or brain waves. Figure 4.2 shows some scrawls produced by the EEG that reflect the frequency and strength of brain waves that occur during the waking state, when we are relaxed, and when we are in one of the stages of sleep.

Brain waves, like other waves, are cyclical. During the various stages of sleep, our brains emit waves of different frequencies and amplitudes. The printouts in Figure 4.2 show what happens during a period of 15 seconds or so. Brain waves high in frequency are associated with wakefulness. The amplitude of brain waves reflects their strength. The strength or energy of brain waves is expressed in the electric unit **volts.**

Figure 4.2 shows five stages of sleep: four stages of **non-rapid-eye-movement (NREM) sleep,** and one stage of **rapid-eye-movement (REM) sleep.** When we close our eyes and begin to relax before going to sleep, our brains emit many **alpha waves.** Alpha waves are low-amplitude brain waves of about eight to thirteen cycles per second. (Through biofeedback training, discussed later in the chapter, people have been taught to relax by purposefully emitting alpha waves.)

As we enter stage 1 sleep, our brain waves slow down from the alpha rhythm and enter a pattern of **theta waves.** Theta waves, which have a frequency of about six to eight cycles per second, are accompanied by slow, rolling eye movements. The transition from alpha waves to theta waves may be accompanied by a **hypnagogic state,** during which we may experience brief hallucinatory, dreamlike images that resemble vivid photographs. These images may be related to creativity. Stage 1 sleep is the lightest stage of sleep. If we are awakened from stage 1 sleep, we may feel that we have not slept at all.

Altered states of consciousness States other than the normal waking state, including sleep, meditation, the hypnotic trance, and the distorted perceptions produced by use of some drugs.

Electroencephalograph An instrument that measures electrical activity of the brain. Abbreviated *EEG.*

Volt A unit of electrical potential.

Non-rapid-eye-movement sleep Stages of sleep 1 through 4. Abbreviated *NREM* sleep.

Rapid-eye-movement sleep A stage of sleep characterized by rapid eye movements, which have been linked to dreaming. Abbreviated *REM* sleep.

Alpha waves Rapid, low-amplitude brain waves that have been linked to feelings of relaxation.

Theta waves Slow brain waves produced during the hypnagogic state.

Hypnagogic state (hip-nuh-GAHDGE-jick). The drowsy interval between waking and sleeping, characterized by brief, hallucinatory, dreamlike experiences.

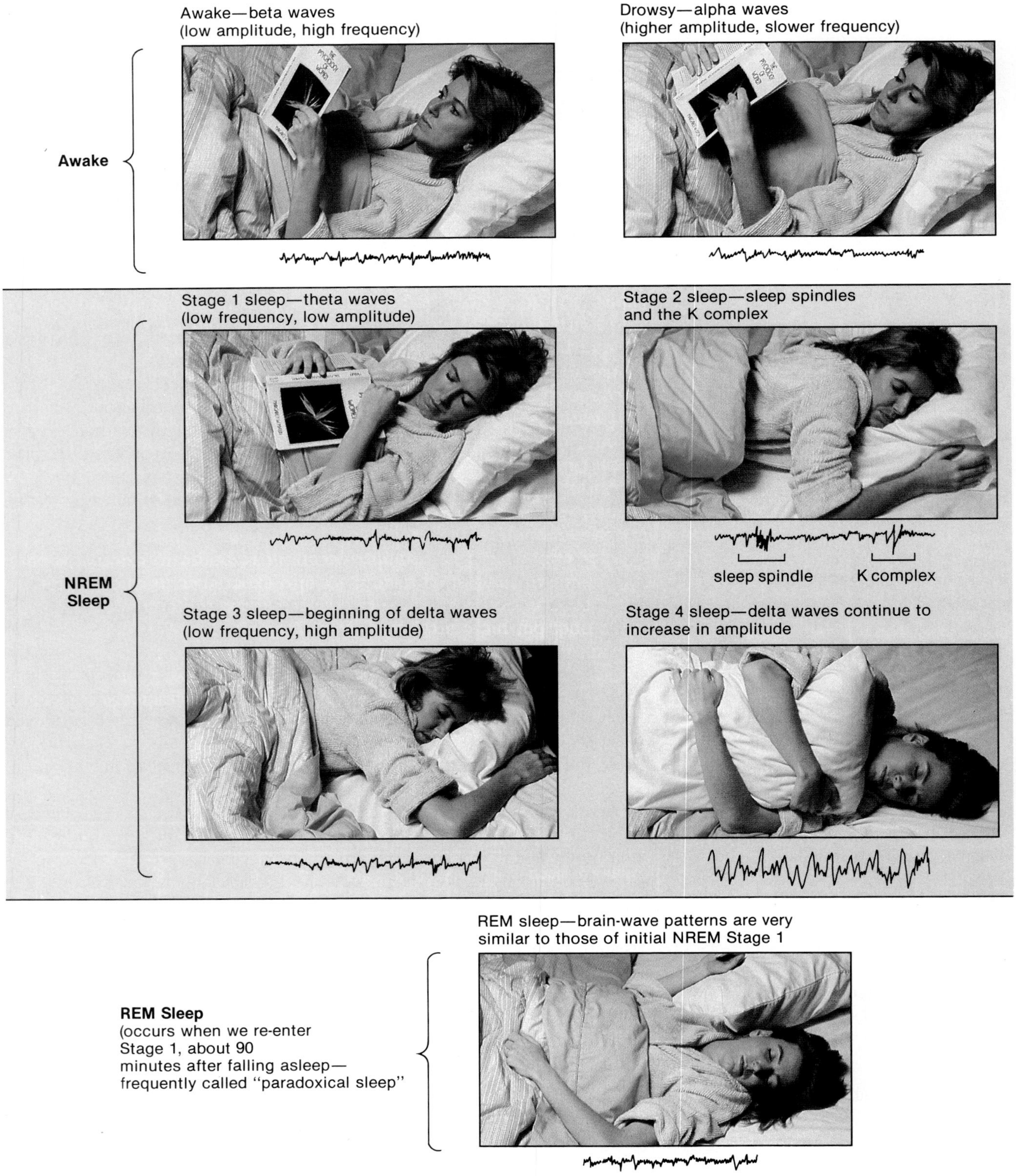

Figure 4.2
The Stages of Sleep.

This figure illustrates typical EEG patterns for the stages of sleep. During REM sleep, EEG patterns resemble those of the lightest stage of sleep, stage 1 sleep. For this reason, REM sleep is often termed *paradoxical sleep*. As sleep progresses from stage 1 to stage 4, brain waves become slower and their amplitude increases. Dreams, including normal nightmares, are most vivid during REM sleep. More disturbing sleep terrors tend to occur during deep stage 4 sleep.

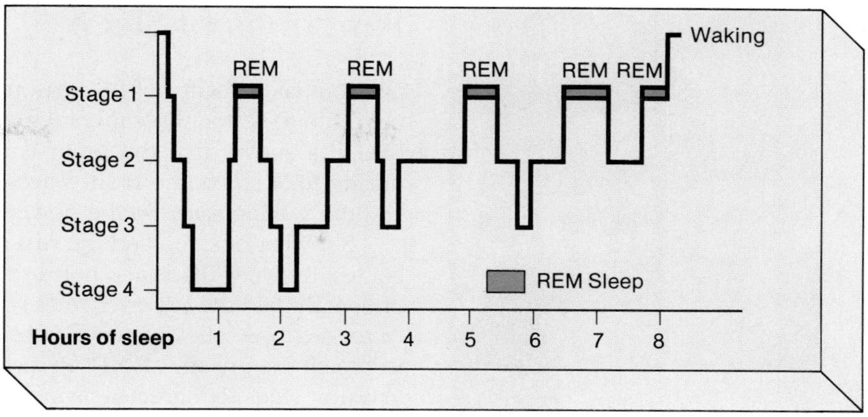

Figure 4.3
Sleep Cycles. This figure illustrates the alternation of REM and non-REM sleep for the typical sleeper. There are about five periods of REM sleep during an eight-hour night. Sleep is deeper earlier in the night, and REM sleep tends to become prolonged toward morning.

After 30 to 40 minutes of stage 1 sleep, we undergo a rather steep descent into sleep stages 2, 3, and 4 (see Figure 4.3). During stage 2, brain waves are medium in amplitude and have a frequency of about four to seven cycles per second, but these are punctuated by **sleep spindles.** Sleep spindles have a frequency of 12 to 16 cycles per second and represent brief bursts of rapid brain activity. During stage 2, we also experience instances of the so-called **K complex.** This complex occurs in response to external stimuli, such as the sound of a book dropped in the room, or internal stimuli, such as muscle tightness in the leg.

During deep-sleep stages 3 and 4, our brains produce slower **delta waves.** During stage 3, the delta waves are of about one to three cycles per second. Delta waves reach relatively great amplitude as compared to other brain waves. Stage 4 is the deepest stage of sleep, from which it is most difficult to be awakened. During stage 4 sleep, the delta waves slow to about one-half to two cycles per second, and their amplitude is greatest.

After perhaps half an hour of deep stage 4 sleep, we begin a relatively rapid journey back upward through the stages until we enter REM sleep (Figure 4.3). REM sleep derives its name from the *r*apid *e*ye *m*ovements, observable beneath our closed lids, that characterize this stage. During REM sleep, we produce relatively rapid, low-amplitude brain waves that resemble those of light stage 1 sleep. REM sleep is also called paradoxical sleep. This is because the EEG patterns observed during REM sleep suggest a level of arousal similar to that of the waking state (Figure 4.2). However, there are important chemical differences between REM sleep and the waking state. During REM sleep, there is a heightened level of acetylcholine in the brain and lowered levels of norepinephrine and serotonin (Schmeck, 1987). REM sleep is also "deep" in the sense that we are difficult to awaken during these periods. When we are awakened during REM sleep, as is the practice in sleep research, about 80 percent of the time we report that we have been dreaming. (We also dream during NREM sleep, but less frequently. We report dreaming only about 20 percent of the time when awakened during NREM sleep.)

As you can see from Figure 4.3, we tend to undergo five trips through the different stages of sleep each night. These trips include about five periods of REM sleep. Our first journey through stage 4 sleep is usually longest. Sleep tends to become lighter as the night wears on. Our periods of REM sleep tend to become longer, and, toward morning, our last period of REM sleep may last close to half an hour.

Now that we have some idea of what sleep is like, let us examine the issue of *why* we sleep.

Sleep spindles Short bursts of rapid brain waves that occur during stage 2 sleep.

K complex Bursts of brain activity that occur during stage 2 sleep and reflect external stimulation.

Delta waves Strong, slow brain waves usually emitted during stage 4 sleep.

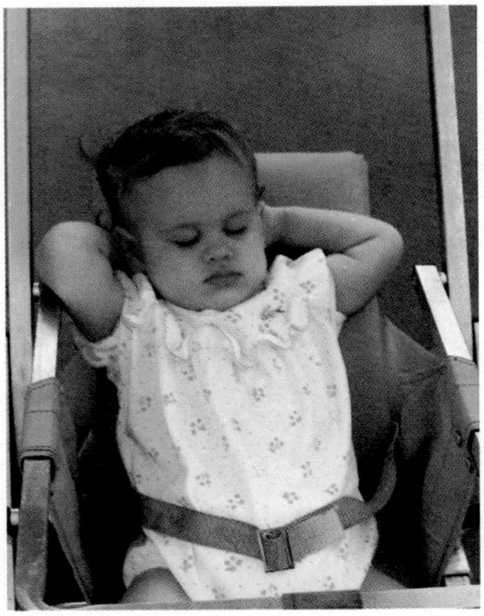

Sleep. Most researchers agree that sleep helps rejuvenate a tired body. There is less agreement about the amount of sleep we need and the possible functions of dreams.

Functions of Sleep

One outdated theory of the reasons for sleep suggested that sleep allowed the brain to rest and recuperate from the stresses of working all day. Yet the EEG has shown that the brain is active all night long. Moreover, at least during REM sleep, the brain waves are quite similar to those of light sleep and the waking state. So the power isn't switched off at night.

But what of sleep and the rest of the body? Most researchers would not contest the view that sleep helps rejuvenate a tired body (Levitt, 1981). Most of us have had the experience of going without sleep for a night and feeling "wrecked" the following day. Perhaps the next evening we went to bed early to "catch up on our sleep." Research also suggests that increased physical exertion leads to a greater proportion of time spent in NREM sleep (Walker et al., 1978). Hartmann (1973) suggests that many proteins are synthesized during NREM sleep and that these proteins may be linked to the restorative effects of sleep. However, no one has yet discovered a relationship between sleep and the restoration of specific chemical substances.

Let us continue our study of the functions of sleep by turning to research concerning long versus short sleepers and the effects of sleep deprivation.

Long versus Short Sleepers Ernest Hartmann (1973) of Tufts University compared people who slept nine hours or more a night (long sleepers) with people who slept six hours or less (short sleepers). He found that short sleepers tended to be more happy-go-lucky. They spent less time ruminating and were energetic, active, and relatively self-satisfied. The long sleepers were more concerned about personal achievement and social causes. They tended to be more creative and thoughtful, but they were also more anxious and depressed. Hartmann also found that, in general, people tend to need more sleep during periods of change and stress, such as a change of jobs, an increase in work load, or an episode of depression. So it may be that sleep helps us recover from the stresses of life.

Truth or Fiction Revisited

It is not true that people who sleep nine hours or more a night tend to be lazy and happy-go-lucky. They are actually more industrious and anxious than short sleepers.

Hartmann also found that long sleepers spend proportionately more time in REM sleep than do short sleepers. Subtracting the amount of REM sleep experienced by both types of sleepers dramatically closed the gap between them. Perhaps REM sleep is at least partially responsible for the restorative function. Since much REM sleep is spent in dreaming, it has been speculated that dreams may somehow promote recovery.

Sleep Deprivation What will happen to you if you miss sleep for one night? For several nights? If you cut down from, say, your normal seven to ten hours to just five and a half? Anecdotal and research evidence offers some suggestions.

In 1959, disc jockey Peter Tripp remained awake for eight days. Toward the end of this episode, he became so paranoid that he could not be given psychological tests (Dement, 1972). However, 17-year-old Randy Gardner remained awake for 264 consecutive hours (eleven days), and he did not show serious psychological disturbance (Levitt, 1981).

In another anecdote, ten of eleven military cadets who were ordered to engage in strenuous activity for 100 hours developed visual hallucinations, and most developed problems in balance and movement (Opstad et al., 1978). But, as noted by Levitt (1981), these cadets were also deprived of rest

Dream Images? In "Winter Night in Vitebsk," Marc Chagall seems to depict images born in dreams.

and food, not just sleep. According to sleep researcher Wilse Webb, carefully controlled experiments with people who remain sleepless for several consecutive days result in few serious disturbances. Most often, participants show temporary problems in attention, confusion, or misperception (Goleman, 1982). These cognitive lapses may reflect brief episodes of borderline sleep. Participants may also show fine hand tremors, droopy eyelids, problems in focusing the eyes, and heightened sensitivity to pain. There are few, if any, horror stories.

Deprivation of REM Sleep In some studies, animals or people have been deprived of REM sleep. Animals deprived of REM sleep learn more slowly and forget what they have learned more rapidly (Hartmann & Stern, 1972; Pearlman & Greenberg, 1973). With people, REM-sleep deprivation is accomplished by monitoring EEG records and eye movements and waking subjects during REM sleep. There is too much individual variation to conclude that people deprived of REM sleep learn more poorly than they otherwise would (McGrath & Cohen, 1978). It does seem, though, that such deprivation interferes with human memory—that is, the retrieval of information that has been learned previously (Cipolli & Salzarulo, 1978; Bloch et al., 1979). In any event, people and lower animals deprived of REM sleep tend to show *REM-rebound.* In other words, they tend to spend more time in REM sleep during subsequent sleep periods. They catch up.

As noted earlier, it is during REM sleep that we tend to dream. Let us now turn our attention to dreams, a mystery about which people have theorized for centuries.

Dreams

Dreams A sequence of images or thoughts that occur during sleep. Dreams may be vague and loosely plotted or vivid and intricate.

Just what is the stuff of **dreams**? Like vivid memories and daytime fantasies, dreams involve imagery in the absence of external stimulation. Some dreams are so realistic and well organized that we feel they must be real—that we simply cannot be dreaming this time. You may have had such a dream on the night before a test. The dream would have been that you had taken the test and now it is all over. (Ah, what disappointment then prevailed when you woke up to realize that such was not the case!) Other dreams are disorganized and unformed.

Dreams are most vivid during REM sleep. Then they are most likely to have clear imagery and coherent plots, even if some of the content is fantastic. Plots are vaguer and images more fleeting during NREM sleep. You may well have a dream every time you are in REM sleep. Therefore, if you sleep for eight hours and undergo five sleep cycles, you may have five dreams. Upon waking, you may think that time seemed to expand or contract during your dreams so that during 10 or 15 minutes, your dream content ranged over days or weeks. But dreams tend to take place in "real time": 15 minutes of events fills about 15 minutes of dreaming. Your dream theater is quite flexible: You can dream in black and white and in full color.

Theories of the Content of Dreams You may recall dreams involving fantastic adventures, but according to Calvin Hall (1966), who has interviewed hundreds of dreamers and recorded the content of thousands of dreams, most dreams are simple extensions of the activities and problems of the day. Hall links dreams to life stresses. If we are preoccupied with illness or death, sexual or aggressive urges, or moral dilemmas, we are likely to dream about them. The characters in our dreams are more likely to be friends and neighbors than spies, monsters, and princes.

The Freudian View Sigmund Freud theorized that dreams reflected unconscious wishes and urges. He argued that through dreams we could express impulses that we would censor during the day. Moreover, he said that the content of dreams was symbolic of unconscious fantasized objects, such as genital organs (see Table 4.1). In Chapter 12 we shall see that a major part of Freud's method of psychoanalysis involved interpretation of his clients' dreams. Freud also believed that dreams "protected sleep" by providing imagery that would help keep disturbing, repressed thoughts out of awareness.

The view that dreams protect sleep has been challenged by the observation that disturbing events of the day tend to be followed by related disturbing dreams—not protective imagery (Foulkes, 1971). Our behavior in dreams is also generally consistent with our waking behavior (Carrington, 1972; Cohen, 1973). Most dreams, then, are unlikely candidates for the expression (even disguised) of repressed urges. The person who leads a moral life tends to dream moral dreams.

Truth or Fiction Revisited

It is not true that we tend to act out our forbidden fantasies in our dreams.

The Activation-Synthesis Model According to the **activation-synthesis model** proposed by J. Allan Hobson and Robert W. McCarley (1977; Schmeck, 1987) of Harvard Medical School, dreams primarily reflect biological, not psychological, activity. According to this view, an abundance of acetylcholine in the brain and a time-triggered mechanism in the pons stimulate a number of responses that lead to dreaming. One is *activation* of the reticular activating system (RAS), which arouses us but not to the point of waking. During the waking state, firing of these cells in the reticular formation is linked to movement, particularly the semiautomatic movements found in walking, running, and other physical acts. During REM sleep, however, there is also general inhibition of motor (muscular) activity, so we don't thrash

Activation-synthesis model The view that dreams reflect activation by the reticular activating system and synthesis by the cerebral cortex.

Table 4.1
Dream Symbols in Psychodynamic Theory

Symbols for the Male Genital Organs				
airplanes	fish	neckties	tools	weapons
bullets	hands	poles	trains	
feet	hoses	snakes	trees	
fire	knives	sticks	umbrellas	
Symbols for the Female Genital Organs				
bottles	caves	doors	ovens	ships
boxes	chests	hats	pockets	tunnels
cases	closets	jars	pots	
Symbols for Sexual Intercourse				
climbing a ladder	entering a room			
climbing a staircase	flying in an airplane			
crossing a bridge	riding a horse			
driving an automobile	riding a roller coaster			
riding an elevator	walking into a tunnel or down a hall			
Symbols for the Breasts				
apples	peaches			

Freud theorized that the content of dreams symbolized urges, wishes, and objects of fantasy that we would censor in the waking state.

about as we dream. In this way, we save ourselves (and our bed partners) some wear and tear. The eye muscles are also stimulated, and they show the rapid eye movement associated with dreaming. In addition, the RAS stimulates neural activity in the parts of the cortex involved in vision, hearing, and memory. The cortex then automatically *synthesizes,* or puts together, these sources of stimulation to yield the substances of dreams.

The activation-synthesis model explains why there is a strong tendency to dream about events of the day: the most current neural activity of the cortex would be that which represented the events or concerns of the day. Even so, Hobson suggests that some dreams may contain "unique stylistic psychological features and concerns" that might provide some insight into an individual's "life strategies," or ways of coping (Schmeck, 1987).

The View of Crick and Mitchison Francis Crick and Graeme Mitchison (1983) propose yet another theory of the function of dreams. They suggest that REM sleep helps the brain "flush out" excessive accumulations of information, in a sense freeing memory space to focus on the issues of the following day.

Nightmares Have you ever dreamed that something heavy was on your chest and watching as you breathed? Or that you were trying to run from a terrible threat but couldn't gain your footing or coordinate your leg muscles?

In the Middle Ages, such nightmares were thought to be the work of demons called incubi and succubi (singular: **incubus** and **succubus).** By and large, they were seen as a form of retribution. That is, they were sent to make you pay for your sins. They might sit on your chest and observe you fiendishly (how else would a fiend observe, if not "fiendishly"?), as suggested in Fuseli's "Nightmare," or they might try to suffocate you. If you were given to sexual fantasies or behavior, they might have sexual intercourse with you.

Nightmares, like most pleasant dreams, are generally products of REM sleep. We shall discuss the more disturbing "night terrors" under the section

Incubus (INK-cue-bus). (1) A spirit or demon thought in medieval times to lie on sleeping people, especially on women for sexual purposes. (2) A nightmare.

Succubus (SUCK-cue-bus). A female demon thought in medieval times to have sexual intercourse with sleeping men.

"Nightmare." In the Middle Ages, nightmares were thought to be the work of demons who were sent to pay sleepers for their sins. In this picture, "Nightmare," by Fuseli, a demon sits upon a woman who is dreaming a nightmare and threatens to suffocate her.

on sleep disorders. First, though, let us consider a novel method being used by some psychologists to help people who suffer from nightmares to create more desirable endings for their dreams.

A CLOSER LOOK

Lucid Dreaming

Along what dream paths would you wander if you could dream whatever you wanted to dream? Have you ever been aware that you were having a dream and tried to control the shapes of the dream images? I have had a number of such dreams, but usually by the time I get things going my way I wake up.

In **lucid dreams,** we seem to be awake within our dreams. We recognize that we are dreaming while the dream is taking place, and we manage to do so without ending the dream or waking up. Dream researcher Stephen LaBerge (1986, 1988) and other psychologists have studied lucid dreaming by interacting with sleepers. In one example, dreamers in REM sleep use prearranged eye movements to signal researchers that they are awake within their dreams (LaBerge et al., 1981). In another, researchers use goggles that flash a red light to dreamers when their eye movements suggest that they are dreaming. According to plan, the red light informs sleepers that they are dreaming and helps them become "awake" within their dreams.

Possible roles for lucid dreaming in fostering creativity and personal growth are being explored. It is also hoped that nightmare sufferers who are taught how to recognize that they are dreaming will be able to reshape the monsters that haunt them in the night.

In the following section, we discuss other kinds of problems that affect us while we are asleep.

Lucid dream A dream in which we seem to be awake and aware that we are dreaming.

Figure 4.4
Narcolepsy. In a narcolepsy experiment the dog barks, nods, then suddenly falls asleep. The causes of narcolepsy are unknown, but it is thought to be a disorder of REM sleep functioning.

Sleep Disorders

There are a number of sleep disorders. Some, like insomnia, are all too familiar. Others, like narcolepsy, seem somewhat exotic. In this section we shall discuss insomnia, narcolepsy, apnea, and the deep-sleep disorders—sleep terrors, bedwetting, and sleepwalking.

Insomnia **Insomnia** refers to three types of sleeping problems: difficulty falling asleep (sleep-onset insomnia), difficulty remaining asleep through the night, and awakening prematurely in the morning. Perhaps 30 million Americans suffer from insomnia (Clark et al., 1981), with women complaining of the disorder more frequently than men.

As a group, people who suffer from insomnia show higher levels of autonomic activity as they try to get to sleep and as they sleep (Haynes et al., 1981; Johns et al., 1971; Monroe, 1967). Persons with sleep-onset insomnia obtain higher anxiety scores on questionnaires and show more muscle tension in the forehead than nonsufferers (Haynes et al., 1974). Personality tests also find poor sleepers to be more depressed and **ruminative** than good sleepers, more concerned about physical complaints, and more shy and retiring (Freedman & Sattler, 1982; Marks & Monroe, 1976; Monroe & Marks, 1977). Insomnia comes and goes with many people, increasing during periods of anxiety and tension.

Insomniacs tend to compound their sleep problems through their efforts to force themselves to get to sleep (Kamens, 1980; Youkilis & Bootzin, 1981). Their concern heightens autonomic activity and muscle tension. You cannot force or will yourself to get to sleep. You can only set the stage for it by lying down and relaxing when you are tired. If you focus on sleep too closely, it will elude you.

Truth or Fiction Revisited

It is true that many people have insomnia because they try too hard to get to sleep at night. *Trying* to get to sleep heightens tension and anxiety, both of which counteract the feelings of relaxation that help induce sleep.

In the section on Psychology and Modern Life, we examine ways in which psychologists help people cope with insomnia.

Narcolepsy **Narcolepsy** (not to be confused with epilepsy) is, in a sense, the mirror image of insomnia. The narcolepsy sufferer falls suddenly, irresistibly asleep. Narcolepsy afflicts as many as 100,000 people in the United States and seems to run in families. The "sleep attack" may last about 15 minutes, after which the person awakens, feeling refreshed. Despite being refreshing, these sleep episodes are dangerous and frightening. They can occur while a person is driving or engaged in work with sharp tools. They also may be accompanied by sudden collapse of muscle groups or even of the entire body (see Figure 4.4)—a condition called sleep paralysis. In sleep paralysis, the person cannot move during the transition from the waking state to sleep, and hallucinations, such as of a person or object sitting on the chest occur.

Although the causes are unknown, narcolepsy is thought to be a disorder of REM-sleep functioning. Stimulants and antidepressant drugs have helped many narcolepsy sufferers.

Apnea **Apnea** is a potentially dangerous sleep disorder that afflicts as many as one million men, primarily the overweight. In apnea, sleepers stop breathing periodically through the night, sometimes as many as 500 times! When

---

Insomnia A term for three types of sleeping problems: (1) difficulty falling asleep, (2) difficulty remaining asleep, and (3) waking early. (From the Latin *in-*, meaning "not," and *somnus,* meaning "sleep.")

Ruminative Given to prolonged turning over of thoughts. (From the Latin *ruminare,* meaning "to chew [the cud]" as a cow does.)

Narcolepsy A sleep disorder characterized by uncontrollable seizures of sleep during the waking state. (From the Greek *narke,* meaning "sleep," and *lepsia,* meaning "an attack.")

Apnea (AP-knee-uh). Temporary stopping of breathing. (From the Greek *a-*, meaning "without," and *pnoie,* meaning "wind.")

this occurs, the sleepers may suddenly sit up, gasp to begin breathing again, then fall back asleep. They are stimulated nearly, but not quite to waking, by the buildup of carbon dioxide.

Causes of apnea may include anatomical deformities that clog the air passageways, such as a thick palate, or a defect in the breathing centers of the brain. Apnea can be treated with **tranquilizers** and, sometimes, by surgery.

Deep-Sleep Disorders: Sleep Terrors, Bed-Wetting, and Sleepwalking

Sleep terrors, bed-wetting, and sleepwalking all occur during deep (stage 3 or 4) sleep, are more common among children, and may reflect immaturity of the nervous system.

Sleep terrors are similar to but more severe than nightmares. Sleep terrors usually occur during deep sleep, whereas nightmares take place during REM sleep. Sleep terrors occur during the first couple of sleep cycles; nightmares more often occur later on (Hartmann, 1981). Experiencing a surge in the heart and respiration rates, the dreamer may suddenly sit up, talk incoherently, and move about wildly. The dreamer is never fully awake, returns to sleep, and may recall a brief image, such as of someone pressing on the chest. In contrast to nightmares, however, memories of the episode are not vivid. Sleep terrors are often decreased by a minor tranquilizer at bedtime, which reduces the amount of time spent in stage 4 sleep.

Bed-wetting is often seen as a stigma that reflects parental harshness or the child's attempt to punish the parents, but this disorder, too, may stem from immaturity of the nervous system. In most cases, bed-wetting resolves itself before adolescence, often by age 8. Behavior-therapy methods that condition children to awaken when about to urinate have been helpful. The "antidepressant" drug *imipramine* often helps by increasing bladder capacity. Often all that is needed, though, is reassurance that no one need be to blame for bed-wetting and that most children "outgrow" the disorder.

Most children occasionally talk in their sleep, and as many as 15 percent walk in their sleep. Sleepwalkers may roam about almost nightly while their parents fret about the accidents that could befall them. Sleepwalkers typically do not remember their excursions, although they may respond to questions while they are up and about. Contrary to myth, there is no evidence that sleepwalkers become violent or grossly disturbed if they are awakened. Mild tranquilizers and maturity typically put an end to sleepwalking.

Truth or Fiction Revisited

It is *not* true that it is dangerous to awaken a sleepwalker.

We have noted that drugs often play a role in the treatment of sleep disorders. But drugs are used recreationally or to "expand consciousness" as well as to treat problems. Let us now turn our attention to a number of such drugs.

Tranquilizers Drugs used to reduce anxiety and tension.

Sleep terrors Frightening dream-like experiences that occur during the deepest stage of NREM sleep. Nightmares, in contrast, occur during REM sleep.

Psychoactive Descriptive of drugs that have psychological effects, such as stimulation or distortion of perceptions.

ALTERING CONSCIOUSNESS THROUGH DRUGS

The world is a supermarket of **psychoactive** substances, or drugs. The United States is flooded with drugs that distort perceptions and change mood—drugs that take you up, let you down, and move you across town.

Some people use drugs because their friends do, or because their parents tell them not to. Some are seeking pleasure, others are seeking inner truth.

Alcohol is the most popular drug on high school and college campuses. Most college students have tried marijuana, and perhaps one in five smokes it regularly. Many Americans take **depressants** to get to sleep at night and **stimulants** to get going in the morning. Karl Marx charged that "religion . . . is the opiate of the people," but heroin is the real opiate of the people. Cocaine was, until recently, the toy of the well-to-do, but price breaks have brought it into the lockers of high school students. Given laws, moral pronouncements, medical warnings, and an occasional horror story, drug use—with the exception of the smokable cocaine derivative, crack—has actually declined somewhat in recent years (Kerr, 1988). But overall, drugs remain a part of American life.

We shall deal with some general issues in substance abuse and dependence and then turn our attention to specific drugs.

Substance Abuse and Dependence

Where does drug use end and abuse begin? The American Psychiatric Association considers use of a substance abusive when it is continued for a period of at least one month despite the fact that it is causing or compounding a social, occupational, psychological, or physical problem (1987, p. 169). If you are missing school or work because you are drunk, or "sleeping it off," your behavior fits the definition of **substance abuse.**

Substance dependence is more severe than substance abuse. Dependence is shown by signs such as increased usage despite knowledge that the substance is interfering with your life and despite desire or efforts to cut down. Dependence is also characterized by orienting your life toward getting and using the substance, by tolerance, by frequent intoxication, and by withdrawal symptoms (American Psychiatric Association, 1987, pp. 166–168). **Tolerance** is the body's habituation to a drug so that with regular usage, higher doses are required to achieve similar effects. Dependence is physiological; there are characteristic withdrawal symptoms, or an **abstinence syndrome,** when the level of usage suddenly drops off. The abstinence syndrome for alcohol includes anxiety, tremors, restlessness, weakness, rapid pulse, and high blood pressure.

When doing without a drug, people who are *psychologically* dependent on it show signs of anxiety (shakiness, rapid pulse, and sweating are three) that overlap abstinence syndromes. Because of these signs, they may believe that they are physiologically dependent on a drug when they are psychologically dependent. Still, symptoms of abstinence from certain drugs are unmistakably physiological. One is **delirium tremens** ("the DTs"), encountered by some chronic alcoholics when they suddenly lower intake.

Depressant A drug that lowers the rate of activity of the nervous system. (From the Latin *de-*, meaning "down," and *premere,* meaning "to press.")

Stimulant A drug that increases activity of the nervous system.

Substance abuse Use of a substance for at least one month even though the substance is causing or compounding problems in meeting the demands of life.

Substance dependence Habitual use of a substance despite knowledge that it is interfering with life and despite efforts to quit or cut down.

Tolerance Habituation to a drug, with the result that increasingly higher doses of the drug are needed to achieve similar effects.

Abstinence syndrome A characteristic cluster of symptoms that results from sudden decrease in an addictive drug's level of usage.

Delirium tremens A condition characterized by sweating, restlessness, disorientation, and hallucinations. The "DTs" occurs in some chronic alcohol users when there is a sudden decrease in usage. (From the Latin *de-*, meaning "from," and *lira,* meaning "line" or "furrow"—suggesting that one's behavior is away from the beaten track or norm.)

Causal Factors in Substance Abuse and Dependence

There are many reasons for substance abuse and dependence. Just a handful include curiosity, conformity to peer pressure, rebelliousness, and escape from boredom or pressure (Brook et al., 1980; Hollister, 1983; Kandel, 1980; Mann et al., 1987; Mittelmark et al., 1987; Wills, 1986).

Psychological and biological theories also account for substance abuse in the following ways.

Psychodynamic Views Psychodynamic explanations of substance abuse propose that drugs help people control or express unconscious needs and impulses. Alcoholism, for example, may reflect the need to remain dependent on an overprotective mother, or the effort to reduce emotional conflicts or to cope with unconscious homosexual impulses.

Learning-Theory Views Social-learning theorists suggest that first use of tranquilizing agents such as Valium and alcohol usually results from observing others or from a recommendation. Expectancies about the effects of a substance are powerful predictors of the use of that substance (Wilson, 1987). Subsequent usage may be reinforced by the drug's positive effects on mood and its reduction of unpleasant sensations such as anxiety, fear, and tension. For people who are physiologically dependent, avoidance of withdrawal symptoms is also reinforcing.

Parents who use drugs such as alcohol, tranquilizers, and stimulants may increase their children's knowledge of drugs and, in effect, show them when to use them—for example, when they are anxious or depressed.

Genetic Predispositions There is some evidence that people may have a genetic predisposition toward physiological dependence on certain substances (Goodwin, 1985; Schuckit, 1987; Vaillant, 1982). For example, the biological children of alcoholics who are reared by adoptive parents seem more likely to develop alcohol-related problems than the natural children of the adoptive parents (Goodwin, 1985).

If there is an inherited tendency toward alcoholism, it may involve bodily reactions to alcohol that show greater tolerance of alcohol. For example, college-age children of alcoholics exhibit better muscular control and visual-motor coordination when they drink (Kolata, 1987). They feel less intoxicated when they drink large quantities of alcohol, and they show lower hormonal response to alcohol.

Let us now consider the effects of some frequently used depressants, stimulants, and hallucinogenics.

Depressants

Depressant drugs generally act by slowing the activity of the central nervous system, although there are a number of other effects specific to each drug. In this section we consider the effects of alcohol, opiates and opioids, barbiturates, and methaqualone.

Alcohol No drug has meant so much to so many as alcohol. Alcohol is our dinnertime relaxant, our bedtime **sedative,** our cocktail-party social facilitator. We celebrate holy days, applaud our accomplishments, and express joyous wishes with alcohol. The young assert their maturity with alcohol; it is used by 85 to 88 percent of the high school population (Johnston, 1988). The elderly use alcohol to stimulate circulation in peripheral areas of the body. Alcohol even kills germs on surface wounds.

No drug has been so abused as alcohol. Ten to 20 million Americans are alcoholics. In contrast, 500,000 use heroin regularly, and 300,000 to 500,000 abuse sedatives. Excessive drinking has been linked to lower productivity, loss of employment, and downward movement in social status

Sedative A drug that soothes or quiets restlessness or agitation. (From the Latin *sedare,* meaning "to settle.")

Two Facets of Alcohol. No drug has meant so much to so many as alcohol. Yet, for many, alcohol is a central problem of life.

(Baum-Baicker, 1984; Mider, 1984; Vaillant & Milofsky, 1982). Yet half of all Americans use alcohol, and despite widespread marijuana use, it is the drug of choice among adolescents.

Effects of Alcohol Although the effects of drugs vary from individual to individual (Erwin et al., 1984), we can generally note that our response to a substance reflects (1) the physiological effects of that substance on us and (2) our interpretations of those effects. Our interpretations of the drug's effects are, in turn, influenced by our expectations.

What do Americans usually expect from alcohol? Adolescent and adult samples tend to report the belief that alcohol reduces tension, diverts one from worrying, enhances pleasure, increases social ability, and transforms experiences for the better (Brown et al., 1980, 1985; Christiansen et al., 1982; Rohsenow, 1983). These are expectations. What *does* alcohol do?

The effects of alcohol vary with the dose and the duration of use. Low doses of alcohol may be stimulating, but higher doses of alcohol have a sedative effect (Niaura et al., 1988), which is why alcohol is classified as a depressant. Ironically, short-term use of alcohol may lessen feelings of depression, but regular use over a year or more may augment feelings of depression (Aneshensel & Huba, 1983). Alcohol relaxes and deadens minor aches and pains. Alcohol also intoxicates: It impairs cognitive functioning, slurs the speech, and reduces motor coordination. Alcohol is implicated in about half of our automobile accidents.

In the following highlight, we consider the physical consequences of drinking. Although there is widespread agreement that heavy drinking is harmful, some researchers suggest that light to moderate drinking may actually be good for us.

A CLOSER LOOK

Effects of Alcohol on Physical Health: Is a Drink a Day Good for You?

As a food, alcohol is fattening. Yet chronic drinkers may be malnourished. Though high in calories, alcohol does not contain nutrients such as vitamins and proteins. Moreover, alcohol can interfere with the body's absorption of a number of vitamins, particularly thiamine, a B vitamin. Thus, chronic drinking can lead to a number of disorders, such as **cirrhosis of the liver,** which has been linked to protein deficiency, and **Wernicke-Korsakoff syndrome,** which has been linked to vitamin B deficiency (Eckhardt et al., 1981). In cirrhosis of the liver, connective fibers replace active liver cells, impeding circulation of the blood.

When alcohol is metabolized in the body, there are increases in levels of lactic and uric acids. Lactic acid has been correlated with anxiety attacks, although there is little reason to think that alcohol causes anxiety. Uric acid can cause gout. Chronic drinking has also been linked to coronary heart disease and high blood pressure (Eckhardt et al., 1981).

Heavy use of alcohol has been linked with cancer of the pancreas (Heuch et al., 1983) and stomach (Gordon & Kannel, 1984; Popham et al., 1984), although light to moderate drinking has not been shown to heighten the risk of stomach cancer.

Possible Benefits of Alcohol: Moderation in All Things? Having noted these problems with alcohol, it might seem ironic that a number of studies suggest that light to moderate drinking *benefits* many people—but it may.

Long-term studies have followed thousands of residents of Hayward, California (Klatsky et al., 1981); Alameda County, California (Berkman et al., 1983); Framingham, Massachusetts (Friedman & Kimball, 1986); and Albany County, New York (Gordon & Doyle, 1987). By and large, they have found that light to moderate male drinkers have fewer heart attacks and strokes and lower mortality rates than nondrinkers and heavy drinkers. A recent nationwide study of 87,526 nurses found that women who had 3 to 15 drinks a week had fewer strokes caused by blocked blood vessels in the brain and fewer heart attacks than nondrinkers or heavier drinkers (Stampfer & Hennekens, 1988). But the women had more strokes caused by bleeding in the brain, a less common kind of stroke.

Why might light drinking be beneficial? Some researchers (e.g., Stampfer & Hennekens, 1988) suggest that light drinking may increase the amount of high-density lipoproteins (HDL) in the blood. HDL, in turn, helps clear blood vessels of blockage by harmful cholesterol.

Recognize that these studies are correlational, not experimental. Therefore, it is possible that the same factors that lead people to light or moderate drinking may also enhance physical health. For example, light to moderate drinkers, as compared to nondrinkers, may be more relaxed, more willing to let go. And, when compared to heavy drinkers, light to moderate drinkers—that is, people who contain their alcohol intake—may also be in greater command of their lives in general.

Scientists who participated in the correlational studies do not suggest that nondrinkers take up light to moderate drinking to reap potential benefits. William Castelli, who took part in the Framingham study, notes that people "can get the benefit [of light to moderate drinking] in other ways, such as by stopping smoking, lowering [their] cholesterol or . . . blood pressure, and [not] run the risk of becoming an alcoholic" (1988).

Cirrhosis of the liver (sir-ROW-sis). A disease caused by protein deficiency in which connective fibers replace active liver cells, impeding circulation of the blood. Alcohol does not contain protein; therefore, persons who drink excessively may be prone to this disease. (From the Greek *kirrhos,* meaning "tawny," referring to the yellow-orange color of the diseased liver.)

Wernicke-Korsakoff syndrome A cluster of symptoms associated with chronic alcohol abuse and characterized by confusion, memory impairment, and filling in gaps in memory with false information (confabulation).

Drinking Your Troubles Away: Drinking as a Strategy for Coping with Stress and Failure Adolescent involvement with alcohol has been linked repeatedly to poor school grades and other negative life events (Chassin et al., 1988; Mann et al., 1987; Wills, 1986). Drinking can, of course, contribute to poor grades and other problems, but drinking may also help reduce the stresses of academic and other problems. Some researchers, in fact, suggest that drinking in order to cope with stress is the most powerful predictor of alcohol abuse (Cooper et al., 1988).

Truth or Fiction Revisited

It is true that some people drink because alcohol provides them with an excuse for failure.

Alcohol lowers self-awareness (Hull, 1981) and impairs information processing (Steele & Josephs, 1988). When we drink, we become less sensitive to personal and social standards and expectations, as well as less aware of our deviation from them. Thus, we are less likely to experience self-criticism, feelings of guilt, and shame for behavior that we would not accept when sober. It is a short step to adopting drinking as a way of life when we seek excuses for doing things that would otherwise be unacceptable.

Let us now examine some experiments that suggest how we use drinking as a strategy in the area of sexual behavior.

Alcohol and Sex A character in Shakespeare's play, *Macbeth,* notes that drink provokes three things: "nosepainting" (rupture of small blood vessels in the nose, turning the nose reddish), sleep, and urine. "Lechery," he adds, "it provokes and unprovokes; it provokes the desire, but takes away the performance." *Does* alcohol stir the sexual appetite? *Does* it inhibit sexual response ("take away the performance")?

Recent studies of response to sexually explicit films suggest that men who *believe* they have drunk alcohol (when they have not) show increases in sexual arousal, as measured by size of erection and subjective feelings of arousal. But men who have *actually* drunk alcohol, without knowing it, show decreased sexual response (Briddell & Wilson, 1976). Similar research shows that alcohol also decreases women's response to sexually explicit films (Wilson & Lawson, 1978). Thus, our beliefs about the effects of alcohol may diverge markedly from its actual effects. The "sexy" feeling we may experience after a few drinks may stem from general feelings of euphoria, decreased sympathetic activity, and our expectations—not from the alcohol itself.

The questionnaire on the next page may offer some insight into your own reasons for drinking—if you do.

Treatment of Alcoholism Treatment of alcoholism has been a frustrating endeavor. *Detoxification,* or helping a physiologically dependent alcoholic safely through the abstinence syndrome, is a generally straightforward medical procedure, requiring about one week (Rada & Kellner, 1979). But assisting the alcoholic to then learn to cope with life's stresses through measures other than drinking is the heart of the problem. Several treatments have been tried, with mixed success.

The drug *disulfuram* (brand name Antabuse) has been used most widely with alcoholics. Mixing Antabuse with alcohol can cause feelings of illness. However, current maintenance doses of Antabuse are usually too low to bring

QUESTIONNAIRE

Why Do You Drink?

Do you drink? If so, why? To enhance your pleasure? To cope with your problems? To help you in your social encounters? Half of all Americans use alcohol for a variety of reasons. Perhaps as many as one user in ten is an alcoholic. College students who expect that alcohol will help them reduce tension are more likely than other students to encounter alcohol-related problems (Brown, 1985).

To gain insight into your reasons for using alcohol, respond to the following items by circling the *T* if an item is true or mostly true for you, or the *F* if an item is false or mostly false for you. Then turn to the answer key in Appendix B.

T F 1. I find it very unpleasant to do without alcohol for some time.

T F 2. Alcohol makes it easier for me to talk to other people.

T F 3. I drink to appear more grown up and more sophisticated.

T F 4. When I drink, the future looks brighter to me.

T F 5. I like the taste of what I drink.

T F 6. If I go without a drink for some time, I am not bothered or uncomfortable.

T F 7. I feel more relaxed and less tense about things when I drink.

T F 8. I drink so that I will fit in better with the crowd.

T F 9. I worry less about things when I drink.

T F 10. I have a drink when I get together with the family.

T F 11. I have a drink as part of my religious ceremonies.

T F 12. I have a drink when a toothache or some other pain is disturbing me.

T F 13. I feel much more powerful when I have a drink.

T F 14. You really can't blame me for the things I do when I have been drinking.

T F 15. I have a drink before a big test, date, or interview when I'm afraid of how well I'll do.

T F 16. I find I have a drink for the taste alone.

T F 17. I've found a drink in my hand when I can't remember putting it there.

T F 18. I'll have a drink when I feel "blue" or want to take my mind off my cares and worries.

T F 19. I can do better socially and sexually after having a drink or two.

T F 20. Drinking makes me do stupid things.

T F 21. Sometimes when I have a few drinks, I can't get to work.

T F 22. I feel more caring and giving after having a drink or two.

T F 23. I drink because I like the look of a drinker.

T F 24. I like to drink more on festive occasions.

T F 25. When a friend or I have done something well, we're likely to have a drink or two.

T F 26. I have a drink when some problem is nagging away at me.

T F 27. I find drinking pleasurable.

T F 28. I like the "high" of drinking.

T F 29. Sometimes I pour a drink without realizing I still have one that is unfinished.

T F 30. I feel I can better get others to do what I want when I've had a drink or two.

T F 31. Having a drink keeps my mind off my problems at home, at school, or at work.

T F 32. I get a real gnawing hunger for a drink when I haven't had one for a while.

T F 33. A drink or two relaxes me.

T F 34. Things look better when I've had a drink or two.

T F 35. My mood is much better after I've been drinking.

T F 36. I see things more clearly when I've been drinking.

T F 37. A drink or two enhances the pleasure of sex and food.

T F 38. When I'm out of alcohol, I immediately buy more.

T F 39. I would have done much better on some things if it weren't for alcohol.

T F 40. When I have run out of alcohol, I find it almost unbearable until I can get some more.

Sources: Items adapted from (1) general discussion of expectancies about alcohol in Christiansen et al. (1982) and (2) smokers' self-testing items analyzed by Leventhal and Avis (1976).

Opiates (OH-pee-ates). A group of addictive drugs derived from the opium poppy that provide a euphoric rush and depress the nervous system.

Narcotics Drugs used to relieve pain and induce sleep. The term is usually reserved for opiates. (From the Greek *narke,* meaning "numbness" or "stupor.")

Analgesia A state of not feeling pain, although fully conscious.

Opioid (OH-pee-oid). A synthetic (artificial) drug similar in chemical composition to opiates.

Morphine An opiate introduced at about the time of the U.S. Civil War.

Heroin An opiate. Heroin, ironically, was used as a "cure" for morphine addiction when first introduced.

about this result, and there is little convincing evidence of the drug's effectiveness (Miller & Hester, 1980).

Many people consider Alcoholics Anonymous (AA), a nonprofessional organization, to offer the most effective treatment for alcoholics. At AA, alcoholics undergo a conversion in identity to that of a "recovering alcoholic." Conversion requires confession of one's drinking problems before a group of alcoholics, and the making of a public commitment not to touch another drop. The new identity becomes confirmed with the passing of each sober day. Recovering alcoholics often help other alcoholics undergo a similar conversion. Group members also offer one another support during periods of temptation.

Although AA commonly cites a success rate in the neighborhood of 75 percent (Wallace, 1985), critics note that figures this high usually include only persons who remain in treatment. As many as 90 percent of those who seek help from AA drop out after a handful of meetings (Miller, 1982).

Behavior therapy is proving to be helpful to many alcoholics. A variety of methods to be explained in depth in Chapter 13 show promising success rates. These include aversion therapy, relaxation training, covert sensitization, instruction in social skills, and self-monitoring (Elkins, 1980; Miller & Mastria, 1977; Olson et al., 1981; Sanchez-Craig et al., 1984). All of these methods have also been used to help people quit and cut down on smoking.

Opiates and Opioids **Opiates** are a group of **narcotics** derived from the opium poppy. The ancient Sumerians gave this poppy its name: It means "plant of joy." The opiates include morphine, heroin, codeine, Demerol, and similar drugs whose major medical application is **analgesia.** Opiates appear to stimulate centers in the brain that lead to pleasure and to physiological dependence (Goeders & Smith, 1984; Ling et al., 1984).

In this section we discuss morphine, heroin, and the **opioid** methadone. Opioids are similar to opiates in chemical structure and effect but are artificial (synthesized in the laboratory).

Morphine **Morphine** was introduced at about the time of the Civil War in the United States and the Franco-Prussian War in Europe. It was used liberally to deaden pain from wounds. Physiological dependence on morphine became known as the "soldier's disease." There was little stigma attached to dependence until morphine became a restricted substance.

Heroin **Heroin** was so named because, when it was derived, it was hailed as the "hero" that would cure physiological dependence on morphine.

"Shooting Up" Heroin. Users of heroin claim that the drug is so pleasurable that it can eradicate any thought of food or sex. Many users remain dependent on heroin because they are unwilling to undergo withdrawal symptoms or to contemplate a life devoid of drugs.

Truth or Fiction Revisited

It is true that heroin was once used as a cure for addiction to morphine. Today, methadone is used to help addicts avert withdrawal symptoms from heroin.

Heroin, like the other opiates, is a powerful depressant that can also provide a euphoric rush. Users of heroin claim that it is so pleasurable it can eradicate any thought of food or sex. Soon after its initial appearance, heroin was used to treat so many problems that it became known as G.O.M. ("God's own medicine").

Morphine and heroin can have distressing abstinence syndromes, beginning with flu-like symptoms and progressing through tremors, cramps, chills alternating with sweating, rapid pulse, high blood pressure, insomnia, vomiting, and diarrhea. However, the syndrome can be quite variable from person to person.

Heroin is illegal. Because the penalties for possession or sale are high, it is also very expensive. For this reason, many physiologically dependent people support their habits through dealing (selling heroin), prostitution, or selling stolen goods. But the chemical effects of heroin do not directly stimulate criminal or aggressive behavior. On the other hand, people who use heroin regularly may be more likely than nonusers to engage in *other* criminal behavior as well. Considering the legal penalties for heroin use, most users are willing to take high risks.

Although regular users develop tolerance for heroin, high doses can cause drowsiness, stupor, altered time perception, and impaired judgment.

Methadone The synthetic narcotic **methadone** has been used to treat physiological dependence on heroin in the same way that heroin was used to treat physiological dependence on morphine. Methadone is slower acting than heroin and does not provide the thrilling rush. Most people treated with it simply swap dependence on one drug for dependence on another. Because they are unwilling to undergo withdrawal symptoms or to contemplate a life style devoid of drugs, they must be maintained on methadone indefinitely.

Barbiturates and Methaqualone **Barbiturates** such as amobarbital, phenobarbital, pentobarbital, and secobarbital are depressants with a number of medical uses, including relief of anxiety and tension, deadening of pain, and treatment of epilepsy, high blood pressure, and insomnia. Barbiturates lead rapidly to physiological and psychological dependence.

Methaqualone, sold under the brand names Quaalude and Sopor, is a depressant similar in effect to barbiturates. Methaqualone also leads to physiological dependence and is quite dangerous.

Psychologists generally oppose using barbiturates and methaqualone for anxiety, tension, and insomnia. These drugs lead rapidly to dependence and do nothing to teach the individual how to alter disturbing patterns of behavior.

Barbiturates and methaqualone are popular as street drugs, because they relax the muscles and produce a mild euphoric state. High doses of barbiturates result in drowsiness, motor impairment, slurred speech, irritability, and poor judgment. A physiologically dependent person who is withdrawn abruptly from barbiturates may experience severe convulsions and die. High doses of methaqualone may cause internal bleeding, coma, and death. Because of additive effects, it is dangerous to mix alcohol and other depressants at bedtime, or at any time.

Stimulants

All stimulants increase the activity of the nervous system. Stimulants' other effects vary somewhat from drug to drug, and some seem to contribute to feelings of euphoria and self-confidence.

Amphetamines **Amphetamines** are a group of stimulants that were first used by soldiers during World War II to help them remain alert through the night. Truck drivers have used them to drive through the night. Amphetamines have become perhaps more widely known through students, who have used them for all-night cram sessions, and through dieters, who use them because they reduce hunger.

Amphetamines and a related stimulant, methylphenidate (Ritalin), increase self-control in **hyperactive** children, increase their attention span,

Methadone (METH-uh-don). An artificial narcotic that is slower acting than, and does not provide the rush of, heroin. Methadone use allows heroin addicts to abstain from heroin without experiencing an abstinence syndrome.

Barbiturate (bar-BICH-ur-it). An addictive depressant used to relieve anxiety or induce sleep.

Methaqualone An addictive depressant. Often called "ludes."

Amphetamines (am-FET-uh-means). Stimulants derived from *a*lpha-*m*ethyl-beta-*ph*enyl-*et*hyl-*amine,* a colorless liquid consisting of carbon, hydrogen, and nitrogen.

Hyperactive More active than normal.

Cocaine (co-CANE). A powerful stimulant.

decrease fidgeting, and lead to academic gains (Abikoff & Gittelman, 1985; Barkley et al., 1984; Kavale, 1982; Rapport, 1984; Whalen et al., 1987). The paradoxical calming effect of stimulants on hyperactive children may be explained by assuming that a cause of hyperactivity is immaturity of the cerebral cortex. Amphetamines might stimulate the cortex to exercise control over more primitive centers in the lower brain. It may be that a combination of stimulants and behavior therapy will prove to be the most effective approach to treating hyperactivity (Hinshaw et al., 1984; Pelham et al., 1983).

Called speed, uppers, bennies (for Benzedrine), and dexies (for Dexedrine), these drugs are often used for the euphoric rush they can produce, especially in high doses. (The so-called antidepressant drugs, which we shall discuss in Chapter 13, do not produce a euphoric rush.) Some people swallow amphetamines in pill form or inject liquid Methedrine, the strongest form, into their veins. They may stay awake and "high" for days on end. Such highs must come to an end. People who have been on prolonged highs sometimes "crash," or fall into a deep sleep or depression. Some people commit suicide when crashing.

People can become psychologically dependent on amphetamines, especially when they are using them to cope with depression. Tolerance develops rapidly, but opinion is mixed as to whether they lead to physiological dependence. High doses may cause restlessness, hallucinations, paranoid delusions, insomnia, loss of appetite, and irritability. In the so-called amphetamine psychosis, there are hallucinations and delusions that mimic the symptoms of paranoid schizophrenia, a psychological disorder that is discussed in Chapter 12.

Cocaine No doubt you've seen commercials claiming that Coke adds life. Given its caffeine and sugar content, "Coke"—Coca-Cola, that is—should provide quite a lift. But Coca-Cola hasn't been "the real thing" since 1906. At that time the manufacturers discontinued use of cocaine in its formula, which is derived from coca leaves—the plant from which the soft drink derived its name.

"Snorting" Cocaine. Cocaine is a powerful stimulant whose use has become widespread because of recent price breaks. Health professionals have become concerned about cocaine's stimulation of sudden rises in blood pressure, its constriction of blood vessels, and its acceleration of the heart rate. Several well-known athletes have recently died from cocaine overdoses.

Truth or Fiction Revisited

It is true that Coca-Cola once "added life" through a powerful but now illegal stimulant. That stimulant is cocaine.

Coca leaves contain **cocaine,** a stimulant that produces a state of euphoria, reduces hunger, deadens pain, and bolsters self-confidence. Cocaine has grown in popularity in recent years, and one survey of young adults (aged about 25) found that 37 percent of males and 24 percent of females had tried it (Kandel et al., 1986). Five million Americans use cocaine regularly (Altman, 1988).

Cocaine is brewed from coca leaves as a "tea," breathed in ("snorted") in powder form, and injected ("shot up") in liquid form. Repeated snorting constricts blood vessels in the nose, drying the skin and, at times, exposing cartilege and perforating the nasal septum. These problems require cosmetic surgery. Of course, people who take cocaine intravenously and share contaminated needles risk becoming infected by the AIDS virus (e.g., Lambert, 1987). The potent derivatives "crack" and "bazooka" have recently received much attention in the media. These derivatives are inexpensive because they are unrefined.

On a physiological level, cocaine stimulates sudden rises in blood pressure, tightening of the blood vessels (with associated decrease of the oxygen supply to the heart), and quickening of the heart rate (Altman, 1988). There are occasional reports of respiratory and cardiovascular collapse, as with the highly publicized deaths of the athletes Len Bias, Don Rogers, and Dave

Croudip. Overdoses can lead to restlessness and insomnia, tremors, headaches, nausea, convulsions, hallucinations, and delusions. Robert Post of the National Institute of Mental Health and his colleagues have reported that cocaine gradually lowers the brain threshold for seizures in laboratory rats (Bales, 1986). That is, individual moderate doses of cocaine had no apparent harmful effect, but there was a cumulative "kindling effect" for brain seizures and, in some cases, sudden death.

Cocaine—also called *snow* and *coke,* like the slang term for the soft drink—has been used as a local anesthetic since the early 1800s. It came to the attention of one Viennese neurologist in 1884, a young chap named Sigmund Freud, who used it to fight his own depression and published an early supportive article, "Song of Praise." Freud's early ardor was soon moderated by awareness that cocaine was habit-forming and could cause hallucinations and delusions.

Dependence Despite media and government claims that cocaine is addictive, some question remains as to whether cocaine does cause physiological dependence. Users may not develop tolerance for the drug, and it is not clear that there is a specific abstinence syndrome for cocaine (Van Dyke & Byck, 1982). There is no doubt, however, that users can readily become psychologically dependent.

Cigarettes All cigarette packs sold in the United States carry messages such as: "Warning: The Surgeon General Has Determined That Cigarette Smoking Is Dangerous to Your Health." Cigarette advertising has been banned on the radio and television. In 1988, Surgeon General C. Everett Koop declared that cigarette smoking is chief preventable cause of death in the United States.

The percentage of American adults who smoke has declined from 42.2 in 1966 to 26.5 in 1986 (Mansnerus, 1988). Nevertheless, about 350,000 still die from smoking-related illnesses each year. This is seven times the number who die from motor-vehicle accidents (Cowley, 1988). Cigarette smoking can cause cancer of the lungs, larynx, oral cavity, and esophagus and may contribute to cancer of the bladder, pancreas, and kidneys. Cigarette smoking is also linked to death from heart disease (Epstein & Perkins, 1988), chronic lung and respiratory diseases, and other illnesses. Pregnant women who smoke risk miscarriage, premature birth, and birth defects.

So it's no secret that cigarette smoking is dangerous. In fact, in the 1980s, peer pressure seems to be favoring *not* smoking. Many people now look upon smoking as a form of "deviant behavior" (Mansnerus, 1988).

Components of Tobacco Smoke: Where There's Smoke, There's Chemicals Tobacco smoke contains *carbon monoxide, hydrocarbons* (or *"tars"*), and *nicotine.*

Oxygen is carried through the bloodstream by **hemoglobin.** When carbon monoxide combines with hemoglobin, it impairs the blood's ability to supply the body with oxygen. One result is shortness of breath. Some **hydrocarbons** have been shown to cause cancer in laboratory animals.

Nicotine is the stimulant in cigarettes. Nicotine can cause cold, clammy skin, faintness and dizziness, nausea and vomiting, and diarrhea—all of which account for the occasional discomforts of the novice smoker. Nicotine also stimulates discharge of the hormone adrenaline. Adrenaline creates a burst of autonomic activity, including rapid heart rate and release of sugar into the blood. It also provides a sort of mental "kick." Nicotine is responsible for the stimulating properties of cigarette smoke, but its effects are short-lived. In the long run it can contribute to fatigue.

Hemoglobin The substance in the blood that carries oxygen.

Hydrocarbons Chemical compounds consisting of hydrogen and carbon.

Nicotine A stimulant found in tobacco smoke. (From the French name for the tobacco plant, *nicotiane.*)

Physiological Dependence Nicotine is the agent that cr iological dependence on cigarettes (Koop, 1988). Regular smo their smoking to maintain fairly even levels of nicotine in their b (Schachter, 1977). Symptoms for withdrawal from nicotine include nervousness, drowsiness, energy loss, headaches, fatigue, irregular bowels, lightheadedness, insomnia, dizziness, cramps, palpitations, tremors, and sweating.

It has also been found that nicotine is excreted more rapidly when the urine is highly acidic. Stress increases the amount of acid in the urine. For this reason, smokers may need to smoke more when under stress to maintain the same blood nicotine level, even though they may *believe* that smoking is helping them cope with stress.

Truth or Fiction Revisited

It is true that cigarette smokers tend to smoke more when they are under stress. That is because nicotine is excreted more rapidly when they are under stress.

In the section on Psychology and Modern Life, we discuss ways of quitting and cutting down on smoking.

Hallucinogenics

Hallucinogenic drugs are so named because they produce hallucinations—that is, sensations and perceptions in the absence of external stimulation. But hallucinogenic drugs may also have additional effects, such as relaxing the individual, creating a sense of euphoria, or, in some cases, causing panic. We shall focus on the effects of marijuana and LSD.

Marijuana **Marijuana** is produced from the *Cannabis sativa* plant, which grows wild in many parts of the world. Marijuana helps some people relax and can elevate their mood. It also sometimes produces mild hallucinations, which is why marijuana is classified as a **psychedelic,** or hallucinogenic, drug. The major psychedelic substance in marijuana is **delta-9-tetrahydrocannabinol,** or THC. THC is found in the branches and leaves of male and female plants, but it is highly concentrated in the **resin** of the female plant. **Hashish,** or "hash," is derived from this sticky resin. Hashish is more potent than marijuana, although the effects are similar.

In the nineteenth century, marijuana was used almost as aspirin is used today for headaches and minor aches and pains. It could be bought without prescription in any drugstore. Today marijuana use and possession are illegal in most states, but medical applications are being explored. Marijuana is known to decrease nausea and vomiting among cancer patients receiving chemotherapy (Grinspoon, 1987). It appears to help **glaucoma** sufferers by reducing fluid pressure in the eye. It may even offer some relief from asthma. However, there are also causes for concern, as noted in 1982 by the Institute of Medicine of the National Academy of Sciences. For example, marijuana impairs motor coordination and perceptual functions used in driving and the operation of other machines. It also impairs short-term memory and slows learning. Although it causes positive mood changes in many people, there are also disturbing instances of anxiety and confusion and occasional reports of psychotic reactions. Marijuana increases the heart rate up to 140–150 beats per minute and, in some people, raises blood pressure. This rise in workload poses a threat to persons with hypertension and cardiovascular disorders.

Hallucinogenic Giving rise to hallucinations.

Marijuana The dried vegetable matter of the *Cannabis sativa* plant. (A Mexican-Spanish word.)

Psychedelic (sigh-kuh-DELL-lick). Causing hallucinations, delusions, or heightened perceptions.

Delta-9-tetrahydrocannabinol (tet-truh-hide-row-can-NAB-in-all). The major active ingredient in marijuana. Abbreviated *THC.* Its name describes its chemical composition.

Resin (RAH-zin). The saplike substance of plants.

Hashish (hah-SHEESH). A drug derived from the resin of *Cannabis sativa.* Often called "hash."

Glaucoma An eye disease characterized by increased fluid pressure within the eye. A cause of blindness. (From the Greek *glaukos,* meaning "gleaming"—referring to the appearance of the diseased eye.)

Today marijuana is used by about 36 percent of high school students, down from a peak of about 51 percent in 1979 (Kerr, 1988).

Psychoactive Effects of Marijuana Marijuana smokers report different sensations at different levels of intoxication. The early stages of intoxication are frequently characterized by restlessness, which gives way to calmness. Fair to strong intoxication is linked to reports of heightened perceptions and increases in self-insight, creative thinking, and empathy for the feelings of others. Strong intoxication is linked to perceiving time as passing more slowly. A song, for example, might seem to last an hour rather than a few minutes. There is increased awareness of bodily sensations, such as heart beat. Smokers also report that strong intoxication heightens sexual sensations. Visual hallucinations are not uncommon. Strong intoxication may cause smokers to experience disorientation.

Some people report that marijuana helps them socialize at parties. However, the friendliness characteristic of early stages of intoxication may give way to self-absorption and social withdrawal as the smoker becomes higher (Fabian & Fishkin, 1981).

There is controversy about whether or not marijuana causes physiological dependence. People can become psychologically dependent on marijuana, as on any other drug, but many psychologists maintain that marijuana does not cause physiological dependence. Tolerance is a sign of dependence, and with marijuana, **reverse tolerance** has been reported. That is, with marijuana, regular usage frequently leads to the need for less of the substance to achieve similar effects. It may be that some of the psychoactive substances in marijuana smoke take a long time to be metabolized by the body. The effects of new doses then would be added to those of the chemicals remaining in the body.

Marijuana and Amotivational Syndrome It has been feared that marijuana can lead to **amotivational syndrome**—that is, that it can destroy achievement motivation, melt away ambition, and cause difficulty in concentrating. These fears have been fueled by correlational evidence that heavy smokers in the college ranks do not strive to succeed as strenuously as do nonsmoking or infrequently smoking classmates. But we cannot confuse correlation with cause and effect. Other studies suggest that people who choose to smoke heavily may already differ from those who do not (Maugh, 1982). For instance, heavy smokers may be more concerned with emotional experience and fantasy than with intellectual performance and self-control. Their approach to life could underlie both relative lack of ambition and regular use of marijuana. Still other research finds no cognitive effects from heavy use of marijuana during a seven-year period (Schaeffer et al., 1981).

Marijuana's entire story has not yet been told. Whereas certain horror stories about marijuana may have been exaggerated, one cannot assume that smoke containing 50 percent more carcinogenic hydrocarbon than tobacco smoke is completely harmless.

LSD **LSD** is the abbreviation for lysergic acid diethylamide, a synthetic hallucinogenic drug. Users of "acid" claim that it "expands consciousness" and opens new worlds. Sometimes people believe they have achieved great insights while using LSD, but when it wears off they often cannot apply or recall these discoveries.

LSD and similar hallucinogenics are used by about 6 percent of the high school population (Johnston, 1988). As a powerful hallucinogenic, LSD produces vivid and colorful hallucinations. LSD "trips" can be somewhat unpre-

Reverse tolerance Requirement of less of a substance to achieve the same effects that were previously attained with higher doses.

Amotivational syndrome Loss of ambition or motivation to achieve.

LSD Lysergic acid diethylamide. A hallucinogenic drug.

Flashbacks Distorted perceptions or hallucinations that occur days or weeks after LSD usage but mimic the LSD experience.

Mescaline A hallucinogenic drug derived from the mescal (peyote) cactus. In religious ceremonies, Mexican Indians chew the buttonlike structures at the tops of the rounded stems of the plant.

Phencyclidine (fen-SIKE-lid-dean). Another hallucinogenic drug whose name is an acronym for its chemical structure. Abbreviated *PCP*.

dictable. Some regular users have only good trips. Others have one bad trip and swear off. Regular users who have had no bad trips argue that people with bad trips were psychologically unstable prior to using LSD. In fairness, Barber's review of the literature (1970) suggests that rare psychotic symptoms are usually limited to people with a history of psychological problems.

Flashbacks Some LSD users have **flashbacks**—distorted perceptions or hallucinations that occur days, weeks, or longer after usage but mimic the LSD trip. It has been speculated that flashbacks stem from chemical changes in the brain produced by LSD, but Heaton and Victor (1976) and Matefy (1980) offer a psychological explanation for flashbacks.

Heaton and Victor (1976) found that users who have flashbacks are more oriented toward fantasy and allowing their thoughts to wander. They are also more likely to focus on internal sensations. If they should experience sensations similar to a past trip, they may readily label them flashbacks and allow themselves to focus on them indefinitely, causing an entire replay of the experience to unfold.

Matefy (1980) found that users who have flashbacks show greater capacity to become fully engrossed in role-playing, and hypothesized that flashbacks may be nothing more than enacting the role of being on a trip. This does not necessarily mean that people who claim to have flashbacks are lying. They may be more willing to surrender personal control in response to internal sensations for the sake of altering their consciousness and having peak experiences. Users who do not have flashbacks prefer to be more in charge of their thought processes and have greater concern for meeting the demands of daily life.

Other Hallucinogenics Other hallucinogenic drugs include **mescaline** (derived from the peyote cactus) and **phencyclidine** (PCP). Regular use of hallucinogenics may lead to tolerance and psychological dependence. But hallucinogenics are not known to lead to physiological dependence. High doses may induce frightening hallucinations, impaired coordination, poor judgment, mood changes, and paranoid delusions.

Let us now consider a number of ways of altering consciousness that do not involve drugs.

Meditation. People use many forms of meditation to try to expand inner awareness and experience inner harmony. The effects of meditation, like the effects of drugs, reflect both the bodily changes induced by meditation *and* the meditator's expectations.

ALTERING CONSCIOUSNESS THROUGH MEDITATION: WHEN EASTERN GODS MEET WESTERN TECHNOLOGY

Back to our mountaintop and our venerable guru. Counting your breaths is one form of meditation. The yogis stare intently at a pattern on a vase or a mandala. The ancient Egyptians stared at an oil-burning lamp—the origin of the fable of Aladdin's magic lamp. Turkish mystics referred to as "whirling dervishes" concentrate on their body movements and the rhythm of their breathing.

Although meditation methods vary, they seem to share the same cognitive thread: Through passive observation, the normal person–environment relationship is altered. Problem-solving, planning, worry, awareness of the events of the day are all suspended. In this way, consciousness—that is, the normal focuses of attention—is altered, and a state of relaxation is often induced. Meditators may report that they have "merged" with the object of meditation (the vase or a repeated phrase, for example) and then transcended it, leading to "oneness with the universe," rapture, or some great insight. Psychology has no way of measuring oneness with the universe, but psychologists can measure other changes, as we shall see. It is reasonable to believe that the effects of meditation, like the effects of drugs, reflect whatever bodily changes are induced by meditation *and* one's expectations about meditation.

Let us now turn our attention to **Transcendental Meditation** (TM), a simplified form of meditation brought to the United States by the Maharishi Mahesh Yogi in 1959. Hundreds of thousands of Americans practice TM by repeating **mantras,** words or sounds that are claimed to have the capacity to help one achieve an altered state of consciousness.

TM

Herbert Benson (1975) of Harvard Medical School studied TM practitioners aged 17 to 41—business people, students, artists. His subjects included people who had practiced TM for anywhere from a few weeks to nine years. Benson found no scientific evidence that TM expanded consciousness, despite the claims of many practitioners. However, TM did produce what Benson labeled a **relaxation response.** During TM, the body's metabolic rate dramatically decreased. The blood pressure of people with hypertension decreased (Benson et al., 1973). In fact, people who meditated twice daily tended to show normalized blood pressure through the entire day. Meditators produced more frequent alpha waves—brain waves associated with feelings of relaxation but infrequent during sleep. Benson's subjects also showed lower heart and respiration rates and a decrease in blood lactate, a substance whose presence has been linked to anxiety.

Truth or Fiction Revisited

It is true that people have managed to bring high blood pressure under control through meditation.

A Challenge to TM Other researchers agree that meditation lowers a person's level of arousal, but they argue that the same relaxing effects can be achieved by engaging in other relaxing activities (West, 1985) or even by resting quietly for the same amount of time (Holmes et al., 1983; Holmes, 1984, 1985). The Holmes group (1983) found no differences between experienced meditators and novice "resters" in heart rate, respiration rate, blood pressure, and sweat in the palms of the hands (that is, galvanic skin response, or GSR). Most critics of meditation do not argue that meditation is useless but rather that meditation may have no special effects as compared with a restful break from a tension-producing routine.

Note that formerly anxious and tense individuals who practice TM have also *chosen* to alter their stress-producing life styles by taking time out for themselves once or twice a day. Just taking this time out may be quite helpful.

The final word on meditation is not yet in (Suler, 1985). Still, if you wish to try meditating, you can try the following instructions.

Transcendental meditation The simplified form of meditation brought to the U.S.A. by the Maharishi Mahesh Yogi. Abbreviated *TM.*

Mantra (MON-truh). A word or sound that is repeated in TM. (A Sanskrit word that has the same origin as the word *mind.)*

Relaxation response Benson's term for a group of responses that can be brought about by meditation. They involve lowered activity of the sympathetic branch of the autonomic nervous system.

A CLOSER LOOK

How to Meditate

There is controversy concerning the effects of meditation. Although psychologists tend to agree that meditation helps us relax and can also normalize our blood pressure, it has not been shown that the effects of meditation are superior to those of resting quietly. However, if you want to gather some first-hand knowledge of the effects of meditation, you can try it out by using the following measures:

1. Begin by meditating once or twice daily for 10 to 20 minutes.
2. What you *don't* do is more important than what you do do. Adopt a passive, "what happens, happens" attitude.
3. Create a quiet, nondisruptive environment. For example, don't directly face a light.
4. Do not eat for an hour beforehand; avoid caffeine for at least two.
5. Assume a comfortable position. Change it as needed. It's okay to scratch or yawn.
6. For a concentrative device, you may focus on your breathing or seat yourself before a calming object such as a plant or burning incense. Benson suggests "perceiving" (rather than mentally saying) the word *one* on every outbreath. This means thinking the word, but "less actively" than usual (good luck). Carrington (1977) suggests thinking or perceiving the word *in* as you are inhaling and *out,* or *ah-h-h,* as you are exhaling. Carrington also suggests mantras such as *ah-nam, shi-rim,* and *ra-mah.*
7. If you are using a mantra, you can prepare for meditation and say the mantra out loud several times. Enjoy it. Then say it more and more softly. Close your eyes and think only the mantra. Allow yourself to perceive, rather than actively think, the mantra. Again, adopt a passive attitude. Continue to perceive the mantra. It may grow louder or softer, disappear for a while and then return.
8. If disruptive thoughts come in as you are meditating, you can allow them to "pass through." Don't get wrapped up in trying to squelch them, or you may raise your level of arousal.
9. Allow yourself to drift. (You won't go too far.) What happens, happens.
10. Above all, take what you get. You cannot force the relaxing effects of meditation. You can only set the stage for it and allow it to happen.

ALTERING CONSCIOUSNESS THROUGH BIOFEEDBACK: GETTING IN TOUCH WITH THE UNTOUCHABLE

There is little we can take for granted in life. A few decades ago, however, psychologists were reasonably secure with the distinction between *voluntary* and *involuntary* functions. Voluntary functions, like lifting an arm or leg,

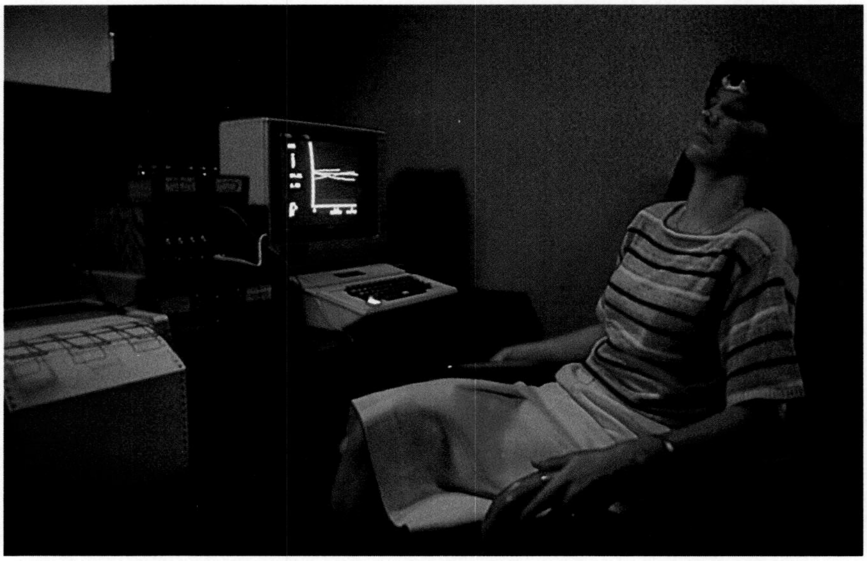

Biofeedback. Biofeedback is a system that provides, or "feeds back," information about a bodily function to an organism. Through biofeedback training, people have learned to gain voluntary control over a number of functions that are normally involuntary.

were conscious. They could be directly willed. But other functions, such as heart rate and blood pressure, were involuntary or autonomic. They were beyond conscious control. We could no more consciously control blood pressure than, say, purposefully emit alpha waves.

Once in a while, to be sure, we heard tales of strange "yoga" experts or other exotics who could make their hair stand literally on end or "will" their cheeks to stop bleeding after a nail had been put through. But such episodes were viewed as horror stories or stage tricks. Serious scientists went back to serious research—except for a handful of pioneering psychologists like Neal E. Miller of Rockefeller University. In the late 1960s, Miller trained laboratory rats to increase or decrease their heart rates voluntarily (Miller, 1969).

Miller implanted electrodes in the rats' pleasure centers. Then some rats were given electric shock whenever their heart rates happened to increase. Other rats received shock when their heart rates went lower. In other words, one group of rats was consistently "rewarded" (that is, shocked) when the rats' heart rates showed an increase. The other group was consistently rewarded for a decrease. After a single 90-minute training session, rats learned to alter their heart rates by as much as 20 percent in the direction for which they had been rewarded.

Miller's research was an early example of **biofeedback training** (BFT). Biofeedback is simply a system that provides, or "feeds back," information about a bodily function to an organism. Miller used electrical stimulation of the brain to feed back information to rats when they had engaged in a targeted bodily response (in this case, raised or lowered their heart rates).

Similarly, people have learned to voluntarily change various bodily functions, including heart rate, that were once considered to be beyond their control. However, electrodes are not implanted in people's brains. Rather, people hear a "blip" or observe some other signal that informs them when the targeted response is being displayed.

Biofeedback training The systematic feeding back to an organism of information about a bodily function so that the organism can gain control of that function. Abbreviated *BFT*.

Truth or Fiction Revisited

It is true that you can learn to increase or decrease your heart rate just by thinking about it. Biofeedback training can help you realize this aim.

Electromyograph An instrument that measures muscle tension. Abbreviated *EMG.* (From the Greek *mys,* meaning "mouse" and "muscle"—reflecting similarity between the movement of a mouse and the contraction of a muscle.)

Hypnosis (hip-NO-sis). A condition in which people appear to be highly suggestible and behave as though they are in a trance. (From the Greek *hypnos,* meaning "sleep.")

Hysterical disorders Disorders in which a bodily function is lost because of psychological rather than biological reasons. (Now referred to as conversion disorders; see Chapter 12.)

BFT is used in many ways. In Chapter 3 we learned how BFT can be used to help people regain control over various functions when nerve pathways have been damaged.

There are also many ways in which BFT helps people combat stress, tension, and anxiety (Budzynski & Stoyva, 1984). In one example, people can learn to emit alpha waves (and feel somewhat more relaxed) through feedback from an EEG. A blip may increase in frequency whenever alpha waves are being emitted. The psychologist's instructions are simply to "make the blip go faster." An **electromyograph** (EMG), which monitors muscle tension, is commonly used to help people become more aware of muscle tension in the forehead and elsewhere and to learn to lower this tension. Through the use of other instruments, people have learned to lower their heart rates, their blood pressure, and the amount of sweat in the palm of the hand. All of these changes are relaxing.

People have also learned to elevate the *temperature* of a finger. Why bother, you ask? It happens that limbs become subjectively warmer when more blood flows into them. Increasing the temperature of a finger—that is, altering patterns of blood flow in the body—helps some people control migraine headaches, which can stem from too great a flow of blood into the head. We shall learn more about migraine headaches in Chapter 11.

ALTERING CONSCIOUSNESS THROUGH HYPNOSIS

Perhaps you have seen films in which Count Dracula hypnotized resistant victims into a stupor. Then he could get on with a bite in the neck with no further nonsense. Perhaps a fellow student labored to place a friend in a "trance" after reading a book on hypnosis. Or perhaps you have seen an audience member hypnotized in a nightclub act. If so, chances are this person acted as if he or she had returned to childhood, imagined that a snake was about to have a nip, or lay rigid between two chairs for a while.

Hypnosis. Only recently has hypnosis become a respectable subject for psychological inquiry. Hypnotized subjects become passive and tend to deploy their attention according to the instructions of the hypnotist.

A Brief History

Hypnosis, a term derived from the Greek word for sleep, has only recently become a respectable subject for psychological inquiry. Hypnosis seems to have begun in its modern form with the ideas of Franz Mesmer in the eighteenth century. Mesmer asserted that the universe was connected by forms of magnetism—which may not be far from the mark. He claimed that people, too, could be drawn to one another by "animal magnetism." (No bullseye here.) Mesmer used bizarre props to bring people under his "spell." He did manage a respectable cure rate for minor ailments. But we skeptics are more likely to attribute his successes to the placebo effect than to animal magnetism.

During the second half of the last century, hypnosis contributed to the formation of psychoanalytic theory. Jean Martin Charcot, a French physician, had believed that **hysterical disorders,** such as hysterical blindness and paralysis, were caused by physical problems. When students were able to stimulate a normal woman to display hysterical symptoms through hypnosis, however, Charcot began to pursue psychological causes for hysterical behavior. One of his students, Pierre Janet, suggested that hysterical symptoms represented subconscious thoughts breaking through a "weakness in the nervous system."

The notion of subconscious roots for hysterical disorders was developed in Vienna, Austria. The physician Josef Breuer discovered that a female patient felt better about personal problems when he encouraged her to talk and express her feelings freely while hypnotized. Sigmund Freud later suggested that hypnosis was one avenue to the unconscious (he believed that dreams were another), and he used hypnosis to uncover what he thought were the unconscious roots of his patients' problems. Under hypnosis, for example, a number of his patients recalled traumatic childhood experiences, such as being seduced by a parent, that they could not remember during the normal state of consciousness.

Hypnotism Today Today hypnotism retains its popularity in nightclubs, but it is also used as an anesthetic in dentistry, childbirth, and even surgery. Psychologists may use hypnosis to teach clients how to relax or help them imagine vivid imagery in techniques like systematic desensitization, which we shall discuss at length in Chapter 13.

The Process of Hypnosis

The state of consciousness called the hypnotic trance is usually induced by asking subjects to narrow attention to a small light, a spot on the wall, an object held by the hypnotist, or just the hypnotist's voice. There are verbal suggestions that the limbs are becoming warm, heavy, and relaxed. (Suggestions of warmth and heaviness can induce blood flow into the limbs and help calm activity of the sympathetic division of the autonomic nervous system. It has been shown that *expecting* certain bodily changes—like changes in heart rate and skin temperature—can actually produce changes in that direction [Pennebaker & Skelton, 1981].) Subjects are also told that they are becoming sleepy or falling asleep.

Hypnosis is *not* sleep, as shown by differences in EEG recordings for the hypnotic trance and the stages of sleep. But the word *sleep* is understood by subjects to suggest a hypnotic trance and has a track record of success.

Hypnotic Suggestibility Hypnosis is most successful with people who understand what is expected of them during the "trance state." People who are readily hypnotized are said to have hypnotic suggestibility. Generally speaking, suggestible subjects have positive attitudes and expectations about hypnosis and want to be hypnotized (Barber et al., 1974).

Truth or Fiction Revisited

It is true that people who are easily hypnotized have positive attitudes toward hypnosis. They look forward to the experience and cooperate fully with the hypnotist.

Like LSD users who claim to experience flashbacks, people with high hypnotic suggestibility enjoy daydreaming and have highly vivid and absorbing imagination styles (Crawford, 1982).

Changes in Consciousness Brought About by Hypnosis

Hypnotists and hypnotized subjects report that hypnosis can bring about some or all of the following changes in consciousness.

Passivity When being hypnotized, or in a trance, subjects await instructions and appear to suspend planning.

Narrowed Attention Subjects may focus on the hypnotist's voice or a spot of light and avoid attending to background noise or intruding thoughts. It is claimed that subjects may not hear a loud noise behind the head if they are directed not to. (However, objective measures of hearing *do* suggest that subjects do not show any reduction in auditory sensitivity; rather they *report* greater deafness [Spanos et al., 1982].)

Hypermnesia Subjects may be instructed to show heightened memory, or **hypermnesia,** by focusing on selected details and then reconstructing an entire memory. This is the method used in police investigations. However, we may ask how accurate these memories are. A number of studies have shown that suggestible subjects "recall" more information under hypnosis than otherwise (Orne et al., 1984) but that this information is frequently incorrect (Dwyan & Bowers, 1983; Nogrady et al., 1985). Nevertheless, hypnotized subjects tend to report the incorrect information with confidence (Sheehan & Tilden, 1983), which may throw off police investigators or juries.

Suggestibility Subjects may respond to suggestions that an arm is becoming lighter and will rise or that the eyelids are becoming heavier and must close. They may act as though they cannot unlock hands clasped by the hypnotist or bend an arm "made rigid" by the hypnotist. Hypnotized subjects serving as witnesses are also highly open to the suggestions of their interviewers. They may incorporate ideas and images presented by interviewers into their "memories" and report them as facts (Laurence & Perry, 1983).

Playing Unusual Roles Most subjects expect to play sleepy, relaxed roles, but they may also be able to play roles calling for increased strength or alertness, such as riding a bicycle with less fatigue than usual (Banyai & Hilgard, 1976). In **age regression,** subjects may play themselves as infants or children. Research shows that many supposed childhood memories and characteristics are played inaccurately. Nonetheless, some subjects show excellent recall of such details as hair style or speech pattern. A subject may speak a language forgotten since childhood.

Perceptual Distortions Hypnotized subjects may act as though hypnotically induced hallucinations and delusions are real. In the "thirst hallucination," for example, subjects act as if they are parched, even if they have just had a drink. Or subjects may behave as though they cannot hear loud noises or smell odors (Zamansky & Bartis, 1985).

Posthypnotic Amnesia Many subjects act as though they cannot recall events that took place under hypnosis, or even recall that they were

---

Hypermnesia (high-purr-KNEE-she-uh). Greatly enhanced memory.

Age regression In hypnosis, taking on the role of childhood, commonly accompanied by vivid recollections of one's past.

hypnotized at all, if so directed. However, subjects can usually recall what occurred if they are hypnotized again and instructed by the hypnotist to do so (Kihlstrom et al., 1985).

The results of at least one experiment suggest that it may be advisable to take the phenomenon of posthypnotic amnesia with a grain of salt. Subjects are more likely to report recalling events while "under a trance" when they are subjected to a lie-detector test and led to believe that they will be found out if they are faking (Coe & Yashinski, 1985).

Posthypnotic Suggestion Subjects may follow instructions according to prearranged cues of which they are supposedly unaware. For instance, a subject may be directed to fall again into a deep trance upon the single command, "Sleep!" Smokers frequently seek the help of hypnotists to break their habits, and they are frequently given the suggestion that upon "waking," cigarette smoke will become aversive. They may also be instructed to forget that this idea originated with the hypnotist.

Theories of Hypnosis

Psychodynamic Theory According to Sigmund Freud's psychodynamic theory, the hypnotic trance represents **regression.** Hypnotized adults suspend "ego functioning," or conscious control of their behavior. They permit themselves to return to childish modes of responding that emphasize fantasy and impulse rather than fact and logic.

Role Theory Theodore Sarbin (1972) offers a **role theory** view of hypnosis (Sarbin & Coe, 1972). He points out that the changes in behavior that are attributed to the hypnotic trance can be successfully imitated when subjects are instructed to behave *as though* they were hypnotized. Also, people cannot be hypnotized unless they are familiar with the hypnotic "role"—the set of behaviors that supposedly constitute the trance. Sarbin is not insisting that hypnotic subjects *fake* the hypnotic role. He is suggesting, instead, that they allow themselves to enact this role under the hypnotist's directions.

Research findings that "suggestible" hypnotic subjects are motivated to enact the hypnotic role (Barber et al., 1974), are good role players, and have vivid and absorbing imagination styles (Crawford, 1982) would all seem to be supportive of role theory.

Neodissociation Theory Ernest Hilgard (1977) explains hypnotic phenomena through **neodissociation theory.** This is the view that we can selectively focus our attention on one thing (like hypnotic suggestions) and still perceive other things "subconsciously." In a sense, we do this all the time. We are not fully conscious, or aware, of everything going on about us. Rather, at any moment we selectively focus on events, like tests, dates, or television shows, that seem important or relevant. Yet while taking a test, we may be peripherally aware of the color of the wall or of the sound of rain.

According to neodissociation theory, when people are hypnotized, they selectively attend to the hypnotist, yet they perceive other events subconsciously or peripherally. When told to forget that they were hypnotized, they focus on other matters. But the experience of hypnosis can be focused on afterward. Let us assume a person in a "trance" is given the posthypnotic suggestion to fall into a trance again upon hearing "Sleep" but not to recall the fact that he or she was given this command. Upon "waking," the person

Regression Return to a form of behavior characteristic of an earlier stage of development. See Chapter 9.

Role theory A theory that explains hypnotic events in terms of the person's ability to act *as though* he or she were hypnotized. Role theory differs from faking in that subjects cooperate and focus on hypnotic suggestions instead of pretending to be hypnotized.

Neodissociation theory A theory that explains hypnotic events in terms of subconscious perception of events. People can focus selectively on hypnotic suggestions but still perceive outside sources of stimulation.

does not focus on the posthypnotic suggestion. However, hearing the command "Sleep!" leads to rapid refocusing of attention and return to the trance. These thoughts are all, in a sense, separated or dissociated from each other. Yet the person's attention can focus rapidly on one, then another.

According to Hilgard, this subconscious level of perception functions as though we had "hidden observers" in us. Hilgard has run experiments in which hypnotized subjects immersed their left hands into buckets of ice water and verbally reported no sensation. Through **automatic writing** with the right hand, these subjects recorded painful coldness. Similarly, subjects have not responded to sudden loud noises when hypnotized, but their hidden observers have recorded them through automatic writing.

Note that role theory and neodissociation theory are not suggesting that the phenomena of hypnosis do not occur. Instead, they suggest that we do not need to explain these events through an altered state of awareness called a trance. Hypnosis may not be special at all. Rather, it is *we* who are special—through our great imaginations, our role-playing ability, and our capacity to divide our consciousness—concentrating now on one event we deem important, concentrating later on another.

Automatic writing Writing about perceived stimulation while the major portion of a person's attention is focused elsewhere.

SUMMARY

1. **What is consciousness?** The term *consciousness* has several meanings, including (1) sensory awareness, (2) direct inner awareness of cognitive processes, (3) personal unity or the sense of self, and (4) the waking state.

2. **What are the stages of sleep?** Electroencephalograph (EEG) records show different stages of sleep as characterized by different brain waves. There are four stages of non-rapid-eye-movement (NREM) sleep and one stage of REM sleep. Stage 1 sleep is lightest, and stage 4 is deepest.

3. **What are the functions of sleep?** Sleep apparently serves a restorative function, but we do not know exactly how sleep restores us or how much sleep we need.

4. **What are dreams?** Dreams are forms of cognitive activity that occur mostly while we are sleeping, and most take place during REM sleep.

5. **What are the sleep disorders?** Sleep disorders include insomnia, which is most often encountered by people who are anxious and tense, narcolepsy, apnea, sleep terrors, bedwetting, and sleepwalking. Sleep terrors usually occur during deep sleep. Bedwetting and sleepwalking are problems of childhood that usually come to an end as the child matures.

6. **What are substance abuse and substance dependence?** Substance abuse is defined as usage that impairs social or occupational functioning. Substance dependence is characterized by physiological dependence, as evidenced by tolerance or by an abstinence syndrome upon withdrawal.

7. **Why do people abuse drugs?** People usually try drugs because of curiosity, but usage can be reinforced by anxiety reduction, feelings of euphoria, and other sensations. People are also motivated to avoid withdrawal symptoms once they become physiologically dependent. Some people may have genetic predispositions to become physiologically dependent on certain substances.

8. **What are depressants?** The group of substances called depressants acts by slowing the activity of the central nervous system.

9. **What are the effects of alcohol?** Alcohol is an intoxicating depressant that leads to physiological dependence. Alcohol provides people with an excuse for failure or for antisocial behavior, but it has not been shown to induce antisocial behavior directly. As a depressant, alcohol also decreases sexual response.

10. **What are the effects of opiates and opioids?** The opiates morphine and heroin are depressants that reduce pain, but they are also bought on the street because of the euphoric rush they provide. Opiates and opioids lead to physiological dependence.

11. **What are the effects of barbiturates?** Barbiturates are depressants used to treat epilepsy, high blood pressure, anxiety, and insomnia. They lead rapidly to physiological dependence.

12. **What are stimulants?** Stimulants are substances that act by increasing the activity of the nervous system.

13. **What are the effects of amphetamines?** Amphetamines are stimulants that produce feelings of euphoria when taken in high doses. But high doses may also cause restlessness, insomnia, psychotic symptoms, and a "crash" upon withdrawal.

14. **What are the effects of cocaine?** As a psychoactive substance, cocaine provides feelings of euphoria and bolsters self-confidence. Cocaine causes sudden rises in blood pressure and constricts blood vessels. Overdoses can lead to restlessness, insomnia, psychotic reactions, and cardiorespiratory collapse.

15. **What are the effects of smoking cigarettes?** Cigarette smoke contains carbon monoxide, hydrocarbons, and the stimulant nicotine. Regular smokers adjust their smoking to maintain a consistent blood level of nicotine, suggestive of physiological dependence. Cigarette smoking has been linked to death from heart disease, cancer, and many other disorders.

16. **What are hallucinogenics?** Hallucinogenic substances produce hallucinations—sensations and perceptions in the absence of external stimulation.

17. **What are the effects of marijuana?** Marijuana is a hallucinogenic whose active ingredients, including THC, often produce heightened and distorted perceptions, relaxation, feelings of empathy, and reports of new insights. Hallucinations are possible.

18. **What are the effects of LSD?** LSD is a hallucinogenic drug that produces vivid hallucinations. So-called LSD flashbacks may reflect psychological factors, like interest in attending to internal sensations and fantasy.

19. **What is meditation?** In meditation, one focuses "passively" on an object or a mantra in order to alter the normal person–environment relationship. In this way, consciousness (that is, the normal focuses of attention) is altered and relaxation is often induced.

20. **What is biofeedback?** Biofeedback is a method for increasing consciousness of bodily functions in which an organism is continuously provided with information about a targeted biological response, such as heart rate or emission of alpha waves. Through biofeedback training, people and lower animals have learned to control a number of autonomic functions consciously.

21. **What is hypnosis?** Hypnosis is an altered state of consciousness in which subjects show passivity, narrowed attention, hypermnesia (heightened memory), suggestibility, assumption of unusual roles, perceptual distortions, posthypnotic amnesia, and posthypnotic suggestion.

22. **How do psychologists explain hypnosis?** Current theories of hypnosis deny the existence of a special trance state. Rather, they emphasize our abilities to assume roles with which we are familiar and to divide our awareness so that we focus now on one event, now on another, as our attention is redirected by the hypnotist.

PSYCHOLOGY AND MODERN LIFE

Insomnia and smoking cigarettes are two of the banes of modern life. As noted in the chapter, insomnia is compounded by anxieties and stress. Life is filled with stressful hassles, changes, and frustrations, as we shall see in Chapter 11. And despite knowledge that cigarette smoking is, as Surgeon General Koop put it, "the chief preventable cause of death," millions of us smoke. We also tend to smoke more when we are under stress.

So in this section we shall outline psychology's contributions in helping people get to sleep and stay asleep and in helping people cut down on and quit smoking.

Coping with Insomnia: How *(and How Not)* to Get to Sleep at Night

In this section we shall consider methods innovated by psychologists to help people get to sleep. First, though, let us take a side trip and discuss sleeping pills.

No question about it: The most common medical method for fighting insomnia in the United States is popping pills. Sleeping pills may be effective—for a while. They generally work by reducing arousal. At first lowered arousal may be effective in itself. Focusing on changes in arousal may also distract you from your efforts to *get* to sleep. Expectation of success may also help.

But there are problems with sleeping pills. First, because you attribute your success to the pill and not to yourself, you create dependency on the pill rather than self-reliance. Second, you develop tolerance for sleeping pills. With regular use you must progress to higher doses to achieve the same effects. Third, high doses of these chemicals can be dangerous, especially if mixed with an alcoholic beverage or two.

Relaxing Recently, psychological methods for coping with insomnia have been developed. Some of these methods reduce tension directly, as in the case of muscle-relaxation exercises. Psychological methods also divert us from the "task" of trying somehow to *get* to sleep, which, of course, is one of the ways in which we keep ourselves awake. Instead, we need only recline when we are tired and allow sleep to happen.

Focusing on releasing muscle tension has been shown to reduce the amount of time needed to fall asleep and the incidence of waking during the night. It increases the number of hours slept and leaves us feeling more rested in the morning (Lick & Heffler, 1977; Weil & Gottfried, 1973). A common method for easing muscle tension is progressive relaxation, which we shall discuss in Chapter 11. Biofeedback training (Haynes et al., 1977) and autogenic training (Nicassio & Bootzin, 1974) have also been used successfully. Biofeedback for falling asleep usually focuses on reducing muscle tensions in the forehead or in the arms, but there has also been some success in teaching people to produce the kinds of brain waves that are associated with relaxation and sleep. In autogenic training, one reduces muscle tension by focusing on suggestions that the limbs are growing warm and heavy and that the breathing is becoming regular.

Coping with Exaggerated Fears You need not be a sleep expert to realize that convincing yourself that the day will be ruined unless you get to sleep *right now* will increase, rather than decrease, bedtime tensions. As noted earlier, sleep does seem to restore us, especially after physical exertion. But we often exaggerate the problems that will befall us if we do not sleep. Here are some beliefs that increase bedtime tension and some alternatives that may be of use to you:

Exaggerated Belief	Alternative Belief
If I don't get to sleep, I'll feel wrecked tomorrow.	Not necessarily. If I'm tired, I can go to bed early tomorrow night.
It's unhealthy for me not to get more sleep.	Not necessarily. Some people do very well on only a few hours of sleep.
I'll wreck my sleeping schedule for the whole week if I don't get to sleep very soon.	Not at all. If I'm tired, I'll just go to bed a bit earlier. I'll get up about the same time with no problem.
If I don't get to sleep, I won't be able to concentrate on that big test/conference tomorrow.	Possibly, but my fears may be exaggerated. I may just as well relax or get up and do something enjoyable for a while.

Avoiding Ruminating in Bed Don't plan or worry about tomorrow in bed. When you lie down for sleep, you may organize thoughts for the day for a few minutes, but then allow yourself to relax or engage in fantasy. If an important idea comes to you, jot it down on a handy pad so that you won't lose it. If thoughts persist, however, get up and follow them elsewhere. Let your bed be a place for relaxation and sleep—not your study. A bed—even a waterbed—is not a think tank.

Establishing a Regular Routine Sleeping late can encourage sleep-onset insomnia. Set your alarm for the same time each morning and get up, regardless of how many hours you have slept. By sticking to a regular time for rising, you'll be indirectly encouraging yourself to get to sleep at a regular time as well.

Using Fantasy Psychologist Jerome Singer (1975) notes that fantasies or "daydreams" are almost universal and may occur naturally as we fall asleep. You can allow yourself to "go with" fantasies that occur at bedtime, or purposefully use fantasies to get to sleep. You may be able to ease yourself to sleep by focusing on a sun-drenched beach, with waves lapping on the shore, or on a walk through a mountain meadow on a summer day. You can construct your own "mind trips" and paint their details finely. With mind trips you conserve fuel and avoid lines at airports.

Quitting and Cutting Down on Smoking

When it comes to stopping smoking, common sense is also good psychology. People who successfully cut their cigarette use by at least 50 percent are more highly motivated and committed to cutting down than would-be reducers (Perri et al., 1977).

Evidence is mixed as to whether it is more effective to cut down gradually or quit all at once. Going cold turkey (quitting all at once) is more effective for some smokers (Flaxman, 1978), but cutting down gradually is more effective for others (Glasgow et al., 1984). Although it is most healthful to quit smoking completely, some smokers who have not been able to quit have learned to reduce their cigarette consumption by at least 50 percent. Also, they have stuck to their lower levels for up to two and a half years (Glasgow et al., 1983, 1985).

Strategies for Quitting Given the determination to quit, you or your friends may find it helpful to try some of the following suggestions:

- Tell your family and friends that you're quitting—make a public commitment.
- Think of specific things to tell yourself when you feel the urge to smoke: how you'll be stronger, free of fear of cancer, ready for the marathon, etc.
- Tell yourself that the first few days are the hardest—after that, withdrawal symptoms weaken dramatically.
- Remind yourself that you're "superior" to nonquitters.
- Start when you wake up, at which time you've already gone eight hours without nicotine.
- Go on a smoke-ending vacation to get away from places and situations in which you're used to smoking.
- Throw out ashtrays and don't allow smokers to visit you at home for a while.
- Don't carry matches or light other people's cigarettes.
- Sit in nonsmokers' sections of restaurants and trains.
- Fill your days with novel activities—things that won't remind you of smoking.
- Use sugar-free mints, cinnamon sticks, or gum as substitutes for cigarettes (don't light them).*
- Buy yourself presents with all that cash you're socking away.

Strategies for Cutting Down

- Count your cigarettes to establish your smoking baseline.
- Set concrete goals for controlled smoking. For example, plan to cut down baseline consumption by at least 50 percent.
- Gradually restrict the settings in which you allow yourself to smoke (see Chapter 13).
- Get involved in activities where smoking isn't allowed or practical.
- Switch to a brand you don't like. Hold your cigarettes with your nondominant hand only.
- Keep only enough cigarettes to meet the (reduced) daily goal. Never buy more than a pack at a time.
- Use sugar-free candies or gum as a substitute for a few cigarettes each day.
- Jog instead of having a cigarette. Or walk, swim, or make love.
- Pause before lighting up. Put the cigarette in an ashtray between puffs. Ask yourself before each puff if you really want more. If not, throw the cigarette away.
- Put the cigarette out before you reach the end. (No more eating the filter.)
- Gradually lengthen the amount of time between cigarettes.
- Imagine living a prolonged, noncoughing life. Ah, freedom!
- As you smoke, picture blackened lungs, coughing fits, the possibilities of cancer and other lung diseases.

And those of you who are seeking an "instant cure" for smoking may be interested in the following information. However, you will see that the "magic" lies in our changing the way in which we interpret or structure our experiences—a method that is used by cognitive therapists.

*There is a nicotine gum available that may be of use to some smokers who are heavily physiologically dependent on nicotine, especially when combined with behavioral techniques (Hall et al., 1985). The gum decreases withdrawal symptoms by providing a source of nicotine, but it does not contain hydrocarbons or carbon monoxide.

Cognitive Restructuring: An Instant Cure for Smoking? Let us assume that you are convinced that smoking is bad for your health and that you would like to quit if you could. Unfortunately, like many others, you question whether you have the willpower.

Well, then, what if there were an instant cure for smoking? A cure that was guaranteed to help you through the abstinence syndrome . . . with just one hitch?

The hitch? Some side effects. For two to three days after taking the cure, some people complain of nervousness and drowsiness, some of headaches, insomnia, or constipation. But these side effects are usually gone within a week. Considering the alternatives—fear of cancer and heart disease, the cost of cigarettes, the humiliation of being unable to quit—wouldn't "the cure" be worth it?

The instant cure exists and is readily available. It's called stopping smoking. I've simply described some common withdrawal symptoms. Sarbin and Nucci (1973) point out that we need not look upon these symptoms as being awful. They are, after all, signs that the body is recovering from the effects of smoking.

Cognitive psychologists suggest that our interpretation of bodily sensations is central in coping with abstinence from any drug. Reinterpretation of sensations of hunger is also helpful in curbing overeating. We can cognitively restructure temporary, unpleasant sensations as signs that we are *winning,* not as disasters that must be avoided at all costs. After all, we wouldn't be experiencing them if we had not marshalled our will power to take action that we believed was good for us.

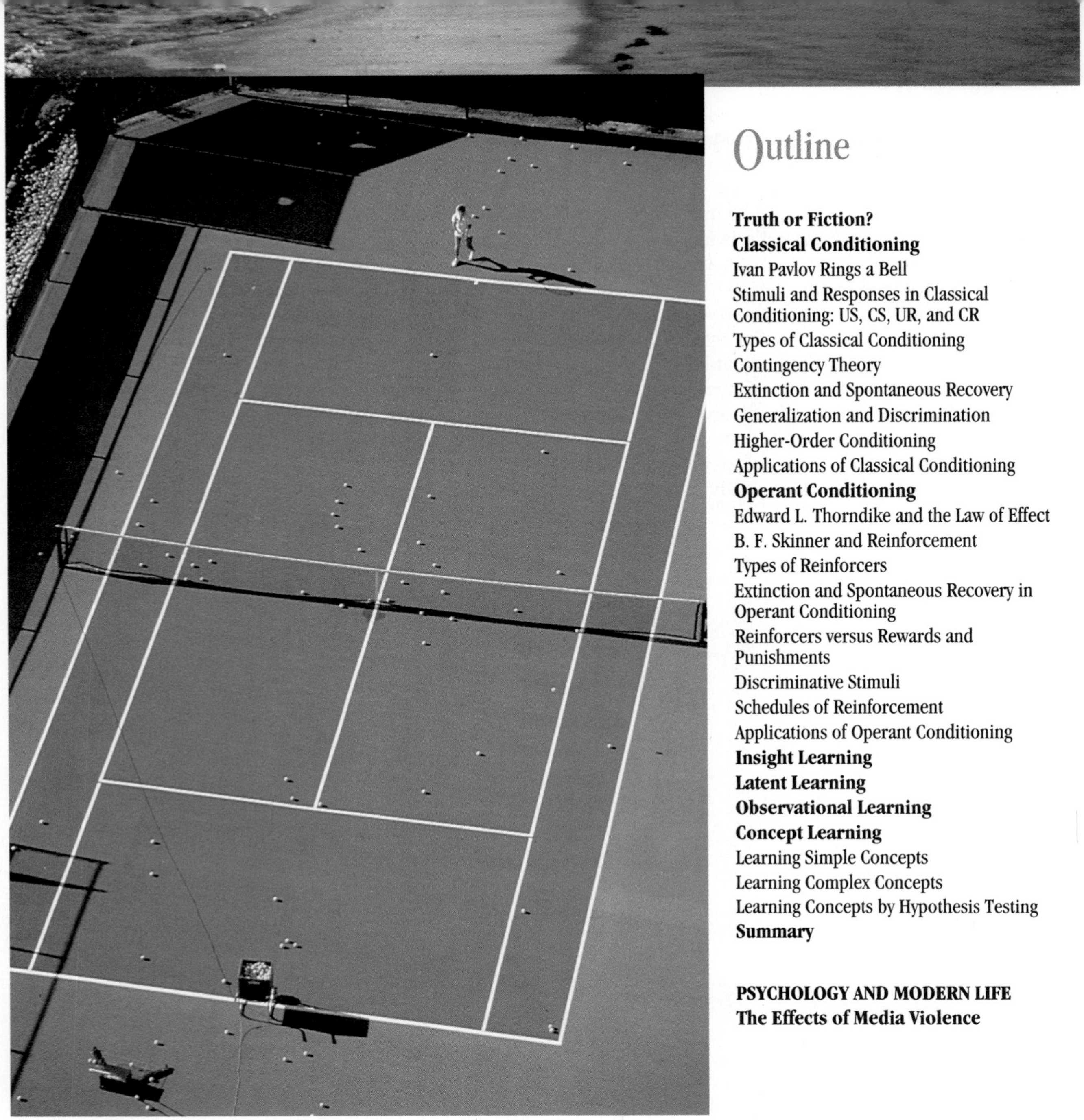

Outline

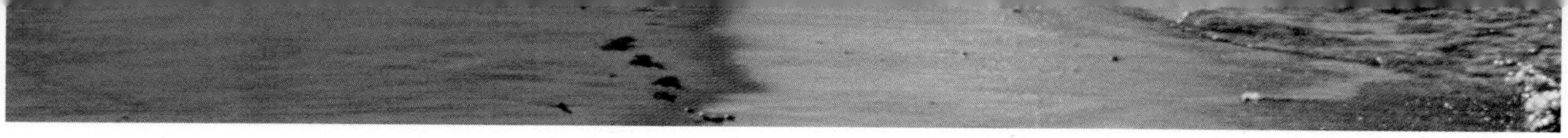

5 Learning

Truth or Fiction?

- □ You can develop an aversion to a food that lasts for months or years on the basis of one nauseating meal.
- □ Dogs can be trained to salivate when a bell is sounded.
- □ Psychologists helped a young boy overcome fear of rabbits by having him eat cookies while a rabbit was brought nearer.
- □ During World War II, a psychologist devised a plan for training pigeons to guide missiles to their targets.
- □ Punishment does not work.
- □ You can "hook" people on gambling by allowing them to win some money in the early stages and then tapering off with the payoffs.
- □ Rats can be trained to climb a ramp, cross a bridge, climb a ladder, pedal a toy car, and do several other tasks—all in proper sequence.
- □ Psychologists successfully fashioned a method to teach an emaciated 9-month-old infant to stop throwing up.
- □ We must make mistakes if we are to learn.
- □ Only people are capable of insight.

When I was a child in The Bronx, my friends and I would go to the movies on Saturday mornings. There would be a serial ("Rocketman" was my favorite) followed by a feature film, and admission was a quarter. We would also eat candy (I loved Nonpareils and Raisinets) and popcorn. One morning my friends dared me to eat two large containers of buttered popcorn by myself. For reasons that I label "youth," I rose to the challenge. Down went an enormous container of buttered popcorn. More slowly—much more slowly—I stuffed down the second. Predictably, I felt bloated and nauseated. The taste of the butter, corn, and salt lingered in my mouth and nose, and my head spun with the repulsive sensations. It was obvious to me that I would have no more popcorn that day. However, I was surprised that I could not face buttered popcorn again for a year.

Years later I learned that psychologists referred to my response to buttered popcorn as a *taste aversion.* Although I could not analyze my reaction in a sophisticated fashion at the time, I recognized that there was something strange about it. As I thought of it then, my "head" was telling me one thing about the popcorn while my "stomach" was telling me another. On a cognitive level, I recognized that my feelings stemmed from eating too much buttered popcorn and that smaller amounts would be safe. But something had also apparently been learned on a "gut level" that overrode my belief that I should be able to eat and enjoy reasonable amounts of buttered popcorn.

Now I know that a **taste aversion** is an example of *classical conditioning.* Classical conditioning leads organisms to anticipate events. An "overdose" of buttered popcorn had made me queasy. Afterward, the sight and odor of buttered popcorn—even the thought of it—was sufficient to make me anticipate nausea. In fact, they induced sensations of nausea in my throat and stomach. My aversion seemed silly at the time, but it is adaptive for organisms to develop taste aversions readily. Often when foods make us ill, it is because they are poisoned or unhealthful for other reasons. A taste aversion serves the adaptive function of keeping us away from them.

After I had acquired my taste aversion, I stayed away from buttered popcorn. My avoidance could be explained in terms of another kind of learning, *operant conditioning,* in which organisms learn to do things, and not to do other things, because of the consequences of their behavior. I stayed away from buttered popcorn in order to avoid anticipated nausea. But we also seek fluids when thirsty, sex when aroused, and an ambient temperature of 68 to 70 degrees Fahrenheit because we anticipate pleasant consequences. Put briefly, classical conditioning focuses on how organisms form anticipations about their environments. Operant conditioning focuses on what they do about them.

By the way, more than 30 years have now passed—how many more is my business. But I still prefer my popcorn *un*buttered today, although I enjoy butter on other foods.

Truth or Fiction Revisited

It is true that you can develop an aversion to a food that lasts for months or years on the basis of one nauseating meal.

Classical and operant conditioning are two forms of learning, which is the subject of this chapter. In lower organisms, much behavior is instinctive, or inborn. Fish are born "knowing" how to swim. Salmon instinctively return to spawn in the streams of their birth after they have matured and spent years roaming the deep seas. Robins instinctively know how to sing the songs of their species and to build nests. Rats instinctively mate and rear their young. Among people, however, the variety and complexity of behavior patterns are largely learned through experience. Experience is essential in our learning to walk and in our acquisition of the languages of our parents and communities. We learn to read, to do mathematical computations, and to symbolically rotate geometric figures. We learn to seek out the foods valued in our cultures when we are hungry. We "get into the habit" of starting our days with coffee, tea, or other beverages. We learn which behavior patterns are deemed socially acceptable and which are considered wrong. And, of course, our families and communities use verbal guidance, set examples, and apply rewards and punishments in an effort to teach us to stick to the straight and narrow.

Sometimes our learning experiences are direct, as was my taste aversion for buttered popcorn. But we can also learn from the experiences of others. For example, I warn my children against the perils of jumping from high

---

Taste aversion A kind of classical conditioning in which a previously desirable or neutral food becomes repugnant because it is associated with aversive stimulation.

places and running wild in the house. (Occasionally they heed me.) We learn about the past, about other peoples, and about how to put things together from books and visual media. And we learn as we invent ways of doing things that have never been done before.

Having noted these various ways of learning, let me admit that the very definition of **learning** stirs controversy in psychology. The concept may be defined in different ways.

From the behaviorist perspective, learning is defined as a relatively permanent change in behavior that arises from experience. Changes in behavior also arise from maturation and physical changes, but they are not considered to reflect learning. The behaviorist definition is operational. Learning is defined in terms of the measurable events or changes in behavior by which it is known. From the behaviorist perspective, buttered popcorn came to evoke nausea because it was temporally associated with nausea. I also learned to avoid popcorn because of the temporal consequences of consuming it—simple and not-so-sweet.

From the cognitive perspective, learning involves processes by which experience contributes to relatively permanent changes in the way organisms mentally represent the environment. Changes in representation may influence but do not cause changes in behavior. From this perspective, learning is *made evident* by behavioral change, but learning is defined as an internal and not directly observable process. From the cognitive perspective, my gorging on buttered popcorn taught me to regard, or mentally represent, buttered popcorn in a different way. My altered image of buttered popcorn then encouraged me to avoid it for a while. But my avoidance was not mechanical or imperative.

Behaviorists do not concern themselves with the ways in which I mentally represent buttered popcorn. (And who can fault them?) They argue that there is no direct way of measuring my mental imagery, only my overt behavior. So why try to embrace imagery in a scientific theory?

Let us now focus on some of the particulars of a number of kinds of learning, beginning with classical conditioning. We shall return to these theoretical matters from time to time as well.

CLASSICAL CONDITIONING

Classical conditioning involves some of the ways in which we learn to associate events. Consider: We have a distinct preference for having instructors grade our papers with A's rather than F's. We are also (usually) more likely to stop our cars for red than green traffic lights. Why? We are not born with instinctive attitudes toward the letters A and F. Nor are we born knowing that red means stop and green means go. We learn the meanings of these symbols because they are associated with other events. A's are associated with instructor approval and the likelihood of getting into graduate school. Red lights are associated with avoiding accidents and traffic citations.

Ivan Pavlov Rings a Bell

Lower animals also learn relationships among events, as Russian physiologist Ivan Pavlov (1849–1936) discovered in research with laboratory dogs. Pavlov was attempting to identify neural receptors in the mouth that triggered a response from the salivary glands. But his efforts were hampered by the

Learning (1) According to behaviorists, a relatively permanent change in behavior that results from experience. (2) According to cognitive theorists, the process by which organisms make relatively permanent changes in the way they represent the environment because of experience. These changes influence the organism's behavior but do not fully determine it.

Ivan Pavlov. Pavlov, his assistants, and a professional salivator (the dog) at a Russian academy early in the century.

dogs' salivating at undesired times, such as when a laboratory assistant inadvertently clanged a food tray.

Because of its biological makeup, a dog will salivate if meat powder is placed on its tongue. Salivation in response to meat powder is unlearned, a **reflex.** Reflexes are elicited by a certain range of stimuli. A **stimulus** is an environmental condition that evokes a response from an organism, such as meat powder on the tongue or a traffic light's changing colors. Reflexes are simple unlearned responses to stimuli. Pavlov discovered that reflexes can also be learned, or conditioned, through association. His dogs began salivating in response to clinking food trays because this noise, in the past, had been paired repeatedly with the arrival of food. The dogs would also salivate when an assistant entered the laboratory. Why? In the past the assistant had brought food.

When we are faced with novel events, we sometimes have no immediate way of knowing whether or not they are important. When we are striving for concrete goals, we often ignore the unexpected, even when the unexpected is just as important, or more important, than the goal. So it was that Pavlov at first saw this uncalled-for canine salivation as an annoyance, a hindrance to his research. But in 1901, he decided that his "problem" was worth looking into. He then set about to show that he could train, or condition, his dogs to salivate when he wished and in response to any stimulus he chose.

Pavlov termed these trained salivary responses "conditional reflexes." They were *conditional* upon the repeated pairing of a previously neutral stimulus (such as the clinking of a food tray) and a stimulus (in this case, food) that predictably evoked the target response (in this case, salivation). Today conditional reflexes are more generally referred to as **conditioned responses** (CRs). They are responses to previously neutral stimuli that are learned, or conditioned.

Pavlov demonstrated conditioned responses by strapping a dog into a harness such as the one in Figure 5.1. When meat powder was placed on the dog's tongue, the dog salivated. Pavlov repeated the process several times, with one difference. He preceded the meat powder by half a second or so with the sounding of a bell on each occasion. After several pairings of meat powder and bell, Pavlov sounded the bell but did *not* follow the bell with the meat powder. Still the dog salivated. It had learned to salivate in response to the bell.

Reflex A simple unlearned response to a stimulus.

Stimulus An environmental condition that elicits a response.

Conditioned response (CR) In classical conditioning, a learned response to a conditioned stimulus.

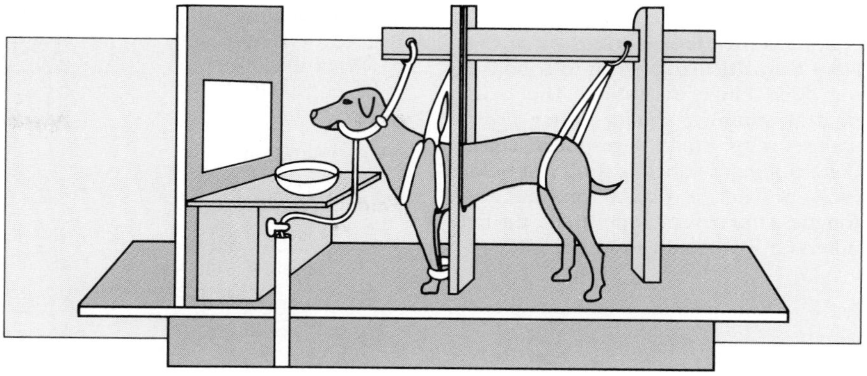

Figure 5.1
Pavlov's Demonstration of Conditioned Reflexes in Laboratory Dogs. From behind the two-way mirror at the left, a laboratory assistant rings a bell and then places meat powder on the dog's tongue. After several pairings, the dog salivates in response to the bell alone. A tube collects saliva and passes it to a vial. The quantity of saliva is taken as a measure of the strength of the animal's response.

Truth or Fiction Revisited

It is true that dogs can be trained to salivate when a bell is rung, a buzzer is sounded, a light is shone, and so on.

Why did the dog learn to salivate in response to the bell? Behaviorists and cognitive psychologists explain the learning process in very different ways.

Behaviorists explain the outcome of **classical conditioning** in terms of the publicly observable conditions of learning. They define classical conditioning as a simple form of learning in which one stimulus comes to evoke the response usually evoked by a second stimulus by being paired repeatedly with the second stimulus. In Pavlov's demonstration, the dog learned to salivate in response to the bell *because* the sounding of the bell had been paired with meat powder. That is, in classical conditioning, the organism forms associations between stimuli because the stimuli are **contiguous.** Behaviorists do *not* say that the dog "knew" that food was on the way. They argue that we cannot speak meaningfully about what a dog "knows." We can only outline the conditions under which targeted behaviors will reliably occur.

Cognitive psychologists view classical conditioning as the learning of relationships among events so as to allow an organism to represent its environment (Rescorla, 1988). In Pavlov's demonstration, the dog salivated in response to the bell because the bell—from the cognitive perspective—had become *represented* as being related to the meat powder. The cognitive focus is on the information gained by organisms. Organisms are viewed as seekers of information who integrate new information with the old in order to refine their representations of the world.

Classical conditioning (1) According to behaviorists, a form of learning in which one stimulus comes to evoke the response usually evoked by a second stimulus by being paired repeatedly with the second stimulus. (2) According to cognitive theorists, the learning of relationships among events so as to allow an organism to represent its environment. Also referred to as *respondent conditioning* or *Pavlovian conditioning.*

Contiguous Next to one another.

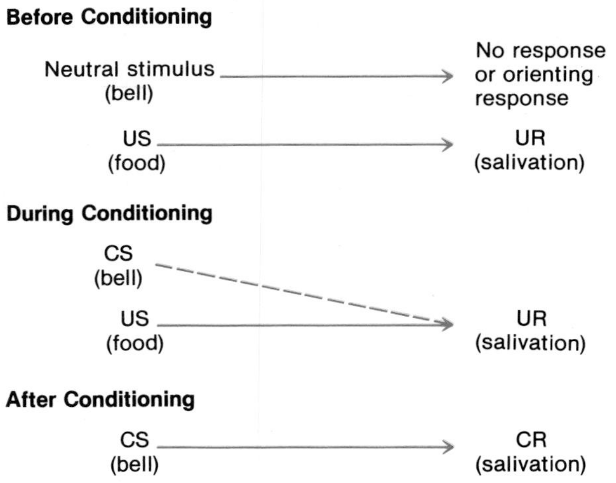

Figure 5.2
A Schematic Representation of Classical Conditioning. Prior to conditioning, food elicits salivation. The bell, a neutral stimulus, elicits either no response or an orienting response. During conditioning, the bell is rung just before meat powder is placed on the dog's tongue. After several repetitions, the bell, now a CS, elicits salivation, the CR.

Stimuli and Responses in Classical Conditioning: US, CS, UR, and CR

In the demonstration just described, the meat powder is an unlearned or **unconditioned stimulus** (US). Salivation in response to the meat powder is an unlearned or **unconditioned response** (UR). The bell was at first a meaningless or neutral stimulus. It might have produced an **orienting reflex** in the dog because of its distinctness. But it was not yet associated with food. Then, through repeated association with the meat powder, the bell became a learned or **conditioned stimulus** (CS) for the salivation response. Salivation in response to the *bell (or CS)* is a learned or conditioned response (CR). A CR is a response similar to a UR, but the response elicited by the CS is by definition a CR, not a UR (see Figure 5.2).

Unconditioned stimulus (US) A stimulus that elicits a response from an organism prior to conditioning.

Unconditioned response (UR) An unlearned response to an unconditioned stimulus.

Orienting reflex An unlearned response in which an organism attends to a stimulus.

Conditioned stimulus (CS) A previously neutral stimulus that elicits a conditioned response because it has been paired repeatedly with a stimulus that already elicited that response.

Simultaneous conditioning A classical conditioning procedure in which the CS and US are presented at the same time, and the CS is left on until the response occurs.

Delayed conditioning A classical conditioning procedure in which the CS is presented several seconds before the US and left on until the response occurs.

Trace conditioning A classical conditioning procedure in which the CS is presented and then removed before the US is presented.

Types of Classical Conditioning

Classical conditioning tends to occur most efficiently when the conditioned stimulus (CS) is presented about 0.5 seconds before the unconditioned stimulus (US). But conditioning can also take place if the CS and US are presented at the same time. In the process referred to as **simultaneous conditioning,** a CS such as a light is presented along with the meat powder and left on until the response (in this case, salivation) occurs. In **delayed conditioning,** the CS (e.g., a light) is presented several seconds before the US (in this case, meat powder) and is left on until the response (salivation) is shown. In a third variation, known as **trace conditioning,** the CS (e.g., a light) is presented and then removed (or turned off) prior to presentation of the US (meat powder). Therefore, only the memory trace of the CS (light) remains to be conditioned to the US.

Conditioning occurs more effectively in delayed conditioning and trace conditioning than in simultaneous conditioning, perhaps because delayed conditioning and trace conditioning are more adaptive. That is, in these cases the CSs signal the consequent appearance of the US. As a result, organisms can learn to make predictions about their environments. Predictability is adaptive because it allows organisms to prepare for future events. When stimuli are presented simultaneously, however, one does not permit useful prediction of the other.

For the same reason, perhaps, learning is still less efficient, and may not take place at all, when the US is presented before the CS. Presenting the US prior to the CS is referred to as **backward conditioning.**

Now that we have considered some of the basics of classical conditioning, let us consider a challenge to the behaviorist view of classical conditioning that is posed by contingency theory.

Contingency Theory

We have already noted that behaviorists and cognitive psychologists interpret the events of the conditioning process in different ways. Behaviorists explain the outcomes of classical conditioning in terms of the contiguous presentation of stimuli. Cognitive psychologists explain classical conditioning in terms of the ways in which stimuli provide organisms with information that allows them to form and revise mental representations of their environments.

Psychologist Robert Rescorla (1967) conducted a series of classical-conditioning experiments with dogs and obtained some results that are difficult to explain without reference to cognitive concepts. Each phase of his work paired a tone (CS) with electric shock (US), but in different ways. With one group of animals, the shock was presented consistently after the tone. That is, the US followed on the heels of the CS, as in Pavlov's studies. The dogs in this group learned to show a fear response when the tone was presented.

A second group of dogs heard an equal number of tones and received an equal number of electric shocks, but the shock never immediately followed the tone. In other words, the tone and shock were unpaired. Now, from the behavioral perspective, the dogs should not have learned to associate the tone and the shock, since one did not presage the other. Actually, the dogs learned quite a lot: They learned that they had nothing to fear when the tone was sounded! The dogs showed vigilance and fear when the laboratory was quiet—for apparently the shock could come at any time—but they were calm in the presence of the tone.

The third group of dogs also received equal numbers of tones and shocks, but these were presented at purely random intervals. Occasionally they were paired, but most often they were not. From the behavioral perspective, intermittent pairing of the tones and shocks should have brought about some learning, but it did not. The animals showed no fear in response to the tone. Rescorla suggests that the animals in this group learned nothing because the tones provided no information about the prospect of being shocked.

Rescorla concluded that contiguity—that is, the co-appearance of two events (the US and the CS)—cannot in itself explain classical conditioning. Instead, learning occurs only when the conditioned stimulus (in this case, the tone) provides information about the unconditioned stimulus (in this case, the shock). According to so-called **contingency theory,** learning occurs because a conditioned stimulus indicates that the unconditioned stimulus is likely to ensue.

Research by Leon Kamin (1969) provides further support for contingency theory. In the first phase of the experiment, Kamin conditioned a group of rats to fear a tone (CS) by pairing it repeatedly with electric shock (US) to the feet. In phase two, he repeatedly paired a compound stimulus consisting of the tone plus a light with the shock. According to traditional explanations

---

Backward conditioning A classical conditioning procedure in which the unconditioned stimulus is presented prior to the conditioned stimulus.

Contingency theory The view that learning occurs when stimuli provide information about the likelihood of the occurrence of other stimuli.

of classical conditioning, the light, like the tone, should have gained the capacity to produce a fear response. (The light, like the tone, was paired repeatedly with the electric shock.) However, the rats did *not* learn to fear the light. Why? Apparently the light *provided no new information about the shock.* The light did not encourage the rats to revise their representation of the environment. The phenomenon whereby a CS (e.g., a tone) overshadows the presentation of a new stimulus (e.g., the light) is referred to as **blocking.** It is somewhat reminiscent of signal-detection theory: Organisms cannot pay equal attention to everything that is happening around them, and they apparently tend to block out stimuli that offer no useful information.

Blocking The phenomenon whereby a new stimulus fails to gain the capacity to signal an unconditioned stimulus (US) when the new stimulus is paired repeatedly with a stimulus that already effectively foretells the US.

Now let us consider some findings concerning taste aversion. We shall try to see why I developed an aversion to buttered popcorn but not to the Rocketman serial—an issue that provides another challenge to the behaviorist view of classical conditioning.

A CLOSER LOOK

Taste Aversion

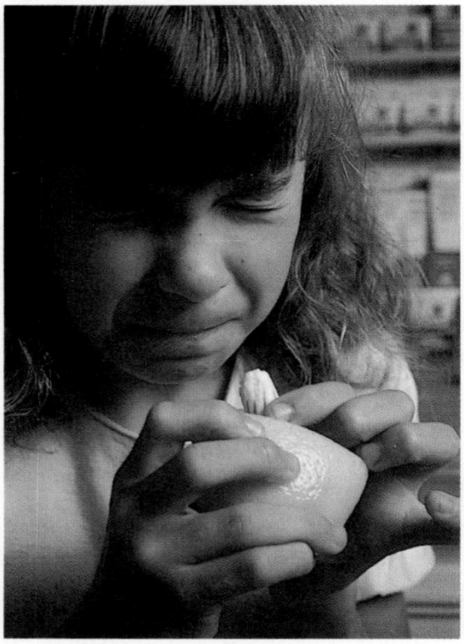

Formation of a Taste Aversion? Taste aversions may be acquired by just one association of the US and the CS. Most kinds of classical conditioning require that the US and CS be contiguous, but in a taste aversion, the US (nausea) can occur hours after the CS (flavor of food).

Taste aversions serve the adaptive function of motivating organisms to avoid potentially harmful foods. Although taste aversions are acquired by association, they differ from other kinds of classical conditioning in a couple of ways. First, only one association may be required. I did not have to go back for seconds at the movies to develop my aversion for buttered popcorn! Second, whereas most kinds of classical conditioning require that the US and CS be contiguous, in taste aversion the US (nausea) can occur hours after the CS (flavor of food).

Sad to say, taste aversion can further impair the health of people being treated with chemotherapy for cancer. The chemotherapy often induces nausea, and a taste aversion can develop for foods eaten earlier in the day. Thus, cancer patients, who may already be losing weight because of their illness, may find that taste aversion compounds the problems associated with lack of appetite. To combat taste aversion in such patients, Ilene Bernstein (1985) recommends giving them unusual foods prior to chemotherapy. If a taste aversion develops, it will then be to the unusual food, and patients' appetites for dietary staples may be unaffected.

Research in taste aversion also challenges the behaviorist view that organisms learn to associate any stimuli that are contiguous. Not all stimuli are created equal. Instead, it seems that organisms are biologically predisposed to develop aversions that are adaptive in their environmental settings. In a classic study, Garcia and Koelling (1966) conditioned two groups of rats. Each group was exposed to the same three-part CS: a taste of sweetened water, a light, and a clicker. Afterward, one group was presented a US of nausea (induced by poison or radiation), and the other group was presented a US of electric shock.

After conditioning, the rats who had been nauseated showed an aversion for sweetened water, but not to the light or clicker. Although all three stimuli had been presented at the same time, *they had acquired only the taste aversion.* After conditioning, the rats who had been shocked avoided both the light and the clicker, *but they did not show a taste aversion to the sweetened water.* For each group of rats, the conditioning that took place was adaptive. In the natural scheme of things, nausea is more likely to stem from poisoned food than from lights or sounds. And so, for nauseated rats, acquiring the taste aversion was appropriate. Sharp pain, in contrast, is more likely to stem from natural events involving lights (fire, lightning) and sharp sounds (twigs snapping, things falling). Therefore, it was more appropriate for the shocked animals to develop an aversion to the light and the clicker than to the sweetened water.

This finding fits in with my experience as well. My nausea led to a taste aversion to buttered popcorn—but not to an aversion to the Rocketman serial (which, in retrospect, was more deserving of nausea) or the movie theater. I returned every Saturday morning to see what would happen next. Yet the serial and the theater, as much as the buttered popcorn, had been associated (contiguous) with my nausea.

Extinction and Spontaneous Recovery

Extinction and *spontaneous recovery* are aspects of conditioning that help organisms adapt by updating their expectations, or revising their representations of the changing environment. A dog may learn to associate a new scent (CS) with the appearance of a dangerous animal. It can then take evasive action when it whiffs the scent. A child may learn to connect hearing a car pull into the driveway (CS) with the arrival of his or her parents (US). Thus the child may come to squeal with delight (CR) when the car is heard.

But times can change. The once dangerous animal may no longer be a threat. (What a puppy perceives to be a threat may lose its power to menace once the dog matures.) After moving to a new house, the child's parents may commute by means of public transportation. The sounds of a car in a nearby driveway may signal a neighbor's, not a parent's, homecoming. When conditioned stimuli (such as the scent or the sound of a car) are no longer followed by unconditioned stimuli (a dangerous animal, a parent's homecoming), they lose their ability to elicit conditioned responses. In this way, the organism adapts to a changing environment.

Extinction In classical conditioning, **extinction** is the process by which conditioned stimuli (CSs) lose the ability to elicit conditioned responses (CRs) because the CSs are no longer associated with unconditioned stimuli (USs). From the cognitive perspective, extinction teaches the organism to modify its representation of the environment because the CS no longer serves its predictive function.

In experiments in the extinction of CRs, Pavlov found that repeated presentations of the CS (or bell) without the US (meat powder) led to extinction of the CR (salivation in response to the bell). Figure 5.3 shows that a dog conditioned by Pavlov began to salivate (show a CR) in response to a bell (CS) after only a couple of pairings—referred to as **acquisition trials**—of the bell with meat powder (the US). Continued pairings of the stimuli led to increased salivation, as measured in number of drops of saliva. After seven or eight trials, salivation leveled off at eleven to twelve drops.

Then salivation to the bell (CR) was extinguished through several trials—referred to as **extinction trials**—in which the CS (bell) was presented without the meat powder (US). After about ten extinction trials, the CR (salivation in response to the bell) was no longer shown.

What would happen if we were to allow a day or two to pass after we had extinguished the CR (salivation response to a bell) in a laboratory dog, and then we again presented the CS (bell)? Where would you place your money? Would the dog salivate or not?

Extinction An experimental procedure in which stimuli lose their ability to evoke learned responses because the events that had followed the stimuli no longer occur. (The learned responses are said to be *extinguished.*)

Acquisition trial In conditioning, a presentation of stimuli such that a new response is learned and strengthened.

Extinction trial In conditioning, a performance of a learned response in the absence of its predicted consequences so that the learned response becomes inhibited.

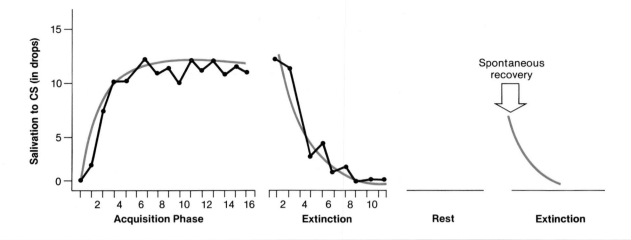

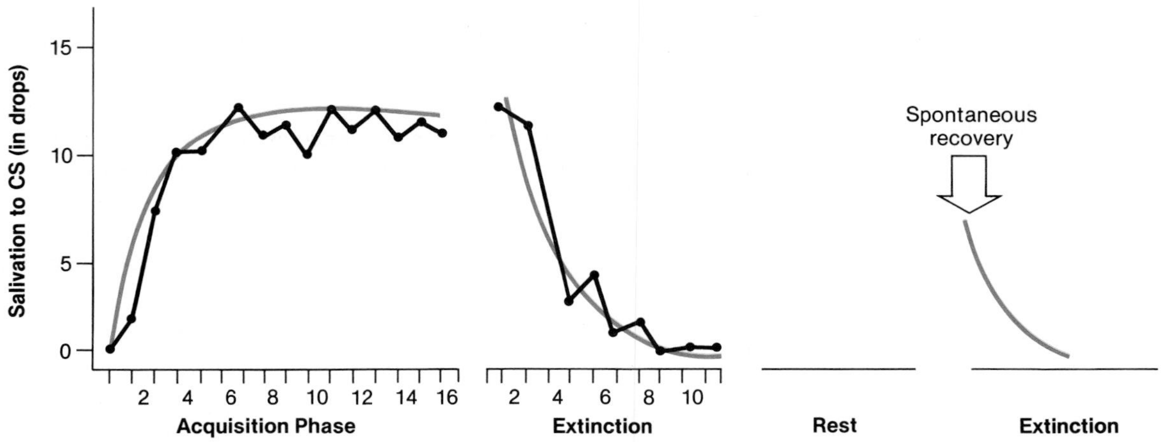

Figure 5.3
Learning and Extinction Curves.

Actual data from Pavlov (1927) compose the jagged line, and the curved lines are idealized. In the acquisition phase, a dog salivates (shows a CR) in response to a bell (CS) after only a few trials in which the bell is paired with meat powder (the US). Afterward, the CR is extinguished in about ten trials in which the CS is not followed by the US. After a rest period, the CR recovers spontaneously. A second series of extinction trials then leads to more rapid extinction of the CR.

If you bet that the dog would again show the CR (salivate in response to the bell), you were correct. Organisms tend to show **spontaneous recovery** of extinguished CRs merely as a function of the passage of time. For this reason, the term *extinction* may be a bit misleading. When a species of animal becomes extinct, all members of that species capable of reproducing have died. The species vanishes permanently. But the experimental extinction of CRs does not lead to the permanent eradication of CRs. Rather, it seems that they inhibit that response. The response does remain available for future performance.

Consider Figure 5.3 again. When spontaneous recovery of the CR does occur, the strength of the response (in this case, the number of drops of saliva) is not as great as it was at the end of the series of acquisition trials. A second set of extinction trials will also extinguish the CR more rapidly than the first series of extinction trials. Although the CR is at first weaker the second time around, pairing the CS with the US once more will build response strength rapidly.

Spontaneous recovery, like extinction, is adaptive. What would happen if the child heard no car in the driveway for several months? It could be that the next time a car entered the driveway, the child would associate the sounds with a parent's homecoming (rather than the arrival of a neighbor). This expectation could be appropriate. After all, *something* had systematically changed in the neighborhood when no car had entered the nearby driveway for so long. In the wilds a waterhole may contain water for only a couple of months during the year. But it is useful for animals to associate the waterhole with the thirst drive from time to time so that they will return to it at the appropriate time.

As time passes and the seasons change, things sometimes follow circular paths and arrive at where they were before. Spontaneous recovery seems to provide a mechanism whereby organisms are capable of rapidly adapting to intermittently recurring situations.

Spontaneous recovery The recurrence of an extinguished response as a function of the passage of time.

Generalization and Discrimination

No two things are exactly alike. Traffic lights are hung at slightly different heights, and shades of red and green differ a little. The barking of two dogs differs, and the sound of the same animal differs slightly from bark to bark. Adaptation requires that we respond similarly to stimuli that are equivalent in function and that we respond differently to stimuli that are not.

Generalization Pavlov noted that responding to different stimuli as though they are functionally equivalent is adaptive for animals. Rustling sounds in the undergrowth differ, but rabbits and deer do well to flee when they perceive any of many varieties of rustling. Sirens differ, but people do well to become vigilant or to pull their cars to the side of the road when any siren is heard.

In a demonstration of **generalization,** Pavlov first conditioned a dog to salivate when a circle was presented. During each acquisition trial, the dog was shown a circle (CS), then given meat powder (US). After several trials, the dog exhibited the CR of salivating when presented with the circle alone. Pavlov demonstrated that the dog also exhibited the CR (salivation) in response to closed geometric figures such as ellipses, pentagons, and even squares. The more closely the figure resembled a circle, the greater the strength of the response (the more drops of saliva that flowed).

Discrimination Organisms must also learn (1) that many stimuli perceived as being similar are functionally different and (2) to respond adaptively to each. During the first couple of months of life, babies can discriminate the voices of their mothers from those of others. They will often stop crying when they hear Mother but not when they hear a stranger's voice.

Pavlov showed that a dog conditioned to salivate in response to circles could be trained *not* to salivate in response to ellipses. The type of conditioning that trains an organism to show a CR in response to a narrow range of stimuli (in this case, circular rather than elliptical geometric figures) is termed **discrimination training.** Pavlov trained the dog by presenting it with circles and ellipses but associating the meat powder (US) with circles only. After a while, the dog no longer showed the CR (salivation) in response to the ellipses. Instead the animal showed **discrimination**. It displayed the CR in response to circles only.

Pavlov then discovered that he could make the dog behave as though it were tormented by increasing the difficulty of the discrimination task. After the dog exhibited stimulus discrimination, Pavlov showed the animal progressively rounder ellipses. Eventually the dog could no longer discriminate them from circles. The animal then put on an infantile show. It urinated, defecated, barked profusely, and snapped at laboratory personnel.

How do we explain the dog's belligerent behavior? In a classic work written half a century ago, *Frustration and Aggression,* a group of behaviorally oriented psychologists suggested that frustration induces aggression (Dollard et al., 1939). Why is failure to discriminate circles from ellipses frustrating? For one thing, in such experiments, rewards—such as meat powder—are usually made contingent on correct discrimination. That is, if the dog errs, it forgoes the meat. Cognitive theorists, however, propose that organisms are motivated to construct realistic maps of the world. In building their overall images of the world, organisms—including dogs—adjust their representations so as to reduce discrepancies and accommodate new information (Rescorla, 1988). In the Pavlovian experiment, the dog lost the ability

---

Generalization In conditioning, the tendency for a conditioned response to be evoked by stimuli that are similar to the stimulus to which the response was conditioned.

Discrimination training Teaching an organism to show a learned response in the presence of only one of a series of similar stimuli, accomplished by alternating the stimuli but following only the one stimulus with the unconditioned stimulus.

Discrimination In conditioning, the tendency for an organism to distinguish between a conditioned stimulus and similar stimuli that do not forecast an unconditioned stimulus.

to meaningfully adjust its representation of the environment as the ellipses grew more circular, and so it was frustrated. Behaviorists counter that it is fruitless to speculate on what goes on in the "mind" of another organism because there is no scientific way to verify our conjectures, whether the organism is a person or a lower animal such as a dog.

In any event, the capacity to make discriminations is important. Most of us would grow concerned if we could no longer make the discriminations necessary for survival. Consider how you might behave if you could barely discriminate between a greenish-red and a reddish-green traffic light, but a person dressed in unmistakable blue was ready to hand you a traffic ticket every time you made an error.

Daily living requires appropriate generalization and discrimination. No two hotels are alike, but when traveling from one city to another it is adaptive to expect to stay in some hotel. It is encouraging that green lights in Washington have the same meaning as green lights in Honolulu. But returning home in the evening requires the ability to discriminate between our homes or apartments and those of others. If we could not readily tell our spouses apart from those of others, we might land in divorce court.

Higher-Order Conditioning

In **higher-order conditioning,** a previously neutral stimulus comes to serve as a CS after being paired repeatedly with a stimulus that has already become a CS. Pavlov demonstrated higher-order conditioning by first conditioning a dog to salivate (show a CR) in response to a bell (a CS). He then paired the shining of a light repeatedly with the bell. After several pairings, shining the light (the higher-order CS) came to elicit the response (salivation) that had been elicited by the bell (the first-order CS).

Consider children who learn that their parents are about to arrive when they hear a car in the driveway. It may be the case that a certain TV cartoon show starts a few minutes before the car enters the driveway. The TV show can begin to elicit the expectation that the parents are coming by being paired repeatedly with the car's entering the driveway. In another example, a boy may burn himself by touching a hot stove. After this experience, the sight of the stove may serve as a CS for eliciting a fear response. And because hearing the word *stove* may evoke a cognitive image of the stove, hearing the word alone may also elicit a fear response.

Applications of Classical Conditioning

Classical conditioning is a major avenue of learning in our daily lives. It is how stimuli come to serve as signals for other stimuli. It is why we come to expect that someone will be waiting outside when the doorbell is rung, or why we expect a certain friend to appear when we hear a characteristic knock. In this section we explore a number of applications of classical conditioning in the areas of child development and behavior modification.

The Bell-and-Pad Method for Bedwetting By the ages of 5 or 6, children normally awaken in response to the sensations of a full bladder. They inhibit urination, which is an automatic or reflexive response to bladder tension, and go to the bathroom. But bedwetters tend not to respond to sensations of a full bladder while asleep. And so they remain asleep and frequently wet their beds.

Higher-order conditioning (1) According to behaviorists, a classical conditioning procedure in which a previously neutral stimulus comes to elicit the response brought forth by a *conditioned* stimulus by being paired repeatedly with that conditioned stimulus. (2) According to cognitive psychologists, the learning of relationships among events, none of which evokes an unlearned response.

By means of the bell-and-pad method, children are taught to wake up in response to bladder tension. They sleep on a special sheet or pad that has been placed on the bed. When the child starts to urinate, the water content of the urine causes an electrical circuit in the pad to be closed. Closing of the circuit triggers a bell or buzzer, and the child is awakened. In terms of principles of classical conditioning, the bell is a *US* that wakes the child (waking up is the *UR*). By means of repeated pairings, stimuli that precede the bell become associated with the bell and also gain the capacity to awaken the child. What stimuli are these? The sensations of a full bladder. In this way, bladder tension (the CS) gains the capacity to awaken the child *even though the child is asleep during the classical conditioning procedure.*

Similar buzzer circuits have also been built into training pants as an aid to toilet training.

The Story of Little Albert: A Case Study in the Classical Conditioning of Emotional Responses In 1920, John B. Watson and his future wife, Rosalie Rayner, published an article describing their demonstration that emotional reactions such as fears can be acquired through principles of classical conditioning. The subject of their demonstration was a lad known in the psychological literature by the name of Little Albert. Albert was a phlegmatic fellow at the age of 11 months, not given to ready displays of emotion. But he did enjoy playing with a laboratory rat. Such are the playmates to be found in psychologists' laboratories.

Using a method that some psychologists have criticized as unethical, Watson startled Little Albert by clanging steel bars behind his head when the infant played with the rat. After seven pairings, Albert showed fear of the rat, even though clanging was suspended. Albert's fear was also generalized to objects similar in appearance to the rat, such as a rabbit and the fur collar on a woman's coat. Albert's conditioned fear of rats may never have become extinguished. Extinction would have required perceiving rats (the conditioned stimuli) without painful consequences (in the absence of the unconditioned stimuli). Fear, however, might have prevented Albert from facing rats. And, as we shall see in the section on operant conditioning, avoiding rats might have been *reinforced* by reduction of fear.

In the chapter on abnormal behavior, we will note that other experiments in conditioning fears (e.g., by English, 1929) have not always been successful. As mentioned in our discussion of taste aversions, it may be that people are more biologically predisposed to learn fears of some objects and situations than others.

In any event, Watson and Rayner did not attempt to reverse, or undo, the effects of Little Albert's conditioning. (Somewhere there may be a gentleman in his 70s who cringes when he sees furry puppies or muffs protecting the hands of girls in winter and, of course, whenever rats are discussed on television.) But, as we shall see in the following sections, other psychologists have used principles of classical conditioning to do just that.

Flooding and Systematic Desensitization Two behavior-therapy methods for reducing fears are based on the classical-conditioning principle of extinction. In one called **flooding,** the client is exposed to the fear-evoking stimulus until fear responses are extinguished. Albert, for example, might have been placed in close contact with a rat until his fears had become fully extinguished. In extinction, the CS (in this case, the rat) is presented repeatedly in the absence of the US (the clanging of the steel bars) until the CR (fear) is no longer evoked.

Although flooding is usually effective, it is unpleasant. (When you are fearful of rats, being placed in a small room with one is not a holiday.) For

Flooding A behavioral fear-reduction technique that is based on principles of classical conditioning. Fear-evoking stimuli (CSs) are presented continuously in the absence of actual harm so that fear responses (CRs) are extinguished.

this reason, behavior therapists frequently prefer to use **systematic desensitization,** in which the client is exposed gradually to fear-evoking stimuli under circumstances in which he or she remains relaxed. For example, while feeling relaxed, Little Albert might have been given the opportunity to look at photos of rats or to see live rats from a distance before they were brought closer. Systematic desensitization will be described more fully in Chapter 13.

Counterconditioning Early in the century, University of California professors Harold Jones and Mary Cover Jones (Jones, 1924) reasoned that if fears could be conditioned by painful experiences, it should be possible to *countercondition* them by pleasant experiences. In **counterconditioning,** a pleasant stimulus is paired repeatedly with a fear-evoking object, in this way counteracting the fear response.

Two-year-old Peter feared rabbits intensely. The Joneses arranged for a rabbit to be gradually brought closer to Peter while he engaged in some of his favorite activities, such as munching merrily away on candy and cookies. As opposed to flooding, the rabbit was not plopped in Peter's lap. Had they done so, the cookies on the plate and those already eaten might have decorated the walls. At first they placed the rabbit in a far corner of the room while Peter munched and crunched. Peter, to be sure, cast a wary eye, but he continued to consume the treat. Gradually the animal was brought closer. Eventually, Peter ate treats and touched the rabbit at the same time. The Joneses theorized that the pleasure of eating was incompatible with fear and thus counterconditioned the fear.

Truth or Fiction Revisted

It is true that psychologists helped a young boy overcome fear of rabbits by having him eat cookies while a rabbit was brought nearer.

Through classical conditioning we learn to associate stimuli so that a simple, usually passive, response made to one is then made in response to the other. In the case of Little Albert, clanging noises were associated with a rat, so the rat came to elicit the fear response brought forth by the noise. However, classical conditioning is only one kind of learning that occurs in these situations. According to O. Hobart Mowrer's two-factor theory of learning, classical conditioning in the study with Little Albert suffices to explain the acquisition of the fear response. But then the boy's voluntary behavior changed. He avoided the rat as a way of reducing his fear. Thus, Little Albert engaged in another kind of learning—operant conditioning.

In operant conditioning, as we see in the next section, organisms learn to engage in certain behaviors because of their effects. The sight of a hypodermic syringe, for example, may elicit a fear response because a person once had a painful injection. The subsequent avoidance of injections is *operant behavior.* It has the effect of reducing fear. In other cases, we engage in operant behavior to attain rewards, not to avoid unpleasant outcomes.

OPERANT CONDITIONING

In **operant conditioning**—also referred to as **instrumental conditioning**—an organism learns to engage in certain behavior because of the effects of that behavior. We begin this section with the historic work of psychologist Edward L. Thorndike. Then we shall examine the more recent work of B. F. Skinner.

Systematic desensitization A behavioral fear-reduction technique in which a hierarchy of fear-evoking stimuli are presented while the person remains relaxed.

Counterconditioning A fear-reduction technique in which pleasant stimuli are associated with fear-evoking stimuli so that the fear-evoking stimuli lose their aversive qualities.

Operant conditioning A simple form of learning in which an organism learns to engage in behavior because it is reinforced.

Instrumental conditioning A term similar to *operant conditioning,* reflecting the fact that the learned behavior is *instrumental* in achieving certain effects.

Edward L. Thorndike

Random trial and error Referring to behavior that occurs in a novel situation prior to learning what behavior is rewarded or reinforced.

Law of effect Thorndike's principle that responses are "stamped in" by rewards and "stamped out" by punishments.

Reinforce To follow a response with a stimulus that increases the frequency of the response.

Edward L. Thorndike and the Law of Effect

In the 1890s, stray cats were mysteriously disappearing from the streets and alleyways of Harlem. Many of them, it turned out, were being brought to the quarters of Columbia University doctoral student Edward Thorndike. Thorndike was using them as subjects in experiments in learning by trial and error.

Thorndike placed the cats in so-called puzzle boxes. If the animals managed to pull a dangling string, a latch would be released, allowing them to jump out and reach a bowl of food.

When first placed in a puzzle box, a cat would try to squeeze through any opening and would claw and bite at the confining bars and wire. It would claw at any feature it could reach. Through such **random trial-and-error** behavior, it might take three to four minutes before the cat would chance on the response of pulling the string. Pulling the string would open the cage and allow the cat to reach the food. When placed back in the cage, it might again take several minutes for the animal to pull the string. But as these trials were repeated, it would take progressively less time for the cat to pull the string. After seven or eight trials, it might pull the string immediately when placed back in the box.

The Law of Effect Thorndike explained the cat's learning to pull the string in terms of his **law of effect.** According to this law, a response (such as string pulling) is "stamped in" or strengthened in a particular situation (such as being inside a puzzle box) by a reward (escaping from the box and eating). Rewards, that is, stamp in S-R (stimulus-response) connections. Punishments, in contrast, "stamp out" stimulus-response connections. Organisms would learn *not* to engage in punished responses. Later we shall see that the effects of punishment on learning are not so certain.

B. F. Skinner and Reinforcement

"What did you do in the war, Daddy?" is a question familiar to many who served during America's conflicts. Some stories involve heroism, others involve the unusual. When it comes to unusual war stories, few will top that of Harvard University psychologist B. F. Skinner. For, as he relates the tale in his autobiography, *The Shaping of a Behaviorist* (1979), one of Skinner's wartime efforts was "Project Pigeon."

During World War II Skinner proposed that pigeons be trained to guide missiles to their targets. In their training, the pigeons would be **reinforced** with food pellets for pecking at targets projected onto a screen (see Figure 5.4). Once trained, the pigeons would be placed in missiles. Pecking at similar targets displayed on a screen within the missile would correct the flight path of the missile, resulting in a "hit" and a sacrificed pigeon. However, plans for building the necessary missile—for some reason called the *Pelican* and not the *Pigeon*—were scrapped. The pigeon equipment was too bulky, and as Skinner lamented, his suggestion was not taken seriously. Apparently the Defense Department concluded that Project Pigeon was for the birds.

B. F. Skinner and some of his associates at the Harvard University laboratory.

Truth or Fiction Revisited

It is true that a psychologist did conceive a plan for training pigeons to guide missiles to their targets during World War II. That psychologist is B. F. Skinner.

Figure 5.4
Project Pigeon. During World War II, B. F. Skinner suggested training pigeons to guide missiles to their targets. In an operant conditioning procedure, the pigeons would be reinforced for pecking at targets projected on a screen. Afterward, in combat, pecking at the on-screen target would keep the missile on course.

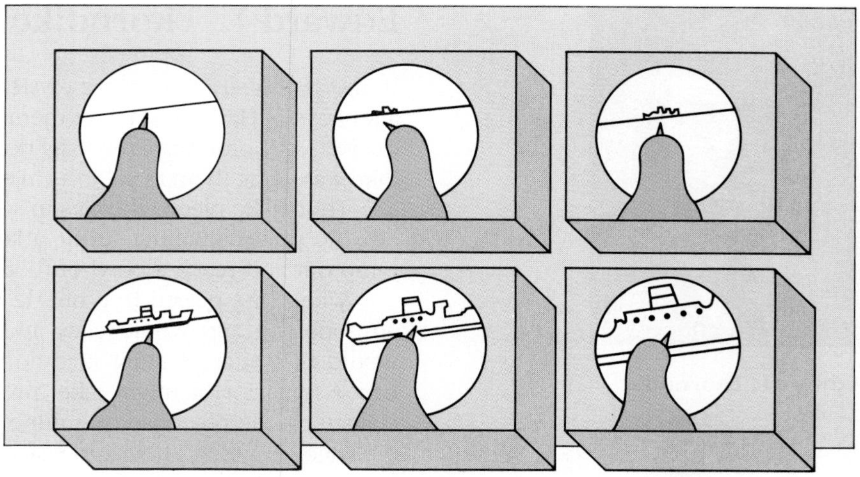

Project Pigeon may have been scrapped, but the principles of learning Skinner applied to the project have found wide applications in operant conditioning. In classical conditioning, an organism learns about the relationships among events. In other words, it learns to associate stimuli. As a laboratory procedure, one previously neutral stimulus (the CS) comes to elicit the response brought forth by another stimulus (the US) because they have been paired repeatedly. In operant conditioning, an organism learns to *do* something because of its effects or consequences.

Operant behavior Voluntary responses that are reinforced.

Operant The same as an operant behavior.

This is **operant behavior,** behavior that operates on, or manipulates, the environment. In classical conditioning, involuntary responses such as salivation or eyeblinks are often conditioned. In operant conditioning, *voluntary* responses such as pecking at a target, pressing a lever, or many of the athletic skills required in playing tennis are acquired, or conditioned.

In operant conditioning, organisms engage in operant behaviors, also known simply as **operants,** that result in presumably desirable consequences such as food, a hug, an A on a test, attention, or social approval. Some children learn to conform their behavior to social codes and rules to earn the attention and approval of their parents and teachers. Other children, ironically, may learn to "misbehave," since misbehavior also results in attention from other people. Children may especially learn to be "bad" when their "good" behavior is routinely ignored.

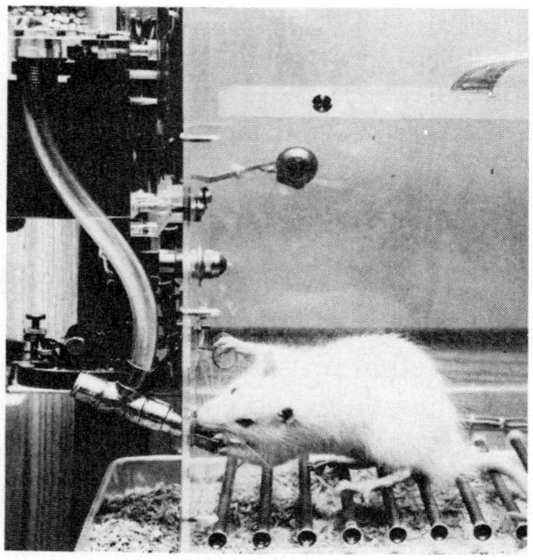

Figure 5.5
The Effects of Reinforcement. One of the luminaries of modern psychology, an albino laboratory rat, earns its keep in a Skinner box. The animal presses a lever because of reinforcement—in the form of food pellets—delivered through the spout of the feeder. The habit strength of this operant can be measured as the frequency of lever pressing.

Units of Behavior, "Skinner Boxes," and Cumulative Recorders In his most influential work, *The Behavior of Organisms,* Skinner made many theoretical and technological innovations. Among them was his focus on discrete behaviors such as lever-pressing as the unit, or type, of behavior to be studied. Whereas other psychologists might focus on how organisms think or "feel," Skinner focused on measurable things that they do. Many psychologists have found Skinner's kinds of behaviors inconsequential, especially when it comes to explaining and predicting human behavior. But Skinner's supporters point out that focusing on discrete behavior creates the potential for helpful behavior changes. For example, in helping people combat depression, one psychologist might focus on people's "feelings" about other people and themselves. The Skinnerian would focus on cataloguing the types of things that "depressed" people *do.* By focusing on directly changing depressive behavior, the person might report that "feelings of depression" were also lifting.

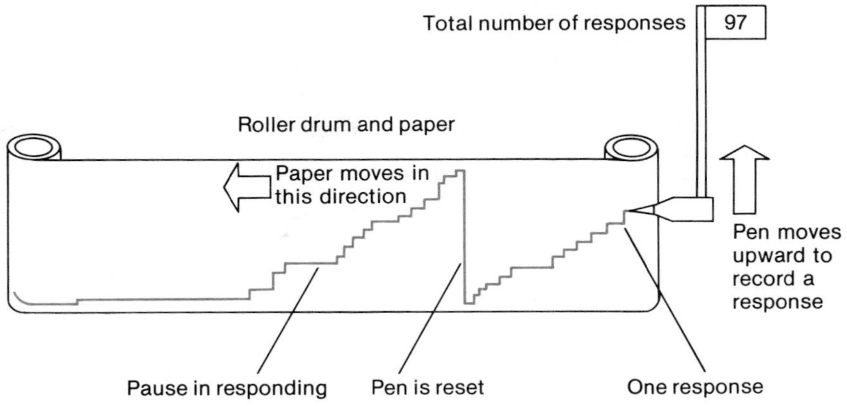

Figure 5.6
The Cumulative Recorder. In the cumulative recorder, paper moves continuously to the left while a pen automatically records each targeted response by moving upward. When the pen reaches the top of the paper, it is automatically reset to the bottom.

To study operant behavior efficiently, Skinner also devised an animal cage that was dubbed the *Skinner box* by psychologist Clark Hull, whose theory of drive-reductionism is discussed in Chapter 8. Such a box is shown in Figure 5.5. The cage is ideal for laboratory experimentation because experimental conditions (treatments) can be carefully introduced and removed, and the results on laboratory animals (defined as changes in the rate of lever pressing) can be carefully observed. The Skinner box is also energy-efficient—in terms of the "energy" of the experimenter. In contrast to Thorndike's puzzle box, a "correct" response does not allow the animal to escape and thus have to be recaptured and placed back in the box.

The rat in Figure 5.5 was deprived of food and placed in a Skinner box with a lever at one end. At first it sniffed its way around the cage and engaged in **random trial-and-error behavior.** In random trial-and-error behavior, responses that meet with favorable consequences tend to occur more frequently; responses that do not meet with favorable consequences tend to be performed less frequently.

The rat's first pressing of the lever was inadvertent. However, because of this action, a food pellet dropped into the cage. The food pellet increased the probability that the rat would press the lever again. The pellet is thus said to have served as a reinforcement for the lever pressing.

Skinner further mechanized his laboratory procedure by making use of a turning drum, or **cumulative recorder,** that had previously been used by physiologists. (See Figure 5.6.) The cumulative recorder provides a precise measure of operant behavior. The experimenter does not even need to be present to record correct responses. In the example used, the lever in the Skinner box is connected to the recorder so that the recording pen moves upward with each correct response. The paper moves continuously to the left at a slow but regular pace. In the sample record shown in Figure 5.6, lever pressings (which record correct responses) were at first few and far between. But after several reinforced responses, lever pressing came fast and furious. When the rat is no longer hungry, the lever pressing will drop off and then stop.

The First "Correct" Response In operant conditioning, it matters little how the first response that is reinforced comes to be made. The organism can happen on it by chance, as in random trial-and-error learning. The organism can also be physically guided into the response. You may command your dog to "Sit!" and then press its backside down until it is in a sitting position. Finally, you reinforce sitting with food or a pat on the head and a kind word.

Random trial-and-error behavior Unplanned, random activity.

Cumulative recorder An instrument that records the frequency of an organism's operants (or "correct" responses) as a function of the passage of time.

B.C.

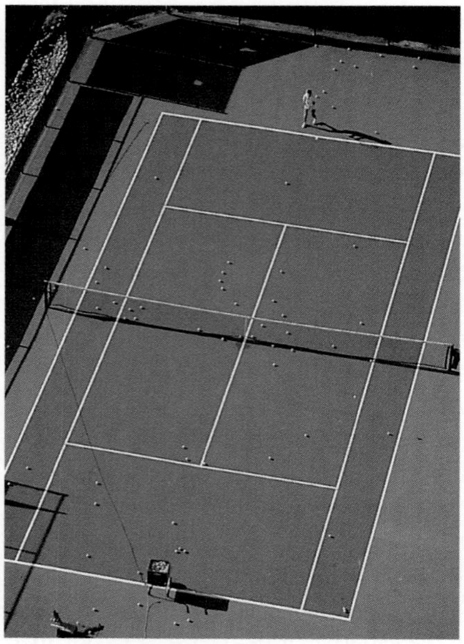

Reinforcement Goes to Court. The tennis player perfects his serve in part by means of trial and error. Knowledge of results reinforces proper strokes.

Animal trainers use physical guiding or coaxing to bring about the first "correct" response. Can you imagine how long it would take to train your dog if you waited for it to sit or roll over and then seized the opportunity to command it to sit or roll over? You would both age significantly in the process.

People, of course, can be verbally guided into desired responses when they are learning tasks such as running a machine, spelling, or adding numbers. But they then need to be informed when they have made the correct response. Knowledge of results is often all the reinforcement that motivated people need to learn new skills.

Types of Reinforcers

Any stimulus that increases the probability that responses preceding it will be repeated serves as a reinforcer. Reinforcers include food pellets when an organism has been deprived of food, water when it has been deprived of liquid, the opportunity to mate, and the sound of a bell that has been previously associated with eating.

Positive and Negative Reinforcers Skinner distinguished between positive and negative reinforcers. **Positive reinforcers** increase the probability that an operant will occur when they are applied. Food and approval usually serve as positive reinforcers. **Negative reinforcers** increase the probability that an operant will occur when they are *removed.* People often learn to plan ahead so that they need not fear that things will go wrong. Fear acts as a negative reinforcer, because *removal* of fear increases the probability that the behaviors preceding it (such as planning ahead or fleeing a predator) will be repeated.

Greater reinforcers prompt more rapid learning than do lesser reinforcers. You will probably work much harder for $1,000 than for $10. (If not, get in touch with me—I have some chores that need to be taken care of.) With sufficient reinforcement, operants become a **habit.** They show a high probability of recurrence in a certain situation.

Primary and Secondary Reinforcers We can also distinguish between primary and secondary, or conditioned, reinforcers. **Primary reinforcers** are effective because of the biological makeup of the organism. Food, water, adequate warmth (positive reinforcers), and pain (a negative reinforcer) all

---

Positive reinforcer A reinforcer that when *presented* increases the frequency of an operant.

Negative reinforcer A reinforcer that when *removed* increases the frequency of an operant.

Habit A learned response that shows a high frequency of recurrence under certain conditions.

Primary reinforcer An unlearned reinforcer.

Figure 5.7
Secondary Reinforcers.

Understanding other people includes being able to predict what they will find reinforcing. In this Dagwood cartoon, Dagwood apparently finds money more reinforcing than the praise of his boss, Mr. Dithers.

serve as primary reinforcers. **Secondary reinforcers** acquire their value through being associated with established reinforcers. For this reason they are also termed **conditioned reinforcers.** We may seek money because we have learned that it may be exchanged for primary reinforcers. Money, attention, social approval—all are conditioned reinforcers in our culture. We may be suspicious of, or not "understand," people who are not interested in money or the approval of others. Part of understanding others lies in being able to predict what they will find reinforcing (see Figure 5.7).

Extinction and Spontaneous Recovery in Operant Conditioning

In operant conditioning, as in classical conditioning, extinction is a process in which stimuli lose the ability to evoke learned responses because the events that had followed the stimuli no longer occur. In classical conditioning, however, the "events" that normally follow and confirm the appropriateness of the learned response (i.e., the conditioned response) are the unconditioned stimuli. In Pavlov's experiment, the meat powder was the event that followed and confirmed the appropriateness of salivation. In operant conditioning, the ensuing events are reinforcers. Thus, in operant conditioning, the extinction of learned responses (i.e., operants) results from repeated performance of operant behavior without reinforcement. After a number of trials, the operant behavior is no longer shown.

When some time is allowed to pass after the extinction process, an organism will usually perform the operant again when placed in a situation in which the operant had been reinforced previously. Spontaneous recovery of learned responses occurs in operant conditioning as well as in classical conditioning. If the operant is reinforced at this time, it quickly regains its former strength. Spontaneous recovery of extinguished operants suggests that they are inhibited or suppressed by the extinction process and not lost permanently.

Secondary reinforcer A stimulus that gains reinforcement value through association with established reinforcers.

Conditioned reinforcer Another term for a secondary reinforcer.

Reinforcers versus Rewards and Punishments

Rewards, like reinforcers, are stimuli that increase the frequency of behavior. But rewards are also considered to be pleasant events. Skinner preferred the concept of reinforcement to that of reward because reinforcement does not suggest trying to "get inside the head" of an organism (person or lower animal) to guess what it would find pleasant or unpleasant. A list of reinforcers is arrived at **empirically,** by observing what sorts of stimuli will increase the frequency of the behavior. However, it should be noted that some psychologists consider the term *reward* to be synonymous with positive reinforcement.

Punishments are aversive events that suppress or decrease the frequency of the behavior they follow.* Punishment can rapidly suppress undesirable behavior and may be warranted in "emergencies," such as when a child tries to run out into the street.

Truth or Fiction Revisited

It is *not* true that punishment doesn't work. Strong punishment suppresses the behavior it follows. The issues pertaining to punishment concern its limitations and its side effects.

Reward A pleasant stimulus that increases the frequency of the behavior it follows.

Empirically By trial or experiment rather than by logical deduction.

Punishment An unpleasant stimulus that suppresses the behavior it follows.

Despite the fact that punishment works, many learning theorists agree that punishment is usually undesirable, especially in rearing children, for reasons such as the following:

1. Punishment does not in itself suggest an alternative acceptable form of behavior.
2. Punishment tends to suppress undesirable behavior only under circumstances in which its delivery is guaranteed. It does not take children long to learn that they can "get away with murder" with one parent, or one teacher, but not with another.
3. Punished organisms may withdraw from the situation. Severely punished children may run away, cut class, or drop out of school.
4. Punishment can create anger and hostility. Adequate punishment will almost always suppress unwanted behavior—but at what cost? A child may express accumulated feelings of hostility against other children.
5. Punishment may generalize too far. The child who is punished severely for bad table manners may stop eating altogether. Overgeneralization is more likely to occur when children do not know exactly why they are being punished and when they have not been shown alternative acceptable behaviors.
6. Punishment may be modeled as a way of solving problems or coping with stress. We shall see that one way that children learn is by observing others. Even though children may not immediately perform the behavior they observe, they may perform it later on, even as adults, when their circumstances are similar to those of the **model.**
7. Finally, children learn responses that are punished. Whether or not children choose to perform punished responses, punishment draws their attention to them.

It is usually preferable to focus on rewarding children for desirable behavior than on punishing them for unwanted behavior. By ignoring their misbehavior, or by using **time out** from positive reinforcement, we can consistently avoid reinforcing children for misbehavior.

To reward or positively reinforce children for desired behavior takes time and care. Simply never using punishment is not enough. First, we must pay attention to children when they are behaving well. If we take their desirable behavior for granted, and act as if we are aware of them only when they misbehave, we may be encouraging misbehavior. Second, we must be certain that children are aware of, and capable of performing, desired behavior. It is harmful and fruitless merely to punish children for unwanted behavior. We must also carefully guide them physically or verbally into making the desired responses and then reward them. We cannot teach children table manners by waiting for them to exhibit proper responses by random trial-and-error and then reinforcing them. If we waited by holding a half-gallon of ice cream behind our backs as a reward, we would have slippery dining room floors long before we had children with table manners.

Model An organism that engages in a response that is then imitated by another organism.

Time out Removal of an organism from a situation in which reinforcement is available when unwanted behavior is shown.

*Recall that *negative reinforcers* are defined in terms of *increasing* the frequency of behavior, although the increase occurs when the negative reinforcer is *removed.* A punishment *decreases* the frequency of a behavior when it is *applied.*

Discriminative Stimuli

B. F. Skinner might not have been able to get his pigeons into the drivers' seats of missiles during the war, but he had no problem training them to respond to traffic lights. Try the following experiment for yourself.

Find a pigeon. Or sit on a park bench, close your eyes, and one will find you. Place it in a Skinner box with a button on the wall. Drop a food pellet into the cage whenever the pigeon pecks the button. (Soon it will learn to peck the button whenever it has not eaten for a while.) Now place a small green light in the cage. Turn it on and off intermittently throughout the day. Reinforce button pecking with food whenever the green light is on but not when the light is off. It will not take long for this clever city pigeon to learn that it will gain as much by grooming itself or squawking and flapping around as it will by pecking the button when the light is off.

The green light will have become a **discriminative stimulus.** Discriminative stimuli act as cues. They provide information about when an operant (in this case, pecking a button) will be reinforced (in this case, by a food pellet being dropped into the cage).

As previously noted, operants that are not reinforced tend to become extinguished. For the pigeon in our experiment, pecking the button *when the light is off* becomes extinguished.

A moment's reflection will suggest many ways in which discriminative stimuli influence our behavior. Would you rather ask your boss for a raise when she is smiling or when she is frowning? Wouldn't you rather answer the telephone when it is ringing? Do you think it is wise to try to get smoochy when your date is blowing smoke in your face or chugalugging a bottle of antacid tablets? One of the factors involved in gaining social skills is learning to interpret social discriminative stimuli (smiles, tones of voice, body language) accurately.

Schedules of Reinforcement

In operant conditioning, some responses are maintained by **continuous reinforcement.** You probably become warmer every time you put on heavy clothing. You probably become less thirsty every time you drink water. Yet if you have ever watched people throwing money down the maws of slot machines, or "one-armed bandits," you know that behavior can also be maintained by **partial reinforcement.**

Some folklore about gambling is based on solid learning theory. You can get a person "hooked" on gambling by fixing the game to allow heavy winnings at first. Then you gradually space out the gambling behaviors that are reinforced until the gambling is maintained by very infrequent winning—or even no winning at all.

Truth or Fiction Revisited

It is true that you can hook people on gambling by allowing them to win some money in the early stages and then tapering off with the payoffs. Partial reinforcement schedules can maintain behavior for a great deal of time, even though it goes unreinforced.

New operants or behaviors are acquired most rapidly through continuous reinforcement or, in some cases, through "one-trial learning" that meets with great reinforcement. So-called **pathological gamblers** often had big wins at the racetrack or casino or in the lottery in their late teens or early

Discriminative stimulus In operant conditioning, a stimulus that indicates that reinforcement is available.

Continuous reinforcement A schedule of reinforcement in which every correct response is reinforced.

Partial reinforcement One of several reinforcement schedules in which not every correct response is reinforced.

Pathological gambler A person who gambles habitually, despite consistent losses.

Fixed-interval schedule A schedule in which a fixed amount of time must elapse between the previous and subsequent times that reinforcement is available.

Variable-interval schedule A schedule in which a variable amount of time must elapse between the previous and subsequent times that reinforcement is available.

Fixed-ratio schedule A schedule in which reinforcement is provided after a fixed number of correct responses.

Variable-ratio schedule A schedule in which reinforcement is provided after a variable number of correct responses.

20s (Greene, 1982). But once the operant has been acquired, it can be maintained by tapering off to a schedule of partial reinforcement.

There are four basic schedules of reinforcement. They are determined by changing either the *interval* of time that must elapse between correct responses before reinforcement is made available or the *ratio* of correct responses to reinforcements. If the interval that must elapse between correct responses, before reinforcement becomes available, is zero seconds, the reinforcement schedule is continuous. A larger interval of time, such as one or thirty seconds, is a partial-reinforcement schedule. A one-to-one (1:1) ratio of correct responses to reinforcements is a continuous-reinforcement schedule. A higher ratio, such as a 2:1 or 5:1 ratio, would be a partial-reinforcement schedule.

The four basic types of schedules of reinforcement are *fixed-interval, variable-interval, fixed-ratio,* and *variable-ratio* schedules.

In a **fixed-interval schedule,** a fixed amount of time, say one minute, must elapse between the previous and subsequent times that reinforcement is made available for correct responses. In a **variable-interval schedule,** varying amounts of time are allowed to elapse between making reinforcement available. In a three-minute variable-interval schedule, the mean amount of time that would elapse between reinforcement opportunities would be three minutes. Each interval might vary, however, from one to five minutes.

With a fixed-interval schedule, an organism's response rate falls off after each reinforcement, then picks up as it nears the time when reinforcement will be dispensed. For example, in a one-minute fixed-interval schedule, a rat will be reinforced with, say, a food pellet for the first operant—for example, the first pressing of a lever—that occurs after a minute has elapsed. After each reinforcement, the rat's rate of lever pressing slows down, but as the end of the one-minute interval draws near, lever pressing increases in frequency, as suggested by Figure 5.8. It is as if the rat has learned that it must wait a while before reinforcement will be made available. The resultant record on the cumulative recorder (Figure 5.8) shows a series of characteristic upward-moving waves or scallops, which is referred to as a *fixed-interval scallop.*

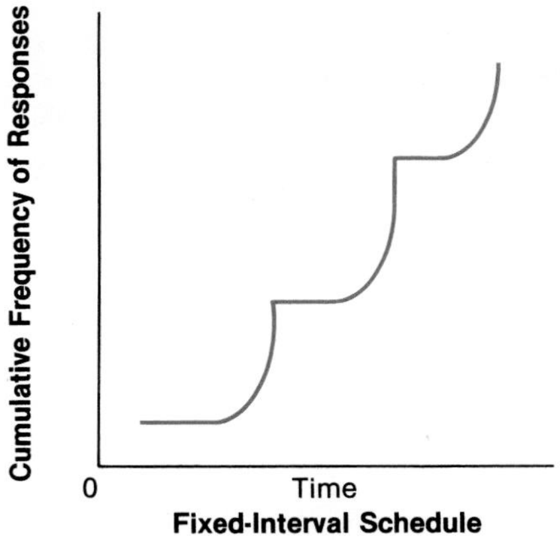

Figure 5.8
The "Fixed-Interval Scallop." Organisms who are reinforced on a fixed-interval schedule tend to slack off in responding after each reinforcement. The rate of response then picks up as they near the time when reinforcement will again become available. The results on the cumulative recorder look like an upward-moving series of waves, or scallops.

In the case of the more unpredictable variable-interval schedule, the response rate is steadier but lower. If the boss calls us in for a weekly report, we will probably work hard to pull the pieces together just before the report is to be given, just as we might cram the night before a weekly quiz. But if we know that the boss might call us in for a report on the progress of a project at any time (variable-interval schedule), we are likely to keep things in a state of reasonable readiness at all times. However, our efforts are unlikely to have the intensity they would in a fixed-interval (e.g., weekly) schedule. Similarly, we are less likely to cram for a series of unpredictable "pop quizzes" than for regularly scheduled quizzes. But we are likely to do at least some studying on a regular basis.

Note the effects of the reduced prices and rebates automobile companies usually offer during the period between July and September to make way for the new models. Aren't they encouraging buyers to wait for the summer and then buy in a flurry?

In a **fixed-ratio schedule,** reinforcement is provided after a fixed number of correct responses has been made. In a **variable-ratio schedule,** reinforcement is provided after a variable number of correct responses has been made. In a 10:1 variable-ratio schedule, the mean number of correct responses that would have to be made before a subsequent correct response would be reinforced is 10, but the ratio of correct responses to reinforcements might be allowed to vary from, say, 1:1 to 20:1 on a random basis.

Figure 5.9
The Shaping Up of Barnabus the Rat. Psychologists at Columbia University (Pierrel & Sherman, 1963) shaped Barnabus to perform a complex behavioral chain by profusely reinforcing each behavior in sequence. The sequence proceeded from last to first, so that each reward would trigger the next behavior in the chain. In these photos you see Barnabus (a) climb a spiral ramp, (b) cross a bridge, (c) climb a ladder, (d) pedal a toy car, (e) climb steps, (f) crawl through a tube, and (g) ride an elevator to return to the starting platform. Finally, Barnabus presses a lever to attain a food pellet (not shown). Complex behavior for a rat?

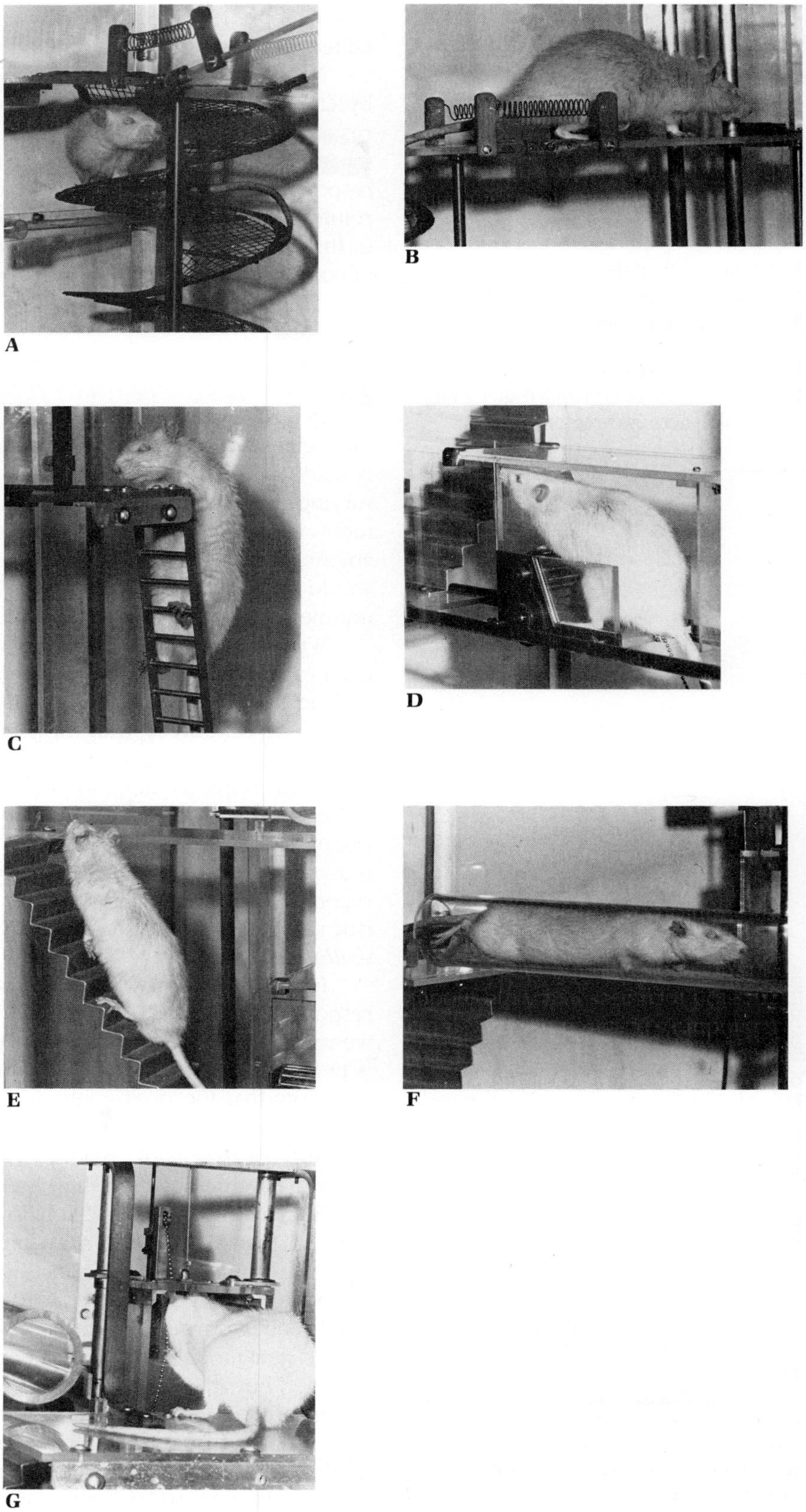

Fixed-ratio and variable-ratio schedules maintain a high response rate. With a fixed-ratio schedule, it is as if the organism learns that it must make several responses before being reinforced. It then "gets them out of the way" as rapidly as possible. Consider the example of piecework. If a worker must sew five shirts to receive a ten dollar bill, he or she is on a fixed-ratio (5:1) schedule and is likely to sew at a uniformly high rate, although there might be a brief pause following each reinforcement. With a variable-ratio schedule, reinforcement can come at any time. This unpredictability also maintains a high response rate. Slot machines tend to pay off on variable-ratio schedules, and players can be seen popping coins into their maws and pulling their "arms" with barely a pause. I have seen players who do not even stop to pick up their winnings. Instead, they continue to smoothly pop in the coins, whether from their original stack or from the winnings tray.

Shaping If you are teaching disco-type maneuvers to people who have never danced, do not wait until they have performed a perfect Latin hustle before telling them they're on the right track. The foxtrot will be back in style before they have learned a thing.

We can teach complex behaviors by **shaping,** or at first reinforcing small steps toward the behavioral goals. In the beginning it may be wise to smile and say "Good" when a reluctant newcomer gathers the courage to get out on the dance floor, even if your feet get flattened by his initial clumsiness. If you are teaching someone to drive a car with a standard shift, at first generously reinforce the learner simply for shifting without stalling.

But as training proceeds, we come to expect more before dispensing reinforcement. We reinforce **successive approximations** to the goal. If you want to train a rat to climb a ladder, first reinforce it (with a food pellet) when it turns toward the ladder. Then wait until it approaches the ladder before using reinforcement. Then do not drop a food pellet into the cage until the rat touches the ladder. In this way the rat will reach the top of the ladder more quickly than if you had waited until the target behavior had first occurred by random trial and error. This method of shaping was used to train one rat, Barnabus, to engage in the complex behavioral sequence shown in Figure 5.9.

Truth or Fiction Revisited

It is true that rats can be trained to climb a ramp, cross a bridge, and so on—all in proper sequence. The operant-conditioning procedure used to do so is called shaping.

Learning to drive a new standard-shift automobile to a new job also involves a complex sequence of operant behaviors. At first we actively seek out all the discriminative stimuli or landmarks that cue us when to turn—signs, buildings, hills, and valleys. We also focus on shifting to a lower gear as we slow down so that the car won't stall. After many repetitions, though, these responses, these chains of behavior, become "habitual" and we need to pay very little attention to them.

Shaping A procedure for teaching complex behaviors that at first reinforces approximations to the target behavior.

Successive approximations Behaviors that are progressively closer to a target behavior.

Applications of Operant Conditioning

Operant conditioning, like classical conditioning, is not just an exotic laboratory procedure. We use operant conditioning every day in our efforts to influence other people. Parents and peers incline children to acquire "sex-appropriate" behavior patterns through the elaborate use of rewards and

Taking the Pledge. Operant conditioning appears to play a role in the socialization of children. Parents and teachers tend to reward children for expressing attitudes that coincide with their own and to punish or ignore them when they express deviant attitudes.

punishments (see Chapter 14). Parents also tend to praise their children for sharing with others and to punish them for being too aggressive. Peers participate in the **socialization** process by playing with children who are generous and nonaggressive and, often, by avoiding those who are not (Rathus, 1988).

Operant conditioning may also play a role in attitude formation (see Chapter 15). Parents tend to reward their children for expressing attitudes that coincide with their own and to punish or ignore them for expressing attitudes that deviate. Many children are also placed in religious schools that provide instruction and a system of rewards and punishments to shape behavior patterns from an early age.

Let us now consider some specific applications of operant conditioning.

Biofeedback Training Biofeedback training (BFT), described in Chapter 4, is based on principles of operant conditioning. Through BFT, people and lower animals have learned to control autonomic responses to attain reinforcement. BFT has been an important innovation in the treatment of health-related problems during the past few decades.

Organisms can gain control of other autonomic functions, such as blood pressure. They also can learn to improve their control over functions that are within the grasp of voluntary manipulation, such as muscle tension. When people receive BFT, reinforcement is in the form of *information*. Perhaps a "bleep" sound changes in pitch or frequency of occurrence to signal that they have modified the autonomic function in the desired direction. People, for example, can learn to emit alpha waves (and feel somewhat more relaxed) through feedback from an electroencephalograph. Through the use of other instruments, people have learned to lower muscle tension, their heart rates, even their blood pressure.

As described in Chapter 3, BFT has also been used with accident patients who have lost neuromuscular control of various parts of the body.

Token Economies Behavior therapists apply operant conditioning to foster desired responses, such as social skills, and to extinguish unwanted behaviors, such as social withdrawal in a mental hospital. Several techniques, such as the use of the **token economy,** are outlined in Chapter 13. In token

---

Socialization Guidance of people into socially desirable behavior by means of verbal messages, the systematic use of rewards and punishments, and other methods of teaching.

Token economy An environmental setting that fosters desired behavior by reinforcing it with tokens (secondary reinforcers) that can be exchanged for other reinforcers.

PSYCHOLOGY GOES TO WORK

Business and Operant Conditioning

We already noted that sales executives are applying a fixed-interval reinforcement schedule when they offer incentives for buying up the remainder of the year's line every summer and fall. In a sense they are suppressing buying at other times, except for those consumers whose current cars are in their death throes or those who cannot exercise self-control.

The so-called frequent-flyer programs offered by airlines are sorts of token economies. In these programs, regular users of airlines are given tokens or vouchers that can be exchanged for free flights later on. Although frequent-flyer programs were originally intended to boost consumer loyalty to specific airlines, they appear to have reinforced flying in general, as measured by a significantly increased rate of flying among recipients (Thompson, 1988).

economies, psychologists give mental patients or prison inmates tokens, such as poker chips, for desired behavior. The tokens reinforce desired behavior because they can be exchanged for television time, desserts, and other desired commodities.

Principles of operant conditioning have also permitted psychologists and educators to develop many beneficial innovations, such as interventions with young children, behavior modification in the classroom, and programmed learning.

Using Avoidance Learning to Save a Baby's Life The techniques of avoidance learning suggested in *Brave New World* have actually found real-life—perhaps real-life-saving—applications with children who are too young or distressed to respond to verbal forms of therapy. In one example, reported by Lang and Melamed (1969), a 9-month-old infant vomited regularly within 10 to 15 minutes after eating. Repeated diagnostic workups had found no medical basis for the problem, and medical treatments were to no avail. When the case was brought to the attention of Lang and Melamed, the infant weighed only nine pounds and was in critical condition, being fed by a pump.

The psychologists monitored the infant for the first physical indications (local muscle tension) that vomiting was to occur. When the child tensed prior to vomiting, a tone was sounded and followed by painful but (presumably) harmless electric shock. After two one-hour treatment sessions, the infant's muscle tensions ceased in response to the tone alone, and vomiting soon ceased altogether. At a one-year follow-up, the infant was still not vomiting and had caught up in weight.

Truth or Fiction Revisited

It is true that psychologists successfully fashioned a method to teach an emaciated 9-month-old infant to stop throwing up. They employed principles of classical and operant conditioning to do so.

How do we explain this remarkable procedure? It appears to be an example of two-factor learning, as theorized by Mowrer (1947). The first factor was classical conditioning. Through repeated pairings, the tone (CS) came to elicit expectation of electric shock (US), so the psychologists could use the painful shock sparingly.

The second factor was operant conditioning. The electric shock and, after classical conditioning, the tone were aversive stimuli. The infant soon learned to suppress the behaviors (muscle tensions) that were followed with aversive stimulation. By so doing, the aversive stimuli were removed. And so, the aversive stimuli served as negative reinforcers.

PSYCHOLOGY GOES TO WORK

Behavior Modification and Education

Remember that reinforcers are defined as stimuli that increase the frequency of behavior—not as pleasant events. Ironically, adults frequently reinforce undesirable behavior in children by attending to them, or punishing them, when they misbehave but by ignoring them when they behave in desirable ways. Similarly, teachers who raise their voices when children misbehave may be unintentionally conferring hero status on their pupils in the eyes of their peers. Some children may go out of their way to earn teacher disapproval, frequently to the teacher's surprise.

Teacher-preparation programs and inservice programs now usually show teachers how to use behavior modification in the classroom in order to reverse these response pattern. Teachers are taught to pay attention to children when they are behaving appropriately and, when possible, to ignore (avoid reinforcing) their misbehavior (Lahey & Drabman, 1981). The younger the school child, the more powerful teacher attention and approval seem to be.

One study of behavior modification in the classroom was designed to change the behavior of three elementary school children who touched others, took others' property, turned around, made noise, and mouthed objects during lessons (Madsen et al., 1968). In this program, the teacher wrote out classroom rules on the blackboard, verbally guiding the children into appropriate responses. The children repeated them aloud. During the early part of training, the teacher left the rules visible while inappropriate behavior was ignored and appropriate behavior was praised. Targeted behavior rapidly decreased.

Similar approaches have reduced aggressive behavior and increased studying in school children. Descriptive praise seems more effective than a simple "Good." Saying "It was very good the way you raised your hand and waited for me to call on you before talking out" reminds the child of the behavior that results in praise and prompts repetition of the desired behavior.

Among older children and adolescents, peer approval is often a more powerful reinforcer than teacher approval. Peer approval may maintain misbehavior, and ignoring misbehavior may only allow peers to become more disruptive. In such cases it may be necessary to separate troublesome children.

Teachers also frequently use time out from positive reinforcement to discourage misbehavior. In this method, children are placed in drab, restrictive environments for a specified time period, usually about 10 minutes, when they behave disruptively. When isolated, they cannot earn the attention of peers or teachers, and no reinforcing activities are present.

It may strike you that these techniques are not startlingly new. Perhaps we all know parents who have ignored their children's misbehavior and have heard of teachers making children "sit facing the corner." What is novel is the focus on (1) avoiding punishment and (2) being consistent so that undesirable behavior is not partially reinforced. It should be noted, however, that punishment can also decrease undesirable behavior in the classroom. For example, after-school detention has been found to reduce disruptive classroom behavior (Brigham et al., 1985).

This learning occurred at an age long before any sort of verbal intervention could have been understood, and it apparently saved the infant's life. Similar procedures have been used to teach very young autistic children to avoid mutilating and otherwise injuring themselves.

Programmed Learning A Harvard University colleague of B. F. Skinner, Fred S. Keller, developed an educational practice called **programmed learning** that is based on operant conditioning. Programmed learning assumes that any complex task, involving conceptual learning as well as motor skills, can be broken down into a number of small steps. These steps can be shaped individually and combined in sequence to form the correct behavioral chain.

Programmed learning does not punish errors. Instead, correct responses are reinforced. All children earn "100," but at their own pace. Programmed learning also assumes that it is the task of the teacher (or program) to structure the learning experience in such a way that errors will not be made.

Truth or Fiction Revisited

It is *not* true that we must make mistakes if we are to learn. This idea that we must make mistakes derives from folklore to the effect that we learn from (bad) experience. However, as pointed out in the chapter, we also learn from good (positively reinforced) experiences and from the experiences of others.

Programmed learning A method of learning in which complex tasks are broken down into simple steps, each of which is reinforced. Errors are not reinforced.

Figure 5.10
A Demonstration of Insight or Just Some Fiddling with Sticks? Gestalt psychologist Wolfgang Köhler ran experiments with chimpanzees that suggest that not all learning is mechanical. This chimp must retrieve a stick outside the cage and attach it to a stick he already has before he can retrieve the distant circular object. While fiddling with two such sticks, Sultan, another chimp, seemed to suddenly recognize that the sticks could be attached. This is an example of learning by insight.

Classical and operant conditioning are relatively simple forms of learning. Much of conditioning's appeal has been that it can be said to meet the behaviorist objective of explaining behavior in terms of public, observable events—in this case, laboratory conditions. Building on this theoretical base, some psychologists have suggested that the most complex human behavior involves the summation of so many instances of conditioning. However, many psychologists believe that conditioning cannot explain all instances of learned behavior, even in laboratory rats. They have turned to other kinds of learning to describe and explain additional findings. These include insight learning, latent learning, observational learning, and concept learning.

INSIGHT LEARNING

During World War I, German Gestalt psychologist Wolfgang Köhler became convinced that not all forms of learning could be explained by conditioning when one of his chimpanzees, Sultan, "went bananas." Sultan had learned to use a stick to rake in bananas placed outside his cage. But now Herr Köhler (pronounced *hair curler)* placed the banana beyond the reach of the stick. He gave Sultan two bamboo poles that could be fitted together to make a single pole long enough to retrieve the delectable reward. The setup was similar to that shown in Figure 5.10.

As if to make this historic occasion more dramatic, Sultan at first tried to reach the banana with one pole. When he could not do so, he returned to fiddling with the sticks. Köhler left the laboratory after an hour or so of frustration (his own as well as Sultan's). An assistant was assigned the thankless task of observing Sultan. But soon afterward, Sultan happened to align the two sticks as he fiddled. Then, in what seemed to be a flash of inspiration, Sultan fitted them together and pulled in the elusive banana.

Köhler was summoned to the laboratory. When he arrived the sticks fell apart, as if on cue. But Sultan regathered them, fit them firmly together, and actually tested the strength of the fit before retrieving another banana.

Köhler was impressed by Sultan's rapid "perception of relationships" and used the term **insight** to describe it. He noted that such insights were not learned gradually through reinforced trials. Rather, they seemed to occur "in a flash" when the elements of a problem had been arranged appropriately. Sultan also proved himself to be immediately capable of stringing several sticks together to retrieve various objects, not just bananas. This seemed to be no mechanical generalization. It appeared that Sultan understood the principle of the relationship between joining sticks and reaching distant objects.

Similarly, psychologist Robert Rescorla (1988) argues that even the events that occur in conditioning suggest that learning is not as mechanical as behaviorists believe. Rescorla suggests that at some point, something akin to insight occurs. That is, animals may fail to grasp the relationships among events during several trials, as measured by display of the targeted response. But then they may suddenly display the intended response, as if something had "clicked."

Soon after Köhler's findings were reported, psychologists in the United States demonstrated that not even the behavior of rats was as mechanical as most behaviorists suggested. E. C. Tolman (1948), a University of California psychologist, showed that rats behaved as if they had acquired **cognitive maps** of mazes. Although they would learn many paths to a food goal, they would typically choose the shortest. If the shortest path was blocked, they would quickly switch to another. The behavior of the rats suggested that they learned *places in which reinforcement was available,* not a series of mechanical motor responses.

Bismarck, one of University of Michigan psychologist N. R. F. Maier's laboratory rats, provided further evidence for learning by insight (Maier & Schneirla, 1935). Bismarck had been trained to climb a ladder to a tabletop where food was placed. On one occasion Maier used a mesh barrier to prevent Bismarck from reaching his goal. But, as shown in Figure 5.11, a second ladder to the table was provided. The second ladder was in clear view of the animal. At first Bismarck sniffed and scratched and made every effort to find a path through the mesh barrier. Then Bismarck spent some time washing his face, an activity that apparently signals frustration in rats. Suddenly Bismarck jumped into the air, turned, ran down the familiar ladder around to the new ladder, ran up the new ladder, and then claimed his just desserts.

It is difficult to explain Bismarck's behavior in terms of conditioning. It seems that Bismarck suddenly perceived the relationships between the elements of his problem so that the solution occurred by insight. He seems to have had what Gestalt psychologists have termed an "Aha!-experience."

Truth or Fiction Revisited

It is *not* true that only people are capable of insight. Lower animals, including apes and rats, have also apparently shown insight in classic experiments.

LATENT LEARNING

Many behaviorists argue that organisms acquire only those responses, or operants, for which they are reinforced. However, E. C. Tolman showed that rats also learn about their environments in the absence of reinforcement.

Tolman trained some rats to run through mazes for standard food goals. Other rats were permitted to explore the same mazes for several days without food goals or other rewards. The rewarded rats could be said to have found

Insight In Gestalt psychology, a sudden perception of relationships among elements of the "perceptual field," permitting the solution of a problem.

Cognitive map A mental representation or "picture" of the elements in a learning situation, such as a maze.

Figure 5.11
Bismarck Uses a Cognitive Map to Claim His Just Desserts. Bismarck has learned to reach dinner by climbing ladder *A.* But now the food goal (*F*) is blocked by a wire mesh barrier *B.* Bismarck washes his face for a while, but then, in an apparent flash of insight, runs back down ladder *A* and up new ladder *N* to reach reinforcement.

Observational Learning. People acquire a vast variety of skills by means of observational learning. Here students learn how to "throw" a pot.

their ways through the mazes with fewer errors (fewer "wrong turns") on each trial run. But, in a sense, the unrewarded rats had no correct or incorrect turns to make, since no response led to a reward.

After the unrewarded rats had been allowed to explore the mazes for ten days, food rewards were placed in a box at the far end of the maze. The previously unrewarded explorers reached the food box as quickly as the rewarded rats after only one or two reinforced trials (Tolman & Honzik, 1950).

Tolman concluded that rats learned about mazes in which they roamed even when they were unrewarded for doing so. He distinguished between learning and performance. Rats would acquire a cognitive map of a maze, and even though they would not be motivated to follow an efficient route to the far end, they would learn rapid routes from end to end, just by roaming about within the maze. Yet this learning might remain hidden, or **latent,** until they were motivated to follow the rapid routes for food goals.

OBSERVATIONAL LEARNING

How many things have you learned from watching other people in real life, in films, and on television? From films and television you may have gathered vague ideas about how to sky dive, ride surfboards, climb sheer cliffs, run a pattern to catch a touchdown pass in the Superbowl, and dust for fingerprints, even if you have never tried these activities.

Social-learning theorist Albert Bandura has run numerous experiments (e.g., Bandura et al., 1963) that show that we acquire operants by observing the behavior of others. We may need some practice to refine the skills we acquire by observation, but we can acquire the required knowledge by observation alone. We may also choose to allow these skills to lie latent. For example, we may not imitate aggressive behavior unless we are provoked and believe that we are more likely to be rewarded than punished for it.

Observational learning may account for most human learning. It occurs when, as children, we observe parents cook, clean, or repair a broken appliance. There is evidence that observational learning for simple "single-action" tasks, such as opening the halves of a toy barrel to look at a barrel inside, occurs as early as 1 year (Abravanel & Gingold, 1985). Observational learning takes place when we watch teachers solve problems on the blackboard or hear them speak in a foreign language. Observational learning is

Latent Hidden or concealed.

Observational learning Acquiring operants by observing others engage in them.

not mechanically acquired through reinforcement. We can learn by observation without engaging in overt responses at all. It appears sufficient to pay attention to the behavior of others.

CONCEPT LEARNING

What's black and white and read all over? This riddle was heard quite often when I was younger. Since the riddle was spoken and involved the colors black and white, you would probably think that "read" meant "red" when you heard it. And so, in seeking an answer, you might scan your memory for an object that was red although it also managed to be black and white. The answer to the riddle, "newspaper," was sure to be met with a good groan.

The word *newspaper* is a **concept.** *Red, black,* and *white* are also concepts—color concepts. Concepts are symbols that stand for groups of objects, events, or ideas that have common properties.

Learning Simple Concepts

Many simple concepts, such as *dog* and *red,* can be taught by association. We can simply point to a dog and say "dog" or "This is a dog" to a child. Dogs are considered to be **positive instances** of the dog concept. **Negative instances**—that is, things that are not dogs—are then shown to the child while one says, "This is *not* a dog."

Things that are negative instances of one concept may be positive instances of another. So, in teaching a child, one may be more likely to say "This is not a dog—it's a cat," than simply, "This is not a dog."

Learning Complex Concepts

More abstract concepts, such as *uncle* or *square root,* may have to be learned through verbal explanations that involve more basic concepts. If one points to *uncles* (positive instances) and *not uncles* (negative instances) repeatedly, a child may eventually learn that uncles are males, or even that they are males that are somehow parts of their extended families. However, it is doubtful that this show-and-tell method would ever teach them that uncles are brothers of a parent. The concept *uncle* is best taught by explanation after the child understands the more basic concepts *parent* (or at least *Mommy* and *Daddy*) and *brother.*

Concepts that are still more abstract, such as *justice, goodness,* and *beauty,* may require complex verbal explanation and the presentation of many positive and negative instances. These concepts are so abstract and instances of them are so varied that no two people may agree on their definition. Or, if their definitions coincide, they may argue over positive versus negative instances. Withholding rent while repairs are being completed may seem just to the tenant but unjust to the landlord. What seems to be a beautiful work of art to me may impress you as meaningless jumbles of color. Thus the phrase, "Beauty is in the eye of the beholder."

Concept A symbol that stands for a group of objects, ideas, or events with common properties.

Positive instance A example of a concept.

Negative instance An idea, event, or object that is *not* an example of a concept. Concept formation is aided by presentation of positive and negative instances.

Figure 5.12
Geometric Forms of the Type Used by Psychologists in Experiments on Concept Formation.

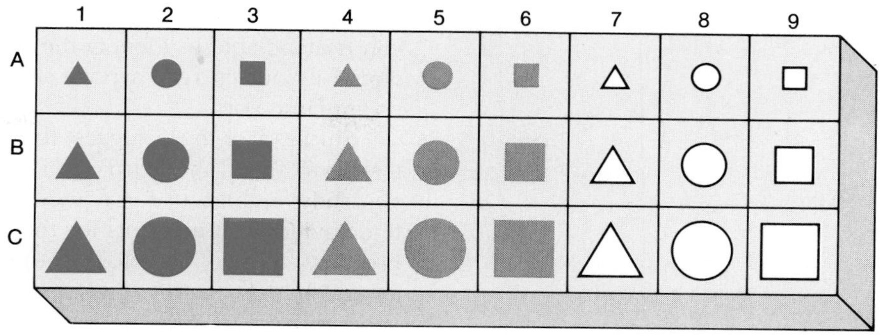

Learning Concepts by Hypothesis Testing

Psychologists have also shown that children are not merely passive recipients of information about the meanings of concepts. They—and we as adults—also engage in the active process of **hypothesis testing** in attempting to ferret out the meanings of concepts.

A parent may point to a small, elongated fish in a tank and tell a child "That's a guppy." The child may hypothesize that "things that move in water" are guppies. Then the parent points to a large fish with flowing fins and says, "That's an angel fish." Now the child will probably modify his or her hypothesis about what makes up a guppy or an angel fish. The child may focus on the shapes, sizes, and colors of the fish and try to generalize to other fish, pointing and asking, "Is this a guppy, too?" The parent will answer yes or no and perhaps begin to explain that guppies are small fish with a sort of cigar shape that come in various colors. The child may then wonder if the small, cigar-shaped fish with the black and white stripes are also guppies and continue to ask, "Is this a guppy, too?" When the parent says, "No, that's a zebra fish," the child may restrict his or her concept of guppies to the fish that are gray or have blue or red patches. The parent's responding yes or no gives the child further feedback as to the accuracy of his or her hypotheses.

Experiments in concept formation through hypothesis testing give us insight into the process (Bourne et al., 1971; Bruner et al., 1956; Horton & Turnage, 1976). Let us try a brief experiment to see how you might acquire the concept *zed*—or learn what "zeds" are so that you can describe their features correctly.

Let us imagine that we sit across a table from one another with a box of plastic shapes between us, arrayed like those shown in Figure 5.12. These are the rules. I ask you to pick pieces out one at a time. Each time, I tell you whether or not it is a zed. When you can state without error which pieces are zeds and which are not, I'll know that you have learned what zeds are.

You select *A1,* the small blue triangle, and I say, "No, that's not a zed." Then you pick out *B2,* and I say, "Yes, that's a zed." Do you pick out your third piece at random or on the basis of hypotheses as to what zeds might be? Have you already eliminated a number of hypotheses? For example, you already have enough information to classify the following hypotheses as false: All zeds are gray; all zeds are white; all zeds are square.

Next you select *B5,* and I say "Yes." What's your latest hypothesis? Next do you pick out *B8*? If you do, I say "No." What do you think? You continue

Hypothesis testing In concept formation, a process in which we attempt to ferret out the meanings or salient features of concepts by testing our assumptions.

to select pieces. *C5* is not a zed. *B4* is, and so is *B3*. But *B7* is not. Would you now be able to identify the remaining zeds without further error? You would if your current hypothesis is that zeds are medium in size and blue or gray in color.

Studies like these suggest that even young children may use hypothesis testing to speed the learning of concepts such as shapes and colors. When you show a child a square and say "This is a square," the child may try to understand what accounts for the squareness of the figure. Is it the figure's boxiness, its size, its color, or the fact that it is closed? After being shown several figures that are identified as squares and several that are not, the child appears to develop a concept of squareness that involves more basic concepts such as *box, straight line,* and [*lines*] *just as long as the others.* Years may pass before the child's definition becomes sophisticated enough to involve concepts such as *a closed geometric figure* that has *four sides equal in length* and *right angles.*

Thus, there are many different kinds of learning. We have touched on a number of them in this chapter. We have seen that psychologists disagree about what learning is, what is learned, and whether organisms are basically active or passive as they participate in the processes of learning. Nonetheless, most psychologists agree that the capacity to learn is at the heart of organisms' abilities to adapt to their environments. Some psychologists also believe that organisms, especially humans, can learn to fashion their environments in ways that enable them to meet their needs better.

It would be of little use to discuss how we learn if we were not capable of remembering what we learn from second to second, from day to day, or, in many cases, for a lifetime. In the next chapter, we turn our attention to the subject of memory. And, in Chapter 7, we shall see how learning is intertwined with language development, problem solving, and a concept that many people think of as learning ability: intelligence.

SUMMARY

1. **What is learning?** Learning is the process by which experience leads to modified representations of the environment and relatively permanent changes in behavior.
2. **What is classical conditioning?** In classical conditioning as a laboratory procedure, a previously neutral stimulus (the conditioned stimulus, or CS) comes to elicit the response evoked by a second stimulus (the unconditioned stimulus, or US) as a result of being paired repeatedly with the second stimulus.
3. **What kinds of classical conditioning procedures are there?** In the most efficient classical conditioning procedure, the CS is presented about 0.5 seconds before the US. Other classical conditioning procedures include trace conditioning; simultaneous conditioning; and backward conditioning, in which the US is presented first.
4. **What is contingency theory?** This is the view that organisms learn associations between stimuli only when stimuli provide new information about one another.
5. **How do extinction and spontaneous recovery occur in classical conditioning?** After a US-CS association has been learned, repeated presentation of the CS (for example, a bell) without the US (meat powder) will extinguish the CR (salivation). But extinguished responses may show spontaneous recovery as a function of the time that has elapsed since the end of the extinction process.
6. **What are generalization and discrimination?** In generalization, organisms show a CR in response to a range of stimuli similar to the CS. In discrimination, organisms learn to show a CR in response to a more limited range of stimuli by pairing only the limited stimulus with the US.

7. **What is the law of effect?** Edward L. Thorndike originated the law of effect, which holds that responses are "stamped in" by rewards and "stamped out" by punishments.

8. **What is operant conditioning?** In operant conditioning, organisms learn to engage in behavior that is reinforced. Initial "correct" responses may be performed by random trial and error or by physical or verbal guiding. Reinforced responses occur more frequently.

9. **What kinds of reinforcers are there?** Positive reinforcers increase the probability that operants will occur when they are applied. Negative reinforcers increase the probability that operants will occur when the reinforcers are removed. Primary reinforcers have their value because of the organism's biological makeup. Secondary reinforcers, like money and approval, acquire their value through association with established reinforcers.

10. **How do extinction and spontaneous recovery occur in operant conditioning?** In operant conditioning, learned responses are extinguished as a result of repeated performance in the absence of reinforcement. As in classical conditioning, spontaneous recovery occurs as a function of the passage of time.

11. **What are rewards and punishments?** Rewards, like reinforcers, increase the frequency of behavior. But rewards differ from reinforcers in that they are pleasant stimuli. Punishments are aversive stimuli that suppress the frequency of behavior.

12. **Why do many learning theorists advise against using punishment in child rearing?** Many learning theorists prefer treating children's misbehavior by ignoring it or using time out from positive reinforcement for several reasons. Punishment fails to teach desirable responses, suppresses behavior only when it is guaranteed, creates hostility, can lead to overgeneralization, and serves as a model for aggression.

13. **What is a discriminative stimulus?** A discriminative stimulus indicates when an operant will be reinforced.

14. **What kinds of schedules of reinforcement are there?** Continuous reinforcement leads to the most rapid acquisition of new responses, but operants are maintained most economically through partial reinforcement. There are four basic schedules of reinforcement. In a fixed-interval schedule, a specific amount of time must elapse since a previous correct response before reinforcement again becomes available. In a variable-interval schedule, the amount of time is allowed to vary. In a fixed-ratio schedule, a fixed number of correct responses must be performed before one is reinforced. In a variable-ratio schedule, this number is allowed to vary.

15. **What is shaping?** In shaping, successive approximations to the target response are reinforced.

16. **What is insight learning?** Insight learning involves a sudden reorganization of perceptual relationships, allowing for the abrupt solution of problems. Classic research with chimpanzees (by Köhler) and rats (by Maier) provide supportive evidence.

17. **What is latent learning?** In latent learning, as demonstrated by Tolman's classic research with rats, organisms can learn (modify their cognitive maps of the environment) in the absence of reinforcement. Moreover, they can gain the capacity for engaging in new behavior even when they do not show the new behavior. According to Tolman, operant conditioning teaches organisms *where* reinforcement may be found, rather than mechanically increasing the frequency of operants.

18. **What is observational learning?** Bandura and other social-learning theorists have shown that people can learn by observing others, without emitting reinforced responses of their own. They may then choose to perform the behaviors they have observed when "the time is ripe"—that is, when they believe that the learned behavior is appropriate or likely to be rewarded.

19. **What are concepts?** Concepts are symbols that stand for groups of objects, events, or ideas that have common properties. Concepts permit us to generalize without experiencing each instance of the concept.

20. **How are concepts learned?** Concepts may be formed through presentation of positive and negative instances, or through explanation using other concepts. People also actively seek to acquire new concepts through hypothesis testing.

PSYCHOLOGY AND MODERN LIFE

The Effects of Media Violence

Most human learning probably occurs by observation. Observational learning extends to observing parents and peers, classroom learning, reading books, and—in one of the more controversial aspects of modern life—learning from media such as television and films. Nearly all of us have been exposed to television, videotapes, and films in the classroom. Children in day-care centers often watch *Sesame Street.* There are filmed and videotaped versions of great works of literature, such as Orson Welles' *Macbeth* or Lawrence Olivier's *Hamlet.* Nearly every school shows films of laboratory experiments. Sometimes we view "canned lectures" by master teachers.

But what of the viewing we do *outside* the classroom? Television is also one of our major sources of informal observational learning. American preschoolers average four hours of viewing a day (Pearl et al., 1982; Singer & Singer, 1981). During the school years, they spend more hours at the television set than in school (Singer, 1983). And many of the shows they watch—from Saturday morning cartoons to evening drama series—brim with violence. Therefore, one of the most important issues that has been raised by psychologists, educators, and parent groups concerns the effects of media violence.

Consider a couple of troubling examples:

In 1974, a 9-year-old California girl was raped with a bottle by four other girls who admitted that they had been given the idea by the television movie *Born Innocent.* The victim's family sued the network and the local station that had screened the film. The courts, however, decided not to award damages. They argued that such a precedent might infringe upon the right of free expression as guaranteed by the First Amendment to the Constitution.

Then there is the 1977 case in which a Florida teenager killed an elderly woman. His lawyers claimed that the boy was not guilty by reason of insanity. They argued that he had become "addicted" to television violence and could no longer differentiate between fantasy and reality. But the courts expect even inveterate television viewers to conform their behavior to the law, and the teenager was found guilty.

There are, of course, many, many more recent reports of young people who get into fights as they depart violent films. Unfortunately, many of these conflicts are lethal.

I have provided some examples of actual and possible influences of media violence. Now let me insert a comment before proceeding. Media violence does not in itself directly *cause* violence. If it did, there would be millions of *daily* incidents in which viewers imitate the aggression that they observe. But most psychologists agree that media violence *contributes* to aggression (NIMH, 1982; Rubinstein, 1983). Let's consider a number of ways in which depictions of violence make this contribution.

What Are the Effects of Media Violence? American preschoolers watch TV an average of four hours a day. Schoolchildren spend more hours at the TV set than in the classroom. With so many shows brimming with violence, psychologists, educators, and parent groups have expressed concern about the possible effects of media violence.

Observational Learning Children learn from observing the behavior of their parents and other adults (Bandura, 1973, 1986). In terms of the social-learning concepts discussed in the chapter, television violence *models* aggressive skills. Acquisition of these skills, in turn, enhances children's aggressive *competencies.* In fact, children are more likely to imitate what their parents do than to heed what they say. If adults say they disapprove of aggression but smash furniture or slap each other when frustrated, children are likely to develop the notion that aggression is the way to handle frustration. Classic experiments have shown that children tend to imitate the aggressive behavior they see on television, whether the models are cartoons or real people (Bandura et al., 1963).

Disinhibition The expression of operants or skills may be inhibited by punishment or by the expectation of punishment. Conversely, media violence may disinhibit the expression of aggressive impulses that would otherwise have been controlled, especially if the media characters "get away" with their violence or are rewarded for it. In fact, "bad guys" were invariably punished in Hollywood movies through most of the 1950s for this reason. Only since the 1960s have many violent characters managed to escape the law in films.

Bandura's research has shown that the probability of aggression increases when the models are similar to the observers and when the models are rewarded for acting aggressively. Viewers have been theorized to be *vicariously* reinforced when they observe another person being reinforced for engaging in operants. And perhaps observers of rewarded aggressors are more likely to come to believe that aggression may be appropriate for them as well.

Increased Arousal Television violence increases the arousal of viewers. In the vernacular, television "works them up." We are more likely to engage in dominant forms of behavior, including aggressive behavior, under high levels of arousal (see Chapter 8).

Habituation We become used to, or habituated to, many stimuli that impinge on us repeatedly. There is evidence that repeated exposure to television violence may decrease viewers' emotional response to real violence (Geen, 1981; Thomas et al., 1977). If children come to perceive violence as the norm, their own attitudes toward violence may become less condemnatory and they may place less value on constraining aggressive urges (Eron, 1987).

A Circular Relationship There also seems to be a circular relationship between viewing media violence and aggressive behavior (Eron, 1982, 1987; Fenigstein, 1979). Yes, television violence contributes to aggressive behavior, but aggressive children are also more likely to tune in and stay tuned to television violence.

Eron and other psychologists found that aggressive children are less popular than nonaggressive children. Eron theorizes that aggressive children watch more television because their peer relationships are less fulfilling and because the high incidence of television violence tends to confirm their encoding of aggressive behavior as being normal (1982, p. 210). And recall my comment that media violence is not the *sole* cause of observer violence. Media violence interacts with other contributors to violence. For example, Eron has found that parental rejection and the use of physical punishment by parents also increases the likelihood of aggression in children (Eron, 1982). Harsh homelife may further confirm the viewer's encoding of the world as a violent place and further encourage reliance on television for companionship.

What To Do The question repeatedly arises as to whether media violence should be curtailed in an effort to stem community violence. Because of constitutional guarantees of free expression, restraints on media depictions of violence are voluntary. Films, perhaps, are more violent than they have ever been, but television stations now and then attempt to downplay the violence in shows intended for children.

Still, our children are going to be exposed to a great deal of media violence—if not in Saturday morning cartoon shows, then in evening dramas and in the news. Or they'll hear about violence from friends, watch children get into fights, or read about violence in the newspapers. Even if all those sources of violence were somehow hidden from view, they would learn of violence in *Hamlet, Macbeth,* and even in the Bible. Thus the notion of limiting exposure to violent models is insufficient. In fact, we might even want our children to learn some aggressive skills so that they can defend themselves.

So, what is there to do? First of all, keep in mind that although media violence contributes to aggressive behavior, it does not automatically trigger aggressive behavior (Eron, 1987). Many other factors, including the quality of the home environment, are involved. A loving, comfortable home life is not likely to further feed into aggressive tendencies. Moreover, Huesmann and his colleagues (1983) have shown that we as parents and educators can do many things to mitigate the impact of media violence. For example, children who watch violent shows are rated by peers as being significantly less aggressive when they are informed of the following:

1. The violent behavior they observe in the media does *not* represent the behavior of most people.
2. The apparently aggressive behaviors they watch are not real. They reflect camera tricks, special effects, and stunts.
3. Most people use other-than-violent means to resolve their conflicts.

In observational learning, the emphasis is on the cognitive. If children consider violence inappropriate for them, they will probably not act aggressively, even if they have acquired aggressive skills.

Outline

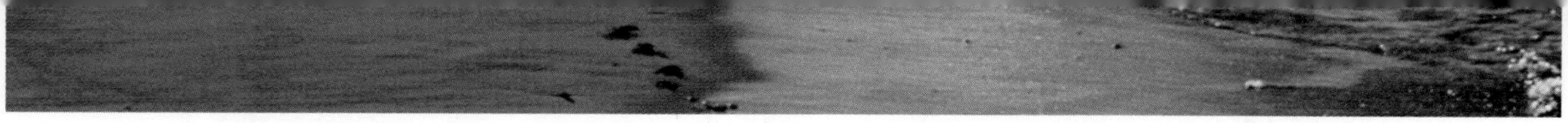

6 Memory

Truth or Fiction?

- □ Some people have photographic memories.
- □ It may be easier for you to recall the name of your first-grade teacher than of someone you just met at a party.
- □ All of our experiences are permanently imprinted on the brain so that proper stimulation can cause us to remember them exactly.
- □ Our memories are distorted by our prejudices.
- □ There is no practical limit to the amount of information you can store in your memory.
- □ Learning must be meaningful if we are to remember it.
- □ We are more likely to recall happy events while we are feeling happy and sad events while we are feeling sad.
- □ We can remember important events that took place at the early ages of 1 or 2.
- □ If a certain part of your brain were damaged, you would retain remembrance of things past, but you would not be able to form new memories.
- □ You can use tricks to improve your memory.

My oldest daughter Jill was talking about how she had run into a friend from elementary school and how they had had a splendid time recalling the goofy things they had done. Her sister Allyn, 6 at the time, was not to be outdone. "I can remember when I was born," she put in.

The family's ears perked up. Being a psychologist, I knew exactly what to say. "You can remember when you were born?" I said.

"Oh, yes," she insisted. "Mommy was there."

So far she could not be faulted. I cheered her on, and she elaborated a remarkably meticulous account of how it had been snowing in the wee hours of a bitter December morning when Mommy had to go to the hospital. You see, she said, her memory was so good that she could also summon up what it had been like *before* she was born. She wove a wonderful patchwork quilt, integrating details we had given her with her own recollections of the events surrounding the delivery of her younger sister, Jordan. All in all, she seemed quite satisfied that she had pieced together a faithful portrait of her arrival on the world stage.

Later in the chapter we shall see that children usually cannot recall events prior to the age of 2 years, much less those of the first hours. But Allyn's tale dramatized the way in which we "remember" many of the things that have happened to us. When it comes to long-term memories, truth can take a back seat to drama and embellishment. Very often our memories are like the bride's apparel—there's something old, something new, something borrowed, and, from time to time, something blue.

Memory is what this chapter is about. Without memory there is no past. Without memory, experience is trivial and learning cannot abide. We shall soon contemplate what psychologists have learned about the ways in which we remember things, but first try to meet the five challenges in the A Closer Look section on the following page.

THREE KINDS OF MEMORY

Memories contain different kinds of information, and some theorists classify memories according to the kind of material they hold (Brewer & Pani, 1984; Tulving, 1972, 1982, 1985). Return to Allyn's "recollection." Of course Allyn could not really remember her own birth. That is, she could not recall the particular event in which she had participated.

Episodic Memory

Memories of the events that happen to a person or take place in the person's presence are referred to as **episodic memory.** Your memory of what you ate for breakfast and of what your professor said in class this afternoon are examples of episodic memory.

What Allyn did recount is more accurately characterized as generalized knowledge than as visions of that important event in her young life. From listening to her parents, and from her personal experience with the events surrounding Jordan's birth, Allyn had gained extensive knowledge of what happens during childbirth. She had erroneously represented this knowledge as a precise portrayal of her birth.

Semantic Memory

Generalized knowledge is referred to as **semantic memory.** *Semantics* concerns meanings, and Allyn was reporting her understanding of the meaning of childbirth rather than an episode in her own life. You "remember" that the United States has 50 states without necessarily visiting all of them and personally adding them up. You "remember" who authored *Hamlet,* although you were not looking over Shakespeare's shoulder as he did so. These, too, are examples of semantic memory.

Your future recollection that there are three kinds of memory is more likely to be semantic than episodic. In other words, you are more likely to

Episodic memory Memories of incidents experienced by a person; of events that occur to a person or take place in the person's presence.

Semantic memory General knowledge as opposed to episodic memory.

A CLOSER LOOK

Five Challenges to Memory

Before we go any further, let's test your memory. If you want to participate, find four sheets of blank paper and number them 1 through 4. Then follow the directions given below.

1. Following are ten letters. Look at them for 15 seconds. Later in the chapter I shall ask you if you can write them on sheet number 1. (No cheating! Don't do it now.)

   THUNSTOFAM

2. Look at these nine figures for 30 seconds. Then try to draw them in the proper sequence on sheet number 2. (Yes, right after you've finished looking at them. We'll talk about your drawings later.)

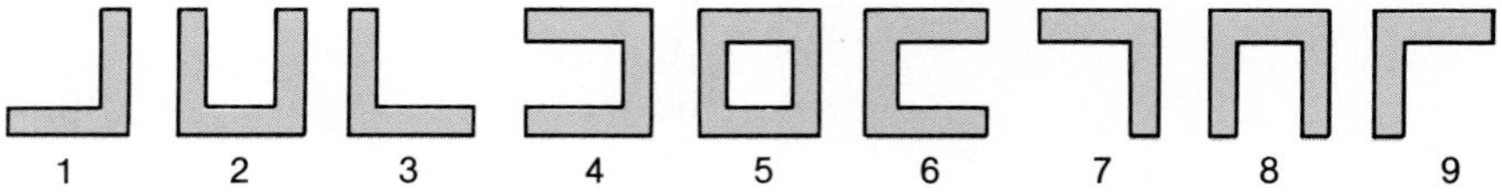

3. Okay, here's another list of letters, 17 this time. Look at the list for 60 seconds and then see whether you can reproduce it on sheet number 3. (I'm being generous this time—a full minute.)

   GMC–BSI–BMA–TTC–IAF–BI

4. Which of these pennies is an accurate reproduction of the Lincoln penny you see every day? This time there's nothing to draw on another sheet; just circle or put a checkmark by the penny you think resembles the ones you throw in the back of the drawer.

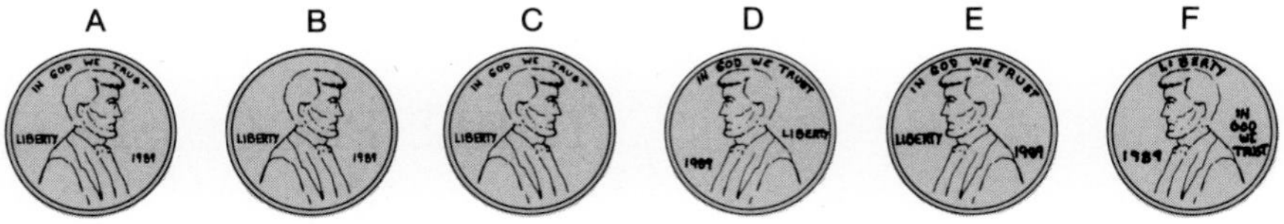

5. Examine the following drawings for one minute. Then copy the names of the figures on sheet number 4. When you're finished, just keep reading. Soon I'll be asking you to draw those figures.

"know" that there are three types of memory than to recall the date on which you learned about them, exactly where you were and how you were sitting, and whether or not you were also thinking about dinner at the time. Tulving (1972) notes that we tend to use the phrase "I remember . . ." when we are referring to episodic memories, as in "I *remember* the blizzard of 1988." But we are more likely to say "I know . . ." in reference to semantic memories, as in "I *know* about—" (or, "I heard about—") "—the blizzard of 1888." Put it another way: You may *remember* that you wrote your mother, but you *know* that Shakespeare wrote *Hamlet.*

Procedural Memory

Procedural Memory. Procedural memory—also referred to as skill memory—involves knowledge of how to do things. Memories of how to ride a bicycle, how to type, how to turn the lights on and off, and how to drive a car are procedural memories. Procedural memories tend to persevere, even when we have not used them for many years. Do we ever forget how to ride a bicycle?

The third type of memory is **procedural memory,** also referred to as *skill memory.* Procedural memory involves knowledge of how to do things. You have learned and "remember" how to ride a bicycle, how to swim or swing a bat, how to type (or in the case of my hunting and pecking, the approximate location of the typewriter keys), how to turn the lights on and off, and how to drive a car. Procedural memories tend to persevere, even when we have not used them for many, many years. For example, it is said that we never forget how to ride a bicycle. On the other hand, procedural memories may concern skills that we cannot readily describe in words. Would you be able to explain to another person just how you manage to keep from falling when you ride a bike? When you're teaching someone how to use a manual shift, do you stick to words or do you move your arm both to remember and to illustrate the technique?

Do you think it would help for a person to have "ESP" to remember the three types of memory? That is, E = episodic, S = semantic, and P = procedural. As we proceed, we shall see that a good deal of information about memory comes in threes. We shall also learn more about **mnemonic devices**, such as "ESP." By the way, is your use of the **acronym** *ESP* to help remember the kinds of memory an instance of episodic, semantic, or procedural memory?

Before proceeding to the next section, why don't you turn to that piece of paper on which you wrote the names of the four figures—that is, sheet number 4—and draw them from memory as exactly as you can. Then hold on to the drawings and we'll talk about them a bit later.

THREE PROCESSES OF MEMORY

Psychologists and computer scientists both speak in terms of the processing of information. Think of using a minicomputer to write a term paper. Once the system is operating, you begin to type in information. You place information into the computer's memory by typing letters on a keyboard. If you were to practice grisly surgery on your computer (which I am often tempted to do) and open up its memory, however, you wouldn't find these letters inside. This is because the computer is programmed to change the letters, the information you have typed, into a form that can be placed in its electronic memory. Similarly, when we perceive information, we must convert it into a form that can be remembered if we are to place it in memory.

Procedural memory Knowledge of ways of doing things; skill memory.

Mnemonic devices Systems for remembering in which items are related to easily recalled sets of symbols, such as acronyms, phrases, or jingles.

Acronym A word that is composed of the first letters of the elements of a phrase.

Encoding Modifying information so that it can be placed in memory. The first stage of information processing.

Encoding

The first stage of information processing, or changing information so that we can place it in memory, is called **encoding.** Information about the world outside reaches our senses as physical and chemical stimulation. When we encode this information, we convert it into psychological formats that can be mentally represented. To do so, we commonly use *visual, auditory,* and *semantic codes.*

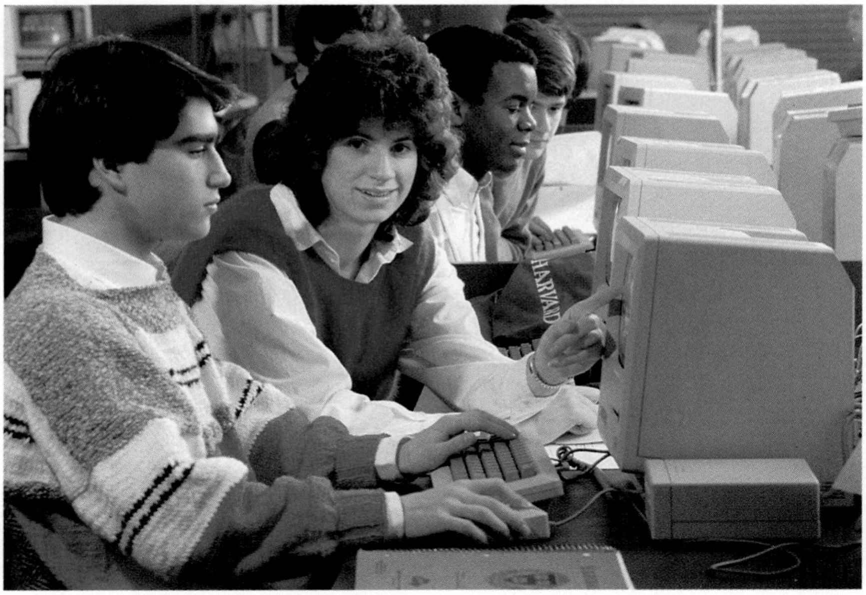

Processing Information. People and computers both process information. The first step in information processing is encoding it, or changing it into a form that enables us to place it in memory. We encode information as we type it into the computer's memory. In what ways do we encode information to enter it into our memories?

Let us illustrate the uses of coding by referring to the list of letters you first saw in the box on challenges to memory. Why not try to write the letters down now on sheet number 1, and then we'll talk about them? Go on, take a minute and then come back.

Okay, now: If you had used a **visual code** to try to remember the list, you would have mentally represented it as a picture. That is, you would have maintained—or attempted to maintain—a mental image of the letters. Some artists and art historians seem to maintain marvelous visual mental representations of works of art, so that they recognize at once whether a photograph of a work is authentic.

You may also have decided to read the list of letters to yourself—that is, to silently say them in sequence: "t," "h," "u," and so on. By so doing, you would have been using an **acoustic code,** or representing the stimuli as a sequence of sounds. You may also have read the list as a three-syllable word, "thun-sto-fam." This is an acoustic code, but it also involves the "meaning" of the letters, in the sense that you are interpreting the list as a word. And so this approach has elements of a semantic code.

Semantic codes represent stimuli in terms of their meaning. How can you use a semantic code to help remember the three colors blue, yellow, and gray? You may recall from Chapter 3 that blue and yellow are complementary, and when we mix lights of complementary colors we attain gray. Using this relationship among the colors to remember them lends the grouping meaning and, for this reason, is an example of a semantic code.

Our ten letters were meaningless in and of themselves. However, they can also serve as an acronym for the familiar phrase "THe UNited STates OF AMerica," an observation that lends them meaning.

Storage

The second process of memory is **storage,** or the maintenance of information over time. If you were given the task of storing the list of letters (told to remember it), how would you attempt to place it in storage? One way would be by **maintenance rehearsal**—by mentally repeating the list, or

Visual code Mental representation of information as a picture.

Acoustic code Mental representation of information as a sequence of sounds.

Semantic code Mental representation of information according to its meaning.

Storage The maintenance of information over time. The second stage of information processing.

Maintenance rehearsal Mental repetition of information in order to keep it in memory.

saying it to yourself. Our awareness of the functioning of our memory, referred to by psychologists as **metamemory,** becomes more sophisticated as we develop. In Chapter 9 we shall see that we become more likely to use rehearsal as we develop.

You could also have condensed the amount of information you were rehearsing by reading the list as a three-syllable word; that is, you could have rehearsed three syllables rather than ten letters. In either case, repetition would have been the key to memory. (We'll talk more about such condensing, or "chunking," very soon.) However, if you had encoded the list semantically, as an acronym for "The United States of America," storage might have been instantaneous and permanent, as we shall see.

Retrieval

The third memory process is **retrieval,** or locating stored information and returning it to consciousness. With well-known information, such as our names and occupations, retrieval is effortless and, for all practical purposes, immediate. But when we are trying to remember massive quantities of information, or information that is not perfectly understood, retrieval can be tedious and not always successful. To retrieve stored information in a computer, we need to know the name of the file. Similarly, retrieval of information from our memories requires knowledge of the proper cues.

If you had encoded THUNSTOFAM as a three-syllable word, your retrieval strategy would involve recollection of the word and rules of decoding. In other words, you would say the "word" thun-sto-fam and then decode it by spelling it out. You might err in that "thun" sounds like "thumb" and "sto" could also be spelled "stow." Using the semantic code, or recognition of the acronym for "The United States of America," could lead to flawless recollection, however.

I stuck my neck out by predicting that you would immediately and permanently store the list if you recognized it as an acronym. Here, too, there would be recollection (of the name of our country) and decoding rules. That is, to "remember" the ten letters, you would have to envision the phrase and read off the first two letters of each word. Since using this semantic code is more complex than simply seeing the entire list (using a visual code), it may take a while to recall (actually, to reconstruct) the list of 10 letters. But by using the phrase you are likely to remember the list of letters perpetually and flawlessly.

Now, what if you were not able to remember the list of ten letters? What could have gone wrong? In terms of the three processes of memory, it could be that you had (1) not encoded the list in a useful way, (2) not entered the encoded information into storage, or (3) stored the information but lacked the proper cues for remembering it—such as the phrase "The United States of America" or the rule for decoding the phrase.

You may have noticed, now that we have been drawn well into the chapter, that I have discussed three kinds of memory and three processes of memory, but I have not yet *defined* memory. No apologies—we weren't ready. Now that we have explored some basic concepts, let us have a try. **Memory** is defined as the processes by which information is encoded, stored, and retrieved. These processes allow us to maintain information over the passage of time. How much time? From a fraction of a second to a lifetime. Memory is responsible for your recollection of the previous word as your eyes scan this page. Memory is equally responsible for your recollection of the names of your elementary school classmates.

Metamemory Self-awareness of the ways in which memory functions, allowing the person to encode, store, and retrieve information effectively.

Retrieval The location of stored information and its return to consciousness. The third stage of information processing.

Memory The processes by which information is encoded, stored, and retrieved.

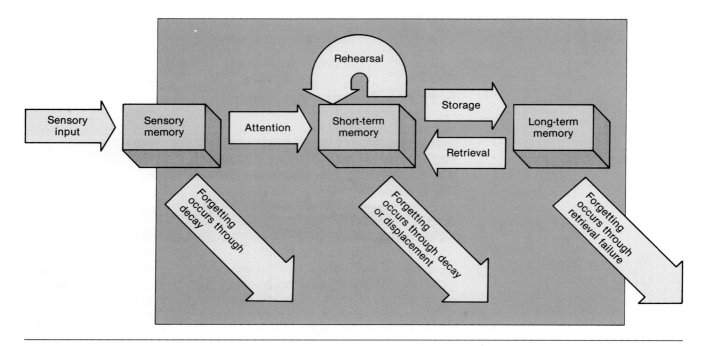

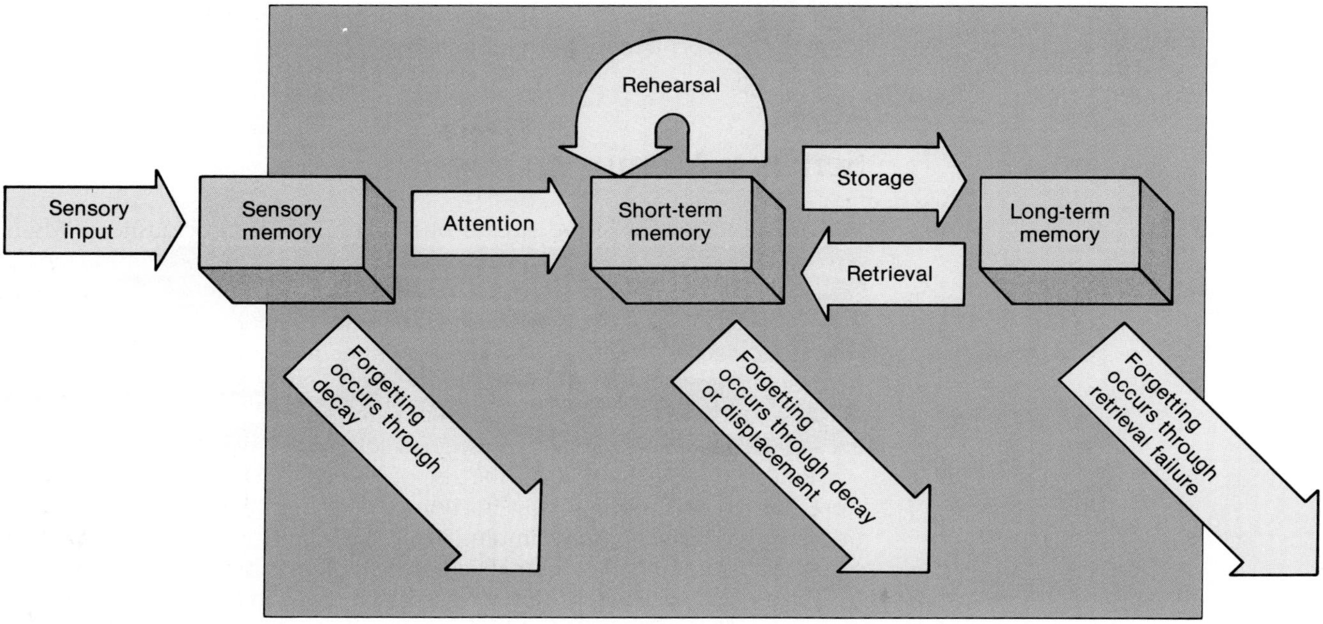

Figure 6.1
Three Stages of Memory.

A number of psychologists hypothesize that there are three distinct stages of memory. Sensory information impacts upon the registers of sensory memory, where memory traces are held briefly before decaying. If we attend to the information, much of it is transferred to short-term memory (STM). Information in STM may decay or be displaced if it is not transferred to long-term memory (LTM). We usually use rehearsal to transfer memories to LTM. Once in LTM, memories may be retrieved through appropriate search strategies. But if information is organized poorly, or if we cannot find cues to retrieve it, it may be lost.

Now let us turn our attention to two psychological models of memory—memory as stages and memory as levels of processing information.

THREE STAGES OF MEMORY

Before the turn of the century, a Harvard University professor was intrigued by the fact that some memories were unreliable, "going in one ear and out the other," whereas others could be recalled for a lifetime:

The stream of thought flows on, but most of its elements fall into the bottomless pit of oblivion. Of some, no element survives the instant of their passage. Of others, it is confined to a few moments, hours, or days. Others, again, leave vestiges which are indestructible, and by means of which they may be recalled as long as life endures.
William James, *Principles of Psychology,* 1890

Yes, the world is a constant display of sights and sounds and other sources of sensory stimulation, but only some of these things are remembered. James observed correctly that we remember various "elements of thought" for different lengths of time, and many not at all. Atkinson and Shiffrin (1968) propose that there are three stages of information processing and that the progress of information through these stages determines whether (and how long) it will be retained (see Figure 6.1). These stages are *sensory memory, short-term memory (STM),* and *long-term memory (LTM).* Let us try to make *sense* of the *short* and the *long* of memory.

Sensory Memory

William James wrote of the stream of thought, or of consciousness. When we look at a visual stimulus, our impressions may seem to be continuous. Actually, they consist of a series of eye fixations referred to as **saccadic eye movement.** These movements jump from one point to another, about four times each second. Yet the visual sensations seem continuous, or streamlike, because of **sensory memory.** Sensory memory is the type or stage of memory first encountered by a stimulus. Although it holds impressions briefly, it is long enough that series of perceptions seem to be connected.

Return to our example of the list of letters: THUNSTOFAM. If the list were flashed on a screen for a fraction of a second, the visual impression, or **memory trace,** of the stimulus would also last for only a fraction of a second afterward. Psychologists speak of the memory trace of the list as being held in a visual **sensory register.** Sensory memory, in other words, consists of registers that can briefly hold information that is entered by means of our senses.

If the letters had been flashed on a screen for, say, one-tenth of a second, your ability to remember them on the basis of sensory memory alone would be meager. Your memory would be based on a single eye fixation, and the trace of the image would vanish before a single second had passed. At the turn of the century, the social psychologist William McDougall (1904) engaged in research in which he presented subjects one to twelve letters arranged in rows—just long enough to allow a single eye fixation. Under these conditions, subjects could typically remember only four or five letters. Thus, recollection of THUNSTOFAM, a list of ten letters arranged into a single row, would probably depend on whether one had successfully transformed or encoded it into a form in which it could be processed by further stages of memory.

George Sperling (1960) modified McDougall's experimental method and showed that there is a difference between what people can see and what they can report. McDougall had used a *whole-report procedure,* in which subjects were asked to report every letter seen in the array. Sperling used a modified *partial-report procedure,* in which subjects were asked to report the contents of one of three rows of letters. In a typical procedure, Sperling flashed three rows of letters like those that follow on a screen for 50 milliseconds (1/20th of a second):

A G R E
V L S B
N K B T

Using the whole-report procedure, subjects could report an average of four letters from the entire display (one out of three). But if Sperling pointed an arrow immediately after presentation at a row he wanted viewers to report, they usually reported most of the letters in the row successfully.

If Sperling presented six letters arrayed in two rows, subjects could usually report either row without error. If subjects were flashed three rows of four letters each—a total of twelve—they reported correctly an average

Saccadic eye movement The rapid jumps made by a person's eyes as they fixate on different points.

Sensory memory The type or stage of memory first encountered by a stimulus. Sensory memory holds impressions briefly, but long enough so that series of perceptions are psychologically continuous.

Memory trace An assumed change in the nervous system that reflects the impression made by a stimulus. Memory traces are said to be "held" in sensory registers.

Sensory register A system of memory that holds information briefly, but long enough so that it can be processed further. There may be a sensory register for every sense.

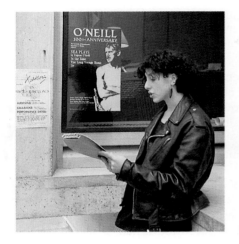

Echoic Memory. The mental representations of auditory stimuli are called echoes, and the sensory register that holds echoes is referred to as echoic memory. By encoding visual information as echoes and rehearsing the echoes, we commit them to memory. The drama student is memorizing the script by encoding typed words as echoes (placing them in echoic memory) and rehearsing them.

of three of four of the designated row, suggesting that about nine letters of the twelve had been perceived.

Sperling found that the amount of time that elapsed before indicating the row to be reported was crucial. If he delayed pointing the arrow for a few fractions of a second after the display, subjects were much less successful in reporting the target row. If he allowed a full second to elapse, the arrow did not aid recall at all. From these data, Sperling concluded that the memory trace of visual stimuli *decays* within a second in the visual sensory register (see Figure 6.1). With a single eye fixation, subjects can *see* most of a display of twelve letters clearly, as shown by their ability to immediately read off most of the letters in a designated row. Yet, as the fractions of a single second are elapsing, the memory trace of the letters is fading. By the time a second has elapsed, the trace has vanished.

Iconic Memory Psychologists believe there is a sensory register for each one of our senses. The mental representations of visual stimuli are referred to as **icons.** The sensory register that holds icons is labeled **iconic memory.** Iconic memories are accurate, photographic memories. So those of us who can see—who mentally represent visual stimuli—have "photographic memories." However, they are very brief. What most of us normally think of as a photographic memory—the ability to retain exact mental representations of visual stimuli over long periods of time—is referred to by psychologists as eidetic imagery, which is discussed in A Closer Look on the next page.

Iconic Memory and Saccadic Eye Movements: Smoothing Out the Bumps in the Visual Ride Saccadic eye movements occur about four times every second. Iconic memory, however, holds icons for up to a second. As a consequence, the flow of visual information seems smooth and continuous. Your impression that the words you are reading flow across the page, rather than jump across in spurts, is a product of your iconic memory. Similarly, you may recall from Chapter 3 that motion pictures present 16 to 22 separate frames, or still images, each second. Iconic memory allows you to perceive the imagery as being seamless (Loftus, 1983).

Echoic Memory The mental representations of auditory stimuli are called **echoes.** The sensory register that holds echoes is referred to as **echoic memory.**

The memory traces of auditory stimuli (that is, echoes) can last for several seconds, many times longer than the traces of visual stimuli (icons). The difference in the duration of traces is probably based on biological differences between the eye and ear. This difference is one of the reasons that acoustic codes aid in the retention of information that has been presented visually—or why saying the letters or syllables of THUNSTOFAM makes the list easier to remember.

Yet echoes, like icons, will fade with the passage of time. If they are to be retained, we must pay attention to them. By selectively attending to certain stimuli, we sort them out from the background noise. For example, in studies on the development of patterns of processing information, young children have been shown photographs of rooms full of toys and then have been asked to recall as many as they can. One such study found that 2-year-old boys are more likely to attend to and remember toys such as cars, puzzles, and trains, whereas 2-year-old girls are more likely to attend to and remember dolls, dishes, and teddy bears (Renninger & Wozniak, 1985). Even by this early age, children's patterns of attention have frequently fallen into stereotypical configurations.

Icon A mental representation of a visual stimulus that is held briefly in sensory memory.

Iconic memory The sensory register that briefly holds mental representations of visual stimuli.

Echo A mental representation of an auditory stimulus that is held briefly in sensory memory.

Echoic memory The sensory register that briefly holds mental representations of auditory stimuli.

A CLOSER LOOK

Eidetic Imagery

Visual stimuli, or icons, persist for remarkably long periods of time among a few individuals. About 5 percent of children can look at a detailed picture, turn away, and several minutes later recall the particulars of the picture with exceptional clarity—as if they were still viewing it. This extraordinary visual memory is referred to as **eidetic imagery** (Haber, 1980). Among the minority of children who have this ability, it declines with age, all but disappearing by adolescence.

Figure 6.2 provides an example of a test of eidetic imagery. Children are asked to look at the first drawing in the series for 20 to 30 seconds, after which it is removed. The children then continue to gaze at a neutral background. Several minutes later the drawing in the center is placed on the backdrop. When asked what they see, many report "a face." A face would be seen only if the children had retained a clear image of the first picture and fused it with the second so that they are, in effect, perceiving the third picture in Figure 6.2 (Haber, 1980).

Eidetic imagery appears remarkably clear and detailed. It seems to be essentially a perceptual phenomenon in which coding is not a factor.

Truth or Fiction Revisited

Those of us who can see actually have photographic, or iconic, memories. However, only a few of us have eidetic imagery, and this capacity usually disappears by adolescence.

Although eidetic imagery is rare, iconic memory, as we see in the following section, universally transforms visual perceptions into smoothly unfolding impressions of the world.

Short-Term Memory

If you focus attention on a stimulus in the sensory register, you will tend to retain it in **short-term memory**—also referred to as **working memory**—for a minute or so after the trace of the stimulus decays. When you are given a phone number by the information operator and then write it down or dial the number, you are retaining the number in your short-term memory. When you are told the name of someone at a party and then use that name immediately in addressing the person, you are retaining the name in short-term memory. In short-term memory, the image tends to fade significantly after 10 to 12 seconds if it is not repeated or rehearsed. It is possible to focus on maintaining a visual image in the short-term memory, but it is more common to encode visual stimuli as sounds, or auditory stimulation. Then the sounds can be rehearsed, or repeated.

As noted, most of us know that a way of retaining information in short-term memory—and possibly storing it permanently—is to rehearse it. When an information operator tells me a phone number, I usually rehearse it continuously while I am dialing it or running around frantically searching for a pencil and a scrap of paper. Most of us also know that the more times we rehearse information, the more likely we are to remember it. We have the capacity (if not the will or the time) to rehearse information and thereby keep it in short-term memory indefinitely.

Eidetic imagery The maintenance of detailed visual memories over several minutes.

Short-term memory The type or stage of memory that can hold information for up to a minute or so after the trace of the stimulus decays. Also called **working memory.**

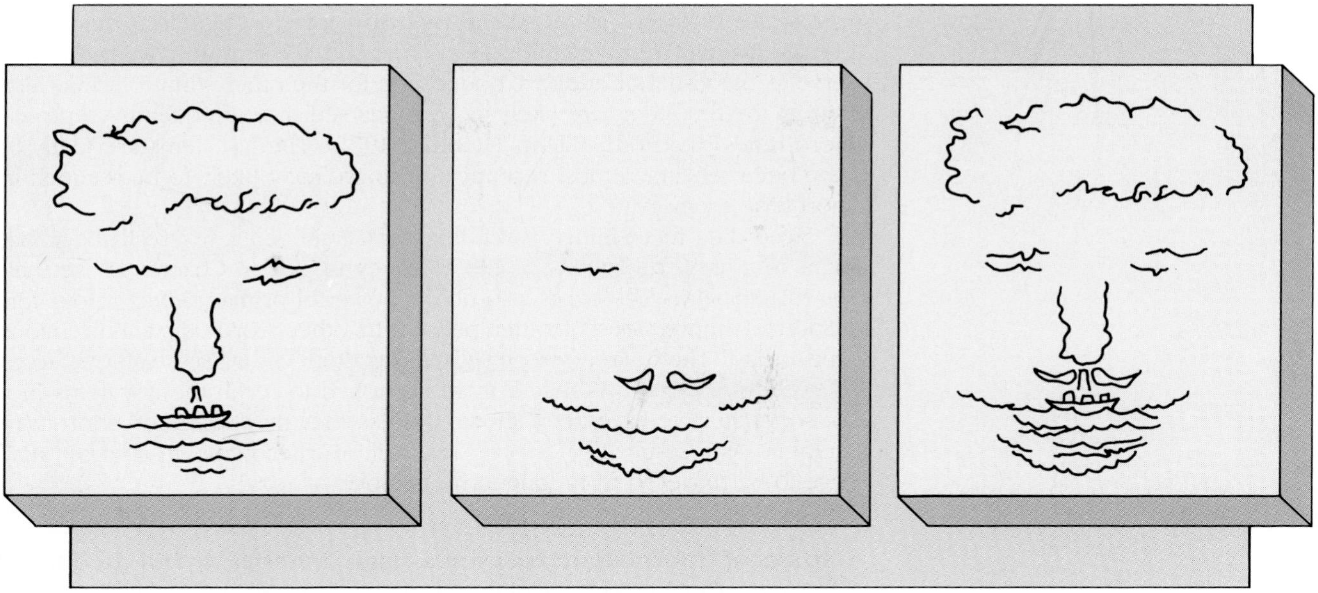

Figure 6.2
A Research Strategy for Assessing Eidetic Imagery.

Children look at the first drawing for 20 to 30 seconds, after which it is removed. Next the children look at a neutral background for several minutes. They are then shown the second drawing. When asked what they see, children with the capacity for eidetic imagery report seeing a face. The face is seen only by children who retain the first image and fuse it with the second, thus perceiving the third image.

Encoding Let us now return to the task of remembering the first list of letters in my challenge to memory. If you had coded the letters as the three-syllable word THUN-STO-FAM, you would probably have recalled them by mentally rehearsing (saying to yourself) the three-syllable "word" and then spelling it out from the sounds. A few minutes later, if someone asked whether the letters had been upper case (THUNSTOFAM) or lower case (thunstofam), you might not have been confident of an answer. You had used an acoustic code to help recall the list, and upper- and lower-case letters sound alike.

Because it can be pronounced, THUNSTOFAM is not too difficult to retain in short-term memory. But what if the list of letters had been TBXLFNTSDK? This list of letters cannot be pronounced as it is. You would have had to find a complex acronym in order to code these letters, and within a fraction of a second—most likely an impossible task. To aid recall, you would probably have chosen to try to repeat or rehearse the letters rapidly—to read each one as many times as possible before the memory trace faded. You might have visualized each letter as you said it and tried to get back to it (that is, to run through the entire list) before it decayed.

Let us assume that you encoded the letters as sounds and then rehearsed the sounds. When asked to report the list, you might mistakenly say T-V-X-L-F-N-T-S-T-K. This would be an understandable error because the incorrect *V* and *T* sounds are similar, respectively, to the correct *B* and *D* sounds.

The Serial-Position Effect Note that you would also be likely to recall the first and last letters in the series, *T* and *K,* more accurately than the others. Why? The tendency to recall more accurately the first and last items in a series is known as the **serial-position effect.** This effect may occur because we pay more attention to the first and last stimuli in a series. They serve as the visual or auditory boundaries for the other stimuli. It may also be that the first items are likely to be rehearsed more frequently (repeated more times) than other items (Rundus, 1971). The last items are likely to have been rehearsed most recently and so are most likely to be retained in short-term memory.

According to cognitive psychologists, the tendency to recall the initial items in a list is referred to as the **primacy effect.** In Chapter 15 we shall see that social psychologists also note a powerful primacy effect in our formation of impressions of other people. In other words, first impressions tend to last. The tendency to recall the last items in a list is referred to as the **recency effect.** As noted, if we are asked to recall the last items in a list soon after we have been shown the list, they may still be in short-term memory. As a result they can be "read off." Earlier items, in contrast, may have to be retrieved from long-term memory.

Chunks of Information: Is Seven a Magic Number or Did the Phone Company Get Lucky? Rapidly rehearsing ten meaningless letters is not an easy task. With TBXLFNTSDK there are ten discrete elements, or **chunks,** of information that must be kept in short-term memory. When we encode *THUNSTOFAM* as three syllables, there are only three chunks to swallow at once—a memory task that is much easier on the digestion.

Psychologist George Miller noted that the average person was comfortable with digesting about seven integers at a time, the number of integers in a telephone number. In an article appearing in the *Psychological Review,* he wrote,

> *My problem is that I have been persecuted by an integer. For seven years this number has followed me around, has intruded in my most private data, and has assaulted me from the pages of our most public journals* (1956).

In public, yet. Most people have little trouble recalling five chunks of information, as in a zip code. Some can remember nine, which is, for all but a few, an upper limit. So seven chunks, plus or minus one or two, is the "magic" number—in Germany (Ebbinghaus, 1885) and China (Yu, 1985) as well as in the English-speaking world.

So how, you ask, do we successfully include the area codes in our recollections of telephone numbers, hence making them ten digits long? The truth of the matter is that we usually don't. We tend to recall the area code as a single chunk of information derived from our general knowledge of where a person lives. (I know that my oldest daughter lives in the 5-1-6 area code—against my wishes, of course. So does my mother, and that's not so bad.) And so, we are more likely to remember (or "know") the ten-digit numbers of acquaintances who reside in locales with area codes we use frequently.

Businesses pay the phone company hefty premiums so that they can attain numbers with two or three zeroes—for example, 592-2000 or 614-3300. These numbers have fewer chunks of information and hence are easier to remember. Customer recollection of business phone numbers increases sales. One financial services company uses the toll-free number CALL-IRA, which reduces the task to two chunks of information that also happen to be meaningfully related (semantically coded) to the nature of the business. Similarly, a clinic in my area that helps people quit smoking arranged for a telephone number that can be reached by dialing the letters NO SMOKE. Do you use meaningful words to assist you in remembering codes that must

---

Serial-position effect The tendency to recall more accurately the first and last items in a series.

Primacy effect The tendency to recall the initial items in a series of items.

Recency effect The tendency to recall the last items in a series of items.

Chunk A stimulus or group of stimuli that are perceived as a discrete piece of information.

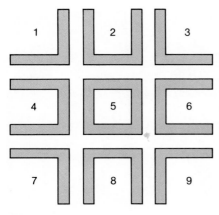

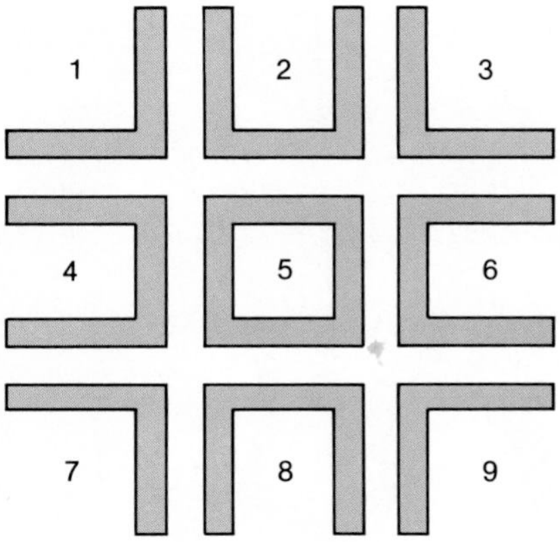

Figure 6.3
A Familiar Grid. The nine drawings in the second challenge to memory form this familiar tic-tac-toe grid when the numbers are placed inside them and they are arranged in numerical order, three shapes to a line. This method for recalling the shapes collapses nine chunks of information into two. One is the tic-tac-toe grid. The second is the rule for decoding the drawings from the grid.

be punched in to use your bank cash card or the combination on a lock? I once used my first address in The Bronx as the combination number of a lock, and now I use one of my publishers' names as the code for my bank cash card. (Was publishing the last bit of information a mistake?)

Return for a moment to the third challenge to memory presented on page 223. Were you able to remember the six groups of letters? Would your task have been simpler if you had grouped them differently? How about moving the dashes forward by a letter, so that they read GM-CBS-IBM-ATT-CIA-FBI? We have exactly the same list of letters, but we suddenly have six chunks of information that can be coded semantically. You may have also been able to generate the list by remembering a rule, such as "big corporations and government agencies."

If we can recall seven or perhaps nine chunks of information, how, then, do children remember the alphabet? The alphabet contains 26 discrete pieces of information. How do children learn to encode the letters of the alphabet, presented visually, as spoken sounds? The 26 letters of the alphabet cannot be pronounced like a word or phrase—despite the existence of that impossible *Sesame Street* song, "Ab k'defkey jekyl m'nop kw'r stoov w'ksizz." There is nothing about the shape of an *A* that suggests its sound. Nor does the visual stimulus *B* sound like a *B*. Children learning the alphabet and learning to associate visually presented letters with their spoken names do so by **rote.** It is mechanical associative learning that requires time and repetition. If you think that learning the alphabet by rote is a simple child's task, now that it is behind you, try learning the Russian or Hebrew alphabet.

Now, if you had recognized THUNSTOFAM as an acronym for the first two letters of each word in the phrase "THe UNited STates OF AMerica," you also would have reduced the number of chunks of information that had to be recalled. You could have considered the phrase to be a single chunk of information, and the rule that you must use the first two letters of each word of the phrase to be another chunk.

Reconsider the second challenge to memory on page 223. You were asked to remember nine chunks of visual information. Perhaps you could have used the acoustic codes "L" and "Square" for chunks three and five, but no obvious codes are available for the seven other chunks. Now look at Figure 6.3. If you had recognized that the elements in the challenge could be arranged as the familiar tic-tac-toe grid, remembering the nine elements might have required two chunks of information. The first would have been the mental image of the grid and the second would have been the rule for decoding: Each element corresponds to the shape of a section of the grid if read like words on a page (from upper left to lower right). The number sequence 1 through 9 would not in itself present a problem, because you learned this series by rote many years ago and have rehearsed it in countless calculations since.

Interference in Short-Term Memory I mentioned that I often find myself running around looking for a pencil and a scrap of paper to write down a telephone number that has been given to me. If I keep on rehearsing the number while I'm looking, I'm okay. But I have also cursed myself repeatedly for failing to keep a pad and pencil by the telephone, and sometimes the mental dressing down interferes with my recollection of the number. (The moral of the story? Avoid self-reproach.) It has also happened that I have actually looked up a phone number for myself and been about to dial it when someone has asked me for the time or where I said we were going to dinner. Unless I say, "Now hold on a minute!" and manage to jot down the number on something, it's back to the phone book. Attending to distracting information, even briefly, prevents me from rehearsing the number, so it falls between the cracks of my short-term memory.

Rote Mechanical associative learning that is based on repetition.

Displacement. Information can be lost to short-term memory by means of displacement. We may have little trouble remembering the names of the first one or two people we meet at a cocktail party. But as introductions continue, new names may displace the old, and we may forget the names of people we met only a few minutes earlier.

In an experiment with college students, Lloyd and Margaret Peterson (1959) demonstrated how prevention of rehearsal can wreak havoc with short-term memory. They asked students to remember three-letter combinations, such as HGB—normally three easy chunks of information. They then had the students count backward from an arbitrary number, such as 181, by threes (that is, 181, 178, 175, 172, and so on). The students were told to stop counting and to report the letter sequence after the passage of the intervals of time shown in Figure 6.4. The percentage of letter combinations recalled correctly fell precipitously within seconds. After 18 seconds of interference, counting had dislodged the letter sequences in almost all of these bright young students' memories.

Psychologists say that the appearance of new information in short-term memory **displaces** the old information. Remember: only a few bits of information at a time can be retained in short-term memory. Klatzky (1980) suggests that we think of short-term memory as being like a shelf or workbench. Once it is full, some things fall off when new items are shoved on. Here we have another possible explanation for the recency effect: The most recently learned bit of information is least likely to be displaced by additional information.

Displacement occurs at cocktail parties, and I'm not referring to the jostling of one's body by others in the crowd. The point is this: When you meet Jennifer or Jonathan at the party, there should be little trouble remembering the name. But then you may meet Tamara or Timothy and, still later, Stephanie or Steven. By that time you may have a hard time dredging up Jennifer or Jonathan—unless, of course, you were very, very attracted to one of them. A passionate response would set the person apart and inspire a good deal of selective attention. Recall signal-detection theory from Chapter 3: If you were enamored enough, we may predict that the person's name (sensory signals) would be "detected" with a vengeance, and perhaps all the ensuing names would dissolve into background noise.

Truth or Fiction Revisited

It is true that it may be easier for you to recall the name of your first-grade teacher than of someone you just met at a party. Your first-grade teacher's name is stored in long-term memory, whereas you may soon be juggling your new acquaintance's name with many others in short-term memory.

Displace In memory theory, to cause chunks of information to be lost from short-term memory by adding new items.

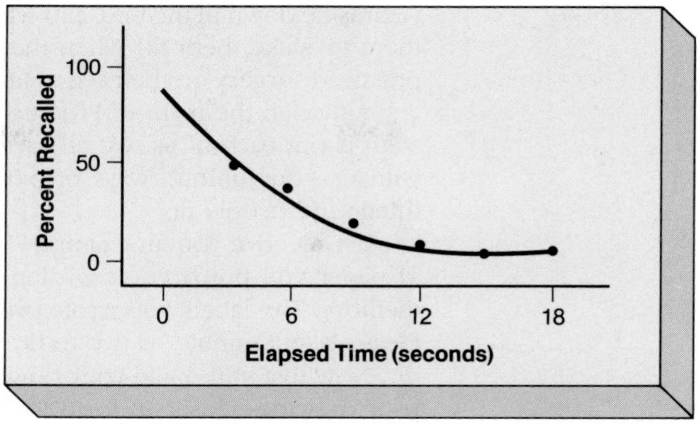

Figure 6.4
The Effect of Interference on Information in Short-Term Memory. In this experiment, college students were asked to maintain a series of three letters in their memories while they counted backwards from an arbitrary number by three's. After just three seconds, retention was cut by half. Ability to recall the letters was almost completely lost by 15 seconds.

Long-Term Memory

Long-term memory is the third stage of processing of information. Think of your long-term memory as a vast storehouse of information containing names, dates, places, what Johnny did to you in second grade, and what Susan said about you when you were 12.

Some psychologists (Sigmund Freud was one) used to believe that nearly all of our perceptions and ideas were stored permanently. Of course, we might not be able to retrieve all of them, but such memories might be "lost" because of the unavailability of the proper cues, or they might be kept beneath the surface of conscious awareness by the forces of **repression.** Adherents to this view often pointed to the work of neurosurgeon Wilder Penfield (1969), which was discussed in Chapter 2. When parts of their brain were electrically stimulated, many of Penfield's patients reported the appearance of images that had something of the feel of memories.

Today most psychologists view this notion as being exaggerated. Memory researcher Elizabeth Loftus, for example, notes that the "memories" stimulated by Penfield's probes were impoverished in detail and not necessarily factual (Loftus & Loftus, 1980; Loftus, 1983).

Truth or Fiction Revisited

It is *not* true that all of our experiences are permanently imprinted on the brain.

Evidence is far from compelling that we store all of our experiences. To the contrary, we appear to be more likely to store incidents that have a greater impact on us—events more laden with personal meaning.

Now let us consider some important questions about long-term memory.

How Accurate Are Long-Term Memories?—Memory as Reconstructive Elizabeth Loftus also notes that memories are distorted by our biases and needs—by the ways in which we conceptualize our worlds. Cognitive psychologists speak of much of our knowledge of the world as being represented in terms of **schemas.**

To understand better what is meant by the schema, consider the problems of travelers who met up with the legendary highwayman of ancient Greece, Procrustes. Procrustes had a quirk. He was not only interested in travelers' pocketbooks but also in their height. He had a concept—a schema—of just how tall people should be, and when people did not fit his schema, they were in for it. You see, Procrustes also had a very famous bed, a bed that comes down to us in history as a "Procrustean bed." He made his

Long-term memory The type or stage of memory capable of relatively permanent storage.

Repression In psychoanalytic theory, the ejection of anxiety-evoking ideas from conscious awareness.

Schema A way of mentally representing the world, such as a belief or an expectation, that can influence perception of persons, objects, and situations.

victims lie down in the bed, and when they were too short for it, he stretched them to make them fit. When they were too long for it, he is said to have practiced surgery on their legs. Many unfortunate passersby failed to survive.

Although the myth of Procrustes may sound absurd, it reflects a quirky truth about each of us. We all carry our cognitive Procrustean beds around with us—our unique ways of perceiving the world—and we try to make things and people fit.

Let me give you an example. Why don't you "retrieve" the fourth sheet of paper you prepared according to the instructions for the challenges to memory. The labels you wrote on the sheet will remind you of the figures. Please take a minute or two to draw them now. Then continue reading.

Now that you made your drawings, turn to Figure 6.5 on page 239. Are your drawings closer in form to those in Group 1 or those in Group 2? I wouldn't be surprised if they were more like those in Group 1. After all, they were labeled like the drawings in Group 1. The labels serve as *schemas* for the drawings—ways of organizing your knowledge of them—and these schemas may have influenced your recollections.

Similarly, Loftus has used pictures in memory tests of a black man holding a hat and a white man carrying a razor. However, when asked what they had seen, people often erroneously recalled the razor as being in the hands of the black man. Our prejudices and biases, in other words, also serve as schemas according to which we organize our perceptions. And again, our schemas color our memories.

Truth or Fiction Revisited

It is true that our memories are indeed distorted by our prejudices, as well as by other kinds of schemas.

The point here is that retrieving information from long-term memory is not like scanning an old photograph. We don't have accurate snapshots in our long-term memories. When we recall the past, we don't just locate and read off faithful mental representations. Instead, memory tends to be **reconstructive** and less than wholly reliable. And we reconstruct our recollections according to our schemas.

Consider another example of the power of schemas in processing information. Loftus and Palmer (1974) showed subjects a film of a car crash and then asked them to fill out questionnaires that included a question about how fast the cars were going at the time. The language of the question varied subtly, however. Some subjects were asked to estimate how fast the cars were going when they "hit" one another. Other subjects were asked to estimate their speed when they "smashed" into one another. Subjects reconstructing the scene on the basis of the cue "hit" estimated a speed of 34 mph. Subjects who watched the same film but reconstructed the scene on the basis of the cue "smashed" estimated a speed of 41 mph! In other words, the use of the word *hit* or *smash* caused subjects to organize their knowledge about the crash in different ways. That is, the words served as diverse schemas that fostered the development of very different ways of processing information about the crash.

Subjects in the same study were questioned again a week later: "Did you see any broken glass?" Since there was no broken glass shown in the film, positive replies were errors. Of subjects who had earlier been encouraged to process information about the accident in terms of one car "hitting" the other, 14 percent incorrectly answered yes. But 32 percent of the subjects who had processed information about the crash in terms of one car "smashing" the other reported, incorrectly, that they had seen broken glass.

As noted in the nearby Psychology Goes to Work section, findings such as these have important implications for the legal profession.

Reconstructive Based on the piecing together of memory fragments with general knowledge and expectations rather than a precise picture of the past.

How Much Information *Can* Be Stored in Long-Term Memory? There is no evidence for any limit to the amount of information that can be stored in long-term memory. New information may replace older information in short-term memory, but there is no evidence that memories in long-term memory are lost by displacement. Long-term memories may last days, years, or for all practical purposes, a lifetime. From time to time it may seem as if we have forgotten, or "lost," a long-term memory, such as the names of elementary or high school classmates. Yet it may be that we cannot find the proper cues to help us retrieve the information. If it is lost, it usually becomes lost only in the same way as when we misplace an object but know that it is still somewhere in the house or apartment. It is lost, but not eradicated or destroyed.

Truth or Fiction Revisited

It is true that there is no practical limit to the amount of information you can store in your memory. At least no limit has been discovered to date.

Transferring Information from Short-Term to Long-Term Memory How is information transferred from short-term to long-term memory? By and large, the more often chunks of information are rehearsed, the more likely they are to be transferred to long-term memory (Rundus, 1971). We noted that repeating information over and over to prevent it from decaying or being displaced is termed *maintenance rehearsal.* Making no attempt to give information meaning by linking it to past learning, maintenance rehearsal is no guarantee of permanent storage (Craik & Watkins, 1973).*

A more effective method is to purposefully relate new material to information that has already been solidly acquired. (Recall that the nine chunks of information in the second challenge were made easier to reconstruct once they were associated with the familiar tic-tac-toe grid in Figure 6.3.) Relating new material to well-known material is known as **elaborative rehearsal** (Postman, 1975). For example, have you seen this word before?

FUNTHOSTAM

Say it aloud. Do you know it? If you had used an acoustic code alone to memorize THUNSTOFAM, the list of letters you first saw on page 223, it might not have been easy to recognize FUNTHOSTAM as an incorrect spelling. Let us assume, however, that by now you have encoded THUNSTOFAM semantically as an acronym for "The United States of America." Then you would have been able to scan the spelling of the words in the phrase "The United States of America" to determine the correctness of FUNTHOSTAM. Of course, you would have found it to be incorrect.

As suggested earlier, pure repetition of a meaningless group of syllables, such as *thun-sto-fam,* would be relying on maintenance rehearsal for permanent storage. The process might be tedious (continued rehearsal) and unreliable. But usage of elaborative rehearsal—tying THUNSTOFAM to the name of a country—might make storage instantaneous and retrieval foolproof.

Truth or Fiction Revisited

It is *not* true that learning must be meaningful if we are to remember it. However, elaborative rehearsal, which is based on meaning, is more efficient than maintenance rehearsal, which is based on repetition.

Elaborative rehearsal A method for increasing retention of new information by relating it to information that is well-known.

* Maintenance rehearsal, however, is responsible for rote learning.

PSYCHOLOGY GOES TO WORK

Eyewitness Testimony and the Legal Profession

Eyewitness Testimony? How trustworthy is eyewitness testimony? Memories are reconstructive rather than photographic, and they can be influenced by prejudice and bias. The wording of questioners also influences the content of the "memory."

Jean Piaget, the famed investigator of children's cognitive development, distinctly remembered an attempt to kidnap him from his baby carriage along the Champs Élysées. He recalled the excited throng, the abrasions on the face of the nurse who rescued him, the police officer's white baton, and the flight of the assailant. Although graphic, Piaget's memories were false. Years afterward, the nurse admitted that she had concocted the tale.

Lawyers, judges, and other legal professionals are vitally concerned about the accuracy of our memories as reflected in eyewitness testimony. Accurate memories are extremely important in the criminal courts, where testimony can lead to judgments of guilt or innocence in capital crimes. Is there reason to believe that the statements of eyewitnesses are any more factual than Piaget's?

There is cause for concern. The words chosen by an experimenter—and those chosen by a lawyer interrogating a witness—influence the reconstruction of memories (Loftus & Palmer, 1973). For example, an attorney for the plaintiff might ask the witness, "How fast was the defendant's car going when it *smashed into* the plaintiff's car?" In such a case, the car might be reported as going faster than if the question had been: "How fast was the defendant's car going when it *hit* the plaintiff's car?" Could the attorney for the defendant claim that use of the word *smashed* biased the witness? What of the jury who heard the word *smashed?* Would they not be biased toward assuming that the driver had been reckless?

There are cases in which the memories of eyewitnesses have been "refreshed" by means of hypnosis. Sad to say (as noted in Chapter 4), hypnosis does more than amplify memories; it can also distort them. One problem is that witnesses may accept and embellish suggestions made by the hypnotist (Press et al., 1981). Another is that imagined events can seem as authentic as true events, and hypnotized people may report fantasized occurrences as compellingly as if they were real (Stark, 1984).

There are also a number of problems concerning the identification of criminals. For one thing, witnesses may pay more attention to the suspect's clothing than to more stable characteristics such as facial features, height, and weight. In one experiment, viewers of a videotaped crime incorrectly identified a man as the criminal because he wore the eyeglasses and T-shirt that had been worn by the perpetrator on the tape. The man who actually committed the crime was identified less often (Sanders, 1984). Criminals seem to be aware of these identification problems because they frequently adjust their appearance before appearing in line-ups (Brigham, 1982).

As you can see, those in the legal profession are faced with a dilemma. It is recognized that our memories are distorted by our schemas—that is, the ways in which we organize experience. The ways in which we are questioned can color our recollections. And perhaps we do not pay as much attention as we should to fixed characteristics when we are trying to identify criminals. On the other hand, suspects are significantly more likely to be convicted when independent witnesses corroborate each other's testimony. In one mock jury study, the facts of a robbery were held constant with one exception: In one condition the victim and a bystander agreed about the guilt of the defendant. In another condition, the victim and the bystander disagreed about who had committed the crime. When the witnesses agreed, 70 percent of the jurors found him guilty. When the witnesses disagreed, only 12.5 percent of them found him guilty.

In sum, eyewitness testimony has its problems. Yet if we were to prevent witnesses to crimes from testifying in the courts, how many criminals would go free?

You may recall that English teachers encouraged you to use new vocabulary words in sentences to help you remember them. Each new usage is an instance of elaborative rehearsal. Usage helps you build extended semantic codes that will help you retrieve their meanings in the future. When I was in high school, foreign-language teachers told us that learning classical languages "exercises the mind" so that we would understand English better. Not exactly. The mind is not analogous to a muscle that responds to exercise. However, the meanings of many English words are based on foreign tongues. A person who recognizes that *retrieve* stems from roots meaning "again" *(re-)* and "find" (*trouver* in French) is less likely to forget that *retrieval* means "finding again" or "bringing back."

Think, too, of all the algebra and geometry problems we were asked to solve in high school. Each problem is an application of a procedure and,

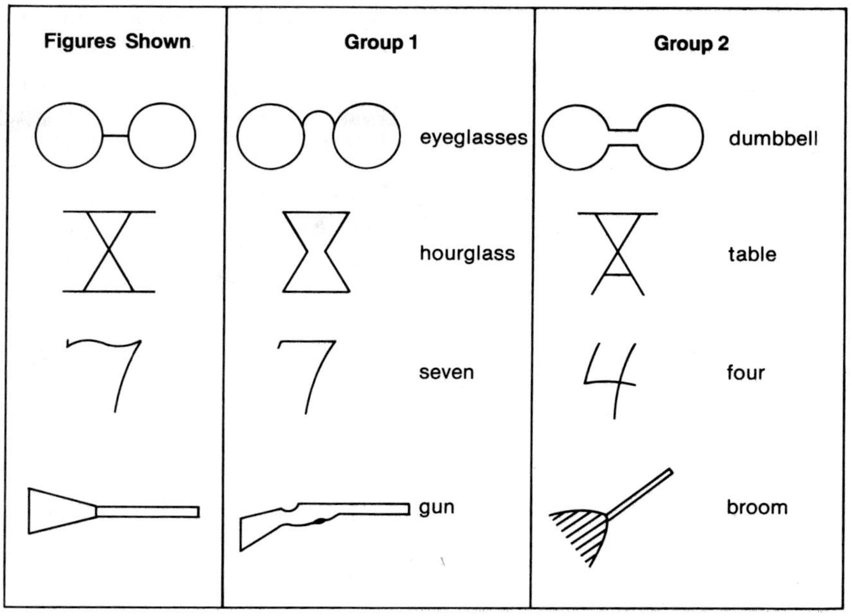

Figure 6.5
Memory as Reconstructive. In their classic experiment, Carmichael, Hogan, and Walter (1932) presented subjects the figures in the left-hand box and made remarks as suggested in the other boxes. For example, the experimenter might say, "This drawing looks like eyeglasses [or a dumbbell]." When subjects later reconstructed the drawings, it was clear that their drawings had been influenced by the experimenters' labels. That is, the experimenters had provided schemas according to which the subjects organized their experiences and reconstructed their memories.

perhaps, of certain formulas and theorems. By repeatedly applying the procedures, formulas, and theorems in different contexts, we rehearse them elaboratively. As a consequence, we are more likely to remember them. Knowledge of the ways in which a formula or an equation is used helps us remember the formula. Also, by building theorem upon theorem in geometry, we relate new theorems to theorems that we already understand. As a result we process information about them more deeply and remember them better.

Before proceeding to the next section, let me ask you to cover the preceding paragraph. Now, which of the following words is correctly spelled: *retrieval* or *retreival?* The spellings sound alike, so an acoustic code for reconstructing the correct spelling would fail. Yet a semantic code, such as the spelling rule "*i* before *e* except after *c*," would allow you to reconstruct the correct spelling: retr*ie*val.

A CLOSER LOOK

Flashbulb Memories

Do you remember the first time you were "in love"? Can you remember how the streets and the trees looked somehow transformed? The vibrancy in your step? How generous you felt? How all of life's problems suddenly seemed to be solved?

Psychologists have learned that we tend to remember more clearly the events that occur under unusual, emotionally arousing circumstances. For example, those of us who are middle-aged and older tend to remember exactly what we were doing at the time we learned that President John F. Kennedy had been shot in November 1963. Younger people tend to recall the events surrounding them on the day the Challenger space shuttle exploded in January 1986. Similarly, we may remember in great detail what we were doing when we learned of a relative's death. All of these are examples of "flashbulb memories," because they preserve experiences in such detail (Brown & Kulik, 1977; Thompson & Cowan, 1986).

Why does the memory become etched when the "flashbulb" goes off? One factor is the distinctness of the memory. It is easier to discriminate stimuli that are markedly different from those that surround them. Such events are salient in themselves, and the feelings that are engendered by them are also rather special. So it is relatively easy to pick them out from the storehouse of memories. But major events, such as the assassination of a president or the loss of a close relative, also tend to have important effects on our lives. As a result, we are likely to dwell on them and form networks of associations to other pieces of information; that is, we are likely to rehearse them elaborately. Our rehearsal sometimes includes great expectations about, or deep fears of, the future.

Organization in Long-Term Memory The storehouse of long-term memory is usually well organized. Items are not just piled on the floor or thrown into closets. We tend to gather information about rats and cats into a certain section of the storehouse, perhaps the animal or mammal section. We put information about oaks, maples, and eucalyptus into the tree section.

Preschoolers tend to organize their memories by grouping objects that share the same function (Lucariello & Nelson, 1985). At first, "toast" is grouped with "peanut butter sandwich" because both are eaten. Only during the early elementary school years are toast and peanut butter sandwich categorized as kinds of foods. Similarly, preschoolers and first graders may associate dogs and cats because they are often found together around the house (Bjorklund & de Marchena, 1984). Dogs and rabbits, however, are usually not placed in the same category until the concept "animal" is used to include them, which may not happen for a few more years.

As we develop, we tend to organize information according to a *hierarchical structure,* as shown in Figure 6.6. A hierarchy is an arrangement of items (or chunks of information) into groups or classes according to common or distinct features. As we work our way up the hierarchy shown in Figure 6.6, we find more encompassing, or **superordinate,** classes to which the items below belong. For example, all mammals are animals, but there are many types of animals other than mammals.*

When items are correctly organized in long-term memory, you are more likely to recall—or know—accurate information about them. For instance, do you remember whether whales breathe underwater? If you did not know that whales are mammals (or, in Figure 6.6, **subordinate** to mammals), or if you knew nothing about mammals, a correct answer might depend on some remote instance of rote learning. That is, you might be depending on chancy episodic memory rather than on reliable semantic memory. For example, you might recall some details from a Public Broadcasting System documentary on whales. If you *did* know that whales are mammals, however, you would also know—or remember—that whales do not breathe underwater. How? You would reconstruct information about whales from knowledge about mammals, the group to which whales are subordinate. Similarly,

Superordinate Descriptive of a higher (including) class or category in a hierarchy.

Subordinate Descriptive of a lower (included) class or category in a hierarchy.

*A note to biological purists: Figure 6.6 is not intended to represent phyla, classes, orders, and so on accurately. Rather, it shows how an individual's classification scheme might be organized.

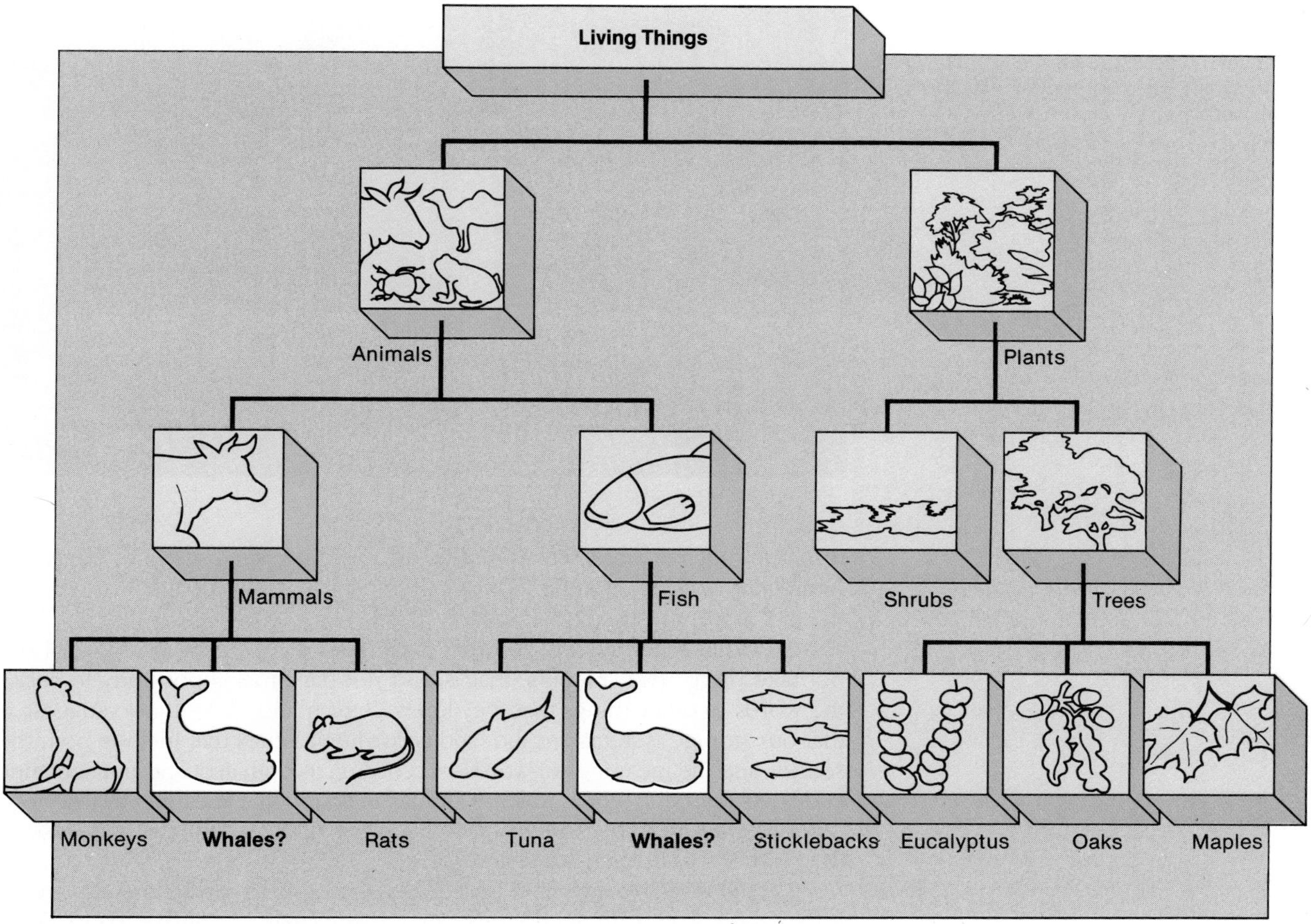

Figure 6.6
The Hierarchical Structure of Long-Term Memory.

Where are whales filed in the hierarchical cabinets of your memory? Your classification of whales may influence your answers to these questions: Do whales breathe underwater? Are they warm-blooded? Do they nurse their young?

you would know, or remember, that whales, because they are mammals, are warmblooded, nurse their young, and are a good deal more intelligent than, say, tunas and sticklebacks, which are fish. Had you incorrectly classified whales as fish, you might have searched your memory and constructed the incorrect answer that they do breathe underwater.

Let us now consider some issues in the retrieval of information from long-term memory: the tip-of-the-tongue phenomenon, state-dependent memory, and context-dependent memory.

Tip-of-the-tongue (TOT) phenomenon The feeling that information is stored in memory although it cannot be readily retrieved. Also called the **feeling-of-knowing experience.**

The Tip-of-the-Tongue Phenomenon Have you ever been so close to retrieving information that it seemed to be "on the tip of your tongue"? Still, you could not quite remember it? This is a frustrating experience, similar to reeling in a fish but having it drop off the line just before it breaks the surface of the water. Psychologists term this experience the **tip-of-the-tongue (TOT) phenomenon,** or the **feeling-of-knowing experience.**

In one TOT experiment, Brown and McNeill (1966) defined some rather unusual words for students, such as *sampan,* which is a small riverboat used in China and Japan. Students were then asked to recall the words they had learned. Some of the students often had the right word "on the tips of their

A Whale Nurses Her Young. Are whales categorized as mammals or fish in your memory? If the answer is fish, the content of this photograph may be of some surprise.

tongues" but reported words similar in meaning, such as *junk, barge,* or *houseboat.* Still other students reported words that sounded similar, such as *Saipan, Siam, sarong,* and *sanching.* Why?

To begin with, the words were unfamiliar, so elaborative rehearsal did not take place. The students, that is, did not have the opportunity to relate the words to other things that they knew. Brown and McNeill also suggested that our storage systems are indexed according to cues that include both the sounds and the meanings of words—according to both acoustic and semantic codes. By scanning words that are similar in sound and meaning to the word that is on the tip of the tongue, we sometimes find a useful cue and retrieve the word for which we are searching.

The feeling-of-knowing experience also seems to reflect incomplete or imperfect learning. In such cases our answers may be "in the ballpark" if not on the mark. In some feeling-of-knowing experiments, subjects are asked trivia questions. When they do not recall an answer, they are then asked to guess how likely it is that they will recognize the right answer if it is among a group of possibilities. People turn out to be very accurate in their estimations about whether or not they will recognize the answer. Similarly, Brown and McNeill found that the students in their TOT experiment proved to be very good at estimating the number of syllables in words they could not recall. The students often correctly guessed the initial sounds of the words and sometimes recognized words that rhymed with them.

Thus, very often our sense that an answer is on the tips of our tongues reflects incomplete knowledge. We may not know the exact answer, but we know something. As a matter of fact, if we have good writing skills, we may present our incomplete knowledge so forcefully that we earn a good grade on an essay question on the topic! At such times, the problem lies not in retrieval but in the original encoding and storage.

Context-Dependent Memory The context in which we acquire information can also play a role in retrieval. I remember walking down the halls of the Bronx apartment building where as a child I had lived many years earlier. I was suddenly assaulted by images of playing under the staircase, of falling against a radiator, of the shrill voice of a former neighbor calling for her child at dinnertime. Have you ever walked the halls of an old school and been assaulted by memories of faces and names that you would have guessed had been lost forever? Have you ever walked through your old neighborhood and recalled the faces of people, or aromas of cooking that were so real you salivated?

These are examples of **context-dependent memory.** Being in the proper context, that is, can dramatically enhance recall (Estes, 1972; Watkins et al., 1976). One fascinating experiment in context-dependent memory included a number of subjects who were "all wet." Members of a university swimming club were asked to learn lists of words either while they were submerged or literally high and dry (Godden & Baddeley, 1975). Students who learned the list underwater showed superior recall of the list when immersed. Those who had rehearsed the list ashore, similarly, showed better retrieval on terra firma.

Other studies have found that students do better on tests when they study in the room where the test is to be given (Smith et al., 1978). When police are interviewing witnesses to crimes, they have the witnesses verbally paint the scene as vividly as possible. People who mentally place themselves back in the context in which they encoded and stored information frequently retrieve it more accurately.

State-Dependent Memory **State-dependent memory** is an extension of context-dependent memory. It sometimes happens that we retrieve information better when we are in a physiological or emotional state that is similar to the one in which we encoded and stored the information. Drugs, for example, alter our physiological response patterns. They can influence the production and uptake of neurotransmitters involved in learning and memory and can modify the general state of alertness of the body. It also happens that material that is learned "under the influence" of a drug may be most readily retrieved when the person is again under the influence of that drug (Overton, 1985).

Our moods may also serve as cues that aid in the retrieval of memories. Feeling the rush of love may trigger images of other times when we had fallen in love. The grip of anger may prompt memories of frustration and rage. Gordon Bower (1981) ran experiments in which happy or sad moods were induced in people by hypnotic suggestion, and the subjects then learned lists of words. People who learned a list while in a happy mood showed better recall when a happy state was induced again. But people who had learned the list when a sad mood had been induced showed superior recall when they were saddened again. Bower suggests that in day-to-day life, a happy mood influences us to focus on positive events. As a result, we will have better recall of these happy events in the future. A sad mood, unfortunately, leads us to focus on and recall the negative. Happiness may feed on happiness, but sadness under extreme circumstances can develop into a vicious cycle.

Truth or Fiction Revisited

It is true that we are more likely to recall happy events while we are feeling happy and sad events while we are feeling sad.

THE LEVELS-OF-PROCESSING MODEL OF MEMORY

Not all psychologists view memory in terms of stages (Denton, 1988). Fergus Craik and Robert Lockhart (1972) suggest that we do not have a sensory memory, a short-term memory, and a long-term memory per se. Instead, our ability to remember things can also be viewed in terms of a single stage or dimension—the degree to which we process information. Put it another way:

Context-dependent memory Information that is better retrieved in the context in which it was encoded and stored, or learned.

State-dependent memory Information that is better retrieved in the physiological or emotional state in which it was encoded and stored, or learned.

According to Craik and Lockhart, we don't form enduring memories by getting information into long-term memory. Rather, memories tend to endure when information is processed deeply—when it is attended to, encoded carefully, pondered, and rehearsed elaboratively or related to things we already know well.

Consider our familiar list of letters, THUNSTOFAM. In an experiment, we could ask one group of people to remember the list by repeating it aloud a few times, a letter at a time. Another group could be informed that it is an acronym for "The United States of America." If several months later each group were shown several similar lists of words and asked to select the correct list, which group do you think would be more likely to pick out THUNSTOFAM from the pack? It ought to be the group given the acronym, because the information in that group would have been processed more deeply. It would have been semantically encoded and rehearsed elaboratively. The group engaging in more superficial information processing would be sticking to acoustic coding and maintenance rehearsal. In another example, consider why so many people have difficulty selecting the accurate drawing of the Lincoln penny. Is it perhaps because they have processed information about the appearance of a penny rather superficially? If they knew they were going to be quizzed about the features of a penny, however, wouldn't they process information about its appearance more deeply? That is, wouldn't they study the features and purposefully note whether the profile is facing left or right, what the lettering says, and where the date goes?

Earlier in the chapter, we noted that 2-year-old boys are more likely to remember stereotypical "boys' toys" in photographs, and girls at the same age are more likely to recall "girls' toys." Why do we find this sex difference? It is probably because cultural conditioning has already encouraged boys to process information about transportation toys more deeply than information about dolls. Girls have been pushed in the opposite direction.

Consider an experiment with children. Pictures of objects that fell into four categories (animals, clothes, furniture, and transportation) were placed on a table before first through sixth graders (Neimark et al., 1971). The children were allowed three minutes to arrange the pictures as they wished and to remember as many of them as they could. Children in older groups made a greater effort to categorize the pictures and showed greater recall of them. However, among children in each grade group, those who categorized the pictures also showed greater recall. By categorizing the pictures, they were engaging in greater semantic coding and elaborative rehearsal; that is, they were processing information about them more deeply.

Also weigh a fascinating experiment with three groups of college students, all of whom were asked to study a picture of a living room for one minute (Bransford et al., 1977). Their examination entailed different approaches, however. Two groups were informed that small *x's* were imbedded in the picture. The first of these groups was asked to find the x's by scanning the picture horizontally and vertically. The second group was informed that the x's could be found in the edges of the objects in the room and was asked to look for them there. The third group was asked, instead, to think about how it would use the objects pictured in the room. As a result of the divergent sets of instructions, the first two groups (the *x* hunters) processed information about the objects in the picture superficially. But the third group rehearsed the objects elaboratively—that is, the group members thought about the objects in terms of their meanings and uses. It should not be surprising that the third group remembered many times more objects than the first two groups.

Nonsense syllables Meaningless sets of two consonants, with a vowel sandwiched in between, that are used to study memory.

Recognition In information processing, the easiest memory task, involving identification of objects or events encountered before.

Recall Retrieval or reconstruction of learned material.

Note that the levels-of-processing model finds uses for most of the concepts employed by those who think of memory in terms of stages. For example, adherents to this model also speak of the basic memory processes (encoding, storage, and retrieval) and of different kinds of rehearsal. The essential difference is that they view memory as consisting of a single dimension or entity that varies according to depth.

We have been discussing remembering for quite some time. Since variety is supposed to be the spice of life, let's consider forgetting for a while.

FORGETTING

What do DAL, RIK, BOF, and ZEX have in common? They are all **nonsense syllables.** Nonsense syllables are meaningless sets of two consonants with a vowel sandwiched in between. They were first used by German psychologist Hermann Ebbinghaus (1850–1909) and have since been used by many psychologists to study memory and forgetting.

Because nonsense syllables are intended to be meaningless, remembering them should depend on simple acoustic coding and maintenance rehearsal rather than on elaborative rehearsal, semantic coding, or other ways of making learning meaningful. Nonsense syllables provide a means of measuring simple memorization ability in studies of the three basic memory tasks of *recognition, recall,* and *relearning.* Studying these memory tasks has led to several conclusions about the nature of forgetting.

Memory Tasks Used in Measuring Forgetting

Recognition There are many ways of measuring **recognition.** In one study of high school graduates, Harry Bahrick and his colleagues (1975) interspersed photos of classmates with four times as many photos of strangers. Recent graduates correctly recognized persons who were former schoolmates 90 percent of the time, whereas subjects who had been out of school for 40 years recognized former classmates 75 percent of the time. A chance level of recognition would have been only 20 percent (one photo in five was of an actual classmate), so even older subjects showed rather solid long-term recognition ability.

Recognition. Recognition is the easiest kind of memory task. In one study, people who had been out of school for 40 years correctly recognized whether or not photos were of former classmates 75 percent of the time.

In many studies of recognition, psychologists ask subjects to read a list of nonsense syllables. The subjects then read a second list of nonsense syllables and indicate whether they recognize any of the syllables as having appeared on the first list. Forgetting is defined as failure to recognize a nonsense syllable that has been read before.

Recognition is the easiest type of memory task. This is why multiple-choice tests are easier than fill-in-the-blank or essay tests. We can recognize or identify photos of former classmates more easily than we can recall their names (Tulving, 1974).

Recall In his own studies of **recall,** another kind of memory task, Ebbinghaus would read lists of nonsense syllables aloud to the beat of a metronome and then see how many he could produce from memory. After reading through a list once, he usually would be able to recall seven nonsense syllables—the typical limit for short-term memory.

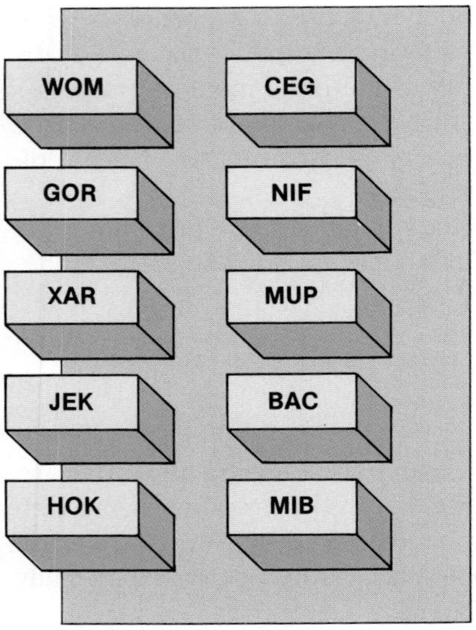

Figure 6.7
Paired Associates. Psychologists often use paired associates, like the above, to measure recall. Retrieving CEG in response to the cue WOM is made easier by an image of a WOMan smoking a "CEG-arette."

Paired associates Nonsense syllables presented in pairs in experiments that measure recall.

Posthypnotic amnesia Inability to recall material presented while hypnotized, following the suggestion of the hypnotist.

Relearning A measure of retention. Material is usually relearned more quickly than it is learned initially.

Method of savings A measure of retention in which the difference between the number of repetitions originally required to learn a list and the number of repetitions required to relearn the list after a certain amount of time has elapsed is calculated.

Savings The difference between the number of repetitions originally required to learn a list and the number of repetitions required to relearn the list after a certain amount of time has elapsed.

Psychologists also often use lists of pairs of nonsense syllables, called **paired associates,** to measure recall. A list of paired associates is shown in Figure 6.7. Subjects read through the lists pair by pair. Later they are shown the first member of each pair and are asked to recall the second. Recall is more difficult than recognition. In a recognition task, one simply indicates whether an item has been seen before or which of a number of items is paired with a stimulus (as in a multiple-choice test). In a recall task, the person must retrieve a syllable, with another syllable serving as a cue.

Retrieval is made easier if the two syllables can be meaningfully linked—encoded semantically—even if the "meaning" is stretched a bit. Consider the first pair of nonsense syllables in Figure 6.7. The image of a WOMan smoking a CEG-arette may make CEG easier to retrieve when the person is presented with the cue WOM.

As we develop throughout childhood, our ability to recall information increases. This memory improvement is apparently linked to our growing ability to process (categorize) stimulus cues quickly (Howard & Polich, 1985). In one study, Robert Kail and Marilyn Nippold (1984) asked 8-, 12-, and 21-year-olds to name as many animals and pieces of furniture as they could during separate seven-minute intervals. The number of items recalled increased with age for both animals and furniture. For all age groups, items were retrieved according to classes. For example, in the animal category, a series of fish might be named, then a series of birds, and so on.

It is easier to recall vocabulary words from foreign languages if you can construct a meaningful link between the foreign and English words (Atkinson, 1975). The *peso,* pronounced *pay-so,* is a unit of Mexican money. A link can be formed by finding a part of the foreign word, such as the *pe-* (pronounced *pay)* in *peso,* and constructing a phrase such as "You pay with money." When you read or hear the word *peso* in the future, you recognize the *pe-* and retrieve the link or phrase. From the phrase, you then reconstruct the translation, "a unit of money."

Some people who have been hypnotized show **posthypnotic amnesia.** They are unable, for example, to recall previously learned word lists (Kihlstrom, 1980). Spanos and his colleagues (1980, 1982) hypothesize that posthypnotic amnesia occurs when hypnotized subjects interpret the suggestion not to recall information as an "invitation" to refrain from attending to retrieval cues. A hypnotized person might be told that he or she would not be able to recall the colors of the spectrum upon awakening. This suggestion might be interpreted as an invitation *not* to focus on the acronym Roy G. Biv.

Relearning: Is Learning Easier the Second Time Around? **Relearning** is a third method of measuring retention. Do you remember having to learn all of the state capitals in grade school? What were the capitals of Wyoming and Delaware? Even when we cannot recall or recognize material that had once been learned, we can relearn it more rapidly the second time, such as Cheyenne for Wyoming and Dover for Delaware. Similarly, as we go through our 30s and 40s we may forget a good deal of our high school French or geometry. Yet we could learn what took months or years much more rapidly the second time around.

To study the efficiency of relearning, Ebbinghaus (1885) devised the **method of savings.** First he recorded the number of repetitions required to learn a list of nonsense syllables or words. Then he recorded the number of repetitions required to relearn the list after a certain amount of time had elapsed. Next he computed the difference between the number of repetitions required to arrive at the **savings.** If a list had to be repeated 20 times before it was learned, and 20 times again after a year had passed, there was no

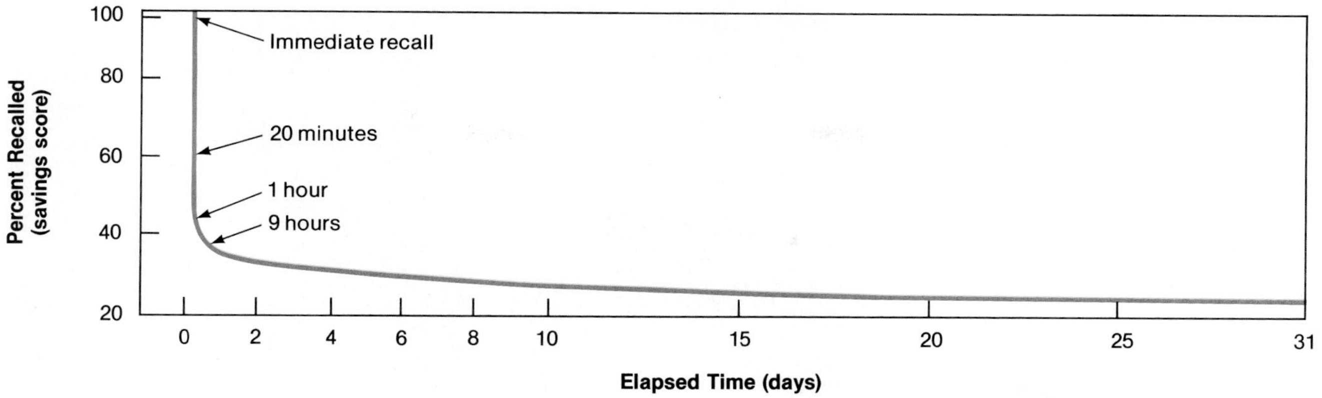

Figure 6.8
Ebbinghaus's Classic Curve of Forgetting.

Recollection of lists of words dropped precipitously during the first hour after learning. Losses of learning then became more gradual. Whereas retention dropped by half within the first hour, it took a month (31 days) for retention to be cut in half again.

savings. Relearning, that is, was as tedious as the initial learning. However, if the list could be learned with only 10 repetitions after a year had elapsed, half the number of repetitions required for learning had been saved. (Ten is half of 20.)

Figure 6.8 is Ebbinghaus's classic curve of forgetting. As you can see, there was no loss of memory as measured by savings immediately after a list had been learned. However, recollection dropped precipitously during the first hour after learning a list. Losses of learning then became more gradual. Whereas retention dropped by half within the first hour, it took a month (31 days) for retention to be cut in half again. In other words, forgetting occurred most rapidly right after material was learned. We continue to forget material as time elapses but at a relatively slower rate.

Before leaving this section, I have one question for you: What are the capitals of Wyoming and Delaware?

Interference Theory

When we do not attend to, encode, and rehearse sensory input, we may forget it through decay of the trace of the image. Material in short-term memory, like material in sensory memory, can be lost through decay. It can also be lost through displacement, as may happen when we try to remember several new names at a party.

According to **interference theory,** we also forget material in short-term and long-term memory because newly learned material interferes with it. The two basic types of interference are *retroactive interference* (also called *retroactive inhibition*) and *proactive interference* (also called *proactive inhibition.*)

Interference theory The view that we may forget stored material because other learning interferes with it.

Retroactive interference The interference of new learning with the ability to retrieve material learned previously.

Retroactive Interference In **retroactive interference,** new learning interferes with the retrieval of old learning. A medical student may memorize the names of the bones in the leg through rote repetition. Later he or she may find that learning the names of the bones in the arm makes it more

Interference. In retroactive interference, new learning interferes with the retrieval of old learning. In proactive interference, older learning interferes with the capacity to retrieve more recently learned material. High school Spanish vocabulary may "pop in," for example, when you are trying to retrieve French or Italian words learned in college.

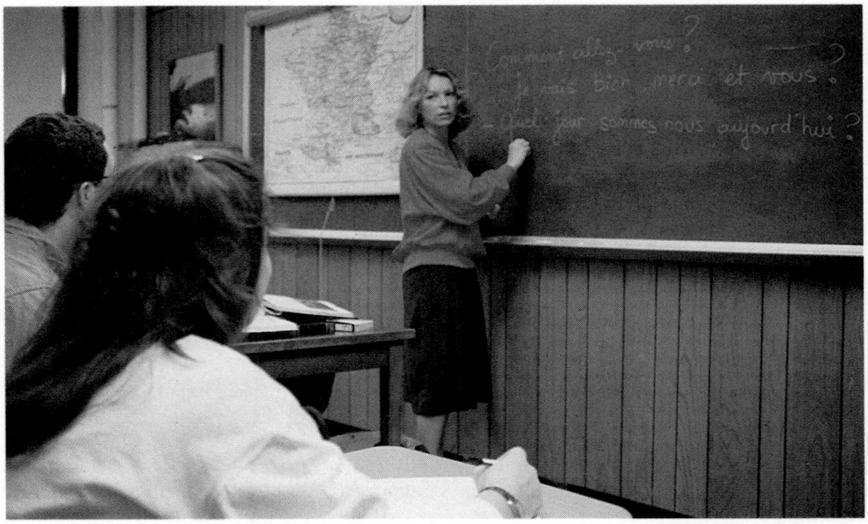

difficult to retrieve the names of the leg bones, especially if the names are similar in sound or in relative location on each limb.

Proactive Interference In **proactive interference,** older learning interferes with the capacity to retrieve more recently learned material. High school Spanish may pop in when you are trying to retrieve college French or Italian words. All three are Romance languages, with similar roots and spellings. Old German vocabulary words probably would not interfere with your ability to retrieve more recently learned French or Italian, because many German roots and sounds differ considerably from those of the Romance languages.

In terms of motor skills, you may learn how to drive a standard shift on a car with three forward speeds and a clutch that must be let up slowly after shifting. Later you learn to drive a car with five forward speeds and a clutch that must be released rapidly. For a while you make a number of errors on the five-speed car because of proactive interference. (Old learning interferes with new learning.) If you return to the three-speed car after driving the five-speed car has become natural, you may stall it a few times. This is because of retroactive interference (new learning interfering with the old).

Repression

According to Sigmund Freud, we are motivated to forget painful memories and unacceptable ideas because they produce anxiety, guilt, and shame. (In terms of operant conditioning, anxiety, guilt, and shame serve as negative reinforcers. We learn to do that which is followed by their removal—in this case, to avoid thinking about certain events and ideas.) In Chapter 12 we shall see that psychoanalysts believe that repression is at the heart of disorders such as **psychogenic amnesia.**

Proactive interference The interference by old learning with the ability to retrieve material learned recently.

Psychogenic amnesia Amnesia thought to stem from psychological conflict or trauma.

Childhood Amnesia

In his clinical investigations of patients' early experiences, Freud discovered that patients could not recall events that happened prior to the age of 3 and that recall was very cloudy through the age of 5. Freud labeled this phenomenon **childhood amnesia.** Many of us have the impression that we have vivid recollections of events during the first two or three years after birth, but studies in which attempts are made to verify these memories by interviewing independent older witnesses show that they are inaccurate (e.g., Sheingold & Tenney, 1982).

Childhood amnesia has nothing to do with the fact that the events are of the distant past. Those of us who are in our 30s, 40s, and older have many vivid memories of childhood events that occurred between the ages of 6 and 10, although they are many decades old. But 18-year-olds show steep declines in memory once they attempt to recall events earlier than the age of 6, even though these events are fewer than 18 years away (Wetzler & Sweeney, 1986).

Freud attributed childhood amnesia to the repression of the aggressive and sexual impulses that he believed young children had toward their parents. However, the events lost to childhood amnesia are not weighted in the direction of such "primitive" impulses; they include the most pedestrian, emotionally bland incidents. The effects of childhood amnesia are too broad, too nonselective, for Freud's hypothesis to hold water.

Childhood amnesia probably reflects the interaction of physiological and cognitive factors rather than psychoanalytic factors. For example, a structure of the limbic system (the **hippocampus**) that is involved in the storage of memories does not become mature until we are about 2 years old. Also, myelination of brain pathways is still occurring for the first several years after birth, contributing to the efficiency of memory functioning for the general processing of information. From a cognitive perspective, children usually cannot use language until about the age of 2. Since they are lacking language, they are impaired in their ability to construct hierarchies of concepts. Therefore, their ability to classify objects and events in their environments is also limited. As a result, their ability to *encode* sensory input—that is, to apply auditory and semantic codes—is severely restricted.

Truth or Fiction Revisited

It is *not* true that we can remember important events that took place at the early ages of 1 or 2. (Really, Allyn, believe me.)

Those early childhood memories that we are so certain we can see today are probably reconstructed and mostly inaccurate. Or else they may stem from a time when we were older than we think.

Anterograde and Retrograde Amnesia

In **anterograde amnesia,** there are memory lapses for the period following a traumatic event, such as a blow to the head, an electric shock, or an operation. In some cases it seems that the trauma interferes with all the processes of memory. The ability to pay attention, the encoding of sensory input, and rehearsal are all impaired. A number of investigators have linked certain kinds of brain damage—such as that to the hippocampus—to amnesia (Corkin et al., 1985; Squire et al., 1984).

Childhood amnesia Inability to recall events that occurred prior to the age of 3.

Hippocampus A structure in the limbic system that plays an important role in the formation of new memories.

Anterograde amnesia Failure to remember events that occur after physical trauma because of the effects of the trauma.

Consider the often-cited case of a man with the initials H.M. As noted in Chapter 2, parts of the brain are sometimes lesioned to help epilepsy patients. In H.M.'s case, a section of the hippocampus was removed (Milner, 1966). Right after the operation, the man's mental functioning appeared to be normal. As time went on, however, it became quite clear that he had severe problems in the processing of information. For example, two years after the operation, H.M. believed that he was 27—his age at the time of the operation. When his family relocated to a new address, H.M. could not find his new home or remember the new address. He responded with appropriate grief to the death of his uncle, yet he then began to ask about his uncle and why he did not visit. Each time he was informed of his uncle's passing, he grieved as though he had first heard of it. All in all, it seems that H.M.'s operation prevented him from transferring information from short-term memory to long-term memory.

In **retrograde amnesia,** the source of trauma prevents people from remembering events that took place before the accident. A football player who is knocked unconscious or a victim of an auto accident may be unable to recall events for several minutes prior to the trauma. The football player may not recall taking to the field. The accident victim may not recall entering the car. It also sometimes happens that the victim cannot remember events that occurred for several years prior to the traumatic incident.

In one well-known case of retrograde amnesia, a man received a head injury in a motorcycle accident (Baddeley, 1982). When he regained consciousness, he had lost memory for all events after the age of 11. In fact, he appeared to believe that he was still 11 years old. During the next few months he gradually recovered more knowledge of his past. He moved toward the present year by year, up until the critical motorcycle ride. But he never did recover the events just prior to the accident. The accident had apparently prevented the information that was rapidly unfolding before him from being transferred to long-term memory.

In terms of stages of memory, it may be that our perceptions and ideas need to **consolidate,** or rest undisturbed for a while, if they are to be transferred to long-term memory (Gold & King, 1974). Let us now turn our attention to some of the biological events that appear to be involved in the formation of memories.

THE BIOLOGY OF MEMORY: FROM ENGRAMS TO ADRENALINE

Psychologists generally assume that mental processes are accompanied by changes in the brain. In Chapter 2 we described some of the ways in which psychologists discover the changes that take place as we, say, solve math problems or listen to music. Psychologists similarly assume that changes in the brain accompany the encoding, storage, and retrieval of information—that is, memory.

Early in the century, many psychologists used the concept of the **engram** in their study of memory. Engrams were hypothesized electrical circuits in the brain that were assumed to correspond to memory traces—a neurological process that was believed to parallel a phenomenological experience. Biological psychologists such as Karl Lashley (1950) spent many fruitless years searching for such circuits or for the structures of the brain in which they might be housed.

During the 1950s and 1960s, research groups headed by James McConnell at the University of Michigan (McConnell et al., 1959, 1970) believed

Retrograde amnesia Failure to remember events that occur prior to physical trauma because of the effects of the trauma.

Consolidation The fixing of information in long-term memory.

Engram (1) An assumed electrical circuit in the brain that corresponds to a memory trace. (2) An assumed chemical change in the brain that accompanies learning. (From the Greek *en-*, meaning "in," and *gramma,* meaning "something that is written or recorded.")

that they had found the elusive engram in ribonucleic acid (RNA). Whereas DNA "remembers" the genetic code from generation to generation, it was thought that the related organic compound, RNA, changed with experience so that personal events and knowledge could be stored and retrieved. RNA came to be dubbed "memory molecules." The McConnell group managed to condition flatworms to scrunch up when a light was shone by pairing the light with electric shock. Then they "taught" naive flatworms this response by feeding them RNA from chopped-up learners. When this research was young and filled with promise, many students joked that perhaps the fastest route to knowledge lay in doing to their professors what the worm researchers had done to their subjects. Unfortunately for this approach—but fortunately for professors—research with RNA could not be replicated by other investigators. And so, psychologists turned elsewhere.

Much contemporary research on the biology of memory focuses on the roles of neurons, neurotransmitters, and hormones.

Changes at the Neural Level

Rats who are reared in richly stimulating environments develop more dendrites and synapses in the cerebral cortex than rats reared in relatively impoverished environments (Rosenzweig et al., 1972). It also has been shown that the level of visual stimulation rats receive is associated with the number of synapses they develop in the visual cortex (Turner & Greenough, 1985). In sum, there is reason to believe that the storage of experience requires that the number of avenues of communication among brain cells be increased.

Thus, changes occur in the visual cortex as a result of visual experience. Changes are also likely to occur in the auditory cortex as a result of heard experiences. Information received through the other senses is just as likely to lead to corresponding changes in the cortical regions that represent them. And so the storage of experiences that are perceived by several senses is likely to involve numerous areas of the brain (Squire, 1986). The recollection of these experiences is also likely to require neural activity in the affected areas of the brain.

Research with sea snails such as *Aplysia* and *Hermissenda* has offered insight into the events that take place at existing synapses when learning occurs. *Aplysia,* for example, has only about 20,000 neurons (compared with humans' *billions*). As a result, researchers have actually been able to study how experience is reflected at the synapses of specific neurons. When sea snails are conditioned, more of the neurotransmitter serotonin is released at certain synapses. As a consequence, transmission at these synapses becomes more efficient as trials (learning) progress (Goelet et al., 1986; Kandel & Schwartz, 1982). Research is underway with mammals to see how far up the evolutionary ladder we may extend these findings.

Many other naturally occurring chemical substances have been shown to play roles in memory. The hormone adrenaline, for example, generally stimulates bodily arousal and activity. It also strengthens memory when it is released into the bloodstream following instances of learning (Delanoy et al., 1982; Laroche & Bloch, 1982; McGaugh, 1983). The neurotransmitter acetylcholine (ACh) is also vital in memory formation, as is highlighted by the study of Alzheimer's disease.

A CLOSER LOOK

Alzheimer's Disease

Alzheimer's disease may afflict 2 to 5 percent of the elderly (Sloane, 1983), and occasionally it besets persons in middle adulthood. The disease is associated with the degeneration of cells in an area of the hippocampus that normally produces large amounts of acetylcholine, or ACh (Coyle et al., 1983). The brain cells, or neurons, that are involved collect plaques (dark areas of cellular "garbage") and die off in large numbers. The affected area of the brain and ACh are involved in the formation of new memories. For this reason, one of the cardinal symptoms of Alzheimer's disease is inability to consolidate new learning (such as recalling a change of address) and disorientation. Memories for remote events are usually less affected, however.

The older the individual, the greater the risk of Alzheimer's disease. The causes of Alzheimer's are unclear, but they may involve some combination of genetic factors, early viral infections, and accumulations of metals such as zinc and aluminum in the brain (Turkington, 1987).

Alzheimer's usually comes on gradually among the elderly, over a period of 8 to 20 years. At first victims note memory loss and frequently get lost—even in their own homes. Eventually they may become highly disoriented; fail to recognize other people, including family members; show childish emotions; and lose the ability to take care of their own hygiene and dress.

Coping with Alzheimer's Disease Researchers are investigating ways of controlling Alzheimer's disease. Some of the ways involve diets low in metals. Others involve drugs or dietary supplements that augment the activity of ACh (Bartus et al., 1982). Still others involve the transplanting of ACh-producing cells into the affected areas of the brain (Kimble et al., 1986).

Elderly people with Alzheimer's or with less dramatic memory problems can make behavioral adjustments. All of us, not only the elderly, profit from keeping pads and pencils near the phone so that we can readily record messages. We can keep calendars and mark down scheduled events, even routine daily events. Persons with memory loss can mark off each day as it passes. Medicine containers with compartments for each day of the week are available at pharmacies. The establishment of daily routines and environmental prompts is of great value to persons who find it difficult to form new memories, such as many of the elderly (Skinner, 1983).

When my mother turned 84, it became necessary for me to put her apartment keys on a chain attached to the straps of her handbag. In this way she could find the keys by running her hand along the chain rather than searching inside the bag. I made her task of locating the keys one of *procedural memory;* she did not have to visualize what she had done with the keys. We can apparently form new procedural memories when we can no longer readily form new episodic or semantic memories.

Another hormone that can play a role in memory is antidiuretic hormone (ADH), also known as vasopressin. Volunteers have received a synthetic form of ADH through nasal sprays and have shown significant improvement in recall (McGaugh, 1983). Excess vasopressin, unfortunately, can have serious side effects, such as constriction of the blood vessels. Research into the effects of similar chemicals, which may have fewer side effects, is under way.

Alzheimer's disease A progressive disease that is associated with degeneration of hippocampal cells that produce acetylcholine and symptomized by confusion and inability to form new memories.

Changes at the Structural Level

As noted in our discussion of the problems that beset H.M. following his epilepsy operation, certain parts of the brain, such as the hippocampus, also appear to be involved in the formation of new memories—or the transfer of information from short-term memory to long-term memory. The hippocampus does not comprise the "storage bins" for memories themselves, because H.M.'s memories prior to the operation were not destroyed. Rather, the hippocampus is involved in relaying incoming sensory information to parts of the cortex. Therefore, it appears to be vital to the storage of new information, even if old information can be retrieved without it (Murray & Mishkin, 1985; Squire, 1986).

In just one of the many surprises that confront and invigorate researchers, it turns out that persons with hippocampal damage can form new procedural memories, even though they cannot form new episodic memories. For example, they can acquire the skill of reading words backwards, even though they cannot recall individual practice sessions (Squire, 1986).

The thalamus, a structure near the center of the brain, appears to be involved in the formation of verbal memories. Part of the thalamus of an unfortunate Air Force cadet, known as N.A., was lesioned in a freak fencing accident. Following the episode, N.A. could no longer form verbal memories. However, his ability to form visual memories was unimpaired (Squire, 1986).

Truth or Fiction Revisited

It is true that if a certain part of your brain were damaged, you would indeed retain remembrance of things past, but you would not be able to form new memories. One such part in the brain is the hippocampus. Another is a section of the thalamus.

And so the encoding, storage, and retrieval of information involves biological activity on several levels. As we learn, new synapses are developed and changes occur at existing synapses. Various parts and structures of the brain are also involved in the formation of different kinds of memories.

The Future of Learning and Memory

Research into the biology of memory is in its infancy, but what an exciting area of research it is. What would it mean to you if you could read for an hour, pop a pill, and cause your new learnings to become consolidated in long-term memory? You would never have to reread the material; it would be at your fingertips for a lifetime. It would save a bit of study time, would it not?

The status of research into the biology of memory parallels that of many other psychological endeavors. We have learned a great deal, but the area of investigation remains in its infancy.

Before we turn to the Psychology and Modern Life section, I'm going to give you a sixth and final challenge to your memory.

A CLOSER LOOK

A Final Challenge to Memory

Now that you've become an expert on memory, I'm going to give you a final challenge—an odd challenge, but one that I bet you'll be able to meet quite well.

At the stroke of midnight on December 31, 2000, I challenge you to remember to say the following list of letters to yourself: T-H-U-N-S-T-O-F-A-M. As you join in the mass reveling of that special New Year's Eve—the one when we usher in the new millennium—repeat that list of letters silently to yourself. Oh, you may also kiss your partner, toot a horn, throw confetti into the air, and any number of other things. But also think T-H-U-N-S-T-O-F-A-M.

Why do I have such confidence in you? Why would I be willing to gamble that you'll be able to set aside other concerns for a few seconds so many years hence? There are two reasons. The first is that you'll surely be able to retrieve the letter list because of your enduring knowledge that it remains an acronym for "The United States of America." The second is that this challenge is so unusual—so distinct from the other happenings in your life—that you may just store it deeply enough to jar your memory a decade into the future.

And if you don't meet this challenge, might you have the nagging thought that there was something you were going to do as the third millennium displaces the second? Might the challenge be—as some psychologists say—right on the tip of your tongue? And on that same New Year's Eve, my daughter Allyn—who will refuse to think T-H-U-N-S-T-O-F-A-M no matter what, will probably still be insisting that she can remember being born.

SUMMARY

1. **What are the three kinds of memory?** These include episodic memory (memory for specific events that one has experienced), semantic memory (general knowledge), and procedural memory (skills).
2. **What are the three processes of memory?** These are encoding, storage, and retrieval. We commonly use visual, auditory, and semantic codes in the process of encoding.
3. **What are the three stages of memory proposed by a number of psychologists?** These include sensory, short-term, and long-term memory.
4. **What are sensory registers?** These hold stimuli in sensory memory. Psychologists believe that information perceived through each sense has a register.
5. **What is the importance of Sperling's research?** Sperling demonstrated that visual stimuli are maintained in sensory memory for only a fraction of a second and that we can see more than we can report.
6. **What are icons and echoes?** Icons are the mental representations of visual stimuli, and echoes are the representations of auditory stimuli. Echoes are maintained several times longer than icons, which is one reason that acoustic encoding helps us remember visual stimuli.
7. **What is the capacity of short-term memory?** We can hold seven chunks of information (plus or minus two) in short-term, or working, memory.
8. **How do psychologists explain the serial-position effect?** We tend to remember the initial items in a list because they are rehearsed most often (the primacy effect). We tend to remember the final items in a list because they are least likely to have been displaced by new information (the recency effect).
9. **How accurate are long-term memories?** Long-term memories are frequently biased because they are reconstructed according to our schemas—that is, our ways of organizing our experiences.

10. **How is information transferred from short-term to long-term memory?** There are two paths: maintenance rehearsal (rote repetition) and elaborative rehearsal (relating information to things known already).

11. **How is knowledge organized in long-term memory?** Knowledge tends to be organized according to a hierarchical structure with superordinate and subordinate concepts. We know things about members of a class when we have information about the class itself.

12. **What are context- and state-dependent memories?** Context dependence refers to the finding that we often retrieve information more efficiently when we are in the context in which we acquired it. State dependence refers to the finding that we often retrieve information better when we are in the same state of consciousness or mood as when we learned it.

13. **What is the levels-of-processing model?** This model views memory in terms of a single dimension—not three stages. It is hypothesized that we can retrieve information more efficiently when we have processed it more deeply.

14. **What are nonsense syllables?** These are meaningless syllables first used by Ebbinghaus as a way of measuring the functions of memory.

15. **How do psychologists measure retention?** Retention is often tested through three types of memory tasks—in order of ascending difficulty, recognition, recall, and relearning.

16. **What is interference theory?** According to interference theory, people forget because learning can interfere with retrieval of other learnings. In retroactive interference, new learning interferes with old learning. In proactive interference, old learning interferes with new learning.

17. **What is repression?** This is Sigmund Freud's concept for motivated forgetting. Freud suggested that we are motivated to forget threatening or unacceptable material.

18. **What is childhood amnesia?** This term refers to inability to remember events from the first couple of years, apparently because of physiological immaturity and lack of language functioning.

19. **What are anterograde and retrograde amnesia?** In anterograde amnesia, a traumatic event, such as hippocampal damage, prevents formation of new memories. In retrograde amnesia, shock or other trauma prevents previously known information from being retrieved.

20. **What biological processes are associated with the processes of memory?** Contemporary research shows that processing of information involves development of synapses, changes at existing synapses, and changes in various sections of the brain—depending on the type of information that is being processed.

PSYCHOLOGY AND MODERN LIFE

Some Methods for Improving Memory

We beleaguered humans have come through an Ice Age, a Stone Age, an Iron Age, and, a bit more recently, an Industrial Revolution. Now we are trying to cope with the so-called Age of Information, in which there has been an exponential explosion of information—much of it scientific. Computers have been developed to process it. We, too, process information, and there is more of it to process than ever before. Fortunately, psychologists have helped devise a number of methods for promoting the retention of information. Let us consider some of them.

Drill and Practice Repetition (rote maintenance rehearsal) helps transfer information from short-term to long-term memory. Maintenance rehearsal may seem rather mechanical for a capable college student, but don't forget that this is how you learned the alphabet and how to count! We write spelling words over and over to remember them. Athletes and gymnasts repeat movements in order to facilitate their procedural memories. When you have formulas down pat, you can use your time pondering when to apply them, not trying to recall them. When the wide receiver has his moves down pat, he can focus on the defenders, and not on his basic patterns.

Some students use flash cards to help them remember facts. For example, they might write "The originator of modern behaviorism is ________ " on one side of the card and "John Broadus Watson" on the flip side.

Relate New Information to What Is Already Known Now we are talking about using elaborative rehearsal. Remember the spelling of "retrieve" by retrieving the rule "*I* before *e* except after c." There are exceptions of course: Remember that "weird" doesn't follow the rule because it's a "weird" word.

We normally expand our knowledge base by relating new items to things already known. Children learn that a cello is like a violin, only bigger. They learn that a bass fiddle is also like a violin, but bigger yet. As noted in the chapter, we remember information about whales by relating whales to other mammals. Similarly, we will better recall information about porpoises and dolphins if we think of them as small whales (and not as friendly, intelligent fish).

The media are filled with stories about people who show abnormal behavior patterns of one kind or another. To help you remember the patterns discussed later on in Chapter 12, think of film or television characters who were portrayed as having the particular problem. Consider how the characters' behaviors were consistent (and inconsistent) with the descriptions in the text (and those offered by your professor). You will better remember the subject matter *and* become a good critic of media portrayals of psychological problems.

Form Unusual, Exaggerated Associations It is easier to recall stimuli that stand out, that separate themselves from the crowd. We pay more attention to them, and they tend to earn more of an emotional response. So sometimes we can better remember information when we create unusual, exaggerated associations to it.

Assume that you are trying to remember the geography of the cerebral cortex, as shown in Figure 2.15. Why not think of what you look like in right profile? (Use your left profile if it is better.) Then imagine a new imaging technique in which we can see through your skull and we find four brightly colored lobes in the right hemisphere of your cerebral cortex. Not only that, but there are little people (homunculi) flapping about in the sensory and motor areas (see Figure 2.15 again). In fact, imagine that you're in a crowded line and someone steps on your toe; thus the homunculus in the sensory cortex has a throbbing toe. This is communicated to the association areas of the cortex, where you decide that you are rather annoyed. The language areas of the cortex think up some choice words, which are relayed to the throat and mouth of the homunculus in the motor cortex, then sent into your throat and mouth. You also send some messages through the motor cortex that tighten your muscles, in readiness to attack.

Then you see that the perpetrator of the crime is a very attractive and apologetic stranger! What part of the occipital lobe is flashing the wonderful images?

The Method of Loci Another example of forming unusual associations is the method of loci (pronounced low-kye). With this method you select a series of related images, such as the parts of your body or the furniture in your home. Then you imagine an item from your shopping list, or another list you want to remember, as being attached to each image. Consider this meaty application: You might be better able to remember your shopping list if you imagine meat loaf in your navel or a strip of bacon draped over your nose.

By placing meat loaf or a favorite complete dinner in your navel, rather than a single item such as chopped beef, you can combine several items into one chunk of information. At the supermarket you recall the (familiar) ingredients for meat loaf and simply recognize whether or not you need each one.

Use Mediation The method of mediation also relies on forming associations: You link two items with a third that ties them together.

What if you are having difficulty remembering that John's wife's name is Tillie? Laird Cermak (1978) suggests that you can mediate between John and Tillie as follows. Reflect that the *john* is a slang term for bathroom. Bathrooms often have ceramic *tiles. Tiles,* of course, sounds like *Tillie.* So it goes: John-bathroom-tiles-Tillie.

I used a combination of mediation and formation of unusual associations to help me remember foreign vocabulary words in high school. For example, the Spanish verb *trabajar* means "to work," in the sense of harassing, laboring, straining. Although "-jar" is pronounced "har," I nevertheless formed a mental image of a "trial by jars" when I laid eyes on the word. I saw myself running the gauntlet with strange enemies pouring jars down upon me until I was so laden that I could barely move. "Now," I thought, "that trial by jars was really *work*!" Trabajar—trial by jars—work. And how about *mujer* (pronounced moo-hair [almost]), meaning "woman"? Women have mo' hair than I do. Woman—mo' hair—mujer. This would no longer work because now nearly all men also have more hair than I, but the association was so outlandish that it has stuck with me.

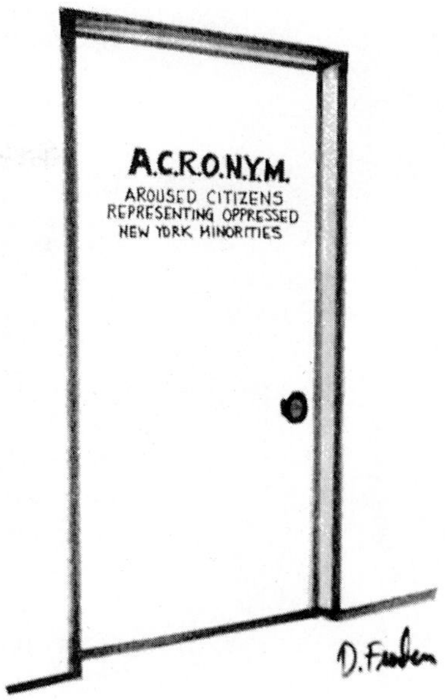

Use Mnemonic Devices Broadly speaking, the methods for jogging memory we have discussed all fall under the heading of *mnemonics,* or systems for remembering information. So-called mnemonic devices usually combine chunks of information into a format like an acronym, jingle, or phrase. For example, recalling the phrase "Every Good Boy Does Fine" has helped many people remember the musical keys E, G, B, D, F. In Chapter 2 we saw that the acronym *SAME* serves as a mnemonic device for distinguishing between afferent and efferent neurons. And in Chapter 3 we noted that most psychology students use the acronym *Roy. G. Biv* to remember the colors of the rainbow, even though your author chose to use the "word" *vibgyor.*

Acronyms have found applications in many disciplines. Consider geography. The acronym *HOMES* stands for the Great Lakes: *H*uron, *O*ntario, *M*ichigan, *E*rie, and *S*uperior. In astronomy, the phrase "*M*ercury's *v*ery *e*ager *m*other *j*ust *s*erved *u*s *n*ine *p*otatoes" helps students recall the order of the planets Mercury, Venus, Earth, Mars, Jupiter, Saturn, Uranus, Neptune, and Pluto.

What about biology? You can remember that Dromedary camels have one hump while Bactrian camels have two by turning the letters *D* and *B* on their sides.

And how can you math students ever be expected to remember the reciprocal of pi (that is, 1 divided by 3.14)? Simple: just remember the question "Can I remember the reciprocal?" and count the number of letters in each word. The reciprocal of pi, it turns out, is 0.318310. (Remember the last two digits as ten, not as one–zero.)

Now, how can you remember how to spell *mnemonics?* Simple—just be willing to grant "aMNesty" to those who cannot.

Truth or Fiction Revisited

It is true that you can use tricks to improve your memory. They all involve forming associations.

Outline

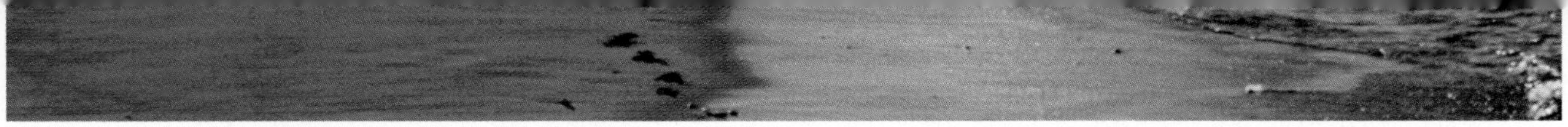

7 Language, Thought, and Intelligence

Truth or Fiction?

- □ Crying is the child's earliest use of language.
- □ Children babble only the sounds of their parents' language.
- □ A 3-year-old says "Daddy goed away" instead of "Daddy went away" because the child does not yet understand rules of grammar.
- □ Black English lacks systematic rules of grammar.
- □ It may be boring, but using the "tried and true" formula is the most efficient way to solve a problem.
- □ The best way to solve a frustrating problem is to keep plugging away at it.
- □ Intelligent people are also creative.
- □ Two children can answer exactly the same items on an intelligence test correctly, yet one can be above average and the other below average in intelligence.
- □ Head Start programs have raised children's IQs.
- □ Psychologists have been able to communicate with chimpanzees and gorillas by means of sign language.

When I was in high school, I remember being taught that human beings differ from other creatures that run, swim, or fly because we are the only ones to use tools and language. Then I learned that lower animals also use tools. Otters use rocks to open clam shells. Chimpanzees toss rocks as weapons and use sticks to dig out grubs for food.

In recent years, our exclusive claim to the use of language has also been questioned, because chimps and gorillas have been taught to use symbols to communicate. Some make signs with their hands. Others use plastic symbols or press keys on a computer keyboard. We shall explore the language of apes in the Psychology and Modern Life section of this chapter.

Language is the communication of thoughts and feelings by means of symbols that are arranged according to rules of grammar. Language makes it possible for one person to communicate large amounts of knowledge to another and for one generation to communicate to another. According to **psycholinguist** Roger Brown, "The important thing about language is that it makes life experiences cumulative; across generations and within one generation, among individuals. Everyone can know much more than he [or she] could possibly learn by direct experience" (1970, p. 212).

Language provides many of the basic units of thought, and thought is central to intelligent behavior. Language is one of our great strengths. Other species may be stronger, run faster, smell more keenly, even live longer, but only we have produced literature, music, mathematics, and science. Language ability has made all this possible.

In this chapter we shall explore the interrelated cognitive processes of language, thought, and intelligence. We shall discuss the structure of language, chronicle language development, and explore theories of language acquisition. This will prepare us for a discussion of how language and thought are intertwined in problem solving. Finally, we shall examine the concept of intelligence.

PROPERTIES OF LANGUAGE: SEMANTICITY, PRODUCTIVITY, AND DISPLACEMENT

Many species have systems of communication. Birds warn other birds of predators. They communicate that they have taken possession of a certain tree or bush through characteristic chirps and shrieks. The "dances" shown by bees inform other bees of the approximate location of a food source or of an invading enemy. Vervet monkeys make sounds that signal the distance and species of predators. But these are all innate, species-specific communication patterns. In contrast to human language, they are largely unmodifiable by experience.

According to Roger Brown (1973), three properties are used today to distinguish between true language and the communications systems of lower animals: *semanticity, productivity,* and *displacement.* **Semanticity** refers to the fact that words serve as symbols for actions, objects, relational concepts (over, in, more, and so on), and other ideas.

Productivity refers to the capacity to combine words into original sentences. An "original" sentence is *not* one that has never been spoken before. Rather, it is a sentence that is produced by the individual instead of being imitated. To produce original sentences, children must have a basic understanding of **syntax,** or the structure of grammar.

Displacement is the capacity to communicate information about events and objects in another time or place.* Language makes possible the efficient transmission of complex knowledge from one person to another and from one generation to another. Displacement permits parents to warn children of their own mistakes. Displacement allows children to tell their parents what they did in school.

Let us now consider some of the basics of language.

*The word *displacement* has a different meaning in Sigmund Freud's psychodynamic theory, as we shall see in Chapter 10.

Psycholinguist A scientist who specializes in the study of the relationships between psychological processes and language.

Semanticity Meaning. The quality of language in which words are used as symbols for objects, events, or ideas.

Productivity The capacity to combine words into original sentences.

Syntax The rules in a language for placing words in proper order to form meaningful sentences.

Displacement The quality of language that permits one to communicate information about objects and events in another time and place.

THE BASICS OF LANGUAGE

The components of language include *phonology* (sounds*), *morphology* (units of meaning), *syntax* (word order), and *semantics* (the meanings of words and groups of words).

Phonology

Phonology is the study of the basic sounds in a language. There are 26 letters in the English alphabet but a larger number of basic sounds or **phonemes.** These include the *t* and *p* in *tip,* which a psycholinguist may designate as the /t/ and /p/ phonemes. The *o* in *go* and the *o* in *gone* are different phonemes. They are spelled with the same letter, but they sound different. English speakers who learn French may be confused because /o/, as in the word *go,* has various spellings in French, including *o, au, eau,* even *eaux.*

Morphology

Morphemes are the smallest units of meaning in a language. A morpheme consists of one or more phonemes in a certain order. Some morphemes such as *dog* and *cat* function as words, but others must be used in combination. The words *dogs* and *cats* each consist of two morphemes. Adding /z/ to *dog* makes the word plural. Adding /s/ to *cat* serves the same function.

An *ed* morpheme at the end of a regular verb places it in the past tense, as with *add* and *added* and with *subtract* and *subtracted.*

Inflections Morphemes such as *s* and *ed* tacked on to the ends of nouns and verbs are referred to as grammatical "markers," or **inflections.** Inflections change the forms of words to indicate grammatical relationships such as *number* (singular or plural) and *tense* (e.g., present or past). Languages have grammatical rules for the formation of plurals, tenses, and other inflections.

Syntax

since feeling is first
who pays any attention
to the syntax of things
will never wholly kiss you . . .
e. e. cummings

The preceding lines from an e. e. cummings poem are intriguing because their syntax permits a variety of interpretations.

Syntax concerns the customary arrangement of words in phrases and sentences in a language. It deals with the ways words are to be strung together, or ordered, into phrases and sentences. The rules for word order are the *grammar* of a language.

Phonology The study of the basic sounds in a language.

Phoneme A basic sound in a language.

Morpheme The smallest unit of meaning in a language.

Inflections Grammatical markers that change the forms of words to indicate grammatical relationships such as number and tense.

*American Sign Language and Signed English, which are languages used by the deaf, are exceptions.

In English, statements usually follow the pattern *subject, verb,* and *object of the verb.* Note this example:

The young boy (subject) → has brought (verb) → the book (object).

The sentence would be confusing if it were written "The young boy *has* the book *brought.*" But this is how the words would be ordered in German. German syntax differs, and in German, a past participle ("brought") is placed at the end of the sentence, whereas the helping verb ("has") follows the subject. Although the syntax of German differs from that of English, children reared in German-speaking homes* acquire German syntax readily.

Semantics

Semantics is the study of meaning. It involves the relationship between language and the objects or events language depicts. Words that sound (and are spelled) alike can have different meanings, depending on their usage. Compare these sentences:

A rock sank the boat.
Don't rock the boat.

In the first sentence, *rock* is a noun and the subject of the verb *sank.* The sentence probably means that the hull of a boat was ripped open by an underwater rock, causing the boat to sink. In the second sentence, *rock* is a verb. The second sentence is usually used as a figure of speech in which a person is being warned not to change things—not to "make waves" or "upset the apple cart."

Or compare these sentences:

The chicken is ready for dinner.
The lion is ready for dinner.
The shark is ready for dinner.

The first sentence probably means that a chicken has been cooked and is ready to be eaten. The second sentence probably means that a lion is hungry or about to devour its prey. Our interpretation of the phrase "is ready for dinner" reflects our knowledge about chickens and lions. Whether we expect a shark to be eaten or to do some eating might reflect our seafood preferences or how recently we had seen the movie *Jaws.*

Semantics The study of the meanings of a language—the relationships between language and objects and events.

*No, homes do not really speak German or any other language. This is an example of idiomatic English; idioms like these are readily acquired by children.

Table 7.1
Milestones in Language Development

Approximate Age	Vocalization and Language
Birth	Cries.
12 weeks	Markedly less crying than at 8 weeks; when talked to and nodded at, smiles, followed by squealing-gurgling sounds usually called cooing, which is vowel-like in character and pitch-modulated; sustains cooing for 15–20 seconds.
16 weeks	Responds to human sounds more definitely; turns head; eyes seem to search for speaker; occasionally some chuckling sounds.
20 weeks	The vowel-like cooing sounds begin to be interspersed with more consonantal sounds; acoustically, all vocalizations are very different from the sounds of the mature language of the environment.
6 months	Cooing changes into babbling resembling one-syllable utterances; neither vowels nor consonants have very fixed recurrences; most common utterances sound somewhat like *ma, mu, da,* or *di.*
8 months	Reduplication (or more continuous repetitions) becomes frequent; intonation patterns become distinct; utterances can signal emphasis and emotions.
10 months	Vocalizations are mixed with sound play such as gurgling or bubble blowing; appears to wish to imitate sounds, but the imitations are never quite successful.*
12 months	Identical sound sequences are replicated with higher relative frequency of occurrence, and words *(mamma* or *dadda)* are emerging; definitely shows signs of understanding some words and simple commands ("Show me your eyes").
18 months	Has a definite repertoire of words—more than 3 but less than 50; still much babbling but now of several syllables with intricate intonation pattern; no attempt at communicating information and no frustration for not being understood; words may include items such as *thank you* or *come here,* but there is little ability to join any of the items into spontaneous two-item phrases; understanding is progressing rapidly.
24 months	Vocabulary of more than 50 items (some children seem to be able to name everything in environment); begins spontaneously to join vocabulary items into two-word phrases; all phrases seem to be own creations; definite increase in communicative behavior and interest in language.
30 months	Fastest increase in vocabulary, with many new additions every day; no babbling at all; utterances have communicative intent; frustrated if not understood by adults; utterances consist of at least two words, although many have three or even five words; sentences and phrases have characteristic child grammar—that is, they are rarely verbatim repetitions of an adult utterance; intelligibility is not very good yet, though there is great variation among children; seems to understand everything that is said to him or her.
3 years	Vocabulary of some 1,000 words; about 80 percent of utterances are intelligible even to strangers; grammatical complexity of utterances is roughly that of colloquial adult language, although mistakes still occur.
4 years	Language is well established; deviations from the adult norm tend to be more in style than in grammar.

*Here we are talking about imitating the sounds of speech. Infants of this age have already imitated the pitch of their parents' sounds quite well for a number of months. The ages in this table are approximations. Parents need not assume that their children will have language problems if they are somewhat behind.

Source: Adapted from E. H. Lenneberg (1967). *Biological Foundations of Language.* New York: Wiley, pp. 128–130.

Noam Chomsky differentiates between the *surface structure* and the *deep structure* of sentences. The **surface structure** involves the superficial grammatical contruction of the sentence. The surface structure of the "ready-for-dinner" sentences is the same. The **deep structure** of a sentence refers to its underlying meaning. The "ready-for-dinner" sentences clearly differ in their deep structure. "Make me a peanut butter and jelly sandwich" has an ambiguous surface structure, allowing different interpretations of its deep meaning—and the typical child's response: "Poof! You're a peanut butter and jelly sandwich!"

Now that we have explored the properties and the basics of language, let us chronicle the "child's task" of acquiring language.

Surface structure The superficial grammatical construction of a sentence.

Deep structure The underlying meaning of a sentence.

Prelinguistic Prior to the development of language.

PATTERNS OF LANGUAGE DEVELOPMENT

Children appear to develop language in an invariant sequence of steps, as outlined in Table 7.1. We begin with the **prelinguistic** vocalizations of crying, cooing, and babbling.

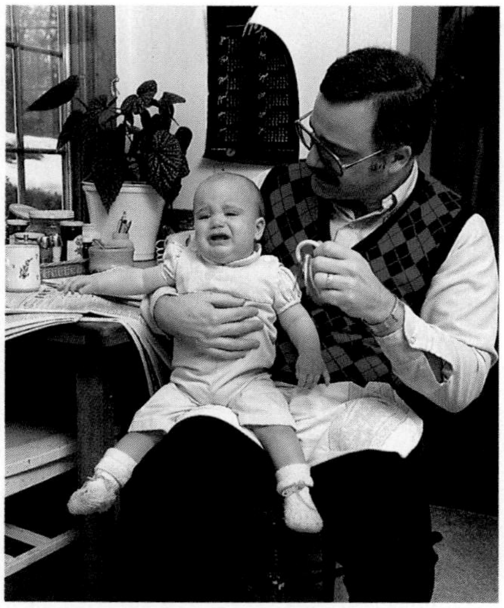

Crying. Crying is a prelinguistic vocalization that most adults find aversive and try to bring to an end.

Prelinguistic Vocalizations

Crying Newborn children, as parents are well aware, have an unlearned but highly effective form of verbal expression: crying and more crying. Studies with the **spectrograph** show that crying is a simple form of vocalizing that is accomplished by blowing air through the vocal tract. Although crying can be prolonged and vigorous and vary in pitch, there are no distinct, well-formed sounds. In addition to serving as a signal that help is needed, crying appears to foster cardiovascular development and increase the capacity of the lungs. These healthful outcomes do not prove that crying is necessary for proper physical development, but parents can at least take comfort in the thought that crying serves some positive functions.

Truth or Fiction Revisited

It is *not* true that crying is the child's earliest use of language. Crying is a prelinguistic event.

Cooing Crying is just about the only sound that infants make during the first month after birth. During the second month, babies also begin **cooing.** Cooing, like crying, is unlearned. Babies use their tongues when they coo, and for this reason coos take on more articulated sounds than cries. Coos are often vowel-like and may resemble repeated "oohs" and "ahs." Cooing appears to be linked to feelings of pleasure or positive excitement. Babies do not coo when they are hungry, tired, or in pain.

Although cries and coos are innate, they can be modified by experience. For example, when parents respond positively to cooing by talking to their babies, smiling at them, and imitating their sounds, cooing tends to increase.

Remember that true language has *semanticity;* that is, sounds (or signs, in the case of sign language) are symbols. Cries and coos do not represent objects or events, so they are prelinguistic. By about 8 months, cooing decreases markedly. By about the fifth or sixth month, children have already begun to babble.

Babbling **Babbling** is the first vocalizing that sounds like human speech. Children babble phonemes of several languages, including the throaty German *ch,* the clicks of certain African tribes, and rolling *r*'s (Atkinson et al., 1970; McNeill, 1970). In their babbling, babies frequently combine consonants and vowels, as in "ba," "ga," and, sometimes, the much valued "dada." "Dada" at first is purely coincidental (sorry, you Dads), despite the family's jubilation over its appearance.

Babbling, like crying and cooing, appears to be inborn. Children from different cultures, where languages sound very different, all seem to babble the same sounds, including many that they could not have heard (Oller, 1981).

Truth or Fiction Revisited

It is *not* true that children babble only the sounds of their parents' language. Children babble sounds heard in languages around the world.

Although it is inborn, babbling can be modified by experience. In one of the classic studies of the effects of reinforcement on babies' vocalizations, Harriet Rheingold and her colleagues (1959) demonstrated that smiling, soft sounds, and pats on the abdomen can increase the frequency of babbling. Infants also babble more when adults imitate them or just attend to their babbling (Haugen & McIntire, 1972).

Spectrograph An instrument that converts sounds to graphs or pictures according to their acoustic qualities.

Cooing Prelinguistic, articulated, vowel-like sounds that appear to reflect feelings of positive excitement.

Babbling The child's first vocalizations that have the sounds of speech.

In verbal interactions, adults often repeat the syllables produced by their babies. They are likely to say "dadada" or "bababa" instead of simply "da" or "ba." Redundancy apparently helps infants discriminate these sounds (Goodsitt et al., 1984) and encourages imitation.

Children seem to single out the types of phonemes used in the home within a few months. By the age of 9 or 10 months, these phonemes are repeated regularly. "Foreign" phonemes begin to drop out, so there is an overall reduction in the variety of phonemes that infants produce.

Development of Vocabulary

To understand vocabulary development, we must first distinguish between *receptive vocabulary* and *expressive vocabulary.* Children's **receptive vocabulary** consists of the words that they can understand, as demonstrated, for example, by following directions ("Show me your nose"). Children's **expressive vocabulary** consists of the words that they use in their speech. Receptive vocabulary growth outpaces expressive vocabulary growth. At any given time, children can understand more words than they can use.

Now let us look at that exciting milestone—a child's first words.

The Child's First Words(!) Ah, that long-awaited first word! What a thrill! What a milestone! Sad to say, many parents miss this milestone. They are not quite sure when their infants utter their first word, often because the first word is not pronounced clearly or because pronunciation varies from usage to usage. *Ball* may be pronounced "ba," "bee," or even "pah" on separate occasions (Ferguson & Farwell, 1975).

Vocabulary acquisition is slow at first. According to Katherine Nelson (1973), it generally takes children three to four months to achieve a ten-word vocabulary after their first word is spoken. By about 18 months, children are producing nearly two dozen words, but, as suggested in Table 7.1, they can understand simple commands using many more words at about 12 months. Many words are quite familiar, such as *no, cookie, mama, hi,* and *eat.* Others, like *allgone* and *bye-bye,* may not be found in the dictionary, but they function as words.

Of children's first 50 words, most are names for people, animals, and objects that move (*Mommy, car, doggy*) or that can be moved (*dolly, milky, diapy*). Others include action words (*bye-bye*), modifiers (*big, hot*), and expressive words (*no, hi, ooh*) (Nelson, 1973, 1981).

Overextension Children try to talk about more objects than they have words for, and so they often extend the meaning of one word to refer to things and actions for which they do not have words. Eve Clark (1973, 1975) studied diaries of infants' language development and found that overextensions are generally based on perceived similarities in function or form between the original object or action and the new one to which the first word is being extended. She provides the example of the word *em,* which one infant originally used to designate a worm and which then became extended to include other small moving animals and objects such as insects and the head of waving grass. At some point many children refer to horses as *doggies.* My daughter Allyn, at age 6, counted by tens as follows: sixty, seventy, eighty, ninety, *tenty.*

Receptive vocabulary The extent of one's knowledge of the meanings of words that are communicated to one by others.

Expressive vocabulary The sum total of the words that one can use in the production of language.

Development of Syntax

Although children first use one-word utterances, these utterances appear to express the meanings found in complete sentences. Roger Brown (1973) calls brief expressions that have the meanings of sentences telegraphic speech. When we as adults write telegrams, we use principles of syntax to cut out all the "unnecessary" words. "Home Tuesday" might stand for "I expect to be home on Tuesday." Similarly, only the "essential" words are used in children's telegraphic speech—in particular, nouns, verbs, and some modifiers.

Let us consider the syntactic features of two types of telegraphic speech: the *holophrase* and *two-word utterances.*

Holophrases Single words that are used to express complex meanings are called **holophrases.** For example, *mama* may be used by the child to signify meanings as varied as "There goes mama," "Come here, mama," and "You are mama." Similarly, *poo-cat* can signify "There is a pussycat," "That stuffed animal looks just like my pussycat," or "I want you to give me my pussycat right now!" Most children readily teach their parents what they intend by augmenting their holophrases with gestures, intonations, and reinforcers. That is, they act delighted when parents do as requested and howl when they do not.

Two-Word Utterances Toward the end of the second year, children begin to speak in telegraphic two-word sentences. In the sentence "That ball," the words *is* and *a* are implied. Two-word utterances seem to appear at about the same time in the development of all languages (Slobin, 1973). Also, the sequence of emergence of the types of two-word utterances (e.g., first, agent-action; then action-object, location, and possession) is the same in languages as diverse as English, Luo (an African tongue), German, Russian, and Turkish (Slobin, 1971, 1983). This apparently universal sequence suggests that innate processes govern language development.

Two-word utterances, although brief, show basic understanding of syntax. The child will say, "Sit chair" to tell a parent to sit in a chair, not "Chair sit." (Apes do not reliably make this distinction.) The child will say, "My shoe," not "Shoe my," to show possession. "Mommy go" means Mommy is leaving, whereas "Go Mommy" expresses the wish for Mommy to go away. For this reason, "Go Mommy" is not heard often.

Toward More Complex Language

Between the ages of 2 and 3, children's sentence structure usually expands to include the words that were missing in telegraphic speech. It is usually during the third year that children add an impressive array of articles *(a, an, the),* conjunctions *(and, but, or),* possessive and demonstrative adjectives *(your, her, that),* pronouns *(she, him, one),* and prepositions *(in, on, over, around, under,* and *through.)* Their grasp of syntax is shown in language oddities such as *your one* instead of *yours* and *his one* instead of, simply, *his.*

It is also usually between the ages of 2 and 3 that children show knowledge of rules for combining phrases and clauses into complex sentences. An early example of a complex sentence is "You goed and Mommy goed, too."

Holophrase A single word used to express complex meanings.

Overregularization The application of regular grammatical rules for forming inflections (e.g., past tense and plurals) to irregular verbs and nouns.

Overregularization One of the more intriguing language developments is **overregularization.** To understand children's use of overregularization, let us first review the formation of the past tense and of plurals in English. We add *d* or *ed* phonemes to regular verbs and *s* or *z* phonemes to regular nouns. Thus, *walk* becomes *walked* and *look* becomes *looked. Pussycat* becomes *pussycats* and *doggy* becomes *doggies.* There are also irregular verbs and nouns. For example, *see* becomes *saw, sit* becomes *sat,* and *go* becomes *went. Sheep* remains *sheep* (plural) and *child* becomes *children.*

At first it seems that children learn a small number of these irregular verbs by imitating their parents. As noted by Stan Kuczaj (1977, 1978), 2-year-olds tend to form them correctly—temporarily! Then they become aware of the syntactic rules for forming the past tense and plurals in English. As a result, they tend to make charming errors (Bowerman, 1982). Some 3- to 5-year-olds, for example, are more likely to say "I seed it" than "I saw it" and more likely to say "Mommy sitted down" than "Mommy sat down." They are likely to talk about the "gooses" and "sheeps" they "seed" on the farm and about all the "childs" they ran into at the playground. This tendency to regularize the irregular is what is meant by overregularization.

Truth or Fiction Revisited

A 3-year-old actually says "Daddy goed away" instead of "Daddy went away" because the child *does* understand rules of grammar. Because of knowledge of grammar, the child is overregularizing the irregular verb "to go."

Some parents recognize that their children were forming the past tense of irregular verbs correctly and that they then began to make errors. The thing to remember is that overregularization *does represent an advance in the development of syntax.* Overregularization reflects knowledge of grammar—not faulty language development. In another year or two, *mouses* will be boringly transformed into *mice,* and Mommy will no longer have *sitted* down. Parents might as well enjoy overregularization while they can.

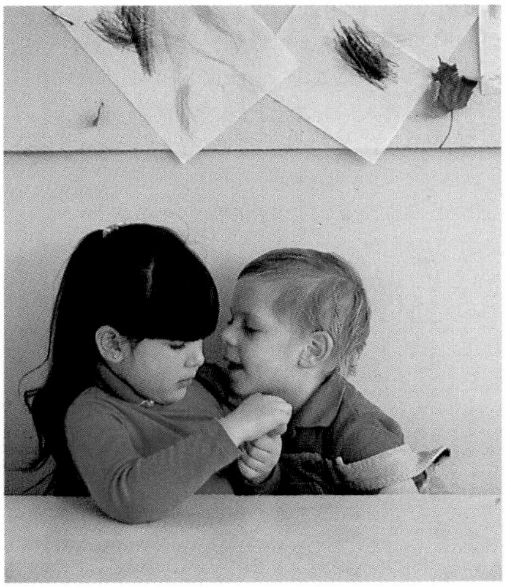

Having a Talk. By the fourth year, children are asking questions, taking turns talking, and holding lengthy conversations. By the age of 6, their vocabularies have expanded to 10,000 words, give or take a few thousand.

Other Developments As language develops beyond the third year, children show increasing facility with the use of pronouns (such as *it* and *she*) and with prepositions (such as *in, before,* or *on*), which represent physical or temporal relationships among objects and events. Children's first questions are telegraphic and characterized by a rising pitch (which signifies a question mark in English) at the end. "More milky?" for example, can be translated into "May I have more milk?" or "Would you like more milk?" or "Is there more milk?"—depending on the context.

It is usually during the third year that the *wh* questions appear. Consistent with the child's general cognitive development, certain *wh* questions *(what, who,* and *where)* appear earlier than others *(why, when, which,* and *how)* (Bloom et al., 1982). *Why* is usually too philosophical for the 2-year-old, and *how* is too involved. Two-year-olds are also likely to be now-oriented, so *when,* too, is of less than immediate concern. By the fourth year, most children are spontaneously producing *why, when,* and *how* questions.

By the fourth year, children are asking questions, taking turns talking, and engaging in lengthy conversations. By the age of 6, their vocabularies have expanded to 10,000 words, give or take a few thousand. By 7 to 9, most children realize that words can have more than one meaning, and they are entertained by riddles and jokes that require semantic sophistication ("What's black and white, but read all over?").

PSYCHOLOGY GOES TO WORK

Educators and Black English

Teachers, school administrators, and speech professionals are frequently in a quandary as to what to do—if anything—about Black English. Black English is spoken by segments of the American black community. It has taken hold most strongly in poor black neighborhoods.

Consider a study in which an audiotape of standard English was played to poor black children who were asked to repeat what they had heard. The taped sentence was "I asked him if he did it, and he said he didn't do it." One 5-year-old girl recast the sentence in Black English as follows: "I asks him if he did it, and he says he didn't did it, but I knows he did" (Anastasiow & Hanes, 1976, p. 3).

As the example suggests, the major differences between Black English and standard English lie in the use of verbs. Tenses are formed differently in Black English. For example, "She-ah hit us" may be used in the place of the standard English "She will hit us." Consider the verb "to be." In Black English, "He be gone" indicates the standard "He has been gone for a long while," and "He gone" signifies "He is gone right now" in standard English.

Some observers have thought that standard English verbs are used haphazardly in Black English, as if the bare bones of English are being adapted and downgraded. As a result, some school systems have reacted to Black English with contempt. Yet, many linguists, such as William Labov (1972), have argued that Black English is just one dialect of English. The grammatical rules of Black English differ from those of standard English. However, Black English has consistent rules, and they allow for the expression of thoughts that are as complex as those permitted by standard English. In other words, Black English is different but not inferior.

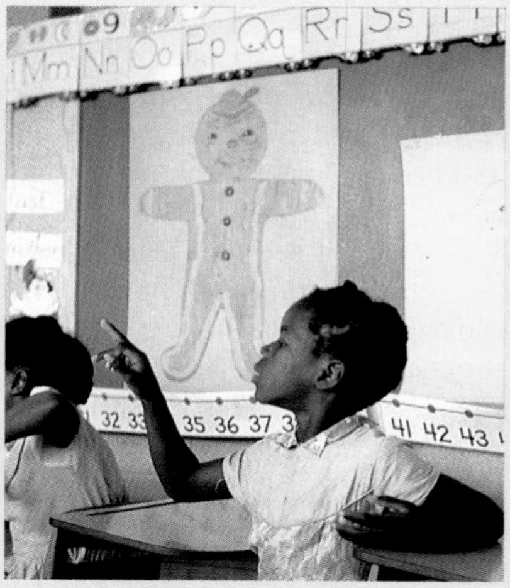

Black English in the Classroom. Teachers, school administrators, and speech professionals are frequently in a quandary as to what to do—if anything—about Black English. Many linguists argue that although the grammatical rules of Black English differ from those of standard English, Black English has consistent rules, and they allow for the expression of thoughts that are as complex.

"To Be or Not to Be": Use of the Verb "to Be" in Black English Let us consider a couple of examples of rules in Black English—rules involving use of the verb "to be" and negation. In standard English, "be" is part of the infinitive form of the verb used in the formation of the future tense, as in "I'll be angry tomorrow." Thus "I be angry" is incorrect. In Black English, "be" is used to denote a continuing state of being. "I am angry" would be perfectly good standard English *and* Black English. But the Black English sentence "I be angry" means in standard English, "I have been angry for a while," and is good Black English.

Black English also *omits* the verb *to be* in some cases (Rebok, 1987), usually when standard English would use a contraction. For example, "She's the one I'm talking about" could be translated as "She the one I talking about." Omitting the verb in Black English is no more careless than contracting it in standard English. Contraction follows a rule of standard English; omission in the example follows a rule of Black English. The Black English sentence is no "simpler" than the standard one.

"Not to Be or Not to Be Nothing": Negation in Black English Black English also differs in the use of the double negative. Consider the sentence, "I don't want no trouble," which is, of course, commendable. Middle-class white children would be corrected for this instance of double negation and encouraged to say either "I don't want any trouble" or "I want no trouble." Double negation is acceptable in Black English, but teachers who use standard English are likely to "jump on" black children who speak this way.

Truth or Fiction Revisited

It is *not* true that Black English is lacking in systematic rules of grammar. Instead, the rules of Black English differ in various ways from those of standard English.

Standard English is spoken by the majority. For this reason, black children who want to succeed will usually find it to their advantage to use standard English—at least in college, on the job, and in similar social situations. However, if the educators who instruct black children realize that Black English is just as complex and rule-governed as standard English, they will treat Black-English–speaking children with greater respect—even as they help provide black children with the "mainstream" linguistic alternative.

Individual Differences in Language Development Although the sequences of development are invariant, there are individual differences in children's rates of language development. There are also sex and social-class differences. Girls are slightly superior to boys in their language development. It appears that children from families of lower socioeconomic status have poorer vocabularies than children from middle- or upper-class families

(Lesser et al., 1965). Knowledge of the meanings of words is the single strongest predictor of overall scores on tests of intellectual functioning. Thus it is not surprising that children from middle- and upper-class families attain higher test scores.

THEORIES OF LANGUAGE DEVELOPMENT

Countless billions of children have acquired the languages spoken by their parents and passed them down, with minor changes, from generation to generation. But how do they do so? In this section we discuss learning-theory, nativist, and cognitive views of language development.

Learning-Theory Views

Learning plays a major role in language development. Children reared in English-speaking homes learn English, not Japanese or Russian. Learning theorists usually explain language development in terms of imitation and reinforcement.

The Role of Imitation From a social-learning perspective, parents serve as **models.** Children learn language, at least in part, by observation and imitation. It seems likely that many vocabulary words, especially nouns and verbs (including irregular verbs) are learned by imitation.

Recall that at first, children accurately repeat the irregular verb forms they observe. This repetition can probably be explained in terms of modeling, but modeling does not explain all the phenomena of learning. Children later begin to overregularize irregular verb forms *because of* knowledge of rules of syntax, not imitation. Nor does imitative learning explain how children can spontaneously utter phrases and sentences they have *not* observed (Rebok, 1987). Parents, for example, are unlikely to model utterances such as "bye-bye sock" and "allgone Daddy," but children do say them.

Sometimes children steadfastly avoid imitating language forms suggested by adults, even when the adults are insistent. Note the following exchange between 2-year-old Ben and a (very frustrated!) adult:

BEN: I like these candy. I like they.
ADULT: You like them?
BEN: Yes. I like they.
ADULT: Say *them.*
BEN: Them.
ADULT: Say "I like *them.*"
BEN: I like them.
ADULT: Good.
BEN: I'm good. These candy good too.
ADULT: Are they good?
BEN: Yes. I like they. You like they? (Kuczaj, 1982, p. 48)

The Role of Reinforcement In his landmark book, *Verbal Behavior,* B. F. Skinner outlined his view of the role of reinforcement in language development: "A child acquires verbal behavior when relatively unpatterned vocalizations, selectively reinforced, assume forms which produce appropriate consequences in a given verbal community" (Skinner, 1957, p. 31).

Models In learning theory, persons who engage in behaviors that are imitated by others.

Skinner allows that prelinguistic vocalizations such as cooing and babbling may be inborn. But parents reinforce children for babbling that approximates the form of real words, such as *da,* which in English resembles *dog* or *daddy.* Children, in fact, do increase their babbling when it results in adults smiling at them, stroking them, and talking back to them.

As the first year progresses, children babble the sounds of their native tongues with increasing frequency. "Foreign" sounds tend to drop out. The behaviorist explains this pattern of changing frequencies in terms of reinforcement (of the sounds of the adults' language) and extinction (of foreign sounds). An alternate (nonbehavioral) explanation is that children actively attend to the sounds in their linguistic environments and are intrinsically motivated to utter them.

From Skinner's (1957, 1983) perspective, children acquire an early vocabulary through shaping. That is, parents require that children's utterances come progressively closer to actual words before they are reinforced. Skinner views multiword utterances as complex stimulus–response chains that are also taught by shaping. As children's utterances increase in length, parents foster correct word order by uttering sentences to their children and reinforcing imitation. As with Ben, when children make grammatical errors, parents recast their utterances correctly. They then reinforce the children for repeating them.

But remember Ben's refusal to be shaped into correct syntax. If the reinforcement explanation were accurate, parents' selective reinforcement of their children's utterances would facilitate their learning of phonetics, syntax, and semantics. We do not have such evidence. For one thing, parents are more likely to reinforce their children for the accuracy, or "truth value," of their utterances than for their grammatical correctness (Brown, 1973). Parents, in other words, generally accept the syntax of their children's vocal efforts. The child who points down and says, "The grass is purple" is not likely to be reinforced, despite correct syntax. But the enthusiastic child who shows her empty plate and blurts out "I eated it all up!" is likely to be reinforced, despite overregularization of *to eat.*

Selective reinforcement of children's pronunciation, in fact, may backfire. Children whose parents reward proper pronunciation but correct poor pronunciation develop vocabulary *more slowly* than children whose parents are more tolerant about pronunciation (Nelson, 1973).

Learning-theory approaches also cannot account for the invariant sequences of language development and for children's spurts in acquisition. Even the types of two-word utterances emerge in a consistent pattern in diverse cultures. Although timing differs from child to child, the types of questions used, passive versus active sentences, and so on all emerge in the same order.

Nativist Views

The nativist view of language development holds that innate or inborn factors cause children to attend to and acquire language in certain ways (Maratsos, 1983). From this perspective, children bring certain neurological "prewiring" to language learning.

There are various nativist views on language development. Among them are the perspectives of David McNeill, Noam Chomsky, and Eric Lenneberg. McNeill's and Chomsky's views are referred to as *psycholinguistic theory.* Lenneberg's theory hypothesizes the existence of a period during which children are particularly sensitive to acquiring the structure of a language.

Psycholinguistic Theory: Is There a Language Acquisition Device? According to **psycholinguistic theory,** language acquisition involves an interaction between environmental influences, such as exposure to parental speech and reinforcement, and an inborn tendency to acquire language (Chomsky, 1968, 1980). Evidence for an inborn tendency is found in the universality of human language abilities and in the invariant sequences of language development.

McNeill (1970) labeled this inborn tendency the **Language Acquisition Device** (LAD). He believed that the LAD is a prewiring of the nervous system that suits it to learn grammar. On the surface, languages differ a great deal. However, the LAD serves children all around the world because languages share what Chomsky refers to as a "universal grammar"—an underlying deep structure or set of rules for turning ideas into sentences. Consider an analogy with computers: According to psycholinguistic theory, the universal grammar that resides in the LAD is the basic operating system of the computer, whereas the particular language that a child learns to use is the word-processing program.

The Sensitive Period Eric Lenneberg (1967) proposes that there is a **sensitive period** for learning language that begins at about 18 to 24 months and lasts until puberty. This "window" for language learning reflects the status of neural maturation. During the sensitive period, neural development (as in the differentiation of brain structures) provides a degree of plasticity that facilitates language learning.

Neural development also provides the basis for cognitive development. By 18 to 24 months, neural maturation permits the child to begin to entertain *preoperational thought,* as we shall see in Chapter 9, and to accelerate developments in vocabulary and syntax. By the time people have reached sexual maturity, brain tissue has also reached adult levels of differentiation. Language learning can occur afterward but is more laborious (Elliot, 1981).

Evidence for a sensitive period is found in recovery from brain injuries in some people. Injuries to the dominant hemisphere can impair or destroy the ability to speak (see Chapter 2). But prior to puberty, brain-injured children frequently recover a good deal of speaking ability. Lenneberg (1967) suggests that in very young children, dominant-hemisphere damage may encourage the development of language functions in the other hemisphere. Adaptation ability wanes in adolescence, however.

In the following section, we shall consider the relationships between language and thought, or cognition.

Cognitive Views

Cognitive views of language development focus on the relationships between cognitive development and language development. Cognitive theorists tend to hold a number of assumptions, including these:

1. Language development is made possible by cognitive analytical abilities (Bates & MacWhinney, 1982; Maratsos, 1983).
2. Children are active agents in language learning. Children's motivation for learning syntax and vocabulary grows out of their "desire to express meanings that conceptual development makes available to them" (Maratsos, 1983).

Jean Piaget believed that cognitive development precedes language development. Piaget (1976) argued that children must first understand **concepts** before they can use words that describe the concepts. This view holds

Psycholinguistic theory The view that language learning involves an interaction chbetween environmental influences and an inborn tendency to acquire language. The emphasis is on the inborn tendency.

Language Acquisition Device In psycholinguistic theory, neural "prewiring" that facilitates the child's learning of grammar. Abbreviated *LAD.*

Sensitive period In linguistic theory, the period from about 18 months to puberty when the brain is thought to be particularly capable of learning language because of plasticity.

Concept A symbol that stands for a group of objects, events, or ideas that share common properties.

that children learn words in order to describe classes or categories that they have already created (Nelson, 1982; Nelson et al., 1977). Children can learn the word *doggy* because they have already perceived the characteristics that distinguish dogs from other things.

The cognitive view of language development is not monolothic. Although many theorists argue that cognitive development precedes language development, others reverse the causal relationship. The opposing point of view holds that children create cognitive classes in order to understand things that are labeled by words (Clark, 1973, 1983). The word can come before the meaning. When children hear the word *dog,* they strive to understand it by searching for characteristics that separate dogs from other things.

Today most cognitive psychologists find something of value in each of these cognitive views (Greenberg & Kuczaj, 1982). In the early stages of language development, concepts often precede words so that many of the infant's words describe classes that have already developed. Later on, however, language is not merely the handmaiden of thought; language also influences thought.

While we as adults continue to struggle with complex concepts to explain language development, 1- and 2-year-olds go right on learning language all around us.

LANGUAGE AND THOUGHT

Theories of language development are of little importance to a 20-month-old who has just polished off her plate of chocolate chip cookies and exclaims "Allgone!" In the previous section, we were concerned with this question: How does the child come to say "Allgone" when she has finished her cookies. Now let us ponder this question: What does her use of "Allgone" suggest about her thought processes? In other words, would the girl have ***known*** that there were no cookies left if she did not have a word to express this idea? Do you always think in words? Can you think ***without*** using language? Would you be able to solve problems without using words or sentences?

The Linguistic-Relativity Hypothesis

Language may not be necessary for all thought, but according to the **linguistic-relativity hypothesis** proposed by Benjamin Whorf (1956), language structures the ways in which we perceive the world. Consider our perceptions of microcomputers. People who understand terms such as *640 K, megabyte,* and *RAM* can think about microcomputers with greater sophistication than those who do not.

According to the linguistic-relativity hypothesis, most English speakers' ability to think about snow may be rather limited when compared to that of the Eskimos. We have only a few words for snow, whereas the Eskimos have many words, related, for example, to whether the snow is hard-packed, falling, melting, or covered by ice. When we think about snow, we have fewer words to choose from and have to search for descriptive adjectives. Eskimos, however, can readily find a single word that describes a complex weather condition. It might then be easier for them to think about this variety of snow in relation to other aspects of their world. Similarly, the Hanunoo people of the Philippines use 92 words for rice, depending on whether the rice is husked or unhusked and on how it is prepared. And we have one word for camel, whereas Arabs have more than 250.

Linguistic relativity hypothesis The view that language structures the way in which we view the world.

In English we have hundreds of words to describe different colors, but those who speak Shona use only three words for colors. People who speak Bassa use only two words for colors (Gleason, 1961), corresponding to light and dark. The Hopi Indians had two words for flying objects, one for birds and an all-inclusive word for anything else that may be found traveling through the air.

Does this mean that the Hopi were limited in their ability to think about bumblebees and airplanes? Are English speakers limited in their ability to think about skiing conditions? Are those who speak Shona and Bassa "color-blind" for practical purposes?

Probably not. People who use only a few words to distinguish colors seem to perceive the same color variations as people with dozens of words (Bornstein & Marks, 1982; Rosch, 1974). For example, the Dani of New Guinea, like the Bassa, have just two words for colors: *mola,* which refers to warm colors, and *mili,* which refers to cool colors. Still, tasks in matching and memory show that the Dani can discriminate the many colors of the spectrum when they are motivated to do so. English-speaking skiers, who are concerned about different skiing conditions, have developed a comprehensive special vocabulary about snow, including the terms *powder, slush, ice, hard-packed,* and *corn snow,* that might enable them to communicate and think about snow with the facility of Eskimos. When a need to expand a language's vocabulary arises, the speakers of that language apparently have little difficulty in meeting the need.

Critics of the linguistic-relativity hypothesis argue that a language's vocabulary only suggests the range of concepts that the speakers of the language have traditionally found important. Yet people can make distinctions for which there are no words. Hopi Indians flying from New York to San Francisco nowadays would not think that they are flying inside a bird or a bumblebee, even if they have no word for airplane.

Although language may not be necessary for all thought, it does help. In the section on problem solving, however, we shall see that our labels for things can sometimes impair our problem-solving abilities.

PROBLEM SOLVING

One of the pleasures I derived from my own introductory psychology course lay in showing friends the textbook and getting them involved in the problems in the section on problem solving. First, of course, I struggled with the problems myself. It's that time, now. And it's your turn. Get some scrap paper, take a breath, and have a go at the following problems. The answers will be discussed in the following pages, but don't peek. *Try* the problems first.

1. Provide the next two letters in the series for each of the following:

a. ABABABAB??
b. ABDEBCEF??
c. OTTFFSSE??

2. Draw straight lines through all the points in part A of Figure 7.1, using only *four* lines. Do not lift your pencil from the paper or retrace your steps. (Answers are given in Figure 7.3.)

3. Move three matches in part B of Figure 7.1 to make four squares of the same size. You must use *all* the matches. (Answer shown on p. 279.)

4. You have three jars, A, B, and C, which hold the amounts of water, in ounces, shown in Table 7.2. For each of the seven problems in Table

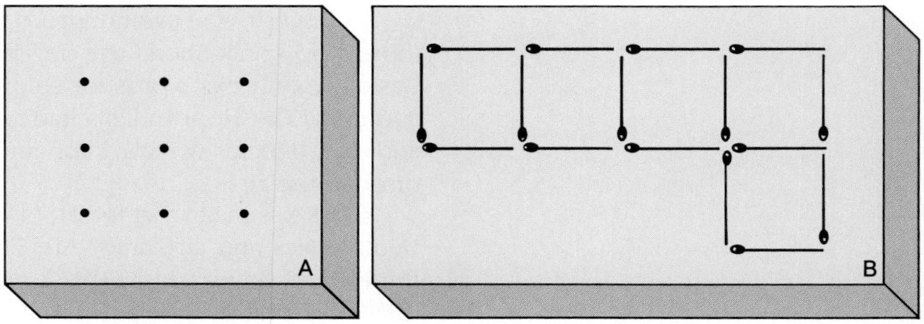

Figure 7.1
Two Problems. Draw straight lines through all the points in Part A, using only four lines. Do not lift your pencil or retrace your steps. Move three matches in Part B to make four squares equal in size. Use all the matches.

7.2, use the jars in any way you wish to arrive at the indicated amount of water. Fill or empty any jar as often as you wish. How do you obtain the desired amount of water in each problem? (The solutions are discussed on p. 276.)

Stages in Problem Solving

If you are like most other problem solvers, you used three steps to solve parts a and b of problem 1. First, you sought to define the elements of the problems by discovering the structure of the *cycles* in each series. Series *1a* has repeated cycles of two letters: *AB, AB,* and so on. Series *1b* may be seen as having four cycles of two consecutive letters: *AB, DE, BC,* and so on.

Then you tried to produce *rules* that governed the advance of each series. In series *1a,* the rule is simply to repeat the cycle. Series *1b* is more complicated, and different sets of rules can be used to describe it. One correct set of rules is that odd-numbered cycles (*1* and *3,* or *AB* and *BC*) simply repeat the last letter of the previous cycle (in this case *B*) and then advance by one letter according to the alphabet. The same rule applies to even-numbered cycles (*2* and *4,* or *DE* and *EF*).

Table 7.2
Water-Jar Problems

	Three Jars Are Present with the Listed Capacity (in Ounces)			
Problem Number	**Jar A**	**Jar B**	**Jar C**	**Obtain This Amount of Water**
1	21	127	3	100
2	14	163	25	99
3	18	43	10	5
4	9	42	6	21
5	20	59	4	31
6	23	49	3	20
7	10	36	7	3

For each problem, how can you use some combination of the three jars given, and a tap, to obtain precisely the amount of water shown?

Adapted from Abraham S. Luchins and Edith H. Luchins, *Rigidity of Behavior* (Eugene: University of Oregon Press, 1959), p. 109.

Then you used your rules to produce the next letters in the series: *AB* in series *1a,* and *CD* in series *1b.* Finally, you evaluated the effectiveness of the rules by checking your answers against the solutions in the preceding paragraphs.

Question: What alternate sets of rules could you have found to describe these two series? Would you have generated the same answers from these rules?

Preparation, Production, Trial, and Evaluation People tend to use four stages in solving problems, whether the problem concerns dieting, selecting a house, or moving matchsticks about to create a design. These stages include (1) preparation, (2) production, (3) trial, and (4) evaluation.

We prepare ourselves to solve a problem by familiarizing ourselves with its elements and clearly defining our goals. We prepare to solve high school algebra and geometry problems by outlining all the givens and trying to picture the answers as best we can. Part of preparation is proper classification of the problem. "Does this problem involve a right triangle? Does it seem to be similar to problems I've solved by using the quadratic equation?"

In parts a and b of problem 1, the search for cycles and for the rules governing the cycles served as preparation for producing possible solutions.

Algorithms versus Heuristics In solving problems, we sometimes turn to *algorithms* or *heuristic devices.* An **algorithm** is a specific procedure for solving a certain type of problem that will lead to the solution if it is used properly. Mathematical formulas, such as the Pythagorean Theorem, are examples of algorithms. They will yield correct answers to problems *as long as the right formula is used.* Finding the right formula to solve a problem may require scanning one's memory for all formulas that contain variables that represent one or more of the elements in the problem. The Pythagorean Theorem, for example, concerns triangles with right angles. Therefore, it is appropriate to consider using this formula for problems concerning right angles but not for others.

Consider anagram problems, in which we try to reorganize groups of letters into words. In seeing how many words we can make from *DWARG,* we can use the algorithm of simply listing every possible letter combination, using from one to all five letters, and then checking to see whether each result is, in fact, a word. The method might be plodding, but it would work.

Heuristics are rules of thumb that help us simplify and solve problems. Heuristics, in contrast to algorithms, do not guarantee a correct solution to a problem, but when they work they tend to allow for more rapid solutions. A heuristic device for solving the anagram problem would be to look for letter combinations that are found in words and then to check the remaining letters for words that include these combinations. In *DWARG,* for example, we can find the familiar combinations *dr* and *gr.* We may then quickly find *draw, drag,* and *grad.* The drawback to this method, however, is that we might miss some words.

Algorithm A systematic procedure for solving a problem that works invariably when applied correctly.

Heuristics Rules of thumb that help us simplify and solve problems.

Means-end analysis A heuristic device in which we try to solve a problem by evaluating the difference between the current situation and the goal.

Truth or Fiction Revisited

It is *not* true that the using the "tried and true" formula (that is, an algorithm) is invariably the most efficient way to solve a problem. Sometimes a heuristic device leads to a more rapid solution.

One type of heuristic device is the **means-end analysis,** in which we evaluate the difference between our current situation and our goals at various steps along the way, and then do what we can to reduce this discrepancy at each step. Let's say that you are lost, but you know that your goal is west of your current location and on the "other side of the tracks." A heuristic device would be to drive toward the setting sun (west) and, at the same time, to remain alert for railroad tracks. If your road comes to an end and you must turn left or right, you can scan the distance in either direction for tracks. If you don't see any, turn right or left, but then, at the next major intersection, turn toward the setting sun again. Eventually you may get there. If not, you could use that most boring of algorithms: Ask people for directions until you find someone who knows the route.

Incubation Let us return to the problems at the beginning of the section. How did you do with problem 1, part c, and problems 2 and 3? If you produced and then tried out solutions that did not meet the goals, you may have become frustrated and thought, "The heck with it! I'll come back to it later." This attitude suggests another avenue to problem solving: **incubation.** An incubator warms chicken eggs for a while so that they will hatch. Incubation in problem solving refers to standing back from the problem for a while as some mysterious process in us seems to continue to work on it. Later, the answer may occur to us as "in a flash." Standing back from the problem might provide us with some distance from unprofitable but persistent mental sets.

Truth or Fiction Revisited

It is *not* necessarily true that the best way to solve a frustrating problem is to keep plugging away at it. It may be better to distance oneself from the problem for a while and allow it to incubate.

Mental Sets

Let us return to problem 1, part c. To try to solve this problem, did you seek a pattern of letters that involved cycles and the alphabet? If so, it may be because parts a and b were solved by this approach.

The tendency to respond to a new problem with the same approach that helped solve earlier, similar-looking problems is termed a **mental set.** Mental sets usually make our work easier, but they can mislead us when the similarity between problems is illusory, as in part c of problem 1. Here is a clue: Part c is no alphabet series. Each of the letters in the series *stands* for something. If you can discover what they stand for (that is, discover the rule), you will be able to generate the ninth and tenth letters. (The answer is in Figure 7.3 on p. 279.)

Let us now have another look at the possible role of incubation in helping us get around hampering mental sets. Consider the seventh water-jar problem. What if we had tried all sorts of solutions involving the three water jars, and none had worked? What if we were then to stand back from this water-jar problem for a day or two? Is it not possible that with a little distance we might suddenly recall a 10, a 7, and a 3—three elements of the problem—and realize that we can arrive at the correct answer by using only two water jars? Our solution might seem too easy, and we might check Table 7.2 cautiously to make certain that the numbers are there as remembered. Perhaps our incubation period would have done nothing more than unbind us from the mental set that the case 7 *ought* to be solved by the formula $B-A-2C$.

While we are discussing mental sets and the water-jar problems, have another look at water-jar case number 6. The formula $B-A-2C$ will solve this problem. Is that how you solved it? Note also that the problem could

Incubation In problem solving, a hypothetical process that sometimes occurs when we stand back from a frustrating problem for a while and the solution "suddenly" appears.

Mental set The tendency to respond to a new problem with an approach that was successfully used with problems similar in appearance.

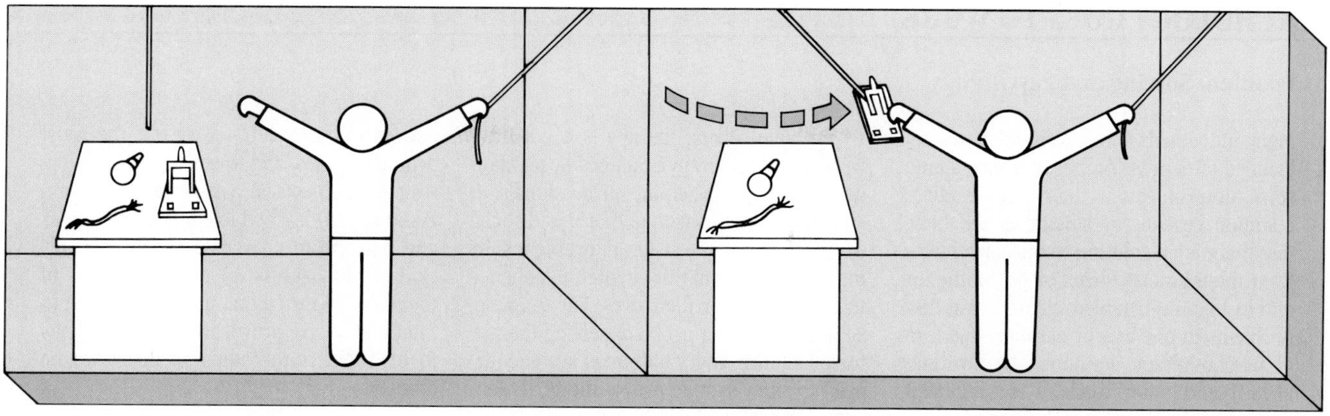

Figure 7.2
The Two-String Problem.

A person is asked to tie two dangling strings together, but he cannot reach them both at once. He is allowed to use any object in the room to help him—paper clips, tissue paper, a pair of pliers, a chair, tape. He can solve the problem by taping the pliers to one string and sending it swinging back and forth. Then he grabs the stationary string and catches the moving string when it swings his way. After removing the pliers, the strings are tied together. Functional fixedness could impede solution of the problem by causing the person to view the pliers as only a grasping tool and not as a weight.

have been solved more efficiently by using the formula $A-C$. If the second formula did not occur to you, it may be because of the mental set you acquired from solving the first five problems.

Functional Fixedness

Functional fixedness may also impair your problem-solving efforts. For example, first ask yourself what a pair of pliers is. Is it a tool for grasping, a paperweight, or a weapon? A pair of pliers could function as any of these, but your tendency to think of it as a grasping tool is fostered by your experience with it. You have probably only used a pair of pliers for grasping things. Functional fixedness is the tendency to think of an object in terms of its name or its familiar usage. Functional fixedness can be similar to a mental set in that it can make it difficult for you to use familiar objects to solve problems in novel ways.

In a classic experiment in functional fixedness, Birch and Rabinowitz (1951) placed subjects in a room with electrical equipment, a switch, and a relay, and asked them to solve the Maier two-string problem. In this problem, a person is asked to tie together two dangling strings. But, as shown in Figure 7.2, they cannot be reached simultaneously.

In the experiment, either the switch or the relay can be used as a weight for one of the strings. If the weighted string is sent swinging, the subject can grasp the unweighted string and then wait for the weighted string to come his or her way. Subjects given prior experience with the switch as an electrical device were significantly more likely to use the relay as the weight. Subjects given prior experience with the intended function of the relay were significantly more likely to use the switch as a weight. Subjects given no prior experience with either device showed no preferences for using one or the other as the weight.

You may know that soldiers in survival training in the desert are taught to view insects and snakes as sources of food rather than as pests or threats.

Functional fixedness The tendency to view an object in terms of its name or familiar usage.

PSYCHOLOGY GOES TO WORK

Problem Solving and Psychology

Many individuals suffer from anxieties and feelings of depression because they cannot solve the problems in their lives. In fact, a common reason for suicide is the belief that there is no solution to one's problems. Even though most forms of psychotherapy aim at helping troubled clients solve their problems in one way or another, one form of psychotherapy developed by Jay Haley (1987) and other workers is specifically termed *problem-solving therapy.*

Problem-solving therapy is a cognitive type of psychotherapy practiced by psychologists and other helping professionals. It encourages clients with personal and social problems to use the stages of problem solving, as discussed in this chapter, to enhance their control over their lives. For example, subjects receiving problem-solving therapy for preventing angry outbursts are encouraged to study sample provocations, to generate various behavioral solutions (alternatives to violence), to try out the most promising ones, and to evaluate their effectiveness. Subjects in a study by Moon and Eisler (1983) learned to control their anger and respond to provocations with socially skillful (nonaggressive) behavior. Many of them also reported that they had learned to interpret social provocations as problems to be solved rather than as insults to be avenged.

But it would be understandable if you chose to show civilian functional fixedness for as long as possible if you were stuck in the desert.

Creativity in Problem Solving

A creative person may be more capable of solving problems to which there are no preexisting solutions, no tried and tested formulas.

Creativity is an enigmatic concept. According to Sternberg (1985), we tend to perceive creative people as follows:

Willing to take chances

Unaccepting of limitations; trying to do the impossible

Appreciating art and music

Capable of using the materials around them to make unique things

Questioning social norms and assumptions

Willing to take an unpopular stand

Inquisitive

A professor of mine once remarked that there is nothing new under the sun, only novel combinations of old elements. To him, the core of creativity was the ability to generate novel combinations of existing elements. My professor's view of creativity was similar to that of many psychologists—that creativity is the ability to make unusual, sometimes remote, associations to the elements of a problem so that new combinations that meet the goals are generated. An essential aspect of a creative response is the leap from the elements of the problem to the novel solution (Amabile, 1983). A predictable solution is not particularly creative, even if it is difficult to arrive at.

Creativity The ability to generate novel solutions to problems.

Convergent thinking A thought process that attempts to narrow in on the single best solution to a problem.

Divergent thinking A thought process that attempts to generate multiple solutions to problems.

Convergent Thinking and Divergent Thinking According to Guilford (1959; Guilford & Hoepfner, 1971), creativity demands divergent thinking rather than convergent thinking. In **convergent thinking,** thought is limited to present facts as the problem solver tries to narrow thinking to find the best solution. In **divergent thinking,** the problem solver associates more fluently and freely to the various elements of the problem. The prob-

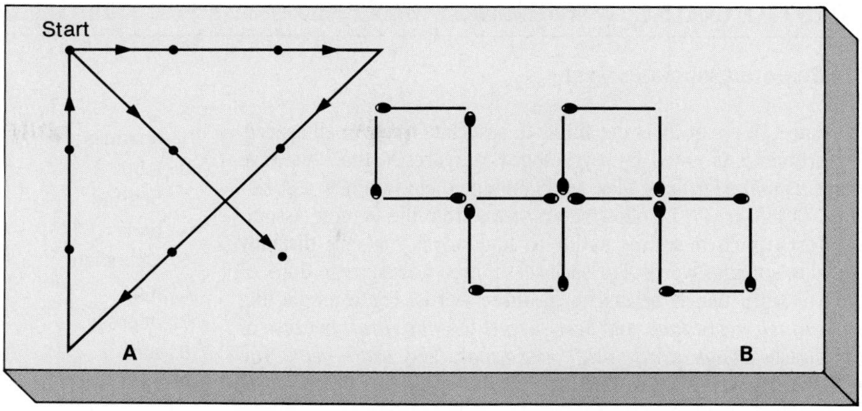

Figure 7.3
Answers to Problems on Page 273. For problem 1C, note that each of the letters is the first letter of the numbers one through eight. Therefore, the two missing letters are *NT*, for *n*ine and *t*en. The solutions to problems 2 and 3 are shown in this illustration.

lem solver allows "leads" to run a nearly limitless course to determine whether they will eventually combine as needed. *Brainstorming* is a popular term for divergent thinking when carried out by a group.

Successful problem solving may require both divergent and convergent thinking. At first divergent thinking generates many possible solutions. Convergent thinking is then used to select the most probable solutions and to reject the others.

Factors in Creativity What factors contribute to creativity? Guilford (1959) noted that creative people show flexibility, fluency (in generating words and ideas), and originality. Getzels and Jackson (1962) found that creative schoolchildren tend to express rather than inhibit their feelings and to be playful and independent. Conger and Petersen (1984) concur that creative people tend to be independent and nonconformist. But independence and nonconformity do not necessarily make a person creative. Stereotypes of the creative personality have led to individual exaggerations of nonconformity.

Nevertheless, creative children are often at odds with their teachers because of their independence. Faced with the chore of managing upward of 30 pupils, teachers too often label quiet and submissive children as "good" children.

Creativity. Henry Moore creates one of his figurative sculptures. What traits are connected with creativity? What is the relationship between intelligence and creativity?

Intelligence and Creativity

Intelligence and creativity sometimes, but not always, go hand in hand. Persons low in intelligence are often low in creativity as well, but high intelligence is no guarantee of creativity. However, it sometimes happens that people of only moderate intelligence excel in creativity, especially in fields like art and music.

Truth or Fiction Revisited

It is *not* necessarily true that intelligent people are also creative. Many intelligent people are relatively unimaginative.

A Canadian study found that highly intelligent ("gifted") boys and girls aged 9 to 11 were as a group more creative than less intelligent children, but not all the gifted children were more creative than their less intelligent peers (Kershner & Ledger, 1985). The girls in the study were significantly more creative than their male agemates, especially on verbal tasks.

QUESTIONNAIRE

The Remote Associates Test

One aspect of creativity is the ability to associate freely to all aspects of a problem. As noted by psychologist Margaret Matlin, "Creative people can take far-flung ideas and combine them into new associations" (1983, p. 251). Following are items from the Remote Associates Test, which measures ability to find words that are distantly related to stimulus words. For each set of three words, try to think of a fourth word that is related to all three words. For example, the words *rough, resistance,* and *beer* suggest the word *draft* because of the phrases *rough draft, draft resistance,* and *draft beer.* The answers are given in Appendix B.

1. charming	student	valiant
2. food	catcher	hot
3. hearted	feet	bitter
4. dark	shot	sun
5. Canadian	golf	sandwich
6. tug	gravy	show
7. attorney	self	spending
8. arm	coal	peach
9. type	ghost	story

Tests that measure intelligence are not useful in measuring creativity. As you will see on the following pages, intelligence-test questions usually require convergent thinking to focus in on the answer. On an intelligence test, an ingenious answer that differs from the designated answer is wrong. Tests of creativity are oriented toward determining how flexible and fluent thinking can be. Here, for example, is an item from a test used by Getzels and Jackson (1962) to measure associative ability, a factor in creativity: "Write as many meanings as you can for each of the following words: (a) duck; (b) sack; (c) pitch; (d) fair." Those who write several meanings for each word, rather than only one, are rated as being potentially more creative.

INTELLIGENCE

What form of life is so adaptive that it can survive in desert temperatures of 120 degrees Fahrenheit or Arctic climes of −40 degrees Fahrenheit? What form of life can run, walk, climb, swim, live underwater for months on end, and fly to the moon and back? I won't keep you in suspense any longer. We are that form of life. Yet our unclad bodies do not allow us to adapt to these extremes of temperature. Brute strength does not allow us to live underwater or travel to the moon. Rather, it is our **intelligence** that permits us to adapt to these conditions and to challenge our physical limitations.

The term *intelligence* is familiar enough. At an early age we gain impressions of how intelligent we are compared to others. We associate intelligence with academic success, advancement on the job, and appropriate social behavior. Psychologists use intelligence as a **trait** that may explain, at least in part, why people do (or fail to do) things that are adaptive and inventive.

Despite our familiarity with the concept of intelligence, it cannot be seen, touched, or measured physically. And so intelligence is subject to various interpretations.

Intelligence A complex and controversial concept. According to David Wechsler, the "capacity . . . to understand the world [and] resourcefulness to cope with its challenges."

Trait A distinguishing characteristic that is presumed to account for consistency in behavior.

Achievement That which is attained by one's efforts and made possible by one's abilities.

THEORIES OF INTELLIGENCE

Psychologists generally distinguish between **achievement** and intelligence. Achievement refers to knowledge and skills gained from experience. It involves specific content, such as English, history, and math. The relationship

Going for a "Walk." Our intelligence permits us to live underwater for months on end or to fly to the Moon and back. Physically we are weaker than many other organisms. But our intelligence permits us to adapt successfully to the physical environment, to create new environments, and to go for leisurely "spacewalks," as shown in this photograph.

between achievement and experience seems obvious: We are not surprised to find that a student who has taken Spanish, but not French, does better on a Spanish achievement test than on a French achievement test.

The meaning of *intelligence* is more difficult to pin down. Most psychologists agree that intelligence somehow provides the cognitive basis for academic achievement. Intelligence is usually perceived as underlying competence or learning ability, whereas achievement involves acquired competencies or performance. However, psychologists disagree about the nature and origins of underlying competence or learning ability.

There are two broad approaches to understanding intelligence: factor and cognitive theories.

Factor Theories

Many investigators have viewed intelligence as consisting of one or more mental abilities, or **factors.**

Spearman's *G* and *S* Factors In 1904, British psychologist Charles Spearman suggested that the behaviors we consider to be intelligent have a common, underlying factor. He labeled this factor **g,** for "general intelligence." *G* represented broad reasoning and problem-solving abilities. Spearman supported this view by noting that people who excel in one area can usually excel in others. But he also noted that even the most capable people are relatively superior in some areas—whether in music or business or poetry.

Factor A cluster of related items, such as those found on an intelligence test.

g Spearman's symbol for general intelligence, which he believed underlay more specific abilities.

Table 7.3
Louis Thurstone's Primary Mental Abilities

Ability	Brief Description
Visual and spatial abilities	Visualizing forms and spatial relationships
Perceptual speed	Grasping perceptual details rapidly, perceiving similarities and differences between stimuli
Numerical ability	Computing numbers
Verbal meaning	Knowing the meanings of words
Memory	Recalling information (words, sentences, etc.)
Word fluency	Thinking of words quickly (rhyming, doing crossword puzzles, etc.)
Deductive reasoning	Deriving examples from general rules
Inductive reasoning	Deriving general rules from examples

For this reason, he suggested that specific, or **s** factors account for specific abilities.

To test his views, Spearman developed a statistical method called **factor analysis.** Factor analysis allows researchers to determine the relationships among large numbers of items, such as those found on intelligence tests. Items that cluster together are labeled *factors.* In his research on relationships among tests of verbal, mathematical, and spatial reasoning, Spearman repeatedly found evidence supporting the existence of *s* factors. The evidence for *g* was more limited.

Thurstone's Primary Mental Abilities American psychologist Louis Thurstone (1938) used factor analysis with various tests of specific abilities and also found only limited evidence for the existence of *g.* Thurstone concluded that Spearman had oversimplified the concept of intelligence. Thurstone's data suggested the presence of nine specific factors, which he labeled **primary mental abilities** (see Table 7.3). Thurstone suggested, for example, that we might have high word fluency, enabling us to rapidly develop lists of words that rhyme yet not enabling us to be efficient at solving math problems (Thurstone & Thurstone, 1963).

This view seems to make sense. Most of us know people who are good at math but poor in English, and vice versa. Nonetheless, some link continues to seem to connect specific mental abilities. The data still show that the person with excellent reasoning ability is likely to have a larger-than-average vocabulary and better-than-average numerical ability.

Guilford's Structure-of-Intellect Model The **structure-of-intellect** (SOI) model proposed by psychologist J. P. Guilford (1959) greatly expands the numbers of factors found in intellectual functioning. Guilford used a combination of factor analysis and logical reasoning to arrive at 120 factors in intellectual functioning. Each of the 120 factors consists of three elements, as shown in Figure 7.4:

1. Operations—the kinds of cognitive processing that are involved
2. Contents—the type of information that is processed
3. Products—the forms that the information takes

Guilford and his associates have developed test items to measure performance in many of the 120 factors. Consider the following examples:

1. Name as many objects as you can that are both white and edible.
2. Give as many sentences as you can that would fit into the form: W________ c________ s________ d________.
   {Example: "Workers can seldom deviate."}

s Spearman's symbol for *specific* factors, or *s factors,* that he believed accounted for individual abilities.

Factor analysis A statistical technique that allows researchers to determine the relationships among large number of items, such as test items.

Primary mental abilities According to Thurstone, the basic abilities that make up intelligence.

Structure-of-intellect model Guilford's three-dimensional model of intelligence, which focuses on the operations, contents, and products of intellectual functioning.

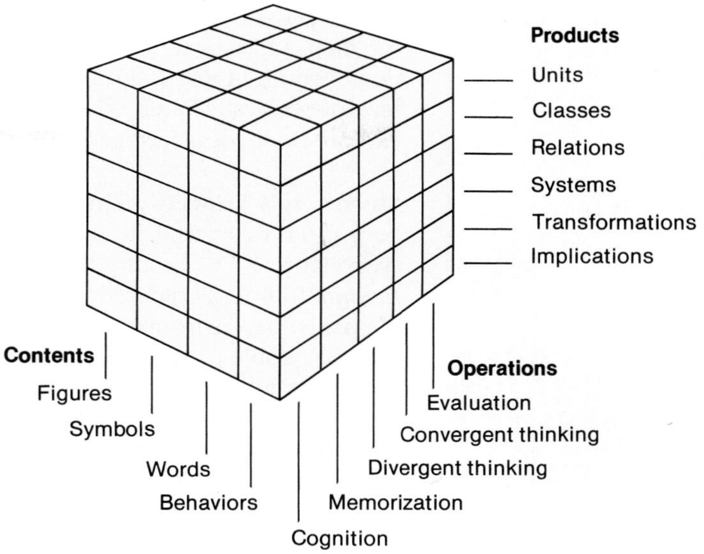

Figure 7.4
Guilford's Structure-of-Intellect Model of Intelligence. Guilford has hypothesized the existence of 120 factors in intelligence.

The operation in each example is divergent thinking. The content of each example consists of words. However, the products differ. The products in the first example consist of single objects, or *units.* The products in example 2 consist of organized sequences of words, or *systems.*

In more recent writings, Guilford (1982) expanded his model to 150 factors. The problem with this approach seems to be that the greater the number of factors generated, the more overlap there is among them.

Cognitive Theories

Cognitive theorists tend to view intelligence in terms of information processing. They focus on how information "flows" through us and is modified by us as we adapt to and act to change our environments. Two of these cognitive theorists are Arthur Jensen and Robert Sternberg.

Jensen's Level I and Level II Jensen's concern has been to explain social-class differences in intelligence. He does so by hypothesizing the existence of two different levels of intelligence: Level I and Level II. Level I intelligence involves associative abilities, which are measured by tasks involving rote learning and memorization. One example would be memorizing a song. Another would be repeating a series of numbers that has been read aloud, such as 7–4–9–6–2–5. Still another would be associating letters and sounds, as in learning the alphabet. Level I skills are not strongly linked to school performance, as measured by academic grades (Rebok, 1987).

Level II intelligence involves conceptual abilities. It includes verbal ability, logical reasoning, and problem-solving skills. All of these are related to cognitive learning and development. They are measured by items that require conceptual thinking ("How are good and bad alike?"), mathematical reasoning ("If two candy bars cost 25 cents, how many candy bars can you buy for one dollar?"), and general comprehension ("Why should pregnant women check with their doctors about the drugs they use?"). Level II skills correlate more strongly with academic grades than Level I skills do.

Jensen argues that all social classes possess adequate degrees of Level I intelligence. However, he controversially asserts that the middle and upper

Robert Sternberg

classes possess more Level II intelligence and that this difference accounts for their superior academic grades and performance in professional positions. Jensen (1969, 1980, 1985) further believes that our potentials at each level are basically inherited and largely unmodifiable by experience. We shall explore these ideas further in the section on the determinants of intelligence.

Sternberg's Triarchic Theory Yale University psychologist Robert Sternberg (1985) constructed a three-level, or **triarchic,** model of intelligence (see Figure 7.5). The three levels are *contextual, experiential,* and *componential.* Individual differences are found at each level. The **contextual level** concerns the environmental setting. It is assumed that intelligent behavior permits people to adapt to the demands of their environments. For example, keeping a job by "adapting" one's behavior to the requirements of one's employer is adaptive. But if the employer is making unreasonable demands, reshaping the environment (by changing the employer's attitudes) or selecting an alternate environment (finding a more suitable job) is also adaptive.

On the **experiential level,** intelligent behavior is defined by the abilities to cope with novel situations and to process information automatically. The ability to quickly relate novel situations to familiar situations (to perceive the similarities and differences) fosters adaptation. Moreover, as a result of experience, we come to solve problems more rapidly. Intelligence and experience in reading permit the child to process familiar words more or less automatically and to decode new words efficiently. In sum, it is "intelligent" to profit from experience.

The **componential level** of intelligence consists of three processes: *metacomponents, performance components,* and *knowledge-acquisition components.* **Metacomponents** concern our awareness of our own intellectual processes. Metacomponents are involved in deciding what problem to solve, selecting appropriate strategies and formulas, monitoring the solution, and changing performance in the light of knowledge of results.

Performance components are the mental operations or skills used in solving problems or processing information. Performance components include encoding information, combining and comparing pieces of information, and generating a solution. Consider Sternberg's (1979) analogy problem:

Washington is to *one* as *Lincoln* is to (a) *five,* (b) *ten,* (c) *fifteen,* (d) *fifty?*

To solve the analogy, we must first correctly *encode* the elements—*Washington, one,* and *Lincoln*—by identifying them and comparing them to other information. We must first encode *Washington* and *Lincoln* as the names of presidents,* and then try to combine *Washington* and *one* in a meaningful manner. Two possibilities quickly come to mind. Washington was the first president, and his picture is on the one dollar bill. We can then generate two possible solutions and try them out. First, what number president was Lincoln? Second, on what bill is Lincoln's picture found? (Do you need to consult a history book or peek into your wallet at this point?)

Knowledge-acquisition components are used in gaining new knowledge. These include encoding information (e.g., Roger Smith as the founder of Rhode Island or as the president of General Motors), combining pieces of information, and comparing new information with what is already known.

Sternberg's model is complex, but it does a promising job of capturing what most investigators mean by intellectual functioning. David Wechsler,

*There are other possibilities. Both are the names of memorials and cities, for example.

Triarchic Governed by three.

Contextual level Those aspects of intelligent behavior that permit people to adapt to their environment.

Experiential level Those aspects of intelligence that permit people to cope with novel situations and process information automatically.

Componential level The level of intelligence that consists of metacomponents, performance components, and knowledge-acquisition components.

Metacomponents Components of intelligence that are based on self-awareness of our intellectual processes.

Performance omponents The mental operations used in processing information.

Knowledge-acquisition components Components used in gaining knowledge, such as encoding and relating new knowledge to existing knowledge.

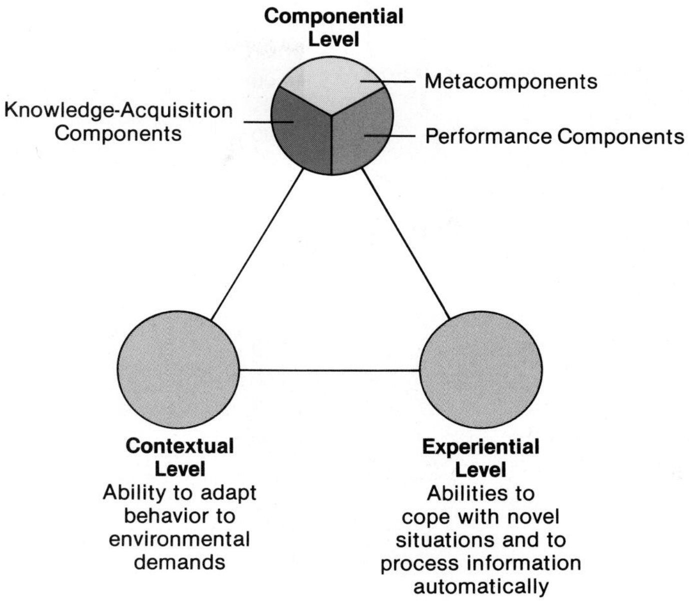

Figure 7.5
Sternberg's Triarchic Model of Intelligence. Robert Sternberg views intelligence as consisting of contextual, experiential, and componential levels. The componential level consists of metacomponents, performance components, and knowledge-acquisition components.

the originator of a series of widely used intelligence tests, described intelligence in terms that are simpler but, I think, consistent with Sternberg's view. Intelligence, wrote Wechler, is the "capacity of an individual to understand the world [and the] resourcefulness to cope with its challenges" (1975, p. 139). Intelligence, to Wechsler, involves accurate representation of the world (which Sternberg discusses as encoding, comparing new information to old information, etc.) and effective problem solving (adapting to one's environment, profiting from experience, selecting the appropriate formulas and strategies, etc.).

MEASUREMENT OF INTELLIGENCE

There may be disagreements about the nature of intelligence, but thousands of intelligence tests are administered by psychologists and educators every day. In this section we first explore some basic characteristics of intelligence tests.

Characteristics of Intelligence Tests

Because important decisions are made on the basis of intelligence tests, they must be *reliable* and *valid.* Psychologists use statistical techniques such as the **correlation coefficient** to determine reliability and validity. For a test to be considered reliable, correlations between a group's test results on separate occasions should be positive and high—about +0.90 (see Table 7.4).

The **reliability** of a measure is its consistency. A measure of height would not be reliable if a person appeared to be taller or shorter every time a measurement was taken. A reliable measure of intelligence, like a good tape measure, must yield similar results on different testing occasions.

Correlation coefficient A number that indicates the direction (positive or negative) and strength of the relationship between two variables.

Reliability Consistency.

Table 7.4
Interpretations of Some Correlation Coefficients

Correlation Coefficient	Interpretation
+1.00	Perfect positive correlation, as between temperature in Fahrenheit and centigrade
+0.90	High positive correlation, adequate for test reliability
+0.60 to +0.70	Moderate positive correlation, usually considered adequate for test validity
+0.30	Weak positive correlation, unacceptable for test reliability or validity
0.00	No correlation between variables (no association indicated)
−0.30	Weak negative correlation
−0.60 to −0.70	Moderate negative correlation
−0.90	High negative correlation
−1.00	A perfect negative correlation

Alfred Binet

There are different ways of showing a test's reliability, all of which rely on the correlation coefficient. One of the most commonly used is **test-retest reliability,** which is shown by comparing scores of tests taken on different occasions.

The **validity** of a test is the degree to which it measures what it is supposed to measure. To determine whether a test is valid, we see whether it actually predicts an outside standard, or external criterion. A proper standard, or criterion, for determining the validity of a test of musical aptitude is the ability to learn to play a musical instrument. Tests of musical aptitude, therefore, should correlate highly with the ability to learn to play a musical instrument. Most psychologists assume that intelligence is one of the factors responsible for academic success. For this reason, intelligence test scores have frequently been correlated with school grades, which serve as one external standard for ascertaining whether the test scores are valid. Other indexes of academic success include scores on achievement tests and teacher ratings of cognitive ability. Intelligence tests generally correlate from about +0.60 to +0.70 with school grades (Lavin, 1965; McCall, 1975; McClelland, 1973).

As noted in Table 7.4, a correlation of about +0.60 to +0.70 is generally considered to be adequate for purposes of assessing test validity. However, such a correlation does not approach a perfect positive relationship. This finding suggests that factors *other* than performance on intelligence tests contribute to academic and occupational success. Motivation to do well and one's general level of personal adjustment are two of them (Anastasi, 1983; Hrncir et al., 1985; Scarr, 1981).

By these standards, the Stanford-Binet Intelligence Scale (SBIS) and the Wechsler scales for children and adults have adequate reliability and validity.

Individual Intelligence Tests

The Stanford-Binet Intelligence Scale The SBIS originated through the work of Frenchmen Alfred Binet and Theophile Simon early in this century. The French public school system sought an instrument that could identify children who were unlikely to profit from the regular classroom so that they could receive special attention. The Binet-Simon scale came into use in 1905. Since that time, it has undergone great revision and refinement.

Test-retest reliability A method for determining the reliability of a test by comparing (correlating) test takers' scores from separate occasions.

Validity The degree to which a test measures what it is supposed to measure.

Table 7.5
Items Similar to Those on the Stanford-Binet Intelligence Scale

Level (Years)	Item
2 Years	1. Children show knowledge of basic vocabulary words by identifying parts of a doll such as the mouth, ears, and hair.
	2. Children show counting and spatial skills along with visual-motor coordination by building a tower of four blocks to match a model.
4 Years	1. Children show word fluency and categorical thinking by filling in the missing words when they are asked questions such as: "Father is a man; mother is a ________?" "Hamburgers are hot; ice cream is ________?"
	2. Children show comprehension by answering correctly when they are asked questions such as: "Why do people have automobiles?" "Why do people have medicine?"
9 Years	1. Children can point out verbal absurdities, as in this question: "In an old cemetery, scientists unearthed a skull which they think was that of George Washington when he was only five years of age. What is silly about that?"
	2. Children show fluency with words, as shown by answering the questions: "Can you tell me a number that rhymes with snore?" "Can you tell me a color that rhymes with glue?"
Adult	1. Adults show knowledge of the meanings of words and conceptual thinking by correctly explaining the differences between word pairs like "sickness and misery," "house and home," and "integrity and prestige."
	2. Adults show spatial skills by correctly answering questions like: "If a car turned to the right to head north, in what direction was it heading before it turned?"

Despite his view that many factors are involved in intellectual functioning, Binet constructed his test to yield a single overall score so that it could be more easily used by the school system. He also assumed that intelligence increased with age. Therefore, older children should get more items right than younger children. Thus, Binet included a series of age-graded questions, as in Table 7.5, and he arranged them in order of difficulty.

The Binet-Simon scale yielded a score called a **mental age,** or MA. The MA shows the intellectual level at which a child is functioning. A child with an MA of 6 is functioning, intellectually, like the average child aged 6. In taking the test, children earned "months" of credit for each correct answer. Their MA was determined by adding the years and months of credit they attained.

Louis Terman adapted the Binet-Simon scale for use with American children. The first version of the *Stanford*-Binet Intelligence Scale (SBIS)* was published in 1916. The SBIS included more items than the original test and was used with children aged 2 to 16. The SBIS also yielded an **intelligence quotient (IQ)** rather than an MA. American educators developed interest in learning the IQs of their pupils. The current version of the SBIS is used with children from the age of 2 upward and with adults.

The IQ reflects the relationship between a child's mental age and actual age, or chronological age (CA). Use of this ratio reflects the fact that the same MA score has different implications for children of different ages. That is, an MA of 8 is an above-average score for a 6-year-old, but an MA of 8 is below average for a 10-year-old. The German psychologist Wilhelm Stern in 1912 suggested use of the IQ to handle this problem.

Stern computed IQ by the formula IQ = (Mental Age/Chronological Age) × 100, or

$$IQ = \frac{MA}{CA} \times 100$$

Mental age The accumulated months of credit that a person earns on the Stanford-Binet Intelligence Scale. Abbreviated *MA.*

Intelligence quotient (IQ) (1) Originally, a ratio obtained by dividing a child's score (or mental age) on an intelligence test by his or her chronological age. (2) Generally, a score on an intelligence test.

*The test is so named because Terman carried out his work at Stanford University.

Table 7.6
Subtests from the Wechsler Adult Intelligence Scale-Revised (WAIS-R)

Verbal Subtests	Performance Subtests
1. *Information:* "What is the capital of the United States?" "Who was Shakespeare?"	7. *Digit Symbol:* Learning and drawing meaningless figures that are associated with numbers.
2. *Comprehension:* "Why do we have zip codes?" "What does 'A stitch in time saves 9' mean?"	8. *Picture Completion:* Pointing to the missing part of a picture.
3. *Arithmetic:* "If 3 candy bars cost 25 cents, how much will 18 candy bars cost?"	9. *Block Design:* Copying pictures of geometric designs using multicolored blocks.
4. *Similarities:* "How are good and bad alike?" "How are peanut butter and jelly alike?"	10. *Picture Arrangement:* Arranging cartoon pictures in sequence so that they tell a meaningful story.
5. *Digit Span:* Repeating a series of numbers forwards and backwards.	11. *Object Assembly:* Putting pieces of a puzzle together so that they form a meaningful object.
6. *Vocabulary:* "What does canal mean?"	

Items for verbal subtests 1, 2, 3, 4, and 6 are similar but not identical to actual test items on the WISC.

David Wechsler

Taking the Wechsler. The Wechsler intelligence scales consist of verbal and performance subtests, such as the one shown in this photograph.

According to this formula, a child with an MA of 6 and a CA of 6 would have an IQ of 100. Children who can handle intellectual problems as well as older children will have IQs above 100. For instance, an 8-year-old who does as well on the SBIS as the average 10-year-old will attain an IQ of 125. Children who do not answer as many items correctly as other children of their age will attain MAs lower than their CAs, and their IQ scores will be below 100.

Today IQ scores on the SBIS are derived by seeing how children's and adults' performances deviate from those of other people of the same age. People who get more items correct than average attain IQ scores above 100, and people who answer fewer items correctly attain scores below 100.

Truth or Fiction Revisited

It is true that two children can answer exactly the same items on an intelligence test correctly, yet one can be above average and the other below average in intelligence. The more intelligent child would be the younger of the two.

We pursue the concept of the so-called deviation IQ in our discussion of the Wechsler scales.

The Wechsler Scales David Wechsler developed a series of scales for use with children and adults. The Wechsler scales group test questions into a number of separate subtests (such as those shown in Table 7.6). Each subtest measures a different type of intellectual task. For this reason, the test shows how well a person does on one type of task (such as defining words) as compared with another (such as using blocks to construct geometric designs). In this way, the Wechsler scales highlight children's relative strengths and weaknesses, as well measure overall intellectual functioning.

As you can see in Table 7.6, Wechsler described some of his scales as measuring *verbal* tasks and others as assessing *performance* tasks. In general, verbal subtests require knowledge of verbal concepts, whereas performance subtests require familiarity with spatial-relations concepts. (Figure 7.6 shows items similar to those found on the performance scales of the Wechsler tests.)

Wechsler also introduced the concept of the deviation IQ. Instead of using mental and chronological ages to compute an IQ, he based IQ scores on how a person's answers compared with (or deviated from) those attained by people in the same age group. The average test result at any age level is

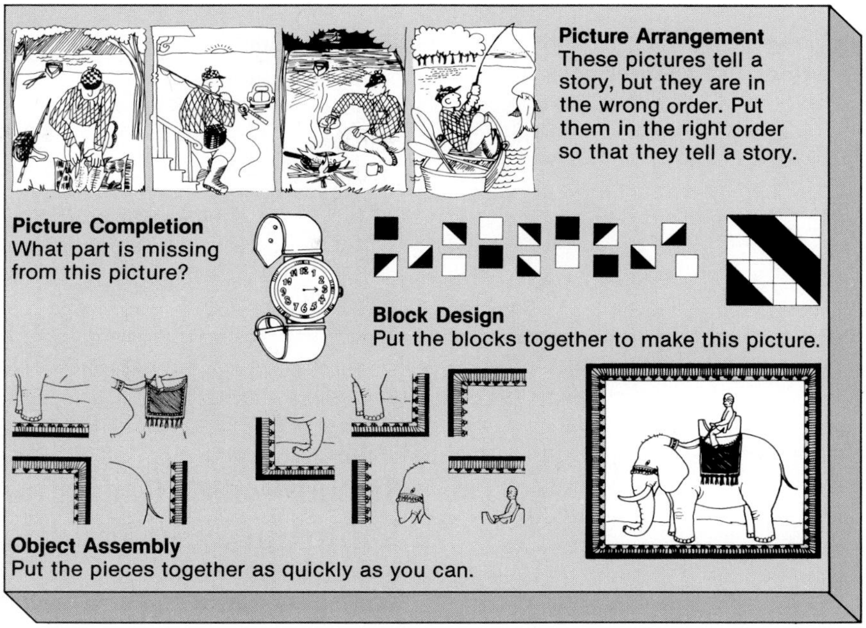

Figure 7.6
Performance Items of an Intelligence Test. This figure shows a number of items that resemble those in the performance subtests of the Wechsler Adult Intelligence Scale.

defined as an IQ score of 100. Wechsler then distributed IQ scores so that the middle 50 percent of them would fall within the "broad average range" of 90 to 110.

As you can see in Figure 7.7, most IQ scores cluster around the average. Only 5 percent of the population have IQ scores of above 130 or below 70. Table 7.7 indicates the labels that Wechsler assigned to various IQ scores and the approximate percentages of the population who attain IQ scores at those levels.

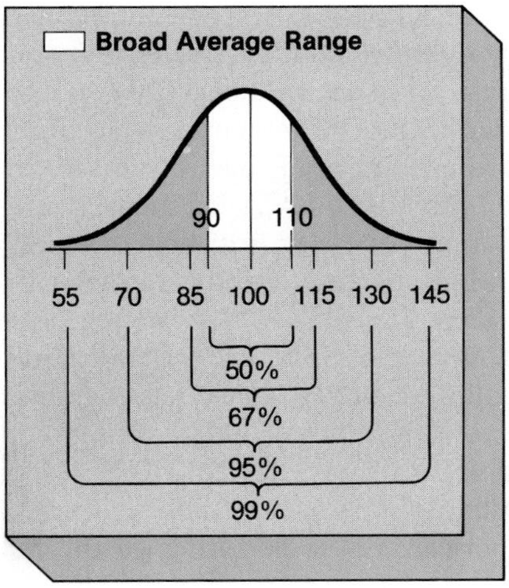

Figure 7.7
Approximate Distribution of IQ Scores. Wechsler defined the deviation IQ so that 50 percent of scores would fall within the broad average range of 90–110. This bell-shaped curve is referred to as a *normal curve* by psychologists. It describes the distribution of many traits, including height.

Group Tests

The SBIS and Wechsler scales are administered to one person at a time. This one-to-one ratio is optimal. It allows the examiner to facilitate performance (within the limits of the standardized directions) and to observe the test taker closely. Thus examiners are alerted to factors that impair performance, such as language difficulties, illness, or a noisy or poorly lit room. But large institutions with few trained examiners, such as the public schools and armed forces, have also wished to estimate the intellectual functioning of their charges. They require tests that can be administered simultaneously to large groups of people.

Group tests for children, first developed during World War I, were administered to 4 million children by 1921, a couple of years after the war had ended (Cronbach, 1975). At first these tests were heralded as remarkable instruments because they eased the huge responsibilities of school administrators. However, as the years passed they came under increasing attack, because many administrators relied on them completely to track children. The administrators did not seek other sources of information about the children's abilities and achievements (Reschly, 1981).

Additional concerns about the measurement of intelligence arise from social-class, racial, and ethnic differences in performance on intelligence tests.

Table 7.7
Variations in IQ Scores

Range of Scores	Percent of Population	Brief Description
130 and above	2	Very superior
120–129	7	Superior
110–119	16	Above average
100–109	25	High average
90–99	25	Low average
80–89	16	Slow learner
70–79	7	Borderline
Below 70	2	Intellectually deficient

Social-Class, Racial, and Ethnic Differences in Intelligence

There is a body of research suggestive of differences between social, racial, and ethnic groups. Lower-class American children attain IQ scores some 10 to 15 points lower than those of middle- and upper-class children. Black children tend to attain IQ scores some 15 to 20 points lower than their **Caucasian** agemates (Hall & Kaye, 1980; Loehlin et al., 1975). As groups, Hispanic American and Native American children also score significantly below the Caucasian norms.

Several studies on IQ have confused the factors of social class and race because disproportionate numbers of blacks, Hispanic Americans, and Native Americans are found among the lower socioeconomic classes. When we limit our observations to particular racial groups, however, we still find an effect for social class. That is, middle-class Caucasians outscore lower-class Caucasians. Blacks, Hispanic Americans, and Native Americans also all outscore lower-class members of their own racial groups.

Research has also discovered differences between Asians and Caucasians. Asian Americans, for example, frequently outscore Caucasian Americans on the math test of the Scholastic Aptitude Test. Students in China (Taiwan) and Japan also outscore Americans on standardized achievement tests in math and science (Stevenson et al., 1986). More than a decade ago, reports were published by British psychologist Richard Lynn (1977, 1982) that the Japanese (residing in Japan) attain higher IQ scores than Caucasian Britishers or Americans. The mean Japanese IQ was 111, which exceeds the top of the high average range in the United States by a point.

The findings concerning Asian and American children have not gone undisputed. Harold Stevenson and his colleagues (1985) gave ten cognitive tasks along with reading and math achievement tests to children from Minneapolis, Minnesota; Taiwan; and Sendai, Japan. They selected 240 children in each of the first five school grades. Although the Asian children attained higher achievement scores than the Americans, their performance on the cognitive tasks was comparable.

The higher scores of Asian students might not reflect differences in underlying competence. They might reflect, instead, different values in the home, the school, or the culture at large. Lynn (1982) suggested that environmental factors such as intensive educational practices have motivated Japanese children to achieve more than their American and European peers. Still, a number of scientists, such as Alan Anderson (1982), an editor of *Nature,* believe that the higher IQ scores of Asians may reflect genetic factors.

Caucasian Descriptive of people whose ancestors came from Europe, North Africa, and the Middle East to North India. Usually referred to as "white people," although skin color actually varies from pale reddish white to olive brown.

The differences in IQ scores between black children and Caucasian children in the United States have stimulated yet hotter disputes and have been studied with greater intensity, as we see in the following section.

The Testing Controversy: Just What Do Intelligence Tests Measure?

I was almost one of the testing casualties. At 15 I earned an IQ test score of 82, three points above the track of the special education class. Based on this score, my counselor suggested that I take up bricklaying because I was "good with my hands." My low IQ, however, did not allow me to see that as desirable.

This testimony, offered by black psychologist Robert L. Williams (1974, p. 32), echoes the sentiments of many psychologists. A recent survey of psychologists and educational specialists by Mark Synderman and Stanley Rothman (1987) found that the majority believe that intelligence tests are somewhat biased against blacks and members of the lower classes. Respondents also believe that elementary and secondary schools rely on them too strongly in making educational placements.

During the 1920s, intelligence tests were misused to prevent the immigration of many Europeans and others into the United States (Kamin, 1982; Kleinmuntz, 1982). For example, test pioneer H. H. Goddard (1917) assessed 178 newly arrived immigrants at Ellis Island and claimed that "83 percent of the Jews, 80 percent of the Hungarians, 79 percent of the Italians, and 87 percent of the Russians were 'feeble-minded' " (Kleinmuntz, 1982, p. 333). Apparently it was of little concern to Goddard that these immigrants by and large did not understand English—the language in which the tests were administered.

Misuse of intelligence tests has led psychologists such as Leon Kamin to complain, "Since its introduction to America the intelligence test has been used more or less consciously as an instrument of oppression against the underprivileged—the poor, the foreign born, and racial minorities" (in Crawford, 1979, p. 664). Despite these historical notes and criticisms, group tests are administered to as many as 10 million children a year in the United States. But some states, such as California, and some cities have outlawed their use as the sole standard for placing children in special classrooms (Bersoff, 1981). Let us explore further some of the controversy concerning the use of both individual and group intelligence tests. Let us consider whether intelligence tests are still misused and misunderstood.

Intelligence tests, as pointed out by critics such as Robert Williams, measure traits that are required in modern, high-technology societies (Anastasi, 1983; Pearlman et al., 1980; Schmidt et al., 1981). The vocabulary and arithmetic subtests on the Wechsler scales, for example, clearly reflect achievements in language skills and computational ability. It is generally assumed that the broad achievements measured by these tests reflect intelligence, but they might also reflect cultural familiarity with the concepts required to answer test questions correctly. In particular, the tests seem to reflect middle-class white culture in the United States (Garcia, 1981).

If scoring well on intelligence tests requires a certain type of cultural experience, the tests are said to have a **cultural bias.** Children reared in black neighborhoods could be at a disadvantage, not because of differences in intelligence but because of cultural differences and economic deprivation.

Cultural bias A factor that provides an advantage for test takers from certain cultural or ethnic backgrounds.

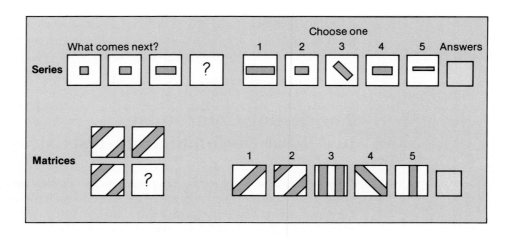

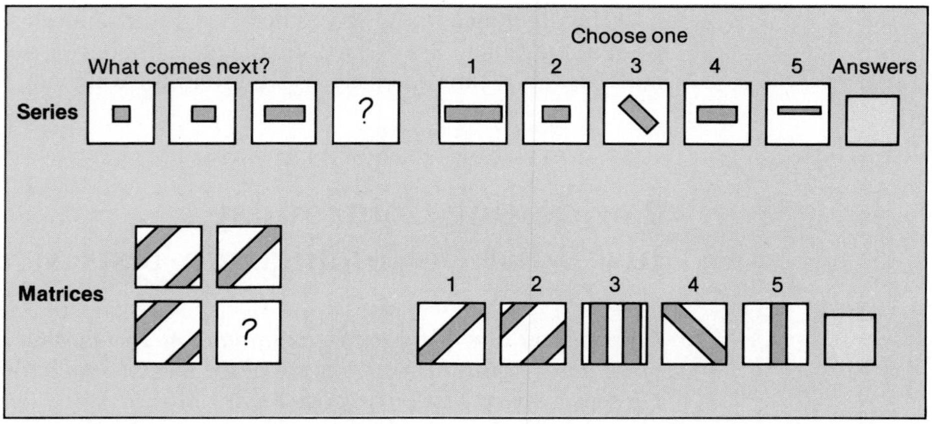

Figure 7.8
Sample Items from Raymond Cattell's Culture-Fair Intelligence Test.

Culture-fair tests attempt to exclude items that discriminate on the basis of cultural background rather than intelligence.

For this reason, psychologists such as Raymond B. Cattell (1949) and Florence Goodenough (1954) have tried to construct **culture-free** intelligence tests.

Cattell's Culture-Fair Intelligence Test evaluates reasoning ability through the child's ability to comprehend the rules that govern a progression of geometric designs, as shown in Figure 7.8. Goodenough's Draw-A-Person test is based on the premise that children from all cultural backgrounds have had the opportunity to observe people and note the relationships between the parts and the whole. Her instructions simply require children to draw a picture of a man or woman.

But culture-free tests have not lived up to their promise. Middle-class white children still outperform blacks, perhaps because they are more likely to be familiar with materials such as blocks and pencils and paper. They are more likely than disadvantaged children to have arranged blocks into various designs (practice relevant to the Cattell test) and more likely to have sketched animals, people, and inanimate objects (practice relevant to the Goodenough test). Too, culture-free tests are not as valid as other intelligence tests: They do not predict academic success as well.

Motivation to do well might also be a cultural factor. Because of socioeconomic differences, black children in the United States often do not have the same motivation as white children to do well on tests. Highly motivated children attain higher scores on intelligence tests than less well–motivated children do (Zigler & Butterfield, 1968). In sum, there may really be no such thing as a culture-free intelligence test.

THE DETERMINANTS OF INTELLIGENCE

In 1969, Arthur Jensen published an article called "How Much Can We Boost IQ and Scholastic Achievement?" in the *Harvard Educational Review*. It gained national visibility because of the assertion that 80 percent of the variability in IQ scores is inherited. This may sound like nothing much to get excited about, but Jensen became the focus of campus demonstrations and was sometimes booed loudly in class. *Why?*

Culture-free Describing a test in which cultural biases have been removed.

It turns out that American blacks score below American Caucasians on intelligence tests. Jensen had asserted that this difference was largely genetically determined. If so, the difference could never be decreased. Protests from the black community were echoed by many whites, including many prominent psychologists and other scientists. Crawford (1979) suggested that Jensen's views met with such opposition because they fly in the face of the belief that American children are supposed to be able to grow up to be whatever they want to be, even president.

What do psychologists know about the **determinants** of intelligence? What are the roles of heredity and environment?

Genetic Influences on Intelligence

Let us return to experiments with laboratory animals to point up some of the difficulties and shortcomings of research on genetic influences on *human* intelligence. Then we shall examine correlational research with human subjects.

In Chapter 2 we saw that rats have been selectively bred for maze-learning ability. Maze-bright parent rats tend to have maze-bright litters, whereas maze-dull parents tend to have maze-dull litters. But, as noted in Chapter 2, we must be cautious in generalizing from rats to people. The (spatial-relations) superiority of the maze-bright rats did not generalize to all learning tasks, even for the rats. And it cannot be emphasized too strongly that maze-learning ability in rats is not comparable to the complex cognitive tasks that define human intelligence. However, the selective-breeding technique provides a model worth noting because it *cannot* be replicated with people for ethical, legal, and practical reasons. Thus research on genetic influences on human intelligence must employ different strategies, such as kinship studies, MZ-DZ twin studies, and adoptee studies.

For example, we can examine the IQ scores of closely and distantly related people who have been reared together or apart. If heredity is involved in human intelligence, closely related people ought to have more similar IQs than distantly related or unrelated people, even when they are reared separately.

Figure 7.9 is a composite of the results of more than 100 studies of IQ and heredity in human beings, as reported by Bouchard and McGue (1981), Henderson (1982), and Erlenmeyer-Kimling and Jarvik (1963). The IQ scores of identical (MZ) twins are more alike than the scores for any other pairs, even when the twins have been reared apart. Correlations between the IQ scores of fraternal (DZ) twins, siblings, and parents and children are weak to moderate. There is no relationship between the IQ scores of unrelated people who are reared separately. This is as it should be, since such pairs share neither heredity nor environment.

Large-scale twin studies are consistent with the data in Figure 7.9. For instance, a study of 500 pairs of MZ and DZ twins in Louisville, Kentucky (Wilson, 1983), found that the correlations in intelligence between MZ twins were about the same as that for MZ twins in Figure 7.9. The correlations in intelligence between DZ twin pairs was the same as that between other siblings.

All in all, these studies appear to provide evidence for a role for heredity in IQ scores. Note, however, that genetic pairs (such as MZ twins) reared together show higher correlations between IQ scores than similar genetic pairs (such as other MZ twins) who were reared apart. This finding holds for MZ twins, siblings, parents and children, and unrelated people. *For this*

Determinants Factors that set limits.

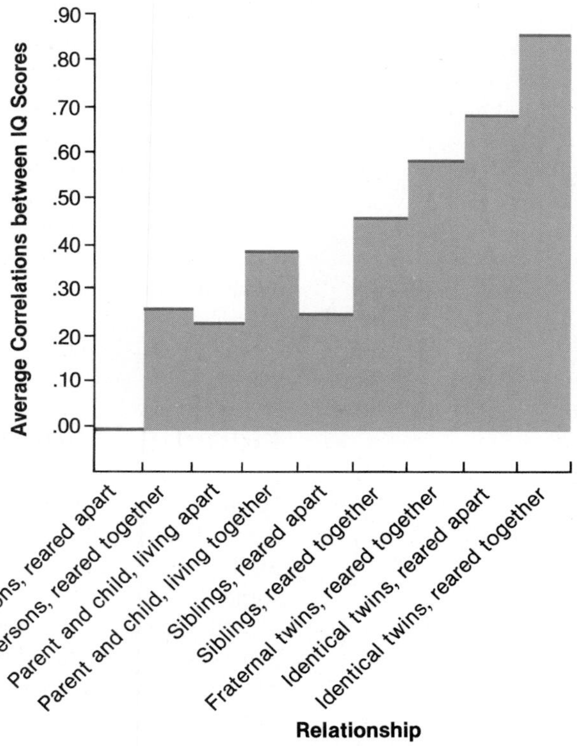

Figure 7.9
Findings of Studies of the Relationship between IQ Scores and Heredity
The data are a composite of hundreds of studies summarized in *Science* (Bouchard & McGue, 1981; Erlenmeyer-Kimling & Jarvik, 1963) and elsewhere (Henderson, 1982). By and large, correlations grow stronger for persons who are more closely related. Persons reared together or living together have more similar IQ scores that persons reared or living apart. Such findings support genetic and environmental hypotheses of the origins of intelligence.

reason, the same group of studies suggests that the environment may play a role in IQ scores.

Another strategy for exploring genetic influences on intelligence is to compare the correlations between adopted children and their biological and adoptive parents. When children are separated from their biological parents at early ages, one can argue that strong relationships between their IQs and those of their natural parents reflect genetic influences. Strong relationships between their IQs and those of their adoptive parents might reflect environmental influences.

Several studies with 1- and 2-year-old children in Colorado (Baker et al., 1983), Texas (Horn, 1983), and Minnesota (Scarr & Weinberg, 1983) have found a stronger relationship between the IQ scores of adopted children and their biological parents than with their adoptive parents.

And so, there may be a genetic influence on intelligence. However, as we shall see, there is also probably an environmental influence.

Environmental Influences on Intelligence

Studies on environmental influences employ various research strategies. One approach simply focuses on the situational factors that determine IQ scores. Remember that an IQ is a score on a test. Thus in some cases, the testing situation itself can explain part of the social-class difference in IQ. In one study, the experimenters (Zigler et al., 1982) simply made children as comfortable as possible during the test. Rather than being cold and impartial, the examiner was warm and friendly, and care was taken to see that the children understood the directions. As one result, children's test anxiety was markedly reduced. As another, the children's IQ scores were six points higher than

Head Start. Preschoolers placed in Head Start programs have made dramatic increases both in readiness for elementary school and in IQ scores.

those for a control group treated in a more indifferent manner, and disadvantaged children made relatively greater gains from the procedure. *By doing nothing more than make testing conditions more optimal for* all *children, we may narrow the IQ gap between white and black children.*

Ironically, the studies of the rats selectively bred for maze-learning ability have also provided evidence for the importance of experience. Cooper and Zubek (1958) provided young rats descended from maze-bright and maze-dull parents with different early environments. Some rats from each group were reared in a dull, featureless environment. Others were reared in rat amusement parks with ramps, ladders, wheels, and toys. Rats reared in the impoverished environment did poorly on maze learning tasks in adulthood, regardless of their parentage. But rats reared in the amusement park later learned mazes relatively rapidly. An enriched early environment narrowed the gap between the performances of rats with maze-dull and maze-bright parents.

The early home environment and styles of parenting also appear to have an effect on IQ (Hoffman, 1985). Children of mothers who are emotionally and verbally responsive, who provide appropriate play materials, who are involved with their children, and who provide varied daily experiences during the early years attain higher IQ scores later on (Bradley & Caldwell, 1976; Elardo et al., 1975, 1977; Gottfried, 1984). The extent of home organization and safety has also been linked to higher IQs at later ages and to higher achievement test scores during the first grade (Bradley & Caldwell, 1984).

Dozens of other studies support the view that the child's early environment is linked to IQ scores and academic achievement. For example, McGowan and Johnson (1984) found that good parent-child relationships and maternal encouragement of independence were both positively linked to Mexican-American children's IQ scores by the age of 3. A number of studies have also found that high levels of maternal restrictiveness and punishment at 24 months are linked to *lower* IQ scores later on (Bee et al., 1982; Yeates et al., 1983).

Government-funded efforts to provide preschoolers with enriched early environments have also led to intellectual gains. Head Start programs, for example, were instituted in the 1960s to enhance the cognitive development and academic skills of poor children. Children in these programs are exposed to letters and words, numbers, books, exercises in drawing, pegs and pegboards, puzzles, toy animals, and dolls, along with other materials and activities that middle-class children can usually take for granted. Studies of Head Start programs provide further evidence that environmental enrichment can enhance the learning ability of children (Darlington et al., 1980; Sprigle & Schaefer, 1985; Zigler & Berman, 1983). For example, in a New York City study, adolescent boys who had participated in Head Start attained average SBIS IQ scores of 99. Boys similar in background, but without preschooling, earned an average SBIS score of 93 (Palmer, 1976). Children whose IQ scores are initially lowest make the greatest gains in these programs (Zigler & Valentine, 1979).

Truth or Fiction Revisited

It is true that Head Start programs have raised children's IQs.

As noted earlier, the Minnesota adoption studies reported by Scarr and Weinberg suggest a genetic influence on intelligence. But the same studies (Scarr & Weinberg, 1976, 1977) also suggest a role for environmental influences. Black children who were adopted during the first year by white parents above average in income and education showed IQ scores some 15 to 25 points higher than those attained by black children reared by their natural parents (Scarr & Weinberg, 1976). Still, the adoptees' average IQ scores, about 106, remained somewhat below those of their adoptive parents' natural children—117 (Scarr & Weinberg, 1977). Even so, the adoptive early environment closed a good deal of the IQ gap.

On Race and Intelligence: A Concluding Note

Many psychologists believe that heredity and environment interact to influence intelligence (Plomin & DeFries, 1980). Forty-five percent of Snyderman and Rothman's (1987) sample of 1,020 psychologists and educational specialists believe that black–white differences in IQ are a "product of both genetic and environmental variation, compared to only 15 percent who feel the difference is entirely due to environmental variation. Twenty-four percent of experts do not believe there are sufficient data to support any reasonable opinion, [and 1 percent] indicate a belief in an entirely genetic determination" (p. 141).

Perhaps we need not be concerned with "how much" of a person's IQ is due to heredity and how much is due to environmental influences. Psychology has traditionally supported the dignity of the individual. It might be more appropriate for us to try to identify children *of all races* whose environments place them at risk for failure and to do what we can to enrich them.

SUMMARY

1. **What is language?** Language is the communication of thoughts and feelings through symbols that are arranged according to rules of grammar. Language has the properties of semanticity, productivity, and displacement.
2. **What are the basic components of language?** The basic components of language include phonology, morphology, syntax, and semantics.
3. **What is phonology?** Phonology is the study of the basic sounds of a language. English has about 46 basic sounds, or phonemes.
4. **What are morphemes?** Morphemes are the smallest units of meaning in a language. Morphemes consist of one or more phonemes pronounced in a particular order.
5. **What is syntax?** Syntax is the system of rules that determines how words are strung together into sentences.
6. **What is semantics?** Semantics concerns the meanings of a language. The surface structure of a sentence refers to its superficial construction, whereas its deep structure refers to the underlying meaning.
7. **What are prelinguistic vocalizations?** Crying, cooing, and babbling are prelinguistic. Newborn children cry and begin to coo by about two months. Babbling, the first vocalizations that have the sound of speech, appears at about six months and contains phonemes found in many languages.
8. **What is telegraphic speech?** Children speak their first words at about a year, and early utterances are telegraphic; that is, they eliminate unessential words. Two-word telegraphic utterances appear toward the end of the second year.
9. **What are overextension and overregularization?** Young children use words in situations for which they have not yet acquired words (that is, they overextend the meanings of words within their grasp). They also overregularize irregular verbs and nouns *because of* their developing grasp of the rules of grammar.
10. **How do psychologists explain language development?** Three kinds of theories are used: learning theories, nativist theories, and cognitive theories. Learning theories focus on the roles of reinforcement and imitation. Nativist theories assume that children bring innate factors to language development that cause them to attend to and perceive language in certain ways. Cognitive theories study the relationships between language development and cognitive development.
11. **What are some of the relationships between thought and language?** Thought is possible without language, but language facilitates thought. Ac-

cording to the linguistic-relativity hypothesis, language structures (and limits) the way in which we perceive the world.

12. **What are the stages of problem solving?** Problem solving involves stages of preparation, production, trial, and evaluation. First we familiarize ourselves with the elements of the problem. Then we try to produce alternate solutions. Finally, we try out promising solutions and evaluate whether they have met our goals.

13. **What are algorithms and heuristic devices?** Algorithms are specific procedures for solving problems (such as formulas) that will work invariably as long as they are applied correctly. Heuristics are rules of thumb that help us simplify and solve problems.

14. **How does incubation help us solve problems?** When we cannot find a solution to a problem, distancing ourselves from the problem sometimes allows the solution to "incubate." Incubation may permit the breaking down of misleading mental sets.

15. **What are mental sets and functional fixedness?** A mental set is the tendency to solve a new problem in a way in which similar problems were solved in the past. Functional fixedness, which is the tendency to perceive an object in terms of its intended function or name, can prevent novel use of familiar objects.

16. **What is creativity?** Creativity is the ability to make unusual and sometimes remote associations to the elements of a problem in order to generate new combinations that meet goals.

17. **What is intelligence?** Achievement is what a person has learned. Intelligence is presumed to underlie achievement and has been defined by Wechsler as "capacity . . . to understand the world . . . and . . . resourcefulness to cope with its challenges."

18. **What are factor theories of intelligence?** These include the theories of Spearman, Thurstone, and Guilford, all of whom believed that intelligence is composed of a number of factors. Spearman believed that a common factor, *g,* underlies all intelligent behavior but that people also have specific abilities, or *s* factors. Thurstone suggested that there are several primary mental abilities, including word fluency and numerical ability. Guilford argued that intelligence includes 120 factors, which involve the operations, products, and contents of thought.

19. **What are cognitive theories of intelligence?** These include the theories of Jensen and Sternberg, who view intelligence in terms of how we process information. Jensen believes that intelligence consists of two levels of information processing—associative (Level I) and conceptual (Level II). Sternberg's triarchic theory views intelligence in terms of contextual, experiential, and componential levels of cognitive functioning.

20. **What are the qualities of useful intelligence tests?** Useful intelligence tests must be reliable and valid, features that are expressed in terms of correlation coefficients. Reliability is the test's consistency. Validity is the degree to which a test measures an external criterion—that which it is supposed to measure.

21. **What is the IQ?** Intelligence tests yield scores called intelligence quotients, or *IQs.* The Stanford-Binet Intelligence Scale, originated by Alfred Binet, derives IQ scores by dividing children's mental age scores by their chronological ages, then multiplying by 100. The Wechsler scales use deviation IQs, which are derived by comparing a person's performance to that of age-mates.

22. **What kinds of items are on intelligence tests?** The Wechsler scales are representative. They contain verbal and performance subtests that measure general information, comprehension, similarities (conceptual thinking), vocabulary, mathematics, block design (copying designs), and object assembly (piecing puzzles together).

23. **What is the controversy over culturally biased tests about?** It turns out that intelligence test scores reflect cultural factors as well as general learning ability. Cultural factors include familiarity with testing, socioeconomic status, familiarity with information concerning the mainstream culture, motivation to do well, and adjustment in the school setting. Efforts have been made to develop culture-fair or culture-free tests.

24. **Where does intelligence come from?** The largest number of psychologists believe that intelligence reflects the interaction of genetic and environmental influences. Evidence from kinship studies, adoptee studies, and other sources suggest roles for both heredity and the environment. Evidence from studies of compensatory-education programs (such as Head Start) shows that enrichment of the child's early environment can narrow the IQ gap between children of lower socioeconomic status and middle-class backgrounds.

PSYCHOLOGY AND MODERN LIFE

Some of us may know people who insist that their dogs understand every word they say. When we look closely, though, we find that the animals respond to their human owners' excitement and a few words or commands such as "Sit," "Lunchtime," or "Out" that have been paired repeatedly with certain acts or events. Nor has anyone had a talking pet cat, horse, or elephant. So, the weight of human history made us skeptical of the first reports that chimpanzees had been taught to use symbols to communicate.

But psychological methods have indeed taught apes to use symbols to communicate. This development has led us to reexamine preexisting ideas about the definition of language. Moreover, it has catalyzed the innovation of techniques for helping retarded people communicate.

Teaching Language to Apes: Going Ape over Language?

Washoe, a female chimp raised by Beatrice and Allen Gardner (1980), was one of the first primates who came to our notice. The Gardners and their assistants raised Washoe from the time she was 1 year of age. Instead of instructing her orally, they used American Sign Language (ASL), which, along with signed English, is a language used by many deaf people in the United States.

By the age of 5, Washoe could use more than 160 signs, including signs for actions (verbs), such as *come, gimme,* and *tickle;* signs for things (nouns), such as *apples, flowers,* and *toothbrush;* and signs for more abstract concepts, such as *more.* She could combine signs to form simple sentences. Washoe's brief sentences were largely telegraphic, like those of young children. Consider these two-word sentences: *More tickle, More banana,* and *More milk*—which doesn't sound like too bad of a way to spend a lazy Sunday afternoon. As time passed, Washoe signed longer sentences, such as *Please sweet drink, Come gimme drink* and *Gimme toothbrush hurry.*

Some observers believe that Washoe's communications showed failings by human standards. For example, we are not certain of the degree to which Washoe and other apes have attended to grammar, as shown by word order (Terrace et al., 1980). Washoe's words were frequently strung in haphazard combinations. One day she might sign *Come gimme toothbrush,* but the next day, *Hurry toothbrush gimme.* Even the language productions of 1-year-old children tend to have reliable word order. Children appear to share an intuitive grasp of grammar, but apes might not. Still, in recent years Washoe and her companions have been observed spontaneously signing to one another, and some mother chimpanzees have taught their infants to use signs to communicate (Bernstein, 1987; Fouts & Fouts, 1985).

Ann and David Premack (1975) taught another female chimp, Sarah, to communicate by arranging symbols on a magnet board. Eventually Sarah learned simple telegraphic sentences like *Place orange dish.* Her word order was less sporadic than Washoe's. The Premacks consider their work with Sarah to be a demonstration of the role of operant conditioning in language learning. Sarah was reinforced for selecting the proper symbols to make a request and for following instructions communicated by symbols.

Still another chimp, Lana, was trained to communicate by means of a keyboard controlled by a computer (Savage-Rumbaugh & Rumbaugh, 1980). Lana learned to manipulate about 100 keys, each of which showed a different symbol. She would press various combinations of keys to communicate simple ideas (Figure 7.10). She also tended to maintain a consistent word order.

Some of the most impressive claims for teaching language to an ape have been made by Francine (Penny) Patterson (1980). Patterson taught a gorilla named Koko to use hundreds of signs, including signs for *friend, airplane, lollipop, belly button,* even *stethoscope.* Patterson also reports that at the ages of 5, 6, and 7, Koko earned scores on intelligence tests just below those of children of comparable ages. She characterizes Koko's use of language as almost "human" in that Koko lies and at times does the exact opposite of what she is told to do. Patterson also reports that Koko has produced some creative insults in ASL—for example, "You dirty toilet devil" and "Rotten stink." Koko, like children, has also created words (signs) of her own, such as tucking her index finger under her arm as a sign for thermometer (Patterson et al., 1987). Apes, like children, name objects. But some linguists argue that Koko, like other apes, shows little understanding of grammar.

Now that we have described the skills of a number of well-known apes, let us wrestle with the issue of whether apes can understand and produce language.

Can Apes Really Understand and Produce Language? There seems to be little doubt that apes can follow commands given to them by means of ASL and other symbol systems. However, psychologist Herbert Terrace (1987a) and other researchers have raised questions about the productivity of apes—that is, whether apes combine signs into original sentences (Terrace et al., 1980). Lana, for example, appeared to learn a number of standard sentences into which she could insert new verbs and nouns, but her productivity was limited.

Terrace (1987b) has concluded that apes cannot master the basics of grammar. He also argues that what looks like spontaneous signing is actually signing for "a variety of concrete incentives"—that is, tricks to gain rewards.

Figure 7.10
Ape Uses Signs to Communicate. Apes at Emory University's Yerkes Primate Center have been taught to express simple ideas by pressing keys on a computer-controlled keyboard.

There are some exceptions, but apes generally use signs in the situations in which they have been taught to use them. What apes produce is very similar to what they have been taught to produce.

In sum, if we consider productivity and facility with grammar to be standards for defining language, some critics argue that apes fall short. However, Michael Maratsos (1983) of the University of Minnesota notes that such strict criteria are relatively new on the scene. "Apes can probably learn to use signs to communicate meanings," Maratsos writes. "As this used to be the old boundary for language, it seems unfair [now] to raise the ante and say that [using signs to communicate meaning] is not really language" (1983, p. 771).

Truth or Fiction Revisited

It is true that psychologists have been able to communicate with chimpanzees and gorillas by means of sign language. But there is no universal agreement as to whether apes perceive and produce language in ways that are comparable to human usage.

Although we have not conclusively answered the question of whether or not apes use language, our discussion of the language of apes affords insight into human facility with language.

Scaling the Walls of Silence: How Apes Have Taught Us to Teach Communications Skills to Humans

Deaf, mute, and retarded since birth, 23-year-old Sandra was written off as a hopeless case. However, in the past few years, the once hostile, violent young woman has been transformed. Today she can request her favorite foods and communicate with her teachers—thanks to the computer-based language that was originally developed to study chimpanzees' abilities to use language.

The language that liberated Sandra is Yerkish, named for the Yerkes Primate Center at Atlanta's Emory University, where it was developed. Invented by psychologist Duane Rumbaugh in the early 1970s, Yerkish consists of a few hundred geometric symbols printed on a computer keyboard (Figure 7.10). Each of the symbols represents a specific English word, such as "apple," "give," "room," "yes," and "no." Sentences are formed by punching a series of keys. Yerkish has been taught to several chimpanzees at the Center.

In the 1980s, Rumbaugh applied what the chimps taught him to see if severely retarded people, lacking in communication skills, could also be taught to communicate by means of symbols on a computer keyboard. With the consent of their families, 14 retarded persons were chosen for the initial projects. Eight of them made significant progress, mastering from two dozen to more than 70 symbols. Instructors begin by teaching their charges the symbol for their favorite food. Correct usage is rewarded with the food. The symbol is then shifted around the keyboard, so that students learn to identify it by shape rather than location. Additional symbols are taught one at a time.

Using Yerkish, the students have learned to communicate so well that many have been placed on a waiting list for a community halfway house. Sandra has fewer temper tantrums and has been moved from the most restrictive to the least restrictive ward in the hospital. Speech pathologist Mary Ann Romski reports, "Retarded people know a lot of things and understand a lot of things that have not been tapped in the past, because they have had no way to tell us." Language, of course, has also probably helped to shape their thinking.

In any event, Rumbaugh notes, "Ten years from now, I hope this looks like a very primitive beginning."

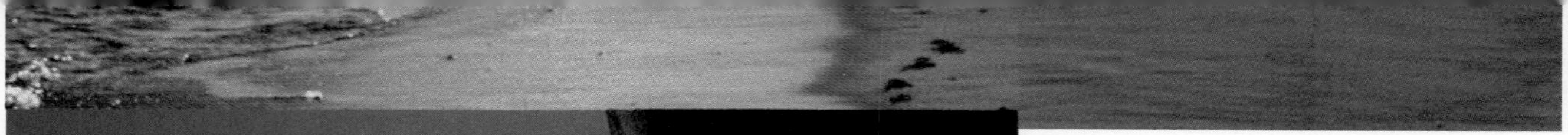

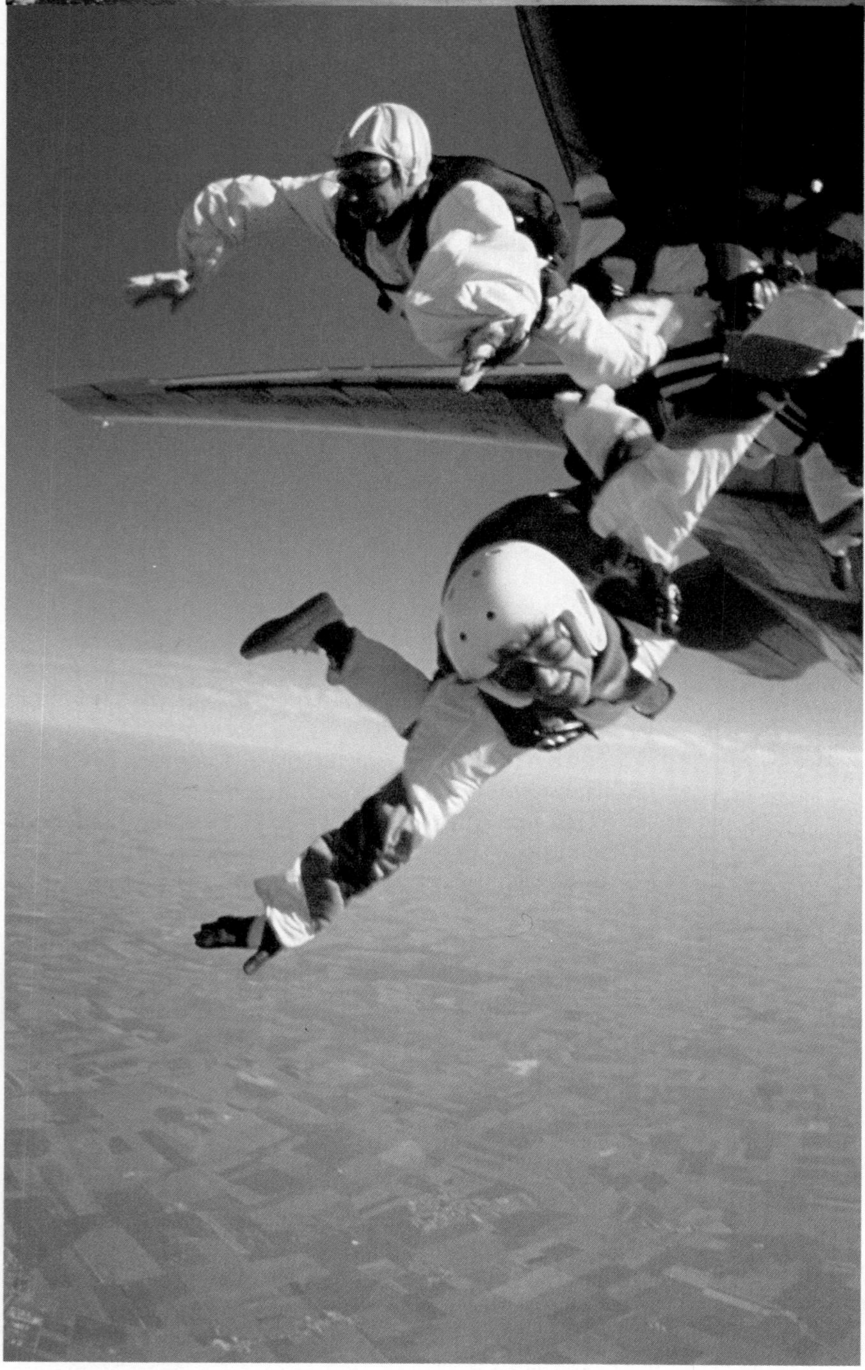

Outline

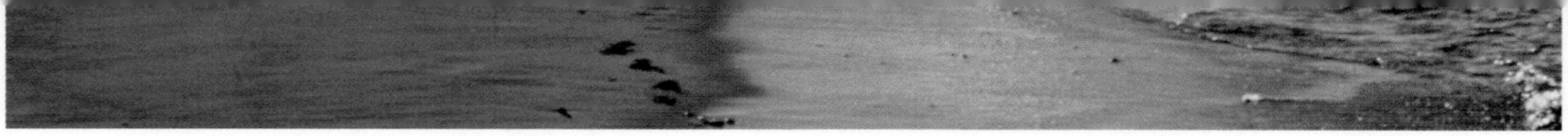

8 Motivation and Emotion

Truth or Fiction?

- □ Salty pretzels can make you thirsty.
- □ "Getting away from it all" by going on a vacation from all sensory input for a few hours is relaxing.
- □ If quarterbacks get too "psyched up" for a big game, their performance on the field may suffer.
- □ A strong need to get ahead is the most powerful predictor of success in climbing the corporate ladder.
- □ Misery loves company.
- □ You may be able to fool a lie detector by squiggling your toes.
- □ Romantic love is found in every culture in the world.
- □ Taking a date to a horror film or for a roller coaster ride may stimulate feelings of passion.
- □ One American adult in five is obese.

When is the last time you came face to face with a tarantula, a laser beam, or an alien from outer space? Actually, if you have been to a movie lately, it may not have been that long ago at all: *Aliens, Star Wars, Raiders of the Lost Ark, Romancing the Stone, First Blood, Star Trek, Close Encounters, Indiana Jones and the Temple of Doom, A View to a Kill, Superman, Conan, The Predator.* In adventure films, characters such as Rambo, James Bond, and Indiana Jones have been pitted against snakes, tarantulas, alligators, mythical monsters, automatic rifles, knives, swords, helicopter gunships, nuclear weapons, laser beams, computers, crazed cultists, floods, hurricanes, blizzards, airplane crashes, shipwrecks, cosmic forces, international forces, occult forces—forces of every flavor and every size.

Most of us lead rather orderly lives, so how do we account for the huge success of these adventure films at the box office? What motivates us to flock to every film from *Gremlins* to *Goonies?*

Adventure! Harrison Ford enacts the role of the dauntless Indiana Jones in this scene from *Raiders of the Lost Ark.* What is the lure of adventure films?

We do not have the final answer to this question. But here are some speculations that have been advanced by psychologists, religious leaders, politicians, film critics, and your friendly neighborhood bartender:

Life is filled with vague anxieties and persistent pressures. Adventure films give us a temporary focus for our fears, anxieties, and frustrations.

Audiences can purge their aggressive impulses by enjoying conflicts in which other people are involved.

We are seeking coping strategies. We learn how to deal with our own frustrations and conflicts by observing the heroes and the heroines.

Adventure films make our own problems seem trivial.

Adventure films heighten awareness of the possibilities of life, giving us hope that we may someday find ourselves in exotic situations.

Most of us lead sedentary lives with uncomfortably low levels of arousal. Adventure films raise our arousal to more optimal levels so that we feel full of vim and vigor.

Afterward, our dates may interpret their high levels of arousal from the movie as attraction to us.

We have an instinctive drive to throw away money.

We're grateful it's not happening to us.

Harrison Ford is cute.

They're fun.

The psychology of motivation is concerned with the *whys* of behavior. Why do we attend adventure films? Why do we eat and drink? Why do some of us ride motorcycles at breakneck speeds? Why do we try new things or strive to get ahead?

In this chapter we explore motivation and the closely related topic of emotion. Adventure films give rise to powerful emotional responses, and it may be that expectation of these responses partly motivates our visit the theater.

Let us begin with a few basic definitions.

MOTIVES, NEEDS, DRIVES, AND INCENTIVES

The word *motive* derives from the Latin *movere,* meaning "to move." **Motives** can be defined as hypothetical states within organisms that activate behavior and propel the organisms toward goals. Why do we say "hypothetical states"? We say so is because motives are not seen and measured directly; as are so many other psychological concepts, they are inferred from behavior. Psychologists assume that behavior does not occur at random. We assume that behavior is caused; the behavior of organisms is assumed to be largely caused by motives. *Needs, drives,* and *incentives* are closely related concepts.

The term **need** has been used in at least two different ways by psychologists. We speak of both physiological needs and psychological needs. Certain physiological needs must be met if we are to survive. They include oxygen, food, drink, pain avoidance, proper temperature, and the elimination of waste products. Some physiological needs, such as hunger and thirst, are states of physical deprivation. For instance, when we have not eaten or drunk for a while, we develop needs for food and water. We speak of the body as having needs for oxygen, fluids, calories, vitamins, minerals, and so on.

Psychological needs include needs for achievement, power, self-esteem, social approval, and belonging, among others. Psychological needs differ from physiological needs in two important ways: First, psychological needs are not necessarily based on states of deprivation; a person with a strong need for achievement may have a history of consistent success. Second, psychological needs may be acquired through experience, or learned, whereas physiological needs reside in the physical makeup of the organism. Because our biological makeups are similar, we would assume that people share similar physiological needs. And because our learning experiences differ, we would expect that people differ markedly in their psychological needs. In the section on social motives, we shall see that this is indeed the case.

Needs are said to give rise to **drives.** Depletion of food gives rise to the hunger drive, and depletion of liquids gives rise to the thirst drive. Physiological drives are the psychological counterparts of physiological needs. When we have gone without food and water, our bodies may *need* these substances; however, our *experience* of drives of hunger and thirst is psychological in nature. Drives arouse us to action. Our drive levels tend to increase with the length of time we have been deprived. We are usually more highly aroused by the hunger drive when we have not eaten for several hours than when we have not eaten for, say, five minutes.

Our psychological needs for approval, achievement, and belonging also give rise to drives. We can be driven to get ahead in the world of business just as surely as we can be driven to eat. For many of us, the drives for achievement and power consume our daily lives.

An **incentive** is an object, person, or situation perceived as being capable of satisfying a need or desirable for its own sake. Money, food, a sexually attractive person, social approval, and attention all can act as incentives that motivate behavior. Needs and incentives can interact to influence the strength of drives. Strong needs combined with enticing incentives create the most powerful drives. Even a person who has just eaten may be tempted

Motive A hypothetical state within an organism that propels the organism toward a goal.

Need A state of deprivation.

Drive A condition of arousal in an organism that is associated with a need.

Incentive An object, person, or situation perceived as being capable of satisfying a need.

by a chocolate dessert. A colleague with whom I eat lunch once said, "That pie looks so good it creates its own drive." A rat will run down a maze more rapidly when it whiffs Limburger cheese than when it has learned to expect Purina Rat Chow. The Limburger cheese acts as an incentive that heightens the hunger drive. A dog will eat steak more rapidly than it will eat Purina Dog Chow. I'll show that I have nothing against the Purina folks by adding that you are probably more motivated to buy Purina Dog Chow when it is on a limited-time-only, half-price sale. That is, you may respond to the financial *incentive*. Consider the role of financial incentives in motivating athletes.

A CLOSER LOOK

Are They Really Motivated? When professional athletes receive lucrative multiyear contracts, do they have sufficient incentive to play their best game after game?

Do Multiyear Contracts Provide Athletes with Sufficient Incentive?

Many professional athletes have multiyear contracts that are not linked to performance. Dave Winfield of the New York Yankees, for example, receives $2 million a year whether he bats .350 or .200 and whether he drives in 100 runs or none. Multiyear contracts became commonplace in professional baseball after a federal arbitration panel ruled that players were no longer bound indefinitely to the teams that originally signed them. This decision made it advantageous for owners to tie up their stars for as many years as possible. And the stars often receive salaries so high, regardless of their performance from season to season, that they will be rich whether they help the team to win or lose.

Richard O'Brien and other psychologists at Hofstra University have gathered statistical evidence to show that long-term contracts take some of the hustle out of professional baseball players—specifically pitchers. The researchers examined the records of 38 pitchers during the three years before and after they signed contracts for at least three years, and they compared their play to that of 38 randomly chosen pitchers who had signed only single-season contracts for the same period.

As long as they had to get their contracts renewed each year, the players who eventually won long-term berths improved steadily, from an average of 3.66 earned runs scored against them per game in 1974 to 2.91 in 1976. After signing their long-term agreements, however, their earned run averages (ERAs) climbed to an average of 4.04 three years later. The pitchers with one-year contracts showed no consistent pattern during the six years.

The researchers recommend that owners combine a base salary with incentive payments for achieving goals such as a specified ERA or batting average. Negotiated performance targets, they say, "would allow equitable rewards for productive seasons for all players."

Former Baltimore Orioles' ace pitcher Jim Palmer provided anecdotal support for that conclusion in a *New York Times* interview. Having a long-term contract himself, Palmer noted that "up until 1975, my next year's salary always depended on every pitch I threw. I never relaxed. I never took anything for granted. It would seem to be hard for some players to have that kind of intensity after signing a multiyear contract. Some players are making a lot more money than they should."

Incentives are only one kind of motive. In the following section, we explore psychological theories of motivation—that is, we ask the question: Just what is so motivating about motives? We shall see that psychologists and others have spawned very different views of the motives that propel us.

A Fixed-Action Pattern. In the presence of another male, the Siamese Fighting Fish assumes an instinctive threatening stance in which the fins and gills are extended. If neither threatening male retreats, there will be conflict.

THEORETICAL PERSPECTIVES ON MOTIVATION

Although psychologists agree that it is important to understand why people and lower animals do things, they do not agree about the nature of motivation. Let us have a brief look at three theoretical perspectives on motivation: instinct theory, drive reductionism, and self-actualization.

Instinct Theory

Animals are born with preprogrammed tendencies to respond to certain situations in certain ways. Birds reared in isolation from other birds build nests during the mating season, even though they have never observed another bird building a nest (or, for that matter, seen a nest). Siamese fighting fish reared in isolation assume stereotypical threatening stances and attack other males when they are introduced into their tanks.

Behaviors such as these are characteristic of particular species (species-specific) and do not rely on learning. They are called **instincts**—inherited dispositions that activate specific behavior patterns that appear to be designed to reach certain goals. Spiders spin webs, and bees "dance" to communicate the location of a food source to other bees. All this activity is inborn; it is genetically transmitted from generation to generation.

Ethologists label instincts **fixed-action patterns** (or FAPs). FAPs occur in response to stimuli that ethologists refer to as **releasers.** As noted in Chapter 3, male members of many species are sexually aroused by pheromones secreted by females. Pheromones "release" the FAP of sexual response.

At the turn of the century, psychologists William James (1890) and William McDougall (1908) argued that people have various instincts that foster self-survival and social behavior. James asserted that we have social instincts such as love, sympathy, and modesty. McDougall catalogued 12 "basic" instincts, including hunger, sex, and self-assertion. Other psychologists have put together longer lists.

Instinct An inherited disposition to activate specific behavior patterns that are designed to reach certain goals.

Ethologist A scientist who studies the behavior patterns characteristic of different species.

Fixed-action pattern An instinct; abbreviated *FAP.*

Releaser In ethology, a stimulus that elicits a FAP.

Drive-reduction theory The view that organisms learn to engage in behaviors that have the effect of reducing drives.

Primary drives Unlearned, or physiological, drives.

Acquired drives Drives that are acquired through experience, or learned.

Self-actualization According to Maslow and other humanistic psychologists, self-initiated striving to become what one is capable of being. The motive to reach one's full potential, to express one's unique capabilities.

The psychoanalyst Sigmund Freud also used the term *instincts* to refer to physiological needs within people. Freud believed that the instincts of sex and aggression give rise to *psychic energy,* which is perceived as a feeling of tension. Tension motivates us to restore ourselves to a calmer, resting state. The behavior patterns we use to reduce the tension are largely learned.

The psychodynamic views of Sigmund Freud also coincide reasonably well with those of a group of learning theorists who presented a drive-reduction theory of learning.

Drive-Reduction Theory

Rewards are defined as pleasant events that increase the frequency of behavior. But what makes them pleasant?

According to **drive-reduction theory,** as framed by psychologist Clark Hull at Yale University in the 1930s, rewards are pleasant because they reduce drives. Hull argued that **primary drives** such as hunger, thirst, and pain trigger arousal (tension) and activate behavior. We learn responses that partially or completely reduce the drives. Through association, we also learn **acquired drives.** We may acquire a drive for money because money enables us to attain food, drink, and homes that protect us from predators and extremes of temperature. We might acquire drives for social approval and affiliation because other people, and their good will, also help us to reduce primary drives, especially when we are infants. In all cases, tension reduction is the goal.

Humanistic Theory

Humanistic psychologists, particularly Abraham Maslow, note that the instinct and drive-reduction theories of motivation are basically defensive. These theories suggest that human behavior occurs in rather mechanical fashion and is aimed toward survival and tension reduction. As a humanist, Maslow asserted that behavior is also motivated by the conscious desire for personal growth. Humanists note that people will tolerate pain, hunger, and many other sources of tension to achieve what they perceive as personal fulfillment.

Abraham Maslow and the Hierarchy of Needs Maslow was fond of asking graduate students, "How many of you expect to achieve greatness in your careers?" He would prod them to extend themselves because he believed that people are capable of doing more than responding to drives. Maslow believed that we are separated from lower animals by our capacity for **self-actualization,** or self-initiated striving to become whatever we believe we are capable of being. In fact, Maslow saw self-actualization to be as essential a human need as hunger.

Maslow (1970) organized human needs into a hierarchy, from physiological needs, such as hunger and thirst, through self-actualization (see Figure 8.1.) He believed that in our lives we would naturally travel up through this hierarchy as long as we did not encounter insurmountable social or environmental hurdles. Maslow was optimistic about human nature. Whereas some psychologists believed in aggressive instincts, Maslow believed that people acted aggressively only when needs were frustrated, particularly the needs for love and acceptance.

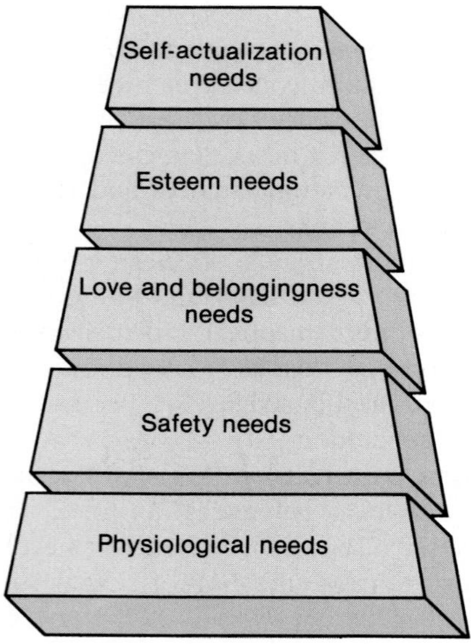

Figure 8.1
Maslow's Hierarchy of Needs. Maslow believed that we progress toward higher psychological needs once basic survival needs have been met. Where do you fit in this picture?

Maslow's needs hierarchy includes the following:

1. *Physiological needs:* hunger, thirst, elimination, warmth, fatigue, pain avoidance, sexual release.
2. *Safety needs:* protection from the environment through housing and clothing, security from crime and financial hardship.
3. *Love and belongingness needs:* love and acceptance through intimate relationships, social groups, and friends. Maslow believed that in a generally well-fed society, such as ours, much frustration stemmed from failure to meet needs at this level.
4. *Esteem needs:* achievement, competence, approval, recognition, prestige, status.
5. *Self-actualization:* fulfillment of our unique potentials. For many individuals, self-actualization involves needs for cognitive understanding (novelty, exploration, knowledge) and aesthetic needs (music, art, poetry, beauty, order).

Evaluation

Instinct theory has been criticized for yielding circular explanations of behavior. If we say that mothers love and care for their children because of a maternal instinct, and then we take maternal care as evidence for such an instinct, we have come full circle. But we have explained nothing. We have only repeated ourselves.

Instincts are also species-specific; that is, they give rise to stereotypical behaviors (FAPs) in all members of a species (or perhaps they apply to all male or to all female adults). There is so much variation in human behavior that it seems unlikely that much of it is instinctive. Consider William James's notion that sympathy is an instinct. Many people are cruel and cold-hearted; are we to assume that they somehow possess less of this instinct? If so, this assumption is incompatible with the definition of an instinct.

Drive-reduction theory appears to apply in many situations involving physiological drives, such as hunger and thirst. But it runs aground when we consider the evidence that we often act to increase, rather than decrease, the tensions acting on us. Even when hungry we might go to lengthy efforts to prepare a meal instead of a snack, although the snack would reduce the hunger drive as well. We drive fast cars, ride roller coasters, and parachute-jump for sport—all activities that heighten rather than decrease arousal. We often seek novel ways of doing things because of the stimulation they afford, shunning the tried and true. Yet the tried and true would lead to tension reduction more reliably. Other psychologists have theorized the existence of so-called "stimulus motives" that surmount the limitations of drive-reduction theory.

Critics of Maslow argue that there is too much individual variation for the hierarchy of motivation to apply to everyone. Some people whose physiological, safety, and love needs are met show little interest in achievement and recognition. Others seek distant, self-actualizing goals while exposing themselves to great danger. Some artists, musicians, and writers devote themselves fully to their art, even at the price of poverty.

In sum, no traditional view of motivation fully accounts for complex human behavior. Instinct theory applies to many species-specific behaviors but not to the diversity of human behavior. Drive-reduction theory applies

Physiological drives Unlearned drives with a biological basis, such as hunger, thirst, and avoidance of pain.

Homeostasis The tendency of the body to maintain a steady state.

Satiety The state of being satisfied; fullness.

Sham False, pretended.

to many physiological drives, but even here there are exceptions. The humanists point out that human motives can be growth-oriented rather than defensive, but there is too much human variation for humanistic theory to apply universally.

Despite the lack of an integrated, satisfying theory of human motivation, there is a wealth of research concerning various types of motivated behavior. Let us first consider drives that arise from physiological needs. Then we shall turn our attention to stimulus motives and social motives.

PHYSIOLOGICAL DRIVES

Physiological needs give rise to **physiological drives**—aroused conditions within the organism that activate behavior that will reduce these needs. Because physiological drives are unlearned, they are also referred to as primary drives. Although sexual behavior allows survival of the species instead of survival of the individual, sex is also considered a primary drive.

Primary drives are inborn, but learning influences the *behavior* that satisfies them. Eating meat or fish, drinking coffee or tea, kissing lips or rubbing noses are all learned preferences.

Homeostasis Physiological drives operate largely according to principles of drive reduction. Mechanisms in the body are triggered when we are in a state of deprivation. These mechanisms then motivate us, through sensations such as hunger, thirst, and cold, to act to restore the balance. The bodily tendency to maintain a steady state is called **homeostasis.**

Homeostasis works much like a thermostat. When the room temperature drops below the set point, the heating system is triggered. The heat stays on until the set point is reached. The body's homeostatic systems involve fascinating interactions between physiological and psychological processes.

In this section we shall explore the drives of hunger and thirst.

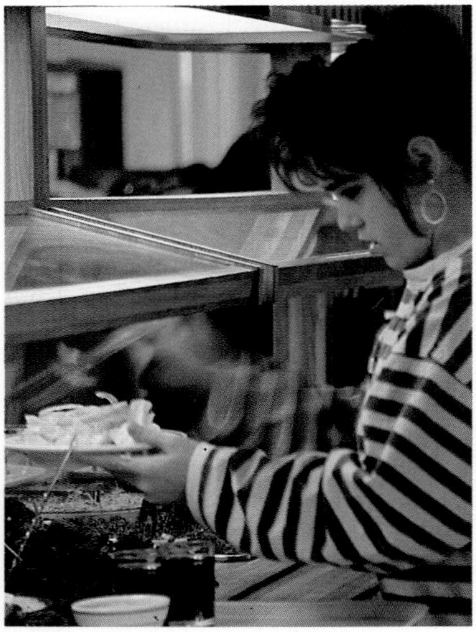

Hunger. Hunger is a physiological drive that motivates us to eat. What makes us feel hungry? What makes us feel satiated? Why do many of us continue to eat when we have already supplied our bodies with the needed nutrients?

Hunger

Some of us bounce up and down in weight because of cycles of binge eating and dieting, but most of us maintain remarkably constant weights over the years (Keesey, 1980). What bodily mechanisms regulate the hunger drive? What psychological processes are at work? Why do many of us continue to eat when we have already supplied our bodies with the needed nutrients?

The Mouth Let us begin with the mouth—an appropriate choice since we are discussing eating. Chewing and swallowing provide some sensations of **satiety.** If they did not, we might eat for a long time after we had taken in enough food; it takes the digestive tract time to metabolize food and provide signals of satiety to the brain by way of the bloodstream.

In classic **sham** feeding experiments with dogs, a tube was implanted in the animals' throats so that any food swallowed fell out of the body. Even though no food arrived at the stomach, the animals stopped feeding after a brief period (Janowitz & Grossman, 1949). However, they resumed feeding sooner than animals whose food did reach the stomach.

Let us proceed to the stomach, too, as we seek further regulatory factors in hunger.

Stomach Contractions An empty stomach will lead to stomach contractions, which we call hunger pangs. These pangs are not as influential as had

Figure 8.2
A Hyperphagic Rat. This rodent winner of the basketball look-alike contest went on a binge after it received a lesion in the ventromedial nucleus (VMN) of the hypothalamus. It is as if the lesion pushed the "set point" for body weight up several notches, and the rat's weight is now about five times normal. But now it eats only enough to maintain its pleasantly plump stature, so you need not be concerned that it will eventually burst. If the lesion had been made in the lateral hypothalamus, the animal might have become the "Twiggy" of the rat world.

once been thought. People and animals whose stomachs have been removed still regulate food intake to maintain a normal weight level. This finding led to the discovery of many other regulatory mechanisms, including blood-sugar level, the hypothalamus, and even receptors in the liver.

Blood-Sugar Level When we are deprived of food, the level of sugar in the blood drops. The deficit is communicated to the hypothalamus (see Chapter 2). The drop in blood sugar apparently indicates that we have been burning energy and need to replenish it by eating.

Experiments with the Hypothalamus: The Search for "Start-Eating" and "Stop-Eating" Centers in the Brain If you were just reviving from a surgical operation, fighting your way through the fog of the anesthesia, food would probably be that last thing on your mind. But when rats are operated on and a **lesion** in the **ventromedial nucleus** (VMN) of the hypothalamus is made, they will grope toward their food supplies as soon as their eyes open. Then they eat vast quantities of Purina Rat Chow or whatever else they can find.

The VMN might function like a stop-eating center in the rat's brain (Novin et al., 1976). If the VMN is electrically stimulated—that is, "switched on"—a rat will stop eating until the current is turned off. When the VMN is lesioned, the rat becomes **hyperphagic.** It will continue to eat until it has about doubled its normal weight (see Figure 8.2). Then it will level off its eating and maintain the higher weight. It is as if the set point of the stop-eating center has been raised to a higher level (Keesey & Powley, 1975, 1986).

VMN-lesioned rats are also more finicky about their food. They will eat more fats or sweet-tasting food, but they will actually eat less if their food is salty or bitter (Kimble, 1988).

The **lateral hypothalamus** might be a start-eating center in the rat's brain. If you electrically stimulate the lateral hypothalamus, the rat will start to eat. If you make a lesion in the lateral hypothalamus, the rat may stop eating altogether—that is, become **aphagic.** However, if you force-feed an aphagic rat for a while, it will begin to eat on its own and level off at a relatively low body weight. You have lowered the rat's set point. It is like turning the thermostat down from, say, 70 degrees Fahrenheit to 40 degrees Fahrenheit.

Receptors in the Liver Other research suggests that receptors in the liver are also important in regulating hunger (Friedman & Stricker, 1976; Schwartz, 1978). These receptors appear to be sensitive to the blood-sugar level. In a state of food deprivation, blood sugar is low, and these receptors send rapid messages to the brain. After a meal the blood-sugar level rises, and the receptors' rate of firing decreases (Novin et al., 1983).

Although many areas of the body work in concert to regulate the hunger drive, this is only part of the story. In human beings, the hunger drive is more complex. Psychological as well as physiological factors play an important role, as we shall see in our discussion of obesity in this chapter's section on Psychology and Modern Life.

Lesion An injury that results in impaired behavior or loss of a function.

Ventromedial nucleus A central area on the underside of the hypothalamus that appears to function as a stop-eating center.

Hyperphagic Characterized by excessive eating.

Lateral hypothalamus An area at the side of the hypothalamus that appears to function as a start-eating center.

Aphagic Characterized by undereating.

Thirst

Our bodies need fluids as well as food to survive. We may survive without food for several weeks, but we will last only for a few days without water. It

Angiotensin A kidney hormone that signals the hypothalamus of bodily depletion of fluids.

Osmoreceptors Receptors in the hypothalamus that are sensitive to depletion of fluid.

has been speculated that thirst is a stronger drive than hunger, because animals who have been deprived of food and water will typically drink before eating when given the opportunity to do both. Critics of this view note that hungry animals must take in fluids to produce saliva and other digestive fluids before eating.

In any event, we maintain rather stable fluid levels. When there is excess fluid, we are not likely to feel thirsty and our bodies form urine. When there is a fluid deficiency, we are likely to experience a thirst drive and our bodies are less likely to form urine.

What are the bodily mechanisms that signal thirst?

The Dry Mouth Theory Because we may experience thirst as dryness in the mouth and throat, it was once thought that receptors in the mouth and throat played a major role in determining thirst or satiety. But classic sham drinking experiments have shown that wetting the mouth and throat does not in itself put an end to thirst (Adolph, 1950; Maddison et al., 1980). In these studies, tubes are implanted in the throats of dogs and monkeys so that any liquid swallowed falls out of the body as rapidly as it is drunk. The resultant behavior is similar to that of the dogs in sham feeding experiments. When these animals are deprived of water, they drink a normal amount and then pause for a few minutes. But they soon return to drinking, unless water is placed in their stomachs. Research suggests that receptors in the kidney and hypothalamus play more central roles in regulating the thirst drive.

Regulation of Thirst in the Kidneys When the body is depleted of fluids, the flow of blood through the kidneys drops off. In response to this decreased flow of blood, the kidneys secrete the hormone **angiotensin.** Angiotensin, in turn, signals the hypothalamus of fluid depletion.

The Role of the Hypothalamus: On Shriveled Cells and Salty Pretzels **Osmoreceptors** in the hypothalamus can also detect fluid depletion from changes that occur within the brain. The brain, like the rest of the body, becomes fluid-depleted. Fluid depletion causes the osmoreceptor cells to shrivel, which in itself may trigger thirst.

Another osmoreceptor signal involves the concentration of chemicals in body fluids. As the volume of water in the body decreases, the concentration of chemicals in the water, such as sodium (which combines with chlorine to make salt) increases. (Think of a pool of salt water evaporating in the sun. The salt does *not* evaporate, only the water, and the remaining water becomes increasingly salty. If all the water were to evaporate, there would be nothing left but a crust of salt.) An increasing concentration of salt can also signal the osmoreceptors that the body's water supply is falling.

In a classic experiment, an injection of a salt solution into a goat's hypothalamus triggered heavy intake of fluids, even though the goat had just drunk its fill (Andersson, 1971). Injection of salt-free water caused the animal *not* to drink, apparently by "fooling" the osmoreceptors into behaving as though there were a higher level of fluids throughout the body. Did you ever wonder why bartenders are usually happy to provide customers with "free" salty peanuts and salty pretzels? As the salt is dissolved into body fluids, the customers become thirsty again, even though they may also be making frequent trips to the bathroom to urinate.

Are Free Pretzels and Peanuts Really Free? Why do bar owners supply patrons with endless supplies of salty pretzels and peanuts? As the salt is dissolved into body fluids, the customer becomes thirsty again, even though he or she may already have had quite a bit to drink.

Truth or Fiction Revisited

It is true that eating salty pretzels can make you thirsty. It heightens the concentration of chemicals in the water in the body.

Antidiuretic hormone A pituitary hormone that conserves body fluids by increasing the reabsorption of urine.

Innate Inborn, unlearned.

The hypothalamus responds to signs of dehydration transmitted by osmoreceptors in at least two ways. First, it signals the pituitary gland to secrete **antidiuretic hormone** (ADH). ADH causes the kidneys to reabsorb urine—a water-conservation measure. Second, the hypothalamus signals the cerebral cortex. As a result, we experience the thirst drive.

Our responses to thirst are varied and largely learned. Some of us go to the tap for water. Others brew coffee or tea. Still others prefer juice or a soft drink. The time of day, social custom, and individual preferences all play a role in deciding which fluids will be drunk.

External cues may also stimulate us to drink, as they can stimulate us to eat, even in the absence of internal cues for thirst. Watching someone squeeze an orange or hearing a cork pop can make us desire orange juice or champagne. We may also drink alcohol to earn the approval of drinking buddies or for whatever incentives the sensations of intoxication may provide.

Receptors in the Mouth and Throat Research using the sham-drinking method does point to a role for receptors in the mouth and throat. Remember that the animals in these experiments pause after they have drunk a normal amount. Thus, at some point the receptors probably signal the hypothalamus, "Stop, enough." But if the central processes that signal dehydration have not been reversed, the animal soon feels thirsty (i.e., drinks) again.

Drinking, like eating, has complex origins. It can be motivated by a combination of internal and external cues.

And so, eating and drinking are largely—though not completely—governed by primary drives. Now let us highlight another area of behavior that many people consider to be governed by a primary drive—maternal behavior. We shall see that psychological research does not support folklore to this effect.

A CLOSER LOOK

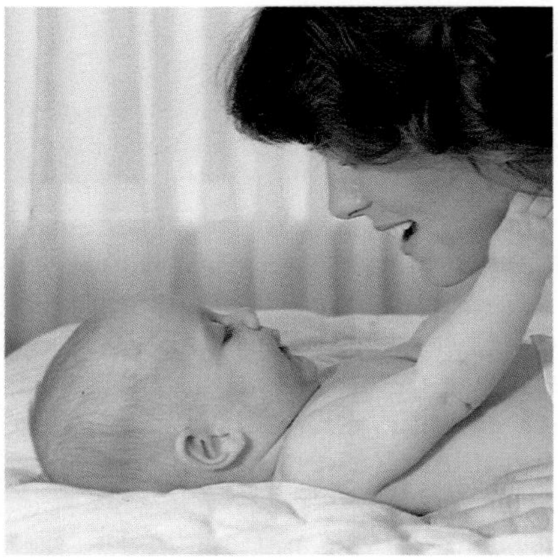

Do Women Make Natural Mothers? Is there a primary maternal drive in people? Is maternal behavior in humans instinctive or learned?

The "Maternal Drive"—Do Women Make Natural Mothers?

It is "common knowledge" that women make natural mothers. Men, on the other hand, are expected to be clumsy at child-rearing tasks such as burping babies, changing diapers, and making faces. Consider the expression, "A mother *knows.*" Somehow a mother is expected to know how to rear children. What are the facts of the matter? *Do* mothers "know"? If so, *how* do they know? Does maternal behavior reflect a primary drive in humans, or is it learned?

The Maternal Drive in Lower Animals In many lower animals, parental behavior is **innate** and governed by hormones. For example, *male* members of some species of fish will guard their young in their mouths at time of danger, at least when under the influence of certain hormones. But when levels of these hormones drop off, their own young will become just another meal if they have not already swum off on their own.

Maternal behavior in rats also appears to be largely under the control of hormones—estrogen, progesterone, and prolactin. Hormones are carried in the bloodstream. When the blood from a rat who has recently given birth is transfused into another female, the second female will also show maternal behaviors (Terkel & Rosenblatt, 1972).

Maternal Behavior among Primates With monkeys, learning plays a more prominent role. At the University of Wisconsin Primate Center, Harry F. Harlow and his colleagues (Harlow & Harlow, 1966; Ruppenthal et al., 1976) reared female rhesus monkeys in isolation. At maturity, the monkeys did not show normal sexual or social behavior patterns. If they bore young, they often showed impatience and lack of interest. This pattern of abuse and neglect was termed the "motherless-mother syndrome." This syndrome suggests that the components of maternal behavior are acquired among primates, and many of them at a tender age.

Gorillas are more advanced primates. Gorilla females reared in captivity often have not had the opportunity to observe adult gorillas behaving in natural social groups. As a consequence, they have to learn how to rear their own offspring by observing others in adulthood, and some have learned by observing human models going through the motions with dolls!

Maternal Behavior among Humans Humans are also primates, the most advanced primates. (We write the textbooks.) With humans, sexual and maternal behaviors must also be learned.

If maternal behaviors are learned, why does child-rearing often seem to come naturally to women but not to men? As noted in Chapter 14, girls are usually given dolls at early ages and are guided into play that prepares them for the child-rearing roles their parents expect them to assume in adulthood. Girls are also expected, more so than boys, to help care for younger siblings and to earn money by babysitting. Given many years of such training, it is not surprising that women seem to take "naturally" to motherhood. If the Chicago Bears had been urged to change siblings' diapers and babysit during adolescence, they, too, might assume maternal behaviors naturally.

Babysitting can be a highly stimulating activity—especially when one does not know what to do. Let us now consider the so-called stimulus motives. We shall see that we tend to require a certain amount of stimulation to feel well and function efficiently, although we may seek this stimulation from very different sources.

STIMULUS MOTIVES

Physical needs give rise to the drives of hunger and thirst. In such cases, organisms are motivated to *reduce* the tension or stimulation that impinges on them. In the case of **stimulus motives,** organisms' goals are to *increase* the amount of stimulation impinging on them. Stimulus motives include sensory stimulation, activity, exploration, and manipulation of the environment.

Stimulus motives, like physiological motives, are generally considered to be innate. People may be motivated to seek the level of stimulation that produces an *optimal level of arousal*—that is, a general level of activity or motivation at which they feel their best and behave most effectively.

Some stimulus motives provide a clear evolutionary advantage. People and lower animals who are motivated to learn about and manipulate the environment are more likely to survive. Learning about the environment increases awareness of resources and of potential dangers, and manipulation permits one to change the environment in beneficial ways. Learning and manipulation increase the chances of survival until sexual maturity and of passing on whatever genetic codes may underlie these motives to future generations.

Stimulus motives Motives to increase the stimulation impinging upon an organism.

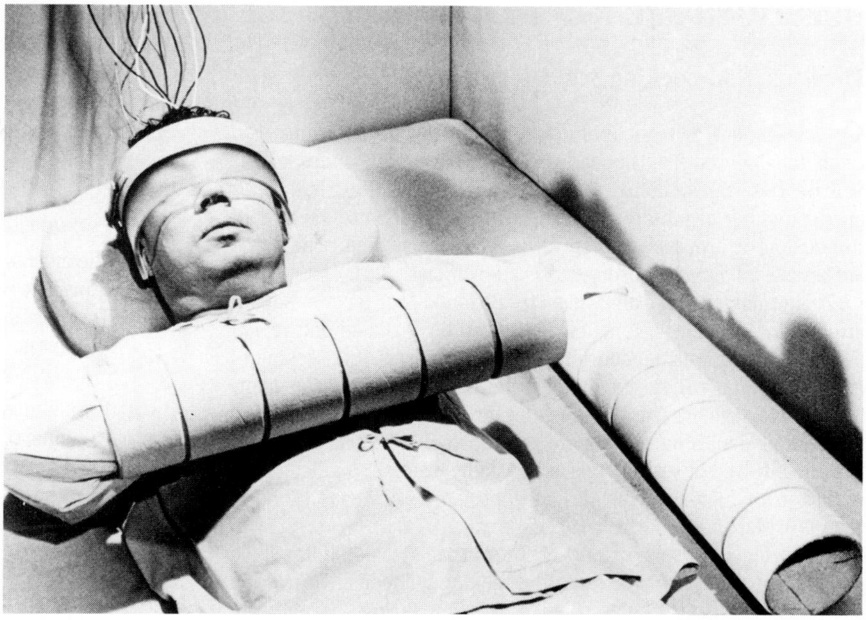

Figure 8.3
A Participant in a Sensory-Deprivation Experiment. He sees, hears, and touches "no evil"—or anything else, for that matter. Experimental conditions such as these do not produce a restful vacation. Instead, volunteers quickly become bored and irritable, and many quit after only a few hours, despite financial incentives. Apparently we have strong motives for sensory stimulation.

Sensory Stimulation and Activity

Sensory deprivation Referring to a research method for systematically decreasing the amount of stimulation that impinges upon sensory receptors.

During the 1950s, some lucky students at McGill University were paid $20 a day (which, with inflation, would be well above $100 today) for doing absolutely nothing. How would you like such "work"? Don't answer too quickly. According to the results of such experiments in **sensory deprivation,** which were run by Bexton, Heron, and Scott (1954), you might find it intolerable.

Student volunteers were placed in isolation booths. In these quiet cubicles, they were blindfolded, their arms were bandaged, and they could hear nothing but the dull, continuous hum of the air conditioning (Figure 8.3). With nothing to do, many students slept for a while. After a few hours of sensory-deprived wakefulness, most students felt bored and irritable. As time went on, they became increasingly uncomfortable. A number of them reported visual hallucinations, usually restricted to simple images of dots and geometric shapes (Zubek, 1973).

Many subjects quit during the first day despite the financial incentive and the desire to contribute to scientific knowledge. Those who remained found it temporarily difficult to concentrate on even the simplest problems after several days of sensory deprivation. All in all, the experimental conditions did not provide a relaxing vacation. Instead, they proved to be a nightmare of boredom and disorientation.

Sky Diving. Why do some people leap into the sky for sport? Do we have innate needs for sensory stimulation and activity? Are we trying to raise our body arousal to more stimulating levels?

Truth or Fiction Revisited

It is *not* true that "getting away from it all" by going on a vacation from all sensory input for a few hours is relaxing. It is more likely to be highly stressful.

Some people seek higher levels of stimulation and activity than others. John is a "couch potato," content to sit by the TV set all evening. Marsha doesn't feel right unless she's out on the tennis court or jogging. Cliff isn't content unless he has ridden his motorcycle over back trails at breakneck speeds, and Janet feels exuberant when she's catching the big wave or diving

QUESTIONNAIRE

The Sensation-Seeking Scale

Are you content to read or watch television all day? Or must you catch the big wave or bounce the bike across the dunes of the Mohave Desert? Psychologist Marvin Zuckerman (1980) has developed a number of sensation-seeking scales that measure the level of stimulation or arousal a person will seek and that predict how well the person will fare in sensory-deprivation studies.

Zuckerman and his colleagues (1978) found four factors that are involved in sensation seeking: (1) seeking of thrill and adventure, (2) disinhibition (that is, tendency to express impulses), (3) seeking of experience, and (4) susceptibility to boredom. Other studies show that people high in sensation seeking are less tolerant of sensory deprivation. Sensation seekers are also more likely to use drugs and become involved in sexual experiences, to be drunk in public, and to volunteer for high-risk activities and unusual experiments (Kohn et al., 1979; Malatesta et al., 1981; Zuckerman, 1974).

A shortened version of one of Zuckerman's scales follows. To gain insight into your own sensation-seeking tendencies, circle the choice, A or B, that best describes you. Then compare your answers to those in the answer key in Appendix B.

1. A. I would like a job that requires a lot of traveling.
   B. I would prefer a job in one location.
2. A. I am invigorated by a brisk, cold day.
   B. I can't wait to get indoors on a cold day.
3. A. I get bored seeing the same old faces.
   B. I like the comfortable familiarity of everyday friends.
4. A. I would prefer living in an ideal society in which everyone is safe, secure, and happy.
   B. I would have preferred living in the unsettled days of our history.
5. A. I sometimes like to do things that are a little frightening.
   B. A sensible person avoids activities that are dangerous.
6. A. I would not like to be hypnotized.
   B. I would like to have the experience of being hypnotized.
7. A. The most important goal in life is to live it to the fullest and experience as much as possible.
   B. The most important goal in life is to find peace and happiness.
8. A. I would like to try parachute-jumping.
   B. I would never want to try jumping out of a plane, with or without a parachute.
9. A. I enter cold water gradually, giving myself time to get used to it.
   B. I like to dive or jump right into the ocean or a cold pool.
10. A. When I go on a vacation, I prefer the change of camping out.
    B. When I go on a vacation, I prefer the comfort of a good room and bed.
11. A. I prefer people who are emotionally expressive even if they are a bit unstable.
    B. I prefer people who are calm and even-tempered.
12. A. A good painting should shock or jolt the senses.
    B. A good painting should give one a feeling of peace and security.
13. A. People who ride motorcycles must have some kind of unconscious need to hurt themselves.
    B. I would like to drive or ride a motorcycle.

---

freefall from an airplane. One's preference for tennis, motorcycling, or skydiving reflects one's geographical location, social class, and learning experiences. But it just may be that the levels of arousal at which we are comfortable would be too high or too low for other people. It also may be that these levels are determined to some degree by innate factors.

Exploration and Manipulation

Have you ever brought a dog or cat into a new home? At first it may show general excitement. New kittens are even known to hide under a couch or bed for a few hours. But then they will begin to explore every corner of the new environment. When placed in novel environments, many animals appear to possess an innate motive to engage in exploratory behavior.

Once they are familiar with the environment, lower animals and people appear to be motivated to seek **novel stimulation.** For example, when they have not been deprived of food for a great deal of time, rats will often explore unfamiliar arms of mazes rather than head straight for the section of the maze in which they have learned to expect food. Animals who have just **copulated** and thereby reduced their sex drives will often show renewed

Novel stimulation (1) An unusual source of arousal or excitement. (2) A hypothesized primary drive to experience new or different stimulation.

Copulate To engage in sexual intercourse.

PSYCHOLOGY GOES TO WORK

Sensation Seeking and Occupational Choice

Sensation seekers desire thrills and adventure, they like to express their impulses, and they are readily bored. What kinds of occupations might be appropriate for sensation seekers? I have listed a few suggestions. Can you think of others?

Actor/actress

Air-traffic controller

Ambulance driver

Bulldozer operator

Commodities broker

Emergency-room physician (nurse, etc.)

Fire fighter

Police officer

Professional athlete (e.g., downhill skier, race-car driver)

Soldier

Taxicab driver

Test pilot (astronaut)

Venture capitalist

interest in sexual behavior when presented with a novel sex partner. Monkeys will learn how to manipulate gadgets for the incentive of being able to observe novel stimulation through a window (see Figure 8.4). Children will spend hour after hour manipulating the controls of video games for no apparent external reward.

The question has arisen whether people and animals seek to explore and manipulate the environment *because* these activities help them reduce primary drives, such as hunger and thirst, or whether they engage in these activities for their own sake. Many psychologists do believe that such stimulating activities are reinforcing in and of themselves. Monkeys do seem to get a kick out of "monkeying around" with gadgets (see Figure 8.5). They learn how to manipulate hooks and eyes and other mechanical devices without any external incentives whatsoever (Harlow et al., 1950). Children engage in prolonged play with "busy boxes"—boxes filled with objects that honk, squeak, rattle, and buzz. They seem to find manipulation of these gadgets pleasurable, even though manipulation does not result in food, ice cream, or even hugs from parents.

The Search for Optimal Arousal

Some drives, such as hunger and thirst, are associated with higher levels of **arousal** within an organism. When we eat or drink to reduce these drives, we are also lowering the associated level of arousal. At other times we act to increase our levels of arousal, as in going to a horror film, engaging in athletic activity, or seeking a new sex partner.

How can we explain the apparently contradictory observations that people and lower animals sometimes act to reduce arousal and other times act to increase arousal? Some psychologists reconcile these differences by suggesting that we are motivated to seek **optimal arousal**—that is, levels of arousal that are optimal for us as individuals at certain times of the day.

Our levels of arousal can vary from quite low (see Figure 8.6), such as when we are sleeping, to quite high, such as when we are frightened or intensely angered. Psychologists also hypothesize that we each have optimal levels of arousal at which we are likely to feel best and function most effectively in various situations. People whose optimal levels of arousal are relatively low may prefer sedentary lives. People whose optimal levels of arousal are high may seek activities such as skydiving and motorcycling, intense

Arousal A general level of activity or motivation in an organism.

Optimal arousal The level of arousal at which we feel and function best.

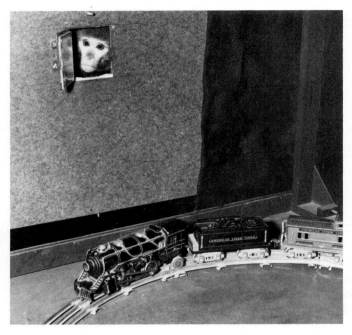

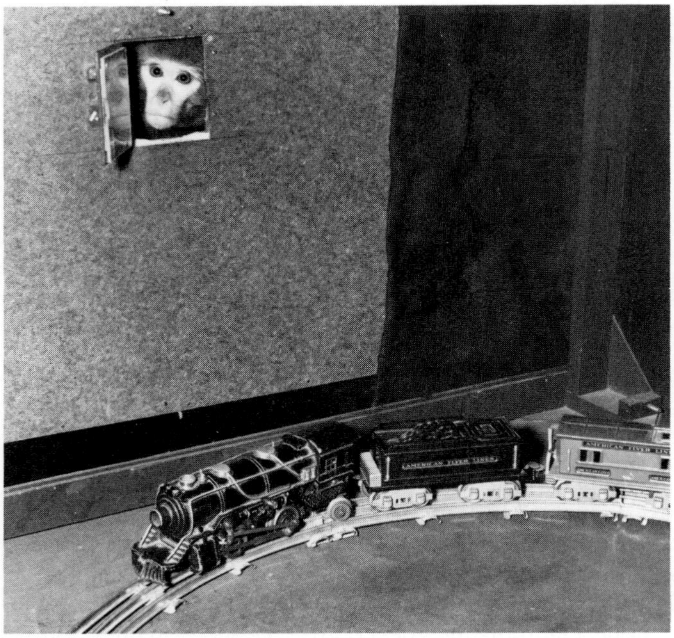

Figure 8.4
The Allure of Novel Stimulation. People and many lower animals are motivated to explore the environment and to seek novel stimulation. This monkey has learned to unlock a door for the privilege of viewing a model train.

Figure 8.5
A Manipulation Drive? These young rhesus monkeys appear to monkey around with gadgets for the sheer pleasure of monkeying around. No external incentives or reinforcements are needed. Children similarly enjoy manipulating gadgets that honk, squeak, rattle, and buzz, even though the resultant honks and squeaks do not satisfy physiological drives such as hunger or thirst.

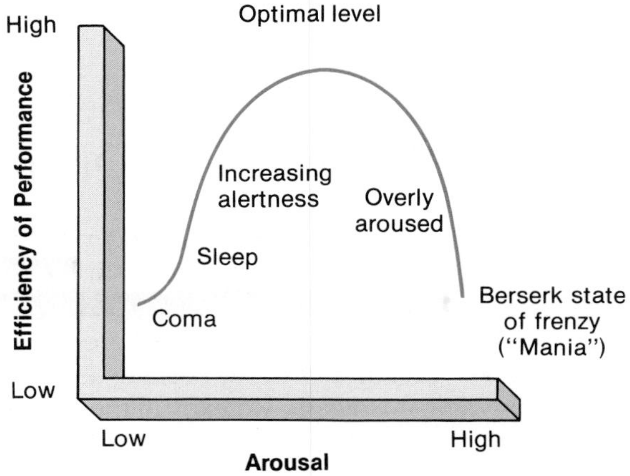

Figure 8.6
Level of Arousal and Efficiency of Performance. Our optimal levels of arousal may differ somewhat, but they tend to lie somewhere in between sleep and a state of panic. People whose optimal levels of arousal are high will seek more stimulation than people whose optimal levels are low.

problem solving (such as a difficult crossword puzzle), or vivid daydreaming. Psychologists Donald Fiske and Salvatore Maddi argue that people behave in ways that increase the impact of stimulation when their levels of arousal are too low and decrease the impact of stimulation when their levels are too high (Maddi, 1980). The types of activity they engage in also depend on such factors as needs for meaningfulness and for variety.

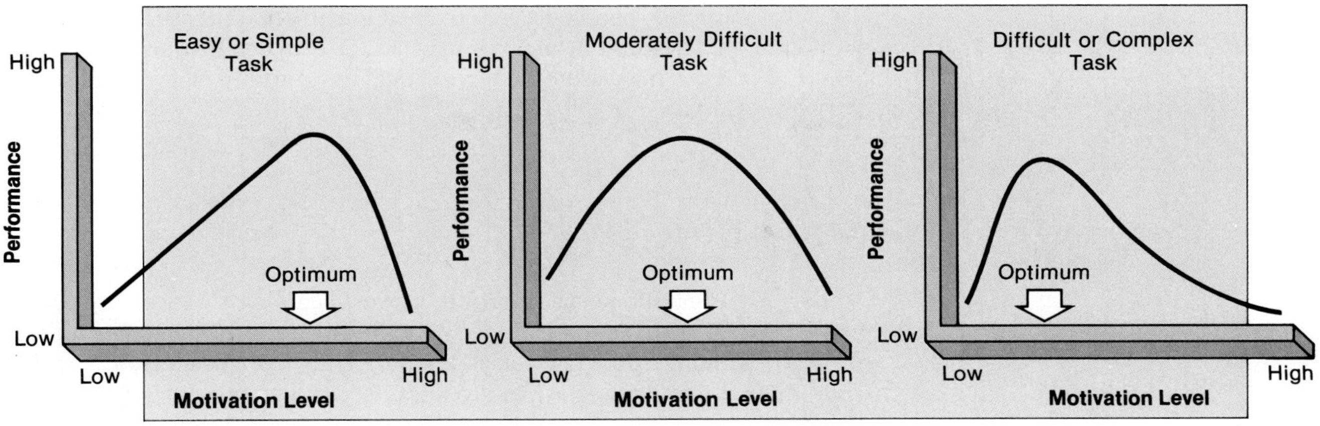

Figure 8.7
The Yerkes-Dodson Law.

A simple task may be facilitated by a high level of arousal or motivation. A highly aroused 118-pound woman is reported to have lifted the front end of a two-ton Cadillac in order to rescue a child. However, a complex task, such as quarterbacking a football team or attempting to solve a math problem, requires attending to many variables at once. For this reason, a complex task is usually carried out more efficiently at a lower level of arousal.

The Yerkes-Dodson Law A former National Football League linebacker was reported to work himself into such a frenzy before a game that other players gave him a wide berth in the locker room. Linebacking is a relatively simple football job, requiring brute strength and something called "desire" more so than does, say, quarterbacking. This particular linebacker was no stronger than many others, but his level of arousal—or desire—helped his team reach the Superbowl on many occasions.

According to the **Yerkes-Dodson law** (see Figure 8.7), a high level of arousal increases performance on a relatively simple task, whether the task is linebacking or solving a series of simple math problems. When a task is complex, it seems to be helpful to keep one's arousal at lower levels. True, there are some complexities to the linebacker's job. Through experience, the linebacker must acquire the capacity to predict, or "read," the play. But the quarterback's job is more complicated. He must call the plays, sometimes change them at the line of scrimmage because of an unexpected defensive realignment, and "keep a cool head" as his receivers try to break into the open and the defenders try to break through the offensive line and tackle him. Similarly, it is worthwhile to try to remain somewhat relaxed on the eve of a demanding (complex) "big test."*

"Cool" linebackers and "hotheaded" quarterbacks don't fare well in the professional ranks. Instead, linebackers must "psych" themselves up, and quarterbacks must "maintain their cool." Some linebackers convince themselves that the players on the opposing team represent the evil in the universe; some quarterbacks approach their job with computerlike level-headedness.

Yerkes-Dodson law The principle that a high level of motivation increases efficiency in the performance of simple tasks, whereas a lower level of motivation permits greater efficiency in the performance of complex tasks.

Truth or Fiction Revisited

It is true that quarterbacks' field performance may suffer if they get too "psyched up" for a big game.

*In later chapters we shall see that our test performance may similarly suffer if we become too aroused. We shall also examine psychological methods for lowering arousal during tests so that we obtain better grades.

What motivates people to get involved in contact sports such as football in the first place? Stimulus motives may be a part of the answer, but learned or social motives may also have a good deal to do with it, as we shall see in the next section.

SOCIAL MOTIVES

Money, achievement, social approval, power, aggression—these are examples of **social motives**. Social motives differ from primary motives in that they are acquired through social learning. But like physiological drives and stimulus motives, social motives arouse us and prompt goal-directed behavior.

Harvard University psychologist Henry Murray (1938) was one of the early researchers into social motives. He referred to social motives as psychological needs and compiled a list of 21 important psychological needs, including needs for achievement, affiliation, aggression, autonomy, dominance, **nurturance,** and understanding. Because we undergo different learning experiences, each of us may develop different levels of these psychological needs or may give them different priorities. Let us now consider some findings concerning the needs for achievement, affiliation, and power and the circumstances that give rise to them.

The Need for Achievement

We all know people who strive persistently to get ahead, to "make it," to earn vast sums of money, to invent, to accomplish the impossible. These people have a high need for achievement, abbreviated ***n* Ach.**

Psychologist David McClelland (1958), also of Harvard University, helped pioneer the assessment of *n* Ach through people's reported fantasies. One assessment method involves use of the **Thematic Apperception Test** (TAT), which was developed by Henry Murray. The TAT contains cards with pictures and drawings that are subject to various interpretations (see Chapter 10). Subjects are shown one or more TAT cards and asked to construct stories about the pictured theme: to indicate what led up to it, what the characters are thinking and feeling, and what is likely to happen.

One TAT card shows a boy with a violin (see Figure 8.8). The picture is somewhat ambiguous: the boy may be staring into space, or his eyes may be almost closed. Consider two stories that could be told about this card:

Story 1: "He's upset that he's got to practice because his instructor is coming by and he hasn't yet learned his lesson for the week. But he'd rather be out playing with the other kids, and he'll probably sneak out to do just that."

Story 2: "He's thinking, 'Someday I'll be the world's greatest violinist. I'll be playing at Lincoln Center and the crowd'll be cheering.' He practices several hours every day."

There are formal standards that enable psychologists to derive *n* Ach scores from stories such as these, but in this case you need not be acquainted with them to see that the second story suggests more achievement motivation than the first. McClelland (1985) has found that motives as measured by the TAT permit the prediction of long-term behavior patterns.

Behavior of Individuals with High *n* Ach Classic studies find that people with high *n* Ach earn higher grades than people of comparable learning ability but low *n* Ach. They are more likely to earn high salaries and be

Social motives Learned or acquired motives.

Nurturance The quality of nourishing, rearing, fostering the development of children, animals, or plants.

***n* Ach** The need for achievement—the need to master, to accomplish difficult things.

Thematic Apperception Test A test devised by Henry Murray to measure needs through fantasy production.

Figure 8.8
Tapping Fantasies in Personality Research. This is a Thematic Apperception Test card that is frequently used to measure the need for achievement. What is happening in this picture? What is the person thinking and feeling? What is going to happen? Your answers to these questions reflect your own needs as well as the content of the picture itself.

promoted than are low-*n*-Ach people with similar opportunities. They perform better at math problems and unscrambling anagrams, such as decoding RSTA into STAR, TARS, ARTS, or RATS.*

McClelland (1965) found that 83 percent of high-*n*-Ach college graduates took positions characterized by risk, decision making, and the chance for great success, such as business management, sales, or businesses of their own making. Seventy percent of the graduates who chose nonentrepreneurial positions showed low *n* Ach. High-*n*-Ach individuals seem to prefer challenges and are willing to take moderate risks to achieve their goals. They see their fate as being in their own hands (McClelland et al., 1953). Workers with higher *n* Ach are also more likely to find satisfaction on the job (Reuman et al., 1984).

A report by industrial psychologist Douglas Bray (1982) finds that factors similar to *n* Ach, including need for advancement and great investment in one's work, are of moderate importance in predicting advancement through the managerial ranks at AT&T. However, two other factors are more important: administrative skills (consisting of organizational ability, decision making, and creativity) and interpersonal skills (leadership, communication ability, and adaptability). *N* Ach is an important element in success, but not the only factor.

Truth or Fiction Revisited

It is *not* true that a strong need to get ahead is the most powerful predictor of success in climbing the corporate ladder. Administrative and interpersonal skills are more important.

Development of *n* Ach Mothers with high *n* Ach tend to encourage their children to think and act independently, whereas low-*n*-Ach mothers tend to be more protective and restrictive. Marion Winterbottom (1958) found that mothers of sons with high *n* Ach made more demands and imposed

*You can count on a psychologist not to miss an opportunity to throw a few rats into his book.

more restrictions on their sons during the early elementary school years than did mothers of sons with low *n* Ach. Even during the preschool years, the mothers of high-*n*-Ach sons demanded that they keep their rooms and possessions neat, that they make their own decisions concerning clothes, that they select their own friends, compete as needed, and undertake difficult tasks and persist at them. But mothers of high-*n*-Ach sons also showed warmth and praised their sons profusely for their accomplishments.

David McClelland and David Pilon (1983) studied *n* Ach among children whose parents' child-rearing practices had been studied 26 to 27 years earlier. It was found that high-*n*-Ach adults were more likely to have had parents who scheduled their feeding as infants (as opposed to allowing feeding on demand) and who were relatively demanding in their toilet-training practices.

In sum, it may be that children who develop high *n* Ach are encouraged to show independence and responsibility at early ages and that their parents respond warmly to their efforts.

The Need for Affiliation

The need for **affiliation,** abbreviated *n* Aff, prompts us to make friends, join groups, and to prefer to do things with others rather than go it alone. *N* Aff contributes to the social glue that creates families and civilizations. In this sense, it is certainly a healthful trait. Yet some people have such strong *n* Aff that they find it painful to make their own decisions or even to be by themselves over extended periods of time. Research by Stanley Schachter suggests that high *n* Aff may indicate anxiety, such as when people "huddle together" in fear of some outside force.

The Schachter Studies on Anxiety and *n* Aff In a classic experiment on the effects of anxiety on *n* Aff, Stanley Schachter (1959) manipulated subjects' anxiety by leading them to believe that they would receive either painful electric shocks (the high-anxiety condition) or mild electric shocks (the low-anxiety condition). Subjects were then asked to wait while the shock apparatus was supposedly being set up. Subjects could choose to wait alone or in a room with others. The majority (63 percent) of subjects who expected a painful shock chose to wait in a room with other people. Only one-third (33 percent) of the subjects who expected a mild shock chose to wait with others.

In a related experiment, Schachter found that "misery loves company," but only company of a special sort. Highly anxious subjects were placed in two social conditions. In the first, they could choose either to wait alone or with other subjects who would also receive painful shocks. Sixty percent of these subjects chose to affiliate—that is, to wait with others. In the second condition, highly anxious subjects could choose to wait alone or with people they believed were not involved with the study. In this second condition, no one chose to affiliate.

Truth or Fiction Revisited

It is true that misery loves company—as long as the company is miserable, too!

Affiliation Association or connection with a group.

PSYCHOLOGY GOES TO WORK

Motivation and Leadership in Business and the Military

For a number of years, Harvard psychologist David McClelland and his colleagues have studied a motivational profile referred to as the *leadership-motive syndrome.* People with this profile show a cluster of needs that includes high needs for power and self-control and low *n* Aff. People high in the leadership-motive syndrome often rise quickly through the military or corporate ranks, assuming that they also have managerial skills. But they also often pay a price.

People with this motivational profile are also at high risk for developing stress-related illnesses, especially when they are under the stress of having their need for power inhibited or frustrated (Fodor, 1984, 1985; McClelland & Jemmott, 1980). On a physiological level, the need for power is often linked to prolonged activity of the sympathetic branch of the autonomic nervous system. Prolonged sympathetic activation can lead to high blood pressure and the breaking down of the body's immune systems (McClelland et al., 1982).

We shall learn more about behavior patterns that lead to stress and illness in Chapter 11. At this point, let us note that David McClelland (1982) suggests that one of contemporary psychology's major achievements has been the development of strategies for coping with this type of behavior. We shall also elaborate on these strategies in Chapter 11.

Why did Schachter's subjects wish to affiliate only with people who shared their misery? Schachter explained their choice through the **theory of social comparison.** This theory holds that in an ambiguous situation—that is, a situation in which we are not certain about what we should do or how we should feel—we will affiliate with people with whom we can compare feelings and behaviors. Schachter's anxious recruits could compare their reactions with those of other "victims," but not with people who had no reason to feel anxious. His highly anxious subjects may also have resented uninvolved people for "getting away free."

The Need for Power

Another social motive is the need for power (*n* Power)—the need to control organizations and other people. High-*n*-Power college students are more likely than others to be members of important committees and to hold prominent offices in student organizations (Beck, 1978). They are more likely than low-*n*-Power individuals to participate in aggressive contact sports and to seek out competitive careers, such as business and—interestingly—psychology.

The need for power has both its positive and negative features, since power can be used either for good or bad purposes. In one recent study, it was found that group leaders with a high need for power may impede group decision making by failing to promote full discussion of all the facts concerning a business situation and by not encouraging full consideration of members' proposals (Fodor & Smith, 1982).

McClelland and Pilon (1983) found that high-*n*-Power adults were more likely than low-*n*-Power adults to have had parents who were permissive toward their children's sexual and aggressive behavior. That is, they were more likely to permit their children to masturbate, to engage in sex play, and to show aggression to their siblings and their parents. Perhaps allowing children to exercise power (to control themselves and others) at an early age encourages them to continue to exercise power as they develop.

Theory of social comparison The view that people look to others for cues about how to behave when they are in confusing or unfamiliar situations.

Table 8.1
Components of Three Common Emotions

Emotion	Components		
	Physiological	Situational	Cognitive
Fear	Sympathetic arousal	Environmental threat	Belief in danger, desire to avoid
Anger	Sympathetic and parasympathetic arousal	Frustration or provocation	Desire to hurt provocateur
Depression	Parasympathetic arousal	Loss, failure, or inactivity	Thoughts of helplessness, worthlessness

Emotions have physiological, situational, and cognitive components.

EMOTION

Emotions color our lives. We are green with envy, red with anger, blue with sorrow. The poets paint a thoughtful mood as a brown study. Positive emotions such as love and desire can fill our days with pleasure, but negative emotions such as fear, depression, and anger can fill us with dread and make each day a chore.

An emotion can at once be a response to a situation (in the way that fear is a response to a threat) and have motivating properties (in the way that anger can motivate us to act aggressively). An emotion can also be a goal in itself. We may behave in ways that will lead us to experience joy or feelings of love.

An **emotion** is a state of feeling that can have physiological, situational, and cognitive components. Although no two people experience emotions in exactly the same way, it is possible to make some generalizations. Fear, for example, involves predominantly **sympathetic** arousal (rapid heartbeat and breathing, sweating, muscle tension), the perception of a threat, and beliefs to the effect that one is in danger (see Table 8.1). Anger may involve both sympathetic and **parasympathetic** arousal (Funkenstein, 1955), a frustrating or provocative situation (such as an insult), and belief that the provocateur ought to be paid back. Depression usually involves predominantly parasympathetic arousal; a situational component of loss, failure, or inactivity; and cognitions of helplessness and worthlessness. Joy, grief, jealousy, disgust, embarrassment, liking—all have physiological, situational, and cognitive components. Generally speaking, the greater the autonomic arousal, the more intense the emotion (Chwalisz et al., 1988).

Let us now consider whether knowledge of emotional responses can be used to detect lies.

Emotion A state of feeling that has physiological, situational, and cognitive components.

Sympathetic Of the sympathetic division of the autonomic nervous system.

Parasympathetic Of the parasympathetic division of the autonomic nervous system.

A CLOSER LOOK

"Lie Detectors"

"Lie detectors" are monitoring devices that are presented as being capable of distinguishing truth from lies. Their usage highlights the theoretical link between autonomic arousal and emotion, but as we shall see, their validity has been questioned.

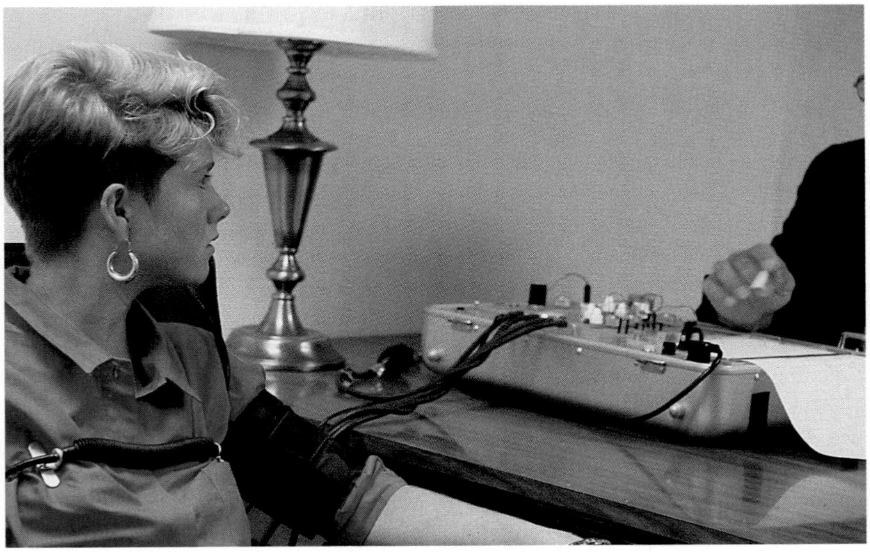

Figure 8.9
What Do "Lie Detectors" Detect? The polygraph monitors heart rate, blood pressure, respiration rate, and sweat in the palms of the hands. Is the polygraph sensitive to lying only? Is it foolproof? Because of the controversy surrounding these questions, many courts no longer admit polygraph evidence.

The use of devices to sort out truth from lies actually has a lengthy, if not laudable, history. As told by Benjamin Kleinmuntz and Julian Szucko (1984, pp. 766–767),

> *The Bedouins of Arabia . . . until quite recently required conflicting witnesses to lick a hot iron; the one whose tongue was burned was thought to be lying. The Chinese, it is said, had a similar method for detecting lying: Suspects were forced to chew rice powder and spit it out; if the powder was dry, the suspect was guilty. A variation of this test was used during the Inquisition. The suspect had to swallow a "trial slice" of bread and cheese; if it stuck to the suspect's palate or throat he or she was not telling the truth.*

These methods may sound primitive, even bizarre, but they are consistent with modern knowledge. Anxiety concerning being caught in a lie is linked to sympathetic arousal, and one sign of sympathetic arousal is lack of saliva, or dryness in the mouth. The emotions of fear and guilt are also linked to sympathetic arousal and, hence, dryness in the mouth.

Modern-day lie detectors, or polygraphs (see Figure 8.9), monitor four indicators of sympathetic arousal while a witness or suspect is being examined: heart rate, blood pressure, respiration rate, and electrodermal response. However, many questions have been raised about the use of the polygraph, especially because it is frequently used in the hiring process in industry and in helping to establish guilt or innocence in the courtroom.

Supporters of the polygraph claim that the device is accurate in more than 90 percent of cases (Podlesny & Raskin, 1977), but conflicting research suggests that polygraphs do not approach this high accuracy rate and that they are sensitive to more than lies (Kleinmuntz & Szucko, 1984; Lykken, 1981; Saxe et al., 1985; U.S. Congress, 1983). In one experiment, subjects were able to reduce the accuracy rate to 25 percent by thinking about exciting or disturbing events during the interview (Smith, 1971). In other studies, subjects have been yet more successful at poking holes in the accuracy rate. They dropped it to about 50 percent by biting their tongues (to produce pain) or pressing their toes against the floor (to tense muscles) while being interviewed (Honts et al., 1985).

Truth or Fiction Revisited

It is true that you may be able to fool a lie detector by squiggling your toes.

In a review of the literature, the government Office of Technology Assessment (OTA) found that there was little or no valid research into the use of the polygraph in preemployment screening, wide-scale "dragnet" investigations (attempts to ferret out the guilty from a large number of subjects), or screening before individuals were given access to classified information (U.S. Congress, 1983). OTA also looked into studies involving investigations of specific indictments. The studies' conclusions varied widely. In 28 studies judged to have adequate methodology, accurate detections of guilt ranged from 35 to 100 percent. Accurate judgments of innocence ranged from 12.5 to 94 percent.

As noted by Leonard Saxe and his colleagues at Boston University (1985), the fact of the matter is that "there is no such thing as a lie detector per se, [but] a number of approaches have been developed that are based on physiological measurement" (p. 355). Because of validity problems, results of polygraph examinations are no longer admitted as evidence in many courtrooms. Polygraph interviews are still often conducted in criminal investigations and in job interviews, but these practices are being questioned as well.

Emotional Development

Now that we have pondered the components of emotions and their physiological assessment, let us consider where they come from. In this section we explore two theories concerning the developmental origins of emotions.

The first, proposed originally by Katherine Bridges (1932), holds that we are born with a single emotion and that other emotions become differentiated as time passes. The second, proposed by Carroll Izard, holds that all emotions are present and adequately differentiated at birth. However, they are not shown all at once. Instead, they emerge in response to the child's developing needs and maturational sequences.

Bridges' and Sroufe's Theory On the basis of her observations of babies, Bridges proposed that newborns experience one emotion—diffuse excitement. By 3 months, two other emotions have differentiated from this general state of excitement—a negative emotion (distress) and a positive emotion (delight). By 6 months, fear, disgust, and anger will have developed from distress. By 12 months elation and affection will have differentiated from delight. Jealousy develops from distress, and joy develops from delight—both during the second year.

Alan Sroufe (1979) has advanced Bridges' theory, focusing on the ways in which cognitive development may provide the basis for emotional development. Jealousy, for example, can not become differentiated without some understanding of the concept of possession. Anger usually results from situations in which our intentions are thwarted. For example, 7-month-old infants show anger when a biscuit is almost placed in their mouths and then removed (Stenberg et al., 1983). It may be that the development of concepts of intentionality (that is, the idea that people can do things "on purpose") and of rudimentary causality (the ability to perceive other people as the causes of frustration) precede the differentiation of anger.

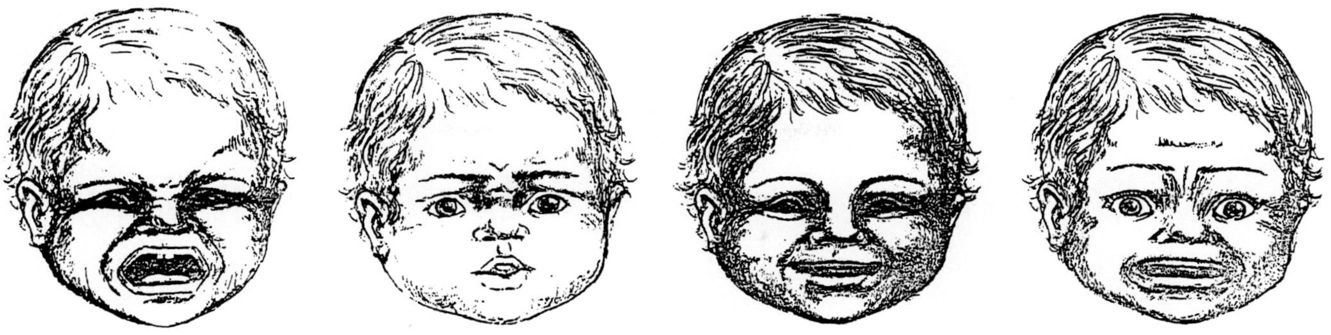

Figure 8.10
Do 1- and 2-Month-Old Infants Show Discrete Emotions? Or Are Emotions More Diffuse among Infants?

Drawings of the facial expressions of infants, as used in Izard's research.

Sroufe also links development of fear of strangers to the perceptual-cognitive capacity to discriminate the faces of familiar people from those of unfamiliar people.

Izard's Theory Carroll Izard (1978, 1979, 1982) proposes that infants are born with discrete emotional states. However, the timing of their appearance is linked to the child's cognitive development and social experiences. For example, in one study, Izard and his colleagues (1983) claim that 2-month-old babies receiving inoculations showed distress, whereas older infants showed anger.

Izard's view may sound very similar to Sroufe's. After all, both researchers are suggesting that there is an orderly unfolding of emotions such that they become more specific as time passes. In keeping with Izard's view, however, other researchers have found that a number of different emotions appear to be shown by infants at ages earlier than those suggested by Bridges and Sroufe. In one study of the emotions shown by babies during their first three months, 99 percent of the mothers interviewed reported that their babies showed the emotion of interest. Ninety-five percent of mothers reported joy; 84 percent, anger; 74 percent, surprise; and 58 percent, fear (Johnson et al., 1982). These figures are based on mothers' reports, and it is possible that the infants were actually showing more diffuse emotions (Murphy, 1983). Perhaps the mothers were "reading" specific emotions "into" the babies based on their own knowledge of appropriate (adult) emotional reactions to the infants' situations. This is a problem that extends to Izard's interpretations of infants' facial expressions.

Izard (1979) claims to have found many discrete emotions at the age of 1 month by using his Maximally Discriminative Facial Movement Scoring System. Figure 8.10 shows some of the infant facial expressions that Izard believes are associated with the basic emotions of anger-rage, disgust, enjoyment-joy, fear-terror, interest-excitement, and sadness-dejection. However, Joseph Campos and his colleagues (1983) suggest that this type of research is fraught with problems. First, these facial expressions seem to be fleeting in young infants, if they are drawn accurately at all. Second, we cannot know the exact relationship between a facial expression and an infant's inner feelings, which of course, are ultimately private events. In other words, even if the drawings accurately represent young infants' facial expressions, we cannot be certain that they express the specific emotions they would suggest in older children and adults.

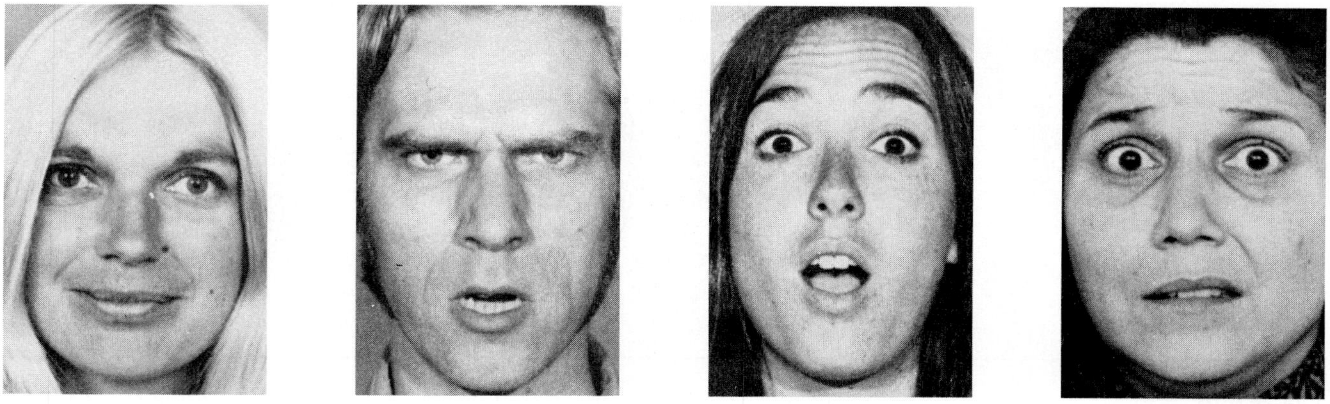

Figure 8.11
The Universality of the Expression of Emotions.

Ekman's research suggests that there are several basic emotions (including those shown in these photographs) whose expression is recognized around the world. These include happiness, anger, surprise, and fear.

In sum, researchers seem to agree that a handful of emotions are shown by infants during the first few months. They agree that other emotions develop in an orderly manner. They agree that emotional development is linked to cognitive development and social experience. They do not agree on exactly when specific emotions are first shown or on whether discrete emotions are present at birth.

Expression of Emotions

Joy and sadness are found in diverse cultures around the world, but how can we tell when other people are happy or despondent? It turns out that the expression of many emotions is also universal (Rinn, 1984). Smiling, for instance, appears to be a universal sign of friendliness and approval (Ekman & Oster, 1979). Baring the teeth, as noted by Charles Darwin (1872) in the last century, may be a universal sign of anger. As the originator of the modern theory of evolution, Darwin believed that the universal recognition of facial expressions would have survival value. For example, facial expressions could signal the approach of enemies even in the absence of language.

Research by psychologist Paul Ekman and his colleagues also supports the universality of the facial expression of emotions. In one study, Ekman (1980) took a number of photographs of people posing the emotions of anger, disgust, fear, happiness, sadness, and surprise, similar to those shown in Figure 8.11, and asked subjects throughout the world to indicate what emotions they depicted. Subjects ranged from European college students to the Fore, an isolated tribe who dwell in the highlands of New Guinea. All groups, including the Fore, who had almost no contact with Western culture, correctly identified the emotions being portrayed. Moreover, even the Fore displayed familiar facial expressions when asked how they would respond if they were the characters in stories that called for basic emotional responses. Ekman and his colleagues (1987) obtained similar results in a study of ten cultures in which subjects were permitted to report that multiple emotions were shown by facial expressions. The subjects generally agreed on which two emotions were being shown and which emotion was most intense.

The Facial-Feedback Hypothesis

We recognize that emotional states are *reflected* by facial expressions, but the **facial-feedback hypothesis** argues that the causal relationship between emotions and facial expressions can also work in the opposite direction. Inducing experimental subjects to smile, for example, leads them to report more positive feelings (Kleinke & Walton, 1982; McCanne & Anderson, 1987) and to rate cartoons as being more humorous (Laird, 1974, 1984). When subjects are induced to frown, they rate cartoons as being more aggressive (Laird, 1974, 1984). When subjects pose expressions of pain, they rate electric shocks as being more painful (Colby et al., 1977; Lanzetta et al., 1976).

Modern-day findings are reminiscent of the observations made by Charles Darwin more than a hundred years ago: "The free expression by outward signs of an emotion intensifies it. On the other hand, the repression, as far as possible, of all outward signs softens our emotions" (Darwin, 1872, p. 22).

What are the possible links between facial feedback and emotion? One link is arousal. Intense contraction of facial muscles, such as those used in signifying fear, heightens arousal (Zuckerman et al., 1981). Our perception of heightened arousal then leads to self-report of heightened emotional activity. Other links may involve changes in brain temperature and the release of neurotransmitters (Ekman, 1985; Zajonc, 1985). Kinesthetic feedback of the contraction of facial muscles may also induce us to perceive heightened emotional activation (McCaul et al., 1982).

Critics of the research on the facial-feedback hypothesis have argued that experimenters have not controlled for subjects' expectation. For example, a subject who is asked to smile is more likely to focus on positive feelings, and vice versa. With this methodological problem in mind, Strack and his colleagues (1988) asked subjects to hold pens in their mouths in certain ways, rather than smile or frown. The method of holding the pen facilitated or inhibited muscles involved in smiling without subject awareness of the purpose of the study. Subjects who held the pens in such a way as to facilitate smiling rated cartoons as being more humorous than subjects who held the pens in the other way. In yet another approach, McCanne and Anderson (1987) suppressed facial response and, as one consequence, decreased subjects' enjoyment of an experimental task. But the researchers admit that the lessened enjoyment might have resulted from distraction from the tasks at hand and not from the suppression of facial muscle activity itself. A reviewer of research on the facial-feedback hypothesis recently analyzed a large body of research and concluded that the effects of modifying facial behavior on self-reported emotional response are small to moderate at best (Matsumoto, 1987).

You may have heard the British expression "to keep a stiff upper lip" as a recommended way of handling stress. It might be that a "stiff" lip suppresses emotional response—as long as the lip is relaxed rather than quivering with fear or tension. But when a lip is stiffened through strong muscle tension, facial feedback may heighten autonomic activity and the perception of emotional response. In the following section, we shall see that the facial feedback-hypothesis is related to the James-Lange theory of emotion.

THEORIES OF EMOTION

Facial-feedback hypothesis The view that stereotypical facial expressions can contribute to stereotypical emotions.

Emotions have physiological, situational, and cognitive components, but psychologists have disagreed about how these components interact to produce feeling states and actions. Some psychologists argue that physiological arousal is a more basic component of emotional response than cognition and that the type of arousal we experience strongly influences our cognitive appraisal and our labeling of the emotion (e.g., Izard, 1984; Zajonc, 1984). Other psychologists argue that cognitive appraisal and physiological arousal are so strongly intertwined that cognitive processes may determine the emotional response (e.g., Lazarus, 1984).

The so-called commonsense theory of emotions is that something happens (situation) that is cognitively appraised (interpreted) by the person and the feeling state (a combination of arousal and thoughts) follows. For example, you meet someone new, appraise that person as being delightful, and feelings of attraction follow. Or you flunk a test, recognize that you're in trouble, and feel down in the dumps.

However, historic and contemporary theories of how the components of emotions interact are at variance with the commonsense view. Let us consider a number of more important theories and see if we can arrive at some useful conclusions.

The James-Lange Theory

Just before the turn of the century, William James suggested that our emotions follow, rather than cause, our overt behavioral responses to events. This view was also proposed by a contemporary of James's, the Danish physiologist Karl G. Lange. For this reason, it is referred to as the James-Lange theory of emotion.

According to James and Lange (see Figure 8.12, part A), certain external stimuli instinctively trigger specific patterns of arousal and action, such as fighting or fleeing. We then become angry *because* we act aggressively. We then become afraid *because* we run away. Emotions are simply the cognitive representations (or by-products) of automatic physiological and behavioral responses.

Walter Cannon (1927) criticized the James-Lange assertion that each emotion has distinct physiological correlates. Cannon argued that the physiological arousal that accompanies emotion A is not as distinct from the arousal that accompanies emotion B as the theory asserts. We can also note that the James-Lange view ascribes a very meager function to human cognition; it denies the roles of cognitive appraisal, personal values, and personal choice.

On the other hand, the James-Lange theory suggests that we can sometimes change our feelings by changing our behavior. In Chapter 12, we shall see how this hypothesis has led to innovative ways of helping people who are depressed.

The Cannon-Bard Theory

Walter Cannon was not content to criticize the James-Lange theory. He (Cannon, 1927) and Philip Bard (1934) suggested that an event would trigger bodily responses (arousal and action) and the experience of an emotion simultaneously. As shown in Figure 8.12 (part B), when an event is perceived (processed by the brain), the brain stimulates autonomic and muscular activity (arousal and action) *and* cognitive activity (experience of the emotion). According to the Cannon-Bard theory, emotions *accompany* bodily responses. Emotions are not *produced by* bodily changes, as in the James-Lange theory.

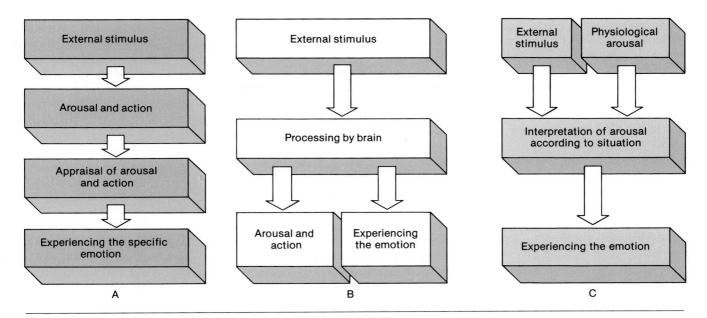

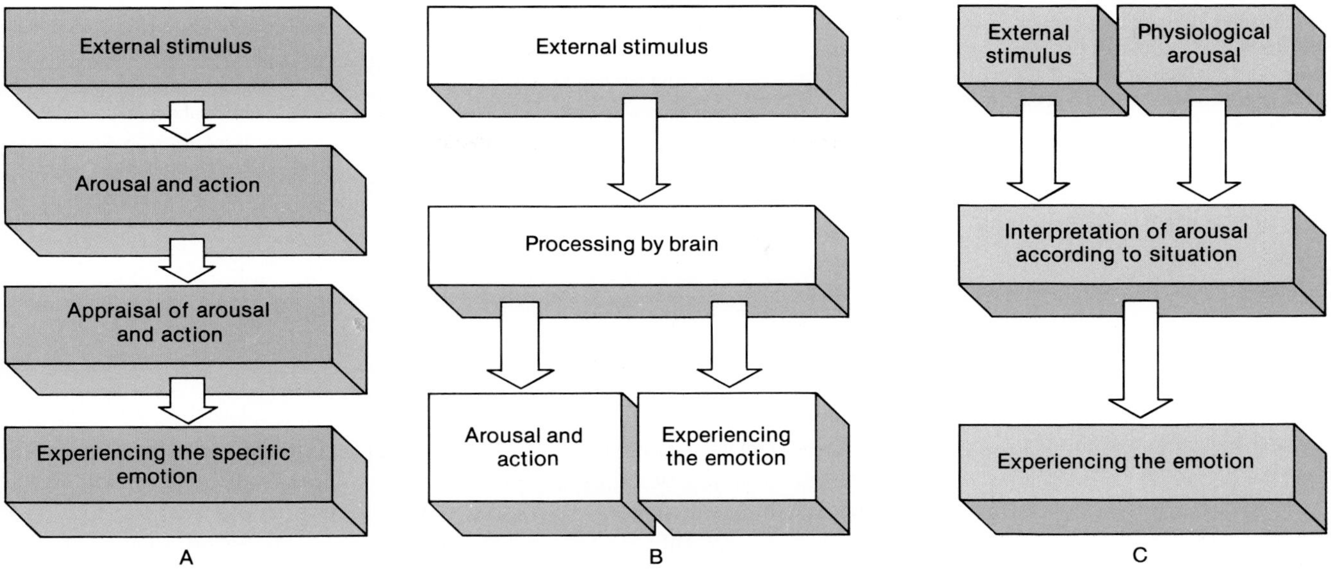

Figure 8.12
What Are the Major Theories of Emotion?

Several theories of emotion have been advanced, each of which proposes a different role for the components of emotional response. According to the James-Lange theory (part A), events trigger specific arousal patterns and actions. Emotions result from our appraisal of our body responses. According to the Cannon-Bard theory (part B), events are first processed by the brain. Body patterns of arousal, action, and our emotional responses are then triggered simultaneously. According to the theory of cognitive appraisal (part C), events and arousal are appraised by the individual. The emotional response stems from the person's appraisal of the situation and his or her level of arousal.

The central criticism of the Cannon-Bard theory focuses on whether bodily responses (arousal and action) and emotions are actually stimulated simultaneously. For example, pain or the perception of danger may trigger arousal before we begin to feel distress or fear. Also, many of us have had the experience of having a "narrow escape" and then becoming aroused and shaky afterward, when we have finally had time to consider the damage that might have occurred.

What is needed is a theory that allows for an ongoing interaction of external events, physiological changes (such as autonomic arousal and muscular activity), and cognitive activities. We do not need to be overly concerned with which comes first—the chicken, the egg, or the egg salad.

The Theory of Cognitive Appraisal

According to Stanley Schachter (1971) and a number of other psychologists, emotions have generally similar patterns of bodily arousal. The essential way in which they vary is along a weak-strong dimension that is determined by one's level of arousal. The label we *attribute* to an emotion largely depends on our cognitive appraisal of our situation. Cognitive appraisal is based on many factors, including our perception of external events and the ways in which other people seem to respond to those events (see Figure 8.12, part C). Given the presence of other people, we engage in *social comparison* (see p. 321) to arrive at an appropriate response.

Table 8.2
Injected Substances and Cognitive Manipulations in the Schachter-Singer Study

Group	Substance	Cognitive Manipulation
1	Adrenaline	No information given about effects
2	Adrenaline	Misinformation given: itching, numbness, etc.
3	Adrenaline	Accurate information: physiological arousal
4	(Inactive)	None

Source: Schachter & Singer, 1962.

In a classic experiment, Schachter and Jerome Singer (1962) showed that arousal can be labeled quite differently, depending on a person's situation. The investigators told subjects that their purpose was to study the effects of a vitamin on vision. Half of the subjects received an injection of adrenaline, a hormone that increases autonomic arousal (see Chapter 2). A control group received an injection of an inactive solution. Subjects given adrenaline then received one of three "cognitive manipulations," as shown in Table 8.2. Group 1 was told nothing about possible emotional effects of the "vitamin." Group 2 was deliberately misinformed; group members were led to expect itching, numbness, or other irrelevant symptoms. Group 3 was informed accurately about the increased arousal they would experience.

After receiving injections and cognitive manipulations, subjects were asked to wait, in pairs, while the experimental apparatus was being set up. Subjects did not know that the person with whom they were waiting was a confederate of the experimenter. The confederates's purpose was to model a response that the subject would believe resulted from the injection.

Some subjects waited with a confederate who acted in a happy-go-lucky manner. He flew paper airplanes about the room and tossed paper balls into a wastebasket. Other subjects waited with a confederate who acted angry, complaining about the experiment, tearing up a questionnaire, and departing the waiting room in a huff. As the confederates worked for their Oscars, real subjects were observed through a one-way mirror.

Subjects in groups 1 and 2 were likely to imitate the behavior of the confederate. Those exposed to the **euphoric** confederate acted jovial and content. Those exposed to the angry confederate imitated that person's complaining, aggressive ways. But groups 3 and 4 were less influenced by the confederate's behavior.

Schachter and Singer concluded that groups 1 and 2 were in an ambiguous situation. The subjects felt arousal from the adrenaline injection but had no basis for attributing it to any event or emotion. Social comparison with the confederate led them to attribute their arousal either to happiness or to anger, whichever was displayed by the confederate. Group 3 expected arousal from the injection with no particular emotional consequences. These subjects did not imitate the confederate's display of happiness or anger because they were not in an ambiguous situation. Group 4 had no physiological arousal for which they needed an attribution, except perhaps for some induced by observing the confederate. Group 4 subjects also failed to imitate the confederate.

Now, happiness and anger are quite different emotions. Happiness is a positive emotion, and anger, for most of us, is a negative emotion. Yet Schachter and Singer suggest that any physiological differences between these two emotions are so slight that opposing cognitive appraisals of the same situation can lead one person to label arousal as happiness and another person to

Euphoric Characterized by feelings of well-being, elation.

label arousal as anger. A supportive experiment suggests that it is similarly possible for people to confuse feelings of fear with feelings of sexual attraction (Dutton & Aron, 1974).

The Schachter-Singer view could not be farther removed from the James-Lange theory, which holds that each emotion has specific and readily recognized body sensations. The truth, it turns out, may lie somewhere in between.

In science it must be possible to attain identical or similar results when experiments are replicated. The Schachter and Singer study has been replicated with *different* results. For instance, in studies by Rogers and Deckner (1975) and Maslach (1978), subjects were less likely to imitate the behavior of the confederate and were more likely to apply negative emotional labels to their arousal, even when exposed to a euphoric confederate.

Evaluation

What do we make of all this? As noted at the outset of our discussion of emotion, emotional responses are activated by physiological, situational, and cognitive factors. Recent research by Paul Ekman and his colleagues (1983) suggests that the patterns of arousal that lead us to believe we are experiencing certain emotions may be more specific than suggested by Schachter and Singer but less specific than suggested by James and Lange. In any event, there are some reasonably distinct patterns of arousal, and these patterns are not fully exchangeable—although we may be confused about our feelings when patterns of arousal rise up in apparently inappropriate situations. This occurs because our situations, and our cognitive appraisals of our situations, are also influential in activating our emotional responses. And when our situations are ambiguous, we may be somewhat more likely to interpret them by social comparison.

In sum, there may be no reason to insist that any particular component of an experience—physiological, situational, or cognitive—is more crucial than others in activating emotional response. Perhaps the most important thing to note is that people are thinking beings who gather information from all three sources in determining their behavioral responses and in pinpointing labels for their emotional responses. The fact that none of the theories we have discussed applies to all people in all situations is comforting. Our emotions are not quite as easily understood or manipulated as theorists have suggested.

Romantic Love. Love is a complex concept, involving many areas of experience—emotional, cognitive, and motivational. Romantic love is an intense, positive emotion that involves sexual attraction, a cultural setting that idealizes love, caring, and the *belief* that one is "in love."

THAT MOST FASCINATING EMOTION: LOVE

Psychological theory and research has expanded our knowledge of emotions, including our knowledge of that deeply stirring emotion, love.

Love is the ideal for which we will make great sacrifice, the emotion that launched a thousand ships in the Greek epic *The Iliad.* For thousands of years, poets have sought to capture love in words. An 18th century poet wrote that his love was like "a red, red rose." In Sinclair Lewis's novel *Elmer Gantry,* love is "the morning and the evening star." Love is beautiful and elusive. Passionate or romantic love can also be earthy and sexy, involving a solid dose of sexual desire.

Psychologists find love to be a complex concept, involving many areas of experience—emotional, cognitive, and motivational (Sternberg & Grajek, 1984). Definitions of romantic love vary. Psychoanalysts generally speak in

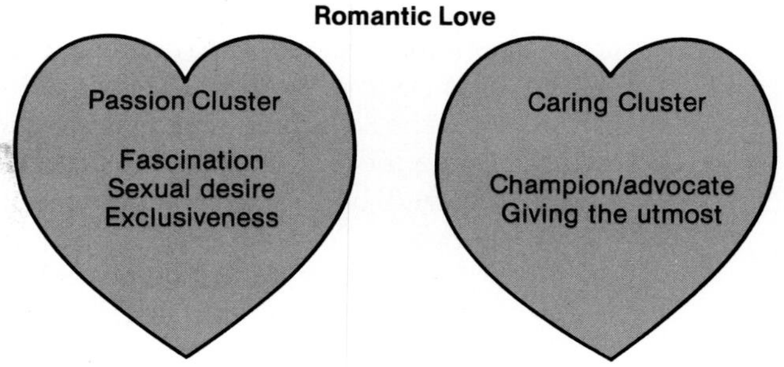

Figure 8.13
Passion and Caring. Romantic love is characterized by two clusters of feelings—a passion cluster and a caring cluster.

terms of global concepts, such as Erich Fromm's "craving for complete fusion . . . with one other person. [Love] is by its very nature exclusive" (1956, p. 44). Erik Erikson also sees love as the merging of two identities. To Erikson, mature love is possible only after one has established ego identity (see Chapter 9).

Other psychologists have avoided unmeasurable concepts like the merging or fusion of identities and define romantic love in terms of the behavior of lovers. According to psychologist Keith Davis (1985), romantic love is characterized by two clusters of behavior patterns: a passion cluster and a caring cluster (see Figure 8.13). The passion cluster contains feelings of fascination, as shown by preoccupation with the loved one; sexual arousal or desire; and the desire for exclusiveness (a special relationship with the loved one). The caring cluster includes championing the interests of the loved one and giving one's utmost to or for the loved one, including sacrificing one's own interests, if necessary. College undergraduates see the desire to help or care for the loved one as being more central to the concept of love than concern about how the loved one can meet one's own needs (Steck et al., 1982). Romantic lovers also idealize one another (Driscoll et al., 1972). They magnify each other's positive features and overlook each other's flaws.

Social psychologists Ellen Berscheid and Elaine Hatfield (Berscheid & Walster, 1978; Walster & Walster, 1978) define love in terms of physiological response and cognitive appraisal of that response. Love, to them, involves intense arousal and some reason to label that arousal love.

Let us define **romantic love** as an intense, positive emotion that involves (1) arousal in the form of sexual attraction; (2) a cultural setting that idealizes love; (3) the actual or fantasized presence of a person considered to be attractive; (4) caring; and (5) the *belief* that one is "in love."

Romantic Love in Contemporary Western Culture: A Role-Playing Approach

To experience romantic love, in contrast to attachment or sexual arousal, one must be exposed to a culture that idealizes the concept. In Western culture, romantic love blossoms within the fairy tales about Sleeping Beauty, Cinderella, Snow White, and all their princes charming. It matures with romantic novels, television tales and films, and the personal tales of friends and relatives about dates and romances (Udry, 1971).

Truth or Fiction Revisited

It is *not* true that romantic love is found in every culture in the world. It is found only in cultures that idealize the concept.

Romantic love An intense, positive emotion that involves sexual attraction, feelings of caring, and the belief that one is in love.

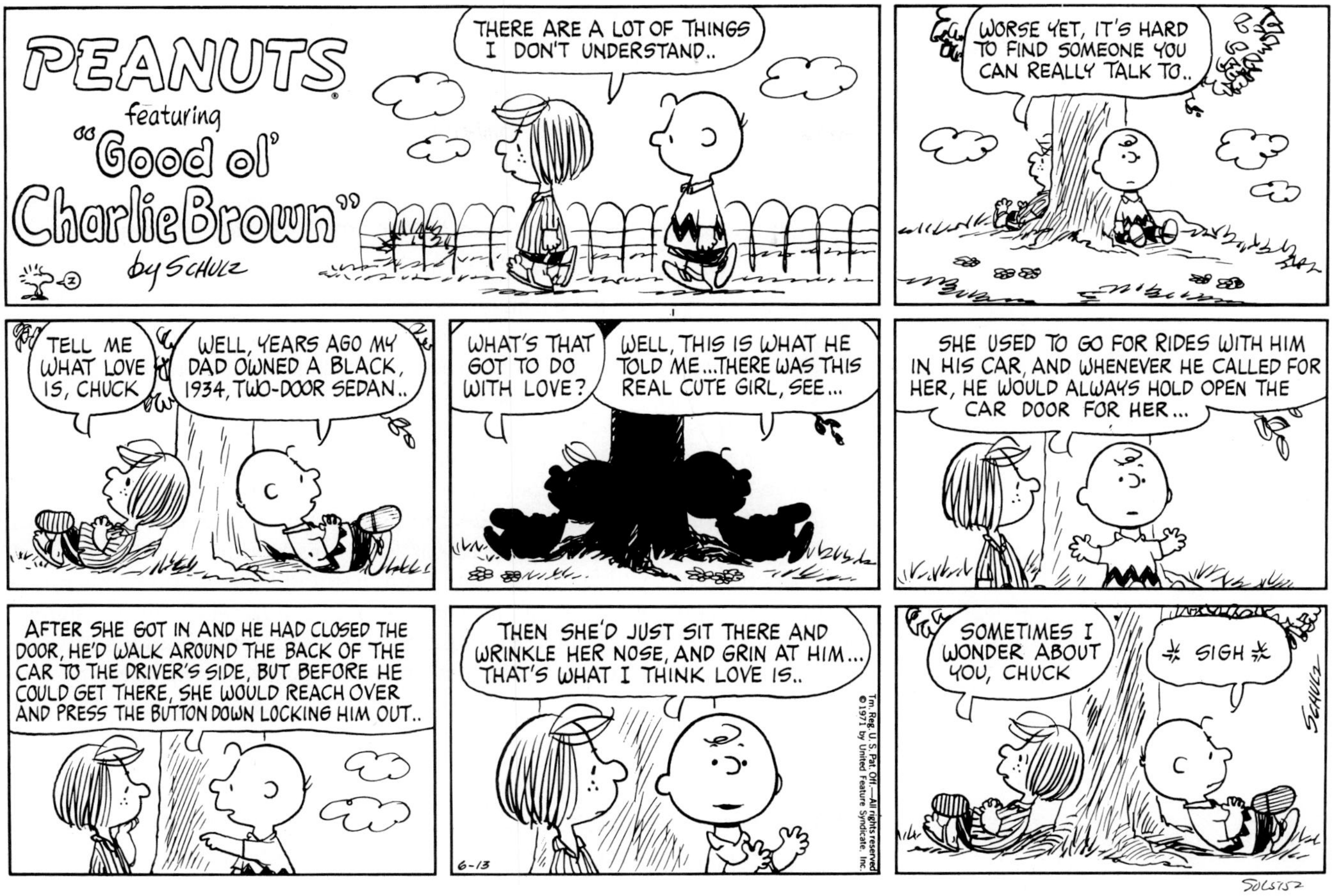

Romantic love may not reflect any natural inner state. A person must have experience with a culture that idealizes the concept of love in order to successfully play the role of a person who is "in love." This does not mean that we are being phony when we enact the role of someone in love—any more than subjects of hypnosis are necessarily being phony when they behave as though they are in a trance. It simply means that we require a clear concept of what a behavior pattern is supposed to be like before we can enact it.

Styles of Love

Psychologists also speak of different "styles" of love. For example, Clyde and Susan Hendrick (1986) of Texas Tech University developed a love-attitude scale that suggests the existence of six styles of love among college students. Following is a list of the styles, with items that identify the style and are similar to the actual items on the love-attitude scale:

1. **Eros,** or romantic love. "My lover fits my ideal," "My lover and I were attracted to one another immediately."
2. **Ludus,** or game-playing love. "I keep my lover up in the air about my commitment," "I get over love affairs pretty easily."

Eros The Greek term for sexual, or romantic, love.

Ludus (LOO-dus). Game-playing love. (A Latin word meaning a "play" or "game.")

3. **Storge,** or friendship-love. "The best love grows out of an enduring friendship."
4. **Pragma**—pragmatic or logical love. "I consider a lover's potential in life before committing myself," "I consider whether my lover will be a good parent."
5. **Mania,** or possessive, excited love. "I get so excited about my love that I cannot sleep," "When my lover ignores me I get sick all over."
6. **Agape,** or selfless love. "I would do anything I can to help my lover," "My lover's needs and wishes are more important than my own."

Storge is translated from the Greek as attachment and nonsexually oriented affection, the emotion that binds friends or parents and children together. *Agape* is similar to generosity and charity. It implies the wish to share one's bounty and is epitomized by anonymous donations to charity. *Eros* is closest in meaning to passionate or romantic love.

Most people who are "in love" combine a number of styles of love in their feelings. Using these six styles of love, the Hendricks (1986) found some interesting sex differences. Male college students are significantly more "ludic" (i.e., game-playing) than females. Female college students are significantly more "storgic" (attached), pragmatic (long-term-relationship oriented), and manicky* (possessive) than males. However, there were no sex differences in terms of eros (passion) or agape (selflessness).

On Love and Arousal: If My Heart Is Pounding, It Must Mean I Love You

The Roman poet Ovid suggested that young men (his interests were admittedly sexist) might open their ladies' hearts by taking them to the gory gladiator contests. The women could attribute the pounding of their hearts and the butterflies in their stomachs to the nearness of their dates and conclude that they were inspired by them. Despite the saying, love does not seem to be "blind"—just a bit nearsighted. Research does suggest that strong arousal in the presence of a reasonably attractive person may lead us to believe that we are experiencing desire (Istvan & Griffitt, 1978). But if the person is decidedly *un*attractive, we may attribute our arousal to revulsion or disgust (White et al., 1981).

Let us consider an experiment in which male college students rated the attractiveness of *Playboy* nudes (Valins, 1966). Each rater was wired so that he could monitor his own heartbeat (he believed) through a microphone and earphone set. Heart sounds accelerated in frequency when certain slides were being shown. In general, subjects rated models as being more attractive when the heartbeats were more rapid.

There was one catch. Valins had doctored the feedback arrangement so that raters were *not* listening to their own heartbeat sounds. Instead, they were hearing heartbeats that were accelerated or slowed down for randomly selected models. The men may have attributed what they believed to be their own hearts racing to the slide being shown. As a consequence, perhaps they believed that this woman *must* be particularly appealing to them.

*Not to be confused with manic-depression, the old term for an abnormal behavior problem to be discussed in Chapter 12.

Storge (STORE-gay). Feelings of attachment, as in friendships or family relationships.

Pragma Logical love. (A Greek word meaning "business.")

Mania In this usage, excited love. (A Greek word meaning "madness." See Chapter 12.)

Agape (ah-gah-pay). Altruistic, generous love. (A Greek word referring to divine love—that is, the type of love that the gods were thought to feel for humans.)

QUESTIONNAIRE

The Love Scale

Are you in love?

The following love scale was developed at Northeastern University in Boston. To compare your own score (or scores, if you have been busy) with those of Northeastern University students, simply think of your dating partner or partners and fill out the scale with each of them in mind. Then compare your scores to those in Appendix B.

Directions: Circle the number that best shows how true or false the items are for you according to this code:

7 = definitely true
6 = rather true
5 = somewhat true
4 = not sure, or equally true and false
3 = somewhat false
2 = rather false
1 = definitely false

1. I look forward to being with ______________ a great deal.
   definitely false 1 2 3 4 5 6 7 definitely true
2. I find ______________ to be sexually exciting.
   definitely false 1 2 3 4 5 6 7 definitely true
3. ______________ has fewer faults than most people.
   definitely false 1 2 3 4 5 6 7 definitely true
4. I would do anything I could for ______________.
   definitely false 1 2 3 4 5 6 7 definitely true
5. ______________ is very attractive to me.
   definitely false 1 2 3 4 5 6 7 definitely true
6. I like to share my feelings with ______________.
   definitely false 1 2 3 4 5 6 7 definitely true
7. Doing things is more fun when ______________ and I do them together.
   definitely false 1 2 3 4 5 6 7 definitely true
8. I like to have ______________ all to myself.
   definitely false 1 2 3 4 5 6 7 definitely true
9. I would feel horrible if anything bad happened to ______________.
   definitely false 1 2 3 4 5 6 7 definitely true
10. I think about ______________ very often.
    definitely false 1 2 3 4 5 6 7 definitely true
11. It is very important that ______________ cares for me.
    definitely false 1 2 3 4 5 6 7 definitely true
12. I am most content when I am with ______________.
    definitely false 1 2 3 4 5 6 7 definitely true
13. It is difficult for me to stay away from ______________ for very long.
    definitely false 1 2 3 4 5 6 7 definitely true
14. I care about ______________ a great deal.
    definitely false 1 2 3 4 5 6 7 definitely true

Total Score for Love Scale: ______

Many sources of stimulation can heighten our levels of arousal, and heightened arousal might just lead us to respond more positively to members of the opposite sex.

Truth or Fiction Revisited

It is true that taking a date to a horror film or for a roller coaster ride may stimulate feelings of passion—by heightening arousal in general.

If you believe that I should not be giving out this information, feel free not to act on it.

SUMMARY

1. **What are motives, needs, drives, and incentives?** A motive is a state within an organism that activates and directs behavior toward a goal. A physiological need is a state of deprivation. Needs give rise to drives, which are psychological in nature and arouse us to action. An incentive is perceived as being capable of satisfying a need.

2. **What is the instinct theory of motivation?** According to the instinct theory of motivation, animals are born with preprogrammed tendencies to behave in certain ways in certain situations. Stimuli called releasers elicit innate fixed action patterns (FAPs).

3. **What is the drive-reduction theory of motivation?** According to the drive-reduction theory of motivation, rewards reduce drives and, as a consequence, we are motivated to learn to engage in behavior that leads to rewards. Drive-reduction theorists differentiate between primary (innate) drives and acquired (learned) drives.

4. **What is the humanistic theory of motivation?** Humanistic psychologists argue that behavior can be growth-oriented as people are motivated to consciously strive for self-fulfillment. Maslow hypothesized that people have a hierarchy of needs, including an innate need for self-actualization. His hierarchy includes physiological needs, safety needs, love and belongingness needs, esteem needs, the need for cognitive understanding, aesthetic needs, and the need for self-actualization.

5. **What are physiological drives?** Physiological or primary drives are unlearned and generally function according to a homeostatic principle—the body's tendency to maintain a steady state.

6. **What factors give rise to the hunger drive?** Hunger is regulated by several internal mechanisms, including stomach contractions, blood-sugar level, receptors in the mouth and liver, and the responses of the hypothalamus. The ventromedial hypothalamus functions as a stop-eating center. Lesions in this area lead to hyperphagia in rats, causing the animals to grow to several times their normal body weight, but their weight eventually levels off. The lateral hypothalamus has a start-eating center. External stimuli, such as the aroma of food, can also trigger hunger.

7. **What factors give rise to the thirst drive?** Thirst is regulated by level of blood flow and the concentration of chemicals, like sodium, in the blood. Dehydration leads the kidneys to produce the hormone angiotensin, which signals the hypothalamus. Osmoreceptors in the hypothalamus detect lowered local flow of blood, which stems from dehydration or increased concentration of sodium. The hypothalamus then stimulates the pituitary to secrete antidiuretic hormone, which increases reabsorption of urine. The hypothalamus also signals the cortex, which prompts the thirst drive.

8. **What are stimulus motives?** Stimulus motives, like physiological motives, are innate, but they involve motives to increase rather than decrease the stimulation impacting upon us. Sensory-deprivation studies show that lack of stimulation is aversive. People and many lower animals have needs for stimulation and activity, for exploration and manipulation. Sensation-seekers may seek thrills, act out on impulses, and be easily bored.

9. **What is optimal arousal?** There is evidence that we are motivated to seek optimal levels of arousal, levels at which we feel best and function most efficiently.

10. **What is the Yerkes-Dodson law?** According to the Yerkes-Dodson law, high levels of motivation facilitate performance on simple tasks but impede performance on complex tasks.

11. **What are social motives?** Social motives are secondary or learned from interaction with other people. They include needs for achievement (*n* Ach), affiliation, and power.

12. **What is the need for achievement?** *N* Ach is the need to accomplish things. People with high *n* Ach attain higher grades and earn more money than people of comparable ability with lower *n* Ach.

13. **What is the need for affiliation?** This is the need to be with other people. The need for affiliation prompts us to join groups and make friends. Anxiety tends to increase our need for affiliation, especially with people who share our predicaments.

14. **What is the need for power?** The need for power is the need to control organizations and other people. People with a frustrated need for power are prone to developing physical illness.

15. **What is an emotion?** An emotion is a state of feeling with physiological, situational, and cognitive components. Emotions motivate behavior and also serve as goals.

16. **How do emotions develop?** There are two theoretical views. According to Bridges and Sroufe, emotions become differentiated as a child develops. According to Izard, several discrete emotions are present at birth.

17. **Are emotions expressed in the same way in different cultures?** They are according to Ekman, whose research shows that there are several basic emotions whose expression is recognized around the world.

18. **What is the facial-feedback hypothesis?** This is the view that posing intense facial expressions can heighten emotional response. Evidence for this hypothesis is somewhat mixed.

19. **What is the James-Lange theory of the activation of emotions?** According to James-Lange theory, emotions have specific patterns of arousal and action that are triggered by certain external events. The emotion follows the overt response.

20. **What is the Cannon-Bard theory of the activation of emotions?** The Cannon-Bard theory proposes that processing of events by the brain gives rise simultaneously to the emotion and to bodily responses. According to this view, emotions accompany bodily responses.

21. **What is the cognitive-appraisal theory of the activation of emotions?** According to Schachter and Singer's theory of cognitive appraisal, emotions have largely similar patterns of arousal. The emotion a person will experience in response to an external stimulus reflects that person's appraisal of the stimulus—that is, the meaning of the stimulus to him or her.

22. **Does research support any of these theories?** Research seems to suggest that although patterns of arousal are more specific than suggested by the theory of cognitive appraisal, cognitive appraisal does play an important role in determining our responses to events.

PSYCHOLOGY AND MODERN LIFE

There is no sincerer love than the love of food.
George Bernard Shaw

The two biggest sellers in any bookstore are the cookbooks and the diet books. The cookbooks tell you how to prepare the food and the diet books tell you how not to eat any of it.
Andy Rooney

We need food to survive, but food means more than survival to many of us. Food is a symbol of family togetherness and caring. We associate food with the nurturance of the parent-child relationship, with visits home during the holidays. Friends and relatives offer food when we enter their homes. Saying no may be interpreted as a personal rejection. Bacon and eggs, coffee with cream and sugar, meat and mashed potatoes—all seem to be part of sharing American values and agricultural abundance.

This nation idealizes slender heroes and heroines. For many of us who measure more-than-up to TV and film idols, food may have replaced sex as the central source of guilt. The obese also encounter more than their fair share of illnesses, including cardiovascular diseases, diabetes, gout, even certain types of cancer (Feist & Brannon, 1988; Sorlie et al., 1980).

Despite the miseries of those who are overweight, consider a few facts:

Forty percent of Americans consider themselves overweight (Burros, 1988), and 35 percent want to lose at least 15 pounds (Toufexis et al., 1986).

One out of five American adults is obese—that is, weighs more than 20 percent above the recommended weight (Wallis, 1985).

Eleven million American adults are severely obese (Wallis, 1985), exceeding their desirable body weight by at least 40 percent.

Twenty-one percent of us are on diets (Burros, 1988), and the number of women on diets exceeds the number of male dieters significantly (Toufexis et al., 1986).

Within one year after dieting, the average dieter regains 36% of the weight that had been lost (Brownell & Wadden, 1986).

Within a few years, at least two-thirds of "successful" dieters regain every pound they have lost—and then some (Toufexis et al., 1986).

Truth or Fiction Revisited

It is true that one American adult in five is obese—and twice as many consider themselves overweight.

Obesity and Weight Control

Because it is such a pervasive problem, the Psychology and Modern Life section of this chapter focuses on obesity and weight control. We shall see that recent psychological research has made major and sometimes startling contributions to our knowledge concerning why so many people are obese and what we can do about it.

Contributors to Obesity Why do so many of us overeat? Is obesity a physiological problem, a psychological problem, or both?

Heredity It is well-known that obesity runs in families. It used to be the conventional wisdom that obese parents encouraged their children to be overweight by having fattening foods in the house and setting poor examples. However, a recent study of Scandinavian adoptees by Stunkard and his colleagues (1986) found that children bear a closer resemblance in weight to their biological parents than their adoptive parents. Heredity, then, appears to play a role. However, we shall see that environmental factors also play a role. Since we are sort of "stuck" with our heredity, that is encouraging. We *can* exert an influence over the situational factors that affect us.

Fat Cells The efforts of obese people to maintain a slender profile might be sabotaged by microscopic units of life within their own bodies: *fat cells.* No, fat cells are not overweight cells. They are adipose tissue, or cells that store fat. Hunger might be related to the amount of fat stored in these cells. As time passes after a meal, the blood-sugar level drops. Fat is then drawn from these cells to provide further nourishment. At some point, referred to as the *set point,* the hypothalamus is signaled of the fat deficiency in these cells, triggering the hunger drive.

People with more adipose tissue than others feel food-deprived earlier, even though they may be equal in weight. This might be because more signals are being sent to the brain. Obese people, and *formerly* obese people, tend to have more adipose tissue than people of normal weight (Braitman et al., 1985). For this reason, many people who have lost weight complain that they are always hungry when they try to maintain normal weight levels.

Fatty tissue also metabolizes food more slowly than muscle. For this reason, a person with a high fat-to-muscle ratio will metabolize food more slowly than a person of the same weight with a lower fat-to-muscle ratio. In other words, two people identical in weight will metabolize food at different rates, according to their bodies' distribution of muscle and fat. Obese people are therefore doubly handicapped in their efforts to lose weight—not only by their extra weight but by the fact that much of their body is composed of adipose tissue.

In a sense, the normal distribution of fat cells could be considered "sexist." The average man is 40 percent muscle and 15 percent fat, whereas the average woman is 23 percent muscle and 25 percent fat. Therefore, if a man and woman with typical distributions of muscle and fat are of the same weight, the woman—who has more fat cells—will have to eat less in order to maintain the same weight.

Compensating Metabolic Forces that Affect Dieters In addition, psychologist Richard Keesey (1986) notes that people who are dieting and people who have lost substantial amounts of weight usually do not eat enough to satisfy the set points in their hypothalamuses. As a consequence, compensating metabolic forces are set in motion; that is, fewer calories are burned.

Fat cells might play a role in triggering internal sensations of hunger, but they cannot compel us to eat. Below we shall review evidence that obese people are actually *less* sensitive than normal-weight people to internal sensations of hunger.

The Perils of Yo-Yo Dieting Repeated cycles of dieting and regaining lost weight—"yo-yo dieting"—might be particularly traumatic to one's set point. Psychologist Kelly Brownell (1986) points out that such cycles might teach the body that it will be intermittently deprived of food, slowing the metabolism whenever future food intake is restricted. For this reason, *to maintain a slim profile, formerly obese people must usually eat much less than people of the same weight who have always been slender.*

Brownell suggests a second effect of yo-yo dieting that hampers repeated dieting efforts:

> *Consider a hypothetical dieter, Christine, who drops from 140 pounds down to 120 pounds. She might lose 15 pounds of fat and 5 pounds of muscle. If she regains the 20 pounds, will she replace all 5 pounds of muscle?* [*Animal studies*] *suggest that she won't, so Christine may replace 18 pounds of fat and only 2 pounds of muscle. She may be the same weight before and after this cycle, but her metabolic rate would be lower after the cycle because she has more fat, which is less metabolically active than muscle (Brownell, 1988, p. 22).*

In other words, it will be more difficult for Christine to merely maintain the 140 pounds the second time around. In fact, if she eats as many calories as she had eaten earlier at 140 pounds, she will probably go above 140. Moreover, now that her body is overall somewhat "less metabolically active," it will be harder for her to lose the same 20 pounds again.

Internal and External Eaters: Out of Sight, Out of Mouth? During the late evening news, just as I am settling in for sleep, a fast-food hamburger or frozen pizza ad assaults me from the TV set. Visions of juicy meat, gooey cheese, and drippy sauce threaten to do me in. My stomach growlings are all the evidence I need that hunger can be triggered by external stimuli, such as the sight of food, as well as by chemical imbalances in the body.

People who respond predominantly to their own internal stimuli are referred to as *internal eaters.* Those who must be tied to the bedpost when they see a food commercial or catch a whiff of kitchen aromas are *external eaters.* Any of us might occasionally respond to an especially appealing incentive, such as a chocolate chocolate-chip cookie. But external eaters are decidedly more swayed by external stimulation.

A number of studies have suggested that overweight people are more likely than the normal-weight to be external eaters (e.g., Schachter & Gross, 1968; Stunkard, 1959). Why might obese people be more responsive than normal-weight people to external stimulation? In considering this question, Stanley Schachter (1971) drew behavioral parallels between the eating patterns of obese people and hyperphagic rats. Many obese people, like hyperphagic rats, are finicky eaters—more sensitive than normal-weight people to the taste of food (Schachter, 1971; Schachter & Rodin, 1974). Obese people, like hyperphagic rats, eat relatively larger quantities of sweet foods, such as vanilla milkshakes, but lower quantities of bitter foods. Obese people and hyperphagic rats also take larger mouthfuls, chew less, and finish their meals more rapidly than those of normal weight (LeBow et al., 1977; Marston et al., 1977). For all these reasons, Schachter speculated that many obese people might be troubled by faulty neural regulation of hunger because of problems in the hypothalamus.

The faulty-neural-mechanism theory has not yet been universally accepted as a factor in obesity in human beings. Moreover, Judith Rodin (1980) has found that numerous people in all weight categories, not only the obese, are external eaters. She also has found that moderately obese people (15 to 25 percent overweight) tend to be external eaters but that extremely obese people (50 percent or more overweight) are less influenced by external cues than the moderately obese. Thus, the links between obesity and responsiveness to external cues are not as powerful as had been thought.

Other factors, such as emotional state, might also play a role in obesity. Dieting efforts may be impeded by negative emotional states such as depression (Baucom

& Aiken, 1981; Ruderman, 1985) and anxiety (Pine, 1985).

But now, here's some good news for people who would like to lose a few pounds. Psychological research has led to a number of helpful suggestions for people who would like to lose some weight and keep it off. Following a self-help manual, like that in this section of the chapter, can be successful (Wing et al., 1982).

It must be noted that excessive thinness is at least as unhealthy as excessive weight, and excessive thinness is becoming more common today, especially among young women. In Chapter 12 we shall focus on the eating disorders of anorexia nervosa and bulimia nervosa, both of which involve dramatic ways of keeping weight down. But now let us turn our attention to psychological knowledge that can be applied by the overweight to lose weight and—just as important—to keep it off.

Methods of Weight Control Research on motivation and on cognitive and behavioral methods of therapy has enhanced our knowledge of healthful ways of losing weight. Sound weight-control programs do not involve sometimes dangerous fad diets (Brownell, 1988), such as fasting, eliminating carbohydrates, or eating excessive amounts of grapefruit or rice. Instead, they involve major changes in life style that include improving nutritional knowledge, decreasing calorie intake, exercising, and modifying behavior (Epstein et al., 1985; Israel et al., 1985; Stalonas & Kirschenbaum, 1985).

Because eating fewer calories is the central method for decreasing weight, we need nutritional knowledge. Knowledge helps assure that we will not deprive ourselves of essential food elements and suggests strategies for losing weight without making us feel overly deprived. For example, taking in fewer calories doesn't only mean eating smaller portions. It includes switching to some lower-calorie foods—relying more on fresh, unsweetened fruits and vegetables (eating apples rather than apple pie); lean meats; fish and poultry; and skim milk and cheese products. It means cutting down on or eliminating butter, margarine, oils, and sugar.

It turns out that the same foods that help us control our weight also tend to be high in vitamins and fiber and low in fats. And so they also lower our risk of developing cardiovascular disorders, cancer, and a number of other illnesses.

Dieting plus exercise is more effective than dieting alone for shedding pounds (Epstein et al., 1984a) and for maintaining weight losses (Perri et al., 1988). Remember that when we restrict calories, our metabolic rates compensate by decreasing (Apfelbaum, 1978; Polivy & Herman, 1985). This decrease can frustrate dieters severely. Some dieters justifiably complain that they reach "plateaus" from which they cannot shed additional pounds unless they literally starve themselves (Brownell, 1988). Exercise burns calories in itself and also helps by increasing our metabolic rate throughout the day, even though we are restricting calories (Donahoe et al., 1984).

We learned that fat (adipose tissue) metabolizes food more slowly than muscle. Exercise builds muscle and consequently heightens the quantity of tissue that will burn calories rapidly. Also, Keesey (1986) hypothesizes that a long-term exercise program may lower the set point for body weight.

Cognitive and behavioral methods have also provided many strategies for losing weight. Here are a number of suggestions for losing weight based on cognitive-behavioral principles:

Establish calorie-intake goals and heighten awareness of whether or not you are meeting them. Get a book that shows how many calories are found in various foods, and keep a diary of your calorie intake.

Use low-calorie substitutes for high-calorie foods. Fill your stomach with celery rather than cheesecake and enchiladas. Eat preplanned low-calorie snacks instead of binging on a jar of peanuts or a container of ice cream.

Establish eating patterns similar to those of internal eaters. Take small bites. Chew thoroughly. Use smaller plates. Put down your utensils between bites. Remove or throw out leftover foods quickly. Take a five-minute break between helpings. Ask yourself whether you're still hungry. If not, stop eating.

Avoid sources of external stimulation (temptations) to which you have succumbed in the past. Shop at the mall with the Alfalfa Sprout, not the Gushy Gloppy Shoppe. Plan your meal before entering a restaurant and avoid ogling that tempting, full-color menu. Attend to your own plate, not to the sumptuous dish at the next table. (Your salad probably looks greener to them, anyhow.) Shop from a list. Walk briskly through the supermarket, preferably after dinner when you're no longer hungry. Don't be sidetracked by pretty packages (fattening things may come in them). Keep out of the kitchen. Study, watch TV, or write letters elsewhere. Keep fattening foods out of the house. Prepare only enough food to remain within your calorie-intake goals.

Exercise to burn more calories and maintain your predieting metabolic rate. Reach for your mate, not your plate (to coin a phrase). Jog rather than eat an unplanned snack. Build exercise routines by a few minutes each week.

Reward yourself for meeting calorie-intake goals—but not with food. Imagine how great you'll look in that new swimsuit next summer. Do not go to see that great new film unless you have met your weekly calorie-intake goal. Each time you meet your weekly calorie-intake goal, put cash in the bank toward a vacation or new camera.

Use imagery to help yourself lose weight. Tempted by a fattening dish? Imagine that it's rotten, that you would be nauseated by it and have a sick taste in your mouth for the rest of the day. Tempted to binge? Strip before the mirror and handle a fatty area of your body. Ask yourself if you *really* want to make it larger or if you would prefer to exercise self-control? When tempted, you can also think of the extra work your heart must do for every pound of extra weight. Imagine your arteries clogging up with dreaded substances (not far off base!).

Mentally rehearse solutions to problem situations. Consider how you will politely refuse when cake is handed out at the office party. Rehearse your next visit to "the relatives"—the ones who tell you how painfully thin you look and try to stuff you like a pig. Imagine how you'll politely (but firmly) refuse seconds, and thirds, despite all their protestations.

Above all, if you slip from your plan for a day, do not blow things out of proportion. Dieters are frequently tempted to binge, especially when they view themselves rigidly either as perfect successes or as complete failures (Polivy & Herman, 1985). Do not tell yourself you're a failure so that you may as well go on a binge. Consider the weekly or monthly trend, not just a single day. And if you do binge, resume dieting the next day. Again, credit yourself for the long-term trend. Do not focus only on the lapse.

Losing weight—and keeping it off—is not easy, but it can be done. Making a personal commitment to losing weight and formulating a workable plan for doing so are two of the keys. And even in the early stages, it is helpful to think of lifelong behavioral changes we can institute to keep weight off—such as modifying our diets, keeping nutritious but low-calorie snacks handy, and exercising regularly.

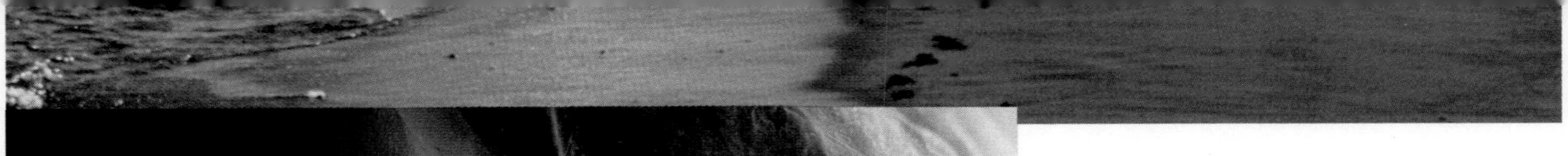

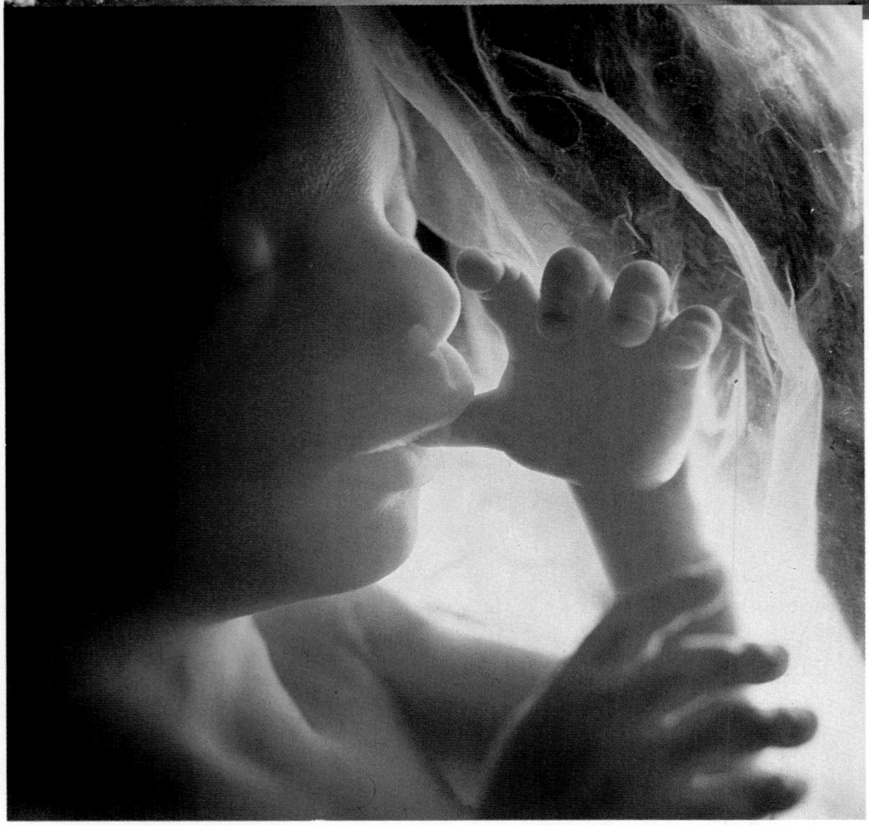

Outline

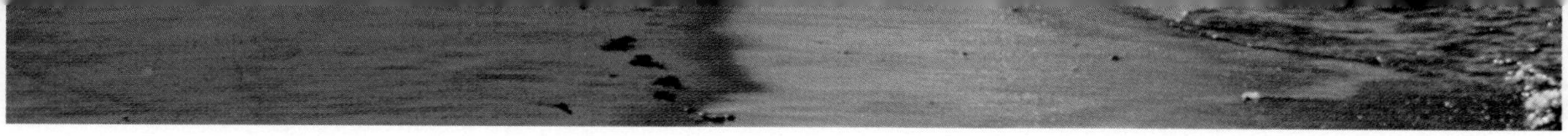

9 Developmental Psychology

Truth or Fiction?

- Fertilization takes place in the uterus.
- Your heart started beating when you were only one-fifth of an inch long and weighed a fraction of an ounce.
- Infants triple their birth weight by the time they reach their first birthdays.
- The way to a baby's heart is through its stomach—that is, babies become emotionally attached to those who feed them.
- The highest level of moral reasoning involves relying on our own views of what is right and wrong.
- Girls are capable of becoming pregnant after they have their first menstrual periods.
- Early maturing boys are more popular than late maturing boys.
- Mothers suffer from the "empty-nest syndrome" when the youngest child leaves home.
- Most elderly people are dissatisfied with their lives.
- Children placed in day care are more aggressive than children cared for in the home.
- Child abusers have frequently been victims of child abuse themselves.

On a summerlike day in October, Elaine and her husband Dennis rush out to their jobs as usual. While Elaine, a buyer for a New York department store, is arranging for dresses from the Chicago manufacturer to arrive in time for the spring line, a very different drama is unfolding in her body. Hormones are causing a follicle (egg container) in one of her ovaries to rupture and release an egg cell, or ovum. Elaine, like other women, possessed from birth all the egg cells she would ever have. How this ovum was selected to ripen and be released this month is unknown. But in any case, Elaine will be capable of becoming pregnant for only a couple of days following ovulation.

When it is released, the ovum begins a slow journey down a four-inch-long fallopian tube to the uterus. It is within this tube that one of Dennis's sperm cells will unite with the egg.

An Exercise Class for Pregnant Women. Years ago, the rule of thumb was that pregnant women were not to exert themselves. Today it is recognized that exercise is healthful for pregnant women, because it promotes cardiovascular fitness and increases muscle strength. Fitness and strength are assets during childbirth—and at other times.

Truth or Fiction Revisited

It is *not* true that fertilization takes place in the uterus. It normally occurs in a fallopian tube.

Like many other couples, Elaine and Dennis engaged in sexual intercourse the night before. But unlike most other couples, their timing and methodology were preplanned. Elaine used a kit bought in a drug store to predict when she would ovulate. She chemically analyzed her urine for the presence of luteinizing hormone, which surges one to two days prior to ovulation. The results suggested that Elaine would be most likely to conceive today.

When Elaine and Dennis made love, he ejaculated hundreds of millions of sperm, with about equal numbers of Y and X sex chromosomes. By the time of conception, only a few thousand had survived the journey to the fallopian tubes. Several bombarded the ovum, attempting to penetrate. Only one succeeded. It carried a Y sex chromosome, so the couple conceived a boy. The fertilized ovum, or **zygote,** is 1/175th of an inch across—a tiny stage for the drama yet to unfold.

Developmental psychologists would be pleased to study the development of Dennis and Elaine's new son from conception throughout his lifetime. There are several reasons for this. One approach to the explanation of adult behavior lies in the discovery of early influences and developmental sequences. An answer to the question of *why* we behave in certain ways lies in outlining the development of behavior patterns over the years. There also is interest in the effects of genetics, early interactions with parents and **siblings,** and the school and the community on traits such as aggressiveness and intelligence.

Developmental psychologists also seek insight into the causes of developmental abnormalities. This avenue of research can contribute to children's health and psychological well-being. For instance, should pregnant women abstain from smoking and drinking? Is it safe for the **embryo** for pregnant women to take aspirin for a headache or tetracycline to ward off a bacterial invasion? Need we be concerned about placing our children in day care? What factors contribute to child abuse? Developmental psychologists are also concerned about issues in adult development. For example, what conflicts and disillusionments can we expect as we journey through our 30s, 40s, and 50s? The information acquired by developmental psychologists can help us make decisions about how we rear our children and lead our own lives.

Of course, there is another very good reason for studying development. Thousands of psychologists enjoy it.

Zygote A fertilized ovum.

Siblings Brothers and sisters.

Embryo The unborn child from the third through the eighth weeks following conception, during which time the major organ systems undergo rapid differentiation.

CONTROVERSIES IN DEVELOPMENTAL PSYCHOLOGY

We have seen throughout this text that psychologists see things in very different ways. Diverse views give rise to controversies in developmental psychology as well.

Arnold Gesell

Does Development Reflect Nature or Nurture?

There is continuing interest in sorting out what human behavior is the result of nature and of nurture. What aspects of behavior originate in a person's genes—that is, nature—and are biologically "programed" to unfold in the child as long as minimal nutrition and social experience are provided? What aspects of behavior can be largely traced to environmental influences such as nutrition and learning—that is, nurture?

Psychologists seek to understand the influences of nature in our genetic heritage, in the functioning of the nervous system, and in the process of **maturation.** Psychologists look for the influences of nurture in our nutrition, cultural and family backgrounds, and opportunities to learn about the world, including early cognitive stimulation and formal education. The American psychologist Arnold Gesell (1880–1961) leaned heavily toward natural explanations of development, arguing that all areas of development are self-regulated by the unfolding of natural plans and processes. John Watson and other behaviorists leaned heavily toward environmental explanations. (Watson, of course, was focusing primarily on adaptive behavior patterns, whereas Gesell was focusing on many aspects of development, including physical and motor growth and development.) But today nearly all researchers would agree, broadly speaking, that nature and nurture interact as children develop.

Is Development Continuous or Discontinuous?

Do developmental changes occur gradually (continuously) or in major qualitative leaps (discontinuously) that dramatically alter our bodies and behavior?

Watson and other behaviorists have viewed human development as being a continuous process in which the effects of learning mount gradually, with no major sudden qualitative changes. Maturational theorists, in contrast, believe that there are periods of life during which development occurs so dramatically that we can speak of it as occurring in **stages.** Maturational theorists point out that the environment, even when enriched, profits us little until we are ready, or mature enough, to develop in a certain direction. For example, newborn babies will not imitate their parents' speech, even when parents speak clearly and deliberately.

Stage theorists such as Sigmund Freud (see Chapter 10) and Jean Piaget saw development as being discontinuous. Both theorists saw biological changes as providing the potential for psychological changes.

Certain aspects of physical development do appear to occur in stages. For example, from the age of 2 to the onset of **puberty,** children gradually grow larger. Then the adolescent growth spurt occurs, ushered in by hormones and characterized by rapid biological changes in structure and function (as in the development of the sex organs) as well as in size. And so, it would appear that a new stage of life has begun. Psychologists disagree more strongly on whether aspects of development such as cognitive development, attachment, and sex typing occur in stages.

Let us now turn to the developments that occur between conception and birth. Although they are literally "out of sight," our most dramatic biological changes occur within this short span of nine months.

Maturation The orderly unfolding of traits, as regulated by the genetic code.

Stage A distinct period of life that is qualitatively different from other stages.

Puberty The period of early adolescence during which hormones spur rapid physical development.

PRENATAL DEVELOPMENT

During the months following conception, the single cell formed by the union of sperm and egg will multiply—becoming two, then four, then eight, and so on. By the time a **fetus** is ready to be born, it will contain more cells than there are stars in the Milky Way galaxy. Prenatal development is divided into three periods: the germinal stage (approximately the first two weeks), the embryonic stage (which lasts from two weeks to about two months after conception), and the fetal stage.

The Germinal Stage

The zygote divides repeatedly as it proceeds on its three- to four-day journey to the uterus. The ball-like mass of dividing cells wanders about the uterus for another three to four days before beginning to become implanted in the uterine wall. Implantation requires another week or so. The period from conception to implantation is called the **germinal stage,** or the **period of the ovum.**

A few days into the germinal stage, cells are separating into groups according to what they will become. Two inner layers of cells are forming what will become the baby. The single outer layer of cells differentiates into membranes that will protect and nourish the embryo, including the umbilical cord; the placenta; the amniotic sac; and the chorion, which will line the placenta. Prior to implantation, the dividing ball of cells is nourished solely by the yolk of the original egg cell, and it does not gain in mass.

The Embryonic Stage

The embryonic stage lasts from implantation until about the eighth week of development. During this stage, the major body organ systems differentiate. Development follows two general trends—**cephalocaudal** and **proximodistal.** As you can note from the relatively large heads of embryos and fetuses during prenatal development (see Figure 9.1), the growth of the head takes precedence over the growth of the lower parts of the body. If you also think of the body as containing a central axis that coincides with the spinal cord, the growth of the organ systems close to this axis (that is, *proximal)* takes precedence over the growth of the extremities *(distal* areas). Relatively early maturation of the brain and the major organ systems allows them to participate in the nourishment and further development of the unborn child.

During the third week after conception, the head and the blood vessels begin to form. During the fourth week, a primitive heart begins to beat and pump blood–in an organism that is one-fifth of an inch long. The heart will continue to beat without rest every minute of every day for perhaps 80 or 90 years.

Truth or Fiction Revisited

It is true that your heart started beating when you were only one-fifth of an inch long and weighed a fraction of an ounce.

Arm buds and leg buds begin to appear toward the end of the first month. Eyes, ears, nose, and mouth begin to take shape. By this time, the nervous system, including the brain, has also begun to develop.

Fetus The unborn child from the third month following conception through childbirth, during which time there is maturation of organ systems and dramatic gains in length and weight.

Germinal stage The first stage of prenatal development during which the dividing mass of cells has not become implanted in the uterine wall.

Period of the ovum Another term for the *germinal stage.*

Cephalocaudal Proceeding from top to bottom.

Proximodistal Proceeding from near to far.

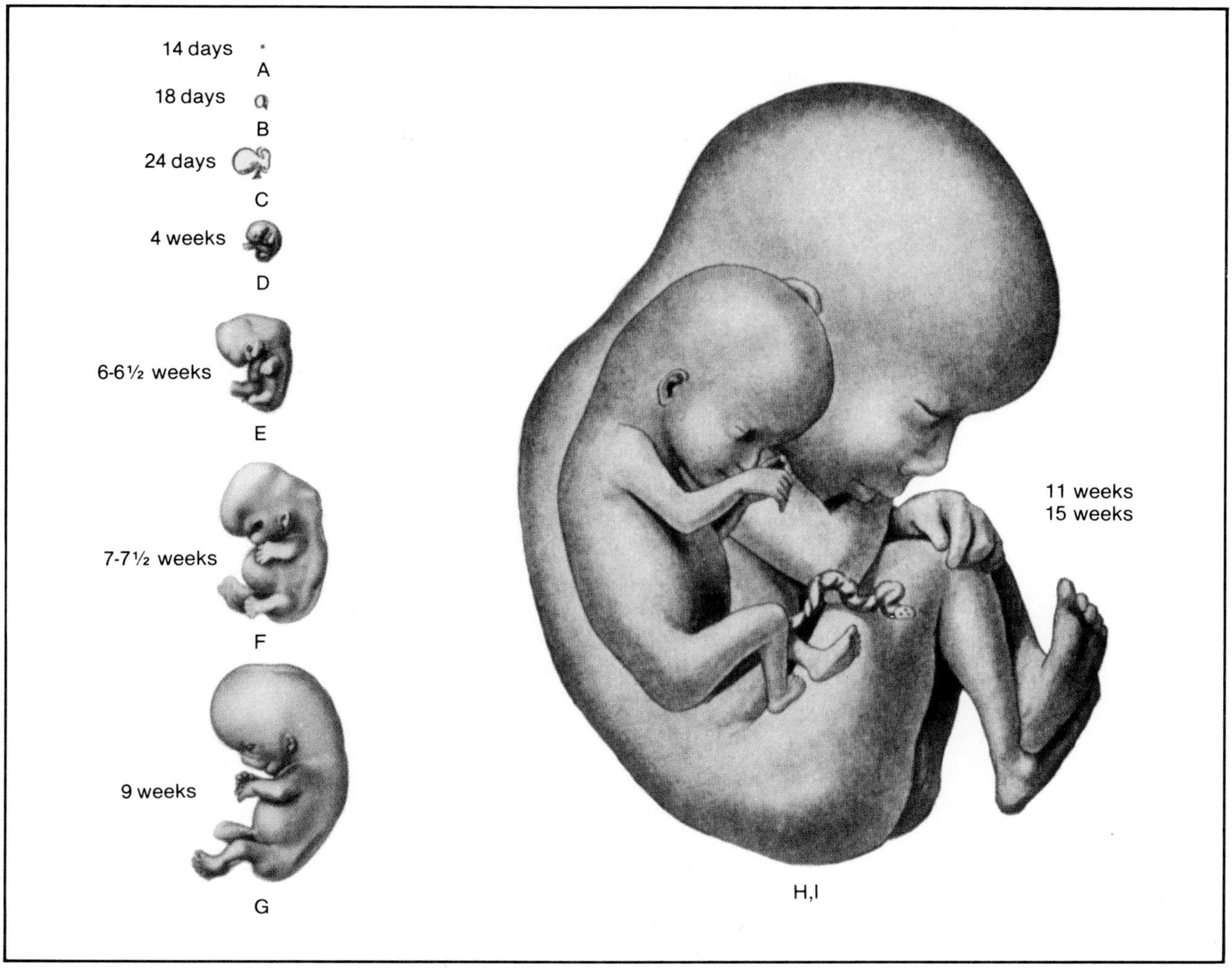

Figure 9.1
Embryos and Fetuses at Various Intervals of Prenatal Development.

The upper arms and legs develop first, followed by the forearms and lower legs. Next come hands and feet, followed at 6 to 8 weeks by webbed fingers and toes. By the end of the second month, the limbs are elongating and separated. The webbing is gone. The head has become rounded and the facial features have become distinct—all in an embryo about one inch long and weighing *1/30th* of an ounce. During the second month, the nervous system begins to transmit messages. By the end of the embryonic period, teeth buds have also formed. The embryo's kidneys are filtering acid from the blood, and its liver is producing red blood cells.

Hormones and Prenatal Sexual Differentiation By about 5 to 6 weeks, when the embryo is only a quarter to a half an inch long, nondescript sex organs have formed. By about the seventh week following conception, the genetic code (XY or XX) begins to assert itself, leading to changes in the internal and external sex organs. If a Y sex chromosome is present, testes will form and begin to produce **androgens,** which prompt further mascu-

Androgens Male sex hormones.

linization of the sexual organs. In the absence of male sex hormones, the embryo will develop female sex organs. Female sex hormones are not needed to induce these changes.

The Amniotic Sac The unborn child—embryo and fetus—develops within an **amniotic sac,** a protective environment in the mother's uterus. The sac is surrounded by a clear membrane and contains amniotic fluid, in which the developing child is suspended. Amniotic fluid serves as a "shock absorber," preventing the child from being damaged by the mother's movements. It also helps maintain an even temperature.

The Placenta The **placenta** is a mass of tissue that permits the embryo (and later on, the fetus) to exchange nutrients and wastes with the mother. The placenta is unique in origin: It grows from material supplied by both mother and embryo. At 3 months it will have become a flattish, round organ about seven inches in diameter and one inch thick—larger than the fetus itself. The fetus is connected to the placenta by the **umbilical cord.** The mother is connected to the placenta by the system of blood vessels in the uterine wall. The umbilical cord develops about five weeks after conception and reaches 20 inches in length.

The circulatory systems of mother and unborn child do not mix. A membrane in the placenta permits only certain substances to pass through. Oxygen and nutrients are passed from the mother to the embryo. Carbon dioxide and other wastes are passed from the child to the mother, where they are removed by the mother's lungs and kidneys. Unfortunately, a number of other substances can pass through the placenta. They include some microscopic disease organisms—such as those that cause syphilis, German measles, and **AIDS**—and some drugs, including aspirin, narcotics, alcohol, and tranquilizers (see Table 9.1).

Ultimately, the placenta passes from the woman's body after the child is delivered. For this reason it is also called the "afterbirth."

The Fetal Stage

The fetal stage lasts from the beginning of the third month until birth. The fetus begins to turn and respond to external stimulation at about the ninth or tenth week. By the end of the third month, all the major organ systems have been formed (Arms & Camp, 1987). The fingers and toes appear to be fully formed. The eyes can be clearly distinguished, and the sex of the fetus can be determined visually.

The fourth through sixth months are characterized by maturation of fetal organ systems and dramatic gains in size. The brain continues to mature, contributing to the fetus's ability to regulate its own basic body functions. During these months, the fetus advances from one *ounce* to two *pounds* in weight and grows three to four times in length, from about 4 to 14 inches. Soft, downy hair grows above the eyes and on the scalp. The skin turns ruddy because of blood vessels that show through the surface. (During the final three months, fatty layers will give the red a pinkish hue.)

In the middle of the fourth month, the mother usually detects the first fetal movements and may suddenly feel that the baby is "alive." By the end of the sixth month, the fetus moves its limbs so vigorously that the mother may complain of being kicked. The fetus opens and shuts its eyes, sucks its thumb, alternates between periods of wakefulness and sleep, and perceives light. It also turns somersaults, which can be clearly perceived by the mother.

Amniotic sac A sac within the uterus that contains the embryo or fetus.

Placenta A membrane that permits the exchange of nutrients and waste products between the mother and her developing child but does not allow the maternal and fetal bloodstreams to mix.

Umbilical cord A tube between the mother and her developing child through which nutrients and waste products are conducted.

AIDS Acquired immune deficiency syndrome. A fatal, sexually transmitted disorder that impairs the body's immune system, rendering the person vulnerable to opportunistic diseases.

Table 9.1
Possible Effects on the Embryo and Fetus of Certain Agents during Pregnancy

Agent	Possible Effect
Accutane	Malformation, stillbirth
Alcohol	Mental retardation, addiction, hyperactivity, undersize
Aspirin (large doses)	Respiratory problems, bleeding
Bendectin	Cleft palate? heart deformities?
Caffeine (coffee, many soft drinks, chocolate, etc.)	Stimulates fetus; other effects uncertain
Cigarettes	Undersize, premature delivery, fetal death
Cocaine	Spontaneous abortion, neurological problems
Diethylstilbestrol (DES)	Cancer of the cervix or testes
Heavy metals (lead, mercury)	Hyperactivity, mental retardation, stillbirth
Heavy sedation during labor	Brain damage, asphyxiation
Heroin, morphine, other narcotics	Addiction, undersize
Marijuana	Early delivery? Neurological problems? Birth defects?
Paint fumes (substantial exposure)	Mental retardation
PCB, dioxin, other insecticides and herbicides	Under study (possible stillbirth)
Progestin	Masculinization of female embryos, heightened aggressiveness?
Rubella (German measles)	Mental retardation, nerve damage impairing vision and hearing
Streptomycin	Deafness
Tetracycline	Yellow teeth, deformed bones
Thalidomide	Deformed or missing limbs
Vitamin A (large doses)	Cleft palate, eye damage
Vitamin D (large doses)	Mental retardation
X rays	Malformation of organs

A variety of chemical and other agents have been found to be harmful to the fetus or are strongly implicated in fetal damage. Pregnant women are advised to consult their physicians about their diets, vitamin supplements, and use of any drugs—including drugs available without a prescription.

A Human Fetus at about Four and a Half Months. The fetus already shows the sucking reflex.

During the seventh to ninth months, fetuses respond to sounds of different frequencies by movements and changes in the heart rate, suggesting that they can discriminate pitch (Bernard & Sontag, 1947). DeCasper and Fifer (1980) carried out an intriguing experiment in which 16 women read aloud the Dr. Seuss book *The Cat in the Hat* twice daily during the final month and a half of pregnancy. After birth, their babies were given pacifiers that could switch on one of two recordings, depending on how they were sucked. Sucking on them in one way would activate recordings of their mothers reading *The Cat in the Hat.* Sucking on them in another way would activate their mothers' readings of another book, *The King, the Mice, and the Cheese,* which was written in very different cadences. The newborns "chose" to hear only *The Cat in the Hat.*

During the last three months, the organ systems of the fetus continue to mature. The heart and lungs become increasingly capable of sustaining independent life. The fetus gains about $5\frac{1}{2}$ pounds and doubles in length. Newborn boys average about $7\frac{1}{2}$ pounds and newborn girls about 7 pounds.

PHYSICAL DEVELOPMENT

Physical development is a complex process that includes gains in height and weight; maturation of the nervous system; and development of bones, muscles, and the sex organs.

A Child-Development Toy Receives an Examination. As children develop, their muscles and neural functions mature, and they learn to coordinate sensory and motor activity. Reflexes such as the grasping reflex drop out of their storehouse of responses and are replaced by voluntary behavior, such as intentional holding and manipulation.

Height and weight are two of the most obvious dimensions of physical growth. The most dramatic gains in height and weight occur during prenatal development. Within nine months, a child develops from a nearly microscopic cell to a **neonate** about 20 inches in length. Weight increases by the billions. During infancy, dramatic gains continue. Babies usually double their birth weight in about five months and triple it by the first birthday. Their height increases by about 10 inches in the first year. Children grow another four to six inches during the second year and gain about four to seven pounds.

Truth or Fiction Revisited

It is true that infants triple their birth weight by the time they reach their first birthdays. They also make dramatic gains in height.

Following the gains of infancy, children gain about two to three inches a year until they reach the adolescent growth spurt. Weight gains also remain fairly even at about four to six pounds per year.

In one of the more fascinating aspects of the development of the nervous system, newborn babies show a number of automatic behavior patterns that are essential to survival—reflexes.

Reflexes

Soon after you were born, a doctor or a nurse probably pressed her fingers against the palms of your hands. Although you would have had no "idea" as to what to do, most likely you grasped the fingers firmly—so firmly that you could have been lifted from your cradle by simply holding on. Grasping at birth is innate, just one of the many **reflexes** with which children are born. Reflexes are simple, unlearned, stereotypical responses that are elicited by specific stimuli. They do not involve higher brain functions but occur automatically, without thinking.

Many reflexes have survival value. The most basic reflex for survival is breathing. The breathing rate is regulated by the oxygen and carbon dioxide content of the blood and other body fluids. We take in oxygen and give off carbon dioxide. Newborns normally take their first breath before the umbilical cord is cut. The breathing reflex continues to work for a lifetime, although we can take conscious control of breathing when we choose to do so.

Because newborn children do not "know" that it is necessary to eat in order to live or to reduce feelings of hunger, it is fortunate that they have **rooting** and sucking reflexes. Neonates will turn their heads (root) toward stimuli that prod or stroke the cheek, chin, or corners of the mouth. They will suck objects that touch their lips. Neonates reflexively withdraw from painful stimuli (the withdrawal reflex), and they draw up their legs and arch their backs in response to sudden noises, bumps, or loss of support while being held (the startle, or Moro, reflex). As noted, they reflexively grasp objects that press against the palms of their hands (the grasp, or palmar, reflex). They spread their toes when the soles of their feet are stimulated (the Babinski reflex). Babies also show sneezing, coughing, yawning, blinking, and many other reflexes. (It is guaranteed that you will learn about the **sphincter** reflex if you put on your best clothes and hold an undiapered neonate on your lap for a while.) Pediatricians learn about the adequacy of newborn children's neural functioning largely by testing their reflexes.

As children develop, their muscles and neural functions mature, and they learn to coordinate sensory and motor activity. Many reflexes tend to

---

Neonate A newly born child.

Reflex A simple unlearned response to a stimulus.

Rooting The turning of an infant's head toward a touch, such as by the mother's nipple.

Sphincter A ringlike muscle that circles a body opening, such as the anus. An infant will exhibit the sphincter reflex (have a bowel movement) in response to intestinal pressure.

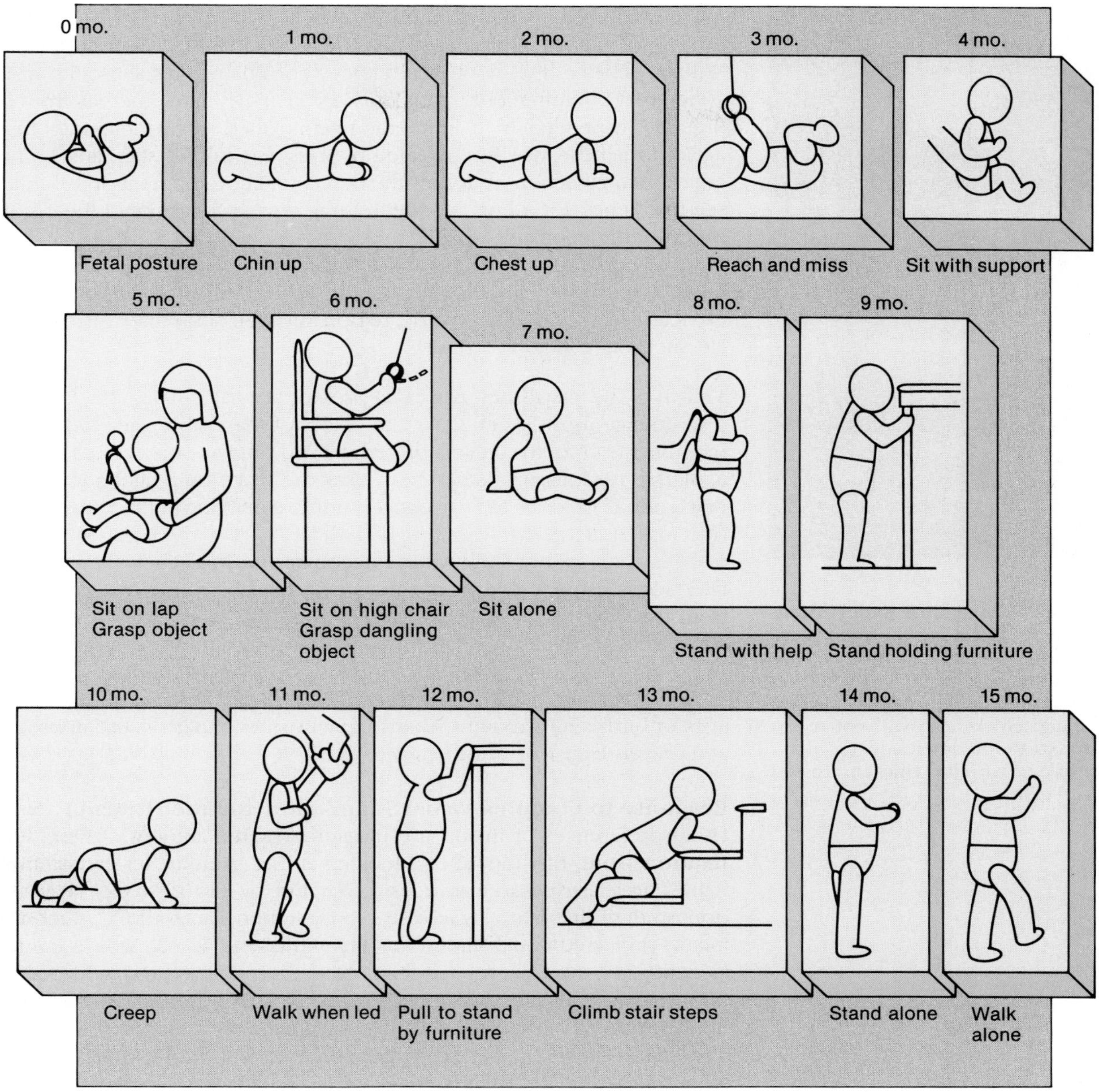

Figure 9.2
Development of Locomotion in Infants.

At birth, infants appear to be bundles of aimless "nervous energy." They have reflexive responses, but they also engage in random muscular movements. Random movement is replaced by purposeful activity as they mature. Infants develop locomotion, or movement from place to place, in an orderly sequence of steps. Practice helps infants learn to coordinate muscles, but maturation is essential. During the first six months, cells in the motor and sensorimotor areas of the brain mature to allow activities like crawling and, later, walking. The times in the figure are approximate: An infant who is a bit behind may develop with no problems at all, and a slightly precocious infant will not necessarily become another Albert Einstein (or Rudolph Nureyev).

drop out of the children's storehouse of responses, and many processes, such as the elimination of wastes, come under voluntary control. Children's locomotor development is chronicled in Figure 9.2.

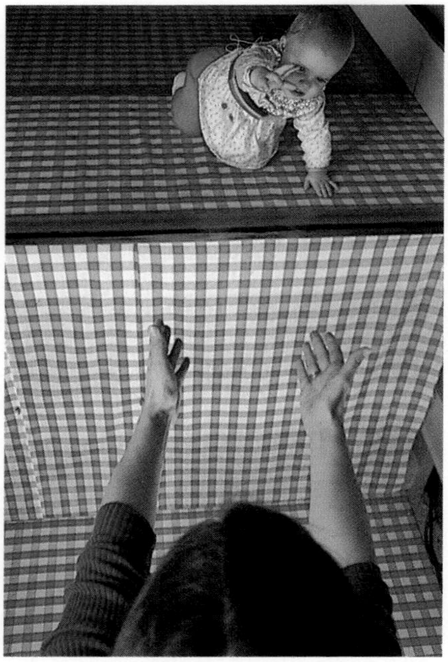

Figure 9.3
The Classic Visual Cliff Experiment. This young explorer has the good sense not to crawl out onto an apparently unsupported surface, even when Mother beckons from the other side. Rats, pups, kittens, and chicks also will not try to walk across to the other side. (So don't bother asking why the chicken crossed the visual cliff.)

Perceptual Development

William James (1890) wrote that the newborn baby must sense the world as "one great booming, buzzing confusion." The neonate emerges from being literally suspended in a temperature-controlled environment to being—again, in James's words—"assailed by eyes, ears, nose, skin, and entrails at once." In this section we follow the perceptual development of the child and see that James, for all his eloquence, might have exaggerated the disorganization of the neonate's world.

Newborn children spend about 16 hours a day sleeping and do not have much opportunity to learn about the world. Still, it seems that they are capable of perceiving the world reasonably well soon after birth (Haber & Hershenson, 1980).

Vision The **pupillary reflex** is present at birth. Infants may be able to discriminate most, if not all, of the colors of the visible spectrum by 2 to 3 months. By 4 months, infants prefer red and blue to other colors (Bornstein & Marks, 1982; Fagan, 1980). Newborns can fixate on a light and within the first couple of days can follow, or track, a moving light with their eyes (McGurk et al., 1977).

Neonates do not show **visual accommodation.** They see as through a fixed-focus camera. One consequence is that objects seven to nine inches from their eyes are seen most clearly. Estimates place their visual acuity at about 20/600 (Banks & Salapatek, 1981). But by about the age of 4 months or so, infants appear to be able to focus on objects about as efficiently as adults can. Their visual acuity makes the most dramatic gains between the ages of birth and 6 months. Gains in acuity then taper off and approximate adult levels by 1 to 5 years.

Response to Complex Visual Stimulation and the Human Face The visual preferences of infants are measured by the amount of time, termed **fixation time,** that they spend looking at one stimulus instead of another. Babies prefer stripes to featureless blobs and, by 8 to 12 weeks, curved lines over straight lines. In classic research by Robert Fantz (1961), 2-month-old infants preferred visual stimuli that resembled the human face as compared to newsprint, a bull's-eye, and featureless disks colored red, white, and yellow. In subsequent research (e.g., Haaf et al., 1983), babies have been shown facelike patterns that differ either according to the number of elements or the degree to which they are organized to match the human face. Five- to ten-week-old babies fixate longer on patterns that have high numbers of elements. The organization of the elements—that is, the degree to which they resemble the face—is less important. By the time infants are 15 to 20 weeks old, the organization of the pattern also matters, and the babies dwell longer on facelike patterns.

And so, it seems that infants have an inborn preference for complex as opposed to simple visual stimulation. However, it may well be that a preference for faces as opposed to other stimuli of equal complexity (and for certain facial expressions) does not emerge until infants have had experience with other people. Nurture as well as nature appears to play a role in infants' preferences.

Depth Perception Infants generally respond to monocular and binocular cues for depth by the time they are able to crawl about (6 to 8 months or so), as well as having the good sense to avoid crawling off ledges and tabletops into open space (Campos et al., 1978). Note the setup (Figure 9.3) in the classic "visual cliff" experiment run by Walk and Gibson (1961). An 8-month-old infant crawls freely above the portion of the glass with a check-

---

Pupillary reflex The automatic adjustment of the irises to permit more or less light to enter the eye.

Visual accommodation Automatic adjustment of the thickness of the lens in order to focus on objects.

Fixation time The amount of time spent looking at a visual stimulus.

erboard pattern immediately beneath but hesitates to crawl over the portion of the glass beneath which the checkerboard has been dropped by about four feet. Since the glass alone would support the infant, this is a "visual" rather than an actual cliff.

Psychologists can assess infants' "emotional" responses to the visual cliff long before the babies can crawl. For example, Joseph Campos and his colleagues (1970) found that 1-month-old infants showed no emotional response, as measured by changes in heart rate, when they were placed face-down on the visual cliff. At the age of 55 days, infants showed decreases in heart rate when so placed, which psychologists interpret as interest. The heart rates of 9-month-olds accelerated when the infants were placed on the cliff, which is interpreted as a fear response. Moreover, eight of ten crawling infants studied by Walk and Gibson refused to venture onto the visually unsupported glass surface, even when their mothers beckoned repeatedly.

The babies observed by Walk and Gibson also avoided the visual cliff when one of their eyes was covered, suggesting that they were able to rely on one-eyed, or monocular, cues to perceive depth.

Hearing Months before they are born, fetuses respond to sounds. Fetuses' middle and inner ears normally reach their mature sizes and shapes before birth (Aslin et al., 1983). Normal neonates hear well unless their middle ears are clogged with amniotic fluid. In such cases, hearing typically improves dramatically within a few hours or days.

Most neonates reflexively turn their heads toward unusual sounds and suspend other activities. Neonates normally respond to sounds of different duration, amplitude, and pitch. By the third day, they can discriminate between tones of 200 and 1,000 cycles per second. Pitch discrimination gradually extends to 20 to 20,000 cycles per second in the adult. But the pitches of the sounds of speech are well within the neonate's capabilities, and babies hear them about as well as adults do (Sinott et al., 1983). Three-day-old babies prefer their mothers' voices to those of other women, but they do not show similar preferences for the voices of their fathers (DeCasper & Fifer, 1980; Prescott & DeCasper, 1981). Remember that by the time they are born, children have had nine months of "experience" in the uterus, and, for a good part of this time, they have been capable of sensing sounds. Because they are predominantly exposed to sounds produced by their mothers, learning may contribute to neonatal preferences.

Smell: The Nose Knows Early Neonates can discriminate distinct odors, such as those of onions and licorice. Infants breathe more rapidly and are more active when presented with powerful odors, and they will turn away from unpleasant odors as early as from 16 hours to 5 days of age (Rieser et al., 1976). Neonates can become used to, or habituated to, even powerful odors, as can adults.

The nasal preferences of newborns are similar to those of older children and adults (Steiner, 1979). Newborn infants spit, stick out their tongues, and literally wrinkle their noses at the odor of rotten eggs. But they smile and show licking motions in response to chocolate, strawberry, vanilla, and honey.

The sense of smell, as the sense of hearing, may provide a vehicle for mother–infant recognition. Neonates respond to the odors of their mothers' breast secretions and underarms. Within the first week, nursing infants turn to look at their mothers' nursing pads (which can be discriminated only by the sense of smell) in preference to those of strange women (MacFarlane, 1977). By 15 days, nursing infants prefer their mothers' **axillary** odors to those of strange women (Cernoch & Porter, 1985).

Axillary Underarm.

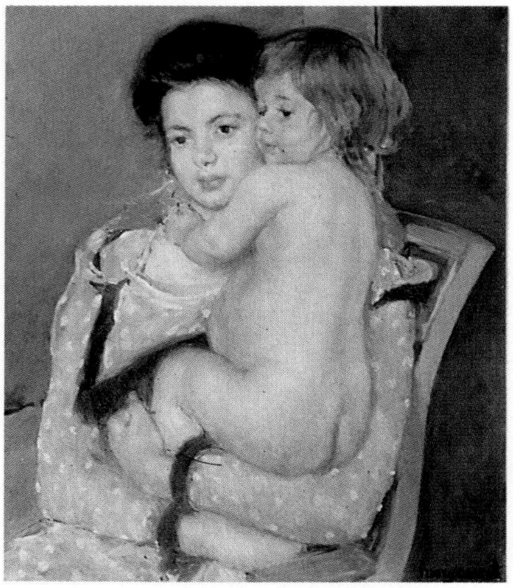

Attachment. This Mary Cassatt painting suggests the feelings of attachment that exist between *Mother and Child.* According to Ainsworth, "Attachment [is] an affectional tie that one person or animal forms between himself and another... that binds them together in space and endures over time."

Taste Shortly after birth, infants show the ability to discriminate taste. They suck liquid solutions of sugar and milk but grimace and refuse to suck salty or bitter solutions. Infants can clearly discriminate sweetness on the day following birth. The tongue pressure of 1-day-old infants sucking on a nipple correlates with the amount of sugar in their liquid diet.

Touch Newborn babies are sensitive to touch. Many reflexes (rooting and sucking are two) are activated by pressure against the skin. Yet newborns are relatively insensitive to pain, which may be adaptive considering the squeezing of the birth process. Sensitivity increases dramatically within a few days.

The sense of touch is an extremely important avenue of learning and communication for babies. Not only do the skin senses provide information, but sensations of skin against skin also appear to provide feelings of comfort and security that may contribute to the formation of affectionate bonds between infants and caregivers, as we shall see in the section on attachment.

ATTACHMENT

Attachment is a slippery concept. Parents and children do not tell one another, "I am attached to you." They speak of feeling love for one another, not attachment. But the concept of attachment is tied directly to behavior. According to Mary Ainsworth, one of the preeminent researchers in the area of attachment, "Attachment may be defined as an affectional tie that one person or animal forms between himself and another specific one—a tie that binds them together in space and endures over time" (1973).

The behaviors that define attachment include (1) attempts to maintain contact or nearness and (2) shows of anxiety when separated. Babies and children try to maintain contact with caregivers to whom they are attached. They engage in eye contact, pull and tug at them, ask to be picked up, and may even jump in front of them in such a way that they will be "run over" if they are not picked up!

Attachment is one measure of the quality of the care that children have received during infancy (Bretherton & Waters, 1985; Sroufe, 1985). **Securely attached** babies cry less frequently than **insecurely attached** babies. They are more likely to show affection toward their mothers, cooperate with them, and use their mothers as a base for exploration.

Stages of Attachment

John Bowlby (1980) is credited with first outlining phases in the development of attachment between infants and caregivers. His views have since been refined by Mary Ainsworth (1989).

Classic cross-cultural studies have provided insight into the stages of attachment. In one, Ainsworth (1967) traveled to Uganda, Africa, and observed infants who ranged in age from 2 to 14 months. She tracked their attachment behaviors over a nine-month period, including their efforts to maintain contact with the mother, their protests when separated, and their use of the mother as a base for exploring the environment. At first the Ugandan infants showed **indiscriminate attachment.** That is, they clearly preferred being held or being with someone to being alone, but they showed no preferences for familiar caregivers. Specific attachment to the mother began to develop at about 4 months and grew intense by about 7 months.

Attachment The enduring affectional tie that binds one person to another.

Secure attachment A type of attachment characterized by positive feelings toward attachment figures and feelings of security.

Insecure attachment A negative type of attachment, in which children show indifference or ambivalence toward attachment figures.

Indiscriminate attachment Showing of attachment behaviors toward any person.

Fear of strangers, if it developed at all, followed by one or two months.

From studies such as these, Mary Ainsworth (1978, 1984, 1985) identified three stages of attachment:

1. The **initial-preattachment phase,** which lasts from birth to about 3 months and is characterized by indiscriminate attachment.
2. The **attachment-in-the-making phase,** which occurs at about 3 or 4 months and is characterized by preference for familiar figures.
3. The **clear-cut-attachment phase,** which occurs at about 6 or 7 months and is characterized by intensified dependence on the primary caregiver—usually the mother.

Bowlby hypothesized a fourth phase occurring between the second and third and characterized by fear of strangers. But because not all children show fear of strangers, this phase is currently omitted.

Theoretical Views of Attachment

Attachment, like so many other behavior patterns, seems to develop as a result of the interaction between nature and nurture.

A Behavioral View of Attachment: Mothers as Reinforcers Early in the century, behaviorists argued that attachment behaviors are learned through conditioning. Caregivers feed their infants and tend to their other physiological needs. Thus, infants associate their caregivers with gratification and learn to approach them to meet their needs. From this perspective, a caregiver becomes a conditioned reinforcer. The feelings of gratification that are associated with meeting basic needs generalize into feelings of security when the caregiver is present.

Harlow's View of Attachment: Mother as a Source of Contact Comfort Research by psychologist Harry F. Harlow cast doubt on the behaviorist view that attachment is learned mechanically. Harlow had noted that infant rhesus monkeys reared without mothers or companions became attached to pieces of cloth in their cages. They maintained contact with them and showed distress when separated from them. Harlow conducted a series of experiments to find out why (Harlow, 1959).

In one study, Harlow placed rhesus monkey infants in cages with two surrogate mothers, as shown in Figure 9.4. One "mother" was made from wire mesh from which a baby bottle was extended. The other surrogate mother was made of soft, cuddly terry cloth. Infant monkeys spent most of their time clinging to the cloth mother, even though "she" did not gratify the need for food (see Figure 9.4). Harlow concluded that monkeys—and perhaps humans—have a primary (unlearned) need for **contact comfort** that is as basic as the need for food. Gratification of the need for contact comfort, rather than food, might be why infant monkeys (and humans) cling to their mothers.

Truth or Fiction Revisited

It is *not* necessarily true that babies become emotionally attached to those who feed them. Contact comfort might be a stronger wellspring of attachment.

Let's put it another way: the path to a monkey's heart may be through its skin, not its stomach.

Initial-preattachment phase The first phase in forming bonds of attachment, characterized by indiscriminate attachment.

Attachment-in-the-making phase The second phase in forming bonds of attachment, characterized by preference for familiar figures.

Clear-cut-attachment phase The third phase in forming bonds of attachment, characterized by intensified dependence on the primary caregiver.

Contact comfort A hypothesized primary drive to seek physical comfort from contact with another.

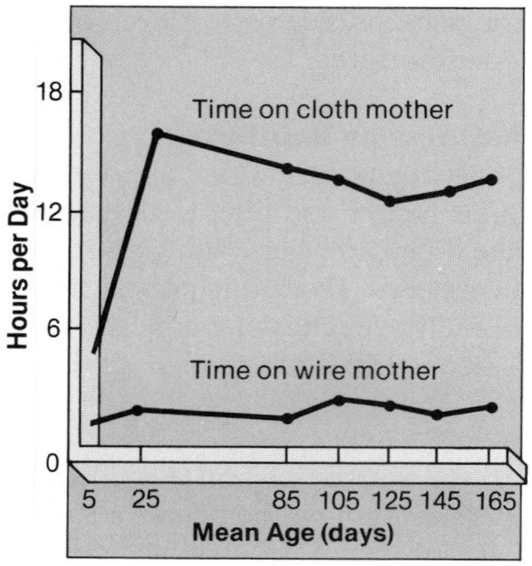

Figure 9.4
Attachment in Infant Monkeys. Although this rhesus monkey infant is fed by the "wire mother," it spends most of its time clinging to the soft, cuddly "terrycloth mother." It knows where to get a meal, but contact comfort is apparently a more central determinant of attachment in infant monkeys (and infant humans?) than is the feeding process.

Figure 9.5
Security. With its terrycloth surrogate mother nearby, this infant rhesus monkey apparently feels secure enough to explore the "bear monster" placed in its cage. But infants with only wire surrogate mothers, or with no mothers, remain cowering in a corner when the bear or other "monsters" are introduced.

Harlow and Zimmerman (1959) found that a surrogate mother made of terry cloth could also serve as a comforting base from which a rhesus infant could explore the environment. Toys such as stuffed bears (see Figure 9.5) and oversized wooden insects were placed in cages with rhesus infants and their surrogate mothers. When the infants were alone or had wire surrogate mothers for companions, they cowered in fear as long as the "bear monster" or "insect monster" was present. But when the terry-cloth mothers were present, the infants clung to them for a while and then explored the intruding "monster." With human infants, too, bonds of mother–infant attachment appear to provide a secure base from which infants feel encouraged to express their curiosity motives.

Imprinting: An Ethological View of Attachment Ethologists note that for many animals, attachment is an inborn fixed action pattern (FAP). The FAP of attachment, like other FAPs, is theorized to occur in the presence of a species-specific releasing stimulus and during a **critical period** of life.

Some animals become attached to the first moving object they encounter. The unwritten rule seems to be, "If it moves, it must be mother." It is as if

Figure 9.6
Imprinting. Quite a following? Konrad Lorenz may not look like Mommy to you, but these goslings became attached to him because he was the first moving object they perceived and followed. This type of attachment process is referred to as imprinting.

the image of the moving object becomes "imprinted" on the young animal, and so the formation of an attachment in this manner is called **imprinting.**

Ethologist Konrad Lorenz (1962, 1981) became well known when pictures of his "family" of goslings were made public (see Figure 9.6). How did Lorenz acquire his following? He was present when the goslings hatched, during their critical periods, and he allowed them to follow him. The critical period for geese and some other animals is bounded, at the younger end, by the age at which they first engage in locomotion and, at the older end, by the age at which they develop fear of strangers. The goslings followed Lorenz persistently, ran to him when frightened, honked with distress at his departure, and tried to overcome barriers between them. If you substitute crying for honking, it all sounds rather human.

If imprinting occurs with children, it cannot follow the mechanics that apply to waterfowl. Not all children develop fear of strangers. When they do, it occurs at about 6 to 8 months of age—*prior to* independent locomotion, or crawling, which usually occurs one or two months later. Human attachments also develop before and long after the middle of the first year of life.

Although there is no evidence for a critical period for the development of attachment among human parents and newborns, some investigators have argued for a weaker "maternal-sensitive" period.

Critical period A period of time when a fixed action pattern can be elicited by a releasing stimulus.

Imprinting A process occurring during a critical period in the development of an organism, in which that organism responds to a stimulus in a manner that will afterward be difficult to modify.

A CLOSER LOOK

Is There a "Maternal-Sensitive" Period for Bonding?

Physicians Marshall Klaus and John Kennell have suggested that there might be a **maternal-sensitive period,** governed by hormones, during which maternal–child "bonding" is most likely to occur. To some extent, their view has captured the public imagination, but let us consider the evidence.

In one study, Kennell and his colleagues (1974) randomly assigned a sample of new mothers and babies to standard hospital procedures or to extended early contact. In the control condition, babies were whisked away to the nursery soon after birth and visited their mothers for half-hour feeding periods throughout the remainder of the stay. The experimental group of mothers and neonates spent five hours a day together throughout the hospital stay.

Two-year follow-ups suggested that extended early contact had benefits for mothers and children (Klaus & Kennell, 1976). Extended-contact mothers were more likely to cuddle, soothe, and enjoy their babies. Their babies outpaced controls in their physical and intellectual development. However,

Maternal-sensitive period A period of time during which a mother, because of hormone levels in the body, is theorized to be particularly disposed toward forming mother–infant bonds of attachment.

the Kennell and Klaus studies and others like them are fraught with methodological problems (Chess & Thomas, 1982; Lamb, 1982; Myers, 1984). For example, the extended-contact mothers knew that they were receiving special treatment. They were a group of poor, unwed mothers who received child-care training from the hospital staff during their extended early contact. Conceiving themselves to be special and receiving the staff training may have led to the benefits we have noted—not the extended early contact itself. In their more recent writings, Klaus and Kennell themselves have admitted that the period immediately following birth provides just one of many opportunities for attachment to develop between caregivers and infants.

Despite flaws in their methodology, Kennell and Klaus's views have nurtured hospital initiation of rooming-in and special "bonding times" for parents, siblings, and newborns. These practices are not necessary for optimal development, but many families enjoy them and they certainly will do no harm.

DIMENSIONS OF CHILD REARING

Investigators of parental approaches to child rearing have found it useful to classify them according to two broad dimensions: warmth–coldness, and restrictiveness–permissiveness. These dimensions are independent. That is, warm parents can be restrictive or permissive. So can cold parents.

Warmth–Coldness Whether or not parents respond to their children with warmth, love, and affection usually reflects their feelings toward their children, not a philosophy of child rearing. Warm parents are affectionate toward their children. They tend to hug and kiss them and to smile at them frequently. They behave in ways that communicate their happiness at having children and their enjoyment in being with them (Sears et al., 1957). Cold parents may not enjoy being with their children and may have few feelings of affection for them. They are likely to complain about their children's behavior, saying that they are naughty or have "minds of their own."

Children of parents who are accepting and warm show fewer behavior problems (Martin, 1975). They are also more likely to develop goals and values similar to their parents' than are children of cold, rejecting parents (Martin, 1975). Maternal affection, when combined with intellectually stimulating mothering, also appears to contribute to competence (Pettit & Bates, 1984).

Restrictiveness–Permissiveness Parents must generally decide how restrictive they will be toward many of their children's behavior patterns. Consider just a brief list: diet; making excessive noise (screaming, screeching, demanding attention) when other children are sleeping or people are trying to converse; playing with dangerous objects or in dangerous areas; damaging property; keeping their rooms and other areas neat; and aggression.

Parents who are highly restrictive tend to impose many rules and to watch their children closely (Sears et al., 1957). Permissive parents impose few if any rules and supervise their children less closely. As a group, they are less concerned about cleanliness.

"Reasoning." The major inductive technique used by parents for enforcing restrictions is "reasoning." Reasoning is explaining why one sort of behavior is good and another is not.

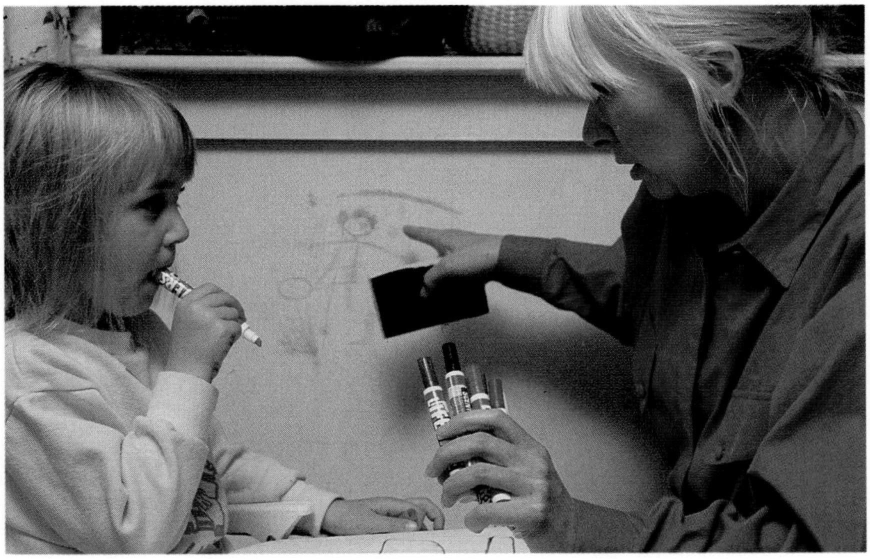

Ways in Which Parents Enforce Restrictions

Regardless of their general approaches to child rearing, most if not all parents are restrictive now and then, even if only when they are teaching their children not to run into the street or to touch the stove. However, parents use different techniques in restricting their children's behavior.

Inductive Techniques **Inductive** methods attempt to provide children with knowledge that will enable them to generate desirable behavior patterns in similar situations. The major inductive technique is "reasoning," or explaining why one sort of behavior is good and another is not.

Power-Assertive Methods Other parents use power or coercion. They tend to believe in physical rewards and punishments. They may give their children presents or special desserts when they are good and spank them when they are not. They often justify physical punishments through aphorisms such as "Spare the rod, and spoil the child." Power-assertive parents also tend to yell at their children rather than reason with them.

A study of abusive mothers found that they used more power-assertive techniques than controls (Oldershaw et al., 1986). They issued more commands and were less flexible, more intrusive, and more inconsistent in their use of parenting techniques than nonabusive mothers. In turn, their children were more noncompliant than the children of control mothers.

Loss of Love Still other parents attempt to control their children by threatening them with loss of love. They tend to isolate or ignore their children when they misbehave. At other times they express great disappointment. Because most children have strong needs for approval and for physical contact with their parents, loss of love can be more threatening than physical punishment.

The literature is not consistent on the effects of these different approaches toward enforcing social demands. Still, there is some evidence that

---

Inductive Going from the particular to the general. Descriptive of ways of enforcing restrictions that teach children the rationales.

the inductive approach can foster compliance and encourage the development of empathy and self-control. Physical rewards and punishments can modify behavior *in the situations in which they are applied,* but it is questionable that they foster empathy. The evidence concerning the effects of the threat of loss of love largely consists of clinical case studies, and their outcomes are not all that consistent. However, it may be that using loss of love, more than the other approaches, fosters feelings of anxiety and self-uncertainty.

COGNITIVE DEVELOPMENT

When she was 2½, my daughter Allyn confused me when she insisted that I continue to play Billy Joel on the stereo. Put aside the issue of her taste in music. My problem stemmed from the fact that when she asked for Billy Joel (the name of the singer), she could be satisfied only by my playing the first song ("Moving Out") on the album. When "Moving Out" ended and the next song, "The Stranger," began to play, she would insist that I play "Billy Joel" again. "That *is* Billy Joel," I would protest. "No! No!" she would insist, "I want Billy Joel!"

We went around in circles until it dawned on me that "Billy Joel," to her, symbolized the song "Moving Out," not the name of the singer. My daughter was conceptualizing *Billy Joel* as a *property* of a given song, not as the name of a person who could sing many songs. From the ages of 2 to 4, children tend to show confusion between symbols and the objects they represent. At their level of cognitive development, they do not recognize that words are arbitrary symbols for objects and events and that people could get together and decide to use different words for things. Instead, they tend to think of words as inherent properties of objects and events.

The developing thought processes of children—their cognitive development—is explored in this section. Cognitive functioning develops over a number of years, and children have ideas about the world that differ considerably from those of adults. Many of these ideas are charming but illogical. Swiss psychologist Jean Piaget (1896–1980) contributed significantly to our understanding of children's cognitive development.

Jean Piaget

Jean Piaget's Cognitive-Developmental Theory

In his early 20s, Jean Piaget obtained a job at the Binet Institute in Paris. His initial task was to develop a standardized version of the Binet intelligence test in French. In so doing, he questioned many children using potential items and became intrigued by their *incorrect* answers. Another investigator might have shrugged them off and forgotten them. Young Piaget realized that there were methods to his children's madness. The wrong answers reflected consistent, if illogical, cognitive processes.

Piaget hypothesized that children's cognitive processes develop in an orderly sequence of stages (1963). Although some children may be more advanced than others at particular ages, the developmental sequence is invariant. Piaget identified four major stages of cognitive development (see Table 9.2): *sensorimotor, preoperational, concrete operational,* and *formal operational.*

Table 9.2
Piaget's Stages of Cognitive Development

Stage	Approximate Age	Description
Sensorimotor	Birth–2 years	Behavior suggests that child lacks language and does not use symbols or mental representations of objects in the environment. Simple responding to the environment (through reflexive schemes) draws to an end, and intentional behavior—such as making interesting sights last—begins. The child develops the object concept and acquires the basics of language.
Preoperational	2–7 years	The child begins to represent the world mentally, but thought is egocentric. The child does not focus on two aspects of a situation at once and therefore lacks conservation. The child shows animism, artificialism, and immanent justice.
Concrete operational	7–12 years	The child shows conservation concepts, can adopt the viewpoint of others, can classify objects in series (for example, from shortest to longest), and shows comprehension of basic relational concepts (such as one object being larger or heavier than another).
Formal operational	12 years and above	Mature, adult thought emerges. Thinking seems to be characterized by deductive logic, consideration of various possibilities before acting to solve a problem (mental trial and error), abstract thought (for example, philosophical weighing of moral principles), and the formation and testing of hypotheses.

Piaget regarded children as natural physicists who actively intend to learn about and manipulate their worlds. In the Piagetan view, children who squish their food and laugh enthusiastically, for example, are often acting as budding scientists. In addition to enjoying a response from parents, they are studying the texture and consistency of their food. (Parents, of course, often wish that their children would practice these experiments in the laboratory, not the dining room.)

Piaget's view differs markedly from the behaviorist view that people merely react to environmental stimuli rather than intending to interpret and act on the world. Piaget saw people as actors, not reactors. Piaget believed that people purposefully form cognitive representations of, and seek to manipulate, the world.

Piaget's Basic Concepts: Assimilation and Accommodation Piaget described human thought or intelligence in terms of *assimilation* and *accommodation.* **Assimilation** is responding to a new stimulus through a reflex or existing habit. Infants, for example, usually try to place new objects in their mouths to suck, feel, or explore. Piaget would say that the child is assimilating a new toy to the sucking **scheme.** A scheme is a pattern of action or a mental structure that is involved in acquiring or organizing knowledge.

Accommodation is the creation of new ways of responding to objects or looking at the world. In accommodation, children transform existing schemes—action patterns or ways of organizing knowledge—in order to incorporate new events. Children (and adults) accommodate to objects and situations that cannot be integrated into existing schemes. The ability to accommodate to novel stimulation advances as a result of both maturation and learning, or experience.

Most of the time, newborn children assimilate environmental stimulation according to reflexive schemes, although adjusting the mouth to contain the nipple is a primitive kind of accommodation. Reflexive behavior, to Piaget, is not characteristic of "true" intelligence. True intelligence involves dealing with the world through a smooth, fluid balancing of the processes of assimilation and accommodation.

Assimilation According to Piaget, the inclusion of a new event into an existing scheme.

Scheme According to Piaget, a hypothetical mental structure that permits the classification and organization of new information.

Accommodation According to Piaget, the modification of schemes so that information inconsistent with existing schemes can be integrated or understood.

The Sensorimotor Stage The newborn infant is capable of assimilating novel stimulation only to existing reflexes (or ready-made schemes), such as the rooting and sucking reflexes. But by the time an infant reaches the age of 1 month, it will already show purposeful behavior by repeating behavior patterns that are pleasurable, such as sucking its hand. During the first month or so, an infant apparently does not connect stimulation perceived through different senses. Crude turning toward sources of auditory and olfactory stimulation has a ready-made look about it that can not be considered purposeful searching. But within the first few months, the infant begins to coordinate vision with grasping so that it simultaneously looks at what it is holding or touching.

A 3- or 4-month-old infant may be fascinated by its own hands and legs. It may become absorbed in watching itself open and close its fists. The infant becomes increasingly interested in acting on the environment to make interesting results (such as the sound of a rattle) last. Behavior becomes increasingly intentional and purposeful. Between 4 and 8 months of age, the infant explores cause-and-effect relationships, such as the thump that can be made by tossing an object or the way kicking can cause a hanging toy to bounce.

Prior to the age of 6 months or so, out of sight is literally out of mind. Objects are not yet mentally represented. For this reason, as you can see in Figure 9.7, a child will make no effort to search for an object that has been removed or placed behind a screen. By the ages of 8 to 12 months, however, infants realize that objects removed from sight still exist and attempt to find them. In this way they show what is known as **object permanence.**

During the second year of life, children begin to show interest in how things are constructed. It may be for this reason that they persistently touch and finger their parents' and their own faces. Toward the end of the second year, children begin to engage in mental trial and error before they try out overt behavior. For instance, when they look for an object you have removed, they will no longer begin their search in the last place it was seen. Rather, they may follow you, assuming that you are carrying the object, even though it is not visible. It is as though they are anticipating failure in searching for the object in the place where it was most recently seen.

Because the first stage of development is dominated by learning to coordinate perception of the self and of the environment with motor (muscular) activity, Piaget termed it the **sensorimotor stage.** The sensorimotor stage comes to a close at about the age of 2 with the acquisition of the basics of language.

The Preoperational Stage The **preoperational stage** is characterized by children's early use of words and symbols to represent objects and the relationships among them. But be warned—any resemblance between the logic of children between the ages of 2 to 7 and your own very often appears to be purely coincidental. Children may use the same words as adults do, but this does not mean that their views of the world are similar to adults' (Piaget, 1971).

For one thing, preoperational children are decidedly **egocentric.** They cannot understand that other people do not see things as they do. They often perceive the world as a stage that has been erected to meet their own needs or for their own amusement. For instance, when asked, "Why does the sun shine?" they may respond, "To keep me warm." Or if you ask, "Why is the sky blue?" they may respond, " 'Cause blue's my favorite color." Preoperational children also show **animism.** That is, they tend to attribute life and intentions to inanimate objects, such as the sun and the moon. They also show **artificialism,** the belief that environmental features like rain and thunder were designed and constructed by people. Again, when asked why the

---

Object permanence Recognition that objects removed from sight still exist, as demonstrated in young children by continued pursuit.

Sensorimotor stage The first of Piaget's stages of cognitive development, characterized by coordination of sensory information and motor activity, early exploration of the environment, and lack of language.

Preoperational stage The second of Piaget's stages, characterized by illogical use of words and symbols, spotty logic, and egocentrism.

Egocentric According to Piaget, assuming that others view the world as one does oneself.

Animism The belief that inanimate objects move because of will or spirit.

Artificialism The belief that natural objects have been created by human beings.

Figure 9.7
Object Permanence.

To the infant at the top, who is in the early part of the sensorimotor stage, out of sight is truly out of mind. Once a sheet of paper is placed between the infant and the toy elephant, the infant loses all interest in the toy. From evidence of this sort, Piaget concluded that the toy is not mentally represented. The bottom series of photos shows a child in a later part of the sensorimotor stage. This child does mentally represent objects and pushes through a towel to reach an object that has been screened from sight.

sky is blue, 4-year-olds may answer, " 'Cause Mommy painted it." Examples of egocentrism, animism, and artificialism are shown in Table 9.3.

To gain further insight into preoperational thinking, first consider these two problems: Imagine that you pour water from a tall, thin glass into a low, wide glass. Now, does the low, wide glass contain more than, less than, or the same amount of water as was in the tall, thin glass? I won't keep you in suspense. If you said the same (with possible minor exceptions for spillage and evaporation), you were correct. Now that you're rolling, here is the other problem. If you flatten a ball of clay into a pancake, do you wind up with more, less, or the same amount of clay? If you said the same, you are correct once more. To arrive at the correct answers to these questions, you must understand the law of **conservation.** This law holds that properties of substances such as mass, weight, and volume remain the same—that is, mass,

Conservation According to Piaget, recognition that properties of substances such as weight and mass remain constant even though their appearance may change.

Table 9.3
Examples of Preoperational Thought

Type of Thought	Sample Questions	Typical Answers
Egocentrism	Why does it get dark out?	So I can go to sleep.
	Why does the sun shine?	To keep me warm.
	Why is there snow?	For me to play in.
	Why is grass green?	Because that's my favorite color.
	What are TV sets for?	To watch my favorite shows and cartoons.
Animism (attributing life to inanimate objects)	Why do trees have leaves?	To keep them warm.
	Why do stars twinkle?	Because they're happy and cheerful.
	Why does the sun move in the sky?	To follow children and hear what they say.
	Where do boats go at night?	They sleep like we do.
Artificialism (assuming that environmental features have been fashioned by people)	What makes it rain?	Someone emptying a watering can.
	Why is the sky blue?	Somebody painted it.
	What is the wind?	A man blowing.
	What causes thunder?	A man grumbling.
	How does a baby get in Mommy's tummy?	Just make it first. (How?) You put some eyes on it, put the head on (etc.).

Source: Adapted from Cowan, 1978; Turner & Helms, 1987.

weight, and volume are *conserved*—even if you change the shape or arrangement of the substances.

Conservation requires the ability to think about, or **center,** on two aspects of a situation at once, such as height and width. Conserving the mass, weight, or volume of a substance requires recognition that a change in one dimension can compensate for a change in another. But the boy in Figure 9.8, who is in the preoperational stage, focuses only on *one dimension at a time.* First he is shown two tall, thin glasses of water and agrees that they have the same amount of water. Then, while he watches, water is poured from one tall glass into a squat glass. Now he is asked which glass has more water. After mulling over the problem, he points to the tall glass. Why? When he looks at the glasses, he is "overwhelmed" by the fact that the thinner glass is taller. The preoperational child focuses only on the most apparent dimension of the situation—in this case, the greater height of the thinner glass. He does not recognize that the gain in width in the new squat glass compensates for the loss in height. By the way, if you ask him whether any water has been added or taken away in the pouring process, he will readily reply no. But if you then repeat the question about which glass has *more* water, he will again point to the taller glass.

If all this sounds rather illogical, that is because it is illogical—or to be precise, preoperational.

After you have tried the experiment with the water, try the following. Make two rows with five pennies each. In the first row, place the pennies about half an inch apart. In the second row, place the pennies two to three inches apart. Ask a 4- to 5-year-old child which row has more pennies. What do you predict the child will answer? Why?

Piaget (1962) found that the moral judgment of preoperational children is usually **objective.** In judging how guilty people are for their misdeeds, preoperational children center on the amount of damage done. Older children and adults, in contrast, usually focus on the intentions or motives of the wrongdoer.

Center According to Piaget, to focus one's attention.

Objective moral judgment According to Piaget, moral judgments that are based on the amount of damage done rather than on the motives of the actor.

Concrete operational stage Piaget's third stage, characterized by logical thought concerning tangible objects, conservation, and subjective morality.

Subjective moral judgment According to Piaget, moral judgments that are based on the motives of the perpetrator.

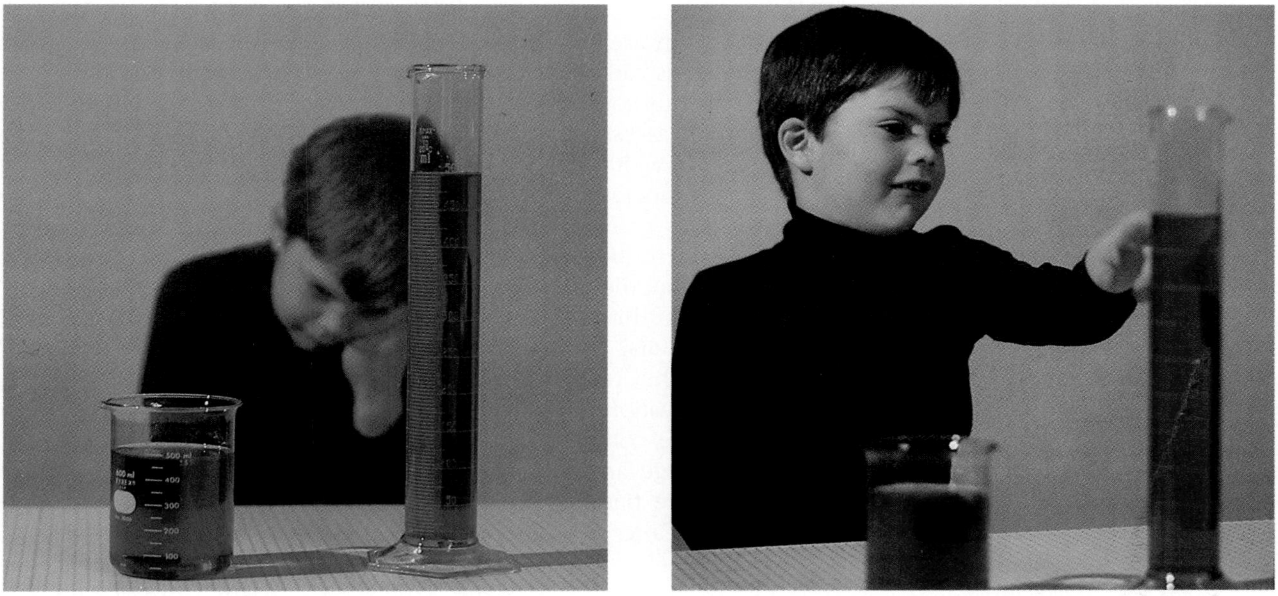

Figure 9.8
Conservation.

The boy in these photographs agreed that the amount of water in two identical containers is equal. He then watched as water from one container was poured into a tall, thin container. In the left-hand photograph, he is examining one of the original containers and the new container. When asked whether he thinks that the amounts of water in the two containers are now the same, he says no. Apparently he is impressed by the height of the new container, and, prior to the development of conservation, he focuses on only one dimension of the situation at a time—in this case, the height of the new container.

The Concrete Operational Stage. Children enter Piaget's stage of concrete operations by about the age of 7. In this stage, children show the beginnings of the capacity for adult logic, but their logical thought tends to involve tangible objects rather than abstract ideas. Concrete operational children can center simultaneously on various aspects of a problem, which makes tasks such as solving puzzles easier.

To demonstrate objective moral judgment, Piaget would tell children stories about people and ask them which character was naughtier and why. Barry, for instance, is helping his mother set the table when he accidentally bangs the dining room door into a tray and breaks nine cups and six plates. Harmon breaks three cups as he sneaks into a kitchen cabinet to find forbidden cookies. Who is naughtier, Barry or Harmon? The typical 4-year-old will say that Barry is naughtier. Why? He broke more china.

The Concrete Operational Stage By about the age of seven, the typical child is entering the stage of **concrete operations.** In this stage, which lasts until about the age of 12, children show the beginnings of the capacity for adult logic. However, their logical thought, or operations, generally involves tangible objects rather than abstract ideas. Concrete operational children can center simultaneously on two dimensions or aspects of a problem. This attainment has implications for moral judgments, conservation, and other intellectual undertakings.

Children now become **subjective** in their moral judgments. They center on the motives of wrongdoers as well as the amount of damage done when assigning guilt. Concrete-operational children judge Harmon more harshly than Barry, since Barry was trying to help his mother when he broke the plates and cups.

Concrete operational children show understanding of the laws of conservation. The boy in Figure 9.8, now a few years older, would say that the squat glass still has the same amount of water. If asked why, he might reply,

"Because you can pour it back into the other one." An answer to this effect also suggests awareness of the concept of **reversibility**—recognition that many processes can be reversed or undone so that things can be restored to their previous condition. Centering simultaneously on the height and the width of the glasses, the boy recognizes that the loss in height compensates for the gain in width.

Concrete operational children can conserve *number* as well as weight and mass. They recognize that there is the same number of pennies in each of the rows described earlier, even though one row may be spread out to look longer than the other.

Children in this stage are less egocentric. They are able to take on the roles of others and to view the world, and themselves, from other peoples' perspectives. They recognize that people see things in different ways because of different situations and different sets of values.

During the concrete operational stage, children's own sets of values begin to emerge and acquire stability. Children come to understand that feelings of love between them and their parents can endure even when someone feels angry or disappointed at the moment.

The Formal Operational Stage The stage of **formal operations** is the final stage in Piaget's theory. It begins at about the time of puberty and is the stage of cognitive maturity. Not all children enter this stage at puberty, and some people never reach it.

Formal operational children (and adults) think abstractly. They become capable of solving geometric problems about circles and squares without reference to what the circles and squares may represent in the real world. Children derive rules for behavior from general principles and can focus, or center, on many aspects of a situation at once in arriving at judgments and solving problems.

In a sense, it is during the stage of formal operations that people tend to emerge as theoretical scientists—even though they may see themselves as having little or no interest in science. As Cowan notes, it is in this stage that children "discover the world of the hypothetical" (1978, p. 249). They become aware that situations can have many different outcomes, and they can think ahead, systematically trying out different possibilities. Children—adolescents by now—also conduct experiments to determine whether their hypotheses are correct. These experiments are not carried out in the laboratory. Rather, adolescents may experiment with different tones of voice, ways of carrying themselves, and ways of treating others to see which sorts of behavior are most effective for them.

Children in this stage can reason deductively, or draw conclusions about specific objects or people once they have been classified accurately. Adolescents can be somewhat proud of their new logical abilities. A new sort of egocentrism can develop in which adolescents emotionally press for acceptance of their logic without recognition of the exceptions or practical problems that are often considered by adults. Consider this **syllogism:** "It is wrong to hurt people. Industry A occasionally hurts people (perhaps through pollution or economic pressures). Therefore, Industry A must be severely punished or dismantled." This thinking is logical. However, by impatiently pressing for immediate major changes or severe penalties, one may not fully consider various practical problems, such as thousands of resultant layoffs.

Evaluation of Piaget's Cognitive-Developmental Theory A number of questions, such as the following, have been raised concerning the accuracy of Piaget's views:

Reversibility According to Piaget, recognition that processes can be undone, that things can be made as they were.

Formal operational stage Piaget's fourth stage, characterized by abstract logical thought; deduction from principles.

Syllogism A form of reasoning in which a conclusion is drawn from two statements or premises.

1. *Was Piaget's timing accurate?* It seems that Piaget's methodology led him to underestimate the abilities of children. American researchers have used different methods, and they have found, for example, that preschoolers are less egocentric and that children are capable of conservation at earlier ages than Piaget believed.

2. *Is cognitive development discontinuous?* The most damaging criticism leveled at Piaget is that cognitive skills such as egocentrism and conservation appear to develop more continuously than Piaget thought—not in general stages. Cognitive psychologist John Flavell (1982) argues that cognitive development is "*not* very stage-like" at all (Flavell, 1982, p. 17). Flavell admits that "later cognitive acquisitions build on or are otherwise linked to earlier ones, and in their turn similarly prepare the ground for later ones" (1982, p. 18). However, the "acquisitions" process may be gradual, not discontinuous.

3. *Are developmental sequences invariant?* Here Piaget's views have fared better. It seems that the sequences of development are indeed invariant, as Piaget believed. I also think it is fair to say that the sequences of development might be more essential to Piaget's theory than their timing.

In sum, Piaget's theoretical edifice has been rocked, but it has not been dashed to rubble. Though research continues to wear away at his timing and at his belief that the stages of cognitive development are continuous, his observations on the sequences of development appear to remain relatively inviolate.

Many psychologists regard Piaget as a towering figure in the study of cognitive development, but it is erroneous to view his approach as the only one. There are many others, including information-processing approaches.

Information-Processing Approaches to Cognitive Development

Whereas Piaget viewed children as budding scientists, psychologists who study **information-processing** view children (and adults) as being similar to computer systems. Children, like computers, attain information ("input") from the environment, store it, retrieve and manipulate it, then respond to it overtly ("output"). One goal of the information-processing approach is to learn how children store, retrieve, and manipulate information—how their "mental programs" develop. Information-processing theorists also study the development of children's strategies for processing information.

Although there may be something to be gained from thinking of children as being computers, children, of course, are not computers. Children are self-aware and capable of creativity and intuition.

Pascual-Leone and Case's View Pascual-Leone and Case have advanced an information-processing view that focuses on children's capacity for memory and their use of cognitive strategies, such as the ways in which they focus their attention (Case, 1978; Case & Sandlos, 1980; Pascual-Leone, 1980; Pascual-Leone et al., 1978). These researchers note, for example, that certain Piagetan tasks require several cognitive strategies instead of one and that young children frequently fail at such tasks because they cannot hold many pieces of information in their short-term or working memories at once. Put another way, 3- and 4-year-old children can solve problems that have only

Information processing An approach to cognitive development that deals with childrens' advances in the input, storage, retrieval, manipulation, and output of information.

one or two steps, whereas older children can retain information from early steps as they proceed to subsequent steps.

Some aspects of development that were thought by Piaget to reflect an increasing capacity for the complexity and quality of thought may actually reflect an increasing capacity for storage and retrieval of information (Gelman & Baillargeon, 1983). Reconsider Piaget's study of children's moral reasoning in the story of the cups. As noted in the previous section, Barry breaks nine cups while trying to help his mother set the dinner table. Harmon breaks three cups while trying to steal a cookie. Who is naughtier: Barry or Harmon?

Most 5-year-olds would say that Barry is naughtier because he broke more cups, whereas 8-year-olds would usually consider Harmon to be naughtier because he was doing something wrong when he broke the cups. Piaget explained this age difference in terms of 5-year-olds' tendencies to focus on the amount of damage done instead of the intentions of the wrongdoer. However, many 5-year-olds say that Barry is naughtier because they can *remember that he broke more cups but not all the details of the two stories.* When the stories are repeated, and an effort is made to make sure that children remember them, even 5-year-olds frequently consider the intentions of the wrongdoer as well as the amount of damage done.

The average adult can keep about seven chunks of information—plus or minus two—in short-term memory at a time. As measured by digit span (see Chapter 7), the typical 3-year-old can work on one chunk of information at a time. At the ages of 5 and 6, the typical child can recall two digits. The ability to recall series of digits improves throughout middle childhood, and 15-year-olds, like adults, can keep about seven chunks of information in short-term memory at once (Pascual-Leone, 1970). Adolescents are typically capable of effectively rehearsing a new phone number to transfer it to long-term memory.

Development of Selective Attention Perhaps the initial cognitive strategy for solving problems is simply to attend to their elements. The ability to focus one's attention and screen out distractions advances steadily through middle childhood (Pick et al., 1975). Younger children (termed "preoperational" by Piaget) tend to focus their attention on one element of a problem at a time—a major reason that they lack conservation. Older children (termed "concrete operational" and "formal operational" by Piaget), in contrast, attend to multiple aspects of the problem at once, which permits them to conserve number, volume, and so on.

A classic experiment by Eleanor Maccoby and John Hagen (1965) illustrates how selective attention develops during middle childhood. The researchers showed children between 6 and 12 years of age pictures of elephants, buckets, scooters, and other objects and instructed them to remember only the colors of the pictures' *backgrounds.* They were told that the subjects themselves were immaterial. Recall of the background colors improved regularly with age, with 12-year-olds recalling about twice as many colors accurately as 6-year-olds. Then the researchers turned the tables on the children by asking them to recall the *subjects* of the pictures. Ironically, the 12-year-olds recalled *fewer* subjects correctly than the 6-year-olds, apparently because of their greater ability to focus their attention according to the original task demands.

Development of Metacognition and Metamemory Children's cognitive functioning is also enhanced by the development of *metacognition* and *metamemory.*

Metacognition refers to children's awareness and purposeful control of cognitive abilities. The ability to formulate problems, awareness of the cognitive processes required to solve a problem, activation of cognitive rules and strategies, keeping one's attention focused on the problem, and checking one's answers are all evidence of the emergence of metacognition.

Pascual-Leone and Case suggest that children's problem-solving abilities are largely made possible by (1) neurological developments that expand the working (short-term) memory and (2) growing automaticity in applying cognitive strategies. The younger child may have to count three sets of two objects each one by one to arrive at a total of six objects. The older child, with a larger working memory, familiarity with multiplication tables, and greater perceptual experience, is likely to arrive automatically at a total of six when three groups of two are perceived. Automaticity in adding, multiplying, and so on allows older children to solve math problems with several steps. Younger children, meanwhile, become occupied at length with individual steps, losing sight of the whole.*

Metamemory refers to the child's awareness of the functioning of his or her memory processes. Older children not only show superiority in information processing; they also show greater insight into how their processing of information works (Brown et al., 1983; Kail, 1984).

Older children also show more knowledge of strategies that can be used to facilitate memory. For example, 2- and 3-year-olds do not use rehearsal when asked to remember a list of items. Four- and five-year-olds will usually use rehearsal if someone else suggests that they repeat the list aloud, but they do not do this spontaneously until about the ages of 6 or 7 (Flavell & Wellman, 1976; Paris et al., 1982).

If you were trying to remember a new phone number, you would know to rehearse it several times or to write it down before doing a series of math problems. Five-year-olds, when asked whether it would make a difference if they jotted down the number before or after doing the math problems, do not reliably report that doing the problems first would matter. Ten-year-olds, however, are aware that new mental activities (the math problems) can interfere with old ones (trying to remember the telephone number) and usually suggest jotting down the number before attempting the math problems.

Let us now turn our attention to Lawrence Kohlberg's theory of moral development and see how children process information that leads to judgments of right and wrong.

Lawrence Kohlberg's Theory of Moral Development

Psychologist Lawrence Kohlberg (1981) originated a theory to explain how children's cognitive development lays the groundwork for different styles of moral reasoning. Before we formally discuss Kohlberg's views, read the following tale used by Kohlberg (1969) in much of his research, and answer the questions that follow.

In Europe a woman was near death from a special kind of cancer. There was one drug that the doctors thought might save her. It was a form of radium that a druggist in the same town had recently discovered. The

Metacognition Awareness and control of one's cognitive abilities, as shown by intentional use of cognitive strategies in solving problems.

Metamemory Knowledge of the functions and processes in one's own memory, as shown by use of cognitive strategies to retain information.

*In Chapter 7 we saw that automaticity in processing information is an element in Robert Sternberg's (1985) theory of intelligence.

Table 9.4
Kohlberg's Levels and Stages of Moral Development

Levels	Stages	Illustrative Responses to Story of Heinz's Stealing of the Drug
Level I: Preconventional level	Stage 1: Obedience and punishment orientation	It isn't really bad to take it—he did ask to pay for it first. He wouldn't do any other damage or take anything else, and the drug he'd take is only worth $200; he's not really taking a $2,000 drug.
	Stage 2: Naively egoistic orientation	Heinz isn't really doing any harm to the druggist, and he can always pay him back. If he doesn't want to lose his wife, he should take the drug because it's the only thing that will work.
Level II: Conventional level	Stage 3: "Good-boy orientation"	Stealing is bad, but this is a bad situation. Heinz isn't doing wrong in trying to save his wife; he has no choice but to take the drug. He is only doing something that is natural for a good husband to do. You can't blame him for doing something out of love for his wife. You'd blame him if he didn't love his wife enough to save her.
	Stage 4: Respect for authority and social order. Orientation to "doing duty" and to showing respect for authority.	The druggist is leading a wrong kind of life if he just lets somebody die like that, so it's Heinz's duty to save her. But Heinz can't just go around breaking laws and let it go at that—he must pay the druggist back and he must take his punishment for stealing.
Level III: Postconventional level	Stage 5: Contractual legalistic orientation	Before you say stealing is wrong, you've got to really think about this whole situation. Of course, the laws are quite clear about breaking into a store. And, even worse, Heinz would know there are no legal grounds for his actions. Yet I can see why it would be reasonable for anybody in this situation to steal the drug.
	Stage 6: Conscience or principled orientation	Where the choice must be made between disobeying a law and saving a human life, the higher principle of preserving life makes it morally right—not just understandable—to steal the drug.

Source: R. J. Rest (1974).

drug was expensive to make, but the druggist was charging ten times what the drug cost him to make. He paid $200 for the radium and charged $2,000 for a small dose of the drug. The sick woman's husband, Heinz, went to everyone he knew to borrow the money, but he could only get together about $1,000, which was half of what it cost. He told the druggist that his wife was dying and asked him to sell it cheaper or let him pay later. But the druggist said: "No, I discovered the drug and I'm going to make money from it." So Heinz got desperate and broke into the man's store to steal the drug for his wife.

What do you think? Should Heinz have tried to steal the drug? Was he right or wrong? As you can see from Table 9.4, the issue is more complicated than a simple yes or no. Heinz's story is an example of a moral dilemma in which a legal or social rule (in this case, laws against stealing) is pitted against a strong human need (Heinz's desire to save his wife). According to Kohlberg's theory, children and adults arrive at yes or no answers for different reasons. These reasons can be classified according to the level of moral development they reflect.

As a stage theorist, Kohlberg argues that the stages of moral reasoning follow an invariant sequence. Different children progress at different rates, and not all children (or adults) reach the highest stage. But children must go through stage 1 before they enter stage 2, and so on. According to Kohlberg, there are three levels of moral development and two stages within each level.

Preconventional level According to Kohlberg, a period during which moral judgments are based largely on expectation of rewards or punishments.

The Preconventional Level In the **preconventional level,** which applies to most children through about the age of 9, children base their moral judgments on the consequences of their behavior. For instance, stage 1 is oriented toward obedience and punishment. Good behavior is seen as that which involves obedience and allows one to avoid punishment.

In stage 2, good behavior is that which will allow people to satisfy their own needs and, sometimes, the needs of others. (Heinz's wife needs the drug; therefore, stealing the drug—the only way of attaining it—is not wrong.)

The Conventional Level In the **conventional level** of moral reasoning, right and wrong are judged by conformity to conventional (family, church, societal) standards of right and wrong. According to the stage 3 "good-boy orientation," it is good to meet the needs and expectations of others. During this stage, moral behavior is seen as being what is "normal"—that is, what the majority does. (Heinz should steal the drug because that is what a "good husband" would do. It is "natural" or "normal" to try to help one's wife. *Or,* Heinz should *not* steal the drug because "good people do not steal.")

In stage 4, moral judgments are based on rules that maintain the social order. Showing respect for authority and doing one's duty are valued highly. (Heinz must steal the drug; it would be his responsibility if he let his wife die. He would pay the druggist when he could.) Many people do not mature beyond the conventional level.

Stage 3 moral judgments are found most frequently among 13-year-olds, and stage 4 judgments most often among 16-year-olds (Kohlberg, 1963). According to a review of the research, juvenile delinquents of the same ages are more likely to show stage 2 moral reasoning (Blasi, 1980). Stage 2 reasoning (viewing right and wrong in terms of satisfying personal needs) is also characteristic of adult offenders who engage in robbery and other "instrumental" crimes (Thornton & Reid, 1982).

The Postconventional Level In the **postconventional level,** moral reasoning is based on the person's own moral standards. In each instance, moral judgments are derived from personal values, not from conventional standards or authority figures. In stage 5's contractual, legalistic orientation, it is recognized that laws stem from agreed-upon procedures and that many laws have great value and should not be violated. But it is also recognized that there are circumstances in which existing laws cannot bind the individual's behavior. (Although it is illegal for Heinz to steal the drug, in this case it is the right thing to do.)

In stage 6's principled orientation, people choose their own ethical principles—such as justice, **reciprocity,** and respect for individuality. Behavior that is consistent with these principles is considered to be right. If a law is seen as being unjust or as contradicting the rights of the individual, it is wrong to obey it.

Postconventional people look to themselves as the highest moral authority. This point has created confusion, because to some it suggests that it is right for people to break the law or ignore social conventions whenever it is convenient. But this interpretation is inaccurate. Kohlberg means that postconventional people are obligated to do what they believe is right, even if it counters social rules or laws or demands personal sacrifice.

Not all people reach the postconventional level of moral reasoning. Postconventional moral judgments were absent among the 7- to 10-year-olds in Kohlberg's (1963) sample of American children. Postconventional judgments are found more frequently during the early and middle teens so that by age 16, stage 5 reasoning is shown by about 20 percent and stage 6 reasoning by about 5 percent of adolescents. However, stage 3 and 4 judgments are made more frequently at all ages, 7 through 16, studied by Kohlberg and other investigators (Colby et al., 1983; Rest, 1983).

Conventional level According to Kohlberg, a period during which moral judgments largely reflect social conventions. A "law and order" approach to morality.

Postconventional level According to Kohlberg, a period during which moral judgments are derived from moral principles and people look to themselves to set moral standards.

Reciprocity Mutual action.

Evaluation of Kohlberg's Theory There is evidence that the moral judgments of children develop toward higher stages in sequence (Snarey et al., 1985), even though most children do not reach postconventional thought. Postconventional thought, when found, first occurs during adolescence. A number of studies (Kuhn et al., 1977; Tomlinson-Keasey & Keasey, 1974) suggests that formal operational thinking is a precedent for postconventional reasoning, which requires the capacities to understand abstract moral principles and to empathize with the attitudes and emotional responses of other people.

Consistent with Kohlberg's theory, children do not appear to skip stages as they progress (Kohlberg & Kramer, 1969; Kuhn, 1976; White et al., 1978). When children are exposed to adult models who engage in a lower type of moral reasoning, they can be induced to express the patterns of judgment characteristic of the earlier stage (Bandura & McDonald, 1963). However, children exposed to examples of moral reasoning above and below that of their own stage generally prefer the higher level of reasoning (Rest, 1976, 1983). Thus the thrust of moral development is from lower to higher stages, even if children can be sidetracked by social influences.

Kohlberg believed that the stages of moral development are universal, following the unfolding of innate sequences. However, stages 1 through 4 are found in about 90 percent of cultures studied around the world, and postconventional thought is found in only 64 percent (Snarey, 1987). Postconventional thinking is virtually absent in tribal and village societies. Critics have suggested that postconventional reasoning, especially stage 6 reasoning, may be more reflective of Kohlberg's philosophical ideals than of a natural stage of cognitive development. Stage 6 reasoning, for example, is based on supposedly "universal" ethical principles. The principles of justice, equality, integrity, and reverence for life may have a high appeal to you, but you were reared in a culture that idealizes them. They are not held universally. They are more reflective of Western cultural influences than of the child's cognitive development. In recognition of these problems, Kohlberg (1985) has virtually dropped stage 6 reasoning from his theory in recent years.

Moreover, some cultures have developed moral principles not covered by Kohlberg's theory (Snarey, 1987). For example, natives of Papua New Guinea and persons living on Israeli kibbutzim have developed a principle of collective moral responsibility. According to one aspect of this principle, Heinz should take the drug because all resources should be available to the community at large.

Truth or Fiction Revisited

It is true, within our culture, that the highest level of moral reasoning involves relying on our own views of what is right and wrong (i.e., postconventional moral reasoning). However, postconventional thought is not found in all cultures, and there is more support for stage 5 reasoning than for stage 6 reasoning.

ADOLESCENCE

Adolescence The period of life bounded by puberty and the assumption of adult responsibilities.

In the last century, psychologist G. Stanley Hall described **adolescence** as a time of *Sturm und Drang*—storm and stress. He attributed the conflicts and distress of adolescence to biological changes. However, anthropologists

Adolescents. In our culture, adolescents are "neither fish nor fowl." Although they may be old enough to reproduce and may be as large as their parents, adolescents are often treated like children.

such as Ruth Benedict (1934) and Margaret Mead (1935) have found cross-cultural evidence that the problems of adolescence reflect cultural influences and expectations rather than hormonal changes or patterns of physical growth.

Adolescence is heralded by puberty, which begins with the appearance of **secondary sex characteristics,** such as the growth of body hair, deepening of the voice in males, and rounding of the breasts and hips in females. Puberty ends when the long bones make no further gains in length so that full height is attained. But adolescence ends with psychosocial markers, such as assumption of adult responsibilities. Adolescence is a psychological concept with biological correlates, but puberty is a biological concept.

The Growth Spurt

The stable growth patterns in height and weight that characterize early and middle childhood come to an abrupt end with the adolescent growth spurt. Girls begin to spurt at about 10 years 3 months and boys at about 11 years 9 months. The spurts last between two and three years, with boys' spurts lasting about a half year longer than girls'. Adolescents add some 8 to 12 inches in height during this period, with boys, as a group, winding up several inches taller and many pounds heavier than girls.

In boys, the muscle mass increases notably in weight, and there are gains in shoulder width and chest circumference. At 20 or 21, men stop growing taller because testosterone prevents the long bones from making further gains in length. Estrogen brakes the female growth spurt earlier than testosterone brakes that of males. Girls deficient in estrogen during their late teens may grow quite tall, but most tall girls reach their heights because of genetically determined variations. Adolescents often eat enormous quantities of food to fuel their growth spurts. Adults fighting the battle of the bulge stare at them in wonder as they wolf down French fries and shakes at the fast-food counter and later go out for pizza.

Secondary sex characteristics Characteristics that differentiate the sexes, such as distribution of body hair and depth of voice, but that are not directly involved in reproduction.

Puberty

At puberty, pituitary hormones in boys stimulate the testes to increase the output of testosterone, causing the penis and testes to grow and pubic hair to appear. By age 13 or 14, erections become frequent and boys may ejaculate. Ejaculatory ability usually precedes the presence of mature sperm by at least a year, so ejaculation is not evidence of reproductive capacity. Axillary, or underarm, hair appears at about 15. At 14 or 15 the voice deepens because of growth of the larynx, or voice box.

In girls, pituitary secretions cause the ovaries to begin to secrete estrogen, which stimulates growth of breast tissue as early as 8 or 9. Estrogen promotes growth of fatty and supportive tissue in the hips and buttocks and widens the pelvis, rounding the hips. Small amounts of androgens produced by the adrenal glands, along with estrogen, stimulate growth of pubic and axillary hair. Estrogen and androgens work together to stimulate the growth of female sex organs. Estrogen production becomes cyclical in puberty and regulates the menstrual cycle. First menstruation, or **menarche,** usually occurs between the ages of 11 and 14. But girls cannot become pregnant until they begin to ovulate, about two years later.

Truth or Fiction Revisited

It is *not* true that girls are capable of becoming pregnant after they have their first menstrual periods. Menarche can precede ovulation by about a year or more.

Menarche is a "dividing time" for females in American society (Matlin, 1987). At menarche, girls come of age. A young girl might play football or lounge around in the home, even in the bedroom, of the boy next door. Now and then her father invites her to sit on his lap. But after menarche, mothers often caution, "You're too big for that now."

Boys who reach physical and sexual maturity early are usually more popular and more likely to be leaders than late-maturing peers (Jones, 1957; Mussen & Jones, 1957). Their edge in sports and the admiration of peers boost their self-worth. But early maturation can hit some boys before they are psychologically prepared to live up to the expectations of others, such as athletic coaches who expect them to excel or peers who want them to fight their battles.

Truth or Fiction Revisited

It is true that early maturing boys are more popular than late maturing boys.

The situation is somewhat reversed for girls. With their tallness and developing bustlines, early-maturing girls are conspicuous. Boys their own age may tease them, and older boys may try to pressure them into sexual activity (Simmons et al., 1983). Early-maturing girls are less poised and sociable than their late-maturing peers but appear to adjust by the high school years (Jones, 1958; Livson & Peskin, 1980).

Adolescent Behavior and Conflicts

In our society, adolescents are "neither fish nor fowl," as the saying goes—neither children nor adults. Although adolescents may be old enough to reproduce and are as large as their parents, they are often treated quite differently. They may not be eligible for driver's licenses until they are 16

Menarche (men-NARK-key). The beginning of menstruation.

or 17, and they cannot attend R-rated films unless accompanied by an adult. They are prevented from working long hours. They are required to remain in school usually through age 16. They may not marry until they reach the "age of consent."

The message is clear. Adolescents are seen as an emotional, impulsive lot. They must be restricted for their own good.

According to Roger Gould's (1975) research with 524 men and women of various age groups, a major concern of 16- to 18-year-olds is a yearning for independence from parental domination. Given the restrictions placed on adolescents, their yearning for independence, and a sex drive heightened by high levels of sex hormones, it is not surprising that many adolescents report frequent conflict with their families.

Ego Identity versus Role Diffusion According to psychoanalyst Erik Erikson, the major challenge of adolescence is the creation of an adult identity. This is accomplished primarily through choosing and developing a commitment to an occupation or a role in life.

Erikson (1963) theorizes that adolescents experience a life crisis of *ego identity versus role diffusion.* If this crisis is resolved properly, adolescents develop a firm sense of who they are and what they stand for. This sense of **ego identity** can carry them through difficult times and color their achievements with meaning. If they do not resolve this life crisis properly, they may experience **role diffusion.** They then spread themselves thin, running down one blind alley after another and placing themselves at the mercy of leaders who promise to give them the sense of identity they cannot mold for themselves.

One aspect of attaining ego identity is learning "how to connect the roles and skills cultivated earlier with the occupational prototypes of the day" (Erikson, 1963, p. 261)—that is, with jobs. But development of ego identity also extends to sexual, political, and religious beliefs and commitments.

Now let us turn our attention to development during adulthood.

ADULT DEVELOPMENT

Development continues throughout a lifetime. Many theorists, including Erik Erikson and Daniel Levinson, believe that adult concerns and involvements are patterned in such a way that we can speak of stages of adult development.

Young Adulthood

Young or early adulthood covers the two decades from ages 20 to 40. Our chronicling of these years is based primarily on the views of Erik Erikson, Daniel Levinson and his colleagues, and the journalist Gail Sheehy.

Erikson's Stage of Intimacy versus Isolation According to Erik Erikson (1963), young adulthood is the stage of **intimacy versus isolation.** Erikson saw the establishment of intimate relationships as being a central task of young adulthood. Young adults who have evolved a firm sense of identity during adolescence are now ready to "fuse" their identities with those of other people through relationships such as marriage and the establishment of abiding friendships.

Erikson warns that we may not be capable of committing ourselves to others in a meaningful way until we have achieved ego identity, or

Ego identity Erikson's term for a firm sense of who one is and what one stands for.

Role diffusion Erikson's term for lack of clarity in one's life roles—a function of failure to develop ego identity.

Intimacy versus isolation Erikson's life crisis of young adulthood, which is characterized by the task of developing abiding intimate relationships.

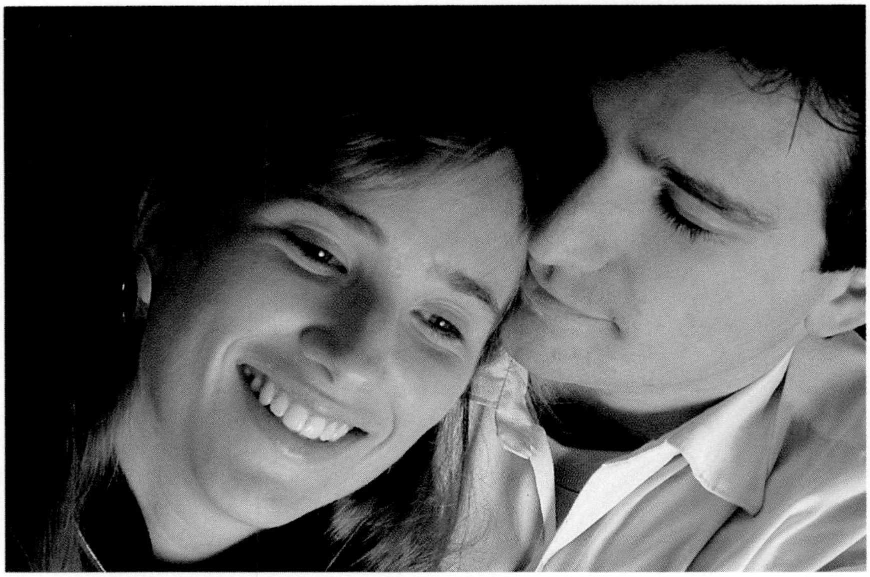

Establishing Intimate Relationships. According to Erik Erikson, establishing intimate relationships is a central task of young adulthood.

"Making It." For many people, young adulthood is characterized by striving to advance in the career world.

established stable life roles. Achieving ego identity in Erikson's theory is the central task of adolescence. Lack of personal stability may be one reason that teenage marriages suffer a much higher divorce rate than those formed in adulthood.

Erikson argues that people who do not reach out to develop intimate relationships risk retreating into isolation and loneliness.

Levinson's Seasons According to Daniel Levinson's in-depth study of 40 men, which was published in 1978 as *The Seasons of a Man's Life,* we enter the adult world in our early 20s (see Figure 9.9). Upon entry, we are faced with the tasks of exploring adult roles (in terms of careers, intimate relationships, etc.) and of establishing some stability in the roles we choose. At this time we also often adopt a **dream,** which serves as a tentative blueprint for our lives and is characterized by the drive to "become" someone, to leave our mark on history.

Sheehy's Passages Surveys show that adults in their 20s tend to be fueled by ambition as they strive to establish their pathways in life (Gould, 1975; Sheehy, 1976). Gail Sheehy labeled the 20s the **Trying 20s**—a period during which people basically strive to advance themselves in the career world.

In one phase of her work, reported in her book *Passages,* Sheehy (1976) interviewed 115 people drawn largely from the middle and upper classes, including many managers, executives, and other professionals. In another phase, she examined 60,000 questionnaires filled out by readers of *Redbook* and *Esquire* magazines, reported in her 1981 book *Pathfinders.* The young adults in her samples were concerned about establishing their pathways in life, finding their places in the world. They were generally responsible for their own support, made their own choices, and were largely free from parental influences.

During the 20s, many of us feel "buoyed by powerful illusions and belief in the power of the will [so that] we commonly insist . . . that what we have chosen to do is the one true course in life" (Sheehy, 1976, p. 33). This "one true course" usually turns out to have many swerves and bends. As we develop, what seemed to be important one year can lose some of its allure in the next. That which we hardly noticed can gain prominence.

Dream In this usage, Levinson's term for the overriding drive of youth to become someone important, to leave one's mark on history.

Trying 20s Sheehy's term for the third decade of life, when people are frequently occupied with advancement in the career world.

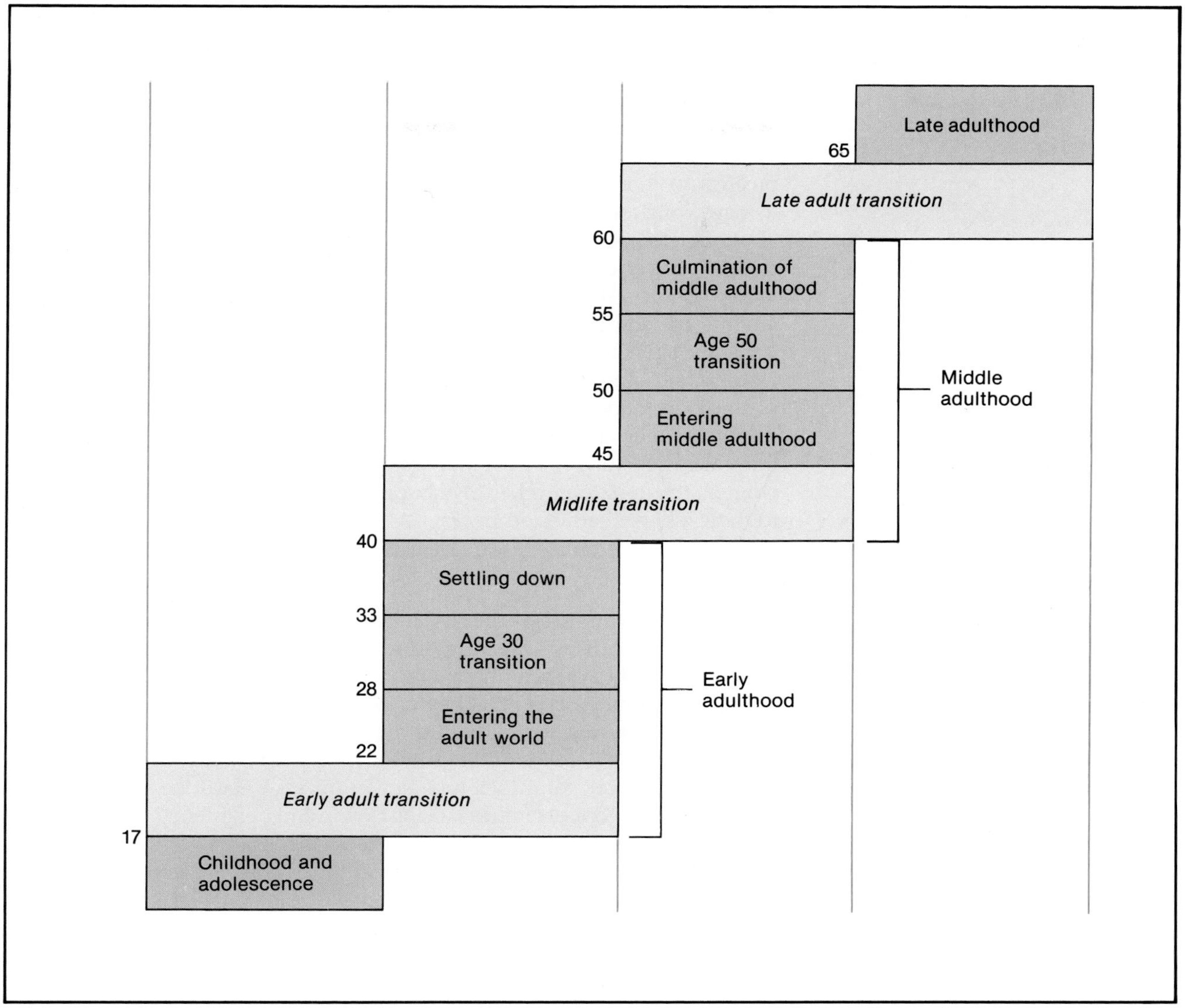

Figure 9.9
The Seasons of a Man's Life.

Daniel Levinson and his colleagues break young, middle, and late adulthood down into a number of developmental periods, including several transitions. Our major tasks as we enter the adult world are to explore and to establish some stability in our adult roles. During the age 30 transition, we reevaluate our earlier choices. How does women's adult development differ from men's?

A CLOSER LOOK

Sex Differences in Developmental Patterns of Young Adulthood

On the basis of his samples drawn from psychiatric clinics, psychiatrist Roger Gould (1975) suggested that men's development seems to be generally guided by needs for individuation (separation from others) and autonomy (self-direction). Psychologists who have focused on the development of women, such as Judith Bardwick (1980) and Carol Gilligan (1982), have found that women are relatively more likely to be guided by changing patterns of attachment and caring. In becoming adults, men are likely to undergo a transition from restriction to control. But women, as pointed out by Gilligan (1982), are relatively more likely to undergo a transition from being cared for to caring for others.

Levinson has recognized that he was remiss in studying only men in earlier years, and he has recently become involved in research into the "seasons" of women's lives. One of his findings is that many young, successful businesswomen differ from their male counterparts in that they are less likely to have long-term business goals: "They want to be independent but they are conflicted about ambition" (cited in Brown, 1987). Some of the conflict stems from concerns about whether ambition is compatible with femininity. Other conflicts stem from practical concerns about balancing a career with a home life and child-rearing.

Although there are very important differences in the development of women and men, a study by Ravenna Helson and Geraldine Moane (1987) of the University of California found that between the ages of 21 and 27, college women do develop in terms of individuation and autonomy. That is, they, like men, tend to assert increasing control over their own lives. College women, of course, are relatively liberated and career-oriented in comparison to their less-well-educated peers.

The Age 30 Transition Levinson labeled the ages of 28 to 33 the **age 30 transition.** For many, this is a period of reassessment of the choices made during the early 20s. A number of researchers have noted that women frequently encounter a crisis that begins between the ages of 27 and 30 (Reinke et al., 1985). During the early 30s, many of the women studied by Helson and Moane (1987) felt exploited by others, alone, weak, limited, and as if they would "never get myself together." Concerns about nearing the end of the fertile years, opportunities closing down, and heightened responsibilities at home and work all make their contributions.

For men and women, the late 20s and early 30s are commonly characterized by self-questioning: "Where is my life going?" "Why am I doing this?" Sheehy (1976) labeled the 30s the **Catch 30s** because of such reassessment. During the 30s, we often find that the life styles we adopted during the 20s do not fit as comfortably as we had anticipated.

One response to the disillusionments of the 30s, according to Sheehy,

> *is the tearing up of the life we have spent most of our 20s putting together. It may mean striking out on a secondary road toward a new vision or converting a dream of "running for president" into a more realistic goal. The single person feels a push to find a partner. The woman who was previously content at home with children chafes to venture into the world. The childless couple reconsiders children. And almost everybody who is married . . . feels a discontent (1976, p. 34).*

Settling Down According to Levinson, the ages of about 33 to 40 are characterized by settling down. Men during this period still strive to forge ahead in their careers, their interpersonal relationships, and their communities. During the latter half of their 30s, men are also concerned about "becoming one's own man." That is, they desire independence and autonomy in their careers and adult relationships. Promotions and pay increases are important as signs of success.

Similarly, Sheehy found that young adults who had successfully ridden out the storm of reassessments of the Catch 30s begin the process of "rooting" at this time. They feel a need to put down roots, to make a financial and emotional investment in their homes. Their concerns become more

Age 30 transition Levinson's term for the ages from 28 to 33, which are characterized by reassessment of the goals and values of the 20s.

Catch 30s Sheehy's term for the fourth decade of life, when many people undergo major reassessments of their accomplishments and goals.

focused on promotion or tenure, career advancement, and long-term mortgages.

Middle Adulthood

Middle adulthood spans the years from 40 to 60 or 65. Some authors, such as Levinson and his colleagues (1978), consider the years from 60 to 65 separately as a transition to late adulthood.

Erikson's Stages of Psychosocial Development Erikson (1963) labels the life crisis of the middle years that of **generativity versus stagnation.** In other words, are we still striving to produce or to rear our children well, or are we marking time, treading water? Generativity by and large requires doing things that we believe are worthwhile. In so doing, we enhance and maintain our self-esteem. Generativity also involves the Eriksonian ideal of helping shape the new generation. This shaping may involve rearing our own children or generally working to make the world a better place.

Levinson's Seasons According to Levinson, there is a **midlife transition** at about 40 to 45 that is characterized by a dramatic shift in psychological perspective. Previously we had thought of our ages largely in terms of the number of years that have elapsed since birth. But once the midlife transition takes place, there is a tendency to think of our ages in terms of the number of years we have left.

Men in their 30s still think of themselves as part of the Pepsi Generation, older brothers to "kids" in their 20s. But at about 40 to 45, some marker event—illness, a change on the job, the death of a friend or of a parent, or being beaten at tennis by one's child—leads men to realize that they are a full generation older than 20-year-olds.

During this transition it strikes men that life may be more than halfway over. There may be more to look back on than forward to. It dawns on men that they'll never be president or chairperson of the board. They'll never play shortstop for the Dodgers. They mourn their own youth and begin to adjust to the specter of old age and the finality of death.

The Midlife Crisis The midlife transition may trigger a crisis referred to as the **midlife crisis.** The middle-level, middle-aged businessperson looking ahead to another 10 to 20 years of grinding out accounts in a Wall Street cubbyhole may encounter severe depression. The housewife with two teenagers, an empty house from 8:00 to 4:00, and a 40th birthday on the way might feel that she is coming apart at the seams. Both feel entrapment and loss of purpose. Some people are propelled into extramarital affairs at this time by the desire to prove to themselves that they remain attractive.

The Dream: Inspiration or Tyranny? Until midlife, the men studied by the Levinson group were largely under the influence of their dream—the overriding drive of youth to "become," to be the great scientist or novelist, to leave one's mark on history. At midlife they found they must come to terms with the discrepancies between their dream and their actual achievements. Middle-aged people who free themselves from their dream find it easier to enjoy the passing pleasures of the day.

Sheehy's Passages Remember that Levinson's study was carried out with men. Women, as suggested by Sheehy and other writers (e.g., Reinke et al.,

---

Generativity versus stagnation Erikson's term for the crisis of middle adulthood, characterized by the task of being productive and contributing to younger generations.

Midlife transition Levinson's term for the ages from 40 to 45, which are characterized by a shift in psychological perspective from viewing ourselves in terms of years lived to viewing ourselves in terms of the years we have left.

Midlife crisis A crisis experienced by many people during the midlife transition when they realize that life may be more than halfway over and they reassess their achievements in terms of their dreams.

"Now, see here, Harley. I was forty once, and I never went through any mid-life crisis!"

Deadline Decade Sheehy's term for the ages of 35 to 45, which are characterized by recognition of mortality, turmoil, and reassessment of youthful dreams.

Menopause The cessation of menstruation.

1985) may undergo a midlife transition a number of years earlier. Sheehy (1976) writes that women enter midlife about five years earlier than men, at about 35 instead of 40. Once they turn 35, women are usually advised to have their fetuses routinely tested for Down syndrome and other chromosomal disorders (see Chapter 2). At age 35, women also enter higher risk categories for side effects from birth-control pills.

Entering midlife triggers a sense of urgency, of a "last chance" to do certain things, and so Sheehy refers to the years between 35 and 45 as the **Deadline Decade.** This decade is characterized by recognition of one's own mortality among women and men. There is reevaluation of youthful illusions and, often, turmoil.

The study of college women by Helson and Moane (1987) suggests that many women in their early 40s may already be emerging from some of the fears and uncertainties that are first confronting men. For example, they found that women at age 43 are more likely than women in their early 30s to feel confident; to exert an influence on their communities; to feel secure and committed; to feel productive, effective, and powerful; and to extend their interests beyond their own families.

Menopause, or the cessation of menstruation, is an occurrence of middle age that we will discuss next.

A CLOSER LOOK

Menopause

Menopause usually occurs during the late 40s or early 50s, although there are wide variations. Menopause is the final stage of a broader female experience, the climacteric, which is caused by a falling off in the secretion of the hormones estrogen and progesterone. The climacteric begins with irregular periods and ends with menopause.* With menopause, ovulation and reproductive capacity also draw to an end. There is some atrophy of breast tissue and a decrease in the elasticity of the skin. There can also be a loss of bone density that leads to osteoporosis in late adulthood.

During the climacteric, some 50 to 85 percent of women encounter symptoms such as hot flashes (uncomfortable sensations characterized by heat and perspiration), insomnia, fatigue, labored breathing, and mood changes as a result. However, in most cases these symptoms are relatively mild, and menopause does not signal the end of a woman's sexual interests (Sarrell & Sarrell, 1984; Skalka, 1984). Physical changes that stem from falloff in hormone production are frequently controlled by estrogen-replacement therapy—although this treatment has side effects and is not used universally. Perhaps a more important issue is the meaning of menopause to the individual. Women who equate menopause with loss of femininity are likely to encounter more distress than those who do not (Rathus, 1983).

The Empty-Nest Syndrome In earlier decades, psychologists placed great emphasis on a concept referred to as the **empty-nest syndrome** that applied to women in particular. It was assumed that women experienced a profound sense of loss when the youngest child went off to college, got married, or moved into an apartment. As noted by Harbeson (1971), "Many married women arrive at middle age without having looked and planned far enough ahead, and experience difficulties in making the transition from motherhood to socially useful occupations" (p. 139). Because of overcommitment to rearing a family and lack of planning for a productive life once the "nest" is empty, women were thought to lose their sense of meaningfulness and to become depressed.

However, research findings paint more of a mixed and optimistic picture. Certainly there can be problems, and these apply to both parents. Perhaps the largest of these is letting go of one's children after so many years of mutual interdependence (Bell, 1983). The stresses of letting go can be compounded when the children are also ambivalent about becoming independent.

But we must also note that many mothers report increased marital satisfaction and personal changes such as greater mellowness, self-confidence, and stability after the children have left home (Reinke et al., 1985). A number of studies have found that middle-aged women show increased dominance and assertiveness, an orientation toward achievement, and greater influence in the worlds of politics and work (Serlin, 1980; Sheehy, 1976). It is as if they are cut free from traditional shackles by the knowledge that their childbearing years are behind them.

In fact, the "empty nest" signals a time of increased freedom for both parents (Dyer, 1983). They have frequently become free of financial worries and are now also free to travel. Slightly more than half the women whose children have left the nest are now in the work force. Some have returned to college.

Truth or Fiction Revisited

Most mothers (and fathers) actually do *not* suffer from the "empty-nest syndrome" when the youngest child leaves home.

Empty-nest syndrome A sense of depression and loss of purpose felt by some parents when the youngest child leaves home.

*There are many other reasons for irregular periods, and women who encounter them are advised to discuss them with their doctors.

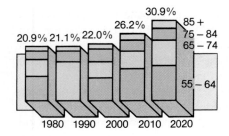

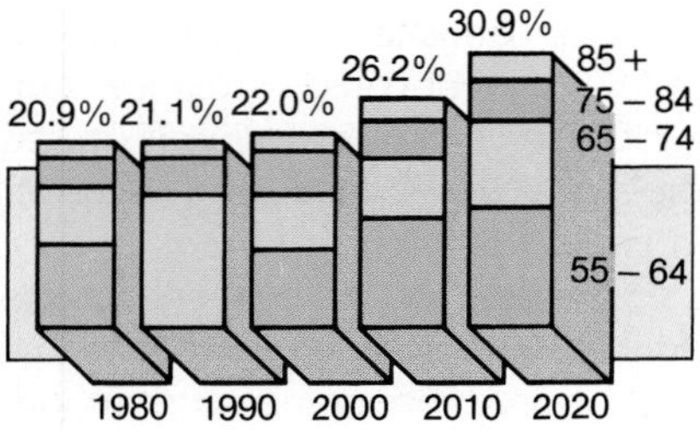

Figure 9.10
The Aging of America. Because of factors such as improved health care, diet, and exercise, Americans are living longer. By the year 2020, for example, about 31 percent of us will be at least 55 years old, as compared to about 21 percent today.

Late Adulthood

Most people say that as you get old you have to give up things. I think you get old because you give up things.

Senator Theodore Francis Green, age 87,
Washington Post, June 18, 1954

How old would you be if you didn't know how old you was?

Satchel Paige, ageless baseball pitcher

The true test of maturity is not how old a person is but how he reacts to awakening in the midtown area in his shorts.

Woody Allen, *Without Feathers*

Late adulthood begins at 65. One reason that developmental psychologists have become concerned about the later years is the so-called demographic imperative (Swensen, 1983). That is, more of us are swelling the ranks of the nation's elderly all the time. Because of improved health care and knowledge of the importance of diet and exercise, more Americans than ever before are 65 or older. In 1900 only one American in 30 was over 65, as compared to one in nine in 1970. By the year 2020, perhaps one American in five will be 65 or older (Eisdorfer, 1983) (Figure 9.10).

Another reason for the increased interest in aging is the recognition that, in a sense, *all* development involves aging. Developmental psychologist Bernice Neugarten (1982) suggests that development and aging are similar, perhaps synonymous, terms.

A third reason for studying the later years is to learn how we can further promote the health and psychological well-being of the elderly.

Physical Development Various changes—some of them problematic—do occur during the later years. Changes in calcium metabolism lead to increased brittleness in the bones and heightened risk of breaks from accidents like falls. The skin becomes less elastic, subject to wrinkles and folds.

The senses become less acute. The elderly see and hear less acutely (Belsky, 1984), and because of a decline in the sense of smell, they may use more spice to flavor their food. The elderly require more time (called **reaction time**) to respond to stimuli. Elderly drivers need more time to respond to traffic lights, other vehicles, and changing road conditions.

As we grow older, our immune systems also function less effectively, leaving us more vulnerable to disease.

Cognitive Development The elderly show some decline in general intellectual ability as measured by scores on intelligence tests. The drop-off is most acute on timed items, such as those on many of the performance scales of the Wechsler Adult Intelligence Scale (see Chapter 7).

Although changes in reaction time, intellectual functioning, and memory are common, we understand very little about *why* they occur (Storandt, 1983). Losses of sensory acuity and of motivation to do well may contribute to lower scores. Elderly psychologist B. F. Skinner (1983) argues that much of the fall-off is due to an "aging environment" rather than an aging person. That is, in many instances the behavior of elderly people goes unreinforced. Note that nursing home residents who are rewarded for remembering recent events show improved scores on tests of memory (Langer et al., 1979; Wolinsky, 1982).

In some cases, supposedly irreversible cognitive changes reflect psychological problems such as depression (Albert, 1981). Such changes are neither primarily cognitive nor irreversible. If the depression is treated effectively, intellectual performance may also improve.

Reaction time The amount of time required to respond to a stimulus.

Theories of Aging Although it may be hard to believe that it will happen to us, everyone who has so far walked the Earth has aged—which may not be a bad fate, considering the alternative. Why do we age? Various factors, some of which are theoretical, apparently contribute to aging.

Heredity plays a role. **Longevity** runs in families. People whose parents and grandparents lived into their 80s and 90s have a better chance of reaching these years themselves.

Environmental factors also influence aging. People who exercise regularly seem to live longer. Disease, stress, obesity, and cigarette smoking can contribute to an early death. Fortunately, we can exert control over some of these factors.

Elderly people show better health and psychological well-being when they do exert control over their own lives (Rodin, 1986; Rodin & Langer, 1977; Wolinsky, 1982). Unfortunately, some elderly people are placed in nursing homes and surrender independence because of a decline in health and finances. But even in the nursing home, they fare better when they are kept well-informed and allowed to make decisions on matters that affect them.

There are several biological theories of aging. The **cellular-aging theory** suggests that the DNA within cells, which carries the individual's genetic code, suffers damage from external factors (like ultraviolet light) and random internal changes. As the person ages, the ability to repair DNA decreases. Damage and other changes eventually accumulate to the point at which affected cells can no longer reproduce or serve their bodily functions. Another view is that waste products within cells eventually accumulate so that many cells become poisoned and are no longer capable of functioning.

Erikson's Stages of Psychosocial Development According to Erikson, late adulthood is the stage of **ego integrity versus despair.** The basic challenge is to maintain the belief that life is meaningful and worthwhile in the face of the inevitability of death. Ego integrity derives from wisdom, as well as from the acceptance of one's life span as occurring at a certain point in the sweep of history and as being limited. We spend most of our lives accumulating things and relationships. Erikson also argues that adjustment in the later years requires the wisdom to be able to let go.

Adjustment among the Elderly Despite the changes that occur with aging, one survey of people aged 70 to 79 found that 75 percent were generally satisfied with their lives (Neugarten, 1971). A more recent study of people retired for from 18 to 120 months found that 75 percent rated retirement as being mostly good (Hendrick et al., 1982). Over 90 percent were generally satisfied with life, and more than 75 percent reported their health as being good or excellent.

Truth or Fiction Revisited

It is *not* true that most elderly people are dissatisfied with their lives.

Adjustment among the elderly, as at any age, is related to financial security and physical health. That is, the sicker we are, the less likely we are to be well adjusted. Also, there is a link between financial status and physical health: poor elderly people are more likely to report ill health than are the financially secure (Birren, 1983). This finding would seem to call for better health care for the aged, and it does. But it may also be that people who have been healthier over the years are also better able to provide for their own financial security.

Longevity A long span of life.

Cellular-aging theory The view that aging occurs because body cells lose the capacity to reproduce and maintain themselves.

Ego integrity versus despair Erikson's term for the crisis of late adulthood, characterized by the task of maintaining one's sense of identity despite physical deterioration.

Among the elderly, as among younger people, there is a relationship between social support and adjustment. Elderly couples are less lonely and happier than the single or the widowed (Barrow & Smith, 1983). Widows with children are also better adjusted than other widows, a prospect that contributes to some people's desire for children. Once retired, couples tend to spend more time together and their relationship tends to improve and take on greater importance (Atchley, 1985; Harris & Cole, 1980).

On Death and Dying Death is the last great taboo. Psychiatrist Elisabeth Kübler-Ross commented on our denial of death in her landmark book *On Death and Dying:*

We use euphemisms, we make the dead look as if they were asleep, we ship the children off to protect them from the anxiety and turmoil around the house if the [person] is fortunate enough to die at home, [and] we don't allow children to visit their dying parents in the hospitals (1969, p. 8).

From her work with terminally ill patients, Kübler-Ross found some common responses to news of impending death. She identified five stages of dying through which many patients pass, and she suggests that elderly people who suspect that death is approaching may undergo similar emotional and cognitive responses. The stages are as follows:

1. *Denial.* In the denial stage, people feel, "It can't be me. The diagnosis must be wrong." As noted by Carroll (1985), denial can be flat and absolute, or it can fluctuate so that now the patient accepts the medical verdict and then the patient starts chatting animatedly about distant plans.

2. *Anger.* Denial usually gives way to anger and resentment toward the young and healthy and, sometimes, toward the medical establishment—"It's unfair. Why me?"

3. *Bargaining.* Next people may try to bargain with God to postpone death, promising, for example, to do good deeds if they are given another six months, another year.

4. *Depression.* With depression come feelings of loss and hopelessness—grief at the specter of leaving loved ones and life itself.

5. *Final acceptance.* Ultimately an inner peace may come, a quiet acceptance of the inevitable. Such "peace" does not resemble contentment; it is nearly devoid of feeling.

Psychologist Edwin Shneidman (1984), who has specialized in the concerns of suicidal and dying individuals, acknowledges the presence of feelings such as those described by Kübler-Ross, but he does not perceive them to be linked in sequence. Instead, Shneidman suggests that dying people show a variety of emotional and cognitive responses that tend to be fleeting or relatively stable, to ebb and flow, and to reflect pain and bewilderment. He also points out that the kinds of responses shown by individuals reflect their personality traits and their philosophies of life.

"Lying Down to Pleasant Dreams . . ." The American poet William Cullen Bryant is best known for his poem "Thanatopsis," which he composed at the age of 18. "Thanatopsis" expresses Erik Erikson's goal of ego integrity—optimism that we can maintain a sense of trust through life. By meeting squarely the challenges of our adult lives, perhaps we can take our leave with dignity. When our time comes to "join the innumerable caravan"—the billions who have died before us—perhaps we can depart life with integrity.

Live, wrote the poet, so that

. . . when thy summons comes to join
The innumerable caravan that moves
To the pale realms of shade, where each shall take
His chamber in the silent halls of death,
Thou go not, like the quarry-slave at night,
Scourged to his dungeon, but, sustained and soothed
By an unfaltering trust, approach thy grave
Like one who wraps the drapery of his couch
About him, and lies down to pleasant dreams.

Bryant, of course, wrote "Thanatopsis" at 18, not at 85, the age at which he died. At that advanced age, his feelings, and his verse, might have differed. But literature and poetry, unlike science, need not reflect reality. They can serve to inspire and warm us.

SUMMARY

1. **Does development reflect nature or nurture?** Development appears to reflect an interaction between nature (genetic factors) and environmental influences (nurture). Nature provides a reaction range for the development of traits, and nurture modifies the expression of traits.

2. **Is development continuous or discontinuous?** Stage theorists such as Freud and Piaget view development as being discontinuous. According to them, we undergo distinct periods of development that differ in quality and follow an orderly sequence. Learning theorists, in contrast, tend to view psychological development as a continuous process.

3. **What are the stages of prenatal development?** These are the germinal, embryonic, and fetal stages. During the germinal stage, the zygote divides as it travels through the fallopian tube and becomes implanted in the uterine wall. The major organ systems are formed during the embryonic stage, and the fetal stage is highlighted by maturation and gains in size.

4. **What are the highlights of physical development?** Physical development occurs most rapidly prenatally and then during the first two years after birth. There is also an adolescent growth spurt during which we make dramatic gains in height and weight.

5. **What are reflexes?** Reflexes are unlearned, stereotypical responses to stimuli that in many cases are essential to infant survival. Examples include breathing, sucking, and swallowing. Many reflexes are replaced by voluntary behavior or simply drop out as the child matures.

6. **How do babies perceive the environment?** Newborn children sleep most of the time. They can see quite well and show greater interest in complex visual stimuli than in simple stimuli. Infants are capable of depth perception by the time they can crawl. Newborns can normally hear and show preferences for their mothers' voices. Newborns can discriminate different odors and tastes and show preferences for pleasant odors and sweet-tasting food.

7. **What are the stages of attachment?** According to Ainsworth, there are three stages of attachment: the initial-preattachment phase, which is characterized by indiscriminate attachment; the attachment-in-the-making phase, which is characterized by preference for familiar figures; and the clear-cut-attachment phase, which is characterized by intensified dependence on the primary caregiver.

8. **What are some of the theories of attachment?** Behaviorists have argued that children become attached to their mothers through conditioning, because their mothers feed them and attend to other needs. Harlow's studies with rhesus monkeys suggest that an innate motive, contact comfort, may be more important than conditioning in the development of attachment. The ethological view of attachment suggests that there are critical developmental periods during which animals such as geese and ducks will become imprinted on, or attached to, an object that they follow.

9. **What are the dimensions of child-rearing?** Two broad, independent dimensions of child-rearing have been found: warmth–coldness, and restrictiveness–permissiveness.

10. **In what ways do parents enforce restrictions?** Three methods have been found: induction, power-assertion, and loss of love.

11. **How did Jean Piaget view children?** Piaget saw children as budding scientists who actively strive to make sense of the perceptual world. He defined intelligence as involving processes of assimilation (responding to events according to existing schemes) and accommodation (changing schemes to permit effective responses to new events).

12. **What are the stages of cognitive development, according to Piaget?** Piaget's view of cognitive development includes four stages: sensorimotor (prior to use of symbols and language); preoperational (characterized by egocentric thought, animism, artificialism, and inability to center on more than one aspect of a situation); concrete operational (characterized by conservation, less egocentrism, reversibility, and subjective moral judgments); and formal operational (characterized by abstract logic).

13. **How do information-processing theorists view cognitive development?** Information-processing theorists view cognitive development in terms of expansion of working memory, growing automaticity in problem solving, development of more sophisticated "mental programs," and increasing self-knowledge of the functioning of one's own cognitive processes (metacognition).

14. **How did Kohlberg view moral development?** Kohlberg focused on the processes of moral reasoning. He hypothesized that these processes develop through three "levels," with two stages within each level. In the preconventional level, judgments are based on expectation of rewards or punishments. Conventional judgments reflect the need to maintain the social order. Postconventional judgments are derived from ethical principles, and the self is seen as the highest moral authority.

15. **What is adolescence?** Adolescence is a period of life that begins at puberty (a biological marker) and ends with assumption of adult responsibilities (a psychosocial marker). Adolescence is often stressful in our society, although cross-cultural evidence suggests that this stress stems from cultural expectations and limitations and not from maturation. Changes that lead to reproductive capacity and secondary sex characteristics are stimulated by testosterone in the male and by estrogen and androgens in the female.

16. **What are some of the major events of young adulthood?** Young adulthood is generally characterized by striving to advance in the business world and the development of intimate ties. Bardwick and Gilligan suggest that men's development is generally guided by a shift from external control to autonomy, whereas women's development is more often guided by a shift from being cared for by others to caring for others. During the late 20s and 30s, many women encounter a crisis that involves concerns about nearing the end of the fertile years, closing opportunities, and heightened responsibilities. Many adults reassess their lives in the 30s and settle down at about age 35.

17. **What are some of the major events of middle adulthood?** Middle adulthood is a time of crisis and further reassessment for many, a time when we must come to terms with the discrepancies between our achievements and the dreams of youth. Some middle-aged adults become depressed when the youngest child leaves home (the so-called "empty-nest syndrome"), but many report increased satisfaction, stability, and self-confidence.

18. **What are some of the changes that occur during late adulthood?** The elderly show less sensory acuity, and reaction time increases. Presumed cognitive deficits may reflect declining motivation or psychological problems like depression.

19. **How well adjusted are the elderly?** Most elderly people rate their life satisfaction and their health as generally good. Adequate financial resources are a major contributor to satisfaction among the elderly.

20. **What factors are involved in longevity?** Heredity plays a role in longevity. We do not know exactly why people age, but environmental factors such as exercise, proper diet, and the maintenance of responsibility can apparently delay aging.

21. **Are there "stages of dying"?** Kübler-Ross identifies five stages of dying among the terminally ill: denial, anger, bargaining, depression, and final acceptance. However, research by other investigators, which finds that psychological reactions to approaching death are more varied than Kübler-Ross suggests, sheds doubt on the notion of stages of dying.

PSYCHOLOGY AND MODERN LIFE

One of the facts of modern life is that most American mothers are in the work force. This includes 41 percent of mothers of children *who are less than 1 year old* (Klein, 1985). The ideals of the women's movement and financial pressures are likely to increase this number. When both parents spend the day on the job, the children must be taken care of by others. As a consequence, 7 to 8 million American preschoolers are now placed in day-care centers. Parents, of course, are very concerned about what happens to them there. And so, as our first topic we will examine the effects of day care and then offer pointers on selecting a day-care center.

Another fact of modern life is that at least 625,000 children in the United States are neglected or abused by parents each year—a figure that is rising (Brown, 1983; National Center on Child Abuse and Neglect, 1982). Thus our second topic in this section is child abuse—why parents abuse their children and what can be done about it.

Day Care. Because more than half of mothers in the U.S.A. are in the work force today, day care is a major influence on the lives of millions of children. Parents are understandably concerned that their children will be provided with positive and stimulating experiences.

Day Care

Day care is a hassle for most parents. In one survey, 56 percent of parents reported having difficulty in arranging for high-quality day care; 54 percent complained that the costs of day care were excessive; 51 percent had problems with the location and hours of their day-care centers; and 25 percent of working mothers had considered quitting their jobs because of these problems (Trost, 1987). What are the effects of day care on parent–child bonds of attachment? On children's social development?

Studies of the effects of day care are actually reasonably encouraging. In their review of the literature, Jay Belsky and Laurence Steinberg (1978) concluded that day care has *not* been shown to interfere with mother–child bonds of attachment.

Day care seems to have positive and negative influences on children's social development. First, the positive: Infants with day-care experience are more peer-oriented and play at higher developmental levels. Day-care children are also more likely to share their toys (Belsky & Steinberg, 1978, 1979). Adolescent boys who had been placed in day care before the age of 5 were rated high in sociability and were liked by their peers (Moore, 1975). So day care may stimulate interest in peers and help in the formation of social skills.

Now, the negative: A number of studies have compared 3- and 4-year-olds who had been in full-time day care for several years with agemates recently placed in day-care centers. The experienced children were more impulsive, more aggressive toward peers and adults, and more egocentric (Caldwell et al., 1970; Lay & Meyer, 1973; Schwartz et al., 1973, 1974). They were also less cooperative and showed less tolerance for frustration.

The negative characteristics found among children placed in day care suggest a common theme: Day care promotes interest in peers and the development of social skills, but children tend not to receive the individual attention or resources they want. Placed in a competitive situation, many become more aggressive to attempt to meet their needs.

Truth or Fiction Revisited

It is true that children placed in day care are more aggressive than children cared for in the home. Perhaps they are so because they must compete for resources.

Even if day care usually fosters impulsivity and aggressiveness, these outcomes are not inevitable. Fewer children per caregiver and more toys would reduce competition. Two obstacles stand in the way of having fewer children per caregiver, of course: money and the scarcity of qualified personnel.

Selecting a Day-Care Center Selecting a day-care center can be an overwhelming task. Standards for day-care centers vary from locale to locale, so licensing is no guarantee of adequate care. To help make a successful choice, parents can weigh factors such as the following:

1. Is the center licensed? By what agency? What standards must be met to acquire a license?
2. What is the ratio of children to caregivers? Everything else being equal, caregivers can do a better

job when there are fewer children in their charge.

3. What are the qualifications of the center's caregivers? How well aware are they of children's needs and patterns of development?
4. How safe is the environment? Do toys and swings seem to be in good condition? Are dangerous objects out of reach? Would strangers have a difficult time breaking in?
5. What is served at mealtime? Is it nutritious and appetizing? Will *your child* eat it?
6. Which caregivers will be responsible for your child? What are their backgrounds? How do they seem to relate to children? To *your* child?
7. What toys, games, books, and other educational materials are provided?
8. What facilities are provided to promote the motor development of your child? How well supervised are children when they use things like swings and tricycles?
9. Are the hours offered by the center convenient for your schedule?
10. Is the location of the center convenient?
11. Do you like the overall environment and "feel" of the center?

Child Abuse

Why do parents abuse their children? A number of factors contribute to child abuse: situational stress, a history of child abuse in at least one of the parent's families of origin, acceptance of violence as a way of coping with stress, failure to become attached to the children, and rigid attitudes about child rearing (Belsky, 1984; Milner et al., 1984; Rosenblum & Paully, 1984). Unemployment is a particularly predisposing source of stress. Child abuse increases during periods of rising unemployment (National Center on Child Abuse and Neglect, 1982; Steinberg et al., 1981).

Stress is also created by crying infants themselves (Green et al., 1987; Murray, 1985). Infants who are already in pain of some kind and relatively difficult to soothe are ironically more likely to be abused (Frodi, 1981, 1985). Abusive mothers are also more likely than nonabusive mothers to assume that their children's stress-producing behavior is intentional, even when it is not (Bauer & Twentyman, 1985).

Sad to say, abused children show an alarming incidence of personal and social problems and abnormal behavior patterns. Maltreatment can disturb basic patterns of attachment. Abused children are less likely than nonabused agemates to venture out to explore the world (Aber & Allen, 1987). Abused children are more likely to be depressed and aggressive than nonabused children, even at preschool ages (Hoffman-Plotkin & Twentyman, 1984; Kazdin et al., 1985).

Child abuse runs in families to some degree. However, *the majority of children who are abused do* not *abuse their own children as adults.* There is no evidence that women who were abused as children are more likely than other women to abuse their own children (Fisher, 1984). But men who were abused as children are somewhat more likely than nonabused men to abuse their own children.

Why does abuse run in families? For one thing, parents serve as role models. If children observe their parents using violence as a means of coping with stress and anger, they are less likely to learn to diffuse anger through techniques such as humor, verbal expression, reasoning, or even "counting to ten." Exposure to violence in their own homes may also lead some children to accept family violence as a norm. Certainly, they can find justifications for violence—if they are seeking them. One is the age-old adage "Spare the rod, spoil the child." Another is the parents' belief that they are hurting their children "for their own good"—to discourage behavior that is likely to get them into trouble.

Truth or Fiction Revisited

It is true that *male* child abusers have frequently been victims of child abuse themselves. However, this relationship does not hold for women. Moreover, male victims of child abuse do not inevitably abuse their own children; the majority of victims do not.

What To Do Dealing with child abuse is frustrating in itself. Social agencies and courts can find it difficult to distinguish between "normal" hitting or spanking and abuse. Because of the American belief that parents have the right to rear their children as they wish, police and courts usually try to avoid involvement in "domestic quarrels" and "family disputes."

However, the alarming incidence of child abuse has spawned new efforts at detection and prevention. Many states require helping professionals such as psychologists and physicians to report any suspicion of child abuse. Many states legally require *anyone* who suspects child abuse to report it to authorities.

Many locales also have Child Abuse Hotlines. Their phone numbers are available from the telephone information service. Private citizens who suspect child abuse may call for advice. Parents who are having difficulty controlling aggressive impulses toward their children are encouraged to use the hotlines. Some hotlines are serviced by groups such as Parents Anonymous, which involve parents who have had similar difficulties and which may help callers diffuse feelings of anger in less harmful ways.

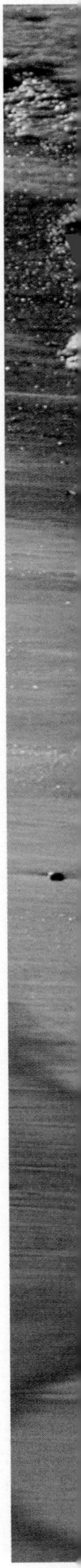

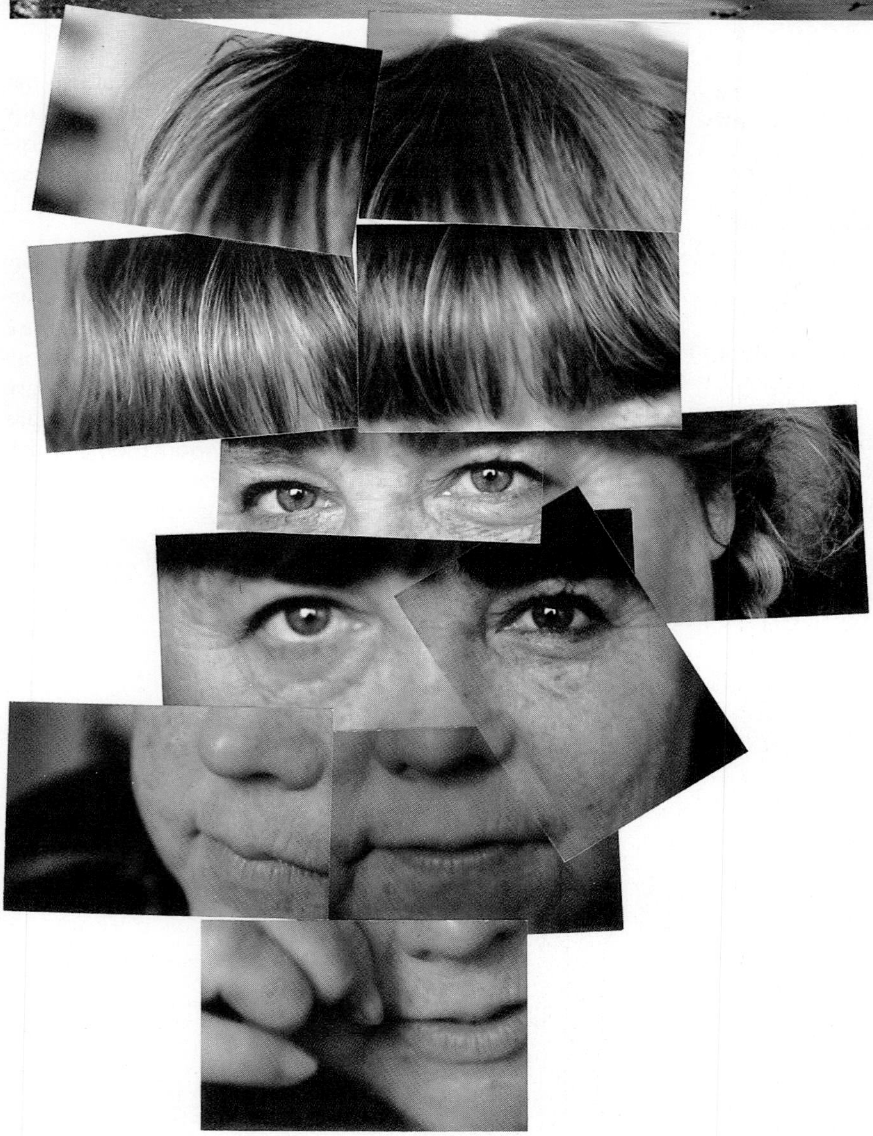

Outline

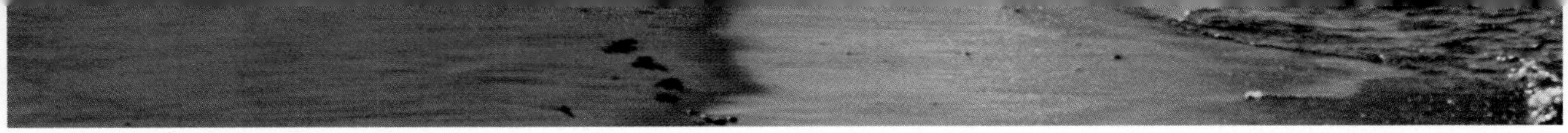

10 Personality: Theories and Measurement

Truth or Fiction?

- □ According to Sigmund Freud, the human mind is like a vast submerged iceberg, only the tip of which rises above the surface into conscious awareness.
- □ According to Freud, biting one's fingernails or smoking cigarettes as an adult is a sign of conflict during very early childhood.
- □ According to Freud, women who compete with men in the business world are suffering from penis envy.
- □ According to Carl Jung, you have inherited mysterious memories that date back to ancient times.
- □ Airline pilots are more emotionally stable than artists.
- □ We are more likely to persist at difficult tasks when we believe that we shall succeed.
- □ Psychologists can determine whether a person has told the truth on a personality test.
- □ There is a psychological test made up of inkblots, and one of them looks like a bat.
- □ A psychologist could write a believable personality report about you without interviewing you, testing you, or, in fact, having any idea who you are.

There is an ancient Islamic tale about the initial encounter of three blind men and an elephant. Each man touched a different part of the elephant, but each was stubborn and claimed that he alone had understood the true nature of the beast. One had grabbed the elephant by the legs and described it as being firm, strong, and upright, like a pillar. To this the blind man who had touched the ear of the elephant objected. From his perspective, the animal was broad and rough, like a rug. The third man had become familiar with the trunk. He was astounded at the gross inaccuracy of the others. Clearly the elephant was long and narrow, he declared, like a hollow pipe.

Each of this trio had come to know the elephant from a different perspective. Each was blind to the beliefs of his fellows and to the real nature of the beast—not only because of his physical limitations, but also because his initial encounter had led him to think of the elephant in a certain way.

So it is that different ways of encountering people have led psychologists to view people from different perspectives. Various theories of human personality have been advanced. Because personality is not something that can be touched directly, theories of personality may differ as widely as the blind men's concepts of the elephant.

Nor do people agree on what the term *personality* means. Some equate personality with liveliness, as in, "She's got a lot of personality." Others characterize a person's personality as consisting of the most striking or dominant traits, as in a "shy personality" or a "happy-go-lucky personality." Personality theorists define **personality** as the reasonably stable patterns of behavior, including thoughts and emotions, that distinguish one person from another (Mischel, 1986). These behavior patterns reflect a person's characteristic ways of adapting to the demands of life. Personality, therefore, deals with the ways in which people's behavior differs. Personality theories may include discussion of internal variables, such as thoughts and emotions, as well as overt behavior.

Personality theories seek to explain how people develop distinctive patterns of behavior and to predict how people with certain patterns will respond to life's demands. In this chapter we explore four major approaches to the study of personality: psychodynamic theories, trait theories, learning theories, and phenomenological theories. Then we discuss psychological methods of measuring personality.

PSYCHODYNAMIC THEORIES

There are several **psychodynamic theories** of personality, but they have a number of things in common. Each teaches that personality is characterized by a dynamic struggle. Drives such as sex, aggression, and the need for superiority come into conflict with laws, social rules, and moral codes. The laws and social rules become internalized. We make them parts of ourselves. After doing so, the dynamic struggle becomes a clashing of opposing *inner* forces. At a given moment, our behavior, as well as our thoughts and emotions, represents the outcome of these inner contests.

Each psychodynamic theory also owes its origin to the thinking of Sigmund Freud.

Sigmund Freud's Theory of Psychosexual Development

He was born with a shock of dark hair—in Jewish tradition, the sign of a prophet. In 1856, in a Czechoslovakian village, an old woman told his mother that she had given birth to a great man. The child was reared with great expectations. His sister, in fact, was prohibited from playing the piano when Freud was reading or reflecting in his room. In manhood, Sigmund Freud himself would be cynical about the prophecy. Old women, after all, would earn greater favors by forecasting good tidings than doom. But the forecast about Freud was not pure fantasy. Few have influenced our thinking about human nature so deeply.

Personality The distinct patterns of behaviors, including thoughts and feelings, that characterize a person's adaptation to life.

Psychodynamic theory Sigmund Freud's perspective, which emphasizes the importance of unconscious motives and conflicts as forces that determine behavior.

Sigmund Freud Freud taught that human personality is characterized by a dynamic struggle as basic physiological drives come into conflict with laws and social codes.

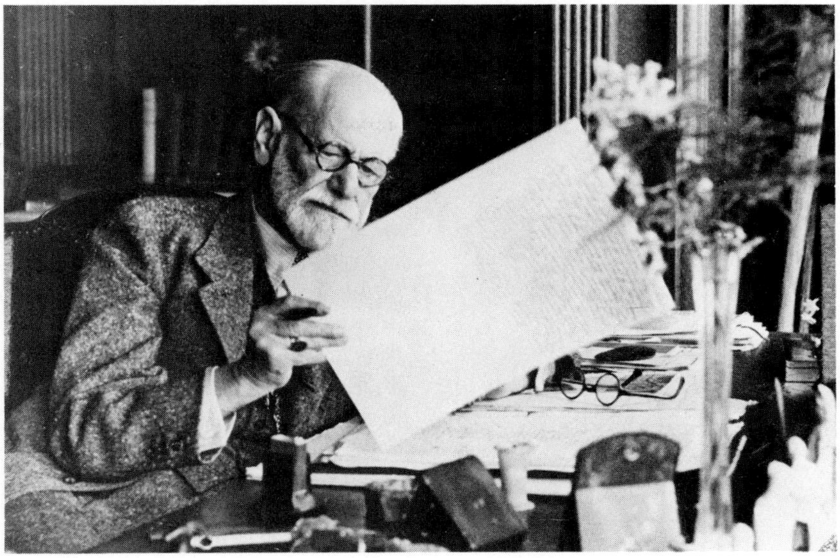

Figure 10.1.
The Human Iceberg According to Freud. According to psychoanalytic theory, only the tip of human personality rises above the surface of the mind into conscious awareness. Material in the preconscious can become conscious if we direct our attention to it, but unconscious material tends to remain shrouded in mystery.

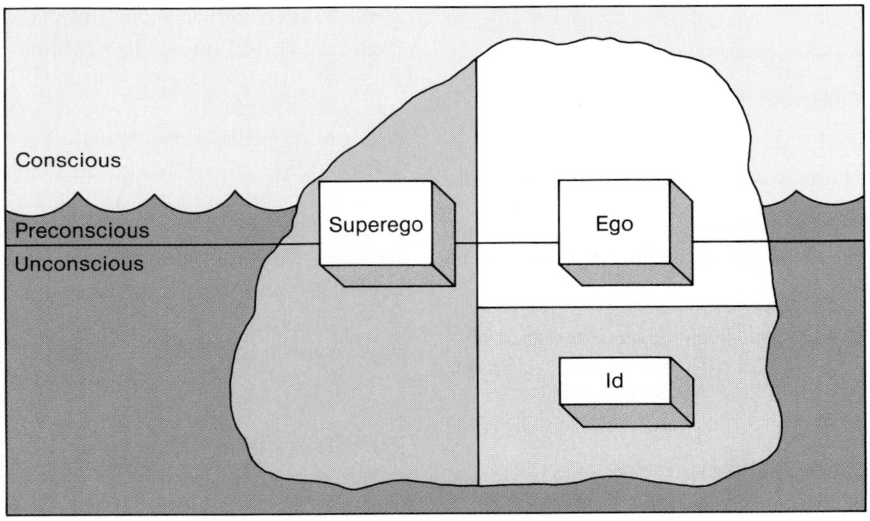

Freud was trained as a physician. Early in his practice, he was astounded to find that some people apparently experienced loss of feeling in a hand or paralysis of the legs in the absence of any medical disorder. These odd symptoms often disappeared once patients had recalled and discussed distressful events and feelings of guilt or anxiety that seemed to be related to the symptoms. For a long time these events and feelings had been hidden beneath the surface of awareness. Even so, they had the capacity to influence patients' behavior.

From this sort of clinical evidence, Freud concluded that the human mind is like an iceberg (see Figure 10.1). Only the tip of an iceberg rises above the surface of the water, while the great mass of it darkens the deep. Freud came to believe that people, similarly, were only aware of a small number of the ideas and impulses that dwelled within their minds. Freud argued that the greater mass of the mind—our deepest images, thoughts, fears, and urges—remained beneath the surface of conscious awareness, where little light illumined them.

Truth or Fiction Revisited

It is true that Freud thought of the mind as being like a vast submerged iceberg, only the tip of which rises above the surface into conscious awareness.

Freud labeled the region that poked through into the light of awareness the **conscious** part of the mind. He called the regions that lay below the surface the preconscious and the unconscious.

The **preconscious** mind contains elements of experience that are presently out of awareness but that can be made conscious simply by focusing on them. The **unconscious** mind is shrouded in mystery. It contains biological instincts such as sex and aggression. Some unconscious urges cannot be experienced consciously because mental images and words could not portray them in all their color and fury. Other unconscious urges may be kept below the surface by repression.

Repression is the automatic ejection of anxiety-evoking ideas from awareness. Repression protects us from identifying impulses we would consider inappropriate in light of our moral values.

The unconscious is the largest part of the mind. Here the dynamic struggle between biological drives and social rules is fiercest. As drives seek expression, and internalized values exert counterpressures, the resultant conflict can precipitate psychological problems and behavioral outbursts. Since we cannot view the unconscious mind directly, Freud developed a method of mental detective work called **psychoanalysis.** In psychoanalysis, people are prodded to talk about anything that "pops" into their minds while they remain comfortable and relaxed. People may gain **self-insight** by pursuing some of the thoughts that pop into awareness. But they are also motivated to evade threatening subjects. The same repression that has ejected unacceptable thoughts from awareness prompts **resistance,** or the desire to avoid thinking about or discussing them. Repression and resistance can make psychoanalysis a tedious process that lasts for years or even decades.

The Structure of Personality When is a structure not a structure? When it is a mental or **psychic structure.** Sigmund Freud labeled the clashing forces of personality psychic structures. They could not be seen or measured directly, but their presence was suggested by observable behavior, expressed thoughts, and emotions. Freud hypothesized the existence of three psychic structures: the *id, ego,* and *superego.*

The **id** is present at birth. It represents physiological drives and is fully unconscious. Freud described the id as "a chaos, a cauldron of seething excitations" (1964, p. 73). The conscious mind might find it inconsistent to love and hate a person at the same time, but Freud believed that conflicting emotions could dwell side by side in the id. In the id, we could feel hatred for our mothers for failing to immediately gratify all of our needs even as we sense love for them.

The id follows what Freud termed the **pleasure principle.** It demands instant gratification of instincts without consideration of law, social custom, or the needs of others.

The **ego** begins to develop during the first year of life, largely because a child's demands for gratification cannot all be met immediately. The ego "stands for reason and good sense" (Freud, 1964, p. 76), for rational ways of coping with frustration. It curbs the appetites of the id and makes plans that are compatible with social convention so that a person can find gratification yet avert the censure of others. The id lets you know that you are

---

Conscious Self-aware.

Preconscious Capable of being brought into awareness by the focusing of attention.

Unconscious In psychodynamic theory, not available to awareness by simple focusing of attention.

Repression A defense mechanism that protects the person from anxiety by ejecting anxiety-evoking ideas and impulses from awareness.

Psychoanalysis In this usage, Freud's method of exploring human personality.

Self-insight Accurate awareness of one's motives and feelings.

Resistance A blocking of thoughts whose awareness could cause anxiety.

Psychic structure In psychodynamic theory, a hypothesized mental structure that helps explain different aspects of behavior.

Id The psychic structure, present at birth, that represents physiological drives and is fully unconscious.

Pleasure principle The governing principle of the id—the seeking of immediate gratification of instinctive needs.

Ego The second psychic structure to develop, characterized by self-awareness, planning, and delay of gratification.

Dr. Jekyll and Mr. Hyde. Freud suggested that each of us is influenced by an id that demands instant gratification without regard for moral scruples and the needs of others. Robert Louis Stevenson had a dream in which a similar idea was expressed, and he developed it into the novel *Dr. Jekyll and Mr. Hyde.* In one film version of the tale, Dr. Jekyll, shown at right, is a loving, considerate person—suggestive of ego functioning. The monstrous Mr. Hyde, shown at left, is suggestive of the id. Stevenson's wife was horrified by the concept and destroyed an early version of the manuscript. But Stevenson was so enthralled by the idea that he rewrote the book.

hungry. The ego formulates the idea of walking to the refrigerator, warming up some enchiladas, and pouring a glass of milk.

The ego is guided by the **reality principle.** It takes into account what is practical and possible, as well as what is urged. Within Freudian theory, it is the ego that provides the conscious sense of self.

Although most of the ego is conscious, some of its business is carried out unconsciously. For instance, the ego also acts as a censor that screens the impulses of the id. When the ego senses that improper impulses are rising into awareness, it may use psychological defenses to deter them from surfacing. Repression is one such psychological defense, or **defense mechanism.** Various defense mechanisms are described in Table 10.1.

The **superego** develops throughout early childhood, usually incorporating the moral standards and values of parents and important members of the community through **identification.** The superego functions according to the **moral principle.** The superego holds forth shining examples of an ideal self and also acts like the conscience, an internal moral guardian. Throughout life, the superego monitors the intentions of the ego and hands out judgments of right and wrong. It floods the ego with feelings of guilt and shame when the verdict is negative.

Reality principle Consideration of what is practical and possible in gratifying needs; the governing principle of the ego.

Defense mechanism In psychodynamic theory, an unconscious function of the ego that protects it from anxiety-evoking material by preventing accurate recognition of this material.

Superego The third psychic structure, which functions as a moral guardian and sets forth high standards for behavior.

Identification In psychodynamic theory, the unconscious assumption of the behavior of another person.

Moral principle The governing principle of the superego, which sets moral standards and enforces adherence to them.

Table 10.1
Some Defense Mechanisms of the Ego, According to Psychodynamic Theory

Defense Mechanism	Definition	Examples
Repression	The ejection of anxiety-evoking ideas from awareness.	A student forgets that a difficult term paper is due. A patient in therapy forgets an appointment when anxiety-evoking material is to be discussed.
Regression	The return, under stress, to a form of behavior characteristic of an earlier stage of development.	An adolescent cries when forbidden to use the family car. An adult becomes highly dependent on his parents following the breakup of his marriage.
Rationalization	The use of self-deceiving justifications for unacceptable behavior.	A student blames her cheating on her teacher for leaving the room during a test. A man explains his cheating on his income tax by saying "Everyone does it."
Displacement	The transfer of ideas and impulses from threatening or unsuitable objects to less threatening objects.	A worker picks a fight with her spouse after being criticized sharply by her supervisor.
Projection	The thrusting of one's own unacceptable impulses onto others so that others are assumed to harbor them.	A hostile person perceives the world as being a dangerous place. A sexually frustrated person interprets innocent gestures of others as sexual advances.
Reaction formation	Assumption of behavior in opposition to one's genuine impulses in order to keep impulses repressed.	A person who is angry with a relative behaves in a "sickly sweet" manner toward that relative. A sadistic individual becomes a physician.
Denial	Refusal to accept the true nature of a threat.	Belief that one will not contract cancer or heart disease although one smokes heavily. "It can't happen to me."
Sublimation	The channeling of primitive impulses into positive, constructive efforts.	A person paints nudes for the sake of "beauty" and "art." A hostile person becomes a tennis star.

Eros In psychodynamic theory, the basic instinct to preserve and perpetuate life.

Libido (1) In psychodynamic theory, the energy of Eros; the sexual instinct. (2) Generally, sexual interest or drive.

Erogenous zone An area of the body that is sensitive to sexual sensations.

Psychosexual development In psychodynamic theory, the process by which libidinal energy is expressed through different erogenous zones during different stages of development.

Oral stage The first stage of psychosexual development, during which gratification is hypothesized to be attained primarily through oral activities.

Weaning Accustoming a child not to suck the mother's breast or a baby bottle.

Fixation In psychodynamic theory, arrested development. Attachment to objects of an earlier stage.

Oral fixation Attachment to objects and behaviors characteristic of the oral stage.

The ego hasn't an easy time of it. It stands between id and superego, braving the arrows of each. It strives to satisfy the demands of the id and the moral sense of the superego. The id may urge, "You are sexually aroused!" But the superego may warn, "You're not married." The poor ego is caught in the middle.

From the Freudian perspective, a healthy personality has found ways to gratify most of the id's demands without seriously offending the superego. Most of the id's remaining demands are contained or repressed. If the ego is not a good problem solver, or if the superego is too stern, the ego will have a hard time of it.

Stages of Psychosexual Development Freud stirred controversy within the medical establishment of his day by arguing that sexual impulses and their gratification were pivotal factors in personality development, even among children. Freud saw children's basic ways of relating to the world, such as sucking their mothers' breasts and moving their bowels, as entailing sexual feelings.

Freud believed that a major instinct, which he termed **Eros,** aimed at preserving and perpetuating life. Eros was fueled by psychological, or psychic, energy, which Freud labeled **libido.** Libidinal energy involved sexual impulses, so Freud considered it to be *psychosexual.* Libidinal energy would be expressed through sexual feelings in different parts of the body, or **erogenous zones,** as the child developed. To Freud, human development involved the transfer of libidinal energy from one zone to another. He hypothesized five periods of **psychosexual development:** oral, anal, phallic, latency, and genital.

Regression. Sometimes anxiety can lead us to regress, or to adopt behavior characteristic of younger people or children. Experiencing extreme anxiety, this woman curls up into a ball and puts her hand to her mouth.

Anal stage The second stage of psychosexual development, when gratification is attained through anal activities.

Anal fixation Attachment to objects and behaviors characteristic of the anal stage.

Anal-retentive Descriptive of behaviors and traits that have to do with "holding in," or self-control.

Anal-expulsive Descriptive of behaviors and traits that have to do with unregulated self-expression, such as messiness.

Sadism Attaining gratification from inflicting pain on or humiliating others.

Phallic stage The third stage of psychosexual development, characterized by a shift of libido to the phallic region.

Clitoris An external female sex organ, which is highly sensitive to sexual stimulation.

Oedipus complex A conflict of the phallic stage in which the boy wishes to possess his mother sexually and perceives his father as a rival in love.

Electra complex A conflict of the phallic stage in which the girl longs for her father and resents her mother.

During the first year of life, a child experiences much of its world through the mouth. If it fits, into the mouth it goes. This is the **oral stage.** Freud argued that oral activities such as sucking and biting bring the child sexual gratification as well as nourishment.

Freud believed that children would encounter conflicts during each stage of psychosexual development. During the oral stage, conflict would center around the nature and extent of oral gratification. Early **weaning** could lead to frustration. Excessive gratification, on the other hand, could lead an infant to expect that it would routinely be handed everything in life. Insufficient or excessive gratification in any stage could lead to **fixation** in that stage and to the development of traits characteristic of that stage. Oral traits include dependency, gullibility, and optimism or pessimism.

Freud theorized that adults with an **oral fixation** could experience exaggerated desires for "oral activities," such as smoking, overeating, alcohol abuse, and nail biting.

Truth or Fiction Revisited

It is true that Freud interpreted biting fingernails or smoking as an adult to be a sign of conflict during very early childhood.

Like the infant whose very survival depends on the mercy of an adult, adults with oral fixations may be disposed toward clinging, dependent interpersonal relationships.

Note that according to psychodynamic theory, people are largely at the mercy of events that occurred long before they can weigh alternatives and make decisions about how to behave. Freud's own "oral fixation," cigar smoking, seems to have advanced the cancer of the mouth and jaw that killed him in 1939.

During the **anal stage,** sexual gratification is attained through contraction and relaxation of the muscles that control elimination of waste products. Elimination, which was controlled reflexively during most of the first year of life, comes under voluntary muscular control, even if such control is not reliable at first. The anal stage is said to begin in the second year of life.

During the anal stage, children learn to delay the gratification of eliminating as soon as they feel the urge. The general issue of self-control may become a source of conflict between parent and child. **Anal fixations** may stem from this conflict and lead to two sets of anal traits. So-called **anal-retentive** traits involve excessive use of self-control. They include perfectionism, a strong need for order, and exaggerated neatness and cleanliness. **Anal-expulsive** traits, on the other hand, "let it all hang out." They include carelessness, messiness, even **sadism.**

Children enter the **phallic stage** during the third year of life. During this stage, the major erogenous zone is the phallic region (the **clitoris** in girls). Parent-child conflict is likely to develop over masturbation, which parents may treat with punishment and threats. During the phallic stage, children may develop strong sexual attachments to the parent of the opposite sex and begin to view the same-sex parent as a rival for the other parent's affections. Boys may want to marry Mommy, and girls may want to marry Daddy.

Feelings of lust and jealousy are difficult for children to handle. Home life would be tense indeed if they were aware of them. So these feelings remain unconscious, although their influence is felt through fantasies about marriage and hostility toward the same-sex parent. Freud labeled this conflict in boys the **Oedipus complex,** after the legendary Greek king who unwittingly killed his father and married his mother. Similar feelings in girls give rise to the **Electra complex.** According to Greek legend, Electra was the daughter of the king Agamemnon. She longed for him after his death and sought revenge against his slayers—her mother and her mother's lover.

The Oedipus and Electra complexes become resolved by about the ages of 5 or 6. Children then repress their hostilities toward and identify with the parent of the same sex. Identification leads to playing the social and sexual roles of the same-sex parent and internalizing that parent's values. Sexual feelings toward the opposite-sex parent are repressed for a number of years. When the feelings emerge during adolescence, they are **displaced,** or transferred, to socially appropriate members of the opposite sex.

By the age of 5 or 6, Freud believed that children would have been in conflict with their parents over sexual feelings for several years. The pressures of the Oedipus and Electra complexes would motivate them to repress all sexual urges. In so doing they would enter **latency,** a period of life during which sexual feelings remain unconscious. They would use this period to focus on schoolwork and to consolidate earlier learning, most notably of appropriate sex-role behaviors. During the latency phase, it would not be uncommon for children to prefer playmates of their own sex.

Freud wrote that we enter the final stage of psychosexual development, or **genital stage,** at puberty. Adolescent males again experience sexual urges toward their mothers and adolescent females toward their fathers. However, the **incest taboo** provides ample motivation for keeping these impulses repressed and displacing them onto other adults or adolescents of the opposite sex. Boys still might seek girls "just like the girl that married dear old Dad." Girls still might be attracted to men who resemble their fathers.

People in the genital stage prefer, by definition, to find sexual gratification through intercourse with a member of the opposite sex. In Freud's view, oral or anal stimulation, masturbation, and homosexual activity would all represent **pregenital** fixations and immature forms of sexual conduct. They would not be consistent with the life instinct Eros.

Displaced Transferred.

Latency A phase of psychosexual development characterized by repression of sexual impulses.

Genital stage The mature stage of psychosexual development, characterized by preferred expression of libido through intercourse with an adult of the opposite sex.

Incest taboo The cultural prohibition against marrying or having sexual relations with a close blood relative.

Pregenital Characteristic of stages less mature than the genital stage.

A CLOSER LOOK

A Career Woman. Most modern psychologists do not accept Freud's suggestion that career women are maladjusted and suffering from unresolved penis envy.

Do Women Who Compete with Men Suffer from Penis Envy?

Psychodynamic theory in many ways has been a liberating force, allowing people to admit the importance of sexuality in their lives. But it has also been argued that Freud's views are repressive toward women. Freud's penis-envy hypothesis, in particular, has stigmatized women who compete with men in the business world as having failed to resolve the Electra complex.

Freud believed that little girls envy boys' penises. Why, they would feel, should boys have something that they do not? As a consequence of this jealousy, girls would resent their mothers for bringing them into the world so "ill-equipped," as Freud wrote in *New Introductory Lectures on Psychoanalysis.* They would then form the wish to marry their fathers as a substitute for not having penises of their own.

Through a series of developmental transformations, the wish to marry the father would evolve into the desire to marry another man and bear children. A baby, especially a male child, would partly gratify the unconscious need to possess something sprouting from the genital region. Freud also equated the penis with power and declared that the well-adjusted woman would also accept her husband's authority, symbolically surrendering the wish to have a penis of her own. Freud warned that retaining the wish for a penis would cause maladjustment. Persistent jealousy would cause women to develop masculine-typed traits such as competitiveness, outspokenness, and, at worst, female homosexuality.

Truth or Fiction Revisited

It is true that Freud believed that women who compete with men in the business world are suffering from penis envy. Feminists and many contemporary psychoanalysts have disparaged this view.

Freud's views on women have been strongly attacked by feminists and by many modern-day psychoanalysts. Karen Horney, for example, contended that little girls do not feel inferior to boys and that the penis-envy hypothesis has not been confirmed by observations of children. Horney argued that Freud's views reflected a Western cultural prejudice against women, not good psychological theory. Horney believed that cultural expectations played a greater role than penis envy in shaping women's self-images. Because of her outspoken opposition to the ways in which the psychoanalytic establishment conceptualized and treated women, Horney was expelled from the staid New York Psychoanalytic Institute early in this century (Quinn, 1987).

Many people want women to remain passive and submissive, emotional, and dependent on men. In Freud's day, oppression of women was even more extreme. Psychodynamic theory, in its original form, supported the belief that motherhood and family life are the only proper avenues of fulfillment for women.

Carl Gustav Jung

Several personality theorists are intellectual heirs of Sigmund Freud. Their theories, like Freud's, include roles for unconscious motivation, for motivational conflict, and for defensive responses to anxiety that involve repression and cognitive distortion of reality (Wachtel, 1982). In other respects, theories differ considerably. We discuss the psychodynamic views of Carl Jung, Alfred Adler, Karen Horney, and Erik Erikson.

Carl Jung

Carl Jung (1875–1961) was a Swiss psychiatrist who had been a member of Freud's inner circle. He fell into disfavor with Freud when he developed his own psychodynamic theory—**analytical psychology.** Jung, like Freud, was intrigued by unconscious processes. He believed that we not only have a *personal* unconscious, which contains repressed memories and impulses, but also an inherited **collective unconscious.** The collective unconscious contains primitive images, or **archetypes,** which are reflections of the history of our species.

Truth or Fiction Revisited

It is true that Jung believed that you have inherited mysterious memories that date back to ancient times.

Archetypes include vague, mysterious mythical images. Examples of archetypes are the All-Powerful God, the young hero, the fertile and nurturing mother, the wise old man, the hostile brother, even fairy godmothers, wicked witches, and themes of rebirth or resurrection. Archetypes themselves remain unconscious, but Jung declared that they influence our thoughts and emotions and render us responsive to cultural themes in stories and films. Archetypes are somewhat accessible through the interpretation of dreams.

Analytical psychology Jung's psychodynamic theory, which emphasizes the collective unconscious and archetypes.

Collective unconscious Jung's hypothesized store of vague racial memories.

Archetypes Basic, primitive images or concepts hypothesized by Jung to reside in the collective unconscious.

A Mandala. To Jung, the mandala is a symbolic expression of the efforts of the Self to provide the personality with wholeness or fullness.

Jung believed that within each of us reside shadowy parts of the personality that may unfold gradually as we mature. He believed that women, who are feminine* in most of their behavior patterns, have an **animus,** a masculine, aggressively competitive aspect of personality. Men, despite their masculinity, possess an **anima,** an aspect of personality that is feminine, soft, supportive, and passive. This is the way in which Jung accounted for the fact that women and men frequently display behaviors that are inconsistent with cultural stereotypes.

Jung downplayed the importance of the sexual instinct. He saw it as but one of several important instincts. Despite all of his interest in the collective unconscious, Jung also granted more importance to conscious motives than Freud did. Jung believed that one of the archetypes is a **Self,** a unifying force of personality that gives direction and purpose to human behavior. According to Jung, the Self aims to provide the personality with wholeness or fullness.

Jung believed that an understanding of human behavior must incorporate the facts of self-awareness and self-direction as well as the impulses of the id and the mechanisms of defense. Yet the same Jung who insisted that importance must be attached to fully conscious functions went even further than Freud in constructing an involved, poetic inner life. Many of Jung's ideas cannot be verified through scientific study. They remain at the level of conjecture, of metaphysical speculation.

Alfred Adler

Alfred Adler

Alfred Adler (1870–1937), another follower of Freud, also believed that Freud had placed too much emphasis on sexual impulses. Adler believed that people are basically motivated by an **inferiority complex.** In some people, feelings of inferiority may be based on physical problems and the need to compensate for them. Adler believed, however, that all of us encounter some feelings of inferiority because of our small size as children, and these feelings give rise to a **drive for superiority.** For instance, the English poet Lord Byron, who had a crippled leg, became a champion swimmer. Beethoven's encroaching deafness may have spurred him on to greater musical accomplishments. Adler as a child was crippled by rickets and suffered from pneumonia, and it may be that his theory developed in part from his own childhood striving to overcome repeated bouts of illness. However, there is no empirical support for the view that all of us harbor feelings of inferiority.

Adler, like Jung, believed that self-awareness plays a major role in the formation of personality. Adler spoke of a **creative self,** a self-aware aspect of personality that strives to overcome obstacles and develop the individual's potential. Because this potential is uniquely individual, Adler's views have been termed **individual psychology.**

Adler founded the first American child guidance clinic in Worcester, Massachusetts, and also introduced the term *sibling rivalry* to describe the jealousies that are found among brothers and sisters.

Animus Jung's term for a masculine archetype of the collective unconscious.

Anima Jung's feminine archetype.

Self In analytical psychology, a conscious, unifying force to personality that provides people with direction and purpose.

Inferiority complex Feelings of inferiority hypothesized by Adler to serve as a central motivating force.

Drive for superiority Adler's term for the desire to compensate for feelings of inferiority.

Creative self According to Adler, the self-aware aspect of personality that strives to achieve its full potential.

Individual psychology Adler's psychodynamic theory, which emphasizes feelings of inferiority and the creative self.

Karen Horney

Karen Horney (1885–1952) was born in Germany and emigrated to the United States before the outbreak of World War II. Horney agreed with Freud that childhood experiences played a major role in the development of adult

*Jung was speaking in terms of traditional sex-role stereotypes, as discussed in Chapter 14.

Karen Horney

Erik Erikson

personality, but, like many other neoanalysts, she believed that sexual and aggressive impulses took a back seat in importance to social relationships. Moreover, she disagreed with Freud that anatomical differences between the sexes led girls to feel inferior to boys.

Horney, like Freud, saw parent-child relationships to be of paramount importance. Small children are completely dependent, and when their parents treat them with indifference or harshness, they develop feelings of insecurity and what Horney terms **basic anxiety.** Children also resent neglectful parents, and Horney theorized that a **basic hostility** would accompany basic anxiety. Horney agreed with Freud that children would repress rather than express feelings of hostility toward their parents because of fear of reprisal and, just as important, fear of driving them away. On the other hand, it should be noted that Horney was more optimistic than Freud about the effects of early childhood traumatic experiences. She believed that genuine and consistent love could mitigate the effects of even the most traumatic childhoods (Quinn, 1987).

Later in life, basic anxiety and repressed hostility would lead to the development of one of three neurotic ways of relating to other people: moving toward others, moving against others, or moving away from others. Of course, it is healthful to relate to other people, but the neurotic person who moves toward others has feelings of insecurity and an excessive need for approval that render him or her compliant and overly anxious to please. People who move against others are also insecure, but they attempt to cope with their insecurity by asserting power and dominating social interactions. People who move away from others cope with their insecurities by withdrawing from social interactions. By remaining aloof from others, they attempt to prevent themselves from getting hurt by them. The price, of course, is perpetual loneliness.

Erik Erikson

Erik Erikson also believed that Freud had placed undue emphasis on sexual instincts, and he asserted that social relationships are more crucial determinants of personality. To Erikson, the general climate of the mother–infant relationship is more important than the details of the feeding process or the sexual feelings that might be stirred by contact with the mother. Erikson also argued that to a large degree we are the conscious architects of our own personalities—a view that grants more powers to the ego than Freud had allowed. Within Erikson's theory, it is possible for us to make real choices. Within Freud's theory, we might think that we are making choices, but we are probably only rationalizing the compromises forced upon us by intrapsychic warfare.

Erikson, like Freud, is known for devising a comprehensive developmental theory of personality. But whereas Freud proposed stages of psycho*sexual development,* Erikson proposed stages of psycho*social* development. In other words, rather than labeling a stage after an erogenous zone, Erikson labeled stages after the traits that might be developed during that stage (see Table 10.2). Each stage is named according to the possible outcomes, which are polar opposites. For example, the first stage of **psychosocial development** is named the stage of trust versus mistrust because of the two possible major outcomes. (1) A warm, loving relationship with the mother (and others) during infancy might lead to a sense of basic trust in people and the world. (2) A cold, nongratifying relationship might generate a pervasive sense of mistrust. Erikson believed that most of us would wind up with some blend of trust and mistrust—hopefully more trust than mistrust.

Basic anxiety Horney's term for lasting feelings of insecurity that stem from harsh or indifferent parental treatment.

Basic hostility Horney's term for lasting feelings of anger that accompany basic anxiety but are directed toward nonfamily members in adulthood.

Psychosocial development Erikson's theory of personality and development, which emphasizes social relationships and eight stages of growth.

Table 10.2
Erik Erikson's Stages of Development

Time Period	Life Crisis	The Developmental Task
Infancy (0–1)	Trust versus mistrust	Coming to trust the mother and the environment—to associate surroundings with feelings of inner goodness
Early childhood (2–3)	Autonomy versus shame and doubt	Developing the wish to make choices and the self-control to exercise choice
Preschool years (4–5)	Initiative versus guilt	Adding planning and "attacking" to choice, becoming active and on the move
Grammar school years (6–12)	Industry versus inferiority	Becoming eagerly absorbed in skills, tasks, and productivity; mastering the fundamentals of technology
Adolescence	Identity versus role diffusion	Connecting skills and social roles to formation of career objectives
Young adulthood	Intimacy versus isolation	Committing the self to another; engaging in sexual love
Middle adulthood	Generativity versus stagnation	Needing to be needed; guiding and encouraging the younger generation; being creative
Late adulthood	Integrity versus despair	Accepting the timing and placing of one's own life cycle; achieving wisdom and dignity

Source: Erikson, 1963, pp. 247–269.

A basic sense of mistrust could mar the formation of relationships for a lifetime unless we came to realize its presence and challenge its suitability.

Adolescent and Adult Development One of Erikson's most important accomplishment is his extension of Freud's five developmental stages to eight. Whereas Freud's developmental theory ends with adolescence, in the form of the genital stage, Erikson's theory includes the changing concerns of adulthood.

For Erikson, the goal of adolescence is the attainment of **ego identity,** not genital sexuality. Adolescents who attain ego identity develop a firm sense of who they are and what they stand for. One aspect of ego identity is learning how to "connect the roles and skills cultivated [during the elementary school years] with the occupational prototypes of the day" (Erikson, 1963, p. 261)—that is, with jobs. But ego identity extends to sexual, political, and religious beliefs and commitments. According to Erikson, adolescents who do not develop a firm sense of identity are especially subject to peer influences and short-sighted hedonism.

Evaluation

Psychodynamic theories have had tremendous appeal. By and large, they are "rich" theories; that is, they involve many concepts and they explain many varieties of human behavior and traits. Let us evaluate them by considering some of their strengths and weaknesses.

Strengths of Psychodynamic Approaches

1. *Psychic Determinism: Toward a More Scientific View of Behavior* One of the basic tenets of psychodynamic theory is that behavior is determined by the outcome of intrapsychic conflict. Today concepts such as "intrapsychic conflict" and "psychic energy" strike many psychologists as being unscientific. In his day, however, Freud fought for the idea

Ego identity A firm sense of who one is and what one stands for.

that human personality and behavior were subject to scientific analysis. Freud's theorizing took place at a time when many people still viewed grave psychological problems as signs of possession by the Devil or evil spirits, as they had during the Middle Ages. Freud argued that psychological disorders stem from problems within the individual—not evil spirits. Freud's thinking contributed to the development of compassion for, and methods of helping, people whose behavior is abnormal.

2. *The Importance of Childhood* Freud's psychodynamic theory also focused the attention of scientists and helping professionals on the far-reaching effects of childhood events. Freud's inquiries helped show how children differ from adults. The developmental theories of Freud and Erikson suggest ways in which early childhood traumas can color our perceptions and influence our behavior for a lifetime. Horney believed that Freud was too pessimistic about the ability of children to recover from trauma and that Freud underestimated the saving powers of love. Yet Freud and other psychodynamic theorists are to be credited for suggesting that personality and behavior *develop*—and that it is important for us as parents to be aware of the emotional needs of our children.

3. *The Importance of "Primitive" Impulses* Freud is in part responsible for "getting people talking" about the importance of sexuality in their lives and about the prevalence of aggressive impulses and urges. Freud has helped us recognize that sexual and aggressive urges are commonplace and that there is a difference between acknowledging these urges and acting on them.

4. *The Role of Cognitive Distortion* Freud also noted that people have defensive ways of looking at the world. He developed a list of defense mechanisms that have become part of everyday parlance. Whether or not we attribute these cognitive distortions to unconscious ego functioning, our thinking is apparently distorted by our efforts to avert anxiety and guilt. If these concepts no longer strike us as being innovative, it is largely because of the influence of Sigmund Freud.

5. *Innovation of Methods of Psychotherapy* In Chapter 13 we shall describe the methods of therapy originated by Freud and other psychodynamic theorists. We shall see that they have helped thousands of people overcome abnormal behavior and develop as individuals.

Weaknesses of Psychodynamic Approaches Despite their richness, psychodynamic theories, particularly the original psychodynamic views of Sigmund Freud, have met with criticism for reasons such as the following:

1. *Overemphasis on Sexuality and Underemphasis on Social Relationships* Some followers of Freud, such as Horney and Erikson, have argued that Freud placed too much emphasis on human sexuality and neglected the importance of social relationships. Other followers, such as Adler and Erich Fromm, have argued that Freud placed too much emphasis on unconscious motives. Adler and Fromm assert that people consciously seek self-enhancement and intellectual pleasures. They do not merely try to gratify the dark demands of the id.

2. *The Lack of Substance of "Psychic Structures"* A number of critics note that "psychic structures" such as the id, ego, and superego have no substance. They are little more than useful fictions—poetic ways to express inner conflict.

Trait An aspect of personality that is inferred from behavior and assumed to give rise to behavioral consistency.

3. *Resistance to Disproof* Sir Karl Popper (1985) has argued that Freud's hypothetical mental processes fail as scientific concepts because they cannot be observed. Nor do they predict observable behavior with precision. Scientific propositions must be capable of being proved false. But, as noted by Popper, Freud's statements about mental structures are unscientific because no conceivable type of evidence can disprove them; any behavior can be explained in terms of these hypothesized (but unobservable) "structures."

4. *Inaccuracies in Developmental Theories* The stages of psychosexual development have not escaped criticism. Children begin to masturbate as early as the first year, not in the phallic stage. As parents know from observing their children play "doctor," the latency stage is not as sexually latent as Freud believed. Much of Freud's thinking concerning the Oedipus and Electra complexes remains speculation.

5. *Possible Biases in the Gathering of Evidence* As noted by philosopher Adolph Grünbaum (1985), Freud's method of gathering evidence from the clinical session is also suspect. Therapists may subtly influence clients to produce what they expect to find. Therapists may also fail to separate reported facts from their own interpretations.

Also, Freud and many other psychodynamic theorists restricted their evidence gathering to case studies with individuals who sought therapy for adjustment problems. Persons seeking therapy do not represent the population at large. They are likely to have more problems than the general population.

One of the richer aspects of the psychodynamic theories is the way in which they account for the development of various traits. Let us now consider trait theories, which address traits from a different perspective.

TRAIT THEORIES

The notion of **traits** is very familiar. If I asked you to describe yourself, you would probably do so in terms of your traits. We also tend to describe other people in terms of traits.

Traits are elements of personality that are inferred from behavior. If you describe a friend as being "shy," it may be because you have observed social anxiety or withdrawal in the friend's encounters. Traits are also assumed to be enduring and to account for consistent behavior in diverse situations. You probably expect your "shy" friend to be retiring in most social confrontations—"all across the board," as the saying goes. The concept of traits also finds a place in other approaches to personality. Recall that throughout Freud's stages of psychosexual development, he linked development of certain traits to children's experiences.

Gordon Allport

Gordon Allport

Psychologist Gordon Allport (1937, 1961) thought of traits as being embedded in our nervous systems. He argued that traits "steer" or guide us to behave consistently. For example, the trait of sociability may steer us to invite friends along when going out, to share confidences in letters, and to make others feel at home at gatherings. A person who "lacks" sociability would be disposed to behave differently in these situations.

Raymond Cattell

More than 50 years ago, Allport and Odbert (1936) catalogued some 18,000 human traits from a search through word lists of the sort found in dictionaries. Some were physical traits, such as short, white, and brunette. Others were behavioral traits, such as shy and emotional. Still others were moral traits, such as honest. This exhaustive list has served as the basis for personality research by many other psychologists, including Raymond Cattell.

Raymond Cattell

Psychologists such as Raymond Cattell (1965) have used statistical techniques to reduce this universe of innumerable traits to smaller lists of traits that show commonality. Cattell also distinguished between surface traits and source traits. **Surface traits** describe characteristic ways of behaving—for example, cleanliness, stubbornness, thrift, and orderliness. We may observe that these traits form meaningful patterns that are suggestive of underlying traits. (Cleanliness, stubbornness, and so on were all referred to as *anal retentive* traits by Freud.)

Cattell refined the Allport catalogue by removing unusual terms and grouping the remaining traits under **source traits**—the underlying traits from which surface traits are derived. Cattell argued that psychological measurement of a person's source traits would enable us to predict his or her behavior in various situations.

Cattell's research led him to suggest the existence of 16 source traits, and these traits can be measured by means of his Sixteen Personality Factors Scale. (See Psychology Goes to Work and Figure 10.2 on the next page.) The "16 PF" is frequently used in psychological research that explores differences between groups of people and individuals.

Hans Eysenck

Hans Eysenck

British psychologist Hans J. Eysenck (1960; Eysenck & Eysenck, 1985) has focused much of his research on the relationships between two important traits: **introversion–extraversion** and emotional stability–instability, the latter otherwise called **neuroticism.** Carl Jung was first to distinguish between introverts and extraverts. Eysenck added the dimension of neuroticism to introversion–extraversion. He has catalogued various personality traits according to where they are "situated" along these dimensions (refer to Figure 10.3). For instance, an anxious person would be high both in introversion and in neuroticism—that is, preoccupied with his or her own thoughts and emotionally unstable.

Eysenck notes that his scheme is reminiscent of that suggested by Hippocrates (ca. 460–377 B.C.), the physician of the Golden Age of Greece. Hippocrates suggested that there are four basic personality types: choleric (quick-tempered), sanguine (warm, cheerful, confident), phlegmatic (sluggish, calm, cool), and melancholic (gloomy, pensive). The terms *choleric, sanguine,* and so on remain in common use. According to Eysenck's dimensions, the choleric type would be extraverted and unstable; the sanguine type, extraverted and stable; the phlegmatic type, introverted and stable; and the melancholic type, introverted and unstable. Hippocrates believed that these types, and mixtures of these types, depend on the balance of the four "basic fluids," or humors, in the body. Yellow bile was associated with a choleric disposition; blood, a sanguine one; phlegm, a phlegmatic disposition; and black bile, a melancholic temperament.

Surface traits Cattell's term for characteristic, observable ways of behaving.

Source traits Cattell's term for underlying traits from which surface traits are derived.

Introversion A source trait characterized by intense imagination and the tendency to inhibit impulses.

Extraversion A source trait characterized by tendencies to be socially outgoing and to express feelings and impulses freely.

Neuroticism Eysenck's term for emotional instability.

PSYCHOLOGY GOES TO WORK

On Source Traits, Pilots, Artists, and Writers

Psychologists have developed a number of tests to measure personality traits. One of the more important tests is Cattell's Sixteen Personality Factors Scale, which measures his so-called source traits. The 16 PF assesses individual differences, but it can also be used to measure group differences among persons in various occupations.

Consider Figure 10.2. It shows the differences, according to the 16 PF, between airline pilots, creative artists, and writers. Notice that the pilots are more stable, conscientious, tough-minded, practical, controlled, and relaxed than the other two groups. The artists and writers are more intelligent, sensitive, and imaginative.

Truth or Fiction Revisited

It is true that airline pilots are generally more emotionally stable than artists, but the artists are more intelligent, sensitive, and imaginative.

You may prefer to have artists at a cocktail party, but pilots—at least those tested by Cattell—seem to have the stable and self-disciplined personality profile you would want to have in charge in the cockpit.

The pilots seem to be "better adjusted" than the writers and artists from a superficial point of view. That is, they are more "stable," more "self-controlled," and less "tense." Yet writers and artists make indispensable contributions to society and, by and large, are willing to pay the emotional price for their more sensitive personalities.

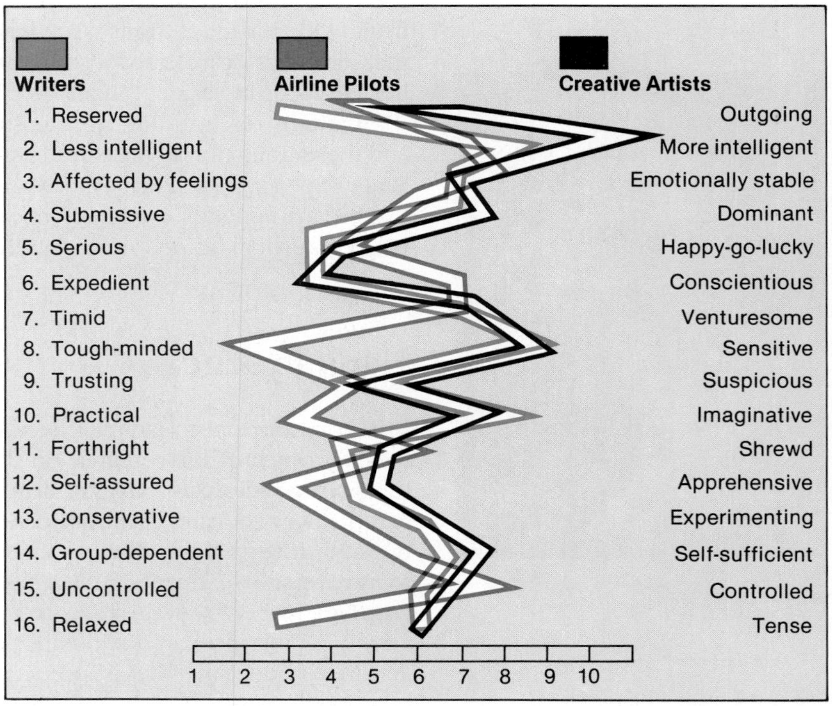

Figure 10.2.
Three Personality Profiles According to Cattell's Personality Factors.
How do the traits of writers, airline pilots, and creative artists compare? Where would you place yourself within these personality dimensions?

Where would you place athletes and artists in terms of the dimensions of introversion–extraversion and neuroticism? Where would you place yourself?

Evaluation

Trait theories, like psychodynamic theories, have their strengths and weaknesses.

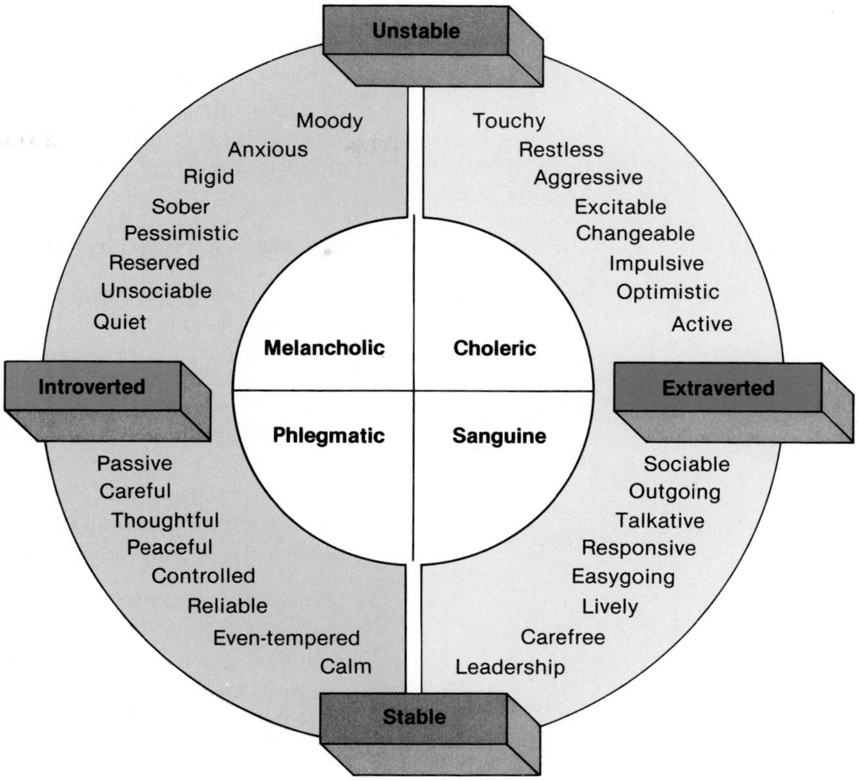

Figure 10.3.
Eysenck's Personality Dimensions and Hippocrates' Personality Types. Various personality traits shown in the outer ring fall within the two major dimensions of personality suggested by Hans Eysenck. The inner circle shows how Hippocrates' four major personality types—choleric, sanguine, phlegmatic, and melancholic—fit within Eysenck's modern dimensions.

Strengths of Trait-Theory Approaches

1. *Developing Psychological Tests* Trait theorists have focused a good deal of their attention on the development of tests to measure traits, such as Cattell's Sixteen Personality Factors Scale. Others are discussed in the section on measurement of personality.

2. *Spawning Theories Concerning the Fit between Personality and Jobs* Because most of us spend some 40 hours a week on the job—and a good deal of the rest of the time thinking about our work!—it is important to our well-being that we "fit" our jobs. The qualities that suit us for various kinds of work can be expressed in terms of our abilities, our personality traits, and our interests. By using interviews and tests to learn about our abilities and our traits, testing and counseling centers can make valuable suggestions about the likelihood for our success and fulfillment in various kinds of jobs.

3. *Identifying of Basic Traits* Freud developed his theories about "oral," "anal," and other traits on the basis of clinical case studies. However, trait theorists have administered broad personality tests to thousands of people and have used sophisticated statistical techniques to identify the basic traits, or factors, that tend to describe us.

   Numerous empirical studies (e.g., Digman & Inouye, 1986; Noller et al., 1987) suggest that there may be five basic personality factors, including a number of those suggested by Eysenck and Cattell. These include the two found by Eysenck: (1) introversion–extraversion and (2) emotional stability–instability (neuroticism). The others are (3) self-control or conscientiousness and (4) tough-mindedness versus sensitivity, as suggested by Cattell, and (5) openness to new experience, which is similar to Cattell's experimenting–conservative dimension.

4. *Pointing Out that Traits Are Reasonably Stable* Research has shown that numerous personality traits are stable over many years. James Conley (1984, 1985), for example, studied psychological tests taken by a sample of adults during the 1930s, the 1950s, and again during the 1980s. Their scores on the traits of extraversion, neuroticism, and impulsiveness showed significant consistency across five decades.

Weaknesses of Trait-Theory Approaches

1. *Trait Theory Is Descriptive, Not Explanatory* Trait theory focuses on describing existing traits rather than tracing their origins or investigating how they may be modified.
2. *Circular Explanations* The explanations provided by trait theory are often criticized as being **circular explanations.** That is, they simply restate what is observed and do not explain what is observed. Saying that John failed to ask Marsha on a date *because* of shyness is an example of a circular explanation; all we have done is to restate John's (shy) behavior as a trait (shyness).
3. *Situational Variability in Behavior* The trait concept requires that traits show stability. Although many personality traits seem to do so, behavior may vary more from situation to situation than trait theory would allow (Bem & Allen, 1974; Mischel, 1977, 1986). People who are high in **private self-consciousness** try to show consistent behavior from situation to situation (Fenigstein et al., 1975; Scheier et al., 1978; Underwood & Moore, 1981), but other people show more variability in behavior.

LEARNING THEORIES

Learning theorists also have studied issues relating to personality. We shall focus on two learning-theory approaches: behaviorism and social-learning theory. Behaviorism is important for its emphasis on the observable, its historical significance, and its continued ability to rally supporters. But today, many if not most learning-theory–oriented psychologists would consider themselves to be social-learning theorists.

Behaviorism

At Johns Hopkins University in 1924, psychologist John B. Watson announced the battle cry of the behaviorist movement:

> *Give me a dozen healthy infants, well-formed, and my own specified world to bring them up in and I'll guarantee to take any one at random and train him to become any type of specialist I might suggest—doctor, lawyer, merchant-chief and, yes, even beggar-man and thief, regardless of his talents, penchants, tendencies, abilities, vocations, and the race of his ancestors* (p. 82).

So it was that Watson proclaimed that situational variables or environmental influences—not internal, person variables—are the important shapers of human preferences and behaviors. As a counterbalance to the psychoanalysts and structuralists of his day, Watson argued that unseen, undetectable mental structures must be rejected in favor of that which can be seen

Circular explanation An explanation that merely restates its own concepts instead of offering additional information.

Private self-consciousness The tendency to take critical note of one's own behavior, even when unobserved by others.

Prosocial Behavior that is characterized by helping others and making a contribution to society.

Social-learning theory. A cognitively oriented learning theory in which observational learning, values, and expectations play major roles in determining behavior.

Person variables Factors within the person, such as generalized expectancies and competencies, that influence behavior.

Expectancies Personal predictions about the outcomes of potential behaviors. "If-then" statements.

Subjective value The desirability of an object or event.

Generalized expectancies Broad expectations that reflect extensive learning and that are relatively resistant to change.

and measured. In the 1930s, Watson's hue and cry was taken up by B. F. Skinner, who agreed that we should avoid trying to see within the "black box" of the organism and emphasized the effect that reinforcements have on behavior.

The views of John B. Watson and B. F. Skinner largely discard the notions of personal freedom, choice, and self-direction. Most of us assume that our wants originate within us. But Skinner suggests that environmental influences, such as parental approval and social custom, shape us into *wanting* certain things and *not wanting* others. To Watson and Skinner, even our telling ourselves that we have free will is determined by the environment as surely as is our becoming startled at a sudden noise.

In his novel *Walden Two,* Skinner (1948) describes a Utopian society in which people are happy and content because they are allowed to do as they please. However, they have been trained or conditioned from early childhood to engage in **prosocial** behavior and to express prosocial attitudes. Because of their reinforcement histories, they *want* to behave in a decent, kind, and unselfish way. They see themselves as being free because society makes no effort to force them to behave as they do as adults.

Skinner elaborated on his beliefs about people and society in *Beyond Freedom and Dignity* (1972). According to Skinner, adaptation to the environment requires acceptance of behavior patterns that ensure survival. If the group is to survive, it must construct rules and laws that foster social harmony. Other people are then rewarded for following these rules and punished for disobeying them. None of us is really free, even though we think of ourselves as coming together freely to establish the rules and as choosing to follow them.

Some object to behaviorist notions because they sidestep the roles of human consciousness and choice. Others argue that people are not so blindly ruled by pleasure and pain. People have rebelled against the so-called necessity of survival by choosing pain and hardship over pleasure or death over life. Many people have sacrificed their own lives to save those of others.

The behaviorist defense might be that the apparent choice of pain or death is forced on the altruist as inevitably as conformity to social custom is forced on others. The altruist was also shaped by external influences, but those influences differed from those that affect most of us.

Julian B. Rotter

Social-Learning Theory

Social-learning theory is a contemporary view of learning developed by Albert Bandura (1977, 1986) and other psychologists. It focuses on the importance of learning by observation and on the role of cognitive activity in human behavior. Social-learning theorists see people as influencing the environment just as the environment influences them. Social-learning theorists agree with behaviorists that discussions of human nature should be tied to observable experiences and behaviors. They assert, however, that variables within the person—**person variables**—must also be considered if we are to understand people.

One goal of all psychological theories is the prediction of behavior. Social-learning theorist Julian B. Rotter (1972) argues that we cannot predict behavior from situational variables alone. Whether or not a person will behave in a certain way also depends on the person's **expectancies** about that behavior's outcomes and the perceived or **subjective values** of those outcomes. **Generalized expectancies** are broad expectations that reflect extensive learning and that are relatively enduring. Their consistency and stability make them the equivalent of traits within social-learning theory.

Model In social-learning theory, an organism who exhibits behaviors that others will imitate or acquire through observational learning.

Competencies Knowledge and skills.

Encode Interpret; tranform.

To social-learning theorists, people are self-aware and engage in purposeful learning. People are not simply at the mercy of the environment. Instead, they seek to learn about their environment. They alter and construct the environment to make reinforcers available.

Social-learning theorists also note the importance of rules and symbolic processes in learning. Children, for example, learn more effectively how to behave in specific situations when parents explain the rules involved. In so-called inductive methods of discipline, parents use specific situations to teach children about general rules and social codes that should govern their behavior. Inductive methods are more effective at fostering desirable behavior than punishment (Rathus, 1988).

Observational Learning Observational learning (also termed **modeling**) refers to the acquisition of knowledge by observing others. For operant conditioning to occur, an organism must engage in a response, and that response must be reinforced. But observational learning occurs even when the learner does not perform the observed behavior pattern. Therefore, direct reinforcement is not required either. Observing others extends to reading about them or perceiving what they do and what happens to them in media such as radio, television, and film.

Our expectations of what will happen if we do something stem from our observations of what happens to others, as well as our own experiences. For example, teachers are more accepting of "calling out" in class from boys than girls (Sadker & Sadker, 1985). As a result, boys frequently expect to be rewarded for calling out in class; girls, however, are more likely to expect to be reprimanded for behaving in what traditionalists might refer to as an "unladylike" manner.

Let us now consider a number of the person variables that account for individual differences in behavior in social-learning theory.

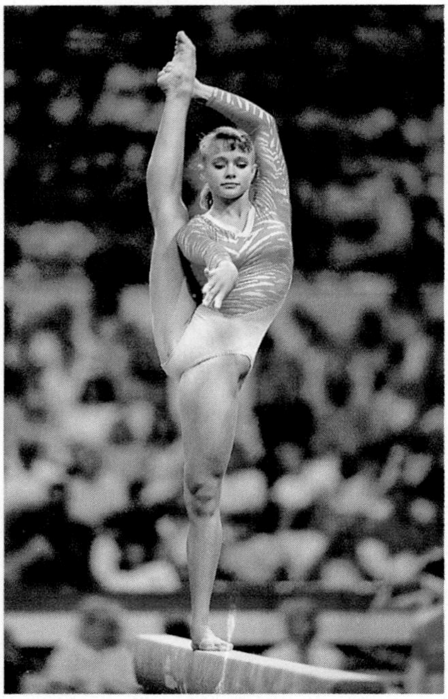

How Do Competencies Contribute to Performance? There are great individual differences in our competencies, based on genetic variation, nourishment, differences in learning opportunities, and other environmental factors. What factors contribute to this girl's performance on the balance beam?

Person Variables in Social-Learning Theory Social-learning theorists view behavior as stemming from a fluid, ongoing interaction between person variables and situational variables. Person variables include competencies, encoding strategies, expectancies, subjective values, and self-regulatory systems and plans (Mischel, 1986, pp. 308–312). See Figure 10.4.

Competencies: What Can You Do? Competencies include knowledge of rules that guide conduct, concepts about ourselves and other people, and skills. Our abilities to actively use information to construct plans and plan overt behavior depend on our competencies.

Competencies include knowledge of the physical world, of cultural codes of conduct, and of the behavior patterns expected in certain situations. They include academic skills, such as reading and writing; athletic skills, such as swimming and tossing a football properly; social skills, such as knowing how to ask someone out on a date; job skills; and many others.

There are individual differences in our competencies, based on genetic variation, nourishment, differences in learning opportunities, and other environmental factors. Generally speaking, people do not perform well at given tasks unless they have the competencies that are required to do so.

Encoding Strategies: How Do You See It? Different people **encode** (symbolize or represent) the same stimuli in different ways, and their encoding strategies are an important factor in their overt behavior. One person might encode a tennis game as a chance to bat the ball back and forth and

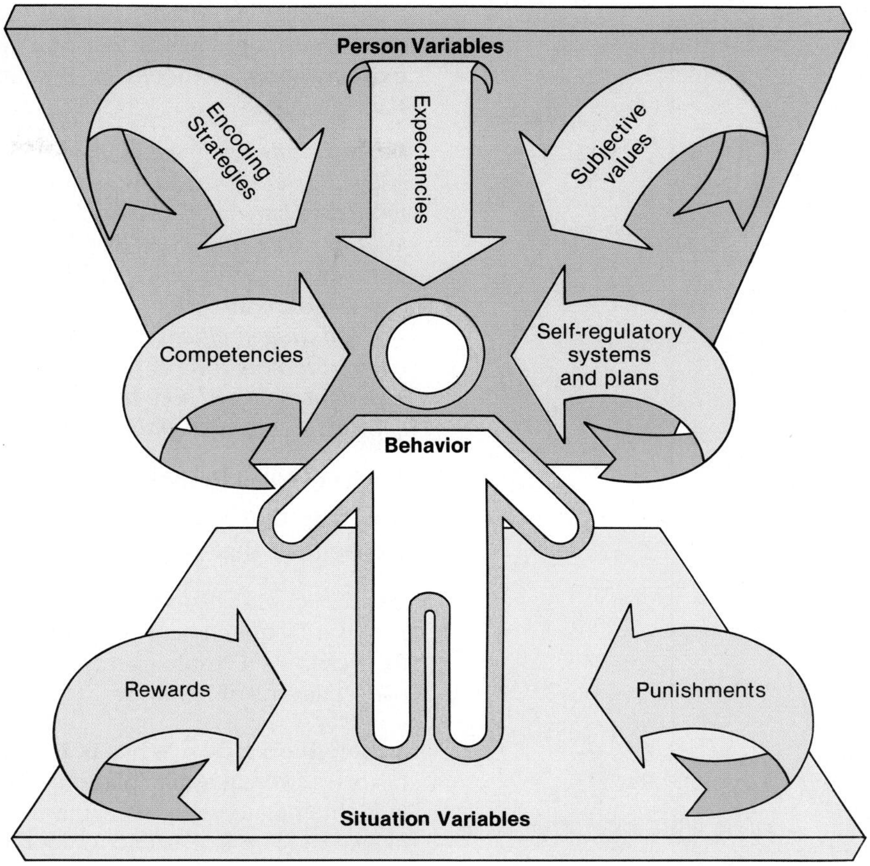

Figure 10.4.
Person Variables and Situational Variables in Social-Learning Theory. According to social-learning theory, person variables and situational variables interact to influence behavior.

have some fun; another might encode the same game as a demand to perfect his or her serve. One person might encode a date that doesn't work out as a sign of his social incompetence; another might encode the dating experience as reflecting the fact that people are not always "made for each other."

In Chapter 12, we shall see how some people make themselves miserable because of encoding strategies that involve irrational beliefs and cognitive distortions. That is, they encode stimuli in self-defeating ways. For example, a linebacker may encode an average day on the field as a failure because he didn't get any sacks. A college student may encode one refusal to accept a date as a disaster that reflects on his worth as a human being. Cognitive and behavior therapists help foster adjustment by challenging their clients to encode stimuli in more productive ways.

Expectancies: What Will Happen? Expectancies are "if-then" statements, or personal predictions about the outcome (or reinforcement contingencies) of engaging in a response. The unique human abilities to manipulate symbols and to ponder events allow us to foresee the potential consequences of our behavior. Expectancies about what will happen if we behave in certain ways are based on our observations of others and on our own experiences in similar situations.

Competencies influence expectancies, and expectancies, in turn, influence motivation to perform. People who believe that they have the competencies required to perform effectively are more likely to try difficult tasks than people who do not believe that they can master them. Albert Bandura (1982) refers to beliefs that one can handle certain tasks as **self-efficacy expectations.** As noted by Bandura and his colleagues Linda Reese and Nancy Adams:

> *In their daily lives people must make decisions about whether to attempt risky courses of action or how long to continue, in the face of difficulties, those they have undertaken. Social-learning theory posits that . . . people tend to avoid situations they believe exceed their coping capabilities, but they undertake and perform assuredly activities they judge themselves capable of managing . . . .*
>
> *Self-judged efficacy also determines how much of an effort people will make and how long they will keep at a task despite obstacles or adverse experiences . . . . Those who have a strong sense of efficacy exert greater effort to master the challenges . . .* (1982, p. 5).

Truth or Fiction Revisited

It is true that we are more likely to persist at difficult tasks when we believe that we shall succeed.

Bandura (1986) also suggests that one of the helpful aspects of psychotherapy is that it frequently changes clients' self-efficacy expectations from "I can't" to "I can." As a result, clients are motivated to try out new—and more adaptive—patterns of behavior.

Subjective Values: What Is It Worth? Because of our different learning histories, we each may place a different value on the same outcome. What is frightening to one person may entice another. What is somewhat desirable to one may be irresistible to another. From the social-learning perspective, in contrast to the behaviorist perspective, we are not controlled by stimuli. Instead, stimuli have various meanings for us, and these meanings are one factor in influencing our behavior.

The subjective value of a particular stimulus or reward is related to our experience with it or similar rewards. Experience may be direct or observational. Because of experience, our feelings about the outcome may be positive or negative. If you became nauseated the last time you drank a glass of iced tea, its subjective value as an incentive may diminish, even on a hot day.

Self-Regulatory Systems and Plans: How Can You Achieve It? Social-learning theory recognizes that one of the features of being human is our tendency to regulate our own behavior, even in the absence of observers and external constraints. We set goals and standards for ourselves, construct plans for achieving them, and congratulate or criticize ourselves, depending on whether or not we reach them.

Self-regulation amplifies our opportunities for influencing our environment. We can select the situations to which we expose ourselves and the arenas in which we shall contend. Based on our expectancies, we may choose to enter the academic or athletic worlds. We may choose marriage or the single life. And, when we cannot readily select our environment, we can to some degree select our responses within an environment—even an aversive one. For example, if we are undergoing an uncomfortable medical procedure, we may try to focus on something else—the cracks in the tiles on the ceiling or an inner fantasy—to reduce the stress.

Self-efficacy expectations Beliefs that one can handle a task.

Evaluation

Learning theorists have made monumental contributions to the scientific understanding of behavior, but they have also left some psychologists dissatisfied. Let us examine several of the strengths and weaknesses of learning-theory approaches.

Strengths of Learning-Theory Approaches

1. *Focus on Observable Behavior* Psychodynamic theorists and trait theorists propose the existence of psychological structures that cannot be seen and measured directly. Learning theorists—particularly behaviorists—have dramatized the importance of referring to publicly observable variables, or behaviors, if psychology is to be accepted as a science.
2. *Focus on the Situation* Psychodynamic theorists and trait theorists focus on internal variables, such as intrapsychic conflict and traits, to explain and predict behavior. Learning theorists have emphasized the importance of environmental conditions, or situational variables, as determinants of behavior.
3. *Outlining the Conditions of Learning* Learning theorists have elaborated on the conditions that foster learning—even automatic kinds of learning. They have shown that involuntary responses, including fear responses, may be conditioned; that we can learn to do things because of reinforcements; and that many broad behavior patterns are acquired by observing others.
4. *Innovation of Therapy Methods* Learning theorists have devised methods for helping individuals solve adjustment problems that probably would not have been derived from any other theoretical perspective. These include the behavioral, extinction-based fear-reduction methods of flooding and systematic desensitization and the operant-conditioning methods of biofeedback training.
5. *General Impact on Psychology* Learning theories have probably had the broadest effect on psychology as a whole. They address issues ranging from learning per se, animal behavior, and motivation to child development, psychological disorders, therapy methods, and even attitude formation and change.

Weaknesses of Learning-Theory Approaches

1. *Problems with Behaviorism* Behaviorism is limited in its ability to explain personality. For example, behaviorism does not describe or explain the richness of inner human experience. We experience thoughts and feelings and peruse our complex inner maps of the world, and behaviorism does not deal with these phenomena. But, to be fair, the "limitations" of behaviorism are self-imposed. Personality theorists have traditionally dealt with thoughts, feelings, and behavior, whereas behaviorism, in its insistence on studying only that which is observable and measurable, deals with behavior alone.
2. *Problems with Social-Learning Theory* Critics of social-learning theory may not accuse its supporters of denying the importance of cognitive activity and feelings. But they may contend that social-learning theory has not derived satisfying statements about the development of traits

Phenomenological Having to do with conscious, subjective experience.

Humanistic Emphasizing the importance of self-awareness and the freedom to make choices.

Gestalt In this usage, a quality of wholeness.

and accounted for self-awareness. Also, social-learning theory—like its intellectual forebear, behaviorism—may not have always paid sufficient attention to genetic variation in explaining individual differences in behavior. Learning theories have done very little to account for the development of traits or personality types.

Social-learning theorists seem to be working on these theoretical flaws. Today's social-learning theorists view people as being active, not as reacting mechanically to environmental pressures (as Watson saw them). Cognitive functioning is an appropriate area of study for social-learning theorists (Bandura, 1986; Wilson, 1982). In the area of abnormal behavior, many social-learning theorists grant that inherited or physiological factors may interact with situational stress to give rise to abnormal behavior.

Now let us consider theories that begin with the assumption of consciousness and dwell on the importance of our cognitive functioning.

PHENOMENOLOGICAL THEORIES

In this section we shall discuss two **phenomenological** approaches to personality: Rogers' self theory and Kelly's psychology of personal constructs. These approaches have a number of things in common: Both propose that the personal experience of events is the most important aspect of human nature. Both propose that we as individuals are our own best experts on ourselves. And both propose that we have unique ways of looking at the world.

Carl Rogers

Carl Rogers' Self Theory

My experience in therapy and in groups makes it impossible for me to deny the reality and significance of human choice. To me it is not an illusion that man is to some degree the architect of himself, . . .

Carl Rogers (1974, p. 119).

The view that people tend to shape themselves through freedom of choice and action is considered to be **humanistic.** Self theory is basically humanistic, but psychologists from other schools may also show a humanistic bent. Erik Erikson's view that we consciously strive to cope with identity crises and to invent ourselves is humanistic. Many social-learning theorists who stress the importance of cognitive person variables as determinants of behavior see themselves as being humanistic.

Rogers defines the self as an "organized, consistent, conceptual **gestalt** composed of perceptions of the characteristics of the 'I' or 'me' and the perceptions of the relationships of the 'I' or 'me' to others and to various aspects of life, together with the values attached to these perceptions" (1959, p. 200). Your self is your center of experience. It is your ongoing sense of who and what you are, your sense of how and why you react to the environment and how you choose to act on the environment. Your choices are made on the basis of your values, and your values are also parts of your self.

To Rogers, the sense of self is inborn, or innate. The self provides the experience of being human in the world. It is the guiding principle behind personality structure and behavior.

Unique. According to humanistic psychologists like Carl Rogers, each of us views the world and ourselves from a unique frame of reference. What is important to one individual may hold little meaning for another.

Self-Actualization Humanistic personality theorists such as Rogers and Abraham Maslow believe that organisms are genetically programed to grow, unfold, and become themselves. This central tendency, termed **self-actualization,** is a characteristic of life itself. Self-actualization renders behavior organized, meaningful, and whole.

The Self-Concept and Frames of Reference Our self-concepts comprise our impressions of ourselves and our evaluations of our adequacy. It may be helpful to think of us as rating ourselves according to various scales or dimensions, such as good–bad, intelligent–unintelligent, strong–weak, and tall–short.

Rogers states that we all have unique ways of looking at ourselves and the world, or unique **frames of reference.** It may be that we each use a different set of dimensions in defining ourselves and that we judge ourselves according to different sets of values. To one person, achievement–failure may be the most important dimension. To another person, the most important dimension may be decency–indecency. A third person may not even think in terms of decency.

Self-Esteem and Positive Regard Rogers assumes that we all develop a need for self-regard, or **self-esteem,** as we develop and become aware of ourselves. At first self-esteem reflects the esteem others hold us in. Parents help children develop self-esteem when they show them **unconditional positive regard**—that is, when they accept them as having intrinsic merit regardless of their behavior at the moment. But when parents show children **conditional positive regard**—accept them only when they behave in a desired manner—children may learn to disown the thoughts, feelings, and behaviors that parents have rejected. Conditional positive regard may lead children to develop **conditions of worth,** or to think that they are worthwhile only if they behave in certain ways.

Because each of us is thought to have a unique potential, children who develop conditions of worth must be somewhat disappointed in themselves. We cannot fully live up to the wishes of others and remain true to ourselves. This does not mean that the expression of the self inevitably leads to conflict. Rogers was optimistic about human nature. He believed that we hurt others or act in antisocial ways only when we are frustrated in our efforts to develop our potential. But when parents and others are loving and tolerant of our differentness, we, too, are loving—even if some of our preferences, abilities, and values differ from those of our parents.

However, children in some families learn that it is bad to have ideas of their own, especially about sexual, political, or religious matters. When they perceive their parents' disapproval, they may come to see themselves as rebels and label their feelings as being selfish, wrong, or evil. If they wish to retain a consistent self-concept and self-esteem, they may have to deny many of their genuine feelings, or disown parts of themselves. In this way the self-concept becomes distorted. According to Rogers, anxiety often stems from partial perception of feelings and ideas that are inconsistent with the distorted self-concept. Since anxiety is unpleasant, such individuals may deny that these feelings and ideas exist.

Psychological Congruence and the Self-Ideal When we accept our feelings as our own, we experience psychological integrity or wholeness. There is a "fit" between our self-concept and our behavior, thoughts, and emotions, which Rogers calls **congruence.**

According to Rogers, the path to self-actualization requires getting in touch with our genuine feelings, accepting them as ours, and acting on them.

Self-actualization In humanistic theory, the innate tendency to strive to realize one's potential.

Frame of reference One's unique patterning of perceptions and attitudes, according to which one evaluates events.

Self-esteem One's evaluation and valuing of oneself.

Unconditional positive regard A persistent expression of esteem for the value of a person but not necessarily an unqualified acceptance of all of the person's behaviors.

Conditional positive regard Judgment of another person's value on the basis of the acceptability of that person's behaviors.

Conditions of worth Standards by which the value of a person is judged.

Congruence According to Rogers, a fit between one's self-concept and one's behaviors, thoughts, and feelings.

George Kelly

This is the goal of Rogers's method of psychotherapy, person-centered therapy, which we discuss in Chapter 13. Here suffice it to say that person-centered therapists provide an atmosphere in which clients can cope with the anxieties of focusing on disowned parts of the self.

Rogers also believes that we have mental images of what we are capable of becoming, or **self-ideals.** We are motivated to reduce the discrepancy between our self-concepts and our self-ideals. As we undertake the process of actualizing ourselves, our self-ideals may gradually grow more complex. Our goals may become higher or change in quality. The self-ideal is something like a carrot dangling from a stick strapped to a burro's head. The burro strives to reach the carrot, as though it were a step or two away, without recognizing that its own progress also causes the carrot to advance. Rogers believes that the process of striving to meet meaningful goals, the good struggle, yields happiness.

George Kelly's Psychology of Personal Constructs

Psychologists see themselves as attempting to gather accurate information about and to predict the behavior of others. But George Kelly (1955) noted with irony that psychologists too often act as though the "others"—that is, the people being studied—are victims of psychic forces, steered by traits or shaped by environmental influences. Nonsense, said Kelly. The main thing to know about people (even experimental subjects!) is that they all function as "scientists." It is human nature to try to understand one's own behavior and the behavior of others. It is human nature to try to find a way to interpret, categorize, and **construe** the world so that one can make accurate predictions about what will lead to what.

Personal Constructs Psychodynamic theorists view personality in terms of motives and internal conflicts. Trait theorists view it in terms of enduring characteristics. Learning theorists views personality in terms of overt behavior and ways of learning. In contrast, phenomenological theorists view personality in terms of the ways in which people view their own experiences.

Kelly (1955, 1958), a phenomenologist, believed that people view their experiences in terms of their **personal constructs.** A personal construct is a psychological dimension according to which we categorize ourselves and others. Extraversion–introversion is a construct that was of importance to Jung and Eysenck. In Chapter 14 we shall see that strong–weak is a construct of more relevance to males than females in our culture.*

According to Freud, people are motivated to behave by basic instincts. According to behaviorists, "motivation" lies in situational variables, such as reinforcers. According to Kelly, people are motivated to understand, anticipate, and control the events in their lives. People try to use constructs that allow them to anticipate and control events.

Alternate Constructions To know the individual, wrote Kelly, we must learn how the individual categorizes and interprets experience—how the

Self-ideal A mental image of what we believe we ought to be.

Construe Interpret.

Personal construct A psychological dimension, such as strong–weak, according to which one evaluates experience.

*Even though women are also likely to use the construct strong–weak in making some evaluations, their own self-esteem is less likely to be wrapped up in how strong they are. One of the reasons that women body-builders remain unusual is that the construct strong–weak is extremely important to their self-evaluations and their evaluations of other women.

individual construes events. People construe the same event in different ways, as in the example offered by Mischel:

> *A boy drops his mother's favorite vase. What does it mean? The event is simply that the vase has been broken. Yet ask the child's psychoanalyst and he may point to the boy's unconscious hostility. Ask the mother and she tells you how "mean" he is. His father says he is "spoiled." The child's teacher may see the event as evidence of the child's "laziness" and chronic "clumsiness." Grandmother calls it just an "accident." And the child himself may construe the event as reflecting his "stupidity"* (1986, pp. 207–208).

Different ways of construing an event—that is, alternate constructions of an event—induce different emotional reactions and, perhaps, different courses of action. In Chapter 12 we shall see why the boy's construing the event as evidence of his "stupidity" could generate depression. Whereas some psychoanalyst might wonder whether the dropping of the vase reflected unconscious motives, George Kelly might point out to the boy that his way of construing the event is not *convenient* for him. Kelly did not believe that there is one true way of construing events. Instead, he believed that when our constructions of events make us miserable and promote maladaptive behavior, we might be well advised to seek an alternative construction.

Role Playing Psychoanalysts see our characters as being formed by early life experiences. Trait theorists see our attributes as being generally stable, steering us to behave in comparable ways in various situations. Some learning theorists view us as creatures of habit; others suggest that "generalized expectancies" may generate stable behavior across diverse situations. Kelly, in contrast, saw people as being capable of continuous change and the enactment of various roles. If the roles we have assumed in life are making us miserable, Kelly believed that we can make broad, sweeping changes in the ways in which we construe the world and behave from day to day.

One avenue to change is through playing another role—attempting to look at the world as through the eyes of a person with another set of beliefs. If we strive to see the world as through the eyes of another, perhaps our constructs will be loosened up and we will be able to generate more convenient ways of looking at, and doing, things.

Evaluation

Strengths of Phenomenological Approaches

1. *Focus on Conscious Experience* We tend to treasure our conscious experiences (our "selves") and those of the people we care about. For lower organisms, to be alive is to move, to process food, to exchange oxygen and carbon dioxide, and to reproduce one's kind. But for human beings, an essential aspect of life is conscious experience—the sense of one's self as progressing through space and time. Phenomenological theorists grant consciousness the cardinal role it occupies in our daily lives.

2. *Phenomenological Theory Sets Us Free* Psychodynamic theories see us largely as victims of our childhoods, whereas learning theories, to some degree, see us as "victims of circumstances"—or, at least, as victims of situational variables. But phenomenological theorists envision us as

Caliper An instrument consisting of a pair of curved movable legs that is used to measure the diameter or thickness of an object.

Phrenology The analysis of personality by measuring the shape and protuberances of the skull.

being free to make choices. Psychodynamic theorists and learning theorists wonder whether our sense of freedom is merely an illusion; phenomenological theorists begin with an assumption of personal freedom.

3. *Innovations in Therapy Methods* The phenomenological theorists we have discussed have made important innovations and contributions to the practice of psychotherapy. Of these, the best-known and most influential innovation is person-centered therapy, the type of therapy originated by Carl Rogers (see Chapter 13). According to a survey of clinical and counseling psychologists (Smith, 1982), Rogers is the single most influential psychotherapist of recent years. Elements of George Kelly's thinking have found their way into cognitive theories of abnormal behavior (see Chapter 12) and into cognitive-therapy approaches (see Chapter 13). As in the example of the boy who broke the vase, it has been shown that the ways in which we construe our failures and shortcomings are linked to our emotional responses. Cognitive therapists point out how our constructions of events create problems for us.

Weaknesses of Phenomenological Approaches

1. *Focus on Conscious Experience* Ironically, the primary strength of the phenomenological approaches—their focus on conscious experience—is also their primary weakness. Conscious experience is private and subjective. Therefore, the validity of formulating theories in terms of consciousness has been questioned.

2. *The Concept of Self-Actualization* The concept of self-actualization—so important to Maslow and Rogers—cannot be proved or disproved. Like an id or a trait, a self-actualizing force cannot be observed or measured directly. It must be inferred from its supposed effects.

   Self-actualization, like trait theory, yields circular explanations for behavior. When we see someone engaged in what seems to be positive striving, we gain little insight by attributing this behavior to a self-actualizing force. We have done nothing to account for the origins of the self-actualizing force. And when we observe someone who is not engaged in growth-oriented striving, it seems arbitrary to "explain" this outcome by suggesting that the self-actualizing tendency has been blocked or frustrated. It could also be that self-actualization is an acquired need, rather than an innate need, and that it is found in some, but not all, of us.

3. *Failure to Account for Traits* Phenomenological theories, like learning theories, have little to say about the development of traits and personality types. Maslow and Rogers assume that we are all unique, but they do not predict the sorts of traits, abilities, and interests we shall develop.

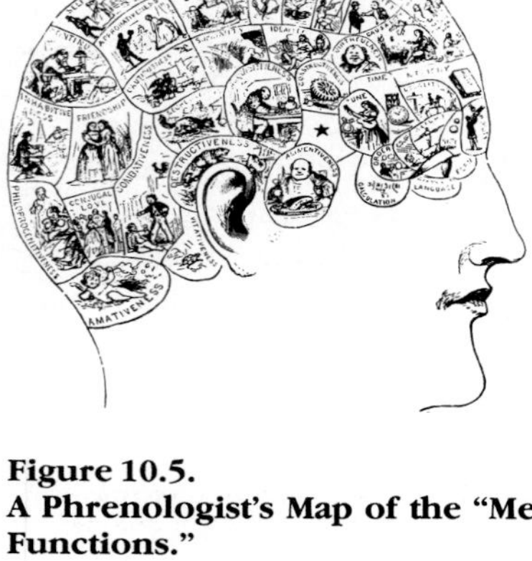

Figure 10.5.
A Phrenologist's Map of the "Mental Functions."

MEASUREMENT OF PERSONALITY

If you had wanted to learn about your personality early in the last century, an "expert" might have measured the bumps on your head with a **caliper.** This method, termed **phrenology,** was based on the erroneous belief that traits, abilities, and mental functions dwelled in specific places in the head and could be measured from the outside. Figure 10.5 shows a "map" of these functions, as used by many phrenologists.

Today's personality measures are more scientific, if not more interesting. They take a sample of behavior, usually in the form of a self-report, to predict future behavior. Standardized interviews can be used, and psychologists even arrange for some routine interviews to be carried out by computer (Erdman et al., 1985). Some measures of personality are **behavior-rating scales,** which assess overt behavior in settings such as the classroom or mental hospital. With behavior-rating scales, trained observers usually check off each occurrence of a specific behavior within a certain time frame—say, a 15-minute period. Standardized objective and projective tests are used more frequently, and they shall be discussed in this section.

Measures of personality are used to make important decisions, such as whether a person is suited for a certain type of work, for a particular class in school, or for a drug to reduce agitation. As part of their admissions process, graduate schools often ask professors to rate prospective students on scales that assess traits like intelligence, emotional stability, and cooperation. Students may take tests of **aptitudes** and interests to gather insight into whether they are suited for certain occupations. It is assumed that students who share the aptitudes and interests of people who are well adjusted in certain positions are also likely to be well adjusted in those positions.

Objective Tests

Objective tests present respondents with a **standardized** group of test items in the form of a questionnaire. Respondents are limited to a specific range of answers. One test might ask respondents to indicate whether items are true or false for them. Another might ask respondents to select the preferred activity from groups of three.

Some tests have a **forced-choice format,** in which respondents are asked to indicate which of two statements is more true for them or which of several activities they prefer. The respondents are not given the option of answering "none of the above." Forced-choice formats are frequently used in interest inventories, which help predict whether one would be well adjusted in a certain occupation. The following item is similar to those found in interest inventories:

I would rather

a. be a forest ranger.
b. work in a busy office.
c. play a musical instrument.

A forced-choice format is also used in the Edwards Personal Preference Schedule, which measures the relative strength of social motives (such as achievement and affiliation) by pitting them against one another consecutively in groups of two.

The Minnesota Multiphasic Personality Inventory The Minnesota Multiphasic Personality Inventory (MMPI) contains 566 items presented in a true-false format. The MMPI was intended to be used by clinical and counseling psychologists to help diagnose abnormal behavior problems (see Chapter 12), and it is the most widely used psychological test in the clinical setting* (Lubin et al., 1985). Accurate measurement of clients' problems

*The MMPI ranks first in use in a composite based on psychiatric hospitals, community mental-health centers, counseling centers, centers for the developmentally disabled, and Veterans Administration medical centers (Lubin et al., 1985).

Behavior-rating scale A systematic means for recording the frequency with which target behaviors occur.

Aptitude A natural ability or talent.

Objective tests Tests whose items must be answered in a specified, limited manner. Tests whose items have concrete answers that are considered correct.

Standardized Given to a large number of respondents so that data concerning the typical responses can be accumulated and analyzed.

Forced-choice format A method of presenting test questions that requires a respondent to select one of a number of possible answers.

Table 10.3
Commonly Used Validity and Clinical Scales of the MMPI

Scale	Abbreviation	Possible interpretations
Validity Scales	?	
Question		Corresponds to number of items left unanswered
Lie	L	Lies or is highly conventional
Frequency	F	Exaggerates complaints or answers items haphazardly
Correction	K	Denies problems
Clinical Scales		
Hypochondriasis	Hs	Has bodily concerns and complaints
Depression	D	Is depressed, guilty; has feelings of guilt and helplessness
Hysteria	Hy	Reacts to stress by developing physical symptoms, lacks insight
Psychopathic deviate	Pd	Is immoral, in conflict with the law; has stormy relationships
Masculinity/femininity	Mf	High scores suggests interests and behavior patterns considered stereotypical of the opposite sex
Paranoia	Pa	Is suspicious and resentful, highly cynical about human nature
Psychasthenia	Pt	Is anxious, worried, high-strung
Schizophrenia	Sc	Is confused, disorganized, disoriented; has unusual ideas
Hypomania	Ma	Is energetic, restless, active, easily bored
Social introversion	Si	Is introverted, timid, shy; lacks self-confidence

should point to appropriate treatment. In recent years, the MMPI has also become the most widely used instrument for personality measurement in psychological research (Costa et al., 1985).

The MMPI has been given to thousands of individuals over the last few decades. This wide usage has permitted psychologists to compare the test records of clients with those of people who are known to have had certain problems. A similar test record is suggestive of the presence of similar problems.

The MMPI is usually scored for the four **validity scales** and ten **clinical scales** described in Table 10.3. The validity scales suggest whether answers are likely to represent the client's thoughts, emotions, and behaviors, although they cannot guarantee that deception will be disclosed.

Truth or Fiction Revisited

It is *not* true that psychologists can invariably determine whether a person has told the truth on a personality test. But validity scales allow them to make educated guesses.

The validity scales in Table 10.3 assess different **response sets,** or biases in answering the questions. People with high L scores, for example, may be attempting to present themselves as excessively moral and well-behaved individuals. People with high F scores may be trying to seem bizarre or are answering haphazardly. In one study, F-scale scores were positively correlated with conceptual confusion, hostility, and presence of **hallucinations** and other unusual thought patterns as measured on a behavior-rating scale (Smith & Graham, 1981). Many personality measures have some kind of validity scale. The clinical scales of the MMPI assess the problems shown in Table 10.3, as well as stereotypical masculine or feminine interests and introversion.

The MMPI scales were constructed empirically on the basis of actual clinical data rather than on the basis of psychological theory. A test-item bank

Validity scales Groups of test items that indicate whether a person's responses accurately reflect that individual's traits.

Clinical scales Groups of test items that measure the presence of various abnormal behavior patterns.

Response set A tendency to answer test items according to a bias—for instance, to make oneself seem perfect or bizarre.

Hallucinations Perceptions in the absence of sensory stimulation that are confused with reality. See Chapter 12.

Figure 10.6.
An MMPI Personality Profile. This profile was attained by a depressed barber. On this form, scores at the standard level of 50 are average for males, and scores above the standard score of 70 are considered abnormally high. The raw score is the number of items answered in a certain direction on a given MMPI scale. K is the correction scale. A certain percentage of the K-scale score is added onto several clinical scales to correct for denial of problems.

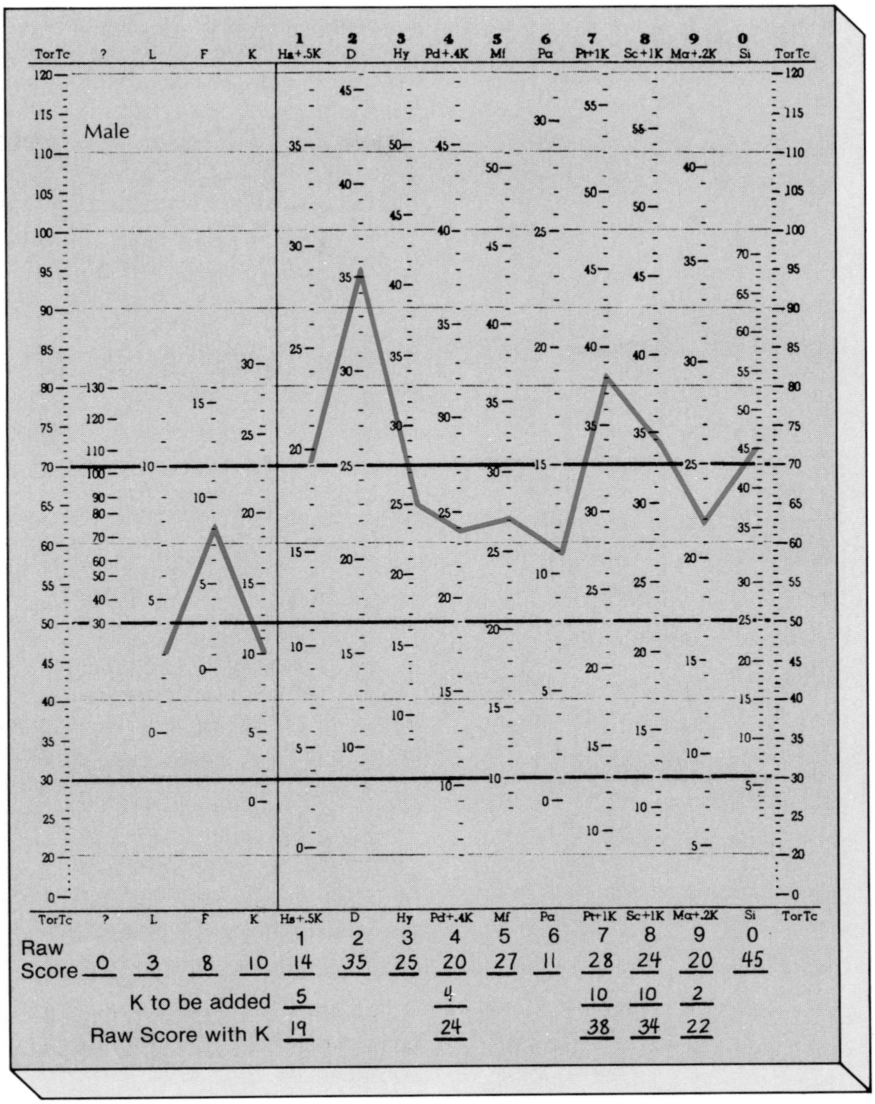

of several hundred items was derived from questions often asked in clinical interviews. Here are some of the items that were used:

My father was a good man.	T F
I am very seldom troubled by headaches.	T F
My hands and feet are usually warm enough.	T F
I have never done anything dangerous for the thrill of it.	T F
I work under a great deal of tension.	T F

The items were administered to clients and psychiatric patients with previously identified symptoms, such as depressive or **schizophrenic** symptoms. Items that successfully set apart people with these symptoms were included on scales named accordingly. Figure 10.6 shows the personality profile of a 27-year-old barber who consulted a psychologist because of depression and difficulty in making decisions. The barber scored abnormally high on the Hs, D, Pt, Sc, and Si scales, suggestive of concern with body functions (Hs), persistent feelings of anxiety and tension (Pt), depression (D), insomnia and fatigue, and some difficulties relating to other people (Sc, Si). Note that the high Sc score does not in itself indicate that the barber is schizophrenic.

Schizophrenic Characteristic of the thought disorder schizophrenia. See Chapter 12.

In addition to the standard validity and clinical scales, investigators of personality have derived many experimental scales, such as those that measure neuroticism, religious orthodoxy, assertiveness, substance abuse, and even well-being (Costa et al., 1985; Johnson et al., 1984; Snyder et al., 1985). The MMPI remains a rich mine for unearthing elements of personality.

The California Psychological Inventory Another personality inventory, the California Psychological Inventory (CPI), is widely used in research to assess 18 dimensions of normal behavior, such as achievement, dominance, flexibility, self-acceptance, and self-control.

Interest Inventories Interest inventories can be of help to high school and college students who are uncertain about their future occupations. Tests such as the Strong-Campbell Interest Inventory (SCII) and the Kuder Occupational Interest Survey (KOIS) are used to predict adjustment in various occupations.

The SCII is used from high school to adulthood and is the most widely used test in counseling centers (Lubin et al., 1985). Most items on the SCII require test takers to indicate whether they like, are indifferent to, or dislike items chosen from the following: occupations (e.g., actor/actress, architect), school subjects (algebra, art), activities (adjusting a carburetor, making a speech), amusements (golf, chess, jazz or rock concerts), and types of people (babies, nonconformists). The preferences of test takers are compared with those of people in various occupations. Areas of general interest (sales, science, teaching, agriculture) and specific interest (mathematician, guidance counselor, beautician) are derived from these comparisons.

The KOIS, like the SCII, is used from high school to adulthood. It consists of triads of activities, such as the following:

a. write a story about a sports event

b. play in a baseball game

c. teach children to play a game

For each triad, the test taker indicates which activities he or she would like most and least. The KOIS predicts adjustment in college majors as well as occupations.

Projective Tests

You may have heard that there is a personality test that asks people what a drawing or inkblot looks like and that people commonly answer "a bat." There are a number of such tests, the best known of which is the Rorschach inkblot test, named after its originator, Swiss psychiatrist Hermann Rorschach (1884–1922).

The Rorschach Inkblot Test The Rorschach test is a **projective test.** In projective techniques, there are no clear, specified answers. People are presented with **ambiguous** stimuli, like inkblots or vague drawings, and may be asked to report what these stimuli look like to them or to tell stories about them. Because there is no one proper response, it is assumed that people *project* their own personalities into their responses. The meanings they attribute to these stimuli are assumed to reflect their personalities as well as the drawings or blots themselves.

Actually, the facts of the matter are slightly different. There may be no single "correct" response to the Rorschach inkblot shown in Figure 10.7, but

Projective test A psychological test that presents ambiguous stimuli onto which the test taker projects his or her own personality in making a response.

Ambiguous Having two or more possible meanings.

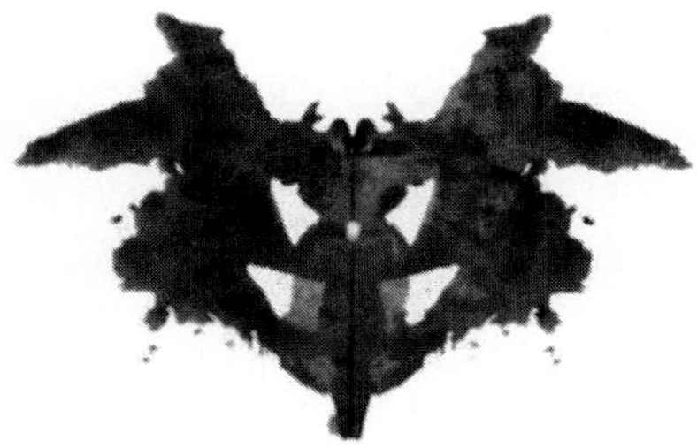

Figure 10.7.
A Rorschach Inkblot. What does this look like? What could it be?

some responses would clearly not be in keeping with the features of the blot. Figure 10.7 could be a bat or a flying insect, the pointed face of an animal, the face of a jack-o'-lantern, or many other things. But responses like "an ice cream cone," "diseased lungs," or "a metal leaf in flames" are not suggested by the features of the blot and may suggest personality problems.

Truth or Fiction Revisited

It is true that there is a psychological test made up of inkblots—the Rorschach inkblot test. And one of them does look somewhat like a bat.

The Rorschach (1921) inkblot test contains ten cards. Five are in black and white and shades of gray. Five use a variety of colors. Subjects are given the cards, one by one, and are asked what they look like or what they could be. The subjects can give no, one, or several responses to each card. They can hold the card upside down or sideways.

Responses are scored according to *location, determinants, content,* and *form level.* The location is the section of the blot chosen—the whole card or a major or minor detail. Determinants include features of the blot like shading, texture, or color that influence the response. The content is the *what* of the response—for instance, a bat, a jack-o'-lantern, or a human torso. Form level indicates whether the response is consistent with the shape of the blot and also indicates the complexity of the response. A response that reflects the shape of the blot is a sign of adequate **reality testing.** A response that richly integrates several features of the blot is a sign of high intellectual functioning. The Rorschach test is thought to provide insight into a person's intelligence, interests, cultural background, degree of introversion or extraversion, level of anxiety, reality testing, and a host of other variables.

Figure 10.8.
A Thematic Apperception Test Card. What is happening in this picture? What are the people thinking and feeling? How will it turn out?

The Thematic Apperception Test The Thematic Apperception Test (TAT) was developed in the 1930s by psychologist Henry Murray at Harvard University. It consists of drawings, like that shown in Figure 10.8, that are open to a variety of interpretations. Subjects are given the cards one at a time and are asked to make up stories about them.

The TAT has been widely used in research into social motives as well as in clinical practice. In an experiment described in Chapter 8, need for achievement was assessed from subjects' responses to a picture of a boy and a violin. The notion is that we are likely to be preoccupied with our own needs to some degree and that our needs will be projected into our responses to ambiguous situations. The TAT is also widely used to assess attitudes toward other people, especially parents, lovers, and spouses.

Evaluation of Measures of Personality

It seems clear that personality measures can provide useful information to help people make decisions about themselves and others. In general, however, psychological tests should not be the sole criteria for making important decisions.

For example, single scales of the MMPI are reasonably accurate measures of the presence of a trait, like depression. But one could not justifiably hospitalize a person for fear of suicide solely on the basis of a high D-scale score on the MMPI. Similarly, combinations of high MMPI scale scores seem to reflect certain clinical pictures in some populations but not in others. A typical study found that a combination of high scores on the D, Pt, and Sc scales was likely to suggest severe disturbance in college males but not in

Reality testing The capacity to perceive one's environment and oneself according to accurate sensory impressions.

college females (Kelley & King, 1979). There is also controversy about whether whites, blacks, and other racial groups score differently on the MMPI, so perhaps special norms should be established for each group (Bertelson et al., 1982; Butcher et al., 1983; Pritchard & Rosenblatt, 1980; Snyder et al., 1985). Interpretation of the MMPI is further clouded by the fact that abnormal validity-scale scores do *not* necessarily invalidate the test for respondents who are highly disturbed.

The Rorschach inkblot test, for all its artistic appeal, has had major difficulties with validation. Although the TAT has been consistently shown to be a useful research tool, its clinical validity has also met with criticism. Despite problems with projective techniques, they continue to be used regularly. The Rorschach inkblot test, in fact, remains the most widely used test in psychiatric hospitals in the 1980s (Lubin et al., 1985).

Psychological tests should not be used as the sole means for making important decisions. But tests that are carefully chosen and interpreted may provide useful information for supplementing other sources of information in making decisions.

SUMMARY

1. **How do psychologists define "personality"?** Personality comprises the reasonably stable patterns of behavior, including thoughts and emotions, that distinguish one person from another. These behavior patterns characterize a person's ways of adapting to the demands of his or her life.

2. **What is the role of conflict in Sigmund Freud's psychodynamic theory?** Psychodynamic theory, originated by Sigmund Freud, assumes that we are driven largely by unconscious motives. Conflict is inevitable as basic instincts of hunger, sex, and aggression come up against social pressures to follow laws, rules, and moral codes. At first this conflict is external, but as we develop it becomes intrapsychic.

3. **What are the psychic structures in psychodynamic theory?** The unconscious id is the psychic structure present at birth. The id represents psychological drives and operates according to the pleasure principle, seeking instant gratification. The ego is the sense of self or "I." The ego develops through experience and operates according to the reality principle. It takes into account what is practical and possible in gratifying the impulses of the id. Defense mechanisms protect the ego from anxiety by repressing unacceptable ideas or distorting reality. The superego is the moral sense, a partly conscious psychic structure that develops largely through identification with others.

4. **What are the stages of psychosexual development?** People undergo psychosexual development as psychosexual energy, or libido, is transferred from one erogenous zone to another during childhood. There are five stages of development: oral, anal, phallic, latency, and genital.

5. **What are "oral" and "anal" traits?** Fixation in a stage may lead to the development of traits associated with that stage. Fixation in the oral stage, for example, may lead to oral traits like dependency and gullibility. Anal fixation may result in cleanliness–messiness or perfectionism–carelessness.

6. **What are the Oedipus and Electra complexes?** In the Oedipus and Electra complexes, which are theorized to occur during the phallic stage, children long to possess the opposite-sex parent and resent the same-sex parent. Eventually, these complexes become resolved by the child identifying with the same-sex parent.

7. **What is Carl Jung's theory?** Jung's psychodynamic theory, called analytical psychology, features a collective unconscious and numerous archetypes, both of which reflect the history of our species.

8. **What is Alfred Adler's theory?** Adler's psychodynamic theory, called individual psychology, features the inferiority complex and the compensating drive for superiority.

9. **What is Karen Horney's theory?** Horney's psychodynamic theory focuses on parent-child relationships and the possible development of feelings of basic anxiety and basic hostility. Later in life, repressed hostility can lead us to relate to others in a neurotic manner.

10. **What is Erik Erikson's theory?** Erikson's psychodynamic theory of psychosocial development highlights the importance of early social relationships rather than the gratification of childhood sexual impulses. Erikson extended Freud's five developmental stages to eight, including stages for periods of adulthood.

11. **What are traits?** Traits are personality elements that are inferred from behavior and that account for behavioral consistency. Trait theory adopts a descriptive approach to personality.

12. **What are Gordon Allport's views?** Allport saw traits as being imbedded in the nervous system and steering behavior.

13. **What are Raymond Cattell's views?** Cattell distinguished between surface traits (characteristic ways of behaving that seem to be linked in an orderly manner) and source traits (underlying traits from which surface traits are derived).

14. **What are Hans Eysenck's views?** Eysenck theorized that there are two broad, independent personality dimensions—introversion–extraversion and emotional stability–instability (neuroticism)—and that our personalities can be described according to combinations of these dimensions.

15. **How do behaviorists view personality?** Behaviorists place emphasis on the situational determinants of behavior. John B. Watson, the father of modern behaviorism, rejected notions of mind and personality altogether. Watson and B. F. Skinner discarded notions of personal freedom and argued that environmental contingencies can shape people into wanting to do the things that the physical environment and society requires of them.

16. **How do social-learning theorists view personality?** Social-learning theory, in contrast to behaviorism, has a strong cognitive orientation and focuses on the importance of learning by observation. Social-learning theorists do not consider only situational rewards and punishments as being important in the prediction of behavior. They also consider the roles of person variables such as competencies, encoding strategies, expectancies, subjective values, and self-regulatory systems and plans.

17. **What are the views of Carl Rogers?** Rogers' phenomenological theory begins with the assumption of the existence of the self. According to Rogers, the self is an organized and consistent way in which a person perceives his or her "I" to relate to others and the world. The self is innate and will attempt to become actualized (develop its unique potential) when the person receives unconditional positive regard. We all have needs for self-esteem. Conditions of worth may lead to a distorted self-concept, disowning parts of the self, and anxiety.

18. **What are the views of George Kelly?** According to Kelly, people are motivated to understand, anticipate, and control the events in their lives. Kelly believed that people view their experiences in terms of their personal constructs—that is, psychological dimensions according to which they categorize themselves and others.

19. **What is personality measurement?** In personality measurement, psychologists take a sample of behavior to predict future behavior.

20. **What are objective tests?** Objective tests present test-takers with a standardized set of test items that they must respond to in specific, limited ways (as in multiple-choice tests or true-false tests). A forced-choice format requires respondents to indicate which of two or more statements is true for them or which of several activities they prefer.

21. **What is the Minnesota Multiphasic Personality Inventory (MMPI)?** The MMPI is the most widely used psychological test in the clinical setting. The MMPI is an objective personality test that uses a true-false format to assess abnormal behavior. It contains validity scales as well as clinical scales and has been validated empirically.

22. **What are projective tests?** Projective tests present ambiguous stimuli and permit the subject a broad range of response.

23. **What is the Rorschach inkblot test?** The foremost projective technique is the Rorschach, in which test-takers are asked to report what inkblots look like or could be. Rorschach responses are scored according to location, determinants (e.g., shading, texture, and color), content, and form level.

24. **What is the Thematic Apperception Test?** The TAT consists of ambiguous drawings that test-takers are asked to interpret. The TAT is widely used in research on social motives as well as in clinical practice.

PSYCHOLOGY AND MODERN LIFE

The study of personality has helped to foster human understanding and has given rise to ways of helping people adjust to the demands of life. In Chapter 13 we shall explore the kinds of therapies spawned by these personality theories. In this section, we see how psychodynamic and cognitive theories offer insight into why some young people are prey to the influences of cults. We also examine the so-called Barnum effect, which has been harnessed by psychologists to encourage clients to believe in themselves and change their behavior for the better.

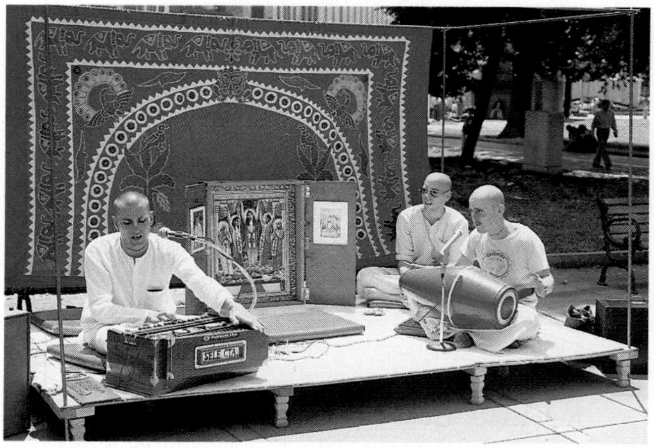

Hare Krishnas. Why do so many young people become Hare Krishnas or "Moonies" or join some other religious cult? Psychodynamic theorists suggest that such religious conversions represent efforts to submit to authoritarian figures—a way of keeping impulses from the id under control. Cognitive theorists might suggest that conversions represent efforts to understand the universe and one's place within.

Cognitive versus Psychodynamic Views of Religious Conversion

Each year thousands of American parents are shocked to learn that their children have become Hare Krishnas or "Moonies" or have joined some other religious cult. They cannot fathom why their children have forsaken not only their early religious teaching but also their families. Now and then we hear of parents who have their own children kidnapped and "deprogramed" in an effort to return them to the family and fold.

Why do people undergo the travail of religious conversion? Are they searching for meaning in life or for an anchor in a sea of troubles? Cognitive and psychodynamic perspectives offer very different hypotheses concerning conversion. From the cognitive perspective, religious conversion reflects a conscious effort to end uncertainty about the nature of humanity and the universe. A person ripe for conversion might be expected to show concern about basic religious and political questions during adolescence.

From the psychodynamic perspective, however, religious conversion represents a defense against an upsurge of unconscious Oedipal hatred directed toward the father (Freud, 1927/1964). By converting to a new religion, a person is submitting to a powerful father figure (God). The external authority figure shores up the convert's own shaky superego and helps keep the lid on impulses from the id. The psychodynamic view suggests that converts have encountered more traumatic events during childhood and adolescence, giving rise to feelings of hostility that can be better controlled through conversion.

In a study of the cognitive and psychodynamic views of religious conversion, Chana Ullman (1982) interviewed 40 religious converts and 30 nonconverts. Ullman had anticipated that her findings would support the cognitive perspective, so she expected that converts would show less tolerance for uncertainty and greater concern about basic religious issues than nonconverts. To her surprise, the converts and nonconverts could not be differentiated according to these variables.

Instead, in keeping with the psychodynamic view, Ullman found that 77 percent of the religious converts, as compared with 23 percent of nonconverts, reported problematic relationships with their fathers, including their fathers' frequent absence. Consider these excerpts from interviews with converts: "My relationship with [my father] was to keep from antagonizing him or causing any trouble," and "He did not understand anything you did, you could do nothing right [and] I started hating him" (Ullman, 1982, p. 192). Converts were also more likely than nonconverts to report traumatic and stressful events during childhood and adolescence.

In addition, 80 percent of the converts reported emotional turmoil before converting through statements such as "I thought I was going crazy" and "I had suicidal thoughts." The same percentage reported that conversion provided relief from anxiety, anger, or depression.

Ullman concluded that stress and anxiety can precipitate religious conversion. Of course, her study cannot directly reveal "unconscious" processes in her subjects, but it strongly suggests that childhood trauma and a rejecting or absent father figure contribute to the likelihood of conversion. As Ullman writes, "In many religious conversion cases, the experience may be seen as an attempt to gain the approval, protection, or guidance of an authority figure, as suggested by the original psychoanalytic hypothesis" (1982, pp. 191–192).

Of course, Ullman's findings cannot apply to all cases of conversion. Nevertheless, they afford some insight into the inner turmoil of modern life and the psychological measures taken by some individuals to cope with it.

Applying the Barnum Effect to Enhance Self-Efficacy Expectations

Before we discuss the Barnum effect, take this brief personality test. Indicate whether each item is mostly true or false for you. Then read the report that follows to learn everything you always wanted to know about your personality but were too intelligent to ask.

1.	I can't unclasp my hands.	T	F
2.	I often mistake my hands for food.	T	F
3.	I never liked room temperature.	T	F
4.	My throat is closer than it seems.	T	F
5.	Likes and dislikes are among my favorites.	T	F
6.	I've lost all sensation in my throat.	T	F
7.	I try to swallow at least three times a day.	T	F
8.	My squirrels don't know where I am tonight.	T	F
9.	Walls impede my progress.	T	F
10.	My toes are numbered.	T	F
11.	My beaver won't go near the water.	T	F

Total number of items marked true (T): ____

If your total number of items marked true was between 0 and 11, the following personality report applies to you:

The personality test you have taken has been found to predict inner potential for change.... In the past it has been shown that people with similar personality scores... have a strong capacity for change.... You have a great deal of unused potential you have not yet turned to your advantage....

The test also suggests that you display ability for personal integration and many latent strengths, as well as the ability to maintain a balance between your inner impulses and the demands of outer reality. Therefore, your personality is such that you have a strong potential for improvement (Halperin & Snyder, 1979, pp. 142–143).

That's you all right, isn't it? I shouldn't be surprised if you thought it sounded familiar. Psychologists Keith Halperin and C. R. Snyder (1979) administered a phony 50-item personality questionnaire to women in an introductory psychology course at the University of Kansas. The items weren't as silly as the ones you answered, which were thrown together by Daniel Wegner (1979) and some friends during their graduate school days. Still, the test was meaningless. The students then rated the same personality report, which included the paragraphs just cited, for accuracy. The average rating was "quite accurate"!

Truth or Fiction Revisited

It is true that a psychologist could write a believable personality report about you without interviewing you, testing you, or even knowing who you are. But the report would have to be rather generalized.

Halperin and Snyder then administered a therapy program to women who had received the phony report and to women who had not. Believe it or not, women who had received the report, which underscored their capacity for change, showed greater improvement from the treatment than women who had not. When you believe that you have the capacity to improve your lot—when your self-efficacy expectations are raised—you are apparently more likely to succeed.

The tendency to believe a generalized (but phony) personality report has been labeled the Barnum effect after circus magnate P. T. Barnum, who once declared that a good circus had a "little something for everybody." It is probably the Barnum effect—the tendency for general personality reports to have a "little something for everybody"—that allows fortune-tellers to make a living. That is, we have enough characteristics in common so that a fortune-teller's "revelations" about our personalities may have the ring of truth.

Some psychologists argue that people who believe broad personality reports are gullible. But Layne (1979) counters that these reports are actually quite accurate, even if they are general. Because we have a variety of traits within ourselves, we may find "a little something" that fits quite well (Johnson et al., 1985).

P. T. Barnum also once declared, "There's a sucker born every minute." But in the case of the Barnum effect, it might be, instead, that most of us recognize general aspects of ourselves and have the ability to improve our lives. We just have to start thinking "I can" instead of "I can't."

Outline

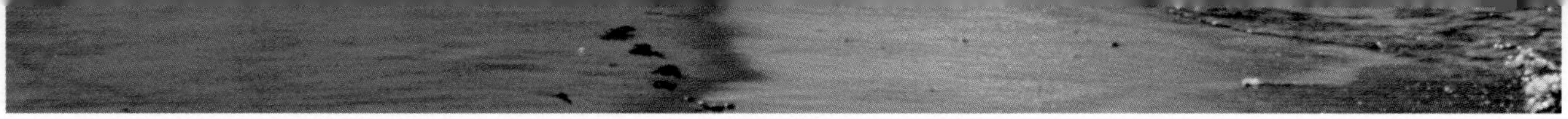

11 Health Psychology

Truth or Fiction?

- □ Too much of a good thing can make you ill.
- □ Commuting on the highway can elevate your blood pressure.
- □ A sense of humor can moderate the impact of stress.
- □ Single men live longer.
- □ At any given moment, countless microscopic warriors within our bodies are carrying out search-and-destroy missions against foreign agents.
- □ Most headaches are caused by muscle tension.
- □ Stress can influence the course of cancer.
- □ Patients are more likely to comply with "doctor's orders" when they are issued by an authoritarian physician.

In 1964, Norman Cousins, former editor of the *Saturday Review,* was hospitalized for a rare and painful collagen illness that is somewhat similar to arthritis. He was not a "good patient." Right from the start he complained about the hospital routines, such as the low-calorie and tasteless diet, the indiscriminate taking of X-rays, and the heavy administration of drugs, including pain-killers (analgesic drugs) and tranquilizers.

Even with all these procedures, his doctors gave him only a slim chance of a full recovery. And so, as he related in his 1979 book, *Anatomy of an Illness,* Cousins decided to take things into his own hands. First, he moved from the hospital setting—which encourages passive compliance with the patient role—to a hotel room. Second, he traded the massive doses of analgesics and other drugs for laughter and vitamins. He watched films of the Marx Brothers and of his favorite TV comedy shows and focused on maintaining a positive attitude. To his physicians' amazement, he made a substantial recovery from his illness.

In 1980, at the age of 65, Cousins had a heart attack. He was brought to the hospital by ambulance, and the first thing he did was take charge of the ride. He refused the analgesic drug morphine, and he asked the driver to keep the siren off and remain within the speed limit. He declined routine medical tests and went home within a few days. As Cousins explained in *The Healing Heart: Antidote to Panic and Helplessness* (1983), he emphasized the use of diet, exercise, and a positive attitude in his return to health.

HEALTH PSYCHOLOGY

Cousins' ways of coping with illness are inspiring to anyone who has resented hospital routines or who has bridled at the physician's authority. They don't seem to have hurt Cousins, and, indeed, they may have helped him recover from his bouts with illness. On the other hand, we do not globally endorse the notion that in rebellion lay the path to recovery; Cousins was more sophisticated about medicine and medical procedures than most of us. He also may have been lucky. His experiences provide us with a fascinating but scientifically uncontrolled case study.

Still, Cousins' experiences dramatize some of the relationships between psychological factors (in Cousins' case, taking control of the situation, maintaining a positive attitude, eating a nutritious diet, and exercising) and physical illness. His experience also seems to be consistent with folklore to the effect that we ought not "give in" to illness. Many of us have hardy relatives who, for example, "refuse" to get sick when people around them are succumbing to the flu.

These issues are also of vital concern to psychologists. The subfield of **health psychology** studies the relationships between psychological factors (e.g., stress, overt behavior, and attitudes) and the prevention and treatment of physical illness. Cousins' own history is a useful springboard for a discussion of health psychology, because in recent years health psychologists have been exploring the ways in which

- stress, behavior patterns, and personality factors heighten the probability of physical illness;
- people moderate the effects of stress;
- stress and **pathogens** interact to influence the immune system;
- people decide to seek medical advice;
- people decide whether or not to comply with medical advice;
- psychological forms of intervention, such as health education (e.g., concerning nutrition, smoking, and exercise) and behavior modification contribute to physical health.

In this chapter we consider a number of issues in health psychology: sources of stress, factors that moderate the impact of stress, the body's response to stress, ways in which stress is related to physical illnesses, and the psychology of being sick. In the section on psychology and modern life, we explore behavior patterns that can enhance our health, including the improvement of physician–patient relationships.

Health psychology The field of psychology that studies the relationships between psychological factors (e.g., attitudes, beliefs, situational influences, and behavior patterns) and the prevention and treatment of physical illness.

Pathogen A microscopic organism (e.g., bacterium or virus) that can cause disease.

SOURCES OF STRESS

In physics, stress is defined as a pressure or force exerted on a body. Tons of rock pressing on the earth, one car smashing into another, a rubber band stretching—all are types of physical stress. Psychological forces, or stresses, also "press," "push," or "pull." We may feel "crushed" by the "weight" of a big decision, "smashed" by adversity, or "stretched" to the point of "snapping."

Daily Hassles. Daily hassles are notable daily conditions and experiences that are threatening or harmful to a person's well-being. What are the daily hassles in your life?

In psychology, **stress** is the demand made on an organism to adapt, to cope, or to adjust. Some stress is healthful and necessary to keep us alert and occupied. Stress researcher Hans Selye (1980) referred to healthful stress as **eustress.** But stress that is too intense or prolonged can overtax our adjustive capacity, dampen our moods (Eckenrode, 1984; Stone & Neale, 1984), and have harmful physical effects. Various sources of stress are to some degree the result of external factors—daily hassles, life changes, pain and discomfort, frustration, and conflict. Others, such as irrational beliefs and Type A behavior, are more clearly self-imposed.

Daily Hassles

It is the last straw that will break the camel's back—so goes the saying. Similarly, stresses can pile atop one another until we can no longer cope. Some of these stresses are **daily hassles,** or notable daily conditions and experiences that are threatening or harmful to a person's well-being (Lazarus, 1984). Others are life changes. Lazarus and his colleagues (1985) analyzed a scale that measures daily hassles and their opposites—**uplifts**—and found that hassles could be grouped as follows:

1. *Household hassles.* For example, preparing meals, shopping, and home maintenance
2. *Health hassles.* For example, physical illness, concern about medical treatment, and the side effects of medication
3. *Time-pressure hassles.* For example, having too many things to do, too many responsibilities, and not enough time
4. *Inner-concern hassles.* For example, being lonely and fearing confrontation

Stress The demand that is made on an organism to adapt.

Eustress (yoo-stress). Stress that is healthful.

Daily hassles Notable daily conditions and experiences that are threatening or harmful to a person's well-being.

Uplifts Notable pleasant daily conditions and experiences.

5. *Environmental hassles.* For example, crime, neighborhood deterioration, and traffic noise
6. *Financial-responsibility hassles.* For example, concern about owing money, such as mortgage payments and loan installments
7. *Work hassles.* For example, job dissatisfaction, not liking one's work duties, and problems with co-workers
8. *Future-security hassles.* For example, concerns about job security, taxes, property investments, stock-market swings, and retirement

These hassles were linked to psychological variables such as nervousness, worrying, inability to get going, feelings of sadness, feelings of aloneness, and so on.

Life Changes: "Going Through Changes"

According to Holmes and Rahe (1967), too much of a good thing can make you ill. You might think that marrying Mr. or Ms. Right, finding a prestigious job, and moving to a better neighborhood all in the same year would propel you into a state of bliss. It might. But the effect of all these events, one on top of the other, could also lead to headaches, high blood pressure, and other ailments. As pleasant as they may be, they all involve major life changes, and life changes are another source of stress.

Life changes differ from daily hassles in two important ways: (1) Many life changes are positive and desirable, whereas all hassles, by definition, are negative. (2) The hassles referred to tend to occur on a daily basis, whereas life changes are relatively more isolated events.

Richard Lazarus and his colleagues (e.g., Kanner et al., 1981) constructed for their research a list of 117 daily hassles. They ask subjects to indicate which hassles they had encountered and how intense they were, according to a three-point intensity scale. Thomas Holmes and Richard Rahe (1967) constructed a scale to measure the impact of life changes by assigning marriage an arbitrary weight of 50 "life-change units." Then they asked people from all walks of life to assign units to other life changes, using marriage as the baseline. Most events were rated as less stressful than marriage, but a few were considered more stressful. More stressful events included death of a spouse (100 units) and divorce (73 units). Changes in work hours and residence (20 units each) were included, regardless of whether they were negative or positive. Positive life changes such as an outstanding personal achievement (28 units) and going on vacation (13 units) also made the list.

Hassles, Life Changes, and Illness It may seem reasonable enough that hassles and life changes—especially negative life changes—have a psychological effect on us, that they may cause us to worry and may generally dampen our moods. But daily hassles (e.g., Kanner et al., 1981) and life changes also appear to be predictors of physical illness. Holmes and Rahe, for example, found that people who "earned" 300 or more life-change units within a year according to their scale were at greater risk for illness. Eight of ten developed medical problems as compared with only one of three people whose life-change-unit totals for the year were below 150. Other researchers have found that high numbers of life-change units amassed within a year are linked to a host of physical and psychological problems, ranging from heart disease and cancer to accidents, school failure, and relapses among persons who show abnormal behavior, such as schizophrenia (Lloyd et al., 1980; Perkins, 1982; Rabkin, 1980; Thoits, 1983).

QUESTIONNAIRE

Social Readjustment Rating Scale

Life changes can be a source of stress. How much stress have you experienced in the past year as a result of life changes? To compare the amount of change-related stress you have encountered with that of other college students, fill out the following questionnaire.

Directions: Indicate how many times (frequency) you have experienced the following events during the past 12 months. Then multiply the frequency (do not enter a number larger than 5) by the number of life-change units (value) associated with each event. Write the product in the column to the right (total). Then add up the points and check the key in Appendix B.

Event	Value	Frequency	Total
1. Death of a spouse, lover, or child	94	______	______
2. Death of a parent or sibling	88	______	______
3. Beginning formal higher education	84	______	______
4. Death of a close friend	83	______	______
5. Miscarriage or stillbirth of pregnancy of self, spouse, or lover	83	______	______
6. Jail sentence	82	______	______
7. Divorce or marital separation	82	______	______
8. Unwanted pregnancy of self, spouse, or lover	80	______	______
9. Abortion of unwanted pregnancy of self, spouse, or lover	80	______	______
10. Detention in jail or other institution	79	______	______
11. Change in dating activity	79	______	______
12. Death of a close relative	79	______	______
13. Change in marital situation other than divorce or separation	78	______	______
14. Separation from significant other whom you like very much	77	______	______
15. Change in health status or behavior of spouse or lover	77	______	______
16. Academic failure	77	______	______
17. Major violation of the law and subsequent arrest	76	______	______
18. Marrying or living with lover against parents' wishes	75	______	______
19. Change in love relationship or important friendship	74	______	______
20. Change in health status or behavior of a parent or sibling	73	______	______
21. Change in feelings of loneliness, insecurity, anxiety, boredom	73	______	______
22. Change in marital status of parents	73	______	______
23. Acquiring a visible deformity	72	______	______
24. Change in ability to communicate with a significant other whom you like very much	71	______	______
25. Hospitalization of a parent or sibling	70	______	______
26. Reconciliation of marital or love relationship	68	______	______
27. Release from jail or other institution	68	______	______
28. Graduation from college	68	______	______
29. Major personal injury or illness	68	______	______
30. Wanted pregnancy of self, spouse, or lover	67	______	______
31. Change in number or type of arguments with spouse or lover	67	______	______
32. Marrying or living with lover with parents' approval	66	______	______

Event	Value	Frequency	Total
33. Gaining a new family member through birth or adoption	65	______	______
34. Preparing for an important exam or writing a major paper	65	______	______
35. Major financial difficulties	65	______	______
36. Change in the health status or behavior of a close relative or close friend	65	______	______
37. Change in academic status	64	______	______
38. Change in amount and nature of interpersonal conflicts	63	______	______
39. Change in relationship with members of your immediate family	62	______	______
40. Change in own personality	62	______	______
41. Hospitalization of yourself or a close relative	61	______	______
42. Change in course of study, major field, vocational goals, or work status	60	______	______
43. Change in own financial status	59	______	______
44. Change in status of divorced or widowed parent	59	______	______
45. Change in number or type of arguments between parents	59	______	______
46. Change in acceptance by peers, identification with peers, or social pressure by peers	58	______	______
47. Change in general outlook on life	57	______	______
48. Beginning or ceasing service in the armed forces	57	______	______
49. Change in attitudes toward friends	56	______	______
50. Change in living arrangements, conditions, or environment	55	______	______
51. Change in frequency or nature of sexual experiences	55	______	______
52. Change in parents' financial status	55	______	______
53. Change in amount or nature of pressure from parents	55	______	______
54. Change in degree of interest in college or attitudes toward education	55	______	______
55. Change in the number of personal or social relationships you've formed or dissolved	55	______	______
56. Change in relationship with siblings	54	______	______
57. Change in mobility or reliability of transportation	54	______	______
58. Academic success	54	______	______
59. Change to a new college or university	54	______	______
60. Change in feelings of self-reliance, independence, or amount of self-discipline	53	______	______
61. Change in number or type of arguments with roommate	52	______	______
62. Spouse or lover beginning or ceasing work outside the home	52	______	______
63. Change in frequency of use of amounts of drugs other than alcohol, tobacco, or marijuana	51	______	______
64. Change in sexual morality, beliefs, or attitudes	50	______	______
65. Change in responsibility at work	50	______	______
66. Change in amount or nature of social activities	50	______	______
67. Change in dependencies on parents	50	______	______
68. Change from academic work to practical fieldwork experience or internship	50	______	______

Event	Value	Frequency	Total
69. Change in amount of material possessions and concomitant responsibilities	50	______	______
70. Change in routine at college or work	49	______	______
71. Change in amount of leisure time	49	______	______
72. Change in amount of in-law trouble	49	______	______
73. Outstanding personal achievement	49	______	______
74. Change in family structure other than parental divorce or separation	48	______	______
75. Change in attitude toward drugs	48	______	______
76. Change in amount and nature of competition with same sex	48	______	______
77. Improvement of own health	47	______	______
78. Change in responsibilities at home	47	______	______
79. Change in study habits	46	______	______
80. Change in number or type of arguments or close conflicts with close relatives	46	______	______
81. Change in sleeping habits	46	______	______
82. Change in frequency of use or amounts of alcohol	45	______	______
83. Change in social status	45	______	______
84. Change in frequency of use or amounts of tobacco	45	______	______
85. Change in awareness of activities in external world	45	______	______
86. Change in religious affiliation	44	______	______
87. Change in type of gratifying activities	43	______	______
88. Change in amount or nature of physical activities	43	______	______
89. Change in address or residence	43	______	______
90. Change in amount or nature of recreational activities	43	______	______
91. Change in frequency of use or amounts of marijuana	43	______	______
92. Change in social demands or responsibilities due to your age	43	______	______
93. Court appearance for legal violation	40	______	______
94. Change in weight or eating habits	39	______	______
95. Change in religious activities	37	______	______
96. Change in political views or affiliations	34	______	______
97. Change in driving pattern or conditions	33	______	______
98. Minor violation of the law	31	______	______
99. Vacation or travel	30	______	______
100. Change in number of family get-togethers	30	______	______

Source: Peggy Blake, Robert Fry, and Michael Pesjack (1984). *Self-assessment and behavior change manual.* New York: Random House, pp. 43–47. Reprinted by permission of Random House, Inc.

Truth or Fiction Revisited

It is true that too much of a good thing—too many positive life changes—can contribute to illness. Changes are stressful and require adjustment.

Although uplifts are defined by Lazarus (1984) as being the opposite of hassles, research has not shown that they are beneficial in terms of health. That is, people who encounter more uplifts do not necessarily have fewer health problems (DeLongis et al., 1982; Zarski, 1984).

Criticisms of the Research Links between Hassles, Life Changes, and Illness

Although the links between daily hassles, life changes, and illness seem to have been supported by a good deal of research, there are a number of limitations:

1. *Correlational Evidence* The links that have been uncovered between hassles, life changes, and illness are correlational rather than experimental (Dohrenwend et al., 1982; Monroe, 1982). Although it may seem logical that the hassles and life changes caused the disorders, they were not manipulated experimentally. Rival explanations of the data are therefore possible. One is that people who are predisposed toward medical or psychological problems encounter more hassles and amass more life-change units. For example, medical disorders may contribute

to sexual problems, arguments with one's spouse or in-laws, changes in living conditions and personal habits, changes in sleeping habits, and so on before they are diagnosed.

2. *Positive versus Negative Life Changes* Other aspects of the research into the relationship between life changes and illness have also been challenged. For instance, positive life changes may be less disturbing than hassles and negative life changes, even when their number of life-change units is high (Lefcourt et al., 1981; Perkins, 1982; Thoits, 1983). A change for the better in the health of a family member is usually less stressful than a change for the worse.

3. *Personality Differences* Another problem with the Holmes and Rahe approach is that different kinds of people respond to life stresses in different ways. For example, people who are easy-going and people who are psychologically hardy—as we shall see later in the chapter—are less likely than their opposites to become ill under the impact of stress.

4. *A Role for Cognitive Appraisal* The degree of stress linked to an event will also reflect the meaning the event has for the individual. Pregnancy, for example, can be a positive or negative life change, depending on whether one wants and is prepared to have a child. We cognitively appraise hassles and life changes (Lazarus et al., 1985). In responding to them, we take into account our values and goals, our beliefs in our coping ability (i.e., our self-efficacy expectations), our social support, and so on.

Despite these methodological flaws, hassles and life changes still require adjustments, and it seems wise for us to be aware of the hassles and life changes in our life-styles.

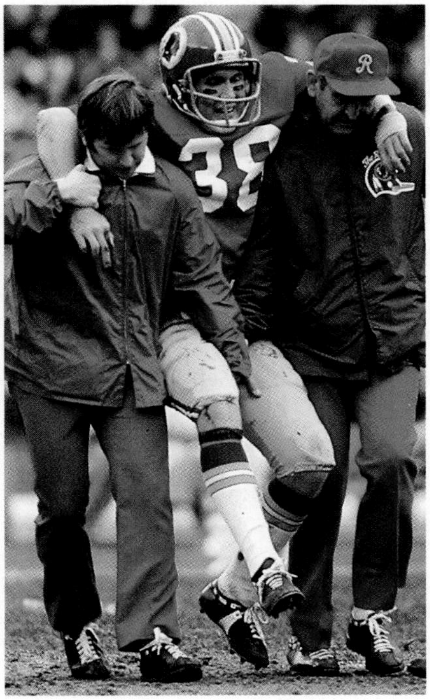

Pain and Discomfort. Pain and discomfort impair performance and coping ability. Athletes report that pain interferes with their ability to run and swim, even when the source of the pain does not directly weaken them.

Pain and Discomfort

Pain and discomfort impair performance and coping ability. Athletes report that pain interferes with their ability to run and swim, even when the source of the pain does not directly weaken them.

In a classic experiment, psychiatrist Curt Richter (1957) dramatized the effects of pain on behavior. First, Richter obtained baseline data by recording the amount of time rats could swim to stay afloat in a tub of water. In water at room temperature, most rats could keep their noses above the surface for about 80 hours. But when Richter blew noxious streams of air into the animal's faces or kept the water uncomfortably hot or cold, the rats could remain afloat for only 20 to 40 hours.

When rats were traumatized before their dunking by having their whiskers noisily cropped off, some managed to remain afloat for only a few minutes. Yet the clipping itself had not weakened them. Rats that were allowed several minutes to recover from the clipping before being launched swam for the usual 80 hours. Psychologists recommend that we space aggravating tasks or chores so that discomfort does not build to the point where it compounds stress and impairs our performance.

Frustration

You may wish to play the line for the varsity football team, but you weigh only 160 pounds or you're a woman. You may have been denied a job or

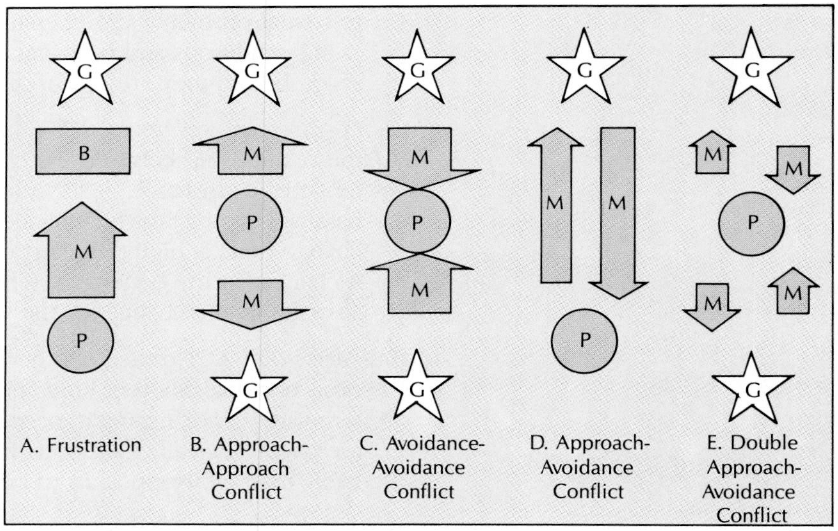

Figure 11.1
Models for Frustration and Conflict. Part A is a model for frustration in which a person (P) has a motive (M) to reach a goal (G) but is frustrated by a barrier (B). Part B shows an approach–approach conflict, in which both goals are desirable, but approaching one requires excluding the other. Part C shows an avoidance–avoidance conflict in which both goals are negative, but avoiding one requires approaching the other. Part D shows an approach–avoidance conflict, in which the same goal has desirable and undesirable properties. Part E shows a double approach–avoidance conflict, which is the simplest kind of *multiple* approach–avoidance conflict. In a multiple approach–avoidance conflict, two or more goals have mixed properties.

educational opportunity because of your ethnic background or favoritism. We all encounter **frustration,** the thwarting of a motive to attain a goal (see Figure 11.1, Part A). Frustration is another source of stress.

Many sources of frustration are obvious. Adolescents are used to being too young to wear makeup, drive, go out, engage in sexual activity, spend money, drink, or work. Age is the barrier that requires them to delay gratification. We may frustrate ourselves as adults if our goals are set too high or if our self-demands are irrational. As Albert Ellis (1977, 1987) notes, if we try to earn other people's approval at all costs, or if we insist on performing perfectly in all of our undertakings, we doom ourselves to failure and frustration.

One of the common frustrations of contemporary life is commuting. Distance, time, and driving conditions are some of the barriers that lie between us and our work or schooling. How many of us fight the highways or crowd ourselves into train cars or buses for an hour or more *before* the workday begins? For most people, the stresses of commuting are mild but persistent (Stokols & Novaco, 1981). Still, lengthy drives on crowded highways are linked to increases in heart rate, blood pressure, and other physical signs of stress, including reports of chest pains. Noise, humidity, and air pollution all contribute to the frustration involved in driving to work.

Truth or Fiction Revisited

It is true that commuting on the highway can elevate your blood pressure.

If you must drive, try to pick times and roads that provide lower volumes of traffic. It may be worth your while to take a longer, more scenic route that has less stop-and-go traffic. Such routes are linked to lower blood pressure and heart rates (Littler et al., 1973).

Anxiety and fear may serve as emotional barriers that prevent us from acting effectively to meet our goals. A high-school senior who wishes to attend an out-of-state college may be frustrated by fear of leaving home. A young adult may not ask an attractive person out on a date because of fear of rejection.

Frustration The thwarting of a motive to attain a goal. The emotion produced by the thwarting of a motive to attain a goal.

Tolerance for Frustration Getting ahead is often a gradual process demanding that we are able to live with some frustration and to delay gratification. Yet our **tolerance for frustration** may fluctuate. Stress heaped upon stress can lower our tolerance, just as Richter's rats, stressed from their close shaves, quickly sank to the bottom of the tub. We may laugh off a flat tire on a good day. However, if it is raining or if we have just waited for an hour in a gas line, the flat may seem like the last straw. People who have encountered frustration but have learned that it is possible to surmount barriers or find substitute goals are more tolerant of frustration than those who have never experienced it, or those who have experienced excesses of frustration.

Conflict

Have you ever felt "damned if you did and damned if you didn't"? Regretted that you couldn't do two things, or be in two places, at the same time? This is **conflict**—being torn in two or more directions by opposing motives. Conflict is frustrating and stressful. Psychologists often break conflicts down into four types: approach-approach, avoidance-avoidance, approach-avoidance, and multiple approach-avoidance.

An **approach-approach conflict** (Figure 11.1, Part B) is the least stressful form of conflict. Here each of two goals is positive and within reach. You may not be able to decide between pizza or tacos, Tom or Dick, or a trip to Nassau or Hawaii. Conflicts are usually resolved by making decisions. People in conflict may **vacillate** until they make a decision.

An **avoidance-avoidance conflict** (Figure 11.1, Part C) is more stressful, because you are motivated to avoid each of two negative goals. However, avoiding one requires approaching the other. You may be fearful of visiting the dentist but also fear that your teeth will decay if you do not. You may not want to contribute to the Association for the Advancement of Lost Causes, but you fear that your friends will consider you cheap or uncommitted if you do not. Each goal is negative in an avoidance-avoidance conflict. When an avoidance-avoidance conflict is highly stressful and no resolution is in sight, some people withdraw from the conflict by focusing their attention on other matters or by suspending behavior altogether. Highly conflicted people have refused to get out of bed in the morning and start the day.

The same goal can produce both approach and avoidance motives, as in the **approach-avoidance conflict** (Figure 11.1, Part D). People and things have their pluses and minuses, their good points and their bad points. Cream cheese pie may be delicious, but oh! the calories. Goals producing mixed motives may seem more attractive from a distance but more repulsive up close. Many couples repeatedly break up, then reunite. When they are apart and lonely, they may recall each other fondly and swear that they could make it work "the next time" if they got together again. But after they again spend time together, they may find themselves facing the same old aggravations and think, "How could I have ever believed this so-and-so would change?"

The most complex form of conflict is the **multiple approach-avoidance conflict,** in which each of several alternative courses of action has its promising and distressing aspects. An example with two goals is shown in Figure 11.1, Part E. This sort of conflict might arise on the eve of an examination, when you are faced with the choice of studying or, say, going to a film. Each alternative has its positive and negative aspects: "Studying's a bore, but I won't have to worry about flunking. I'd love to see the movie, but I'd just be worrying about how I'll do tomorrow."

Tolerance for frustration Ability to withstand frustration.

Conflict Being torn in different directions by opposing motives. Feelings produced by being in conflict.

Approach-approach conflict A type of conflict in which the goals that produce opposing motives are positive and within reach.

Vacillate Move back and forth.

Avoidance-avoidance conflict A type of conflict in which the goals are negative, but avoidance of one requires approach of the other.

Approach-avoidance conflict A type of conflict in which the same goal produces approach and avoidance motives.

Multiple approach-avoidance conflict A type of conflict in which each of a number of goals produces approach and avoidance motives.

Similarly, should you take a job or go on for advanced training when you complete your college program? This is another double approach-avoidance conflict. If you opt for the job, cash will soon be jingling in your pockets, but later you might wonder if you have the education to reach your potential. By furthering your education, you may have to delay the independence and gratification that are afforded by earning a living, but you may find a more fulfilling position later on.

Irrational Beliefs: Ten Doorways to Distress

New York psychologist Albert Ellis (1977, 1985, 1987) notes that our beliefs about events, as well as the events themselves, can be a source of stress. Consider a case in which one is fired from a job and is anxious and depressed about it. It may seem logical that losing the job is responsible for all the misery, but Ellis points out how beliefs about the loss compound misery.

Let us examine this situation according to Ellis's A–B–C approach: Losing the job is an *activating event* (A). The eventual outcome, or *consequence* (C), is misery. But between the activating event (A) and the consequences (C) lies a set of *beliefs* (B), such as the following: "This job was the most important thing in my life," "What a no-good failure I am," "My family will starve," "I'll never find a job as good," "There's nothing I can do about it." Beliefs such as these compound misery, foster helplessness, and divert us from planning and deciding what to do next. For example, the belief "There's nothing I can do about it" fosters helplessness. The belief "What a no-good failure I am" internalizes the blame and is also an exaggeration that might be based on perfectionism. The belief "My family will starve" is also probably an exaggeration.

We can diagram the situation like this:

Activating events → Beliefs → Consequences

Anxieties about the future and depression over a loss are normal and to be expected. However, the beliefs of the person who lost the job tend to **catastrophize** the extent of the loss and to contribute to anxiety and depression. By heightening emotional reaction to the loss and fostering feelings of helplessness, these beliefs also impair coping ability. They lower people's self-efficacy expectations and divert their attention from attempting to solve their problems.

Ellis proposes that many of us harbor a number of the ten following irrational beliefs. We carry them with us; they are our personal doorways to distress. They can give rise to problems in themselves, and, when problems assault us from other sources, these beliefs can magnify their effect. How many of these beliefs do you harbor? Are you sure?

1. You must have sincere love and approval almost all the time from the people who are important to you. (One study found that the irrational belief that one must be loved by, and earn the approval of, practically everyone was endorsed by 65 percent of anxious subjects as compared with only 2 percent of nonanxious subjects [Newmark et al., 1973].)

2. You must prove yourself to be thoroughly competent, adequate, and achieving. Or you must at least have real competence or talent at something important.

3. Things must go the way you want them to go. Life proves to be awful, terrible, and horrible when you don't get your first choices in everything. (College men who believe that it is awful to be turned down

Catastrophize To interpret negative events as being disastrous; to "blow out of proportion."

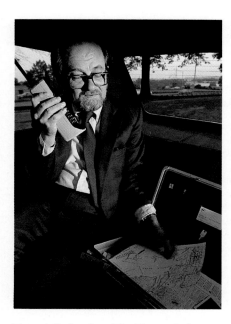

Type A Behavior. The Type A behavior pattern is characterized by a sense of time urgency, competitiveness, and hostility.

for a date show more social anxiety than men who are less likely to catastrophize rejection [Gormally et al., 1981].)

4. Other people must treat everyone fairly and justly. When people act unfairly or unethically, they are terrible and rotten.
5. When there is danger or fear in your world, you must be preoccupied with it and upset by it.
6. People and things should turn out better than they do. It's awful and horrible when you don't find quick solutions to life's hassles.
7. Your emotional misery comes almost completely from external pressures that you have little or no ability to control. Unless these external pressures change, you must remain miserable.
8. It is easier to evade life's responsibilities and problems than to face them and undertake more rewarding forms of self-discipline.
9. Your past influenced you immensely and must therefore continue to determine your feelings and behavior today.
10. You can achieve happiness by inertia and inaction, or by just enjoying yourself from day to day.

Ellis points out that it is understandable that we would want the approval of others, but it is irrational to believe that we cannot survive without it. It would be nice to be competent in everything we do, but it's unreasonable to expect it. Sure, it would be nice to serve and volley like a tennis pro, but most of us haven't the time or natural ability to perfect the game.

Our next topic is Type A behavior. But before proceeding, complete the questionnaire on the following page.

Type A Behavior

Whereas some people create or compound the stress they experience through irrational beliefs, others create stress through the **Type A behavior** pattern. Type A people are highly driven, competitive, impatient, and aggressive (Matthews et al., 1982; Holmes & Will, 1985). They feel rushed and under pressure and keep one eye glued firmly on the clock. They are not only prompt but also frequently early for appointments (Strahan, 1981). They eat, walk, and talk rapidly and become restless when they see others working slowly (Musante et al., 1983). They attempt to dominate group discussions (Yarnold et al., 1985). Type A people find it difficult to surrender control or to share power (Miller et al., 1985; Strube & Werner, 1985). As a consequence, they are often reluctant to delegate authority in the workplace, and in this way they increase their own workloads. Type A people also "accentuate the negative": They are merciless in their self-criticism when they fail at a task (Brunson & Matthews, 1981), and they seek out negative information about themselves in order to better themselves (Cooney & Zeichner, 1985).

Type A people find it difficult just to go out on the tennis court and bat the ball back and forth. They watch their form, perfect their strokes, and demand regular self-improvement. The irrational belief that they must be perfectly competent and achieving in everything they undertake seems to be their motto.

Type B people, in contrast, relax more readily and focus more on the quality of life. They are less ambitious and less impatient, and they pace themselves. Type A people perceive time as passing more rapidly than Type

Type A behavior Behavior characterized by a sense of time urgency, competitiveness, and hostility.

QUESTIONNAIRE

Are You Type A or Type B?

Complete the questionnaire by placing a checkmark under the Yes if the behavior pattern described is typical of you and under the No if it is not. Try to work rapidly and leave no item blank. Then read the section on Type A behavior on the previous page and turn to the scoring key in Appendix B.

DO YOU:	YES	NO
1. Strongly accent key words in your everyday speech?	____	____
2. Eat and walk quickly?	____	____
3. Believe that children should be taught to be competitive?	____	____
4. Feel restless when watching a slow worker?	____	____
5. Hurry other people to get on with what they're trying to say?	____	____
6. Find it highly aggravating to be stuck in traffic or waiting for a seat at a restaurant?	____	____
7. Continue to think about your own problems and business even when listening to someone else?	____	____
8. Try to eat and shave, or drive and jot down notes at the same time?	____	____
9. Catch up on your work on vacations?	____	____
10. Bring conversations around to topics of concern to you?	____	____

DO YOU:	YES	NO
11. Feel guilty when you spend time just relaxing?	____	____
12. Find that you're so wrapped up in your work that you no longer notice office decorations or the scenery when you commute?	____	____
13. Find yourself concerned with getting more *things* rather than developing your creativity and social concerns?	____	____
14. Try to schedule more and more activities into less time?	____	____
15. Always appear for appointments on time?	____	____
16. Clench or pound your fists, or use other gestures, to emphasize your views?	____	____
17. Credit your accomplishments to your ability to work rapidly?	____	____
18. Feel that things must be done *now* and quickly?	____	____
19. Constantly try to find more efficient ways to get things done?	____	____
20. Insist on winning at games rather than just having fun?	____	____
21. Interrupt others often?	____	____
22. Feel irritated when others are late?	____	____
23. Leave the table immediately after eating?	____	____
24. Feel rushed?	____	____
25. Feel dissatisfied with your current level of performance?	____	____

Bs do, and they work more quickly (Yarnold & Grimm, 1982). Type A people earn higher grades and more money than Type Bs of equal intelligence (Glass, 1977). Type A people also seek greater challenges than Type Bs (Ortega & Pipal, 1984).

PSYCHOLOGICAL MODERATORS OF THE IMPACT OF STRESS

There is no one-to-one relationship between the amount of stress we experience and physical illness or psychological distress. Physical factors account for some of the variability in our responses: Some people apparently inherit predispositions toward specific disorders. Yet psychological factors also play a role. They can influence, or *moderate,* the effects of sources of stress.

In this section we discuss a number of psychological moderators of stress.

Self-Efficacy Expectations

Self-efficacy expectations Our beliefs that we can bring about desired changes through our own efforts.

Social-learning theorists (e.g., Bandura, 1982) argue that our **self-efficacy expectations**—that is, our perceptions of our capacities to bring about change—have important influences on our abilities to withstand stress. For

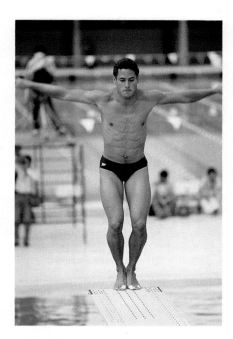

Self-Efficacy Expectations and Performance. Outstanding athletes tend to have high self-efficacy expectations. That is, they believe in themselves. High self-efficacy expectations—beliefs that we can cope—moderate the amount of stress impacting upon us.

example, when we are faced with fear-inducing objects, it has been shown experimentally that high self-efficacy expectations are accompanied by *low* levels of adrenaline and norepinephrine in the bloodstream (Bandura et al., 1985). Adrenaline is secreted by the adrenal medulla when we are under stress, and it generally arouses the body by means such as accelerating the heart rate. As a result, we may experience shakiness, "butterflies in the stomach," and feelings of nervousness. Overarousal can impair our ability to solve complex stress-related problems by elevating our motivation well beyond optimal levels and by distracting us from the tasks at hand. So, people with higher self-efficacy expectations have biological as well as psychological reasons for remaining calmer.

Normal people have higher levels of perceived self-efficacy than psychiatric patients, further suggesting the importance of self-efficacy expectations to psychological well-being (Rosenbaum & Hadari, 1985). Moreover, persons who have greater perceived mastery over events respond more positively to treatment for depression than those who do not (Hoberman et al., 1988).

People in whom high self-efficacy expectations are experimentally induced complete tasks more successfully than people with comparable ability but lower self-efficacy expectations. Moreover, subjects with high self-efficacy expectations show lower emotional arousal as they work, allowing them to maintain more of a task orientation. A combination of high self-efficacy expectations *and a detailed plan* helps overweight college students lose weight (Schifter & Ajzen, 1985). People with higher self-efficacy expectations are less likely to relapse after they have lost weight or quit smoking (Condiotte & Lichtenstein, 1981; Marlatt & Gordon, 1980). They are more effective in athletic competition (Weinberg et al., 1980), and they are more likely to seriously consider nontraditional and challenging career options (Betz & Hackett, 1981). They are also more likely to profit from psychotherapy for problems such as depression (Steinmetz et al., 1983). Women with higher self-efficacy expectations are more likely to persist without medication in controlling pain during childbirth (Manning & Wright, 1983).

When the factors of intelligence and aptitudes are held constant, it appears that people with higher self-efficacy expectations regulate problem-solving behavior more effectively and bounce back more readily from failure. In these ways it seems that life's challenges may be less stressful for them.

Psychological Hardiness

Psychological hardiness is another factor that apparently helps people resist stress. The research on psychological hardiness is largely indebted to the pioneering work of Suzanne Kobasa (1979) and her colleagues, who studied business executives who resisted illness despite heavy loads of stress. In one phase of her research, Kobasa administered a battery of psychological tests to hardy and nonhardy executives and found that the hardy executives differed from the nonhardy in three important ways (Kobasa et al., 1982, pp. 169–170):

1. Hardy individuals were high in *commitment.* That is, they showed a tendency to involve themselves in, rather than experience alienation from, whatever they were doing or encountering.

2. Hardy individuals were high in *challenge.* They believed that change rather than stability was normal in life. They appraised change as an interesting incentive to personal growth, not as a threat to security.

Psychological hardiness A cluster of traits that buffer stress and are characterized by commitment, challenge, and control.

"A Merry Heart Doeth Good Like a Medicine." Finding humor even in difficult situations helps us handle stress. Sigmund Freud regarded humor as "the highest of [the] defensive processes," and empirical research bears out his assumption.

3. Hardy individuals were also high in perceived *control* over their lives. They felt and behaved as though they were influential rather than helpless in facing the various rewards and punishments of life. In terms suggested more than two decades ago by social-learning theorist Julian Rotter (1966), psychologically hardy people tend to have an internal **locus of control.**

According to Kobasa, hardy people are more resistant to stress because they see themselves as *choosing* to be in their stress-producing situations. They also interpret, or encode, the stress impacting upon them as making life more interesting, not as compounding the pressures to which they are subjected. Their activation of control allows them to regulate to some degree the amount of stress they will encounter at any given time (Maddi & Kobasa, 1984). Of the three aspects of psychological hardiness that help people resist stress, Hull and his colleagues (1987) argue that commitment and control are the ones that make the most difference.

Kobasa and Pucetti (1983) suggest that psychological hardiness helps individuals resist stress by providing buffers between themselves and stressful life events. Buffering gives people the opportunity to draw on social supports (Ganellen & Blaney, 1984) and to use successful coping mechanisms, such as controlling what they will be doing from day to day. Type A individuals who show psychological hardiness are more resistant to illness, including coronary heart disease, than Type A individuals who do not (Booth-Kewley & Friedman, 1987; Friedman & Booth-Kewley, 1987; Kobasa et al., 1983; Krantz et al., 1988; Rhodewalt & Agustsdottir, 1984).

As noted, a sense of control is one of the essential factors in psychological hardiness. You may wish to complete the following questionnaire on locus of control to see whether you tend to believe that you are in charge of your own life.

Sense of Humor: Does "A Merry Heart Doeth Good Like a Medicine"?

The idea that humor lightens the burdens of the day and helps us cope with stress has been with us for millennia (Lefcourt & Martin, 1986). Consider the biblical maxim "a merry heart doeth good like a medicine" (Proverbs 17:22).

Locus of control The place (locus) to which an individual attributes control over the receiving of reinforcers—either inside or outside the self.

QUESTIONNAIRE

Locus of Control Scale

Psychologically hardy people tend to have an internal locus of control. They believe that they are in control of their own lives. Persons with an external locus of control, in contrast, tend to see their fates as being out of their hands.

Are you more of an "internal" or more of an "external"? To learn more about your perception of your locus of control, respond to the following questionnaire developed by Nowicki and Strickland (1973).

Place a checkmark in either the Yes or the No column for each question, and, when you are finished, turn to the answer key in Appendix B.

	YES	NO
1. Do you believe that most problems will solve themselves if you just don't fool with them?	______	______
2. Do you believe that you can stop yourself from catching a cold?	______	______
3. Are some people just born lucky?	______	______
4. Most of the time do you feel that getting good grades meant a great deal to you?	______	______
5. Are you often blamed for things that just aren't your fault?	______	______
6. Do you believe that if somebody studies hard enough he or she can pass any subject?	______	______
7. Do you feel that most of the time it doesn't pay to try hard because things never turn out right anyway?	______	______
8. Do you feel that if things start out well in the morning it's going to be a good day no matter what you do?	______	______
9. Do you feel that most of the time parents listen to what their children have to say?	______	______
10. Do you believe that wishing can make good things happen?	______	______
11. When you get punished does it usually seem it's for no good reason at all?	______	______
12. Most of the time do you find it hard to change a friend's opinion?	______	______
13. Do you think cheering more than luck helps a team win?	______	______
14. Did you feel that it was nearly impossible to change your parents' minds about anything?	______	______
15. Do you believe that parents should allow children to make most of their own decisions?	______	______
16. Do you feel that when you do something wrong there's very little you can do to make it right?	______	______
17. Do you believe that most people are just born good at sports?	______	______
18. Are most other people your age stronger than you are?	______	______

	YES	NO
19. Do you feel that one of the best ways to handle most problems is just not to think about them?	______	______
20. Do you feel that you have a lot of choice in deciding who your friends are?	______	______
21. If you find a four-leaf clover, do you believe that it might bring you good luck?	______	______
22. Did you often feel that whether or not you did your homework had much to do with what kind of grades you got?	______	______
23. Do you feel that when a person your age is angry with you, there's little you can do to stop him or her?	______	______
24. Have you ever had a good-luck charm?	______	______
25. Do you believe that whether or not people like you depends on how you act?	______	______
26. Did your parents usually help you if you asked them to?	______	______
27. Have you ever felt that when people were angry with you it was usually for no reason at all?	______	______
28. Most of the time, do you feel that you can change what might happen tomorrow by what you did today?	______	______
29. Do you believe that when bad things are going to happen they are just going to happen no matter what you try to do to stop them?	______	______
30. Do you think that people can get their own way if they just keep trying?	______	______
31. Most of the time do you find it useless to try to get your own way at home?	______	______
32. Do you feel that when good things happen they happen because of hard work?	______	______
33. Do you feel that when somebody your age wants to be your enemy there's little you can do to change matters?	______	______
34. Do you feel that it's easy to get friends to do what you want them to do?	______	______
35. Do you usually feel that you have little to say about what you get to eat at home?	______	______
36. Do you feel that when someone doesn't like you there's little you can do about it?	______	______
37. Did you usually feel it was almost useless to try in school because most other children were just plain smarter than you were?	______	______
38. Are you the kind of person who believes that planning ahead makes things turn out better?	______	______
39. Most of the time, do you feel that you have little to say about what your family decides to do?	______	______
40. Do you think it's better to be smart than to be lucky?	______	______

In *Anatomy of an Illness,* Norman Cousins (1979) reported that ten minutes of belly laughter had a powerful anesthetic effect on his pain. It allowed him to sleep for at least two hours without analgesic medication. Laughter also might have reduced his inflammation, a finding that has led some writers to speculate that laughter might stimulate the output of endorphins within the body. But the benefits of humor also might be explained in terms of the sudden cognitive shifts they entail and the emotional changes that accompany them (Dixon, 1980).

Until recently, the benefits of humor were largely speculative and anecdotal. But an important psychological study of the moderating effects of humor on stress was run by Canadian psychologists Rod Martin and Herbert Lefcourt (1983). The researchers administered a negative-life-events checklist and a measure of mood disturbance to college students. The mood-disturbance measure also yielded a stress score. The students were also given self-report scales concerning their sense of humor and behavioral assessments of their ability to produce humor under stressful conditions. Overall, there was a significant relationship between negative life events and stress scores: High accumulations of negative life events predicted higher levels of stress. However, students who had a greater sense of humor and who produced humor in difficult situations were less affected by negative life events than other students.

Truth or Fiction Revisited

It is true that a sense of humor can moderate the effects of stress. In the experiment run by Martin and Lefcourt, humor apparently played its conjectured stress-buffering role.

Predictability

It appears that being able to predict the onset of a stressor moderates its impact on us. Predictability allows us to brace ourselves for the inevitable and, in many cases, permits us to plan ways of coping with it. People who have accurate knowledge of medical procedures and what they will feel cope with pain more effectively than people who do not (e.g., Shipley et al., 1978; Staub et al., 1971). Experiments also show that crowding is less aversive when we are forewarned about how crowding might make us feel (Baum et al., 1981; Fisher & Baum, 1980; Paulus & Matthews, 1980; Langer & Saegert, 1977).

There is also a relationship between the desire to assume control over one's situation and the usefulness of information about impending stressors (Lazarus & Folkman, 1984). Predictability is of greater benefit to **"internals"**—that is, to people who wish to exercise control over their situations—than to **"externals."**

Animal Research Animal research tends to support the view that there are advantages to predictability, especially when predictability allows one to exercise direct control over a stressor (Weinberg & Levine, 1980). Providing laboratory rats with a signal that a stressor is approaching apparently buffers its impact.

In one study, Weiss (1972) placed three sets of rats matched according to age and weight into individual soundproof cages, as shown in Figure 11.2. The rat on the left received electric shock following a signal. It could then terminate the shock by turning the wheel. The rat in the center was shocked in tandem with the rat to the left, but it received no warning signal and could do nothing to terminate the shock. The rat to the right received no signal and no electric shock. However, it was placed in the identical apparatus, including having electrodes attached to its tail, to control for any effects of this unnatural environment.

"Internals" People who perceive the ability to attain reinforcements as being largely within themselves.

"Externals" People who perceive the ability to attain reinforcements as being largely outside themselves.

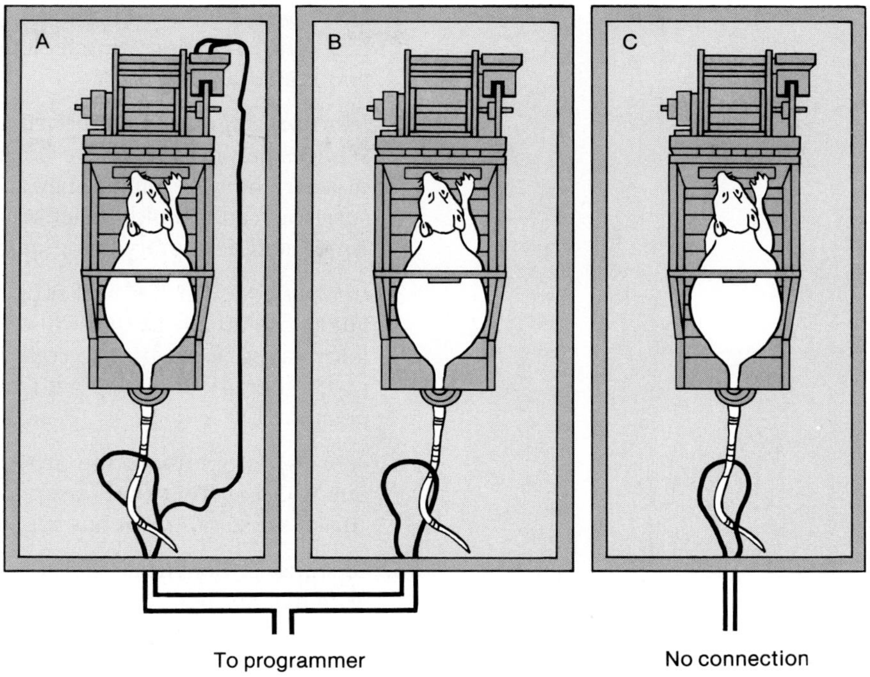

Figure 11.2
The Experimental Set-Up in the Weiss Study on Ulcer Formation in Rats. The rat to the left is signaled prior to receiving electric shock and can terminate the shock by turning the wheel. The rat in the center receives a shock of the same intensity and duration but is not warned of its onset and cannot terminate it. The rat to the right receives no signal and no shock.

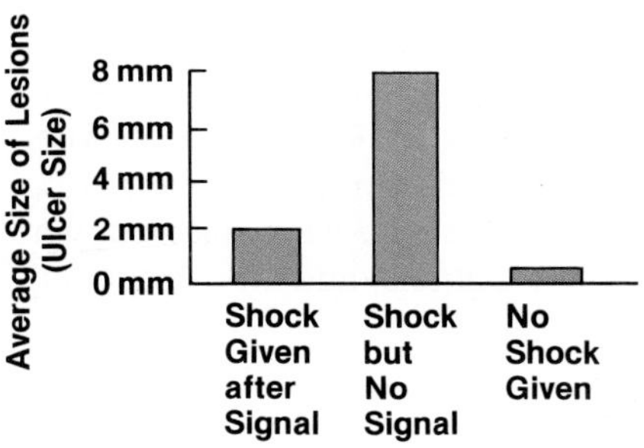

Figure 11.3
Effects of Predictability and Ability to Control a Stressor on Ulcer Formation in Rats. Rats who received no signals or shocks formed hardly any ulcers. Rats who received shocks but could not predict or terminate them showed the most ulcer formation. Rats who were warned of impending shocks and could terminate them showed more ulcer formation than rats who were not shocked, but not nearly as much ulceration as rats who could not predict the onset of shocks.

As shown in Figure 11.3, shock led to ulceration in the rats—the definition of stressful experience in this study. The rats to the right, which received no signal and no shock, showed hardly any ulceration. Rats that received shock without warning showed the greatest amount of ulceration. Rats given warning signals and allowed to terminate the shock also developed ulcers, but to a significantly lesser degree.

The Weiss study suggests that inescapable stressors may be less harmful when they are predictable and when we act purposefully upon their arrival. The predictability of a stressor is to some degree a situational variable. But if we learn what we can about the sources of stress in our lives—concurrent and impending—and commit ourselves to regulating them as best we can, we may, like Weiss's warned subjects, be able to brace ourselves and plan effective responses.

Social Support

Social support, like psychological hardiness, seems to buffer the effects of stress (Cohen & Wills, 1985; Pagel & Becker, 1987; Rook & Dooley, 1985). Although social support is a situational variable, it should be noted that we can choose whether we shall seek support. Some children who thrive despite environmental hardships show an uncanny knack for seeking out the support of adults—before their fourth birthdays (Farber & Egeland, 1987). Social support, in turn, helps the child behave more resiliently.

Writing in the context of handling stress on the job, James House (1981, 1984) identifies four kinds of social support that can help us cope with stress. Fiore (1980) adds a fifth. Altogether, these forms of social support include the following:

1. *Emotional concern.* Emotional concern involves listening to people's problems and expressing feelings of sympathy, caring, understanding, and reassurance.
2. *Instrumental aid.* Instrumental aid includes the material supports and services that make adaptive behavior possible. For example, after a disaster, the government may arrange for low-interest loans so that survivors can rebuild. Relief organizations may provide foodstuffs, medicines, and temporary living quarters.
3. *Information.* This form of support involves giving people cognitive guidance and advice that will enhance their abilities to cope. Seeking of information about how to cope is a primary motivation for undertaking psychotherapy or talking with experienced grandparents and religious personnel.
4. *Appraisal.* Appraisal is the provision of feedback from others on how one is doing. This kind of support involves helping people interpret, or "make sense of," what has happened to them.
5. *Socializing.* Beneficial effects are derived from socializing itself, even in ways that are not oriented toward solving problems (Fiore, 1980). Examples include simple conversation, recreation, even going shopping with another person.

Research shows that social support moderates the effects of stress in situations ranging from problems at work to technological disasters. Consider the nuclear accident at the Three Mile Island nuclear plant in Pennsylvania. Nearby residents who had solid networks of social support—close relatives and friends with whom they could share the experience—reported less stress than those who did not (Fleming et al., 1982).

People who receive social support may even live longer, as was found in studies of Alameda County, California (Berkman & Syme, 1979; Berkman & Breslow, 1983) and Tecumseh, Michigan (House, Robbins & Metzner, 1982). In the Tecumseh study, adults were followed during a 12-year period. The mortality rate was significantly lower for men who were married, who regularly attended meetings of voluntary associations, and who frequently engaged in social leisure activities.

Truth or Fiction Revisited

It is *not* true that single men live longer than married men. Actually, the reverse is true.

PHYSIOLOGICAL RESPONSES TO STRESS

How is it that too much of a good thing—or that anxiety, frustration, or conflict—can make us ill? Why do Type A people have higher blood pressure than Type Bs? We do not have all the answers yet, but those we have suggest that the body, under stress, is like a clock with an alarm system that does not shut off until its energy is dangerously depleted.

General Adaptation Syndrome

The body's response to different stressors shows some similarities, whether the stressor is a bacterial invasion, a perceived danger, a major life change, an inner conflict, or a wound. Selye (1976) has labeled this response the

Table 11.1
Components of the Alarm Reaction

Corticosteroids are secreted	Muscles tense
Adrenaline is secreted	Blood shifts from internal organs to the skeletal musculature
Norepinephrine is secreted	Digestion is inhibited
Respiration rate increases	Sugar is released from the liver
Heart rate increases	Blood coagulability increases
Blood pressure increases	

The alarm reaction is triggered by various types of stressors. It is defined by release of corticosteroids and adrenaline and by activity of the sympathetic branch of the autonomic nervous system. It prepares the body to fight or flee from a source of danger.

general adaptation syndrome (GAS). The GAS consists of three stages: an alarm reaction, a resistance stage, and an exhaustion stage.

The Alarm Reaction The **alarm reaction** is triggered by perception of a stressor. This reaction mobilizes or arouses the body in preparation for defense. Cannon (1929) had earlier termed this alarm system the **fight-or-flight reaction.** The alarm reaction involves a number of body changes that are initiated by the brain and further regulated by the endocrine system and the sympathetic division of the autonomic nervous system (ANS). Let us consider the roles of these two body systems.

There is a "domino effect" in the endocrine system when a stressor is perceived. The hypothalamus secretes corticotrophin-releasing hormone (CRH), which, in turn, stimulates the pituitary gland to secrete adrenocorticotrophic hormone (ACTH). ACTH then acts upon the adrenal cortex, causing it to release cortisol and other steroids that help the body respond to stress by fighting inflammation and allergic reactions (such as difficulty in breathing).

Two other hormones that play a major role in the alarm reaction are secreted by the adrenal medulla. The sympathetic division of the ANS activates the adrenal medulla, causing a mixture of adrenaline and norepinephrine to be released. The mixture arouses the body to cope with threats and stress by accelerating the heart rate and causing muscle tissue and the liver to release glucose (sugar). In this way energy is provided for the fight-or-flight reaction, which was inherited from a time when many stressors were life-threatening. This reaction activates the body so that it is prepared to fight or flee from a predator. Many of the bodily changes that occur in the fight-or-flight reaction are outlined in Table 11.1. Historically, the reaction was triggered by a predator at the edge of a thicket or by a sudden rustling in the undergrowth. Today it is also aroused when you chafe at the bit in stop-and-go traffic or learn that your mortgage payments are going to be increased. Once the threat is removed, the body returns to a lower state of arousal.

Because cortisol and adrenaline are secreted in response to stress, the amount of these substances in the body serves as an objective measure of stress (see, for example, Brantley et al., 1988). In their research, psychologists frequently use the amount of cortisol in the saliva or urine and the amount of adrenaline in the urine as biological measures of stress.

Our ancestors lived in situations in which the alarm reaction would not be activated for long. They fought or ran quickly or, to put it bluntly, they died. Sensitive alarm reactions contributed to survival.

The Resistance Stage In any event, if the alarm reaction mobilizes the body and the stressor is not removed, we enter the adaptation stage, or

General adaptation syndrome Selye's term for a hypothesized three-stage response to stress. Abbreviated *GAS*.

Alarm reaction The first stage of the GAS, which is triggered by the impact of a stressor and characterized by sympathetic activity.

Fight-or-flight reaction A hypothesized innate adaptive response to the perception of danger.

resistance stage, of the GAS. The levels of endocrine and sympathetic activity are not as high as in the alarm reaction, but they are still greater than normal. In this stage the body attempts to restore lost energy and repair whatever damage has been done.

The Exhaustion Stage If the stressor is still not adequately dealt with, we may enter the final or **exhaustion stage** of the GAS. Our individual capacities for resisting stress vary, but all of us, even the strongest of Richter's rats, eventually become exhausted when stress persists indefinitely. Our muscles become fatigued, and we deplete our bodies of resources required for combating stress. With exhaustion, the parasympathetic division of the ANS may predominate. As a result, our heartbeats and respiration rates slow down, and many of the body responses that had characterized sympathetic activity are reversed. It might sound as if we would profit from the respite, but remember that we are still under stress—and possibly an external threat. Continued stress in the exhaustion stage may lead to what Selye terms "diseases of adaptation"—from allergies and hives to ulcers and coronary heart disease—and, ultimately, to death.

Let us now consider the effects of stress on the body's immune system. Our discussion will pave the way for understanding the links between various psychological factors and physical illnesses.

THE IMMUNE SYSTEM

Given the complexities of our bodies and the fast pace of scientific change, it is common for us to think of ourselves as being highly dependent on trained professionals, such as physicians, to cope with illness. Yet we actually do most of this coping by ourselves, by means of our **immune systems.**

Functions of the Immune System

The immune system has several functions that help us combat disease.

Destruction of Pathogens One way in which we combat physical disorders is by producing white blood cells that routinely engulf and kill pathogens such as bacteria, fungi, and viruses; wornout body cells; and even cells that have changed into cancerous cells. White blood cells are technically termed **leukocytes.** Leukocytes carry on microscopic warfare. They engage in search-and-destroy missions in which they "recognize" and then eliminate foreign agents and unhealthy cells.

Recognition of Pathogens A second function of the immune system is to "remember" foreign agents so that future combat will be more efficient. The foreign agents that are recognized and destroyed by leukocytes are called **antigens.** Some leukocytes, as noted, actually kill antigens, but others operate by producing **antibodies,** or specialized proteins, that bind to their antigens and mark them for destruction. The immune system "remembers" how to battle these antigens by maintaining them in the bloodstream, often for many years.*

*Vaccination involves the introduction of a weakened form of an antigen (usually a bacteria or a virus) into the body, stimulating the production of antibodies. Antibodies can confer immunity for many years, in some cases for a lifetime. Smallpox has been eradicated by means of vaccination, and scientists are searching for a vaccine against the AIDS virus.

Resistance stage The second stage of the GAS, characterized by prolonged sympathetic activity in an effort to restore lost energy and repair damage. Also called the *adaptation stage.*

Exhaustion stage The third stage of the GAS, characterized by weakened resistance and possible deterioration.

Immune system The system of the body that recognizes and destroys foreign agents (antigens) that invade the body.

Leukocytes (LOO-ko-sites). White blood cells. (Derived from the Greek words *leukos,* meaning "white," and *kytos,* literally meaning "a hollow," but used to refer to cells.)

Antigen A substance that stimulates the body to mount an immune-system response to it. (The contraction for *anti*body *gen*erator.)

Antibodies Substances formed by white blood cells that recognize and destroy antigens.

Inflammation **Inflammation** is a third function of the immune system. When injury occurs, blood vessels in the area first contract (to stem bleeding) but then dilate. Dilation increases the flow of blood to the damaged area, causing the redness and warmth that characterize inflammation. The increased blood supply also brings in large numbers of white blood cells to combat invading microscopic life forms, such as bacteria, that might otherwise use the local damage as a point of entry into the body.

Truth or Fiction Revisited

It is true that countless microscopic warriors within our bodies are carrying out search-and-destroy missions against foreign agents at any given moment. They are white blood cells.

Effects of Stress on the Immune System

Psychologists, biologists, and medical researchers have recently been exploring a new field of study that addresses the relationships between psychological factors and the immune system: **psychoneuroimmunology** (Schindler, 1985). One of the major concerns of psychoneuroimmunology is the effect of stress on the immune system.

One of the reasons that stress eventually exhausts us is that it stimulates us to produce steroids. Steroids suppress the functioning of the immune system. Suppression has negligible effects when steroids are secreted intermittently, but persistent secretion impairs the functioning of the immune system by decreasing inflammation and interfering with the formation of antibodies. As a consequence, susceptibility to various kinds of illnesses increases.

Empirical Findings Concerning Stress–Immune-System Relationships Research supports the hypothesized links between stress and the immune system. It also demonstrates the moderating effects of psychological factors such as control, the need for power, and social support.

An experiment with laboratory rats and electric shock mirrored the method of Weiss (1972), as described earlier. But this time the dependent variable was activity of the immune system, not ulcer formation (Laudenslager et al., 1983). The rats were exposed to inevitable electric shocks, but, as in the Weiss study, one group of rats could terminate the shock. Rats who could *not* exert control over the stressor showed immune-system deficits, but the rats who could terminate the shock showed no deficiency.

One study with people focused on dental students (Jemmott et al., 1983). Students showed lower immune-system functioning, as measured by lower levels of antibodies in the saliva, during stressful school periods than immediately following vacations. Moreover, students with many friends showed less suppression of the immune system than students with few friends. Social support, that is, apparently buffered school stresses.

Another study with students found that the stress of examinations depressed immune-system response to the Epstein-Barr virus, which causes fatigue and other problems (Kiecolt-Glaser et al., 1984). Moreover, students who were lonely showed greater suppression of the immune system than students who had more social support. In a study of elderly people, it was found that a combination of relaxation training, which decreases sympathetic activity, and training in coping skills *improves* immune-system functioning (Kiecolt-Glaser et al., 1985). We shall discuss relaxation training in the section on lowering arousal.

Inflammation Increased blood flow to an injured area of the body, resulting in redness, warmth, and an increased supply of white blood cells.

Psychoneuroimmunology The field that studies the relationships between psychological factors (e.g., attitudes and overt behavior patterns) and the functioning of the immune system.

Let us now turn our attention to some major physical illnesses and examine the roles of stress and the immune system in succumbing to them.

PSYCHOLOGICAL FACTORS AND PHYSICAL ILLNESS

Psychological factors such as stress and our behavior patterns are implicated in the development and course of a number of illnesses. In this section we focus on the relationships between psychological factors and illnesses such as headaches, cardiovascular disorders, and cancer.

Headaches

Headaches are among the most common stress-related physical ailments. According to Bonica (1980), 45 million Americans suffer from severe headaches.

Muscle-Tension Headache The single most frequent kind of headache is the muscle-tension headache. We are likely to contract muscles in the shoulders, neck, forehead, and scalp during the first two stages of the GAS. Persistent stress can lead to persistent contraction of these muscles, giving rise to muscle-tension headaches. Such headaches usually come on gradually. They are most often characterized by dull, steady pain on both sides of the head and feelings of tightness or pressure.

Migraine Headache Most other headaches, including the severe migraine headache, are vascular in nature—that is, stemming from changes in the blood supply to the head. **Migraine headaches** have preheadache phases during which the arteries that supply the head with blood are constricted, decreasing blood flow, and headaches phases, during which the arteries are dilated, increasing the blood flow. There is often a warning "aura" accompanying the preheadache phase that may be characterized by visual problems and perception of unusual odors. The attacks themselves are often attended by intensified sensitivity to light; loss of appetite, nausea, and vomiting; sensory and motor disturbances, such as loss of balance; and changes in mood. The so-called common migraine headache is identified by sudden onset and throbbing on one side of the head. The so-called classic migraine is known by sensory and motor disturbances that precede the pain. The origins of migraine headaches are not clearly understood. It is believed, however, that they can be induced by barometric pressure; pollen; specific drugs; the chemical monosodium glutamate (MSG), which is often used to enhance the flavor of food; chocolates; aged cheeses; beer, champagne, and red wines; and the hormonal changes of the period prior to and during menstruation. Type A behavior may also be an important contributor to migraine headaches. In one study, 53 percent of 30 migraine sufferers showed the Type A behavior pattern, as compared with 23 percent of 30 muscle-tension headache sufferers (Rappaport et al., 1988).

Regardless of the original source of the headache, we can unwittingly propel ourselves into a vicious cycle: Headache pain is a stressor that can lead us to increase, rather than relax, muscle tension in the neck, shoulders, scalp, and face.

Migraine headaches Throbbing headaches that are connected with changes in the supply of blood to the head.

Headache. Headaches are among the most common stress-related physical ailments. The most common headache is the muscle-tension headache, which is usually caused by contraction of muscles in the shoulders, neck, forehead, and scalp. Muscle tightness in these areas is characteristic of the first two stages of the general adaptation syndrome.

Truth or Fiction Revisited

It is true that most headaches are caused by muscle tension. And those that are not can be exacerbated by muscle tension.

Treatment Aspirin and ibuprofen frequently decrease pain, including headache pain, by inhibiting the production of the prostaglandins that help initiate transmission of pain messages to the brain. Behavioral methods can also help. Progressive relaxation focuses on decreasing muscle tension and has been shown to be highly effective in relieving muscle-tension headaches (Blanchard et al., 1985, 1987; Teders et al., 1984). Biofeedback training that alters the flow of blood to the head has been used effectively to treat migraine headache (Blanchard et al., 1980, 1982, 1985, 1987). People who are sensitive to MSG or red wine can ask that MSG be left out of their dishes and can switch to a white wine.

Why, under stress, do some of us develop ulcers, others develop hypertension, and still others suffer no physical problems? In the following sections we see that there may be an interaction between stress and predisposing biological and psychological differences between individuals (Davison & Neale, 1986; Walker, 1983).

Hypertension

Ten to 30 percent of Americans are afflicted by **hypertension,** or abnormally high blood pressure (Seer, 1979). When high blood pressure has no identifiable causes, it is referred to as *essential hypertension.* Arousal of the sympathetic division of the ANS heightens the blood pressure, and, when we are very stressed, we may believe that we can feel our blood pressure "pounding through the roof." But such ideas are usually misleading. Although most people believe that they would be able to recognize symptoms of hypertension, most of the time they cannot (Baumann & Leventhal, 1985;

Hypertension High blood pressure.

Meyer et al., 1985). Thus, it is important for us to have our blood pressure checked regularly.

Hypertension predisposes victims to other cardiovascular disorders such as arteriosclerosis, heart attacks, and strokes (Berkman et al., 1983). Blood pressure rises in situations in which people must be constantly on guard against threats, whether in combat, in the work place, or in the home. Blood pressure appears to be higher among blacks than whites. It is also higher among both blacks and whites who tend to hold in, rather than express, feelings of anger (Diamond, 1982; Harburg et al., 1973).

Treatment High blood pressure can frequently be controlled by means of medication, but because of the lack of symptoms, many patients do not take their medicine reliably. Dietary components, particularly sodium (salt), can heighten the blood pressure.

Behavioral methods such as progressive relaxation have shown promise in the treatment of hypertension (Agras et al., 1983). As noted in Chapter 4, meditation also seems to lower the blood pressure of many hypertensive individuals (Benson et al., 1983).

One study with a group of 496 patients whose blood pressure had been normalized by medication for five years highlighted the powerful potential of dietary behavior modification in the treatment of hypertension (Langford et al., 1985). The patients were taken off their medication and assigned to either a general weight-loss diet or a sodium-restricted diet; 72 percent of those in the weight-loss group and 78 percent of those in the sodium-restricted group were able to maintain their blood pressure at normal levels without medication.

Cardiovascular Disorders

Cardiovascular disorders are the cause of nearly half the deaths in the United States (U.S. Department of Health and Human Services, 1984). Cardiovascular diseases include heart disease and disorders of the circulatory system, the most common of which is stroke.

There are several risk factors for cardiovascular disease:

1. *Family history.* People whose families show a history of cardiovascular disease are more likely to develop cardiovascular disease themselves (Feist & Brannon, 1988).
2. *Physiological conditions.* Such conditions include obesity, hypertension, and high levels of **serum cholesterol.**
3. *Patterns of consumption.* Such patterns include heavy drinking, smoking (Epstein & Perkins, 1988), overeating, and eating food high in cholesterol, such as animal fats and coconut oils (Jeffery, 1988).
4. *Type A behavior.* Evidence is mixed as to whether the Type A behavior pattern—or one or more of its components—places people at risk for cardiovascular disorders. Still, it is worthy of consideration.
5. *Work overload.* Overtime work, assembly-line labor, and exposure to conflicting demands all make their contributions (Jenkins, 1988).
6. *Chronic fatigue and emotional strain.*
7. *A physically inactive life-style.*

Cardiovascular disorders Diseases of the cardiovascular system, including heart disease, hypertension, and arteriosclerosis.

Serum cholesterol Cholesterol found in the blood.

Hypertension and high serum cholesterol levels are risk factors in cardiovascular disorders. As noted earlier in the chapter, Type A people seek difficult challenges. Unfortunately, Type A people respond to challenge with higher blood pressure than Type Bs do (Holmes et al., 1984). In addition, Type Bs smoke less and have lower serum cholesterol levels.

Type A Behavior: Conflicting Evidence Many studies have shown that Type A people are at greater risk for heart disease than Type Bs (e.g., Bernardo et al., 1985; Cohen & Reed, 1985; DeBacker et al., 1983; French-Belgian Collaborative Group, 1982; Weiss & Richter-Heinrich, 1985). Eight- and ten-year longitudinal studies of people in Framingham, Massachusetts, found that men and women who showed the Type A behavior pattern were overall about twice as likely as their Type B counterparts to develop coronary heart disease (Haynes et al., 1980, 1983). Male Type A white-collar workers were about three times as likely as male Type B white-collar workers to develop coronary heart disease. Younger Type A women showed about 2.5 times the risk for coronary heart disease as compared with young Type B women, but the Type A–Type B difference in risk declined with age.

On the other hand, some studies have found no difference in the incidence of heart attacks and death rates between Type A and Type B men (Fischman, 1987; Matthews & Haynes, 1986). The so-called Multiple Risk Factor Intervention Trial (MRFIT), which followed 12,700 men from 1973 to 1982, is one such study. In fact, Ragland and Brand (1988) reported that Type A men were actually at *lower risk* for recurrent heart attacks than Type B men. Ragland and Brand followed the survival patterns of 257 heart attack victims over a dozen years and found that the death rate for the 160 Type A patients in the group was 19.1 per thousand person-years. (A person-year is number of patients multiplied by number of years of survival.) In comparison, the death rate for the 71 Type B patients in the group was 31.7 per thousand person-years. That is, five Type Bs died for every three Type A people who died.

We cannot satisfactorily explain the discrepancies in studies of the cardiovascular risks of Type A behavior. Meyer Friedman, one of the originators of the Type A concept, argues that the MRFIT study did a poor job of interviewing subjects and assigning them to Type A or Type B categories (Fischman, 1987). We can also note that the Ragland and Brand research addresses only recurrent heart attack victims, not initial victims.

Because the global concept of Type A behavior has not been satisfactorily linked to cardiovascular disease, some investigators are looking into the cardiovascular risks of various components of the Type A behavior pattern, such as hostility (Barefoot et al., 1983; Chesney & Rosenman, 1985; Fischman, 1987; Friedman et al., 1985; Shekelle et al., 1983; Wright, 1988). Some of these researchers suggest that a factor related to hostility—expecting the worst from people, or cynicism—is the culprit. Others point to the possible cardiovascular consequences of holding in rather than expressing anger (e.g., Dembroski et al., 1985; Spielberger et al., 1985).

Of course, there is no one-to-one relationship between any behavior pattern and heart disease (Jenkins, 1988; Krantz et al., 1988). Different people's cardiovascular systems react to stress differently. People termed **hot reactors** by Eliot and Buell (1983), for example, respond to stress with accelerated heart rate and constriction of blood vessels in peripheral areas of the body, whereas others do not. And some people, including some Type A people, moderate the effects of stress successfully through psychological means, as we shall see in the section on psychology and modern life.

Hot reactors People who respond to stress with accelerated heart rate and constriction of blood vessels in peripheral areas of the body.

Behavior Modification for Reducing Risk Factors Once cardiovascular disease has been diagnosed, there are a number of medical treatments, including surgery and medication. However, persons who have not encountered cardiovascular disease (as well as those who have) can profit from behavior modification that is intended to reduce the risk factors. These methods include the following:

1. *Stopping smoking.* (See methods in Chapter 4.)
2. *Weight control.* (See methods in Chapter 8.)
3. *Reducing hypertension.*
4. *Lowering serum cholesterol.* The major method involves cutting down on foods high in cholesterol, but exercise may also help.
5. *Modifying Type A behavior.* Studies suggest that behavioral programs described in the section on psychology and modern life can modify Type A behavior patterns and decrease the risk of heart attacks, even for people who have previously suffered heart attacks (Friedman & Ulmer, 1984; Roskies et al., 1986).
6. *Exercise.*

Ulcers

Ulcers may afflict one person in ten and cause as many as 10,000 deaths each year in the United States (Whitehead & Bosmajian, 1982). People who develop ulcers under stress often have higher pepsinogen levels than those who do not (Weiner et al., 1957), and heredity may contribute to pepsinogen level (Mirsky, 1958). Research with laboratory rats suggests that intense approach-avoidance conflict may also contribute to ulcers (Sawrey et al., 1956; Sawrey & Weisz, 1956).

Asthma

Asthma is a respiratory disorder in which the main tubes of the windpipe—the bronchi—contract, making it difficult to breathe. Asthma attacks can be triggered by an allergic reaction, by stress, by emotional responses such as anger, even by laughing too hard (Brody, 1988). In most cases the initial asthma attack follows on the heels of a respiratory infection (Alexander, 1981). Asthma sufferers can experience attacks in response to the suggestion that their air flow will become constricted (Luparello et al., 1971), suggesting that worrying about an attack can help bring one on. There are some reports (e.g., Rathus, 1973b) in which asthma sufferers have been helped by cognitive behavioral methods in which they enhance their self-efficacy expectations concerning their ability to cope with asthma and engage in relaxed, regular breathing regimens.

Cancer

The term *cancer* refers not just to one illness but to a number of disorders that afflict plants and animals as well as people. These disorders show the common feature of the development of abnormally changed, or mutant, cells that reproduce rapidly and rob the body of nutrients. Cancerous cells may take root anywhere, such as the blood (leukemia), bones, digestive tract, lungs, and genital organs. If not controlled early, the cancerous cells may metastasize—that is, establish colonies elsewhere in the body.

With all the talk of environmental toxins and the assorted hazards of contemporary life, one might expect that cancer rates have been skyrocketing. This is not the case. According to the National Institutes of Health (1985), cancers of the bladder, prostate, colon, and rectum have been stable since the 1940s. Cancer of the stomach has been declining. Lung cancer increased markedly between the 1940s and 1980 but has recently leveled off. However, a recent rise in cases among women has offset a decline among men. Smoking seems to be the culprit. Women who have entered the work force and taken managerial positions have increased their smoking. Men, however, have been decreasing their consumption of cigarettes.

Risk Factors As with cardiovascular and many other disorders, people can inherit dispositions toward developing cancer (Moolgavkar, 1983). However, many behavior patterns markedly heighten the risk for cancer, such as smoking, drinking alcohol (especially in women), ingesting animal fats, sunbathing (which because of ultraviolet light causes skin cancer [Levy, 1985]), and, perhaps, stress.

Stress and Cancer In recent years, researchers have begun to uncover links between stress and cancer (Justice, 1985). For example, a study of children with cancer by Jacob and Charles (1980) revealed that a significant percentage had encountered severe life changes within a year of the diagnosis, often involving the death of a loved one or the loss of a close relationship.

There are also numerous studies that connect stressful life events to the onset of cancer among adults. However, this research has been criticized because it tends to be retrospective (Krantz et al., 1985). That is, cancer patients are interviewed about events preceding their diagnoses and about their psychological well-being prior to the onset of the disease. Self-reports are confounded by problems in memory and other inaccuracies. Moreover, as noted earlier in the chapter, the causal relationships in such research are clouded. For example, development of the illness might have precipitated many of the stressful events. Stress, in other words, might have been the result of the illness rather than the cause.

Experimental research that could not be conducted with humans has been conducted with rats and other animals. In one type of study, animals are injected with cancerous cells or with viruses that cause cancer and then exposed to various conditions. In this way, it can be determined which conditions influence the likelihood that the animals' immune systems will be able to fend off the antigens. Such experiments with rodents suggest that once cancer has affected the individual, stress can influence its course. In one study, for example, rats were implanted with small numbers of cancer cells so that their own immune systems would have a chance to successfully combat them (Visintainer et al., 1982). Some of the rats were then exposed to inescapable shocks, whereas others were exposed to escapable shocks or to no shock. The rats exposed to the most stressful condition—the inescapable shock—were half as likely as the other rats to reject the cancer and two times as likely to die from it.

In a study of this kind with mice, Riley (1981) studied the effects of a cancer-causing virus that can be passed from mothers to offspring by means of nursing. This virus typically produces breast cancer in 80 percent of female offspring by the time they have reached 400 days of age. Riley placed one group of female offspring at risk for cancer in a stressful environment of loud noises and noxious odors. Another group was placed in a less stressful environment. At the age of 400 days, 92 percent of the mice who developed under stressful conditions developed breast cancer, as compared to 7 percent of the controls. Moreover, the high-stress mice showed increases in levels of steroids, which depress the functioning of the body's immune system, and lower blood levels of disease-fighting antibodies. However, the "bottom line" in this experiment is of major interest: By the time another 200 days had elapsed, the low-stress mice had nearly caught up to their high-stress peers in the incidence of cancer. Stress appears to have hastened along the inevitable for many of these mice, but the ultimate outcomes were not overwhelmingly influenced by stress.

So it may be that although stress influences the timing of the onset of certain diseases, such as cancer, genetic predispositions toward disease and powerful antigens will eventually do their damage.

Truth or Fiction Revisited

It is true that stress can influence the course of cancer. Whether or not stress ever affects the ultimate outcome remains an open question.

Health psychologists have also found that the feelings of depression and helplessness that often accompany the diagnosis of cancer can interfere with recovery among humans (Goldberg & Tull, 1984; Levy et al., 1985), perhaps by suppressing the immune system. For example, a ten-year follow-up of breast cancer patients found a significantly higher survival rate for patients who met their diagnosis with anger and a "fighting spirit" rather than with helplessness or stoic acceptance (Pettingale et al., 1985). Hospitalization itself is highly stressful because it reduces the patient's sense of control over his or her own fate (Peterson & Raps, 1984), and, if handled insensitively, it might further depress the patient's own ability to fight illnesses.

Although the prospect of cancer is frightening to most of us, we are not helpless in the face of it. Here are a number of the things we can do:

1. We can control our exposure to behavioral risk factors for cancer;
2. We can go for regular medical checkups so that we discover cancer early;
3. We can regulate the amount of stress impacting upon us; and
4. If we are struck by cancer, we can fight the disease vigorously rather than be passive victims.

Health psychologists are also investigating the role of chronic stress in inflammatory diseases such as arthritis; premenstrual distress; digestive diseases such as colitis; and even metabolic diseases such as diabetes and hypoglycemia. The relationships among behavior patterns, attitudes, and illness are complex and under intense study. With some stress-related illnesses, it may be that stress determines whether or not the person will contract the disease at all. In others, it may be that an optimal environment merely delays the inevitable or that a stressful environment merely hastens the onset of the inevitable. Then, too, in different illnesses stress may have different effects on the patient's ability to recover.

Despite healthful behavior patterns, all of us become sick from time to time. In the following section we explore what psychologists have learned about the ways in which we conceptualize and respond to sickness.

THE PSYCHOLOGY OF BEING SICK

Individual differences truly hit home when it comes to our behavior during illness. Some of us refuse to go to the doctor unless we are incapable of moving. Others rush off to the doctor at the drop of a hat. Some of us deny pain and other symptoms. Others exaggerate pain. Some of us view chronic disorders such as essential hypertension and diabetes as temporary setbacks. Others see them as the lingering problems that they are. Some of us make good use of visits to the doctor. Others do not. Some of us comply with medical advice. Others do not.

In this section we first review factors that determine whether or not we seek help when we feel ill and the ways in which we conceptualize illness. Then we consider "the sick role" that is enacted in our society. Finally, we discuss patient–physician interactions and the issues involved in whether or not we comply with medical advice.

Factors that Determine Willingness to Seek Health Care

You've heard the expression, "Do as I say, not as I do." This saying applies to illness behavior, because people are much more willing to advise others to go to the doctor than they are to go themselves (Feldman, 1966). Reluctance to seek health care is related to fear of what the doctor might find; to social and demographic factors, such as gender, socioeconomic status, and ethnic background; to characteristics of the symptoms; and to the ways in which we conceptualize illness (see Figure 11.4).

Women, for example, are more likely to seek medical help than men, even when we consider visits for pregnancy and childbirth (Rosenstock & Kirscht, 1979). The gender difference may reflect the traits associated with the rugged, independent, stereotypically masculine sex role in our society, as we shall see in Chapter 14. Men, in other words, are expected to be self-sufficient. According to a U.S. Department of Health, Education, and Welfare (1979) report, people of higher socioeconomic status are more willing than persons of lower status to seek medical help, even though poor people are more likely to become ill and to eventually be hospitalized.

Mechanic (1978) found that four symptom characteristics also help determine whether we shall seek medical help:

1. *Visibility of the symptom.* For example, everything else being equal, a rash or a cut on the face is more likely to cause concern than a rash or a cut on the torso or the legs.
2. *Perceived severity of the symptom.* More severe symptoms prompt greater concern and are more likely to induce a visit to the doctor.
3. *Interference of symptoms with the person's life.* We are more likely to see the doctor when symptoms, say, make it difficult to eliminate, engage in sexual activity, eat, or move around.
4. *Frequency and persistence of the symptoms.* Symptoms that come on frequently and persist are more likely to prompt a visit to the doctor than intermittent symptoms.

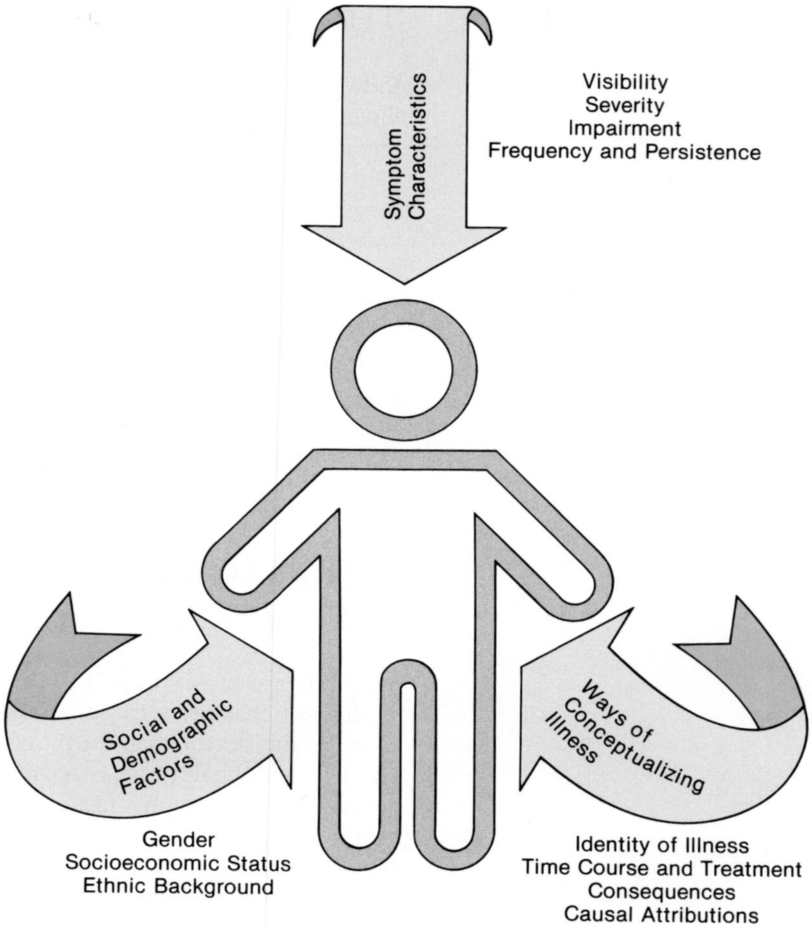

Figure 11.4
Factors that Influence the Decision to Seek Medical Advice. Social and demographic factors, symptom characteristics, and the ways in which we conceptualize the illness are factors in the decision to seek—or not to seek—medical advice.

Ways in Which We Conceptualize Illness

The ways in which we conceptualize illness are important because they, too, influence whether or not we will behave in health-enhancing ways. Howard Leventhal and his colleagues (1980, 1984; Meyer et al., 1985) have identified four components of our conceptualizations of illness:

1. *Identity of the Illness.* Our ideas about what is wrong with us provide a framework for the interpretation of symptoms. Severe chest pains, for example, can be symptoms of a heart attack, a spasm of the esophagus (the muscular tube through which food passes on the way to the stomach), indigestion, and other problems. We have a tendency to attribute symptoms to minor, common illnesses because such illnesses are more likely to be within our experiences (Lau & Russell, 1983). A proper label is the basis for proper illness behavior, such as seeking help or complying with treatment.
2. *Time Course of the Illness and the Treatment.* Accurate conceptualization of the course of a disease is important to maintaining an adequate treatment regimen. Even though professionals may tell them otherwise, people tend to erroneously view hypertension, diabetes, and bipolar affective disorder (see Chapter 12) as acute, temporary problems. These

and many other disorders can require protracted adherence to a therapeutic regimen.

3. *Consequences of the Illness.* Sometimes we do not seek medical advice for symptoms because the illnesses they suggest are minor, as in the case of cold symptoms. But we also might avoid seeking advice about symptoms such as a lump in the breast or blood in the urine because they suggest the possibility of life-threatening disorders.
4. *Causal Attributions for the Illness.* Causal attributions for illnesses are important because they influence preventive behavior as well as the seeking of proper treatment. If we attribute cardiovascular disorders and cancer purely to genetic factors, we might throw up our hands in despair at being able to influence their onsets and ignore our nutritional and activity patterns. However, recognition that there are multiple risk factors for such illnesses can motivate us to engage in daily healthful behavior patterns.

The Sick Role

Thus, various factors influence our determination of whether we are sick and, if so, what type of illness we have. Sociologist Talcott Parsons (1978) has noted that once we consider ourselves to be sick, we tend to enact "the sick role." The sick role is based on three assumptions: first, that we are not to blame for being sick; second, that being sick relieves us of our normal responsibilities; and three, that sick people do what is required to get well.

The notion that we are not to blame for being sick is complex and in many cases only partly true. For example, if we are struck by a pathogen such as the AIDS virus, shall we attribute illness to the virus *or to our own behavior, which exposed us to the virus and, in many cases, might have been prevented?* Before the AIDS virus was isolated, people could not have known what behavior patterns would increase the likelihood of exposure. But today, pathways such as sharing contaminated needles and having sexual relations with affected persons have been widely publicized. We can say, therefore, that in the majority of cases the pathogen and the behavior of the person are jointly responsible. With cancer and cardiovascular disorders there are certainly genetic risk factors, but our nutritional and activity patterns also play a role.

Depending on the illness, sick people may not be expected to go to school, work, mow the grass, or care for the children. Some people find it difficult to take on this aspect of the sick role and insist on continuing to work as much as they can. Others are all too willing to be relieved of their responsibilities! This aspect of the sick role sometimes backfires in the case of abnormal behavior. As we shall see in Chapter 13, many persons with abnormal behavior are helped rather than hurt by remaining in the community and not being hospitalized. Living at home and remaining at work keep them in touch with the realities of daily life and bolster their self-efficacy expectations. The responsibility-relieving aspect of the sick role is also one of the reasons that many psychologists object to the so-called medical model of abnormal behavior, which includes elements of the sick role.

The desire to get well is expected of sick people. In order to get well, people must frequently interact with medical experts and comply with medical advice. Let us now turn our attention to physician–patient interactions and to the issue of compliance.

Compliance with Medical Instructions and Procedures

Once we have been to see the doctor, how many of us comply with medical instructions and procedures? In a review of the literature, Sackett and Snow (1979) concluded that about 75 percent of us keep appointments we have made, but only about half of us keep appointments scheduled by the professional. More of us will take medicines to cure illnesses than to prevent them: 77 percent of us will take medicine over the short term to cure an illness, whereas 63 percent of us will take medicine to prevent it. Over the long-term, compliance drops to about 50 percent, which is especially troublesome for disorders such as hypertension, in which there may be no symptoms and protracted treatment can be required. Similarly, it has been found that only about 50 percent of patients stick to clinical exercise programs following the first six months (Dishman, 1982).

Some factors that determine compliance reside with the physician. Patients are more likely to adhere to advice from physicians who are perceived as being competent, friendly, warm, and concerned (DiNicola & DiMatteo, 1984). Patients are less likely to comply with instructions from physicians whom they perceive as being authoritarian and condescending (Gastorf & Galanos, 1983).

Truth or Fiction Revisited

It is *not* true that patients are more likely to comply with "doctor's orders" when they are issued by an authoritarian physician.

There was a time when medical training was almost completely technical, but research findings like these have prompted medical schools to train students in ways of relating to patients as people.

Health psychologists have found that patients are more likely to comply with medical instructions when illness is severe (Becker & Maiman, 1980) and when they believe that the instructions will work. Women, for example, are more likely to engage in breast self-examination when they believe that they will really be able to detect abnormal growths (Alagna & Reddy, 1984). Diabetes patients are more likely to use insulin when they believe that their regimens will help control their blood-sugar levels (Brownlee-Duffeck et al., 1987).

Physicians often prescribe drugs and other treatment regimens without explaining to patients the purposes of the treatments and their possible complications. This approach can backfire. When it comes to taking prescribed drugs, patients frequently tend not to take them or to take them incorrectly (Haynes et al., 1979). Patients are particularly likely to discontinue medications when they encounter side effects, especially unexpected side effects. Therefore, specific instructions coupled with accurate information about potential side effects appears to be most useful in inducing compliance (Baron & Byrne, 1987; Keown et al., 1984).

Cultural factors are also involved in compliance. It has been shown, for example, that Hispanic Americans are more likely to comply with medical instructions when they are issued by personnel who have an understanding of Hispanic-American culture. A study in Zimbabwe, Africa, points out that some people do not comply with medical regimens because of belief in nonscientific but traditional methods of healing (Zyazema, 1984).

As in so many other areas of life, social support is helpful in fostering compliance with medical instructions and procedures. One study, for example, found that men with supportive spouses are more likely to change

PSYCHOLOGY GOES TO WORK

Health Psychology Shows the Medical Profession How To Enhance Physician–Patient Interactions

Because of the anxiety the symptoms of illnesses provoke, most people try not to think about them when they first appear (Suls & Fletcher, 1985). By the time people visit the physician, they are frequently quite anxious about these symptoms. Anxiety during the physician-patient interview sometimes causes patients to forget to mention certain symptoms and to forget to ask questions that had been on their minds. Health psychologists have found that having patients take a few minutes before their visits to mull over their questions leads them to ask more questions and heightens their satisfaction with the interview (Roter, 1984; Thompson, 1988). Nurses and physicians can encourage patients to jot down their questions in the waiting room by offering them pads of paper and directly suggesting that they do so.

Health psychologists have found many other ways in which physicians and patients can increase the effectiveness and satisfaction of their interactions. One area involves the physician's so-called bedside manner. For example, in an experiment to determine which aspects of a physician's nonverbal behavior contributed to patient satisfaction, Harrigan and Rosenthal (1983) manipulated behaviors such as leaning forward versus sitting back. It was found that patients evaluated physicians most positively when they leaned forward rather than sat back, nodded their heads in response to patient verbalizations, and kept their arms open rather than folded. Patients are also more satisfied when their doctors encourage them to ask questions (Thompson, 1988). Patient satisfaction is not a frivolous goal—it has a direct bearing on wellness. Patients who find their doctors to be warm and interested, and who gather the information they need to know about their illnesses and treatments, are more likely to comply with medical advice.

So it seems that there are a number of things that the medical profession (and we!) can do to enhance the physician–patient relationship and to improve the prospects of profiting from medical advice.

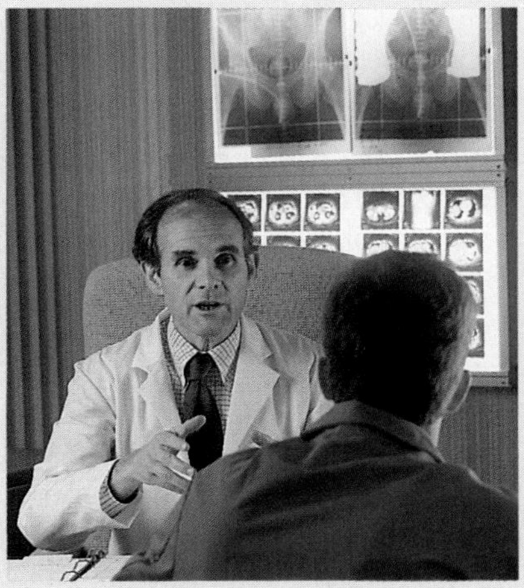

A Physician–Patient Interaction. Patients are more satisfied with visits to the doctor, and more likely to comply with medical advice, when the physician is caring and friendly. Health psychologists have also learned that patients need to understand why treatments have been prescribed. Patients are more likely to follow regimens when they believe that they will be effective.

their nutritional and activity patterns to avert cardiovascular disorders (Doherty et al., 1983).

In this chapter we have dealt primarily with physical disorders. In the following chapter we turn our attention to psychological disorders—also referred to as patterns of abnormal behavior.

SUMMARY

1. **What is health psychology?** Health psychology is an emerging field of psychology that studies the relationships between psychological factors (e.g., overt behavior, emotions, stress, beliefs, and attitudes) and the prevention and treatment of physical illness.

2. **What is stress?** Stress is the demand made on an organism to adjust. Whereas some stress is desirable (eustress) to keep us alert and occupied, too much stress can tax our adjustive capacities and contribute to physical illness.

3. **What are some sources of stress?** Sources of stress include daily hassles, life changes, pain, frustration, conflict, irrational beliefs, and Type A behavior. Type A behavior is characterized by aggressiveness, a sense of time urgency, and competitiveness.

4. **What psychological factors moderate the impact of stress?** These include positive self-efficacy expectations, psychological hardiness, a sense of humor, predictability of stressors, and social support.

Self-efficacy expectations—our beliefs that we can cope successfully—encourage us to persist in difficult tasks and to endure pain and discomfort. Psychological hardiness is characterized by commitment, challenge, and control.

5. **What is the general adaptation syndrome (GAS)?** The GAS is a body response triggered by perception of a stressor and consists of three stages: the alarm, resistance, and exhaustion stages.

6. **What is the role of the endocrine system in the body's response to stress?** In response to stress, the hypothalamus and pituitary glands secrete hormones that stimulate the adrenal cortex to release cortisol and other steroids. Corticosteroids help the body resist stress by fighting inflammation and allergic reactions. Adrenaline and norepinephrine are also secreted by the adrenal medulla, and adrenaline arouses the body by activating the sympathetic division of the autonomic nervous system.

7. **What is the role of the autonomic nervous system (ANS) in the body's response to stress?** The sympathetic division of the ANS is highly active during the alarm and resistance stages of the GAS, and this activity is characterized by rapid heartbeat and respiration rate, release of stores of sugar, muscle tension, and other responses that spend the body's stores of energy. The parasympathetic division of the ANS predominates during the exhaustion stage of the GAS, and its activity is characterized by responses, such as digestive processes, that help restore the body's reserves of energy.

8. **What are the functions of the immune system?** The first function of the immune system is to engulf and kill pathogens, wornout body cells, and cancerous cells. The second function of the immune system is to "remember" pathogens to facilitate future combat against them. The third function is to facilitate inflammation, which increases the numbers of white blood cells brought to a damaged area.

9. **What are the effects of stress on the immune system?** By stimulating the release of corticosteroids, stress depresses the functioning of the immune system. (For example, steroids counter inflammation.)

10. **What kinds of headaches are there, and how are they related to stress?** The most common kinds are muscle-tension headaches and migraine headaches. Stress causes and compounds headache pain by stimulating muscle tension.

11. **What is hypertension, and how is it related to stress?** Hypertension is elevated blood pressure. Persistent hypertension in the absence of external stressors is called essential hypertension. Stress increases the blood pressure by activating the sympathetic division of the ANS.

12. **What are the risk factors for cardiovascular disorders?** They include family history; physiological conditions such as hypertension and high levels of serum cholesterol; behavior patterns such as heavy drinking, smoking, eating fatty foods, and Type A behavior; work overload; chronic tension and fatigue; and physical inactivity.

13. **What are the risk factors for cancer?** Risk factors for cancer include family history, smoking, drinking alcohol, eating animal fats, sunbathing, and stress.

14. **What behavioral measures contribute to the prevention and treatment of cancer?** The following measures do: controlling our exposure to behavioral risk factors for cancer; going for regular medical checkups; regulating the amount of stress impacting upon us; and vigorously fighting cancer if we are afflicted.

15. **What factors influence willingness to seek health care when we are ill?** Factors that influence willingness to bring symptoms to the attention of a health professional include visibility of the symptoms, perceived severity of the symptoms, interference of the symptoms with our lives, and frequency and persistence of the symptoms.

16. **How do we conceptualize illness?** There are four components to our conceptualization of illness: the identity of the illness, the time course of the illness and the treatment, the consequences of the illness, and our causal attributions for the illness. Our conceptualization of the illness influences whether or not we will seek medical attention and comply with medical advice.

17. **What are the components of the sick role in our society?** The sick role has three components: first, that we are not to be blamed for being sick; second, that sickness relieves us of responsibilities; and third, that we should desire to get well and take steps in that direction.

18. **What factors influence compliance with medical instructions and procedures?** Factors that influence compliance include the physician's bedside manner (we are more likely to comply with advice from competent, friendly, concerned physicians), belief that the advice will be effective, ability to cope with side effects, cultural factors, and social support.

PSYCHOLOGY AND MODERN LIFE

What do these things have in common: (1) Telling yourself that you can live with another person's disappointment, (2) taking a deep breath and telling yourself to relax, (3) taking the scenic route to work, and (4) jogging for half an hour? These are all methods psychologists have suggested for helping us cope with the stresses of modern life.

Ways of Coping with Stress

Stress takes many forms and can have a harmful effect on our psychological well being and physical health. Let us highlight a number of ways of coping with stress: controlling irrational thoughts, lowering arousal, modifying the Type A behavior pattern, and—a method that you might find somewhat surprising—exercising. We shall see that exercise has psychological as well as physical benefits.

Controlling Irrational Thoughts Consider the following experiences to see whether you encounter pressures from your own thoughts:

1. You have difficulty with the first item on a test and become absolutely convinced that you will flunk?
2. You want to express your genuine feelings but think that you might make another person angry or upset?
3. You haven't been able to get to sleep for 15 minutes and assume that you will lie awake the whole night and feel "wrecked" in the morning?
4. You're not sure what decision to make, so you try to put your conflicts out of your mind by going out, playing cards, or watching TV?
5. You decide not to play tennis or go jogging because your form isn't perfect and you're in less than perfect condition?

If you have had these or similar experiences, it may be because you harbor a number of the irrational beliefs identified by Albert Ellis (see pages 438–439). These beliefs may make you overly concerned about the approval of others (experience 2 in the preceding list) or perfectionistic (experience 5). They may lead you to think that you can best relieve yourself of certain dilemmas by pretending that they do not exist (experience 4) or that a minor setback will invariably lead to greater problems (experiences 1 and 3).

How, then, do we change irrational or catastrophizing thoughts? The answer is deceivingly simple: We change these thoughts by changing them. However, change may require some work, and before we can change our thoughts, we must first become aware of them.

Meichenbaum's Three Steps for Controlling Catastrophizing Thoughts Cognitive psychologist Donald Meichenbaum (1976, 1983) suggests a three-step procedure for controlling the irrational and catastrophizing thoughts that often accompany feelings of pain, anxiety, frustration, conflict, or tension:

1. Develop awareness of these thoughts through careful self-examination. Study the examples at the beginning of this section or in Table 11.2 to see if these experiences and thought patterns apply to you. (Also carefully read Ellis's irrational beliefs on pages 438–439 and ask yourself whether any of them tend to govern your behavior.) When you encounter anxiety or frustration, pay careful attention to your thoughts. Are they helping to point toward a solution, or are they compounding your problems?
2. Prepare thoughts that are incompatible with the irrational and catastrophizing thoughts, and practice saying them firmly to yourself. (If nobody is nearby, why not say them firmly aloud?)
3. Reward yourself with a mental pat on the back for effective changes in beliefs and thought patterns.

Lowering Arousal As noted in the chapter, stress tends to trigger high levels of activity of the sympathetic division of the autonomic nervous system—or, briefly, arousal. Arousal is a sign that something may be wrong, a message to survey the situation and take appropriate action. But once you are aware that a stressor is acting upon you and have developed a plan to cope with it, it is no longer helpful to have blood pounding so fiercely through your arteries. Psychologists and other scientists have developed many methods for teaching people to lower excessive arousal. They include meditation, biofeedback (both discussed in Chapter 4), and progressive relaxation.

Meditation appears to facilitate adjustment to stress without decreasing awareness. In this way it does not reduce perception of potential threats. In one experiment, Orne-Johnson (1973) exposed meditators and nonmeditators to unpredictable loud noises. Meditators stopped showing a stress reaction, as measured by the amount of sweat in the palms of the hands, earlier than nonmeditators. In another experiment, Goleman and Schwartz (1976) used heart rate and sweat to measure stress reactions to a film that explicitly portrayed accidents and death. Meditators showed a greater alarm reaction than nonmeditators when the contents of the film were announced, but they recovered to normal levels of arousal more rapidly during the showings. Meditators in this study thus showed greater alertness to potential threat—a factor that could allow them to develop a plan for dealing with a stressor more rapidly—but also showed more ability to control arousal.

Table 11.2
Controlling Irrational Beliefs and Thoughts

Irrational Thoughts	Incompatible (Coping) Thoughts
"Oh, my God, I'm going to lose all control!"	"This is painful and upsetting, but I don't have to go to pieces."
"This will never end."	"This will come to an end, even if it's hard to see right now."
"It'll be awful if Mom gives me that look."	"It's more pleasant when Mom's happy with me, but I can live with it if she isn't."
"How can I go out there? I'll look like a fool."	"So you're not perfect; that doesn't mean that you're going to look stupid. And so what if someone thinks you look stupid? You can live with that, too. Just stop worrying and have some fun."
"My heart's going to leap out of my chest! How much can I stand?"	"Easy—hearts don't leap out of chests. Stop and think! Distract yourself. Breathe slowly, in and out."
"What can I do? There's nothing I can do!"	"Easy—stop and think. Just because you can't think of a solution right now doesn't mean there's nothing you can do. Take it a minute at a time. Breathe easy."

Do irrational beliefs and catastrophizing thoughts compound the stress you experience? Cognitive psychologists suggest that you can cope with stress by becoming aware of self-defeating beliefs and thoughts and replacing them with rational, calming beliefs and thoughts.

In research on biofeedback training (BFT) and stress, Sirota and his colleagues (1976) trained college women to slow their heart rates voluntarily, after which they reported a painful electric shock to be less stressful. College students at another campus reduced speech anxiety through BFT that taught them to control their heart rates (Gatchel & Proctor, 1976).

Meditation seems to focus on the cognitive components of a stress reaction, whereas biofeedback can be directed at various physiological functions, such as heart rate and muscle tension. Progressive relaxation focuses on reducing muscle tension, although the instructions to slow down the breathing and to develop mental imagery—for example, feelings of heaviness in the limbs—foster other responses that are incompatible with the alarm reaction. But all three methods lower arousal, enhance self-efficacy expectations, and promote an internal locus of control.

Progressive Relaxation University of Chicago physician Edmund Jacobson (1938), the originator of progressive relaxation, noted that people tense their muscles when they are under stress, compounding their discomfort. Jacobson developed the method of *progressive relaxation* to teach people how to relax these tensions. In this method, people purposefully tense a muscle group before relaxing it. This sequence allows them to (1) develop awareness of their muscle tensions and (2) differentiate between feelings of tension and relaxation. The method is "progressive" because people move on, or progress, from one muscle group to another.

Progressive relaxation lowers the arousal of the alarm reaction (Paul, 1966b). It has been found to be useful for stress-related physical illnesses ranging from headaches (Blanchard et al., 1985, 1987; Teders et al., 1984) to hypertension (Agras et al., 1983; Taylor et al., 1977). You can experience muscle relaxation in the arms by doing the following:

Settle down in a reclining chair, dim the lights, and loosen any tight clothing. Use the instructions given below, which were written by Joseph Wolpe and Arnold Lazarus (1966, p. 177). The instructions can be memorized (slight variations from the text will do no harm), tape-recorded, or read aloud by a friend. For instructions concerning relaxation of the entire body, consult a behavior therapist or other helping professional familiar with the technique.

Settle back as comfortably as you can. Let yourself relax to the best of your ability. . . . Now, as you relax like that, clench your right fist, just clench your fist tighter and tighter, and study the tension as you do so. Keep it clenched and feel the tension in your right fist, hand, forearm . . . and now relax. Let the fingers of your right hand become loose, and observe the contrast in your feelings. . . . Now, let yourself go and try to become more relaxed all over. . . . Once more, clench your right fist really tight . . . hold it, and notice the tension again. . . . Now let go, relax; your fingers straighten out, and you notice the difference once more. . . . Now repeat that with your left fist. Clench your left fist while the rest of your body relaxes; clench that fist tighter and feel the tension . . . and now relax. Again enjoy the contrast. . . . Repeat that once more, clench the left fist, tight and tense. . . . Now do the opposite of tension—relax and feel the difference. Continue relaxing like that for a while. . . . Clench both fists tighter and together, both fists tense, forearms tense, study the sensations . . . and relax; straighten out your fingers and feel that relaxation. Continue relaxing your hands and forearms more and more. . . . Now bend your elbows and tense your biceps, tense them harder and study the tension feelings . . . all right, straighten out your arms, let them relax and feel that difference again. Let the relaxation develop. . . . Once more, tense your biceps; hold the tension and observe it carefully. . . . Straighten the arms and relax; relax to the best of your ability. . . . Each time, pay close attention to your feelings when you tense up and when you relax. Now straighten your arms, straighten them so that you feel most tension in the triceps muscles along the back of your arms; stretch your arms and feel that tension. . . . And now relax. Get your arms back into a comfortable position. Let the relaxation proceed on its own. The arms should feel comfortably heavy as you allow them to relax. . . . Straighten the arms once more so that you feel the tension in the triceps muscles; straighten them. Feel that tension . . . and relax. Now let's concentrate on pure relaxation in the arms without any tension. Get your arms comfortable and let them relax further and further. Continue relaxing your arms even further. Even when your arms seem fully relaxed, try to go that extra bit further; try to achieve deeper and deeper levels of relaxation.

Knowledge of ways of coping with self-defeating thoughts and of reducing arousal can help us cope with test anxiety.

Coping with Test Anxiety How many times have you heard these complaints? "I just know I'm going to flunk." "I study hard and memorize everything, but when I get in there my mind goes blank." "I don't know what's wrong with me—I just can't take tests." "The way I do on standardized tests, I'll never get into graduate school." Test anxiety is a frustrating handicap. When we study diligently, test anxiety seems a particularly cruel obstacle to good grades.

Yet we are not born with test anxiety. Test anxiety appears to reflect a combination of high arousal and self-defeating thoughts, including critical self-evaluations. People with high test anxiety show high levels of arousal during tests and are likely to report signs of sympathetic arousal such as dryness in the mouth and rapid heart rate (Galassi et al., 1981). On a cognitive level, these people have more negative thoughts and are more self-critical than people with low or moderate test anxiety, even when they are performing just as well (Galassi et al., 1984; Holroyd et al., 1978; Meichenbaum & Butler, 1980). Moreover, they allow their self-criticisms, and negative thoughts of the sort shown in Table 11.3, to *distract* them from working effectively on their tests (Arkin et al., 1982; Bandura, 1977; Sarason, 1984). As you can see in Table 11.4, many of these thoughts catastrophize the test-taking situation, and, in many instances, they are irrational.

Because test anxiety is often linked to anxiety-evoking, distracting thoughts, it is appropriate to cope with test anxiety by challenging these thoughts and returning one's attention to the test itself (Goldfried, 1988).

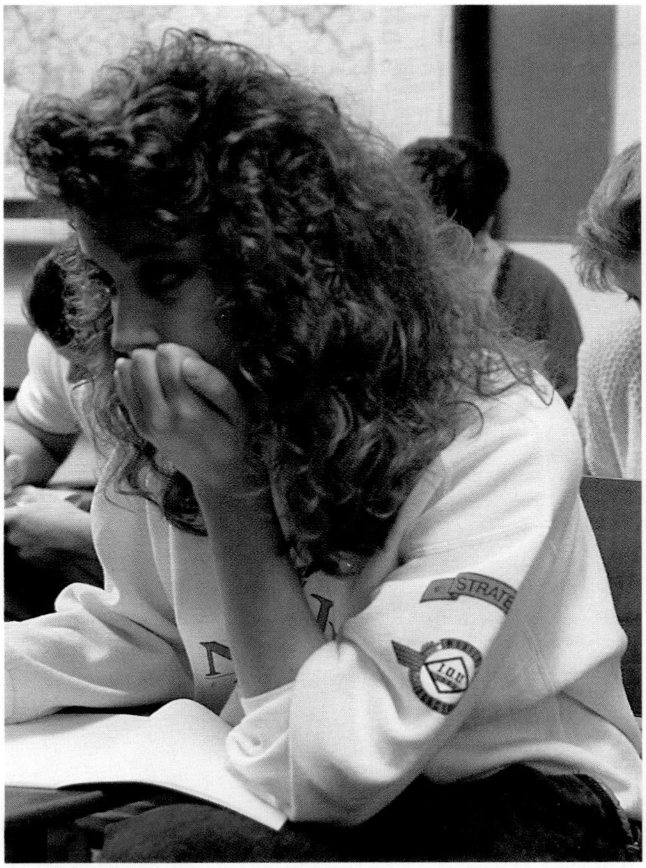

Test Anxiety. Test anxiety reflects a combination of high arousal and self-defeating thoughts, including critical self-evaluation. Test-anxious students have more negative thoughts and are more self-critical than people with low or moderate test anxiety, even when they perform just as well. Moreover, they allow their negative thoughts to distract them from the test items.

College students on several campuses have reduced test anxiety and improved their test grades through such a method—cognitive restructuring.

Participants in one study of this method (Goldfried et al., 1978) pinpointed their self-defeating thoughts by imagining themselves in the testing situation and then searching for the mental villains. They then restructured their responses to these thoughts by constructing rational alternative thoughts, as shown in Table 11.4. They practiced the rational alternatives and gave themselves mental pats on the back for improved performance. The method led to significantly higher grades.

Controlling catastrophizing thoughts along with lowering the arousal of your alarm reaction reduces the effect of the stressor, whether it is pain, anxiety, or feelings of frustration. These methods give you the chance to develop a plan for effective action. When effective ac-

Table 11.3
Percent of Positive and Negative Thoughts for University Students with Low or High Test Anxiety

Thought	Low Test Anxiety (Percent)	High Test Anxiety (Percent)
Positive Thoughts		
Will do all right on test	71	43
Mind is clear, can concentrate	49	26
Feel in control of my reactions	46	23
Negative Thoughts		
Wish I could get out or test was over	46	65
Test is hard	45	64
Not enough time to finish	23	49
Work I put into studying won't be shown by my grade	16	44
Stuck on a question and it's making it difficult to answer others	13	34
Mind is blank or can't think straight	11	31
Going to do poorly on test	11	28
Think how awful it will be if I fail or do poorly	11	45

Highly test-anxious students report fewer positive thoughts and more negative thoughts while taking tests. Moreover, their negative thoughts are linked to signs of sympathetic arousal such as dryness in the mouth and rapid heart rate.

Source of data: Galassi, Frierson & Sharer, 1981, pp. 56, 58.

Table 11.4
Rational Alternatives to Irrational Cognitions Concerning Test Taking

Irrational Thoughts	Rational Alternatives
"I'm the only one who's going so bananas over this thing."	"Nonsense, lots of people have test anxiety. Just don't let it take your mind off the test itself."
"I'm running out of time!"	"Time is passing, but just take it item by item and answer what you can. Getting bent out of shape won't help."
"This is impossible! Are all the items going to be this bad?"	"Just take it item by item. They're all different. Don't assume the worst."
"I just can't remember a thing!"	"Just slow down and remember what you can. Take a few moments and some things will come back to you. If not, go on to the next item."
"Everyone else is smarter than I am!"	"Probably not, but maybe they're not distracting themselves from the test by catastrophizing. Just do the best you can and take it easy. Breathe easy, in and out."
"I've got to get out of here! I can't take it anymore!"	"Even if you feel that you need to leave now and then, you don't have to act on it. Just focus on the test items, one by one."
"I just can't do well on tests."	"That's only true if you believe it's true. Back to the items, one by one."
"There are a million items left!"	"Quite a few, but not a million. Just take them one by one and answer as many as you can. Focus on each item as it comes, not on the number of items."
"Everyone else is leaving. They're all finished before me."	"Fast work is no guarantee of good work. Even if most of them do well, it doesn't have to mean that you *won't* do well. Take all the time you need. Back to the items, one by one."
"If I flunk, everything is ruined!"	"You won't be happy if you fail, but it won't be the end of the world either. Just take it item by item and don't let worrying distract you. Breathe easy, in and out."

To restructure your cognitions concerning test taking, prepare rational alternatives to your irrational thoughts and rehearse them. Don't let catastrophizing distract you from the test items.

tion is not possible, controlling your thoughts and your level of arousal can still enhance your capacity to tolerate discomfort.

Modifying the Type A Behavior Pattern Type A behavior is identified by a sense of time urgency, hostility, and hard-driving, self-destructive behavior patterns. Cardiologist Meyer Friedman (one of the originators of the Type A concept) and registered nurse Diane Ulmer reported in 1984 on some of the results of the San Francisco Recurrent Coronary Prevention Project (RCPP). The RCPP was designed to help Type A heart-attack victims modify their behavior in an effort to avert future attacks. After three years, participants placed in a treatment group in which they learned to reduce Type A behavior patterns had only one-third as many recurrent heart attacks as participants placed in a control group.

The three broad RCPP guidelines were alleviating participants' sense of time urgency, their hostility, and their self-destructive tendencies. Of course, subjects were also counseled to give up smoking, eat a low-fat diet, and establish a peaceful environment. The buffering effects of a sense of humor were noted, too.

Alleviating Your Sense of Time Urgency Stop driving yourself—get out and walk. Too often we jump out of bed to the sound of an abrasive alarm, hop into a shower, fight commuter crowds, and arrive at class or work with no time to spare. Then we become involved in our hectic day. For Type A people, the day begins urgently and never lets up.

The first step in coping with a sense of time urgency is confronting and replacing the beliefs that support it. Friedman and Ulmer (1984) note that Type A individuals tend to harbor the following beliefs:

1. "My sense of time urgency has helped me gain social and economic success" (p. 179). *The idea that impatience and irritation contribute to success, according to Friedman and Ulmer, is absurd.*
2. "I can't do anything about it" (p. 182). The belief that we cannot change ourselves is self-defeating and irrational, as noted by cognitive psychologist Albert Ellis (see Chapter 13). *Even in late adulthood, note Friedman and Ulmer, old habits can be discarded and new habits can be acquired.*

Friedman and Ulmer (1984) also use many exercises to help combat the sense of time urgency. Note this sampling:

1. Engage in more social activities with family and friends.
2. Spend a few minutes each day recalling events from the distant past. Check old photos of family and friends.

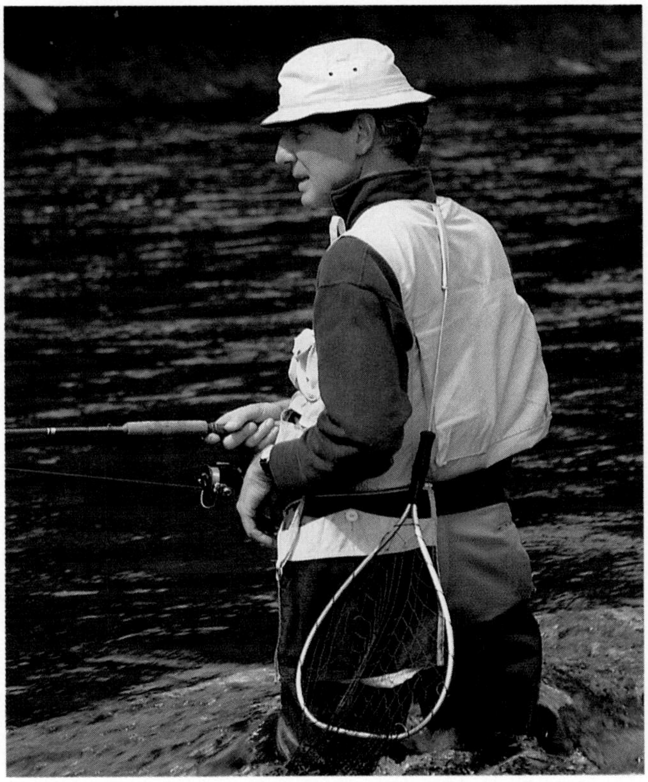

Coping with the Type-A Sense of Time Urgency. The San Francisco Recurrent Coronary Prevention Project has helped many Type A heart-attack victims modify their behavior in an effort to avert future attacks. Type A individuals modify their behavior to alleviate their sense of time urgency, their hostility, and their "self-destructive tendencies," such as smoking, gorging on high-fat foods, and drinking heavily.

3. Read books—literature, drama, politics, biographies, science, nature, science fiction. (Not books on business or on climbing the corporate ladder!)
4. Visit museums and art galleries for their aesthetic value—not for speculation on the price of paintings.
5. Go to the movies, ballet, and theater.
6. Write letters to family and friends.
7. Take a course in art, or begin violin or piano lessons.
8. Remind yourself daily that life is by nature unfinished and you do not need (and should not want) to have all your projects finished on a given date.
9. Ask a family member what he or she did that day, and actually *listen* to the answer.

University of Colorado psychologist Richard Suinn (1976, 1982) adds the following suggestions for alleviating the sense of time urgency:

10. Get a nice-sounding alarm clock!
11. Move about slowly when you awake. Stretch.
12. Drive more slowly. This saves energy, lives, and traffic citations. It's also less stressful than racing the clock.
13. Don't wolf lunch. Get out; make it an occasion.
14. Don't tumble words out. Speak more slowly. Interrupt less frequently.
15. Get up earlier to sit and relax, watch the morning news with a cup of tea, or meditate. This may mean going to bed earlier.
16. Leave home earlier and take a more scenic route to work or school. Avoid rush-hour jams.
17. Don't car-pool with last-minute rushers. Drive with a group that leaves earlier or use public transportation.
18. Have a snack or relax at school or work before the "day" begins.
19. Don't do two things at once. Avoid scheduling too many classes or appointments back to back.
20. Use breaks to read, exercise, or meditate. Limit intake of stimulants like caffeine. Try decaffeinated coffee (tasty when brewed, not instant).
21. Space chores. Why have the car and typewriter repaired, work, shop, and drive a friend to the airport all in one day?
22. If rushed, allow unessential work to go till the next day.
23. Set aside some time for yourself: for music, a hot bath, exercise, relaxation. (If your life will not permit this, get a new life.)

Alleviating Your Hostility Friedman and Ulmer (1984) note that hostility, like time urgency, is supported by a number of irrational beliefs. So it is up to us to begin again by recognizing our irrational beliefs and replacing them with new beliefs. Irrational beliefs that support hostility include the following:

1. "I need a certain amount of hostility to get ahead in the world" (p. 222). *Becoming readily irritated, aggravated, and angered does not contribute to getting ahead.*
2. "I can't do anything about my hostility" (p. 222). Is any comment necessary?
3. "Other people tend to be ignorant and inept" (p. 223). Surely some of them are, but the world is what it is, and, as Albert Ellis points out, we just expose ourselves to aggravation by demanding that other people be what they are not.
4. "I don't believe I can ever feel at ease with doubt and uncertainty" (p. 225). There are ambiguities in life; certain things remain unpredictable. Becoming irritated and aggravated doesn't make things less uncertain.
5. "Giving and receiving love is a sign of weakness" (228). This belief is rugged individualism carried to the extreme, and it can isolate us from social support.

Friedman and Ulmer (1984) also offer a number of suggestions in addition to replacing irrational beliefs:

1. Tell your spouse and children that you love them.
2. Make some new friends.
3. Let friends know that you stand ready to help them.
4. Get a pet. (Take care of it!)
5. Don't talk to another person about subjects on which you know that the two of you hold divergent and set opinions.
6. When other people do things that fall short of your expectations, consider the situational factors such as level of education or cultural background that might limit or govern their behavior. Don't assume that they "will" the behavior that distresses you.
7. Look for the beauty and joy in things.
8. Stop cursing so much.
9. Express appreciation for the help and encouragement of others.
10. Play to lose, at least some of the time. (Ouch?)
11. Say "Good morning" in a cheerful manner.

12. Look at your face in the mirror at various times during the day. Search for signs of aggravation and anger and ask yourself if you need to look like that.

Alleviating Your Self-Destructive Tendencies Friedman and Ulmer (1984) assert that Type A individuals harbor (frequently unconscious) wishes to destroy themselves. We cannot accept this view without evidence, but there is no doubt that many of us overeat, gorge on high-fat foods, drink heavily, fail to exercise, and work 16-hour workdays month after month with full knowledge that such behavior can be harmful.

Here we are advised to monitor our behavior throughout the day and to determine whether it is health-enhancing or health-impairing. If we are doing things that are health-impairing, are we going to continue them or modify them? If we're not going to modify them, why not? Are we going to tell ourselves we cannot change? Do we think so little of ourselves that we do not think it is worth it to change our behavior?

A little honest self-reflection is in order.

Exercising: Run for Your Life? Exercise, particularly aerobic exercise, can enhance our psychological well being and help us cope with stress as well as foster physical health. *Aerobic exercise* is any kind of exercise that requires a sustained increase in the consumption of oxygen. Kenneth Cooper (1982, 1985), the originator of the term *aerobic,* suggests that at least five minutes of continued effort is required to obtain the "training effects" of aerobic exercise—that is, to promote cardiovascular fitness. Aerobic exercises include but are not limited to running and jogging, running in place, walking (at more than a "leisurely pace"), aerobic dancing, jumping rope, swimming, bicycle riding, basketball, racquetball, and cross-country skiing.

Anaerobic exercises, in contrast, involve short bursts of muscle activity. Examples of anaerobic exercises are weight training, use of Nautilus-type equipment, calisthenics (which usually allow rest periods between exercises), and sports such as baseball, in which there are infrequent bursts of strenuous activity. Anaerobic exercises can strengthen muscles and improve flexibility.

Physiological Benefits of Exercise The major physiological effect of exercise is the promotion of *fitness.* Fitness is a complex concept (Kuntzleman, 1978) that includes muscle strength; muscle endurance; suppleness or flexibility; cardiorespiratory, or aerobic, fitness; and changes in body composition so that the ratio of muscle to fat is increased, usually as a result of both building muscle and reducing fat.

Cardiovascular fitness, or "condition," means that the body can use greater amounts of oxygen during vigorous activity and pump more blood with each heart beat (Pollock et al., 1978). Because the conditioned athlete's heart pumps more blood with each beat, he or she usually has a slower pulse rate—that is, fewer heart beats per minute. However, during aerobic exercise, the person may double or even triple his or her resting heart rate for many minutes at a time.

As noted in the chapter, stress has cardiovascular costs. Research suggests that sustained physical activity not only fosters fitness but also reduces the risks of cardiovascular disorders, as measured by incidence of heart attacks and mortality rates. A well-known English study by Jeremy Morris and his colleagues (1953) correlated the incidence of cardiovascular disorders and physical activity among transportation and postal workers. Conductors aboard London's double-decker buses, who moved about the buses collecting fares, had about half the heart attacks of the more sedentary drivers. Among postal workers, mail carriers had significantly fewer heart attacks than clerks.

Ralph Paffenbarger (1972) and his colleagues surveyed some 3,700 San Francisco longshoremen and found that those who handled heavy cargo had only about 60 percent as many heart attacks as those engaged in less strenuous activity. To date, Paffenbarger and his colleagues (1978, 1984, 1986) have been tracking some 17,000 Harvard University alumni by means of university records and questionnaires and correlating the group's incidence of heart attacks with their levels of physical activity. As shown in Figure 11.5, the incidence of heart attacks among the alumni declines as the physical activity level rises to burning about 2,000 calories a week—the exercise equivalent of jogging about 20 miles a week. But above 2,000 calories, the incidence of heart attacks begins to climb again, although not steeply. Inactive alumni run the highest risks of heart attacks, and alumni who burn at least 2,000 calories a week through exercise live two years longer, on the average, than their less active counterparts.

Of course there is an important limitation to the Morris and Paffenbarger studies: They are correlational, not experimental. It is possible that persons in better health choose to engage in, and enjoy, higher levels of physical activity. If such is the case, then their lower incidence of heart attacks and their lower mortality rates would be attributable to their initial superior health, not to physical activity.

However, an experiment with monkeys appears to confirm the cardiovascular benefits of sustained activity (Kramsch et al., 1981). Three groups of nine monkeys each were assigned at random to the following conditions: a sedentary group of monkeys who received a low-fat diet; another sedentary group switched to a diet high in fats and cholesterol after 12 months; and an active group of monkeys who gradually worked up to an hour

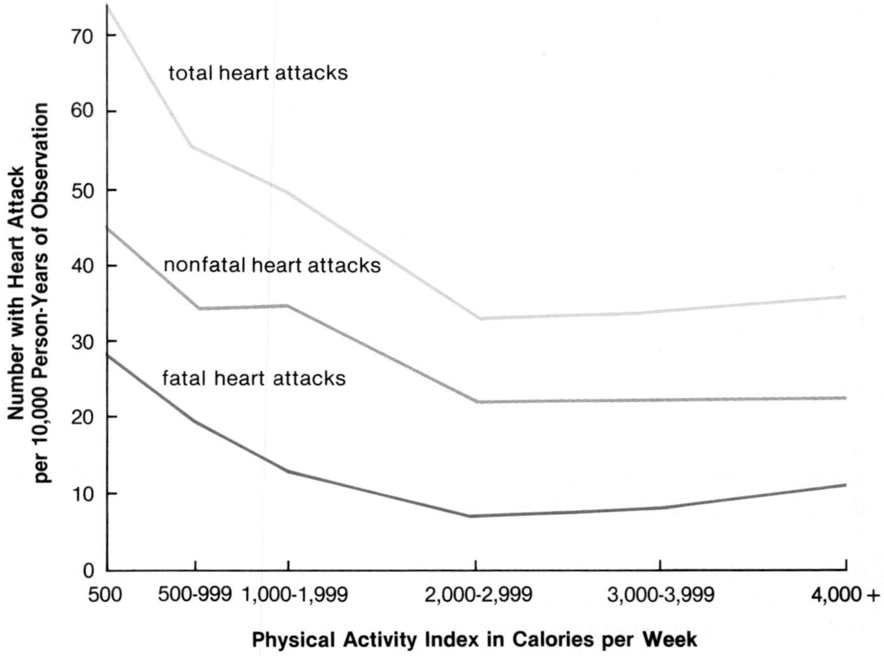

Figure 11.5
Incidence of Heart Attacks and Level of Physical Activity. Paffenbarger and his colleagues have correlated the incidence of heart attacks with level of physical activity among 17,000 Harvard alumni. The incidence of heart attacks declines as the activity level rises to burning about 2,000 calories a week by means of physical activity. Above 2,000 calories a week, however, the incidence of heart attacks begins to climb gradually again, although not steeply.

of exercise on a treadmill three times weekly, and who were also switched to the diet high in fats and cholesterol. The animals were monitored over a 42-month period. It turns out that the monkeys who exercised on the treadmill had lower levels of health-impairing cholesterol than their sedentary counterparts. Moreover, arteriosclerosis and sudden death were significantly more frequent occurrences within the sedentary groups.

Psychological Benefits of Exercise Psychologists have been keenly interested in the effects of exercise on psychological variables such as depression. Articles have appeared on exercise as "therapy"—for example, "running therapy" (Greist, 1984).

Depression is characterized by inactivity and feelings of helplessness. Aerobic exercise is, in a sense, the "opposite" of inactivity, and success at it might also help alleviate feelings of helplessness. In a notable experiment, McCann and Holmes (1984) assigned mildly depressed college women at random to aerobic exercise, a progressive-relaxation placebo, and a no-treatment control group. The relaxation group showed some improvement, but aerobic exercise made dramatic inroads on students' depression. Other experiments also suggest that aerobic exercise alleviates feelings of depression, at least among mildly and moderately depressed individuals (Buffone, 1984; Greist, 1984).

Still other research suggests that sustained exercise alleviates feelings of anxiety (Long, 1984) and boosts feelings of self-esteem (Sonstroem, 1984).

Getting Started So, how about you? Are you considering climbing aboard the exercise bandwagon? If so, consider the following suggestions:

1. Unless you have engaged in sustained and vigorous exercise recently, seek the advice of a medical expert. If you smoke, have a family history of cardiovascular disorders, are overweight, or are over 40, get a stress test.
2. Consider joining a beginners aerobics class. Group leaders are not usually experts in physiology, but at least they "know the steps." You'll also be among other beginners and derive the benefits of social support.
3. Get the proper equipment to facilitate performance and help avert injury.
4. Read up on the activity you are considering. There are many excellent books on the market, such as the recent Kenneth Cooper (1982, 1985) books on aerobic exercise, that will give you an idea of how to get started and how fast you can expect to progress.
5. Try to select activities that you can sustain for a lifetime. Don't worry about building yourself up rapidly. Enjoy yourself, and your strength and endurance will progress on their own. If you do not enjoy what you're doing, you're not likely to stick to it.

6. Keep a diary or log and note your progress. If running, note the paths or streets you follow, the distance you run, the weather conditions, and any remarkable details that come to mind. Check your notes now and then to remind yourself of enjoyable paths and experiences.
7. If you feel severe pain, don't try to exercise "through" it. Soreness is to be expected for beginners (and some old-timers now and then). In that sense, soreness, at least when intermittent, is normal. But sharp pain is abnormal and a sign that something is wrong.
8. Have fun!

Modern life has its stresses, and none of us is completely immune to them. However, psychological knowledge can help us recognize the sources of stress in our life and cope with them.

Outline

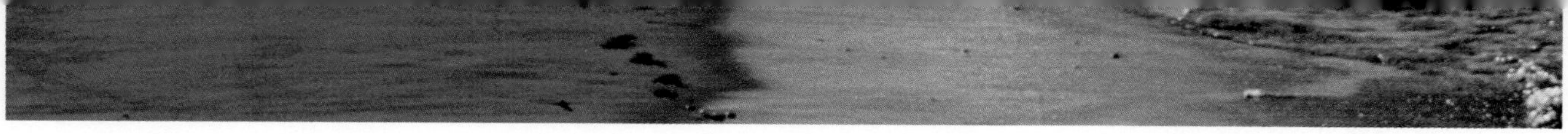

12 Abnormal Behavior

Truth or Fiction?

- □ A man shot the president of the United States in front of millions of television witnesses, yet was found not guilty by a court of law.
- □ In the Middle Ages, innocent people were drowned to prove that they were not possessed by the Devil.
- □ Stressful experiences can lead to recurrent nightmares.
- □ Some people have more than one personality, and the personalities may have different allergies and eyeglass prescriptions.
- □ People have lost the use of their legs or eyes under stress, even though there was nothing medically wrong with them.
- □ Some college women control their weight by going on cycles of binge eating and self-induced vomiting.
- □ It is abnormal to feel depressed.
- □ People who threaten suicide are only seeking attention.
- □ In some abnormal behavior problems, people see and hear things that are not actually there.
- □ Strip-teasers are exhibitionists.

The Ohio State campus lived in terror throughout the long fall of 1978. Four college women were abducted, were forced to cash checks or obtain money with their instant-cash cards, then were raped. A mysterious phone call led to the arrest of a 23-year-old drifter, William, who had been dismissed from the Navy.

William was not the boy next door.

Several psychologists and psychiatrists who interviewed William concluded that ten personalities—eight male and two female—resided within him (Keyes, 1982). His personality had been "fractured" by an abusive childhood. The personalities showed distinct facial expressions, vocal patterns, and memories. They even performed differently on personality and intelligence tests.

Arthur, the most rational personality, spoke with a British accent. Danny and Christopher were normal, quiet adolescents. Christene was a 3-year-old girl. It was Tommy, a 16-year-old, who had enlisted in the Navy. Allen was 18 and smoked. Adelena, a 19-year-old lesbian personality, had committed the rapes. Who had made the mysterious phone call? Probably David, aged 9, an anxious child personality.

The defense claimed that William was suffering from **multiple personality.** Several distinct personalities dwelled within him. Some were aware of the others; some believed that they were the sole occupants. Billy, the core personality, had learned to sleep as a child to avoid the abuse of his father. A psychiatrist asserted that Billy had also been "asleep," in a "psychological coma," during the abductions. Therefore Billy should be found innocent by reason of **insanity.**

On December 4, 1978, Billy was found not guilty by reason of insanity. He was committed to an institution for the mentally ill and released in 1984.

In 1982, John Hinckley was also found not guilty of the assassination attempt on President Reagan's life by reason of insanity. Expert witnesses testified that he was suffering from **schizophrenia.** Hinckley, too, was committed to an institution for the mentally ill.

Truth or Fiction Revisited

It is true that a man shot the president of the United States in front of millions of television witnesses and was found not guilty by a court of law—not guilty by reason of insanity.

Multiple personality and schizophrenia are two patterns of abnormal behavior. In this chapter we first define what is meant by abnormal behavior. Then we examine various broad explanations for, or models of, abnormal behavior. With the exception of the demonological and medical models, models of abnormal behavior overlap with the major approaches to understanding human personality discussed in Chapter 10. In our discussion of the demonological model, we shall see that if William had lived in Salem, Massachusetts, in 1692, just 200 years after Columbus set foot in the New World, he might have been hanged or burned as a witch. At that time most people assumed that abnormal behavior was caused by possession by the Devil. Nineteen people lost their lives that year in that colonial town for allegedly practicing the arts of Satan.

We then discuss various patterns of abnormal behavior, including anxiety disorders, dissociative disorders, somatoform disorders, eating disorders, mood disorders, schizophrenia, personality disorders, and sexual disorders.

WHAT IS ABNORMAL BEHAVIOR?

There are various patterns of abnormal behavior. Some are characterized by anxiety or depression, but many of us are anxious or depressed now and then without our behavior being considered abnormal. It is normal to be anxious before a big date or on the eve of a midterm examination. It would be appropriate to be depressed if a friend is upset with you or if you have done poorly on a test or in a job.

So when are feelings such as anxiety and depression considered abnormal? For one thing, anxiety and depression might be considered abnormal when they are not appropriate to our situations. It is not normal to be depressed when everything is going well or to be distraught when entering an elevator or looking out of a fourth-story window. The magnitude of the

Multiple personality A disorder in which a person appears to have two or more distinct personalities, which may alternate in controlling the person.

Insanity A legal term descriptive of a person judged to be incapable of recognizing right from wrong or of conforming his or her behavior to the law.

Schizophrenia A psychotic disorder characterized by loss of control of thought processes and inappropriate emotional responses.

problem might also suggest abnormal behavior. Whereas some anxiety is to be expected before a momentous interview, feeling that your heart is pounding so intensely that it might leap out of your chest—and then avoiding the interview—are not. Nor is sweating so profusely that your clothing literally becomes soaked.

Most psychologists would agree that behavior is abnormal when it meets some combination of the following criteria:

1. *It is unusual.* Although people who show abnormal behavior are in a minority, infrequent behavior is not abnormal in and of itself. There is only one president of the United States at a given time, yet that person is not considered to be abnormal (usually). Only one person holds the record for running or swimming the fastest mile. That person is different from you and me, but he or she is not abnormal.

   Although rarity or statistical deviance is not sufficient for behavior to be labeled abnormal, it helps. Most people do not see or hear things that are not there, and "seeing things" and "hearing things" are considered abnormal. We must also consider the situation: Although many of us feel panicked now and then because we recall that a term paper or report is due within a day or two, most of us do not have panic attacks "out of the blue." And so, unpredictable panic attacks might also be considered abnormal.

2. *It is socially unacceptable.* Each society has standards or norms for acceptable behavior in a given context. In our society, walking naked is normal in a locker room but abnormal on a crowded boulevard. Similarly, what is abnormal for one generation can be normal for another. Living together without benefit of marriage was almost unheard of a generation ago, but it raises few eyebrows today.

   Also, what is normal in one society may be abnormal in another. Citizens of our society who assume that strangers will be hostile and try to take advantage may be considered overly suspicious, even **paranoid.** But among the Mundugumor, a cannibalistic tribe studied by the anthropologist Margaret Mead (1935), perpetual suspicion was justified. Strangers, even male members of the same household, *were* hostile.

3. *One's perception or interpretation of reality is faulty.* We've heard it said that it's all right to say that you talk to God through prayer, but if you say that God talks back, you may be committed to a mental institution. Our society considers it normal to be inspired by religious beliefs but abnormal to believe that God is literally speaking to you. "Hearing voices" and "seeing things" are considered to be **hallucinations.** Similarly, **ideas of persecution,** such as believing that the Mafia or the CIA or the communists are "out to get you," are considered signs of disorder. (Unless they *are* out to get you, of course.)

4. *One is in severe personal distress.* Anxiety, depression, exaggerated fears, and other psychological states cause personal distress, and severe personal distress may be considered abnormal. But, as noted earlier, anxiety and depression may also be appropriate responses to one's situation, as in a real threat or a loss. In such cases, they are not abnormal unless they persevere indefinitely, long after the source of distress has been removed or after most people would have adjusted.

5. *One's behavior is self-defeating.* Behavior that leads to misery rather than happiness and fulfillment may be considered disordered. From this perspective, chronic drinking that interferes with work and family life, and cigarette smoking that impairs health, are abnormal.

Paranoid Characterized by oversuspiciousness and delusions of grandeur or persecution.

Hallucination A perception in the absence of sensory stimulation that is confused with reality.

Ideas of persecution Erroneous beliefs that one is being victimized or persecuted.

Trephining. Our ancestors may have "air-conditioned" skulls in an effort to treat abnormal behavior. The threat of trephining certainly could have encouraged conformity to social norms.

6. *It is dangerous.* Behavior that is dangerous to the self or others is considered abnormal. People who threaten or attempt suicide may be considered abnormal, as may people who threaten or attack others.

MODELS OF ABNORMAL BEHAVIOR

There are a number of models of, or ways of explaining, abnormal behavior. In this section we consider the demonological, medical (organic and psychodynamic versions), learning, and cognitive models.

The Demonological Model: "The Devil Made Me Do It"

Throughout human history, the **demonological model** has been the prevalent model for explaining abnormal behavior. For example, archaeologists have unearthed human skeletons dating to the Stone Age with egg-sized holes in the skull. The holes offer evidence that our ancestors believed that abnormal behavior reflected invasion by evil spirits and used the brutal method of breaking a pathway through the skull—called **trephining**—to provide those irascible spirits an outlet. New bone growth suggests that some "patients" actually survived the ordeal.

Did trephining work? Well, most of the time it terminated the disturbing behavior. And the "patient." Threat of trephining probably also persuaded many people to conform their behavior to group or tribal norms as best they could.

The ancient Greeks by and large believed that the gods punished humans by causing confusion and madness. An exception was Hippocrates, the Greek physician of the Golden Age of art and literature (fourth century B.C.). Hippocrates made the radical suggestion that abnormal behavior was caused by

Demonological model The view that abnormal behavior reflects invasion by evil spirits or demons.

Trephining The prehistoric practice of venting the skull with the intention of providing evil spirits a passage out of the head.

an abnormality of the brain. The notion that bodily processes could affect thoughts, feelings, and behaviors was to lie dormant for about 2,000 years.

During the Middle Ages in Europe, as well as during the early days of American civilization along the rocky coast of Massachusetts, the demonological model was in full sway. It was generally believed that abnormal behavior was a sign of possession by agents or spirits of the Devil. Possession could stem from retribution, or God's having the Devil possess your soul as punishment for sins. Wild agitation and confusion were attributed to retribution. Possession was also believed to result from deals with the Devil in which people traded their souls for earthly power or wealth. Such traders were called witches. Witches were held responsible for unfortunate events ranging from a neighbor's infertility to a poor crop.

In either case you were in for it. An exorcist, whose function was to persuade these spirits to find better pickings elsewhere, might pray at your side and wave a cross at you. If the spirits didn't call it quits, you might be beaten or flogged. If your behavior was still unseemly, there were other remedies, such as the rack, which had powerful influences on behavior.

In the fifteenth century, Pope Innocent VIII ordered that witches be put to death. In the same century two Dominican monks published a manual, *The Hammer of Witches,* that advised peasants about how they could recognize witches in their own neighborhoods. At least 200,000 accused witches were killed during the next two centuries. Europe was no place to practice strange ways. The goings-on at Salem, Massachusetts, were trivial in comparison.

There were ingenious "diagnostic" tests to ferret out possession. One was a water float test for purity, based on the principle that pure metals sink to the bottom during smelting, but impurities float to the surface. Suspects who sank to the bottom and drowned were judged to be pure. Suspects who managed to keep their heads above water were assumed to be "impure" and in league with the Devil. Then they were in real trouble. This ordeal is the origin of the phrase, "Damned if you do and damned if you don't."

Truth or Fiction Revisited

It is true that innocent people were drowned in the Middle Ages as a way of proving that they were not possessed by the Devil.

Although contemporary models of abnormal behavior may not have the curious characteristics of the demonological model, they have more scientific merit.

The Medical Model: Organic and Psychodynamic Versions

According to the **medical model,** abnormal behavior patterns are symptoms of underlying disorders. Symptoms are noted for diagnostic purposes, but the underlying disorders must be treated if abnormal behavior is to abate. There are two versions of the medical model: the organic version and the psychodynamic version.

Medical model The view that abnormal behavior is symptomatic of an underlying illness.

Medical Model: Organic Version According to the organic version of the medical model, abnormal behavior patterns reflect underlying biological or biochemical problems, not evil spirits. In 1883, Emil Kraepelin published a textbook of psychiatry in which he elaborated the medical model. Kraepelin argued that there were specific kinds of psychological disorders that, within

Table 12.1
Some Commonly Used Terms Concerning Abnormal Behavior that Are Derived from the Medical Model

Mental Illness	Mental Hospital
Mental Health	Prognosis
Symptoms	Treatment
Syndrome	Therapy
Diagnosis	Cure
Mental Patient	Relapse

the medical model, are often referred to as mental illnesses. (See Table 12.1 for a list of many of the commonly used terms concerning psychological disorders that reflect the widespread influence of the medical model.) Each mental illness is believed to have specific biological origins.

Throughout history, researchers have looked to various parts of the body as possible sites for abnormalities that might contribute to psychological disorders. The ancient Greeks, as a matter of fact, attributed premenstrual syndrome to a wandering uterus. In more recent years, researchers have looked, usually in vain, at the size of various structures in the brain and for a number of different substances in the blood. Today psychologists and medical researchers frequently look for such biological abnormalities in neurotransmitters, the chemicals that conduct "messages" from one cell in the nervous system, or neuron, to another. In many cases, as we shall see later in this chapter, such messages may be too strong. In other cases they may be too weak. And in some cases there are subtle interactions between different neurotransmitters, or between neurotransmitters and a person's situational experiences.

Kraepelin argued that each mental illness, just like each physical illness, was typified by its own cluster of symptoms, or **syndrome.** Each mental illness or pattern of abnormal behavior had a specific outcome, or course, and would presumably respond to a characteristic form of treatment, or therapy.

Contemporary supporters of the organic version of the medical model point to various sources of evidence. For one thing, a number of mental disorders run in families and might, therefore, be transmitted from generation to generation by way of DNA, the material that contains our genetic codes. For another, chemical imbalances in the brain and elsewhere produce behavioral effects such as those found in problems like severe depression and schizophrenia, as we shall see later in the chapter.

According to the organic version of the medical model, treatment requires medical expertise and involves controlling or curing the underlying biological or biochemical problem. The biological therapies discussed in Chapter 13 are largely based on the medical model.

The organic version of the medical model was a major advance over demonology. It led to the view that mentally ill people should be treated by qualified professionals rather than be punished. Compassion replaced hatred, fear, and persecution.

There are some problems with the organic version of the medical model, however. For one thing, biological causes have not been found for each pattern of abnormal behavior. For another, as noted in Chapter 11, the medical model suggests that the mentally ill, like the physically ill, may not be responsible for their problems and limitations. In the past, this view often led to hospitalization and suspension of responsibility (as in work and maintenance of a family life) among the mentally ill. Thus removed from the real

Syndrome A cluster or group of symptoms suggestive of a particular disorder.

world, the abilities of the mentally ill often declined further instead of returning to normal. But today even most adherents to the medical model encourage patients to remain in the community and maintain as much responsibility as they can. Finally, treatments derived from other models have been shown to be of help with several patterns of abnormal behavior, as we shall see in Chapter 13.

Medical Model: Psychodynamic Version Whereas the organic version of the medical model suggests that abnormal behavior reflects underlying biological problems, Sigmund Freud's psychodynamic model argues that abnormal behavior is symptomatic of underlying psychological problems or conflicts. In keeping with Freud's theory of psychosexual development, the underlying problem is usually assumed to be unconscious conflict of childhood origins. Abnormal behavior patterns are viewed as being "symptoms" of the underlying conflict. Frequently, as in the case of persistent anxiety, they are assumed to be symptomatic of difficulty in repressing primitive sexual and aggressive impulses.

Within Freudian theory, **neurotic** behavior and anxiety stem from the leakage of primitive impulses. Anxiety represents the impulse itself and fear of what might happen if the impulse were acted upon. In the case of **psychosis,** impulses are assumed to have broken through so that behavior falls under the control of the id instead of the ego or superego. According to psychodynamic theory, treatment (other than a sort of "band-aid" therapy) requires resolving the unconscious conflicts that underlie abnormal behavior.

Learning Models

Learning theorists do not necessarily see abnormal behavior as being symptomatic of underlying problems. Rather, they see abnormal behavior itself as being the problem. To a large degree, abnormal behavior is believed to be acquired in the same ways normal behaviors are acquired—for example, by means of conditioning and observational learning. Why, then, do some people show abnormal behavior? From the behaviorist perspective, one reason is found in situational variables. That is, the learning or reinforcement histories of persons with abnormal behavior might differ from those of most of us. But from the social-learning perspective, differences in person variables such as competencies, encoding strategies, self-efficacy expectations, and self-regulatory systems might also account for abnormal behavior.

A person who lacks social skills might never have had the chance to observe skillful models. Or it might be that a minority subculture reinforced behaviors that are not approved by the majority. Punishment for early exploratory behavior or childhood sexual activity might lead to adult anxieties over independence or sexuality. Inconsistent discipline (haphazard rewarding of desirable behavior and unreliable punishment of misbehavior) might lead to antisocial behavior. Children whose parents ignore or abuse them might come to pay more attention to their fantasies than the outer world, leading to schizophrenic withdrawal and inability to distinguish reality from fantasy. Deficits in competencies, encoding strategies, and self-regulatory systems might heighten schizophrenic problems. Because learning theorists do not believe that behavior problems necessarily reflect biological problems or unconscious conflict, they often try to change or modify the problems directly, such as by means of behavior therapy (see Chapter 13).

Neurotic Of neurosis. Within psychodynamic theory, neuroses are a group of disorders theorized to stem from unconscious conflict.

Psychosis A major disorder in which a person lacks insight and has difficulty meeting the demands of daily life and maintaining contact with reality.

The Cognitive Model

Cognitive theorists focus on the cognitive events—such as thoughts, expectations, and attitudes—that accompany and in some cases underlie psychological disorders.

One cognitive approach to understanding disordered behavior involves information processing. Information-processing theorists compare the processes of the mind to those of the computer, and they think in terms of cycles of input (based on perception), storage, retrieval, manipulation, and output of information. They view psychological disorders as disturbances in the cycle. Disturbances might be caused by the blocking or distortion of input or by faulty storage, retrieval, or manipulation of information. Any of these can lead to lack of output or distorted output (e.g., bizarre behavior). Schizophrenic individuals, for example, frequently jump from topic to topic in a disorganized fashion, which information-processing theorists might explain as problems in manipulation of information.

Other cognitive theorists (Albert Ellis [1977, 1987] is one) view anxiety problems as stemming from irrational beliefs and attitudes, such as an overwhelming desire for social approval and perfectionism. Aaron Beck attributes numerous instances of depression to "cognitive errors" such as self-devaluation, interpretation of events in a negative light, and general pessimism (Beck et al., 1979). Some cognitive psychologists, as we shall see, attribute many cases of depression to cognitions to the effect that one is helpless to change things for the better.

Social-learning theorists such as Albert Bandura (1986) and Walter Mischel (1986) attribute importance to encoding strategies, self-regulatory systems, and expectancies in explaining and predicting behavior. For example, expectancies that we shall not be able to carry out our plans (low self-efficacy expectancies) sap motivation and generate feelings of hopelessness—two facets of depression (Bandura, 1982).

Many psychologists look to more than one model to explain and treat psychological disorders. These psychologists are deemed **eclectic.** For example, many social-learning theorists believe that some psychological disorders stem from biochemical factors or the interaction of biochemistry and learning. They are open to combining behavior therapy with drugs to treat problems such as schizophrenia and **bipolar disorder.** Psychodynamic theorists might also be eclectic. They might believe that schizophrenic disorganization reflects control of the personality by the id and argue that only long-term psychotherapy can help the ego achieve supremacy. But they might still be willing to use drugs to calm agitation on a temporary basis.

We shall refer to these models in our discussion of the major categories of abnormal behavior. But let us first consider some issues in their classification.

CLASSIFYING ABNORMAL BEHAVIOR

Toss some people, apes, seaweed, fish, and sponges into a room—preferably a well-ventilated room. Stir slightly. What do you have? It depends on how you classify this hodgepodge.

Classify them as plants versus animals and you lump the people, chimpanzees, fish, and, yes, sponges together. Classify them as stuff that carries on its business on land or underwater, and we throw in our lots with just the chimps. How about those that swim and those that don't? Then the chimps, the fish, and some of us are pigeonholed together.

Eclectic Selecting from various systems or theories.

Bipolar disorder A disorder in which the mood alternates between two extreme poles (elation and depression). Also referred to as *manic-depression.*

Our ways of classifying things reflect the factors we deem important. The most widely used classification scheme for abnormal behavior patterns is the *Diagnostic and Statistical Manual* of the American Psychiatric Association, third edition, revised version, published in 1987—the DSM–III–R for short. Psychiatrists are medical doctors, not psychologists. The DSM–III–R sorts abnormal behavior patterns largely on the basis of observable commonalities, which seems logical enough. However, the medical model was widely adopted by the authors of previous editions, and the assumption that abnormal behaviors reflected certain underlying problems led them to group things differently. One consequence was the category of the "neuroses." I mention this because the terms *neurosis* and *neurotic* are widely used by nonprofessionals, and without some explanation, it might seem strange that they have largely been abandoned. Neuroses were grouped not because of observable commonalities but because of theoretical speculation that they shared common origins. From the psychodynamic perspective, all neuroses—no matter how different they might appear to be on the surface—stemmed from unconscious neurotic conflict. Each neurosis was thought to reflect a way of coping with unconscious fear that primitive impulses might break loose. As a result, sleepwalking was included as a neurosis, since psychoanalysts assumed that sleepwalking contained impulses by permitting their partial expression during the night. But now that the focus is on the observable, sleepwalking is considered to be a disorder of childhood and is no longer grouped with other disorders that were previously considered neuroses (Millon, 1983). Despite the increased focus on observable behavior, psychologists in general still find that the DSM has a distinct medical flavor (Smith & Kraft, 1983).

We must also consider the reliability and validity of the categories listed in the DSM–III–R. The reliability of a diagnosis, such as multiple personality, is its consistency, usually measured as the degree of agreement among professionals who make diagnoses. Reliability studies based on earlier versions of the DSM were disappointing. For example, the percentage of agreement between a pair of psychiatrists was 53 percent for the diagnosis of schizophrenia and from 38 to 63 percent for the mood disorders (Beck et al., 1962). But with the DSM–III's greater emphasis of observable behaviors, the agreement rates for schizophrenia and mood disorders have risen to 81 percent and 83 percent, respectively (Spitzer et al., 1979). The validity of a diagnosis is the degree to which it reflects an *actual* disorder. For example, there is question as to whether the kinds of depression listed in the DSM–III–R are all subtypes of one basic kind of depression, or whether there are several types of depression, each with different origins and in need of a different kind of treatment. Many questions remain unanswered about the validity of the DSM categories, although validity studies are under way (Spitzer, 1981).

Finally, it should be noted that some mental-health professionals, like psychiatrist Thomas Szasz (1961), believe that the disorders described in the DSM are really "problems in living" and not disorders at all—at least in the sense that high blood pressure, cancer, and influenza are disorders. Szasz argues that considering people with problems in living as being "sick" is degrading to them and also encourages them to evade their responsibilities to themselves and others.* Moreover, Szasz (1984) argues that since sick people are encouraged to obey doctors' orders, labeling persons with problems as "sick" accords too much power to mental-health professionals. Instead, the troubled persons need to be encouraged to take greater responsibility for solving their own problems.

*In the previous chapter's discussion of "the sick role," it was noted that people who are sick are forgiven failure to meet the needs of daily life until they get well.

Table 12.2
The Multiaxial Classification System of the DSM–III–R

Axis	Type of Information	Brief Description
Axis I	Clinical Syndromes	The patterns of abnormal behavior ("mental disorders") that impair functioning and are stressful to the individual
	"V Codes"	Conditions that are not attributable to a mental disorder but are nonetheless a focus of attention or treatment, such as academic, vocational, or social problems
Axis II	Developmental Disorders	Disorders that generally begin in childhood or adolescence and persist in stable form into adult life, such as mental retardation, autism, and specific developmental disorders in academic skills, language and speech, or motor skills
	Personality Disorders	Deeply ingrained, maladaptive ways of perceiving others and behavior that are stressful to the individual or those who relate to the individual. Notable personality traits can be listed here, even when no personality disorder per se is diagnosed.
Axis III	Physical Disorders and Conditions	Chronic and acute illnesses, injuries, allergies, and so on that affect functioning and treatment, such as cardiovascular disorders, athletic injuries, and allergies to medication
Axis IV	Severity of Psychosocial Stressors	Stressors that occurred during the past year that may have contributed to the development of a new mental disorder or the recurrence of a prior disorder or that may have exacerbated an existing disorder, such as divorce occurring during a depressive episode. Stressors can be marital, parental, occupational, financial, legal, developmental, physical, and so on.
Axis V	Global Assessmen' of Functioning	Overall judgment of current functioning and the highest level of functioning in the past year according to psychological, social, and occupational criteria

Based on DSM–III–R (1987), pp. 3–21.

Thus, the DSM–III–R is not perfect, even though it focuses more on observable behaviors than previous editions. Questions remain as to the reliability and validity of the diagnostic pictures it describes. And some critics, like Szasz, even challenge the value of the classification system on broader philosophical grounds. Yet, in our consideration of the patterns of abnormal behavior, we shall refer to the DSM–III–R. My use of the DSM–III–R is a convenience, not an endorsement, however. In future years psychologists may publish their own classification system, and it will doubtless show a greater departure from the medical model.

The DSM–III–R is *multiaxial.* It provides for classifying problems according to five kinds of information, or axes. As shown in Table 12.2, abnormal behavior patterns are described either on Axis I or II. Axis I contains the disorders discussed in this chapter, with the exception of personality disorders. Problems with substance abuse are also placed on Axis I. Clinicians frequently find that persons showing abnormal behavior problems, such as alcoholism, have personality problems that have ramifications for treatment. Axis III covers physical illnesses and conditions that may have an impact on understanding or treating the abnormal behavior problems.

Axes IV and V yield additional information that can affect the client's prognosis (outlook for improvement) and treatment plan. Axis IV permits the clinician to estimate the severity of the psychosocial stressors affecting the client, and Axis V calls for a judgment of the client's current level of functioning and highest level of functioning (social, occupational, recreational, etc.) in the past year. Other things being equal, clients who encounter severe stressors and show recent high levels of functioning have better prognoses. That is, they are most likely to respond positively to treatment. Situational stressors and reactions to them can often be changed, and the client has a solid record of recent performance to which to return.

Let us now consider the more prominent patterns of abnormal behavior listed on Axes I and II.

Anxiety. Anxiety is characterized by nervousness, fears, feelings of dread and foreboding, and physical signs such as rapid heartbeat and sweating.

ANXIETY DISORDERS

Anxiety disorders have subjective and physical features (Beck et al., 1988). Subjective features include fear of the worst happening, fear of losing control, nervousness, and inability to relax. Physical features reflect arousal of the sympathetic division of the autonomic nervous system. They entail trembling, sweating, a pounding or racing heart, elevated blood pressure (a flushed face), and faintness. Anxiety is an appropriate response to a threat. Anxiety can be abnormal, however, when its extent is out of proportion to the threat, or when it "comes out of the blue"—that is, when events do not seem to warrant it. The anxiety disorders include phobic, panic, generalized anxiety, obsessive-compulsive, and post-traumatic stress disorders.

Phobias

There are several types of phobias, including *simple phobia, social phobia,* and *agoraphobia.* According to the DSM–III–R (American Psychiatric Association, 1987), **simple phobias** are excessive, irrational fears of specific objects or situations. **Social phobias** are persistent fears of scrutiny by others or of doing something that will be humiliating or embarrassing. Stage fright and speech anxiety are common social phobias.

One simple phobia is fear of elevators. Some people will not enter elevators, despite the hardships they suffer (such as walking six flights of steps) as a result. Yes, the cable *could* break. The ventilation *could* fail. One *could* be stuck waiting in midair for repairs. But these problems are uncommon, and it does not make sense for most of us to repeatedly walk flights of stairs to elude them. Similarly, some people with simple phobias for hypodermic needles will not receive injections, even when they are the advised remedy for profound illness. Injections can be painful, but most people with phobias for needles would gladly suffer an excruciating pinch if it would help them fight illness. Other simple phobias include **claustrophobia** (fear of tight or enclosed places), **acrophobia** (fear of heights), and fear of mice, snakes, and other creepy-crawlies.

Phobias can seriously disrupt one's life. A person may know that a phobia is irrational yet still experience acute anxiety and avoid the phobic article or circumstance.

Fears of animals and imaginary creatures are common among children, and **agoraphobia** is among the most widespread phobias of adults. Agoraphobia is derived from the Greek meaning "fear of the marketplace," or of being out in open, busy areas. Persons with agoraphobia fear being in places from which it might be difficult to escape or in which help might be unavailable if they become disquieted. In practice, people who receive this label are often loath to venture out of their homes, especially when they are alone. They find it trying or infeasible to hold jobs or to sustain an ordinary social life.

Simple phobia Persistent fear of a specific object or situation.

Social phobia An irrational, excessive fear of public scrutiny.

Claustrophobia Fear of tight, small places.

Acrophobia Fear of high places.

Agoraphobia Fear of open, crowded places.

Panic disorder The recurrent experiencing of attacks of extreme anxiety in the absence of external stimuli that usually elicit anxiety.

Panic Disorder

Panic disorder is an abrupt attack of acute anxiety that is not triggered by a specific object or situation. Panic sufferers experience symptoms such as shortness of breath, heavy sweating, quaking, and pounding of the heart

(Anderson et al., 1984; Barlow et al., 1985; Norton et al., 1985). It is not unusual for them to think that they are having a heart attack. According to the DSM–III–R, there may also be choking sensations; nausea; numbness or tingling; flushes or chills; chest pain; and fear of dying, going crazy, or losing control. There is a stronger bodily component to the anxiety experienced by people with panic disorders than to that encountered by people with other anxiety disorders (Barlow et al., 1985). Panic attacks may last from a minute or two to an hour or more, and afterwards victims usually feel spent.

Forty to 50 percent of us experience panic now and then (Norton & Rhodes, 1983), but the DSM–III–R diagnoses panic disorder when there have been four attacks in a four-week period or an attack has been followed by a month of dread of another attack. When we use these criteria, panic disorders affect only about 1 percent of the population (Meyers et al., 1984).

Because panic attacks seem to descend from nowhere, some sufferers remain in the home most of the time for fear of having an attack in public. In such cases, sufferers are diagnosed as having *panic disorder with agoraphobia.*

Generalized Anxiety Disorder

The central feature of **generalized anxiety disorder** is persistent anxiety of at least one month's duration. As in the panic disorder, the anxiety cannot be attributed to a phobic object, situation, or activity. Rather, it seems to be free-floating. Symptoms may include motor tension (shakiness, inability to relax, furrowed brow, fidgeting); autonomic overarousal (sweating, a dry mouth, a racing heart, light-headedness, frequent urinating, diarrhea); feelings of dread and foreboding; and excessive vigilance, as shown by distractibility, insomnia, and irritability.

Obsessive-Compulsive Disorder

An **obsession** is a recurrent thought or image that seems irrational and beyond control. Obsessions are so compelling and recurrent that they disrupt daily life. They may include doubts about whether one has locked the doors and shut the windows; impulses, such as the wish to strangle one's spouse; and images, such as one mother's repeated fantasy that her children had been run over by traffic on the way home from school. In another case, a 16-year-old boy found "numbers in my head" whenever he was about to study or take a test. A housewife became obsessed with the idea that she had contaminated her hands with Sani-Flush and that the contamination was spreading to everything she touched.

A **compulsion** is a seemingly irresistible urge to engage in an act, often repeatedly, such as prolonged, elaborate washing after using the bathroom. The impulse is recurrent and forceful, interfering with daily life. Some men, called *exhibitionists,* report experiencing the compulsion to expose their genitals to women strangers. The woman who felt contaminated by Sani-Flush engaged in intricate hand-washing rituals. She spent three to four hours daily at the sink and complained, "My hands look like lobster claws."

Generalized anxiety disorder Feelings of dread and foreboding and sympathetic arousal of at least one month's duration.

Obsession A recurring thought or image that seems beyond control.

Compulsion An apparently irresistible urge to repeat an act or engage in ritualistic behavior, such as hand-washing.

A Traumatic Experience from the Vietnam War. Physical threats and other traumatic experiences can lead to post-traumatic stress disorder (PTSD). PTSD is characterized by intrusive memories of the experience, recurrent dreams about it, and the sudden feeling that it is, in fact, recurring (as in "flashbacks").

Post-Traumatic Stress Disorder

Post-traumatic stress disorder (PTSD) is defined as intense and persistent feelings of anxiety and helplessness that are caused by a traumatic experience, such as a physical threat to oneself or one's family, destruction of one's community, or the witnessing of the death of another person. PTSD has troubled many Vietnam war veterans, victims of rape, and persons who have seen their homes and communities inundated by floods or swept away by tornadoes. In some cases, PTSD occurs six months or more after the event.

The precipitating event is incessantly reexperienced, as in the form of intrusive memories, recurrent dreams, and the sudden feeling that the event is, in fact, repeating (as in "flashbacks" to the event).

Truth or Fiction Revisited

It is true that stressful experiences can lead to recurrent nightmares.

Typically the sufferer attempts to avoid thoughts and activities connected to the traumatic event. He or she may also display sleep problems, irritable outbursts, difficulty concentrating, extreme vigilance, and an intensified "startle" response. When traumatic events take place, it appears that being part of a supportive social network can mitigate their impact (Stretch, 1985, 1987).

Post-traumatic stress disorder A disorder which follows a psychologically distressing event that is outside the range of normal human experience and which is characterized by symptoms such as intense fear, avoidance of stimuli associated with the event, and reliving of the event.

Theoretical Views

According to the psychodynamic model, phobias symbolize conflicts of childhood origin. Psychodynamic theory explains generalized anxiety as persistent difficulty in maintaining repression of primitive impulses. Psychoanalysts view obsessions as the leakage of unconscious impulses, and they view compulsions as acts that allow people to keep such impulses partly repressed.

Some learning theorists suggest that phobias might be conditioned fears that were acquired in early childhood and whose origins are beyond memory. Avoidance of feared stimuli is reinforced by reduction of anxiety.

Seligman and Rosenhan (1984) suggest that there is an interaction between organic factors and conditioning that biologically predisposes us to acquire phobias to certain classes of stimuli. We are genetically prepared to be conditioned to certain stimuli, and, for this reason, this view is termed **prepared conditioning.** We would not inherit specific fears, according to this view, but evolutionary forces would have favored the survival of individuals who were biologically predisposed toward acquiring fears of large animals, snakes, heights, entrapment, sharp objects, and strangers. In laboratory experiments, people have been shown photographs of various objects and then have been given electric shock (Hugdahl & Ohman, 1977; Ohman et al., 1976). Subjects do seem to have been more "prepared" to acquire fear reactions to some stimuli (e.g., spiders and snakes) than others (e.g., flowers and houses) as measured by galvanic skin response to subsequent presentations of these stimuli. But these experiments do not show that the subjects were *biologically* prepared to develop fear responses to stimuli such as snakes and spiders. Keep in mind that subjects were reared in a society in which many people react negatively to these "creepy crawlies." So, their learning experiences, not genetic factors, might have readied them to fear these stimuli.

Similarly, a number of social-learning theorists have noted a role for observational learning in acquiring fears (Bandura et al., 1969). If parents squirm, grimace, and shudder at mice, blood, or dirt on the kitchen floor, children might encode these stimuli as being awful and imitate their behavior. Social-learning theorists suggest that generalized anxiety is often nothing more than fear that has been associated with situations so broad that they are not readily identified, such as social relationships or personal achievement. Social-learning and cognitive theorists suggest that anxiety can be maintained by thinking that one is in a terrible situation and is helpless to change it. Psychoanalysts and social-learning theorists broadly agree that compulsive behavior reduces anxiety.

Social-learning and cognitive theorists note that obsessions and compulsions serve the purpose of diverting attention from more important and threatening issues, such as "What am I to do with my life?" They also note that when anxieties are acquired at a young age, we might later interpret them as enduring traits and label ourselves as "people who fear ________" (you fill it in). Then we live up to the labels. We also entertain thoughts that heighten and perpetuate anxiety (Meichenbaum & Jaremko, 1983), such as "I've got to get out of here," or "My heart is going to leap out of my chest." Such ideas intensify physical signs of anxiety, disrupt planning, magnify the aversiveness of stimuli, motivate avoidance, and decrease self-efficacy expectations concerning ability to control the situation. Belief that we shall not be able to handle a threat heightens anxiety (Bandura, 1981; Bandura et al., 1982), whereas belief that we are in control lessens anxiety (Miller, 1980).

Organic factors might play a role in anxiety disorders. For one thing, anxiety disorders tend to run in families (Turner et al., 1987). In one study, Sandra Scarr and her colleagues (1981) compared the **neuroticism** test scores of adopted adolescents to those of their natural and adoptive parents. Scarr found that scores of parents and their natural children correlated more highly than those of parents and adopted children. Studies such as these suggest a stronger role for heredity than for environmental influences. A recent twin study found that the **concordance** rate for anxiety disorders is higher among pairs of identical than fraternal twins (Torgersen, 1983).

Prepared conditioning The view that we are genetically predisposed — or "prepared"—to become conditioned to certain classes of stimuli.

Neuroticism A personality trait characterized largely by persistent anxiety.

Concordance Agreement.

Thus, a predisposition toward anxiety—perhaps in the form of a highly reactive autonomic nervous system—might be inherited. Why might a nervous system be "highly reactive"? One possibility is that receptor sites in the brain are not sensitive enough to gamma-aminobutyric acid (GABA), an inhibitory neurotransmitter that may help quell anxiety reactions. The **benzodiazepines**, a class of drugs that are effective in reducing anxiety, are thought to work by increasing the action of GABA. In the case of people with panic disorder, receptors might trigger attacks in response to blood levels of lactic acid and carbon dioxide that do not disturb other people (Fishman & Sheehan, 1985).

Many cases of anxiety disorders might reflect the interaction of organic and psychological factors. For example, some combination of biological preparedness to respond negatively to specific classes of stimuli, a highly reactive nervous system, and early experience might explain many cases of phobia. Also, in the case of panic attacks, it may be that organic imbalances initially trigger the attacks, but subsequent fear of attacks—and of the bodily cues that signal the onset of attacks—might heighten the discomfort of ensuing attacks and give sufferers the impression that there is nothing they can do about them. An attitude of helplessness increases fear. So panic sufferers can be helped by psychological methods that provide ways of reducing physical discomfort—including regular breathing—and that show them that there are, after all, things they can do to cope with attacks (Barlow, 1986). The origins of many patterns of abnormal behavior seem quite complex, involving the interaction of biological and psychological factors.

DISSOCIATIVE DISORDERS

The DSM–III–R lists four major **dissociative disorders:** *psychogenic amnesia, psychogenic fugue, multiple personality,* and *depersonalization.* In each case there is a disturbance in the normal functions of identity, memory, or consciousness that make the person feel whole.

Psychogenic Amnesia

In **psychogenic amnesia,** there is sudden inability to recall important personal information. Memory loss cannot be attributed to organic problems, such as a blow to the head or alcoholic intoxication. Thus it is *psycho*genic. In the most common example, the person cannot recall events for a number of hours after a stressful incident, as in warfare or in the case of the uninjured survivor of an accident. In generalized amnesia, people forget their entire lives. Amnesia may last for hours or years. Termination of amnesia is also sudden.

People sometimes claim that they cannot recall engaging in socially unacceptable behavior, promising to do something, and so on. Claiming to have a psychological problem such as amnesia in order to escape responsibility is known as **malingering.** Current research methods do not guarantee that we can distinguish malingerers from people with dissociative disorders.

Benzodiazepines A class of drugs that reduce anxiety. Minor tranquilizers.

Dissociative disorders Disorders in which there are sudden, temporary changes in consciousness or self-identity.

Psychogenic amnesia A dissociative disorder marked by loss of memory or self-identity. Skills and general knowledge are usually retained.

Malingering Pretending to be ill in order to escape duty or work.

Psychogenic Fugue

In **psychogenic fugue,** the person shows loss of memory for the past, travels abruptly from his or her home or place of work, and takes a new identity. Either the person does not think about the past, or that person reports a past filled with sham memories that are not known to be erroneous. Following recovery, the events that occurred during the fugue are not recalled.

Multiple Personality Disorder

Multiple personality is the name given to William's disorder as described at the beginning of the chapter. In this disorder, two or more "personalities," each with distinct traits and memories, "occupy" the same person, with or without awareness of the others. Different personalities might even have different eyeglass prescriptions (American Psychiatric Association, 1987).

Braun (1988) reports cases in which assorted personalities showed different allergic responses. In one patient, a personality named Timmy was not sensitive to orange juice. But when other personalities who alternated control over him drank orange juice, they would break out with hives. Hives would also erupt after Timmy drank orange juice if another personality emerged while the juice was being digested. And if Timmy re-appeared when the allergic reaction was present, the itching of the hives would cease at once, and the water-filled blisters would start to subside. In other cases reported by Braun, different personalities in one person might show various responses to the same medicine. Or one personality might exhibit color blindness while others had intact color vision. If such cases are accurately reported, they provide a fascinating demonstration of the varieties of behavior patterns and ways of perceiving the world that are possible for persons with comparable biological makeup.

Truth or Fiction Revisited

It does seem to be true that some people do have more than one personality, with different allergies and eyeglass prescriptions.

A few celebrated cases have been portrayed in the popular media. In one that became the subject of the film *The Three Faces of Eve,* a timid housewife named Eve White harbored two other personalities: Eve Black, a sexually aggressive, antisocial personality; and Jane, an emerging personality who was able to accept the existence of her primitive impulses yet show socially appropriate behavior. Finally, the three faces merged into one—Jane. Ironically, Jane (Chris Sizemore, in real life) reportedly split into 22 personalities later on. Another well-publicized case is that of Sybil, a woman with 16 personalities who was played by Sally Field in a film.

Psychogenic fugue A dissociative disorder in which one experiences amnesia, then flees to a new location and establishes a new lifestyle.

Depersonalization disorder Persistent or recurrent feelings that one is not real or is detached from one's own experiences or body.

Depersonalization Disorder

Depersonalization is the persistent feeling that one is not real. Persons with the disorder may feel detached from their own bodies, as if they are observing their thought processes from the outside. Or they may feel that they are functioning on automatic pilot or as if in a dream.

Multiple Personality. In the film *The Three Faces of Eve,* Joanne Woodward played three personalities in the same woman: the shy, inhibited Eve White (lying on couch); the flirtatious and promiscuous Eve Black (in dark dress); and a third personality (Jane) who could accept her sexual and aggressive impulses and still maintain her sense of identity.

Theoretical Views

According to psychodynamic theory, dissociative disorders entail massive use of repression to avert recognition of improper impulses. In psychogenic amnesia and fugue, the person forgets a profoundly disturbing event or impulse. In multiple personality, the person expresses unacceptable impulses through alternate personalities. In depersonalization, the person stands outside—removed from the turmoil within.

Learning theorists generally regard dissociative disorders as conditions in which people learn *not to think* about disturbing acts or impulses in order to avoid feelings of guilt and shame. Technically speaking, *not thinking about these matters* is reinforced* by *removal* of the aversive stimuli of guilt and shame.

Social-learning theory suggests that many people come to role-play people with multiple personality through observational learning. This is not exactly the same thing as pretending or malingering, because people can "forget to tell themselves" that they have assumed a role. Reinforcers are made available by role-playing individuals with multiple personality: drawing attention to oneself and escaping responsibility for unacceptable behavior are two (Spanos et al., 1985; Thigpen & Cleckley, 1984). According to Nicholas Spanos and his colleagues (1985), films and TV shows such as *The Three Faces of Eve* and *Sybil* have "provided detailed examples of the symptoms and course of multiple personality" (p. 363). That is, some of us have learned how to enact the role of the person with multiple personality by watching TV.

One cognitive perspective explains dissociative disorders in terms of deployment of attention. Perhaps all of us are capable of dividing our awareness so that we become unaware, at least temporarily, of events that we usually focus more attention on. Perhaps the marvel is *not* that attention can be divided, but that human consciousness normally integrates experience into a meaningful whole.

*This is an example of negative reinforcement, because the frequency of behavior—in this case, the frequency of diverting one's attention from a certain topic—is increased by *removal* of a stimulus—in this case, by removal of feelings of, say, guilt or shame.

SOMATOFORM DISORDERS

In **somatoform disorders,** people show or complain of physical problems, such as paralysis, pain, or the persistent belief that they have a serious disease, yet no evidence of a physical abnormality can be found. In this section we shall discuss two somatoform disorders: *conversion disorder* and *hypochondriasis.*

Conversion Disorder

Conversion disorder is characterized by a major change in or loss of physical functioning, although there are no medical findings to explain the loss of functioning. The symptoms are not intentionally produced; that is, the person is not faking.

If you lost the ability to see at night, or if your legs became paralyzed, you would understandably show concern. But some victims of conversion disorder show indifference to their symptoms, a remarkable feature referred to as **la belle indifférence.** Conversion disorder is so named because it appears to "convert" a source of stress into a physical difficulty.

During World War II, a number of bomber pilots developed night blindness. They could not carry out their nighttime missions, although no damage to the optic nerves was found. In rare cases, women with large families have been reported to become paralyzed in the legs, again with no medical findings.

Truth or Fiction Revisited

It is true that some people have lost the use of their legs or eyes under stress, even though nothing was medically wrong with them.

Hypochondriasis

Persons with **hypochondriasis** have the persistent belief that they are suffering from profound illness, even though no medical evidence can be found. Sufferers often become preoccupied with minor physical sensations and maintain an unrealistic belief that something is wrong despite medical reassurance. "Hypochondriacs" may go from doctor to doctor, seeking the one who will find the causes of the sensations. Fear may disrupt work or home life.

Hypochondriasis is supposed to be found more often among elderly people. However, as pointed out by Paul Costa and Robert McCrae (1985) of the National Institute on Aging, real health changes tend to occur with age, and most complaints are probably accurate reflections of people's changing health status.

Theoretical Views

Instances of conversion disorder are rare and short in duration, but their existence led the young Sigmund Freud to believe that subconscious processes were at work in people. The psychodynamic view of conversion disorders is that the symptoms produced by the victim protect the victim

Somatoform disorders Disorders in which people complain of physical (somatic) problems, even though no physical abnormality can be found.

Conversion disorder A disorder in which anxiety or unconscious conflicts are "converted" into physical symptoms that often have the effect of helping the person cope with anxiety or conflict.

La belle indifférence A French term descriptive of the lack of concern sometimes shown by people with conversion disorders.

Hypochondriasis Persistent belief that one has a medical disorder despite lack of medical findings.

from feelings of guilt or shame or from another source of stress. Conversion disorders, like dissociative disorders, often seem to serve a purpose. The "blindness" of the pilots may have afforded them respite from stressful missions, or may have allowed them to evade the guilt from bombing civilian populations. The paralysis of a woman who prematurely commits herself to a large family and a life at home may prevent her from doing housework or from engaging in sexual intercourse and becoming pregnant again. She "accomplishes" certain ends without having to identify them or make decisions.

There is evidence that some hypochondriacs use their complaints as a self-handicapping strategy (Smith et al., 1983). That is, they are more likely to complain of feeling ill in situations in which illness can serve as an excuse for poor performance. In other cases, focusing on physical sensations and possible problems may serve the function of taking the person's mind off other life problems—just like the obsessive-compulsive woman's focusing on her supposed contamination by Sani-Flush might have served the function of diverting her thoughts from issues concerning her unfulfilling daily behavior patterns. However, every effort should be made to uncover real medical problems among presumed hypochondriacs. Now and then, a supposed hypochondriac dies from something all too real.

EATING DISORDERS

Did you know that today the eating habits of the "average" American woman are characterized by dieting? For this reason, efforts to restrict the intake of food have become the norm. However, the eating disorders that we discuss in this section are characterized by gross disturbances in patterns of eating. They include *anorexia nervosa* and *bulimia nervosa.*

Anorexia Nervosa

There is a saying that you can never be too rich or too thin. Excess money may be pleasant enough, but one certainly can be too thin, as in the case of **anorexia nervosa.** Anorexia is a life-threatening disorder characterized by refusal to maintain a healthful body weight, intense fear of being overweight, a distorted body image, and, in females, **amenorrhea.** Anorectic persons usually weigh less than 85 percent of their expected body weight.

By and large, anorexia afflicts girls and young women. Nearly one in 200 school-aged girls has trouble gaining or maintaining weight (Crisp et al., 1976), and the incidences of anorexia nervosa and bulimia nervosa have increased markedly since the 1950s (Boskind-White & White, 1986; Strober, 1986). Anorectic females outnumber anorectic males by estimates of from 9:1 to 20:1. Onset is most often in adolescence, between the ages of 12 and 18.

Anorectic girls may be full height but weigh 60 pounds or less. They may drop 25 percent or more of their body weight in a year. Severe weight loss triggers amenorrhea (Sullivan, 1988). The girl's general health declines, and she may experience slowed-down heart rate, low blood pressure, constipation, dehydration, and a host of other problems (Kaplan & Woodside, 1987). About 5 percent of anorectic girls die from weight loss (Hsu, 1986; Szmukler & Russell, 1986).

In the typical pattern, girls notice some weight gain after menarche and decide that it must come off. However, dieting—and, often, exercise—continue at a fever pitch. They go on long after girls reach normal body weights,

Anorexia nervosa An eating disorder characterized by maintenance of an abnormally low body weight, intense fear of weight gain, a distorted body image, and, in females, amenorrhea.

Amenorrhea Absence of menstruation.

even after family members and others have told them that they are losing too much. Anorectic girls almost always adamantly deny that they are wasting away. They may point to their fierce exercise regimens as proof. Their body images are distorted. Whereas others perceive them as "skin and bones," they frequently sit before the mirror and see themselves as getting to where they want to be. Or they may focus on nonexistent "remaining" pockets of fat.

Although the thought of eating can be odious to anorectic girls, now and then they may feel quite hungry. Many anorectics become obsessed with food and are constantly "around it." They may engross themselves in cookbooks, take on the family shopping chores, and prepare elaborate dinners for others.

On a Binge. Bulimia nervosa is defined as recurrent cycles of binge eating and the taking of dramatic measures, such as self-induced vomiting, to purge the food. Many more women than men suffer from the eating disorders of anorexia nervosa and bulimia nervosa.

Bulimia Nervosa

The case of Nicole provides a vivid account of a young woman with **bulimia nervosa**:

Nicole awakens in her cold dark room and already wishes it was time to go back to bed. She dreads the thought of going through this day, which will be like so many others in her recent past. She asks herself the question every morning, "Will I be able to make it through the day without being totally obsessed by thoughts of food, or will I blow it again and spend the day binging"? She tells herself that today she will begin a new life, today she will start to live like a normal human being. However, she is not at all convinced that the choice is hers (Boskind-White & White, 1983, p. 29).

It turns out that this day Nicole begins by eating eggs and toast. Then she binges on cookies; doughnuts; bagels smothered with butter, cream cheese, and jelly; granola; candy bars; and bowls of cereal and milk—all within 45 minutes. Then she cannot take in any more food and turns her attention to purging what she has eaten. She goes to the bathroom, ties back her hair, turns on the shower to mask any noise she will make, drinks a glass of water, and makes herself vomit. Afterward she vows, "Starting tomorrow, I'm going to change." But she knows that tomorrow it will probably be the same story.

Truth or Fiction Revisited

It is true that some college women do control their weight by going on cycles of binge eating followed by self-induced vomiting. They are said to have bulimia nervosa.

Bulimia nervosa is defined as recurrent cycles of binge eating, especially of foods rich in carbohydrates,* and the taking of dramatic measures to purge the food, once consumed. These measures include self-induced vomiting, fasting or strict dieting, use of laxatives, and vigorous exercise. As with anorexia, there is overconcern about body shape and weight. The disorder usually begins in adolescence or early adulthood, and it afflicts women more so than men by about a 10:1 ratio (American Psychiatric Association, 1987).

Bulimia is even more common than anorexia. It has been estimated to affect 5 percent of the population (Nagelman et al., 1983). Bulimia has become of great concern on college campuses. About half of college women

Bulimia nervosa An eating disorder characterized by recurrent episodes of binge eating followed by purging as well as by persistent overconcern with body shape and weight.

*For example, candy, cookies, cakes. Meats contain protein and fat and are of relatively less interest to bulimic bingers.

admit to at least an occasional cycle of binging and purging (Herzog, 1982a, 1982b). Foreyt (1986) estimates that perhaps 15 percent of the college-age female population could be considered bulimic! Could it be that we are heading toward an era in which eating disorders, at least from a statistical perspective, are no longer deviant?

Theoretical Views

Numerous hypotheses concerning the origins of anorexia nervosa and bulimia nervosa have been advanced. Psychoanalysts, for example, have suggested that anorexia may represent an unconscious effort by the girl to remain prepubescent. The frequent link between anorexia and menarche seems to provide some support for this view. Anorexia allows the girl to circumvent growing up, separating from the family, and assuming adult responsibilities. Severe weight loss also prevents the rounding of the breasts and the hips. Thus, some investigators hypothesize that anorectic girls are conflicted about their sexuality and the prospect of pregnancy in particular.

Some learning theorists have proposed that anorexia is a phobia concerning the possibility of gaining weight. An irrational fear of gaining weight might reflect cultural idealization of the slender female. As noted by psychologists Janet Polivy and C. Peter Herman (1987), this cultural ideal has become so ingrained that "normal" eating for American women today is characterized by dieting! Such an ideal might contribute to distortion of the body image. Women college students generally see themselves as being significantly heavier than the figure that is most attractive to males, and heavier still than the "ideal" female figure (Fallon & Rozin, 1985).

Other theorists focus on family relationships as a causal factor and note that self-starvation has a brutal effect on parents (Bemis, 1978). They suggest that adolescents may use refusal to eat as a weapon against their parents.

Over the years, anorexia nervosa and bulimia nervosa have generally been attributed to psychological origins. However, a great deal of recent research has also implicated biological factors. For example, it has been speculated that some eating disorders might reflect problems in the hypothalamus. It has been shown that when the neurotransmitter norepinephrine acts upon a segment of the hypothalamus, it stimulates animals to eat, and these animals show preference for carbohydrates (Kaplan & Woodside, 1987; Leibowitz, 1986; Mitchell & Eckert, 1987). The neurotransmitter serotonin, in contrast, appears to induce feelings of satiation, thereby suppressing the appetite and particularly the desire for carbohydrates (Halmi et al., 1986; Kaplan & Woodside, 1987). So a biological condition that would increase the effect of serotonin could have a negative impact on the desire to eat, as in anorexia. One could also speculate that a biological condition that decreased the effect of serotonin, which normally suppresses appetite for carbohydrates, could result in periodic carbohydrate binging, as found in bulimia.

These hypotheses are under intense study, as are hypotheses concerning a possible role for still another transmitter—dopamine (Kaplan & Woodside, 1987). It is of major interest that "antidepressant" medications, which work by increasing the quantities of norepinephrine and serotonin available to the brain, have increased the appetite in a number of anorectic individuals. They have also controlled cycles of binge eating and vomiting (Halmi et al., 1986; Hughes et al., 1986; Walsh et al., 1984). However, antidepressants have not helped all anorectic and bulimic patients who try them.

MOOD DISORDERS

The mood disorders are characterized by disturbance in expressed emotions. The disruption generally involves depression or elation. As noted earlier, it must be kept in mind that most instances of depression are perfectly normal, or "run-of-the-mill." I am not suggesting that run-of-the-mill depression is to be ignored. My point is that if you have failed an important test, if a business investment has been lost, or if your closest friend becomes ill, it is understandable and fitting for you to feel depressed about it. In fact, it would be odd if you were *not* affected by adversity.

Truth or Fiction Revisited

It is *not* abnormal to feel depressed when one's situation is depressing.

As with the anxiety disorders, feelings of depression are considered to be abnormal when they are magnified far beyond one's circumstances or when there is no apparent justification for them. In this section we discuss two mood disorders: *major depression* and *bipolar disorder,* which involves feelings of elation as well as depression.

Major Depression

Depression is the "common cold" of psychological problems, according to Seligman (1973)—the most common psychological problem we face. People with run-of-the-mill depression may feel sad, blue, or "down in the dumps." They may complain of lack of energy, loss of self-esteem, difficulty concentrating, loss of interest in other people and usually enjoyable activities, pessimism, crying, and thoughts of suicide.

People with **major depression** usually share these feelings, but they tend to be more intense. In addition, people with major depression may show poor appetite and serious weight loss, agitation or **psychomotor retardation,** inability to concentrate and make decisions, complaints of "not caring" anymore, and recurrent suicide attempts.

Persons with major depression may also show faulty perception of reality, or so-called psychotic symptoms. Psychotic symptoms include delusions of unworthiness, guilt for imagined wrongdoings, and even ideas that one is rotting away from disease. There may also be hallucinations, such as of the Devil administering just punishment or of strange bodily sensations.

Bipolar Disorder

In bipolar disorder, formerly known as manic-depression, there are mood swings from elation to depression. These cycles seem to be unrelated to external events. In the elated, or **manic** phase, people might show excessive excitement or silliness, carrying jokes too far. They might show poor judgment, sometimes destroying property, and might be argumentative (Depue et al., 1981). Roommates might avoid them, finding them abrasive. Manic people often speak rapidly ("pressured speech") and jump from topic to topic, showing **rapid flight of ideas.** It is hard to "get a word in edgewise." They might show extreme generosity by making unusually large contributions to charity or giving away expensive possessions. They might not be able to sit still or to sleep restfully.

Major depression A severe depressive disorder in which the person may show loss of appetite, psychomotor symptoms, and impaired reality testing.

Psychomotor retardation Slowness in motor activity and (apparently) in thought.

Manic Elated, showing excessive excitement.

Rapid flight of ideas Rapid speech and topic changes, characteristic of manic behavior.

Depression is the other side of the coin. Bipolar depressed people often sleep more than usual and are lethargic. People with major (or unipolar) depression are more likely to show insomnia and agitation (Davison & Neale, 1986). Bipolar depressed individuals also exhibit social withdrawal and irritability.

Some persons with bipolar disorder attempt suicide "on the way down" from the elated phase of the disorder. They report that they will do almost anything to escape the depths of depression that they realize lie ahead.

Theoretical Views

As noted, depression is a normal reaction to loss or to exposure to unpleasant events. Negative life events such as marital discord, physical discomfort, incompetence, failure at work, and pressure at work all contribute to feelings of depression (Coyne et al., 1987; Eckenrode, 1984; Lewinsohn & Amenson, 1978; Stone & Neale, 1984). We are most likely to be depressed by undesirable events for which we feel responsible, such as academic problems and dropping out of school; financial problems; unwanted pregnancy; social problems, arguments, and fights; and conflict with the law (Hammen & Mayol, 1982). But many people recover from losses less readily than the rest of us. When compared to nondepressed people, depressed individuals are less likely to use problem-solving to alleviate the stresses acting upon them, and they have fewer supportive relationships to draw upon (Asarnow et al., 1987; Billings et al., 1983; Nezu & Ronan, 1985; Pagel & Becker, 1987; Schotte & Clum, 1987).

Most researchers, as we shall see, believe that bipolar disorder has an organic basis (Klein & Depue, 1985).

Psychodynamic Views Psychoanalysts suggest various explanations for depression. In one, depressed people are overly concerned about hurting others' feelings or losing their approval. As a result, they hold in rather than express feelings of anger. Anger becomes turned inward and is experienced as misery and self-hatred. From the psychodynamic perspective, bipolar disorder may be seen as alternating dominance of the personality by the superego and the ego. In the depressive phase of the disorder, the superego dominates, flooding the individual with exaggerated ideas of wrongdoing and associated feelings of guilt and worthlessness. After a while, the ego defends itself by rebounding and asserting supremacy, accounting for the elation and self-confidence that in part characterize the manic phase. Later, in response to the excessive display of ego, feelings of guilt return, again plunging the person into depression.

Learning Views Social-learning theorists note similarities in behavior between people who are depressed and laboratory animals who go unreinforced for instrumental behavior. Inactivity and loss of interest result in each. Lewinsohn (1975) theorizes that many depressed people lack skills that might lead to rewards. Some depressed people are nonassertive (Gotlib, 1984); others do have the social skills of nondepressed people, but they do not reinforce (credit) themselves as much for showing these skills (Gotlib, 1982). In any event, research by Michel Hersen and his colleagues (1984) suggests that social-skills training can ameliorate feelings of depression in many individuals.

Research has also found links between depression and **learned helplessness.** In one study, Seligman (1975) taught dogs that they were helpless

Learned helplessness Seligman's model for the acquisition of depressive behavior, based on findings that organisms in aversive situations learn to show inactivity when their operants are not reinforced.

to escape an electric shock by preventing them from leaving a cage in which they received repeated shock. Later a barrier to a safe compartment was removed, allowing the animals a way out. But when they were shocked again, the dogs made no effort to escape. Apparently they had learned that they were helpless. Seligman's dogs were also, in a sense, reinforced for doing nothing. That is, the shock *eventually* stopped when the dogs were showing helpless behavior—inactivity and withdrawal. "Reinforcement" might have increased the likelihood of repeating their "successful behavior"—that is, doing nothing—in a similar situation. This helpless behavior resembles that of depressed people.

Cognitive Factors The concept of learned helplessness bridges social-learning and cognitive approaches in that it is an attitude, an expectancy. There are many other potential cognitive factors in depression. For example, perfectionists set themselves up for depression through irrational self-demands. They are likely to fall short of their (unrealistic) expectations and, as a consequence, to feel depressed (Vestre, 1984). Feelings of unattractiveness contribute to unhappiness, and depressed people tend to have negatively distorted self-images. Depressed people, for example, are less likely than nondepressed people to be satisfied with their bodies, and they see themselves as being less attractive, even when they are not (Noles et al., 1985).

Our psychological well-being is reduced by focusing on negative outcomes of stressful events (Goodhart, 1985). Depressed people tend to respond to stress and to interpret shortcomings in particularly negative ways (Cochran & Hammen, 1985; Hammen et al., 1985; Persons & Rao, 1985). Depressed people tend to be self-critical (Zuroff & Mongrain, 1987), to attribute problems to factors that they are helpless to change (Lam et al., 1987), and to be generally pessimistic about the future (Alloy & Ahrens, 1987; Pyszczynski et al., 1987). They expect good things to happen to other people but not to them.

Failure and Attributional Style Seligman and his colleagues note that when things go wrong, we may think of the causes of failure as *internal* or *external, stable* or *unstable, global* or *specific*. Let us explain these various **attributional styles** through the example of having a date that does not work out. An internal attribution involves self-blame, as in "I really loused it up," whereas an external attribution places the blame elsewhere (as in "Some couples just don't take to each other," or, "She was the wrong sign for me"). A stable attribution ("It's my personality") suggests a problem that cannot be changed, whereas an unstable attribution ("It was the head cold") suggests a temporary condition. A global attribution of failure ("I have no idea what to do when I'm with people") suggests that the problem is quite large. A specific attribution ("I have problems making small talk at the very outset of a relationship") chops the problem down to a manageable size. Many depressed people overgeneralize the importance of a single failure (Carver & Ganellen, 1983; Carver et al., 1985).

Research shows that depressed people are more likely than nondepressed people to attribute the causes of their failures to internal, stable, and global factors—factors that lead them to see themselves as being more helpless to change things for the better (Blumberg & Izard, 1985; Miller et al., 1982; Peterson et al., 1981; Pyszczynski & Greenberg, 1985; Raps et al., 1982; Seligman et al., 1979, 1984). Individuals who see themselves as being more capable of controlling events (less helpless to make changes) respond more adaptively in stressful social interactions (Sacks & Bugental, 1987); they speak more frequently and are more pleasant and less hostile toward unresponsive conversants. As a result, they are less likely to fail in their social interactions

Attributional style One's tendency to attribute one's behavior to internal or external factors, stable or unstable factors, and so on.

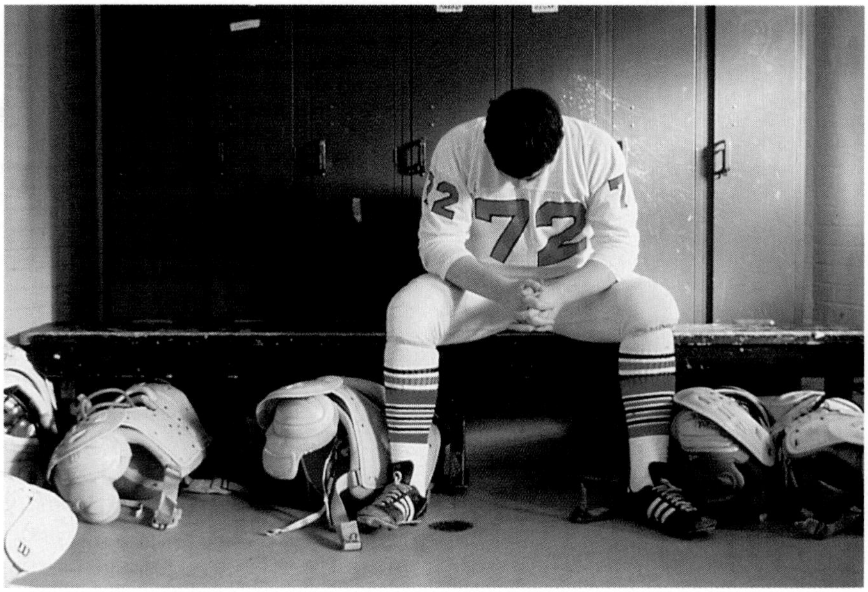

Why Did He Miss That Tackle? This football player is compounding his feelings of depression by attributing his shortcomings on the field to factors that he cannot change. For example, he tells himself that he missed the tackle because of stupidity and lack of athletic ability. He ignores the facts that his coaching was poor and that his teammates failed to come to his support.

and become depressed by them. Depressed people exaggerate the blame they deserve and view their problems as being all but impossible to change. Is it any wonder that they are more likely than nondepressed people to feel helpless?

Organic Factors Researchers are also searching for organic factors in the mood disorders. Mood swings tend to run in families, and there is a higher concordance rate for bipolar disorder among identical than fraternal twins (Klein et al., 1985; Smith & Winokur, 1983). A recent study of an Amish community in Pennsylvania by Janice Egeland and her colleagues (1987) traced the distribution of bipolar disorder among the members of an extended family with a high incidence of the problem. The research group isolated a segment of DNA (gene) on chromosome 11, which was transmitted to children half the time and apparently was present in all family members who showed bipolar disorder. However, only about 80 percent of those who possessed this "genetic vulnerability" actually displayed the disorder. So, genetic factors probably create a predisposition for bipolar disorder but do not, in and of themselves, guarantee its appearance. Maybe depressive cognitions and other stressors heighten the probability that the disorder will be manifested.

Perhaps the genetic vulnerability manifests itself in terms of the actions of neurotransmitters. Much research has focused on the role of the neurotransmitter norepinephrine. Rats with lowered levels of norepinephrine show behavior similar to that of depressed people (Ellison, 1977). They are less aggressive than colony-mates and appear to be apathetic and withdrawn. They lie around listlessly in their burrows. Their appetites decrease and they lose weight.

Interactions between biological factors (such as level of norepinephrine) and psychological factors (such as learned helplessness) might exacerbate feelings of depression. For example, Martin Seligman (1975) and Jay Weiss (1982) have found that dogs who had learned that they were helpless to escape electric shocks showed a decrease in the amount of norepinephrine available to the brain. Thus, helplessness *and* inactivity are linked to low norepinephrine levels. The relationship might be a vicious cycle: a depressing situation might decrease the action of norepinephrine, and this chemical change might compound depressive behavior. Manic behavior, in contrast, appears to reflect heightened action of norepinephrine.

As will be noted in Chapter 13, people whose depression reaches psychotic proportions often respond to antidepressant drugs. One effect of these drugs is to raise norepinephrine levels; another might be to enhance the sensitivity of norepinephrine receptors. The apparent actions of antidepressant drugs therefore suggest further evidence of a role for norepinephrine in depression. Moreover, the metal lithium, which is the major chemical treatment for bipolar disorder, apparently flattens out manic-depressive cycles by moderating levels of norepinephrine.

Some researchers argue that the neurotransmitter serotonin also plays a role in mood disorders (e.g., Berger, 1978). It has been speculated that deficiencies in serotonin may create a general disposition toward mood disorders. A deficiency of serotonin *combined with* a deficiency of norepinephrine might be linked with depression. But a deficiency of serotonin combined with excessive levels of norepinephrine might produce manic behavior.

Although the exact causes of depression remain clouded to some degree, we know all too well that for some people suicide is one of the possible outcomes of depression. We discuss that distressing topic next.

Suicide

Consider a number of facts about suicide:

Suicide is more common among college students than among nonstudents. About 10,000 college students attempt suicide each year.

Suicide is the second leading cause of death among college students.

Nearly 200,000 people attempt suicide each year in the United States. About one in ten succeeds.

Three times as many women as men attempt suicide, but three times as many men succeed.

Men prefer to use guns or to hang themselves, but women prefer to use sleeping pills.

Young blacks and Native Americans are more than twice as likely as whites to commit suicide.

Suicide is especially common among physicians, lawyers, and psychologists, although it is found among all occupational groups and at all age levels.

No other cause of death leaves such feelings of guilt, distress, and puzzlement in friends and relatives.

Why do people take their own lives? It seems that the great majority of suicides are linked to depression (Leonard, 1977; Schotte & Clum, 1982). Although most people who attempt suicide show hopelessness and despair, they do not appear to be out of touch with reality (Leonard, 1974).

Strongly suicidal people report finding life more dull, empty, and boring than do less or nonsuicidal people. Suicidal people feel more anxious, excitable, submissive, angry, guilt-ridden, helpless, and inadequate than others (Mehrabian & Weinstein, 1985; Neuringer, 1982). All in all, things look hopeless to them (Cole, 1988; Petrie & Chamberlain, 1983). According to psychologist Edwin Shneidman (1985, 1987) of the UCLA Neuropsychiatric Institute, suicide attempters usually experience unendurable psychological pain and attempt to end awareness of their suffering. In a Boston University study, college women who had attempted suicide were more likely than their peers to implicate their parents as a source of the pain that led to the attempt (Cantor, 1976). They were also less likely to feel able to ask parents or others for help when they felt desperate or under great stress.

Suicide attempts are more frequent following stressful life events, especially "exit events" (Slater & Depue, 1981). Exit events involve loss of social support—as in the death of a spouse, close friend, or relative; divorce or separation; a family member's leaving home; or the loss of a close friend. People who consider suicide in response to stress have also been found to be less capable of solving problems than those who do not consider suicide (Schotte & Clum, 1987). That is, they are less likely to find ways of changing the stressful circumstances.

Some suicides are quite logical (Shneidman & Farberow, 1970), as in the case of a terminally ill patient in unrelenting pain whose spouse has died and who feels like a burden to the family. Suicide may also be ceremonial, as in the case of Japanese Samurai warriors who chose suicide over dishonor. A few suicides stem from thought disorders, as in paranoid schizophrenia or a "bad trip" induced by drugs.

Now let us consider a number of myths about suicide—and the realities.

Myths about Suicide Some believe that people who threaten suicide are only seeking attention. The serious just "do it." Actually, 70 to 80 percent of suicides gave clear clues concerning their intentions prior to the act (Cordes, 1985; Leonard, 1977).

Truth or Fiction Revisited

It is *not* true that people who threaten suicide are only seeking attention. Many attempt to take their lives.

Some believe that those who fail at suicide attempts are only seeking attention. But 75 percent of successful suicides had made previous attempts (Cohen et al., 1966). Contrary to myth, discussion of suicide with a depressed person does not prompt suicide. In fact, extracting a promise that the person will not commit suicide before calling or visiting a mental-health worker seems to have prevented suicides.

Some believe that only "insane" people (meaning people who are out of touch with reality) would take their own lives. However, Shneidman points out that suicidal thinking is not necessarily a sign of psychosis, neurosis, or personality disorder; instead, the contemplation of suicide reflects a narrowing of the range of options that people think are available to them (Cordes, 1985). Finally, most people with suicidal thoughts, contrary to myth, will *not* act on them. Suicidal thoughts at a time of great stress are not uncommon.

In the section on Psychology and Modern Life, we shall consider ways of preventing suicide.

SCHIZOPHRENIA

Joyce was 19. Her boyfriend Ron brought her into the emergency room because she had slit her wrists. When she was interviewed, her attention wandered. She seemed distracted by things in the air, or something she might be hearing. It was as if she had an invisible earphone.

She explained that she had cut her wrists because the "hellsmen" had told her to. Then she seemed frightened. Later she said that the hellsmen had warned her not to reveal their existence. She had been afraid that they would punish her for talking about them.

Ron told the emergency-room physician that Joyce had been living with him for about a year. At first they had been together in a small apartment in town. But Joyce did not want to be near other people and had convinced him to rent a bungalow in the country. There she would make fantastic drawings of goblins and monsters during the days. Now and then she would become agitated and act as if invisible things were giving her instructions.

"I'm bad," Joyce would mutter, "I'm bad." She would begin to jumble her words. Ron would then try to convince her to go to the hospital, but she would refuse. Then the wrist-cutting would begin. Ron thought he had made the cottage safe by removing knives and blades. But Joyce would always find something.

Then Joyce would be brought to the hospital, have stitches put in, be kept under observation for a while, and medicated. She would explain that she cut herself because the hellsmen had told her that she was bad and must die. After a few days she would deny hearing the hellsmen, and she would insist on leaving the hospital.

Ron would take her home. The pattern continued.

When the emergency-room physician examined Joyce's wrists and heard that she believed she had been following the orders of "hellsmen," he began to suspect that she was suffering from schizophrenia. Schizophrenia touches every aspect of victims' lives. Schizophrenia is characterized by disturbances in (1) thought and language, (2) perception and attention, (3) motor activity, and (4) mood and by (5) withdrawal and **autism.**

Schizophrenia is known primarily by disturbances in thought, which are inferred from verbal and other overt behavior. Schizophrenic persons may show *loosening of associations.* Unless we are daydreaming or deliberately allowing our thoughts to "wander," our thinking is normally tightly knit. We start at a certain point, and the things that come to mind (the associations) tend to be logically and coherently connected. But schizophrenics often think in an illogical, disorganized manner. Their speech may be jumbled, combining parts of words or making rhymes in a meaningless fashion. Schizophrenics may also jump from topic to topic, conveying little useful information. Nor do they usually have insight that their thoughts and behavior are abnormal.

Many schizophrenics have **delusions**—for example, delusions of grandeur, persecution, or reference. In the case of delusions of grandeur, a person may believe, for example, that he is Jesus or a person on a special mission, or he may have grand, illogical plans for saving the world. Delusions tend to be unshakable, despite disconfirming evidence. Persons with delusions of persecution may believe that they are sought by the Mafia, CIA, FBI, or some other group or agency. A woman with delusions of reference expressed the belief that national news broadcasts contained coded information about her. A man with such delusions complained that neighbors had "bugged" his walls with "radios." Other schizophrenics may have delusions to the effect that they have committed unpardonable sins, that they are rotting away from a hideous disease, or that they or the world do not really exist.

The perceptions of schizophrenics often include hallucinations—imagery in the absence of external stimulation that the schizophrenic cannot distinguish from reality. Joyce believed that she heard "hellsmen." Others may see colors or even obscene words spelled out in midair. Auditory hallucinations are most common.

Autism Self-absorption. Absorption in daydreaming and fantasy.

Delusions False, persistent beliefs that are unsubstantiated by sensory or objective evidence.

The "Son-of-Sam Killer." David Berkowitz, the "Son-of-Sam Killer," smiles benignly upon his arrest in 1977. Does his response to arrest seem appropriate? Because of his inappropriate emotional responses and his claim that a dog had urged him to commit his crimes, many mental-health professionals considered him to be schizophrenic.

Truth or Fiction Revisited

It is true that in some abnormal behavior problems, people see and hear things that are not actually there. Schizophrenia is an example.

Motor activity may become wild and excited or may slow to a **stupor.** There may be strange gestures and peculiar facial expressions. Emotional response may be flat or blunted, or inappropriate—as in giggling at bad news. Schizophrenics tend to withdraw from social contacts and become wrapped up in their own thoughts and fantasies.

Many people diagnosed as schizophrenic show only a few of these symptoms. The DSM–III–R takes the view that schizophrenics at some time or another show delusions, problems with associative thinking, and hallucinations, but not necessarily all at once. There are also different kinds or types of schizophrenia, and different symptoms predominate with each type.

Types of Schizophrenia

The DSM–III–R lists three major types of schizophrenia: *disorganized, catatonic,* and *paranoid.*

Disorganized Type **Disorganized schizophrenics** show incoherence, loosening of associations, disorganized behavior, disorganized delusions, and vivid, abundant hallucinations that are often sexual or religious. One 23-year-old female disorganized schizophrenic remarked "I see 'pennis' " when I interviewed her. She pointed vaguely into the air before her. Asked to spell *pennis,* she replied irritatedly: "P-e-n-i-s." Apparently her social background was so inhibited that she had never heard the word for the male sex organ spoken aloud, and so she mispronounced it. Extreme social impairment is common among disorganized schizophrenics. They also often show silliness and giddiness of mood, giggling and nonsensical speech. They may neglect their appearance and hygiene and may lose control of their bladder and their bowels.

Stupor A condition in which the senses and thought are dulled.

Disorganized schizophrenics Schizophrenics who show disorganized delusions and vivid hallucinations.

Catatonic Type **Catatonic schizophrenics** show striking impairment in motor activity. Impairment is characterized by slowing of activity into a stupor that may change suddenly into an agitated phase. Catatonic individuals may hold unusual, even difficult postures for hours, even as their limbs grow swollen or stiff. A striking symptom is **waxy flexibility,** in which they maintain positions into which they have been manipulated by others. Catatonic individuals may also show **mutism,** but afterward they usually report that they heard what others were saying at the time.

Paranoid Type **Paranoid schizophrenics** have systematized delusions and, frequently, related auditory hallucinations (American Psychiatric Association, 1987). They usually show delusions of grandeur and persecution, but they may also show delusions of jealousy, in which they believe that a spouse or lover has been unfaithful. They may show agitation, confusion, and fear, and may experience vivid hallucinations that are consistent with their delusions. The paranoid schizophrenic often constructs a complex or systematized delusion involving themes of wrongdoing or persecution.

A rarely used, related diagnostic category is **paranoia** (or "delusional [paranoid] disorder," according to the DSM–III–R). People may receive this diagnosis if they show a permanent, "unshakable" delusional system that does not have the bizarreness typical of schizophrenia. Persons with the disorder do not show the confused, jumbled thinking suggestive of schizophrenia. Hallucinations, when present, are not prominent. Daily functioning in paranoia and in some cases of paranoid schizophrenia may be minimally impaired, or not impaired at all, as long as the person does not act on the basis of his or her delusions.

Theoretical Views

Psychologists have investigated various factors that may contribute to schizophrenia.

Psychodynamic Views According to the psychodynamic model, schizophrenia is the overwhelming of the ego by sexual or aggressive impulses from the id. The impulses threaten the ego and cause intense intrapsychic conflict. Under this threat, the person regresses to an early phase of the oral stage in which the infant has not yet learned that it and the world are separate. Fantasies become confused with reality, giving birth to hallucinations and delusions. Primitive impulses may carry more weight than social norms.

Critics point out that schizophrenic behavior is not that similar to infantile behavior. Moreover, psychoanalysts have not been able to predict a schizophrenic outcome on the basis of theoretically predisposing early experiences.

Learning Views Learning theorists explain schizophrenia through conditioning and observational learning. From this perspective, people show schizophrenic behavior when it is more likely than normal behavior to be reinforced. This may occur when the person is reared in a socially unrewarding or punitive situation; inner fantasies then become more reinforcing than social realities.

In the mental hospital, patients may learn what is "expected" of them by observing other patients. Hospital staff may reinforce schizophrenic behavior by paying more attention to patients who behave bizarrely. This view is consistent with folklore that the child who disrupts the class earns more attention from the teacher than the "good" child.

Catatonic schizophrenics Schizophrenics who show striking impairment in motor activity.

Waxy flexibility A symptom of catatonic schizophrenia in which persons maintain postures into which they are placed.

Mutism Refusal to talk.

Paranoid schizophrenia A type of schizophrenia characterized primarily by delusions—commonly of persecution—and by vivid hallucinations.

Paranoia A major but rare disorder in which a person shows a persistent delusional system but not the confusion of the schizophrenic.

Critics note that many of us grow up in socially punitive settings but seem to show immunity to extinction of socially appropriate behavior. Others acquire schizophrenic behavior patterns without having had the opportunity to observe other schizophrenics. In Chapter 13, we shall see that behavioral methods, derived from principles of learning, *can* decrease socially undesirable responses, but there is little evidence that they can make major changes in the expression of thought disorders.

Genetic Factors Schizophrenia, like many other psychological disorders, runs in families. Children of schizophrenic parents are at greater than average risk for showing certain problems at early ages. In the so-called *New York Project,* for example, it was found that 12- and 13-year-old children of schizophrenics have more difficulty in social relationships, more emotional instability, and less academic motivation than their age-mates (Watt et al., 1982).

Schizophrenic persons constitute about 1 percent of the population, but children with two schizophrenic parents have about a 35 percent chance of becoming schizophrenic (Rosenthal, 1970). Twin studies also find a higher concordance rate for the diagnosis among pairs of identical twins, whose genetic codes are the same, than among pairs of fraternal twins, who are no more closely related genetically than other siblings. In their review of twin studies, Davison and Neale (1986) reported concordance rates ranging from 6 to 86 percent for identical twin pairs and from 2 to 34 percent for fraternal twin pairs.

The studies reviewed by Davison and Neale (1986) did not generally control for environmental influences. Children reared in the same family have similar environments. Moreover, parents (and others) often expect (and encourage) identical behavior in identical twins. To overcome this problem, studies of adopted children have been undertaken to determine whether their natural or adoptive parents exert a greater influence on the likelihood of their being judged schizophrenic (e.g., Heston, 1966; Wender et al., 1974). In such studies, the biological parent typically places the child at greater risk than the adoptive parent—even though the child has been reared by the adoptive parent. In more recent research, a number of cases of schizophrenia were linked to an abnormally functioning gene or cluster of genes on chromosome 5 (Sherrington et al., 1988).

Whereas evidence for a genetic role in schizophrenia seems strong, heredity cannot be the sole factor. If it were, there would be a 100 percent concordance rate for schizophrenia between pairs of identical twins. Genetic factors probably create a predisposition toward schizophrenia that interacts with other factors to produce schizophrenic behavior. Heredity might transmit biochemical factors, such as those discussed in the following section.

The Dopamine Theory of Schizophrenia Over the years, numerous substances have been thought to play a role in schizophrenic disorders. Much current theory and research focus on the neurotransmitter **dopamine.**

The dopamine theory of schizophrenia evolved from observation of the effects of **amphetamines,** a group of stimulants. Researchers are confident that amphetamines act by increasing the quantity of dopamine in the brain. High doses of amphetamines lead to behavior that mimics paranoid schizophrenia in normal people, and even low doses exacerbate the symptoms of schizophrenics (Snyder, 1980). A second source of evidence for the dopamine theory lies in the effects of a class of drugs called **phenothiazines.** Research suggests that the phenothiazines, which are often effective in treating schizophrenia, work by blocking the action of dopamine receptors (Creese et al., 1978; Turkington, 1983).

It does not appear that schizophrenic persons produce more dopamine than others but that they *utilize* more of the substance (Davison & Neale,

---

Dopamine A neurotransmitter implicated in schizophrenia.

Amphetamines Stimulants whose abuse can trigger symptoms that mimic schizophrenia.

Phenothiazine A member of a family of drugs that are effective in treatment of many cases of schizophrenia.

1986). Why? It could be that they have a greater number of dopamine receptors in the brain or that their dopamine receptors are hyperactive (Lee & Seeman, 1977; Mackay et al., 1982; Snyder, 1984). Postmortem studies of schizophrenics' brains have yielded evidence consistent with both possibilities.

Future research may suggest that schizophrenia can have multiple causes. In some cases it might be that genetic biochemical factors predispose borderline individuals to develop schizophrenic disorders in response to stressors. In such cases, biological predispositions would interact with situational factors to produce the disorder. But other people might be so severely handicapped by biochemical factors that they will develop schizophrenia under the most positive environmental conditions.

PERSONALITY DISORDERS

Personality disorders, like personality traits, are characterized by enduring patterns of behavior. Personality disorders, however, are inflexible and maladaptive. They impair personal or social functioning and are a source of distress to the individual or to others.

There are a number of personality disorders, including the *paranoid, schizotypal, schizoid,* and *antisocial personality disorders.* The defining trait of the **paranoid personality disorder** is the tendency to interpret other people's behavior as being deliberately threatening or demeaning. Although persons with the disorder do not show grossly disorganized thinking, they are mistrustful of others, and their social relationships suffer for it. They may be suspicious of coworkers and supervisors, but they can generally hold onto jobs.

Schizotypal personality disorder is characterized by pervasive peculiarities in thought, perception, and behavior, such as excessive fantasy and suspiciousness, feelings of being unreal, or odd usage of words (American Psychiatric Association, 1987, pp. 340–342). The bizarre psychotic behaviors that characterize schizophrenia are absent, so this disorder is schizo*typal* instead of schizophrenic. Because of their oddities, persons with the disorder are often maladjusted on the job.

The **schizoid personality** is defined by indifference to social relationships and flatness in emotional responsiveness. Schizoid personalities are "loners" who do not develop warm, tender feelings for others. They have few friends and rarely get married. Some schizoid personalities do very well on the job, as long as continuous social interaction is not required. Hallucinations and delusions are absent.

Personality disorders Enduring patterns of maladaptive behavior that are a source of distress to the individual or others.

Paranoid personality disorder A disorder characterized by persistent suspiciousness but not involving the disorganization of paranoid schizophrenia.

Schizotypal personality disorder A disorder characterized by oddities of thought and behavior but not involving bizarre psychotic symptoms.

Schizoid personality disorder A disorder characterized by social withdrawal.

Antisocial personality disorder The diagnosis given a person who is in frequent conflict with society yet who is undeterred by punishment and experiences little or no guilt and anxiety.

The Antisocial Personality

Persons with **antisocial personality disorders** persistently violate the rights of others, show indifference to commitments, and encounter conflict with the law (Table 12.3). In order for the diagnosis to be used, the person must be at least 18 years old (American Psychiatric Association, 1987). Cleckley (1964) notes that persons with antisocial personalities often show a superficial charm and are at least average in intelligence. Perhaps their most striking feature, given their antisocial behavior, is their lack of guilt and low

Table 12.3 Characteristics of the Antisocial Personality

Persistent violation of the rights of others
Irresponsibility
Lack of formation of enduring relationships or loyalty to another person
Failure to maintain good job performance over the years
Failure to develop or adhere to a life plan
History of truancy
History of delinquency
History of running away
Persistent lying
Sexual promiscuity
Substance abuse
Impulsivity
Inability to tolerate boredom
At least 18 years of age
Onset of antisocial behavior by age 15

Source: DSM–III–R (1987).

level of anxiety. They seem to be largely undeterred by punishment. Though they have usually received punishment from parents and others for their misdeeds, they continue their impulsive, irresponsible styles of life.

Theoretical Views Various factors appear to contribute to antisocial behavior, including an antisocial father, parental lack of love and rejection during childhood, and inconsistent discipline.

Antisocial personalities tend to run in families. Studies of adoptees have found higher incidences of antisocial behavior among the biological than the adoptive relatives of persons with the disorder (Cadoret, 1978; Hutchings & Mednick, 1974; Mednick, 1985).

Some researchers have attributed antisocial personality disorder to an extra Y sex chromosome. Males with an XYY sex chromosomal structure (sometimes referred to as **supermales**) were thought to have a predisposition toward aggressiveness and crime. Supermales as a group are somewhat taller and more heavily bearded than XY males, but only about 1.5 percent of male delinquents and criminals tested show the XYY structure (Rosenthal, 1970). Moreover, most supermales do not engage in crime or violence.

One promising avenue of research concerns the observation that antisocial personalities are unlikely to show guilt for their misdeeds or be deterred by punishment. It is suggested that low levels of guilt and anxiety reflect lower-than-normal levels of arousal, which, in turn, have at least a partial genetic basis (Lykken, 1957, 1982). Experiments on this issue show, for example, that antisocial subjects do not learn as rapidly as others equal in intelligence when the payoff is avoidance of impending electric shock. But when the antisocial subjects' levels of arousal are increased by injections of adrenaline, they learn to avoid punishment as rapidly as others (Schachter & Latané, 1964; Chesno & Kilmann, 1975).

A lower-than-normal level of arousal does not guarantee the development of an antisocial personality. It might also be necessary for a person to be reared under conditions that do not foster the self-concept of one who abides by law and social custom. Punishment for deviation from the norm would then be unlikely to induce feelings of guilt and shame. The individual might be "undeterred" by punishment.

Supermale A male with XYY chromosomal structure.

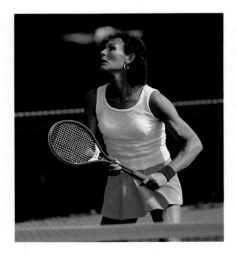

Transsexualism. Physician Richard Raskin underwent sex reassignment surgery and became Renée Richards. For a while, Renée competed as a woman on the women's tennis circuit. More recently, Renée served as a coach to Martina Navratlova.

SEXUAL DISORDERS

The DSM–III–R lists various sexual disorders, including *paraphilias* and *sexual dysfunctions*. We shall also discuss the **gender-identity disorder** of transsexualism in this section.* In a gender-identity disorder, one's assigned sex (as based on anatomic sex and recorded on the birth certificate) is inconsistent with one's gender identity (one's psychological sense of being male or being female). In the **paraphilias,** people show sexual arousal in response to unusual or bizarre objects or situations. **Sexual dysfunctions** are characterized by lack of sexual "appetite" or problems in becoming sexually aroused and reaching orgasm. We shall discuss sexual dysfunctions in Chapter 14.

Transsexualism

About 30 years ago, headlines were made when an ex-GI, now known as Christine Jorgensen, had a "sex-change operation" in Denmark. Since that time some 2,500 American transsexuals, including tennis player Dr. Renée Richards, have undergone sex-reassignment surgery. Sex-reassignment surgery is cosmetic. It does not actually change gender by implanting reproductive organs of the opposite sex. Instead, it creates the appearance of the external genitals of the opposite sex—more successfully with male-to-female than with female-to-male transsexuals. After these operations, transsexuals can engage in sexual intercourse but they cannot have children.

Transsexualism is a towering adjustment problem, because it is the persistent feeling that one is of the wrong sex. Transsexuals wish to be rid of their own genitals and to live as members of the opposite sex. Although transsexuals are sexually attracted to members of their own sex, they do not see themselves as homosexuals. This is because they view nature's assignment as a mistake. They see themselves as being "trapped" inside the body of the wrong sex.

The causes of transsexualism are unclear. Socialization patterns might affect transsexuals who are reared by parents who had wanted children of the opposite sex and who thus encourage cross-sex dressing and patterns of play. But it is also possible that some transsexuals have been influenced by prenatal hormonal imbalances. It might be that the brain can be "masculinized" or "feminized" by sex hormones during certain stages of prenatal development. Perhaps the brain is influenced in one direction, even as the genitals are being differentiated in the other direction (Money, 1987).

Results are mixed concerning transsexuals who undergo sex reassignment. Female-to-male transsexuals are somewhat better adjusted than male-to-female transsexuals (Abramowitz, 1986). Most female-to-male transsexuals rate their adjustment as positive and are solid workers and tax payers (Person & Ovesey, 1974; Randall, 1969). Despite difficulties in surgically constructing structures that serve as external male sex organs, a group of 22 female-to-male transsexuals were generally satisfied postoperatively with their new bodies (Fleming et al., 1982). A follow-up study of 116 transsexuals (both female-to-male and male-to-female) at least one year after surgery found that most were pleased with the results and that the majority were acceptably adjusted (Blanchard et al., 1985). One study of 42 postoperative male-to-

Gender-identity disorder A disorder in which a person's anatomic sex is inconsistent with his or her gender identity (or sense of being male or female).

Paraphilias Disorders in which people show sexual arousal in response to unusual or bizarre objects or situations.

Sexual dysfunctions Persistent problems in achieving or maintaining sexual arousal or in reaching orgasm.

Transsexualism A gender-identity disorder in which a person feels trapped in the body of the wrong sex.

*The DSM–III–R classifies transsexualism as a "disorder usually first evident in infancy, childhood, or adolescence."

female transsexuals found that all but one would repeat the surgery, and the great majority found sexual activity to be more pleasurable as a "woman" (Bentler, 1976). However, about 10 percent of male-to-female transsexuals seem to encounter serious adjustment problems (Abramowitz, 1986).

Paraphilias

Paraphilias are characterized by sexual response to unusual objects or situations. The American Psychiatric Association (1987) uses the following diagnoses when people act on these urges or—if they do not act on them—when they are markedly distressed by them.

Fetishism **Fetishism** is sexual response to an inanimate object, such as an article of clothing, or to a bodily part, such as the feet. Sexual gratification is often achieved through masturbating in the presence of the object. Fetishes for undergarments and for objects made of leather, rubber, or silk are not uncommon.

Transvestic Fetishism **Transvestic fetishism** is recurrent, persistent dressing in clothing usually worn by a woman in order to achieve sexual excitement in a heterosexual male. Transvestism may range from wearing a single female undergarment in private to sporting full dress at a transvestite club. Most transvestites are married and engage in sexual activity with their wives, but they seek additional sexual gratification through dressing as women.

Zoophilia **Zoophilia,** or *bestiality,* is sexual contact with animals as a preferred or exclusive means of achieving sexual arousal. Thus, a child or adolescent who shows some sexual response to an episode of rough-and-tumble play with the family pet is not likely to be showing zoophilia.

Pedophilia **Pedophilia** is actual or fantasized sexual activity with children as a preferred means of becoming sexually aroused. Most episodes involve exhibitionism or fondling rather than sexual intercourse.

Exhibitionism **Exhibitionism** is the repetitive act of exposing one's genitals to a stranger in order to surprise or shock, rather than sexually arouse, the victim. The exhibitionist is usually not interested in actual sexual contact with the victim. He may masturbate while fantasizing about or actually exposing himself.

Professional strip-teasers and scantily clad swimmers do not fit the definition of exhibitionists. Both groups might seek to sexually arouse, but usually not to shock, observers. In fact, the main motive of the strip-teaser might be to earn a living.

Exhibitionism and voyeurism are nearly completely limited to males.

Truth or Fiction Revisited

It is *not* true that strip-teasers are exhibitionists. The aims of the exhibitionist are very different.

Voyeurism **Voyeurism** is repetitive watching of unsuspecting strangers while they are undressing or engaging in sexual activity as the preferred or exclusive means of achieving sexual arousal. We may enjoy observing spouses undress, or the nudity in an R-rated film, without being diagnosed

---

Fetishism A variation of choice in sexual object in which a bodily part (e.g., a foot) or an inanimate object (e.g., an undergarment) elicits sexual arousal and is preferred to a person.

Transvestic fetishism Recurrent, persistent dressing in clothing worn by the opposite sex for purposes of sexual excitement.

Zoophilia Sexual contact with animals as a preferred means of achieving sexual arousal.

Pedophilia Sexual contact with children as the preferred source of sexual excitement.

Exhibitionism The compulsion to expose one's genitals in public.

Voyeurism Attainment of sexual gratification through observing others undress or engage in sexual activity.

as voyeurs. In voyeurism, the "victim" does not know that he or she is being watched, and the voyeur prefers looking to doing.

Sexual Masochism **Sexual masochism** is named after the Austrian storyteller Leopold von Sacher-Masoch, who portrayed sexual satisfaction as deriving from pain or humiliation. The sexual masochist must receive pain or humiliation to achieve sexual gratification. It has been suggested that many masochists experience guilt about sex, but they can enjoy sex as long as they see themselves as being appropriately punished for it.

Sexual Sadism **Sexual sadism** is named after the infamous Marquis de Sade, a Frenchman who wrote stories about the pleasures of achieving sexual gratification by inflicting pain or humiliation on others. In sadism, the person may not be able to become sexually excited unless he or she inflicts pain on the partner.

Theoretical Views According to psychodynamic theory, paraphilias are defenses against anxiety. The exhibitionist, for example, has unconscious castration anxiety. His victim's shock at his exposure reassures him that he does, after all, have a penis. Fetishism, pedophilia, and so on protect him from fear of failure in adult heterosexual relationships and provide him with sexual outlets.

Rathus (1983) offers a social-learning view of fetishism and other paraphilias. First, a fantasized or actual event—such as becoming excited when a woman happens upon a person who is urinating behind a bush—prompts that person to encode the unusual object or situation as being sexually arousing. As a consequence, second, the person acquires the expectancy that the object or situation will increase the pleasure of sexual activity. Expectancies about an outcome can be powerful influences on behavior, and so, third, the object is used in actuality or fantasy to heighten sexual arousal. Fourth, recognition of the deviance of the fantasy or act may cause feelings of anxiety or guilt. These feelings, if not extreme, may enhance emotional arousal in the presence of the deviant object or activity. Heightened emotional response might then be *attributed* to the deviant object or activity. Fifth, orgasm reinforces the preceding behaviors and fantasies. Sixth, orgasm also confirms the stimulating properties attributed to the deviant object or activity. Seventh, in cases in which a person is anxious about normal sexual relationships, the deviant object or activity might become the major or sole sexual outlet.

Although the causes of many patterns of abnormal behavior remain in dispute, a number of therapy methods have been devised to deal with them. Those methods are the focus of Chapter 13.

Sexual masochism Attainment of sexual gratification by means of receiving pain or humiliation.

Sexual sadism Attainment of sexual gratification by means of inflicting pain or humiliation on sex partners.

SUMMARY

1. **What is abnormal behavior?** Behavior is likely to be labeled abnormal when it is unusual, is socially unacceptable, involves faulty perception of reality, or is personally distressful, dangerous, or self-defeating.
2. **What are the major models of abnormal behavior?** These are the demonological, medical, psychodynamic, learning-theory, and cognitive models. Demonologists view abnormal behavior as a sign of possession. Adherents to the medical model see abnormal behavior as symptomatic of underlying organic disorders. Psychodynamic theorists view it as symbolizing psychological conflicts. Social-learning theorists see abnormal behaviors as being acquired through principles of learning or as problems in person variables. Cognitive theorists tend to explain abnormal behavior patterns as problems in processing information or as reflections of self-defeating beliefs and attitudes.

3. **What are the anxiety disorders?** Anxiety disorders are characterized by motor tension, feelings of dread, and overarousal of the sympathetic branch of the ANS. Anxiety disorders include irrational, excessive fears, or phobias; panic disorder, which is characterized by sudden attacks in which people typically fear that they may be losing control or going crazy; generalized or "free-floating" anxiety; obsessive-compulsive disorders, in which people are troubled by intrusive thoughts or impulses to repeat some activity; and post-traumatic stress disorder (PTSD), in which a stressful event is followed by persistent fears and intrusive thoughts about the event.

4. **How do psychologists explain anxiety disorders?** Psychoanalysts tend to view anxiety disorders as representing problems in maintaining repression of primitive impulses. Many learning theorists view phobias as conditioned fears. The concept of prepared conditioning refers to the view that we may be biologically predisposed to acquire certain kinds of phobias. Anxiety disorders tend to run in families, and some psychologists suggest that biochemical factors that create a predisposition toward anxiety disorders may be inherited.

5. **What are the dissociative disorders?** Dissociative disorders are characterized by a sudden temporary change in consciousness or self-identity. They include psychogenic amnesia, or "motivated forgetting" of personal information; psychogenic fugue, which involves forgetting plus fleeing and adopting a new identity; multiple personality, in which a person behaves as if more than one distinct personality occupies the body; and depersonalization, which is characterized by feelings that one is not real or that one is standing outside one's body and observing one's thought processes.

6. **What are the somatoform disorders?** In somatoform disorders, people show or complain of physical problems, although no evidence of a medical abnormality can be found. The somatoform disorders include conversion disorder and hypochondria. In a conversion disorder, there is loss of a body function with no organic basis. Some people with conversion disorder show la belle indifférence, or lack of concern about their disorder. Hypochondriacs insist that they are suffering from illnesses, although there are no medical findings.

7. **What is anorexia nervosa?** Anorexia nervosa is an eating disorder characterized by dramatic weight loss and intense fear of being overweight. Anorectic females also show amenorrhea; that is, they stop menstruating. Anorectic women have a distorted body image in which they view themselves as being overweight when others perceive them as being dangerously thin. Theoretical views of anorexia include hypotheses that the disorder might reflect organic problems in the hypothalamus or concerns about assuming the role of an adult woman.

8. **What is bulimia nervosa?** In bulimia nervosa, the individual also fears becoming overweight but goes on eating binges, especially of carbohydrates. Binging is followed by severe weight-loss methods such as fasting or self-induced vomiting.

9. **What are the mood disorders?** Mood disorders are characterized by disturbances in expressed emotions. Major depression is characterized by persistent feelings of sadness, loss of interest, feelings of worthlessness or guilt, inability to concentrate, and physical symptoms that may include disturbances in the regulation of eating and sleeping. Feelings of unworthiness and guilt may be so excessive that they are considered delusional. In bipolar disorder there are mood swings from elation to depression and back. Manic people also tend to show pressured speech and rapid flight of ideas.

10. **How do psychologists explain the mood disorders?** Recent research emphasizes the possible roles of learned helplessness, attributional styles, and neurotransmitters in depression. Depressed people are more likely than normal people to make internal, stable, and global attributions for failures. It might be that a deficiency in the neurotransmitter serotonin creates a predisposition toward mood disorders. A concurrent deficiency of norepinephrine might contribute to depression, whereas a concurrent excess of norepinephrine might contribute to manic behavior.

11. **Why do people commit suicide?** Most suicides reflect feelings of depression and hopelessness, and they tend to follow "exit events," such as loss of a spouse or close friend, divorce, or a family member's leaving home.

12. **What is schizophrenia?** Schizophrenia is characterized by disturbances in: (1) thought and language, such as loosening of associations and delusions; (2) perception and attention, as found in hallucinations; (3) motor activity, as shown by stupor or by excited behavior; and (4) mood, as in flat or inappropriate emotional responses. It is also characterized by withdrawal and autism.

13. **What are the subtypes of schizophrenia?** There are three major types of schizophrenia: disorganized, catatonic, and paranoid. Disorganized schizophrenia is characterized by disorganized delusions and vivid, abundant hallucinations. Catatonic schizophrenia is characterized by impaired motor activity, as in stupor, and by waxy flexibility. Paranoid schizophrenia is characterized by paranoid delusions.

14. **How do psychologists explain schizophrenia?** There is a tendency for schizophrenia to run in families, suggestive of genetic factors. According to the dopamine theory, schizophrenics might utilize more of the neurotransmitter dopamine than normal people do because of a greater-than normal number of dopamine receptors in the brain. Schizophrenic people also might have greater sensitivity to dopamine than normal people do.

15. **What are the personality disorders?** Personality disorders are inflexible, maladaptive behavior patterns that impair personal or social functioning and are a source of distress to the individual or others. The defining trait of the paranoid personality is suspiciousness. Persons with schizotypal personality disorders show oddities of thought, perception, and behavior. Social withdrawal is the major characteristic of the schizoid personality. Persons with antisocial personality disorders persistently violate the rights of others and encounter conflict with the law. They show little or no guilt or shame over their misdeeds and are largely undeterred by punishment.

16. **How do psychologists explain antisocial personality?** Research suggests that antisocial personalities might develop from some combination of inconsistent discipline, an antisocial father, and lower-than normal levels of arousal, which would help explain why persons with the disorder are undeterred by punishment.

17. **What is transsexualism?** In transsexualism, the person feels trapped in the body of the wrong sex and seeks to have surgery so that his or her external genitals will take on the appearance of those of the opposite sex. Transsexualism is considered a gender identity disorder.

18. **What are the paraphilias?** In the paraphilias, people are sexually aroused by unusual or bizarre objects or situations. The paraphilias include fetishism; transvestic fetishism, or cross-dressing; pedophilia, or sexual preference for children; exhibitionism; voyeurism; sexual masochism, in which gratification involves personally experiencing pain or humiliation; and sexual sadism, in which gratification involves hurting or humiliating one's partner.

PSYCHOLOGY AND MODERN LIFE

As noted in the chapter, depression is the "common cold" of psychological problems—the emotional problem that besets us most frequently in modern life. In this section, we discuss psychological methods for coping with the inactivity, feelings of sadness, and cognitive distortions that characterize depression. Then we consider a related problem, suicide, by placing you in a situation that can be distressing for professionals as well as lay people: Someone tells you that he or she is thinking about suicide. What is there to do?

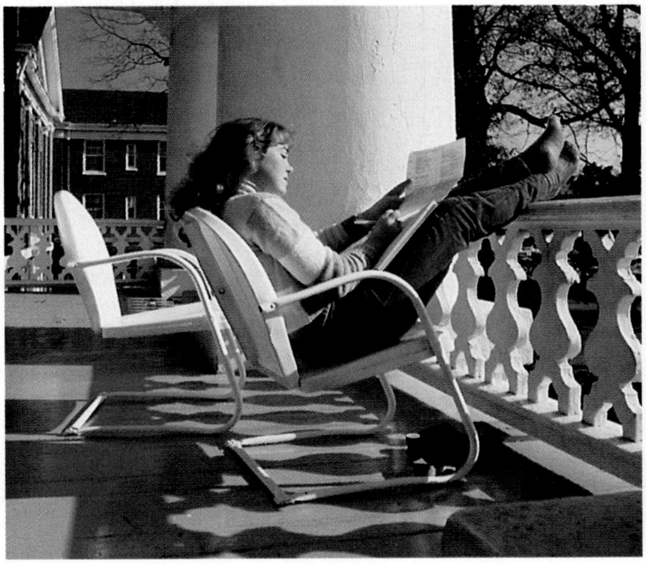

A Pleasant Event. **Simply sitting in the sun is the kind of pleasant event that helps many people combat feelings of depression.**

Coping with Depression

People who feel that their situations may fit the picture of a major depressive episode or bipolar disorder are advised to talk over their problems with their instructors or with a helping professional. However, there are many strategies that we can use to cope with lingering feelings of depression that accompany losses, failures, or persistent pressures. These include using pleasant events, modifying depressing thoughts, exercising, and using assertive behavior.

Using Pleasant Events to Lift Your Mood Becky's romance had recently disintegrated, and she was now at a low ebb, weepy and withdrawn. Depression is an appropriate emotional response to a loss, but after weeks of moping, Becky's friends became concerned. After much argument, they finally prevailed on her to accompany them to a rock concert. It took Becky a while to break free from her own ruminations and begin to focus on the music and the electricity of the crowd, but then Becky found herself clapping and shouting with her friends. Depressive feelings did not return until the following morning. At that time Becky thought, "Well, what could I expect? I was really depressed *underneath it all.*"

Becky's thoughts were understandable, if irrational. She had a right to feel sad that her romance had ended. But after several weeks had passed, her belief that sadness was the only emotion she ought to feel was irrational. (She also seemed to believe that her feelings were subject to the whims of others and that there was nothing she could do to elevate her mood as long as her love life was in a shambles.) For Becky, the rock concert was incompatible with depression. She could not listen to the punk rock group, The Naked and the Dead, and remain miserable.* Although her friends were helpful, it is unfortunate that they, and not Becky, were responsible for placing her in the audience. Becky eventually profited from the experience, but she attributed her improvement to good friends, not to her own resources. Again, her own mood was attributed to, and dependent upon, the behavior of others.

In any event, there is a significant relationship between our moods and our activities. Pressures and failures can trigger feelings of depression, but it also seems that the opposite may hold true: It may be possible to generate feelings of happiness and joy by means of pleasant events. Peter Lewinsohn and his colleagues (Lewinsohn & Graf, 1972; Lewinsohn & Libet, 1972) had subjects track their activities and feelings of depression for 30 days, using checklists they mailed to the researchers on a daily basis. Lewinsohn and Graf (1973) found 49 items from 160-item checklists that contributed to a positive mood in at least 10 percent of subjects. Some are listed in Table 12.4. The researchers classify them into three groups: (1) activities that counteract depression by producing positive, or incompatible, emotional responses; (2) social interactions; and (3) ego-supportive activities or events. "Ego-supportive" activities help raise self-efficacy expectations.

Will pleasant events do the trick for you? Experiments in using pleasant events for the purpose of lifting one's mood have shown mixed results. Reich and Zautra (1981) found that engaging in pleasant activities en-

*Your author, however, *would* be able to accomplish this feat.

Table 12.4
Activities Linked to Positive Feelings in the Lewinsohn and Graf Study

Activities Producing Incompatible Emotional Responses	Social Interactions	Ego-Supportive Activities or Events
Thinking about something good in the future	Being with happy people	Doing a project in my own way
Listening to music	Having a frank and open conversation	Planning trips or vacations
Being relaxed	Having coffee, tea, a Coke with friends	Reading stories, novels, poems, or plays
Wearing clean clothes	Watching people	Planning or organizing something
Breathing clean air	Being told I am loved	Doing a job well
Sitting in the sun	Meeting someone new of the same sex	Learning to do something new
Watching wild animals	Being with friends	
Seeing beautiful scenery	Smiling at people	
	Expressing my love to someone	
	Having a lively talk	
	Kissing	
	Having sexual relations	
	Complimenting or praising someone	

Lewinsohn and Graf (1973) found that many activities seem to contribute to positive feelings and raise self-efficacy expectations. How frequently do you do things like these for yourself?

hanced feelings of well-being but relieved distress only for people under considerable stress. In another study (Biglan & Craker, 1982), pleasant activities increased the activity level of four depressed women but did not improve self-reports of mood. Research involving athletic activities is more encouraging, as we shall see later.

If you have been down in the dumps for a while, it may help you to engage in activities that are incompatible with depression. You can systematically use pleasant events to lift your mood—or to enrich the quality of your daily life—through the following steps:

1. Check off items that appeal to you on the Pleasant Events Schedule (see the nearby questionnaire).
2. Engage in at least three pleasant events each day.
3. Record your pleasant activities in a diary. Add other activities and events that struck you as being pleasant, even if they were unplanned.
4. Toward the end of each day, rate your response to each activity using a scale like the following:

   +3 Wonderful
   +2 Very nice
   +1 Somewhat nice
   0 No particular response
   −1 Somewhat disappointing
   −2 Rather disappointing
   −3 The pits

5. After a week or so, check the activities and events in the diary that received positive ratings.
6. Make a point of repeating highly positive activities and continue to experiment with new ones.

QUESTIONNAIRE

The Pleasant Events Schedule—A List of Turn-Ons

Walking, loving, reading, collecting, redecorating—different people enjoy different things. Here is a list of 116 activities and events enjoyed by many people. One hundred fourteen are derived from research by MacPhillamy and Lewinsohn (1971). The last two are a contemporary update. You can use the 116 items to get in touch with what turns you on by rating them according to the scale given below. Then you may want to enrich the quality of your life by making sure you fit one or more of them in daily.

2 = very pleasant
1 = pleasant
0 = not pleasant

1 1. Being in the country
2 2. Wearing expensive or formal clothes
2 3. Making contributions to religious, charitable, or political groups
0 4. Talking about sports
2 5. Meeting someone new

2 6. Going to a rock concert
0 7. Playing baseball, softball, football, or basketball
2 8. Planning trips or vacations
2 9. Buying things for yourself
2 10. Being at the beach
2 11. Doing art work (painting, sculpture, drawing, moviemaking, etc.)
0 12. Rock climbing or mountaineering
1 13. Reading the Scriptures
0 14. Playing golf
2 15. Rearranging or redecorating your room or house
2 16. Going naked
0 17. Going to a sports event
0 18. Going to the races
2 19. Reading stories, novels, poems, plays, magazines, newspapers
2 20. Going to a bar, tavern, club
2 21. Going to lectures or talks
2 22. Creating or arranging songs or music
2 23. Boating
1 24. Restoring antiques, refinishing furniture
2 25. Watching television or listening to the radio
2 26. Camping
2 27. Working in politics
0 28. Working on machines (cars, bikes, radios, television sets)
0 29. Playing cards or board games
0 30. Doing puzzles or math games
2 31. Having lunch with friends or associates
0 32. Playing tennis
0 33. Driving long distances
0 34. Woodworking, carpentry
2 35. Writing stories, novels, poems, plays, articles
0 36. Being with animals
0 37. Riding in an airplane
0 38. Exploring (hiking away from known routes, spelunking, etc.)
2 39. Singing
2 40. Going to a party
2 41. Going to church functions
2 42. Playing a musical instrument
0 43. Snow skiing, ice skating
0 44. Wearing informal clothes, "dressing down"
2 45. Acting
2 46. Being in the city, downtown
____ 47. Taking a long, hot bath
____ 48. Playing pool or billiards
____ 49. Bowling
____ 50. Watching wild animals
____ 51. Gardening, landscaping
____ 52. Wearing new clothes
____ 53. Dancing
____ 54. Sitting or lying in the sun
____ 55. Riding a motorcycle
____ 56. Just sitting and thinking
____ 57. Going to a fair, carnival, circus, zoo, amusement park
____ 58. Talking about philosophy or religion
____ 59. Gambling
____ 60. Listening to sounds of nature
____ 61. Dating, courting
____ 62. Having friends come to visit
____ 63. Going out to visit friends
____ 64. Giving gifts
____ 65. Getting massages or backrubs
____ 66. Photography
____ 67. Collecting stamps, coins, rocks, etc.
____ 68. Seeing beautiful scenery
____ 69. Eating good meals
____ 70. Improving your health (having teeth fixed, changing diet, having a checkup, etc.)
____ 71. Wrestling or boxing
____ 72. Fishing
____ 73. Going to a health club, sauna
____ 74. Horseback riding
____ 75. Protesting social, political, or environmental conditions
____ 76. Going to the movies
____ 77. Cooking meals
____ 78. Washing your hair
____ 79. Going to a restaurant
____ 80. Using cologne, perfume
____ 81. Getting up early in the morning
____ 82. Writing a diary
____ 83. Giving massages or backrubs
____ 84. Meditating or doing yoga
____ 85. Doing heavy outdoor work
____ 86. Snowmobiling, dune buggying
____ 87. Being in a body-awareness, encounter, or "rap" group
____ 88. Swimming
____ 89. Running, jogging
____ 90. Walking barefoot
____ 91. Playing frisbee or catch
____ 92. Doing housework or laundry, cleaning things
____ 93. Listening to music
____ 94. Knitting, crocheting
____ 95. Making love
____ 96. Petting, necking
____ 97. Going to a barber or beautician
____ 98. Being with someone you love
____ 99. Going to the library
____ 100. Shopping
____ 101. Preparing a new or special dish
____ 102. Watching people
____ 103. Bicycling
____ 104. Writing letters, cards, or notes
____ 105. Talking about politics or public affairs
____ 106. Watching attractive women or men
____ 107. Caring for houseplants
____ 108. Having coffee, tea, or Coke, etc., with friends
____ 109. Beachcombing
____ 110. Going to auctions, garage sales, etc.
____ 111. Water skiing, surfing, diving
____ 112. Traveling
____ 113. Attending the opera, ballet, or a play
____ 114. Looking at the stars or the moon*
____ 115. Using a microcomputer
____ 116. Playing videogames

*Source of first 114 items: Adapted from D. J. MacPhillamy & P. M. Lewinsohn, *Pleasant Events Schedule, Form III-S*, University of Oregon, Mimeograph, 1971.

Challenging Irrational, Depressing Thoughts: Seeing the Cognitive Errors of Your Ways

Public opinion is a weak tyrant compared with our own private opinion. What a man thinks of himself, that it is which determines, or rather indicates his fate.
Henry David Thoreau, *Walden*

Depressed people tend to have excessive needs for social approval and to be perfectionistic in their self-demands (Vestre, 1984). They also tend to blame themselves for failures and problems, even when they are not at fault. They *internalize* blame and see their problems as being *stable* and *global*—as all but impossible to change. Depressed people also make the cognitive errors of tending to *catastrophize* their problems and to *minimize* their accomplishments (Beck, 1976).

Consider Table 12.5. Column 1 illustrates a number of (often) irrational, depressing thoughts. How many of them have you had? Column 2 indicates the type of cognitive error being made (such as internalizing or catastrophizing), and column 3 shows examples of more rational, less depressing alternatives.

You can pinpoint your own irrational, depressing thoughts by focusing on what you are thinking whenever you feel low. Try to pay particular attention to the rapid, fleeting thoughts that can trigger mood changes. It helps to jot down the negative thoughts. Then challenge their accuracy. Do you characterize difficult situations as being impossible and hopeless? Do you expect too much from yourself and therefore minimize your achievements? Do you internalize more than your fair share of blame?

You can use the guidelines in Table 12.5 to classify your own cognitive errors. Also use the table as a guide in constructing rational alternatives to your own depressing thoughts. Jot down the rational alternatives next to each irrational thought, and review them now and then. When you are alone, read the irrational thought aloud, then follow it by saying, firmly, "No, that's irrational!" Then read aloud the rational alternative twice, *emphatically*.

After you have thought or read aloud the rational alternative, think or say things like, "That makes a bit more sense! That's a more accurate view of things! It feels better now that I have things in proper perspective."

Irrational thoughts do not just happen, nor are you stuck with them. You can learn to exert control over your thoughts and, in this way, to exert a good deal of control over your feelings—whether the feelings are of anxiety, depression, or anger.

Exercise Exercise, particularly sustained exercise, frequently has a positive effect on the moods of depressed people, as noted in Chapter 11. Aerobic exercises such as running, jogging, swimming, bicycle riding, or fast walking appear to alleviate feelings of depression in many cases (Doyne et al., 1983; Folkins & Sime, 1981; Klein et al., 1985). As noted in the chapter, depression may be linked to deficiencies in norepinephrine, serotonin, and even endorphins. It has been speculated that sustained exercises may achieve mood-enhancing effects by increasing levels of these substances (Dimsdale & Moss, 1980; Carr et al., 1981), although these hypotheses have not yet been borne out empirically. In any event, anaerobic exercise in the form of weight-training has also been shown to be of help to depressed college students (Doyne et al., 1987).

Assertive Behavior Because we humans are social creatures, our social interactions are very important to us. Nonassertive behavior patterns, as measured by scores on the Rathus Assertiveness Schedule (see Chapter 13), are linked to feelings of depression (Gotlib, 1984). Learning to express our feelings and relate effectively to others, on the other hand, has been shown to alleviate feelings of depression (Hersen et al., 1984). Assertive behavior permits more effective interactions with our families, friends, co-workers, and strangers—thereby removing sources of frustration and increasing the social support we receive. Expressions of positive feelings—saying we love someone or simply saying "Good morning" brightly—helps reduce feelings of hostility and paves the way for further social involvement.

Suicide Prevention

Imagine that you are having a heart-to-heart talk on campus with one of your best friends, Jamie. Things haven't been going well, you know. Jamie's grandmother died a month ago, and they were very close. Jamie's coursework has been suffering, and things have also been going downhill with the person Jamie has been seeing regularly. But you are not prepared when Jamie looks you straight in the eye and says, "I've been thinking about this for days, and I've decided that the only way out is to kill myself."

If someone tells you that he or she is considering suicide, you may feel frightened and flustered or feel that an enormous burden has been placed on you. It has. In such a case, your objective should be to encourage the person to consult a professional mental health worker, or to consult a worker yourself, as soon as possible. But if the person refuses to talk to anyone else and you feel that you can't break free for a consultation, there are a number of things you can do:

Table 12.5
Irrational, Depressing Thoughts and Rational Alternatives

Irrational Thought	Type	Rational Alternative
"There's nothing I can do."	Catastrophizing, minimizing, stabilizing	"I can't think of anything to do right now, but if I work at it, I may."
"I'm no good."	Internalizing, globalizing, stabilizing	"I did something I regret, but that doesn't make me evil or worthless as a person."
"This is absolutely awful."	Catastrophizing	"This is pretty bad, but it's not the end of the world."
"I just don't have the brains for college."	Stabilizing, globalizing	"I guess I really need to go back over the basics in that course."
"I just can't believe I did something so disgusting!"	Catastrophizing	"That was a bad experience. Well, I won't be likely to try that again soon."
"I can't imagine ever feeling right."	Stabilizing, catastrophizing	"This is painful, but if I try to work it through step by step, I'll probably eventually see my way out of it."
"It's all my fault."	Internalizing	"I'm not blameless, but I wasn't the only one involved. It may have been my idea, but he/she went into it with his/her eyes open."
"I can't do anything right."	Globalizing, stabilizing, catastrophizing, minimizing	"I sure screwed this up, but I've done a lot of things well, and I'll do other things well."
"I hurt everybody who gets close to me."	Internalizing, globalizing, stabilizing	"I'm not totally blameless, but I'm not responsible for the whole world. Others make their own decisions, and they have to live with the results, too."
"If people knew the real me, they would have it in for me."	Globalizing, minimizing (the positive in yourself)	"I'm not perfect, but nobody's perfect. I have positive as well as negative features, and I am entitled to self-interests."

Many of us create or compound feelings of depression because of cognitive errors such as those in this table. Have you had any of these irrational, depressing thoughts? Are you willing to challenge them?

1. Draw the person out. Edwin Shneidman, cofounder of the Los Angeles Suicide Prevention Center, suggests asking questions such as "What's going on?" "Where do you hurt?" "What would you like to see happen?" (1985, p. 11). Questions such as these may encourage people to express frustrated psychological needs and provide some relief. They also give you time to assess the danger and think.
2. Be empathetic. Show that you understand how upset the person is. Do *not* say, "Don't be silly."
3. Suggest that measures other than suicide might be found to solve the problem, even if they are not evident at the time. Shneidman (1985) suggests that suicidal people can typically see only two solutions to their problems—either death or a magical resolution of their problems. Therapists thus attempt to "widen the mental blinders" of suicidal people.
4. Ask how the person intends to commit suicide. People with concrete plans and the weapon are at greater risk. Ask if you might hold on to the weapon for a while. Sometimes the person says yes.
5. Suggest that the person go *with you* to obtain professional help *now*. The emergency room of a general hospital, the campus counseling center or infirmary, or the campus or local police will do. Some campuses have "hot lines" you can call. Some cities have suicide prevention centers with hot lines that people can use anonymously.
6. Extract a promise that the person will not commit suicide before seeing you again. Arrange a concrete time and place to meet. Get professional help as soon as you are apart.
7. Do *not* tell people threatening suicide that they're silly or crazy. Do *not* insist on contact with specific people, like parents or a spouse. Conflict with these people may have led to the suicidal thinking.

Above all, remember that your primary objective is to consult a helping professional. Don't "go it alone" for one moment more than you have to.

Outline

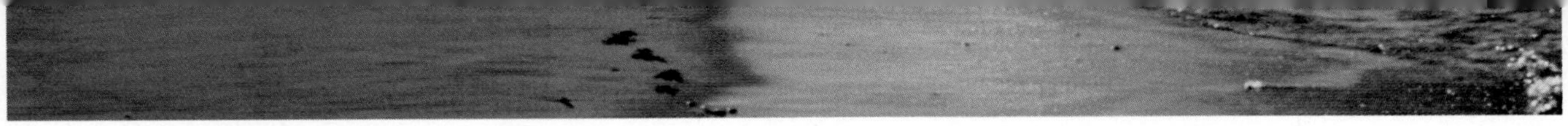

13 Methods of Therapy

Truth or Fiction?

- □ People in Merry Old England used to visit the local insane asylum for a fun night out on the town.
- □ To be of help, psychotherapy must continue for months, perhaps years.
- □ Some psychotherapists interpret clients' dreams.
- □ Other psychotherapists encourage their clients to take the lead in the therapy session.
- □ Still other psychotherapists tell their clients precisely what to do.
- □ Lying around in your reclining chair and fantasizing can be an effective way of confronting your fears.
- □ Smoking cigarettes can be an effective treatment for helping people to . . . stop smoking cigarettes.
- □ You might be able to gain control over bad habits merely by keeping a record of where and when you practice them.
- □ Individual therapy is preferable to group therapy for people who can afford it.
- □ The originator of a surgical technique intended to reduce violence learned that it was not always successful—when one of his patients shot him.
- □ Drugs are never of help in treating people with abnormal behavior.

Brad is having an uplifting experience—literally. Six people who minutes ago were perfect strangers have cradled him in their arms and raised him into midair. His eyes are closed. Gently they rock him back and forth and carry him about the room.

Brad is no paralyzed hospital patient. He has just joined an encounter group. He hopes to be able to learn to relate to other people as individuals, not as passing blurs on the street or as patrons asking him to cash payroll checks at the bank where he works as a teller. The group leader had directed that Brad be carried about to help him break down his defensive barriers and establish trust in others.

Brad had responded to a somewhat flamboyant ad in the therapy section of the classifieds in New York's *Village Voice:*

Come to life! Stop being a gray automaton in a mechanized society! Encounter yourself and others. New group forming. First meeting free. Call 212–555–0599. Qualified therapist.

Like many who seek personal help, Brad had little idea how to go about it. His group experience might or might not work out. For one thing, he has no idea about the qualifications of the group leader and did not know enough to ask. If he had answered other ads in the *Voice,* including some placed by highly qualified therapists, his treatment might have been quite different. Brad could have been:

Lying on a couch talking about anything that pops into awareness and exploring the hidden meanings of a recurrent dream.

Sitting face to face with a gentle, accepting therapist who places the major burden for what happens during therapy directly on Brad's shoulders.

Listening to a frank, straightforward therapist insist that his problems stem from self-defeating attitudes and beliefs, such as an overriding need to be liked and approved of.

Role-playing the beginning of a social relationship, including smiling at a new acquaintance, making small talk, and looking the person squarely in the eye.

These methods, although quite different, all represent psychotherapies. In order to make sense of what is happening to Brad—and of all the things that are not happening to him—in this chapter we first define *psychotherapy.* We consider the history of therapy and examine several of the major current psychotherapies, including psychodynamic, phenomenological, cognitive, behavior, and group therapies. After exploring these approaches to psychotherapy, we shall turn our attention to *biological therapies,* including drug therapy (also called *chemotherapy*), electroconvulsive shock therapy, and psychosurgery.

WHAT IS THERAPY?

The form of psychotherapy practiced by a psychologist or another helping professional is related to that practitioner's theory of personality or theoretical model of abnormal behavior. Treatment is not, or ought not be, a matter of chance.

Although there are many different kinds of psychotherapy, they have a number of things in common. **Psychotherapy** is defined as a systematic interaction between a therapist and a client that brings psychological principles to bear on influencing the client's thoughts, feelings, or behavior in order to help the client overcome abnormal behavior, adjust to problems in living, or develop as an individual.

Quite a mouthful? True. But note the essentials:

1. *Systematic Interaction* Psychotherapy is a systematic interaction between a client and a therapist. The client's needs and goals and the therapist's theoretical point of view interact to determine how the therapist and client relate to one another.

Psychotherapy A systematic interaction between a therapist and a client that brings psychological principles to bear on influencing the client's thoughts, feelings, or behavior in order to help that client overcome abnormal behavior or adjust to problems in living.

2. *Psychological Principles* Psychotherapy brings psychological principles to bear on the client's problems or goals. Psychotherapy is based on psychological theory and research in areas such as personality, learning, motivation, and emotion. Psychotherapy is not based on, say, religious or biological principles, although there is no reason why psychotherapy cannot be compatible with both.

3. *Thoughts, Feelings, and Behavior* Psychotherapy influences clients' thoughts, feelings, and overt behavior. Psychotherapy can be aimed at any or all of these aspects of human psychology.

4. *Abnormal Behavior, Adjustment Problems, and Personal Growth* Psychotherapy is used with at least three types of clients. First there are people who have been diagnosed as showing patterns of abnormal behavior, such as anxiety disorders, mood disorders, or schizophrenia. When these disorders are severe, as in the case of major depression or schizophrenia, biological therapies can play a major role in treatment. Still, psychotherapy is frequently used to help the individual in areas of personal, social, or vocational concern.

   Then there are people who seek help in adjusting to problems such as social shyness, weight problems, loss of a spouse, or career confusion. In such cases there is usually no need for biological approaches. Finally, many individuals use psychotherapy, especially psychodynamic and phenomenological therapies, not because they are seeking help in solving problems, but because they want to learn more about themselves and to reach their full potential as individuals, creative artists, parents, and members of social groups.

History of Therapies

Ancient and medieval "treatments" of psychological disorders often reflected the demonological model. As such, they tended to involve cruel practices such as exorcism and death by hanging or burning, as was practiced some 300 years ago. In Europe and the United States, some people who could not meet the demands of everyday life were also thrown into prisons. Others begged in city streets, stole produce and food animals from farms, or entered marginal societal niches occupied by prostitutes and petty thieves. A few might have found their ways to monasteries or other retreats that offered a kind word and some support. Generally speaking, they died early.

Asylums **Asylums** often had their origins in European monasteries. They were the first institutions meant primarily for persons with psychological disorders. Their functions were human warehousing, not treatment. Asylums mushroomed in population until the daily stresses created by noise, overcrowding, and unsanitary conditions undoubtedly heightened the problems they were meant to ameliorate. Inmates were frequently chained and beaten. Some were chained for decades.

The word *bedlam* is derived from the name of the London asylum St. Mary's of Bethlehem, which opened its gates in 1547. Here the unfortunate were chained between the inner and outer walls, whipped, and allowed to lie in their own waste. And here the ladies and gentlemen of the British upper class might go for a stroll on a lazy afternoon to take in the sights. The admission for such amusement? One penny.

Asylum An institution for the care of the mentally ill.

St. Mary's of Bethlehem. This institution is the source of the term *bedlam.*

The Unchaining of the Patients at La Bicêtre. Frenchman Philippe Pinel sparked the humanitarian reform movement by unchaining the patients at this Parisian asylum.

Truth or Fiction Revisited

It is true that the English were wont to visit the local insane asylum as a source of entertainment. St. Mary's of Bethlehem was the best known.

Humanitarian reform movements began in the eighteenth century. In Paris, Philippe Pinel unchained the patients at the asylum known as La Bicêtre. The populace was amazed that most patients, rather than running amok, profited from kindness and greater freedom. Many could eventually function in society once more. Reform movements were later led by the Quaker William Tuke in England and by Dorothea Dix in America.

Mental Hospitals Mental hospitals gradually replaced asylums in the United States. In the mid-1950s, more than a million people resided in state, county, Veterans Administration, or private facilities. Treatment, not warehousing, is the function of the mental hospital. Still, because of high patient

Table 13.1
Functions of the Community Mental Health Center

Outpatient treatment
Short-term hospitalization
Partial hospitalization (e.g., patient sleeps in the hospital and works outside during the day)
Crisis intervention
Community consultation and education about abnormal behavior

The Community Mental-Health Centers Act provided funds for community agencies that attempt to intervene in mental-health problems as early as possible and to maintain mental patients in the community.

populations and understaffing, many patients have received little attention. Even today, with somewhat improved conditions, it is not unusual for one psychiatrist to be responsible for the welfare of several hundred patients on a weekend.

The Community Mental-Health Movement Since the 1960s, efforts have been made to maintain as many mental patients as possible in the community. The Community Mental-Health Centers Act of 1963 provided funds for creating hundreds of community mental-health centers, in which patients would be charged according to their ability to pay, in order to accomplish this goal. These centers attempt to maintain new patients as outpatients, to serve patients from mental hospitals who have been released into the community, and to provide other services as listed in Table 13.1. Today, about 63 percent of the nation's chronic mentally ill live in the community, not the hospital (Morganthau et al., 1986).

Critics note that many people who had resided in hospitals for decades were suddenly discharged to "home" communities that seemed foreign and frightening. Many discharged patients do not receive adequate follow-up care in the community (Morganthau et al., 1986). Perhaps a third to a half of the nation's homeless reflect the process of deinstitutionalization (Cordes, 1984; Fustero, 1984). Some former hospital inhabitants try to return to the protected world of the hospital and become trapped in a "revolving door" between the hospital and the community (Cordes, 1984).

The outlook for maintaining new patients in the community, rather than hospitalizing them, looks brighter. In a review of ten experiments in which seriously disturbed patients were randomly assigned either to hospitalization or outpatient care, Kiesler (1982) did not find one case in which the outcomes of hospitalization were superior. The outpatient alternative was usually superior in terms of the patient's maintaining independent living arrangements, staying in school, and finding employment.

Let us now consider the different kinds of therapies available today.

PSYCHODYNAMIC THERAPIES

Psychodynamic therapies are based on the thinking of Sigmund Freud, the founder of psychodynamic theory. Broadly speaking, they are based on the view that our problems largely reflect early childhood experiences and internal conflicts. According to Freud, as noted in Chapter 10, this internal conflict involves the shifting of psychic, or libidinal, energy among the three psychic structures—the id, ego, and superego. The sway of psychic energy determines our behavior, and, when primitive urges threaten to break through from the id or when the superego floods us with excessive guilt, it prompts the establishment of defenses and creates distress. Freud's psychodynamic therapy method—psychoanalysis—aims to modify the flow of energy among these structures, largely to bulwark the ego against the torrents of energy loosed by the id and the superego. With impulses and feelings of guilt and shame placed under greater control, clients are emotionally freed to develop more adaptive behavior patterns.

Not all psychodynamically oriented therapists view internal conflict in terms of unconscious forces, however. In this section we first outline Freud's psychoanalytic methods for shoring up the ego, frequently referred to as "traditional" psychoanalysis. Then we examine more modern psychoanalytic approaches, and we see that their concepts of conflict and their methods differ from those of Freud.

Traditional Psychoanalysis: Where Id Was, There Shall Ego Be

Canst thou not minister to a mind diseas'd,
Pluck out from the memory a rooted sorrow,
Raze out the written troubles of the brain,
And with some sweet oblivious antidote
Cleanse the stuff'd bosom of that perilous stuff
Which weighs upon the heart?

Shakespeare, *Macbeth*

In this passage from *Macbeth,* Macbeth asks a physician to minister to Lady Macbeth after she has gone mad. In the play, her madness is in part caused by current events—namely, her guilt for participating in murders designed to seat her husband on the throne of Scotland. But there are also hints of more deeply rooted and mysterious problems, such as conflicts about infertility.

If Lady Macbeth's physician had been a traditional psychoanalyst, he might have asked her to lie down on a couch in a slightly darkened room. He would have sat just behind her and encouraged her to talk about anything that came to mind, no matter how trivial, no matter how personal. To avoid interfering with her self-exploration, he might have said little or nothing for session after session. That would have been par for the course. A traditional **psychoanalysis,** you see, can extend for months, or years.

Psychoanalysis is the clinical method devised by Freud for plucking "from the memory a rooted sorrow," for razing "out the written troubles of the brain." Psychoanalysis is the method used by Freud and his followers to "cleanse . . . that perilous stuff which weighs upon the heart"—to provide insight into the conflicts presumed to lie at the roots of a person's problems. Insight involves a number of things: knowledge of the experiences that lead to conflicts and maladaptive behavior; identification and labeling of feelings and conflicts that lie below conscious awareness; and objective evaluation of one's beliefs and ideas, feelings, and overt behavior.

Psychoanalysis also seeks to allow the client to express emotions and impulses that are theorized to have been dammed up by the forces of repression. Freud was fond of saying, "Where id was, there shall ego be." In part he meant that psychoanalysis could shed light on the inner workings of the mind. But Freud did not believe that we ought, or needed to, become conscious of all of our conflicts and primitive impulses. Instead, he sought to replace impulsive and defensive behavior with coping behavior. He believed that impulsive behavior reflected the urges of the id. Defensive behavior, such as timidly avoiding confrontations, represented the ego's compromising

Psychoanalysis Freud's method of psychotherapy.

A View of Freud's Consulting Room at Berggasse 19 in Vienna. Freud would sit in the chair by the head of the couch while a client free associated. The cardinal rule of free association is that no thought is to be censored.

efforts to protect the client from these impulses and the possibility of retaliation. Coping behavior would allow the client to partially express these impulses, but in socially acceptable ways. In so doing, the client would find gratification but avoid social and self-condemnation.

In this way a man with a phobia for knives might discover that he had been repressing the urge to harm someone who had taken advantage of him. He might also find ways to confront his antagonist verbally. A woman with a conversion disorder—for example, paralysis of the legs—could see that her disability allowed her to avoid unwanted pregnancy without guilt. She might also realize her resentment at being pressed into a stereotypical feminine sex role and decide to expand her options.

Freud also believed that psychoanalysis permitted the client to spill forth the psychic energy theorized to have been repressed by conflicts and guilt. He called this spilling forth **abreaction,** or **catharsis**. Abreaction would provide feelings of relief by alleviating some of the forces assaulting the ego.

Free Association Early in his career as a therapist, Freud found that hypnosis allowed his clients to focus on repressed conflicts and talk about them. The relaxed "trance state" provided by hypnosis seemed to allow clients to break through to topics of which they were otherwise unaware. But Freud also found that many clients denied the accuracy of this material once they were out of the trance. Other clients found these revelations to be premature and painful. So Freud turned to **free association,** a more gradual method of breaking down the walls of defense that blocked insight into unconscious processes.

In free association, the client is made comfortable, as by lying on a couch, and is asked to talk about any topic that comes to mind. No thought is to be censored—that is the cardinal rule. Psychoanalysts ask their clients to wander "freely" from topic to topic, but they do not believe that the process *within* the client is fully free. Repressed impulses press for release. A client may begin to free associate with meaningless topics, but pertinent repressed material may eventually surface.

Abreaction In psychoanalysis, expression of previously repressed feelings and impulses to allow the psychic energy associated with them to spill forth.

Catharsis Another term for *abreaction.*

Free association In psychoanalysis, the uncensored uttering of all thoughts that come to mind.

However, the ego persists in trying to repress unacceptable impulses and threatening conflicts. As a result, clients might show **resistance** to recalling and discussing threatening ideas. Clients might claim "My mind is blank" when they are about to entertain such thoughts. They might accuse the analyst of being demanding or inconsiderate. They might "forget" their appointment when threatening material is due to be uncovered.

The therapist observes the dynamic struggle between the compulsion to utter and resistance. Through discreet remarks, the analyst subtly tips the balance in favor of uttering. A gradual process of self-discovery and self-insight ensues. Now and then the analyst offers an **interpretation** of an utterance, showing how it suggests resistance or deep-seated feelings and conflicts.

Dream Analysis Freud considered dreams the "royal road to the unconscious." The psychodynamic theory of dreams holds that they are determined by unconscious processes as well as by the remnants, or "residues," of the day. Unconscious impulses tend to be expressed in dreams as a form of **wish fulfillment.**

But unacceptable sexual and aggressive impulses are likely to be displaced onto objects and situations that reflect the client's era and culture. These objects become symbols of the unconscious wishes. For example, long, narrow dream objects might be **phallic symbols,** but whether the symbol takes the form of a spear, rifle, "stick shift," or spacecraft partially reflects one's cultural background.

In psychodynamic theory, the perceived content of the dream is called its shown or **manifest content.** Its presumed hidden or symbolic content is referred to as its **latent content.** A man might dream that he is flying. Flying is the manifest content of the dream. Freud usually interpreted flying as being symbolic of erection, so issues concerning sexual potency might make up the latent content of such a dream.

Freud often asked clients to jot down their dreams upon waking so that they could be interpreted during the psychoanalytic session.

Transference Freud found that his clients responded not only to his appearance and behavior but also to what these characteristics meant to clients. A young woman might see Freud as a father figure and displace, or transfer, her feelings toward her own father onto Freud. Another woman might view him as a lover and act seductively or suspiciously. Men also showed **transference.** A man, like a woman, might view Freud as a father figure, but a man also might respond to Freud as a competitor.

Freud discovered that transference was a two-way street. Freud could also transfer his feelings onto his clients—perhaps viewing a woman as a sex object or a young man as a rebellious son. He called this placing of clients into roles in his own life **countertransference.**

Transference and countertransference lead to unjustified expectations of new people and can foster maladaptive behavior. We might relate to our spouses as to our opposite-sex parents and demand too much (or too little) from them. Or we might accuse them unfairly of harboring wishes and secrets we attribute to our parents. We might not give new friends or lovers "a chance" when we have been mistreated by someone who played a similar role in our lives or our fantasies.

In any event, psychoanalysts are trained to be **opaque** concerning their own behavior and feelings. This is so that they will not encourage client transference or express their own feelings of countertransference. Then, when the client acts accusingly, seductively, or otherwise inappropriately toward the analyst, the analyst can plead not guilty of encouraging the client's

---

Resistance The tendency to block the free expression of impulses and primitive ideas—a reflection of the defense mechanism of repression.

Interpretation An explanation of a client's utterance according to psychoanalytic theory.

Wish fulfillment A primitive method used by the id to attempt to gratify basic instincts.

Phallic symbol A sign that represents the penis.

Manifest content In psychodynamic theory, the reported content of dreams.

Latent content In psychodynamic theory, the symbolized or underlying content of dreams.

Transference In psychoanalysis, the generalization to the analyst of feelings toward a person in the client's life.

Countertransference In psychoanalysis, the generalization to the client of feelings toward a person in the analyst's life.

Opaque In psychoanalysis, descriptive of the analyst, who hides personal feelings.

behavior and suggest that it reflects historical events and fantasies. In this way, transference behavior becomes grist for the therapeutic mill.

Analysis of client transference is an important element of therapy. It provides client insight and encourages more adaptive social behavior. Yet it might take months or years for transference to develop fully and be resolved, which is one reason that psychoanalysis can be a lengthy process.

Modern Psychodynamic Approaches

Some psychoanalysts still adhere faithfully to Freud's protracted techniques. They continue to practice traditional psychoanalysis. In recent years, however, briefer, less intense forms of psychodynamic therapy have also been devised (Koss et al., 1986; Zaiden, 1982). Briefer methods make it possible for therapists to practice "psychoanalytically oriented" therapy with clients who cannot afford protracted therapy or whose schedules will not permit it. Also, frankly, many of these therapists believe that protracted therapy is not needed or justifiable in terms of the ratio of cost to benefits.

Truth or Fiction Revisited

It is *not* true that psychotherapy need go on for months or years in order to be of help.

Although some modern psychodynamic therapies continue to focus on revealing unconscious material and on breaking through psychological defenses or resistance, there are a number of differences with traditional psychoanalysis. One of them is that client and therapist usually sit face to face, as opposed to the client's reclining on a couch. The therapist is also usually more directive than the traditional psychoanalyst. Modern psychoanalytically oriented therapists frequently suggest productive behavior patterns instead of fostering self-insight only. Finally, there is usually more focus on the ego and the ways in which the ego acts as the "executive" of personality. Accordingly, there is less emphasis on the role of the id. For this reason, many modern psychodynamic therapists are considered **ego analysts.**

Ego Analysis Many of Freud's followers, the "second generation" of psychoanalysts—from Jung and Adler to Horney and Erikson—believed that Freud had placed too much emphasis on sexual and aggressive impulses and underestimated the importance of the ego. Freud, for example, aimed to establish conditions under which clients could spill forth psychic energy and eventually shore up the position of the ego. Erikson, in contrast, spoke to clients directly about their values and concerns and encouraged them to consciously fashion desired traits and behavior patterns. Freud saw clients as perpetual victims of the past and doubted their ability to fully overcome childhood trauma. Karen Horney, on the other hand, saw clients as being capable of overcoming early abuse and deprivation through self-understanding and productive adult relationships (Quinn, 1987). Even Freud's own daughter, the psychoanalyst Anna Freud (1895–1982), was more concerned with the ways in which the ego perceived the world and met clients' needs than she was with unconscious forces and conflicts.

Margaret Mahler and Object Relations: On Becoming Your Own Person One popular contemporary psychodynamic approach, developed by psychoanalysts such as Melanie Klein and Margaret Mahler (1976), focuses on the "objects" of children's primitive impulses. These objects include their parents and other people in whom children invest powerful emotions.

Ego analyst A psychodynamically oriented therapist who focuses on the conscious, coping behavior of the ego instead of the hypothesized, unconscious functioning of the id.

Margaret Mahler

In psychodynamic theory, we tend to **introject,** or incorporate into our own personalities, elements of the people who are important to us. Introjection is more powerful when we are afraid of losing others by death or because of their disapproval of us. (We might fear that people who disapprove of us will leave us.) Thus we might be particularly prone toward bringing inward elements of the people who *disapprove* of us or who see things differently. Ironically, we take within the harsh parent more so than the generous parent.

After introjection occurs, symbolic representations (images and memories) of these people come to influence our perceptions and behavior. And so, according to this point of view, referred to as **object-relations theory,** we are likely to experience internal conflict as the ways of looking at things and the values of introjected people do battle with our own. Some of our perceptions may be distorted or seem unreal to us; some of our impulses and behavior may seem unlike us, as if they come out of the blue. People in such conflict have difficulty telling where the influences of other people end and their "real selves" begin. Margaret Mahler (1897–1985) helped her clients separate their own ideas and feelings from those of the introjected objects so that they could develop as individuals—as their own persons.

Today there are many psychodynamic therapies, many approaches that show the influence of Sigmund Freud. As a group they continue to use terms such as *conflict* and *ego,* but they differ in the prominence they ascribe to unconscious forces and in their perception of the role of the ego.

Let us now turn our attention to phenomenological approaches to therapy. Like Mahler, many phenomenological therapists also find that clients can have difficulty telling where the influences of others end and their real selves begin.

PHENOMENOLOGICAL THERAPIES

Whereas psychodynamic therapies focus on internal conflicts and unconscious processes, phenomenological therapies focus on the quality of clients' subjective, conscious experience. Whereas psychodynamic therapies tend to focus on the past, and particularly on early childhood experiences, phenomenological therapies usually focus on what clients are experiencing today—on "the here and now."

Having noted these differences, we must point out that they are frequently differences in *emphasis.* The happenings of the past have a way of influencing the mental activity and overt behavior of the present. Carl Rogers, the originator of person-centered therapy, recognized that early childhood experiences tended to give rise to the conditions of worth that troubled his clients in the here and now. Rogers and Fritz Perls, the originator of Gestalt therapy, recognized that early incorporation of other people's values often leads clients to "disown" parts of their own personalities in the here and now.

Let us now consider person-centered therapy, transactional analysis, and Gestalt therapy and discuss some of these ideas in more detail.

Person-Centered Therapy: Removing Roadblocks to Self-Actualization

Person-centered therapy was originated by Carl Rogers (1951), who was rated as the most influential psychotherapist in the Smith (1982) survey.

Introjection In psychodynamic theory, the bringing within oneself of the personality of another individual.

Object-relations theory The psychodynamic view that focuses on the potentially conflicting properties of internalized objects (e.g., personalities of loved ones).

Person-centered therapy Carl Rogers' method of psychotherapy, which emphasizes the creation of a warm, therapeutic atmosphere that frees clients to engage in self-exploration and self-expression.

Person-Centered Therapy. By showing the qualities of unconditional positive regard, empathic understanding, genuineness, and congruence, person-centered therapists create an atmosphere in which clients can explore their feelings.

Rogers believed that we are free to make choices and control our destinies, despite the burdens of our pasts.

Rogers also believed that we have natural tendencies toward health, growth, and fulfillment. Given this view, Rogers wrote that psychological problems arise from roadblocks placed in the path of our own self-actualization. Because others show us selective approval when we are young, we learn to disown the disapproved parts of ourselves. We don masks and facades to earn social approval. We might learn to be seen but not heard—not even heard, or examined fully, by ourselves. As a result we might experience stress and discomfort and the feeling that we—or the world—are not real.

Person-centered therapy aims to provide insight into the parts of us that we have disowned so that we can feel whole. It stresses the importance of a warm, therapeutic atmosphere that encourages client self-exploration and self-expression. Therapist acceptance of the client is thought to lead to client self-acceptance and self-esteem. Self-acceptance frees the client to make choices that foster development of his or her unique potential.

Person-centered therapy is nondirective.* The client takes the lead, listing and exploring problems. The therapist reflects or paraphrases expressed feelings and ideas, helping the client to get in touch with deeper feelings and to follow the strongest leads in the quest for self-insight.

Truth or Fiction Revisited

It is true that some psychotherapists encourage their clients to take the lead in the therapy session. Person-centered therapists provide an example.

*Although Rogers believed that therapy should be nondirective, he admitted, "Sometimes I'll give in to a client and give a little advice. But then the client will say, 'I've already tried that' " (Bennett, 1985, p. 3).

It should also be noted that person-centered therapy is practiced widely in college and university counseling centers, not just to help students experiencing, say, anxieties or depression but also to help them make decisions. Many college students have not yet made career choices, for example, or wonder whether they should become involved with particular people or in sexual activity. Person-centered therapists facilitate decision making by providing an encouraging atmosphere in which clients can verbally explore various choices and paths. The point is that person-centered therapists do not tell clients what to do. Instead, they help clients arrive at their own decisions.

The effective person-centered therapist also shows four qualities: *unconditional positive regard, empathic understanding, genuineness,* and *congruence.* In showing **unconditional positive regard** for clients, person-centered therapists respect clients as important human beings with unique values and goals. Clients are provided with a sense of security that encourages them to follow their own feelings. Psychoanalysts might hesitate to encourage clients to freely express their impulses because of the fear that primitive sexual and aggressive forces might be unleashed. But person-centered therapists believe that people are basically *pro*social. If people follow their own feelings, rather than act defensively, they should not be abusive or *anti*social.

Empathic understanding is shown by accurately reflecting the client's experiences and feelings. Therapists try to view the world through their clients' **frames of reference** by setting aside their own values and listening closely.

Whereas psychoanalysts are trained to be opaque, person-centered therapists are trained to show **genuineness.** Person-centered therapists are open about their feelings. It would be harmful to clients if their therapists could not truly accept and like them, even though their values might differ from those of the therapists. Rogers admitted that he sometimes had negative feelings about clients, usually boredom; he usually expressed these feelings rather than hold them in (Bennett, 1985). Person-centered therapists must also be able to tolerate differentness, because they believe that every client is different in important ways.

Person-centered therapists also try to show **congruence,** or a fit between their thoughts, feelings, and behavior. Congruence gives us access to inner experience (Kahn, 1985). Person-centered therapists serve as models of integrity to their clients.

Unconditional positive regard Acceptance of the value of another person, although not necessarily acceptance of all of that person's behaviors.

Empathic understanding Ability to perceive a client's feelings from the client's frame of reference. A quality of the good person-centered therapist.

Frame of reference One's unique patterning of perceptions and attitudes, according to which one evaluates events.

Genuineness Recognition and open expression of the therapist's own feelings.

Congruence A fit between one's self-concept and behaviors, thoughts, and emotions.

Transactional analysis A form of psychotherapy that deals with how people interact and how their interactions reinforce attitudes, expectations, and "life positions." Abbreviated *TA.*

Parent In TA, a moralistic ego state.

Child In TA, an irresponsible, emotional ego state.

Adult In TA, a rational, adaptive ego state.

Transaction In TA, an exchange between two people.

Complementary In TA, descriptive of a transaction in which the ego states of two people interact harmoniously.

Transactional Analysis: I'm OK— You're OK—We're All OK

Although **transactional analysis** (TA) is considered a phenomenological therapy because of its focus on clients' subjective experiences, it is also rooted in the psychodynamic tradition. According to Thomas Harris, author of *I'm OK—You're OK* (1967), many of us suffer from inferiority complexes of the sort described by the psychoanalyst Alfred Adler. Even though we have become adults, we might continue to see ourselves as dependent children. We might think other people are "OK" but not see ourselves as being OK.

Within TA, *I'm not OK—You're OK* is one of four basic "life positions," or ways of perceiving relationships with others. A major goal of TA is to help people adopt the life position *I'm OK—You're OK,* in which they accept others and themselves. Unfortunately, people tend to adopt "games," or styles of relating to others that are designed to confirm one of the unhealthy life positions: I'm OK—You're not OK, I'm not OK—You're OK, or I'm not OK—You're not OK.

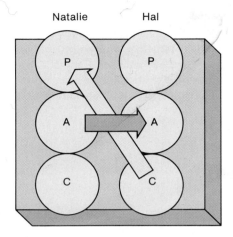

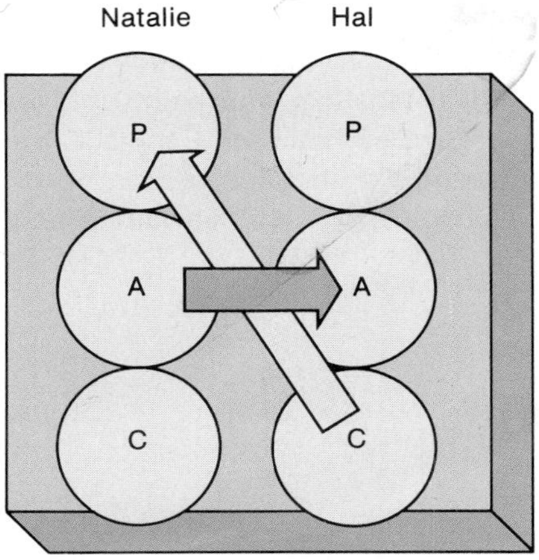

Figure 13.1
A Crossed Transaction. Transactions are social exchanges. "Crossed" transactions hamper communication. In this crossed transaction, Natalie asks Hal, "Did you have a good time tonight?" Hal replies, "Why do you wanna know?" Thus communication is broken off.

Psychiatrist Eric Berne, the originator of TA and author of the well-known book *Games People Play* (1976), described our personalities as containing three "ego states": **Parent, Child,** and **Adult.** The "parent" is a moralistic ego state. The "child" is an irresponsible and emotional ego state. The "adult" is a rational ego state. It is easy to confuse the child ego state with the id, the adult ego state with the ego, and the parent ego state with the superego. But note that these are three hypothesized *ego states,* or ways of coping. As we saw in Chapter 10, the id is unconscious and so is some of the functioning of the superego. In TA, however, we are capable of being fully conscious of the child and parent ego states, which is another reason why TA is considered to be a phenomenological rather than psychodynamic therapy.

Many interpersonal troubles occur because people tend to relate to each other as parents, children, or adults. A social exchange between two people is called a **transaction.** A transaction is said to fit, or be **complementary,** when a social exchange follows the same lines. In one type of complementary transaction, people relate as adults. Yet a transaction can also be complementary, even if it is upsetting, when two people relate as parent and child (Parent: "You shouldn't have done that"; Child: "I'm sorry, I promise it won't happen again"). Communication breaks down when the social exchange between the parties does not follow complementary lines (as in Figure 13.1).

NATALIE (adult to adult): Did you have a good time tonight?
HAL (child to parent): Why do you wanna know?

Or:

BILL (adult to adult): Nan, did you see the checkbook?
NAN (parent to child): A place for everything and everything in its place!

TA is often carried out with couples who complain of communication problems. It encourages people to relate to each other as adults.

A CLOSER LOOK

Games People Play

Eric Berne

Eric Berne, the originator of transactional analysis (TA), noted that many of us play games that help us maintain unhealthful life positions. For example, a common marital game is "If It Weren't for You" (Berne, 1976). People who play this game marry domineering mates who prevent them from going into things they would not have the courage to do anyhow, such as taking a more challenging job or moving to a new city. But by playing "If It Weren't for You," they can blame their mates for their shortcomings and excuse their own timidity.

TA is one of the types of psychotherapy that focuses on the present—the here and now—rather than the past. It is assumed that we have the capacity to change, despite painful incidents in the past, and that excessive focusing on the past is a diversion. But Berne found that some clients play a psychoanalytically oriented game that he termed "Archaeology." Archaeologists dig in the ruins of ancient civilizations. In this game, people dig into the ruins of their pasts to unearth the decisive event that could explain why they are having problems today. Why? Craig DeGree and C. R. Snyder (1985) of the University of Kansas have found that many of us emphasize the adversity of our early experiences when we are faced with the possibility of failure today, so the discovery of the details of a traumatic background might serve as a fitting excuse for failure.

In therapy groups, Berne noted, some clients take advantage of the Freudian view that no thought is to be censored by playing the game of "Self-Expression." In this game, a client uses vulgar language and paints a lurid scene, while other group members play "liberated" roles and applaud his or her "honesty." One might ask, of course, why a liberated person needs to be vulgar. Some of the other games people play have intriguing and reasonably self-explanatory titles:

- "Look How Hard I've Tried"
- "I'm Only Trying to Help You"
- "Why Does This Always Happen to Me?"
- "Now I've Got You, You Son of a Bitch!"
- "See What You Made Me Do"
- "You Got Me into This"
- "Kick Me"

Fritz Perls

Gestalt Therapy: Getting It Together

Like Rogers' person-centered approach, **Gestalt therapy,** originated by Fritz Perls (1893–1970), aims to help individuals integrate conflicting parts of the personality. Perls used the term *Gestalt* to signify his interest in providing the conflicting parts of the personality an integrated form or shape. He aimed to have his clients become aware of inner conflict, accept the reality of conflict rather than deny it or keep it repressed, and make productive choices despite misgivings and fear.

Although Perls' ideas about conflicting personality elements owe much to psychodynamic theory, his form of therapy, unlike psychoanalysis, focuses on the here and now. In Gestalt therapy, clients undergo exercises to heighten awareness of current feelings and behavior rather than to explore the past. Perls also believed, along with Carl Rogers, that people are free to make choices and to direct their personal growth. Unlike person-centered therapy, however, Gestalt therapy is highly directive. The therapist leads the client through planned experiences.

One Gestalt technique that increases awareness of internal conflict is the **dialogue.** Clients undertake verbal confrontations between opposing wishes and ideas. An example of these clashing personality elements is "top dog" and "underdog." One's top dog might conservatively suggest, "Don't take chances. Stick with what you have or you might lose it all." One's frustrated underdog might then rise up and assert, "You never try anything. How will you ever get out of this rut if you don't take on new challenges?" Heightened awareness of the elements of conflict can clear the path toward resolution, perhaps through compromise.

Body language also provides insight into conflicting feelings. Clients might be instructed to attend to the ways in which they furrow their eyebrows and tense their facial muscles when they express ideas that they think they support. In this way they often find that their body language asserts feelings that they have been denying.

To increase clients' understanding of opposing points of view, Gestalt therapists might encourage them to argue in favor of ideas opposed to their own. They might also have clients role-play people who are important to them to become more in touch with their points of view.

Gestalt therapy Fritz Perls's form of psychotherapy, which attempts to integrate conflicting parts of the personality through directive methods designed to help clients perceive their whole selves.

Dialogue A Gestalt therapy technique in which clients verbalize confrontations between conflicting parts of their personality.

Whereas psychodynamic theory views dreams as the "royal road to the unconscious," Perls saw the stuff of dreams as disowned parts of the personality.

Truth or Fiction Revisited

It is true that some psychotherapists interpret clients' dreams. Psychoanalysts and Gestalt therapists are two examples.

Perls would often ask clients to role-play the elements in their dreams to get in touch with these parts. In *Gestalt Therapy Verbatim*, Perls—known to clients and friends alike as Fritz—describes a session in which a client, Jim, is reporting a dream:

JIM: I just have the typical recurring dream which I think a lot of people might have if they have a background problem, and it isn't of anything I think I can act out. It's the distant wheel—I'm not sure what type it is—it's coming towards me and ever-increasing in size. And then finally, it's just above me and it's no height that I can determine, it's so high. And that's—

FRITZ: If you were this wheel, . . . what would you do with Jim?

JIM: I am just about to roll over Jim. (1971, p. 127)

Perls encourages Jim to undertake a dialogue with the wheel. Jim comes to see that the wheel represents fears about taking decisive action. Through this insight, the "wheel" becomes more manageable in size, and Jim is able to use some of the "energy" that he might otherwise have spent in worrying to begin to take charge of his life.

Let us now turn our attention to another group of therapies that are concerned with subjective experience and the here and now—cognitive therapies. But whereas phenomenological therapists tend to focus on clients' "personalities," cognitive therapists tend to focus on mental processes, such as thoughts, strategies for interpreting experience, plans, problem-solving techniques, and attitudes—especially self-defeating attitudes.

COGNITIVE THERAPIES

There Is Nothing Either Good or Bad,
but Thinking Makes It So
Shakespeare, *Hamlet*

In these lines from *Hamlet,* Shakespeare did not mean to suggest that injuries and misfortunes are painless or easy to cope with. Rather, he meant that our cognitive appraisals of unfortunate circumstances can heighten our discomfort and impair our coping ability. In so doing, Shakespeare was providing a kind of motto for cognitive therapists.

Cognitive therapies are the newest kinds of therapies presented in this book. Although there are many cognitively oriented therapists and more than one type of cognitive therapy, cognitive therapists would generally agree with Carl Rogers that people are free to make choices and develop in accord with their concepts of what they are capable of becoming. Cognitive therapists would also agree with Fritz Perls that it is appropriate for clients to focus on the here and now. Cognitive therapists, like Perls, are also reasonably directive in their approaches.

Cognitive therapists tend to focus on the beliefs, attitudes, and automatic types of thinking that create and compound their clients' problems. Cognitive

---

Cognitive therapy A form of therapy that focuses on how clients' cognitions (expectations, attitudes, beliefs, etc.) lead to distress and may be modified to relieve distress and promote adaptive behavior.

Albert Ellis

therapists, like psychodynamic and phenomenological therapists, are interested in fostering client self-insight, but they aim to heighten clients' insight into their *current cognitions,* not those in the distant past. Cognitive therapists also aim to directly *change* maladaptive cognitions to reduce negative feelings, to provide more accurate perceptions of the self and others, and to orient the client toward solving problems.

Let us have a look at some of the major cognitive therapists and at some of their approaches and methods.

Albert Ellis's Rational-Emotive Therapy

Albert Ellis is the founder of **rational-emotive therapy** and the second most influential psychotherapist in the Smith (1982) survey. As explained in Chapter 11, Ellis (1977, 1985, 1987) points out that our beliefs about events, as well as the events themselves, shape our responses to them. Moreover, many of us harbor a number of irrational beliefs that can give rise to problems or magnify their impact. Two of the most important ones are the belief that you must have the love and approval of people who are important to you and the belief that you must prove yourself to be thoroughly competent, adequate, and achieving.

Ellis's methods are active and directive. Rather than sitting back like the traditional psychoanalyst and occasionally offering an interpretation, Ellis urges clients to seek out their irrational beliefs, which can be fleeting and hard to catch. He then shows clients how their beliefs lead to misery and directly challenges them to change their beliefs. According to Ellis, we need less misery and less blaming but more action.

Aaron Beck's Cognitive Therapy: Correcting Cognitive Errors

Psychiatrist Aaron Beck (1976, 1985) also focuses on clients' cognitive distortions. He questions patients in a manner that encourages them to see the irrationality of their own ways of thinking—how, for example, their minimizing of their accomplishments and their pessimistic assuming that the worst will happen heightens feelings of depression. Beck, like Ellis, notes that our cognitive distortions can be fleeting and automatic, difficult to detect. His therapy methods help clients pin down these self-defeating thoughts.

Beck notes in particular the pervasive influence of four basic types of cognitive errors that contribute to clients' miseries:

1. Clients may *selectively perceive* the world as a harmful place and ignore evidence to the contrary
2. Clients may *overgeneralize* on the basis of a few examples. For example, they may perceive themselves as worthless because they were laid off at work or as grossly unattractive because they were refused a request for a date
3. Clients may *magnify,* or blow out of proportion, the importance of negative events. As noted in the discussion of Ellis's views, clients may catastrophize flunking a test by assuming they will flunk out of college, or catastrophize losing a job by believing that they will never work again and that serious harm will befall their families

Rational-emotive therapy Albert Ellis's form of cognitive psychotherapy, which focuses on how irrational expectations create anxiety and disappointment and which encourages clients to challenge and correct these expectations.

Aaron Beck

4. Clients may engage in *absolutist thinking,* or looking at the world in black and white rather than in shades of gray. In doing so, a rejection on a date takes on the meaning of a lifetime of loneliness; a discomforting illness takes on life-threatening proportions.

The concept of pinpointing and modifying errors may become more clear from reading an excerpt from a case in which a 53-year-old engineer was treated with cognitive therapy for severe depression. The engineer had left his job and become inactive. As reported by Beck and his colleagues, the first treatment goal was to foster physical activity—even things like raking leaves and preparing dinner—because activity is incompatible with depression. Then:

[The engineer's] cognitive distortions were identified by comparing his assessment of each activity with that of his wife. Alternative ways of interpreting his experiences were then considered.

In comparing his wife's résumé of his past experiences, he became aware that he had (a) undervalued his past by failing to mention many previous accomplishments, (2) regarded himself as far more responsible for his "failures" than she did, and (3) concluded that he was worthless since he had not succeeded in attaining certain goals in the past. When the two accounts were contrasted, he could discern many of his cognitive distortions. In subsequent sessions, his wife continued to serve as an "objectifier."

In midtherapy, [he] compiled a list of new attitudes that he had acquired since initiating therapy. These included:

1. *"I am starting at a lower level of functioning at my job, but it will improve if I persist."*
2. *"I know that once I get going in the morning, everything will run all right for the rest of the day."*
3. *"I can't achieve everything at once."*
4. *"I have my periods of ups and downs, but in the long run I feel better."*
5. *"My expectations from my job and life should be scaled down to a realistic level."*
6. *"Giving in to avoidance [e.g., staying away from work and social interactions] never helps and only leads to further avoidance."*

He was instructed to re-read this list daily for several weeks even though he already knew the content (Rush et al., 1975).

Re-reading the list of productive attitudes is a variation of the cognitive technique of having clients rehearse or repeat accurate and rational ideas so that they come to replace cognitive distortions and irrational beliefs. The engineer gradually became less depressed in therapy and returned to work and an active social life. Along the way he learned to combat inappropriate self-blame for problems, perfectionistic expectations, magnifications of failures, and overgeneralizations from failures.

Becoming aware of cognitive errors and modifying catastrophizing thoughts helps provide us with coping ability under stress. In the discussion of depression in Chapter 12, it was noted that internal, stable, and global attributions of failure lead to depression and feelings of helplessness. Cognitive therapists also alert clients to cognitive errors such as these so that the clients can change their attitudes and pave the way for more effective overt behavior.

Cognitive Restructuring: "No, No, Look at It This Way"

In cognitive restructuring, clients are shown how their interpretations of events lead to maladaptive responses. Then they are helped to rethink their situations so that they can generate more adaptive overt behavior (Goldfried, 1988; Meichenbaum & Deffenbacher, 1988). Consider the example of aggressive people who see themselves as simply "exploding" at the slightest provocation. To them, the explosion is an automatic response to another person's insult. But the fact is that in people, aggressive behavior is not automatic, even when they are sorely annoyed—it involves thought processes and decision making (Berkowitz, 1983).

Still, many people claim that they "just explode" and are unaware of the thoughts that mediate provocations and their reactions. Cognitive therapists have devised a number of methods to help people get in touch with fleeting thoughts, such as "running movies." Consider this example: Imagine that you are pushing a cart down an aisle in a supermarket. Someone pushes into you, so hard that it seems purposeful, and then says, "What the hell's the matter with you? Why don't you watch where you're going!"

What would you think? Would you think, "This so-and-so can't treat me this way! People can't be allowed to act like that!" If so, you would have made the cognitive errors of taking this person's rudeness personally and expecting others to live up to your own standards. Irrational beliefs and cognitive errors intensify negative feelings and prompt maladaptive behavior. They might prompt you to violence, to behavior you might regret afterward.

In running a movie about the supermarket incident, a client would relive this upsetting experience in the imagination to search out fleeting thoughts that might otherwise barely be noticed. In an important experiment, Novaco (1974) showed how running movies, cognitive restructuring, and relaxation training helped explosive men and women deal with the supermarket-type of provocation more effectively. His strategy included three phases: education, planning, and application training. In phase 1, participants were shown how anger is intensified by the irrational beliefs that one must expect flawless behavior from others and that an insult is a threat to one's self-esteem. In phase 2, they were taught relaxation skills* and alternatives for their irrational beliefs. In phase 3, participants imagined provocations and practiced using rational beliefs and relaxation to arrive at adaptive, nonviolent responses. Subjects made dramatic gains in coping with provocations in socially acceptable ways. Many attributed their gains to reconceptualizing provocations as problems demanding solutions rather than as threats requiring violent responses.

Before leaving our discussion of cognitive therapy, it should be noted that many theorists consider cognitive therapy to be a collection of techniques that belong within the province of behavior therapy, which is discussed in the following section. Some members of this group prefer the name "cognitive *behavior* therapy"; others argue that the term *behavior therapy* is broad enough to include cognitive techniques. However, there is a difference in focus between many cognitive therapists and behavior therapists. To behavior therapists, the purpose of dealing with client cognitions is to change *overt* behavior. Cognitive therapists agree that cognitive change leads to overt behavioral change and also see the value of tying treatment outcomes to observable behavior. But cognitive therapists tend to assert that cognitive change is in itself an important goal.

*Relaxation training is usually considered a behavior-therapy technique, but it has been adopted by therapists of many orientations.

Joseph Wolpe

Arnold Lazarus

BEHAVIOR THERAPY: ADJUSTMENT IS WHAT YOU DO

Behavior therapy—also called *behavior modification*—is the direct promotion of desired behavioral change by means of systematic application of principles of learning. As suggested in the section on cognitive therapy, many behavior therapists incorporate cognitive processes in their theoretical outlook and cognitive procedures in their methodology (Wilson, 1982). For example, techniques such as systematic desensitization, covert sensitization, and covert reinforcement ask clients to focus on visual imagery. However, behavior therapists insist that their methods be established by experimentation (Wolpe, 1985) and that therapeutic outcomes be assessed in terms of observable, measurable behavior.

Behavior therapists rely heavily on principles of conditioning and observational learning. They help clients discontinue self-defeating behavior patterns, such as overeating, smoking, and phobic avoidance of harmless stimuli. They also help clients acquire adaptive behavior patterns, such as the social skills required to start social relationships and to say no to insistent salespeople.

Behavior therapists might help clients gain "insight" into maladaptive behavior in the sense of fostering awareness of the circumstances in which it occurs. But they do not foster insight in the psychoanalytic sense of unearthing the early childhood origins of problems and the symbolic meanings of maladaptive behavior patterns. Behavior therapists, like psychoanalysts and person-centered therapists, may also build warm, therapeutic relationships with clients, but they see the special efficacy of behavior therapy as deriving from specific, learning-based procedures (Wolpe, 1985).

About 17 percent of the clinical and counseling psychologists surveyed by Smith (1982) labeled themselves behavioral or cognitive-behavioral in orientation—the largest group of therapists who identified with a specific orientation. Behavior therapists Joseph Wolpe and Arnold Lazarus were ranked fourth and fifth among the ten most influential psychotherapists (Smith, 1982, p. 807).

Let us look at a number of behavior-therapy techniques.

Systematic Desensitization

Adam has a phobia for receiving injections. His behavior therapist treats him as he reclines in a comfortable padded chair. In a state of deep muscle relaxation, Adam observes slides projected on a screen. A slide of a nurse holding a needle has just been shown three times, 30 seconds at a time. Each time Adam has shown no anxiety. So now a slightly more discomforting slide is shown: one of the nurse aiming the needle toward someone's bare arm. After 15 seconds, our armchair adventurer notices twinges of discomfort and raises a finger as a signal (speaking might disturb his relaxation). The projector operator turns off the light, and Adam spends two minutes imagining his "safe scene"—lying on a beach beneath the tropical sun. Then the slide is shown again. This time Adam views it for 30 seconds before feeling anxiety.

Adam is undergoing **systematic desensitization,** a method for reducing phobic responses originated by psychiatrist Joseph Wolpe (1958, 1973) (see Figure 13.2). Systematic desensitization is a gradual process. Clients learn to handle increasingly disturbing stimuli while anxiety to each one is being counterconditioned. About 10 to 20 stimuli are arranged in a sequence or **hierarchy** according to their capacity to elicit anxiety. In imagination or by being shown photos, the client travels gradually up through this hierarchy,

Behavior therapy Systematic application of the principles of learning to the direct modification of a client's problem behaviors.

Systematic desensitization Wolpe's method for reducing fears by associating a hierarchy of images of fear-evoking stimuli with deep muscle relaxation.

Hierarchy An arrangement of stimuli according to the amount of fear they evoke.

Figure 13.2
Systematic Desensitization. In systematic desensitization, clients engage in deep muscle relaxation while the therapist presents a graduated series of fear-evoking stimuli.

approaching the target behavior. In Adam's case the target behavior was the ability to receive an injection without undue anxiety.

Joseph Wolpe developed systematic desensitization on the assumption that maladaptive anxiety responses, like other behaviors, are learned or conditioned. He reasoned that they can be unlearned by counterconditioning or by extinction (see Chapter 5). In counterconditioning, a response that is incompatible with anxiety is made to appear under conditions that usually elicit anxiety. Muscle relaxation is incompatible with anxiety. For this reason Adam's therapist is teaching Adam to experience relaxation in the presence of (usually) anxiety-evoking slides of needles. (Muscle relaxation is usually achieved by means of *progressive relaxation,* which was described in Chapter 11 as a method for lowering the arousal that attends anxiety reactions.)

Remaining in the presence of phobic imagery, rather than running from it, is also likely to enhance our self-efficacy expectations (Galassi, 1988).

Truth or Fiction Revisited

It is true that lying around in your recliner and fantasizing can be an effective way of confronting your fears—if you are using the method of systematic desensitization.

The Symptom-Substitution Controversy Psychoanalysts have argued that phobias are symptoms of unconscious conflicts and that systematic desensitization of a "symptom" might only lead to the appearance of another symptom—that is, to **symptom substitution.** To behavior therapists, maladaptive behavior *is* the problem, not just a symptom of the problem. Evidence suggests that systematic desensitization is effective in 80 to 90 percent of cases (Paul, 1969a; Smith & Glass, 1977; Marks, 1982), and symptom substitution has not been found to be a problem (Deffenbacher & Suinn, 1988).

Symptom substitution The emergence of a second symptom when the first symptom is relieved.

Participant modeling A behavior-therapy technique in which a client observes and imitates a person who approaches and copes with feared objects or situations.

Participant Modeling A behavioral alternative to systematic desensitization is **participant modeling,** which relies on observational learning. In this method, clients observe and then imitate people who do approach and cope with the objects or situations they fear. Bandura and his colleagues (1969) found that participant modeling worked as well as systematic desen-

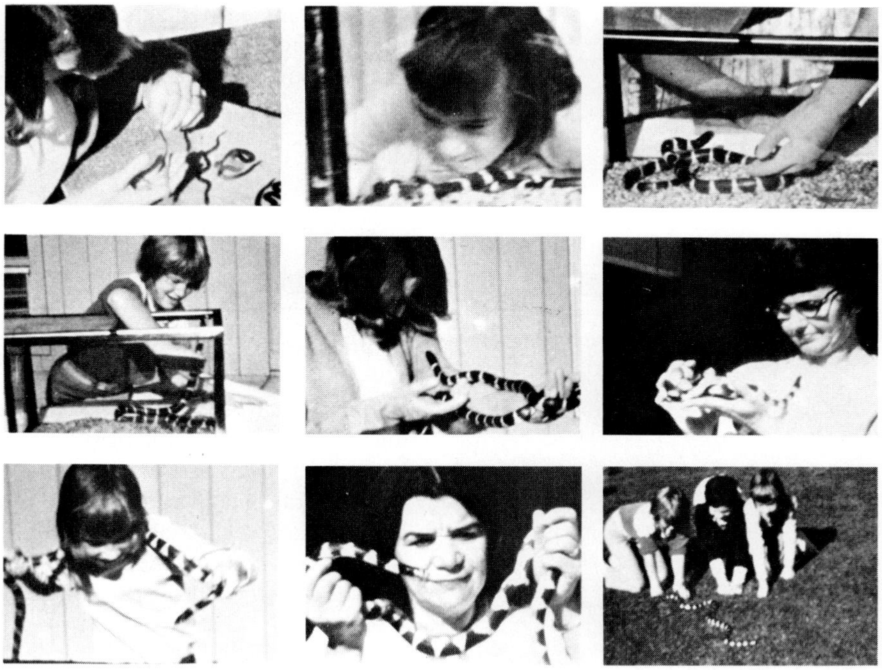

Figure 13.3
Participant Modeling. Participant modeling is a behavior-therapy technique that is based on principles of observational learning. In these photos, people with fear of snakes observe and then imitate models who are unafraid. Parents often try to convince children that something tastes good by eating it before them and saying "Mmm!"

sitization, and more rapidly, in reducing fear of snakes (see Figure 13.3). Participant modeling, like systematic desensitization, is likely to increase self-efficacy expectations in coping with feared stimuli.

Aversive Conditioning

You might have read or seen the filmed version of the futuristic Anthony Burgess novel, *A Clockwork Orange.* Alex, the antisocial "hero," finds violence and rape to be superb pastimes. When he is caught, he is given the chance to undergo an experimental reconditioning program rather than serve a prison term. In this program, he watches films of violence and rape while vomiting under the influence of a nausea-inducing drug. After his release, he feels ill whenever he contemplates violence. Unfortunately, Beethoven's music, which he had previously enjoyed, accompanies the films and feelings of nausea. So Alex acquires an aversion for Beethoven as well.

In the novel, Alex undergoes a program of **aversive conditioning**—also called *aversion therapy*—which is actually used quite frequently today, although not in prisons. It is one of the more controversial procedures in behavior therapy. In aversive conditioning, painful or aversive stimuli are paired with unwanted impulses, such as desire for a cigarette or desire to engage in antisocial behavior, to make the goal less appealing. For example, to help people control alcohol intake, tastes of different alcoholic beverages can be paired with drug-induced nausea and vomiting or with electric shock (Wilson et al., 1975).

Aversive conditioning has been used with some success in treating problems as divergent as paraphilias (Rathus, 1983), cigarette smoking (Lichtenstein, 1982; Walker & Franzoni, 1985), and retarded children's self-injurious behavior. In one large-scale study of aversive conditioning in the treatment of alcoholism, 63 percent of the 685 people treated remained abstinent for one year afterward, and about a third remained abstinent for at least three

Aversive conditioning A behavior-therapy technique in which undesired responses are inhibited by pairing repugnant or offensive stimuli with them.

years (Wiens & Menustik, 1983). It may seem ironic that punitive aversive stimulation is sometimes used to stop children from punishing themselves, but people sometimes hurt themselves to obtain sympathy and attention from others. If self-injury leads to more pain than anticipated and no sympathy, it might be discontinued.

A CLOSER LOOK

Aversive Conditioning. In aversive conditioning, unwanted behaviors take on a noxious quality as a result of pairing them repeatedly with aversive stimuli. Overexposure is making cigarette smoke aversive to the smoker in this photograph.

Using Aversive Conditioning to Help Clients Quit Smoking

Several aversive-conditioning techniques are used to help people quit smoking. In one, rapid smoking, the would-be quitter inhales every six seconds. In another, the hose of an everyday hair dryer is hooked up to a chamber with several lit cigarettes. Smoke is blown into the quitter's face as he or she also smokes a cigarette. In a third, branching pipes are used so that the smoker draws in smoke from two or more cigarettes simultaneously. In all of these methods, overexposure renders once-desirable cigarette smoke aversive. The quitter becomes motivated to avoid, rather than seek, cigarettes and stops smoking on a preplanned date. Many reports have shown a quit rate of 60 percent or higher at six-month follow-ups.

Rapid smoking is the most widely researched aversion method for treating cigarette smoking (Lichtenstein, 1982). Rapid smoking is popular, because it is as effective as other methods and the apparatus—the quitter's own cigarettes—is readily available. But in addition to producing discomfort, rapid smoking raises the blood pressure, decreases the blood's capacity to carry oxygen, and produces heart abnormalities, as shown by the electrocardiogram (Lichtenstein & Glasgow, 1977). Nevertheless, a two-year follow-up study of cardiac and pulmonary patients found no negative effects from rapid smoking (Hall et al., 1984)—and, when we consider the positive benefits of quitting smoking for these patients, rapid smoking elicits hope.

Truth or Fiction Revisited

It is true that smoking cigarettes can be an effective treatment for helping people to stop smoking cigarettes. The trick is to inhale enough smoke so that it is aversive rather than enjoyable.

Operant Conditioning

We usually prefer to relate to people who smile at us rather than ignore us, and to take courses in which we do well rather than fail. We tend to repeat behavior that is reinforced. Behavior that is not reinforced tends to become extinguished. Behavior therapists have used these principles of operant conditioning with psychotic patients as well as clients with milder problems.

The staff at one mental hospital was at a loss about how to encourage withdrawn schizophrenic patients to eat regularly. Ayllon and Haughton (1962) observed that the staff were exacerbating the problem by coaxing patients into the dining room, even feeding them. Increased staff attention apparently reinforced the patients' uncooperativeness. Some rules were changed. Patients who did not arrive at the dining hall within 30 minutes after serving were locked out. Staff could not interact with patients at mealtime. With uncooperative behavior no longer reinforced, patients quickly changed their eating habits. Patients were then required to pay one penny to enter the dining hall. Pennies were earned by interacting with other patients and showing other socially appropriate behaviors. These target behaviors also increased in frequency.

Many psychiatric wards and hospitals now use **token economies** in which tokens, such as poker chips, must be used by patients to purchase TV-viewing time, extra visits to the canteen, or private rooms. The tokens are reinforcements for productive activities such as making beds, brushing teeth, and socializing. Whereas token economies have not eliminated all symptoms of schizophrenia, they have enhanced patient activity and cooperation. Tokens have also been used successfully in programs designed to modify the behavior of children with conduct disorders. For example, Schneider and Byrne (1987) gave children tokens for helpful behaviors such as volunteering and removed tokens for behaviors such as arguing and inattention.

The operant-conditioning method of **successive approximations** is often used to help clients build good habits. Let us use a (not uncommon!) example: You wish to study three hours an evening but can only maintain concentration for half an hour. Rather than attempting to increase study time all at once, you could do so gradually, say, by five minutes an evening. After every hour or so of studying, you could reinforce yourself with five minutes of people-watching in a busy section of the library.

Assertiveness Training

Are you a person who can't say no? Do people walk all over you? Brush off those footprints and get some assertiveness training! Over the years, large numbers of people have done just that. Assertiveness training helps clients decrease social anxieties, but it is also one of the therapy methods that has been used to optimize the functioning of individuals without problems.

Assertive behavior can be contrasted with both *nonassertive* (submissive) behavior and *aggressive* behavior. Assertive people express their genuine feelings, stick up for their legitimate rights, and refuse unreasonable requests. But they do not insult, threaten, or belittle. Assertive people also do not shy away from meeting and constructing relationships with new people, and they express positive feelings such as liking and love.

Assertiveness training decreases social anxiety and builds social skills through techniques such as self-monitoring, modeling, and behavior rehearsal. In **self-monitoring,** the client keeps a record of upsetting social encounters in order to pinpoint instances of social avoidance, clumsiness, and feelings of frustration. The therapist **models** more effective social behavior and encourages the client to rehearse this behavior as the therapist provides **feedback.** The therapist attends to the client's posture, facial expressions, and tone of voice as well as to the content of what is being said.

The therapist may also point out that various irrational beliefs can impede progress. Beliefs to the effect that it is awful to earn the disapproval of others or to fumble at the first few attempts at behavioral change are likely to increase, rather than decrease, social anxieties. Clients need to learn to reward themselves for small but consistent gains rather than condemn themselves for imperfection.

Assertiveness training is effective in groups. Group members can role-play important people—such as parents, spouses, or potential dates—in the lives of other members. The trainee then can engage in **behavior rehearsal** with the role-player.

The nearby Questionnaire will afford you insight into how assertive you are in various situations.

Token economy A controlled environment in which people are reinforced for desired behaviors with tokens (such as poker chips) that may be exchanged for privileges.

Successive approximations In operant conditioning, a series of behaviors that gradually become more similar to a target behavior.

Self-monitoring Keeping a record of one's own behavior to identify problems and record successes.

Model To engage in behavior patterns that are imitated by others.

Feedback In assertiveness training, information about the effectiveness of a response.

Behavior rehearsal Practice.

QUESTIONNAIRE

The Rathus Assertiveness Schedule

How assertive are you? Do you stick up for your rights, or do you allow others to walk all over you? Do you say what you feel or what you think other people want you to say? Do you initiate relationships with attractive people, or do you shy away from them?

One way to gain insight into how assertive you are is to take the following self-report test of assertive behavior. Once you have finished, turn to Appendix B to find out how to calculate and interpret your score.

Directions: Indicate how well each item describes you by using this code:

3 = very much like me
2 = rather like me
1 = slightly like me
−1 = slightly unlike me
−2 = rather unlike me
−3 = very much unlike me

_____ 1. Most people seem to be more aggressive and assertive than I am.*
_____ 2. I have hesitated to make or accept dates because of "shyness."*
_____ 3. When the food served at a restaurant is not done to my satisfaction, I complain about it to the waiter or waitress.
_____ 4. I am careful to avoid hurting other people's feelings, even when I feel that I have been injured.*
_____ 5. If a salesperson has gone to considerable trouble to show me merchandise that is not quite suitable, I have a difficult time saying "No."*
_____ 6. When I am asked to do something, I insist upon knowing why.
_____ 7. There are times when I look for a good, vigorous argument.
_____ 8. I strive to get ahead as well as most people in my position.
_____ 9. To be honest, people often take advantage of me.*
_____ 10. I enjoy starting conversations with new acquaintances and strangers.
_____ 11. I often don't know what to say to attractive persons of the opposite sex.*
_____ 12. I will hesitate to make phone calls to business establishments and institutions.*
_____ 13. I would rather apply for a job or for admission to a college by writing letters than by going through with personal interviews.*
_____ 14. I find it embarrassing to return merchandise.*
_____ 15. If a close and respected relative were annoying me, I would smother my feelings rather than express my annoyance.*
_____ 16. I have avoided asking questions for fear of sounding stupid.*
_____ 17. During an argument I am sometimes afraid that I will get so upset that I will shake all over.*
_____ 18. If a famed and respected lecturer makes a comment which I think is incorrect, I will have the audience hear my point of view as well.
_____ 19. I avoid arguing over prices with clerks and salespeople.*
_____ 20. When I have done something important or worthwhile, I manage to let others know about it.
_____ 21. I am open and frank about my feelings.
_____ 22. If someone has been spreading false and bad stories about me, I see him or her as soon as possible and "have a talk" about it.
_____ 23. I often have a hard time saying "No."*
_____ 24. I tend to bottle up my emotions rather than make a scene.*
_____ 25. I complain about poor service in a restaurant and elsewhere.
_____ 26. When I am given a compliment, I sometimes just don't know what to say.*
_____ 27. If a couple near me in a theater or at a lecture were conversing rather loudly, I would ask them to be quiet or to take their conversation elsewhere.
_____ 28. Anyone attempting to push ahead of me in a line is in for a good battle.
_____ 29. I am quick to express an opinion.
_____ 30. There are times when I just can't say anything.*

Reprinted from Rathus, 1973, pp. 398–406.

Self-Control Techniques

Does it sometimes seem that mysterious forces are at work? Forces that delight in wreaking havoc with your New Year's resolutions and other efforts to take charge of bad habits? Just when you go on a diet, that juicy Big Mac stares at you from the TV set. Just when you resolve to balance your budget, that sweater goes on sale. Behavior therapists have developed a number of self-control techniques to help people cope with such temptations.

Functional analysis A systematic study of behavior in which one identifies the stimuli that trigger it and the reinforcers that maintain it.

Functional Analysis of Behavior Behavior therapists usually begin by doing a **functional analysis** of the problem behavior. In this way, they help

Table 13.2
Excerpts from Brian's Diary of Nail Biting for April 14

Incident	Time	Location	Activity (Thoughts, Feelings)	Reactions
1	7:45 AM	Freeway	Driving to work, bored, not thinking	Finger bleeds, pain
2	10:30 AM	Office	Writing report	Self-disgust
3	2:25 PM	Conference	Listening to dull financial report	Embarrassment
4	6:40 PM	Living room	Watching evening news	Self-disgust

A functional analysis of problem behavior, like nail biting, increases awareness of the environmental context in which it occurs, spurs motivation to change, and, in highly motivated people, might lead to significant behavioral change.

determine the stimuli that trigger problem behavior and the reinforcers that maintain it. In a functional analysis, you use a diary to jot down each instance of the behavior. You note the time of day, location, your activity (including your thoughts and feelings), and reactions (yours and others').

Functional analysis serves a number of purposes. For example, it makes you more aware of the environmental context of your behavior and can increase your motivation to change. In studies with highly motivated people, functional analysis alone has been found to increase the amount of time spent studying (Johnson & White, 1971) and talking in a therapy group (Komaki & Dore-Boyce, 1978) and to decrease cigarette consumption (Lipinski et al., 1975).

Truth or Fiction Revisited

It is true that you may be able to gain control over bad habits merely by keeping a record of where and when you practice them. The record may help motivate you, make you more aware of the problems, and suggest strategies for behavior change.

Brian used functional analysis to master his nail biting. Table 13.2 shows a few items from his notebook. He discovered that boredom and humdrum activities seemed to serve as triggers for nail biting. He began to watch out for feelings of boredom as signs to practice self-control. He also made some changes in his life so that he would feel bored less often.

There are numerous self-control strategies aimed at (1) the stimuli that trigger behavior, (2) the behaviors themselves, and (3) reinforcers.

Strategies Aimed at Stimuli that Trigger Behavior

Restriction of the stimulus field. Gradually exclude the problem behavior from more environments. For example, for a while, first do not smoke while driving, then extend not smoking to the office. Or practice the habit only outside the environment in which it normally occurs. Psychologist J. Dennis Nolan's (1968) wife had tried to quit smoking several times—to no avail. Finally the Nolans applied restriction of the stimulus field by limiting her smoking to one place—a "smoking chair." The rule was that Ms. Nolan could smoke as much as she wanted to, but only in that chair. Also, smoking was the only activity permitted in the chair. The chair was set in a "stimulus-deprived" corner of the basement so that smoking would become dissociated from its usual triggers, such as watching television, reading, and conversing. Ms. Nolan's awareness of the details of her habit increased, and she had more opportunity to reflect on her reasons for cutting down. Her smoking fell off, and, after a few weeks of humiliating trips to the basement, she quit altogether.

Avoidance of powerful stimuli that trigger habits. Avoid obvious sources of temptation. People who go window-shopping often wind up buying more than windows. If eating at The Pizza Glutton tempts you to forget your diet, eat at home or at The Celery Stalk instead.

Stimulus control. Place yourself in an environment in which desirable behavior is likely to occur. Maybe it's difficult to lift your mood directly at times, but you can place yourself in the audience of that uplifting concert or film. It might be difficult to force yourself to study, but how about rewarding yourself for spending time in the library?

Strategies Aimed at Behavior

Response prevention. Make unwanted behavior difficult or impossible. Impulse buying is curbed when you shred your credit cards, leave your checkbook home, and carry only a couple of dollars. You can't reach for the strawberry cream cheese pie in your refrigerator if you have left it at the supermarket (that is, have not bought it).

Competing responses. Engage in behaviors that are incompatible with the bad habits. It is difficult to drink a glass of water and a fattening milkshake simultaneously. Grasping something firmly is a useful competing response for nail biting or scratching.

Chain breaking. Interfere with unwanted habitual behavior by complicating the process of engaging in it. Break the chain of reaching for a readily available cigarette and placing it in your mouth by wrapping the pack in aluminum foil and placing it on the top shelf in the closet. Rewrap the pack after taking one. Put your cigarette in the ashtray between puffs, or put your fork down between mouthfuls of dessert. Ask yourself if you really want more.

Successive approximations. Gradually approach targets through a series of relatively painless steps. Increase studying by only five minutes a day. Decrease smoking by pausing for a minute when the cigarette is smoked halfway, or by putting it out a minute before you would wind up eating the filter. Decrease your daily intake of food by 50 to 100 calories every couple of days, or else cut out one type of fattening food every few days.

Strategies Aimed at Reinforcements

Reinforcement of desired behavior. Why give yourself something for nothing? Make pleasant activities, like going to films, walking on the beach, or reading a new novel, contingent upon meeting reasonable, daily behavioral goals. Put one dollar away toward that camera or vacation trip each day you remain within your calorie limit.

Response cost. Heighten awareness of the long-term reasons for dieting or cutting down on smoking by punishing yourself for not meeting a daily goal or for practicing a bad habit. Make out a check to your most hated cause and mail it at once if you bite your nails or inhale that cheesecake.

"Grandma's method." Remember Grandma's method for inducing children to eat their vegetables? Simple: No veggies, no dessert. In this method, desired behaviors, like studying and teethbrushing, can be increased by insisting that they be done before you carry out a favored or frequently occurring activity. For example, don't watch television unless you have studied first. Don't leave the apartment until you've brushed your teeth.

Group Therapy. Group therapy has a number of advantages over individual therapy for many clients. It's economical, provides a fund of information and experience for clients to draw upon, elicits group support and reassurance, and provides the opportunity to relate to other people. On the other hand, some clients do require individual attention.

You can also place reminders of new attitudes you're trying to acquire on little cards and read them regularly. For example, in quitting smoking, you might write "Every day it becomes a little easier" on one card and "Your lungs will turn pink again" on another, place these cards and others in your wallet, and read them like clockwork before you leave the house.

Covert sensitization. Create imaginary horror stories about problem behavior. Psychologists have successfully reduced overeating and smoking by having clients imagine that they become acutely nauseated at the thought of fattening foods or that a cigarette is made from vomit. Some horror stories are not so "imaginary." Deliberately focusing on heart strain and diseased lungs every time you overeat or smoke, rather than ignoring these long-term consequences, might also promote self-control.

Covert reinforcement. Create rewarding imagery for desired behavior. When you have achieved a behavioral goal, fantasize about how wonderful you are. Imagine friends and family patting you on the back. Fantasize about the *Playboy* or *Playgirl* centerfold for a minute.

Truth or Fiction Revisited

It is true that some psychotherapists outline behavioral prescriptions for their clients (or "tell their clients precisely what to do"). Behavior therapists as well as Gestalt therapists and some cognitive therapists provide examples.

GROUP THERAPIES

When a psychotherapist has several clients with similar problems—whether anxiety, depression, adjustment to divorce, or lack of social skills—it often makes sense to treat these clients in groups of 6 to 12 rather than conduct individual therapy sessions. The methods and characteristics of the group will reflect the needs of the members and the theoretical orientation of the leader. For example, in a psychoanalytic group, clients might interpret one anothers' dreams. In a person-centered group, they might provide an accepting atmosphere for self-exploration. Clients in a TA group might comment on the games played by others. Behavior-therapy groups might undergo joint desensitization to anxiety-evoking stimuli or model and rehearse social skills.

There are several advantages to group therapy:

1. Group therapy is economical. It allows the therapist to work with several clients simultaneously.
2. As compared with one-to-one therapy, group therapy provides a greater fund of information and experience for clients to draw upon. The helping professionals who lead groups might have greater group skills and psychological knowledge than individual group members, but the group members will have a large fund of life experiences.
3. Appropriate behavior receives group support. Clients usually appreciate approval from their therapists, but a spontaneous outpouring of approval from peers might seem to be more appropriate since they will be attaining future approval from peers, not a therapist.
4. When we run into troubles, it is easy to imagine that we are different from other people and possibly inferior. Group members frequently learn that other people have had similar problems, similar self-doubts, similar failure experiences.
5. Group members who show improvement provide hope for other members.
6. Many individuals seek therapy because of problems in relating to other people; and people who seek therapy for other reasons are also frequently socially inhibited. Members of therapy groups have the opportunity to rehearse social skills with one another in a relatively nonthreatening atmosphere.

Truth or Fiction Revisited

It is *not* true that individual therapy is always preferable to group therapy for people who can afford it. Group therapy offers advantages, such as the shared experience and support of group members.

Many types of therapy can be conducted either individually or in groups. Encounter groups and family therapy can be conducted in group-format only.

Encounter Groups

Encounter groups are not appropriate for treating serious psychological problems. Rather, they are intended to promote personal growth by heightening awareness of one's own needs and feelings and those of others. This goal is sought through intense confrontations, or encounters, between strangers. Like ships in the night, group members come together out of the darkness, touch one another briefly, then sink back into the shadows of one anothers' lives. But something is thought to be gained from the passing.

Encounter groups stress interactions between group members in the here and now. Discussion of the past may be outlawed. Interpretation is out. Expression of genuine feelings toward others is encouraged. When group members think that a person's social mask is phony, they might descend en masse to rip it off.

Professionals recognize that encounter groups can be damaging when they urge overly rapid disclosure of intimate matters, or when several members attack one member in unison. Responsible leaders do not tolerate these abuses and try to keep groups moving in growth-enhancing directions.

Encounter group A type of group that aims to foster self-awareness by focusing on how group members relate to each other in a setting that encourages open expression of feelings.

Family Therapy

In **family therapy,** one or more families constitute the group. Family therapy may be undertaken from various theoretical viewpoints. One is the "systems approach," for which much credit is to be given to family therapist Virginia Satir (1967). In Satir's method, the family system of interaction is studied and modified to enhance the growth of family members and of the family unit as a whole.

It is often found that family members with low self-esteem cannot tolerate different attitudes and behaviors from other family members. Faulty family communications also create problems. It is also not uncommon for the family to present an "identified patient"—that is, the family member who has *the* problem and is *causing* all the trouble. Yet family therapists usually assume that the identified patient is a scapegoat for other problems within and among family members. It is a sort of myth: Change the bad apple, or identified patient, and the barrel, or family, will be functional once more.

The family therapist—who is often a specialist in this field—attempts to teach the family to communicate more effectively and to encourage growth and the eventual autonomy, or independence, of each family member. In doing so, the family therapist will also show the family how the identified patient has been used as a focus for the problems of other members of the group.

There are many other types of groups: couples groups, marathon groups, sensitivity-training groups, and psychodrama groups, to name just a few.

EVALUATION OF METHODS OF PSYCHOTHERAPY AND BEHAVIOR THERAPY

Now that we have explored some of the types of psychotherapy in use today, we must tackle a very important issue: Does psychotherapy *work?* Many of us know people who swear by the therapy they have received, but very often the evidence they provide is shaky—for example, "I was a wreck before, but now . . . ," or "I feel so much better now." Anecdotes like these may be encouraging, but we have no way of knowing what would have happened to these same people if they had not gone for help. As pointed out by Hans Eysenck (1952) in an evaluation that "shook up" psychotherapists, many people feel better about their problems as time goes on, with or without therapy. Sometimes, happily, problems seem to go away by themselves. At other times, people find solutions to their problems on their own. Then, too, we hear many stories of how therapy was to no avail, and sometimes we hear of people hopping fruitlessly from therapist to therapist.

Let us now consider some of the problems in evaluating therapy methods scientifically.

Problems in Running Experiments on Psychotherapy As noted in Chapter 1, the ideal method for evaluating the effectiveness of a treatment—such as a method of therapy—is the experiment. However, it is not always easy to run experiments in the realm of therapy. Consider the case of psychoanalysis. In well-run experiments, subjects are assigned to experimental and control groups at random. Thus, it could be argued that a sound experiment to evaluate psychoanalysis would require randomly assigning people seeking therapy to psychoanalysis and to a control group or to a number of other kinds of therapy for comparison. Yet a subject might have to remain in

Family therapy A form of therapy in which the family unit is treated as the client.

traditional psychoanalysis for years to attain results. How could control subjects be kept in briefer forms of therapy or in a no-treatment control group for a comparable period of time? Moreover, some people seek psychoanalysis per se rather than psychotherapy in general. Would it be ethical to assign them at random to other treatments or to a no-treatment control group? Clearly not (Basham, 1986; Parloff, 1986). Could it even be done? That is, could clients requesting psychoanalysis be deceived into thinking that a cognitive or behavioral form of therapy is psychoanalysis? Probably not, and no ethical helping professional would want to deceive a client in such a manner. So we run into obstacles with the subjects we can place in our experimental and control groups, just as we do when we try to define a comparable duration of treatment for various kinds of therapies.

Recall also that in an ideal experiment, subjects are blind as to the treatment they receive. In the Lang (1975) experiment on the effects of alcohol discussed in Chapter 1, subjects were blind as to whether or not they had received the treatment—alcohol. In this way, the researchers could control for subjects' expectations about the effects of alcohol. It follows that in an ideal experiment evaluating therapy, subjects would be blind as to the type of therapy they are receiving—or as to whether they are receiving a placebo. But can we conceal the type of therapy clients are receiving? And would we want to?

Problems in Measuring the Outcomes of Therapy Also consider the problems we run into in measuring the outcomes of various kinds of therapies. Since behavior therapists define their goals in behavioral terms—such as a formerly phobic individual being able to receive an injection or look out of a 20th-story window—behavior therapists do not encounter too many problems in this area. But what of the cognitive therapist who seeks to alter the ways in which clients interpret the world, or to replace irrational beliefs with rational beliefs? We cannot directly measure a mental picture of the world or the presence of a rational belief; instead, we must assess what clients say and do, such as their self-reports on the effectiveness of therapy or their lowered anxiety.

In addition, consider the problems we can encounter with therapies such as psychoanalysis and person-centered therapy. The goals for such therapies may include fostering self-insight, becoming one's own person, and actualizing unique talents. As a matter of fact, many well-adjusted individuals undertake psychoanalysis and person-centered therapy in order to learn about themselves, not to "get better." Because each person's self-insights and growth potentials are by nature unique, we may not be able to measure just how much insight has been gained or how well clients have separated their perceptions and values from those of others.

Are Clinical Judgments Valid? Because of problems such as these, many psychodynamically and phenomenologically oriented therapists claim—understandably so—that clinical judgment must be the basis for evaluating the effectiveness of therapy. Unfortunately, therapists have a stake in believing that their clients profit from treatment. Therapists are not unbiased judges, even though they may try to be.

Analyses of Therapy Effectiveness Despite these evaluation problems, research into the effectiveness of psychodynamic, person-centered, and other therapies has been reasonably encouraging (Lambert et al., 1986; Smith et al., 1980). The largest gains from therapy occur within the first few months (Howard et al., 1986), and these gains appear to be lasting (Nicholson & Berman, 1983).

In an averaging technique referred to as *meta-analysis,* Mary Lee Smith and Gene Glass analyzed the results of dozens of outcome studies on types of therapies and concluded that people who received psychodynamic therapy showed greater well being, on the average, than 70 to 75 percent of those who were left untreated (Smith & Glass, 1977; Smith et al., 1981). Similarly, nearly 75 percent of the clients receiving person-centered therapy were better off than people who were left untreated. There also seems to be a consensus that psychodynamic and person-centered therapies are most effective with well-educated, highly verbal, and strongly motivated clients who report problems with anxiety, depression (of light to moderate proportions), and interpersonal relationships (Abramowitz et al., 1974; Luborsky & Spence, 1978; Wexler & Butler, 1976). Neither form of therapy appears to be successful with psychotic disorders such as major depression, bipolar disorder, and schizophrenia.

Smith and Glass (1977) found that people who received TA were better off than about 72 percent of those left untreated, and people who received Gestalt therapy showed greater well-being than about 60 percent of those left untreated. In sum, the effectiveness of psychoanalysis, person-centered therapy, and TA is reasonably comparable; Gestalt therapy falls somewhat behind.

Does Therapy Help Because of the Method or Because of the Therapist? Despite Smith and Glass's positive findings, critics of psychoanalysis and person-centered therapy, such as behavior therapist Joseph Wolpe (1985), assert that it has not been shown that their benefits can be attributed to the therapy methods per se. There are common factors in many types of therapy, such as showing warmth, encouraging exploration, and combating feelings of hopelessness and helplessness (Bandura, 1986; Klein & Rabkin, 1984; Rounsaville et al., 1987). It has also been shown that the clients of more competent therapists fare better than clients of less proficient therapists (O'Malley et al, 1988). Therefore, the benefits of therapy could stem largely from the relationship with the therapist. If so, the method itself might have little more value than the famed "sugar-pill" placebo does in combating physical ailments.

What Is the Experimental Treatment in Psychotherapy Outcome Studies? This point raises another important issue in the evaluation of psychotherapeutic methods: What, exactly, is the experimental "treatment" being evaluated? Several therapists may say that they are practicing psychoanalysis, but they differ as individuals and in their training. Moreover, no clients present precisely the same set of problems. Treatment techniques interact with client problems so that no two clients receive exactly the same treatment from the same therapist. For all these reasons, it is difficult to specify just what is happening in the therapeutic session (Luborsky & DeRubeis, 1984; Vallis et al., 1986). Many of the positive outcomes found by Smith and Glass could be attributed to the benefits of a close client–therapist relationship—benefits that could be derived from almost any sort of therapy. These considerations extend to the evaluation of types of psychotherapy other than psychoanalysis.* For reasons like these, psychologists in recent years have been introducing detailed treatment manuals into their therapy-outcome studies (e.g., Luborsky & DeRubeis, 1984). Even so, there remains

*Even behavior therapists, who tend to stick closer to the therapeutic "script" than many other kinds of therapists, establish relationships with clients and combat demoralization, encouraging them to take charge of their own lives.

some variability in the practitioners who use the manuals and in the clients themselves.

In any event, during the 1940s and 1950s, psychotherapy was almost synonymous with psychoanalysis. Few other approaches to psychotherapy had an impact on psychologists or on public awareness (Garfield, 1981, 1982). But today, according to a survey of clinical and counseling psychologists, only 14 percent of psychotherapists have a psychodynamic orientation (Smith, 1982). Sigmund Freud, once the model for almost all therapists, is currently rated third in influence, following Carl Rogers and Albert Ellis. The largest group of psychotherapists (41 percent) consider themselves eclectic (Smith, 1982, p. 804).

"Well, I'm sorry if my remarks hurt your feelings, but I think it's a little unfair of you to blame me. *I said those things on the advice of a highly qualified therapist."*

What's Wrong with This Cartoon? Psychologists of many theoretical persuasions do, in fact, encourage clients to express their feelings. "Qualified" therapists, however, also prompt clients to take responsibility for their own behavior—not to attribute their misdeeds to the influence of other people.

Evaluation of Cognitive Therapies There is an increasing body of evidence that cognitive factors play an important role in psychological disorders and adjustment problems (e.g., Blackburn et al., 1981; DeRubeis, 1983; Murphy et al., 1984; Rush et al., 1982; Simons et al., 1986). They are especially pertinent to feelings of anxiety and depression that are acquired through experience. This is abundantly clear in phobias, in which the client believes that an object or situation is awful and must be avoided at all costs, and in depressive reactions that are linked to cognitive distortions.

Smith and Glass (1977) did not include cognitive therapies in their meta-analysis because many of these approaches are relatively new. Also, behavior therapists incorporate many of them, so it can be difficult to sort out which aspects—cognitive or otherwise—of behavior-therapy treatments are most effective. Nonetheless, a number of studies show that modification of irrational beliefs decreases emotional distress (Lipsky et al., 1980; Smith, 1983). Also, researchers who have analyzed the recent studies that compare cognitive, psychodynamic, and phenomenological approaches to the treatment of anxiety and depression have generally found that cognitive approaches foster greater improvements (Andrews & Harvey, 1981; Shapiro & Shapiro, 1982). In fact, there is some evidence that cognitive therapy is helpful in severe cases of depression that are usually considered responsive only to biological therapies (Simons et al., 1986).

Evaluation of Behavior Therapy Behavior therapy has provided various strategies for treating anxiety, mild depression, social-skills deficits, and problems in self-control. These strategies have proved effective for most clients in terms of quantifiable behavioral change. Behavior therapists have also been innovative with a number of problems, such as phobias and sexual dysfunctions, for which there had not previously been effective treatments. Overall, Smith and Glass (1977) found behavior-therapy techniques to be somewhat more effective than psychodynamic or phenomenological methods. About 80 percent of those people receiving behavior-therapy treatments, such as systematic desensitization and strategies for self-control, showed greater well-being than people who were left untreated (as compared to percentages in the low to middle 70s for psychodynamic and phenomenological approaches).

In analyses of studies that directly compare treatment techniques, behavior-therapy, psychodynamic, and phenomenological approaches have been found to be about equal in overall effectiveness (Berman et al., 1985; Smith et al., 1980). However, psychodynamic and phenomenological approaches seem to foster greater self-understanding, whereas behavior-therapy techniques (including cognitive-behavioral techniques) show superior results in treatment of problems such as phobias and sexual dysfunctions. Behavior therapy has also been effective in helping manage institutionalized populations, including schizophrenics and the mentally retarded. However, there is little evidence that behavior therapy alone is effective in treating the thought disorders involved in severe psychotic disturbance (Wolpe, 1985).

So, it is not enough to ask which type of therapy is most effective. We must ask, instead, which type of therapy is most effective for a particular problem. What are its advantages? What are its limitations? Clients might successfully use systematic desensitization to overcome stagefright, as measured by actual ability to get up and talk before a group of people. But if clients also want to know why they have stagefright, behavior therapy alone will not be fully satisfactory. (Behavior therapists would counter that insight-oriented therapists would merely construct a tale about the origins of the problem that is consistent with their theory but that ultimate truth would elude them [and their clients] anyhow.)

Also, the treatment manuals for behavioral techniques tend to be more specific than those for psychodynamic and phenomenological methods. Thus, the benefits of behavior therapy may be more attributable to the techniques themselves than to the personal qualities and general skills of the therapist. This is a relative and not an absolute issue: As Wolpe (1985) noted, behavior therapists generally establish at least a warm working relationship with clients, so the usefulness of the techniques themselves cannot be totally divorced from therapist factors.

Today, overall, research on the outcomes of the various psychotherapies is much more encouraging than that reported by Eysenck back in 1952.

BIOLOGICAL THERAPIES

In the 1950s, Fats Domino popularized the song "My Blue Heaven." Fats was singing about the sky and happiness. But today, "blue heavens" is one of the street names for the ten-milligram dose of one of the most widely prescribed drugs: Valium. The **minor tranquilizer** Valium became popular because it reduces feelings of anxiety and tension. The manufacturer also once claimed that people could not become addicted to Valium nor could they readily kill themselves with overdoses. Today Valium appears to be more dangerous. Some people who have been used to taking high doses of Valium are reported to go into convulsions when use is suspended. And, now and then, someone dies from mixing Valium with alcohol, or someone shows unusual sensitivity to the drug.

Psychiatrists and other physicians prescribe Valium and other drugs as chemical therapy, or **chemotherapy,** for various forms of abnormal behavior. In this section we discuss chemotherapy, *electroconvulsive therapy,* and *psychosurgery,* three biological or medical approaches to treating abnormal behavior.

Chemotherapy

In this section we discuss minor tranquilizers, major tranquilizers, antidepressants, and lithium.

Minor Tranquilizers Valium (diazepam) is but one of many (many) minor tranquilizers. Some of the others are Librium, Miltown, Atarax, Serax, and Equanil. These drugs are usually prescribed for outpatients who complain of anxiety or tension, although many people also use them as sleeping pills. Valium and other tranquilizers are theorized to depress the activity of

Minor tranquilizer A drug that relieves feelings of anxiety and tension.

Chemotherapy The use of drugs to treat disordered behavior.

"It's no use, Marvin. We tried tenderness and we tried Valium and you're still impossible."

parts of the central nervous system (CNS). The CNS, in turn, decreases sympathetic activity, reducing the heart rate, respiration rate, and feelings of nervousness and tension (Caplan et al., 1983).

With regular usage, unfortunately, people come to tolerate small dosages of these drugs very quickly. Dosages must be increased for the drug to remain effective.

Another problem associated with many minor tranquilizers is **rebound anxiety.** Many patients who have been using these drugs regularly report that their anxiety returns in exacerbated form once they discontinue them. Some users might simply be experiencing fear of doing without the drugs. For others, rebound anxiety might reflect biochemical processes that are poorly understood (Chouinard et al., 1983).

Valium, interestingly, is usually ineffective with panic disorder, suggesting that panic has quite different bodily correlates than other anxiety disorders. Antidepressant medications, discussed later, do often help panic sufferers, giving rise to speculation that panic might involve faulty metabolism of norepinephrine (Fishman & Sheehan, 1985).

Major Tranquilizers Schizophrenic patients are likely to be treated with **major tranquilizers,** or "antipsychotic" drugs. Many of them, including Thorazine, Mellaril, and Stelazine, belong to the chemical class of **phenothiazines** and are thought to act by blocking the action of dopamine in the brain. Research along these lines supports the dopamine theory of schizophrenia (see Chapter 12).

Rebound anxiety Strong anxiety that can attend the suspension of usage of a tranquilizer.

Major tranquilizer A drug that decreases severe anxiety or agitation in psychotic patients or in violent individuals.

Phenothiazines A family of drugs that act as major tranquilizers and that are effective in treating many cases of schizophrenic disorders.

Antidepressant Acting to relieve depression.

Monoamine oxidase inhibitors Antidepressant drugs that work by blocking the action of an enzyme that breaks down norepinephrine and serotonin. Abbreviated *MAO inhibitors.*

Tricyclic antidepressants Antidepressant drugs that work by preventing the reuptake of norepinephrine and serotonin by transmitting neurons.

Sedative Relieving nervousness or agitation.

In most cases, major tranquilizers reduce agitation, delusions, and hallucinations (May, 1975; Watson et al., 1978). Major tranquilizers account in large part for the lessened need for various forms of restraint and supervision (padded cells, straitjackets, hospitalization, and so on) used with schizophrenic patients. More than any other single form of treatment, major tranquilizers have allowed hundreds of thousands of patients to lead largely normal lives in the community, to hold jobs and maintain family lives.

Unfortunately, in many cases the blocking of dopamine action leads to symptoms like those of Parkinson's disease, including tremors and muscular rigidity, as described in Chapter 2 (Calne, 1977; Kimble, 1988). These side effects can usually be controlled by drugs that are used for Parkinsonism. In some patients, however, long-term use of phenothiazines leads to motor problems that are not readily controlled (Jus et al., 1976).

Antidepressants So-called **antidepressant** drugs are often given to patients with major depression, but, as noted in Chapter 12, they are also helpful with some people who suffer from anorexia nervosa and bulimia nervosa. Problems in the regulation of norepinephrine and serotonin may be involved in eating disorders as well as depression. Antidepressants are believed to work by increasing the amount of these neurotransmitters available in the brain, which can have an effect on both kinds of disorders.

There are two types of antidepressant drugs. Each type increases the brain concentrations of norepinephrine and serotonin in a different way. **Monoamine oxidase (MAO) inhibitors** block the activity of an enzyme that breaks down norepinephrine and serotonin. Nardil and Parnate are examples of MAO inhibitors. **Tricyclic antidepressants** prevent reuptake of norepinephrine and serotonin by the axon terminals of the transmitting neurons. As a result, the neurotransmitters remain in the synaptic cleft for a greater amount of time, enhancing the probability that they will dock at receptor sites on receiving neurons. Tofranil and Elavil are examples of tricyclic antidepressants.

Antidepressants tend to alleviate the physical aspects of depression. For example, they tend to increase the patient's activity level and to reduce eating and sleeping disturbances (Lyons et al., 1985; Weissman et al., 1981). In this way patients may become more receptive to psychotherapy, which addresses the cognitive and social aspects of depression. Research suggests that a combination of chemotherapy and psychotherapy is more effective in treating depression than is chemotherapy alone (Beckham & Leber, 1985; Conte et al., 1986).

Severely depressed people often have insomnia, and it is not unusual for antidepressant drugs, which have a strong **sedative** effect, to be given at bedtime. Typically, antidepressant drugs such as Tofranil and Elavil must "build up" to a therapeutic level, which might take ten days to three weeks. Because overdoses of antidepressants can be lethal, some patients are hospitalized during the build-up period to prevent suicide attempts.

Now let us highlight another interesting antidepressant medication: coffee.

A CLOSER LOOK

Coffee as a Self-Medication for Depression

Millions of Americans assault the morning blahs and the midafternoon doldrums by downing cups of coffee, that tasty drink that also happens to contain the stimulant caffeine. Millions of Britishers ritualistically down their after-

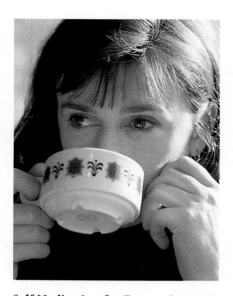

Self-Medication for Depression? Millions of us assault the morning blahs and the midafternoon doldrums by downing cups of coffee containing caffeine. Some of us also apparently use the stimulant caffeine to self-medicate ourselves for feelings of depression.

noon tea, another beverage containing caffeine. Legend has it that shepherds at an Arabian monastery watched as their goats chewed on the beans (which, botanically, are berries) of the *Coffea arabica* plant and then proceeded to frisk sleeplessly through the night. The abbot, sensing a way to remain awake through the evening prayers, experimented with brewing a beverage from the berries. Today the coffee plant is cultivated on many continents, and coffee and tea joust for world-wide supremacy.

We need no proof of the lift provided by coffee, but Emory University anthropologist/physician Melvin Konner suggests that millions of us might also be self-medicating ourselves for depression by imbibing. Physicians have long used 5 to 10 cups (500 to 1,000 milligrams of caffeine) a day to help in treatment of low blood pressure and asthma, but many of us may also use these "therapeutic dosages" to help cope with lethargy and feelings of sadness.

How does caffeine work? Research by Solomon Snyder at Johns Hopkins Medical School shows that molecules of caffeine are similar in structure to molecules of adenosine, a naturally occurring substance in the nervous system (Konner, 1988). Adenosine, it seems, fits into receptor sites on, and suppresses the activity of, neurons that would normally elevate the mood and increase alertness. Caffeine molecules also fit into these receptor sites, and by doing so they lock adenosine out. But caffeine molecules do not suppress the activity of these cells. Caffeine, that is, lets these neurons "do their thing," and keeps adenosine, the "party pooper," out the door.

Are there dangers to the caffeine high? Are depressing side effects found in stimulant's clothing? Perhaps. For one thing, some of us are more susceptible to "coffee jitters" than others. Coffee is also acidic and so can be harmful to the digestive tract and contribute to ulcers. (Anti-acid medications help.) Coffee raises the blood pressure, and persons with cardiovascular conditions are advised to consult their physicians about it. Moreover, there are some unresolved questions about drinking coffee—or "too much" coffee—during pregnancy. (Check with your obstetrician.)

Yet for most of us, two to four cups of coffee a day pose no documented risks, and millions of us are apparently going to continue to fight the blahs with caffeine.

Lithium In a sense, the ancient Greeks and Romans were among the first to use the metal lithium as a psychoactive drug. They would prescribe mineral water for patients with bipolar disorder. They had no inkling as to why this treatment sometimes helped, but it might have been because mineral water contains lithium. A salt of the metal lithium (lithium carbonate), in tablet form, flattens out cycles of manic behavior and depression for most sufferers, apparently by moderating the level of norepinephrine available to the brain. Because of its moderating effects on norepinephrine, lithium is also being studied as a treatment for eating disorders, although its side effects might be more dangerous for people with anorexia nervosa than for people with bipolar disorder (Mitchell & Eckert, 1987).

Because lithium is more toxic than most drugs, the dose must be carefully monitored during early phases of therapy by repeated analysis of blood samples. It might be necessary for persons with bipolar disorder to use lithium indefinitely, just as a medical patient with diabetes must continue insulin to control the illness. Lithium also has been shown to have the side effects of impairing memory and depressing motor speed (Shaw et al., 1987). Memory impairment is reported as the primary reason that patients discontinue lithium (Jamison & Akiskal, 1983).

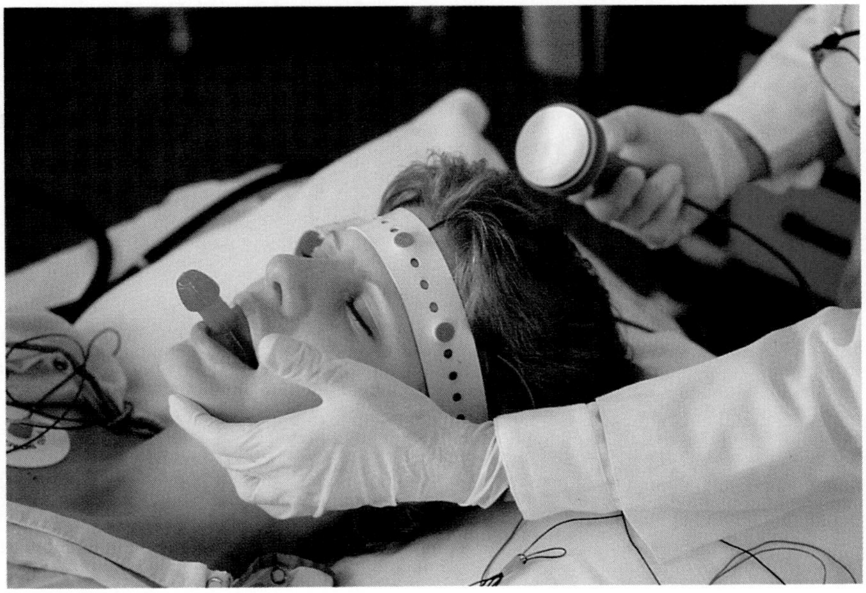

Electroconvulsive Therapy. In ECT, electrodes are placed on each side of the patient's head and a current is passed in between. A seizure is induced in this way. ECT is used mainly in cases of major depression when antidepressant drugs fail. ECT is quite controversial: Many believe that it is barbaric, and there are side effects.

Electroconvulsive Therapy

Electroconvulsive therapy (ECT) was introduced by Italian psychiatrist Ugo Cerletti in 1939 for use with psychiatric patients. Cerletti had noted that some slaughterhouses used electric shock to render animals unconscious. The shocks also produced convulsions, and Cerletti erroneously believed, as did other European researchers of the period, that convulsions were incompatible with schizophrenia and other major disorders.

After the advent of major tranquilizers, use of ECT was generally limited to treatment of people with major depression. The discovery of antidepressants has limited use of ECT even further—to patients who do not respond to these drugs. But even as a therapy of last resort, ECT is still used with about 60,000 to 100,000 people a year in the United States (Sackeim, 1985).

ECT patients typically receive one treatment three times a week for several weeks. Electrodes are attached to the temples, and an electrical current strong enough to produce a convulsion is passed between them. The shock induces unconsciousness, so patients would not recall it. Still, patients are usually put to sleep with a sedative prior to treatment. In the past, ECT patients flailed about wildly during the convulsions, sometimes breaking bones. Today they are given muscle-relaxing drugs, and convulsions are barely perceptible to onlookers. ECT is not given to patients with high blood pressure or heart ailments.

ECT is controversial for many reasons. First, many professionals are distressed by the thought of passing electric shock through the head and producing convulsions, even if they are suppressed by drugs. Second are the side effects. ECT disrupts recall of recent events. Although memory functioning usually seems near normal for most patients a few months after treatment, some patients appear to suffer permanent memory impairment (Roueche, 1980). Third, nobody knows *why* ECT works. For reasons such as these, ECT was outlawed in Berkeley, California, by voter referendum in 1982. This decision was later overturned in the courts, but it remains of interest because it marked the first time that a specific treatment found its way to the ballot box.

Electroconvulsive therapy Treatment of disorders like major depression by passing an electric current (that causes a convulsion) through the head. Abbreviated *ECT.*

Psychosurgery

Psychosurgery is more controversial than ECT. The best-known modern technique, the **prefrontal lobotomy,** has been used with severely disturbed patients. In this method, a picklike instrument is used to crudely sever the nerve pathways that link the prefrontal lobes of the brain to the thalamus. The prefrontal lobotomy was pioneered by the Portuguese neurologist Antonio Egas Moniz and was brought to the United States in the 1930s. As pointed out by Valenstein (1986), the theoretical rationale for the operation was vague and misguided, and Moniz's reports of success were exaggerated. Nevertheless, the prefrontal lobotomy was performed on more than a thousand mental patients by 1950 in an effort to reduce violence and agitation. Anecdotal evidence of the method's unreliable outcomes is found in an ironic footnote to history: One of Dr. Moniz's failures shot him, leaving a bullet lodged in his spine and paralyzing his legs.

Truth or Fiction Revisited

It is true that the originator of a surgical technique intended to reduce violence—the prefrontal lobotomy—was indeed shot by one of his patients.

The prefrontal lobotomy also has a host of side effects, including hyperactivity and distractibility, impaired learning ability, overeating, apathy and withdrawal, epileptic-type seizures, reduced creativity, and, now and then, death. Because of these side effects and because of the advent of major tranquilizers, the prefrontal lobotomy has been largely discontinued in the United States.

In recent years, a number of more refined psychosurgery techniques have been devised for various purposes. Generally speaking, they focus on smaller areas of the brain and leave less damage in their wake than does the prefrontal lobotomy. As pointed out by Elliot Valenstein (1980), these operations have been performed to treat problems ranging from aggression to depression, psychotic behavior, chronic pain, and epilepsy. Follow-up studies of these contemporary procedures find that slightly more than half of them result in marked improvement (Corkin, 1980; Mirsky & Orzack, 1980). Moreover, no major neurological damage was attributable to these operations.

Evaluation of the Biological Therapies

There is little question that major tranquilizers, antidepressants, and lithium help many people with severe psychiatric disorders. These drugs enable thousands of formerly hospitalized patients to enter or return to the community and lead productive lives. Moreover, their potential for helping persons with eating disorders looks promising. The problems related to these drugs often concern their dosage and side effects.

Minor tranquilizers are frequently abused by overuse. Many people request them to dull the arousal that stems from anxiety-producing life-styles or interpersonal problems. Rather than make the often painful decisions required to confront their problems and change their lives, these people find it easier to pop a pill. At least for a while. Then the dosage must be increased if the drug is to remain effective, and substance dependence becomes a possibility. Another problem is that many family physicians, even some psychiatrists, find it easier to prescribe minor tranquilizers than to help patients examine their lives and change anxiety-evoking conditions. The physician's lot is not eased by the fact that many patients want pills, not conversation.

Psychosurgery Surgery intended to promote psychological changes or to relieve disordered behavior.

Prefrontal lobotomy The severing or destruction of a section of the frontal lobe of the brain.

Truth or Fiction Revisited

It is *not* true that drugs are never of help to people with abnormal behavior problems, particularly schizophrenia and severe mood disorders. On the other hand, psychologists discourage use of drugs to cope with the anxieties, tensions, and problems of daily life.

In spite of the controversies that surround ECT, there is evidence that it brings many immobilized patients out of their depression when antidepressant drugs fail (Janicak et al., 1985; NIMH, 1985; Scovern & Kilmann, 1980). Moreover, ECT patients have a lower mortality rate following treatment than depressed people who do not receive ECT (Martin et al., 1985), a finding that may in part be attributable to a lower suicide rate. There are also suggestions that memory impairment is minimized by giving patients the lowest dose of electricity required to produce seizures (Daniel & Crovitz, 1983a; Sackeim et al., 1985). Also encouraging is the development of unilateral ECT, in which the electrodes are attached to only one side of the brain. With unilateral ECT, there seems to be no decrease in effectiveness, but the side effects, such as memory impairment, are lessened (Daniel & Crovitz, 1983b; Squire, 1977; Squire & Slater, 1978). Unfortunately, the unilateral method has not filtered down to the majority of psychiatrists. In 1985, 75 percent of those who practiced ECT were still using the original method (NIMH, 1985).

In sum, biological forms of therapy, particularly chemotherapy, seem to be desirable for some major disorders that do not respond to psychotherapy or behavior therapy alone. Yet common sense as well as research evidence suggest that psychological methods of therapy are preferable with problems such as anxiety, mild depression, and interpersonal conflict. No chemical can show a client how to change an idea or to solve an interpersonal problem. Chemicals can only dull the pain of failure and put off the day when the client must deal with reality. ECT and psychosurgery are probably still to be considered experimental. Their use seems appropriately limited to severe cases in which all else fails.

SUMMARY

1. **What is psychotherapy?** Psychotherapy is a systematic interaction between a therapist and client that brings psychological principles to bear in helping the client overcome psychological disorders or adjust to problems in living. Behavior therapy is a kind of therapy that relies on psychological principles of learning (e.g., conditioning and observational learning) to help clients directly develop adaptive behavior patterns and discontinue maladaptive behavior patterns.

2. **What are the goals of traditional psychoanalysis?** The goals are to provide self-insight, allow the spilling forth (catharsis) of psychic energy, and replace defensive behavior with coping behavior.

3. **What are the methods of traditional psychoanalysis?** Methods include free association, dream analysis, and resolution of the transference relationship between the therapist and client.

4. **How do modern psychodynamic approaches differ from traditional psychoanalysis?** Modern approaches are briefer and more directive, and the therapist and client usually sit face to face.

5. **What are the goals and traits of the person-centered therapist?** The person-centered therapist uses nondirective methods to help clients overcome obstacles to self-actualization. Therapists show unconditional positive regard, empathic understanding, genuineness, and congruence.

6. **What are the goals and methods of transactional analysis (TA)?** TA helps people adopt healthy life positions ("I'm OK—You're OK"); fosters complementary transactions, or exchanges; encourages people to interact as adults rather than as children or parents; and alerts people to the "games" they play in order to retain self-defeating life positions.

7. **What are the goals and methods of cognitive therapies?** Cognitive therapies aim to provide clients with insight into irrational beliefs and cognitive distortions and to replace these cognitive errors with rational beliefs and accurate perceptions. Ellis notes that clients often show one or more of his ten irrational beliefs, including excessive needs for approval and perfectionism. Beck notes that clients may become depressed because of their minimizing of accomplishments, catastrophizing of failures, and general pessimism.

8. **What is systematic desensitization?** This is a behavior-therapy method that counterconditions fears by gradually exposing clients to a hierarchy of fear-evoking stimuli while the clients remain deeply relaxed.

9. **What is aversive conditioning?** This is a behavior-therapy method for discouraging undesirable behavior by repeatedly pairing the goals (e.g., alcohol, cigarette smoke, deviant sex objects) with aversive stimuli so that the goals become aversive rather than tempting.

10. **What is operant conditioning?** This is a behavior-therapy method that fosters adaptive behavior through successive approximations and reinforcement and that extinguishes maladaptive behavior, usually by ignoring it.

11. **What is assertiveness training?** This is a behavior-therapy method for fostering social skills and decreasing social anxieties that uses techniques such as modeling, coaching, role-playing, feedback, and behavior rehearsal.

12. **What are self-control methods?** These are behavior-therapy methods for adopting desirable behavior patterns and breaking bad habits. They focus on modifying the antecedents (stimuli that act as triggers) and consequences (reinforcers) of behavior and on modifying the behavior itself.

13. **What are the advantages of group therapy?** Group therapy is more economical than individual therapy. Moreover, group members profit from each other's social support and funds of experiences.

14. **Does psychotherapy work?** Apparently it does. Complex statistical analyses show that people receiving most forms of psychotherapy fare better than people left untreated. Psychodynamic and person-centered approaches are particularly helpful with highly verbal and motivated individuals. Cognitive and behavior therapies are probably most effective, and behavior therapy also helps in the management of retarded and severely disturbed populations.

15. **What are the uses of chemotherapy?** Major tranquilizers often help schizophrenic individuals, apparently by blocking the action of dopamine. Antidepressants often help severely depressed people, apparently by raising the levels of norepinephrine and serotonin available to the brain. Lithium often helps persons with bipolar disorder, apparently by moderating levels of norepinephrine.

16. **What is electroconvulsive therapy (ECT)?** ECT passes an electrical current through the temples, inducing a seizure and frequently relieving severe depression. ECT is controversial because of side effects such as loss of memory and because nobody knows why it works.

17. **What is psychosurgery?** Psychosurgery is an extremely controversial method for alleviating severe agitation by severing nerve pathways in the brain. The best-known psychosurgery technique, the prefrontal lobotomy, has been largely discontinued because of side effects.

PSYCHOLOGY AND MODERN LIFE

Ways of Getting Help

Many of us decide that we would like some help in coping with the pressures of modern life. Throughout history, persons in many roles have helped us to feel better and to solve our problems—including friends, parents and grandparents, priests and ministers, witch doctors, palm readers, and wise men (and women). Persons in these roles are often still of help, although I would advise against leafing through the yellow pages for witch doctors and palm readers. But sometimes we want the advice of a highly trained helping professional; and sometimes we pass a self-help book that catches our eye. Once we've made the decision to seek a therapist, how can we know to whom we can safely turn? And what of the question that is bound to pop into mind when we're browsing through a bookstore or the book rack at the check-out counter of the supermarket: Dare we rely on a self-help book?

Finding a Qualified Therapist

The helping professionals who are qualified to help us cope with the pressures of modern life include psychologists, counselors, psychiatrists, social workers, and psychiatric nurses, among others.

Unfortunately, many states allow almost anyone to use the label *therapist.* This label indicates nothing about one's education and experience. People seeking effective therapy should never be shy about asking helping professionals about their education and supervised experience. Here are some of the people who are genuinely qualified to help:

1. *Psychologists* Psychologists have at least a master's degree, and in most states must have a doctoral degree (Ph.D, Ed.D., Psy.D.), to use the label *psychologist.* The state will typically weigh the adequacy of the individual's education and supervised experience in psychology before granting a license to practice psychology. Psychologists use interviews, behavioral observations, and psychological tests to diagnose psychological disorders and adjustment problems, and they use psychotherapy to treat them. Most psychologists have been trained extensively in research methods. They are more likely than other helping professionals to be critically acquainted with psychological theory. Psychologists work with people with various disorders and adjustment problems, and they also help clients develop as individuals.
2. *Counselors* Counselors usually have degrees in education, such as the Ed.M. (Master of Education) or Ed.D. (Doctor of Education). Their graduate programs will have included supervised counseling experience, and in many states counselors are licensed. Counselors are frequently found in school settings, such as college and university testing and counseling centers. Many counselors specialize in areas such as academic, vocational, marriage, and family counseling or therapy. Counselors typically specialize in adjustment problems or career development and do not work with individuals with severe psychological disorders.
3. *Psychiatrists* A psychiatrist is a licensed physician. Psychiatrists earn medical degrees such as the M.D. (Doctor of Medicine) or D.O. (Doctor of Osteopathy), and then they undertake a psychiatric residency during which time they learn to apply medical skills, such as prescribing drugs, to treating psychological disorders. Psychiatrists, like psychologists, may practice psychotherapy. Most psychiatrists rely on interviews for diagnostic purposes but may refer patients to psychologists for psychological testing.
4. *Psychiatric Social Workers* Psychiatric social workers have an M.S.W. (Master of Social Work) or D.S.W. (Doctor of Social Work) degree and supervised experience in helping people adjust. Many offer psychotherapy, but social workers do not use psychological tests or prescribe medical treatments. Like counselors, many specialize in marital or family problems.
5. *Psychoanalysts* Once only physicians were admitted to psychoanalytic training, but today many psychologists and social workers also practice this form of therapy, which was originated by Sigmund Freud. The practice of psychoanalytic therapy typically requires years of training beyond the doctoral level and completion of one's own psychoanalysis. Psychoanalysts usually focus on problems such as anxiety, depression, and difficulties in forming and maintaining productive social relationships.

Coping with Self-Help Books *How To Be Your Own Best Friend; Don't Say Yes When You Want to Say No; The Art of Sensual Massage; Don't Be Afraid; Mind Power; Dianetics; Dr. Atkins' Diet Revolution; Our Bodies, Our Selves; Toilet Training in a Day; The Relaxation Response; Treating Type A Behavior and Your Heart; Becoming Orgasmic; The Scarsdale Diet; Looking Out for Number One*—these are a bare shelfful of the hundreds of self-help books that have flooded the marketplace in recent years. People who are shy, anxious, depressed, heavy, stressed, and confused scan the bookstores and the check-out counter racks of supermarkets every day in hopes of finding the one book that will hold the answer.

When we are looking for help through books, how are we to know what to buy? How can we separate the

Self-Help, Anyone? With such a bewildering array of self-help books on the shelves, readers are appropriately concerned about how to separate the self-help wheat from the chaff.

helpful wheat from the useless and sometimes harmful chaff? How can we be intelligent consumers of these works?

The fact of the matter is that there are no easy answers. Many of us are used to believing most of the things we see in print, and anecdotes about how John lost 60 pounds in 60 days and how Joni blossomed from a wallflower into a social butterfly in one month have a powerful allure—especially when we are needy. Moreover, in a nation where self-help books are displayed one aisle over from the U.S. government-inspected meats, the books might have the aura of a government stamp as well.

Not so. The price we pay for the protection of the First Amendment of the Constitution is that nearly anything can wind up in print. Authors can make the most extravagant claims without fear of imprisonment. They can lie about the effectiveness of the newest fad diet without fear of prosecution just as easily as they can lie about their latest communion with the departed Elvis Presley or their most recent kidnapping by the occupants of a U.F.O.

So how can you protect yourself? How would you be able to tell, for example, that *Don't Be Afraid, Toilet Training in a Day,* and *Mind Power* were authored by respected psychologists, whereas *Looking Out for Number One* was written by a professional writer and book publisher? How would you know that *The Relaxation Response* is well researched, whereas the research reported in *Dr. Atkins' Diet Revolution* is controversial?

I don't have all the answers, but here are some hints:

1. First of all, don't judge the book by its cover or its title. Good books as well as bad books tend to have catchy titles and exciting covers. After all, dozens, perhaps hundreds of books are competing for your attention, so all publishers try to do something "snazzy" with the covers.
2. Avoid books that make extravagant claims. No method helps everyone who tries it. Also, very few methods work overnight (*Toilet Training in a Day* might be an exception). No healthful diet, for example, allows you to lose a pound or more a day. Unfortunately, as noted by William D. Phillips, editor-in-chief at Little, Brown, "People want the instant cure. A book that guarantees you will lose 10 pounds in two days will sell faster than one that says it will take six months" (Hinds, 1988).
3. Check authors' educational credentials. Be suspicious if the author's title is just "Dr.", and it is placed before the name. The degree could be a phony doctorate purchased through the mail; it could be issued by a religious cult rather than a university or professional school. It is better if the "doctor" puts Ph.D., Psy.D., Ed.D., or M.D. after his or her name rather than "Dr." in front of it.
4. Check authors' current affiliations. Again there are no guarantees, but psychologists who are affiliated with colleges and universities and physicians who are affiliated with medical schools might have more to offer than those who are not.
5. Consider authors' complaints about the conservatism of professional groups to be a red flag. If authors boast about how they are ahead of their time and berate the psychological and medical "establishments" for reactionary pigheadedness, be suspicious. Although it's true that great discoveries are now and then met with opposition, such as the discovery that the Earth revolves around the sun, most psychologists and physicians are committed to change and advancement of their sciences. They are open to new ideas, as long as the ideas are supported by scientific evidence.
6. Check the evidence reported in the book. Bad books usually use anecdotal evidence or superficially reported case studies. By and large, the techniques that authors claim will help should have been tested by experiments with many subjects. Moreover, the subjects should have been assigned at random to treatment groups and control groups, and measures should have been taken to control for subjects' expectations.

7. Check the reference citations for the evidence. Solid, legitimate psychological and medical research is reported in the journals found in the reference list of this textbook. To get published in these journals, research reports must be submitted to peer reviewers—respected psychologists and physicians—and judged to be valid. If the publications in the book's reference list are suspicious, or if there is no bibliography, you be suspicious, too.
8. Another strategy is to ask your instructor for advice. A faculty member in an academic department is likely to be able to point out which books can help and which can hurt.
9. Read textbooks and professional books, such as this book, instead of self-help books. For knowledge about healthful dieting, read a health psychology or nutrition textbook used in a course in your college. For exercise advice, read a textbook used in teaching physical education courses. Roam the college bookstore for appropriate textbooks and professional books. Don't be scared by technical terms—these books usually have helpful glossaries.
10. You can also consult a member of a respected helping profession for ideas and for help.

There are no guarantees and no quick fixes. Nevertheless, by exercising a few precautions, you can find a qualified therapist and you can become a more sophisticated consumer of self-help books.

Outline

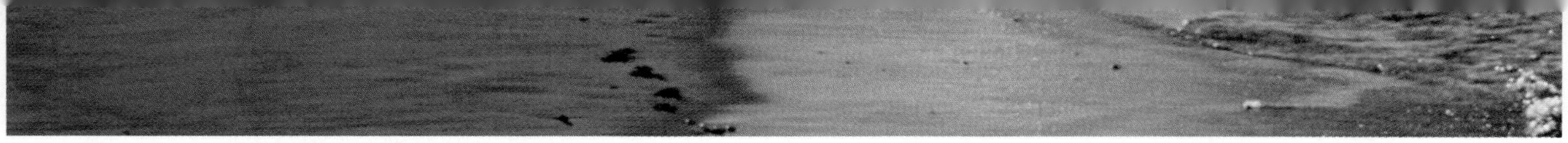

14 Human Sexuality

Truth or Fiction?

- □ Men behave more aggressively than women do
- □ Homosexuals suffer from hormonal imbalances.
- □ Pornographic films cause crimes of violence against women.
- □ Any healthy woman can successfully resist a rapist if she really wants to.
- □ Orgasm is a reflex.
- □ People who truly love each other enjoy the sexual aspects of their relationship.
- □ If the symptoms of sexually transmitted diseases go away by themselves, medical treatment is not necessary.
- □ Only homosexuals and substance abusers are at risk for contracting AIDS.

Offshore from the misty coasts of Ireland lies the small island of Inis Beag. From the air it is a green jewel, warm and inviting. At ground level, things are somewhat different.

For example, the residents of Inis Beag do not believe that women experience orgasm. The woman who chances to find pleasure in sex is considered deviant (Messenger, 1971). Premarital sex is all but unknown. Women engage in sexual relations in order to conceive children and to appease their husbands' carnal cravings. But they need not worry about being called on for frequent performances since the men of Inis Beag believe, erroneously, that sex saps their strength. Sex on Inis Beag is carried out in the dark—literally and figuratively, and with the nightclothes on. The man lies on top in the so-called missionary position. In accord with local concepts of masculinity, he ejaculates as fast as he can. Then he rolls over and falls asleep.

If Inis Beag does not sound like your cup of tea, you may find the atmosphere of Mangaia more congenial. Mangaia is a Polynesian pearl of an island, lifting languidly from the blue waters of the Pacific. It is on the other side of the world from Inis Beag—in more ways than one.

On Being Male and Being Female. Sexual behavior per se is only one aspect of human sexuality. Psychologists are also concerned about the stereotypes of "masculinity" and "femininity" and how they affect behavior. A great deal of research has been done on sex differences in cognition and personality and how they develop. There are also many issues in sexual motivation and sexual response.

From an early age, Mangaian children are encouraged to get in touch with their sexuality through masturbation (Marshall, 1971). Mangaian adolescents are expected to engage in sexual intercourse. They may be found on secluded beaches or beneath the listing fronds of palms, diligently practicing techniques learned from village elders.

Mangaian women are expected to reach orgasm several times before their partners do. Young men want their partners to reach orgasm and compete to see who is more effective at bringing young women to multiple orgasms.

HUMAN SEXUAL BEHAVIOR IN PERSPECTIVE: A TALE OF TWO CULTURES

The residents of Inis Beag and Mangaia have similar anatomic features but vastly different attitudes toward sex. Their attitudes influence their patterns of sexual behavior and the pleasure they find—or do not find—in sex. Like eating, sexual activity is a natural function. Yet no other natural function has found such varied expression. No other natural function has been influenced so strongly by religious and moral beliefs, by cultural tradition, folklore, and superstition.

This chapter is about human sexuality, but we shall see that sexual behavior per se is only one aspect of the issues involved in this area of psychological research. For example, we begin our discussion by exploring the behavior patterns that compose the stereotypes of "masculinity" and "femininity." Then we examine research on sex differences in cognition and personality and consider the biological and psychological factors that contribute to the development of these differences. Next we turn our attention to a number of issues in sexual motivation, including sex hormones, pornography, homosexuality, and rape. We examine sexual anatomy and response, and we see that women and men may be more alike in their sexual response than you may have thought. We consider sexual dysfunctions and their treatment. In response to increased concern about sexually transmitted diseases, including AIDS, we consider these diseases, as well as their treatment and prevention, in the section on psychology and modern life.

SEX ROLES AND STEREOTYPES

"Why Can't a Woman Be More Like a Man?" You may recognize this song from the musical *My Fair Lady*. In the song, Henry Higgins laments that women are emotional and fickle, whereas men are logical and dependable. The excitable woman is a **stereotype**—a fixed, conventional idea about a group. The logical man is also a stereotype. Stereotypes shape our expectations: We assume that all group members share the stereotypes we attribute to the group.

Cultural expectations of men and women involve complex clusters of stereotypes, called **sex roles,** that define the ways in which men and women are expected to behave. Lay persons tend to see the traditional feminine stereotype as dependent, gentle, helpful, kind, mild, patient, and submissive (Cartwright et al., 1983). The typical masculine sex-role stereotype is perceived as tough, protective, and gentlemanly (Myers & Gonda, 1982). Females are more often viewed as being warm and emotional, whereas males are more frequently seen as being independent and competitive. Women are

Stereotype A fixed, conventional idea about a group.

Sex roles Complex clusters of ways in which males and females are expected to behave.

more often expected to care for the kids and cook the meals (Deaux & Lewis, 1983). Men are usually expected to head the family and put bread on the table.

In a well-known study of the cultural conception of masculine and feminine sex roles, Inge Broverman and her colleagues (1972) first had undergraduate psychology students list traits and behaviors that they thought set men apart from women. A list of 122 traits, each of which was mentioned at least twice, was generated. Each trait was made into a bipolar scale, such as:

Not at all aggressive . . . . . Very aggressive

Another group of students indicated which pole of the scale was more descriptive of the "average" man or woman. Only 41 of the 122 traits achieved a 75 percent agreement rate, and they are shown in Table 14.1.

Further analysis broke the list down into two broad factors. One centered around competency in the realm of objects, including the business world (which we label "instrumentality"). The second involved emotional warmth and expression of feelings (the Brovermans' "warmth-expressiveness cluster"). Other samples then rated the items as more desirable for men or women. In general, masculine traits in the instrumentality cluster were rated as more desirable for men, whereas feminine traits in this cluster were rated as more desirable for women.

As pointed out by Alice Eagly and Valerie Steffen (1984), these stereotypes largely reflect the traditional distribution of men into breadwinning roles and women into homemaking roles. When the wife works, she is less likely to be perceived as sharing stereotypical feminine traits—that is, as long as she works because of choice and not because of financial necessity (Atkinson & Huston, 1984).

Regardless of their exact origins, these cultural stereotypes exact enormous costs, which we consider in the following section.

Costs of Sex-Role Stereotyping

Sex-role stereotypes exact costs in terms of education, activities, careers, our psychological well-being, and our interpersonal relationships.

Costs in Terms of Education Stereotyping has historically worked to the disadvantage of women. In past centuries, girls were considered to be unsuited to education. Even the great Swiss-French philosopher Jean-Jacques Rousseau, who was in the forefront of an open approach to education, believed that girls were basically irrational and naturally disposed to childrearing and homemaking tasks—certainly not to commerce, science, and industry.

In the United States today, boys and girls are looked upon as being about equal in overall learning ability. Yet there remain some differences in expectations that limit the horizons of both sexes.

Consider reading. Psychologists have many hypotheses about why girls, as a group, read better than boys, and some involve biological factors. But it might also be that cultural factors, and stereotyping in particular, play a role in sex differences in reading. Evidence for this view is found in the fact that sex differences in reading tend to disappear or be reversed in other cultures (Matlin, 1987). Reading is stereotyped as a feminine activity in the United States and Canada, and girls surpass boys in reading skills in these countries. Yet boys score higher than girls on most tests of reading in Nigeria and England, where boys have traditionally been expected to outperform

Table 14.1
Stereotypical Sex-Role Traits

Instrumentality Cluster (Masculine Pole Perceived as More Desirable)

Feminine	Masculine
Not at all aggressive	Very aggressive
Not at all independent	Very independent
Very emotional	Not at all emotional
Does not hide emotions at all	Almost always hides emotions
Very subjective	Very objective
Very easily influenced	Not at all easily influenced
Very submissive	Very dominant
Dislikes math and science very much	Likes math and science very much
Very excitable in a minor crisis	Not at all excitable in a minor crisis
Very passive	Very active
Not at all competitive	Very competitive
Very illogical	Very logical
Very home-oriented	Very worldly
Not at all skilled in business	Very skilled in business
Very sneaky	Very direct
Feelings easily hurt	Feelings not easily hurt
Not at all adventurous	Very adventurous
Has difficulty making decisions	Can make decisions easily
Cries very easily	Never cries
Almost never acts as a leader	Almost always acts as a leader
Not at all self-confident	Very self-confident
Very uncomfortable about being aggressive	Not at all uncomfortable about being aggressive
Not at all ambitious	Very ambitious
Unable to separate feelings from ideas	Easily able to separate feelings from ideas
Very dependent	Not at all dependent
Very conceited about appearance	Never conceited about appearance
Thinks women are always superior to men	Thinks men are always superior to women
Does not talk freely about sex with men	Talks freely about sex with men

Warmth-Expressiveness Cluster (Feminine Pole Perceived as More Desirable)

Feminine	Masculine
Doesn't use harsh language at all	Uses very harsh language
Very talkative	Not at all talkative
Very tactful	Very blunt
Very gentle	Very rough
Very aware of feelings of others	Not at all aware of feelings of others
Very religious	Not at all religious
Very interested in own appearance	Not at all interested in own appearance
Very neat in habits	Very sloppy in habits
Very quiet	Very loud
Very strong need for security	Very little need for security
Enjoys art and literature	Does not enjoy art and literature at all
Easily expresses tender feelings	Does not easily express tender feelings at all

Based on responses from 74 college men and 80 college women. Adapted from I. K. Broverman et al. (1972), Sex-role stereotypes: A current appraisal. *Journal of Social Issues, 28*(2), p. 63.

girls in academic pursuits, including reading. Similarly, math and spatial-relations skills are sex-typed as masculine in North America, and boys tend to outperform girls in these areas.

Bucking the Stereotypes. Many contemporary women and men are bucking the stereotypes and pursuing careers in fields that previously were reserved for the opposite sex.

Costs in Terms of Activities and Careers Children show preferences for sex-stereotyped activities and toys by the ages of 2 or 3. Then, if they should stray from sex-typed activities, their peers are sure to let them know of the "errors of their ways."

Children not only develop stereotypical attitudes toward play activities at an early age; they also acquire clear ideas about what is "man's work" and what is "woman's work." Consider a study of 2- and 3-year-olds' stereotypes about the workplace. To learn about the children's ideas, the researchers Gettys and Cann (1981) showed the children male and female dolls and asked them to point to the one that held a particular job. Even by this age, 78 percent of the children thought that the male doll was the construction worker. In contrast, only 23 percent pointed to the male doll as a teacher.

Once we enter the workplace, we also find inequities that are based on gender. And here too, it is women who suffer most. For example, women earn less than men for comparable work. Women are less likely than men to be promoted into responsible managerial positions. Once in managerial positions, women often feel pressured to be "tougher" than men in order to seem as tough. They also feel pressured to pay more attention to their appearance than men do, because co-workers pay more attention to what they wear, how they crop their hair, and so forth.

Women are also expected to engage in traditionally feminine tasks, such as making the coffee or cleaning up after the conference lunch, as well as the jobs they were hired to do. Finally, women usually have the dual responsibility of being the major caretaker for the children.

Costs in Terms of Psychological Well-Being and Interpersonal Relationships Stereotyping also interferes with our psychological well-being and our interpersonal relationships. Women who fully accept the traditional feminine sex role appear to have lower self-esteem than women who also show masculine-type traits (Flaherty & Dusek, 1980; Spence et al., 1975). They are also likely to believe that women are to be seen and not heard. Therefore, they are unlikely to assert themselves by making their needs and wants known. As a consequence, they are likely to encounter frustration.

Men who accept the traditionally masculine sex role are less likely to feel comfortable performing the activities involved in caring for children, such as bathing them, dressing them, and feeding them (Bem, 1975; Bem et al., 1976; Helmreich et al., 1979). Such men are less likely to ask for help—including medical help—when they need it (Rosenstock & Kirscht, 1979). They are also less likely to be sympathetic and tender and to express feelings of love in their marital relationships (Coleman & Ganong, 1985).

We have been considering the effects of sex-role *stereotypes* on our perceptions and expectations of men and women. Now let us turn our attention to research concerning *actual* sex differences in behavior and personality.

SEX DIFFERENCES: VIVE LA DIFFÉRENCE OR VIVE LA SIMILARITÉ?

Sex-role stereotypes reflect public impressions. What are the actual differences in cognition and personality between the sexes?

Differences in Cognitive Abilities

It was once believed that males were more intelligent than females because of their greater knowledge of world affairs and their skill in science and industry. We now recognize that greater male knowledge and skill reflected not differences in intelligence but the systematic exclusion of females from world affairs, science, and industry.

Girls seem to acquire language somewhat faster than boys. Girls make more prelinguistic vocalizations and utter their first word a half month earlier (Harris, 1977). They acquire additional words more rapidly, and their pronunciation is clearer (Nelson, 1973; Schachter et al., 1978). Differences increase throughout the high-school years (Maccoby & Jacklin, 1974). Female students excel in spelling, punctuation, reading comprehension, solving verbal analogies (such as Washington : one :: Lincoln : ?), and solving anagrams (scrambled words). Also, far more American boys than girls have reading problems, ranging from reading below grade level to severe disabilities in reading.

On the other hand, many males seem to catch up to females in verbal skills. Among high-school students taking the Scholastic Aptitude Tests in 1988, for example, males outscored females by an average score of 435 to 422 (Carmody, 1988).

Males apparently excel in visual-spatial abilities. Beginning in adolescence, boys usually outperform girls on tests of spatial ability (Maccoby & Jacklin, 1974; Petersen, 1980). These tests assess skills such as mentally rotating figures in space (see Figure 14.1) and finding figures embedded within larger designs (see Figure 14.2).

Males apparently excel in mathematics, too. Maccoby and Jacklin (1974) found that boys and girls show similar math ability until late childhood. Boys begin to outperform girls at about the age of 12, and consistent sex differences appear at about 15 (Meece et al., 1982).

Consider sex differences on the mathematics test of the Scholastic Aptitude Test (SAT). The mean score is 500, and about two-thirds of the test-takers received scores between 400 and 600. Twice as many boys as girls attain scores over 500 (Benbow & Stanley, 1980). *Thirteen* times as many boys as girls attain scores over 700 (Benbow & Stanley, 1983).

In sum, it does appear that within our culture, girls show greater verbal abilities than boys, but boys may catch up by college age. Males apparently show greater spatial and math abilities than females. However, three factors should caution us not to attach too much importance to these cognitive sex differences:

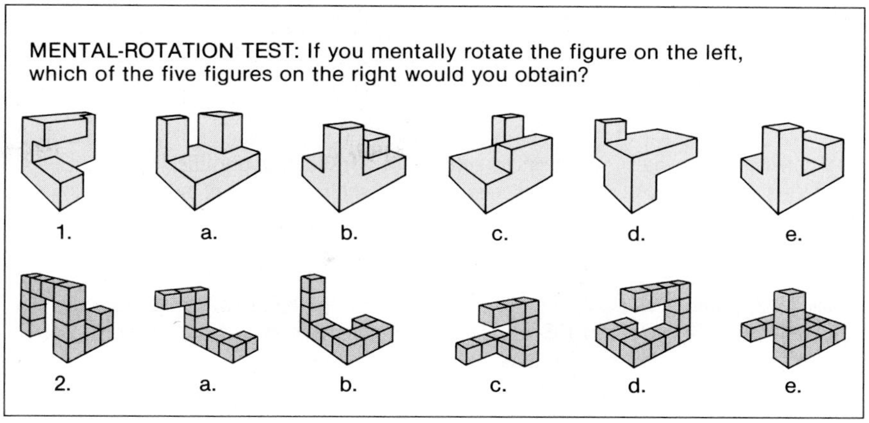

Figure 14.1
Rotating Figures in Space. Males as a group outperform females on spatial-relations tasks, such as rotating figures in space and picturing the results. However, females do as well as males when they receive some training in the task.

1. First, in most cases they are small (Deaux, 1984; Hyde, 1981).
2. Second, these sex differences are *group* differences. Variation in these skills is larger *within* than between the sexes. Millions of females outdistance the "average" male in math and spatial abilities.
3. Third, the small differences that appear to exist may largely reflect cultural expectations and environmental influences (Tobias, 1982). Spatial and math abilities are stereotyped as masculine in our culture. Female introductory psychology students given just three hours of training in various visual-spatial skills, such as rotating geometric figures, showed no performance deficit in these skills when compared to men (Stericker & LeVesconte, 1982).

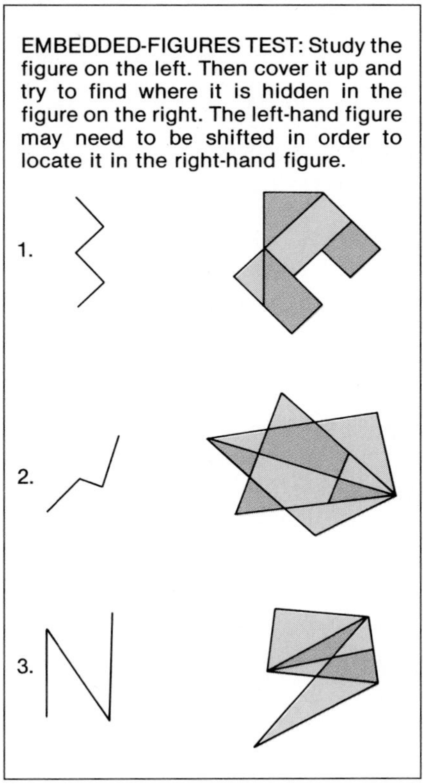

EMBEDDED-FIGURES TEST: Study the figure on the left. Then cover it up and try to find where it is hidden in the figure on the right. The left-hand figure may need to be shifted in order to locate it in the right-hand figure.
1.
2.
3.

Figure 14.2
Items from an Embedded-Figures Test.

Differences in Aggressiveness

In most cultures, it is the males who march off to war and who battle for glory and shaving-cream–commercial contracts. Most psychological studies of aggression have found that male children and adults behave more aggressively than females (Frodi et al, 1977; Maccoby & Jacklin, 1980; White, 1983).

Truth or Fiction Revisited

It is true that men behave more aggressively than women.

Ann Frodi and her colleagues (1977) reviewed 72 studies concerning sex differences in aggression and found that females are more likely to act aggressively under some circumstances than others:

1. Males are more likely than females to report physical aggression in their behavior, intentions, and dreams.
2. Females are more likely to feel anxious or guilty about behaving aggressively. These feelings tend to inhibit aggression.
3. Females behave as aggressively as males when they have the means to do so and believe that their behavior is justified.
4. Females are more likely to empathize with the victim—to put themselves in the victim's place.

PSYCHOLOGY GOES TO WORK

Sex Differences and Careers in Math and Engineering

Women are less likely than men to enter careers in mathematics and engineering. Although women now make up more than a third of graduates in medicine and law, the number of women engineering graduates has expanded from about 4 percent in 1976 to only about 14 percent in 1986 (Adelson, 1988). Why the discrepancy? It is partly because math and engineering are perceived as being inconsistent with the feminine sex role. Many little girls are dissuaded from thinking about professions such as engineering and architecture because they are given dolls, not firetrucks and blocks, to play with. Many boys are likewise deterred from child-care and nursing professions because others look askance at them when they reach for dolls.

However, males also outperform females in math and spatial-relations tasks. Why? We cannot completely rule out the possibility of biological differences, but math and spatial-relations skills are also clearly related to the number of math courses taken (Fennema & Sherman, 1977). Children are likely to practice spatial skills in geometry and related courses, and boys take more math courses in high school than girls (Meece et al., 1982). Math courses open doorways to occupations in the natural sciences, engineering, and economics, among many others. There are several reasons why American boys are more likely than American girls to feel "at home" with math:

1. Fathers are more likely than mothers to help children with math homework (Meece et al., 1982; Raymond & Benbow, 1986).
2. Advanced math courses are more likely to be taught by men (Fox, 1982).
3. Teachers often show higher expectations for boys in math courses (Meece et al., 1982).
4. Teachers of math courses spend more time instructing and interacting with boys than girls (Meece et al., 1982).

Given these typical experiences with math, we should not be surprised that by junior high, boys view themselves as more competent in math than girls do, even when they receive identical grades (Meece et al., 1982). Boys are more likely to have positive feelings about math, and girls are more liable to have math anxiety (Tobias & Weissbrod, 1980). It becomes increasingly hard to convince high-school and college women to take math courses, even when they show superior math ability (Eccles, 1985; Fox et al., 1985; Paulsen & Johnson, 1983).

If women are to find their places in professions related to mathematics and engineering, we may need to provide more female role models in these professions to break down the stereotype that those occupations are meant for men, and we will have to encourage girls to take more courses in math.

5. Sex differences in aggression decrease when the victim is anonymous. Anonymity may prevent females from empathizing with their victims.

Differences in Communication Styles

Despite the stereotype of women as gossips and "chatterboxes," research in communication styles suggests that males in many situations spend more time talking than women. Males are also more likely to introduce new topics and to interrupt (Brooks, 1982; Deaux, 1985; Hall, 1984). Yet females do seem more willing to reveal their feelings and personal experiences (Cozby, 1973). Females are less likely than males to curse—with the exception of women who are bucking sex-role stereotypes.

TOWARD PSYCHOLOGICAL ANDROGYNY: THE MORE TRAITS THE MERRIER?

Most of us think of masculinity and femininity as opposite poles of a continuum (Storms, 1980). We assume that the more masculine people are, the less feminine they are, and vice versa. Thus a man who shows the "feminine" traits of nurturance, tenderness, and emotionality might be considered less

Table 14.2
Vive la Différence? Just How Different Are the Sexes?

Differences Borne Out by Most Research Studies	Differences about which There is Doubt	Assumed Differences that Research Has Shown to Be False
Males tend to be more aggressive than females.	Females have greater verbal ability than males.*	Males are more logical and analytical than females.
Males have greater visual-spatial ability than females.	Females are more timid and anxious than males.	Females are more suggestible than males.
Males have greater ability in mathematics than females.	Males are more active than females.	Males have higher self-esteem than females.
	Males are more competitive than females.	Females lack achievement motivation.
	Males are more dominant than females.	Females are more talkative than males.
	Females are more sociable than males.	

*This stereotype apparently remains true for children. However, males frequently catch up as they reach adulthood.

masculine than other men. Women who compete with men in the business world are seen as being not only more masculine than other women but also less feminine.

Are Masculinity and Femininity Opposites on the Same Continuum or Independent Dimensions? Today, many psychologists assert that masculinity and femininity make up independent personality dimensions. That is, people (male or female) who score high on measures of masculine traits need not score low on feminine traits. People who show stereotypical masculine *instrumentality* can also show stereotypical feminine *warmth-expressiveness* (see Table 14.1). People who have both instrumentality and warmth-expressiveness traits are said to show **psychological androgyny.** People high in instrumentality *only* are stereotypically masculine. People high in warmth-expressiveness *only* are stereotypically feminine. People who are low in both instrumentality and warmth-expressiveness are "undifferentiated" according to the stereotypical sex-role dimensions. Undifferentiated people seem to encounter distress. Undifferentiated women, for example, are viewed less positively than either more feminine or more masculine women, even by their friends (Baucom & Danker-Brown, 1983). Undifferentiated women are also less satisfied with their marriages (Baucom & Aiken, 1984).

Psychological Androgyny, Well-Being, and Adjustment Now let us consider research findings that consider the ways in which psychological androgyny contributes to our well-being and adjustment. First of all, research is mixed as to whether psychologically androgynous people are physically healthier than highly masculine or feminine people (Hall & Taylor, 1985). There is a good deal of evidence, however, that androgynous people are relatively well-adjusted, apparently because they can summon both "masculine" and "feminine" traits to express their talents and desires and to meet the demands of their situations.

In terms of Erik Erikson's concepts of **ego identity** and intimacy, androgynous college students are more likely than feminine, masculine, and undifferentiated students to show a combination of "high identity" and "high intimacy" (Schiedel & Marcia, 1985). That is, they are more likely to show a firm sense of who they are and what they stand for (identity), and they have a greater capacity to form intimate, sharing relationships.

Psychological androgyny Possession of instrumental and warmth–expressiveness traits.

Ego identity Erikson's term for a firm sense of who one is and what one stands for.

Psychologically androgynous people of both sexes show "masculine" independence under group pressures to conform and "feminine" nurturance in interactions with a kitten or a baby (Bem, 1975; Bem et al., 1976). They feel comfortable performing a wider range of activities, including (the "masculine") nailing of boards and (the "feminine") winding of yarn (Bem & Lenney, 1976; Helmreich et al., 1979). In adolescence, they report greater interest in pursuing nontraditional occupational roles (Motowidlo, 1982). They show greater maturity in moral judgments, greater self-esteem (Flaherty & Dusek, 1980; Spence et al., 1975), and greater ability to bounce back from failure (Baucom & Danker-Brown, 1979). They are more likely to try to help others in need. Androgynous people are more willing to share the leadership in mixed-sex groups. Masculine people attempt to dominate such groups, and feminine people tend to be satisfied with taking a back seat (Porter et al., 1985). Androgynous women rate stressful life events as being less undesirable than do feminine women (Shaw, 1982).

So-called feminine traits apparently contribute to marital happiness, whether shown by women or men. Not only is husbands' happiness positively related to their wives' femininity; wives' happiness is also positively related to their husbands' femininity (Antill, 1983). Wives of psychologically androgynous husbands are far happier than women whose husbands adhere to a strict, stereotypical masculine sex role. Androgynous men are more tolerant of their wives' or lovers' faults and more likely to express loving feelings than are "macho" males (Coleman & Ganong, 1985). And women, like men, appreciate sympathetic, tender spouses who love children.

Challenges to Androgyny There have been several challenges to the concept of psychological androgyny and its apparent benefits. One concerns the supposed self-esteem benefits of androgyny. On the basis of an analysis of 35 studies on the relationship between sex roles and self-esteem, Bernard Whitley (1983) argues that the self-esteem benefits of psychological androgyny do *not* derive from the combination of masculine and feminine traits. Instead, they reflect the presence of "masculine" traits, whether they are found in males or females. That is, traits such as independence and assertiveness contribute to high self-esteem in both sexes.

Some feminists, for theoretical and political reasons, have criticized the view that psychological androgyny is a worthwhile goal. The basic problem, from the feminist perspective, is that psychological androgyny is defined as the possession of both masculine and feminine personality traits. However, this very definition relies on the presumed rigidity of masculine and feminine sex-role stereotypes. Feminists such as Bernice Lott (1981, 1985) would prefer to see the dissolution of these stereotypes.

ON BECOMING A MAN OR A WOMAN: THE DEVELOPMENT OF SEX DIFFERENCES

And so, there are a number of sex differences in cognition, personality, and overt behavior. They include minor differences in cognitive functioning and differences in activity levels and preferences, aggressiveness, and communication styles. In this section we consider the biological and psychological factors that appear to contribute to the development of these sex differences.

Biological Influences

Biological views on sex differences tend to focus on two issues: brain organization and sex hormones.

Brain Organization A number of studies suggest that we can speak of "left brain" versus "right brain" functions. Language skills seem to depend more on left-brain functioning, whereas right-brain functioning may be more involved in spatial relations and in aesthetic and emotional responses. The brain hemispheres may be even more specialized in males than in females (Bryden, 1982).

Evidence for this view derives from adults who receive brain injuries. Men with damage to the left hemisphere are more likely to show verbal deficits than women with similar damage (McGlone, 1980). Men with damage to the right hemisphere are more likely to show spatial-relations deficits than similarly injured women.

Sex differences in brain organization might in part explain why women exceed men in verbal skills that require some spatial organization, such as reading, spelling, and crisp articulation of speech. But men might be superior at more specialized spatial-relations tasks, such as interpreting road maps and visualizing objects in space.

Prenatal Sex Hormones Sex hormones are responsible for prenatal differentiation of sex organs. Prenatal sex hormones may also "masculinize" or "feminize" the brain by creating predispositions that are consistent with some sex-role stereotypes (Diamond, 1977; Money, 1977, 1987).

Diamond takes an extreme view. She suggests that **in-utero** brain masculinization can cause tomboyishness and assertiveness—even preferences for trousers over skirts and for playing with "boys' toys." Money agrees that predispositions may be created in utero but argues that social learning plays a stronger role in the development of gender identity, personality traits, and preferences. Money claims that social learning is powerful enough to counteract many prenatal predispositions.

Some evidence for the possible role of hormonal influences derives from animal studies. For example, male rats are generally superior to females in maze-learning ability, a task that requires spatial skills. However, female rats who are exposed to androgens in the uterus or soon after birth learn maze routes as rapidly as males (Beatty, 1979; Goy & McEwen, 1982).

Sex Hormones at Puberty Sex hormones also spur sexual maturation during adolescence, and there are some interesting suggestions that sexual maturation is linked to development of cognitive skills. Girls usually reach sexual maturity earlier than boys. Researchers have found that late maturers, whether boys or girls, show the "masculine pattern" of exceeding early maturers on math and spatial-relations tasks (Sanders & Soares, 1986; Sanders et al., 1982; Waber et al., 1985). Early-maturing boys exceed late-maturing boys in verbal skills and also show the "feminine pattern" of higher verbal than math and spatial-relations skills (Newcombe & Bandura, 1983). Thus early maturation seems to favor development of verbal skills, whereas late maturation may favor development of math and spatial-relations skills.

In-utero Inside the uterus.

Adult Hormone Levels In more recent research, Donald Baucom and his colleagues (1985) found relationships between levels of testosterone and personality traits among women college students. Eighty-four female undergraduates took a number of paper-and-pencil tests, including masculinity and femininity scales and Sandra Bem's Sex Role Inventory. Their testosterone levels were determined from samples of saliva. Masculine-sex-typed, androgynous, and undifferentiated women all had higher testosterone levels than feminine-sex-typed women. Women with higher testosterone levels perceived themselves as more enterprising, unconventional, spontaneous, and resourceful than women with lower testosterone levels—but also as less "civilized," rational, helpful, and warm. All in all, high concentrations of testosterone were linked to stereotypical masculine behaviors.

Schindler (1979) found a link between women's testosterone levels and their needs and vocational choices. Women with high testosterone levels showed higher needs for achievement and autonomy, as measured by the Edwards Personal Preference Schedule, than women with lower concentrations. Women lawyers showed higher testosterone levels than women teachers, nurses, and athletes. Why women athletes had lower testosterone levels than lawyers is unclear, although it is known that strenuous exercise lowers estrogen levels in women (Sullivan, 1988).

Despite their intriguing findings, keep in mind that the Baucom and Schindler studies were correlational, not experimental. Although testosterone levels were linked to "masculine" traits, needs, and vocations, we cannot conclude that testosterone gave rise to this personality and behavior pattern. Perhaps the traits and behavior patterns influenced hormone levels, or perhaps other, undetected factors gave rise to both.

Let us now consider psychological views of the development of sex differences.

Psychodynamic Theory

Sigmund Freud explained the acquisition of sex roles in terms of **identification.** Freud believed that gender identity remains flexible until the resolution of the Oedipus and Electra complexes at about the age of 5 or 6. Appropriate sex-typing requires that boys identify with their fathers and surrender the wish to possess their mothers. Girls have to surrender the wish to have a penis and identify with their mothers.

However, boys and girls develop stereotypical preferences for toys and activities much earlier than might be predicted by psychodynamic theory. Even within their first year, boys are more explorative and independent. Girls are relatively more quiet, dependent, and restrained (Goldberg & Lewis, 1969). By 18 to 36 months, girls are more likely to play with soft toys and dolls and to dance. Eighteen- to 36-month-old boys are more likely to play with hard objects, blocks, and toy cars, trucks, and airplanes (Fagot, 1974).

Let us consider the ways in which social-learning and cognitive theories account for sex-typing.

Identification In psychodynamic theory, the process of incorporating within ourselves the behaviors and our perceptions of the thoughts and feelings of others. In social-learning theory, a broad, continuous learning process in which children are influenced by rewards and punishments to strive to imitate adults of the same sex.

Social-Learning Theory

Social-learning theorists explain the acquisition of sex roles and sex differences in terms of observational learning, identification*, and socialization.

*But the social-learning concept of identification differs from the psychodynamic concept, as noted in this section.

Acquiring Sex Roles. What biological and psychological factors contribute to the acquisition of sex roles? Social-learning theory focuses on the roles of imitation of the behavior patterns of same-sex adults and reinforcement by parents and peers.

Children learn much of what is considered masculine or feminine by observational learning, as suggested by an experiment conducted by David Perry and Kay Bussey (1979). In this study, children learned how behaviors are sex-typed by observing the *relative frequencies* with which men and women performed them. However, the adult role models expressed arbitrary preferences for one item from each of 16 pairs of items—pairs such as oranges versus apples and toy cows versus toy horses—as 8- and 9-year-old boys and girls observed. Then the children were asked to show their own preferences. Boys selected an average of 14 of 16 items that agreed with the "preferences" of the men. Girls selected an average of only three of 16 items that agreed with the choices of the men.

Social-learning theorists view identification as a broad, continuous learning process in which children are influenced by rewards and punishments to imitate adults of the same sex—particularly the parent of the same sex (Bronfenbrenner, 1960; Kagan, 1964; Storms, 1979). In identification, as opposed to imitation, children do not simply imitate a certain behavior pattern. They also try to become broadly like the model.

Socialization also plays a role. Parents and other adults—even other children—inform children about how they are expected to behave. They reward children for behavior they consider sex-appropriate. They punish (or fail to reinforce) children for behavior they consider inappropriate. Girls, for example, are given dolls while they still sleep in cribs. They are encouraged to rehearse care-taking behaviors in preparation for traditional feminine adult roles.

The Role of Parents Mothers usually bear the major responsibility for the day-to-day nurturance of children (Belsky et al., 1984; Feldman et al., 1984). Mothers tend to provide the supportive and empathic functions—the "emotional glue"—that keeps the family integrated as a unit (Johnson, 1983; Orlofsky, 1983). Yet fathers are more likely to communicate norms for sex-typed behaviors (Lamb, 1981; Power, 1985). Fathers tend to encourage instrumental behavior in their sons and warm, expressive behavior in their daughters (Block, 1979).

Socialization The process of guiding people into socially acceptable behavior patterns by means of information, rewards, and punishments.

The Social Learning of Sex Differences in Aggressive Behavior Concerning the greater aggressiveness of boys, Maccoby and Jacklin note the following:

> *Aggression in general is less acceptable for girls, and is more actively discouraged in them, by either direct punishment, withdrawal of affection, or simply cognitive training that "that isn't the way girls act." Girls then build up greater anxieties about aggression, and greater inhibitions against displaying it (1974, p. 234).*

Girls frequently learn to respond to social provocations by feeling anxious about the possibility of acting aggressively, whereas boys are generally encouraged to retaliate (Frodi et al., 1977).

Several experiments highlight the importance of social-learning factors in female aggressiveness. Studies by Albert Bandura and his colleagues (1963) found that boys are more likely than girls to imitate film-mediated aggressive models, because the social milieu more often frowns upon aggressiveness in girls. Other investigators find that the development of aggressive behavior in females is influenced by situational variables, such as the nature of the provocation and the possibility that someone will disapprove of them (Taylor & Epstein, 1967; Richardson et al., 1979).

In the Taylor and Epstein study, aggressive behavior was measured by the strength of the electric shock selected for delivery to another person. Subjects used a fearsome looking console (see Figure 15.3) to take turns shocking other participants in the study when they failed to respond quickly enough to a stimulus. Subjects could select the strength of the shock themselves. When men set low or moderate shock levels for women subjects, the women generally chose somewhat lower shock levels for the men when their turn came. In this way, they adhered to the feminine stereotype of nonaggressiveness. But when the men violated the **sex norm** of treating women favorably by setting high levels of shock for them, the women retaliated by setting shock levels that were equally high. Apparently the women decided that what was sauce for the gander was sauce for the goose. If men could violate sex norms and treat women aggressively, women, too, could violate sex norms and respond just as aggressively.

The development of aggressive behavior in girls is also influenced by the responses of those who monitor their behavior and reward or punish them. In the Richardson study, college women competed with men in responding quickly to a stimulus over four blocks of trials, with six trials in each block. They could not see their opponents. The loser of each trial received an electric shock whose intensity was set by the opponent. Women competed under one of three experimental conditions: public, private, or with a supportive other. In the public condition, another woman observed the subject silently. In the private condition, there was no observer. In the supportive-other condition, another woman urged the subject to retaliate strongly when her opponent selected high shock levels. As shown in Figure 14.3, women in the private and supportive-other conditions selected increasingly higher levels of shock in retaliation. Presumably, the women subjects assumed that an observer—though silent—would frown on aggressive behavior. This assumption is likely to reflect the women's own early socialization experiences. Women who were unobserved or urged on by a supportive other apparently felt free to violate the sex norm of nonaggressiveness when their situations called for aggressive responses.

In sum, social-learning theory has done an admirable job of outlining the ways in which rewards, punishments, and modeling foster "sex-appropriate" behavior patterns. Critics of social-learning theory do not challenge the validity of experiments such as those we have reported. Instead, they focus on theoretical issues such as, *How do reinforcers influence us?* Do

Sex norm An expectation about what sort of behavior is considered to be appropriate in social interactions between males and females.

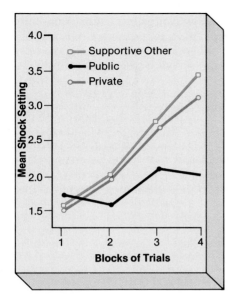

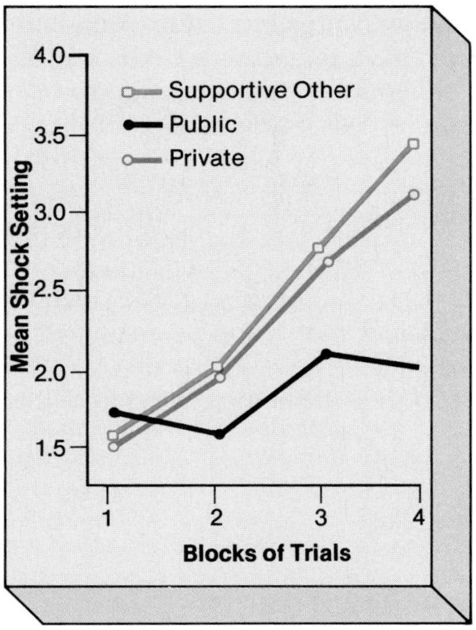

Figure 14.3
Shock Settings Chosen by Women in Retaliation against Male Opponents in the Richardson Study. In this study, women behaved as aggressively as men when they were alone or when urged on by another person. Women apparently behave aggressively when (a) they are provoked, (b) they have the means for doing so, and (c) the social milieu is supportive rather than condemnatory of aggression from them.

Gender identity One's concept of being male or female. (The first stage in the cognitive-developmental theory of the assumption of sex roles.)

Gender stability The concept that one's gender is a permanent feature.

Gender constancy The concept that one's gender remains the same, despite superficial changes in appearance or behavior.

reinforcers mechanically increase the frequency of behavior, or do they provide us with information that we process in making decisions? Let us consider two cognitive-theory approaches to sex-typing that will shed some light on this matter: cognitive-developmental theory and gender-schema theory.

Cognitive-Developmental Theory

Lawrence Kohlberg (1966) has proposed a cognitive-developmental view of sex-typing. Whereas social-learning theory balances environmental (situational) influences and person variables, cognitive theories tip the balance in favor of viewing children as more active participants in the development of sex roles and sex differences. According to cognitive-developmental theory, these developments occur in stages and are entwined with the child's general cognitive development.

Rewards and punishments influence children's choices of toys and activities, but from the cognitive perspective, rewards do not mechanically strengthen stimulus–response connections. Instead, rewards provide children with information about when they are behaving in ways that other people deem appropriate. For this reason, even at the ages of 21 to 25 months, girls respond more positively to rewards from other girls. Boys at this age respond more positively to rewards from other boys (Fagot, 1985a). Rewards are a source of information that is processed in terms of the gender of the rewarder; their effects are not mechanical.

Thus there is a role for rewards and punishments in cognitive theories: They provide information. But Kohlberg views the essential aspects of sex-typing to be the emergence of three concepts: *gender identity, gender stability,* and *gender constancy.*

The first step in sex-typing is attaining **gender identity,** or knowledge of being male or female. Gender identity appears to begin with sexual assignment, or labeling the child a boy or girl. Sexual assignment reflects the child's anatomic sex and usually occurs at birth. Gender identity is so important to parents that they may want to know "Is it a boy or a girl?" before they begin to count fingers and toes.

Most children acquire a firm gender identity by the age of 36 months (Marcus & Corsini, 1978; McConaghy, 1979; Money, 1977). By this age, most children can also tell anatomic sex differences (Ruble & Ruble, 1980).

At age 4 or 5, most children develop the concept of **gender stability.** They recognize that people retain their genders for a lifetime. Girls no longer believe that they will grow up to be daddies, and boys no longer think they can become mommies. According to cognitive-developmental theory, the emergence of gender stability contributes to the organization of sex-stereotyped behavior (Siegal & Robinson, 1987).

By the age of 7 or 8, most children develop the more sophisticated concept of **gender constancy.** Children with gender constancy recognize that gender does not change, even if people modify their dress or their behavior patterns. Gender, that is, remains constant despite rearrangement of superficial appearances. A woman who crops her hair short remains a woman. A man who cries remains a man.

Studies in the United States, Samoa, Nepal, Belize, and Kenya have found that the concepts of gender identity, gender stability, and gender constancy do emerge in the order predicted by Kohlberg (Munroe et al., 1984; Slaby & Frey, 1975).

According to cognitive-developmental theory, once children have established concepts of gender stability and constancy, they will be motivated to behave in ways that are consistent with their genders. Once girls understand that they will remain female, they will show a preference for "feminine" activities. As shown by Perry and Bussey (1979), 8- and 9-year-olds actively seek information about which behavior patterns are "masculine" and which are "feminine." Then they tend to imitate the "sex-appropriate" patterns.

However, there are problems with the ages at which sex-typed play emerges. Numerous studies have shown that many children prefer sex-typed toys such as cars and dolls at the age of 2 (Huston, 1983). At this age, children are likely to have a sense of gender identity, but gender stability and gender constancy remain some years away (Fagot, 1985b). Therefore, gender identity alone seems to provide a child with sufficient motivation to assume sex-typed behavior patterns.

Another cognitive view, gender-schema theory, attempts to address this shortcoming.

Gender-Schema Theory: An Information-Processing Approach

Gender-schema theory holds that children use gender as one way of organizing their perceptions of the world (Bem, 1981, 1985; Martin & Halverson, 1981). Gender has a great deal of prominence, even to young children (Maccoby, 1988). Therefore, children mentally group people of the same gender together.

Gender-schema theory borrows elements from social-learning theory and from cognitive-developmental theory. As in social-learning theory, children learn "appropriate" behavior patterns by observation. But children's active cognitive processing of information also contributes to their sex-typing.

Consider the example of the strength–weakness construct or dimension. Children learn that strength is linked to the male sex-role stereotype and weakness to the female stereotype. They also learn that some dimensions, such as strength–weakness, are more relevant to one gender than the other—in this case, to males. Bill will learn that the strength he displays in weight training or wrestling affects the way others perceive him. Most girls do not find this dimension to be important, unless they are competing in sports such as gymnastics, tennis, or swimming. Even so, boys are expected to compete in these sports, and girls are not. Jane is likely to find that her gentleness and neatness are more important in the eyes of others than her strength.

Thus, children learn to judge themselves according to the traits, or constructs, considered to be relevant to their genders. In so doing, their self-concepts become blended with the gender schema of their culture. The gender schema provides standards for comparison. Children whose self-concepts are consistent with their society's gender schema are likely to have higher self-esteem than children whose self-concepts are not.

From the viewpoint of gender-schema theory, gender identity is sufficient to prompt "sex-appropriate" behavior. As soon as children understand the labels *boy* and *girl,* they have a basis for blending their self-concepts with the gender schema of their society. Children with gender identity will actively seek information about the gender schema. Their self-esteem will soon become wrapped up in the ways in which they measure up to the gender schema.

A number of recent studies support the view that children process information according to the gender schema (Cann & Newbern, 1984; List et al., 1983). Boys, for example, show better memory for "masculine" toys and objects, whereas girls show better memory for "feminine" objects and toys (Bradbard & Endsley, 1984).

Gender-schema theory The view that one's knowledge of the gender schema in one's society (the distribution of behavior patterns that are considered appropriate for men and women) guides one's assumption of sex-typed preferences and behavior patterns.

In sum, brain organization and sex hormones may contribute to sex-typed behavior patterns and play a role in verbal ability, math skills, and aggression. Yet the effects of social learning may be strong enough to counteract most prenatal biological influences. Social-learning theory does an excellent job of outlining the environmental factors that influence children to assume "sex-appropriate" behavior patterns. However, social-learning theory may pay insufficient attention to children's active roles as seekers of information. Cognitive-developmental theory views children as active, but it may overestimate the roles of gender stability and gender constancy in sex-typing. Gender-schema theory integrates the strengths of social-learning theory and cognitive-developmental theory. It also highlights the ways in which children process information so as to blend their self-concepts with the gender schema of their culture.

SEXUAL MOTIVATION

We may describe people as "hungering" or "thirsting" for sex. Yet the sex drive differs from the hunger and thirst drives in that sex may be necessary for the survival of the species but not for the survival of the individual (despite occasional claims to the effect, "I'll simply *die* unless you . . .").

There are, however, important similarities among these drives. All three can be triggered by external cues as well as internal processes. The sex drive, for example, can be triggered by the sight (or memory) of an attractive person, a whiff of perfume, provocative photographs, even a wink.

In Chapter 3 we noted that chemicals detected through the sense of smell—pheromones—play an important role in sexual behavior among lower animals and may play a minor role in the sexual behavior of some humans. In this section we focus on various issues concerning sexual motivation, including the organizing and activating effects of sex hormones, homosexuality, pornography, and rape.

Organizing and Activating Effects of Sex Hormones

Sex hormones have many effects. They promote biological sexual differentiation, regulate the menstrual cycle, and influence sexual behavior.

Sexual behavior among many lower animals is almost completely governed by hormones (Crews & Moore, 1986). They predispose lower animals toward masculine or feminine mating patterns (a directional or **organizing effect**). Hormones also influence the sex drive and facilitate sexual response **(activating effects).**

Consider the influences of sex hormones on the mating behavior of rats. Male rats who have been castrated at birth—and thus deprived of **testosterone**—make no effort to mate as adults. But when they receive *female* sex hormones in adulthood, they become receptive to the sexual advances of other males and assume female mating stances (Harris & Levine, 1965). Male rats who are castrated in adulthood do not engage in sexual activity. However, if they receive injections of testosterone, which replaces the testosterone that would have been secreted by their own testes, they resume stereotypical male sexual behavior patterns.

The sex organs of female rodents exposed to large doses of testosterone in utero (which occurs naturally when they share the uterus with many

Organizing effects The directional effects of sex hormones—for example, along stereotypically masculine or feminine lines.

Activating effects The arousal-producing effects of sex hormones that increase the likelihood of dominant sexual responses.

Testosterone A male hormone that promotes development of male sexual characteristics and that has activating effects on sexual arousal.

brothers or artificially as a result of hormone injections) become masculinized in appearance. Such females are also predisposed toward masculine mating behaviors. If they are given additional testosterone as adults, they attempt to mount other females about as often as males do (Goy & Goldfoot, 1975). Prenatal testosterone might have organized the brains of these females in the masculine direction, predisposing them toward masculine sexual behaviors in adulthood. Testosterone in adulthood would then activate the masculine behavior patterns.

Testosterone is also important in the behavior of human males. Men who are castrated or given drugs that decrease the amount of androgens in the blood stream (antiandrogens) usually show gradual loss of sexual desire and of the capacities for erection and orgasm. Still, many castrated men remain sexually active for years, suggesting that for many people, fantasies, memories, and other cognitive stimuli are as important as hormones in sexual motivation. Beyond minimal levels, there is no clear link between testosterone level and sexual arousal. For example, sleeping men are *not* more likely to have erections during surges in the testosterone level (Schiavi et al., 1977).

Female mice, rats, cats, and dogs are receptive to males only during **estrus,** when female sex hormones are plentiful. During estrus, female rats respond to males by hopping, wiggling their ears, and arching their backs with their tails to one side, thus making penetration possible. But, as noted by Kimble (1988),

> *if we were to observe this same pair of animals one day* [*after estrus*], *we would see very different behaviors. The male would still be interested (at least at first), but his advances would not be answered with hopping, ear wiggling, and* [*back arching*]. *The female would be much more likely to "chatter" her teeth at the male (a sure sign of hostility if you are a rat). If the male were to be slow to grasp her meaning, she might turn away from him and kick him in the head, mule fashion. Clearly, it is over between them (p. 271).*

Women, in contrast, are sexually responsive during all phases of the menstrual cycle, even during menstruation itself, when hormone levels are low, and after **menopause.** Androgens influence female as well as male sexual response (Davidson et al., 1985; Sherwin et al., 1985). Women whose adrenal glands and ovaries have been removed (so that they no longer produce androgens) may gradually lose sexual interest and the capacity for sexual response. An active and enjoyable sexual history seems to ward off loss of sexual capacity, suggestive of the importance of cognitive and experiential factors in human sexual motivation.

The message is that sex hormones do play a role in human sexual behavior but that our sexual behavior is far from mechanical. Sex hormones initially promote the development of our sex organs, and as adults, we need minimal levels of sex hormones to become sexually aroused. However, psychological factors also influence our sexual behavior. In human sexuality, biology apparently is not destiny.

Estrus The periodic sexual excitement of many female mammals, during which they can conceive and are receptive to the sexual advances of males.

Menopause The cessation of menstruation.

Homosexuality The sexual orientation characterized by preference for sexual activity and the formation of romantic relationships with members of one's own sex.

Homosexuality

Homosexuality, or a homosexual orientation, is an erotic response to members of one's own sex. Sexual activity with member's of one's own sex is not in itself evidence of homosexuality. It may reflect limited sexual opportunities or even ritualistic cultural practices, as in the case of the New Guinean Sambian people. American adolescent males may masturbate one another

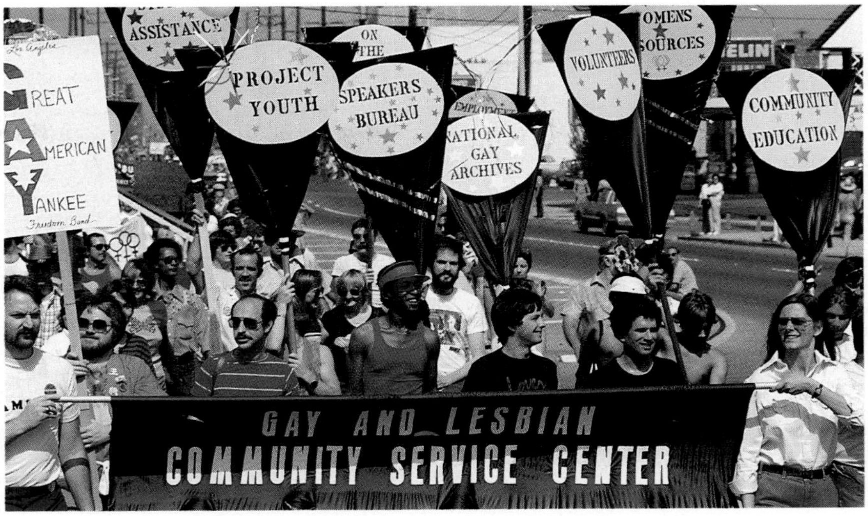

Gay Rights. In recent years, gay males and lesbians have become more open about their sexual orientations and have demanded equal rights.

while fantasizing about girls. Men in prisons may similarly turn to each other as sexual outlets. Sambian male youths engage exclusively in homosexual practices with older males, since it is believed that they must drink "men's milk" to achieve the fierce manhood of the head hunter (Money, 1987). But their behavior turns exclusively **heterosexual** once they reach marrying age.

Kinsey and his colleagues (1948, 1953) estimated that as many as 37 percent of the men and 13 percent of the women in his sample had at least one homosexual *encounter*, but only about 4 percent of his male subjects and 1 to 3 percent of his female subjects reported a homosexual *orientation*. About 2 percent of the men and 1 percent of the women in a more recent survey reported a homosexual orientation (Hunt, 1974).

Origins of Homosexuality The origins of homosexuality are complex and controversial. Developmentally speaking, about two gay males in three report gender nonconformity as children. That is, they preferred playing with girls and "girls' toys" to transportation toys, guns, and rough-and-tumble play. These preferences frequently led to their being called "sissies" (Adams & Chiodo, 1983; Bell et al., 1981; Green, 1987). On the other hand, about one in three homosexuals shows gender conformity—for example, "masculine" aggressiveness. Some homosexuals have played professional football. Let us consider a number of psychological and biological theories concerning the origins of homosexuality.

Psychodynamic theory ties homosexuality to identification with male or female figures. Identification, in turn, is related to resolution of the Oedipus and Electra complexes. In men, faulty resolution of the Oedipus complex would stem from a "classic pattern" in which there is a "close-binding" mother and a "detached-hostile" father. Boys reared in such a family environment would identify with their mothers and not their fathers. Psychodynamic theory has been criticized, however, because many gay males have had excellent relationships with both parents. Also, the childhoods of many heterosexuals fit the "classic pattern."

From a learning-theory point of view, as set forth by Kinsey and others, early reinforcement of sexual behavior (as by orgasm achieved through interaction with members of one's own sex) can influence one's sexual orientation. But many gay males and lesbians are aware of their orientations before they have overt sexual contacts (Bell et al., 1981), so we cannot attribute

Heterosexual A person whose sexual orientation is characterized by preference for sexual activity and the formation of romantic relationships with members of the opposite sex.

their orientations to early reinforcement of sexual behavior by persons of the same sex. Nor can we point to the power of observational learning. In a society that denigrates homosexuality, children are unlikely to develop the expectancy that homosexual behavior will be reinforcing for them. In other words, they are unlikely to strive to imitate homosexual models. And remember the Sambian youth: Even repeated homosexual experiences do not sway them from their eventual exclusive heterosexuality.

Biological theories focus on genetic and hormonal factors. It was once thought that homosexuality might be genetically transmitted. Kallmann (1952) found a 95 percent **concordance** rate for homosexuality among the **probands** of 40 identical twin pairs, but only 12 percent among pairs of fraternal twins. However, more recent studies have found much lower concordance rates for identical twins (Eckert et al., 1986; Ellis & Ames, 1987; McConaghy & Blaszczynski, 1980). Although genetic factors may partly determine sexual orientation, psychologist John Money of Johns Hopkins University, who has specialized in sexual behavior, concludes that homosexuality is "not under the direct governance of chromosomes and genes" (1987, p. 384).

Because sex hormones influence the mating behavior of lower animals, it has been wondered whether gay males might be deficient in testosterone or whether lesbians might have lower-than-normal levels of estrogen and higher-than-normal levels of androgens in their bloodstreams. However, homosexuality has not been reliably linked to current (adult) levels of male or female sex hormones (Feder, 1984).

Truth or Fiction Revisited

It is *not* true that homosexuals suffer from hormonal imbalances.

There are other hypotheses about possible links between hormones and sexual orientation. For example, some gay males may be more sensitive to the small quantities of estrogen that all men produce, even though they do not secrete greater amounts of estrogen (Gladue et al., 1984).

Another possibility concerns the prenatal effects of sex hormones. Prenatal sex hormones can masculinize or feminize the brains of laboratory animals in the ways that they direct the development of brain structures. So it is possible that the brains of some gay males have been prenatally feminized and that the brains of some lesbians have been prenatally masculinized (Money, 1987). Even so, Money argues that prenatal hormonal influences would not induce a robotlike sexual orientation in humans and that socialization—or early learning experiences—would probably also play a role.

The causes of human homosexuality are mysterious and complex. The current status of the research suggests that they might involve genetic factors—which, in turn, affect secretion of prenatal hormones—*and* postnatal socialization experiences. But the exact interaction of these influences has eluded detection.

Adjustment of Homosexuals Despite the slings and arrows of an often outraged society, it seems that homosexuals are about as well adjusted as heterosexuals. Saghir and Robins (1973) could not distinguish gay males from heterosexuals in terms of anxiety, depression, and psychosomatic complaints like headaches and ulcers. Adelman (1977) found that professionally employed lesbians were somewhat more socially isolated than professional heterosexual women but could not otherwise be differentiated. Other studies find no more anxiety, tension, and depression among lesbians than among heterosexual females. Siegelman (1978, 1979) concludes that the similarities between lesbians and heterosexual women outweigh the differences.

Concordance Agreement.

Proband The family member first studied or tested.

Pornography. What are the effects of pornography? Does pornography inspire antisocial behavior?

Bell and Weinberg (1978) found that the adjustment of San Francisco homosexuals was linked to their lifestyles. Homosexual "close couples" who live as if they are married appear to be as well-adjusted as married people. Homosexuals who lead other lifestyles show various levels of adjustment. Older homosexuals who live by themselves and have few, if any, sexual contacts tend to be poorly adjusted (as are many heterosexuals who lead a similar lifestyle).

Pornography

Since the late 1960s, when the Supreme Court ruled that prohibiting **explicit** sexual materials violated freedom of expression, **pornography** has been a boom industry in the United States. Some people complain that the availability of pornography has led to a breakdown in moral standards. Women's groups have argued that pornography inspires crimes of violence against women. In this section we review research bearing on two important questions concerning pornography: What are the effects of pornography? Does pornography inspire antisocial behavior?

What Are the Effects of Pornography? In the 1960s, Congress created a presidential Commission on Obscenity and Pornography to review research on pornography and conduct its own studies. The commission concluded that married couples exposed to pornography reported feeling sexually aroused but were not motivated to try observed sexual activities that were "deviant" for them (Abelson et al., 1970). More recent studies with participants ranging from middle-aged couples to college students have attained similar results (Brown et al., 1976; Hatfield et al., 1978; Heiby & Becker, 1980; Herrell, 1975; Schmidt et al., 1973). Observers were sexually aroused and might have been motivated to masturbate or engage in sexual activity with their usual sex partners. But they did not lose self-control or become notably distressed or disturbed.

Explicit Frank, revealing; leaving nothing implied or to the imagination.

Pornography Explicit, uncensored portrayals of sexual activity that are intended to excite the observer sexually.

In a more recent study, undergraduates of both sexes were exposed to six pornographic films a week during a six-week period (Zillmann & Bryant, 1983). Generally speaking, the students became **habituated** to pornography, as shown by lessened sexual response to new pornographic films by the end of the study. The films included examples of **sadomasochism** and sex with animals, and by the end of the study, the students also showed less revulsion toward these activities. Overexposure to deviant sex can apparently **desensitize** the viewer.

It is folklore that men are most sexually responsive to explicit, hardcore sexual materials and fantasies. Women, it is believed, are more romantic and thus more likely to be sexually aroused by affectionate, soft-core themes. But psychologist Julia Heiman (1975) found that **hard-core** erotica is not for men only. She played audiotapes with romantic or sexually explicit content while college students' responses were measured by the **penile strain gauge** and the **vaginal photoplethysmograph.** She found that explicit sex, with or without romantic trappings, was sexually arousing to both women and men.

Does Pornography Inspire Crimes of Violence Against Women? In recent years, **feminists** and others have argued that pornography degrades women and supports stereotypes of women as being submissive to the needs of men (Blakely, 1985). They have charged that materials that depict sexual and other types of violence against women encourages male viewers to abuse women. Experiments appear to support their concerns, even though normal men and women are usually more sexually aroused by films that portray affectionate sex than by films displaying sex with aggression (Malamuth, 1981).

In one study (Donnerstein, 1980), 120 college men were either provoked or treated neutrally by a male or female confederate of the experimenter. Subjects were then shown neutral, erotic, or aggressive-erotic films. In the last film, a man forced himself into a woman's home and raped her. Subjects were then given the opportunity to be aggressive against the male or female confederate of the experimenter through a fake electric-shock apparatus. The measure of aggression was the intensity of the shock chosen. As expected, provoked subjects selected higher shock levels. However, even nonprovoked men who were shown aggressive-erotic films showed greater aggression toward women confederates. And provoked men who were shown aggressive-erotic films chose the highest shock levels against women.

Another study (Malamuth et al., 1980) found that college men and women usually reported greater sexual response to a story about mutually desired sex than to a story about rape. But in variations of the study, Malamuth and his colleagues portrayed the rape victim as experiencing an involuntary orgasm, with or without pain. The addition of the involuntary orgasm raised students' self-reports of sexual arousal to levels that equaled the response to mutually desired sex. Women subjects were most responsive when the woman in the story did not have pain, but men were most aroused when she did. The researchers speculate that the woman's orgasm legitimized the violence. Thus, sexual response in the observers was **disinhibited.** The story may have reinforced the cultural myth that some women need to be dominated and will be "turned on" by an overpowering man. Exposure to aggressive-erotic films may increase violence, even among normal college men (Donnerstein & Linz, 1984).

The Attorney General's Commission Report A review of such research by the Attorney General's Commission on Pornography concluded in 1986

Habituate A process during which one's response to a stimulus decreases because of continued exposure.

Sadomasochism Activities involving attainment of gratification by the inflicting and the receiving of pain and humiliation.

Desensitize To cause to lose sensitivity to a stimulus.

Hard-core Unyielding, unqualified; suggestive of explicit sex in the absence of a romantic context.

Penile strain gauge An instrument that measures the size of erection and provides an index of sexual arousal in the male.

Vaginal photoplethysmograph An instrument that measures sexual arousal in women as a function of vaginal blood pressure.

Feminists People (of both sexes) who seek social change and legislation to reverse discrimination against women and to otherwise advance the concerns of women.

Disinhibit In social-learning theory, to stimulate a response that is normally inhibited by showing a model engaging in that response.

that explicit sexual materials are a cause of violence against women. A follow-up workshop organized by the Surgeon General C. Everett Koop (1987) made three points about depictions of sexual *aggression:*

1. "Pornography that portrays sexual aggression as pleasurable to the victim increases the acceptance of the use of coercion in sexual relations."
2. "Acceptance of coercive sexuality appears to be related to sexual aggression."
3. "In laboratory studies measuring short-term effects, exposure to violent pornography increases punitive behavior toward women" (p. 945).

A Critique of the Commission's Report As noted by Donnerstein and Linz (1987), the Attorney General's Report (1986) misses the point because commission members *did not separate the effects of explicit sexual materials from those of violent materials.* There remains no evidence that explicit sexual materials *in the absence of violence* stimulate antisocial behavior.

Truth or Fiction Revisited

It is *not* true that pornographic films per se have been shown to provoke violence against women. However, pornographic films that contain violent themes may do so.

Donnerstein and Linz conclude, "It is not sex, but violence that is an obscenity in our society" (1986, p. 56). The same critique can be made of Koop's (1987) remarks; that is, they do not distinguish between pornography and violent pornography. As a matter of fact, the only statement that Koop's (1987) workshop could agree on concerning the effects of nonviolent pornography on adults is that "prolonged use of pornography increases beliefs that less common sexual practices are more common" (p. 945).

The Bottom Line In sum, if legislation were to be considered to answer the legitimate concerns of women who argue against the availability of *violent* pornography, it may be that the Swedish approach of outlawing portrayals of *violence* rather than of sexual behavior per se would be more on target. Curtailment of *nonviolent* pornography would have to be based purely on moral grounds; scientific methods have failed to demonstrate that it has a harmful effect on adults. Interestingly, only a minority of Americans would support legislation to make explicit erotic materials illegal, but about 75 percent of us would outlaw pornography that combines sex with violence (Harris, 1988).

Yet any legislation that would curtail the production or sale of pornographic materials might impede freedom of expression. Such legislation could be found in conflict with the First Amendment and therefore unconstitutional (Blakely, 1985). Even the feminist community is split on the issue of banning pornography. Some feminist writers, such as Kate Millett, argue that "we're better off hanging tight to the First Amendment so that we have freedom of speech" (Press et al., 1985). Moreover, Linz, Donnerstein, and Penrod (1987) argue that educational programs may be able to decrease many of the negative effects of sexual violence in the media. The question of what (if anything) should and can be done about pornography is a controversial issue that is likely to remain with us for some time to come. As the debate rages on, it may be useful to separate moral issues from scientific issues—and moral judgments from scientific findings.

Rape

Rape is the seeking of sexual gratification without another person's consent. There are more than 90,000 reported cases of rape in the United States each year (Allgeier & Allgeier, 1984). Since it has been estimated that only one rape in five is reported, it may be that as many as 450,000 rapes actually take place annually.

Nine percent of a sample of 6,159 college women reported that they had given in to sexual intercourse as a result of threats or physical force (Koss et al., 1987). Up to 2 million instances of forced sex may occur within marriage each year, although women are not likely to define forced sex by their husbands as rape.

If we add to these figures instances in which women are subjected to forced kissing and petting, the numbers grow more alarming. For example, nearly 70 percent of 282 women in one college sample had been assaulted (usually by dates and friends) at some time since entering college (Kanin & Parcell, 1977). At a major university, 40 percent of 201 male students surveyed admitted to using force to unfasten a woman's clothing, and 13 percent reported that they had forced a woman to engage in sexual intercourse (Rapaport & Burkhart, 1984). Forty-four percent of the college women in the Koss study (Koss et al., 1987) reported that they had "given in to sex play" because of a "man's continual arguments and pressure."

Why Do Men Rape Women? Why do men coerce women into sexual activity? Many social scientists argue that sexual motivation often has little to do with it. Rape, they argue, is more often a man's way of expressing anger toward, or power over, women (e.g., Groth & Birnbaum, 1979). In fact, many rapists have long records as violent offenders (Amir, 1971). With some rapists, violence also appears to enhance sexual arousal, so they are motivated to combine sex with aggression (Quinsey et al., 1984).

Does Our Culture Socialize Men into Becoming Rapists? Many social critics also assert that our culture socializes men into becoming rapists (Burt, 1980). Males, who are often reinforced for aggressive and competitive behavior, could be said to be asserting culturally expected dominance over women. Sexually coercive college males, as a group, are more likely to believe that aggression is a legitimate form of behavior than are noncoercive college males (Rapaport & Burkhart, 1984).

Are Women Socialized into Becoming Victims? Women, on the other hand, may be socialized into the victim role. The stereotypical feminine role encourages passivity, nurturance, warmth, and cooperation. Women are often taught to sacrifice for their families and not to raise their voices. Thus a woman may be totally unprepared to cope with an assailant. She may lack aggressive skills and believe that violence is inappropriate for women. Mary Beth Myers and her colleagues (1984) found that rape victims are less dominant and self-assertive than nonvictims—that is, their behavior is more consistent with what society expects of women. Victimization is not a random process, and women who appear vulnerable are apparently more likely than others to be attacked (Myers et al., 1985).

Rape Myths Many people, including professionals who work with rapists and victims, believe a number of myths about rape. These include "Only bad girls get raped," "Any healthy woman can resist a rapist if she wants to," and "Women only cry rape when they've been jilted or have something to cover up" (Burt, 1980, p. 217). These myths tend to deny the impact of the assault and also to place blame on the victim rather than on her assailant. They

---

Rape Sexual interaction with a person without that person's consent.

QUESTIONNAIRE

Cultural Myths that Create a Climate that Supports Rape

Martha Burt (1980) has compiled a number of statements concerning rape. Read each statement and indicate whether you believe it to be true or false by circling the T or the F. Then turn to the key in Appendix B to learn of the implications of your answers.

T F 1. A woman who goes to the home or apartment of a man on their first date implies that she is willing to have sex.

T F 2. Any female can get raped.

T F 3. One reason that women falsely report a rape is that they frequently have a need to call attention to themselves.

T F 4. Any healthy woman can successfully resist a rapist if she really wants to.

T F 5. When women go around braless or wearing short skirts and tight tops, they are just asking for trouble.

T F 6. In the majority of rapes, the victim is promiscuous or has a bad reputation.

T F 7. If a girl engages in necking or petting and she lets things get out of hand, it is her own fault if her partner forces sex on her.

T F 8. Women who get raped while hitchhiking get what they deserve.

T F 9. A woman who is stuck-up and thinks she is too good to talk to guys on the street deserves to be taught a lesson.

T F 10. Many women have an unconscious wish to be raped, and may then unconsciously set up a situation in which they are likely to be attacked.

T F 11. If a woman gets drunk at a party and has intercourse with a man she's just met there, she should be considered "fair game" to other males at the party who want to have sex with her too, whether she wants to or not.

T F 12. Many women who report a rape are lying because they are angry and want to get back at the man they accuse.

T F 13. Many, if not most, rapes are merely invented by women who discovered they were pregnant and wanted to protect their reputation.

---

contribute to a social climate that is too often lenient toward rapists and unsympathetic toward victims.

Truth or Fiction Revisited

It is *not* true that a healthy woman can successfully resist a rapist if she really wants to. Feminists argue that myths such as this foster a social climate that supports rape.

You may take the following questionnaire if you want to learn whether you harbor some of the more common myths.

Rape Prevention Given the incidence of rape, it is useful to be aware of things that can be done to prevent rape. *The New Our Bodies, Ourselves,* written by the Boston Women's Health Book Collective (1984), lists numerous suggestions that may be of help: Establish signals and arrangements with other women in an apartment building or neighborhood. List only first initials in the telephone directory or on the mailbox. Use dead-bolt locks. Keep windows locked and obtain iron grids for first-floor windows. Keep entrances and doorways brightly lit. Have keys ready for the front door or the car. Do not walk alone in the dark. Avoid deserted areas. Never allow a strange man into your apartment or home without verifying his credentials. Drive with the car windows up and the door locked. Check the rear seat of the car before entering. Avoid living in an unsafe building. Do not pick up hitchhikers (including women). Do not talk to strange men in the street. Shout "Fire!" not "Rape!" People crowd around fires but avoid scenes of violence.

THE SEXUAL RESPONSE CYCLE

Sexual dysfunctions Problems in becoming sexually aroused or reaching orgasm.

During the 1960s, William Masters and Virginia Johnson became renowned for their research in human sexual response and **sexual dysfunctions.**

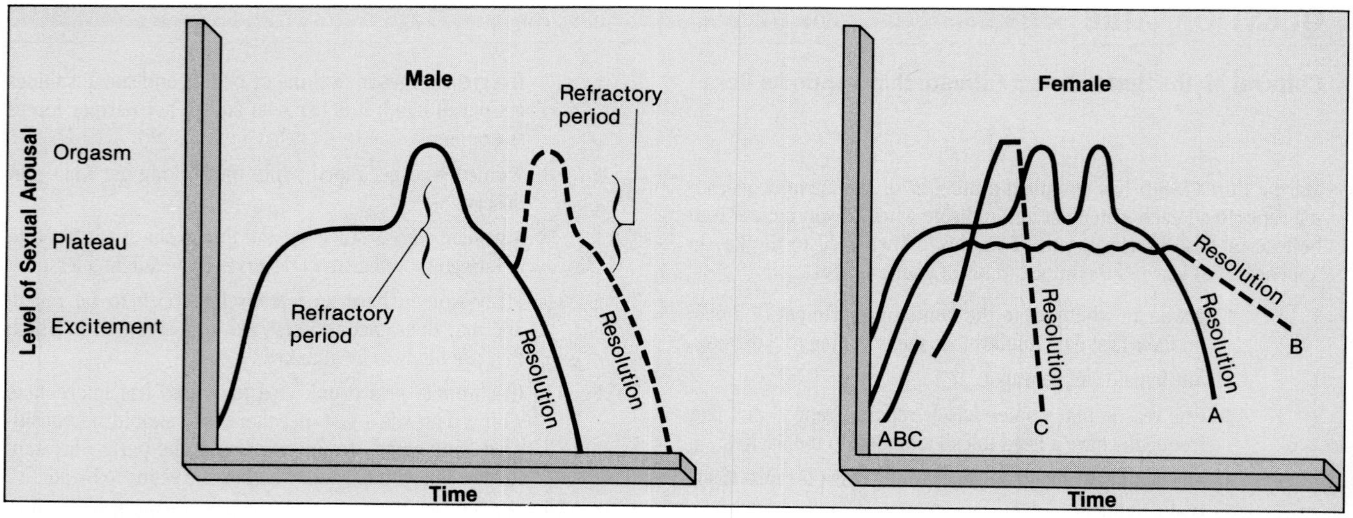

Figure 14.4
The Sexual Response Cycle.

Men and women both undergo four phases of sexual response: excitement, plateau, orgasm, and resolution. For men, a refractory period follows orgasm, during which they usually cannot become aroused to the point where they have further orgasms. However, some men (as shown by the broken line) can have two consecutive ejaculations when they are young. Pattern B with women portrays a plateau phase that is not followed by orgasm, whereas Pattern C portrays the occurrence of orgasm without a preceding plateau phase. Pattern A portrays multiple orgasms. (Source: Masters & Johnson, 1966.)

They disdained the standard questionnaire and interview approaches to sex research. Instead, they arranged for volunteers to engage in sexual activity in the laboratory while their physiological responses were monitored.

Masters and Johnson (1966) found that sexual stimulation leads to many types of responses. Two of them are largely reflexive: **myotonia,** or muscle tension; and **vasocongestion,** or the flow of arterial blood into the genitals and other parts of the body, such as the breasts. These responses, and others, can be described in terms of a **sexual response cycle** that applies to both men and women. The four phases of this cycle are the excitement, plateau, orgasm, and resolution phases (Figure 14.4).

Myotonia Muscle tension.

Vasocongestion Accumulation (congestion) of blood, particularly in the genital region.

Sexual response cycle A four-phase process that describes response to sexual stimulation in males and females.

Excitement phase The first phase of the sexual response cycle, characterized by erection in the man and by vaginal lubrication and clitoral swelling in the woman.

Sex flush A reddish hue on body surfaces that is caused by vasocongestion.

The Excitement Phase

The **excitement phase** is the first phase of physiological response to sexual stimulation. The heart rate, blood pressure, and respiration rate increase. In the male, blood vessels in chambers of loose tissue within the penis dilate reflexively to allow blood to flow in, resulting in erection.

In the female, the breasts swell and the nipples become erect. Blood engorges the genital region and the clitoris expands. The inner part of the vagina lengthens and dilates. Within 10 seconds to half a minute, vaginal lubrication reflexively appears. A **sex flush,** or mottling of the skin, may appear late in this phase.

The Plateau Phase

The **plateau phase** describes a heightening of sexual arousal that prepares the body for orgasm. The heart rate, blood pressure, and respiration rate continue to rise. In the man, further engorgement causes the ridge around the head of the penis to turn deep purple. The testes increase in size and elevate in order to allow a full ejaculation.

In the woman, the outer vagina becomes so engorged that its diameter is reduced about one-third. Engorgement of the area around the clitoris causes the clitoris to "withdraw" beneath a fold of skin called the clitoral hood. Further swelling of the breasts causes the nipples to appear to have become smaller, although they have not. The sex flush becomes pronounced.

The Orgasm Phase

During orgasm, breathing, blood pressure, and heart rate reach a peak, and there are involuntary muscle contractions throughout the body. In the man, muscles at the base of the penis contract and expel semen through the penis. In the woman, muscles surrounding the outer third of the vagina contract rhythmically. Most authorities agree that there is no female ejaculation, just vaginal lubrication.* For both sexes, the initial contractions are most intense and are spaced at about 0.8-second intervals (five contractions every four seconds). Subsequent contractions are weaker and are spaced farther apart.

Following orgasm, men enter a **refractory period** during which they are unresponsive to further sexual stimulation, although some men are capable of reaching orgasm twice before sexual arousal subsides. Women can experience numerous or **multiple orgasms,** as many as 50 in rapid succession. This capacity has given some women the feeling that they ought not be satisfied with only one—the flip side of the old myth that sexual pleasure is meant for men only. In sex, as in other areas of life, our oughts and shoulds often place arbitrary demands on us that evoke anxiety and feelings of inadequacy.

Orgasm is a reflex. We can set the stage for it by receiving adequate sexual stimulation of a physical and cognitive nature (by focusing on the attractiveness of our partner, erotic fantasies, and so forth), but we cannot force or will an orgasm to happen. Efforts to force orgasm can be counterproductive, as we shall see in our discussion of the sexual dysfunctions.

Truth or Fiction Revisited

It is true that orgasm is a reflex.

The Resolution Phase

After an orgasm that is not followed by additional sexual stimulation, a **resolution phase** occurs in which the body gradually returns to its resting state. The heart rate, blood pressure, and respiration rate all return to normal

*See Ladas and her colleagues (1982) for a divergent view.

Plateau phase An advanced state of sexual arousal that precedes orgasm.

Refractory period A period of time following orgasm during which the male is not responsive to further sexual stimulation.

Multiple orgasms The experiencing of additional orgasms because of sexual stimulation during the resolution stage. Two or more orgasms in rapid succession.

Resolution phase The final phase of the sexual response cycle, during which body functions gradually return to their prearoused state.

levels. Blood that has engorged the genitals is dispelled from this region throughout the body.

If a lengthy plateau phase is not followed by orgasm (as in pattern B in Figure 14.4), genital engorgement may take longer to dissipate, leading to pelvic tension or discomfort in both men and women.

SEXUAL DYSFUNCTIONS AND SEX THERAPY

Many of us will be troubled by a sexual dysfunction at some time or other. Masters and Johnson (1970) estimated that at least half the marriages in this nation are sexually dysfunctional. The incidence of sexual dysfunctions may be higher among single people, because singles are less likely to feel secure in their sexual relationships and to be familiar with their partner's sexual needs.

Types of Sexual Dysfunctions

The sexual dysfunctions that we shall discuss are labeled as follows in the DSM–III–R (American Psychiatric Association, 1987): *hypoactive sexual desire disorder, female sexual arousal disorder, male erectile disorder, inhibited orgasm, premature ejaculation, dyspareunia,* and *vaginismus.*

In **hypoactive sexual desire disorder,** the person shows lack of interest in sexual activity and frequently reports an absence of sexual fantasies. The diagnosis exists because of the assumption that sexual fantasies and interests are normal response patterns that may be blocked by anxiety or other factors.

In the female, as noted earlier, sexual arousal is characterized by lubrication of the vaginal walls that makes entry by the penis possible. Sexual arousal in the male is characterized by erection of the penis. Almost all women now and then have difficulty becoming or remaining lubricated. Almost all men have occasional difficulty attaining or maintaining an erection through intercourse. The diagnoses of **female sexual arousal disorder** and **male erectile disorder** are used when these problems are persistent or recurrent.

In **inhibited orgasm,** the man or woman, although sexually excited, is persistently delayed in reaching orgasm or does not reach orgasm at all. Inhibited orgasm is more common among women than men. In some cases, an individual can reach orgasm without difficulty while engaging in sexual relations with one partner but not with another.

In **premature ejaculation,** the male persistently ejaculates with minimal sexual stimulation, too soon to permit his partner or himself to enjoy sexual relations fully.

In **dyspareunia,** sexual intercourse is associated with recurrent pain in the genital region. **Vaginismus** is involuntary spasm of the muscles surrounding the vagina, making sexual intercourse painful or impossible.

Hypoactive sexual desire disorder A sexual dysfunction characterized by lack of interest in sexual activity.

Female sexual arousal disorder A sexual dysfunction characterized by difficulty in becoming sexually aroused, as defined by vaginal lubrication, or in sustaining arousal long enough to engage in satisfying sexual relations.

Male erectile disorder A sexual dysfunction characterized by difficulty in becoming sexually aroused, as defined by achieving erection, or in sustaining arousal long enough to engage in satisfying sexual relations.

Inhibited orgasm A sexual dysfunction in which one has difficulty reaching orgasm, although one has become sexually aroused.

Premature ejaculation Ejaculation that occurs prior to the couple's desires.

Dyspareunia Painful coitus.

Vaginismus Involuntary contraction of the muscles surrounding the vagina, which makes entry difficult or impossible.

Causes of Sexual Dysfunctions

Perhaps 10 to 20 percent of sexual dysfunctions stem from disease. Hypoactive sexual desire, for example, can reflect diabetes and diseases of the heart and lungs. Fatigue can dampen sexual desire and inhibit orgasm. Fatigue-

The Importance of Communication. Sexual relationships are usually no better than other aspects of relationships. Communication problems are linked to sexual as well as general marital dissatisfaction. Sex therapists help couples open lines of communication.

related incidents will be isolated unless we attach too much meaning to them and become overly concerned about future sexual performance. Depressants such as alcohol, narcotics, and tranquilizers can also impair sexual response.

Old-fashioned stereotypes suggest that although men may find sex to be pleasurable, sex is a duty for women. Women who share these sex-negative attitudes may not be fully aware of their sexual potentials. They may also be so anxious about sex that the attitudes become a self-fulfilling prophecy. Men, too, may be handicapped by misinformation and sexual taboos.

Physically or psychologically painful sexual experiences can cause future sexual response to be blocked by anxiety. Rape victims may encounter sexual adjustment problems such as vaginismus or inhibited orgasm. Masters and Johnson (1970) report cases of men with erectile problems who had anxiety-evoking encounters with prostitutes.

As noted earlier, a sexual relationship is usually no better than other aspects of the relationship or marriage (Perlman & Abramson, 1982). Communication problems are linked to general marital dissatisfaction. Couples who have problems expressing their sexual desires are at a disadvantage in teaching their partners how to provide pleasure.

Sexual competencies, like other competencies, are based on knowledge and skill, and competencies are based largely on learning. We learn what makes us and others feel good through trial and error, by talking and reading about sex, and, perhaps, by watching sex films. Many people do not acquire sexual competencies because of lack of knowledge and experimentation—even within marriage.

Albert Ellis (1977) and other cognitive psychologists point out that irrational beliefs and attitudes contribute to sexual dysfunctions. If we believe that we need others' approval at all times, we may catastrophize the importance of one disappointing sexual episode. If we demand that each sexual encounter be perfect, we set ourselves up for inevitable failure.

In most cases of sexual dysfunction, the physical and psychological factors we have outlined lead to yet another psychological factor—**performance anxiety,** or fear of whether we shall be able to perform sexually. People with performance anxiety may focus on recollections of past failures and expectations of another disaster rather than lose themselves in their erotic sensations and fantasies (Barlow, 1986). Performance anxiety can make it difficult for a man to attain erection, yet spur him to ejaculate prematurely. Performance anxiety can also prevent a woman from becoming adequately lubricated or can contribute to vaginismus.

Performance anxiety Fear about whether one will be able to perform adequately.

Truth or Fiction Revisited

It is *not* true that people who love each other automatically enjoy sexual relations. Sexual dysfunctions can occur even when the relationship is loving. Fortunately we now have treatments for sexual dysfunctions, and a good overall relationship between sex partners facilitates therapy.

As we see in the next section, sex therapy fosters sexual competencies by enhancing sexual knowledge and encouraging sexual experimentation under circumstances in which performance anxiety is unlikely to be aroused.

Sex Therapy

When Kinsey was making his surveys of sexual behavior in the 1940s, there was no effective treatment for the sexual dysfunctions. However, various treatments based on the social-learning model, collectively called sex therapy, have been developed during the past few decades. Sex therapists assume that sexual dysfunctions can be treated by directly modifying the problem behavior that occurs in the bedroom. Treatment of most dysfunctions is enhanced by the cooperation of a patient's sex partner, so it may be necessary to work on the couple's relationship before sex therapy is undertaken.

Sex therapy focuses on (1) reducing performance anxiety, (2) changing self-defeating expectations, and (3) fostering sexual skills or competencies. Both sex partners are frequently involved in therapy, although, as we shall see, individual treatment may be preferable in some cases. The sex therapists, often a male and female therapy team, educate the couple and guide them through a series of homework assignments. Masters and Johnson have a standard two-week treatment format that they use with couples who live in residence at their clinic during this period. However, most therapists do not require clients to live at the clinic. And, in many instances, bibliotherapy—or treatment of problems through self-help manuals—has also been of help (e.g., Dodge et al., 1982).

Let us look at a sample of the techniques that have been effective in treating arousal and erectile disorders, premature ejaculation, and inhibited orgasm.

Arousal and Erectile Disorders In sex therapy, women who have trouble becoming lubricated and men with problems in achieving erection learn that they need not "do" anything to become sexually aroused. They need only receive sexual stimulation under relaxed circumstances so that anxiety does not inhibit their natural reflexes.

To reduce performance anxiety, the partners engage in contacts that do not demand lubrication or erection. They may start with so-called sensate focus exercises in which they massage one another without touching the genitals. Each partner learns to "pleasure" the other and to "be pleasured" by receiving and giving verbal instructions and guiding the other's hands. Communication skills as well as sexual skills are thus acquired. After a couple of sessions, sensate focus extends to the genitals. When the person achieves sexual excitement, the couple does not immediately attempt coitus, because this might recreate performance anxiety. Once excitement is attained reliably, the couple engages in a graduated series of sexual activities, culminating in intercourse.

Masters and Johnson (1970) report that this technique resulted in a "reversal" of erectile disorders in men in about 72 percent of the couples they treated. But it should be noted that Masters and Johnson have been criticized for their evaluation of the effectiveness of their treatments. Their shortcomings include (1) failure to operationally define degrees of improvement in clients and (2) inadequate follow-up of treated clients to determine whether treatment "reversals" remain reversed (Adams, 1980; Zilbergeld & Evans, 1980).

Premature Ejaculation Sensate focus exercises are also often used in treatment of premature ejaculation so that couples may learn to give and receive pleasure under relaxed, rather than sexually demanding, circumstances. Then, when the couple is ready to begin sexual interaction, Masters and Johnson (1970) teach them the "squeeze technique," in which the tip of the penis is squeezed when the man feels he is about to ejaculate. This method, which can be learned only through personal instruction by sex therapists, prevents ejaculation. Gradually the man learns to prolong coitus without ejaculating. Masters and Johnson report this technique was successful with 182 of 196 men treated.

In 1956, urologist James Semans suggested a simpler method called the "stop-and-go" technique, in which a man simply suspends sexual stimulation whenever he feels he is about to ejaculate. With this method, too, the man gradually learns to prolong sexual stimulation without ejaculating.

Inhibited Orgasm in the Female Women who have never experienced orgasm often harbor beliefs that sex is dirty and may have been taught never to touch themselves. They are anxious about their sexuality and have not had the chance to learn, through trial and error, what types of sexual stimulation will excite them and bring them to climax.

Masters and Johnson have treated women with inhibited orgasm by working with the couples involved, but other sex therapists suggest that it is preferable to use masturbation (Andersen, 1981; Barbach, 1975; Heiman & LoPiccolo, 1987; McMullen & Rosen, 1979). Masturbation provides women with a chance to learn about their own bodies and to give themselves pleasure without depending on a sex partner. Masturbation programs instruct women about their own sexual anatomy and encourage them to experiment with self-caresses at their own pace. Women gradually learn to bring themselves to orgasm as pleasure helps countercondition sexual anxiety. Once they can masturbate to orgasm, additional treatment can facilitate orgasm with a partner.

When inhibited orgasm reflects a woman's relationship with or feelings about her sex partner, treatment requires dealing with the couple—if the woman chooses to maintain the relationship. Masters and Johnson again begin with sensate focus exercises to decrease performance anxiety, open communication channels, and enhance the couple's sexual skills. During genital massage and then coitus, the woman guides her partner in the caresses and movements that she finds sexually exciting. Psychologically, the woman's taking charge helps free her from traditional stereotypes of the passive female and grants her permission to enjoy sex. Masters and Johnson (1970) report that the dysfunctions of 81 percent of 183 women treated for this problem were reversed.

Sex therapists tend to agree that success rates for treating these problems would be enhanced if everyone they worked with were fully committed to change. This observation applies to every area of life. Aren't we generally more successful at those undertakings to which we are fully committed—whether we're talking about giving up smoking, improving our marriages, or going after a graduate degree?

SUMMARY

1. **What is a sex-role stereotype?** A stereotype is a fixed, conventional idea about a group, and a sex role is a cluster of stereotypes attributed to one of the sexes.

2. **What are the stereotypical masculine and feminine roles in our society?** In our society, the masculine sex-role stereotype includes aggressiveness, independence, logic, and competence in the business world or the realm of objects (instrumentality). The feminine sex-role stereotype includes nurturance, passivity, and dependence (warmth–expressiveness traits).

3. **What cognitive sex differences are there?** Girls generally excel in verbal abilities, whereas males excel in math and spatial-relations abilities.

4. **What sex differences are there in aggression?** Boys are more aggressive than girls under most circumstances. Aggressiveness in girls may be inhibited by lesser physical strength, by anxiety (caused by aggression's inconsistency with the feminine sex-role stereotype), and by empathy with the victim.

5. **What sex differences are there in communication styles?** In group settings, men talk and interrupt more often than women do.

6. **What is psychological androgyny?** Psychological androgyny is the possession of the clusters of traits referred to as instrumentality and warmth-expressiveness.

7. **Does psychological androgyny foster adjustment and personal development?** Apparently so. Psychologically androgynous people show both independence and nurturance, depending on the situation. They have higher self-esteem and greater ability to bounce back from failure.

8. **How do biological sex differences contribute to sex differences in personality and behavior?** Brain lateralization, prenatal hormonal influences, and the timing of pubertal changes may all play roles.

9. **What is the psychoanalytic view of sex typing?** According to psychoanalytic theory, sex typing largely stems from resolution of the conflicts of the phallic stage.

10. **What is the social-learning view of sex typing?** Social-learning theory explains sex typing in terms of observational learning, identification, and socialization.

11. **What is the cognitive-developmental view of sex typing?** Cognitive-developmental theory views sex typing in terms of the emergence of gender identity, gender stability, and gender constancy. It is thought that the development of gender stability fosters the organization of sex-typed behavior.

12. **What is the gender-schema view of sex typing?** Gender-schema theory proposes that children use the gender schema of their society to organize their perceptions and that children attempt to blend their self-concepts with the gender schema.

13. **What are the effects of sex hormones?** Sex hormones promote biological sexual differentiation, regulate the menstrual cycle, and have organizing (directional) and activating (motivational) effects on sexual behavior.

14. **What is homosexuality?** Homosexuality is a sexual orientation in which people are sexually aroused by, and interested in forming romantic relationships with, people of their own sex.

15. **What are the effects of pornography?** Pornography appears to sexually arouse women as well as men, but there is no reliable evidence that pornography contributes to antisocial behavior.

16. **Why do people commit rape?** Rape appears to be motivated more by anger and the desire to exercise power over women than by sexual needs. Social critics argue that our culture socializes men into becoming rapists and women into assuming the role of victim.

17. **What is the sexual-response cycle?** For both sexes, the sexual response cycle consists of four phases: excitement, plateau, orgasm, and resolution.

18. **What are sexual dysfunctions?** Sexual dysfunctions are problems in becoming sexually aroused or reaching orgasm. Dysfunctions include hypoactive sexual desire, female sexual arousal disorder, male erectile disorder, inhibited orgasm, premature ejaculation, dyspareunia, and vaginismus.

19. **What are the causes of sexual dysfunctions?** Sexual dysfunctions now and then reflect physical factors, such as disease, but most reflect psychosocial factors such as traditional sex-negative beliefs, psychosexual trauma, troubled relationships, lack of sexual skills, and irrational beliefs. Any of these may lead to performance anxiety, which compounds sexual problems.

20. **What is sex therapy?** Sex therapy is a group of cognitively and behaviorally oriented techniques that treat sexual dysfunctions by (1) reducing performance anxiety, (2) changing self-defeating expectations, and (3) fostering sexual competencies.

PSYCHOLOGY AND MODERN LIFE

Sexually Transmitted Diseases

Sexually transmitted diseases (STDs) are one of the more pervasive and disturbing aspects of modern life, but, as shown by the remarks of one young woman, it can be clumsy to protect oneself:

> *It's one thing to talk about "being responsible about STD" and a much harder thing to do it at the very moment. It's just plain hard to say to someone I am feeling very erotic with, "Oh, yes, before we go any further, can we have a conversation about STD?" It's hard to imagine murmuring into someone's ear at a time of passion, "Would you mind slipping on this condom or using this cream just in case one of us has STD?" Yet it seems awkward to bring it up beforehand, if it's not yet clear between us that we want to make love with one another (*Our Bodies, Ourselves, *1984, p. 267).*

Although AIDS has deeply embedded itself in our consciousness in the past few years, there are a number of other STDs that are also of concern, or ought to be—including gonorrhea, syphilis, and herpes. In this section we discuss the causes and courses of a number of STDs, and we explore behavior patterns that influence the risk of contracting them. In the case of the AIDS virus, which so far has eluded medical efforts to develop a vaccine or a cure, prevention is the only real weapon we have (Kaplan, 1987; Reinisch, 1988). For that reason, a major focus of this section will be on safe(r) sex—"safe(r)" rather than "safe" because when we engage in sexual activity with another person, there are few guarantees. Let us consider these STDs more closely.

Bacterial Infections Some STDs, including gonorrhea, syphilis, and chlamydia, are caused by bacteria.

Gonorrhea Gonorrhea is the second most common STD in the United States, with 1.8 million new cases per year reported by the Centers for Disease Control (1988). Gonorrhea is caused by the *Neisseria gonorrhoeae* bacterium and generally is spread by vaginal, oral, or anal intercourse.

Symptoms among males include a penile discharge that begins about three to five days after infection. At first the discharge is clear, but within a day it turns yellow to yellow-green, thickens, and becomes puslike. The urethra becomes inflamed, and urination is accompanied by a burning sensation.

One of the tragedies of gonorrhea is that most women do not experience symptoms in the early stages of the disease. For this reason they are likely to go untreated. But when left untreated, gonorrhea spreads through the genital and urinary systems of both sexes, leading to fertility problems and others. Gonorrhea is one cause of pelvic inflammatory disease (PID) in women, which is symptomized by painful, irregular periods; pain in the lower abdomen; headaches; nausea; and fever.

Gonorrhea is diagnosed from samples of discharges and is treated (and almost always cured) by antibiotics such as penicillin. In recent years, strains of gonorrhea have appeared that are resistant to penicillin, but they are usually cured by higher doses of penicillin or by other antibiotics.

Syphilis Syphilis afflicts some 85,000 Americans each year and is caused by the *Treponema pallidum* bacterium. Like gonorrhea, syphilis is transmitted by genital, oral, or anal contact with an infected person.

Syphilis undergoes four stages of development. The first, or primary, stage is characterized by formation of a painless chancre (a hard, round, ulcerlike lesion with raised edges) that appears at the site of infection two to four weeks after contact. The chancre will disappear within a few weeks, but if untreated, syphilis will continue to work under the skin. The secondary stage begins a few weeks to a few months later and is symptomized by a skin rash consisting of painless, reddish raised bumps that darken after a while and burst, oozing a discharge. There can also be sores in the mouth, painful swelling of joints, a sore throat, headaches, and fever, so a sufferer may assume that he or she has "the flu." These symptoms also disappear, and then syphilis enters the latent stage and may lie dormant for from 1 to 40 years. Some people eventually encounter the final, or tertiary, stage of the disease, which can cause large ulcers and damage the cardiovascular and central nervous systems. The painter Paul Gauguin died from tertiary syphilis.

Because the symptoms of the first two stages of syphilis inevitably disappear, victims are tempted to pretend that they are no longer in danger and to avoid seeing the doctor. This is unfortunate, because syphilis can be diagnosed by a simple blood test (called a VDRL) and eradicated by penicillin. If you have had suspicious symptoms and they have disappeared, get a VDRL. Syphilis can be treated at any stage of development.

Truth or Fiction Revisited

It is *not* true that medical treatment is unnecessary if the symptoms of sexually transmitted diseases go away by themselves. Gonorrhea and syphilis, for example, can both continue to harm the body after symptoms have abated.

Chlamydia *Chlamydia* is caused by the *Chlamydia trachomatis* bacterium. The incidence of chlamydial

infections has been mushrooming and in recent years has reached 4 million new infections a year (Leary, 1988). The incidence is especially high among college students.

The symptoms of chlamydia are similar to those of gonorrhea, but most often they are milder. In men there is burning urination and a discharge; the testes may feel heavy and the scrotum sore. In women, chlamydia can cause frequent and painful urination, PID, and disruption of the menstrual cycle. It is treated by antibiotics such as tetracycline and erythromycin. Penicillin usually does not help.

Rarer Bacterial Infections Less common sexually transmitted bacterial infections, such as chancroid, granuloma inguinale, and lymphogranuloma venerium, have also been on the rise in recent years (Leary, 1988). Because they are uncommon, they are less likely to be properly diagnosed. Each is characterized by genital or rectal ulcers or by enlarged lymph nodes in the groin. Each is treated with antibiotics.

Viral Infections Among the STDs transmitted by viruses are genital herpes, AIDS, and genital warts.

Herpes There are several kinds of herpes, and each is caused by a variant of the *Herpes simplex* virus. The most common type is the HSV-1 virus, which is usually limited to nongenital areas and causes "cold sores" or "fever blisters" on the lips or in the mouth. The HSV-2 virus causes genital herpes, or painful blisters and sores on and around the genitals. HSV-1 can also infect the genitals and HSV-2 the mouth—particularly when there is oral–genital contact.

In 1986, the Centers for Disease control reported that about 100 million Americans had been infected by the HSV-1 virus and that nearly 10 million had genital herpes. The HSV-1 virus is easily spread by kissing, drinking from the same cup, sharing towels, and so forth. The HSV-2 virus is usually only spread by sexual intercourse and oral and anal sex, and there are about 500,000 new cases a year (Leary, 1988).

Genital herpes is symptomized by reddish, painful bumps, or papules, in the genital region. These papules then turn into small, painful blisters filled with infectious fluid. The blisters become pus-filled and rupture. A person may also have muscle aches, headaches, swollen lymph nodes, fever, burning urination, and, in the case of women, a vaginal discharge. The blisters crust over and heal in 10 to 16 days, but 30 to 70 percent of victims have recurrent episodes. Genital herpes is most contagious when the individual is showing symptoms, but it can also be transmitted between episodes (Centers for Disease Control, 1985; Mertz et al., 1985).

Women appear to be in greater danger than men from genital herpes. Whereas men usually have only the discomfort to contend with, some infected women develop cervical cancer. Women may also infect babies with genital herpes during childbirth, which can damage or kill them (Sweet, 1985). Babies at risk can be born by Caeserean section.

Genital herpes is diagnosed visually during an eruption of the disorder or by a sample of fluid taken from the base of a sore. At this time there is no cure for herpes, but the drug acyclovir and some newer drugs appear to offer symptom relief. Loose clothing, warm baths, and aspirin may also be helpful.

Acquired Immune Deficiency Syndrome (AIDS) The virus that causes AIDS is transmitted by heterosexual vaginal intercourse, anal intercourse, sharing contaminated hypodermic needles (as when a group of people "shoots up" a drug), transfusions of contaminated blood, and childbirth (Baum & Nesselhof, 1988; Hall, 1988; Peterson & Marin, 1988). As of this writing it has not been demonstrated that the AIDS virus is transmitted by oral–genital sex, because victims who have engaged in oral–genital sex have also engaged in other sexual activities that are known to transmit the AIDS virus. Nor has it yet been shown that the virus can be spread by kissing, but small amounts of the virus have been found in victims' saliva. As of this writing, there is no evidence that using public toilets, holding or hugging an infected person, living in the same house, or going to the same school transmits the virus (Koop, 1988).

The AIDS virus has an affinity for, and kills, white blood cells called T-helper lymphocytes, or T4 lymphocytes, that are found in the immune system. T-helper lymphocytes are the cells that recognize pathogens and "instruct" other white blood cells—called B lymphocytes—to make antibodies. As a result of depletion of T-helper lymphocytes, the body is left vulnerable to various "opportunistic" diseases. These are diseases that do not stand much of a chance of developing in persons whose immune systems are intact (Hall, 1988).

To date the AIDS virus has infected fewer Americans than the gonorrhea and syphilis bacteria and the genital herpes virus. However, the AIDS virus has been of more concern for a number of reasons. One is that despite a handful of people who have survived the illness for five years, AIDS may eventually be fatal to all people who develop full-blown cases. As of today, a minority of infected Americans have developed full-blown cases. The medical community has not reached a consensus of opinion as to what percentage of those infected will ultimately develop AIDS or what the upper boundaries of the incubation period might be. In other words, we don't know how long an infected person can go before developing AIDS. There are estimates of several years.

Infected people who develop AIDS frequently come down with a mononucleosislike illness anywhere from a week to several months after infection. Symptoms include fever, fatigue, and swollen glands. There may also be headaches, nausea, and a rash. These symptoms usu-

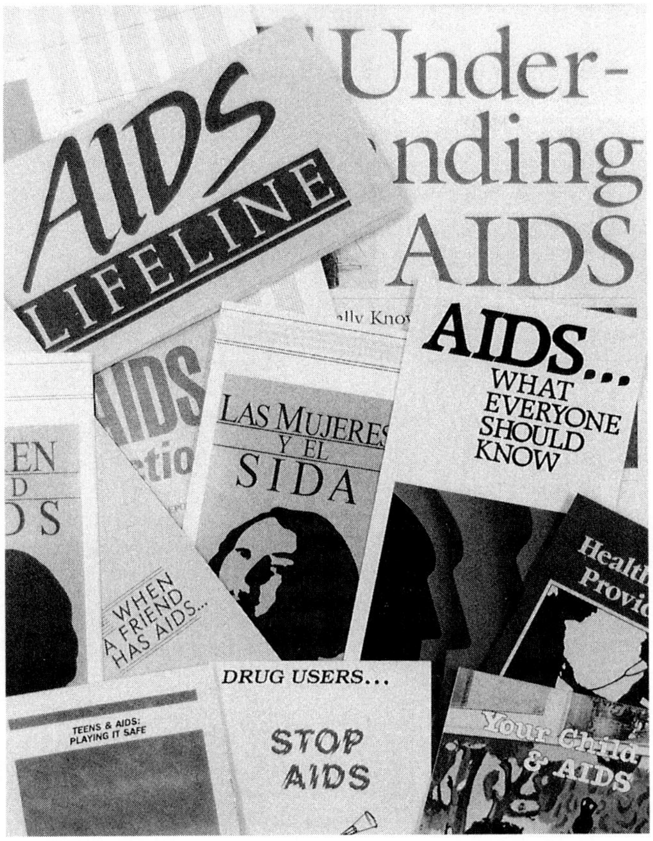

AIDS. **We have been inundated with information on AIDS. Although the prospects of being infected with the AIDS virus are frightening, burying our heads in the sand is no answer. Some behavior patterns are considered to be completely safe, and others are known to be high-risk. We can learn about them and modify our behavior to minimize the likelihood of infection.**

ally disappear within days or weeks. Some weeks or months later, the person may develop AIDS-related complex, or ARC, which is characterized chiefly by swollen lymph glands. Weeks or months afterward, the person may develop the full-blown case, which is characterized by fatigue, fever, weight loss, swollen glands, and diarrhea. Opportunistic infections may now take hold, such as various kinds of cancer (Kaposi's sarcoma, a cancer of the blood cells, has been seen in many gay males who contract AIDS) and a kind of pneumonia (*PCP*) that is characterized by coughing and shortness of breath.

Because AIDS is of such concern, it might be helpful to point out those who are at greatest risk for contracting the disease (Mays & Cochran, 1988; Reinisch et al., 1988; Stall et al., 1988):

1. Gay males. The San Francisco and New York gay communities have been particularly hard hit (Boffey, 1988). The Federal Centers for Disease Control reported in 1988 that about 64 percent of cases of AIDS were among homosexual or bisexual males (*New York Times,* 1988).
2. Intravenous (IV) drug abusers—about 18 percent of cases.
3. Sex partners of IV drug abusers.
4. Babies born to sex partners of IV drug abusers.
5. Prostitutes.
6. Men who visit prostitutes.
7. Sex partners of men who visit infected prostitutes.
8. People receiving transfusions of blood—for example, surgery patients and hemophiliacs. However, this avenue of infection has become increasingly unlikely because of the medical community's awareness that blood supplies may be contaminated.

Although people on this list may be at greatest risk, others cannot assume that they have nothing to worry about (Kaplan, 1987).

Truth or Fiction Revisited

It is *not* true that only homosexuals and substance abusers are at risk for contracting AIDS. We all need to be aware of the risk factors and to take appropriate precautions.

Infection by the AIDS virus is diagnosed by blood tests that show antibodies to the virus or the virus itself. As of this writing, tests that show the presence of the virus itself are under development; existing tests are more likely to reveal the presence of antibodies. It can take several months after infection for antibodies to develop, so repeated tests may be in order. Also, presence of HIV antibodies is not proof that one is infected with the virus itself. Some babies, for example, apparently acquire antibodies from the bloodstreams of infected mothers without being infected by the virus. This may sound confusing, but the bottom line is this: If you have a couple of negative blood tests a few months apart, and you do not engage in high-risk behavior between the tests, you're unlikely to be infected.

Unfortunately, there is not yet a vaccine for the AIDS virus or a cure for AIDS. And as of this writing, the outlook for a breakthrough is not encouraging (Kolata, 1988). A number of antiviral drugs are under investigation, singly and in combination. However, these drugs can have severe side effects and the results are mixed at best. For these reasons, the only logical way to cope with AIDS is *prevention,* as we shall see in the section on safe(r) sex.

Genital Warts Genital, or venereal, warts are caused by a virus and affect 1 million Americans each year (Leary, 1988). On dry-skin areas, warts are hard and yellow-gray; on moist areas, they are soft and pinkish.

Warts can be burned off (by a doctor!), vaporized, frozen, surgically removed, or treated with podophyllin.

Other Sexually Transmitted Diseases There are a number of other STDs that it is useful to know about. We can mention a few of them, but readers are advised to consult health or human sexuality textbooks, their physicians, or their college or university counseling or health centers for more information.

A yeast infection, or *moniliasis,* is caused by a fungus. Symptoms include vaginal irritation and a white, cheesy vaginal discharge. The condition can be cured by vaginal creams or suppositories.

Trichomoniasis, or "trich," is caused by a protozoan (a one-celled animal). Symptoms include irritation of the vulva and a white or yellow vaginal discharge with an unpleasant odor. It is treated with metronidazole (brand name Flagyl) in both sexes.

Pubic lice, or "crabs," are body lice that can be spread by bringing pubic hair into contact or sharing bedding or clothing. Lice cause itching and can be seen with the naked eye. They are killed by gamma benzene hexachloride (brand name Kwell) or A-200 pyrinate.

Now that we have learned some of the things that can happen when we contract STDs, perhaps it will seem that the best way to cope with STDs is not to contract them in the first place (Reinisch, 1988). So let us turn our attention to safe(r) sex in the age of AIDS.

Safe(r) Sex in the Age of AIDS Ways of preventing STDs are not the most pleasant things to talk about. As Helen Singer Kaplan notes in the beginning of her book about AIDS, she is used to telling people, "Enjoy, it's okay to have sexual feelings . . . Sex is a natural function . . . Sex is not dirty or harmful . . . Don't give your kids sexual hangups!" (1987, p. 11).

Sexual feelings are just as normal as they ever were, and sex is still a natural function. Unfortunately, the bacteria, viruses, and other pathogens that give rise to STDs are also natural functions—that is, they occur naturally in our world and their biological effects on us are also natural. Because of these pathogens, sex can be harmful. And although we may not want to give our children, or our readers, "sexual hangups," it is wise to consider a number of precautions that lower the risks.

Here, then, are a few things that can be done.

1. *Refusing to deny the prevalence and harmful nature of STDs.* Many people try to put STDs out of their minds and "wing it" when it comes to sex. So the first and perhaps most important step in protecting oneself against STDs is psychological: keeping them in mind—refusing to play the dangerous game that involves pretending (at least for the moment) that they do not exist.
2. *Being selective.* Engaging in sexual activity only with well-known people who do not belong to the high-risk groups for AIDS.
3. *Inspecting one's partner's genitals.* Visually examining one's partner's genitals for blisters, discharges, chancres, rashes, warts, and lice while engaged in foreplay. An unpleasant odor is a warning sign.
4. *Washing one's own genitals before and after contact.* Washing beforehand helps protect one's partner, and washing promptly afterward with soap and water helps remove some pathogens. Urinating afterward might be of some help, particularly to men, since the acidity of urine can kill some pathogens in the urethra.

5. *Using spermicides.* Spermicides are marketed as birth-control devices, but many creams, foams, and jellies kill pathogens as well as sperm (Centers for Disease Control, 1985a; Lourea et al, 1986). One can check with a pharmacist.
6. *Using condoms.* Latex condoms protect the man from vaginal (or other) body fluids and protect the woman from having infected semen enter the vagina. Condoms are particularly effective in preventing gonorrhea, syphilis, and AIDS (Conant et al., 1986; Heiman & LoPiccolo, 1987; Koop, 1988). Combining condoms with spermicides is even more effective.
7. *Consulting a physician about medication.* It can be helpful to use antibiotics after unprotected sex to guard against certain infections, but medication will not shield one from herpes or AIDS. Also, routine use of antibiotics may do nothing more than make them less effective when they are really needed.
8. *Having regular medical checkups.* These include blood tests. In this way one can learn about and treat disorders whose symptoms have gone unnoticed. But again, this method is to no avail against herpes and AIDS.
9. *When in doubt, stopping.* If one is not sure that sex is safe, one can stop and mull things over or seek expert advice.

By taking reasonable precautions, we can enjoy the natural function of sex, prevent sex from being harmful, and, perhaps, avoid too many "hangups" about STDs.

Outline

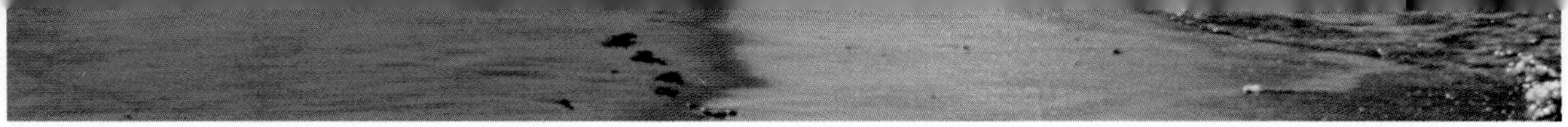

15 Social Psychology

Truth or Fiction?

- □ Airing a television commercial repeatedly hurts sales.
- □ We appreciate things more when we have to work for them.
- □ First impressions have powerful effects on our social relationships.
- □ We take others to task for their misdeeds but tend to see ourselves as victims of circumstances when our conduct falls short of our ideals.
- □ Beauty is in the eye of the beholder.
- □ People are perceived as being more attractive when they are smiling.
- □ Most people would refuse to deliver painful electric shocks to an innocent party, even under strong social pressure.
- □ Many people are late to social gatherings because they are conforming to a social norm.
- □ Group decisions tend to represent conservative compromises of the opinions of the group members.
- □ Nearly 40 people stood by and did nothing while a woman was being stabbed to death.

Candy and Stretch. A new technique for controlling weight gains? No, these are the names Bach and Deutsch (1970) give two people who have just met at a camera club that doubles as a meeting place for singles.

Candy and Stretch stand above the crowd—literally. Candy, an attractive woman in her early 30s, is almost 6 feet tall. Stretch is more plain-looking, but wholesome, in his late 30s, and 6 feet 5 inches.

Stretch has been in the group for some time. Candy is a new member. Let's listen in on them as they make conversation during a coffee break. As you will see, there are some differences between what they say and what they are thinking:

	They Say	They Think
Stretch:	Well, you're certainly a welcome addition to our group.	(Can't I ever say something clever?)
Candy:	Thank you. It certainly is friendly and interesting.	(He's cute.)
Stretch:	My friends call me Stretch. It's left over from my basketball days. Silly, but I'm used to it.	(It's safer than saying my name is David Stein.)
Candy:	My name is Candy.	(At least my nickname is. He doesn't have to hear Hortense O'Brien.)
Stretch:	What kind of camera is that?	(Why couldn't a girl named Candy be Jewish? It's only a nickname, isn't it?)
Candy:	Just this old German one of my uncle's. I borrowed it from the office.	(He could be Irish. And that camera looks expensive.)
Stretch:	May I? (He takes her camera, brushing her hand and then tingling with the touch.) Fine lens. You work for your uncle?	(Now I've done it. Brought up work.)
Candy:	Ever since college. It's more than being just a secretary. I get into sales, too.	(So okay, what if I only went for a year. If he asks what I sell, I'll tell him anything except underwear.)
Stretch:	Sales? That's funny. I'm in sales, too, but mainly as an executive. I run our department. I started using cameras on trips. Last time I was in the Bahamas. I took—	(Is there a nice way to say used cars? I'd better change the subject.) (Great legs! And the way her hips move—)
Candy:	Oh! Do you go to the Bahamas, too? I love those islands.	(So I went just once, and it was for the brassiere manufacturers' convention. At least we're off the subject of jobs.)
Stretch:		(She's probably been around. Well, at least we're off the subject of jobs.)
	I did a little underwater work there last summer. Fantastic colors. So rich in life.	(And lonelier than hell.)
Candy:		(Look at that build. He must swim like a fish. I should learn.)
	I wish I'd had time when I was there. I love the water.	(Well, I do. At the beach, anyway, where I can wade in and not go too deep.)

And so begins a relationship. Candy and Stretch have a drink and talk, sharing their likes and dislikes. Amazingly, they seem to agree on everything—from cars to clothing to politics. The attraction is very strong, and neither is willing to risk turning the other off by disagreeing.

They spend the weekend together and feel that they have fallen in love. They still agree on everything they discuss, but they scrupulously avoid one topic: religion. Their religious differences became apparent when they exchanged last names. But that doesn't mean they have to talk about it.

They also put off introducing each other to their parents. The O'Briens and the Steins are narrow-minded about religion. If the truth be known, so are Candy and Stretch. They narrow their relationships to avoid tension with one another, and as the romance develops, they feel progressively isolated from family and friends.

What happens in this tangled web of deception? Candy becomes pregnant. After some deliberation, and not without misgivings, the couple decides to get married. Do they live happily ever after? We cannot say—"ever after" hasn't arrived yet.

We do not have all the answers, but we have some questions. Candy and Stretch's relationship began with a powerful attraction. What is *attraction?* How do we determine who is attractive? Candy and Stretch pretended to share each other's attitudes? What are *attitudes?* Also, why were they so reluctant to disagree?

Candy and Stretch were both a bit prejudiced about religion. What is *prejudice?* Why didn't they introduce each other to their parents? Did they fear that their parents would want them to *conform* to their own standards? Would their parents try to *persuade* them to limit dating to people of their own religions? Would they *obey?*

Attraction, attitudes, prejudice, conformity, persuasion, obedience—these topics are the province of the branch of psychology called **social psychology.** Social psychologists study the nature and causes of our thoughts, feelings, and behaviors in social situations (Baron & Byrne, 1987). The social psychological topics we discuss in this chapter include attitudes, social perception, attraction, social influence, and group behavior.

ATTITUDES

Psychologists are a rather independent bunch, so it is not surprising to find different definitions of **attitudes.** Some view attitudes primarily as enduring cognitive evaluations (e.g., Petty & Cacioppo, 1986). Others consider attitudes to be feelings that have an evaluative, cognitive component. But most social psychologists today adhere to the **ABC model of attitudes,** which views attitudes in terms of affect (feelings), behavior, and cognitions (Breckler, 1984). They see attitudes as enduring systems of beliefs, feelings, and behavioral tendencies toward people, groups, religion and religious groups, politics, and so on.

The A–B Problem

Our definition of attitude implies that our behavior is consistent with our beliefs and our feelings. When we are free to do as we wish, it often is. But, as indicated by the term **A–B problem,** the link between attitudes (A) and behavior (B) tends to be weak. In their review of the literature, Ajzen and Fishbein (1977) found that global attitudes toward groups of people, politics, and religion (such as whether one is prejudiced toward blacks or whether one is a Republican or a Christian) do not predict specific behavior patterns very well. For example, knowing that James is a Republican does not guarantee that he will vote invariably for Republicans, or even that he will bother to vote.

A number of factors influence the likelihood that we can predict behavior from attitudes:

1. *Specificity.* We can better predict specific behavior from specific attitudes than from global attitudes (Baron & Byrne, 1987). We can better predict church attendance by knowing people's attitudes toward the importance of regular church attendance than by knowing, more globally, whether they are Christian.
2. *Strength of attitudes.* Strong attitudes are more likely to determine behavior than weak attitudes (Fazio et al., 1982). A person who believes

Social psychology The field of psychology that studies the nature and causes of individual thoughts, feelings, and overt behavior in social situations.

Attitude An enduring system of beliefs, feelings, and behavioral tendencies concerning people, objects, or ideas.

ABC model of attitudes The view that attitudes are composed of affect (feelings), behavioral tendencies, and cognitions.

A–B problem The issue of how well we can predict behavior on the basis of attitudes.

Can We Predict How These People Will Vote? Can we predict behavior, such as voting behavior, from knowledge of people's attitudes? Actually, as indicated by the term *A–B problem,* the link between attitudes (A) and behavior (B) tends to be weak.

that the nation's destiny depends on Republicans taking control of Congress is more likely to vote than a person who leans toward Republicanism but does not believe that the outcome of elections makes much difference.

3. *Vested interest.* People are more likely to act on their attitudes when they have a vested interest in the outcome (Sivacek & Crano, 1982). People are more likely to vote for (or against) unionization of their workplace, for example, when they believe that their job security depends on the outcome.
4. *Accessibility.* People are more likely to express their attitudes when they are accessible—that is, when they are brought to mind (Fazio, 1986; Fazio et al., 1986). This is why politicians attempt to "get out the vote" by means of media blitzes just prior to an election. It does politicians little good to have supporters who forget them on election day. Attitudes that have strong emotional impact are more accessible (Wu & Shaffer, 1987), which is one reason that politicians strive to get their adherents "worked up" over the issues they wish to promote.

Candy and Stretch avoided discussing matters on which they differed. One motive might have been to avoid heightening the *accessibility* of their clashing attitudes. By keeping them under the table, perhaps Candy and Stretch would be less likely to act on them and go their separate ways.

Origins of Attitudes

You were not born a Republican or a Democrat. You were not born a Catholic or a Jew—although your parents may have practiced one of these religions when you came along. Political, religious, and other attitudes are learned.

Conditioning Conditioning may play a role in the acquisition of attitudes. Laboratory experiments have shown that attitudes toward national groups can be influenced simply by associating them with positive words (such as *gift* or *happy*) or negative words (such as *ugly* and *failure*) (Lohr & Staats, 1973). Parents often reward children for saying and doing things that are consistent with their own attitudes. Children may be given approval for wearing Daddy's "No nukes" button or carrying Mommy's "My body is my own" placard. Experiments have shown that people who are rewarded consistently for favorable descriptions of even nonexistent groups will later express more positive attitudes toward these groups (Kerpelman & Himmelfarb, 1971). How much more positive would they be if the groups did indeed exist?

Observational Learning Attitudes formed through direct experience may be stronger and easier to recall (Fazio & Cooper, 1983), but we also acquire attitudes from friends and the mass media. The approval or disapproval of peers molds adolescents to prefer short or long hair, blue jeans or preppy sweaters. Television shows us that body odor, bad breath, and the frizzies are dreaded diseases—and, perhaps, that people who use harsh toilet paper are somehow un-American.

Cognitive Appraisal Yet all is not so mechanical. Now and then we also evaluate information and attitudes on the basis of evidence. We may revise stereotypes on the basis of new information (Weber & Crocker, 1983). We are especially likely to scrutinize our attitudes when we know that we shall have to justify them to people who may dissent (Tetlock, 1983).

Still, initial attitudes tend to serve as cognitive anchors. They help mold the ways in which we perceive the world and interpret events. Thus attitudes we encounter later are often judged in terms of how much they "deviate" from the initial set. Accepting larger deviations appears to require greater adjustments in information processing (Quattrone, 1982). For this reason, perhaps, great deviations are apt to be resisted. Yet attitudes can be changed by persuasion, as we shall see in the following section.

Changing Attitudes through Persuasion

Richard Petty and John Cacioppo (1986) have devised the **elaboration likelihood model** for understanding the processes by which people examine the information in persuasive messages. According to this view, there are at least two routes to persuading others to change attitudes—that is, two ways of responding to, or elaborating, persuasive messages. The first, or central route, views elaboration and possible attitudinal change as resulting from conscientious consideration of arguments and evidence. The second, or peripheral route, involves elaboration of the objects of attitudes by associating them with positive or negative cues. Cues include rewards (such as a smile or a hug) and punishments (such as parental disapproval) and factors such as the trustworthiness and attractiveness of the communicator.

Advertisements, which are a form of persuasive communication, also rely on central and peripheral routes. Some ads focus on the quality of the product (central route), whereas others attempt to associate the product with appealing images (peripheral route) (Fox, 1984). Ads for Total cereal, which highlight its nutritional benefits, provide information about the quality of the product (Snyder & DeBono, 1985). So too do the "Pepsi challenge" taste-test ads, which claim that Pepsi tastes better than Coca-Cola. The Marlboro cigarette ads, in contrast, focus on the masculine, rugged image of the "Marlboro man"* and offer no information about the product itself (Snyder & DeBono, 1985).

Elaboration likelihood model The view that persuasive messages are evaluated (elaborated) on the basis of central and peripheral cues.

*The actor in the original TV commercials died from lung cancer in 1987.

The success of most persuasive communications often relies on a combination of central and peripheral cues, such as speech content and voice quality (O'Sullivan et al., 1985). In this section we shall examine one central factor in persuasion—the nature of the message itself—and three peripheral factors: (1) the person delivering the message, (2) the context in which the message is delivered, and (3) the audience. We shall also examine two methods of persuasion used frequently, for example, by persons seeking charitable contributions and by salespersons: the foot-in-the-door technique and low-balling.

The Persuasive Message: Say What? Say How? Say How Often? How do we respond when TV commercials are repeated until we have memorized every dimple on the actors' faces? Research suggests that familiarity breeds content, not contempt.

You might not be crazy about *zabulons* and *afworbus* at first, but Zajonc (1968) found that people began to react favorably toward these bogus Turkish words on the basis of repeated exposure. Political candidates who become well known to the public through regular TV commercials attain more votes (Grush, 1980). People respond more favorably to abstract art (Heingartner & Hall, 1974), classical music (Smith & Dorfman, 1975), and photographs of blacks (Hamm et al., 1975) and of college students (Moreland & Zajonc, 1982) on the basis of repetition. Love for classical art and music may begin through exposure in the nursery, not the college appreciation course.

Truth or Fiction Revisited

It is *not* true that airing a commercial repeatedly hurts sales. Repeated exposure frequently leads to liking and acceptance.

The more complex the stimuli, the more likely it is that frequent exposure will have favorable effects (Saegert & Jellison, 1970; Smith & Dorfman, 1975). The 100th playing of a Bach concerto may be less tiresome than the 100th performance of a pop tune.

Two-sided arguments, in which the communicator recounts the arguments of the opposition in order to refute them, can be especially effective when the audience is at first uncertain about its position (Hass & Linder, 1972). Theologians and politicians sometimes expose their followers to the arguments of the opposition. By refuting them one by one, they impart to their followers a kind of psychological immunity to them. Swinyard found that two-sided product claims, in which advertisers admitted their product's weak points in addition to highlighting its strengths, were most believable (in Bridgwater, 1982).

It would be nice to think that people are too sophisticated to be persuaded by an **emotional appeal.** However, grisly films of operations on cancerous lungs are more effective than matter-of-fact presentations for changing attitudes toward smoking (Leventhal et al., 1972). Films of bloodied gums and decayed teeth are also more effective than logical discussions for boosting toothbrushing (Dembroski et al., 1978). Fear appeals are most effective when they are strong, when the audience believes the dire consequences, and when the recommendations seem sensible (Mewborn & Rogers, 1979). Induced feelings of guilt as well as fear promote persuasion (Regan et al., 1972; Wallington, 1973).

Audiences also tend to believe arguments that appear to run counter to the vested interests of the communicator (Wood & Eagly, 1981). People may pay more attention to a whaling-fleet owner's claim than to a conservationist's that whales are becoming extinct. If the president of Chrysler or General Motors conceded that Toyotas and Hondas were superior, you can bet that we would prick up our ears.

Emotional appeal A type of persuasive communication that influences behavior on the basis of feelings that are aroused instead of rational analysis of the issues.

Can You Take Beauty to the Bank? Advertisers use both central and peripheral cues to hawk their wares. What factors contribute to the persuasiveness of messages? To the persuasiveness of communicators?

The Persuasive Communicator: Whom Do You Trust? Would you buy a used car from a person convicted of larceny? Would you attend weight-control classes run by a 350-pound leader? Would you leaf through fashion magazines featuring homely models? Probably not. Research shows that persuasive communicators show expertise (Hennigan et al., 1982), trustworthiness, attractiveness, or similarity to their audiences (Baron & Byrne, 1987).

Television news anchorpersons enjoy high prestige. One study (Mullen et al., 1987) found that before the 1984 presidential election, Peter Jennings of ABC News had shown significantly more favorable facial expressions when reporting on Ronald Reagan than on Walter Mondale. Tom Brokaw of NBC and Dan Rather of CBS had not shown favoritism. The researchers also found that viewers of ABC News voted for Reagan in greater proportions than viewers of NBC or CBS News. It is tempting to conclude that viewers were subtly persuaded by Jennings to vote for Reagan—and maybe this happened in a number of cases. But Sweeney and Gruber (1985) have shown that viewers do not simply absorb, spongelike, whatever the tube feeds them. Instead, they show **selective avoidance** and **selective exposure.** They tend to switch channels when they are faced with news coverage that counters their own attitudes. They also seek communicators whose outlooks coincide with their own. And so, Jennings may have swayed his audience's attitudes toward Reagan, but it may also be that Reaganites favored Jennings over Brokaw and Rather.

The Context of the Message: "Get 'Em in a Good Mood" You are too shrewd to let someone persuade you by buttering you up, but perhaps someone you know would be influenced by a sip of wine, a bite of cheese, and a sincere compliment. Seduction attempts usually come at the tail end of a date—after the Szechuan tidbits, the nouveau Fresno film, the disco party, and the wine that was sold at its time. An assault at the outset of a date would be viewed as . . . well, an assault. Experiments suggest that food and pleasant music boost acceptance of persuasive messages (Galizio & Hendrick, 1972; Janis et al., 1965).

It is also counterproductive to call your dates fools when they differ with you—even though their ideas are bound to be foolish if they do not concur

Selective avoidance Diverting one's attention from information that is inconsistent with one's attitudes.

Selective exposure Deliberately seeking and attending to information that is consistent with one's attitudes.

with yours. Agreement and praise are more effective at encouraging others to embrace your views (Baron, 1971; Byrne, 1971). Appear sincere, or else your compliments will look manipulative. (It seems unsporting to hand out this information.)

The Persuaded Audience: Are You a Person Who Can't Say No? Why do some people have "sales resistance," whereas others enrich the lives of every door-to-door salesperson? It may be that people with high self-esteem and low social anxiety are more likely to resist social pressure (Santee & Maslach, 1982). However, Baumeister and Covington (1985) challenge the view that persons with low self-esteem are more open to persuasion. Persons with high self-esteem may also be persuaded, but they may be less willing to confess that others have influenced them. Knowledge of the areas that a communicator is addressing also tends to lessen persuadability (Wood, 1982).

A study by Schwartz and Gottman (1976) reveals the cognitive nature of the social anxiety that can make it hard for some of us to refuse requests. Schwartz and Gottman found that people who comply with unreasonable requests are more apt to report thinking, "I was worried about what the other person would think of me if I refused," "It is better to help others than to be self-centered," or "The other person might be hurt or insulted if I refused." People who did not comply reported thoughts such as, "It doesn't matter what the other person thinks of me," "I am perfectly free to say no," or "This request is an unreasonable one" (p. 916).

The Foot-in-the-Door Technique You might suppose that contributing money to door-to-door solicitors for charity will get you off the hook. That is, they'll take the cash and leave you alone for a while. Actually, the opposite is true: The next time they mount a campaign, they may call on generous you to go door to door! Organizations compile lists of persons they can rely on. Giving an inch apparently encourages others to go for a yard. They have gotten their "foot in the door."

Consider a classic experiment on the **foot-in-the-door technique** by Freedman and Fraser (1966). Groups of women received phone calls from a consumer group requesting that they let a six-man crew drop by their homes to catalog the products they used. It could take hours to conclude the job. Only 22 percent of one group acceded to this irksome entreaty. But 53 percent of another group of women assented to a visit from this wrecking crew. Why was the second group more compliant? The pliant group had been phoned a few days earlier and had agreed to answer a few questions about the soap products they used. They had been primed for the second request. The caller had gotten a "foot in the door." The foot-in-the-door technique has also been shown to be effective in persuading people to make charitable contributions (Pliner et al., 1974) and to sign petitions (Baron, 1973).

The results of a study by Snyder and Cunningham (1975) suggest that people who have acceded to a small request become more likely to consent to a larger one because they come to see themselves as the "type of person" who helps others in this fashion. Regardless of how the foot-in-the-door technique works, if you want to say no, it may be easier to do so (and stick to your guns) the first time a request is made instead of later.

Low-Balling Have you ever had a salesperson promise you a low price for merchandise, committed yourself to buy at that price, and then had the salesperson tell you that he or she had been in error or that the supervisor had not agreed to the price? Have you then cancelled the order or stuck to your commitment?

Foot-in-the-door technique A method for inducing compliance in which a small request is followed by a larger request.

You might have been a victim of **low-balling,** also called "throwing the low ball." In this method, you are persuaded to make a commitment on favorable terms, and the persuader then claims that he or she must revise the terms. Perhaps the car you agreed to buy for $11,400 did not have both the automatic transmission and air conditioning you thought it had. Perhaps the yen or the mark had just gone up against the dollar, and the price of the car had to be raised accordingly.

Low-balling places us in cognitive conflict: we have one cognition to the effect that we have made a commitment and another cognition to the effect that the terms have been altered (or perhaps that we are being "suckered"). Let us examine the role of cognitive conflict further by considering balance theory and cognitive-dissonance theory.

Balance Theory

According to **balance theory,** we are motivated to maintain harmony among our perceptions, beliefs, and attitudes (Heider, 1958). When people we like share our attitudes, there is balance and all is well. It works the other way as well: If we like Peter Jennings and he expresses an attitude, our own cognitions will remain in balance if we agree with him. For this reason, we are likely to develop favorable attitudes toward unfamiliar objects that Jennings seems to endorse. If we dislike other people, we might not care very much about their attitudes. They may disagree with us, but this state of **nonbalance** leaves us indifferent (Newcomb, 1981).

But when someone we care about expresses a discrepant attitude, we are likely to be concerned. The relationship will survive if we like chocolate and our friend prefers vanilla, but what if the discrepancy concerns an important attitude about religion, politics, or raising children? Now a state of **imbalance** exists. What if Peter Jennings, whom we like, reports favorably on an object we dislike? Now there is an uncomfortable state of imbalance. Candy was Catholic and Stretch Jewish. Each was painfully aware of the imbalance in religious choice. How did they handle the imbalance? At first they misperceived the other's religion. Later they tried to sweep it under the rug.

Cognitive-Dissonance Theory

According to cognitive-dissonance theory, which was originated by Leon Festinger (Festinger, 1957; Festinger & Carlsmith, 1959), people dislike inconsistency. As with balance theory, we do not like to think that our attitudes (cognitions) are inconsistent. Nor do we like to think that our attitudes are incompatible with our behavior. Awareness that two cognitions are dissonant, or that our cognitions and our behavior are contradictory, is sufficient to motivate us to reduce the discrepancy. Cognitive dissonance is an unpleasant state (Fazio & Cooper, 1983) that is accompanied by heightened arousal (Croyle & Cooper, 1983). Thus, one motive for eliminating cognitive dissonance may be to reduce our arousal to a more optimal level.

In the first and one of the best-known studies on cognitive dissonance, one group of subjects received $1.00 for telling someone else that a just-completed boring task was very interesting (Festinger & Carlsmith, 1959). A second group of subjects received $20.00 to describe the chore positively. Both groups were paid to engage in **attitude-discrepant behavior**—that is, behavior that ran counter to their actual thoughts and feelings. After "selling" the job to others, the subjects were asked to rate their own liking for

---

Low-balling A method in which extremely attractive terms are offered to induce a person to make a commitment. Once the commitment is made, the terms are revised.

Balance theory The view that people have a need to organize their perceptions, opinions, and beliefs in a harmonious manner.

Nonbalance In balance theory, a condition in which persons whom we dislike do not agree with us.

Imbalance In balance theory, a condition in which persons whom we like disagree with us.

Attitude-discrepant behavior Behavior that runs counter to one's thoughts and feelings.

PSYCHOLOGY GOES TO WORK

Social Psychology and Advertising

Advertising professionals, in running their ad campaigns, make liberal use of the findings of social psychologists. For example, advertisers know that an emotional appeal stimulates behavior and jogs the memory. Could this be the reason for toothpaste commercials that combine fear and humor in order to encourage children to fight the "cavity creeps"? And how about those commercials that remind us that we have only two days before that incredible sale comes to an end?

Health professionals enjoy high status in our society and are deemed experts. It is not surprising that toothpaste ads boast that their products have the approval of the American Dental Association or that a specific pain killer is the brand "doctors recommend most."

Even though we are reared not to judge books by their covers, we are more likely to find attractive people persuasive. Corporations do not gamble millions on the physically unappealing to hawk their products. Some advertisers seek out a blend of attractiveness and plain, simple folksiness with which the audience can identify. Ivory Soap commercials sport "real" people with appealing features who are so freshly scrubbed that you may think you can smell Ivory Soap emanating from the TV set.

And why do advertisers urge their clients to spend millions to recruit "America's favorite TV Daddy," Bill Cosby, to sell Jello, or Michael Jackson or Lionel Ritchie to extol the virtues of Pepsi? Balance theory suggests why advertisers seek Cosby and Jackson. If we have positive feelings about Bill Cosby and Michael Jackson, and if they then express positive feelings about Jello and Pepsi, perhaps our own attitudes toward Jello and Pepsi will grow more positive. Perhaps we'll even spend our hard-earned cash on them.

it. Ironically, the group paid *less* rated the task as significantly more interesting. *Why?*

From a learning-theory point of view, this result would be confusing. After all, shouldn't we learn to like that which is highly rewarding? But cognitive-dissonance theory would predict this "less-leads-to-more effect" for the following reason: The cognitions "I was paid very little" and "I told someone that this assignment was interesting" are dissonant. You see, another concept in cognitive-dissonance theory is **effort justification.** Subjects in studies such as this one are helped to justify their behavior by concluding that their attitudes may not have been as discrepant with their behavior as they had originally believed.

Truth or Fiction Revisited

It is true that we tend to appreciate things more when we have to work for them. This is another example of the principle of effort justification.

Consider another situation. Cognitive dissonance would be created if we were to believe that our preferred candidate was unlikely to win the American presidential election. One cognition would be that our candidate is better for the country or, at an extreme, would "save" the country from harmful forces. A second and dissonant cognition would be that our candidate does not have a chance to win. Research shows that in the presidential elections from 1952 to 1980, people by a four-to-one margin helped reduce such dissonance by expressing the belief that their candidate would win (Granberg & Brent, 1983). They frequently held these beliefs despite lopsided polls to the contrary. Among highly involved but poorly informed people, the margin of self-deception was still higher.

Concerning Candy and Stretch, cognitive-dissonance theory may predict that their discovery that they held different religious views could have *strengthened* rather than destroyed their relationship. Why? After discovering the other's religion, each might have thought, "Stretch (Candy) must be *very* important to me if I can feel this way about him (her), knowing that he (she) is Jewish (Catholic)."

Let us consider the case of Patty Hearst to see how cognitive-dissonance theory may account for attitudinal changes.

Effort justification The tendency to seek justification (reasons) for strenuous efforts.

A CLOSER LOOK

Effects of Attitude-Discrepant Behavior. Patty Hearst as the "urban guerrilla" Tania (top), and on her way to testify in court (bottom). After her abduction by extremists, Patty was forced into attitude-discrepant revolutionary behavior. Engaging in antisocial acts such as armed robbery appears to have converted her self-identity from that of a typical (though wealthy) college student to that of a revolutionary. After her capture, her identity appeared to revert back to that of Patty. Patty's experience raises a challenging question: How can any of us know where the influences of others end and our "real selves," or true identities, begin?

The Strange Case of Patty Hearst

The kidnapping of newspaper heiress Patty Hearst provides a case study in how attitude-discrepant behavior can influence our thoughts and feelings. The Patty Hearst case also raises a question about how we can tell where our "real selves" or identities leave off and the influences of others begin.

In February 1974, newspaper heiress Patty Hearst, an undergraduate student at Berkeley, was abducted by a revolutionary group known as the Symbionese Liberation Army (SLA). Early messages from the SLA directed the Hearst family to distribute millions of dollars' worth of food to the poor if they wished their daughter to live. There was no suggestion that Patty was a willing prisoner.

But a couple of months later, SLA communiqués contained statements by Patty that she had willingly joined the group. Patty declared her revolutionary name to be Tania and sent a photograph in which she wore a guerrilla outfit and held a machine gun. She expressed contempt for her parents' capitalist values and called them pigs. However, her family did not believe that Patty's attitudes had really changed. They had reared her for 20 years. She had been with the SLA for only two months. Surely her statements were designed to earn good treatment from her captors.

In April, Patty and other SLA members robbed a San Francisco bank. Patty was videotaped brandishing a rifle. She was reported to have threatened a guard. But, the Hearsts maintained, the rifle could have been unloaded. Patty might still have been acting out of fear of losing her life. Then Patty became involved in another incident. She acted as a cover for SLA members William and Emily Harris, firing an automatic rifle as they fled from a store they had robbed. Patty seemed to be unsupervised at the time.

Patty and the Harrises were captured in San Francisco late in 1975. At first Patty was defiant. She gave a revolutionary salute and identified herself as Tania. But once she was in prison, her identity appeared to undergo another transformation. She asked to be called Patty. At her trial she seemed quite remorseful. The defense argued that had it not been for the social influence of the SLA, Patty would never have engaged in criminal behavior or adopted revolutionary values. When President Jimmy Carter commuted Patty's sentence in 1979, releasing her from prison, he was operating under an admission from Patty's prosecutors that they, too, believed that Patty would not have behaved criminally without having been abducted by the SLA and experiencing dread in the days that followed.

How is it that a college undergraduate with typical American values came to express attitudes that were opposed to her lifelong ideals?

It may be that such conversions in identity can be explained through cognitive-dissonance theory. After Patty's kidnapping, she was exposed to fear and fatigue and forced into attitude-discrepant behavior. She had to express agreement with SLA values, engage in sexual activity with SLA members, and train for revolutionary activity. As Patty described it many years later, "They raped me mentally, physically and emotionally" (Hearst, 1988). As long as she clung firmly to her self-identity as Patty, these repugnant acts created great cognitive dissonance. But by adopting the suggested revolutionary identity of Tania, Patty could look upon herself as "liberated" rather than as a frightened captive or criminal. In this way her cognitive dissonance would be reduced, and her behavior would no longer be so stressful. Supportive research shows that we do draw conclusions about our attitudes from our decisions to engage in particular behavior (Fazio et al., 1982; Nisbett & Ross, 1980).

So, cognitive-dissonance theory leads to the hypothesis that we can change people's attitudes by somehow getting them to behave in a manner consistent with the attitudes we wish to promote. Research shows that people may indeed change attitudes when attitude-discrepant behavior is rewarded (Calder et al., 1973; Cooper, 1980). It is at once a frightening and promising concept. For instance, it sounds like a prescription for totalitarianism. Yet it also suggests that prejudiced individuals who are prevented from discriminating—who are compelled, for example, by open-housing laws to allow people from different ethnic backgrounds to buy homes in their neighborhoods—may actually become less prejudiced.

In the following section we discuss the troubling topic of prejudice.

Prejudice

Iowa schoolteacher Jane Elliot taught her all-white class of third graders some of the effects of prejudice. She separated the class into blue-eyed and brown-eyed children. The brown-eyed children were labeled inferior, made to wear collars that marked their group, and denied classroom privileges. After a few days of discrimination, the brown-eyed children lost self-esteem and earned poorer grades. They cried often and expressed the wish to stay at home. Then the pattern was reversed. Blue-eyed children were assigned the inferior status. After a few days they, too, learned how upsetting it is to be victims of discrimination.

Prejudice is an attitude toward a group that leads people to evaluate members of that group negatively. On a cognitive level, prejudice is linked to expectations that the target group will behave poorly, say, in the workplace, or by engaging in criminal behavior. On an affective level, prejudice is associated with negative feelings such as dislike or hatred. Behaviorally, prejudice is associated with avoidance, aggression, and as we shall see, discrimination. There is an interaction among our cognitions, emotional responses, and behavior patterns. In one experiment, for example, white people given the opportunity to act aggressively toward other people showed apparent broad-mindedness by acting less aggressively toward blacks than toward other whites—when the subjects were in a nonangered condition. But white subjects in an angered condition acted more aggressively toward blacks than toward whites. Heightened arousal and feelings of anger might have aroused persistent, underlying prejudices against blacks (Rogers & Prentice-Dunn, 1981).

Discrimination One form of negative behavior that results from prejudice is called **discrimination.** Many groups have been discriminated against in the United States—Jews, Catholics, blacks, Native Americans, Hispanic Americans, Asian Americans, homosexuals, and women, to name a few. Discrimination takes many forms, including denial of access to jobs, housing, and the voting booth. Many people have forgotten that black men gained the right to vote decades before women did.

Stereotypes Are Jews shrewd and ambitious? Are blacks superstitious and musical? Are men macho? If you believe such ideas, you are falling for a **stereotype**—a prejudice about a group that can lead you to interpret observations in a biased fashion. For example, sex-role stereotypes persist in American society. As a result, men are generally perceived as being assertive, dominant, aggressive, and independent, whereas women are generally per-

Prejudice The belief that a person or group, on the basis of assumed racial, ethnic, sexual, or other features, will possess negative characteristics or perform inadequately.

Discrimination The denial of privileges to a person or group because of prejudice.

Stereotype A fixed, conventional idea about a group.

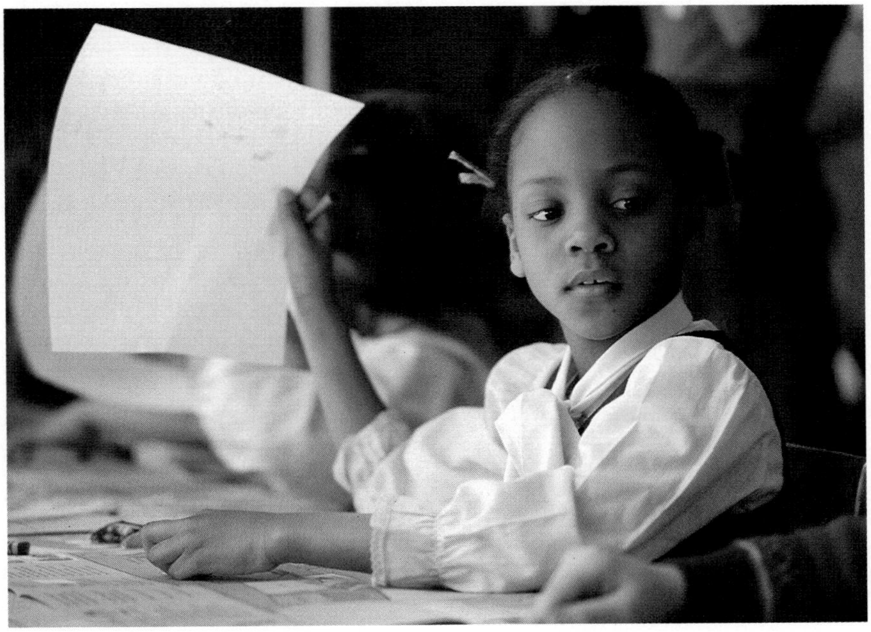

Stereotyping. How well is this child performing on her test? An experiment by Darley and Gross showed that our expectations concerning a child's performance on a test are linked to our awareness of that child's socioeconomic background.

ceived as being gentle, compassionate, sensitive, and nurturant (Martin, 1987). These stereotypes at once tend to pressure men into socially combative roles and to limit women to supportive, dependent roles.

One experiment showed how social-class stereotypes can help advantaged children but influence teachers and other people to underrate the abilities of disadvantaged children. Subjects watched videotapes of a girl taking an academic test. One group of subjects was told that she came from a high socioeconomic background, and as a consequence, they rated her performance as superior. Other subjects were told that she came from a low socioeconomic background. They watched the same videotape but rated her performance as below grade level (Darley & Gross, 1983).

In studies of stereotypes (Sagar & Schofield, 1980; Smedley & Bayton, 1978), whites viewed middle-class blacks as ambitious, intelligent, conscientious, and responsible but saw *lower-class* blacks as ignorant, rude, dangerous, and self-pitying. Blacks shared whites' negative impressions of lower-class individuals of the other race. But blacks also negatively evaluated *middle-class* whites as biased, sly, and deceitful, even though they also considered middle-class whites to be conscientious and ambitious.

Sources of Prejudice The sources of prejudice are many and varied. Let us briefly consider several possible contributors:

1. *Assumptions of dissimilarity.* As we shall see later in the chapter, we are apt to be attracted to and like people who share our attitudes. In forming impressions of others, we are influenced by attitudinal similarity and dissimilarity as well as by race (Goldstein & Davis, 1972; Rokeach et al., 1960). People of different religions and races often have different backgrounds and values, giving rise to dissimilar attitudes.
2. *Social conflict.* There is also a lengthy history of social and economic conflict between people of different races and religions. Conflict and competition lead to negative attitudes (Sherif, 1966).
3. *Authoritarianism.* Based on psychoanalytic theory and their interpretation of the **Holocaust,** some social scientists (e.g., Adorno et al., 1950)

Holocaust The name given the Nazi murder of millions of Jews during World War II.

have argued that racial and religious minorities serve as **scapegoats** for majority groups. The Germans, for instance, submitted to Nazi **authoritarianism** because they had been raised to submit to authority figures. They then displaced unconscious hostility toward their fathers onto Jews. These Freudian concepts have been criticized by many psychologists, but authoritarian people do appear to harbor more prejudices than nonauthoritarians (e.g., Stephan & Rosenfield, 1978).

4. *Social learning.* As noted, children tend to acquire some attitudes from others, especially parents, through identification and socialization. Children often broadly imitate their parents, and parents often reinforce their children for doing so. In this way, prejudices are likely to be transferred from generation to generation.

5. *Information processing.* As attitudes, prejudices act as cognitive filters through which we perceive the social world. Prejudices influence the processing of social information. In other words, when we observe the behavior of group members against whom we are prejudiced, we tend to pay special attention to, and to remember, instances of behavior that are consistent with our prejudices (Bodenhausen & Wyer, 1985; Dovidio et al., 1986; Fiske & Taylor, 1984). If you believe that Jews are stingy, you might be more likely to recall a Jew's negotiation of a price than a Jew's charitable donation. If you believe that Californians are "airheads," you might be more likely to recall TV images of surfing than of scientific conferences at Caltech and Berkeley.

   People also tend to divide the social world into two categories: "us" and "them." People usually view those who belong to their own groups—the "ingroup"—more favorably than those who do not—the "outgroup" (Hemstone & Jaspars, 1982; Wilder & Thompson, 1980). Moreover, there is a tendency for us to assume that outgroup members are more alike, or homogeneous, in their attitudes and behaviors than members of our own groups (Judd & Park, 1988; Park & Rothbart, 1982). Our relative isolation from outgroups does not encourage us to break down our stereotypes.

Let us now turn our attention to some of the factors involved in the formation of our impressions of other people.

SOCIAL PERCEPTION

Getting to know you,
Getting to know all about you . . .

So goes the song from *The King and I.* How do we get to know other people, get to know all about them? In this section we shall explore some factors that contribute to **social perception:** primacy and recency effects, attribution theory, and body language. Then we shall survey the determinants of interpersonal attraction.

Primacy and Recency Effects: The Importance of First Impressions

Why do you wear your best outfit to a job interview? Why do defense attorneys dress their clients neatly and cut their hair before they are seen by the jury? Because first impressions are important.

Scapegoat A person or group on whom the blame for the mistakes or crimes of others is cast.

Authoritarianism Belief in the importance of unquestioning obedience to authority.

Social perception A subfield of social psychology that studies the ways in which we form and modify impressions of others.

When I was a teenager, a young man was accepted or rejected by his date's parents the first time they were introduced. If he was considerate and made small talk, her parents would allow the couple to stay out past curfew, even to watch submarine races at the beach during the early morning hours. If he was boorish or uncommunicative, he was a cad forever. Her parents would object to him, no matter how hard he worked to gain their favor later on.

First impressions often make or break us. This is the **primacy effect.** As noted in Chapter 10, we infer traits from behavior. If we act considerately at first, we are labeled considerate. The trait of consideration is used to explain and predict our future behavior. If after being labeled considerate, one keeps a date out past curfew, this lapse is likely to be seen as an exception to a rule—as excused by circumstances or external causes. But if at first one is seen as inconsiderate, several months of considerate behavior may be perceived as a cynical effort to "make up for it."

In a classic experiment on the primacy effect, Luchins (1957) had subjects read different stories about "Jim." The stories consisted of one or two paragraphs. One-paragraph stories portrayed Jim as friendly or unfriendly. These paragraphs were also used in the two-paragraph stories but were presented to different subjects in opposite order. Of subjects reading only the "friendly" paragraph, 95 percent rated Jim as friendly. Of those who read just the "unfriendly" paragraph, 3 percent rated him as friendly. Seventy-eight percent of those who read two-paragraph stories in the "friendly-unfriendly" order labeled Jim as friendly. But when they read the paragraphs in the reverse order, only 18 percent rated Jim as friendly.

Truth or Fiction Revisited

It is true that first impressions have powerful effects on our social relationships.

How can we encourage people to pay more attention to more recent impressions? Luchins accomplished this by allowing time to elapse between presenting the paragraphs. In this way, fading memories allowed more recent information to take precedence. This is the **recency effect.** Luchins found a second way to counter first impressions: He simply counseled subjects to avoid snap judgments and to weigh all the evidence.

Attribution Theory

At the age of 3, one of my daughters believed that a friend's son was a boy because he *wanted* to be a boy. Since she was 3 at the time, this error in my daughter's **attribution** for the boy's gender is charming and understandable. But we as adults tend to make somewhat similar attribution errors. No, we do not believe that people's preferences have much to do with their gender, but as we shall see, we may tend to exaggerate the role of conscious choice in other aspects of their behavior.

An assumption about why people do things is called an attribution for behavior. Our inference of the motives and traits of others through the observation of their behavior is called the **attribution process.** We now focus on attribution theory, or the processes by which people draw conclusions about the factors that influence one another's behavior.

Attribution theory is very important, because our attributions lead us to perceive others either as purposeful actors or as victims of circumstances.

Primacy effect The tendency to evaluate others in terms of first impressions.

Recency effect The tendency to evaluate others in terms of the most recent impression.

Attribution A belief concerning why people behave in a certain way.

Attribution process The process by which people draw inferences about the motives and traits of others.

Dispositional and Situational Attributions Social psychologists describe two types of attributions—dispositional attributions and situational attributions. In making **dispositional attributions,** we ascribe a person's behavior to internal factors, such as personality traits and free will. In making **situational attributions,** we attribute a person's actions to external factors, such as social influence or socialization.

Knowledge of the attribution process helps us understand additional events surrounding the Patty Hearst case. For example, when Patty was sent to prison, her sentence was harsh because the court believed that she had willfully chosen to break the law. The court, that is, had ascribed Patty's behavior to dispositional factors—to her personality and to choice. When President Carter commuted Patty Hearst's sentence, he was acting on the belief that Patty had been a victim of circumstances. Carter ascribed Patty's behavior largely to external, situational factors.

Perhaps the most fascinating aspect of the Patty Hearst case concerns Patty's attributions for her own behavior. In the early stages of her kidnapping, she was coerced into attitude-discrepant behavior and no doubt attributed her participation to external, situational factors. But persistent coercion somehow led her to modify her self-identity so that she became "radicalized." At that point, she apparently ascribed her behavior to internal, dispositional factors and might have wondered how she had been duped by American society for all the years prior to her "awakening."

The Fundamental Attribution Error We have a tendency to attribute too much of other people's behavior to internal factors such as choice. This bias in the attribution process is what social psychologists refer to as the **fundamental attribution error.** Apparently, when we observe the behavior of others, we focus excessively on their actions and too little on the contexts within which their actions take place. But we do tend to be more aware of the networks of forces acting on ourselves.

The Actor-Observer Effect When we see ourselves and others engaging in behavior that we do not like, we tend to see the others as willful actors but to perceive ourselves as victims of circumstances. The tendency to attribute the behavior of others to internal, dispositional factors and our own behavior to external, situational influences is called the **actor-observer effect** (Jellison & Green, 1981; Jones, 1979; Reeder, 1982; Safer, 1980).

Let us consider an example of the actor-observer effect. When parents and children argue about the children's choice of friends or dates, the parents infer traits from behavior and tend to perceive their children as stubborn, difficult, and independent. But the children also infer traits from behavior and may perceive their parents as bossy and controlling. Parents and children alike attribute the others' behavior to internal causes. That is, they make dispositional attributions about the behavior of others.

How do the parents and children perceive themselves? The parents probably see themselves as being forced into combat by their children's foolishness. If they become insistent, it is in response to their children's stubbornness. The children probably see themselves as responding to peer pressures and, perhaps, to sexual urges that may have come from within but do not seem "of their own making."

Truth or Fiction Revisited

It is true that we tend to hold others responsible for their misdeeds but to see ourselves as victims of circumstances when our conduct falls short of our ideals. This bias in the attribution process is referred to as the actor-observer effect.

Dispositional attribution An assumption that a person's behavior is determined by internal causes, such as personal attitudes or goals.

Situational attribution An assumption that a person's behavior is determined by external circumstances, such as the social pressure found in a situation.

Fundamental attribution error The tendency to assume that others act predominantly on the basis of their dispositions, even when there is evidence suggesting the importance of their situations.

Actor-observer effect The tendency to attribute our own behavior to situational factors but to attribute the behavior of others to dispositional factors.

Table 15.1
Factors Leading to Internal or External Attributions of Behavior

	Internal Attribution	External Attribution
Consensus	Low: Few people behave this way.	High: Most people behave this way.
Consistency	High: The person behaves this way frequently.	High: The person behaves this way frequently.
Distinctiveness	Low: The person behaves this way in many situations.	High: The person behaves this way in few situations.

We are more likely to attribute behavior to internal, dispositional factors when it is low in consensus, high in consistency, and low in distinctiveness. In the example given in the text, we will be most likely to attribute a complaint about one's food to external factors if other people also complain (high consensus) and if the complainer usually does not (high distinctiveness).

The Self-Serving Bias There is also a **self-serving bias** in the attribution process. We are likely to ascribe our successes to internal, dispositional factors but our failures to external, situational influences (Baumgardner et al., 1986; O'Malley & Becker, 1984; Van der Plight & Eiser, 1983). When we have done well on a test or impressed a date, we are likely to credit these outcomes to our intelligence and charm. But when we fail, we are likely to ascribe them to bad luck, an unfairly demanding test, or our date's bad mood.

It seems that we extend the self-serving bias to others in our perceptions of why we win or lose when we gamble. A study by Gilovich (1983) found that when we win bets on football games, we tend to attribute our success to the greater ability of the winning team (a dispositional factor). But when we lose our bets, we tend to ascribe the game's outcome to a fluke, such as an error by a referee—that is, to some unforeseeable external factor.

An ironic twist to the self-serving bias is that we tend to see ourselves as less self-centered than others (Rempel et al., 1985).

Factors Contributing to the Attribution Process: Consensus, Consistency, and Distinctiveness According to Harold Kelley (1979; Kelley & Michela, 1980), our attribution of behavior to internal or external causes can be influenced by three factors: *consensus, consistency,* and *distinctiveness.* When few people act in a certain way—that is, when **consensus** is low—we are likely to attribute behavior to dispositional (internal) factors. Consistency refers to the degree to which the same person acts in the same way on other occasions. Highly consistent behavior can be attributed either to dispositional or situational factors. Distinctiveness is the extent to which the person responds differently in different situations. If the person acts similarly in different situations, distinctiveness is low, and we are likely to attribute his or her behavior to dispositional factors.

Let us apply the criteria of consensus, consistency, and distinctiveness to a hypothetical situation adapted from Baron and Byrne (1987) involving a friend in a restaurant. She takes one bite of her blueberry cheese taco and calls loudly for the waiter. She argues that her food is inedible and demands that it be replaced. The question is whether she complained as a result of internal causes (e.g., because she is difficult to please) or external causes (i.e., because the food really is bad). Under the following circumstances, we are likely to attribute her behavior to internal, dispositional causes: (1) No one else at the table is complaining, so consensus is low. (2) She has returned food on other occasions, so consistency is high. (3) She complains in other restaurants also, so distinctiveness is low (see Table 15.1).

But under the following circumstances, however, we are likely to attribute her behavior to external, situational causes: (1) Everyone else at the table

Self-serving bias The tendency to view one's successes as stemming from internal factors and one's failures as stemming from external factors.

Consensus General agreement.

Body Language. By observing people's body language, we can frequently tell whether or not they like or dislike one another. What about this couple? What aspects of their nonverbal behavior provide cues about their attitudes and feelings?

is also complaining, so consensus is high. (2) She has returned food on other occasions, so consistency is high. (3) She usually does not complain at restaurants, so distinctiveness is high. Given these conditions, we are likely to believe that the blueberry cheese taco really is awful and our friend is justifiedly responding to the circumstances.

Body Language

Body language is an important factor in our perception of others. At an early age we learn that the ways people carry themselves provide cues to how they feel and are likely to behave. You may have noticed that when people are "uptight," their bodies may also be rigid and straight-backed. People who are relaxed are more likely, literally, to "hang loose." It seems that various combinations of eye contact, posture, and distance between people provide broadly recognized cues to their moods and feelings toward their companions (Schwartz et al., 1983).

When people face us and lean toward us, we may assume that they like us or are interested in what we are saying. If we are privy to a conversation between a couple and observe that the woman is leaning toward the man but that the man is sitting back and toying with his hair, we are likely to infer that he is not having any of what she is selling (Clore et al., 1975; DePaulo et al., 1978).

Touching also communicates. Women are more likely than men to touch other people when they are interacting with them (Stier & Hall, 1984). In one touching experiment, Kleinke (1977) showed that appeals for help can be more effective when the distressed person engages in physical contact with people being asked for aid. A woman received more dimes for phone calls when she touched the person she was asking for money on the arm. In another experiment, waitresses received higher tips when they touched patrons on the hand or the shoulder while making change (Crusco & Wetzel, 1984).

Body language can also be used to establish and maintain territorial control (Brown & Altman, 1981), as anyone who has had to step aside because a football player was walking down the hall can testify. Werner and her colleagues (1981) found that players in a game arcade used touching as a way of signaling others to keep their distance. Solo players engaged in more touching than did groups, perhaps because they were surrounded by strangers.

Gazing and Staring: The Eyes Have It We usually feel that we can learn much from eye contact. When others "look us squarely in the eye," we may assume that they are being assertive or open with us. Avoidance of eye contact may suggest deception or depression (Knapp, 1978; Siegman & Feldstein, 1977). In a study designed to validate a scale to measure romantic love, Rubin (1970) found that couples who attained higher "love scores" also spent more time gazing into each other's eyes.

Gazes are different, of course, from persistent hard stares. Hard stares are interpreted as provocations or signs of anger (Ellsworth & Langer, 1976). Adolescent males sometimes engage in staring contests as an assertion of dominance. The male who looks away first loses.

In a series of field experiments, Phoebe Ellsworth and her colleagues (1972) subjected drivers stopped at red lights to hard stares from riders of motor scooters (see Figure 15.1). Recipients of the stares crossed the intersection more rapidly than nonrecipients when the light changed. Greenbaum and Rosenfeld (1978) found that recipients of hard stares from a man seated

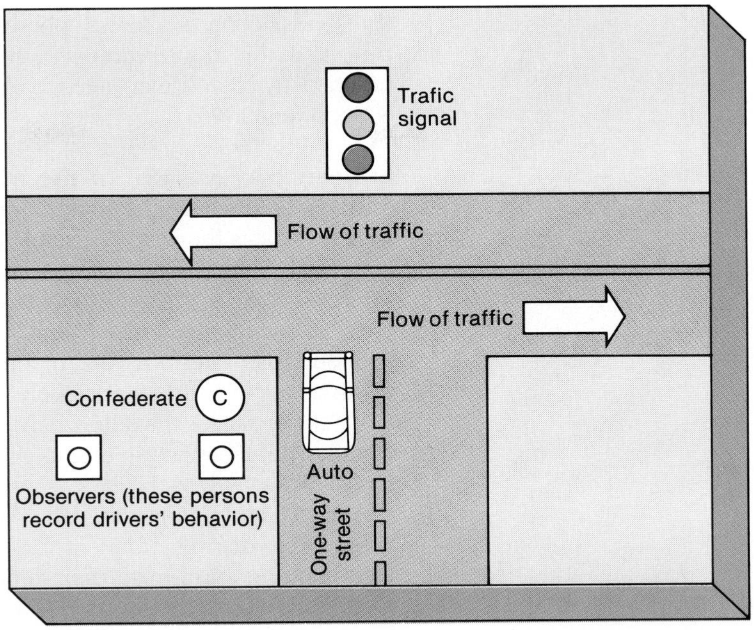

Figure 15.1
Diagram of an Experiment in Hard Staring and Avoidance. In the Greenbaum and Rosenfeld study, the confederate of the experimenter stared at some drivers and not at others. Those stared at drove across the intersection more rapidly once the light turned green. Why?

near an intersection also drove off more rapidly after the light turned green. Other research shows that recipients of hard stares show higher levels of physiological arousal than people who do not receive the stares (Strom & Buck, 1979). Did you ever leave a situation in which you were stared at in order to lower feelings of arousal and avoid the threat of danger?

"Looking Good." How important is physical attractiveness? What are our stereotypes of attractive people? Do we see them as being more successful? As making better spouses and parents?

Attraction In social psychology, an attitude of liking or disliking (negative attraction).

INTERPERSONAL ATTRACTION

Whether we are discussing the science of physics, a pair of magnetic toy dogs, or a couple in a singles bar, **attraction** is a force that draws bodies together. In psychology and sociology, attraction is also thought of as a force that draws bodies, or people, together—an attitude of liking or disliking (Berscheid, 1976). Magnetic "kissing" dogs are usually constructed so that the heads attract one another, but (unlike their flesh-and-blood counterparts) a head and tail repel one another. We shall see that when there is a matching of the heads—that is, a meeting of the minds—people are also attracted to one another. And, as with the toy dogs, when we believe that another person's opinions are, well, asinine, we are repelled.

Many factors contribute to interpersonal attraction: physical attractiveness, attitudinal similarity, complementarity, reciprocity, propinquity, parental opposition, our general feelings in another person's presence, and whether he or she seems "hard to get."

Physical Attractiveness: How Important Is Looking Good?

You might like to think that we are all so intelligent and sophisticated that we rank physical appearance low on the roster of qualities we seek in a date—below sensitivity and warmth, for example. But in experimental "Coke dates" and computer dates, physical appearance has been found to be the central factor in attraction and consideration of partners for future dates, sexual activity, and marriage (Byrne et al., 1970; Green et al., 1984; Hatfield & Sprecher, 1986).

Is Beauty in the Eye of the Beholder? What determines physical attractiveness? Are our standards subjective—that is, "in the eye of the beholder"—or is there widespread agreement on what is appealing?

It may be that there are no universal standards for beauty (Ford & Beach, 1951), but there are some collective standards for physical attractiveness in our society. Tallness is an asset for men in our culture, although college women favor dates who are medium in height (Graziano et al., 1978). Tall women are beheld less positively. Undergraduate women prefer their dates to be about six inches taller than they are, whereas undergraduate men, on the average, fancy women who are about 4½ inches shorter (Gillis & Avis, 1980).

Stretch and Candy were tall. Since we tend to connect tallness with social dominance, many women of Candy's height may be concerned that their stature will compromise their femininity. Some fear that shorter men are disinclined to ask them out. A few walk with a slight hunch, trying to downplay their height.

Plumpness is valued in many cultures. Grandmothers who worry that their granddaughters are starving themselves often come from cultures in which stoutness is an acceptable or desirable feature.* In current Western society, both sexes find slenderness engaging (Lerner & Gellert, 1969). Women generally favor men with a V-taper, whose backs and shoulders are medium wide but whose waists, buttocks, and legs taper from medium thin to thin (Lavrakas, 1975; Horvath, 1981).

Truth or Fiction Revisited

It is *not* true that beauty is in the eye of the beholder, despite the familiarity of the adage. There are actually cultural standards for beauty that are adhered to rather strongly.

Both sexes perceive overweight people as unappealing (Harris et al., 1982), but there are fascinating sex differences in perceptions of the most desirable body shape. Male college undergraduates as a group believe that their current physique is similar to the ideal male physique and to the build women find most appealing (Fallon & Rozin, 1985). Women undergraduates, in contrast, generally see themselves as being notably heavier than the figure that is most attractive to males, and heavier still than the ideal female figure (see Figure 15.2). Both mothers and fathers of college students see themselves as being heavier than their ideal weights (Rozin & Fallon, 1988). However, both sexes err in their estimates of the other's preferences. Men of both generations actually prefer women to be heavier than women presume—somewhere between the girth of the average woman and what the woman thinks is most pleasing. And women of both generations fancy men who are somewhat slimmer than the men assume.

A flat-chested look was a hallmark of the enchanting profile of the 1920s "flapper" era, but substantial busts are considered to be more attractive today. Men desire women with larger-than-average breasts, medium-length legs, and small to medium buttocks (Wiggins et al., 1968). Yet social psychologists have found that we tend to attribute certain personality traits to large-busted

*But, as we saw in the discussion of anorexia nervosa in Chapter 12, some granddaughters *are* literally starving themselves today.

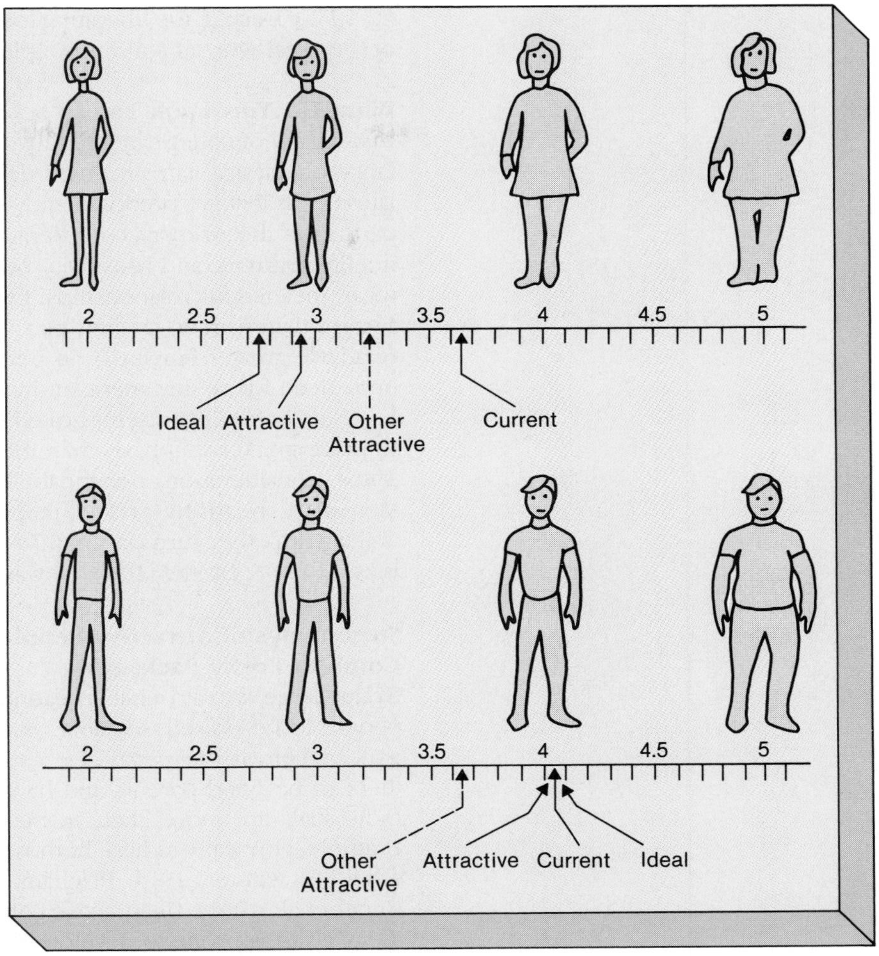

Figure 15.2
Can You Ever Be Too Thin? Research suggests that most college women believe that they are heavier than they ought to be. However, men actually prefer women to be a bit heavier than women assume the men would like them to be.

women. They are perceived as less intelligent, competent, moral, and modest than women with smaller breasts (Kleinke & Staneski, 1980). This is clearly a case in which people overattribute a feature to dispositional factors!

How Behavior Patterns Influence Perceptions of Physical Attractiveness Men and women are both perceived as being more attractive when they are posing happy faces than sad faces (Mueser et al., 1984). Thus there is ample reason to, as the song goes, "put on a happy face" when you are meeting people or looking for a date.

Truth or Fiction Revisited

It is true that people are perceived as being more attractive when they are smiling.

Other aspects of behavior also play a role in impressions of physical attractiveness. Women viewing videotapes of prospective dates preferred men who acted outgoing and self-expressive (Riggio & Wolf, 1984). College men who showed dominance (defined in this experiment as control over a social interaction with a professor) in a videotape were rated as more attractive by female viewers than men who did not (Sadalla et al., 1987). But college men viewing videotapes responded negatively to women who showed self-assertion and social dominance (Riggio & Wolf, 1984; Sadalla et al., 1987). Despite the liberating forces of recent years, the cultural stereotype of the ideal woman still finds a place for demureness.

What Do You Look For in a Long-Term, Meaningful Relationship? In a survey of college men and women, Nevid (1984) found that the importance of physical attractiveness depends on the type of relationship. In relationships that are predominantly sexual, the physical attractiveness of one's partner is the primary consideration. Psychological traits such as honesty, fidelity, warmth, and sensitivity become relatively more important in long-term, meaningful relationships. Overall, however, men are relatively more swayed than women by their partners' physical characteristics. Women place relatively greater emphasis on personal qualities such as warmth, assertiveness, need for achievement, and wit.

Nevid's findings are replicated in studies on mate selection. Women tend to place greater emphasis than men on characteristics such as professional status, consideration, dependability, kindness, and fondness for children. Men place relatively greater emphasis on physical attractiveness, cooking ability (can't they turn on the microwave oven themselves?), and even thriftiness (Buss & Barnes, 1986; Howard et al., 1987).

Stereotypes of Attractive People: Do Good Things Come in Pretty Packages?
By and large, we rate what is beautiful as good. We expect physically attractive people to be poised, sociable, popular, mentally healthy, and fulfilled. We expect them to be persuasive and hold prestigious jobs. We even expect them to be good parents and have stable marriages. Physically unattractive individuals are more likely to be rated as outside of the mainstream—for example, politically radical, homosexual, or psychologically disordered (Berscheid & Walster, 1974; Brigham, 1980; Dion et al., 1972; O'Grady, 1982; Unger et al., 1982). Unattractive college students are even more likely to rate themselves as prone to developing problems and psychological disorders.

These stereotypes seem to have some basis in reality. For one thing, it seems that more attractive individuals are less likely to develop psychological disorders and that the disorders of unattractive individuals are more severe (e.g., Archer & Cash, 1985; Farina et al., 1986; Burns & Farina, 1987). For another, physical attractiveness is positively correlated with educational achievement, occupational prestige, and higher income (Umberson & Hughes, 1984).

One way to interpret the data on the correlates of physical attractiveness is to assume that these links are all innate. In other words, we can believe that beauty and competence genetically go hand in hand. We can believe that biology is destiny and throw up our hands in despair. But a more useful way to interpret these data is to assume that we can do things to make ourselves more attractive and also more successful and fulfilled. Recall that smiling is linked to attractiveness. So is having a decent physique or figure (which is something we can work on) and attending to good grooming and the ways in which we dress. So don't give up the ship.

Then, too, us mere mortals may feel better by noting that attractive people are seen as more vain and self-centered and more likely to have extramarital affairs (Dermer & Thiel, 1975). Yet even these negative assumptions have a positive side. After all, don't they mean that we think attractive people have more to be self-centered about and that their affairs reflect their greater sexual opportunities?

Attractive people are also more likely to be found innocent of crimes in mock jury experiments and observational studies (Michelini & Snodgrass, 1980). When found guilty, they are handed down less severe sentences (Efran, 1974; Stewart, 1980). Perhaps we assume that more attractive people are less likely to need to resort to deviant behavior to achieve their goals. Even when they have erred, perhaps they will have more opportunity for personal growth and be more likely to change their evil ways.

The beautiful are also perceived as more talented. In one experiment, students rated essays as being higher in quality when their authorship was attributed to a more attractive woman (Landy & Sigall, 1974).

Attractive children learn early of the high expectations of others. Even during the first year of life, adults tend to rate physically attractive babies as good, smart, likeable, and unlikely to cause their parents problems (Stephan & Langlois, 1984). Parents, teachers, and other children expect attractive children to do well in school and to be popular, well behaved, and talented. Because our self-esteem reflects the admiration of others, it is not surprising that the physically attractive have higher self-esteem (Maruyama & Miller, 1975).

The Matching Hypothesis: Who Is "Right" for You? Have you ever refrained from asking out an extremely attractive person for fear of rejection? Do you feel more comfortable when you approach someone who is a bit less attractive?

If so, you're not alone. Although we may rate highly attractive people as being most desirable, we will not necessarily be left to blend in with the wallpaper. According to the **matching hypothesis,** we tend to ask out people who are similar to ourselves in physical attractiveness rather than the local Tom Selleck or Kim Basinger look-alike (Berscheid et al., 1971).

The major motive for asking out "matches" seems to be fear of rejection by more attractive people. Shanteau and Nagy (1979) asked female undergraduates to choose between two possible male dates on the basis of physical attractiveness (as suggested by a photograph) and the probability that the man would accept the date request (as suggested by statements attached to the photographs varying from "Sure thing" to "No chance"). Women preferred not to pursue men who were either very unattractive or very unlikely to accept the date. Moderately attractive men who were "highly likely" to accept the date were chosen most often. In a second phase of the experiment, women were asked to choose a date on the basis of the photograph alone. Again, most women chose moderately attractive men, suggesting that they *assumed* that the more attractive a man was, the less likely he would be to accept the date.

People also tend to select mates more or less equal in attractiveness to themselves (Murstein, 1972; Murstein & Christy, 1976). Yet we tend to rate our mates as slightly more attractive than ourselves—as if we had somehow "gotten the better of the deal" (Murstein, 1972). Can our good luck be explained in terms of biases in the attribution process? We may be very aware of our own struggles to present ourselves to the world each day but may more or less take our mates' appearance for granted. Although our mates, as we, may labor to make themselves attractive, we are likely to attribute their attractiveness as "coming from within." But when we perceive ourselves, we tend to focus on all the external influences (exercise, hair shaping, makeup, etc.) that add to our appeal.

There are exceptions. Now and then we find a beautiful woman married to a plain man, or vice versa. How do we explain it? According to Bar-Tal and Saxe (1976), we may assume that such men are wealthy (as in the Jackie Kennedy–Aristotle Onassis match), highly intelligent, or otherwise successful. We seek an unseen factor that will maintain the sense of balance in the match.

The matching hypothesis does not apply to physical attractiveness only. We are also more likely to get married to people who are similar to us in their psychological needs (Meyer & Pepper, 1977), personality traits (Buss,

Matching hypothesis The view that people tend to choose persons similar to themselves in attractiveness and attitudes in the formation of interpersonal relationships.

1984; Lesnik-Oberstein & Cohen, 1984), and attitudes, as we shall see in the next section.

Now let us turn our attention to other factors, including attitudinal similarity, that influence feelings of attraction.

Attitudinal Similarity: "Birds of a Feather Flock Together"

It has been observed since ancient times that we tend to like people who agree with us (Jellison & Oliver, 1983). The more dogmatic we are, the more likely we are to reject people who disagree with us (Palmer & Kalin, 1985). Attitudinal similarity is a powerful contributor to the formation of both friendships and love relationships.

The strong physical attraction Candy and Stretch felt for one another motivated them to pretend that their preferences, tastes, and opinions coincided. They entered into an unspoken agreement not to discuss their religious differences. Research also suggests that birds of a feather flock together—especially when they are good-looking. College students are most attracted to dates who are physically appealing and express similar attitudes (Byrne et al., 1970). In the Byrne study, ratings of physically attractive dates with dissimilar attitudes approximated those of unattractive dates with similar attitudes. Unattractive dates who held dissimilar attitudes were least desirable.

There is also evidence that we may tend to *assume* that physically attractive people share our attitudes (Marks et al., 1981). Can this be a sort of wish fulfillment? When physical attraction is very strong, as it was with Candy and Stretch, perhaps we like to think that all the kinks in a relationship will be small or capable of being ironed out. Similarly, we tend to assume that preferred presidential candidates share our political and social attitudes (Brent & Granberg, 1982). We may even fail to remember statements they make that conflict with our attitudes (Johnson & Judd, 1983). Then, once they are in office, we may become disillusioned when they swerve from our expectations.

Not all attitudes are necessarily equal. Men on computer dates at the University of Nevada were more influenced by sexual than religious attitudes (Touhey, 1972). But women were more attracted to men whose religious views coincided with their own. These findings suggest that the women may have been less interested than the men in a physical relationship but more concerned about creating a family with cohesive values. Studies show that attitudes toward religion and children are more important in mate selection than characteristics such as kindness and professional status (e.g., Buss & Barnes, 1986; Howard et al., 1987).

Similarity in tastes and distastes is also important in the development of relationships, including friendships. For example, May and Hamilton (1980) found that college women rated photos of male strangers as more attractive when they were listening to music that they like (in most cases, rock) as compared to music that they don't like (in this experiment, avant-garde classical). If a dating couple's taste in music does not overlap, one member may look more appealing at the same time the second is losing appeal in the other's eyes—and all because of what is on the stereo. Does this mean that you find out what music your date likes and make sure to play it when you're together? Certainly not if you're interested in a long-term relationship! It could be rather distressing to wind up with music you hate blaring from the stereo for the next 50 years.

Complementarity: Every Comic Needs a Straight Man, or Woman

There are some occasions on which opposites do attract. In terms of sex roles, the historical attraction between man and woman has been viewed as a natural intermingling of the active and the passive, the dominant and the submissive. Now that stereotypical sex roles are fading, it is no longer easy to predict whether someone will be active or dominant on the basis of gender. But a dominant person may still often be attracted to someone who is submissive. A needy person may be attracted to someone who is giving. These are examples of **complementarity,** in which opposing traits reinforce each other so that each person benefits from the interaction.

Although dominant people may be more comfortable with friends and lovers who let them take the lead, the evidence that people form relationships on this basis is sketchy (Nias, 1979). Friends and lovers may be more likely to develop complementary relationships as they interact over the years (Rubin, 1973).

In any event, relationships characterized by dominance–submissiveness may run aground when the submissive party decides that he or she is tired of playing the doormat. The formerly submissive wife of a domineering husband may decide that the times are a-changing and begin to assert herself.

Reciprocity: If You Like Me, You Must Have Excellent Judgment

Has anyone told you how good-looking, brilliant, and mature you are? That your taste is refined? That all in all, you are really something special? If so, have you been impressed by his or her fine judgment?

In his 1937 classic *How to Win Friends and Influence People,* Dale Carnegie advised that we could make others like us by greeting them with enthusiasm and pouring on the praise. When we feel admired and complimented, we tend to return these feelings and behaviors. This is **reciprocity.** Research supports the view that we are prone to like people who do favors for us, compliment us, and tell us that they like us (Baron, 1971; Byrne, 1971). Men tend to be attracted to women who engage them in conversation, maintain eye contact, and lean toward them while speaking, even when their attitudes are dissimilar (Gold et al., 1984).

Propinquity: "Simply Because You're Near Me"

Why did Sarah Abrams walk down the aisle with Allen Ackroyd and not Danny Schmidt? Sarah and Danny actually had more in common. But Sarah and Al exchanged smoldering glances all throughout 11th-grade English because their teacher had used an alphabetical seating chart. Danny sat diagonally across the room and had to content himself with passing romantic notes to Andrea Sugarman. Sarah Abrams, to him, was only a name he heard called when attendance was taken.

Attraction is more likely to develop between people who are placed in frequent contact with one another. This is the effect of nearness, or **propinquity.** The development of friendships as well as romances are influenced

Complementarity The tendency to be attracted to people with opposing traits.

Reciprocity In interpersonal attraction, the tendency to return feelings and attitudes that are expressed about us.

Propinquity Nearness.

by propinquity. Students are more likely to develop friendships when they sit next to one another (Segal, 1974). Homeowners are most likely to become friendly with next-door neighbors, especially those with adjacent driveways (Whyte, 1956). Apartment dwellers tend to find friends among those who live nearby on the same floor (Nahemow & Lawton, 1975). Even infants respond more positively to strangers after a few meetings (Levitt, 1980). Adults report increased liking for a photograph of a stranger simply as a result of being exposed to the picture several times (Moreland & Zajonc, 1982).

The Romeo and Juliet Effect

Would parental opposition drive a wedge between you and your love, or would you fight to maintain the relationship? In the Shakespearean play, the young lovers, Romeo and Juliet, drew closer against the bloody backdrop of a family feud. But that was literature. What about real life?

Psychologists sought an answer through a survey of dating and married couples at the University of Colorado (Driscoll et al., 1972). Student questionnaires suggested that parental opposition intensified feelings of love between couples during the first six to ten months of the relationship. But parental opposition did not affect feelings between married couples.

During the early stages of a relationship, parental opposition may intensify needs for security within a couple so that they cling together more strongly. For couples who have already made a strong commitment, as in a lengthy courtship or a marriage, parental opposition may become irrelevant.

Playing Hard to Get: "I Only Have Eyes for You"

We tend to reciprocate feelings of attraction, but what if a person who professes to be attracted to you is equally attracted to everybody? Are you more impressed when the other person has eyes for you only?

Elaine Walster and her colleagues (1973) recruited male subjects for an experiment in which they were given the opportunity to rate and select dates. They were given phony initial reactions of their potential dates to them and to the other men in the study. One woman was generally hard to get. She reacted indifferently to all the men. Another woman was uniformly easy to get. She responded positively to all male participants. A third showed the fine judgment of being attracted to the rater only. Men were overwhelmingly more attracted to this woman—the one who had eyes only for them. She was selected for dates 80 percent of the time.

Now that we have seen how our feelings of attraction are influenced by physical features, attitudinal similarity, and so on, let us consider the psychology of social influence.

SOCIAL INFLUENCE

Most of us would be reluctant to wear blue jeans to a funeral, to walk naked on city streets, or, for that matter, to wear clothes at a nudist colony. Other people and groups can exert enormous pressure on us to behave according to their wishes or according to group norms. **Social influence** is the area of social psychology that studies the ways in which people alter the thoughts, feelings, and behaviors of others. Earlier in the chapter we learned how attitudes can be changed through persuasion or by inducing attitude-discrepant behavior. We also know a good deal about the ways in which people try to manipulate one another. For example, we are more likely to use "charm" to elicit desired behavior than to suppress behavior, and we are more likely to use force or the "silent treatment" to discourage unwanted behavior (Buss et al., 1987). In this section we shall describe a couple of classic experiments to show various ways in which people have influenced others to engage in destructive obedience and to conform to social norms.

Obedience to Authority

Richard Nixon resigned the presidency of the United States in August 1974. For two years, the business of the nation had almost ground to a halt while Congress investigated the 1972 burglary of a Democratic party campaign office in the Watergate office and apartment complex. It turned out that Nixon supporters had authorized the break-in. Nixon himself might have been involved in the cover-up of this connection later on. For two years, Nixon and his aides had been investigated by the press and by Congress. Now it was over. Some of the bad guys were thrown in jail. Nixon was exiled to the beaches of southern California. The nation returned to work. The new president, Gerald Ford, declared, "Our national nightmare is over."

But was it over? Have we come to grips with the implications of the Watergate affair?

According to the late Stanley Milgram (*APA Monitor,* January 1978), a prominent Yale University psychologist, the Watergate cover-up, like the Nazi slaughter of the Jews, was made possible through the compliance of people who were more concerned about the approval of their supervisors than about their own morality. Otherwise they would have refused to abet these crimes. The broad question is: How pressing is the need to obey authority figures at all costs?

The Milgram Studies: Shocking Stuff at Yale

Stanley Milgram also wondered how many of us would resist authority figures who made immoral requests. To find out, he ran a series of experiments at Yale University. In an early phase of his work, Milgram (1963) placed ads in New Haven newspapers for subjects for studies on learning and memory. He enlisted 40 men ranging in age from 20 to 50—teachers, engineers, laborers, salespeople, men who had not completed elementary school, men with graduate degrees. The sample was a cross section of the male population of this Connecticut city.

Let us suppose you had answered an ad. You would have shown up at the university for a fee of $4.50, for the sake of science and your own curiosity. You might have been impressed. After all, Yale was a venerable institution that dominated the city. You would not have been less impressed by the elegant labs, where you would have met a distinguished behavioral scientist dressed in a white laboratory coat and another newspaper recruit—like you. The scientist would have explained that the purpose of the experiment was to study the *effects of punishment on learning.* The experiment

Social influence The area of social psychology that studies the ways in which people influence the thoughts, feelings, and behavior of others.

Figure 15.3
The "Aggression Machine." In the Milgram studies on obedience to authority, pressing levers on the "aggression machine" was the operational definition of aggression.

would require a "teacher" and a "learner." By chance you would be appointed the teacher and the other recruit the learner.

You, the scientist, and the learner would enter a laboratory room with a rather threatening-looking chair with dangling straps. The scientist would secure the learner's cooperation and strap him in. The learner would express some concern, but this was, after all, for the sake of science. And this was Yale University, was it not? What could happen to a person at Yale?

You would follow the scientist to an adjacent room from which you would do your "teaching." This teaching promised to be effective. You would punish the learner's errors by pressing levers marked from 15 to 450 volts on a fearsome-looking console (see Figure 15.3). Labels described 28 of the 30 levers as running the gamut from "Slight Shock" to "Danger: Severe Shock." The last two levers resembled a film unfit for anyone under age 17: They were rated simply "XXX." Just in case you had no idea what electric shock felt like, the scientist gave you a sample 45-volt shock. It stung. You pitied the fellow who might receive more.

Your learner was expected to learn word pairs. Pairs of words would be read from a list. After hearing the list once, the learner would have to produce the word that was paired with the stimulus word. He would do so by pressing a switch that would signify his choice from a list of four alternatives. The switch would light one of four panels in your room. If it was the correct panel, you would proceed to the next stimulus word. If not, you would deliver an electric shock. With each error, you would increase the voltage of the shock (Figure 15.4).

You would probably have some misgivings. Electrodes had been strapped to the learner's wrists, and the scientist had applied electrode paste to "avoid blisters and burns." You were also told that the shocks would cause "no permanent tissue damage," although they might be extremely painful. Still, the learner was going along, and after all, this was Yale.

The learner answered some items correctly and then made some errors. With mild concern you pressed the levers up through 45 volts. You had tolerated that much yourself. Then a few more mistakes were made. You

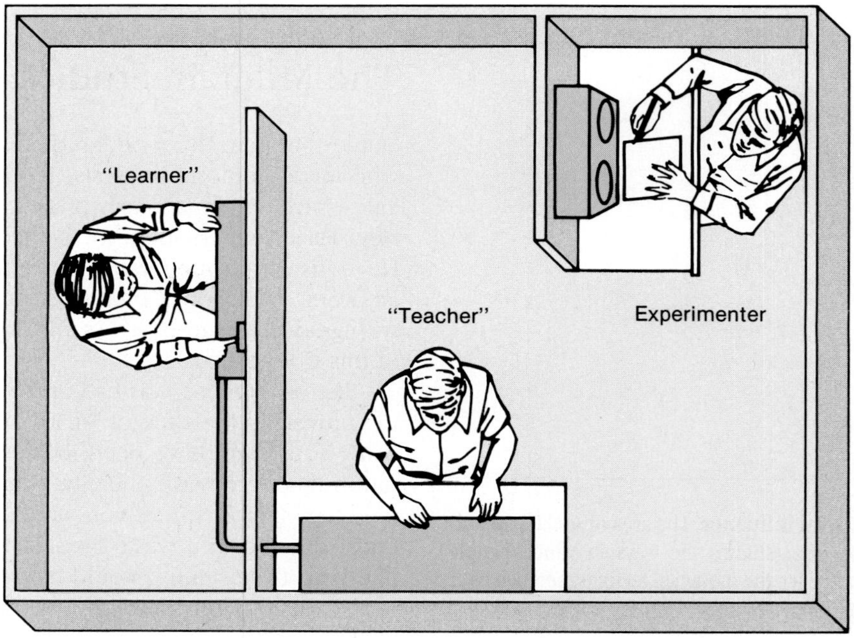

Figure 15.4
The Experimental Set-Up in the Milgram Studies. When the "learner" makes an error, the experimenter prods the "teacher" to deliver a painful electric shock.

A "Learner" in the Milgram Studies on Obedience to Authority. This learner could be in for quite a shock.

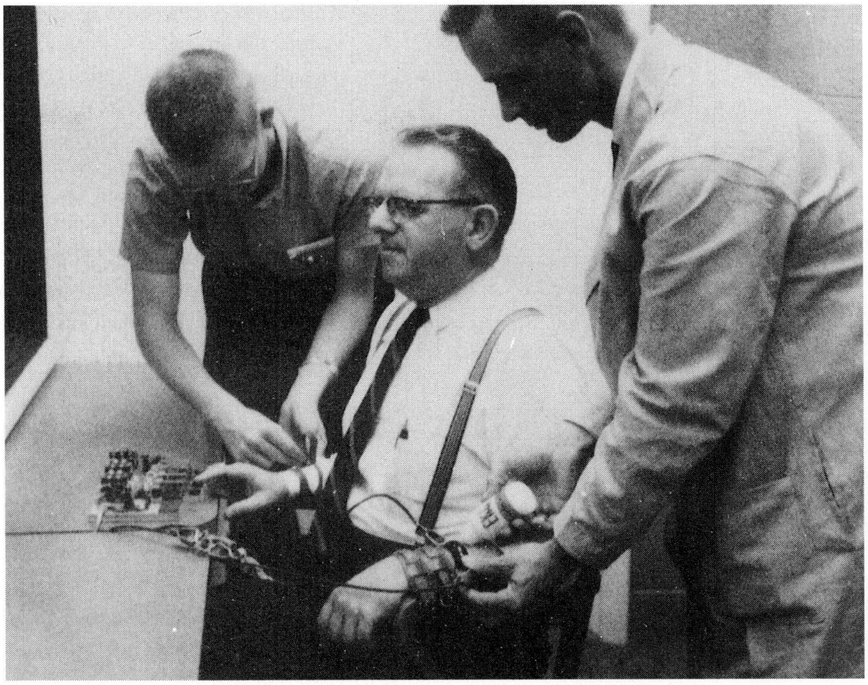

pressed the 60-volt lever, then 75. The learner made another mistake. You paused and looked at the scientist. He was reassuring: "Although the shocks may be painful, there is no permanent tissue damage, so please go on." Further errors were made, and quickly you were up to a shock of 300 volts. But now the learner was pounding on the other side of the wall! Your chest tightened and you began to perspire. Damn science and the $4.50, you thought. You hesitated and the scientist said, "The experiment requires that you continue." After the delivery of the next stimulus word, there was no answer at all. What were you to do? "Wait for five to ten seconds," the scientist instructed, "and then treat no answer as a wrong answer." But after the next shock, there was again that pounding on the wall! Now your heart was racing and you were convinced that you were causing extreme pain and discomfort. Was it possible that no lasting damage was being done? Was the experiment that important, after all? What to do? You hesitated again. The scientist said, "It is absolutely essential that you continue." His voice was very convincing. "You have no other choice," he said, "you *must* go on." You could barely think straight, and for some unaccountable reason you felt laughter rising in your throat. Your finger shook above the lever. What were you to do?

On Truth at Yale Milgram (1963, 1974) found out what most people would do. Of the 40 men in this phase of his research, only 5 refused to go beyond the 300-volt level, at which the learner first pounded the wall. Nine more "teachers" defied the scientist within the 300-volt range. But 65 percent of the participants complied with the scientist throughout the series, believing that they were delivering 450-volt, XXX-rated shocks.

Were these newspaper recruits simply unfeeling? Not at all. Milgram was impressed by their signs of stress. They trembled, they stuttered, they bit their lips. They groaned, they sweated, they dug their fingernails into their flesh. There were fits of laughter, though laughter was inappropriate. One salesperson's laughter was so convulsive that he could not continue with the experiment.

Milgram wondered if college students, heralded for independent thinking, would show more defiance. But a replication of the study with Yale undergraduates yielded similar results. What about women, who were supposedly less aggressive than men? Women, too, shocked the learners—and all this in a nation that values independence and the free will of the individual. Our "national nightmare" may not be over at all.

Truth or Fiction Revisited

It is *not* true that most people would refuse to deliver distressing electric shocks to an innocent party. When they are under strong social pressure, the majority will deliver such shocks.

Nor should we take too much comfort in the finding that a minority of individuals refused to follow the experimenter's orders. *Not one teacher attempted to extricate the unfortunate learner from the experiment. Not one teacher barged into the administrative offices at Yale and demanded that they investigate and put an end to the experiment* (Ross, 1988).

On Deception at Yale You are probably skeptical enough to wonder whether the teachers in the Milgram study actually shocked the learners when they pressed the levers on the console. They didn't. The only real shock in this experiment was the 45-volt sample given to the teachers. Its purpose was to lend credibility to the procedure.

The learners in the experiment were actually confederates of the experimenter. They had not answered the newspaper ads but were in on the truth from the start. Teachers were the only real subjects. They were led to believe that they were chosen at random for the teacher role, but the choosing was rigged so that newspaper recruits would always become teachers.

As you can imagine, many psychologists have questioned the ethics of deceiving participants in the Milgram studies. As discussed in Chapter 1, psychologists use deception only when research could not be run without it and when they believe that the benefits of the research outweigh potential harm. Regardless of the propriety of Milgram's research, we must acknowledge that it has highlighted some hard truths about human nature.

The Big Question: Why? We have shown that most people obey the commands of others, even when pressed to perform immoral tasks. But we have not answered the most pressing question: *Why?* Why did Germans "just follow orders" and commit atrocities? Why did "teachers" obey orders from the experimenter? We do not have all the answers, but we can offer a number of hypotheses:

1. *Socialization.* Despite the expressed American ideal of independence, we are socialized to obey others (such as parents and teachers) from the time we are little children.
2. *Lack of social comparison.* In Milgram's experimental settings, experimenters showed command of the situation, whereas teachers (subjects) were on the experimenter's ground and very much on their own. Being on their own, they did not have the opportunity to compare their ideas and feelings with those of people in the same situation. So they were less likely to have a clear impression of what to do.
3. *Perception of legitimate authority.* The phase of Milgram's research just described took place within the hallowed halls of Yale University. Subjects there might have been overpowered by the reputation and authority of the setting. An experimenter at Yale might have appeared to be very much the legitimate authority figure—as might a government official or a high-ranking officer in the military. Further research showed

that the university setting contributed to compliance but was not fully responsible for it. The percentage of subjects complying with the experimenter's demands dropped from 65 percent to 48 percent when Milgram (1974) replicated the study in a dingy storefront in a nearby town. In the less prestigious setting, slightly fewer than half the subjects were willing to administer the highest levels of shock. At first glance this finding might seem encouraging. But the main point of the Milgram studies is precisely that most of us remain willing to engage in morally reprehensible acts at the behest of a legitimate-appearing authority figure.

4. *The foot-in-the-door technique.* The foot-in-the-door technique might also have contributed to the obedience of the teachers (Gilbert, 1981). That is, after they had begun the process of delivering graduated shocks to learners, perhaps they found it progressively more difficult to extricate themselves from the project. Soldiers, similarly, are first taught to obey unquestioningly in innocuous matters such as dress and drill. By the time they are ordered to risk their lives, they have been saluting smartly and following commands for quite some time.

5. *Inaccessibility of values.* Earlier in the chapter, we saw that people are more likely to behave in ways that are consistent with their attitudes when their attitudes are readily available, or accessible. Moral values opposed to harming innocent people are attitudes. As the subjects in the Milgram experiments became more and more aroused, their attitudes might have become less accessible.

6. *Buffers.* Several buffers decreased the effect of the learners' suffering on the teachers. Learners (confederates of the experimenter), for example, were in another room. When they were in the same room with teachers—that is, when subjects had full view of their victims—the compliance rate dropped from 65 to 40 percent (Miller, 1986). Moreover, when the subject was given the duty of holding the learner's hand on the shock plate, the compliance rate dropped to 30 percent. In modern warfare, opposing soldiers tend to be separated by great distances. It is one thing to press a button to launch a missile or to aim a piece of artillery at a distant troop carrier or a distant ridge. It is another thing to hold the weapon to the victim's throat.

And so, there are numerous theoretical expl ınations for obedience. Regardless of the exact nature of the forces that acted on the subjects in the Milgram studies, Milgram's research has alerted us to a real and present danger—the tendency of most people to obey an authority figure, even when the figure's demands contradict their own moral attitudes and values. It has happened before. Unhappily, unless we remain alert, it may happen again. Who are the authority figures in your life? How do you think you would have behaved if you had been a teacher in the Milgram studies? Are you sure?

In the section on conformity, we describe another classic study, and you may again try to imagine how you would behave if you were involved in it.

Conformity

Conform To changes one's attitudes or overt behavior to adhere to social norms.

Social norms Explicit and implicit rules that reflect social expectations and influence the ways people behave in social situations.

Earlier we noted that most of us would be reluctant to wear blue jeans to a funeral, to walk naked on city streets, or to wear clothes at a nudist colony. We are said to **conform** when we change our behavior to adhere to social norms. **Social norms** are widely accepted rules that indicate how we are

The Experimental Set-Up in the Asch Experiment in Conformity. The experimenter is at the right, and the unsuspecting subject is seated sixth from the left. All other "subjects" are actually in league with the experimenter.

expected to behave under certain circumstances (Moscovici, 1985). Rules that require us to whisper in libraries and to slow down when driving past a school are examples of explicit social norms. Other social norms are unspoken, or implicit (Zuckerman et al., 1983). One unspoken social norm is to face front in elevators. Another is to be fashionably late for social gatherings.

Truth or Fiction Revisited

It is true that many people are late to social gatherings because they are conforming to a social norm—in this case, the norm of "fashionable lateness."

The tendency to conform to social norms is often a good thing. Many norms have evolved because they favor comfort and survival. Yet group pressure can also promote maladaptive behavior, as in pressure to wear coats and ties in summer in buildings cooled only to, say, 78 degrees Fahrenheit. At that high temperature, the only motive for conforming to a dress code may be to show that we have been adequately socialized and are not threats to social rules.

Let us look at a classic experiment on conformity run by Solomon Asch in the early 1950s. Then we shall examine factors that promote conformity.

Seven Line Judges Can't Be Wrong: The Asch Study

Do you believe what you see with your own eyes? Seeing is believing, is it not? Not if you were a participant in the Asch (1952) study.

You would enter a laboratory room with seven other subjects for an experiment on visual discrimination. If you were familiar with psychology experiments, you might be surprised: There were no rats and no electric-shock apparatus in sight, only a man at the front of a room with some cards with lines drawn on them.

The eight of you would be seated in a series. You would be given the seventh seat, a minor fact at the time. The man would explain the task. There was a single line on the card on the left. Three lines were drawn on the card at the right (Figure 15.5). One line was the same length as the line on the

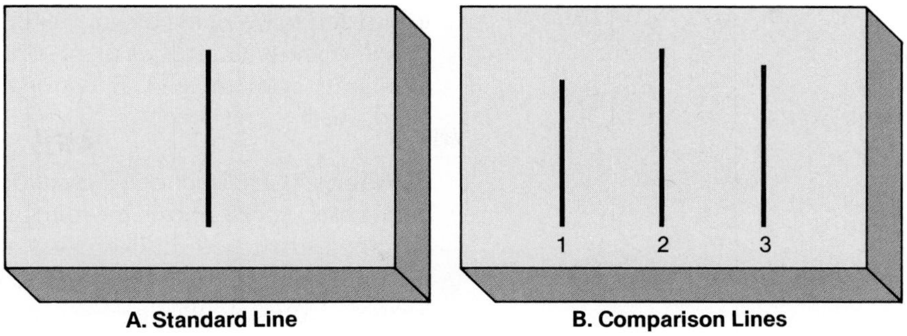

Figure 15.5
Cards Used in the Asch Study on Conformity. Which line on card B—1, 2, or 3—is the same length as the line on card A? Line 2, right? But would you say "2" if you were a member of a group and six people answering ahead of you all said "3"? Are you sure?

other card. You and the other subjects need only call out, one at a time, which of the three lines—1, 2, or 3—was the same length. Simple.

You would try it out. Those to your right spoke out in order: "3," "3," "3," "3," "3," "3." Now it was your turn. Line 3 was clearly the same length as the line on the first card, so you said "3." Then the fellow after you chimed in: "3." That's all there was to it. Then two other cards were set up in the front of the room. This time line 2 was clearly the same length as the line on the first card. The answers: "2," "2," "2," "2," "2," "2." Your turn again: "2," you said, and perhaps your mind began to wander. Your stomach was gurgling a bit. That night you would not even mind dorm food particularly. The fellow after you said, "2."

Another pair of cards was held up. Line 3 was clearly the correct answer. The six people on your right spoke in turn: "1," "1 . . ." Wait a second! ". . . 1," "1—" You forgot about dinner and studied the lines briefly. No, 1 was too short, by a good half an inch. But ". . . 1," "1," and suddenly it was your turn. Your hands had quickly become sweaty and there was a lump in your throat. You wanted to say 3, but was it right? There was really no time and you had already paused noticeably: "1," you said, "1," the last fellow confirmed matter-of-factly.

Now your attention was riveted on the chore. Much of the time you agreed with the other seven line judges, but sometimes you did not. And for some reason beyond your understanding, they were in perfect agreement, even when they were wrong—assuming that you could trust your eyes. The experiment was becoming an uncomfortable experience, and you began to doubt your judgment.

The discomfort in the Asch study was caused by the pressure to conform. Actually, the other seven recruits were confederates of the experimenter. They prearranged a number of incorrect responses. The sole purpose of the study was to see whether you would conform to the erroneous group judgments.

How many of Asch's subjects caved in? How many went along with the crowd rather than assert what they thought to be the right answer? Seventy-five percent. *Three of four agreed with the majority wrong answer at least once.*

What about you? Would you wear blue jeans if everyone else wore slacks and skirts? A number of more recent experiments (Wheeler et al., 1978) show that the tendency to conform did not go out with the Fabulous Fifties.

Factors Influencing Conformity

Several personal and situational factors prompt conformity to social norms. Personal factors include the desires to be liked by other members of the group and to be right (Insko, 1985), low self-esteem, high self-consciousness, social shyness (Krech et al., 1962; Santee & Maslach, 1982), gender, and familiarity with the job. Situational factors include group size and social support.

Gender There has been a great deal of controversy about whether women conform to social norms more than men do. Old-fashioned stereotypes portray men as rugged individualists and women as civilizing influences, so it is not surprising that women have been generally perceived as more conformist. Experimental findings over the past several decades have at first glance tended to support this view. A sophisticated statistical analysis of the literature up through the middle 1970s, for example, suggested that women by and large were more conformist than men (Cooper, 1979).

On the other hand, several studies suggest that sex differences are complex and not quite so predictable. For example, an experiment run by Sandra Bem (1975) of Cornell University found that women who accept the sex-role stereotype of the passive, dependent female are more likely than men to conform. But other women can be as self-assertive and independent as men. Another fascinating experiment on sex differences was run by social psychologist Alice Eagly and her colleagues (1981). The Eagly group found that men conform to group opinions as frequently as women do when their conformity or independence will be private. But when their conformity would be made known to the group, they conform less often than women do, apparently because nonconformity is more consistent with the masculine sex-role stereotype of independence. Ironically enough, men may be motivated to act independently in order to conform to the male sex-role stereotype of rugged individualism. It's a little bit like "doublethink" in the Orwell novel *1984:* "Nonconformity is conformity."

Social psychologists Robert Baron and Donn Byrne (1987) take issue with Cooper's (1979) findings and assert that "it now seems clear that there are no important differences between males and females in terms of the tendency to conform" (p. 233). But Baron and Byrne admit that many people still perceive women as being easier to "push around." They offer the explanation that we usually see people of lower social status as being more conformist and that women, sad to say, are often afforded lower social standing in the United States—in society at large and especially in the work force. In other words, the view of women as being lower in social standing often stems from the traditional distribution of men into breadwinning roles and women into homemaking roles (Eagly & Steffen, 1984). And women in the work force, as a group, earn less than men.

Familiarity with Task Demands Familiarity with the task at hand promotes self-reliance (Eagly, 1978). In one experiment, for example, Sistrunk and McDavid (1971) found that women were more likely to conform to group pressure on tasks involving identification of tools (such as wrenches) that were more familiar to men. Men were more likely to conform on duties involving identification of cooking utensils, with which women, in our society, are usually more familiar.

Group Size Situational factors include the number of people who hold the majority opinion and the presence of at least one other person who shares the discrepant opinion. Probability of conformity, even to incorrect group judgments, increases rapidly as a group grows to five members. It then increases at a slower rate up to eight members (Gerard et al., 1968; Wilder, 1977), at which point maximum probability of conformity is reached.

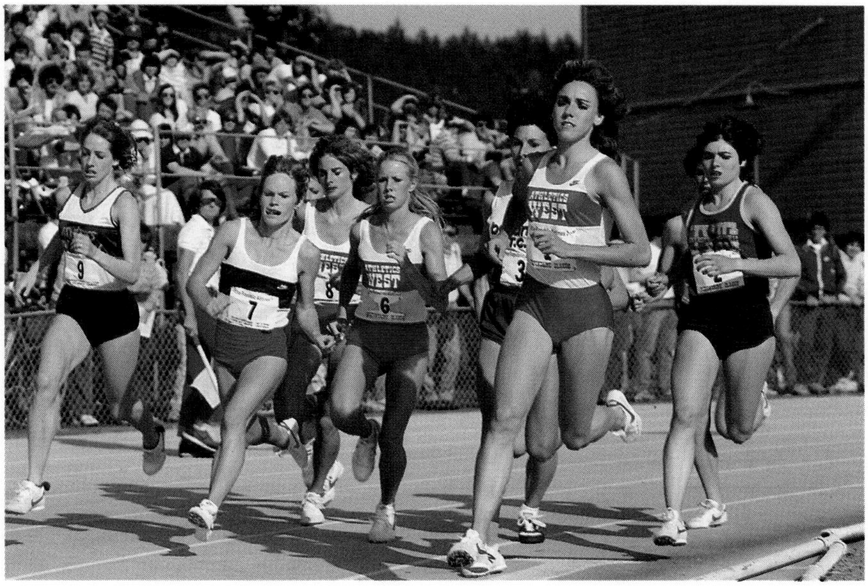

Social Facilitation. Runners tend to move more rapidly when they are members of a group. Does the presence of others raise our levels of arousal or give rise to evaluation apprehension?

Social Support Finding just one other person who supports your minority opinion is apparently enough to encourage you to stick to your guns (Morris et al., 1977). In a variation of the Asch experiment, recruits were provided with just one confederate who agreed with their minority judgments (Allen & Levine, 1971). Even though this confederate seemed to have a visual impairment, as evidenced by thick glasses, his support was sufficient to lead actual subjects not to conform to incorrect majority opinions.

A final note: it has been shown that people who value being right more than being liked by others are less likely to conform to group pressure (Insko et al., 1985). Which is more important to you?

Studies in conformity highlight some of the ways in which we are influenced by groups. In the following section, we shall discuss other aspects of group behavior.

GROUP BEHAVIOR

To be human is to belong to groups. Families, classes, religious groups, political parties, circles of friends, bowling teams, sailing clubs, conversation groups, therapy groups—to how many groups do you belong? How do groups influence the behavior of individuals?

In this section we shall look at a number of aspects of group behavior: social facilitation, group decision making, mob behavior, and the bystander effect.

Social Facilitation

Social facilitation The process by which a person's performance is increased when other members of a group engage in similar behavior.

One effect of groups on individual behavior is **social facilitation,** or the effects on performance that result from the presence of others. Bicycle riders and runners tend to move more rapidly when they are members of a group.

This effect is not limited to humans: Dogs and cats eat more rapidly when others are present. Even roaches run more rapidly when other roaches are present (Zajonc, 1980).

According to psychologist Robert Zajonc (1980), the presence of others influences us by increasing our levels of arousal, or motivation. When our levels of arousal are highly increased, our performance of simple, dominant responses is facilitated, but our performance of complex, recently acquired responses may be impaired. For this reason, a well-rehearsed speech may be delivered more masterfully before a larger audience, but our performance in an offhand speech or at a question-and-answer session may be hampered by a large audience.

Social facilitation may be influenced by **evaluation apprehension** as well as level of arousal (Bray & Sugarman, 1980; Markus, 1981). Our performance before a group may be affected not only by the physical presence of others but also by our concern that they are evaluating our performance. When giving a speech, we may "lose our thread" if we become distracted by the audience and begin to focus too much on what they may be thinking of us (Seta, 1982). If we believe that we have begun to flounder, our evaluation apprehension may skyrocket, and as a consequence, our performance may deteriorate further.

The presence of others can also decrease performance when we are not acting *before* a group but are anonymous members *of* a group (Latané et al., 1979; Williams et al., 1981). Workers, for example, may "goof off" or engage in "social loafing" on humdrum jobs when they believe that they will not be found out and held accountable. There is then no evaluation apprehension. There may also be **diffusion of responsibility** in groups. That is, each person may feel less responsibility to help because others are present. Group members may also reduce their efforts if an apparently capable member makes no contribution but tries to "ride free" on the efforts of other group members (Kerr, 1983). The belief that other group members are not likely to work as hard as oneself also contributes to social loafing (Jackson & Harkins, 1985).

Group Decision Making

In 1986 and 1987, President Ronald Reagan's popularity took a drubbing when it was alleged that he had authorized the sale of American weapons to Iran to try to gain the release of American hostages being held by pro-Iranian groups in Lebanon. This occurred at a time when the American public was very hostile toward Iran. Reagan had also sworn he would never negotiate with terrorists and had branded Iran a "terrorist nation." The decision to trade weapons for hostages apparently resulted from heated discussions in the White House during which the secretaries of state and defense took one position and the national security adviser took another position.

How do group decisions get made? Social psychologists have discovered a number of rules, or **social decision schemes,** that seem to govern group decision making (Baron & Byrne, 1987; Davis et al., 1984; Kerr & MacCoun, 1985; Vinocur et al., 1985). Note the following examples:

1. *The majority-wins scheme.* In this commonly used scheme, the group arrives at the decision that was initially supported by the majority. This scheme appears to guide decision making most often when there is no objectively correct decision. An example would be a decision about what car model to build when the popularity of various models has not been tested in the "court" of public opinion.

Evaluation apprehension Concern that others are evaluating our behavior.

Diffusion of responsibility The spreading or sharing of responsibility for a decision or behavior within a group.

Social decision schemes Rules for predicting the final outcome of group decision making on the basis of the members' initial positions.

"And now at this point in the meeting I'd like to shift the blame away from me and onto someone else."

2. *The truth-wins scheme.* In this scheme, the group comes to recognize that one approach is objectively correct as more information is provided and opinions are discussed. For example, a group deciding whether to use SAT scores in admitting students to college would profit from information about whether these scores actually predict college success.

3. *The two-thirds majority scheme.* This scheme is frequently adopted by juries, who tend to convict defendants when two-thirds of the jury initially favors conviction.

4. *The first-shift rule.* In this scheme, the group tends to adopt the decision that reflects the first shift in opinion expressed by any group member. If a car-manufacturing group is equally divided on whether or not to produce a convertible, it may opt to do so after one group member initially opposed to the idea changes her mind. If a jury is deadlocked, the members may eventually follow the lead of the first juror to change his position.

Now let us consider whether group members are likely to make compromise decisions or to take relatively extreme viewpoints as a result of diverse initial positions.

Polarization and the Risky Shift

We might think that a group decision would be more conservative than an individual decision. After all, shouldn't there be an effort to compromise, to "split the differences"? We might also expect that a few mature individuals would be able to balance the opinions of daredevils. But, in general, groups do not seem to work in these ways.

Consider the **polarization** effect. As an individual, you might recommend that your company risk $50,000 to develop or market a new product. Other company executives, polled individually, might risk similar amounts. But if you were gathered for a group decision, it is likely that you would recommend either an amount well above this figure or nothing at all (Myers & Lamm, 1976). This group effect is called polarization, or the taking of an extreme position. Yet if you had to gamble on which way the decision would go, you would do better to place your money on movement toward the higher sum—that is, to bet on a **risky shift.** Why?

One possibility is that a group member may reveal information the others had not been aware of and that this information clearly points in one direction or the other. With doubts removed, the group becomes polarized, moving decidedly in the appropriate direction. It may also be that social facilitation occurs in the group setting and that increased motivation prompts more extreme decisions.

But why do groups tend to take greater, not smaller, risks than those that would be ventured by their members as individuals? One answer is diffusion of responsibility (Burnstein, 1983; Myers, 1983). If the venture flops, it will not be you alone to blame. Remember the self-serving bias: You can always say (and tell yourself) that the failure was, after all, a group decision. And if the venture pays off handsomely, you can attribute the outcome to your cool analysis and trumpet abroad your influential role in the group decision-making process.

Truth or Fiction Revisited

It is not true that group decisions are conservative. Group decisions actually tend to be riskier than the average decision that would be made by each group member acting as an individual—probably because of diffusion of responsibility.

Groupthink

A problem that sometimes arises in group decision making is called **groupthink.** Groupthink is usually instigated by a dynamic group leader. As noted by the originator of the term, Irving Janis (1982), groupthink is usually unrealistic and fueled by the perception of external threats to the group or to those the group wishes to protect. The perception of external threat heightens group cohesiveness and serves as a source of stress. When under stress, group members tend not to consider all their options carefully (Keinan, 1987). Flawed decisions are therefore a common outcome.

When the U.S. government sold weapons to Iran during the mid-1980s, profits from the sales were diverted—possibly illegally—to support the "contras," a group attempting to unseat the Sandinista government of the Central American country of Nicaragua. Although we do not know all the details of the plan to divert profits from the arms sales, it seems that the decision to do so was made by a small group including members of the National Security Council (Colonel Oliver North and Admiral John Poindexter) and, possibly, the director of the CIA, William Casey. Five characteristics of groupthink noted by Janis might have played a role in this decision, which resulted in several indictments and a congressional investigation:

1. *Feelings of invulnerability.* The group might have believed that it was beyond the reach of the law because its actions were being carried out by powerful individuals close to the president.

Polarization In social psychology, taking an extreme position or attitude on an issue.

Risky shift The tendency to make riskier decisions as a member of a group than as an individual acting independently.

Groupthink A process in which group members are influenced by cohesiveness and a dynamic leader to ignore external realities as they make decisions.

2. *Group belief in its rightness.* The group apparently believed it was in the right because (1) it was carrying out the president's expressed desire to find ways to support the contras, and (2) it was arming the contras against a leftist government.

3. *The discrediting of information opposed to the group's decision.* At the time the group decided to divert funds, it was illegal for the U.S. government to provide funds or weapons to the contras. The group apparently discredited the law by (1) deciding that it was inconsistent with the best interests of the United States and (2) enlisting private citizens to divert profits from sales to the contras so that the U.S. government was not directly involved.

4. *Pressures on group members to conform.* Here we must be more speculative. It can be noted, however, that North and Poindexter repeatedly testified that they were carrying out the expressed wishes of President Reagan (i.e., to help the contras), even though Reagan was unaware of the diversion of funds from arm sales to Iran. In this sense, they were conforming to the president's wishes. Moreover, most group members were convinced of the need to help the contras as a way of combating Communism in the Western Hemisphere.

5. *Stereotyping of members of the outgroup.* The group apparently viewed persons who would oppose them as Communist "sympathizers"; "knee-jerk liberals"; and, in the case of the Congress that had made helping the contras illegal, "slow-acting," "vacillating" (i.e., voting to aid the contras in one bill and prohibiting aid to the contras in another), and "irresolute."

These characteristics of the groupthink process apparently led the group to overestimate its power, to view itself as singlehandedly protecting the United States from the Communist threat in this hemisphere, and to make a decision that nearly brought the Reagan administration crashing down.

Mob Behavior and Deindividuation

Gustave Le Bon (1960), the French social thinker, branded mobs and crowds irrational, like a "beast with many heads." Mob actions such as race riots and lynchings sometimes seem to operate on a psychology of their own. Do mobs elicit the beast in us? How is it that mild-mannered people will commit mayhem as members of a mob? In seeking an answer, let us examine a lynching and the baiting type of crowd that often seems to attend threatened suicides.

The Lynching of Arthur Stevens In *Social Learning and Imitation,* Neal Miller and John Dollard (1941) vividly described a southern lynching. Arthur Stevens, a black, was accused of murdering his lover, a white woman, when she wanted to break up with him. Stevens was arrested and confessed to the crime. The sheriff feared violence and moved Stevens to a town 200 miles distant during the night. But his location was uncovered. The next day, a mob of a hundred persons stormed the jail and returned Stevens to the scene of the crime.

Outrage spread from person to person like a plague bacillus. Laborers, professionals, women, adolescents, and law-enforcement officers alike were infected. Stevens was tortured, emasculated, and murdered. His corpse was dragged through the streets. Then the mob went on a rampage in town, chasing and assaulting other blacks. The riot ended only when troops were sent in to restore law and order.

Deindividuation When we act as individuals, fear of consequences and self-evaluation tend to prevent antisocial behavior. But as members of a mob, we may experience **deindividuation,** a state of reduced self-awareness and lowered concern for social evaluation (Mann et al., 1982). Many factors lead to deindividuation, including anonymity, diffusion of responsibility, arousal due to noise and crowding (Zimbardo, 1969), and focus of individual attention on the group process (Diener, 1980). Individuals also tend to adopt the emerging norms and attitudes of the group (Turner & Killian, 1972). Under these circumstances, crowd members behave more aggressively than they would as individuals.

Police know that mob actions are best averted early, by dispersing the small groups that may gather into a crowd. On an individual level, perhaps we can resist deindividuation by instructing ourselves to stop and think whenever we begin to feel highly aroused as group members. If we dissociate ourselves from such groups when they are in the formative process, we shall be more likely to retain critical self-evaluation and avoid behavior that we shall later regret.

The Baiting Crowd in Cases of Threatened Suicide As individuals, we often feel compassion when we observe people who are so distressed that they are considering suicide. Why is it, then, that when people who are considering suicide threaten to jump from a ledge, the crowd often baits them, urging them on?

Such baiting occurred in 10 of 21 cases of threatened suicide studied by Leon Mann (1981). Analysis of newspaper reports suggested a number of factors that might have prompted deindividuation among crowd members, all contributing to anonymity: The crowds were large. It was dark (past 6 P.M.). The victim and the crowd were distant from one another (with the victim, for example, on a high floor). Baiting by the crowd was also linked to high temperatures (the summer season) and a long duration of the episode, suggestive of stress and fatigue among crowd members.

Helping Behavior and the Bystander Effect: Some Watch While Others Die

In 1964, the nation was shocked by the murder of 28-year-old Kitty Genovese in New York City. Murder was not unheard of in the Big Apple, but Kitty had screamed for help as her killer had repeatedly stabbed her. Nearly 40 neighbors had heard the commotion. Many watched. Nobody helped. Why? As a nation, are we a callous bunch who would rather watch than help when others are in trouble? Penn State psychologist R. Lance Shotland notes that in the two decades since the murder (Dowd, 1984), more than 1,000 books and articles have been written attempting to explain the behavior of bystanders in crises. According to Stanley Milgram, the Genovese case "touched on a fundamental issue of the human condition. If we need help, will those around us stand around and let us be destroyed or will they come to our aid?" (in Dowd, 1984).

Truth or Fiction Revisited

It is true that some 40 people stood by and did nothing while a woman was being stabbed to death. Their failure to come to her aid has been termed the *bystander effect.*

Deindividuation The process by which group members may discontinue self-evaluation and adopt group norms and attitudes.

Whom Do You Help? Psychologists have dressed the same person in different ways in experiments to determine how appearance influences our decisions to help others.

What factors determine whether we help others who are in trouble?

The Helper: Who Helps? Some psychologists (e.g., Hoffman, 1981) suggest that **altruism** is a part of human nature. In keeping with sociobiological theory, they argue that self-sacrifice will sometimes help guarantee that a close relative will succeed. In this way, self-sacrifice is actually selfish from a genetic point of view: It helps us perpetuate a genetic code similar to our own in future generations.

Most psychologists focus on the roles of a helper's mood and personality traits. By and large, we are more likely to help others when we are in a good mood (Berkowitz, 1987; Manucia et al., 1984; Rosenhan et al., 1981). Yet we may help others when we are miserable ourselves if our own problems work to increase our empathy or sensitivity to the plights of others (Batson et al., 1981; Thompson et al., 1980). People with a high need for approval may act altruistically to earn approval from others (Satow, 1975). People who are empathic, who can take the perspective of others, are also likely to help (Archer et al., 1981).

There are many reasons why bystanders frequently do not come to the aid of others in distress. First, if bystanders do not fully understand what they are seeing, they may not recognize that an emergency exists. That is, the more ambiguous the situation, the less likely it is that bystanders will try to help (Shotland & Heinold, 1985). Second, the presence of others may lead to diffusion of responsibility so that no one assumes responsibility for helping others (as we shall see in a following section). Third, if bystanders are not certain that they possess the competencies to take charge of the situation, they may also stay on the sidelines for fear of making a social blunder and being subject to ridicule (Pantin & Carver, 1982)—or for fear of getting hurt themselves.

Bystanders who believe that others get what they deserve may rationalize not helping by thinking that a person would not be in trouble unless this outcome was just (Lerner et al., 1975). A sense of personal responsibility increases the likelihood of helping. Such responsibility may stem from having made a verbal commitment to help (e.g., Moriarty, 1975) or from having been designated by others as being responsible for carrying out a helping chore (Maruyama et al., 1982).

The Victim: Who Is Helped? Although sex roles have been changing, it is traditional for men to help women in our society. Latané and Dabbs (1975) found that women were more likely than men to receive help, especially from men, when they dropped coins in Atlanta (a southern city) than in Seattle or Columbus (northern cities). The researchers explain this difference by noting that traditional sex roles persevere more strongly in the South.

Women are also more likely than men to be helped when their cars have broken down on the highway or they are hitchhiking (Pomazal & Clore, 1973). There may be sexual overtones to some of this altruism. Women are most likely to be helped by males when they are attractive and when they are alone (Benson et al., 1976; Snyder et al., 1974).

As in the research on interpersonal attraction, similarity also seems to promote helping behavior. Poorly dressed people are more likely to succeed in requests for a dime with poorly dressed strangers, and well-dressed people are more likely to get money from well-dressed strangers (Hensley, 1981).

Situational Determinants of Helping: "Am I the Only One Here?" It may seem logical that a group of people would be more likely to have come to the aid of Kitty Genovese than a lone person. After all, a group could more effectively have overpowered her attacker. Yet research by Darley and

Altruism Unselfish concern for the welfare of others.

Latané (1968) suggests that a lone person may have been more likely to try to help her.

In their experiment, male subjects were performing meaningless tasks in cubicles when they heard a (convincing) recording of a person apparently having an epileptic seizure. When the subjects thought that four other persons were immediately available to help, only 31 percent made an effort to help the victim. But when they thought that no one else was available, 85 percent of them tried to offer aid. As in other areas of group behavior, it seems that diffusion of responsibility inhibits helping behavior in groups or crowds. When we are in a group, we are often willing to let George (or Georgette) do it. When George isn't around, we are more willing to help others ourselves.

Note that in most studies on the bystander effect, the bystanders are strangers (Latané & Nida, 1981). Research shows that bystanders who are acquainted with victims are more likely to respond to the social norm of helping others in need (Rutkowski et al., 1983). And aren't we more likely to give to charity when asked directly by a co-worker or supervisor in the socially exposed situation of the office as compared to a letter received in the privacy of our own homes?

We are more likely to help others when we can clearly see what is happening (for instance, if we can see clearly that the woman whose car has broken down is alone) and when the environment is familiar to us (e.g., when we are in our home town rather than a strange city).

Helping behavior and the bystander effect highlight the fact that we are members of a vast, interdependent social fabric. The next time you see a stranger who is in need of help, what will you do? Are you sure?

SUMMARY

1. **What do social psychologists do?** Social psychologists study the factors that influence our thoughts, feelings, and behaviors in social situations.

2. **What are attitudes?** According to the ABC model, attitudes are enduring systems of beliefs with emotional (affective), behavioral, and cognitive components. The so-called A–B problem (attitude–behavior problem) refers to the finding that people frequently do not always behave in ways that are consistent with their attitudes. Attitudes may be acquired through conditioning, observational learning, and cognitive appraisal.

3. **What is the elaboration likelihood model for understanding persuasive messages?** According to this model, persuasion occurs through central and peripheral routes. Change occurs through the central route by means of consideration of arguments and evidence. Peripheral routes involve associating the objects of attitudes with positive or negative cues, such as attractive communicators.

4. **What factors affect the persuasiveness of messages?** Repeated messages generally "sell" better than messages delivered once. People tend to show greater response to emotional appeals than to purely factual presentations, especially when emotional appeals offer concrete advice for avoiding negative consequences. Persuasive communicators tend to show expertise, trustworthiness, attractiveness, or similarity to the audience.

5. **What is the foot-in-the-door technique?** In this technique, people are asked to accede to large requests after they have acceded to smaller requests. Perhaps initial compliance causes them to view themselves as people who help others by acceding to requests.

6. **What is balance theory?** According to balance theory, we are motivated to maintain harmony among our perceptions, beliefs, and attitudes. When people we care about express attitudes that differ from ours,

we are in a state of imbalance, and we are motivated to try to restore the balance.

7. **What is cognitive-dissonance theory?** According to cognitive-dissonance theory, which is similar to balance theory, people dislike inconsistency between their attitudes and their behavior. Attitude-discrepant behavior apparently induces cognitive dissonance, which people can then reduce by changing their attitudes. People also engage in effort justification; that is, they tend to justify attitude-discrepant behavior to themselves by concluding that their attitudes may differ from what they thought they were.

8. **What is prejudice?** Prejudice is an attitude toward a group that includes negative evaluations, negative affect, and avoidance behavior or discrimination. Sources of prejudice include attitudinal dissimilarity (or the assumption that members of outgroups hold different attitudes), social conflict, social learning, authoritarianism, and the tendency to divide the social world into two categories: "us" and "them."

9. **What is the importance of first impressions?** First impressions can last (the primacy effect) because we tend to label or describe people in terms of the initial behavior we see. However, recent impressions (the recency effect) can become important when time passes between observations.

10. **What is the attribution process?** Our inference of the motives and traits of others through the observation of their behavior is called the attribution process. In dispositional attributions, we attribute people's behavior to internal factors, such as their personality traits and decisions. In situational attributions, we attribute people's behavior to their circumstances or external forces.

11. **What factors determine our attributions?** Our attribution of behavior to internal or external causes is influenced by the behavior's consensus, consistency, and distinctiveness. We are likely to attribute behavior to internal factors when it is low in consensus (few people act that way), high in consistency (the person behaves that way consistently), and low in distinctiveness (the person acts similarly in different situations).

12. **What are some of the biases in the attribution process?** According to the actor-observer effect, we tend to attribute the behavior of others to internal, dispositional factors, whereas we tend to attribute our own behavior to external, situational factors. The so-called fundamental attribution error is the tendency to attribute too much of other people's behavior to dispositional factors.

13. **What can we infer from body language?** At an early age, we learn to read body language. People who feel positively toward one another position themselves close together and touch. Gazing into another's eyes can be a sign of love, but a hard stare is an aversive challenge.

14. **What is interpersonal attraction?** In social psychology, attraction is an attitude of liking (positive attraction) or disliking (negative attraction).

15. **What factors contribute to attraction?** In our culture, slenderness is found to be attractive in both men and women, and tallness is valued in men. We are more attracted to good-looking people, and we tend to assume that attractive people are more likely to be talented and less likely to engage in criminal behavior. Attitudinal similarity, propinquity, reciprocity, parental opposition, and playing hard to get can all enhance feelings of attraction.

16. **What is the matching hypothesis?** According to the matching hypothesis, we tend to seek dates and mates at our own level of attractiveness, largely because of fear of rejection.

17. **Will people obey authority figures who command them to engage in improper behavior?** Most people comply with the demands of authority figures, even when these demands seem immoral, as shown in the Milgram studies on obedience. Factors contributing to obedience include socialization, lack of social comparison, perception of legitimate authority figures, the foot-in-the-door technique, inaccessibility of values, and buffers between perpetrator and victim.

18. **What factors contribute to conformity?** Personal factors such as low self-esteem, high self-consciousness, and shyness contribute to conformity. Group size is also a factor.

19. **What is social facilitation?** Social facilitation refers to the effects on performance that result from the presence of others. The presence of others may facilitate performance for reasons such as increased arousal and evaluation apprehension. However, when we are anonymous group members, task performance may fall off; this phenomenon is referred to as social loafing.

20. **How do group decisions differ from individual decisions?** Group decisions tend to be more polarized and risky than individual decisions, largely because groups diffuse responsibility.

21. **How do groups make decisions?** Social psychologists have identified several decision-making schemes, including the majority-wins scheme, the truth-wins scheme, the two-thirds majority scheme, and the first-shift rule.

22. **What is groupthink?** Groupthink is an unrealistic kind of decision making that is fueled by the perception of external threats to the group or to those the group wishes to protect. Groupthink is facilitated by feelings of invulnerability, group belief in its rightness, the discrediting of information opposed to the group's decision, pressures on group members to conform, and stereotyping of members of the outgroup.

23. **How do social psychologists explain mob behavior?** Highly emotional crowds may induce attitude-discrepant behavior through the process of deindividuation, which is a state of reduced self-awareness and lowered concern for social evaluation.

24. **What is the bystander effect?** According to the bystander effect, we are unlikely to aid others in distress when we are members of crowds. Crowds tend to diffuse responsibility. We are more likely to help people in need when we think we are the only one available, when we have a clear view of the situation, and when we are not afraid that we shall be committing a social blunder or endanger ourselves.

PSYCHOLOGY AND MODERN LIFE

Enhancing Social Interactions

We are social creatures, and we interact with other people every day—or nearly every day—of our lives. In this section, we will apply principles of social psychology and suggest a number of ways in which we can enhance our social interactions. For example, in the chapter we discussed methods of persuasion, and I assume that you will be better able to see through the peripheral cues that make advertisements so appealing. In this section, we offer advice on responding to the sales practice of low-balling. We offer advice on what to do about prejudice. We also explore ways of marshalling findings on social perception—namely, ways of making a solid first impression and of recognizing and coping with biases in the attribution process. In the chapter we warned of the pressures we can feel when we are given commands by authority figures or when we would counter social norms. Perhaps the warning will encourage us to behave in ways that are consistent with our own values despite the social influences acting on us.

Handling Low-Balling Imagine that you're shopping for a new stereo set. You know just what you want, and you see it advertised by a discount store at the (excellent) price of $350. You rush to the store and find a salesperson.

"Uh-oh," says the salesperson, shaking his head. "These sets have been going fast. I'll have to check on whether it's in stock. Give me a couple of minutes." Then he disappears into the back.

Fifteen minutes pass and you're getting fidgety. But then the salesperson returns—looking more upbeat. You are optimistic.

"I looked everywhere," he says, "and we're all out of the speakers." You have a sinking feeling. "But I checked with my manager," he continues, "and she says we can give you the same amplifier and turntable with more powerful speakers for $425. That's a bargain when you consider the sound you'll be getting."

You're no sucker, so you ask, "Won't you be getting them in stock again?"

"Sure," says the salesperson, "but not at $350. The dollar's been going down against the yen, and Japanese electronics are going up every day. Look, we don't want you to be unhappy. Believe me, at $425, the set with bigger speakers is a very good deal."

You want the set, but you don't need bigger speakers. And the price in the paper was $350 with the speakers you wanted.

You may be a victim of low-balling. In this kind of low-balling, the customer is lured into the store by a good price on unavailable merchandise and then offered substitute goods at a higher price. Sad to say, this is not a rare sales practice. What can you do about it? There is no single right answer, but here are some possibilities:

You might say, "I think you had better let me talk to that manager myself. Please show me the way." (If the salesperson hems and haws, or if he says he'll "bring the manager out to you" in a few minutes, it might be that he had not spoken to the manager but was following a preplanned tactic.)

You could also say, "Thank you for looking. I'll find the set I want at a decent price elsewhere." (This lets the salesperson know you're not going to be suckered, and perhaps you will find that set elsewhere—at a good price.)

Or you could simply walk out. You won't have a stereo, but you will be happier with yourself than you would by paying for the larger speakers.

Coping with Prejudice and Discrimination Prejudice has existed throughout history, and I doubt that miracle cures are at hand to eradicate it fully. However, a number of measures have met with success. In many cases, it is easier to deal with discrimination, the behavioral manifestation of prejudice. For example, laws now prohibit denial of access to jobs, housing, and other social necessities on the basis of race, religion, handicaps, and related factors.

Let us consider several things that can be done:

1. *Role Reversal: An Immunization Technique?* A study by Weiner and Wright (1973) tested the implications of Jane Elliot's informal demonstration with blue- and brown-eyed children. White third-graders were assigned at random to "Green" or "Orange" groups and identified with armbands. First, the "Green" people were labeled inferior and denied social privileges. After a few days, the pattern was reversed. Children in a second class did not receive the "Green–Orange treatment" and served as a control group.

   Following this treatment, children from both classes were asked whether they wanted to go on a picnic with black children from another school. Ninety-six percent of the "Green–Orange" group expressed desire to go on the picnic, as compared with 62 percent of the controls. The experience of prejudice and discrimination apparently led the "Green–Orange" children to think that it is wrong to discriminate on the basis of color. Perhaps being discriminated against made the children more mindful of the sensitivities and feelings of members of outgroups.

2. *Intergroup Contact.* A stereotype is a fixed, conventional schema about a *group* of people. Negative stereotypes can lead us to avoid other groups, but

intergroup contact can break down stereotypes. Contact reveals that groups consist of individuals who are not, after all, homogeneous. They have different abilities, interests, personalities, attitudes, and even prejudices (Amir, 1976; Stephan, 1978).

Research has shown that intergroup contact can reduce prejudice when it is handled in a certain way (Clore et al., 1978; Kennedy & Stephan, 1977; Wilder & Thompson, 1980; Worchel et al., 1977). First, the individuals should work toward common goals rather than compete. Competition can stir up feelings of antipathy. Second, the individuals should come from similar socioeconomic backgrounds so that they have a number of things in common. Third, contacts should be informal. Highly structured contacts cause participants to feel distant from one another. Finally, prolonged contact is more effective than brief contact.

3. *Seeking Compliance with the Law.* On a more personal level, it may sometimes be appropriate to demand legal support if we have been discriminated against on the basis of race, religion, or other ethnic factors.
4. *Self-Examination.* Very often we say or do things that remind us that we have certain prejudices. Recently a Catholic acquaintance said "That damned Jew" when someone disappointed him. I asked if he had ever been disappointed by a Catholic, and, of course, the answer was yes. I then asked, "Did you call him 'That damned Catholic'?" Of course he hadn't. The thought had not occurred to him. Individuals of all groups have done, or might do, things that disappoint or disturb us. In such cases we need not deny the harm, but we should remember to attribute the behavior to them as *individuals,* not as *group representatives.*

Making a Positive First Impression As noted in the chapter, the first impressions we make on others, and the first impressions others make on us, are important to our interpersonal relationships. First impressions contribute to the concepts we form of others. Here are some things you can do to enhance the first impressions you make on others:

1. Become more aware of the first impressions you make on others. When you meet people for the first time, remember that they are forming person schemas about you. Once these schemas are formed, they are resistant to change.
2. When you apply for a job, your first impression may reach your prospective employer before you walk in the door. It is in the form of your vita or résumé. Make sure that it is neat and that some of your more important accomplishments are presented right at the beginning.

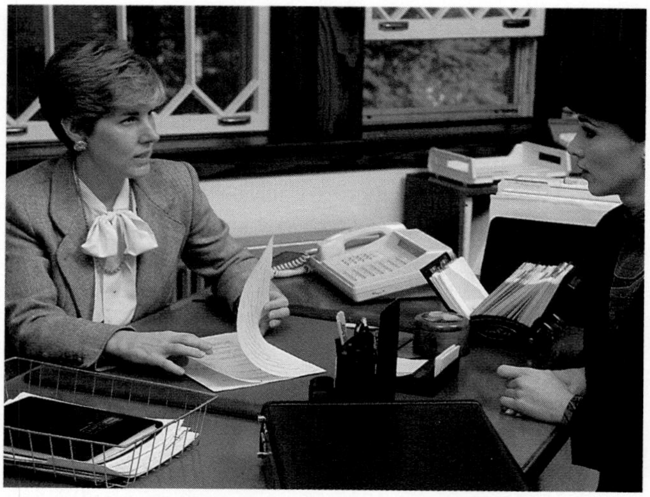

Making a Good First Impression. First impressions count. This is why defense attorneys deck out their clients in their Sunday finery and why the rest of us try to be neat and well-groomed for job interviews.

3. There's no harm in planning and rehearsing your first few remarks for a date or a job interview. Imagine the situation and, in the case of a job interview, things you are likely to be asked. If you have some relatively smooth statements prepared, along with a nice smile, you are more likely to be thought of as socially competent, and competence is respected.
4. Smile. As noted in the chapter, you're more attractive when you smile.
5. Be well dressed for job interviews, college interviews, first dates, or other important appointments.
6. When you write answers to essay questions, be concerned about your penmanship. It is the first thing your instructor notices when looking at your paper.
7. In class, seek eye contact with your instructors and look interested. That way, if you do poorly on a couple of quizzes, your instructor might think of you as a "basically good student who made a couple of errors" rather than "a poor student who is revealing his/her shortcomings." (Don't tell your instructor that this paragraph is in this book. Maybe he/she won't notice.)
8. The first time you talk to your instructor outside of class, be reasonable and sound interested in his/her subject.
9. When you pass someone in a race, put on a huge burst of speed. That way your competitor may think that trying to catch you will be futile.
10. Ask yourself if you are being fair to other people in your life. If your date's parents are a bit cold

toward you the evening of your first date, maybe it's because they don't know you and are concerned about their son/daughter's welfare. If you show them that you are treating their son/daughter decently, they may very well come around. Don't assume that they're basically prunefaces.

Attribution Theory and Conflict Resolution: Seeing Where the Other Person Is "Coming From" There are many biases in the attribution process, and some of them hinder our ability to discern other people's motives. As a result, we may blame them when blame is undue, and we may generate conflict. These biases even cloud our perceptions of ourselves.

Our review of theory and research concerning the attribution process leads to a few suggestions for construing things in more productive ways:

1. Avoid jumping to the conclusion that others are always to blame for their behavior. People may not always be completely responsible for their behavior. Nevertheless, we are biased to attribute too much of other people's behavior to dispositional factors (i.e., to make the fundamental attribution error). People are influenced by situational variables as well as by dispositional, person variables. Just a handful of these include financial hardship, physical illness, social pressures, academic stresses and strains, role models, the promise of reward, and the threat of punishment.

   So, when we do not like other people's behavior, we might try to empathize with them and imagine from their own perspective the pressures that are affecting them. As a result, we may understand them better, and we may also find factors that can be changed in an effort to induce more appropriate behavior.

2. Avoid jumping to the conclusion that we are *never* to blame for our behavior. We have also seen that we tend to be highly aware of the situational forces that act on us and influence our behavior. We tend to focus on external factors to the point that we often ignore our own dispositional factors—for example, the role of decision making in our own behavior. In other words, from time to time we place the responsibility for our own behavior—and our own behavioral changes—in the hands of others. For example, do you ever say to yourself, "How can I be expected to relax and unwind when I'm going to this pressure cooker of a college?" "How can I be happy when John/Mary treats me this way?" "How can I enjoy myself when I'm broke?" "How can I get out from under when my boss treats me this way?" "John/Mary will never understand me." Situational and dispositional variables may interact to influence our behavior patterns, but when we focus on the situational variables alone, we may lose sight of our own involvement in maladaptive behavior.

3. Recognize that other people may tend to blame us for things that are not our fault. Other people are also subject to biases in the attribution process. For example, they may attribute too much of our behavior to dispositional, internal factors. Our parents, employers, professors, lovers, and friends may think that we are being stubborn, mean, or even stupid when we do not accede to their requests. When in conflict with others, it is useful to explain the forces that we perceive to be acting on us—to give other people the information that will permit them to empathize with us.

4. Recognize that other people often see themselves as being coerced into their behavior. Remember that to some degree we tend to see ourselves as victims of circumstances, as compelled by our situations.

It is helpful to try to perceive events from the perspective of other people, including one's adversaries. When we realize that other people can feel forced into their behavior, just as we can, we can begin to focus on the forces that compel us all—not just on our own problems. Perhaps that is one of the great lessons of social psychology.

Outline

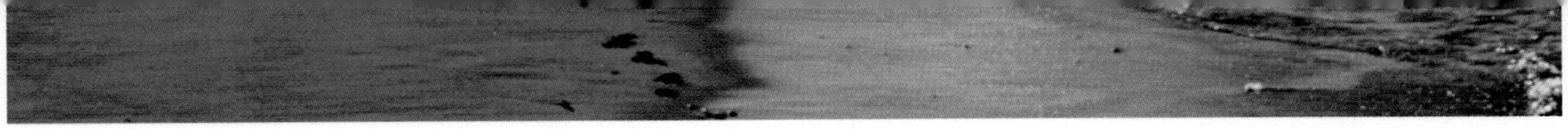

16 Applied Psychology

Truth or Fiction?

- Evaluators tend to rate workers on the basis of how well they like them rather than on their performance on the job.
- Efficient, skillful employees are evaluated more highly than hard-working employees who must struggle to get the job done.
- Stressed workers have more accidents on the job.
- Psychologists help design computer keyboards and aircraft controls.
- Television commercials must be likable if they are to influence us to buy the advertised products.
- Auto fumes can lower your children's IQ.
- Psychologists help police handle hostage crises.
- You can improve your athletic performance by imagining yourself making the right moves.
- Teachers who know more about a subject do a better job of teaching it.

Columnist Russell Baker once wrote, "The goal of all inanimate objects is to resist man and ultimately to defeat him." He must know my stove personally. Each morning it tries to do me in. It has four burners, two in back and two in front, but the burner controls are lined up in a neat row. Unless I strain my eyes looking for the tiny "F" or "B" that shows which one governs which burner, I wind up minutes later with a pot of cold water and a red-eyed burner glaring wrathfully at me. Then I hop into my shower—the one with the single knob that is turned clockwise for hot (or is it cold?) and counter-clockwise for cold (or is it hot?). Each morning I risk burning or freezing as I relearn which is which.

Next I encounter my car, whose "smart sticks" are much smarter than I. I usually turn on the lights when it begins to rain and the windshield wipers to welcome the twilight. I know that if I turn one of them clockwise (or is it counterclockwise?), I get intermittent wiping, and if I turn it counterclockwise (or is it clockwise?), I get rapid wiping, but I'm not sure which. To gas up, I have to release the gas tank-cover. Unfortunately, the control is out of sight on the floor to the side of the driver's seat, next to two others that feel just like it. So I'm as likely to pop open the hood or the trunk as the door to the gas tank. (The attendant always smiles.)

If I were not a psychologist, I would think that I'm just inept. But as a professional, I recognize all these problems as shortcomings in human-factors engineering. The field called human factors, or human factors in engineering, ensures that equipment and facilities are compatible with human behavior patterns and mental processes—that is, they are reasonably easy to work, or work in, and safe (Norman, 1988). But the machines surrounding me were either designed by sadists or left to chance.

Many industrial/organizational psychologists further specialize in human factors. Human-factors design is one example of **applied psychology.** There are many kinds of applied psychologists, but they all have some things in common: They all use psychological knowledge and methods to solve problems in the world outside the laboratory. All of them apply knowledge from psychology's basic areas—for example, knowledge of biology and behavior, sensation and perception, learning, memory, motivation, and personality—to meet broad needs. Clinical psychologists are the largest subgroup of applied psychologists. Clinical psychologists apply psychological knowledge from areas such as biology, learning, motivation, and personality to the evaluation and treatment of problems in abnormal behavior. Counseling psychologists apply psychological knowledge to help people with academic, vocational, and adjustment problems. Health psychologists, as we saw in Chapter 11, apply psychological knowledge to the prevention and treatment of illness. In this chapter we explore a number of other areas of applied psychology, including industrial/organizational psychology and the related fields of human factors and consumer psychology, environmental psychology, community psychology, forensic psychology, sports psychology, and educational psychology. In each case we shall discuss the ways in which basic psychological knowledge is applied to solve human problems.

INDUSTRIAL/ORGANIZATIONAL PSYCHOLOGY

It has been said that the business of the United States is business. From broad questions concerning the economy to the details of our own workplaces, earning a living—and the way we feel about earning a living—are vital concerns.

Over the years psychologists have become increasingly involved in the questions that confront the workplace. **Industrial/organizational (I/O) psychologists** are employed by corporations and other groups to help in matters such as the following:

- Devising psychological tests for recruitment of people for industrial positions
- Interviewing individuals who are being recruited for industrial positions
- Measuring performance on the job
- Motivating workers to increase productivity
- Enhancing job satisfaction
- Helping organizations function more efficiently

Applied psychology The application of fundamental psychological methods and knowledge to the investigation and solution of human problems.

Industrial psychology The field of psychology that studies the relationships between people and work.

Organizational psychology The field of psychology that studies the structure and functions of organizations.

- Identifying and modifying stressors in the workplace
- Making person–machine systems "user friendly" and efficient
- Studying and modifying the behavior of consumers

Currents in Contemporary Industrial/ Organizational Psychology

I/O psychology is born of several movements and contains many currents (Landy, 1985). First is the twentieth-century testing movement, which has focused on the measurement of individual differences in personality and aptitudes. The assumption is that there are relationships among a person's intelligence, personality traits (e.g., sociable or shy, domineering or self-abasing), and specific aptitudes (e.g., mechanical or musical) on the one hand and the requirements of various jobs on the other. People whose personal attributes fit the requirements of their jobs are better adjusted in their work and more productive.

Second is the human-relations (or human-potential) movement, which conveys the thinking of the humanistic psychologists Carl Rogers and Abraham Maslow. Rogers argued that we possess unique talents and abilities and that, ideally, the environment ought to encourage each of us to develop our bents (see Chapter 10). When this philosophy is translated into the workplace, one inference is that the workplace, like other arenas of life, should provide an opportunity for individuals to reach their potential, express unique talents, and find self-fulfillment. Historically, workers had been bound to their companies by loyalty and extrinsic rewards such as money and job status. Traditional values prompted workers to endure discomforts on the job as long as they brought home enough to support their families. But in recent years, according to pollster Daniel Yankelovitch (1981), workers have set family and self-loyalty above loyalty to their employers. Many of today's workers demand opportunities for self-development and self-fulfillment from their jobs, not just bread on the table.

Third is the industrial-engineering movement, which has sparked interest in efficient, user-friendly person–machine systems and has prompted psychologists to become involved in human factors.

Many I/O psychologists also apply the behavioral and cognitive perspectives. For example, since the 1960s they have applied principles of learning and behavior modification to the workplace. Behavioral principles have been used in industry, for example, to train workers in step-by-step fashion, to modify problem work behaviors, and to make sure that workers are rewarded for targeted behaviors. When required work behaviors are made explicit and the reinforcers (e.g., raises, bonuses, promotions, and time off) for completing tasks are spelled out, morale rises and complaints about favoritism decrease. In recent years, companies as diverse as Chase Manhattan, Proctor & Gamble, Ford, Standard Oil of Ohio, Emery Air Freight, General Electric, B. F. Goodrich, and Connecticut General Life Insurance have used behavior modification in some form.

I/O psychology is currently undergoing a "cognitive revolution" (e.g., Landy & Farr, 1983). The influences of cognitive psychology are being felt in issues ranging from biases in the appraisal of worker performance to the ways in which workers' information-processing capacities impact on the design of work environments. For example, as we shall see later, supervisors tend to rate employees according to how much they like them and to evaluate "hard workers" more positively than other workers, even if they accomplish less.

We shall consider some of the functions and findings of I/O psychologists in the areas of job recruitment, training, and evaluation.

Recruitment and Placement

Sometimes people get hired for reasons that are irrelevant to actual potential to perform in the job. Now and then people are hired because they are physically attractive (Cash & Kilcullen, 1985). On other occasions, nepotism reigns, and relatives or friends of friends get chosen. But by and large, in recruiting personnel, businesses attempt to find employees who are capable of doing the job and who are likely to be reasonably satisfied with it. Employees who are satisfied with their jobs have lower absenteeism and turnover (quit) rates. I/O psychologists facilitate recruitment procedures by analyzing jobs, specifying the skills and personal attributes that are needed in a position, and constructing tests and interview procedures that are likely to determine the presence of these skills and attributes among candidates. These procedures can enhance both job satisfaction and productivity (Hunter & Schmidt, 1983; Katzell & Guzzo, 1983).

Personnel Tests Personnel tests most likely to be used by organizations include tests of (1) intellectual abilities, (2) spatial and mechanical abilities, (3) perceptual accuracy, (4) motor abilities, and (5) personality and interests. An effort is made to correlate test performances with specific job requirements. For this reason, in assessing intellectual abilities, many employers are more concerned about candidates' verbal and numerical abilities than their overall level of intellectual functioning, as might be measured by the Wechsler scales.

Tests of mechanical comprehension are appropriate for many factory workers, construction workers, and of course, mechanics. They include items such as indicating which of two pairs of shears would cut metal better. Spatial-relations ability is needed in any job that requires the ability to visualize objects in three dimensions. Examples include drafting, clothing design, and architecture. Tests of perceptual accuracy are useful for clerical positions, such as bank tellers and secretaries. Some items on these tests require that respondents compare columns of letters, words, or numbers and indicate which do or do not match. Tests of motor abilities are useful for jobs that require strength, coordination of the limbs, rapid reaction time, or dexterity. Moving furniture, driving certain kinds of equipment, and sewing all require some motor skills.

The relationships between personality and performance in a job are somewhat less clear. It seems logical that one might wish to hire a candidate for a sales position who has a strong need to persuade others. However, many businesses have used personality tests to measure the candidates' general "stability," and this use has sometimes been criticized as an invasion of privacy.

Interest Inventories Psychologists have devised a number of interest inventories, such as the Strong/Campbell Interest Inventory and others, that predict adjustment in various occupations. Brown (1983) summarizes the validity data for such tests by noting that about half the people who score high in an occupational area choose that area, or a closely related area, for their occupation.

Interest in an occupation does not attest to presence of the aptitudes required to excel in that occupation. However, there are many types of jobs in a broad occupational area. Consider medicine. There are medical technicians (X-ray technicians, blood analysts, etc.), nurses, physical therapists, physicians, and many other specific occupations. Assessment of interests and aptitudes can help one zero in on a potentially fulfilling career.

On-the-Job Training. Employee training is the most commonly reported way of enhancing productivity. Training provides workers with appropriate skills, equips them to solve job problems, reduces stress, and enhances their feelings of self-worth.

Training and Instruction

I/O psychologists are versed in principles of learning, and worker training and instruction is the most commonly reported way of enhancing productivity (Katzell & Guzzo, 1983). Training provides workers with appropriate skills. Equipping them to solve job problems also reduces the stress they will encounter and enhances their feelings of self-worth. For reasons such as these, more than 90 percent of American corporations offer some kind of systematic training (Goldstein & Buxton, 1982).

Training programs usually follow when managers identify a need for improved performance in a given job. A formal needs assessment has three components: (1) organizational analysis, (2) task analysis, and (3) person or worker analysis.

Organizational analysis is appraisal of the goals and resources of the corporation or other institution. Consider IBM. The goals of IBM include such varied items as selling computers, identifying future markets, and pure scientific development (advancement of the sciences for their own sake, although commercial opportunities are certainly acted upon). The resources of IBM include factory workers, managers, sales personnel, doctoral-level scientists, and so on.

Task analysis involves appraisal of the duties (breaking them down into subparts) of a person in a given job title. For example, a police officer is expected to carry out duties ranging from operating vehicles under varied weather conditions and transporting prisoners to chasing animals, counseling juveniles, giving street directions, controlling crowds, and using weapons. Person analysis deals with the question of who should be trained. Trainees can include persons already in a job and new recruits.

Learning objectives are usually established on the basis of the needs analysis. Learning objectives are designed to give employees the skills, the knowledge, and sometimes the attitudes that they will need to perform well on the job. Why attitudes? A factory worker might resist wearing protective devices, even when taught how to do so, if he has the attitude that safety devices are for sissies. I have observed barehanded gardeners injuring themselves on thorns and barehanded construction clean-up workers injuring themselves on glass shards, nails, and so on all because of the self-defeating attitude that "real men" don't use protective gloves.

Once objectives are established, psychologists help devise ways to gain and maintain the workers' attention, to present materials in step-by-step fashion, to promote retention, and to evaluate the effectiveness of the training program.

Appraisal of Workers' Performance

Workers fare better and productivity is enhanced when workers receive individualized guidance and reinforcers are based on accurate appraisal of their performance. Criticism of workers' performance is necessary if workers are to improve, and it is important that criticisms be delivered constructively. Poor use of criticism is the greatest cause of conflict at work. It saps workers' motivation and belief in their own ability to perform adequately (Baron,

Organizational analysis Evaluation of the goals and resources of an organization

Task analysis The breaking down of a job or behavior pattern into its component parts.

1988). Workers respond best to criticisms that are specific, prompt, and delivered considerately (Ilgen, 1988).

Biases in the Appraisal Process In an ideal world, appraisal of workers' performances would be based solely on how well they do their jobs. And it does turn out that managers give the largest salary increments to workers whose objective performances are rated most positively (Alexander & Barrett, 1982). However, research into appraisal of performance shows that several biases are at work in the process.

One is a tendency for supervisors to focus on the *worker* rather than the worker's performance. Raters form general impressions of workers and then may evaluate them on the basis of these impressions rather than on how well they carry out their tasks (Williams, 1986).

Truth or Fiction Revisited

It is true that evaluators do tend to rate workers on the basis of how well they like them rather than on their performance on the job.

The tendency to rate workers according to general impressions (for example, of liking or disliking) is an example of the **halo effect.** The halo effect is often overcome when raters are instructed to focus on how well the worker carries out specific tasks.

Behavioral I/O psychologists suggest that the criteria for appraisal be totally objective—based on publicly observable behaviors that are outlined to workers and supervisors beforehand. Ideally, workers are rated according to whether or not they engage in targeted behavior patterns. Workers are not penalized for intangibles such as "poor attitude." Of course, workers cannot be rated according to objective standards unless a comprehensive task analysis of a job is undertaken.

A second bias in the appraisal procedure is the tendency to evaluate workers according to how much effort they put into their work (Knowlton & Mitchell, 1980).

Truth or Fiction Revisited

It is *not* true that efficient, skillful employees are evaluated more highly than hard-working employees who must struggle to get the job done! Supervisors actually tend to focus on the extent of employees' efforts, sometime to a greater degree than their actual performance.

Hard work is not necessarily good work. (Do you think that students who work harder than you should be given higher grades on tests, even when you get the answers right and they make errors?) It is more productive, again, to focus on how well workers perform targeted behaviors and to evaluate the workers on this basis.

We tend to overestimate the role of dispositional (internal) factors in our attributions for other people's behavior, as noted in Chapter 15. This attribution error extends into the workplace. For example, American workers have been criticized in recent years for flagging productivity. That is, as productivity in Japan and some other nations began to surpass our own, there was a tendency to assume that American were lazy. More perceptive critics of the workplace have noted that situational factors, such as the aid of robots, have contributed to the (apparent) lagging of American workers. Similarly, in individual cases there is also a tendency to exaggerate the roles of skill and motivation in performance and to minimize the role of situational factors (Gioia & Sims, 1985; Heerwagen et al., 1985).

Halo effect The tendency for one's general impression of a person to influence one's perception of aspects of, or performances by, that person.

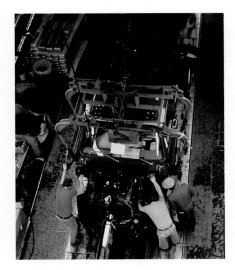

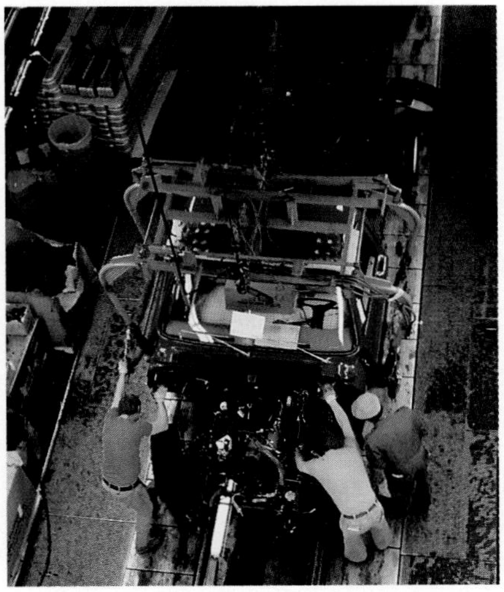

The Assembly Line. Although the assembly line is an integral part of contemporary industrial life, many workers sing the "assembly-line blues." Assembly-line workers may repeat one task hundreds of times a day and never see the finished product. Experimental work-redesign programs are helping many such workers—and their companies.

Both situational and dispositional factors play roles in workers' satisfaction. Let us now consider a number of them.

Enhancing Job Satisfaction

Businesses are interested in employee satisfaction for humanitarian and self-serving reasons. That is, managers are people, and many of them want their employees to be satisfied. But from a self-serving perspective, satisfied employees also have better attendance records and are less likely to quit. Absenteeism and turnover cost companies money. Products get put together more slowly, and new workers may spend more time in training than on the job. So I/O psychologists have studied various factors that contribute to job satisfaction.

Goal Setting Workers should know exactly what is demanded of them. Too often goals are vague. Workers are told that they should "work hard" or "be serious" about their jobs, but hard work and seriousness are ill defined. Lack of understanding of what is expected creates anxiety and hampers performance. Behaviorally oriented I/O psychologists point out that workers who know what is required of them can better conform their behavior to supervisors' expectations. Setting concrete goals at high but attainable levels can render work challenging but keep stress within acceptable limits.

Financial Compensation I/O psychologists offer advice about the potentials and pitfalls of rewards. When possible, performance should be linked to financial reward. It can be demoralizing when productive workers earn no more than nonproductive workers. If financial incentives are to be used, however, productivity must be assessed objectively. If assessment is subjective, workers may become demoralized because of actual or suspected favoritism.

Some I/O psychologists suggest that supervisors handle problem performances in a manner consistent with principles of behavior modification. As noted in Chapter 5, punishment of unacceptable behavior does not in itself teach acceptable behavior, and it can also create hostility. It is preferable, through careful assessment and training, to provide workers with the skills to perform adequately and then to reinforce the targeted work behaviors.

Work Redesign I/O psychologists understand the importance of creating settings in which workers can feel pride and a sense of closure. An assembly-line worker may repeat one task hundreds of times a day and never see the finished product. To make factory work more meaningful, workers at one Volvo assembly plant in Sweden have been organized into small groups that elect leaders and distribute tasks among themselves. In another work-redesign program, workers move along the assembly line with "their" truck chassis, which gives them the satisfaction of seeing their product take shape (Blackler & Brown, 1978). In an experiment at Motorola, one worker builds an entire pocket radio pager and signs the product when finished. The janitorial staff members at a Texas Instruments worksite meet in small groups to set goals and distribute cleaning tasks among themselves. Texas Instruments reports a cleaner plant, lowered costs, and decreased turnover (Dickson, 1975).

The concept of the **quality circle,** practiced widely in Japan, has also been catching on in the United States. Ironically, this method, in which workers meet regularly to discuss problems and suggest solutions, was

Quality circle A regularly scheduled meeting in which a group of workers discusses problems and suggests solutions in order to enhance the quality of products.

brought to Japan after World War II by H. Edwards Deming, an American. I/O psychologists note that quality circles give workers a greater sense of control over their jobs and increase their commitment to the company (Lawler & Mohrman, 1985; Marks, 1986). Moreover, workers are often in the best position to perceive problems that impede performance.

Work Schedules When there is no company reason for maintaining a rigid 9:00-to-5:00 schedule, workers frequently profit from **flextime,** or being able to modify their own schedules to meet their personal needs. In one variation on flextime, workers put in four ten-hour workdays rather than five eight-hour days (Ronen, 1981). Flextime lowers absenteeism and enables workers to better meet personal and family needs as well as company needs (Cohn, 1988; Narayanan & Nath, 1982).

At Honeywell, a "mothers' shift" allows women to coordinate their work schedules with their children's school hours. Mothers also may have college students fill in for them during their children's summer vacations. Are we ready for a "fathers' shift"?

In job sharing, multiple workers fill one job, which permits them to carry out family responsibilities and also meets company needs. For example, at Steelcase, 40 workers share 20 jobs. Since job sharing was introduced, absenteeism among working mothers has declined (Cohn, 1988).

Our focus on recruitment, training, appraisal, and job satisfaction has been largely on the worker within the organization. But in their efforts to enhance efficiency and productivity, I/O psychologists also focus on the broader nature of organizations themselves, as we see in our discussion of organizational theory.

Organizational Theory

Organizations are composed of people, but like most institutions, organizations have their own characters. These include formal characteristics such as the chain of command, channels of communication, and policies concerning hiring, compensation, and retirement. But corporations also have informal characteristics, such as "personalities," which may be impersonal and cold, warm and familylike, authoritarian, or relatively permissive.

The traits of individuals involve relatively stable ways of responding to the demands of life. The formal and informal characteristics of organizations also constitute "traits"—consistent ways in which organizations respond to economic, political, and other challenges to organizational life. As with individuals, we may speak of corporations as adapting or failing to adapt to environments (such as economic environments) and as growing and thriving or as acting sick and dying or disintegrating.

Adaptation to new economic environments certainly requires the imaginative responses of individuals within organizations. But organizational changes may also be required if businesses are to remain competitive. For example, during the 1980s we became accustomed to hearing of corporations heightening competitiveness by stripping away layers of middle management (thereby cutting costs) and, as a consequence, becoming "leaner and meaner." Many formerly staid corporations changed their personalities and acquired "lean and hungry" looks.

As with other areas of psychology, there are different theoretical approaches to organizing businesses. Three broad approaches are in sway today: *classic organization theory, contingency theories,* and *human-relations theories.*

Flextime A modification of one's work schedule from the standard 9:00 to 5:00 in order to enable one to better meet personal needs.

Classic Organization Theories **Classic organization theories** tend to propose that there is one best way to structure an organization—from the skeleton outward. That is, organization is based on the required levels of authority and supervision.

Classic organization theories frequently rely on a **bureaucracy,** which ideally frees workers from the injustices of favoritism and nepotism and enables them to make long-range plans. Other elements of classic organization theories include the division of labor and the delegation of authority. The computer firm Texas Instruments has a classic organization and "sends down orders from the top" (*The New York Times,* 1987, p. D8).

Contingency Theories of Organization **Contingency theories** hold that there are many valid ways to structure organizations, and that organizational approaches are *contingent on* factors such as organizational goals, workers' characteristics, and the overall political or economic environment. For example, a classic bureaucracy might make sense when timeliness and accuracy in production are central corporate objectives. When scientific innovation is the major goal, however, a less centralized, authoritarian organization might be more facilitative. For reasons such as these, IBM—which has many functions and goals, including production and scientific innovation—structures its internal organization in different ways. Production workers may be given concrete goals. Scientists engaged in basic research are given extensive resources and are pretty much left to their own devices. Product developers, in contrast, often compete for scarce resources, and only a minority of new product ideas survive internal reviews.

Human-Relations Theories of Organization **Human-relations theories** begin their structuring with the individual—the worker. They argue that the behavior of the organization cannot be predicted or controlled without taking into account the characteristics and needs of the individual worker. From this perspective, efficient organizational structure will reflect the cognitive processes of individuals as these processes are applied to problem solving, decision making, and the quests for self-expression and self-fulfillment. Let us consider three human-relations approaches: McGregor's *Theory Y,* Argyris's developmental theory, and Ouichi's *Theory Z.*

Theory Y Douglas McGregor's (1960) **Theory Y** is based on the assumption that workers are motivated to take responsibility for their work behavior and that worker apathy and misbehavior stem from shortcomings of the organization. Theory Y holds that management's central task is to structure the organization so that organizational goals will be congruent with workers' goals. Workers cannot be expected to be productive if their personal goals are at odds with those of the organization.

Argyris's Developmental Theory Chris Argyris (1972) notes a number of developmental principles and suggests that organizations are structured efficiently when they allow their workers to develop. For example, Argyris notes that individuals develop in the following ways:

- From passive to active organisms
- From dependent to independent organisms
- From organisms capable of dealing with concrete issues to organisms capable of dealing with abstract issues, and
- From organisms with few abilities to organisms with many abilities

---

Classic organization theories Theories that hold that organizations should be structured from the skeleton (governing body) outward.

Bureaucracy An administrative system characterized by departments and subdivisions whose members frequently are given long tenure and inflexible work tasks.

Contingency theories Theories that hold that organizational structure should depend on factors such as goals, workers' characteristics, and the overall economic or political environment.

Human-relations theories Theories that hold that efficient organizations are structured according to the characteristics and needs of the individual worker.

Theory Y McGregor's view that organizational goals should be congruent with workers' goals.

PSYCHOLOGY GOES TO WORK

Fighting the Assembly-Line Blues

Because people undergo broad developmental processes, certain kinds of work environments are inherently flawed for many if not for all workers. For example, assembly-line work does not allow workers to function independently and to express multiple abilities. Thus tension may be created on the job, leading to apathy, absenteeism, and turnover. As noted earlier, many companies have instituted methods such as work redesign so that workers can have a sense of control and can develop.

At Steelcase, Inc., the Grand Rapids, Michigan, office-furniture company, workers receive a moderate hourly wage but can earn virtually unlimited incentive pay for each chair they upholster or each slab of metal they cut (Cohn, 1988). Many workers raise their base income by 35 percent or more in this way. Profit sharing enhances productivity and also allows workers to nearly double their income if the company does well. Therefore, workers encourage each other to keep up the pace on the assembly line. Colleagues who are nonproductive are referred to as "bonus busters."

Steelcase, Inc. also has a "cafeteria style" benefits plan that lets workers feel they are in charge of their future. Workers can apply their benefits to an assortment of medical plans, dental plans, and off-site day care programs. Unused benefits can be taken home in cash or salted away to augment retirement income.

Theory Z Ouchi's (1981) **Theory Z** combines some of the positive features of the Japanese workplace with some of the realities of the American workplace in an effort to foster loyalty to the company and heighten productivity. Perhaps the most salient feature of many Japanese workplaces is their *paternalism*—that is, offering security through lifetime employment, involvement of workers' families in company activities, and the subsidizing of housing and education for workers' families. Many American firms, in contrast, lay off workers with every economic downturn. Ouchi's theory compromises by suggesting that American firms offer long-term (if not lifetime) employment when possible. Restructuring to avoid layoffs would enhance workers' loyalty—as is the case with IBM.

Traditionally there is high division of labor and specialization in the American workplace, leading to feelings of being "cubbyholed" and lack of a sense of control over the whole product. Japanese career paths tend to be relatively nonspecialized, allowing for sideways movement and variety. Again, a compromise of a moderately specialized career path is suggested. In the traditional American workplace, decision making and responsibility are in the hands of relatively few supervisors. In Japan, decision making tends to be consensual and responsibility collective. In Japan, moreover, managers often eat with laborers and share their bathrooms. The importing of the quality circle and the creation of other methods for enhancing employees' sense of participation in the decision-making process are also consistent with the compromises of Theory Z. Although the Japanese are highly competitive in the world marketplace, managers within given firms tend to reach decisions by means of consensus, in contrast to the typical American "winner-take-all" approach. And so, another Theory-Z Japanese import is a consensus management system, in which managers tend to feel that "nobody has lost."

Professional psychologists are highly concerned with the dignity of the individual. For this reason, they tend to gravitate toward organizational structures that allow for the self-development and satisfaction of the individual worker. In many cases, this leaning also heightens productivity.

In the next section we highlight an issue in which health psychology and I/O psychology overlap: stress in the workplace.

Theory Z Ouchi's view that adapts positive features of the Japanese workplace to the U.S. workplace.

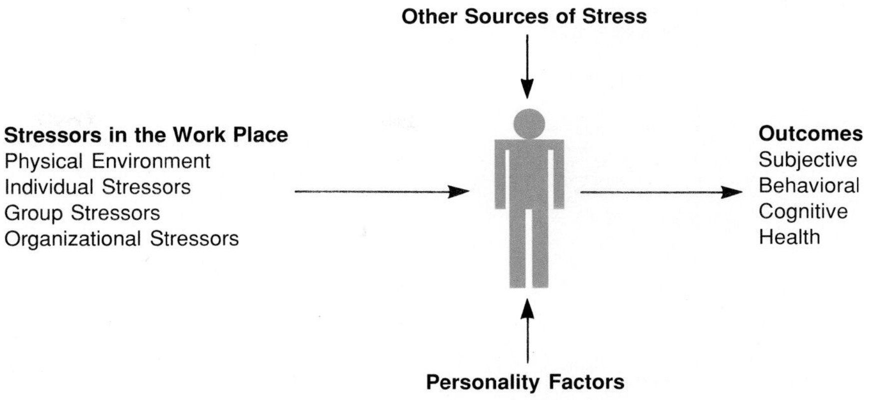

Figure 16.1
A Model for the Effects of Stress in the Workplace. Various sources of stress, such as those emanating from relationships with co-workers, the physical environment, and organizational policies, affect the worker. Workplace stressors can also interact with stresses from home and personality factors to produce negative outcomes.

Stress and Work

Most of us don't "punch out" and leave our work behind us. When we figure in commutation, preparation, lunch time, continuing education, and just thinking about the job, many of us invest more than half our waking hours in our work. So stress on the job can dominate our lives and aggravate stress at home. Frustrations and resentments over work can tire us and set our tempers on short fuses. They can intensify family conflicts (Gibson et al., 1985). In a vicious cycle, marital conflict may then magnify problems in the workplace.

The left-hand part of Figure 16.1 shows how various features of the workplace can contribute to stress (Ivancevich & Matteson, 1980). Among the aspects of the physical environment that can produce stress are poor lighting, air pollution (including cigarette or cigar smoke produced by co-workers and clients), crowding, noise, and extremes of temperature. Individual stressors include work overload, boredom, conflict about one's work (e.g., being ordered to give an offender psychological treatment when one believes that he or she should be treated purely as a criminal), excessive responsibility, and lack of forward movement. Group stressors include irritating relationships with supervisors, subordinates, and peers.

Organizational stressors include lack of opportunity to participate in decision making, ambiguous or conflicting company policies, too much or too little organizational structure, low pay, racism, and sexism. There are many others (Holt, 1982).

The central part of Figure 16.1 shows the worker and the sources of stress that may be acting on him or her. For example, marital or inner conflict may compound any conflicts encountered in the workplace. A Type-A personality may turn an easy, routine task into a race against the clock. Irrational needs for excessive approval may diminish the effect of rewards.

The right-hand side of the figure suggests a number of possible outcomes from the interaction of these sources of stress. On a subjective level, stressed workers can experience anxiety, depression, frustration, fatigue, boredom, and loss of self-esteem (Gibson et al., 1985). Behaviorally, stressed workers may become accident prone, engage in excessive eating or smoking, turn to alcohol or other drugs (Bensinger, 1982; Milam & Ketcham, 1981; Peyser, 1982), and show temperamental outbursts.

Truth or Fiction Revisited

It is true that stressed workers have more accidents on the job.

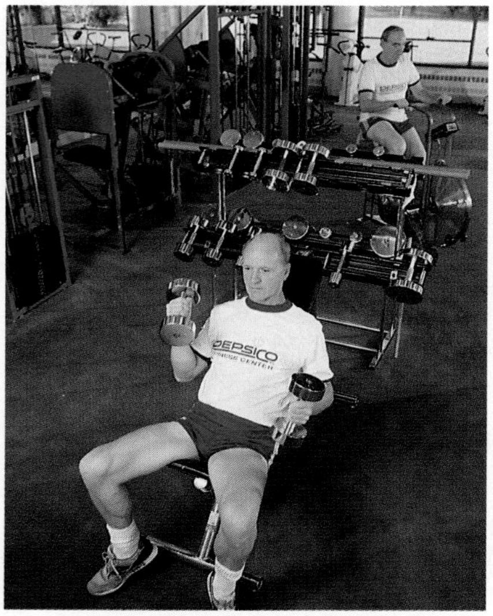

Working Out in the Workplace. Many companies realize that employee stress decreases job satisfaction and contributes to high absenteeism and turnover. They are finding ways to help workers handle stress, including providing facilities for physical development and fitness.

On a cognitive level, stress decreases attention span, impairs concentration, and interferes with decision making. Physiological effects include high blood pressure and the "diseases of adaptation" discussed in Chapter 11. The organizational effects of stress include absenteeism, alienation from co-workers, decreased productivity, turnover, and loss of commitment and loyalty to the organization (Gibson et al., 1985; McKenna et al., 1981).

I/O psychologists have identified measures that can abate stress in the workplace. They often begin with an objective analysis of the workplace to determine whether physical conditions are hampering rather than enhancing the quality of work life. A good deal of job stress arises from a mismatch between job demands and the employee's abilities and needs (Chemers et al., 1985). I/O psychologists help companies enhance screening (e.g., interviewing and psychological testing) to recruit employees whose personalities are compatible with job requirements. They also help companies provide the training and education to impart skills that will enable workers to perform effectively. Through task analysis, they make job requirements specific and clear.

Social support moderates the effect of stress, as noted in Chapter 11. I/O psychologists point out that workers need to feel that their supervisors will support them when they have complaints or suggestions (Gottlieb, 1983; Rocco et al., 1980). I/O psychologists have shown companies how to help workers manage stress through counseling and supportive therapy, education about health, and gymnasiums (Glasgow & Terborg, 1988). Control Data, IBM, Johnson & Johnson, Kimberly-Clark, Xerox, Pepsi-Cola, Weyerhauser, and Rockwell International, for example, encourage employees to use nearby health facilities or have invested in gyms with jogging tracks and exercise cycles.

As noted earlier, the way some of the objects around me are designed provides me with a good deal of unneeded stress. In the next section we consider some of the functions of psychologists who specialize in human factors.

HUMAN FACTORS

I was griping about the ways in which displays are *coded.* The controls of my stove, shower, and car hassle me because they are arbitrary, inconvenient, and, to some degree, dangerous. To use the vernacular, they are "user-*un*friendly." Psychologists in **human factors** apply knowledge of biology, sensation and perception, learning, memory, and motivation in enhancing the efficiency and safety of person–machine systems and work environments.

Criteria for Evaluating Person–Machine Systems and Work Environments

In evaluating the efficiency and safety of stoves and other kinds of equipment, human-factors psychologists use performance criteria, physiological criteria, subjective criteria, and accident and injury criteria (McCormick & Ilgen, 1985).

Performance standards involve the quality of the performance made possible by the design. For example, how rapidly can the task (such as finding the proper water temperature in the shower!) be carried out? Can it be performed without making errors? (Am I likely to turn on the correct burner of the stove?)

Human factors The field that studies the efficiency and safety of person–machine systems and work environments.

An Intimidating Display. Display panels of modern instruments can be overwhelming unless their coding is helpful. I/O psychologists attribute the following characteristics to good coding: detectability, discriminability, compatibility, meaningfulness, standardization, and multidimensionality.

Physiological standards involve the physical changes caused by operating the equipment. For example, are switches difficult to throw? Does working in a certain factory raise the blood pressure or damage the lungs? Does the screen of the computer monitor cause eye strain?

Subjective criteria include psychological factors such as boredom and job satisfaction. We saw that for many people, assembly-line work is boring and nonsatisfying. There can be high absenteeism and turnover in such humdrum positions. Keyboards are more enjoyable to work when they make responsive clacks; quiet keyboards are frustrating. And computer programmers attempt to choose pleasing color combinations for the screen. (My screen now shows white letters against a crisp blue background that reminds me of the noon sky in New Mexico.)

And, of course, the degree to which designs foster or prevent accidents and injuries is crucial. Are we at risk of burning our hands (or our houses down!) when we cannot readily find the control that governs the burner? Fortunately, I have not yet been injured in the shower, but making the water hotter when I think I am cooling it down could have dangerous consequences. How many times do we injure ourselves by using dangerous tools? Part of the problem may lie in failure to follow rules of safety. But tools are also often designed less safely than they could be.

Criteria for Evaluating the Coding in Displays

I don't want you to think that I'm obsessed with my stove, so I'll talk about word processing for a minute. My current "enhanced" computer keyboard has nicely marked keys that say "Insert" and "Delete." With my previous (unenhanced) keyboard, I had to press a function key simultaneously with keys for regular letters. But it wasn't too difficult because the "D" key was used for deleting and the "S" key, which is next to it, was used for inserting. Think of the designer's quandary: Should the "S" or "I" key be used to insert material? The "I" key begins with the proper letter, but the "S" key sat next to the "D" key and in the section of the keyboard that housed all the codes. It worked out fine.

The "Men" and "Women" restroom signs are adequate for people who read English, and "Caballeros" and "Damas" are helpful for speakers of Spanish. But the universal nonverbal code is a stick figure of a man or woman. Here the code (the figure) is inherently related to the function of the design. That is, one door is meant for men to walk through, the other for women. Consider, however, an arbitrary code that is growing in popularity: Decaffeinated coffee is almost always served from pots that are color-coded orange. If you think about it logically, perhaps decaffeinated coffee should be color-coded green or blue. As noted in Chapter 3, orange is a warm color, and oranges and reds are more likely than greens and blues to be used to signal increases in intensity or danger. Since caffeine is the "dangerous" substance, shouldn't caffeinated coffee be coded orange or red? Nevertheless, common practice seems to overcome logic.

I/O psychologists attribute the following characteristics to good coding (McCormick & Ilgen, 1985):

- *Detectability.* Good codes are readily detected or sensed. I had difficulty detecting the gas-tank cover release lever because it was out of sight (down along the side of my seat).
- *Discriminability.* Good codes can be discriminated from other symbols of the kind. My gas-tank cover release switch was next to the hood and trunk releases, and the three were similar in design—not easy to tell apart.

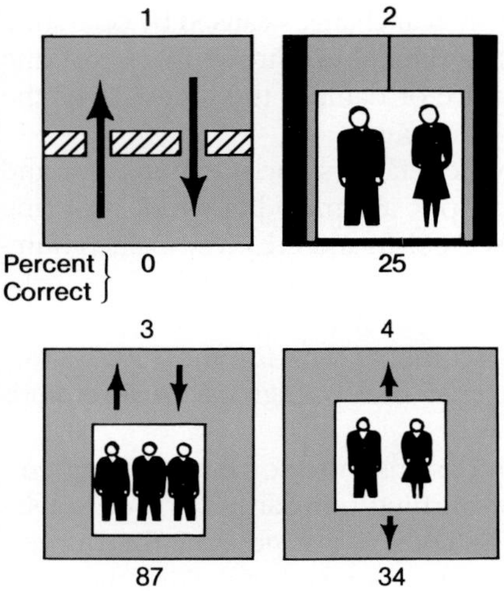

Figure 16.2
Elevator Symbols. Psychologists in human factors evaluate symbols' effectiveness at communicating ideas. Which of these symbols best signifies an elevator to you?

- *Compatibility.* Good codes are consistent with our expectations. The stick figure of a man is compatible with our expectation that the room being coded is the "men's room." For reasons noted, however, the color orange is incompatible with *de*caffeinated coffee.
- *Meaningfulness.* When possible, good codes symbolize the information in question. The stick figure of the man symbolizes men. The "Do not enter" symbol is a meaningful barrier. However, the meaning of orange as the symbol for decaffeinated coffee runs contrary to the color's "meaning."
- *Standardization.* When possible, the same code should be used universally. Growing consistency in usage is the saving grace of using the color orange to signify decaffeinated coffee. Using green to mean go and red to mean stop is universal in traffic lights.
- *Multidimensionality.* Codes are made easier to recognize when they employ two or more dimensions. Traffic stop signs, for example, employ a hexagonal shape and are red in color. A green stop sign would confuse drivers and create hazardous crossings. Red traffic lights are always on top: Top to bottom, they are arranged red, amber, green. You may not ever think about this array, but if you drove up to an intersection with a different grouping, it wouldn't feel right, and there might be accidents.

Psychologists who engage in human-factors design, like other psychologists, are empirically oriented. In addition to deriving design concepts from psychological theory, they try them out before implementing them. Consider, for example, the four designs in Figure 16.2. Which telegraphs itself as the best symbol for an elevator? As you can see from the numbers beneath the designs, the third was identified as the symbol for an elevator by 87 percent of subjects in one study (Mackett-Stout & Dewar, 1981). *None* correctly identified the symbol on the left. From this type of research, the more effective designs would be selected. And if no code were correctly identified by the great majority of subjects, perhaps designers would return to the drawing board.

Figure 16.3 provides some other examples of good symbols. Part A of Figure 16.4 shows my problem with the electric stove: The burners are grouped in a square, but the controls form a line. In his book *The Psychology of Everyday Things,* psychologist Donald Norman (1988) agrees with me that if the controls were in a square pattern that corresponded to the arrangement of the burners (see Part B of Figure 16.4), I wouldn't be heating the air and

Figure 16.3
Visual-Code Symbols. Psychologists in human factors apply knowledge of sensation and perception in the design of effective visual-code symbols.

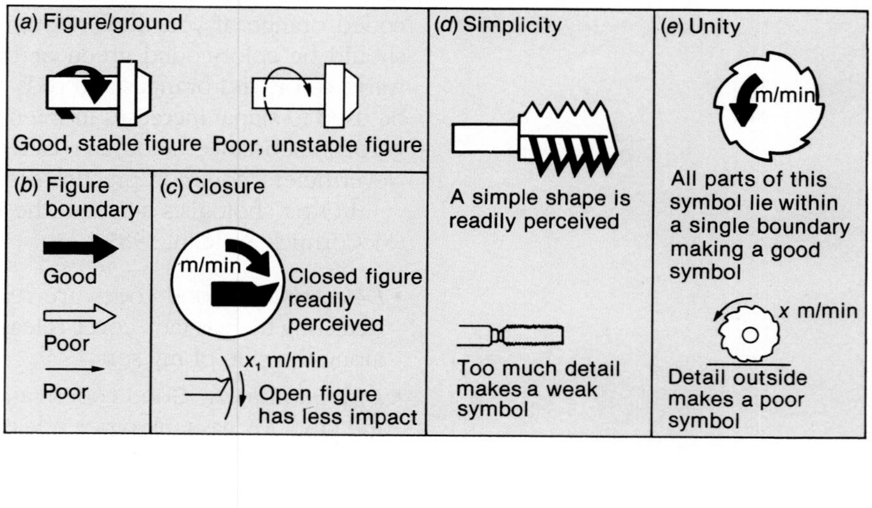

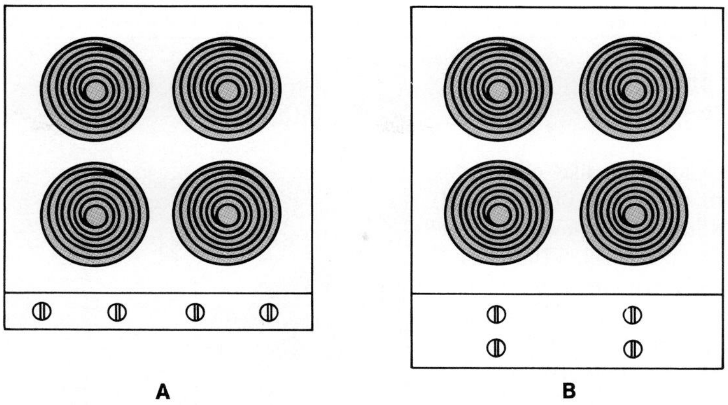

Figure 16.4
Two Stove-Top Configurations. Well-designed regulation systems are readily interpreted by users (are "user-friendly.") Which control regulates which burner? Is it easier to determine which regulates which in stove top A or stove top B?

pouring ice-cold water over my poor wife's tea bags. Finally, note how the shape-coded cockpit control knobs in Figure 16.5 discourage a pilot from accidentally activating the wrong mechanism.

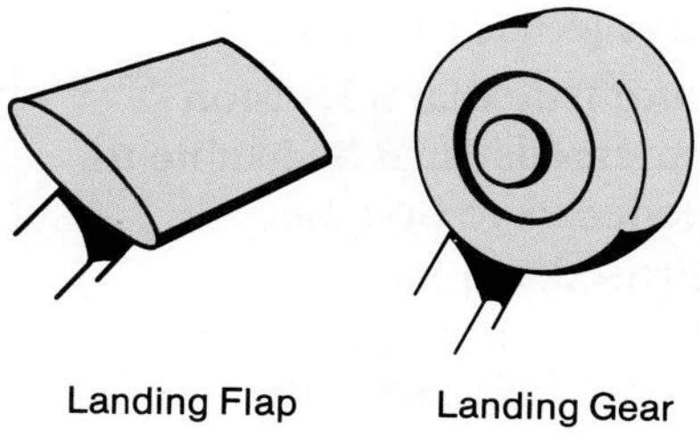

Figure 16.5
Shape-Coded Control Knobs. How does the shape of each airplane control knob help signal its function?

Truth or Fiction Revisited

It is true that psychologists help design computer keyboards, aircraft controls, and many other person–machine systems. These psychologists work in human factors.

Human-factors engineering can make our devices and machines safer and more user-friendly. In a following section, we shall explore some of the ways in which environmental psychologists are learning more about our relationships with our physical environment—in the workplace and elsewhere.

CONSUMER PSYCHOLOGY

Consumer psychology applies psychological methods to the investigation and modification of consumer behavior and mental processes. We encounter topics of concern to consumer psychologists every day. Here is just a brief list:

- Why are consumers loyal to one brand or another? For example, why do consumers buy Miller Beer or Budweiser?
- What qualities or characteristics do consumers associate with various brands? For example, what are consumers' impressions of American cars versus Japanese cars?
- How can consumer attitudes toward products be modified? How can brand images be enhanced? For example, how can consumers be persuaded that the reliability of American cars and electronic devices is improving? Why did Pepsico hire Mike Tyson to endorse Diet Pepsi?*
- What is the best way to market a new product? Should there be a national advertising blitz, or should the product first be tested in a local market?

Consumer psychology The field of psychology that studies the nature, causes, and modification of consumer behavior and mental processes.

*Apparently to counter the image that diet soft drinks are appropriate for women only.

PSYCHOLOGY GOES TO WORK

Psychology and Marketing Research

Consumer psychologists, like other psychologists, are empirically oriented, and their methods have had a powerful effect on marketing personnel. They have shown marketing managers how to test hypotheses concerning the effectiveness of advertising, marketing, and so on through *marketing research*. In this method, a consumer population is *targeted*—for example, "yuppies," babyboomers, or teenagers. Representative samples are then drawn from the target population, and their responses to product names, ads, packages, and the products themselves are measured. So-called taste tests of soft drinks apply methods used by psychologists who study sensation and perception. Consumer psychologists find ways of having drinkers indicate their preferences for the flavors of various beverages. Subjects may simply report that they prefer brand A over the notorious brand X. Or they may rate each drink on, for example, scales from one to ten according to variables such as sweetness, stimulation, general liking, and so on.

In applying principles of social psychology, consumer psychologists also study the factors that enhance advertisements' persuasiveness. For example, does sex sell? Are

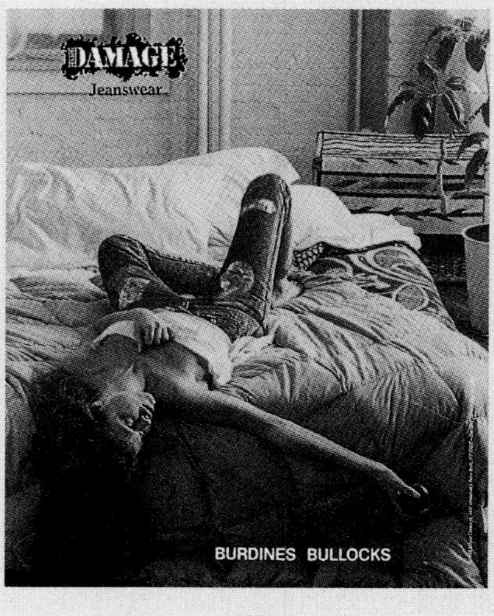

An Enticing Advertisement. Ads such as this certainly gain readers' attention. The question is whether readers remember the product and when to use it or whether the ad actually distracts readers from this information.

cars made more appealing to viewers when an attractive woman drives them or yearns for the male driver? And what about all those sexy jeans ads? Consumer psychologists have found that when ads are too sexy, they may catch the eye, but you may forget the product (LaChance et al., 1978).

Social psychologists have found that an attitude of liking—toward people—is associated with behavioral tendencies to approach people. But do attitudes toward advertisements transfer into approach or avoidance tendencies toward the products? Not necessarily. For example, consumer psychologists have found that it doesn't matter whether a commercial is likable or irritating. What is important is that the viewer can remember the product and when to use it (Baron & Byrne, 1987).

Truth or Fiction Revisited

It is *not* true that television commercials must be likable to influence us to buy the advertised products. It is sufficient that they prompt the viewer to remember the product and when to use it.

Many TV viewers hated the "Tastes great!–Less filling!" commercials, but the commercials markedly increased sales of Lite Beer.

Task Analysis of Consumer Behavior

Consumer psychologists have undertaken task analyses of consumer behavior and found that it often involves a number of steps: deciding to make a purchase, selecting the brand, shopping, buying the product, and evaluating how well it meets one's needs (Robertson et al., 1984). Consumer psychologists study ways of intervening at each stage in order to enhance the probability that consumers will decide to make a purchase and choose a certain brand. Advertising, for example, is used not only to help consumers tell brands apart but also to encourage them to make a purchase. Packaging similarly helps consumers distinguish between brands, and, if the packages are "pretty" enough, consumers may assume that "good things come in" them. First impressions count in the supermarket as well as in the world of interpersonal relationships.

ENVIRONMENTAL PSYCHOLOGY

Environmental psychologists study the ways in which people and the physical environment influence each other (Holahan, 1986). As people, we have needs that must be met to some degree if we are to remain physically and psychologically healthy. Environmental conditions such as temperature and population density affect our capacities to meet our needs. People also influence the environment. We have pushed back forests and driven many species to extinction or near extinction. In recent years, our impact has mushroomed, as the controversies over the greenhouse effect, the diminution of the ozone layer, and acid rain clearly show. Many of us have an aesthetic interest in the environment and appreciate the remaining bastions of wilderness. But protecting the environment also ultimately means protecting ourselves—for it is in the environment that we flourish or fade away.

Environmental psychology The field of psychology that studies the ways in which people and the environment influence one another.

Therefore, one concern of environmental psychologists is the study of ways to persuade people to consider the damage that they may be doing to the environment. But in this section we shall forego the soap box and explore some findings of environmental psychologists concerning the effects of atmospheric conditions, noise, heat, and crowding on us.

A CLOSER LOOK

Let the Sun Shine In

Environmental psychologists have discovered that our dispositions may vary with the sunshine. To some degree we become bright and open, or grim and cloudy, as the skies do. We tend to be more cooperative and generous when the sun shines down on us.

In one phase of a study by Cunningham (1979), student passers-by at the University of Minnesota were asked to fill out a drawn out public-opinion poll. They were more likely to accede when the sun was shining than when the day was cloudy but equal in temperature. Temperature, wind velocity, and humidity also played roles. Cooperation peaked when the temperature was an agreeable 65 degrees Fahrenheit and slackened when the thermometer moved up or down. Wind velocity was positively linked to cooperation in the summer, when cooling breezes are appreciated, but negatively linked in winter, when the wind-chill factor chilled the hearts of passers-by. Students were more cooperative when the air was dry. High humidity dampened participation.

Sunshine streaming in through restaurant windows may also warm customers' hearts, as measured by the size of tips. In another phase of the Cunningham study, waitresses at a Chicago restaurant with large windows tracked their tips for several weeks. The temperature and humidity in the restaurant were kept constant during the period. But when the sun shone, it shone into the restaurant as well, and tips were significantly larger.

If misfortune should befall us so that we are in need of help, let us hope that the sun is shining, the temperature is 65 degrees F, and the humidity is low. Now let us see what might have happened to waitresses' tips if trucks had been clamoring noisily outside the restaurant.

At the Disco. Couples may enjoy high noise levels (up to 140 dB) at the discotheque. Less desirable noises of only 80 dB, however, can decrease feelings of attraction, put a damper on helping behavior, and contribute to aggressive behavior.

Noise: Of Muzak, Rock 'n' Roll, and Low-Flying Aircraft

Environmental psychologists apply knowledge of sensation and perception in an effort to design environments that induce positive emotional responses and contribute to human performance. Thus they may suggest sound-proofing of certain environments or the use of pleasant background sounds, such as music or recordings of water in natural environments (rain, the beach, brooks, and so on). However, noise, especially loud noise, can be aversive. How do you react when chalk is scraped on the blackboard or when an airplane screeches low overhead?

The decibel (dB) is used to express the loudness of noise. The hearing threshold is defined as zero dB. Your school library is probably about 30 to 40 dB. A freeway is about 70 dB. One hundred forty dB is painfully loud, and 150 dB can rupture your eardrums. After eight hours of exposure to 110 to 120 dB, your hearing may be damaged (rock groups play at this level). High noise levels can lead to increases in blood pressure, neurological and intestinal disorders (National Academy of Sciences, 1981), ulcers (Colligan & Murphy, 1982), and other stress-related illnesses.

High noise levels also impair the efficiency of daily functioning, fostering forgetfulness, perceptual errors, even dropping things (Smith & Stansfield, 1986). Children who are exposed to greater traffic noise on the lower floors of apartment complexes (Cohen et al., 1973) or to loud noise from low-flying airplanes at their schools (Cohen et al., 1980, 1986) may encounter stress, hearing loss, and impairments in learning and memory. Time to adjust and subsequent noise abatement do not seem to reverse their cognitive and perceptual deficits (Cohen et al., 1981).

Couples may enjoy high noise levels at the disco, but less desirable noises of 80 dB seem to decrease feelings of attraction, causing couples to space themselves farther apart. Loud noise also puts a damper on helping behavior. People are less likely to help pick up a dropped package when the background noise of a construction crew is at 92 dB than when it's at 72 dB (Page, 1977). They're even less willing to make change for a quarter.

If you and your date have had a fight and are then exposed to a sudden blowout, look out. Angered people are more likely to behave aggressively when exposed to a sudden noise of 95 dB than one of 55 dB (Donnerstein & Wilson, 1976).

Temperature

Environmental psychologists also study the ways in which temperature can facilitate or impair behavior and mental processes. When a car's engine is too hot, there may be great demands on the circulatory system, causing the water to overheat and the radiator to pop its cap. Extremes of heat can also make excessive demands on our bodies' circulatory systems, leading to conditions such as dehydration, heat exhaustion, heat stroke, and, in severe enough cases, a heart attack.

When it is too cold, the body responds by attempting to generate and retain heat. The metabolism increases; we shiver; blood vessels in the skin constrict, decreasing flow of blood to the periphery of the body, where its warmth can be transmitted more easily to the outside.

Despite their obvious differences, both hot and cold temperatures are aversive events with some similar consequences, the first of which is in-

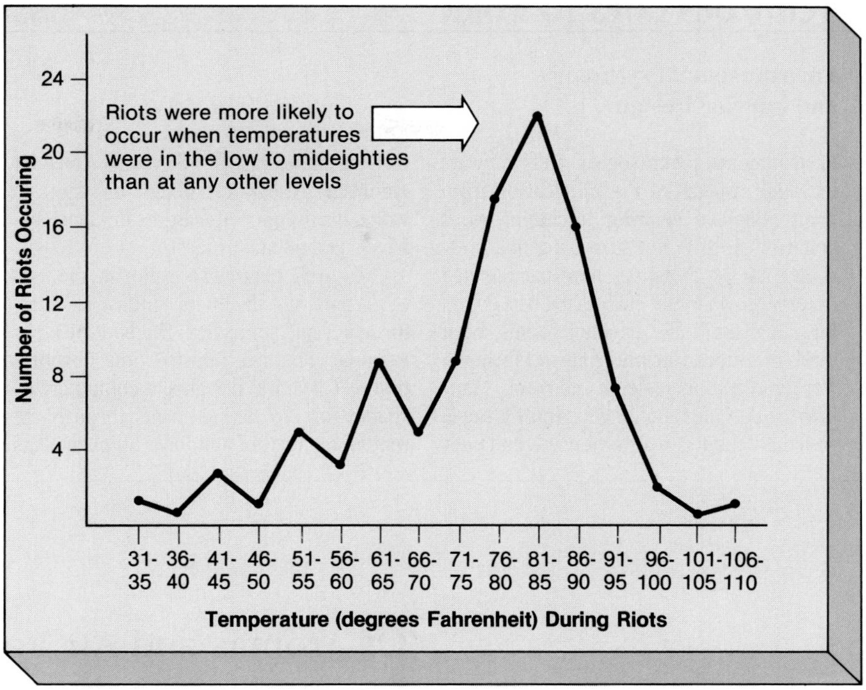

Figure 16.6
The "Long, Hot Summer" Effect. Most riots of the 1960s occurred when temperatures were in the uncomfortable range of the mid-80s Fahrenheit. When the weather turns hot, we are apparently more likely to become "hot under the collar" as well.

creased arousal. Beyond this, it is difficult to generalize (Bell, 1982). However, a number of studies suggest that moderate shifts in temperature are mildly arousing and so may facilitate learning and performance, increase feelings of attraction, and have other positive effects. But extreme temperatures cause performance and activity levels to deteriorate.

Environmental psychologists, applying knowledge concerning the psychology of motivation, point out that small increments in arousal tend to get our attention, motivate us to perform, and facilitate the performance of tasks. But great increments in arousal, as can result from major deviations from ideal temperatures, are aversive in their own right and hinder the performance of complex tasks. We are motivated to reduce major discrepancies from ideal temperatures by means of clothing, air conditioning, or traveling to more amenable climes. If the pain and discomfort caused by such temperatures become too high, however, we may lose motivation to behave effectively in addition to suffering the consequences of the temperature extremes themselves.

The "Long, Hot Summer" Effect High temperatures may encourage aggression. Campus and city riots broke out regularly during the broiling summers of the 1960s (Figure 16.6). Each spring, news commentators wondered whether we would be in for another "long, hot summer." Yet it may sometimes be too hot for a riot. The U.S. Riot Commission (1968) found that riots erupted only rarely in temperatures exceeding 100 degrees Fahrenheit.

More recent studies have shown that in Houston, the aggressive crimes of murder and rape are most likely to occur when the temperature is 94.3 degrees (Anderson & Anderson, 1984). The frequency of car honking at a traffic light increased along with the temperature in Phoenix (Kenrick & MacFarlane, 1986). The point at which heat may begin to damper aggression is in question.

PSYCHOLOGY GOES TO WORK

Environmental Psychology and Interior Design

Environmental psychologists study the ways in which aspects of the physical environment influence behavior, including work behavior. So it is not surprising that environmental psychologists have participated in research on issues such as the best colors for office walls and hospital rooms, what kinds of sounds (including music) facilitate work and getting to sleep, and so on. Many interior designers no longer simply grapple with their clients' expressed needs and their own aesthetic tastes—they also consider empirical research findings on ways in which environmental features influence behavior and mental processes.

Researchers are also exploring the uses of scents to facilitate industrial performance and spur sales (Hinds, 1988). For example, Shimizu Construction Corporation of Tokyo has designed a computerized system for circulating scents through the ventilation ducts of buildings. Shimizu plans a cypress aroma for display areas of a convention center, cinnamon for restrooms, and lavender and peppermint for offices and conference rooms! 3M Company of Minneapolis predicts that odor promotions will invade supermarket aisles as they have magazine pages.

In future years will we shop in the supermarkets that have the lowest prices or the supermarkets with the most aromatic aisles?

Of Aromas and Air Pollution: Facilitating, Fussing, and Fuming

Environmental psychologists also investigate the psychological effect of odors. In the nearby box, we note how some of their findings have influenced interior designers.

Environmental psychologists also explore the effects of air pollution. Auto fumes, industrial smog, cigarette smoke, fireplaces, burning leaves—these are but a few of the sources of contamination. The lead in auto fumes may impair children's intellectual functioning in the same way that eating lead paint does (Fogel, 1980).

Truth or Fiction Revisited

It is true that auto fumes can lower children's IQs—that is, impair their intellectual functioning, as measured by intelligence tests.

Carbon monoxide, a colorless, odorless gas found in cigarette smoke and auto fumes, decreases the capacity of the blood to carry oxygen. Carbon monoxide impairs learning ability and perception of the passage of time (Beard & Wertheim, 1967). It may also contribute to highway accidents.

Air pollution can kill more directly. In December 1952, stagnation of industrial smog over London was linked to 3,500 deaths, with sulfur dioxide considered to be the specific culprit (Goldsmith, 1968). Residents of Los Angeles, New York, and various other major cities are accustomed to warnings to remain indoors or to be inactive in order to reduce air consumption when atmospheric inversions allow smog to accumulate.

There is mounting evidence that odorous air pollutants, like other forms of aversive stimulation, decrease feelings of attraction and heighten aggression (Fisher et al., 1984). In people sensitive to it, even the atmospheric electricity that accompanies changing weather patterns can decrease feelings of attraction and lead to tension, irritability, and crimes of violence (Baron, 1987; Baron et al., 1985; Charry & Hawkinshire, 1981; Rotton & Frey, 1985).

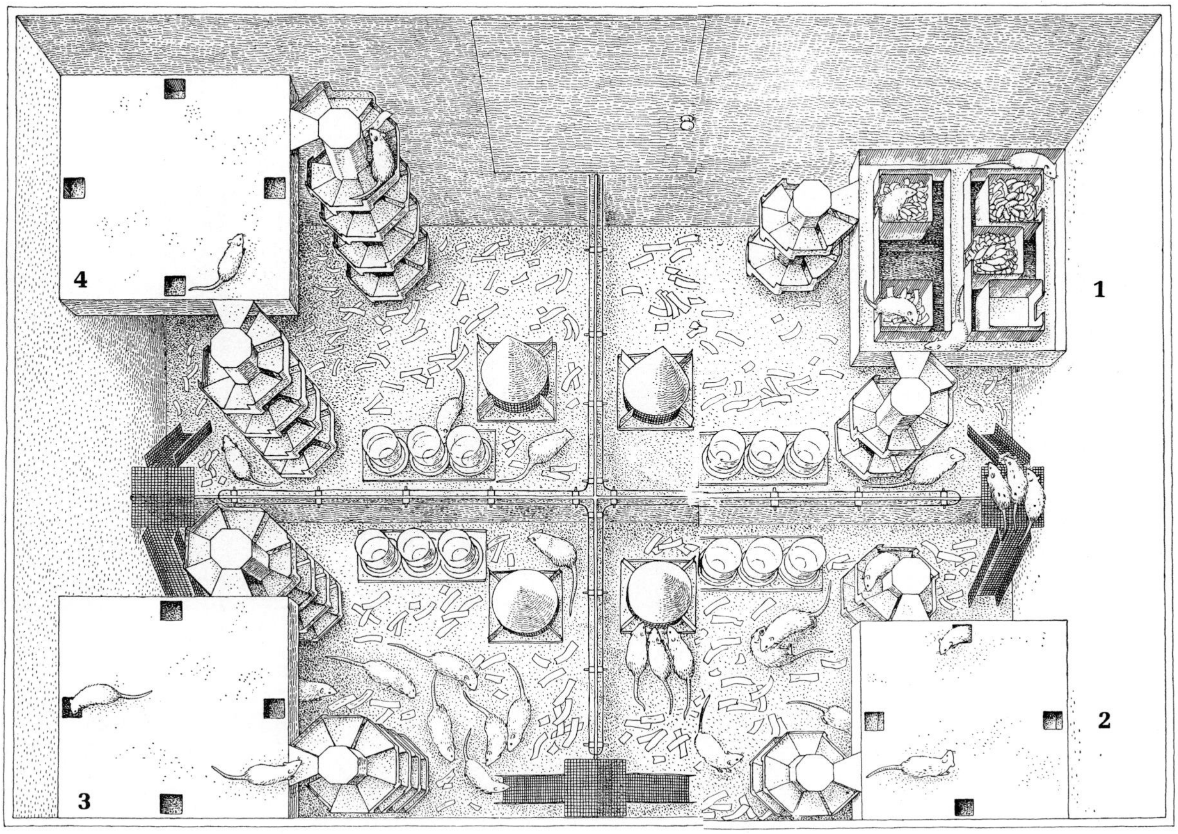

Figure 16.7
Calhoun's "Rat Universe."

In Calhoun's rat universe, an unlimited food supply and avenues of communication made compartments 2 and 3 into "behavioral sinks." (There was no access between compartments 1 and 4, so they did not become thoroughfares). Behavioral sinks were characterized by overpopulation, breakdown of the social order, and a higher mortality rate. What is the difference between high density and crowding? Are some human cities behavioral sinks?

Crowding and Personal Space

Sometimes you do everything you can for rats. You give them all they can eat, sex partners, a comfortable temperature, and protection from predators like owls and pussycats. And how do they reward you? By acting like, well, rats.

Calhoun's "Rat Universe" John Calhoun (1962) allowed rats to reproduce with no constraints except for the limited space of their laboratory environment (Figure 16.7). At first all was bliss in rat city. The males scurried about, gathered females into harems, and defended territories. They did not covet their neighbors' wives. They rarely fought. The females, unliberated, built nests and nursed their young. They resisted the occasional advance of the passing male.

But unrestricted population growth proved to be the snake in rat paradise. Beyond a critical population, the mortality rate rose. Family structure

Figure 16.8
Type of Film and Appraisal of High-Density Seating. In the study by Worchel and Brown (1984), viewers seated inappropriately closely or at appropriate distances watched four kinds of films. Of subjects seated too closely, those who could attribute their arousal to the film were less likely to experience crowding than those who could not.

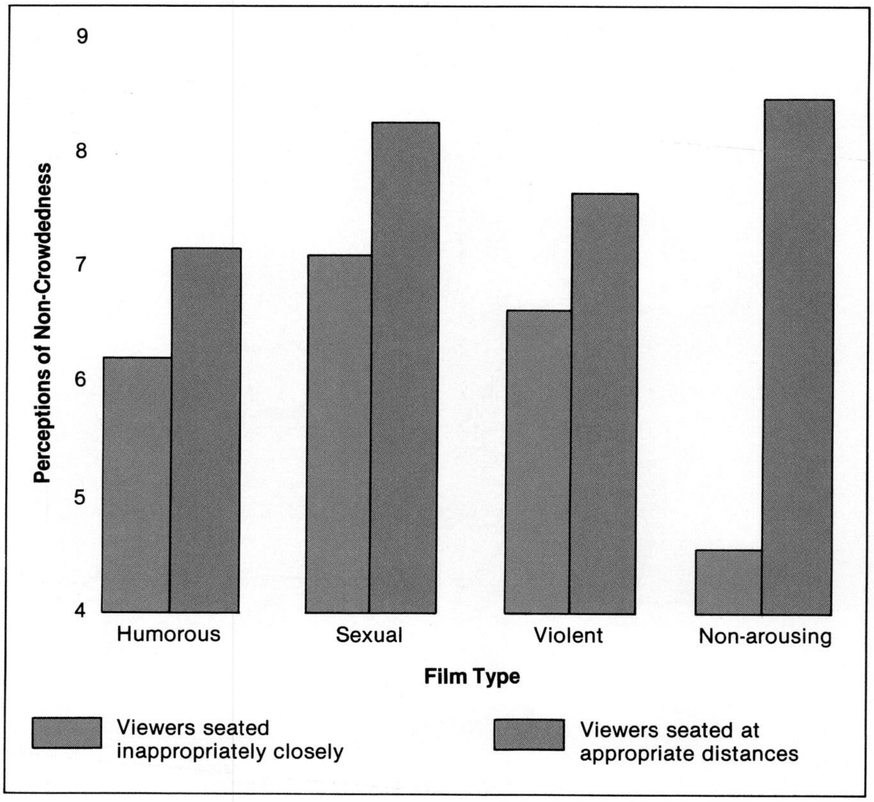

broke down, packs of delinquent males assaulted inadequately defended females. Some males shunned all social contact. Some females avoided sexual advances and huddled with fearsome males. Upon dissection, many rats showed biological signs of stress such as unhealthful changes in organs and gland malfunctions.

High Density versus Crowding Environmental psychologists distinguish between "density" and "crowding" (Baron & Byrne, 1987). They use *density* to refer to the number of people in an area and *crowding* to suggest a high-density social situation that is aversive.

Is Crowding Okay as Long as There's Sex, Aggression, and Laughs? All instances of density are not equal. Whether we feel crowded or not depends on who is thrown in with us and our interpretation of the situation, as we shall see in the discussion of personal space. Environmental psychologists apply principles of information processing and social psychology in explaining why.

A fascinating experiment illustrates the importance of cognitive factors—in this case, attributions for arousal—in transforming high density into crowding. Worchel and Brown (1984) arranged for small groups of subjects to watch films under conditions in which they were spaced comfortably apart or uncomfortably close. There were four different films. Three were arousing (either humorous, sexual, or violent), and one was unarousing.

As shown in Figure 16.8, subjects who sat more closely together generally felt more crowded than those seated farther apart. Note that those who were seated at appropriate distances from one another uniformly rated the seating arrangements as uncrowded. Among those who were seated inappropriately closely, subjects who saw the unarousing film felt most crowded. Subjects who saw the arousing films felt less crowded. Why? The researchers suggest that subjects who were packed in could *attribute* their arousal to the content of the films. Subjects who watched the unarousing film could not, so they were likely to attribute their arousal to the seating arrangements.

Psychological Moderators of the Impact of High Density In Chapter 11 we saw that a sense of control over our situations can enhance our psychological hardiness. Examples from everyday life suggest that a sense of control—of choice—over the situation also helps us cope with the stress of being packed in. When we are at a concert, a disco, or a sports event, we may encounter higher density than we do in those frustrating registration lines. But we may be having a wonderful time. Why? We have *chosen* to be at the concert and are focusing on our good time (unless a tall or noisy person sits in front of us). We feel in control.

Another example: Women seem to find high density less aversive than men do. This may be because women feel freer to express their discomfort (Karlin et al., 1976). Men who conform to the rugged, independent masculine stereotype tend to keep a "stiff upper lip." Women may form a supportive social network under the same circumstances in which men remain isolated. And social support also moderates the effect of stress.

We tend to moderate the effects of high density in subway cars and other mass-transportation vehicles by ignoring fellow passengers and daydreaming about pleasant events or situations at work, by reading newspapers and books, and by finding humor in the situation. Some of us manage to catch a snooze and yet wake up in time to get off at our stops.

Crowding on Campus Consider some campus examples of high-density arrangements that are sensed as crowding. You may have been shoehorned with several roommates into a dorm room intended for two. In such situations, students are more likely to withdraw from social interaction (Paulus, 1979). They are less satisfied with their roommates and rate them as less cooperative (Baron et al., 1976). Crowded prison inmates show higher blood pressure, more mental disorders, and a higher mortality rate than uncrowded prisoners (Fisher et al., 1984).

There is also a "tripling effect." When three students live together, a coalition frequently forms between two of them so that the third feels isolated. The isolated person finds the crowding more aversive than his or her roommates do (Aiello et al., 1981; Reddy et al., 1982). Findings such as these suggest that with humans, it is not crowding per se that is so aversive. Instead, it may be the sense that one does not have *control* over the situation.

Architecture can do much to eliminate the feelings of stress that often attend crowding. Students in suite arrangements, who share a common gathering place and bathroom, find their roommates more cooperative and encounter less stress than do students who live along a lengthy central hall (Baum & Davis, 1980). The suite arrangement allows them to exercise more control over their social contacts.

Figure 16.9 shows how Baum and Davis (1980) altered the plan of a dormitory floor. The drawing on the left shows the pre-intervention layout—including a long central corridor populated by many students. The drawing on the right shows that the psychologists converted centrally located bedrooms into a lounge area. Students in the altered arrangement had their own bathroom and shorter corridors. The decline in the numbers of students jostling each other in the halls decreased stress and led to the formation of more cohesive relationships among neighbors.

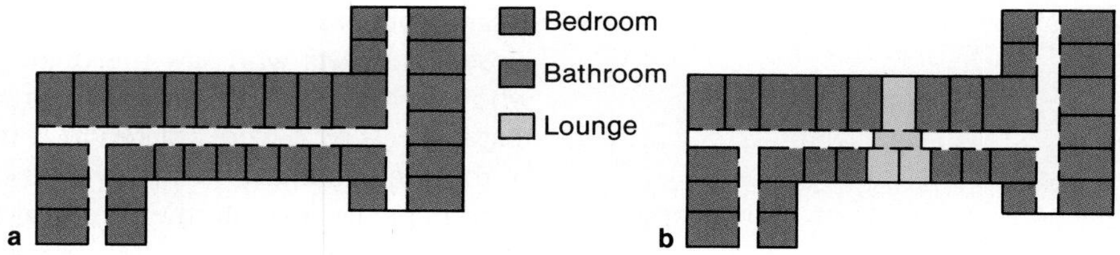

Figure 16.9
Architectural Design Has an Impact on Crowding. Baum and Davis (1980) divided a dormitory floor (Part A) with unlocked doors that opened onto a central lounge area (as in Part B). Students living on the divided floor were more open to social contacts and reported less stress from crowding than students living on a comparable undivided floor.

Some Effects of City Life As compared with suburbanites and rural folk, people who live in a big city encounter greater stimulus overload and fear of crime. Overwhelming crowd stimulation, bright lights, shop windows, and so on cause them to narrow their perceptions to a particular face, destination, or job.

City dwellers are less willing to shake hands with (Milgram, 1977), make eye contact with (Newman & McCauley, 1977), or help strangers (Glass & Singer, 1972; Milgram, 1970). People who move to the city from more rural areas adjust by becoming more deliberate in their daily activities (Franck et al., 1974). They plan ahead to take safety precautions, and they increase their alertness to potential dangers.

Farming, anyone?

Personal Space: "Don't Burst My Bubble, Please" One adverse effect of crowding is the invasion of **personal space.** Personal space is an invisible boundary, something like a bubble, that surrounds you. You are likely to become anxious and, perhaps, angry when others invade your space, as in someone sitting down across from or next to you in an otherwise empty cafeteria or standing too close in an elevator.

Personal space appears to serve protective and communicative functions. Violent people are likely to expect violent reactions from others, and violent prisoners require three times the personal space sought by nonviolent prisoners (Kinzel, 1970). Anxious people position themselves farther from others than do nonanxious people (Karabenick & Meisels, 1972). We need more personal space when we are in small rooms with others (White, 1975) or indoors rather than outdoors (Pempus et al., 1975). We apparently seek a safe distance from others when escape or exit could be a problem. Persons who feel that they are in control of their lives apparently require less personal space than people who do not (Duke & Nowicki, 1972). Perhaps they feel more competent to handle potential threats.

As a form of communication, the distance between people limits the possible interactions (Hall, 1968). Up to 1½ feet permits an intimate relationship in which touch is important, as in lovemaking, comforting, and contact sports like wrestling. Close friends and everyday acquaintances tend to remain from 1½ to 4 feet apart. Impersonal business contacts remain 4 to 12 feet apart, and formal contacts, as between performer and audience or lawyer and judge, remain at least 12 feet apart.

People sit and stand closer to people of the same race, similar age, or similar socioeconomic status. Dating couples come closer together as the attraction between them increases. Females seek more space between themselves and strangers of the opposite sex than males do (Rüstemli, 1986). Men are made more uncomfortable by strangers who sit across from them, whereas women feel more "invaded" by strangers who sit next to them. In libraries, men tend to pile books protectively in front of them. Women strategically place books and coats to discourage others from taking adjacent seats (Fisher et al., 1984). Consider the possibilities for miscommunicating

---

Personal space An invisible boundary that surrounds a person and serves protective functions.

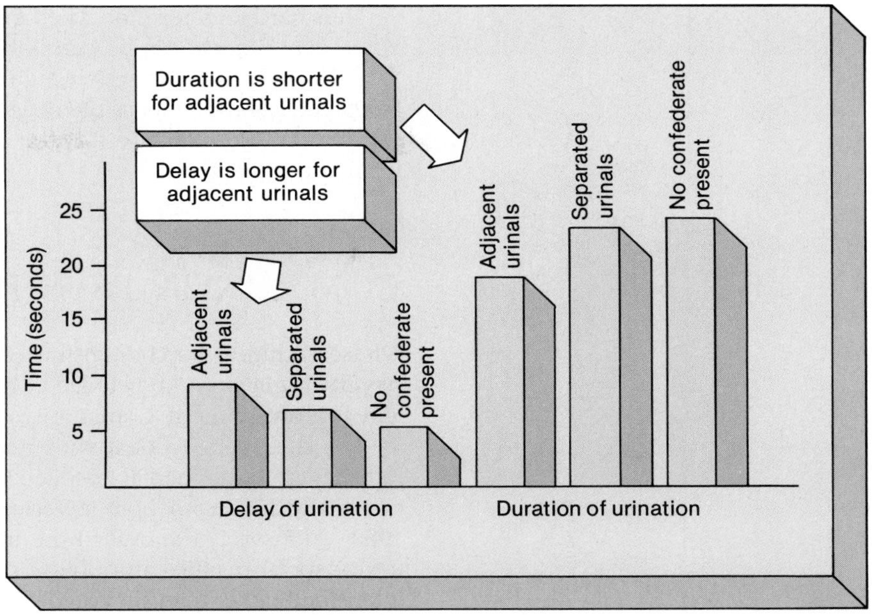

Figure 16.10
Effects of the Restroom "Space Invaders." The graph shows that men whose personal space was invaded by a person using the adjacent urinal showed (1) delay of onset and (2) shorter duration of urination. Both effects are interpreted as signs of stress.

your intentions to the opposite sex. A man might seat himself next to a woman rather than across from her in order to avoid threatening her. Yet she might find his behavior forward and offensive.

Perhaps such communications problems have a bright side. They help keep a number of psychologists in business.

"Space Invaders" and Arousal, *or* Psychology Goes to the John *Up periscope!* was the thrilling cry of submarine warfare during World War II. These cigar-shaped vessels poked their periscopes above the water to search for prey without alerting their victims.

Recently a periscope was used in a less dramatic but more unusual theater of action: a men's room. Psychologists (Middlemist et al., 1976) were pioneering an ingenious method for seeing whether personal space invasions lead to stress, as reflected by higher levels of arousal. High arousal, you see, interferes with urinating. When people are aroused, it takes them longer to begin to urinate (there is "delay of onset"), and the duration of urinating is shorter.

The men's room had three urinals and a toilet stall. When a male subject was about to urinate in the urinal next to the stall, his personal space was invaded by another male who was a confederate of the experimenter. The "space invader" would use either the urinal adjacent to the subject or the one at the far end of the row. While this drama was taking place, an unseen experimenter in the innocent-looking stall used a periscope to observe time of onset and duration of urination. Sure enough, close encounters led to increased delay of onset and shorter duration of urination—the target signs of heightened arousal (Figure 16.10).

This experiment received some acid commentary from other psychologists. Gerald Koocher (1977), for one, complained that it invaded the privacy as well as the space of the subjects. The subjects might also have suffered psychological damage if they had known they were being observed. Middlemist and his colleagues (1977) replied that men in a pilot study reported no concern when they were told that they had been secretly observed while urinating.

It is hard to determine whether some experiments are ethically justified. Some experiments can be run only by secretly observing or deceiving subjects. In each case we must weigh the value of the potential knowledge to be gained against the possible negative consequences to the people involved.

In any case, I'm sure that the restroom down the hall from you is free from experimenters.

COMMUNITY PSYCHOLOGY

Whereas clinical psychologists treat psychological problems, **community psychologists** use knowledge of biology, learning, motivation, and personality to prevent them. Community mental-health centers (CMHCs) were created in the 1960s to deal with psychological problems in the community rather than in the mental hospital. Hospitalization has not been shown to be of help with most people suffering from psychological problems (Kiesler, 1982). Moreover, removal of the individual from the community can sever ties to social realities and obligations. As a result, problems are sometimes intensified rather than alleviated. Some functions of the CMHC were designed to maintain patients in the community: Partial hospitalization allows the patient to sleep in a community hospital and work outside during the day. Through community consultation and education, problems may be averted or identified during their formative stages.

Levels of Prevention

Prevention takes place at three levels: primary, secondary, and tertiary. **Primary prevention** aims to deter problems before they start. There is not much that community psychologists can do about genetic predispositions toward psychological problems. However, as noted in Chapter 12, genetic predispositions tend to interact with psychological and social factors to spawn problems. These factors include unemployment, lack of education, drug abuse, teenage pregnancy, marital conflict, and substandard housing. And so, by consulting with community leaders, agencies and institutions, and lawmakers, community psychologist try to change stressful conditions that contribute to abnormal behavior. Community psychologists apply knowledge of developmental psychology, abnormal psychology, and social psychology when they consult with groups such as Big Brothers and Boys' Clubs to help avert delinquency among high-risk youth. Many community psychologists follow a so-called systems approach: They study the ways in which the criminal-justice, educational, welfare, and mental-health systems can work together to foster psychological well-being among groups at risk.

The aim of **secondary prevention** is to catch psychological problems in their formative stages and to stay their advancement. Groups such as Parents Anonymous and suicide prevention centers provide ways for distressed people to express their concerns before child abuse gets out of hand or they kill themselves. Community psychologists also work with teachers and others to sensitize them to early signs of psychological problems or abuse.

Tertiary prevention deals with psychological problems that have ripened. There is much overlap between psychological treatment, as in psychotherapy and behavior therapy, and tertiary prevention. However, in tertiary prevention there is a community emphasis: The focus is on rallying community forces to shore up patients' ties to family and vocational life.

Community psychology A field of psychology, related to clinical psychology, that focuses on the prevention of psychological problems and the maintenance of distressed persons in the community.

Primary prevention In community psychology, the deterrence of psychological problems.

Secondary prevention In community psychology, the early detection and treatment of psychological problems.

Tertiary prevention In community psychology, the treatment of ripened psychological problems.

Halfway houses, partial hospitalization, and consultation with employers and family groups are as likely to be used as the methods of therapy outlined in Chapter 13.

The overall effectiveness of community psychology demands complex evaluation. The methods of therapy discussed in Chapter 13 are helpful in CMHCs, just as they are in other clinics and private practice. But, as noted in Chapter 13, there are some sad stories concerning patients who were released into the community without adequate follow-up care. Many of the nation's homeless are former hospital patients. Questions have also been raised about the success of primary prevention as a means of reducing the prevalence of psychological problems in the community (Cowen, 1983). Of course, it could be that communities have not yet invested enough resources in follow-up care and in primary prevention to make the difference. The principles behind community psychology appear to remain sensible.

FORENSIC PSYCHOLOGY

Forensic psychologists apply psychological knowledge to the functioning of the criminal justice system. A number of forensic psychologists apply knowledge concerning social psychology and information processing in the investigation of the legal process. They study the use of eyewitness testimony, which, as we saw in Chapter 6, has many shortcomings. They also investigate ways in which the behavior of judges, attorneys, and defendants influence jury decisions.

Many forensic psychologists are employed by law-enforcement agencies. They apply knowledge of personality, personality assessment, and the psychology of learning to facilitate the recruitment and training of police officers. There is a high burnout rate among police officers, and some psychologists apply therapy methods to help police find ways of coping with stress. They apply knowledge of abnormal behavior and social psychology to help train police to handle special problems—for example, assessing of the dangerousness of persons they suspect of crimes or are trying to apprehend, and handling suicide threats, hostage crises, and family disputes.

Truth or Fiction Revisited

It is true that psychologists help police handle hostage crises.

The Insanity Plea

Some forensic psychologists apply knowledge of abnormal behavior in the evaluation of persons who commit illegal acts. They testify about defendants' competence to stand trial or participate in their own defense, as well as about whether defendants should be found not guilty by reason of insanity. In Chapter 12 I mentioned a couple of cases in which individuals were found not guilty of crimes by reason of insanity. One involved William, who was diagnosed as suffering from multiple personality in 1978. The other person involved, John Hinckley, was found not guilty in 1982 of an assassination attempt on President Reagan. Hinckley was diagnosed as schizophrenic. In both cases the defendants were committed to institutions for the mentally ill rather than given prison sentences. William was discharged a number of years ago, but Hinckley remains hospitalized.

In pleading insanity, lawyers use the so-called M'Naghton rules, named after Daniel M'Naghton, who tried to assassinate the British prime minister,

Forensic psychology The field that applies psychological knowledge within the criminal justice system.

The Insanity Plea. The insanity plea is one of the issues that concerns forensic psychologists. Would-be presidential assassin John Hinckley (left) is just one of the many who have evaded criminal responsibility through the insanity plea. The defense claimed that Hinckley was living in a fantasy world that involved actress Jodie Foster (right), who played a young prostitute in the film *Taxi Driver.*

Sir Robert Peel, in 1843. M'Naghton was suffering from delusions that Peel was persecuting him, and he killed Peel's secretary in the attempt. The court found M'Naghton not guilty by reason of insanity, referring to what have become the M'Naghton rules. The "rules" are that the accused do not understand what they are doing at the time of the act, do not realize it is wrong, or are not competent to conform their behavior to legal standards. Some of the implications of the M'Naghton rules are highlighted by the Hinckley case.

The Hinckley Case The Hinckley case epitomizes some of the problems with the M'Naghton rules for determining guilt or innocence. After all, we cannot know with certainty whether other people know right from wrong or understanding the implications of their behavior at any given moment. We can only observe them and draw our own conclusions. In the typical insanity defense, defense attorneys employ expert witnesses—usually psychologists and psychiatrists—who, on the basis of interviews or previous knowledge of the defendant, usually testify that the accused was insane at the time of the act. The prosecution typically presents opposing testimony from other experts that the accused was sane at the time of the act.

Such back-and-forth testimony characterized the Hinckley trial. Hinckley claimed that his assassination attempt was designed to impress movie actress Jodie Foster. The defense argued that Hinckley was suffering from schizophrenia when he shot Reagan and was therefore insane. He was portrayed as a "mental cripple" living in a "fantasy world." In the film *Taxi Driver,* Foster had played a New York street prostitute who was saved by the movie's schizophrenic hero, played by Robert De Niro. Inspired by the film, Hinckley had even sought streetwalkers who seemed in need of help.

The prosecution then brought to the stand witnesses who testified that Hinckley had recognized the wrongfulness of his act. Because well-trained professionals often have opposing views about people's mental states, which are private events, the public voices skepticism concerning the insanity plea.

Criminals who are found not guilty by reason of insanity are usually committed to mental institutions rather than given prison terms. They are eligible for release when they are no longer behaving abnormally. The possibility of release leads the public to fear that "sick" people will be walking the streets if they can contain their symptoms for a while. In an Associated Press-NBC News poll, 87 percent of a national sample said they feared that many murderers used the insanity plea to avoid imprisonment.

The American Psychological Association (1984) takes the position that social and political pressures to repeal the insanity plea should be resisted. The APA proposes a review of the scientific research on the appropriateness and effects of the insanity plea and the support of new research, as needed. As noted by Rogers (1987), the public is not always perturbed when obviously disturbed people are found not guilty by reason of insanity. Instead, the public's ire is aroused when morally repugnant people are found not guilty or when the victim is a public figure of Reagan's stature.

SPORTS PSYCHOLOGY

Among the welter of a spirited tennis crowd, I overheard a conversation between two women:

> "Do you think there's anything I could do to learn how to play like Steffi Graf?"
>
> "The first thing you've got to do is get Steffi Graf's genes."
>
> A pause. Then: "But she's wearing a skirt."

Clothes may make the man, or woman, but probably not the athlete. Why does Steffi Graf outplay nearly every other woman on the tennis circuit? There is a combination of reasons, including motivation, dedication, long hours of training, superb coaching—as well as her ability to cope with stardom and the crowds. And, yes, "genes"—not jeans. Heredity plays a role in terms of her physical strength, her coordination, her reaction time, and her eyesight.

Task Analysis of Athletic Performances

Sports psychologists apply psychological methods and knowledge to the study and modification of the behavior and mental processes of people involved in sports. Sports psychologists do task analyses of athletic performances just as I/O psychologists do task analyses of work performances. That is, they break athletic performances down into their components in an effort to discover ways of enhancing the performance of each component. In doing so, they apply knowledge about biology (the facts concerning human limits and health hazards), motivation, learning (for example, the roles of cognitive understanding, repetition, and reinforcement), self-efficacy expectations ("I can do it"), and coping with stress. They apply this knowledge and knowledge about group processes to help coaches. Many amateur and professional teams have psychologists as well as coaches.

Note some of the issues that sports psychologists deal with:

- How can athletes focus their attention on their own performance and not on the crowd or on competing athletes?
- How can athletes use cognitive strategies such as mental practice and positive visualization to enhance performance?

Sports psychology The field of psychology that studies the nature, causes, and modification of the behavior and mental processes of people involved in sports.

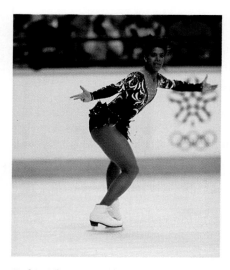

Debi Thomas. U.S. Olympic figure skater Debi Thomas had toiled for many years in preparation for the 1988 winter games. Then, when her opportunity to take the gold medal arose, she "choked." One of the functions of sports psychologists is to help athletes handle choking through techniques like relaxation and positive visualization.

- What is the role of emotions in performance? For example, do tennis pro John McEnroe's on-court cursing and arguing spark his achievement motivation and concentration, or do they distract him and cost him matches?
- What are the relationships between sports and mental health?
- How can knowledge of group behavior be applied to enhance team cohesiveness?
- How can psychologists help athletes handle "choking"?

Let us consider this last issue further—the problem of "choking."

How Sports Psychologists Help Athletes Handle "Choking"

American Olympic figure skater Debi Thomas had toiled for many years preparing for the 1988 Winter games. For several hours every day, she perfected her form on the ice—in addition to being a full-time college student. Then, when her opportunity to take the gold medal arose, she "choked." She fell not once but several times, shattering her hopes of outskating her European nemesis, Katerina Witt.

A critical outing also had a devastating effect one fall on Penn State place kicker Herb Menhardt. Penn State was facing its second loss in three games. With a fourth down on the Iowa 37-yard line and 50 seconds to play, coach Paterno took a chance on the untested Menhardt, a first-year student. As 75,000 anxious Penn State fans looked on at Beaver Stadium, Menhardt hooked the 54-yard-kick wide to the left, leaving Iowa with a 7–6 victory. As a result, Matt Bahr got the starting place-kicking job, which eventually landed him with the Pittsburgh Steelers.

Choking during an athletic contest, as when taking a test, is especially cruel. The athlete, like the student, may have sweated long hours preparing for a crucial performance. Then it's over in a matter of seconds or minutes, and it may devastate one's self-esteem and taint one's entire life.

Fortunately, Menhardt had an opportunity to work with sports psychologists Charles Stebbins and Kevin Hickey. They taught him a variety of coping skills. Some were largely perceptual and physical—such as helping him develop his peripheral vision, sense of balance, and response time. They taught him relaxation skills, as described in Chapter 11. Menhardt learned to breathe deeply and regularly under stress. He was shown how to relax muscle groups as he repeated the self-command, "Relax."

Positive Visualization

Like many other performers, Menhardt was also shown how to use the technique of positive visualization. He envisioned himself going through the motions in a critical game situation. He pictured blocking the crowd out of his mind and focusing on the ball. He moved fluidly toward the ball as if in a trance—as if he and the performance were one—and booted the ball flawlessly through the posts.

Truth or Fiction Revisited

It is true that you may be able to improve your athletic performance by imagining yourself making all the right moves. This is an example of the technique of positive visualization.

Educational psychology The field of psychology that studies the nature, causes, and enhancement of teaching and learning.

And after his new combination of athletic, behavioral, and cognitive training, Menhardt returned to the team and made a last-second 54-yard goal against North Carolina State. He gave Penn State the winning margin: 9–6. That season he went on to convert 14 field goals in 20 attempts and all of his 28 kicks after touchdowns.

Peak Performance

Menhardt was now engaging in what sports psychologists refer to as "peak performances." In their review of the literature, Browne and Maloney (1984) found that such performances are characterized by intense concentration; ability to screen out the crowd and, when appropriate, the competitors (successful field-goal kickers and quarterbacks do not usually "hear footsteps" or focus on the opposition's defenders rushing in); a sense of power and control over the situation; lack of pain and fatigue; and the sense that time has slowed down, as if the performance is being carried out in slow motion. Great hitters in baseball have fine eyesight and timing. They report that they can "see" the ball very well and that when they are at their peak, even fast balls seem to linger in the air as they come across the plate—so that to them, a fast ball might not seem very swift at all.

It also seems that peak performances can elude athletes who pursue them intentionally, or who "try too hard." A useful comprehensive prescription includes training adequately—that is, enhancing endurance and fine-tuning physical skills, learning how to regulate one's breathing and relax muscle groups that are unessential to performance, and spending some practice time picturing oneself performing flawlessly under adverse conditions.

We could say that sports psychology is about educating athletes to enhance their performance. Let us now turn our attention to educational psychology, which is concerned with the enhancement of learning in general.

EDUCATIONAL PSYCHOLOGY

In a sense, discussion of educational psychology brings this book full circle. After all, educating students in psychology is what it is all about.

Educational psychologists apply knowledge from many areas of psychology to the processes of teaching and learning (Woolfolk, 1987). They apply knowledge of developmental psychology to determine when children are ready to undertake certain kinds of learning and whether teaching practices can be modified to meet the special needs of elderly persons. They apply knowledge of learning and memory to present instructional materials in ways that will foster comprehension and retention (e.g., semantic coding and elaborative rehearsal). They apply knowledge of motivation to find ways to encourage students to become involved with and attend to subject matter. They apply knowledge of test construction and statistics to the development of tests that assess aptitudes and achievement. They apply knowledge of social psychology to enhance teacher–student and student–student relationships in the classroom.

Let us survey some of the concerns of educational psychologists.

A Class Act. Educational psychologists help instructors find ways of teaching effectively. For example, they connect various teaching methods to the outcomes of learning (e.g., whether students are expected to show changes in their attitudes, motor skills, verbal information, intellectual skills, or cognitive strategies for processing information).

Teaching Practices

Educational psychologists help instructors find ways of teaching effectively. A first step is the analysis of the outcomes of learning—that is, whether students are expected to show changes in their attitudes, motor skills, verbal information, intellectual skills (e.g., knowing how to add and subtract), or cognitive strategies for processing information (e.g., paying attention and rehearsing information). A number of psychologists, such as Jerome Bruner (1960), argue in favor of **discovery learning;** that is, they claim that children should be placed in resource-rich environments and be allowed to work on their own to discover basic principles. Others, like David Ausubel (1977), prefer to rely on **expository teaching,** or the orderly setting forth of facts and ideas.

In teaching concepts, Rosch (1975) suggests that children learn best when adults point out the best examples, or prototypes, of the concepts. For example, a sparrow is a better prototype of the concept *bird* than is an ostrich, which does not fly. Psychologists also help teachers develop ways of teaching problem solving and critical thinking. Let us consider some of the activities of educational psychologists, beginning with their contributions to classroom management.

Classroom Management

Educational psychologists also study ways of motivating and managing students in the classroom setting. For example, Wlodkowski (1982) suggests that teachers can develop ways of motivating students if they ask themselves how they can help foster positive attitudes toward learning activities and how the activities can help meet students' needs. How can teachers marshall students' needs for achievement and mastery? There is also a link between teacher expectations and how well students do (Rathus, 1988). Therefore, it is important for teachers to challenge each student appropriately and not to assume that a student will perform badly because of his or her background

Discovery learning Bruner's view that children should work on their own to discover basic principles.

Expository teaching Ausubel's method of presenting material in an organized form, moving from broad to specific concepts.

or "attitude." Teacher expectations have ways of becoming **self-fulfilling prophecies.**

Woolfolk (1987, pp. 332–333) suggests that teachers can help motivate students in the following ways:

1. By making the classroom and the lesson interesting and inviting
2. By assuring that students can fulfill their needs for affiliation and belonging
3. By making the classroom a safe and pleasant place
4. By recognizing that students' backgrounds can give rise to various patterns of needs
5. By helping students take appropriate responsibility for their successes and failures
6. By encouraging students to perceive the links between their own efforts and their achievements
7. By helping students set attainable short-term goals

Classrooms are special environments crowded with people, learning resources, tasks, and time pressures (Doyle, 1986). Everything seems to happen at once, and some events—such as the burning out of a light bulb or a child's becoming ill—can make them unpredictable places. Despite the unpredictables, classrooms become more manageable when concrete procedures and rules are spelled out to students (Emmer et al., 1984; Evertson et al., 1984). For example, elementary school students need to be given rules concerning being polite and helpful, taking care of the school, avoiding aggressive behavior, keeping the bathroom neat, and behaving properly in the cafeteria. Young students need concrete examples. Saying "Be good" is not sufficient; children need multiple examples of "good" behavior spelled out. Class procedures involve ways in which students are expected to enter and leave the room, whether or not they must raise their hands and be called on before they participate in class discussion, and how they will find out about and hand in assignments. Teachers who communicate procedures and rules clearly and who insist that they be followed during the early weeks of school usually encounter fewer behavior problems as the year progresses.

Planning and Teaching

Educational psychologists also point out the importance of teachers' setting **instructional objectives.** Communication of objectives helps students focus on the essential aspects of the material that is presented. Objectives can be general (the student should be able to reason in solving simple math problems) and specific (the student should be able to add single digits when written in the form, $3 + 5 = x$). A classification system, or **taxonomy,** of instructional objectives divides them into three domains: *cognitive, affective* (emotional), and *psychomotor* (concerning the development of physical abilities and skills). Examples of objectives in the cognitive domain include acquisition of knowledge, comprehension of subject matter, and ability to apply concepts to solve problems.

Educational psychologists conduct research into which teaching formats best enable teachers to meet instructional objectives. For example, in the **recitation** approach, teachers pose questions that students answer. Other basic teaching formats include the lecture approach, group discussion, seatwork and homework, and individualized instruction. In the latter format, students are taught on a one-to-one basis and then given time to read about

Self-fulfilling prophecy An expectation that is confirmed because of the behavior of those who hold the expectation.

Instructional objective A clear statement of what is to be learned.

Taxonomy Classification system.

Recitation A teaching format in which teachers pose questions that are answered by students.

or apply the subject matter on their own. It is interesting to note that individualized instruction, which is usually prized because of the presumably ideal teacher-to-student ratio, has *not* been shown to be superior for elementary and secondary students. Perhaps it leaves immature students too much time on their own. However, individualized instruction does seem to be beneficial to college students (Bangert et al., 1983), who are presumably better capable of managing their time.

There are some interesting findings concerning teacher characteristics and student learning. For example, it has *not* been shown that teachers who know more about a subject do a better job of teaching it, particularly at the elementary level. However, students of teachers who know more about classroom management and who present material in a clear, organized fashion apparently learn more than students of poor managers and disorganized teachers (Cantrell et al., 1977; Hines et al., 1985).

Truth or Fiction Revisited

It is *not* necessarily true that teachers who know more about a subject do a better job of teaching it—at least in the lower grades. Teacher communication skills and organization seem to be just as important, if not more important, than knowledge of content areas with young children. The situation may differ in college, where students are more capable of organizing subject matter for themselves.

Effective teachers are also sensitive to the needs of students of different ages and students with different aptitudes.

Teaching Exceptional Students

Just as no two people are quite alike, no two students are alike. However, the term **exceptional student** is usually applied to students whose needs are special because of physical and health problems, communication problems, behavior disorders, specific learning disabilities, mental retardation, or—at the other intellectual extreme—giftedness. Educational psychologists have studied ways of maximizing instructional effectiveness with exceptional students and of integrating them into regular classrooms when possible so that they will not suffer from losses in self-esteem.

The practice of placing exceptional students in educational environments that are as normal as possible is referred to as **mainstreaming.** Since the passage of Education for All Handicapped Children Act in 1975, exceptional children have been afforded the **least restrictive placement**—that is, put in settings that are as normal and as much in the mainstream of education as possible. On the other hand, educational psychologists have also labored to develop instructional methods that will benefit exceptional children who receive supplementary instruction or who must be placed in special classes.

Exceptional students The term applied to students whose educational needs are special because of physical and health problems, communication problems, behavior disorders, specific learning disabilities, mental retardation, or intellectual giftedness.

Mainstreaming The practice of placing exceptional students in educational environments that are as normal as possible.

Least restrictive placement Placement of exceptional students in settings that are as normal and as much in the mainstream of education as possible, in accord with the Education for All Handicapped Children Act.

Tests and Grades

Educational psychologists are also concerned about the development of methods for assessing students and assigning grades. Assessment includes the kinds of standardized tests that are used to measure intelligence (e.g., the Wechsler and Stanford-Binet scales), aptitudes (e.g., the SATs and GREs), achievement in specific subjects (e.g., the California Achievement Tests and the advanced tests of the GREs), and problems that have an effect on learning (e.g., perceptual and motor problems, as measured by the Bender Gestalt Test). Such tests are used by schools to assess broad learning ability and to see how well children are reading or computing math problems as compared to agemates. They are used by colleges to make decisions about whether test-takers will be admitted to colleges and graduate programs.

Such tests can be **norm-referenced** or **criterion-referenced.** Students' performances on norm-referenced tests are compared with the average performance of others. In other words, how well one does on the Wechsler scales or on the GREs depends on how well one performs relative to other people who take the tests. On the Wechsler scales for children, test-takers' performances are compared to a nationwide sample that represents their agemates. Norms for the GRE are based on numbers of items answered correctly by young adults interested in pursuing graduate education—a rather select group.

In criterion-referenced testing, test-takers' scores are compared to a fixed performance standard. In other words, criterion-referenced testing might be used to determine whether or not one can use long division, type 60 words a minute, or speak Spanish fluently. A good score on the norm-referenced GRE advanced test in Spanish means that you answered more questions correctly than the average test-taker, not that you can understand or speak Spanish. A road test for a driver's license is a criterion-referenced test; either you can drive successfully according to the set standard or you can't.

Educational psychologists are also interested in classroom evaluation and testing. They study the reliability and validity of various kinds of tests, such as multiple-choice tests versus essay tests. They have found, for example, that long tests are more reliable than brief tests. They have learned that the grading of multiple-choice tests is more objective, or fair, than the grading of essay tests. The grading of essays (and course grades themselves), like the appraisal of workers, can be influenced by the halo effect—that is, the teacher's general impression of the student. However, the consistency of essay test grades can be enhanced by writing a model answer and then assigning points to its various parts (Gronlund, 1985). Covering students' names while grading also increases fairness (but penmanship can also affect grades!).

Educational psychologists also investigate the effects of grading. Grades provide students with more than just feedback about how much they have achieved. They also have an effect on students' self-esteem and motivation. For that reason, some teachers try to encourage students they perceive as underachievers by grading them on their (presumed) abilities and not on their actual achievements. In elementary schools, teachers are frequently allowed to give children two grades for the same subject matter area: One reflects achievement and the other is based on "judgment calls" and intangibles such as effort.

What grade will you earn for this course? Will it be determined by norm-referenced testing or criterion-referenced testing? Will your grade reflect the amount of work you have put into the course? Will it influence your attitude toward psychology? What do you think? Shakespeare wrote, "What a piece of work is man!" What has this course taught you about our favorite "piece of work"?

Norm-referenced testing A testing approach in which scores are derived by comparing the number of items answered correctly with the average performance of others.

Criterion-referenced testing A testing approach in which scores are based on whether or not one can perform up to a set standard.

SUMMARY

1. **What is applied psychology?** Applied psychology refers to a number of fields of psychology, such as industrial/organizational or environmental psychology, that apply fundamental psychological methods and knowledge to the investigation and solution of human problems.

2. **What is industrial/organizational (I/O) psychology?** I/O psychologists apply psychological expertise to assist in worker recruitment, training, and appraisal; enhance job satisfaction; and structure organizations to function efficiently.

3. **How do I/O psychologists facilitate recruitment?** I/O psychologists facilitate recruitment procedures by analyzing jobs in order to specify the skills and personal attributes that are required. They also construct personnel tests and interview procedures to assess the presence of these skills and attributes.

4. **How do I/O psychologists facilitate training?** Training programs usually follow when managers identify a need for improved performance in a given job. Steps in devising training programs include assessing needs, establishing learning objectives, devising methods for gaining and maintaining attention, presenting material, and evaluating program effectiveness.

5. **What have I/O psychologists learned about employee appraisal?** Appraisal of a workers' performance is a cognitive process that is subject to distortions. For example, workers may be judged on the basis of general impressions instead of work performance. Also, "hard workers" tend to be evaluated more favorably than workers who work at a less intense pace, even when the less intense workers outperform the hard workers.

6. **What techniques have been devised by I/O psychologists to enhance worker satisfaction?** Various techniques have been devised for enhancing job satisfaction. They include goal setting, tying financial compensation to specific performances, work redesign, and modifying work schedules.

7. **What are the various approaches to organizational theory?** There are three basic approaches to organizational theory: the classic approach, which tends to rely on a bureaucracy, division of labor, and delegation of authority; contingency approaches, which tie organizational structures to organizational objectives and environmental demands; and human-relations approaches, which place the worker first.

8. **What are the major human-relations approaches?** Three important human-relations theories are McGregor's Theory Y, which is based on the assumption that workers are motivated to take responsibility for their work behavior; Argyris's view that organizations are structured efficiently when they allow their workers to develop; and Ouchi's Theory Z, which combines some of the positive features of the Japanese workplace with some of the realities of the American workplace.

9. **What is human-factors psychology?** This is the field that ensures that equipment and facilities are compatible with human behavior patterns and mental processes—that is, they are reasonably easy to work, or work in, and safe.

10. **What criteria do human-factors psychologists use in evaluating person–machine systems and work environments?** They use performance criteria, physiological criteria, subjective criteria, and accident and injury criteria.

11. **What criteria do human-factors psychologists use for evaluating the coding in displays?** They consider the displays' detectability, discriminability, compatibility, meaningfulness, standardization, and multidimensionality.

12. **What is consumer psychology?** Consumer psychology applies psychological methods to the investigation and modification of consumer behavior and mental processes.

13. **What kinds of questions are considered by consumer psychologists?** They consider issues such as why consumers are loyal to one brand over another, the qualities or characteristics that consumers associate with various brands, and how consumer attitudes toward products can be modified.

14. **What is environmental psychology?** Environmental psychologists study the ways in which people and the physical environment influence one another. They investigate the ways in which factors such as noise, temperature, pollution, and population density affect human behavior and mental processes.

15. **What have environmental psychologists learned about crowding?** Crowding is high population density that is perceived as aversive. Crowding is stressful and leads people to rate others as less cooperative. We seek a certain amount of personal space, which seems to serve both protective

and communicative functions. Invasions of our personal space can lead to anxiety and irritation.

16. **What is community psychology?** Community psychology is related to clinical psychology but focuses on the prevention of psychological problems and the maintenance of distressed individuals in the community.

17. **What kinds of prevention are there?** Primary prevention is the modification of the community environment to preclude the emergence of problems. Secondary prevention is the early detection and treatment of problems. Tertiary prevention is the treatment of developed problems.

18. **What is forensic psychology?** Forensic psychology is the application of psychological knowledge to the functioning of the criminal justice system.

19. **What kinds of issues are dealt with by forensic psychologists?** Forensic psychologists study ways in which witnesses, judges, defendants, and attorneys affect the legal process. Forensic psychologists participate in the recruitment, training, and counseling of police personnel. They also testify as to the competence of defendants to participate in their own defense.

20. **What is sports psychology?** Sports psychology is the application of psychological methods and knowledge to the study and modification of the behavior and mental processes of people involved in sports.

21. **What kinds of issues do sports psychologists deal with?** In addition to task analysis of athletic performances, sports psychologists are concerned with issues such as how athletes can use cognitive strategies such as mental practice and positive visualization to enhance performance, how sports contribute to mental health, how team cohesiveness can be enhanced, how coaching methods can be improved, how athletes can handle "choking," and how athletes can attain peak performance.

22. **What is educational psychology?** Educational psychologists apply knowledge from many areas of psychology to the processes of teaching and learning.

23. **How do educational psychologists contribute to teaching practices?** They analyze the outcomes of learning and the effects of different kinds of teaching, such as discovery learning and expository teaching.

24. **How do educational psychologists contribute to classroom management?** They study ways of motivating and managing students in the classroom setting. They relate instructional methods to students' needs and point out the value of concrete school rules and procedures.

25. **How do educational psychologists contribute to planning and teaching?** They explain how to use instructional objectives according to a taxonomy. They conduct research into which teaching formats best enable teachers to meet their objectives. Basic teaching formats include the recitation approach, the lecture approach, group discussion, seatwork and homework, and individualized instruction.

26. **What are exceptional students?** Exceptional students are students whose needs are special because of physical and health problems, communication problems, behavior disorders, specific learning disabilities, mental retardation, or—at the other intellectual extreme—giftedness.

27. **How do educational psychologists help educators meet the needs of exceptional students?** They study ways of maximizing instructional effectiveness with exceptional students and of integrating them into regular classrooms when possible so that they will not suffer from losses in self-esteem.

28. **What role do educational psychologists play in the development of methods of testing and grading?** Educational psychologists distinguish between standardized and nonstandardized tests and between norm-referenced and criterion-referenced scoring systems. They study the reliability and validity of classroom testing procedures, and they investigate the uses and effects of grades.

PSYCHOLOGY AND MODERN LIFE

Career Selection

. . . if one advances confidently in the direction of his dreams, and endeavors to live the life which he has imagined, he will meet with a success unexpected in common hours.

Henry David Thoreau, *Walden*

"Any child can grow up to be President." "My child—the doctor." "You can do anything, if you set your mind to it." America—land of opportunity. America—land of decision anxiety.

In societies with caste systems, such as Old England or India, children grew up to do what their parents did. They assumed that they would follow in their parents' footsteps. The caste system saved people the necessity of deciding what they would "do" with themselves. Unfortunately, it also squandered special talents and made a mockery of personal freedom.

And what we "do" is most important. "*What* do you do?" is a more important question at social gatherings than "*How* do you do?" It is usually the first question raised in small talk. Occupational prestige is central to general social standing in modern America. But, more importantly, the day-to-day consequences of our occupational choices are key factors in our psychological adjustment and well-being.

So this section focuses on a very important application of industrial/organizational psychology—the selection of a career. Career choices are likely to be of central concern to many students as they undertake their college years. In fact, as suggested in Chapter 9's discussion of adult development, many of us change our minds about our careers in our 20s, 30s, or even our 40s.

Coping Styles and Career Selection: Vocational "Types" In making realistic career decisions, we try to select careers that will fit us. Trait theory has given rise to ways of thinking about person–environment fit. A proper fit, in terms of our aptitudes, our interests, and our personality traits, will enhance our satisfaction from day to day.

Put it another way: it might matter little that we are bringing home a good salary if we feel trapped in our jobs and hate getting up in the morning to face them. Also, if we do not have a good person–environment fit with our jobs, we will find them more stressful and we are unlikely to be motivated to do our best in them (Chemers et al., 1985). And, when our performance is poor or mediocre, we are not likely to get ahead.

There are a number of different approaches to predicting whether or not we are likely to adjust well to various job environments or occupations. By and large, they all involve some kind of matching of our traits to the job. John Holland (1975) has developed a theory of matching in which various coping styles are linked to a fit in certain kinds of occupations. In his research, Holland has identified six coping styles:

1. *Realistic.* Persons with a realistic coping style tend to be concrete in their thinking, mechanically oriented, and interested in jobs that involve motor activity. Examples include farming; unskilled labor, such as attending gas stations; and skilled trades, such as construction and electrical work.
2. *Investigative.* Investigative people tend to be abstract in their thinking, creative, and introverted. They are frequently well adjusted in research and college and university teaching.
3. *Artistic.* Artistic individuals tend to be creative, emotional, interested in subjective feelings, and intuitive. They tend to gravitate toward the visual arts and the performing arts.
4. *Social.* Socially oriented people tend to be extroverted and socially concerned. They frequently show high verbal ability and strong needs for affiliating with others. Jobs such as social work, counseling, and teaching children often fit them well.
5. *Enterprising.* Enterprising individuals tend to be adventurous and impulsive, domineering, and extroverted. They gravitate toward leadership and planning roles in industry, government, and social organizations.
6. *Conventional.* Conventional people tend to enjoy routines. They show high self-control, needs for order, and the desire for social approval; they are not particularly imaginative. Jobs that suit them include banking, accounting, and clerical work.

Many occupations call for combinations of these coping styles. For example, a copywriter in an advertising agency might be both artistic and enterprising. Clinical and counseling psychologists tend to be investigative, artistic, and socially oriented. Military people and beauticians tend to be realistic and conventional. (But military leaders who plan major operations and form governments are also enterprising; and individuals who create new hair styles and fashions are also artistic.)

Holland has created the Vocational Preference Inventory in order to assess these coping styles, but they are also measured by more widely used vocational tests, such as the Strong/Campbell Interest Inventory.

Now that we have seen the value of making realistic career choices—that is, of finding a good person–environment fit in our occupations—let us turn our attention to ways in which psychology can help us make effective choices. Two of them involve using the balance sheet and using psychological tests.

Using the Balance Sheet to Make Career Decisions

Psychologist Irving Janis has applied the balance sheet—which is normally used to weigh assets and liabilities in business—to personal decision making. In using a balance sheet, we list the pluses and minuses of making a certain decision in terms of tangible gains and losses for ourselves and others, and self- and social approval and disapproval, as in Table 16.1. Seniors at Yale found that the balance sheet helped heighten awareness of gaps in information they needed to make wise career decisions (Janis & Wheeler, 1978). The balance sheet can also help you weigh your goals, pinpoint potential sources of frustration, and plan how to get more information or how to surmount obstacles.

Deborah, a first-year liberal arts major, wondered whether she should strive to become a physician. There were no physicians in her family with whom to discuss the idea. As reported by Rathus and Nevid (1989), a psychologist in her college counseling center advised her to fill out the balance sheet shown in Table 16.1 in order to help weigh the pluses and minuses of medicine.

Deborah's balance sheet helped her see that she needed dozens of pieces of information to decide. For example, how would she react to intense, prolonged studying? What were her chances of being accepted by a medical school? How did the day-to-day nitty-gritty of medical work fit her coping style and her psychological needs? Could she handle the disapproval of those who still believed that medicine—or at least specialties such as surgery—should remain a male preserve?

Deborah's need for information is not peculiar to those contemplating medicine. We all need to consider the types of questions raised in Table 16.2.

As part of her information-gathering process, Deborah's vocational counselor used several psychological tests, including a Wechsler Adult Intelligence Scale (WAIS). Deborah's WAIS score was in the 130s, so she learned that her general level of intellectual functioning was on a par with that of people who performed well in medicine.

The balance sheet suggested that Deborah had only superficially asked herself about how she would enjoy being a physician. She had recognized that physicians are generally admired, and she assumed that she would have feelings of pride. But would the work of a physician be consistent with her coping style? Would her psychological needs be met? The counselor provided helpful personality information through the Strong/Campbell Interest Inventory (SCII) and the Edwards Personal Preference Schedule (EPPS). The EPPS pairs a number of statements expressive of psychological needs, and test takers indicate which of each pair of statements is more descriptive of them. In this way it can be determined, for example, whether test takers have a stronger need for dominance than for deference (taking direction from others), or a strong need for order or to be helped by others.

Psychology Contributes to Career Selection. Psychology helps people make career decisions in many ways, such as providing information about the "fit" between their aptitudes and personalities and the requirements of occupations. Psychologists also point out that we can predict future behavior by sampling current behavior. If the young woman in this photograph enjoys her internship with a veterinarian, veterinary medicine may be right for her.

Table 16.1
Deborah's Balance Sheet for the Alternative of Taking Premedical Studies

Areas of Consideration	Positive Anticipations	Negative Anticipations
Tangible gains and losses for Deborah	1. Solid income	1. Long hours and years of demanding study 2. Anxiety about acceptance by medical school 3. High financial debt
Tangible gains and losses for others	1. Solid income for family	1. Little time for family life
Self-approval or self-disapproval	1. Pride in being a physician	
Social approval	1. Other people admire doctors	1. Disapproval of people who still believe that medicine—or certain medical specialties—should remain a male preserve

Deborah's balance sheet for this alternative showed that although she knew that other people admired physicians, she had not considered how she would feel about herself as a physician. It encouraged her to seek further information about her personal psychological needs.

Table 16.2
Types of Information Needed to Make Satisfying Career Decisions

1. *Intellectual and Educational Appropriateness: Is your intended career compatible with your own intellectual and educational abilities and background?*

Have you taken any preprofessional courses that lead to the career? Have you done well in them? What level of intellectual functioning is shown by people already in the career? Is your own level of intellectual functioning comparable? What kinds of special talents and intellectual skills are required for this career? Are there any psychological or educational tests that can identify where you stand in your possession of these talents or in the development of these skills? If you do not have these skills, can they be developed? How are they developed? Is there any way of predicting how well you can do at developing them? Would you find this field intellectually demanding and challenging? Would you find the field intellectually sterile and boring?

Information Resources: College or university counseling or testing center, college placement center, private psychologist or vocational counselor, people working in the field, professors in or allied to the field.

2. *Intrinsic Factors: Is your intended career compatible with your coping style, your psychological needs, and your interests?*

Does the job require elements of the realistic coping style? Of the investigative, artistic, social, enterprising, or conventional coping styles? What is your coping style? Is there a good person–job-environment fit? Is the work repetitious, or is it varied? Do you have a strong need for change (perpetual novel stimulation), or do you have a greater need for order and consistency? Would you be working primarily with machinery, with papers, or with other people? Do you prefer manipulating objects, doing paper work, or interacting with other people? Is the work indoors or outdoors? Are you an "indoors" or an "outdoors" person? Do you have strong needs for autonomy and dominance, or do you prefer to defer to others? Does the field allow you to make your own decisions, permit you to direct others, or require that you closely take direction from others? Do you have strong aesthetic needs? Is the work artistic? Are you Type A or Type B, or somewhere in between? Is this field strongly competitive or more relaxed?

Information Resources: Successful people in the field. (Do you believe you are similar to people in the field? Do you have common interests? Do you like people in the field and enjoy their company.) Written job descriptions. Psychological tests of personality (e.g., coping style and psychological needs) and interests.

3. *Extrinsic Factors: What is the balance between the investment you would have to make in the career and the probable payoff?*

How much time, work, and money would you have to invest in your educational and professional development to enter this career? Do you have the financial resources? If not, can you get them? (Do the sacrifices you would have to make to get them—such as long-term debt—seem worthwhile?) Do you have the endurance? The patience? What will the market for your skills be like when you are ready to enter the career? In 20 years? Will the financial rewards adequately compensate you for your investment?

Information Resources: College financial-aid office, college placement office, college counseling center, family, people in the field.

The SCII suggested that Deborah would enjoy investigative work, science (including medical science), and mathematics. However, she was not particularly socially oriented. Well-adjusted physicians usually show a combination of investigative and social coping styles.

The EPPS showed relatively strong needs for achievement, order, dominance, and endurance. All these factors meshed well with premedical studies—the long hours, the willingness to delay gratification, and the desire to learn about things—to make them fit together and work properly. The EPPS report dovetailed with the SCII's report to the effect that Deborah was not particularly socially oriented in her coping style. The EPPS suggested that Deborah had a low need for nurturance—that is, for caring for others and promoting their well-being.

With this information in hand, Deborah recognized that she really did not sense any strong desire to help others through medicine. Her medical interests might be purely academic. But after some reflection, she chose to pursue premedical studies, and she decided to expand her college work in chemistry and other sciences in order to lay the groundwork for alternative careers in medically related sciences. The courses promised to be of interest even if she did not develop a strong desire to help others or was not accepted by medical school.

How to Make a Positive Impression at a Job Interview After you have chosen and prepared for a career, you will be applying for a job. And at some point you will be invited to a job interview.

The interview is a combination of a social occasion and a test. First impressions and neatness count, so dress well and look your best. When other things are held equal, people who look their best usually get the job (Cash & Kilcullen, 1985).

Maintain direct eye contact with your interviewer, but look alert, cooperative, and friendly—don't stare. Recall from Chapter 15 that a hard stare is perceived as an aversive challenge.

As noted in Chapter 1, one good way to prepare for an academic test is to try to anticipate your instructor's questions. Similarly, anticipating an interviewer's questions will help prepare you for the interview—just as anticipating reporters' questions helps prepare the president for press conferences. Once you have arrived at a list of potential questions, rehearse answers to them. Practice them aloud, perhaps recruiting a friend to role-play the interviewer.

Keep in mind that you don't have to do all the talking in the interview. Be patient. Allow the interviewer to tell you about the job and the organization without feeling that you must jump in. Look interested. Nod now and then. Don't champ at the bit.

Now, back to the questions. Some of the interviewer's questions will be specific to your field, and I can't help you anticipate those. But others are more likely to be found in any interview, and some of them follow.

All right, the person ahead of you leaves and it's your turn for an interview! Here are the questions? What should you answer?

1. "How are you today?" My recommendation: *Don't* get cute or fancy. Say something like, "Fine, thank you. How're you?"
2. "How did you learn about the opening?" My recommendation: *Don't* say, "I indicated that in my application." Yes, you probably did specify this on your application or in the cover letter for your résumé, but your interviewer may not be familiar with the letter or may want to follow standard procedure anyhow. So answer concisely.
3. "What do you know about our organization?" Your interviewer wants to learn whether you actually know something about the organization or applied everywhere with equal disinterest. Do your homework and show that you know quite a bit about the organization. Suggest how the organization is an ideal setting for you to reach your vocational goals.
4. "What are you looking for in this job?" This is another opportunity to show that you have concrete goals, and that's what interviewers are looking for. Mention things like the opportunity to work with noted professionals in your field, the organizational personality (organizations, like people, can be conceptualized as having personalities), the organization's leadership in its field, and so on. *Don't* say "It's close to home." You can say that you know that salaries are good, but also refer to opportunities for personal growth and self-fulfillment.
5. "What do you plan to be doing ten years from now?" Your interviewer wants to hear that you have a clear cognitive map of the corporate ladder and that your career goals are consistent with company needs. Preplan a coherent answer but also show flexibility—perhaps that you're interested in exploring a couple of branches of the career ladder. This will show your interviewer that you're not rigid and that you recognize that the organization will affect your concept of your future.
6. "Are you willing to relocate after a year or two if we need you in another office/plant?" Your interviewer wants to hear that you would be willing—that your ties to the company would be more important than your geographical ties.
7. "What are your salary needs?" Entry-level salaries in many positions are fixed, especially in large organizations. But if this question is asked, *don't* fall into the trap of thinking you're more likely to get the job if you ask for less. Mention a reasonably high—not ridiculously high—figure. You can also mention the figure "with an explanation"—reemphasizing your experience and training. Good things don't come in cheap packages.
8. "What is the first thing you would do if you were to take the job?" Your interviewer probably wants to know (a) if you're an active, take-charge type of person and (b) whether you do have an understanding of what is required. *Don't* say you'd be shocked or surprised. Say something like, "I'd get to know my supervisors and coworkers to learn the details of the organization's goals and expectations for the position." Or it might be appropriate to talk about organizing your workspace or evaluating and ordering equipment, depending on the nature of the occupation.
9. "Do you realize that this is a very difficult (or time-consuming) job?" It is or it isn't, but the interviewer doesn't want to hear that you think the job's a snap. The interviewer wants to hear that you will dedicate yourself to your work and that you have boundless energy.
10. "What do you see as your weaknesses?" Trap time! *Don't* make a joke and say that you can't get along with anyone or know nothing about the job! Your interviewer is giving you a chance to show that you are arrogant by denying weaknesses or to drop some kind of bombshell—that is, admit to a self-disqualifying problem. Don't do either. Turn the question into an opportunity for emphasizing strengths. Say something like, "I think my weakness is that I have not already done this job (or worked for your organization), so we cannot predict with certainty what will happen. But I'm a fast learner and pretty flexible, so I'm confident that I'll do a good job."
11. "Do *you* have any questions?" Having intelligent questions is a sign that you are interested and can handle the job. Prepare a few good questions before the interview.
12. Finally, what do you say when the interview is over? Say something like, "Thank you for the interview. I look forward to hearing from you."

Now that you are on your way, I leave you with my best wishes. You will find that your college years, your career, your leisure activities, and your relationships are what you make of them. And over the years you will find that psychology is, in fact, deeply entwined with most aspects of modern life. Perhaps this book will continue to grow with you as you take on new life roles. Perhaps advanced psychology courses will deepen your wisdom or even pave the way for a career in psychology. Perhaps in one of these courses we shall meet again.

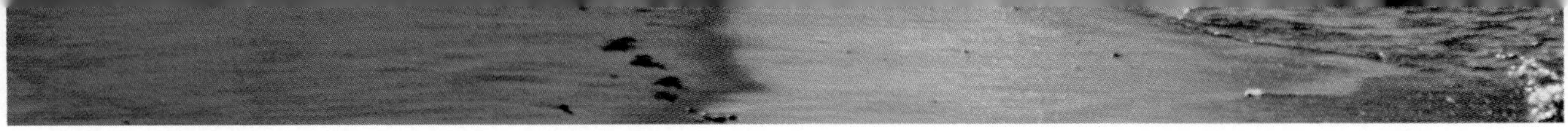

Appendix A Statistics

Imagine that some visitors from outer space arrive outside Madison Square Garden in New York City. Their goal this dark and numbing winter evening is to learn all they can about the inhabitants of planet Earth. They are drawn inside the Garden by lights, shouts, and warmth. The spotlighting inside rivets their attention to a wood-floored arena where the New York Apples are hosting the California Quakes in a briskly contested basketball game.

Our visitors use their sophisticated instruments to take some measurements of the players. Some surprising statistics are sent back to the planet of their origin: It appears that (1) 100 percent of Earthlings are male, and (2) the height of Earthlings ranges from six feet one inch to seven feet two inches.

Statistics is the name given the science concerned with obtaining and organizing numerical measurements or information. Our imagined visitors have sent home some statistics about the sex and size of human beings that are at once accurate and misleading. Although they accurately measured the basketball players, their small **sample** of Earth's **population** was quite distorted. Fortunately for us Earthlings, about half of us are female. And the **range** of heights observed by the aliens, of six feet one to seven feet two, is both restricted and too high. People vary in height by more than one foot and one inch. And our **average** height is not between six one and seven two but a number of inches below.

Statistics Numerical facts assembled in such a manner that they provide significant information about measures or scores. (From the Latin word *status,* meaning "standing" or "position.").

Sample Part of a population.

Population A complete group from which a sample is selected.

Range A measure of variability; the distance between extreme measures or scores.

Average Central tendency of a group of measures, expressed as means, median, and mode.

Psychologists, like our imagined visitors, are vitally concerned with measuring human as well as animal characteristics and traits—not just physical characteristics like sex and height but also psychological traits like intelligence, aggressiveness, anxiety, or self-assertiveness. By observing the central tendencies (averages) and variations in measurements from person to person, psychologists can state that some person is average or above average in intelligence, or that another person is less assertive than, say, 60 percent of the population.

But psychologists, unlike our aliens, are careful in their attempts to select a sample that accurately represents the entire population. Professional basketball players do not represent the human species. They are taller, stronger, and more agile than the rest of us, and they make more shaving-cream commercials.

In this appendix we shall survey some of the statistical methods used by psychologists to draw conclusions about the measurements they take in research activities. First we shall discuss *descriptive statistics* and learn what types of statements we can make about the height of basketball players and some other human traits. Then we shall discuss the *normal curve* and learn why basketball players are abnormal—at least in terms of height. We shall explore *correlation coefficients* and provide you with some less-than-shocking news: More intelligent people attain higher grades than less intelligent people. Finally, we shall have a brief look at *inferential statistics* and see why we can be bold enough to say that the difference in height between basketball players and other people is not just a chance accident, or fluke. Basketball players are in fact *statistically significantly* taller than the general population.

DESCRIPTIVE STATISTICS

Being told that someone is a "ten" is not very descriptive unless you know something about how possible scores are distributed and how frequently one finds a ten. Fortunately—for tens, if not for the rest of us—one is usually informed that someone is a ten on a scale of one to ten and that ten is the positive end of the scale. If this is not sufficient, one will also be told that tens are few and far between—rather unusual statistical events.

This business of a scale from one to ten is not very scientific, to be sure, but it does suggest something about **descriptive statistics.** We can use descriptive statistics to clarify our understanding of a distribution of scores, such as heights, test grades, IQs, or increases or decreases in measures of sexual arousal following the drinking of alcohol. For example, descriptive statistics can help us to determine measures of central tendency, or averages, and to determine how much variability there is in the scores. Being a ten loses some of its charm if the average score is an eleven. Being a ten is more remarkable in a distribution whose scores range from one to ten than in one that ranges from nine to ten.

Let us now examine some of the concerns of descriptive statistics: the *frequency distribution, measures of central tendency* (types of averages), and *measures of variability.*

The Frequency Distribution

A **frequency distribution** takes scores, or items of raw data; puts them into order, as from lowest to highest; and groups them according to class intervals. Table A.1 shows the rosters for a recent California Quakes–New York Apples basketball game. The members of each team are listed according to the numbers on their uniforms. Table A.2 shows a frequency distribution of the heights of the players of both teams combined, with a class interval of one inch.

It would also be possible to use three-inch class intervals, as in Table A.3. In determining how large a class interval should be, a researcher attempts to collapse that data into a small enough number of classes to ensure that they will appear meaningful at a glance. But the researcher also attempts to maintain a large enough number of categories to ensure that important differences are not obscured.

Descriptive statistics The branch of statistics that is concerned with providing information about a distribution of scores.

Frequency distribution An ordered set of data that indicates how frequently scores appear.

Table A.1
Rosters of Quakes versus Apples at New York

California		New York	
2 Callahan	6′-7″	3 Roosevelt	6′-1″
5 Daly	6′-11″	12 Chaffee	6′-5″
6 Chico	6′-2″	13 Baldwin	6′-9″
12 Capistrano	6′-3″	25 Delmar	6′-6″
21 Brentwood	6′-5″	27 Merrick	6′-8″
25 Van Nuys	6′-3″	28 Hewlett	6′-6″
31 Clemente	6′-9″	33 Hollis	6′-9″
32 Whittier	6′-8″	42 Bedford	6′-5″
41 Fernando	7′-2″	43 Coram	6′-2″
43 Watts	6′-9″	45 Hampton	6′-10″
53 Huntington	6′-6″	53 Ardsley	6′-10″

A glance at the rosters for a recent California Quakes—New York Apples basketball game shows you that the heights of the team members, combined, ranged from six feet one inch to seven feet two inches. Are the heights of the team members representative of those of the general male population?

Table A.2
Frequency Distribution of Heights of Basketball Players, with a One-inch Class Interval

Class Interval	Number of Players in Class
6-1 to 6-1.9	1
6-2 to 6-2.9	2
6-3 to 6-3.9	2
6-4 to 6-4.9	0
6-5 to 6-5.9	3
6-6 to 6-6.9	3
6-7 to 6-7.9	1
6-8 to 6-8.9	2
6-9 to 6-9.9	4
6-10 to 6-10.9	2
6-11 to 6-11.9	1
7-0 to 7-0.9	0
7-1 to 7-1.9	0
7-2 to 7-2.9	1

Table A.3
Frequency Distribution of Heights of Basketball Players, with a Three-inch Class Interval

Class Interval	Number of Players in Class
6-1 to 6-3.9	5
6-4 to 6-6.9	6
6-7 to 6-9.9	7
6-10 to 7-0.9	3
7-1 to 7-3.9	1

Table A.3 obscures the fact that no players are six feet four inches tall. If the researcher believes that this information is extremely important, a class interval of one inch may be maintained.

Figure A.1 shows two methods for representing the information in Table A.3 with graphs. Both in frequency **histograms** and frequency **polygons,** the class intervals are typically drawn along the horizontal line, or X-axis, and the number of scores (persons, cases, or events) in each class is drawn along the vertical line, or Y-axis. In a histogram, the number of scores in each class interval is represented by a rectangular solid so that the graph resembles a series of steps. In a polygon, the number of scores in each class interval is plotted as a point, and the points are then connected to form a many-sided geometric figure. Note that class intervals were added at both ends of the horizontal axis of the frequency polygon so that the lines could be brought down to the axis to close the geometric figure.

Histogram A graphic representation of a frequency distribution that uses rectangular solids. (From the Greek *historia,* meaning "narrative," and *gramma,* meaning "writing" or "drawing.")

Polygon A closed figure. (From the Greek *polys,* meaning "many," and *gõnia,* meaning "angle.")

Figure A.1
Two Graphical Representations of the Data in Table A.3

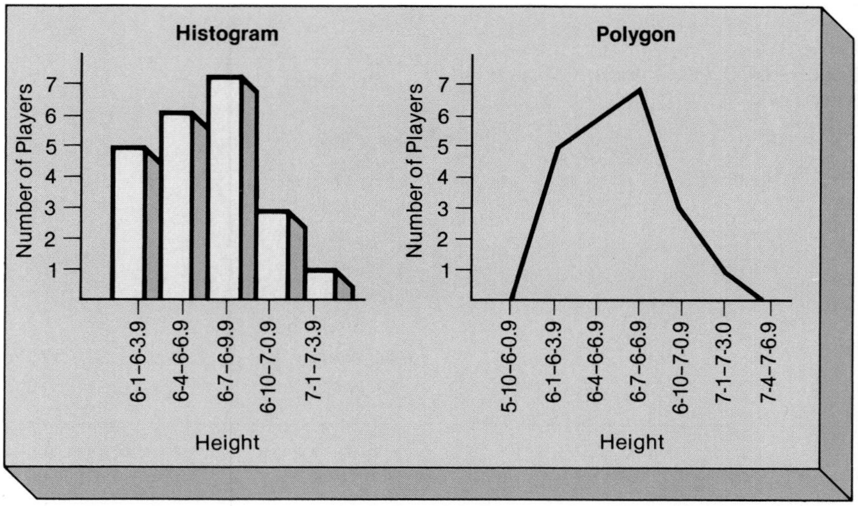

Measures of Central Tendency

There are three types of measures of central tendency, or averages: *mean, median,* and *mode.* Each tells us something about the way in which the scores in a distribution may be summarized by a typical or representative number.

The **mean** is what most people think of as "the average." The mean is obtained by adding up all the scores in a distribution and then dividing this sum by the number of scores. In the case of our basketball players, it would be advisable first to convert all heights into one unit, such as inches (6′1″ becomes 73″, and so on). If we add all the heights in inches, then divide by the number of players, or 22, we obtain a mean height of 78.73″, or 6′6.73″.

The **median** is the score of the middle case in a frequency distribution. It is the score beneath which 50 percent of the cases fall. In a distribution with an even number of cases, such as the distribution of the heights of the 22 basketball players in Table A.2, the median is determined by finding the mean of the two middle cases. Listing these 22 cases in ascending order, we find that the eleventh case is 6′6″ and the twelfth case is 6′7″. Thus the median is (6′6″ + 6′7″)/2, or 6′6½″.

In the case of the heights of the basketball players, the mean and the median are similar, and either serves as a useful indicator of the central tendency of the data. But suppose we are attempting to determine the average savings of 30 families living on a suburban block. Let us assume that 29 of the 30 families have savings between $8,000 and $12,000, adding up to $294,000. But the thirtieth family has savings of $1,400,000! The mean savings for a family on this block would thus be $56,467. A mean can be greatly distorted by one or two extreme scores, and for such distributions the median is a better indicator of the central tendency. The median savings on our hypothetical block would lie between $8,000 and $12,000 and so would be more representative of the central tendency of savings. Studies of the incomes of American families usually report median rather than mean incomes just to avoid the distortions that would result from treating incomes of the small numbers of multimillionaires in the same way as other incomes.

The **mode** is simply the most frequently occurring score in a distribution. The mode of the data in Table A.1 is 6′9″ because this height occurs most often. The median class interval for the data in Table A.3 is 6′6½″ to

Mean A type of average calculated by dividing the sum of scores by the number of scores. (From the Latin *medius,* meaning "middle.")

Median The score beneath which 50 percent of the cases fall. (From the Latin *medius,* meaning "middle.")

Mode The most frequently occurring number or score in a distribution. (From the Latin *modus,* meaning "measure.")

Figure A.2
A Bimodal Distribution This hypothetical distribution represents students' scores on a test. The mode at the left represents the central tendency of students who did not study, and the mode at the right represents the mode of students who did study.

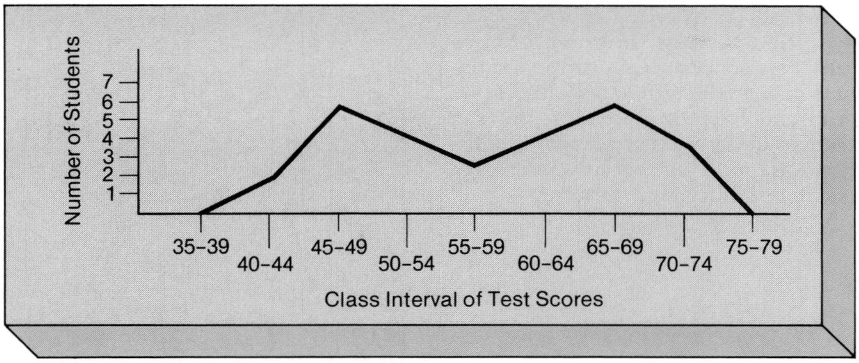

6′9½″. In these cases the mode is somewhat higher than the mean or median height.

In some cases the mode is a more appropriate description of a distribution than the mean or median. Figure A.2 shows a **bimodal** distribution, or a distribution with two modes. In this hypothetical distribution of the test scores, the mode at the left indicates the most common class interval for students who did not study, and the mode at the right indicates the most frequent class interval for students who did. The mean and median test scores would probably lie within the 55–59 class interval, yet use of that interval as a measure of central tendency would not provide very meaningful information about the distribution of scores. It might suggest that the test was too hard, not that a number of students chose not to study. One would be better able to visualize the distribution of scores if it is reported as a bimodal distribution. Even in similar cases in which the modes are not exactly equal, it might be more appropriate to describe a distribution as being bimodal or even multimodal.

Measures of Variability

Measures of variability of a distribution inform us about the spread of scores, or about the typical distances of scores from the average score. Measures of variability include the *range* of scores and the *standard deviation.*

The **range** of scores in a distribution is defined as the difference between the highest score and the lowest score, and it is obtained by subtracting the lowest score from the highest score. The range of heights in Table A.2 is 7′2″ minus 6′1″, or 1′1″. It is important to know the range of temperatures if we move to a new climate so that we may anticipate the weather and dress appropriately. A teacher must have some understanding of the range of abilities or skills in a class in order to teach effectively. Classes of gifted students or slow learners are formed so that teachers may attempt to devise a level of instruction that will better meet the needs of all members of a particular class.

The range is an imperfect measure of variability because of the manner in which it is influenced by extreme scores. In our earlier discussion of the savings of 30 families on a suburban block, the range of savings is $1,400,000 to $8,000, or $1,392,000. This tells us little about the typical variability of savings accounts, which lie within a restricted range of $8,000 to $12,000. The **standard deviation** is a statistic that indicates how scores are distributed about a mean of a distribution.

Bimodal Having two modes.

Range The difference between the highest and the lowest scores in a distribution.

Standard deviation A measure of the variability of a distribution, attained by the formula

$$\sqrt{\frac{\text{Sum of } d^2}{N}}$$

Figure A.3
Hypothetical Distributions of Student Test Scores Each distribution has the same number of scores, the same mean, and even the same range, but the standard deviation is greater for the distribution on the left because the scores tend to be farther from the mean.

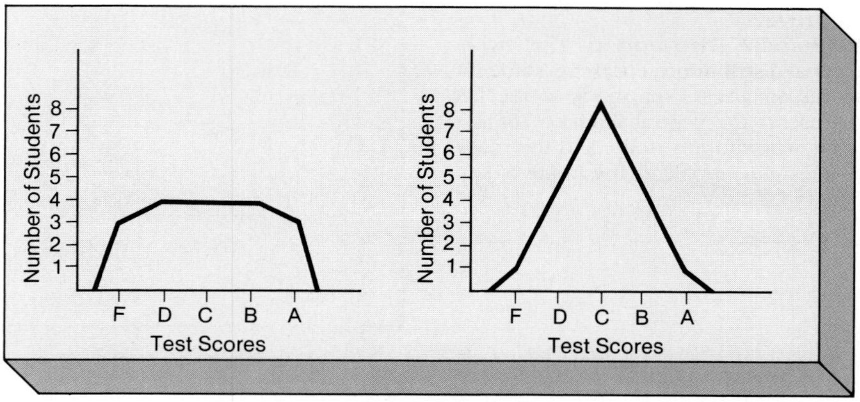

The standard deviation considers every score in a distribution, not just the extreme scores. Thus the standard deviation for the distribution on the right in Figure A.3 would be smaller than that of the distribution on the left. Note that each distribution has the same number of scores, the same mean, and the same range of scores. But the standard deviation for the distribution on the right is smaller than that of the distribution on the left because the scores tend to cluster more closely about the mean.

The standard deviation (S.D.) is calculated by the following formula:

$$\text{S.D.} = \sqrt{\frac{\text{Sum of } d^2}{N}}$$

where d equals the deviation of each score from the mean of the distribution, and N equals the number of scores in the distribution.

Let us find the mean and standard deviation of the IQ scores listed in column 1 of Table A.4. To obtain the mean, we add all the scores, attain 1,500, and then divide by the number of scores (15) to obtain a mean of 100. We obtain the deviation score (d) for each IQ score by subtracting the score from 100. The d for an IQ of 85 equals 100 minus 85, or 15, and so on. Then we square each d and add these squares. The S.D. equals the square root of the sum of squares (1,426) divided by the number of scores (15), or 9.75.

As an additional exercise, we can show that the S.D. of the test scores on the left (in Figure A.3) is greater than that for the scores on the right by assigning the grades points according to a 4.0 system. Let A = 4, B = 3, C = 2, D = 1, and F = 0. The S.D. for each distribution of test scores is computed in Table A.5. The greater S.D. for the distribution on the left indicates that the scores in that distribution are more variable, or tend to be farther from the mean.

THE NORMAL CURVE

Normal distribution A symmetrical distribution in which approximately 68 percent of cases lie within a standard deviation of the mean.

Many human traits and characteristics, such as height and intelligence, seem to be distributed in a pattern known as a normal distribution. In a **normal distribution,** the mean, median, and mode all fall at the same data point or score. Scores cluster most heavily about the mean, fall off rapidly in either direction at first (as shown in Figure A.4), and then taper off more gradually.

Table A.4
Hypothetical Scores Attained from an IQ Testing

IQ Score	d (Deviation Score)	d^2 (Deviation Score Squared)
85	15	225
87	13	169
89	11	121
90	10	100
93	7	49
97	3	9
97	3	9
100	0	0
101	−1	1
104	−4	16
105	−5	25
110	−10	100
112	−12	144
113	−13	169
117	−17	289

Sum of IQ scores = 1,500 Sum of d^2 scores = 1,426

$$\text{Mean} = \frac{\text{Sum of scores}}{\text{Number of scores}} = \frac{1{,}500}{15} = 100$$

$$\text{Standard Deviation (S.D.)} = \sqrt{\frac{\text{Sum of } d^2}{\text{Number of Scores}}} = \sqrt{\frac{1{,}426}{15}} = \sqrt{95.07} = 9.75$$

Table A.5
Computation of Standard Deviations for Test-score Distributions in Figure A.3

Distribution at Left:			Distribution at Right:		
Grade	d	d^2	Grade	d	d^2
A (4)	2	4	A (4)	2	4
A (4)	2	4	B (3)	1	1
A (4)	2	4	B (3)	1	1
B (3)	1	1	B (3)	1	1
B (3)	1	1	B (3)	1	1
B (3)	1	1	C (2)	0	0
B (3)	1	1	C (2)	0	0
C (2)	0	0	C (2)	0	0
C (2)	0	0	C (2)	0	0
C (2)	0	0	C (2)	0	0
C (2)	0	0	C (2)	0	0
D (1)	−1	1	C (2)	0	0
D (1)	−1	1	C (2)	0	0
D (1)	−1	1	D (1)	−1	1
D (1)	−1	1	D (1)	−1	1
F (0)	−2	4	D (1)	−1	1
F (0)	−2	4	D (1)	−1	1
F (0)	−2	4	F (0)	−2	4

Distribution at Left:
Sum of grades = 36
Mean grade = 36/18 = 2
Sum of d^2 = 32

$$\text{S.D.} = \sqrt{\frac{32}{18}} = 1.33$$

Distribution at Right:
Sum of grades = 36
Mean grade = 36/18 = 2
Sum of d^2 = 16

$$\text{S.D.} = \sqrt{\frac{16}{18}} = 0.94$$

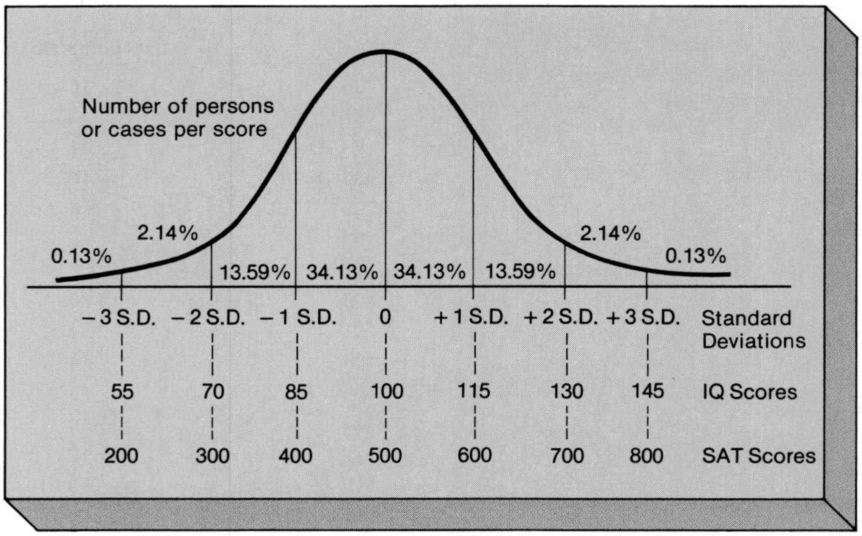

Figure A.4
A Bell-Shaped or Normal Curve In a normal curve, approximately 68 percent of the cases lie within a standard deviation (S.D.) from the mean, and the mean, median, and mode all lie at the same score. IQ tests and scholastic aptitude tests have been constructed so that distributions of scores approximate the normal curve.

The curve in Figure A.4 is bell-shaped. This type of distribution is also called a **normal curve.** It is hypothesized to reflect the distribution of variables in which different scores are determined by chance variation. Height is thought to be largely determined by chance combinations of genetic material. A distribution of the heights of a random sample of the population approximates normal distributions for men and women, with the mean of the distribution for men a few inches higher than the mean for women.

Test developers traditionally assumed that intelligence was also randomly or normally distributed among the population. For that reason, they constructed intelligence tests so that scores would be distributed as close to "normal" as possible. In actuality, IQ scores are also influenced by environmental factors and chromosomal abnormalities, so the resultant curves are not perfectly normal. Most IQ tests have means defined as scores of 100 points, and the Wechsler scales are constructed to have standard deviations of 15 points, as shown in Figure A.4. This means that 50 percent of the Wechsler scores fall between 90 and 110 (the "broad average" range), about 68 percent (or two of three) fall between 85 and 115, and more than 95 percent fall between 70 and 130—that is, within two S.D.s of the mean. The Stanford-Binet Intelligence Scale has an S.D. of 16 points.

The Scholastic Aptitude Tests (SATs) were constructed so that the mean scores would be 500 points, and an S.D. would be 100 points. Thus a score of 600 would equal or excel that of some 84 to 85 percent of the test takers. Because of the complex interaction of variables determining SAT scores, the distribution of SAT scores is not exactly normal either. The normal curve is an idealized curve.

THE CORRELATION COEFFICIENT

What is the relationship between intelligence and educational achievement? Between cigarette smoking and lung cancer in human beings? Between introversion and frequency of dating among college students? We cannot run experiments to determine whether the relationships between these variables are causal, because we cannot manipulate the independent variable. For example, we cannot randomly assign a group of people to cigarette smoking

Normal curve Graphic presentation of a normal distribution, showing a bell shape.

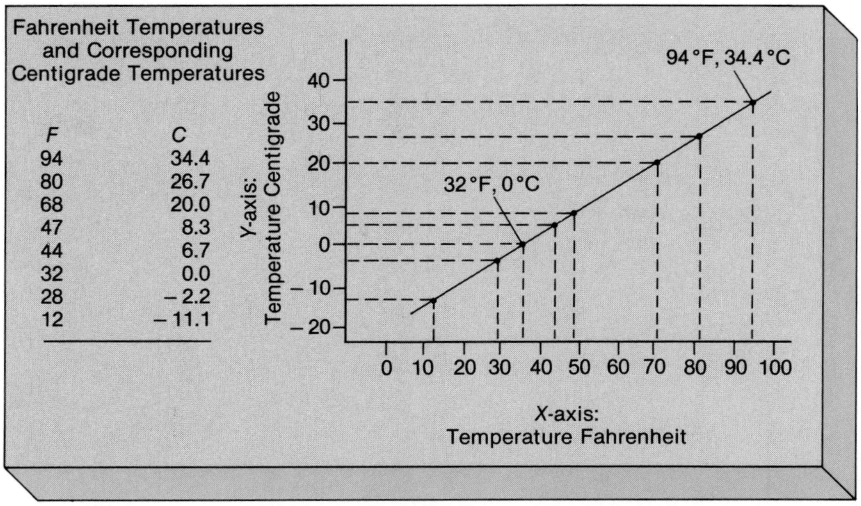

Figure A.5
A Scatter Diagram Showing the Perfect Positive Correlation between Fahrenheit Temperatures and the Corresponding Centigrade Temperatures Scatter diagrams have *X* and *Y* axes, and each point is plotted by finding the spot where an *X* value and the corresponding *Y* value meet.

and another group to nonsmoking. People must be permitted to make their own choices, and so it is possible that the same factors that lead people to choose to smoke may also lead to lung cancer. However, the **correlation coefficient** may be used to show that there is a relationship between smoking and cancer. If a strong correlation is shown between the two variables, and we add supportive experimental evidence with laboratory animals who are assigned to conditions in which they inhale tobacco smoke, we wind up with a rather convincing indictment of smoking as a determinant of lung cancer.

The correlation coefficient is a statistic that describes the relationship between two variables. It varies from +1.00 to −1.00; therefore, a correlation coefficient of +1.00 is called a perfect positive correlation, a coefficient of −1.00 is a perfect negative correlation, and a coefficient of 0.00 shows no correlation between variables. To examine the meanings of different correlation coefficients, let us first discuss the *scatter diagram.*

The Scatter Diagram

A **scatter diagram,** or scatter plot, is a graphic representation of the relationship between two variables. As shown in Figure A.5, a scatter diagram is typically drawn with an *X* axis (horizontal) and *Y* axis (vertical).

Let us assume that we have two thermometers. One measures temperature according to the Fahrenheit scale and one measures temperature according to the centigrade scale. Over a period of several months, we record the temperatures Fahrenheit and centigrade at various times of the day. Then we randomly select a sample of eight Fahrenheit readings and jot down the corresponding centigrade readings, as shown in Figure A.5.

Figure A.5 shows a perfect positive correlation. One variable increases as the other increases, and the points on the scatter diagram may be joined to form a straight line. We usually do not find variables forming a perfect positive (or perfect negative) correlation, unless they are related according to a specific mathematical formula. The temperatures Fahrenheit and centigrade are so related (degrees Fahrenheit = 9/5 degrees centigrade + 32).

A positive correlation of about +0.80 to +0.90, or higher, between scores attained on separate testings is usually required to determine the **reliability** of psychological tests. Intelligence tests such as the Stanford-Binet

Correlation coefficient A number between −1.00 and +1.00 that indicates the degree of relationship between two variables.

Scatter diagram A graphic presentation showing the plotting of points defined by the intersections of two variables.

Reliability Consistency; see Chapter 6.

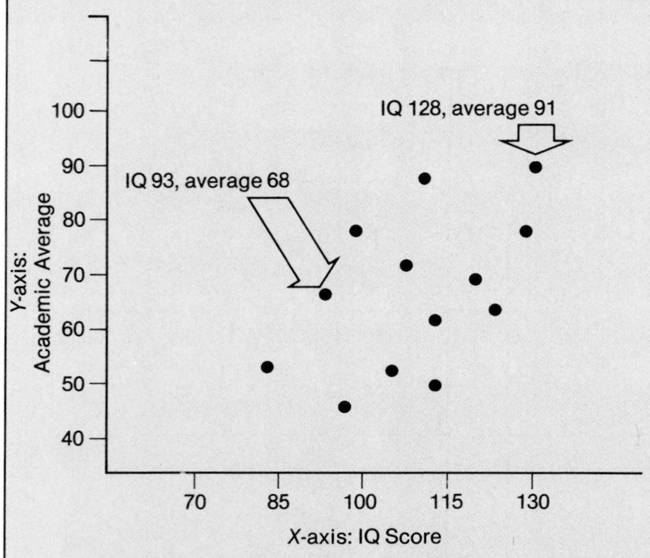

Figure A.6
A Hypothetical Scatter Diagram Showing the Relationship Between IQ Scores and Academic Averages Such correlations usually fall between +0.60 and +0.70, which is considered an adequate indication of validity for intelligence tests, since such tests are intended to predict academic performance.

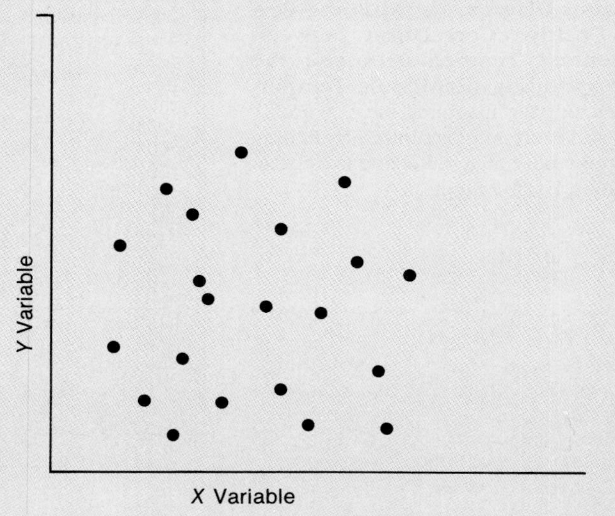

Figure A.7
A Scatter Diagram Showing a Correlation Coefficient of 0.00 between the *X* and *Y* Variables.

Intelligence Scale and the Wechsler scales have been found to yield **test-retest reliabilities** that meet these requirements. Somewhat lower correlation coefficients are usually accepted as indicators that a psychological test is **valid** when test scores are correlated with scores on an external criterion. Figure A.6 shows a hypothetical scatter diagram that demonstrates the relationship between IQ scores and academic averages for children in grade school. The correlation coefficient that would be derived by mathematical formula would be between +0.60 and +0.70. Remember that correlation does not show cause and effect. Figure A.6 suggests a relationship between the variables but cannot be taken as evidence that intelligence causes achievement.

Figure A.7 shows a scatter diagram in which there is a correlation coefficient of about 0.00 between the *X* and *Y* variables, suggesting that they are fully independent of each other. A person's scores on spelling quizzes taken in California ought to be independent of the daily temperatures in Bolivia. Thus we would expect a correlation coefficient of close to 0.00 between the variables.

Figure A.8 shows a scatter diagram in which there is a perfect negative correlation between two variables: As one variable increases, the other decreases systematically.

Correlations between 0.80 and 1.00 are considered to be very high (whether they are positive or negative). Correlations between 0.60 and 0.80 are high, between 0.40 and 0.60 moderate, from 0.20 to 0.40 weak, and between 0.00 and 0.20 very weak.

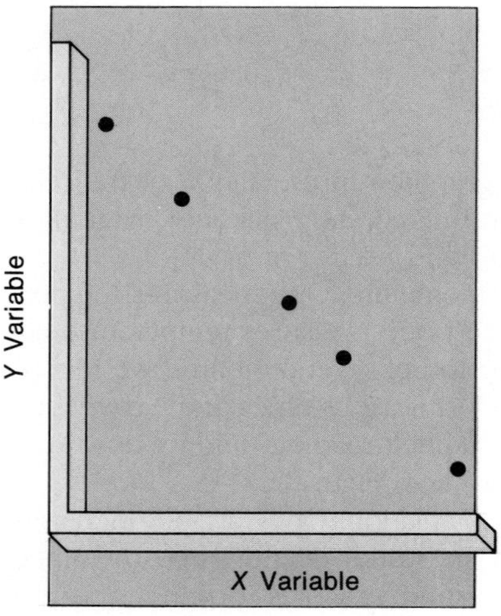

Figure A.8
A Scatter Diagram Showing a Correlation Coefficient of −1.00 between the *X* and *Y* Variables, or a Perfect Negative Relationship.

Test-retest reliability Consistency of a test as determined by a comparison of scores on repeated testings.

Validity The degree to which a test measures what it is supposed to measure; see Chapter 6.

Infer To draw a conclusion, to conclude. (From the Latin *in,* meaning "in," and *ferre,* meaning "to bear.")

Inferential statistics The branch of statistics concerned with the confidence with which conclusions drawn about samples may be extended to the populations from which they were drawn.

It cannot be overemphasized that correlation coefficients do not show cause and effect. For instance, a relationship between intelligence and academic performance, as shown in Figure A.9, could be explained by suggesting that the same cultural factors that lead some children to do well on intelligence tests also lead them to do well on academic tasks. According to this view, intelligence does not cause high academic performance. Instead, a third variable determines both intelligence and academic performance.

However, many psychologists undertake correlational research as a first step in attempting to determine causal relationships between variables. Correlation does not show cause and effect; yet a lack of correlation between two variables suggests that it may be fruitless to undertake experimental research to determine whether they are causally related.

INFERENTIAL STATISTICS

In a study reported in Chapter 6, children enrolled in a Head Start program earned a mean IQ score of 99, whereas children similar in background who were not enrolled in Head Start earned a mean IQ score of 93. Is this difference of six points in IQ significant, or does it represent chance fluctuation of scores? In a study reported in Chapter 1, subjects who believed they had drunk alcohol chose higher levels of electric shock to be applied to persons who had provoked them than did subjects who believed they had not drunk alcohol. Did the difference in level of shock chosen reflect an actual difference between the two groups of subjects, or could it have been a chance fluctuation? Inferential statistics help us make decisions about whether differences found between such groups reflect real differences or just fluctuations.

Figure A.9 shows the distribution of heights of a thousand men and a thousand women selected at random. The mean height for men is greater than the mean height for women. Can we draw the conclusion, or **infer,** that this difference in heights represents the general population of men and women? Or must we avoid such an inference and summarize our results by stating only that the sample of a thousand men in the study had a higher mean height than that of the sample of a thousand women in the study?

If we could not draw inferences about populations from studies of samples, our research findings would be very limited indeed—limited only to the specific subjects studied. However, the branch of statistics known as **inferential statistics** uses mathematical techniques in such a way that we can make statements about populations from which samples have been drawn, with a certain level of confidence.

Statistically Significant Differences

In determining whether differences in measures taken of research samples may be applied to the populations from which they were drawn, psychologists use mathematical techniques that indicate whether differences are statistically significant. Was the difference in IQ scores for children attending and those not attending Head Start significant? Did it represent only the children participating in the study, or can it be applied to all children represented by the sample? Is the difference between the height of men and the height of women in Figure A.10 statistically significant? Can we apply our findings to all men and women?

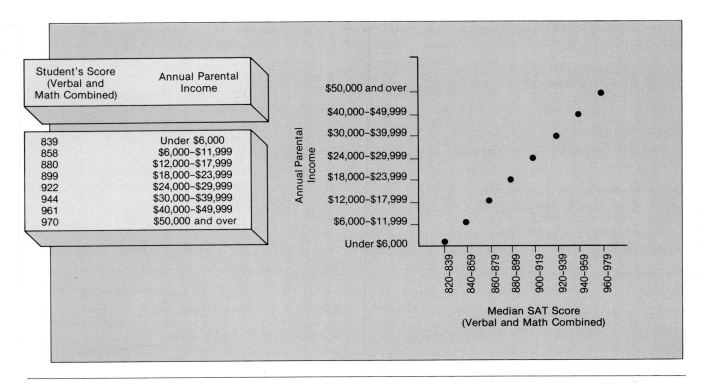

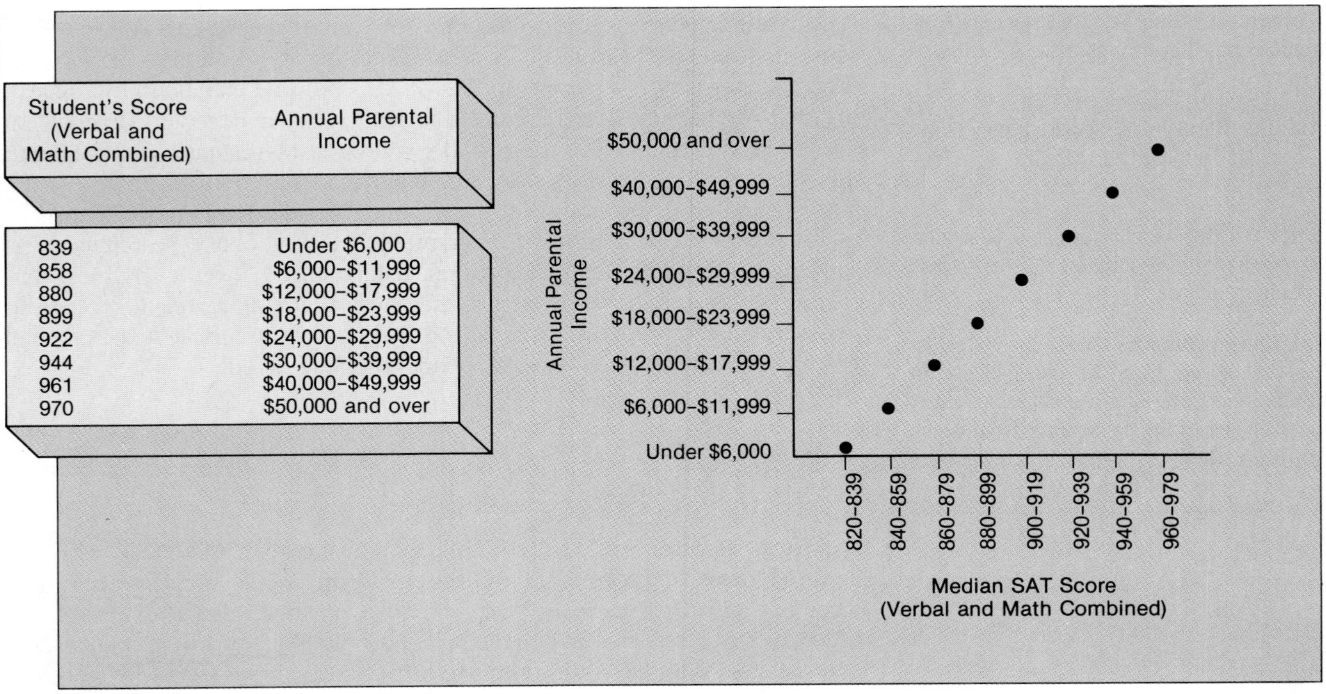

Figure A.9
A Scatter Diagram Showing the Relationship between the Income of a Student's Family and the Student's Score on the Scholastic Aptitude Test (SAT) Taken during 1980–1981. Scores are a combination of scores on the Verbal and Mathematics subtests and may vary from 400–1600. Scores shown are for white students only. SAT scores predict performance in college. Note the strong positive correlation between SAT scores and parental income. Does the relationship show that a high-income family is better able to expose children to concepts and skills measured on the SAT? Or that families who transmit genetic influences that may contribute to high test performance also tend to earn high incomes? Correlation is *not* cause and effect. For this reason, the data cannot answer these questions.

Figure A.10
Distribution of Heights for Random Samples of Men and Women Inferential statistics permit us to apply our findings to the populations sampled.

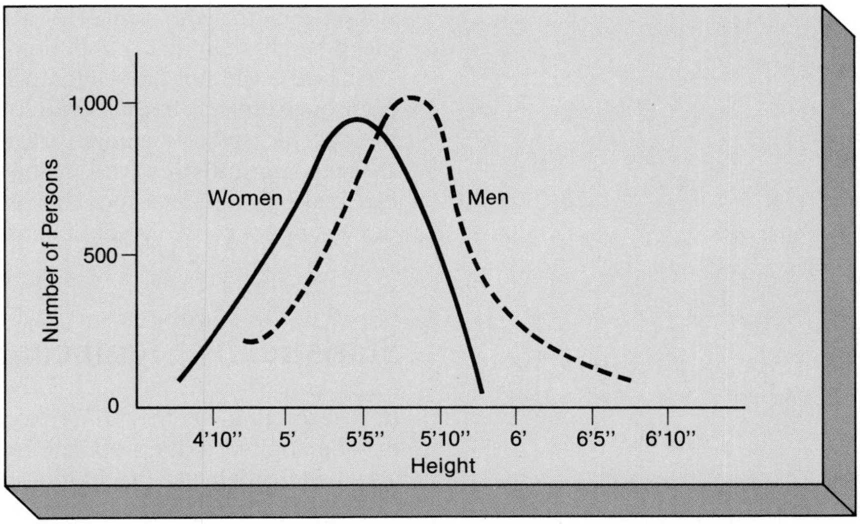

Psychologists use formulas involving the means and standard deviations of sample groups to determine whether group differences are statistically significant. As you can see in Figure A.11, the farther apart the group means are, the more likely it is that the difference between them is statistically

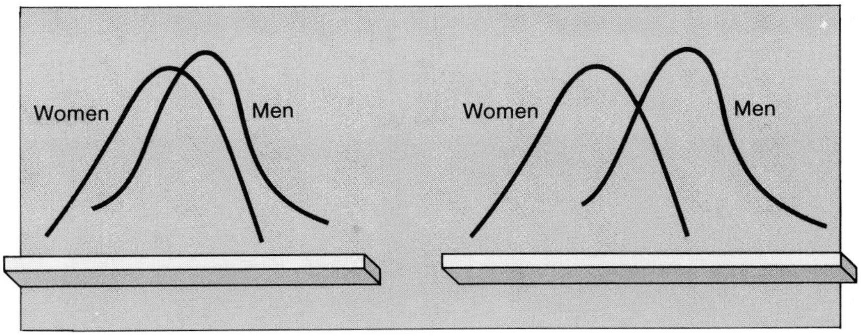

Figure A.11 Psychologists use group means and standard deviations to determine whether the difference between group means is statistically significant. The difference between the means of the groups on the right is greater and thus more likely to be statistically significant.

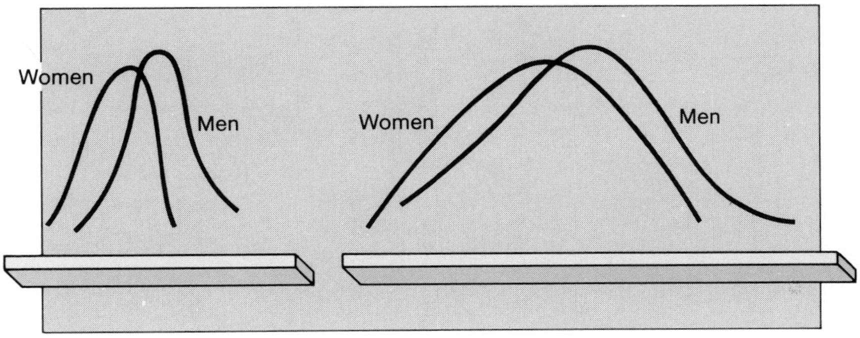

Figure A.12 The variability of the groups on the left is smaller than the variability of the groups on the right. Thus it is more likely that the difference between the means of the groups on the left is statistically significant.

significant. This makes a good deal of common sense. After all, if you were told that your neighbor's car had gotten one-tenth of a mile more per gallon of gasoline than your car had last year, you might assume that this was a chance difference. But if the differences were farther apart, say fourteen miles per gallon, you might readily believe that this difference reflected an actual difference in driving habits or efficiency of the automobiles.

As you can see in Figure A.12, the smaller the standard deviations (a measure of variability) of the two groups, the more likely it is that the difference of the means is statistically significant. As an extreme example, if all women sampled were exactly 5′5″ tall, and all men sampled were exactly 5′10″, we would be highly likely to assume that the difference of five inches in group means is statistically significant. But if the heights of women varied from 2′ to 14′, and the heights of men varied from 2′1″ to 14′3″, we might be more likely to assume that the five-inch difference in group means could be attributed to chance fluctuation.

Samples and Populations

Inferential statistics are mathematical tools that psychologists apply to samples of scores to determine whether they can generalize their findings to populations of scores. Thus they must be quite certain that the samples involved actually represent the populations from which they were drawn.

As you learned in Chapter 1, psychologists often use the techniques of random sampling and stratified sampling of populations in order to draw representative samples. If the samples studied do not accurately represent their intended populations, it matters very little how sophisticated the statistical techniques of the psychologist may be. We could use a variety of statistical techniques on the heights of the New York Apples and California Quakes, but none would tell us much about the height of the general population.

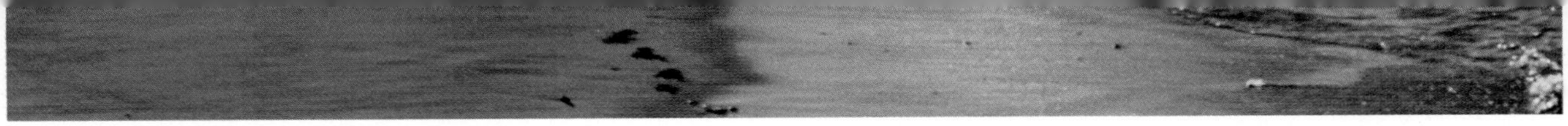

Appendix B Answer Keys for Questionnaries

Scoring Key for the "Social Desirability Scale" (Chapter 1, page 30)

Place a check mark on the appropriate line of the scoring key each time your answer agrees with the one listed on the scoring key. Add the check marks and place the total number of check marks on the line marked "Total Score."

1. T___	**12.** F___	**23.** F___
2. T___	**13.** T___	**24.** T___
3. F___	**14.** F___	**25.** T___
4. T___	**15.** F___	**26.** T___
5. F___	**16.** T___	**27.** T___
6. F___	**17.** T___	**28.** F___
7. T___	**18.** T___	**29.** T___
8. T___	**19.** F___	**30.** F___
9. F___	**20.** T___	**31.** T___
10. F___	**21.** T___	**32.** F___
11. F___	**22.** F___	**33.** T___

TOTAL SCORE ______

Interpreting Your Score LOW SCORERS (0–8). About one respondent in six earns a score between 0 and 8. Such respondents answered in a socially *undesirable* direction much of the time. It may be that they are more willing than most people to respond to test items truthfully, even when their answers might meet with social disapproval.

AVERAGE SCORERS (9–19). About two respondents in three earn scores between 9 and 19. They tend to show an average degree of concern for the social desirability of their responses, and it may well be that their actual behavior represents an average degree of conformity to social rules and conventions.

HIGH SCORERS (20–33). About one respondent in six earns a score between 20 and 33. These respondents may be highly concerned about social approval and respond to test items in such a way as to avoid the disapproval of people who may learn of their responses. Their actual behavior may show high conformity to social rules and conventions.

Scoring Key for the "Why Do You Drink?" Questionnaire (Chapter 4, page 162)

Why do you drink? Score your questionnaire by seeing how many items you answered for each of the following reasons for drinking. Consider the key to be *suggestive* only. For example, if you answered several items in a manner indicative of the *addiction* factor, it may be wise to seriously examine what your drinking means to you. But do not interpret a few test-item scores as binding evidence of addiction.

Addiction
1. T
6. F
32. T
38. T
40. T

Anxiety/Tension Reduction
7. T
9. T
12. T
15. T
18. T
26. T
31. T
33. T

Pleasure/Taste
2. T
5. T
16. T
27. T
28. T
35. T
37. T

Transforming Agent
2. T
4. T
19. T
22. T
28. T
30. T
34. T
36. T

Social Reward
3. T
8. T
23. T

Celebration
10. T
24. T
25. T

Religion
11. T

Social Power
2. T
13. T
19. T
30. T

Scapegoating (Using alcohol as an excuse for failure or social misconduct)
14. T
15. T
20. T
21. T
39. T

Habit
17. T
29. T

Scoring Key for the "Remote Associates Test" (Chapter 7, page 280)

1. Prince
2. Dog
3. Cold
4. Glasses
5. Club
6. Boat
7. Defense
8. Pit
9. Writer

Table B.1
Love-Scale Scores of Northeastern University Students

Condition	N*	Mean Scores
Absolutely in love	56	89
Probably in love	45	80
Not sure	36	77
Probably not in love	40	68
Definitely not in love	43	59

*N = Number of students

Scoring Key for "The Sensation-Seeking Scale" (Chapter 8, page 314)

Because this is a shortened version of a questionnaire, no norms are available. However, answers in agreement with the following key point in the direction of sensation seeking:

1. A
2. A
3. A
4. B
5. A
6. B
7. A
8. A
9. B
10. B
11. A
12. A
13. B

Norms for "The Love Scale" (Chapter 8, page 335)

The Love Scale was validated with a sample of 220 undergraduates, aged 19–24 (mean age = 21), from Northeastern University. Students were asked to indicate whether they were "absolutely in love," "probably in love," "not sure," "probably not in love," or "definitely not in love" with a person they were dating. Then they answered the items on the Love Scale with the same person in mind.

Table B.1 shows the mean score for each category. Mean scores for men and women in each of the five categories did not differ, so they were lumped together. If your Love-Scale score for your date is 84, it may be that your feelings lie somewhere in between those of Northeastern University students who claimed that they were "probably in love" and "absolutely in love."

Be warned: A number of students broke into arguments after taking the Love Scale—their "love" for one another differed by a few points! Please do not take the scale so seriously. Such scales are fun, but they will not hold up in court as grounds for divorce. Rely on your feelings, not on your scores.

Answer Key for the "Social Readjustment Rating Scale" (Chapter 11, page 433)

Add all the scores in the Total column to arrive at your final score.

FINAL SCORE ______

Interpretation Your final score is indicative of the amount of stress you have experienced during the past 12 months:

Final Score	Amount of Stress
From 0 to 1,500	Minor stress
1,501–3,500	Mild stress
3,501–5,500	Moderate stress
5,501 and above	Major stress

Research has shown that the probability of encountering physical illness within the *following* year is related to the amount of stress experienced during the *past* year. That is, college students who experienced minor stress have a 28 percent chance of becoming ill; mild stress, a 45 percent chance; moderate stress, a 70 percent chance; and major stress, an 82 percent chance. Moreover, the seriousness of the illness also increases with the amount of stress.

It should be recognized that these percentages reflect previous research with college students. Do not assume if you have encountered a great deal of stress that you are "doomed" to illness. Also keep in mind that a number of psychological factors moderate the effect of stress. For example, psychologically hardy college students could theoretically withstand the same amount of stress that could enhance the risk of illness for nonhardy individuals.

Answer Key for the "Are You Type A or B?" Questionnaire (Chapter 11, page 440)

As described in Chapter 11, Type A's are ambitious, hard driving, and chronically discontent with their current achievements. Type B's, in contrast, are more relaxed and more involved with the quality of life.

The questionnaire was developed from descriptions of Type A people by Friedman and Ulmer (1984), Matthews and her colleagues (1982), and Musante et al. (1983). Yesses suggest the Type A behavior pattern, which is marked by a sense of time urgency and constant struggle. In appraising your type, you need not be overly concerned with the precise number of "yes" answers; we have no normative data for you. But as Freidman and Rosenman (1974, p. 85) note, you should have little trouble spotting yourself as "hard core" or "moderately afflicted"—that is, if you are honest with yourself.

Answer Key for the "Locus of Control Scale" (Chapter 11, page 443)

Place a check mark in the blank space in the scoring key that follows each time your answer agrees with the answer in the key. The number of checkmarks is your total score.

Scoring Key:

1. Yes ____	**11.** Yes ____	**21.** Yes ____	**31.** Yes ____
2. No ____	**12.** Yes ____	**22.** No ____	**32.** No ____
3. Yes ____	**13.** No ____	**23.** Yes ____	**33.** Yes ____
4. No ____	**14.** Yes ____	**24.** Yes ____	**34.** No ____
5. Yes ____	**15.** No ____	**25.** No ____	**35.** Yes ____
6. No ____	**16.** Yes ____	**26.** No ____	**36.** Yes ____
7. Yes ____	**17.** Yes ____	**27.** Yes ____	**37.** Yes ____
8. Yes ____	**18.** Yes ____	**28.** No ____	**38.** No ____
9. No ____	**19.** Yes ____	**29.** Yes ____	**39.** Yes ____
10. Yes ____	**20.** No ____	**30.** No ____	**40.** No ____

TOTAL SCORE ______

Interpreting Your Score LOW SCORERS (0–8). About one respondent in three earns a score of from 0 to 8. Such respondents tend to have an internal locus of control. They see themselves as being responsible for the reinforcements they attain (and fail to attain) in life.

AVERAGE SCORERS (9–16). Most respondents earn from 9 to 16 points. Average scorers may see themselves as partially in control of their lives. Perhaps they see themselves as being in control at work but not in their social lives—or vice versa.

HIGH SCORERS (17–40). About 15 percent of respondents attain scores of 17 or above. High scorers tend to see life largely as a game of chance and success as a matter of luck or the generosity of others.

Scoring Key for the "Rathus Assertiveness Schedule" (Chapter 13, page 540)

Tabulate your score as follows: For these items followed by an asterisk (*), change the signs (plus to minus; minus to plus). For example, if the response to an asterisked item was 2, place a minus sign (−) before the two. If the response to an asterisked item was −3, change the minus sign to a plus sign (+) by adding a vertical stroke. Then add up the scores of the 30 items.

Scores on the assertiveness schedule can vary from +90 to −90. The following table will show you how your score compares to those of 764 college women and 637 men from 35 campuses across the United States. For example, if you are a woman and your score was 26, it exceeds that of 80 percent of the women in the sample. A score of 15 for a male exceeds that of 55–60 percent of the men in the sample.

Women's Scores	Percentile	Men's Scores
55	99	65
48	97	54
45	95	48
37	90	40
31	85	33
26	80	30
23	75	26
19	70	24
17	65	19
14	60	17
11	55	15
8	50	11
6	45	8
2	40	6
−1	35	3
−4	30	1
−8	25	−3
−13	20	−7
−17	15	−11
−24	10	−15
−34	5	−24
−39	3	−30
−48	1	−41

Source: Nevid and Rathus (1978).

Answer Key for "Cultural Myths that Create a Climate that Supports Rape" Questionnaire (Chapter 14, page 585)

Actually, each item, with the exception of number 2, represents a cultural myth that tends to support rape. Agreement with any of these items shows an endorsement of such a myth.

GLOSSARY

A

A–B problem The issue of how well we can predict behavior on the basis of attitudes.

ABC model of attitudes The view that attitudes are composed of affect (feelings), behavioral tendencies, and cognitions.

Abreaction In psychodynamic theory, the expression of previously repressed feelings and impulses in order to allow the psychic energy associated with them to spill forth.

Absolute refractory period A phase following a neuron's firing during which an action potential cannot be triggered.

Absolute threshold The minimal amount of energy that can produce a sensation.

Abstinence syndrome A characteristic cluster of symptoms that results from sudden decrease in the level of usage of a drug on which one is physiologically dependent.

Accommodation According to Piaget, the modification of existing concepts or schemas so that new information can be integrated or understood.

Acetylcholine A neurotransmitter that controls muscle contractions. Abbreviated *ACh.*

Achievement Accomplishment; that which is attained by one's efforts and presumed to be made possible by one's abilities.

Acoustic code Mental representation of information as a sequence of sounds.

Acquired drives Drives that are acquired through experience, or learned.

Acquisition trial In conditioning, a presentation of stimuli such that a new response is learned and strengthened.

Acronym A word that is composed of the first letters of the elements of a phrase.

Acrophobia Fear of high places.

Action potential The electrical impulse that provides the basis for the conduction of a neural impulse along an axon of a neuron.

Activating effects The arousal-producing effects of sex hormones that increase the likelihood of dominant sexual responses.

Activation-synthesis model The view that dreams reflect activation by the reticular activating system and synthesis by the cerebral cortex.

Active coping A response to stress that manipulates the environment or changes the response patterns of the individual to permanently remove the stressor or to render it harmless.

Actor-observer effect In attribution theory, the tendency to attribute our own behavior to situational factors but to attribute the behavior of others to dispositional factors.

Acupuncture The ancient Chinese practice of piercing parts of the body with needles to deaden pain and treat illness.

Adaptation stage See *resistance stage.*

ADH Abbreviation of antidiuretic hormone.

Adipose tissue Tissue that contains fat.

Adjustment The process of responding to stress.

Adolescence The stage of development bounded by the advent of puberty and the capacity to assume adult responsibilities.

Adrenal medulla The inner part of the adrenal gland, which produces adrenaline.

Adrenal cortex The outer part of the adrenal gland, which produces steroids.

Adrenaline A hormone produced by the adrenal medulla that stimulates the sympathetic division of the autonomic nervous system. Also called *epinephrine.*

Adrenocorticotrophic hormone A pituitary hormone that regulates the adrenal cortex. Abbreviated *ACTH.*

"Adult" In transactional analysis, a rational, adaptive ego state.

Aerobic exercise Exercise that requires sustained increase in oxygen consumption.

Affective disorders Disorders characterized primarily by prolonged disturbances of mood or emotional response. (Now referred to as *mood disorders.*)

Afferent neuron A neuron that transmits messages from sensory receptors to the spinal cord and brain. Also called *sensory neuron.*

Affiliation The social motive to be with others and to cooperate.

Afterimage The lingering impression made by a stimulus that has been removed.

Agape Altruistic, generous love. A Greek word referring to divine love—that is, the type of love that the gods were thought to feel for humans.

Age regression In hypnosis, taking on the role of childhood, frequently accompanied by vivid recollections of the early years.

Agoraphobia Fear of open, crowded places.

AIDS-related complex A stage in the development of AIDS characterized mainly by swollen lymph glands.

AIDS Acronym for *acquired immune deficiency syndrome.* A disorder of the immune system caused by a virus and characterized by suppression of the immune response, leaving the body prey to opportunistic diseases.

Alarm reaction The first stage of the general adaptation syndrome, which is triggered by the impact of a stressor and characterized by heightened sympathetic activity.

Alcoholism Drinking that persistently impairs personal, social, or physical well-being.

Algorithm A specific procedure, such as a formula, for solving a problem that will work invariably if it is applied correctly.

All-or-none principle The principle that a neuron fires an impulse of the same strength whenever its action potential has been triggered.

Allele Each member of a pair of genes.

Alpha waves Rapid, low-amplitude brain waves that have been linked to feelings of relaxation.

Altered states of consciousness States other than the normal waking state, including sleep, meditation, the hypnotic trance, and the distorted perceptions that can be caused by use of certain drugs.

Alternate-form reliability The consistency of a test as determined by correlating scores attained on one form of the test with scores attained on another form. The Scholastic Aptitude Tests and Graduate Record Exams, for example, have many forms.

Altruism Selflessness; unselfish concern for the welfare of others.

Alzheimer's disease A progressive disease that is associated with degeneration of hippocampal cells that produce acetylcholine. It is symptomized by the inability to form new memories and the loss of other cognitive functions.

Ambiguous Having two or more possible meanings.

Amenorrhea Absence of menstruation.

American Sign Language The communication of meaning through the use of symbols that are formed by moving the hands and arms and associated gestures. Abbreviated *ASL.*

Amino acid Protein involved in metabolism.

Amniocentesis A method for tapping amniotic fluid and examining fetal chromosomes that have been sloughed off, making it possible to determine the presence of genetic abnormalities and the sex of the fetus.

Amniotic fluid Fluid within the amniotic sac, formed largely from the fetus's urine, that protects the fetus from jarring or injury.

Amniotic sac A sac within the uterus that contains the embryo or fetus.

Amotivational syndrome Loss of ambition or motivation to achieve.

Amphetamines Stimulants like Dexedrine and Benzedrine that are derived from *a*lpha-*m*ethyl-beta-*ph*enyl-*et*hyl-*amine.* Abuse can trigger symptoms that mimic schizophrenia.

Amplitude Height. The extreme range of a variable quantity.

Amygdala A part of the limbic system that apparently facilitates stereotypical aggressive responses.

Anabolic steroids Steroids, the chief of which is testosterone, that promote the growth of muscle tissue by creating protein and other substances. Anabolic steroids also foster feelings of invincibility. See also *corticosteroids.*

Anaerobic exercise Exercise that does not require sustained increase in oxygen consumption, such as weight lifting.

Anal-expulsive A Freudian personality type characterized by unregulated self-expression, such as messiness.

Anal fixation In psychodynamic theory, attachment to objects and behaviors characteristic of the anal stage.

Anal-retentive A Freudian personality type characterized by self-control, such as excessive neatness and punctuality.

Anal stage In psychodynamic theory, the second stage of psychosexual development, in which gratification is obtained through anal activities like eliminating wastes.

Analgesia A state in which one does not feel pain but is fully conscious.

Analogous colors Colors that lie next to one another on the color wheel and form harmonious families.

Analyst A person who practices psychoanalysis, Freud's method of psychotherapy.

Analytical psychology Jung's psychodynamic theory, which emphasizes archetypes, a collective unconscious, and a unifying force of personality called the Self.

Androgenital syndrome A hormonal disorder in which prenatal exposure to androgens masculinizes the external genitals of genetic females.

Androgens Male sex hormones.

Anger (1) A negative emotion frequently characterized by a provocation, cognitions that one has been taken advantage of and should seek revenge, and aggressive behavioral tendencies. (2) The second stage in Kübler-Ross's theory of dying.

Angiotensin A kidney hormone that signals the hypothalamus of depletion of body fluids.

Anima Jung's feminine archetype.

Animism The belief, characteristic of preoperational thought, that inanimate objects move because of will or spirit.

Animus Jung's masculine archetype.

Anorexia nervosa An eating disorder characterized by maintenance of an abnormally low body weight, intense fear of weight gain, a distorted body image, and, in females, amenorrhea.

Anosmia Lack of sensitivity to a specific odor.

ANS Abbreviation for *autonomic nervous system.*

Antecedent An event or thing that occurs before another.

Anterograde amnesia Failure to remember events that occur after physical trauma because of the effects of the trauma.

Antibodies Substances formed by white blood cells that recognize and destroy antigens.

Antidepressant drug A drug that acts to relieve depression.

Antidiuretic hormone A pituitary hormone that conserves body fluids by increasing the reabsorption of urine. Abbreviated *ADH.*

Antigen A substance that stimulates the body to mount an immune-system response to it. (The contraction for *anti*body *gen*erator.)

Antisocial personality disorder The diagnosis given a person who is in frequent conflict with society yet is undeterred by punishment and experiences little or no guilt and anxiety. Also referred to as psychopathy or sociopathy.

Anvil A bone of the middle ear.

Anxiety A psychological state characterized by tension and apprehension, foreboding and dread.

Aphagic Characterized by undereating.

Aphasia Impaired ability to comprehend or express oneself through speech.

Apnea Temporary discontinuation of breathing during sleep.

Applied research Research conducted in an effort to find solutions to particular problems.

Applied psychology The application of fundamental psychological methods and knowledge to the investigation and solution of human problems.

Approach-approach conflict Conflict involving two positive but mutually exclusive goals.

Approach-avoidance conflict Conflict involving a goal with positive and negative features.

Aptitude A natural ability or talent.

Archetypes In Jung's personality theory, primitive images or concepts that reside in the collective unconscious.

Arousal (1) A general level of activity or preparedness for activity in an organism. (2) A general level of motivation in an organism.

Arteriosclerosis A disease characterized by thickening and hardening of the arteries.

Artificialism The belief, characteristic of preoperational thought, that natural objects have been created by human beings.

Assertiveness training A collection of behavior-therapy techniques (modeling, feedback, behavior rehearsal, etc.) that teach clients to express feelings, seek fair treatment, and improve social skills.

Assimilation According to Piaget, the inclusion of a new event into an existing concept or schema.

Association areas Parts of the cerebral cortex involved in learning, thought, memory, and language.

Asthma Recurrent attacks of difficult breathing and wheezing.

Astigmatism A visual disorder in which vertical and horizontal contours cannot be focused on simultaneously.

Asylum (1) An early institution for the care of the mentally ill. (2) A safe place, or refuge.

Attachment The enduring affectional tie that binds one person to another.

Attachment-in-the-making phase The second phase in forming bonds of attachment, characterized by preference for familiar figures.

Attitude An enduring system of beliefs, feelings, and behavioral tendencies concerning people, objects, or ideas.

Attitude-discrepant behavior Behavior that is inconsistent with an attitude and may have the effect of modifying an attitude.

Attraction A force that draws bodies or people together. In social psychology, an attitude of liking (positive attraction) or disliking (negative attraction).

Attribution A belief about why people behave in a certain way.

Attributional style One's tendency to attribute one's behavior to internal or external factors, stable or unstable factors, and so on.

Attribution process The process by which people draw conclusions about the motives and traits of others.

Auditory Having to do with hearing.

Auditory nerve The axon bundle that transmits neural impulses from the organ of Corti to the brain.

Authoritarianism Belief in the importance of unquestioning obedience to authority.

Autism (1) Self-absorption. Absorption in daydreaming and fantasy. (2) A childhood disorder marked by problems such as failure to relate to others, lack of speech, and intolerance of change.

Autogenic training A method for reducing tension involving repeated suggestions that the limbs are becoming warmer and heavier and that one's breathing is becoming more regular.

Autokinetic effect The tendency to perceive a stationary point of light in a dark room as moving.

Automatic writing Writing about perceived stimulation while the major portion of a person's attention is focused elsewhere.

Autonomic nervous system The division of the peripheral nervous system that regulates glands and involuntary activities like heartbeat, respiration, digestion, and dilation of the pupils. Abbreviated *ANS*. Also see *sympathetic* and *parasympathetic* branches of the ANS.

Autonomy Self-direction. The social motive to be free, unrestrained, and independent.

Autonomy versus shame and doubt Erikson's second stage of psychosocial development, during which the child develops (or does not develop) the wish to make choices and the capacity to exercise self-control.

Autosomes Chromosomes that look alike and possess information about the same sets of traits. One autosome is received from the father and the corresponding autosome is received from the mother.

Average The central tendency of a group of measures, expressed as *mean, median,* or *mode*.

Aversive conditioning A behavior-therapy technique in which a previously desirable or neutral stimulus is made obnoxious by being paired repeatedly with a repugnant or offensive stimulus.

Avoidance-avoidance conflict Conflict involving two negative goals in which avoidance of one requires approach of the other.

Avoidance learning An operant conditioning procedure in which an organism learns to exhibit an operant that permits it to avoid an aversive stimulus.

Axon A long, thin part of a neuron that transmits impulses to other neurons from branching structures called terminals.

B

B lymphocytes The white blood cells of the immune system that produce antibodies.

Babbling The child's first verbalizations that have the sound of speech.

Babinski reflex An infant's fanning of the toes in response to stimulation of the sole of the foot.

Backward conditioning A classical conditioning procedure in which the unconditioned stimulus is presented prior to the conditioned stimulus.

Balance sheet An outline of positive and negative expectations concerning a course of action. An aid to effective decision making.

Balance theory The view that people have a need to organize their perceptions, opinions, and beliefs in a harmonious manner.

Barbiturate An addictive depressant used to relieve anxiety or induce sleep.

Bargaining The third stage in Kübler-Ross's theory of dying, in which the terminally ill try to bargain with God to postpone death, usually by offering to do good deeds in exchange for time.

Barnum effect The tendency to believe in the accuracy of a generalized personality report or prediction about oneself.

Basal ganglia Ganglia located in the brain between the thalamus and the cerebrum that are involved in motor coordination.

Basic anxiety Horney's term for enduring feelings of insecurity that stem from harsh or indifferent parental treatment.

Basic hostility Horney's term for enduring feelings of anger that accompany basic anxiety but that are directed toward nonfamily members in adulthood.

Basilar membrane A membrane to which the organ of Corti is attached. The basilar membrane lies coiled within the cochlea.

Behavior The observable or measurable actions of people and lower animals.

Behavioral competencies Skills.

Behavioral medicine An interdisciplinary field in which psychological principles are applied to the treatment of health problems.

Behavior genetics The study of the genetic transmission of structures and traits that give rise to behavior.

Behaviorism The school of psychology that defines psychology as the study of observable behavior and investigates the relationships between stimuli and responses.

Behaviorist A psychologist who believes that psychology should address observable behavior and the relationships between stimuli and responses.

Behavior modification Use of principles of learning to change behavior in desired directions.

Behavior rating scale A systematic means of recording the frequency with which target behaviors occur. (An alternative to self-report methods of personality testing.)

Behavior rehearsal Practice.

Behavior therapy Use of the principles of learning in the direct modification of problem behavior.

Benzodiazepines A class of drugs that reduce anxiety. Minor tranquilizers.

Bimodal Having two modes.

Binocular cues Stimuli that suggest depth by means of simultaneous perception by both eyes. Examples: retinal disparity and convergence.

Biofeedback training The systematic feeding back to an organism of information about a body function so that the organism can gain control of that function. Abbreviated *BFT.*

Biological psychologist A psychologist who studies the relationships between biological processes and behavior.

Bipolar cells Neurons that conduct neural impulses from rods and cones to ganglion cells.

Bipolar disorder A disorder in which the mood inappropriately alternates between extremes of elation and depression. Formerly called *manic-depression.*

Blind spot The area of the retina where axons from ganglion cells meet to form the optic nerve. It is insensitive to light.

Blind In experimental terminology, unaware of whether one has received a treatment.

Blocking In conditioning, the phenomenon whereby a new stimulus fails to gain the capacity to signal an unconditioned stimulus (US) when the new stimulus is paired repeatedly with a stimulus that already effectively foretells the US.

Breathalyzer A device that measures the quantity of alcohol in the body by analyzing the breath.

Brief reactive psychosis A psychotic episode of less than two weeks in duration that follows a known stressful event.

Brightness constancy The tendency to perceive an object as being just as bright even though lighting conditions change the intensity with which it impacts on the eye.

Broca's aphasia A speech disorder caused by damage to Broca's area of the brain. It is characterized by slow, laborious speech and by difficulty articulating words and forming grammatical sentences.

Bulimia nervosa An eating disorder characterized by recurrent episodes of binge eating followed by purging and by persistent overconcern with body shape and weight.

Bureaucracy An administrative system characterized by departments and subdivisions whose members frequently are given long tenure and inflexible work tasks.

C

Cannon-Bard theory The theory of emotion that holds that events are processed by the brain and that the brain induces patterns of activity and autonomic arousal *and* cognitive activity—that is, the experiencing of the appropriate emotion.

Carcinogen An agent that gives rise to cancerous changes.

Cardinal trait Allport's term for pervasive traits that steer practically all of a person's behavior.

Cardiovascular disorders Diseases of the cardiovascular system, including heart disease, hypertension, and arteriosclerosis.

Case study A carefully drawn biography that may be obtained through interviews, questionnaires, psychological tests, and, sometimes, historical records.

Catalyst An agent that hastens or facilitates a reaction. (A term borrowed from chemistry.)

Catastrophize To exaggerate or magnify the noxious properties of negative events; to "blow out of proportion."

Catatonic schizophrenia A subtype of schizophrenia characterized by striking impairment in motor activity.

Catch Thirties Sheehy's term for the fourth decade of life, which is frequently characterized by major reassessment of one's accomplishments and goals.

Catecholamines A number of chemical substances produced from an amino acid that are important as neurotransmitters (dopamine and norepinephrine) and as hormones (adrenaline and norepinephrine).

Catharsis The free expression or spilling forth of feelings. Also called *abreaction.*

Caucasian Descriptive of people whose ancestors came from Europe, North Africa, and the Middle East to North India. Usually referred to as "white people," although skin color actually varies from pale reddish white to olive brown.

Cellular-aging theory The view that aging occurs because body cells lose the capacity to reproduce and maintain themselves.

Center According to Piaget, to focus one's attention.

Central fissure The valley in the cerebral cortex that separates the frontal and parietal lobes.

Central nervous system The brain and spinal cord.

Central traits Characteristics that are outstanding and noticeable but not necessarily all-pervasive.

Cephalocaudal Proceeding from top to bottom.

Cerebellum A part of the hindbrain involved in muscle coordination and balance.

Cerebral cortex The wrinkled surface area of the cerebrum, often called "gray matter" because of the appearance afforded by the many cell bodies.

Cerebrum The large mass of the forebrain, which consists of two hemispheres.

Chain breaking A behavior-therapy self-control technique in which one disrupts problematic behavior by complicating its execution.

Chemotherapy The use of drugs to treat abnormal behavior patterns.

"Child" In transactional analysis, an irresponsible, emotional ego state.

Childhood amnesia Inability to recall events that occurred before the age of 3.

Chorionic villus sampling The detection of genetic abnormalities by sampling the membrane that envelopes the amniotic sac and the fetus within. Abbreviated *CVS.*

Chromosomes Genetic structures consisting of genes that are found in the nuclei of the body's cells.

Chronological age A person's actual age—as contrasted to *mental age.*

Chunk A stimulus or group of stimuli that are perceived or encoded as a discrete piece of information.

Circular explanation An explanation that merely repeats its own concepts instead of offering additional information.

Cirrhosis of the liver A disease caused by protein deficiency in which connective fibers replace active liver cells, impairing circulation of the blood. Alcohol does not contain protein; therefore, people who drink excessively may be prone to acquiring this disease.

Classic organization theories Theories that hold that organizations should be structured from the skeleton (governing body) outward.

Classical conditioning (1) According to cognitive theorists, the learning of relations among events so as to allow an organism to represent its environment. (2) According to behaviorists, a form of learning in which one stimulus comes to evoke the response usually evoked by a second stimulus by being paired repeatedly with the second stimulus. Also referred to as *respondent conditioning* or *Pavlovian conditioning.*

Claustrophobia Fear of tight, small places.

Clear-cut-attachment phase The third phase in forming bonds of attachment, characterized by intensified dependence on the primary caregiver.

Client-centered therapy The former name for *person-centered therapy.*

Clinical scales Groups of test items that measure the presence of various abnormal behavior patterns, as on the Minnesota Multiphasic Personality Inventory.

Clitoris An external female sex organ, which is highly sensitive to sexual stimulation.

Closure The tendency to perceive a broken figure as being complete or whole.

Cocaine A powerful stimulant derived from coca leaves that is usually snorted, brewed, or injected.

Cochlea The inner ear; the bony tube that contains the basilar membrane and the organ of Corti.

Cognitive Having to do with mental processes such as sensation and perception, memory, intelligence, language, thought, and problem solving.

Cognitive dissonance theory The view that we are motivated to make our cognitions or beliefs consistent.

Cognitive map A mental representation or picture of the elements in a learning situation, such as a maze.

Cognitive therapy A form of psychotherapy that focuses on how clients' cognitions (expectations, attitudes, beliefs, etc.) lead to distress and may be modified to relieve distress and promote adaptive behavior.

Coitus Sexual intercourse.

Collective unconscious Jung's hypothesized store of vague racial memories and archetypes.

Color constancy The tendency to perceive an object as being the same color even as lighting conditions change its appearance.

Comatose In a coma, a state resembling sleep from which it is difficult to be aroused.

Common fate The tendency to perceive elements that move together as belonging together.

Community psychology A field of psychology, related to clinical psychology, that focuses on the prevention of psychological problems and the maintenance of distressed persons in the community.

Companionate love A type of nonsexual love based on intimacy, respect, and trust.

Competencies Within social-learning theory, knowledge and skills.

Competing response In behavior therapy, a response that is incompatible with an unwanted response.

Complementary (1) In sensation and perception, descriptive of colors of the spectrum which, when combined, produce white or nearly white light. (2) In transactional analysis, descriptive of a transaction in which the ego states of two people interact harmoniously.

Componential level According to Sternberg, the level of intelligence that consists of metacomponents, performance components, and knowledge-acquisition components.

Compulsion An apparently irresistible urge to repeat an act or engage in ritualistic behavior, such as hand-washing.

Computerized axial tomography Formation of a computer-generated image of the anatomical details of the brain by passing a narrow X-ray beam through the head and measuring from different angles the amount of radiation that passes through. Abbreviated *CAT scan.*

Concept A symbol that stands for a group of objects, events, or ideas that share common properties.

Concordance Agreement.

Concrete operational stage Piaget's third stage of cognitive development, characterized by logical thought processes concerning tangible objects, conservation, reversibility, and subjective morality.

Conditional positive regard In self theory, judgment of another person's basic value as a human being on the basis of the acceptability of that person's behaviors.

Conditioned reinforcer Another term for *secondary reinforcer.*

Conditioned response In classical conditioning, a learned response to a previously neutral stimulus. A response to a conditioned stimulus. Abbreviated *CR.*

Conditioned stimulus A previously neutral stimulus that elicits a conditioned response because it has been paired repeatedly with a stimulus that had already elicited that response. Abbreviated *CS.*

Conditioning A simple form of learning in which responses become associated with stimuli. See *classical conditioning* and *operant conditioning.*

Conditions of worth Standards by which the value of a person, or the self, is judged.

Conduction deafness The forms of deafness in which there is loss of conduction of sound through the middle ear.

Cone A cone-shaped photoreceptor in the eye that transmits sensations of color.

Confederate In experimental terminology, a person who pretends to be a subject in a study but who is in league with the experimenter.

Confidential Secret, not to be disclosed.

Conflict (1) Being torn in different directions by opposing motives. (2) Feelings produced by being in conflict.

Conform To changes one's attitudes or overt behavior to adhere to social norms.

Conformity Behavior that is in accordance with group norms and expectations.

Congruence In self-theory, a fit between one's self-concept and one's behaviors, thoughts, and feelings. A quality shown by the person-centered therapist.

Conscious Aware, in the normal waking state.

Consciousness A complex and controversial concept in psychology. Consciousness has several meanings in addition to the normal waking state; see *sensory awareness, direct inner awareness,* and *self.*

Consensus General agreement.

Conservation According to Piaget, recognition that certain properties of substances remain constant even though their appearance may change. For example, the weight and mass of a ball of clay remain constant (are conserved) even if the ball is flattened into a pancake.

Consolidation The fixing of information in long-term memory.

Consonant In harmony.

Construe Interpret.

Consultation The provision of professional advice or services.

Consumer psychology The field of psychology that studies the nature, causes, and modification of consumer behavior and mental processes.

Contact comfort (1) The pleasure attained from physical contact with another. (2) A hypothesized primary drive to seek physical comfort through physical contact with another.

Context-dependent memory Information that is better retrieved in the context in which it was encoded and stored, or learned.

Contextual level According to Sternberg, those aspects of intelligent behavior that permit people to adapt to their environment.

Contiguous Next to one another.

Contingency theory (1) In conditioning, the view that learning occurs when stimuli provide information about the likelihood of the occurrence of other stimuli. (2) In industrial/organizational psychology, a theory that hold that organizational structure should depend on factors such as goals, workers' characteristics, and the overall economic or political environment.

Continuity As a rule of perceptual organization, the tendency to perceive a series of stimuli as having unity.

Continuous reinforcement A schedule of reinforcement in which every correct response is reinforced. See *partial reinforcement.*

Control subject A participant in an experiment who does not receive the experimental treatment but for whom all other conditions are comparable to those of experimental subjects.

Conventional level According to Kohlberg, a period of moral development during which moral judgments largely reflect social conventions. A "law-and-order" approach to morality.

Convergence A binocular cue for depth based on the inward movement of the eyes as they attempt to focus on an object that is drawing nearer.

Convergent thinking A thought process that attempts to narrow in on the single best solution to a problem.

Conversion disorder A disorder in which anxiety or unconscious conflicts are "converted" into physical symptoms that often have the effect of helping the person cope with the anxiety or conflicts.

Cooing Prelinguistic, articulated, vowel-like sounds that appear to reflect feelings of positive excitement.

Copulate To engage in sexual intercourse.

Cornea Transparent tissue that forms the outer surface of the eyeball.

Corpus callosum A thick bundle of fibers that connects the two hemispheres of the cerebrum.

Correlation coefficient A number ranging from $+1.00$ to -1.00 that expresses the strength and direction (positive or negative) of the relationship between two variables.

Correlational research A method of scientific investigation that studies the relationships between variables. Correlational research can imply but cannot show cause and effect, because no experimental treatment is introduced.

Corticosteroids Steroids produced by the adrenal cortex that regulate carbohydrate metabolism and increase resistance to stress by fighting inflammation and allergic reactions. Also called *cortical steroids.*

Cortisol A hormone (steroid) produced by the adrenal cortex that helps the body cope with stress by counteracting inflammation and allergic reactions.

Counterconditioning A behavior-therapy technique which involves the repeated pairing of a stimulus that elicits a problematic response (such as fear) with a stimulus that elicits an antagonistic response (such as relaxation instructions) so that the first stimulus loses the capacity to evoke the problematic response. See also *systematic desensitization* and *aversive conditioning.*

Countertransference In psychoanalysis, the generalization to the client of feelings toward another person in the analyst's life.

Covert reinforcement A behavior-therapy self-control technique in which one creates pleasant imagery to reward desired behavior.

Covert sensitization A behavior-therapy self-control technique in which one creates aversive imagery and associates it with undesired behavior.

CR Conditioned response.

Creative self According to Adler, the self-aware aspect of personality that strives to achieve its full potential.

Creativity The ability to generate novel solutions to problems. A trait characterized by originality, ingenuity, and flexibility.

Cretinism A condition caused by thyroid deficiency in childhood and characterized by mental retardation and stunted growth.

Criteria Plural of *criterion.*

Criterion A standard; a means for making a judgment.

Criterion-referenced testing A testing approach in which scores are based on whether or not one can perform up to a set standard.

Critical period A period in an organism's development during which it is capable of certain types of learning.

CS Conditioned stimulus.

Cultural bias A factor hypothesized to be present in intelligence tests that provides an advantage for test-takers from certain cultural or ethnic backgrounds but that does not reflect actual intelligence.

Culture-fair Describing a test in which there are no cultural biases. On such a test, test-takers from different cultural backgrounds would have an equal opportunity to earn scores that reflect their true abilities.

Cumulative incidence The occurrence of an event or act by a given time or age.

Cumulative recorder An instrument used in operant conditioning laboratory procedures to automatically record the frequency of targeted responses.

D

Daily hassles Notable daily conditions and experiences that are threatening or harmful to a person's well-being.

Dark adaptation The process of adjusting to conditions of lower lighting by increasing the sensitivity of rods and cones.

Debrief To receive information about a procedure that has been completed.

Decibel A unit expressing the loudness of a sound. Abbreviated *dB.*

Deep structure The underlying meaning of a sentence as determined by interpretation of the meanings of the words.

Defense mechanisms In psychodynamic theory, unconscious functions of the ego that protect it from anxiety-evoking material by preventing accurate recognition of this material.

Defensive coping A response to stress that reduces the stressor's immediate effect, but frequently at some cost to the individual. Defensive coping may involve self-deception and does not change the environment or the person's response patterns to permanently remove or modify the effects of the stressor. Contrast with *active coping.*

Deindividuation The process by which group members may discontinue self-evaluation and adopt group norms and attitudes.

Delayed conditioning A classical conditioning procedure in which the CS is presented several seconds before the US and left on until the response occurs.

Delirium tremens A condition characterized by sweating, restlessness, disorientation, and hallucinations that occurs in some chronic users of alcohol when there is a sudden decrease in the level of drinking. Abbreviated *DTs.*

Delta waves Strong, slow brain waves usually emitted during stage 4 sleep.

Delta-9-tetrahydrocannabinol The major active ingredient in marijuana. Abbreviated *THC.*

Delusions False, persistent beliefs that are unsubstantiated by sensory or objective evidence.

Delusions of grandeur Erroneous beliefs that one is a grand person, like Jesus or like a secret agent on a special mission.

Delusions of persecution Erroneous beliefs that one is being threatened or persecuted.

Dendrites Rootlike structures attached to the soma of a neuron that receive impulses from other neurons.

Denial (1) A defense mechanism in which threatening events are misperceived to be harmless. (2) The first stage in Kübler-Ross's theory of dying.

Dependent variable A measure of an assumed effect of an independent variable. An outcome measure in a scientific study.

Depersonalization disorder Persistent or recurrent feelings that one is not real or is detached from one's own experiences or body.

Depolarization The reduction of the resting potential of a cell membrane from about −70 millivolts toward zero.

Depressant A drug that lowers the nervous system's rate of activity.

Depression (1) A negative emotion frequently characterized by sadness, feelings of helplessness, and a sense of loss. (2) The fourth stage in Kübler-Ross's theory of dying.

Descriptive statistics The branch of statistics that is concerned with providing descriptive information about a distribution of scores.

Desensitization The type of sensory adaptation in which we become less sensitive to constant stimuli. Also called *negative adaptation.*

Determinant A factor that defines or sets limits.

Deviation IQ A score on an intelligence test that is derived by determining how far an individual's score deviates from the norm. On the Wechsler scales, the mean IQ score is defined as 100, and approximately two of three scores fall between 85 and 115.

Diabetes A disorder caused by inadequate secretion or utilization of insulin and characterized by excess sugar in the blood.

Diagnosis A decision or opinion about the nature of a diseased condition.

Dialogue A Gestalt therapy technique in which clients verbalize confrontations between conflicting parts of their personality.

Dichromat A person who is sensitive to the intensity of light and to red and green or blue and yellow and who thus is partially colorblind.

Difference threshold The minimal difference in intensity that is required between two sources of energy so that they will be perceived as being different.

Differentiation The modification of tissues and organs in structure, function, or both during the course of development.

Diffusion of responsibility The spreading or sharing of responsibility for a decision or behavior among the members of a group.

Direct coping See *active coping.*

Direct inner awareness One of the definitions of consciousness: Knowledge of one's own thoughts, feelings, and memories, without use of sensory organs.

Discovery learning Bruner's view that children should work on their own to discover basic principles.

Discrimination (1) In conditioning, the tendency for an organism to distinguish between a conditioned stimulus and similar stimuli that do not forecast an unconditioned stimulus. (2) In social psychology, the denial of privileges to a person or a group on the basis of prejudice.

Discrimination training Teaching an organism to show a conditioned response to only one of a series of similar stimuli by pairing that stimulus with the unconditioned stimulus and presenting similar stimuli in the absence of the unconditioned stimulus.

Discriminative stimulus In operant conditioning, a stimulus that indicates that reinforcement is available.

Disinhibit In social learning theory, to trigger a response that is usually inhibited, generally as a consequence of observing a model engage in the behavior without negative consequences.

Disorganized schizophrenia A subtype of schizophrenia characterized by disorganized delusions and vivid hallucinations. Formerly *hebephrenic schizophrenia.*

Disorientation Gross confusion. Loss of awareness of time, place, and the identity of people.

Displacement (1) In information processing, the causing of chunks of information to be lost from short-term memory by adding too many new items. (2) In psychodynamic theory, a defense mechanism that involves the transference of feelings or impulses from threatening or unacceptable objects onto unthreatening or acceptable objects. (3) As a property of language, the ability to communicate information about events in other times and places.

Dispositional attribution An assumption that a person's behavior is determined by internal causes, such as personal attitudes or goals. Contrast with *situational attribution.*

Dissociative disorder A disorder in which there is a sudden, temporary change in consciousness or self-identity, such as psychogenic amnesia, psychogenic fugue, or multiple personality.

Dissonant Incompatible, discordant.

Divergent thinking A thought process that attempts to generate multiple solutions to problems. Free and fluent associations to the elements of a problem.

Dizygotic twins Twins who develop from separate zygotes. Fraternal twins. Abbreviated *DZ twins.* Contrast with *monozygotic twins.*

DNA Deoxyribonucleic acid. The substance that carries the genetic code and makes up genes and chromosomes.

Dominant trait In genetics, a trait that is expressed. See *recessive trait.*

Dopamine A neurotransmitter that is involved in Parkinson's disease and theorized to play a role in schizophrenia.

Double approach-avoidance conflict Conflict involving two goals, each of which has positive and negative aspects.

Double-blind study A study in which neither the subjects nor the persons measuring results know who has received the treatment.

Down syndrome A chromosomal abnormality caused by an extra chromosome in the 21st pair ("trisomy 21") and characterized by slanted eyelids and mental retardation. Also called *mongolism.*

Dream A form of cognitive activity—usually a sequence of images or thoughts—that occurs during sleep. Dreams may be vague and loosely plotted or vivid and intricate.

Drive A condition of arousal within an organism that is associated with a need.

Drive for superiority Adler's term for the desire to compensate for feelings of inferiority.

Drive-reduction theory The view that organisms are motivated to learn to engage in behaviors that have the effect of reducing drives.

DSM-III-R The third edition, revised version, of the *Diagnostic and Statistical Manual of the Mental Disorders,* published by the American Psychiatric Association in 1987.

Duct Passageway.

Duplicity theory A combination of the place and frequency theories of pitch discrimination.

Dyslexia A severe reading disorder characterized by problems such as letter reversals, reading as if one were seeing words reflected in a mirror, slow reading, and reduced comprehension.

Dyspareunia Persistent or recurrent pain during or after sexual intercourse.

E

Eardrum A thin membrane that vibrates in response to sound waves, transmitting them from the outer ear to the middle and inner ears.

Echo A mental representation of an auditory stimulus that is held briefly in sensory memory.

Echoic memory The sensory register that briefly holds mental representations of auditory stimuli.

Eclectic Selecting from various systems or theories.

ECT Acronym for *electroconvulsive therapy.*

Educational psychology The field of psychology that studies the nature, causes, and enhancement of teaching and learning.

Efferent neuron A neuron that transmits messages from the brain or spinal cord to muscles or glands. Also called *motor neuron.*

Effort justification In cognitive-dissonance theory, the tendency to seek justification (acceptable reasons) for strenuous efforts.

Ego In psychodynamic theory, the second psychic structure to develop. The ego is governed by the reality principle and its functioning is characterized by self-awareness, planning, and capacity to tolerate frustration and delay gratification.

Ego analyst A psychodynamically oriented therapist who focuses on the conscious, coping behavior of the ego instead of the hypothesized unconscious functioning of the id.

Egocentric According to Piaget, assuming that others view the world as oneself does. Unable or unwilling to view the world as through the eyes of others.

Ego-dystonic homosexuality Homosexuality that is inconsistent with one's self-concept and therefore causes personal distress.

Ego identity Erikson's term for the sense of who one is and what one stands for.

Ego identity versus role diffusion Erikson's fifth stage of psychosocial development, which challenges the adolescent to connect skills and social roles to career objectives.

Ego integrity Erikson's term for a firm sense of identity during the later years, characterized by the wisdom to accept the fact that life is limited and the ability to let go.

Ego integrity versus despair Erikson's eighth stage of psychosocial development, which challenges persons to accept the limits of their own life cycles during the later years.

Eidetic imagery The maintenance of detailed visual memories over several minutes.

Elaboration likelihood model The view that persuasive messages are evaluated (elaborated) on the basis of central and peripheral cues.

Elaborative rehearsal A method for increasing retention of new information by relating it to information that is well-known.

Electra complex In psychodynamic theory, a conflict of the phallic stage in which the girl longs for her father and resents her mother.

Electroconvulsive therapy Treatment of disorders like major depression by passing an electric current that causes a convulsion through the head. Abbreviated *ECT.*

Electroencephalograph An instrument that measures electrical activity of the brain (brain waves). Abbreviated *EEG.*

Electromyograph An instrument that measures muscle tension. Abbreviated *EMG.*

Elicit To bring forth, evoke.

Embryo The unborn child from the third through the eighth weeks following conception, during which time the major organ systems undergo rapid differentiation.

Embryonic period The period of prenatal development between the period of the ovum and fetal development, approximately from the third through the eighth weeks following conception.

Embryo transfer Transfer of an embryo from the fallopian tube of its mother into the uterus of another woman, where it becomes implanted and develops.

Emetic Causing vomiting.

Emotion A state of feeling that has physiological, situational, and cognitive components.

Emotional appeal A type of persuasive communication that influences behavior on the basis of feelings that are aroused instead of rational analysis of the issues.

Empathic understanding Ability to perceive a client's feelings from the client's frame of reference. A quality of a good person-centered therapist.

Empathy Ability to understand and share another person's feelings.

Empirical Experimental. Emphasizing or based on observation and measurement, in contrast to theory and deduction.

Empty-nest syndrome A sense of depression and loss of purpose felt by some parents when the youngest child leaves home.

Encoding Modifying information so that it can be placed in memory. The first stage of information processing.

Encounter group A structured group process that aims to foster self-awareness by focusing on how group members relate to each other in a setting that encourages frank expression of feelings.

Endocrine system The body's system of ductless glands that secrete hormones and release them directly into the bloodstream.

Endorphins Neurotransmitters that are composed of amino acids and are functionally similar to morphine.

Engram (1) An assumed electrical circuit in the brain that corresponds to a memory trace. (2) An assumed chemical change in the brain that accompanies learning.

Enkephalins Types of endorphins that are weaker and shorter-acting than beta-endorphin.

Enuresis Lack of bladder control at an age by which control is normally attained.

Environmental psychology The field of psychology that studies the ways in which people and the physical environment influence one another.

Epilepsy Temporary disturbances of brain functions that involve sudden neural discharges.

Epinephrine A hormone produced by the adrenal medulla that stimulates the sympathetic division of the ANS. Also called *adrenaline.*

Episodic memory Memories of incidents experienced by a person; of events that occur to a person or take place in the person's presence.

Equilibrium Another term for the vestibular sense.

Erogenous zone An area of the body that is sensitive to sexual sensations.

Eros (1) The Greek concept of love closest in meaning to romantic love, emphasizing sexual desire. (2) In psychodynamic theory, the basic life instinct, which aims toward the preservation and perpetuation of life.

Erotica Sexual material that stimulates a sexual response.

Estrogen A generic term for several female sex hormones that promote growth of female sexual characteristics and regulate the menstrual cycle.

Estrus The periodic sexual excitement of many female mammals, during which they are capable of conceiving and are receptive to sexual advances by males.

Ethical Moral; referring to one's system of deriving standards for determining what is moral.

Ethologist A scientist who studies behavior patterns that are characteristic of various species.

Euphoria Feelings of extreme well-being, elation.

Eustress Stress that is healthful.

Evaluation apprehension Concern that others are evaluating our behavior.

Exaltolide A musky substance that is suspected to be a sexual pheromone.

Exceptional students The term applied to students whose educational needs are special because of physical and health problems, communication problems, behavior disorders, specific learning disabilities, mental retardation, or intellectual giftedness.

Excitatory synapse A synapse that influences receiving neurons in the direction of firing by increasing depolarization of their cell membranes.

Excitement phase The first phase of the sexual response cycle, characterized by erection in the man and by vaginal lubrication and clitoral swelling in the woman.

Exhaustion stage The third stage of the general adaptation syndrome, characterized by parasympathetic activity, weakened resistance, and possible deterioration.

Exhibitionism A paraphilia in which a person feels the compulsion to seek sexual excitement by exposing his genitals in public.

Expectancies A person variable in social-learning theory. Personal predictions about the outcomes of potential behaviors—"if-then" statements.

Experiential level According to Sternberg, those aspects of intelligence that permit people to cope with novel situations and process information automatically.

Experiment A scientific method that seeks to discover cause-and-effect relationships by introducing independent variables and observing their effects on dependent variables.

Experimental subject (1) A subject receiving a treatment in an experiment, in contrast to a *control subject.* (2) More generally, a participant in an experiment.

Explicit Frank, revealing; leaving nothing implied or to the imagination.

Expository teaching Ausubel's method of presenting material in an organized form, moving from broad to specific concepts.

Expressive vocabulary The sum total of the words that one can use in the production of language.

External eater A person who eats predominantly in response to external stimuli, such as the time of day, the smell of food, or the presence of people who are eating. See *internal eater.*

"Externals" People who have an external locus of control—who perceive the ability to attain reinforcements as largely outside themselves.

Extinction An experimental procedure in which stimuli lose their ability to evoke learned responses because the events that had followed the stimuli no longer occur. (The learned responses are said to be *extinguished.*)

Extinction trial In conditioning, a performance of a learned response in the absence of its predicted consequences so that the learned response becomes inhibited.

Extrasensory perception Perception of external objects and events without sensation. Abbreviated *ESP.* A controversial area of investigation.

Extraversion A source trait in which one's attention is directed to persons and things outside the self, often associated with a sociable, outgoing approach to others and the free expression of feelings and impulses. Opposite of *introversion.*

F

Facial-feedback hypothesis The view that stereotypical facial expressions can contribute to the experiencing of stereotypical emotions.

Factor A cluster of related items, such as those found on an intelligence test.

Factor analysis A statistical technique that allows researchers to determine the relationships among large number of items, such as test items.

Fallopian tube A tube that conducts ova from an ovary to the uterus.

Family therapy A form of therapy in which the family unit is treated as the client.

Farsighted Capable of seeing distant objects with greater acuity than nearby objects.

Fat cells Cells that store fats. Also called *adipose tissue.*

Fear A negative emotion characterized by perception of a threat, sympathetic nervous system activity, and avoidance tendencies.

Feedback Information about one's own behavior.

Feeling-of-knowing experience See *tip-of-the-tongue phenomenon.*

Female sexual arousal disorder A sexual dysfunction characterized by difficulty in becoming sexually aroused, as defined by vaginal lubrication, or sustaining arousal long enough to engage in satisfying sexual relations.

Feminists People (of both sexes) who seek social change and legislation to reverse discrimination against women and to otherwise advance the concerns of women.

Fetishism A paraphilia; a variation of choice of sexual object in which the person prefers a body part (like a foot) or an inanimate object (like an undergarment) to sexual relations with another person.

Fetus The unborn child from the third month following conception through childbirth, during which time there is maturation of organ systems and dramatic gains in length and weight.

Fight-or-flight reaction Cannon's term for a hypothesized innate adaptive response to the perception of danger.

Final acceptance The fifth stage in Kübler-Ross's theory of dying, which is characterized by lack of feeling.

Fissure Valley—referring to the valleys in the wrinkled surface of the cerebral cortex.

Fixation In psychodynamic theory, arrested development. Attachment to objects of an earlier stage.

Fixation time The amount of time spent looking at a visual stimulus. A measure of interest in infants.

Fixed-action pattern An instinct; abbreviated *FAP.*

Fixed-interval schedule A partial reinforcement schedule in which a fixed amount of time must elapse between the previous and subsequent times that reinforcement is made available.

Fixed-ratio schedule A partial reinforcement schedule in which reinforcement is made available after a fixed number of correct responses.

Flashbacks Distorted perceptions or hallucinations that occur days or weeks after usage of a hallucinogenic drug (usually LSD) but that mimic the effects of the drug.

Flashbulb memories Memories that are preserved in great detail because they reflect intense emotional experiences.

Flat affect Monotonous, dull emotional response.

Flextime A modification of one's work schedule from the standard 9:00 to 5:00 in order to enable one to better meet personal needs.

Flooding A behavioral fear-reduction technique that is based on principles of classical conditioning. Fear-evoking stimuli (CSs) are presented continuously in the absence of actual harm so that fear responses (CRs) are extinguished.

Foot-in-the-door technique A method of persuasion in which compliance with a large request is encouraged by first asking the recipient of the request to comply with a smaller request.

Forced-choice format A method of presenting test questions that requires a respondent to select one of a number of possible answers.

Foreclosure In Erikson's theory, adoption of a set of beliefs without undergoing an identity crisis—for instance, accepting parental or peer values without serious examination or questioning.

Forensic psychology The field that applies psychological knowledge within the criminal justice system.

Formal operational stage Piaget's fourth stage of cognitive development, characterized by abstract logical and theoretical thought and deduction from principles.

Fovea A rodless area near the center of the retina where vision is most acute.

Frame of reference In self theory, one's unique patterning of perceptions and attitudes, according to which one evaluates events.

Free association In psychoanalysis, the uncensored uttering of all thoughts that come to mind.

Free-floating anxiety Chronic, persistent anxiety. Anxiety that is not tied to particular events.

Frequency distribution An ordered set of data that indicates how frequently scores appear.

Frequency theory The theory that the pitch of a sound is reflected in the frequency of the neural impulses that are generated in response.

Frontal lobe The lobe of the cerebral cortex that is involved with movement and that lies to the front of the central fissure.

Frustration (1) The thwarting of a motive. (2) The emotion produced by the thwarting of a motive.

Functional analysis A systematic study of behavior in which one identifies the stimuli that trigger it (antecedents) and the reinforcers that maintain it (consequences).

Functional fixedness The tendency to view an object in terms of its name or familiar usage; an impediment to creative problem solving.

Functionalism The school of psychology, founded by William James, that emphasizes the uses or functions of the mind.

Functional psychosis A psychotic disorder that is hypothesized to stem from psychological conflict.

Fundamental attribution error A bias in social perception characterized by the tendency to assume that others act predominantly on the basis of their dispositions, even when there is evidence suggesting the importance of their situations.

G

g Spearman's symbol for general intelligence, a general factor that he hypothesized underlay more specific abilities.

Galvanic skin response A sign of sympathetic arousal detected by the amount of sweat in the hand. The greater the amount of sweat, the more electricity is conducted across the skin, suggesting greater sympathetic arousal. Abbreviated *GSR.*

Ganglia Plural of *ganglion.* A group of neural cell bodies found elsewhere in the body other than the brain or spinal cord.

Ganglion cells Neurons whose axons form the optic fiber.

Ganglion See *ganglia.*

GAS Abbreviation for general adaptation syndrome.

Gay male A male homosexual.

Gender constancy The concept that one's gender remains the same, despite superficial changes in appearance or behavior.

Gender identity One's sense of being male or female. (The first stage in the cognitive-developmental theory of the assumption of sex roles.)

Gender-identity disorder A disorder in which a person's anatomic sex is inconsistent with his or her sense of being male or female.

Gender-schema theory The view that gender identity plus knowledge of the distribution of behavior patterns into masculine and feminine roles motivates and guides the sex typing of the child.

Gender stability The concept that one's gender is a permanent feature.

Gene The basic building block of heredity, which consists of deoxyribonucleic acid (DNA).

General anesthetics Methods that control pain by putting a person to sleep.

General adaptation syndrome Selye's term for a theoretical three-stage response to stress. Abbreviated *GAS.*

Generalization (1) The process of going from the particular to the general. (2) In conditioning, the tendency for a conditioned response to be evoked by stimuli that are similar to the stimulus to which the response was conditioned.

Generalized anxiety disorder Feelings of dread and foreboding and sympathetic arousal of at least one month's duration.

Generalized expectancies In social-learning theory, broad expectations that reflect extensive learning and that are relatively resistant to change.

Generativity versus stagnation Erikson's seventh stage of psychosocial development; the middle years during which persons find (or fail to find) fulfillment in expressing creativity and in guiding and encouraging the younger generation.

Genetic counseling Advice or counseling that concerns the probability that a couple's offspring will have genetic abnormalities.

Genetics The branch of biology that studies heredity.

Genital stage In psychodynamic theory, the fifth and mature stage of psychosexual development, characterized by preferred expression of libido through intercourse with an adult of the opposite sex.

Genotype The sum total of one's traits as inherited from one's parents.

Genuineness Recognition and open expression of one's feelings. A quality of the good person-centered therapist.

German measles A disease that can cause nerve damage to a fetus.

Germinal stage The first stage of prenatal development during which the dividing mass of cells has not become implanted in the uterine wall.

Gestalt psychology The school of psychology that emphasizes the tendency to organize perceptions into wholes, to integrate separate stimuli into meaningful patterns.

Gestalt therapy Fritz Perls's form of psychotherapy, which attempts to integrate conflicting parts of the personality through directive methods designed to help clients perceive their whole selves.

Glaucoma An eye disease characterized by increased fluid pressure within the eye. A cause of blindness.

Glial cells Cells that nourish and insulate neurons, direct their growth, and remove waste products from the nervous system.

Glucagon A pancreatic hormone that increases the levels of sugar and fat in the blood.

Gonorrhea A sexually transmitted disease that can inflame the pelvic region.

Gout A disease characterized by swelling of joints and severe pain, especially in the big toe.

Grasp reflex An infant reflex in which an object placed on the palms or soles is grasped. Also called *palmar* or *plantar reflex.*

Gray matter In the spinal cord, the neurons and neural segments that are involved in spinal reflexes. They are gray in appearance. Also see *white matter.*

Groupthink A process in which group members, as they make decisions, are influenced by cohesiveness and a dynamic leader to ignore external realities.

Growth hormone A pituitary hormone that regulates growth.

Growth-hormone releasing factor A hormone produced by the hypothalamus that causes the pituitary to secrete growth hormone.

GSR Abbreviation for galvanic skin response.

H

Habit A response to a stimulus that becomes automatic with repetition.

Habituate To become accustomed to a stimulus, as determined by no longer showing a response to the stimulus.

Hallucination A sensory experience in the absence of sensory stimulation that is confused with reality.

Hallucinogenic Giving rise to hallucinations.

Halo effect The tendency for one's general impression of a person to influence one's perception of aspects of, or performances by, that person.

Hammer A bone of the middle ear.

Hard-core Unyielding, unqualified; suggestive of explicit sex in the absence of a romantic context.

Hashish A psychedelic drug derived from the resin of *Cannabis sativa.* Often called "hash."

Hassle A source of annoyance or aggravation.

Health psychology The field of psychology that studies the relationships between psychological factors (e.g., attitudes, beliefs, situational influences, and overt behavior patterns) and the prevention and treatment of physical illness.

Hebephrenic schizophrenia See *disorganized schizophrenia.*

Hemoglobin The substance in the blood that carries oxygen.

Heredity The transmission of traits from one generation to another through genes.

Heroin A powerful opiate that provides a euphoric "rush" and feelings of well-being.

Hertz A unit expressing the frequency of sound waves. One Hertz, or *1 Hz,* equals one cycle per second.

Heterosexual A person whose sexual orientation is characterized by preference for sexual activity and the formation of romantic relationships with members of the opposite sex.

Heterozygous Having two different alleles.

Heuristic device A rule of thumb that helps us simplify and solve problems.

Higher-order conditioning (1) According to cognitive psychologists, the learning of relations among events, none of which evokes an unlearned response. (2) According to behaviorists, a classical conditioning procedure in which a previously neutral stimulus comes to elicit the response brought forth by a *conditioned* stimulus by being paired repeatedly with that conditioned stimulus.

Hippocampus A part of the *limbic system* of the brain that plays an important role in the formation of new memories.

Histogram A graphic representation of a frequency distribution that uses rectangular solids.

Holocaust The name given the Nazi murder of millions of Jews during World War II.

Holophrase A single word used to express complex meanings.

Homeostasis The tendency of the body to maintain a steady state, such as body temperature or level of sugar in the blood.

Homosexuality The sexual orientation characterized by preference for sexual activity and the formation of romantic relationships with members of one's own sex.

Homozygous Having two identical alleles.

Homunculus Latin for "little man." A homunculus within the brain was once thought to govern human behavior.

Hormone A substance secreted by an endocrine gland that promotes development of body structures or regulates bodily functions.

Hot reactors People who respond to stress with accelerated heart rate and constriction of blood vessels in peripheral areas of the body.

Hue The color of light, as determined by its wavelength.

Human factors The field that studies the efficiency and safety of person–machine systems and work environments.

Humanistic psychology The school of psychology that assumes the existence of the self and emphasizes the importance of consciousness, self-awareness, and the freedom to make choices.

Human-relations theories Theories that hold that efficient organizations are structured according to the characteristics and needs of the individual worker.

Hydrocarbons Chemical compounds consisting of hydrogen and carbon.

Hyperactive More active than normal.

Hyperactivity A disorder found most frequently in young boys, characterized by restlessness and short attention span. It is thought to reflect immaturity of the nervous system.

Hyperglycemia A disorder caused by excess sugar in the blood that can lead to coma and death.

Hypermnesia Greatly enhanced memory.

Hyperphagic Characterized by excessive eating.

Hypertension High blood pressure.

Hyperthyroidism A condition caused by excess thyroxin and characterized by excitability, weight loss, and insomnia.

Hypnagogic state The drowsy interval between waking and sleeping, characterized by brief, hallucinatory, dreamlike experiences.

Hypnosis A condition in which people appear to be highly suggestible and behave as though they are in a trance.

Hypoactive sexual desire disorder Persistent or recurrent lack of sexual fantasies and of interest in sexual activity.

Hypochondriasis Persistent belief that one has a medical disorder despite the lack of medical findings.

Hypoglycemia A metabolic disorder that is characterized by shakiness, dizziness, and lack of energy. It is caused by a low level of sugar in the blood.

Hypothalamus A bundle of nuclei below the thalamus involved in the regulation of body temperature, motivation, and emotion.

Hypothesis An assumption about behavior that is tested through research.

Hypothesis testing In concept formation, an active process in which we try to ferret out the meanings of concepts by testing our assumptions.

Hypothyroidism A condition caused by a deficiency of thyroxin and characterized by sluggish behavior and a low metabolic rate.

Hysterical disorder, conversion type Former term for *conversion disorder.*

I

Icon A mental representation of a visual stimulus that is held briefly in sensory memory.

Iconic memory The sensory register that briefly holds mental representations of visual stimuli.

Id In psychodynamic theory, the psychic structure that is present at birth and that is governed by the pleasure principle. The id represents physiological drives and is fully unconscious.

Idealize To think of as being perfect, without flaws.

Ideas of persecution Erroneous beliefs that one is being victimized or persecuted.

Identification (1) In psychodynamic theory, unconscious incorporation of the personality of another person. (2) In social-learning theory, a broad, continuous process of imitation during which children strive to become like role models.

Identity achievement Resolution of an identity crisis through development of a stable set of beliefs or a course of action.

Identity crisis According to Erikson, a period of inner conflict during which one examines his or her values and makes decisions about life roles.

Identity diffusion See *role diffusion.*

Illusions Sensations that give rise to misperceptions.

Imbalance In balance theory, an uncomfortable condition in which persons whom we like disagree with us.

Immune system The system of the body that recognizes and destroys foreign agents (antigens) that invade the body.

Imprinting A process that occurs during a critical period in an organism's development, in which that organism forms an attachment that will afterwards be difficult to modify.

Incentive An object, person, or situation perceived as being capable of satisfying a need.

Incest taboo The cultural prohibition against marrying or having sexual relations with a close blood relative.

Incidence The extent to which an event occurs.

Incubation In problem solving, a hypothetical process that sometimes occurs when we stand back from a frustrating problem for a while and the solution suddenly appears.

Incubus (1) A spirit or demon thought in medieval times to lie on sleeping people, especially on women, for sexual purposes. (2) A nightmare.

Incus A bone of the middle ear. Latin for "anvil."

Independent variable A condition in a scientific study that is manipulated so that its effects may be observed.

Indiscriminate attachment The showing of attachment behaviors toward any person.

Individual psychology Adler's psychodynamic theory, which emphasizes feelings of inferiority and the creative self.

Individuation The process by which one separates from others and gains control over one's own behavior.

Inductive Going from the particular to the general; for example, descriptive of a disciplinary technique in which the individual is taught the principle involved and not merely punished.

Industrial psychology The field of psychology that studies the relationships between people and work.

Industry versus inferiority Erikson's fourth stage of psychosocial development, in which the child is challenged to master the fundamentals of technology during the primary-school years.

Infant A very young organism, a baby.

Infer Draw a conclusion.

Inference Conclusion.

Inferential statistics The branch of statistics concerned with the confidence with which conclusions drawn about samples may be extended to the populations from which they were drawn.

Inferiority complex Feelings of inferiority hypothesized by Adler to serve as a central source of motivation.

Inflammation Increased blood flow to an injured area of the body, resulting in redness, warmth, and increased supply of white blood cells.

Inflections Grammatical markers that change the forms of words to indicate grammatical relationships such as number and tense.

Information processing The processes by which information is encoded, stored, and retrieved.

Informed consent Agreement to participate in research after receiving information about the purposes of the study and the nature of the treatments.

Inhibited orgasm Persistent or recurrent delay in or absence of orgasm in a sexually excited person who has been engaging in sexually stimulating activity.

Inhibited sexual desire Lack of interest in sexual activity, usually accompanied by absence of sexual fantasies.

Inhibited sexual excitement Persistent lack of sexual response during sexual activity.

Inhibitory synapse A synapse that influences receiving neurons in the direction of not firing by encouraging changes in their membrane permeability in the direction of the resting potential.

Initial-preattachment phase The first phase in forming bonds of attachment, characterized by indiscriminate attachment.

Initiative versus guilt Erikson's third stage of psychosocial development, during which the child is challenged to add planning and "attacking" to the exercise of choice.

Innate Existing at birth. Unlearned, natural.

Innate fixed-action pattern An instinct.

Inner ear The cochlea.

Insanity A legal term descriptive of a person judged to be incapable of recognizing right from wrong or of conforming his or her behavior to the law.

Insecure attachment A negative type of attachment, in which children show indifference or ambivalence toward attachment figures.

Insight (1) In Gestalt psychology, the sudden perception of relationships among elements of the perceptual field, allowing the sudden solution of a problem. (2) In psychotherapy, awareness of one's genuine motives and feelings.

Insomnia A term for three types of sleeping problems: (1) difficulty falling asleep; (2) difficulty remaining asleep; and (3) waking early.

Instinct An inherited disposition to activate specific behavior patterns that are designed to reach certain goals.

Instinctive Inborn, natural, unlearned.

Instructional objective A clear statement of what is to be learned.

Instrumental conditioning Another term for operant conditioning, reflecting the fact that in operant conditioning, the learned behavior is instrumental in achieving certain effects.

Instrumental learning See instrumental conditioning.

Insulin A pancreatic hormone that stimulates the metabolism of sugar.

Intellectualization A defense mechanism in which threatening events are viewed with emotional detachment.

Intelligence A complex and controversial concept: (1) Learning ability, as contrasted with achievement. (2) Defined by David Wechsler as the "capacity . . . to understand the world [and the] resourcefulness to cope with its challenges." (3) Defined operationally as the trait or traits required to perform well on an intelligence test.

Intelligence quotient (1) Originally, a ratio obtained by dividing a child's mental age on an intelligence test by his or her chronological age. (2) Generally, a score on an intelligence test. Abbreviated *IQ.*

Interactionism An approach to understanding behavior that emphasizes specification of the relationships among the various determinants of behavior instead of seeking the first cause of behavior.

Interference theory The view that we may forget stored material because other learning interferes with it.

Internal eaters People who eat predominantly in response to internal stimuli, like hunger pangs. See *external eater.*

"Internals" People who have an internal locus of control—who perceive the ability to attain reinforcements as being largely within themselves.

Interneuron A neuron that transmits a neural impulse from a sensory neuron to a motor neuron.

Interpersonal attraction See *attraction.*

Interposition A monocular cue for depth based on the fact that closer objects obscure vision of objects behind them.

Interpretation In psychoanalysis, an analyst's explanation of a client's utterance according to psychodynamic theory.

Intimacy versus isolation Erikson's sixth stage of psychosocial development; the young adult years during which persons are challenged to commit themselves to intimate relationships with others.

Intonation The use of pitches of varying levels to help communicate meaning.

Intoxication Drunkenness.

Intrapsychic Referring to the psychodynamic movement of psychic energy among the psychic structures hypothesized by Sigmund Freud.

Introjection In psychodynamic theory, the bringing within oneself of the personality of another individual.

Introspection An objective approach to describing one's mental content.

Introversion A trait characterized by intense imagination and the tendency to inhibit impulses. Opposite of *extraversion.*

Intuitive The direct learning or knowing of something without conscious use of reason.

In utero A Latin phrase meaning "in the uterus."

Involuntary Automatic, not consciously controlled—referring to functions like heartbeat and dilation of the pupils.

IQ Intelligence quotient. A score on an intelligence test.

Iris A muscular membrane whose dilation regulates the amount of light that enters the eye.

J

James-Lange theory The theory that certain external stimuli trigger stereotypical patterns of activity and autonomic arousal. Emotions are the cognitive representations of this behavior and arousal.

Job sharing Sharing of a full-time job by two or more workers.

Just noticeable difference The minimal amount by which a source of energy must be increased or decreased so that a difference in intensity will be perceived.

K

Kinesthesis The sense that provides information about the positions and motion of parts of the body.

Klinefelter's syndrome A chromosomal disorder found among males. It is caused by an extra X sex chromosome and is characterized by infertility and mild mental retardation.

Knobs Swellings at the ends of axon terminals. Also referred to as *bulbs* or *buttons.*

Knowledge-acquisition components According to Sternberg, components of intelligence that are used in gaining knowledge, such as encoding and relating new knowledge to existing knowledge.

Korsakoff's syndrome See *Wernicke-Korsakoff's syndrome.*

L

La belle indifférence A French term descriptive of the lack of concern shown by some persons with conversion disorder.

LAD Acronym for *language acquisition device.*

Language The communication of information through symbols that are arranged according to rules of grammar.

Language acquisition device In psycholinguistic theory, neural "prewiring" that is theorized to facilitate the child's learning of grammar.

Larynx The structure in the throat that contains the vocal cords.

Latency stage In psychodynamic theory, the fourth stage of psychosexual development, during which sexual impulses are repressed.

Latent content In psychodynamic theory, the symbolized or underlying content of dreams.

Latent learning Learning that is not exhibited at the time of learning but is shown when adequate reinforcement is introduced.

Lateral fissure The valley in the cerebral cortex that separates the temporal lobe from the frontal and parietal lobes.

Lateral hypothalamus An area at the side of the hypothalamus that appears to function as a start-eating center.

Law of effect Thorndike's principle that responses are "stamped in" by rewards and "stamped out" by punishments.

Leadership-motive syndrome A cluster of needs that includes strong needs for power and self-control and a low need for affiliation.

Learned helplessness Seligman's model for the acquisition of depressive behavior, based on findings that organisms in aversive situations learn to show inactivity when their operants are not reinforced.

Learning (1) According to cognitive theorists, the process by which organisms make relatively permanent changes in the way they represent the environment because of experience. These changes influence the organism's behavior. (2) According to behaviorists, a relatively permanent change in behavior that results from experience.

Least restrictive placement Placement of exceptional students in settings that are as normal and as much in the mainstream of education as possible, in accord with the Education for All Handicapped Children Act.

Lens A transparent body between the iris and the vitreous humor of the eye that focuses an image onto the retina.

Lesbian Female homosexual.

Lesion An injury that results in impaired behavior or loss of a function.

Leukocytes The white blood cells of the immune system.

Libido (1) In psychodynamic theory, the energy of Eros, the sexual instinct. (2) Generally, sexual interest or drive.

Lie detector See *polygraph.*

Life-change units Numbers assigned to various life events that indicate the degree of stress they cause.

Light Electromagnetic energy of various wavelengths. The part of the spectrum of energy that stimulates the eye and produces visual sensations.

Limbic system A group of brain structures that form a fringe along the inner edge of the cerebrum. These structures are involved in memory and motivation.

Linguistic relativity hypothesis The view that language structures the way in which we perceive the world. As a consequence, our thoughts would be limited by the concepts available in our languages.

Linguists Scientists who study the structure, functions, and origins of language.

Locus of control The place (locus) to which an individual attributes control over the receiving of reinforcements—either inside or outside the self.

Long-term memory The type or stage of memory capable of relatively permanent storage.

Love A strong, positive emotion with many meanings. See, for example, *romantic love* and *attachment.*

Low-balling A sales method in which extremely attractive terms are offered to induce a person to make a commitment. Once the commitment is made, the terms are revised.

LSD Lysergic acid diethylamide. A hallucinogenic drug.

Lucid dream A dream in which we seem to be awake and aware that we are dreaming.

Ludus Game-playing love.

Lysergic acid diethylamide A hallucinogenic drug. Abbreviated *LSD.*

M

Mainstreaming The practice of placing exceptional students in educational environments that are as normal as possible.

Maintenance rehearsal Mental repetition of information in order to keep it in memory.

Major depression A severe mood disorder in which the person may show loss of appetite, psychomotor symptoms, and impaired reality testing.

Major tranquilizer A drug that decreases severe anxiety or agitation in psychotic patients or in violent individuals.

Male erectile disorder A sexual dysfunction characterized by difficulty in becoming sexually aroused, as defined by achieving erection, or in sustaining arousal long enough to engage in satisfying sexual relations.

Malingering Pretending to be ill in order to escape duty or work.

Malleus A bone of the middle ear. Latin for "hammer."

Mania (1) Excited love. (A Greek word meaning "madness.") (2) A state characterized by elation and restlessness.

Manic depression Former term for *bipolar disorder.*

Manifest content In the psychodynamic theory of dreams, the reported or perceived content of dreams.

Mantra A word or sound that is repeated in transcendental meditation as a means of narrowing consciousness and inducing relaxation.

Marijuana The dried vegetable matter of the *Cannabis sativa* plant. A mild hallucinogenic drug that is most frequently taken in by smoking.

Masochism The attainment of gratification, frequently sexual, through the receiving of pain or humiliation.

Masturbation Self-stimulation of the sexual organs.

Matching hypothesis The view that people tend to choose persons similar to themselves in attractiveness and attitudes in the formation of interpersonal relationships.

Maternal-sensitive period A theoretical period of time during which a mother, because of hormone levels in the body, is thought to be particularly disposed toward forming mother–infant bonds of attachment.

Maturation Changes that result from heredity and minimal nutrition but that do not appear to require learning or exercise. A gradual, orderly unfolding or developing of new structures or behaviors as a result of heredity.

Mean A type of average calculated by dividing the sum of scores by the number of scores.

Means-end analysis A heuristic device in which we try to solve a problem by evaluating the difference between the current situation and the goal.

Median A type of average defined as the score beneath which 50 percent of the cases fall.

Mediation In information processing, a method of improving memory by linking two items with a third that ties them together.

Medical model The view that abnormal behavior is symptomatic of underlying illness.

Meditation A systematic narrowing of attention that slows the metabolism and helps produce feelings of relaxation.

Medulla An oblong-shaped area of the hindbrain involved in heartbeat and respiration.

Meiosis A process of reduction division in which sperm and ova are formed, each of which contains 23 chromosomes.

Memory The processes by which information is encoded, stored, and retrieved.

Memory trace An assumed change in the nervous system that reflects the impression made by a stimulus. Memory traces are said to be "held" in sensory registers.

Menarche The onset of menstruation.

Menopause The cessation of menstruation.

Menstrual synchrony The convergence of the menstrual cycles of women who spend time in close quarters.

Menstruation The monthly shedding of the uterine lining by non-pregnant women.

Mental age The accumulated months of credit that a test-taker earns on the Stanford Binet Intelligence Scale.

Mental set (1) Readiness to respond to a situation in a set manner. (2) In problem solving, a tendency to respond to a new problem with an approach that was successful with problems similar in appearance.

Mescaline A hallucinogenic drug derived from the mescal (peyote) cactus. In religious ceremonies, Mexican Indians chew the button-like structures at the tops of the rounded stems of the plant.

Metabolism In organisms, a continuous process that converts food into energy.

Metacognition Awareness and control of one's cognitive abilities, as shown by the intentional use of cognitive strategies in solving problems.

Metacomponents According to Sternberg, components of intelligence that are based on self-awareness of our intellectual processes.

Metamemory Self-awareness of the ways in which memory functions, as shown by use of cognitive strategies to foster the effective encoding, storing, and retrieval of information.

Metaphor The use of words or phrases characteristic of one situation in another situation. A figure of speech that dramatizes a description by applying imagery from another situation.

Methadone An artificial narcotic that is slower acting than, and does not provide the rush of, heroin. Methadone allows heroin addicts to abstain from heroin without experiencing an abstinence syndrome.

Methaqualone An addictive depressant often referred to as "ludes."

Method of constant stimuli A psychophysical method for determining thresholds in which the researcher presents stimuli of various magnitudes and asks the subject to report detection.

Method of loci A method of retaining information in which chunks of new material are related to a series of well-established or well-known images.

Method of savings A measure of retention in which the difference between the number of repetitions originally required to learn a list and the number of repetitions required to relearn the list after a certain amount of time has elapsed is calculated.

Microspectrophotometry A method for analyzing the sensitivity of single cones to lights of different wavelengths.

Middle ear The center part of the ear that contains three small bones, the "hammer," "anvil," and "stirrup."

Midlife crisis A crisis felt by many people at about age 40 when they realize that life may be halfway over and they feel trapped in meaningless life roles.

Migraine headache A throbbing headache, usually occurring on one side of the head, that stems from change in the blood supply to the head. It is often accompanied by nausea and impaired vision.

Mind That part of consciousness involved in perception and awareness.

Minor tranquilizer A drug that relieves feelings of anxiety and tension.

Mitosis The process of cell division by which the identical genetic code is carried into new cells in the body.

Mnemonics A system for remembering in which items are related to easily recalled sets of symbols, such as acronyms, phrases, or jingles.

Mode A type of average defined as the most frequently occurring score in a distribution.

Model In social-learning theory: (1) As a noun, an organism that engages in a response that is imitated by another organism. (2) As a verb, to engage in behavior patterns that are imitated by others.

Modeling A behavior-therapy technique in which the therapist or a group member engages in a behavior that is imitated by a client.

Modifier genes Genes that alter the action of the phenotypical expression of other genes.

Mongolism A term for Down syndrome that is no longer used, because it is recognized as being racially offensive.

Monoamine oxidase inhibitors Antidepressant drugs that work by blocking the action of an enzyme that breaks down norepinephrine and serotonin. Abbreviated *MAO inhibitors.*

Monochromat A person who is sensitive to the intensity of light only and thus color-blind.

Monocular cues Stimuli that suggest depth and that can be perceived with only one eye, such as perspective and interposition.

Monozygotic twins Twins who develop from the same zygote, thus carrying the same genetic instructions. Identical twins. Abbreviated *MZ twins.* See *dizygotic twins.*

Moral principle In psychodynamic theory, the governing principle of the superego, which sets moral standards and enforces adherence to them.

Moro reflex An infant reflex characterized by arching of the back and drawing up of the legs in response to a sudden, startling stimulus. Also called the *startle reflex.*

Morpheme The smallest unit of meaning in a language.

Morphine A narcotic derived from opium that reduces pain and produces feelings of well-being.

Morphology The study of the units of meaning in a language.

Motherese Adaptation of language for use in speaking to young children, characterized by features such as repetition and high-pitched sounds.

Motion parallax A monocular cue for depth based on the perception that nearby objects appear to move more rapidly in relation to our own motion.

Motive A hypothetical state within an organism that propels the organism toward a goal.

Motor cortex The section of cerebral cortex that lies in the frontal lobe, just across the central fissure from the sensory cortex. Neural impulses in the motor cortex are linked to muscular responses.

Multiple approach-avoidance conflict A type of conflict in which a number of goals each produces approach and avoidance motives.

Multiple orgasms The experiencing of one or more additional orgasms as a result of sexual stimulation during the resolution phase. Two or more orgasms in rapid succession.

Multiple personality A dissociative disorder in which a person appears to have two or more distinct personalities. The personalities may alternate in controlling the person.

Mutation Sudden variations in the genetic code that usually occur as a result of environmental influences.

Mutism Refusal to talk.

Myelination The process by which Schwann cells wrap the axons of neurons, producing myelin coatings.

Myelin sheath A fatty substance produced by Schwann cells that encases and insulates axons, permitting more rapid transmission of neural impulses.

Myotonia Muscle tension.

N

***n* Ach** The need for achievement; the need to master, to accomplish difficult things.

***n* Aff** The need for affiliation; the need to be associated with groups.

Narcolepsy A sleep disorder characterized by uncontrollable seizures of sleep during the waking state.

Narcotics Drugs used to relieve pain and induce sleep. The term is usually reserved for opiates.

Native-language approach A method of teaching a second language in which children are at first taught in the language spoken in the home.

Naturalistic observation A method of scientific investigation in which organisms are observed carefully and unobtrusively in their natural environments.

Nature In behavior genetics, inherited influences on behavior, as contrasted with *nurture.*

Nearsightedness Inability to see distant objects with the acuity with which a person with normal vision can see distant objects.

Need A state of deprivation.

Need for achievement The need to master, to accomplish difficult things.

Need for affiliation The need for affiliation; the need to be associated with groups.

Negative correlation A relationship between two variables in which one variable increases as the other variable decreases.

Negative feedback Descriptive of a system in which information that a quantity (e.g., of a hormone) has reached a set point suspends action of the agency (e.g., a gland) that gives rise to that quantity.

Negative instance In concept formation, events that are *not* examples of a concept.

Negative reinforcer A reinforcer that increases the frequency of operant behavior when it is removed. Pain, anxiety, and disapproval usually, but not always, function as negative reinforcers. See *positive reinforcer.*

Neodissociation theory A theory that explains hypnotic events in terms of an ability to divide our awareness so that we can focus on hypnotic instructions and, at the same time, perceive outside sources of stimulation.

Neo-Freudians Theorists in the psychodynamic tradition who usually place less emphasis than Freud did on the importance of sexual impulses and unconscious determinants of behavior. Instead, they place more emphasis than Freud did on conscious motives and rational decision making.

Neonate A newborn child.

Nerve A bundle of axons from many neurons.

Neural impulse The electrochemical discharge of a neuron, or nerve cell.

Neural tube A hollowed-out area in the embryo from which the nervous system will develop.

Neuroendocrine reflex A reflex that involves the nervous system and the endocrine system, such as the ejection of milk.

Neuron A nerve cell.

Neuropeptide A short chain of amino acids (peptide) that functions as a neurotransmitter.

Neurosis One of a number of disorders characterized chiefly by anxiety, feelings of dread and foreboding, and avoidance behavior and theorized to stem from unconscious conflict. (Contemporary systems of classifying abnormal behavior deemphasize this concept.)

Neurotic anxiety In psychoanalysis, feelings of anxiety that stem from unconscious concern that unacceptable ideas or impulses may break loose into consciousness or may be expressed in behavior.

Neuroticism (1) A trait in which a person is given to anxiety, feelings of foreboding, inhibition of impulses, and avoidance behavior. (2) Eysenck's term for emotional instability—a definition that is not fully consistent with other usages of the word.

Neurotransmitter A chemical substance that is involved in the transmission of neural impulses from one neuron to another.

Nicotine A stimulant found in tobacco smoke.

Night terrors See *sleep terrors.*

Nightmare A frightening dream that usually occurs during rapid-eye-movement (REM) sleep.

Node of Ranvier A noninsulated segment of an otherwise myelinated axon.

Noise (1) In signal-detection theory, any unwanted signal that interferes with perception of the desired signal. (2) More generally, a combination of dissonant sounds.

Non-rapid-eye-movement sleep Stages of sleep 1 through 4, which are not characterized by rapid eye movements. Abbreviated *NREM sleep.*

Nonbalance In balance theory, a condition in which persons whom we dislike do not agree with us.

Nonconscious Descriptive of bodily processes, such as the growing of hair, of which we cannot become conscious. We may know that our hair is growing, but we cannot directly experience the biological process.

Nonsense syllables Meaningless sets of two consonants, with a vowel sandwiched in between, that are used to study memory.

Norepinephrine A neurotransmitter whose action is similar to that of the hormone *epinephrine* and which may play a role in depression.

Normal curve A graphic presentation of a normal distribution, showing a bell shape.

Normal distribution A symmetrical distribution in which approximately two-thirds of the cases lie within a standard deviation of the mean. A distribution that represents chance deviations of a variable.

Normative data Information concerning the behavior of a population.

Norm-referenced testing A testing approach in which scores are derived by comparing the number of items answered correctly with the average performance of others.

Novel stimulation (1) New or different stimulation. (2) A hypothesized primary drive to experience new or different stimulation.

Noxious Harmful, injurious.

Nuclear magnetic resonance Formation of a computer-generated image of the anatomical details of the brain by measuring the signals that these structures emit when the head is placed in a strong magnetic field.

Nuclei Plural of *nucleus.* A group of neural cell bodies found in the brain or spinal cord.

Nurturance The quality of nourishing, rearing, and fostering the development of children, animals, or plants.

Nurture In behavior genetics, environmental influences on behavior, including factors like nutrition, culture, socioeconomic status, and learning. Contrast with *nature.*

O

Objective Of known or perceived objects rather than existing only in the mind; real.

Objective morality According to Piaget, objective moral judgments assign guilt according to the amount of damage done rather than on the motives of the actor.

Objective tests Tests whose items must be answered in a specified, limited manner. Tests that have concrete answers that are considered to be correct.

Object permanence Recognition that objects removed from sight still exist, as demonstrated in young children by continued pursuit.

Object-relations theory The psychodynamic view that focuses on the potentially conflicting properties of internalized objects (e.g., personalities of loved ones).

Observational learning In social-learning theory, the acquisition of expectations and skills by observing the behavior of others. As opposed to operant conditioning, skill acquisition by means of observational learning occurs without the emission and reinforcement of a response.

Obsession A recurring thought or image that seems to be beyond control.

Occipital lobe The lobe of the cerebral cortex that is involved in vision. It lies below and behind the parietal lobe and behind the temporal lobe.

Odor The characteristic of a substance that makes it perceptible to the sense of smell. An odor is a sample of the molecules of the substance being sensed.

Oedipus complex In psychodynamic theory, a conflict of the phallic stage in which the boy wishes to possess his mother sexually and perceives his father as a rival in love.

Olfactory Having to do with the sense of smell.

Olfactory membrane A membrane high in each nostril that contains receptor neurons for the sense of smell.

Olfactory nerve The nerve that transmits information about odors from olfactory receptors to the brain.

Opaque (1) Not permitting the passage of light. (2) In psychoanalysis, descriptive of the analyst, who is expected to hide his or her own feelings from the client.

Operant behavior Voluntary responses that are reinforced.

Operant conditioning A simple form of learning in which an organism learns to engage in behavior because it is reinforced.

Operational definition A definition of a variable in terms of the methods used to create or measure the variable.

Opiate An addictive drug derived from the opium poppy that provides a euphoric rush and depresses the nervous system.

Opioid A synthetic (artificial) drug similar in chemical structure and effects to opiates.

Opponent-process theory The theory that color vision is made possible by three types of cones, some of which respond to red or green light, some to blue or yellow light, and some to the intensity of light only.

Optic nerve The nerve that transmits sensory information from the eye to the brain.

Optimal arousal A level of arousal at which an organism has the greatest feelings of well-being or functions most efficiently.

Oral fixation In psychodynamic theory, attachment to objects and behaviors characteristic of the oral stage.

Oral stage The first stage in Freud's theory of psychosexual development, during which gratification is obtained primarily through oral activities like sucking and biting.

Organ of Corti The receptor for hearing, which lies on the basilar membrane in the cochlea. Called the command post of hearing, it contains the receptor cells that transmit auditory information to the auditory nerve.

Organic psychosis A psychotic disorder that is known to stem from biochemical abnormalities.

Organic model The view that abnormal behavior is caused by biochemical or physiological abnormalities.

Organizational analysis Evaluation of the goals and resources of an organization.

Organizational psychology The field of psychology that studies the structure and functions of organizations.

Organizing effects The directional effects of sex hormones—for example, along stereotypical masculine or feminine lines.

Orgasm The height or climax of sexual excitement, involving involuntary muscle contractions, release of sexual tensions, and, usually, intense subjective feelings of pleasure.

Orienting reflex An unlearned response in which an organism attends to a stimulus.

Osmoreceptors Receptors in the hypothalamus that are sensitive to depletion of fluid in the body.

Osteoporosis A condition caused by calcium deficiency and characterized by brittleness of the bones.

Outer ear The funnel-shaped outer part of the ear that transmits sound waves to the eardrum.

Oval window A membrane that transmits vibrations from the stirrup of the middle ear to the inner ear.

Ovaries The female reproductive organs located in the abdominal cavity. The ovaries produce egg cells (ova) and the hormones estrogen and progesterone.

Overextension Overgeneralizing the use of words into situations in which they do not apply (characteristic of the speech of young children).

Overregularization The formation of plurals and past tenses of irregular nouns and verbs according to rules of grammar that apply to regular nouns and verbs (characteristic of the speech of young children).

Overtones Tones higher in frequency than those played on an instrument. Overtones result from vibrations throughout the instrument.

Ovulation The releasing of an egg cell (ovum) from an ovary.

Oxytocin A pituitary hormone that stimulates labor (childbirth).

P

Paired associates Nonsense syllables presented in pairs in experiments that measure recall. After viewing pairs, participants are shown one member of each pair and asked to recall the other.

Palmar reflex See *grasp reflex.*

Pancreas A gland behind the stomach whose secretions, including insulin, influence the level of sugar in the blood.

Panic disorder The recurrent experiencing of attacks of extreme anxiety in the absence of external stimuli that usually elicit anxiety.

Paradoxical intention Achieving one's goals by undertaking an apparently opposing course of action.

Paradoxical sleep Another term for rapid-eye-movement sleep, reflecting the fact that brain waves found during REM sleep suggest a level of arousal similar to that shown during the waking state.

Paranoia A rare psychotic disorder in which a person shows a persistent delusional system but not the confusion of the paranoid schizophrenic.

Paranoid personality disorder A disorder characterized by persistent suspiciousness but not the disorganization of paranoid schizophrenia.

Paranoid schizophrenia A subtype of schizophrenia characterized primarily by delusions—commonly of persecution—and by vivid hallucinations.

Paraphilia A disorder in which the person shows sexual arousal in response to unusual or bizarre objects or situations.

Parasympathetic nervous system The branch of the autonomic nervous system that is most active during processes that restore the body's reserves of energy, like digestion and relaxation. See *sympathetic division.*

"Parent" In transactional analysis, a moralistic ego state.

Parietal lobe The lobe of the cerebral cortex that lies behind the central fissure and that is involved in body senses.

Partial reinforcement One of several types of reinforcement schedules in which correct responses receive intermittent reinforcement, as opposed to *continuous reinforcement.*

Participant modeling A behavior-therapy technique in which a client observes and imitates a person who approaches and copes with feared objects or situations.

Passionate love See *romantic love.*

Pathogen An organism such as a bacterium or virus that can cause disease.

Pathological gambler A person who gambles habitually despite consistent losses. A compulsive gambler.

PCP Phencyclidine; a hallucinogenic drug.

Peak experience In humanistic theory, a brief moment of rapture that stems from the realization that one is on the path toward self-actualization.

Pedophilia A paraphilia in which sexual contact with children is the preferred source of sexual excitement.

Pelvic inflammatory disease Inflammation of the woman's abdominal region that is caused by pathogens such as the gonorrhea bacterium and characterized by fever, local pain, and, frequently, fertility problems.

Penile strain gauge An instrument that measures the size of erection, an objective measure of sexual response.

Penis envy In psychodynamic theory, jealousy of the male sexual organ attributed to girls in the phallic stage.

Pepsinogen A substance that helps the body digest proteins.

Perceived self-efficacy In social-learning theory, a person's belief that he or she can achieve goals through his or her own efforts.

Perception The process by which sensations are organized into an inner representation of the world. A psychological process through which we interpret sensory information.

Perceptual organization The tendency to integrate perceptual elements into meaningful patterns.

Performance anxiety Fear concerning whether or not one will be able to perform adequately.

Performance components According to Sternberg, the mental operations used in processing information.

Period of the ovum Up to the first two weeks following conception, before the developing ovum (now fertilized) has become securely implanted in the uterine wall. Another term for the *germinal stage.*

Peripheral nervous system The part of the nervous system consisting of the somatic nervous system and the autonomic nervous system.

Permeability The degree to which a membrane allows a substance to pass through it.

Personal construct According to Kelly, a psychological dimension, such as strong–weak, according to which one evaluates experience.

Personal space A psychological boundary that surrounds a person and permits that person to maintain a protective distance from others.

Personality The distinct patterns of behaviors, including thoughts and feelings, that characterize a person's adaptation to the demands of life.

Personality disorder An enduring pattern of maladaptive behavior that is a source of distress to the individual or to others.

Personality structure One's total pattern of traits.

Person-centered therapy Carl Rogers' method of psychotherapy, which emphasizes the creation of a warm, therapeutic atmosphere that frees clients to engage in self-expression and self-exploration.

Person variables In social-learning theory, determinants of behavior that lie within the person, including competencies, encoding strategies, expectancies, subjective values, and self-regulatory systems and plans.

Perspective A monocular cue for depth based on the convergence (coming together) of parallel lines as they recede into the distance.

pH A chemical symbol expressing the acidity of a solution.

Phallic stage In psychodynamic theory, the third stage of psychosexual development, characterized by shifting of libido to the phallic region and by the Oedipus and Electra complexes.

Phallic symbol In psychodynamic theory, a sign that represents the penis.

Phencyclidine A hallucinogenic drug whose name is an acronym for its chemical structure. Abbreviated *PCP.*

Phenomenological Having to do with subjective, conscious experience.

Phenothiazines A family of drugs that act as major tranquilizers and that are effective in treating many cases of schizophrenic disorders.

Phenotype The sum total of one's traits at a given point in time, as influenced by heredity and environmental factors.

Phenylketonuria A genetic abnormality, transmitted by a recessive gene, in which one is unable to metabolize phenylpyruvic acid, leading to mental retardation. Abbreviated *PKU.*

Pheromones Chemical secretions detected by the sense of smell that stimulate stereotypical behaviors in other members of the same species.

Philia A Greek word meaning feelings of friendship. A form of love.

Phi phenomenon The perception of movement as a result of sequential presentation of visual stimuli, as with lights going on and off in a row on a theater marquee.

Phobic neurosis See *phobic disorder.*

Phobic disorder Excessive, irrational fear. Fear that is out of proportion to the actual danger and that interferes with one's life. Formerly called *phobic neurosis.*

Phoneme A basic sound in a language.

Phonology The study of the basic sounds in a language.

Photographic memory See *iconic memory.*

Photoreceptors Cells that respond to light. See *rod* and *cone.*

Phrenology An unscientific method of analyzing personality by measurement of the shapes and protuberances of the skull.

Physiological Having to do with the biological functions and vital processes of organisms.

Physiological dependence Addiction to a drug.

Physiological drives Unlearned drives with a biological basis, like hunger, thirst, and avoidance of pain. Also called *primary drives.*

Physiological psychologists Same as biological psychologists.

Pitch The highness or lowness of a sound, as determined by the frequency of the sound waves.

Pituitary gland The body's master gland, located in the brain, that secretes growth hormone, prolactin, antidiuretic hormone, and others.

Placebo A bogus treatment that controls for the effects of expectations. A so-called "sugar pill."

Place theory The theory that the pitch of a sound is determined by the section of the basilar membrane that vibrates in response to it.

Placenta A membrane that permits the exchange of nutrients and waste products between the mother and her developing child but that does not allow the maternal and fetal bloodstreams to mix.

Plantar reflex See *grasp reflex.*

Plateau phase An advanced state of sexual arousal that precedes orgasm.

Pleasure principle In psychodynamic theory, the principle that governs the id; the demanding of immediate gratification of instinctive needs.

Polarization (1) In physiological psychology, the readying of a neuron for firing by creating an internal negative charge in relation to the body fluid outside the cell membrane. (2) In social psychology, the taking of an extreme position or attitude on an issue.

Polygenic Determined by more than one gene.

Polygraph An instrument that is theorized to be sensitive to whether or not an individual is telling lies by assessing four measures of arousal: heart rate, blood pressure, respiration rate, and galvanic skin response (GSR). Also called a *lie detector.*

Pons A structure of the hindbrain involved in respiration.

Population A complete group of organisms or events.

Pornography Explicit, uncensored portrayals of sexual activity that are intended to sexually excite the observer.

Positive correlation A relationship between variables in which one variable increases as the other variable also increases.

Positive instance In concept formation, an example of a concept.

Positive reinforcer A reinforcer that increases the frequency of operant behavior when it is presented. Food and approval are usually, but not always, positive reinforcers. See *negative reinforcer.*

Positron-emission tomography Formation of a computer-generated image of the neural activity of parts of the brain by tracing the amount of glucose used by the various parts. Abbreviated *PET scan.*

Possession According to superstitious belief, a psychological state induced by demons or the Devil as a result of retribution or of making a pact with the Devil in which a person shows abnormal behavior.

Postconventional level According to Kohlberg, a period of moral development during which moral judgments are derived from moral principles and people look to themselves to set moral standards.

Posthypnotic amnesia Inability to recall material presented while hypnotized, following the suggestion of the hypnotist.

Post-traumatic stress disorder A disorder that follows a psychologically distressing event that is outside the range of normal human experience. It is characterized by symptoms such as intense fear, avoidance of stimuli associated with the event, and reliving of the event.

Pragma Logical love.

Pragmatics The practical aspects of communication. Adaptation of language to fit the social context.

Preconscious In psychodynamic theory, descriptive of material of which one is not currently aware but which can be brought into awareness by focusing one's attention. Also see *unconscious.*

Preconventional level According to Kohlberg, a period of moral development during which moral judgments are based largely on expectation of rewards and punishments.

Prefrontal lobotomy A form of psychosurgery in which a section of the frontal lobe of the brain is severed or destroyed.

Pregenital In psychodynamic theory, characteristic of stages less mature than the genital stage.

Prejudice The unfounded belief that a person or group—on the basis of assumed racial, ethnic, sexual, or other features—will possess negative characteristics or perform inadequately.

Prelinguistic Prior to the development of language.

Premature ejaculation Ejaculation that occurs before the couple are satisfied with the duration of coitus.

Premenstrual syndrome A cluster of symptoms—which may include tension, irritability, depression, and fatigue—that some women experience before menstruating.

Prenatal Prior to birth.

Preoperational stage The second of Piaget's stages of cognitive development, characterized by illogical use of words and symbols, egocentrism, animism, artificialism, and objective moral judgments.

Presbyopia Brittleness of the lens, a condition that impairs visual acuity for nearby objects.

Primacy effect (1) In information processing, the tendency to recall the initial items in a series of items. (2) In social psychology, the tendency to evaluate others in terms of first impressions.

Primary colors Colors that we cannot produce by mixing other hues; colors from which other colors are derived.

Primary drives Unlearned drives; physiological drives.

Primary mental abilities According to Thurstone, the basic abilities that compose human intelligence.

Primary narcissism In psychodynamic theory, the type of autism that describes the newborn child who has not learned that he or she is separate from the rest of the world.

Primary prevention In community psychology, the deterrence of psychological problems before they start.

Primary reinforcer A stimulus that has reinforcement value without learning. Examples: food, water, warmth, and pain. See *secondary reinforcer.*

Primary sex characteristics Physical traits that distinguish the sexes and that are directly involved in reproduction.

Primate A member of an order of mammals including monkeys, apes, and human beings.

Prism A transparent triangular solid that breaks down visible light into the colors of the spectrum.

Private self-consciousness The tendency to take critical note of one's own behavior, even when unobserved by others.

Proactive interference Interference from previously learned material in one's ability to retrieve or recall recently learned material. See *retroactive interference.*

Proband The family member first studied or tested.

Procedural memory Knowledge of ways of doing things; skill memory.

Productivity A property of language; the ability to combine words into unlimited, novel sentences.

Progesterone A sex hormone that promotes growth of the sexual organs and helps maintain pregnancy.

Prognosis A prediction of the probable course of a disease.

Programmed learning A method of learning, based on operant conditioning principles, in which complex tasks are broken down into simple steps. The proper performance of each step is reinforced. Incorrect responses go unreinforced but are not punished.

Progressive relaxation Jacobson's method for reducing muscle tension, which involves alternate tensing and relaxing of muscle groups throughout the body.

Projection In psychodynamic theory, a defense mechanism in which unacceptable ideas and impulses are cast out or attributed to others.

Projective test A psychological test that presents questions to which there is no single correct response. A test that presents ambiguous stimuli into which the test-taker projects his or her own personality in making a response.

Prolactin A pituitary hormone that regulates production of milk and, in lower animals, maternal behavior.

Propinquity Nearness.

Prosocial Behavior that is characterized by helping others and making a contribution to society.

Proximity Nearness. The perceptual tendency to group together objects that are near one another.

Proximodistal Proceeding from near to far.

Psychedelic Causing hallucinations or delusions, or heightening perceptions.

Psychiatrist A physician who specializes in the application of medical treatments to abnormal behavior.

Psychic structure In psychodynamic theory, a hypothesized mental structure that helps explain various aspects of behavior. See *id, ego,* and *superego.*

Psychoactive Describing drugs that give rise to psychological effects.

Psychoanalysis The school of psychology, founded by Sigmund Freud, that emphasizes the importance of unconscious motives and conflicts as determinants of human behavior. Also the name of Freud's methods of psychotherapy and clinical investigation.

Psychodynamic Descriptive of Freud's view that various forces move within the personality, frequently clashing, and that the outcome of these clashes determines behavior.

Psychogenic amnesia A dissociative disorder marked by loss of episodic memory or self-identity. Skills and general knowledge are usually retained.

Psychogenic fugue A dissociative disorder in which one experiences amnesia, then flees to a new location and establishes a new identity and life-style.

Psycholinguist A psychologist who studies how we perceive and acquire language.

Psycholinguistic theory The view that language learning involves an interaction between environmental influences and an inborn tendency to acquire language. The emphasis is on the innate tendency.

Psychological androgyny Possession of both instrumental and warmth–expressiveness traits.

Psychological dependence Repeated use of a substance as a way of dealing with stress.

Psychological hardiness A cluster of traits that buffer stress and that are characterized by commitment, challenge, and control.

Psychology The science that studies behavior and mental processes.

Psychomotor retardation Slowness in motor activity and, apparently, in thought.

Psychoneuroimmunology The field that studies the relationships between psychological factors (e.g., attitudes and overt behavior patterns) and the functioning of the immune system.

Psychopath Another term for a person who shows an antisocial personality disorder.

Psychophysics The study of the relationships between physical stimuli, like light and sound, and their perception.

Psychophysiological Psychosomatic.

Psychosexual development In psychodynamic theory, the process by which libidinal energy is expressed through different erogenous zones during different stages of development.

Psychosexual trauma A distressing sexual experience that may have lingering psychological effects.

Psychosis A major psychological disorder in which a person shows impaired reality testing and has difficulty meeting the demands of everyday life.

Psychosocial development Erikson's theory of personality and development, which emphasizes the importance of social relationships and conscious choice throughout eight stages of development, including three stages of adult development.

Psychosomatic Having to do with physical illnesses that have psychological origins or that are intensified by stress.

Psychosurgery Biological treatments in which specific areas or structures of the brain are destroyed in order to promote psychological changes or to relieve disordered behavior.

Psychotherapy A systematic interaction between a therapist and a client that brings psychological principles to bear on influencing the client's thoughts, feelings, or behaviors in order to help that client overcome abnormal behavior or adjust to problems in living.

Puberty The period of early adolescence during which hormones spur rapid physical development.

Punishment An unpleasant stimulus that suppresses the frequency of the behavior it follows.

Pupil The apparently black opening in the center of the iris, through which light enters the eye.

Pupillary reflex The automatic adjusting of the irises to permit more or less light to enter the eye.

Pure research Research conducted without concern for immediate applications.

Q

Quality circle A regularly scheduled meeting in which a group of workers discusses problems and suggests solutions in order to enhance the quality of products.

R

Radical behaviorist A person who does not believe in the existence of mind, consciousness, and other mentalistic concepts.

Rage response Stereotypical aggressive behavior that can be brought forth in lower animals by electrical stimulation of the brain.

Random sample A sample drawn in such a manner that every member of a population has an equal chance of being selected.

Random trial-and-error In operant conditioning, refers to behavior that occurs prior to learning what behavior is reinforced. The implication is that in a novel situation, the organism happens upon the first correct (reinforced) response by chance.

Range A measure of variability; the distance between extreme measures or scores in a distribution.

Rape Sexual interaction with a person without that person's consent.

Rapid smoking A type of aversive conditioning in which cigarettes are inhaled every six seconds, making the smoke aversive.

Rapid flight of ideas Rapid speech and topic changes, characteristic of manic behavior.

Rapid-eye-movement sleep A stage of sleep characterized by rapid eye movements that have been linked to dreaming. Abbreviated *REM sleep*. Also called *paradoxical sleep*.

Rational-emotive therapy Albert Ellis's form of cognitive psychotherapy, which focuses on how irrational expectations create anxiety and disappointment and which encourages clients to challenge and correct these expectations.

Rationalization In psychodynamic theory, a defense mechanism in which an individual engages in self-deception, finding justifications for unacceptable ideas, impulses, or behaviors.

Reaction formation In psychodynamic theory, a defense mechanism in which unacceptable impulses and ideas are kept unconscious through the exaggerated expression of opposing ideas and impulses.

Reaction time The amount of time required to respond to a stimulus.

Readiness In developmental psychology, referring to a stage in the maturation of an organism when it is capable of engaging in a certain response.

Reality principle In psychodynamic theory, the principle that guides ego functioning; consideration of what is practical and possible in gratifying needs.

Reality testing The capacity to form an accurate mental representation of the world, including socially appropriate behavior, reasonably accurate knowledge of the motives of others, undistorted sensory impressions, and self-insight.

Rebound anxiety Strong anxiety that can attend the suspension of usage of a tranquilizer.

Recall Retrieval or reconstruction of learned material.

Recency effect (1) In information processing, the tendency to recall the last items in a series of items. (2) In social psychology, the tendency to evaluate others in terms of the most recent impression.

Receptive vocabulary The extent of one's knowledge of the meanings of words that are communicated to one by others.

Receptor site A location on a dendrite of a receiving neuron that is tailored to receive a neurotransmitter.

Recessive trait In genetics, a trait that is not expressed when the gene or genes involved have been paired with *dominant* genes. However, recessive traits are transmitted to future generations and expressed if paired with other recessive genes. See *dominant trait.*

Reciprocity (1) Mutual action. Treating others as one is treated. (2) In interpersonal attraction, the tendency to return feelings and attitudes that are expressed about us.

Recitation A teaching format in which teachers pose questions that are answered by students.

Recognition In information processing, a relatively easy memory task in which one identifies objects or events as having been encountered previously.

Reconstructive memories Memories that are based on the piecing together of memory fragments with general knowledge and expectations rather than a precise picture of the past.

Reflex A simple, unlearned response to a stimulus.

Refractory period (1) In discussion of the nervous system, a period following firing during which a neuron's action potential cannot be triggered. (2) In human sexuality, a period following orgasm when a male is insensitive to further sexual stimulation.

Regression In psychodynamic theory, return to a form of behavior characteristic of an earlier stage of development. As a defense mechanism, regression to less mature behavior is a means of coping with stress.

Reinforcement A stimulus that follows a response and increases the frequency of that response. See *positive* and *negative, primary* and *secondary* reinforcers.

Relative refractory period A phase following the absolute refractory period during which a neuron will fire in response to stronger-than-usual messages from other neurons.

Relaxation response Benson's term for a cluster of responses brought about by meditation that lower the activity of the sympathetic division of the autonomic nervous system.

Relearning A measure of retention. Material is usually relearned more quickly than it is learned initially.

Releaser In ethology, a stimulus that elicits an instinctive response.

Reliability In psychological measurement, consistency. Also see *validity.*

Remediation The process of helping people overcome deficiencies.

Replication The repetition or duplication of scientific studies in order to double-check their results.

Repression In psychodynamic theory, the ejection of anxiety-provoking ideas, impulses, or images from awareness, without the awareness that one is doing so. A defense mechanism.

Resistance During psychoanalysis, a blocking of thoughts the awareness of which could cause anxiety. The client may miss sessions or verbally abuse the analyst as threatening material is about to be unearthed.

Resistance stage The second stage of the general adaptation syndrome, characterized by prolonged sympathetic activity in an effort to restore lost energy and repair damage. Also called the *adaptation stage.*

Resolution phase The final stage of the sexual response cycle, during which the body returns gradually to its resting state.

Response A movement or other observable reaction to a stimulus.

Response cost A behavior-therapy self-control technique in which one uses self-punishment for practicing a bad habit or failing to meet a goal.

Response prevention A behavior-therapy self-control technique in which one makes unwanted behaviors difficult or impossible.

Response set A tendency to answer test items according to a bias—for example, with the intention of making oneself appear perfect or bizarre.

Resting potential The electrical potential across the neural membrane when it is not responding to other neurons.

Restriction of the stimulus field A behavior-therapy self-control technique in which a problem behavior is gradually restricted from more environments.

Reticular activating system A part of the brain involved in attention, sleep, and arousal. Abbreviated *RAS.*

Retina The area of the inner surface of the eye that contains rods and cones.

Retinal disparity A binocular cue for depth based on the difference of the image cast by an object on the retinas of the eyes as the object moves closer or farther away.

Retrieval The location of stored information and its return to consciousness. The third stage of information processing.

Retroactive interference The interference by new learning in one's ability to retrieve material learned previously. See *proactive interference.*

Retrograde amnesia Failure to remember events that occur prior to physical trauma because of the effects of the trauma.

Reversibility According to Piaget, recognition that processes can be undone, leaving things as they were before. Reversibility is a factor in conservation of the properties of substances. See *conservation* and *concrete operational stage.*

Reward A pleasant stimulus that increases the frequency of the behavior it follows.

Risky shift The tendency to make riskier decisions as a member of a group than as an individual acting independently.

Rod A rod-shaped photoreceptor in the eye that is sensitive to the intensity of light. Rods permit "black-and-white" vision.

Role diffusion According to Erikson, a state of confusion, insecurity, and susceptibility to the suggestions of others; the probable outcome if ego identity is not established during adolescence.

Role theory A theory that explains hypnotic events in terms of the person's ability to act *as though* he or she were hypnotized. Role theory differs from faking in that subjects cooperate and focus on hypnotic suggestions instead of cynically pretending to be hypnotized.

Romantic love An intense, positive emotion that involves arousal, a cultural setting that idealizes love, an attractive person, feelings of caring, and the belief that one is in love. Also called *passionate love.*

Rooting (1) A reflex in which an infant turns its head toward a touch, such as by the mother's nipple. (2) In adult development, the process of establishing a home, which frequently occurs in the second half of the 30s.

Rorschach Inkblot Test A projective personality test that presents test-takers the task of interpreting inkblots.

Rote Mechanical associative learning that is based on repetition.

"Roy G. Biv" A mnemonic device for remembering the colors of the visible spectrum.

Rumination Turning or chewing over thoughts repeatedly in one's mind.

S

s Spearman's symbol for specific or "s" factors, which he believed accounted for individual abilities.

Saccadic eye movement The rapid jumps made by a reader's eyes as they fixate on different points in the text.

Sadism The attainment of gratification, frequently sexual, from inflicting pain on or humiliating others.

Sadomasochism Activities involving attainment of gratification by the infliction and reception of pain and humiliation.

"SAME" The mnemonic device for remembering that *s*ensory neurons are called *a*fferent neurons and that *m*otor neurons are termed *e*fferent neurons.

Sample Part of a population.

Satiety The state of being satisfied; fullness.

Saturation The degree of purity of a color, as measured by its freedom from mixture with white or black.

Savings The difference between the number of repetitions originally required to learn a list and the number of repetitions required to relearn the list after a certain amount of time has elapsed.

Scapegoat A person or group upon whom the blame for the mistakes or crimes of others is cast.

Scatter diagram A graphic presentation formed by plotting the points defined by the intersections of two variables.

Schachter-Singer theory The theory of emotion that holds that emotions have generally similar patterns of bodily arousal, and that the label we attribute to an emotion depends on our level of arousal and our cognitive appraisal of our situation.

Schema A way of mentally representing the world, such as a belief or an expectation, that can influence perception of persons, objects, and situations.

Schizoid personality disorder A disorder characterized by social withdrawal.

Schizophrenic disorder A psychotic disorder of at least six months' duration in which thought processes and reality testing are impaired and emotions are not appropriate to one's situation. Also see *schizophreniform disorder, brief reactive psychosis,* and *schizotypal personality.*

Schizophreniform disorder A disorder whose symptoms resemble schizophrenia but that is relatively brief (two weeks to less than six months in duration).

Schizotypal personality disorder A disorder characterized by oddities of thought and behavior but not involving bizarre psychotic symptoms. Formerly called *simple schizophrenia.*

Schwann cell A type of glial cell that wraps around the axons of neurons to form myelin.

Scientific method A four-step method for obtaining scientific evidence in which a hypothesis is formed and tested.

Secondary colors Colors derived by mixing primary colors.

Secondary prevention In community psychology, the early detection and treatment of psychological problems.

Secondary reinforcer A stimulus that gains reinforcement value through association with other, established reinforcers. Money and social approval are secondary reinforcers. Also called *conditioned reinforcer.* See *primary reinforcer.*

Secondary sex characteristics Physical traits that differentiate the sexes, such as the depth of the voice, but that are not directly involved in reproduction.

Secondary traits Allport's term for traits that appear in a limited number of situations and govern a limited number of responses.

Secure attachment A type of attachment characterized by positive feelings toward attachment figures and feelings of security.

Sedative A drug that soothes or quiets restlessness or agitation.

Selective avoidance Diverting one's attention from information that is inconsistent with one's attitudes.

Selective exposure The deliberate seeking of and attending to information that is consistent with one's attitudes.

Self The totality of one's impressions, thoughts, and feelings. The center of consciousness that organizes sensory impressions and governs one's perceptions of the world.

Self-actualization According to Maslow and other humanistic psychologists, self-initiated striving to become what one is capable of being. The motive to reach one's full potential, to express one's unique capabilities.

Self-efficacy expectations Our beliefs that we can bring about desired changes through our own efforts.

Self-esteem One's evaluation of and the placement of value on oneself.

Self-fulfilling prophecy An expectation that is confirmed because of the behavior of those who hold the expectation.

Self-ideal A mental image of what we believe we ought to be.

Self-insight In psychodynamic theory, accurate awareness of one's own motives and feelings.

Self-monitoring A behavior-therapy technique in which one keeps a record of his or her behavior in order to identify problems and record successes.

Self-report (1) A subject's testimony about his or her own thoughts, feelings, or behaviors. (2) A method of investigation in which information is obtained through the report of the subject.

Self-serving bias The tendency to view one's successes as stemming from internal factors and one's failures as stemming from external factors.

Self theory The name of Carl Rogers' theory of personality, which emphasizes the importance of self-awareness, choice, and self-actualization.

Semantic code Mental representation of information according to its meaning.

Semanticity Meaning. The property of language in which words are used as symbols for objects, events, or ideas.

Semantic memory General knowledge, as opposed to episodic memory.

Semantics The study of the relationships between language and objects or events. The study of the meaning of language.

Semicircular canals Structures of the inner ear that monitor body movement and position.

Sensate-focus exercises Planned sex-therapy sessions in which couples take turns giving and receiving physical pleasure.

Sensation The stimulation of sensory receptors and the transmission of sensory information to the central nervous system.

Sensitive period In linguistic theory, the period from about 18 months to puberty when the brain is thought to be particularly capable of learning language because of plasticity.

Sensitization The type of sensory adaptation in which we become more sensitive to stimuli that are low in magnitude. Also called *positive adaptation.*

Sensorimotor stage The first of Piaget's stages of cognitive development, characterized by coordination of sensory information and motor activity, early exploration of the environment, and lack of language.

Sensory adaptation The processes by which organisms become more sensitive to stimuli that are low in magnitude and less sensitive to stimuli that are constant or ongoing in magnitude.

Sensory awareness One of the definitions of consciousness: Knowledge of the environment through perception of sensory stimulation.

Sensory cortex The section of the cerebral cortex that lies in the parietal lobe, just behind the central fissure. Sensory stimulation is projected in this section of cortex.

Sensory deprivation (1) In general, insufficient sensory stimulation. (2) A research method for systematically decreasing the stimuli that impinge on sensory receptors.

Sensory memory The type or stage of memory first encountered by a stimulus. Sensory memory holds impressions briefly, but long enough so that series of perceptions are psychologically continuous.

Sensory-neural deafness The forms of deafness that result from damage to hair cells or the auditory nerve.

Sensory register A system of memory that holds information briefly, but long enough so that it can be processed further. There may be a sensory register for every sense.

Septum A part of the limbic system that apparently restrains stereotypical aggressive responses.

Serial position effect The tendency to recall more accurately the first and last items in a series.

Serotonin A neurotransmitter, deficiencies of which have been linked to affective disorders, anxiety, and insomnia.

Serum cholesterol A fatty substance (cholesterol) in the blood (serum) that has been linked to heart disease.

Set point A value that the body attempts to maintain. For example, the body tries to maintain a certain weight by adjusting the metabolism.

Sex chromosomes The 23rd pair of chromosomes, which determine sex.

Sex flush A reddish hue on body surfaces that is caused by vasocongestion during sexual excitement.

Sexism The prejudgment that a person, on the basis of his or her sex, will possess negative traits or perform inadequately.

Sex norms Social rules or conventions that govern the ways in which males and females interact.

Sex role A complex cluster of behaviors that characterizes traditional male or female behaviors.

Sex therapy A number of cognitive and behavioral methods that seek to reverse sexual dysfunctions by reducing performance anxiety, reversing defeatist expectations, and fostering sexual competencies.

Sex typing The process by which people acquire a sense of being male or female and acquire the traits considered typical of males or females.

Sexual apathy Lack of interest in sexual activity.

Sexual dysfunctions Persistent or recurrent problems in achieving or maintaining sexual arousal or in reaching orgasm.

Sexual masochism Attainment of sexual gratification by means of receiving pain or humiliation.

Sexual response cycle A four-phase process that describes response to sexual stimulation in males and females.

Sexual sadism Attainment of sexual gratification by means of inflicting pain or humiliation on sex partners.

Shadowing A monocular cue for depth based on the fact that opaque objects block light and produce shadows.

Sham False, pretended.

Shape constancy The tendency to perceive an object as being the same shape even though its retinal images changes in shape as the object rotates.

Shaping In operant conditioning, a procedure for teaching complex behaviors that at first reinforces approximations to these behaviors.

Short-term memory The type or stage of memory that can hold information for up to a minute or so after the trace of the stimulus decays. Also called *working memory*.

Siblings Brothers and sisters.

Signal-detection theory In psychophysics, the view that the perception of sensory stimuli is influenced by the interaction of physical, biological, and psychological factors.

Significant others Persons who have a major influence on one's psychosocial development, including parents, peers, lovers, and children.

Similarity As a rule of perceptual organization, the tendency to group together objects that are similar in appearance.

Simple schizophrenia See *schizotypal personality disorder*.

Simple phobia Persistent fear of a specific object or situation.

Simultaneous conditioning A classical conditioning procedure in which the CS and US are presented at the same time, and the CS is left on until the response occurs.

Situational attribution An assumption that a person's behavior is determined by external circumstances, such as social pressure. Contrast with *dispositional attribution*.

Situational variables In social-learning theory, external determinants of behavior, such as rewards and punishments.

Size constancy The tendency to perceive an object as being the same size even as the size of its retinal image changes according to its distance.

Skewed distribution A slanted distribution, drawn out toward the low or high scores.

Sleep spindles Short bursts of rapid brain waves that occur during stage 2 sleep.

Sleep terrors Frightening, dream-like experiences that usually occur during deep stage 4 sleep.

Sleep-onset insomnia Difficulty falling asleep.

Social-comparison theory The view that people look to others for cues about how to behave in confusing situations.

Social decision schemes Rules for predicting the final outcome of group decision making on the basis of the initial positions of the members.

Social facilitation The process by which a person's performance is increased when other members of a group engage in similar behavior.

Social influence The area of social psychology that studies the ways in which people influence the thoughts, feelings, and behavior of others.

Socialization Guidance of people—and children in particular—into socially desirable behavior by means of verbal messages, the systematic use of rewards and punishments, and other methods of teaching.

Social-learning theory A cognitively-oriented learning theory that emphasizes observational learning and the roles of person and situational variables in determining behavior.

Social loafing The process by which a person's performance is decreased as a function of being a member of a group.

Social motives Learned or acquired motives, such as the needs for achievement and affiliation.

Social norms Explicit and implicit rules that reflect social expectations and influence the ways people behave in social situations.

Social phobias Irrational fears that involve themes of public scrutiny.

Social perception A subfield of social psychology that studies the ways in which we form and modify impressions of others.

Social psychology The field of psychology that studies the nature and causes of people's thoughts, feelings, and behavior in social situations.

Sociobiology A biological theory of social behavior that assumes that the underlying purpose of behavior is to ensure the transmission of an organism's genes from generation to generation.

Sociopath Another term for a person who shows an antisocial personality disorder.

Soma A cell body.

Somatic nervous system The division of the peripheral nervous system that connects the central nervous system (brain and spinal cord) with sensory receptors, muscles, and the surface of the body.

Somatoform disorders Disorders in which people complain of physical (somatic) problems, although no physical abnormality can be found. See *conversion disorder* and *hypochondriasis.*

Source traits Cattell's term for underlying traits from which surface traits are derived.

Spectrograph An instrument that converts sounds to graphs or pictures according to their acoustic qualities.

Sphincter A ringlike muscle that circles a body opening, such as the anus. An infant will exhibit the sphincter reflex (have a bowel movement) in response to intestinal pressure.

Spinal cord A column of nerves within the spine that transmits messages from the sensory receptors to the brain and from the brain to muscles and glands throughout the body.

Spinal reflex A simple, unlearned response to a stimulus that may involve only two neurons.

Split-brain operation An operation in which the corpus callosum is severed, usually in an effort to control epileptic seizures.

Split-half reliability A method for determining the internal consistency of a test (an index of reliability) by correlating scores attained on half the items with scores attained on the other half of the items.

Spontaneous recovery Generally, the recurrence of an extinguished response as a function of the passage of time. In classical conditioning, the eliciting of a conditioned response by a conditioned stimulus after some time has elapsed following the extinction of the conditioned response. In operant conditioning, the performance of an operant in the presence of discriminative stimuli after some time has elapsed following the extinction of the operant.

Sports psychology The field of psychology that studies the nature, causes, and modification of the behavior and mental processes of people involved in sports.

Stage In developmental psychology, a distinct period of life that is qualitatively different from other stages. Stages follow one another in an orderly sequence.

Standard deviation A measure of the variability of a distribution, obtained by taking the square root of the sum of difference scores squared, divided by the number of scores.

Standardization The process of setting standards for a psychological test, accomplished by determining how a population performs on it. Standardization permits psychologists to interpret individual scores as deviations from a norm.

Standardized tests Tests for which norms are based on the performance of a wide range of individuals.

Stapes A bone of the middle ear. Latin for "stirrup."

Startle reflex See *Moro reflex.*

State anxiety A temporary condition of anxiety that may be attributed to one's situation. Contrast with *trait anxiety.*

State-dependent memory Information that is better retrieved in the physiological or emotional state in which it was encoded (stored) or learned.

Statistically significant difference As indicated by inferential statistics, a difference between two groups that is not likely to result from chance fluctuation.

Statistics Numerical facts assembled in such a manner that they provide useful information about measures or scores.

Stereotype A fixed, conventional idea about a group.

Steroids A family of hormones that includes testosterone, estrogen, progesterone, and corticosteroids.

Stimulant A drug that increases the activity of the nervous system.

Stimulation deafness The forms of deafness that result from exposure to excessively loud sounds.

Stimuli Plural of *stimulus.*

Stimulus (1) A feature in the environment that is detected by an organism or that leads to a change in behavior (a response). (2) A form of physical energy, such as light or sound, that impinges on the sensory receptors.

Stimulus control A behavior-therapy self-control technique in which one places oneself in an environment in which desired responses are likely to occur.

Stimulus discrimination The eliciting of a conditioned response by only one of a series of similar stimuli.

Stimulus generalization The eliciting of a conditioned response by stimuli that are similar to the conditioned stimulus.

Stimulus motives Motives to increase the stimulation impinging on an organism.

Stirrup A bone of the middle ear.

Storage The maintenance of information over time. The second stage of information processing.

Storge Feelings of attachment, as in friendships or family relationships.

Strabismus A visual disorder in which the eyes point in different directions and thus do not focus simultaneously on the same point.

Stratified sample A sample drawn in such a way that known subgroups within a population are represented in proportion to their numbers in the population.

Stress The demand made on an organism to adjust or adapt.

Stressor An event or stimulus that acts as a source of stress.

Stroboscopic motion A visual illusion in which the perception of motion is generated by presentation of a series of stationary images in rapid succession.

Structuralism The school of psychology, founded by Wilhelm Wundt, that argues that the mind consists of three basic elements—sensations, feelings, and images—which combine to form experience.

Structure-of-intellect model Guilford's three-dimensional model of intelligence, which focuses on the operations, contents, and products of intellectual functioning.

Stupor A condition in which the senses and thought processes are dulled.

Subject A participant in a scientific study. Many psychologists consider this term dehumanizing and no longer use it in reference to human participants.

Subjective Of the mind; personal; determined by thoughts and feelings rather than by external objects.

Subjective morality According to Piaget, subjective moral judgments assign guilt according to the motives of the actor. See *objective morality.*

Subjective value The desirability of an object or event.

Sublimation In psychodynamic theory, a defense mechanism in which primitive impulses—usually sexual or aggressive—are channeled into positive, constructive activities.

Subordinate Descriptive of a lower (included) class or category in a hierarchy. Contained by another class. Opposite of *superordinate.*

Substance dependence Habitual use of a drug as characterized by physiological dependence.

Successive approximations In operant conditioning, a series of behaviors that gradually become more similar to a target behavior.

Superego In psychodynamic theory, the psychic structure that is governed by the moral principle, sets forth high standards for behavior, and floods the ego with feelings of guilt and shame when it falls short.

Supermale A man with XYY chromosomal structure, who is likely to have a heavier beard and be slightly taller than the average male.

Superordinate Descriptive of a higher (including) class or category in a hierarchy. Containing another class. Opposite of *subordinate.*

Suppression The deliberate, or conscious, placing of certain ideas, impulses, or images out of awareness. Contrast with *repression.*

Surface structure The superficial construction of a sentence as defined by the placement of words.

Surface traits Cattell's term for characteristic, observable ways of behaving. See *source traits.*

Surrogate Substitute.

Survey A method of scientific investigation in which large samples of people are questioned.

Syllogism A form of reasoning in which a conclusion is drawn from two statements or premises.

Symbol Something that stands for or represents another thing.

Sympathetic nervous system The branch of the autonomic nervous system that is most active when the person is engaged in behavior or experiencing feeling states that spend the body's reserves of energy, such as fleeing or experiencing fear or anxiety.

Symptom substitution The exchange of one symptom for another. The term refers to the psychodynamic argument that a phobia is a symptom of an underlying disorder (that is, unconscious conflict) and that the removal of the phobia through behavioral techniques may lead to the emergence of another symptom of the disorder.

Synapse A junction between a terminal knob of a transmitting neuron and a dendrite or soma of a receiving neuron.

Syndrome A cluster of symptoms characteristic of a disorder.

Syntax The rules in a language for placing words in proper order to form meaningful sentences.

Syphilis A sexually transmitted disease.

Systematic desensitization A behavior-therapy fear-reduction technique in which a hierarchy of fear-evoking stimuli are presented while the person remains in a state of deep muscle relaxation.

T

TA Abbreviation for *transactional analysis.*

Tactile Of the sense of touch.

Target behavior Goal.

Task analysis The breaking down of a job or behavior pattern into its component parts.

Taste aversion A kind of classical conditioning in which a previously desirable or neutral food comes to be perceived as repugnant because it is associated with aversive stimulation.

Taste buds The sensory organs for taste. They contain taste cells and are located on the tongue.

Taste cells Receptor cells that are sensitive to taste.

TAT Thematic Apperception Test.

Taxonomy Classification system.

Telegraphic speech Speech in which only the essential words are used, as in a telegram.

Temporal lobe The lobe of the cerebral cortex that is involved in hearing. It lies below the lateral fissure, near the temples.

Terminal A small branching structure found at the tip of an axon.

Territory In sociobiology, the particular area acquired and defended by an animal, or pair of animals, for purposes of feeding and breeding.

Tertiary colors Colors derived by mixing primary and adjoining secondary colors.

Tertiary prevention In community psychology, the treatment of ripened psychological problems. (See *primary* and *secondary prevention.*

Test-retest reliability A method for determining the reliability of a test by comparing (correlating) test-takers' scores on separate occasions.

Testes The male reproductive organs that produce sperm and the hormone testosterone.

Testosterone A male sex hormone (steroid) that is produced by the testes and promotes growth of male sexual characteristics and sperm.

Texture gradient A monocular cue for depth based on the perception that nearby objects appear to have rougher or more detailed surfaces.

Thalamus An area near the center of the brain that is involved in the relay of sensory information to the cortex and in the functions of sleep and attention.

Thanatos In psychodynamic theory, the death instinct.

THC Delta-9-tetrahydrocannabinol. The major active ingredient in marijuana.

The Dream Levinson's term for the overriding drive of youth to become someone important, to leave one's mark on history.

T-helper lymphocytes The white blood cells of the immune system that recognize invading pathogens. Also called *T4-helper lymphocytes.*

Thematic Apperception Test A projective test devised by Henry Murray to measure needs through the production of fantasy.

Theory A formulation of relationships underlying observed events. A theory involves assumptions and logically derived explanations and predictions.

Theory of social comparison The view that people look to others for cues about how to behave when they are in confusing or unfamiliar situations.

Theory Y McGregor's view that organizational goals should be congruent with workers' goals.

Theory Z Ouchi's view that adapts positive features of the Japanese workplace to the U.S. workplace.

Theta waves Slow brain waves produced during the hypnagogic state.

Threshold The point at which a stimulus is just strong enough to produce a response.

Thyroxin The thyroid hormone that increases the metabolic rate.

Timbre The quality or richness of a sound. The quality that distinguishes the sounds of one musical instrument from those of another.

Time out In operant conditioning, a method for decreasing the frequency of undesired behaviors by removing an organism from a situation in which reinforcement is available as a consequence of showing the undesired behavior.

Tip-of-the-tongue phenomenon The feeling that information is stored in memory although it cannot be readily retrieved. Also called the *feeling-of-knowing experience.*

TM Transcendental meditation.

Token economy A controlled environment in which people are reinforced for desired behaviors with tokens (such as poker chips) that may be exchanged for privileges.

Tolerance Habituation to a drug, with the result that increasingly higher doses of the drug are required to achieve similar effects.

Tolerance for frustration Ability to delay gratification, to maintain self-control when a motive is thwarted.

Total immersion A method of teaching a second language in which all instruction is carried out in the second language.

Trace conditioning A classical conditioning procedure in which the CS is presented and then removed before the US is presented.

Trait A distinguishing quality or characteristic of personality that is inferred from behavior and assumed to account for consistency in behavior.

Trait anxiety Anxiety as a personality variable, or persistent trait. Contrast with *state anxiety.*

Tranquilizers Drugs used to reduce anxiety and tension.

Transaction In transactional analysis, an exchange between two people.

Transactional analysis A form of psychotherapy that deals with how people interact and how their interactions reinforce attitudes, expectations, and "life positions." Abbreviated *TA.*

Transcendental meditation The simplified form of meditation brought to the United States by the Maharishi Mahesh Yogi in which one focuses on a repeated mantra. Abbreviated *TM.*

Transference In psychoanalysis, the generalization to the analyst of feelings toward another person in the client's life.

Transsexualism A gender identity disorder in which the person feels trapped inside a body of the wrong sex.

Transvestic fetishism Recurrent, persistent dressing in clothing worn by the opposite sex for purposes of sexual excitement.

Trauma An injury or wound.

Treatment In experiments, a condition received by participants so that its effects may be observed.

Trial In conditioning, a presentation of the stimuli.

Triarchic Governed by three. (Referring to Sternberg's triarchic theory of intelligence.)

Trichromat A person with normal color vision.

Trichromatic theory The theory that color vision is made possible by three types of cones, some of which respond to red light, some to green, and some to blue.

Tricyclic antidepressants Antidepressant drugs that work by preventing the reuptake of norepinephrine and serotonin by transmitting neurons.

Trimester A period of three months.

Trisomy 21 Another term for Down syndrome.

Trust versus mistrust The first of Erikson's stages of psychosocial development, during which the child comes to (or not to) develop a basic sense of trust in others.

Trying Twenties Sheehy's term for the third decade of life, which is frequently characterized by preoccupation with advancement in the career world.

Turner's syndrome A chromosomal disorder found among females that is caused by having a single X sex chromosome and is characterized by infertility.

Two-point threshold The least distance by which two rods touching the skin must be separated before the subject will report that there are two rods, not one, on 50 percent of occasions.

Type In personality theory, a group of traits that cluster in a meaningful way.

Type A behavior Behavior characterized by a sense of time urgency, competitiveness, and hostility.

U

Ulcer An open sore, as in the lining of the stomach.

Umbilical cord A tube between the mother and her fetus through which nutrients and waste products are conducted.

Unconditional positive regard In self theory, a consistent expression of esteem for the basic value of a person, but not necessarily an unqualified endorsement of all that person's behaviors. A quality shown by the person-centered therapist.

Unconditioned response An unlearned response. A response to an unconditioned stimulus. Abbreviated *UR.*

Unconditioned stimulus A stimulus that elicits a response from an organism without learning. Abbreviated *US.*

Unconscious In psychodynamic theory, descriptive of ideas and feelings that are not available to awareness, in many instances because of the *defense mechanism* of *repression.*

Unobtrusive Not interfering.

Uplifts Notable pleasant daily conditions and experiences.

UR Unconditioned response.

US Unconditioned stimulus.

Uterus The hollow organ within women in which the unborn child develops.

V

Vaccination Purposeful infection with a small amount of an antigen so that in the future the immune system will recognize and efficiently destroy the antigen.

Vacillate Move back and forth.

Vaginal photoplethysmograph An instrument that measures sexual arousal in women as a function of vaginal blood pressure.

Vaginismus Persistent or recurrent spasm of the muscles surrounding the outer part of the vaginal barrel, making entry difficult or impossible.

Validity The degree to which a test or instrument measures or predicts what it is supposed to measure or predict. Also see *reliability.*

Validity scale A group of test items that suggests whether or not the results of a test are valid—whether a person's test responses accurately reflect his or her traits.

Variable A condition that is measured or controlled in a scientific study. A variable can be altered in a measurable manner.

Variable-interval schedule A partial reinforcement schedule in which a variable amount of time must elapse between the previous and subsequent times that reinforcement is available.

Variable-ratio schedule A partial reinforcement schedule in which reinforcement is provided after a variable number of correct responses.

Vasocongestion Accumulation (congestion) of blood, particularly in the genital region.

Vasopressin Another term for *antidiuretic hormone.*

Ventromedial nucleus A central area on the underside of the hypothalamus that appears to function as a stop-eating center. Abbreviated *VMN.*

Vestibular sense The sense that provides information about the position of the body relative to gravity. Also referred to as the sense of equilibrium.

Vicarious Taking the place of another person or thing. In vicarious learning, we learn from the experiences of others.

Visible light The band of electromagnetic energy that produces visual sensations.

Visual accommodation Automatic adjustment of the thickness of the lens in order to focus on objects.

Visual acuity Keenness or sharpness of vision.

Visual capture The tendency of vision to dominate the other senses.

Visual code Mental representation of information as a picture.

Volley principle A modification of the *frequency theory* of pitch perception. The hypothesis that groups of neurons may be able to achieve the effect of firing at very high frequencies by "taking turns" firing—that is, by firing in volleys.

Volt A unit of electrical potential.

Voyeurism A paraphilia in which the person prefers to seek sexual excitement through secret observation of others undressing or engaged in sexual activity.

W

Waxy flexibility A symptom of catatonic schizophrenia in which the person maintains a posture or position into which he or she is placed.

Weaning Accustoming the child not to suck the mother's breast or a baby bottle.

Weber's constant The fraction of the intensity by which a source of physical energy must be increased or decreased so that a difference in intensity will be perceived.

Wernicke-Korsakoff's syndrome An alcohol-related disorder that is characterized by loss of memory and that is thought to reflect nutritional deficiency.

Wernicke's aphasia An aphasia caused by damage to Wernicke's area of the brain. It is characterized by difficulty comprehending the meaning of spoken language and by the production of language that is grammatically correct but confused or meaningless in content.

White matter In the spinal cord, axon bundles that carry messages back and forth from and to the brain.

White noise Discordant sounds of many frequencies, which often produce a lulling effect.

Wish fulfillment In psychodynamic theory, a primitive method used by the id—such as in fantasy and dreams—to attempt to gratify basic impulses.

Working memory See *short-term memory.*

Y

Yerkes-Dodson law The principle that a high level of arousal increases performance on a relatively simple task, whereas a low level of arousal increases performance on a relatively complex task.

Z

Zoophilia A paraphilia in which the person prefers sexual contact with animals for purposes of sexual excitement. Also called *bestiality.*

Zygote A fertilized egg cell or ovum.

REFERENCES

Abel, E. L. (1980). Fetal alcohol syndrome: Behavioral teratology. *Psychological Bulletin, 87,* 29–50.

Abelson, H., Cohen, R., Heaton, E., & Slider, C. (1970). Public attitudes toward and experience with erotic materials. In *Technical Reports of the Commission on Obscenity and Pornography,* Vol. 6. Washington, DC: U.S. Government Printing Office.

Aber, J. L., & Allen, J. P. (1987). Effects of maltreatment of young children on young children's socioemotional development: An attachment theory perspective. *Developmental Psychology, 23,* 406–414.

Abikoff, H., & Gittelman, R. (1985). The normalizing effects of methylphenidate on the classroom behavior of ADDH children. *Journal of Abnormal Child Psychology, 13,* 33–44.

Abraham, G. (1981). Premenstrual tension. *Current Problems in Obstetrics and Gynecology,* 1–39.

Abramowitz, C. V., Abramowitz, S. I., Roback, H. B., & Jackson, C. (1974). Differential effectiveness of directive and nondirective group therapies as a function of client internal-external control. *Journal of Consulting and Clinical Psychology, 42,* 849–853.

Abrams, K. I., & Bennet, J. W. (1981). Changing etiological perspectives in Down's syndrome: Implications for early intervention. *Journal of the Division for Early Childhood, 2,* 109–112.

Abravanel, E., & Gingold, H. (1985). Learning via observation during the second year of life. *Developmental Psychology, 21,* 614–623.

Abravanel, E., & Sigafoos, A. D. (1984). Exploring the presence of imitation during early infancy. *Child Development, 55,* 381–392.

Adair, J. G., Dushenko, T. W., & Lindsay, R. C. L. (1985). Ethical regulations and their impact on research practice. *American Psychologist, 40,* 59–72.

Adams, A., Carnine, D., & Gersten, R. (1982). Instructional strategies for studying context area texts in the intermediate grades. *Reading Research Quarterly, 18,* 27–53.

Adams, H. E., & Chiodo, J. (1983). Sexual deviations. In H. E. Adams & P. B. Sutker (Eds.), *Comprehensive handbook of psychopathology.* New York: Plenum Publishing Co.

Adams, V. (1980). Sex therapies in perspective. *Psychology Today, 14*(8), 35–36.

Adelman, M. R. (1977). A comparison of professionally employed lesbians and heterosexual women on the MMPI. *Archives of Sexual Behavior, 6,* 193–202.

Adelson, A. (1988, March 9). Women still finding bias in engineering. *The New York Times,* p. D6.

Adelson, J. (1982). Still vital after all these years. *Psychology Today, 16*(4), 52–59.

Adickes, E., & Shuman, R. (1981). Fetal muscles and alcohol. *Journal of Pediatric Pathology.*

Adolph, E. F. (1950). Thirst and its inhibition in the stomach. *American Journal of Physiology, 161,* 374–386.

Adorno, T. W., Frenkel-Brunswick, E., & Levinson, D. J. (1950). *The authoritarian personality.* New York: Harper.

Agras, W. S., Southam, M. A., & Taylor, C. B. (1983). Long-term persistence of relaxation-induced blood pressure lowering during the working day. *Journal of Consulting and Clinical Psychology, 51,* 792–794.

Aiello, J. R., & Thompson, D. E. (1980). Personal space, crowding, and spatial behavior in a cultural context. In I. Altman, J. F. Wohlwill, & A. Rapoport (Eds.), *Human behavior and environment,* Vol. 4. New York: Plenum Publishing Co.

Ainsworth, M. D. S. (1963). The development of infant–mother interaction among the Ganda. In D. M. Foss (Ed.), *Determinants of infant behavior,* Vol. 2. New York: Wiley.

Ainsworth, M. D. S. (1979). Infant–mother attachment. *American Psychologist, 34,* 932–937.

Ainsworth, M. D. S. (1984). Attachment. In N. S. Endler & J. McV. Hunt (Eds.), *Personality and the behavioral disorders,* Vol. 1, 2d ed. New York: Wiley.

Ainsworth, M. D. S. (1985). Patterns of infant–mother attachments: Antecedents and effects on development. *Bulletin of the New York Academy of Medicine, 61,* 771–791

Ainsworth, M.D.S. (1989). Attachments beyond infancy. *American Psychologist, 44,* 709–716.

Ainsworth, M. D. S., Blehar, M. C., Waters, E., & Wall, S. (1978). *Patterns of attachment: A psychological study of the strange situation.* Hillsdale, NJ: Erlbaum.

Akil, H. (1978). Endorphins, beta-LPH, and ACTH: Biochemical pharmacological and anatomical studies. *Advances in Biochemical Psychopharmacology, 18,* 125–139.

Akil, H., Mayer, D. J., & Liebeskind, J. L. (1976). Antagonism of stimulation-produced analgesia. *Science, 191,* 961–962.

Albert, M. S. (1981). Geriatric neuropsychology. *Journal of Consulting and Clinical Psychology, 49,* 835–850.

Alemi, B., et al. (1981). Fat digestion in very low-birth-weight infants: Effects of addition of human milk to low-birth-weight formula. *Pediatrics, 68,* 484–489.

Alexander, A. B. (1981). Asthma. In S. N. Haynes & L. Gannon (Eds.), *Psychosomatic disorders: A psychophysiological approach to etiology and treatment.* New York: Praeger Books.

Alexander, R. A., & Barrett, G. U. (1982). Equitable salary increase judgments based upon merit and nonmerit considerations: A cross-national comparison. *International Review of Applied Psychology, 31,* 443–454.

Allen, V. L., & Levine, J. M. (1971). Social support and conformity: The role of independent assessment of reality. *Journal of Experimental Social Psychology, 7,* 48–58.

Allgeier, A. A., & Byrne, D. (1973). Attraction toward the opposite sex as a determinant of physical proximity. *Journal of Social Psychology, 90,* 213–219.

Allgeier, E. R., & Allgeier, A. A. (1984). *Sexual interactions.* Lexington, MA: Heath.

Allon, N., & Fishel, D. (1979). Singles bars. In N. Allon (Ed.), *Urban life styles.* Dubuque: Brown.

Alloy, L. B., & Ahrens, A. H. (1987). Depression and pessimism for the future: Biased use of statistically relevant information in predictions for self versus others. *Journal of Personality and Social Psychology, 52,* 366–378.

Allport, G. W. (1937). *Personality: A psychological interpretation.* New York: Holt, Rinehart and Winston.

Allport, G. W. (1961). *Pattern and growth in personality.* New York: Holt, Rinehart and Winston.

Allport, G. W., & Oddbert, H. S. (1936). Trait names: A psycholexical study. *Psychological Monographs, 47,* 2–11.

Altman, L. K. (1988, January 12). AIDS researchers frustrated in hunt for genetic factors. *The New York Times,* p. C3.

Altman, L. K. (1988, January 26). Cocaine's many dangers: The evidence mounts. *The New York Times,* p. C3.

Amabile, T. M. (1982). Social psychology of creativity: A consensual assessment technique. *Journal of Personality and Social Psychology, 43,* 997–1013.

Amabile, T. M. (1983). The social psychology of creativity: A componential conceptualization. *Journal of Personality and Social Psychology, 45,* 357–376.

Amato, P. R. (1983). Helping behavior in urban and rural environments: Field studies based on taxonomic organization of helping episodes. *Journal of Personality and Social Psychology, 45,* 571–586.

American College of Obstetricians and Gynecologists. (1985, January). *Dysmenorrhea.*

American Psychiatric Association (1987). *Diagnostic and statistical manual of the mental disorders–Third Edition–Revised.* Washington, DC: American Psychiatric Press, Inc.

American Psychological Association (1981). Ethical principles of psychologists. *American Psychologist, 36,* 633–638.

American Psychological Association (1984). Text of position on insanity defense. *APA Monitor, 15*(3), 11.

Amir, M. (1971). *Patterns in forcible rape.* Chicago: University of Chicago Press.

Amoore, J. E. (1970). *The molecular basis of odor.* Springfield, IL: Thomas.

Anastasi, A. (1983). Evolving trait concepts. *American Psychologist, 38,* 175–184.

Andersen, B. L. (1981). A comparison of systematic desensitization and directed masturbation in the treatment of primary orgasmic dysfunction in females. *Journal of Consulting and Clinical Psychology, 49,* 568–570.

Anderson, A. (1982). The great Japanese IQ increase. *Nature, 297,* 180–181.

Anderson, C. W., Nagle, R. J., Roberts, W. A., & Smith, J. W. (1981). Attachment to substitute caregivers as a function of center quality and caregiver involvement. *Child Development, 52,* 53–61.

Anderson, D. J., Noyes, R., Jr., & Crowe, R. (1984). A comparison of panic disorder and generalized anxiety disorder. *American Journal of Psychiatry, 141,* 572–575.

Anderson, J. R. (1976). *Language, memory, and thought.* Hillsdale, NJ: Erlbaum.

Anderson, J. R. (1985). *Cognitive psychology and its implications,* 2d ed. San Francisco: W. H. Freeman.

Andersson, B. (1971). Thirst—and brain control of water balance. *American Scientist, 59,* 408.

Andrews, G., & Harvey, R. (1981). Does psychotherapy benefit neurotic patients? *Archives of General Psychiatry, 38,* 1203–1208.

Aneshensel, C. S., & Huba, G. J. (1983). Depression, alcohol use, and smoking over one year: A four-wave longitudinal causal model. *Journal of Abnormal Psychology, 92,* 134–150.

Antill, J. K. (1983). Sex role complementarity versus similarity in married couples. *Journal of Personality and Social Psychology, 52,* 260–267.

APA Monitor, February 1978, p. 4.

APA Monitor, January 1978, pp. 5, 23.

Apfelbaum, M. (1978). Adaptation to changes in caloric intake. *Progress in Food and Nutritional Science, 2,* 543–559.

Archer, D., Iritani, B., Kimes, D. D., & Barrios, M. (1983). Face-ism: Five studies of sex differences in facial prominence. *Journal of Personality and Social Psychology, 45,* 725–735.

Archer, R. L., Diaz-Loving, R., Gollwitzer, P. M., Davis, M. H., & Foushee, H. C. (1981). The role of dispositional empathy and social evaluation in the empathic mediation of helping. *Journal of Personality and Social Psychology, 40,* 786–796.

Archer, R. P., & Cash, T. F. (1985). Physical attractiveness and maladjustment among psychiatric patients. *Journal of Social and Clinical Psychology, 3,* 170–180.

Argyris, C. (1972). *The applicability of organizational psychology.* Cambridge: Cambridge University Press.

Arkin, R. M., Detchon, C. S., & Maruyama, G. M. (1982). Roles of attribution, affect, and cognitive interference in test anxiety. *Journal of Personality and Social Psychology, 43,* 1111–1124.

Arms, K., & Camp, P. S. (1987). *Biology, 3d ed.* Philadelphia: Saunders College Publishing.

Asarnow, J. R., Carlson, G. A., & Guthrie, D. (1987). Coping strategies, self-perceptions, hopelessness, and perceived family environments in depressed and suicidal children. *Journal of Consulting and Clinical Psychology, 55,* 361–366.

Asch, S. E. (1952). *Social psychology.* Englewood Cliffs, NJ: Prentice-Hall.

Aslin, R. N., & Banks, M. S. (1978). Early visual experience in humans: Evidence for a critical period in the development of binocular vision. In S. Schneider, H. Liebowitz, H. Pick, & H. Stevenson (Eds.), *Psychology: From basic research to practice.* New York: Plenum Publishing Co.

Aslin, R. N., Pisoni, D. B., & Jusczyk, P. W. (1983). Auditory development and speech perception in infancy. In P. H. Mussen (Ed.), *Handbook of child psychology, 4th ed.* New York: Wiley.

Atchley, R. C. (1985). *Social forces and aging: An introduction to social gerontology.* Belmont, CA: Wadsworth.

Atkins, C. J., Kaplan, R. M., Timms, R. M., Reinsch, S., & Lofback, K. (1984). Behavioral exercise programs in the management of chronic obstructive pulmonary disease. *Journal of Consulting and Clinical Psychology, 52,* 591–603.

Atkinson, J., & Huston, T. L. (1984). Sex role orientation and division of labor early in marriage. *Journal of Personality and Social Psychology, 46,* 330–345.

Atkinson, K., MacWhinney, B., & Stoel, C. (1970). An experiment on recognition of babbling. In *Papers and reports on child language development.* Stanford, CA: Stanford University Press.

Atkinson, R. C. (1975). Mnemotechnics in second-language learning. *American Psychologist, 30,* 821–828.

Atkinson, R. C., & Shiffrin, R. M. (1968). Human memory: A proposed system and its control processes. In K. Spence (Ed.), *The psychology of learning and motivation,* Vol. 2. New York: Academic Press.

Attorney General's Commission on Pornography: Final Report. (1986, July). Washington, DC: U.S. Department of Justice.

Ausubel, D. P. (1977). The facilitation of meaningful verbal learning in the classroom. *Educational Psychologist, 12,* 162–178.

Ayllon, T., & Haughton, E. (1962). Control of the behavior of schizophrenic patients by food. *Journal of the Experimental Analysis of Behavior, 5,* 343–352.

Azjen, I., & Fishbein, M. (1977). Attitude-behavior relations: A theoretical analysis and review of empirical research. *Psychological Bulletin, 84,* 888–918.

Azjen, I., & Fishbein, M. (1980). *Understanding attitudes and predicting social behavior.* Englewood Cliffs, NJ: Prentice-Hall.

Bach, G. R., & Deutsch, R. M. (1970). *Pairing.* New York: Peter H. Wyden.

Bagozzi, R. P. (1981). Attitudes, intentions, and behaviors: A test of some key hypotheses. *Journal of Personality and Social Psychology, 41,* 607–627.

Bahrick, H. P., Bahrick, P. O., & Wittlinger, R. P. (1975). Fifty years of memory for names and faces: A cross-sectional approach. *Journal of Experimental Psychology: General, 104,* 54–75.

Bakeman, R., Lumb, J. R., Jackson, R. E., & Smith, D. W. (1986). AIDS-risk group profiles in whites and members of minority groups. *New England Journal of Medicine, 315,* 191–192.

Baker, L. A., DeFries, J. C., & Fulker, D. W. (1983). Longitudinal stability of cognitive ability in the Colorado adoption project. *Child Development, 54,* 290–297.

Bales, J. (1986). New studies cite drug use dangers. *APA Monitor, 17*(11), 26.

Bales, J. (1988). Computers "an adjunct" to animals. *APA Monitor, 19*(11), 10.

Bandura, A. (1973). *Aggression: A social learning analysis.* Englewood Cliffs, NJ: Prentice-Hall.

Bandura, A. (1977). *Social learning theory.* Englewood Cliffs, NJ: Prentice-Hall.

Bandura, A. (1978). The self system in reciprocal determinism. *American Psychologist, 33,* 344–358.

Bandura, A. (1981). Self-referrant thought: A developmental analysis of self-efficacy. In J. H. Flavell & L. Ross (Eds.), *Social cognitive development: Frontiers and possible futures.* Cambridge: Cambridge University Press.

Bandura, A. (1982). Self-efficacy mechanism in human agency. *American Psychologist, 37,* 122–147.

Bandura, A. (1986). *Social foundations of thought and action: A social-cognitive theory.* Englewood Cliffs, NJ: Prentice-Hall.

Bandura, A., Blanchard, E. B., & Ritter, B. (1969). The relative efficacy of desensitization and modeling approaches for inducing behavioral, affective, and cognitive changes. *Journal of Personality and Social Psychology, 13,* 173–199.

Bandura, A., & McDonald, F. J. (1963). Influence of social reinforcement and the behavior of models in shaping children's moral judgments. *Journal of Abnormal and Social Psychology, 67,* 274–281.

Bandura, A., Reese, L., & Adams, N. E. (1982). Microanalysis of action and fear arousal as a function of differential levels of perceived self-efficacy. *Journal of Personality and Social Psychology, 43,* 5–21.

Bandura, A., & Rosenthal, T. L. (1966). Vicarious classical conditioning as a function of fear arousal. *Journal of Personality and Social Psychology, 3,* 54–62.

Bandura, A., Ross, D., & Ross, S. A. (1963a). A comparative test of the status envy, and the secondary reinforcement theories of identificatory learning. *Journal of Abnormal and Social Psychology, 67,* 527–534.

Bandura, A., Ross, S. A., & Ross, D. (1963b). Imitation of film-mediated aggressive models. *Journal of Abnormal and Social Psychology, 66,* 3–11.

Bandura, A., Taylor, C. B., Williams, S. L., Medford, I. N., & Barchas, J. D. (1985). Catecholamine secretion as a function of perceived coping self-efficacy. *Journal of Consulting and Clinical Psychology, 53,* 406–414.

Bangert, R., Kulik, J., & Kulik, C. (1983). Individualized systems of instruction in secondary schools. *Review of Educational Research, 53,* 143–158.

Banks, M. S., & Salapatek, P. (1981). Infant pattern vision: A new approach based on the contrast selectivity function. *Journal of Experimental Child Psychology, 31,* 1–45.

Banks, M. S., & Salapatek, P. (1983). Infant visual perception. In M. M. Haith & J. J. Campos (Eds.), *Handbook of child psychology,* Vol. 2. New York: Wiley.

Banmen, J., & Vogel, N. (1985). The relationship between marital quality and interpersonal sexual communication. *Family Therapy, 12,* 45–58.

Banyai, E. I., & Hilgard, E. R. (1976). A comparison of active-alert hypnotic induction with traditional relaxation induction. *Journal of Abnormal Psychology, 85,* 218–224.

Barbach, L. G. (1975). *For yourself: The fulfillment of female sexuality.* Garden City, NY: Doubleday.

Barber, T. X. (1970). *LSD, marihuana, yoga, and hypnosis.* Chicago: Aldine.

Barber, T. X. (1984). Hypnosis, deep relaxation, and active relaxation: Data, theory, and clinical applications. In R. L. Woolfolk & P. M. Lehrer (Eds.), *Principles and practice of stress management.* New York: Guilford Press.

Barber, T. X., Spanos, N. P., & Chaves, J. F. (1974). *Hypnosis, imagination, and human potentialities.* New York: Pergamon Press.

Bard, P. (1934). The neurohumoral basis of emotional reactions. In C. A. Murchison (Ed.), *Handbook of general experimental psychology.* Worcester, MA: Clark University Press.

Bardwick, J. M. (1971). *Psychology of women: A study of biocultural conflicts.* New York: Harper & Row.

Bardwick, J. M. (1980). The seasons of a woman's life. In D. G. McGuigan (Ed.), *Women's lives: New theory, research, and policy.* Ann Arbor: University of Michigan, Center for Continuing Education of Women.

Barefoot, J. C., Dahlstrom, W. G., & Williams, R. B., Jr. (1983). Rapid communication, hostility, CHD incidence, and total mortality: A 25-year follow-up study of 225 physicians. *Psychosomatic Medicine, 45,* 59–63.

Barkley, R. A., Karlsson, J., Strzelecki, E., & Murphy, J. V. (1984). Effects of age and Ritalin dosage on the mother–child interactions of hyperactive children. *Journal of Consulting and Clinical Psychology, 52,* 750–758.

Barlow, D. H. (1986). Causes of sexual dysfunction: The role of anxiety and cognitive interference. *Journal of Consulting and Clinical Psychology, 54,* 140–148.

Barlow, D. H. (1986). Behavioral conception and treatment of panic. *Psychopharmacology Bulletin, 22,* 802–806.

Barlow, D. H., Vermilyea, J., Blanchard, E. B., Vermilyea, B. B., DiNardo, P. A., & Cerny, J. A. (1985). The phenomenon of panic. *Journal of Abnormal Psychology, 94,* 291–297.

Barnard, K. E., & Bee, H. L. (1983). The impact of temporally patterned stimulation on the development of preterm infants. *Child Development, 54,* 1156–1167.

Barnes, M. L., & Buss, D. M. (1985). Sex differences in the interpersonal behavior of married couples. *Journal of Personality and Social Psychology, 48,* 654–661.

Barnett, R. C., & Baruch, G. K. (1985). Women's involvement in multiple roles and psychological distress. *Journal of Personality and Social Psychology, 49,* 135–145.

Baron, R. A.. (1971). Behavioral effects of interpersonal attraction: Compliance with requests from liked and disliked others. *Psychonomic Science, 25,* 325–326.

Baron, R. A. (1973). The "foot-in-the-door" phenomenon: Mediating effects of size of first request and sex of requester. *Bulletin of the Psychonomic Society, 2,* 113–114.

Baron, R. A. (1983). "Sweet smell of success"? The impact of pleasant artificial scents on evaluations of job applicants. *Journal of Applied Psychology, 68,* 709–713.

Baron, R. A. (1983). *Behavior in organizations.* Boston: Allyn and Bacon.

Baron, R. A. (1987). Effects of negative ions on interpersonal attraction. *Journal of Personality and Social Psychology, 52,* 547–553.

Baron, R. A. (1988). Cited in D. Goleman, Why job criticism fails: Psychology's new findings. *The New York Times,* July 26, 1988, pp. C1, C15.

Baron, R. A., & Byrne, D. (1987). *Social psychology: Understanding human interaction,* 5th ed. Boston: Allyn and Bacon.

Baron, R. A., Mandel, D. R., Adams, C. A., & Griffen, L. M. (1976). Effects of social density in university residential requirements. *Journal of Personality and Social Psychology, 34,* 434–446.

Baron, R. A., Russell, G. W., & Arms, R. L. (1985). Negative ions and behavior: Impact on mood, memory, and aggression among Type A and Type B persons. *Journal of Personality and Social Psychology, 48,* 746–754.

Barr, H. M., Streissguth, A. P., Martin, D. C., & Herman, C. S. (1984). Infant size at 8 months of age: Relationship to maternal use of alcohol, nicotine, and caffeine during pregnancy. *Pediatrics, 74,* 336–341.

Barrow, G. M., & Smith, P. A. (1983). *Aging, the individual, and society,* 2d ed. St. Paul: West.

Bar-Tal, D., & Saxe, L. (1976). Perceptions of similarly and dissimilarly physically attractive couples and individuals. *Journal of Personality and Social Psychology, 33,* 772–781.

Bartus, R. T., Dean, R. L., III, Beer, R., & Lippa, A. S. (1982). The cholinergic hypothesis of geriatric memory dysfunction. *Science, 217,* 408–417.

Baruch, G., Barnett, R., & Rivers, C. (1983). *Lifeprints.* New York: McGraw-Hill.

Basham, R. B. (1986). Scientific and practical advantages of comparative design in psychotherapy outcome research. *Journal of Consulting and Clinical Psychology, 54,* 88–94.

Bates, E., Bretherton, I., Beeghly-Smith, M., & McNew, S. (1982). Social bases of language development: A reassessment. In H. W. Reese & L. P. Lipsitt (Eds.), *Advances in child development and behavior,* Vol. 16. New York: Academic Press.

Bates, E., & MacWhinney, B. (1982). A functionalist approach to grammatical development. In L. Gleitman & H. E. Wanner (Eds.), *Language acquisition: The state of the art.* Cambridge: Cambridge University Press.

Batson, C. D., Duncan, B. D., Ackerman, P., Buckley, T., & Birch, K. (1981). Is empathic emotion a source of altruistic motivation? *Journal of Personality and Social Psychology, 40,* 290–302.

Baucom, D. H., & Aiken, P. A. (1981). Effect of depressed mood on eating among obese and nonobese dieting and nondieting persons. *Journal of Personality and Social Psychology, 41,* 577–585.

Baucom, D. H., & Aiken, P. A. (1984). Sex role identity, marital satisfaction, and response to behavioral marital therapy. *Journal of Consulting and Clinical Psychology, 52,* 438–444.

Baucom, D. H., Besch, P. K., & Callahan, S. (1985). Relationship between testosterone concentration, sex role identity, and personality among females. *Journal of Personality and Social Psychology, 48,* 1218–1226.

Baucom, D. H., & Danker-Brown, P. (1979). Influence of sex roles on the development of learned helplessness. *Journal of Consulting and Clinical Psychology, 47,* 928–936.

Baucom, D. H., & Danker-Brown, P. (1983). Peer ratings of males and females possessing different sex role identities. *Journal of Personality Assessment, 44,* 334–343.

Bauer, R. H., & Fuster, J. M. (1976). Delayed-matching and delayed-response deficit from cooling dorsolateral prefrontal cortex in monkeys. *Journal of Comparative and Physiological Psychology, 90,* 293–302.

Bauer, W. D., & Twentyman, C. T. (1985). Abusing, neglectful, and comparison mothers' responses to child-related and non-child-related stressors. *Journal of Consulting and Clinical Psychology, 53,* 335–343.

Baum, A., & Davis, G. E. (1980). Reducing the stress of high-density living: An architectural intervention. *Journal of Personality and Social Psychology, 38,* 471–481.

Baum, A., & Nesselhof, S. E. A. (1988). Psychological research and the prevention, etiology, and treatment of AIDS. *American Psychologist, 43,* 900–906.

Baumann, L. J., & Leventhal, H. (1985). "I can tell when my blood pressure is up, can't I?" *Health Psychology, 4,* 203–218.

Baum-Baicker, C. (1984). Treating and preventing alcohol abuse in the workplace. *American Psychologist, 39,* 454.

Baumeister, R. F., & Covington, M. V. (1985). Self-esteem, persuasion, and retrospective distortion of initial attitudes. *Electronic Social Psychology, 1,* 1–22.

Baumgardner, A. H., Heppner, P. P., & Arkin, R. M. (1986). Role of causal attribution in personal problem solving. *Journal of Personality and Social Psychology, 50,* 636–643.

Baumrind, D. (1985). Research using intentional deception: Ethical issues revisited. *American Psychologist, 40,* 165–174.

Baumrind, D. (1986). Sex differences in moral reasoning: Response to Walker's (1984) conclusion that there are none. *Child Development, 57,* 511–521.

Beal, C. R., & Flavell, J. H. (1983). Young speakers' evaluation of their listeners' comprehensions in a referential communication task. *Child Development, 54,* 148–153.

Beal, C. R., & Flavell, J. H. (1984). Development of the ability to distinguish communicative attention and literal message meaning. *Child Development, 55,* 920–928.

Beard, R. R., & Wertheim, G. A. (1967). Behavioral impairment associated with small doses of carbon monoxide. *American Journal of Public Health, 57,* 2012–2022.

Beardslee, W. R., Bemporad, J., Keller, M. B., & Klerman, G. L. (1983). Children of parents with major affective disorder: A review. *American Journal of Psychiatry, 140,* 825–832.

Beatty, W. W. (1979). Gonadal hormones and sex differences in nonreproductive behaviors in rodents: Organizational and activational influences. *Hormones and Behavior, 12,* 112–163.

Beauchamp, G. (1981). Paper presented to the Conference on the Determination of Behavior by Chemical Stimuli. Hebrew University, Jerusalem.

Beck, A. T. (1976). *Cognitive therapy and the emotional disorders.* New York: International Universities Press.

Beck, A. T. (1985). Theoretical perspectives on clinical anxiety. In A. H. Tuma, & J. D. Maser (Eds.), *Anxiety and the anxiety disorders.* Hillsdale, NJ: Erlbaum.

Beck, A. T., Epstein, N., Brown, G., & Steer, R. A. (1988). An inventory for measuring clinical anxiety: Psychometric properties. *Journal of Consulting and Clinical Psychology, 56,* 893–897.

Beck, A. T., Rush, A. J., Show, B. F., & Emery, G. (1979). *Cognitive therapy of depression.* New York: Guilford Press.

Beck, A. T., Ward, C. H., Mendelson, M., Mock, J. E., & Erbaugh, J. K. (1962). Reliability of psychiatric diagnoses II: A study of consistency of clinical judgments and ratings. *American Journal of Psychiatry, 119,* 351–357.

Beck, J., Elsner, A., & Silverstein, C. (1977). Position uncertainty and the perception of apparent movement. *Perception and psychophysics, 21,* 33–38.

Beck, R. C. (1978). *Motivation: Theories and principles.* Englewood Cliffs, NJ: Prentice-Hall.

Becker, M. H., & Maiman, L. A. (1980). Strategies for enhancing patient compliance. *Journal of Community Health, 6,* 113–135.

Beckham, E. E., & Leber, W. R. (1985). The comparative efficacy of psychotherapy and pharmacotherapy for depression. In E. E. Beckham & W. R. Leber (Eds)., *Handbook of depression: Treatment, assessment, and research.* Homewood, IL: Dorsey Press.

Beckman, L. J., & Houser, B. B. (1982). The consequences of childlessness on the social-psychological well-being of older women. *Journal of Gerontology, 37,* 243–250.

Beckwith, L., & Parmelee, A. H., Jr. (1986). EEG patterns of preterm infants, home environment, and later IQ. *Child Development, 57,* 777–789.

Bee, H. L., et al. (1982). Prediction of IQ and language skill from perinatal status, child performance, family characteristics, and mother–infant interaction. *Child Development, 53,* 1134–1156.

Behrman, R. E., & Vaughn, V. C., III. (1983). *Pediatrics.* Philadelphia: W. B. Saunders Co.

Beit-Hallahmi, B., & Rabin, A. I. (1977). The kibbutz as a social experiment and as a child-rearing laboratory. *American Psychologist, 32,* 532–544.

Bell, A. P., & Weinberg, M. S. (1978). *Homosexualities: A study of diversity among men and women.* New York: Simon and Schuster.

Bell, A. P., Weinberg, M. S., & Hammersmith, S. K. (1981). *Sexual preference: Its development in men and women.* Bloomington, IN: University of Indiana Press.

Bell, P. A. (1982, August). Theoretical interpretations of heat stress. Paper presented to the American Psychological Association, Washington, DC.

Bell, R. R. (1983). *Marriage and family interaction,* 6th ed. Homewood, IL: Dorsey.

Belsky, J. (1980). Child maltreatment: An ecological integration. *American Psychologist, 35,* 320–335.

Belsky, J. (1984). The determinants of parenting: A process model. *Child Development, 55,* 83–96.

Belsky, J. (1984). *The psychology of aging: Theory, research, and practice.* Monterey, CA: Brooks/Cole.

Belsky, J., Gilstrap, B., & Rovine, M. (1984). The Pennsylvania and infant family development project, I: Stability and change in mother–infant and father–infant interaction in a family setting at one, three, and nine months. *Child Development, 55,* 692–705.

Belsky, J., & Steinberg, L. D. (1978). The effects of day care: A critical review. *Child Development, 49,* 929–949.

Belsky, J., & Steinberg, L. D. (1979, July–August). What does research teach us about day care? A follow-up report. *Children Today,* pp. 21–26.

Belsky, J., Steinberg, L. D., & Walker, A. (1982). The ecology of day care. In M. E. Lamb (Ed.), *Nontraditional families: Parenting and child development.* Hillsdale, NJ: Erlbaum.

Bem, D. J. (1972). Self-perception theory. In L. Berkowitz (Ed.), *Advances in experimental social psychology,* Vol. 6. New York: Academic Press.

Bem, D. J., & Allen, A. (1974). On predicting some of the people some of the time: The search for cross-situational consistencies in behavior. *Psychological Review, 81,* 506–520.

Bem, S. L. (1974). The measurement of psychological androgyny. *Journal of Consulting and Clinical Psychology, 42,* 151–162.

Bem, S. L. (1975). Sex role adaptability: One consequence of psychological androgyny. *Journal of Personality and Social Psychology, 31,* 634–643.

Bem, S. L. (1981). Gender schema theory: A cognitive account of sex typing. *Psychological Review, 88,* 354–364.

Bem, S. L. (1983). Gender schema theory and its implications for child development: Raising gender-aschematic children in a gender-schematic society. *Signs: Journal of Women in Culture and Society, 8,* 598–616.

Bem, S. L. (1985). Androgyny and gender schema theory: A conceptual and empirical integration. In T. B. Sonderegger (Ed.), *Nebraska symposium on motivation.* Lincoln, NE: University of Nebraska Press.

Bem, S. L., & Lenney, E. (1976). Sex typing and the avoidance of cross-sexed behaviors. *Journal of Personality and Social Psychology, 33,* 48–54.

Bem, S. L., Martyna, W., & Watson, C. (1976). Sex typing and androgyny: Further explorations of the expressive domain. *Journal of Personality and Social Psychology, 34,* 1016–1023.

Bemis, K. M. (1978). Current approaches to the etiology and treatment of anorexia nervosa. *Psychological Bulletin, 85,* 593–617.

Benbow, C. P., & Stanley, J. C. (1980). Sex differences in mathematical ability: Fact or artifact? *Science, 210,* 1029–1031.

Benbow, C. P., & Stanley, J. C. (1983). Sex differences in mathematical reasoning ability: More facts. *Science, 229,* 1029–1030.

Benedek, E., & Vaughn, R. (1982). Voluntary childlessness. In M. Kirkpatrick (Ed.), *Women's sexual experience.* New York: Plenum Publishing Co.

Benedict, R. (1934). *Patterns of culture.* Boston: Houghton Mifflin.

Bennett, D. (1985). Rogers: More intuition in therapy. *APA Monitor, 16*(10), 3.

Bennett, W., & Gurin, J. (1982). *The dieter's dilemma: Eating less and weighing more.* New York: Basic Books.

Bensinger, P. B. (1982, November–December). Drugs in the workplace. *Harvard Business Review,* 48–60.

Benson, H. (1975). *The relaxation response.* New York: Morrow.

Benson, H., Manzetta, B. R., & Rosner, B. (1973). Decreased systolic blood pressure in hypertensive subjects who practiced meditation. *Journal of Clinical Investigation, 52,* 8.

Benson, P. L., Karabenick, S. A., & Lerner, R. M. (1976). Pretty pleases: The effects of physical attractiveness, race, and sex on receiving help. *Journal of Experimental Social Psychology, 12,* 409–415.

Bentler, P. M. (1976). A typology of transsexualism: Gender identity theory and data. *Archives of Sexual Behavior, 5,* 567–584.

Bentler, P. M., & Speckart, G. (1981). Attitudes "cause" behaviors: A structural equation analysis. *Journal of Personality and Social Psychology, 40,* 226–238.

Berg, J. H., & Peplau, L. A. (1982). Loneliness: The relationship of self-disclosure and androgyny. *Personality and Social Psychology Bulletin, 8,* 624–630.

Berger, P. A. (1978). Medical treatment of mental illness. *Science, 200,* 974–981.

Berkman, L. F., & Breslow, L. (1983). *Health and ways of living: The Alameda County Study.* New York: Oxford University Press.

Berkman, L. F., & Syme, S. L. (1979). Social networks, host resistance, and mortality: A nine-year follow-up study of Alameda County residents. *American Journal of Epidemiology, 109,* 186–204.

Berkowitz, L. (1983). Aversively stimulated aggression: Some parallels and differences in research with animals and humans. *American Psychologist, 38,* 1135–1144.

Berkowitz, L. (1987). Mood, self-awareness, and willingness to help. *Journal of Personality and Social Psychology, 52,* 721–729.

Berkowitz, L., & Donnerstein, E. (1982). External validity is more than skin deep: Some answers to criticisms of laboratory experiments. *American Psychologist, 37,* 245–257.

Berkowitz, W. R., Nebel, J. C., & Reitman, J. W. (1971). Height and interpersonal attraction: The 1960 mayoral election in New York City. Paper presented to the American Psychological Association, Washington, DC.

Berman, J. S., Miller, R. C., & Massman, P. J. (1985). Cognitive therapy versus systematic desensitization: Is one therapy superior? *Psychological Bulletin, 97,* 451–461.

Bernardo, M., DeFlores, T., Valdes, M., Mestre, L., & Fernandez, G. (1985, May). Type A personality in a coronary disease sample. Paper presented at the Fourth World Congress of Biological Psychiatry, Philadelphia.

Berne, E. (1976a). *Beyond games and scripts.* New York: Grove Press.

Berne, E. (1976b). *Games people play.* New York: Ballantine Books.

Bernstein, B. E. (1977). Effect of menstruation on academic performance among college women. *Archives of Sexual Behavior, 6,* 289–296.

Bernstein, E. (1987). Reply to Terrace. *American Psychologist, 42,* 272–273.

Bernstein, I. L. (1985). Learned food aversions in the progression of cancer and its treatment. In N. S. Braverman & P. Bernstein (Eds.), *Experimental assessments and clinical application of conditioned food aversions. Annals of the New York Academy of Sciences, 443.*

Bernstein, W. M., Stephenson, B. O., Snyder, M. L., & Wicklund, R. A. (1983). Causal ambiguity and heterosexual affiliation. *Journal of Experimental Social Psychology, 19,* 78–92.

Berntzen, D., & Götestam, K. G. (1987). Effects of on-demand versus fixed-interval schedules in the treatment of chronic pain with analgesic compounds. *Journal of Consulting and Clinical Psychology, 55,* 213–217.

Berscheid, E. (1976). Theories of interpersonal attraction. In B. B. Wolman & L. R. Pomeroy (Eds.), *International encyclopaedia of neurology, psychiatry, psychoanalysis, and psychology.* New York: Springer.

Berscheid, E., Dion, K., Walster, E., & Walster, G. W. (1971). Physical attractiveness and dating choice: A test of the matching hypothesis. *Journal of Experimental Social Psychology, 7,* 173–189.

Berscheid, E., & Walster, E. (1974a). A little bit about love. In T. L. Huston (Ed.), *Foundations of interpersonal attraction.* New York: Academic Press.

Berscheid, E., & Walster, E. (1974b). Physical attractiveness. In L. Berkowitz (Ed.), *Advances in experimental social psychology,* Vol. 7. New York: Academic Press.

Berscheid, E., & Walster, E. (1978). *Interpersonal attraction.* Reading, MA: Addison-Wesley.

Bersoff, D. N. (1981). Testing and the law. *American Psychologist, 36,* 1159–1166.

Bertelson, A. D., Marks, P. A., & May, G. D. (1982). MMPI and race: A controlled study. *Journal of Consulting and Clinical Psychology, 50,* 316–318.

Betz, N. E., & Hackett, G. (1981). The relationships of career-related self-efficacy expectations to perceived career options in college women and men. *Journal of Counseling Psychology, 28,* 399–410.

Bexton, W. H., Heron, W., & Scott, T. H. (1954). Effects of decreased variation in the sensory environment. *Canadian Journal of Psychology, 8,* 70–76.

Biglan, A., & Craker, D. (1982). Effects of pleasant-activities manipulation on depression. *Journal of Consulting and Clinical Psychology, 50,* 436–438.

Billings, A. G., Cronkite, R. C., & Moos, R. H. (1983). Social-environmental factors in unipolar depression: Comparisons of depressed patients and nondepressed controls. *Journal of Abnormal Psychology, 92,* 119–133.

Biran, M., & Wilson, G. T. (1981). Treatment of phobic disorders using cognitive and exposure methods: A self-efficacy analysis. *Journal of Consulting and Clinical Psychology, 49,* 886–899.

Birch, H. G., & Rabinowitz, H. S. (1951). The negative effect of previous experience on productive thinking. *Journal of Experimental Psychology, 42,* 121–125.

Birren, J. E. (1983). Aging in America: Roles for psychology. *American Psychologist, 38,* 298–299.

Bjorklund, A., & Stenevi, U. (1984). Intracerebral neural implants: Neuronal replacement and reconstruction of damaged circuitries. *Annual Review of Neuroscience, 7,* 279–308.

Bjorklund, D. F., & de Marchena, M. R. (1984). Developmental shifts in the basis of organization in memory: The role of associative versus categorical relatedness in children's free recall. *Child Development, 55,* 952–962.

Blackburn, I. M., et al. (1981). The efficacy of cognitive therapy in depression: A treatment trial using cognitive therapy and pharmacotherapy, each alone and in combination. *British Journal of Psychiatry, 139,* 181–189.

Blackler, F. H. M., & Brown, C. A. (1978). *Job redesign and management control: Studies in British Leyland and Volvo.* New York: Praeger Books.

Blakeley, M. K. (1985). Is one woman's sexuality another woman's pornography? The question behind a major legal battle. *Ms., 13*(10), 37–47, 120–123.

Blanchard, E. B., Andrasik, F., Ahles, T. A., Teders, S. J., & O'Keefe, D. M. (1980). Migraine and tension headache: A meta-analytic review. *Behavior Therapy, 11,* 613–621.

Blanchard, E. B., Andrasik, F., Neff, D. F., Arena, J. G., Ahles, T. A., Jurish, S. E., Pallmeyer, T. P., Saunders, N. L., Teders, S. J., Barron, K. D., & Rodichok, L. D. (1982). Biofeedback and relaxation training with three kinds of headache: Treatment effects and their prediction. *Journal of Consulting and Clinical Psychology, 50,* 562–575.

Blanchard, E. B., Andrasik, F., Evans, D. D., Neff, D. F., Appelbaum, K. A., & Rodichok, L. D. (1985). Behavioral treatment of 250 chronic headache patients: A clinical replication series. *Behavior Therapy, 16,* 308–327.

Blanchard, E. B., Andrasik, F., Guarnieri, P., Neff, D. F., & Rodichok, L. D. (1987). Two-, three-, and four-year follow-up on the self-regulatory treatment of chronic headache. *Journal of Consulting and Clinical Psychology, 55,* 257–259.

Blanchard, R., Steiner, B. W., & Clemmensen, L. H. (1985). Gender dysphoria, gender reorientation, and the clinical management of transsexualism. *Journal of Consulting and Clinical Psychology, 53,* 295–304.

Blasi, A. (1980). Bridging moral cognition and moral action: A critical review of the literature. *Psychological Bulletin, 88,* 1–45.

Bloch, V., Hennevin, E., & Leconte, P. (1979). Relationship between paradoxical sleep and memory processes. In M. A. B. Braszier (Ed.), *Brain mechanisms in memory and learning: From the single neuron to man.* New York: Raven Press.

Block, J. (1983). Differential premises arising from differential socialization of the sexes: Some conjectures. *Child Development, 54,* 1335–1354.

Block, J., & Block, J. (1951). An investigation of the relationship between intolerance of ambiguity and ethnocentrism. *Journal of Personality, 19,* 303–311.

Bloom, L., Lahey, L., Hood, L., Lifter, K., & Fiess, K. (1980). Complex sentences: Acquisition of syntactic connectives and the semantic relations they encode. *Journal of Child Language, 7,* 235–261.

Bloom, L., Merkin, S., & Wootten, J. (1982). *Wh*-questions: Linguistic factors that contribute to the sequence of acquisition. *Child Development, 53,* 1084–1092.

Blumberg, S. H., & Izard, C. E. (1985). Affective and cognitive characteristics of depression in 10- and 11-year-old children. *Journal of Personality and Social Psychology, 49,* 194–202.

Bodenhausen, G. V., & Wyer, R. S. (1985). Effects of stereotypes on decision making and information-processing strategies. *Journal of Personality and Social Psychology, 48,* 267–282.

Boffey, P. M. (1988, February 14). Spread of AIDS abating, but deaths will still soar. *The New York Times,* pp. 1, 36.

Bolles, R. C., & Faneslow, M. S. (1982). Endorphins and behavior. *Annual Review of Psychology, 33,* 87–101.

Bonica, J. J. (Ed.) (1980). *Pain.* New York: Raven Press.

Booth, A., & Edwards, J. N. (1985). Age at marriage and marital instability. *Journal of Marriage and the Family, 47,* 67–75.

Booth-Kewley, S., & Friedman, H. S. (1987). Psychological predictors of heart disease: A quantitative review. *Psychological Bulletin, 101,* 343–362.

Borgida, E., & Campbell, B. (1982). Belief relevance and attitude-behavior consistency: The moderating role of personal experience. *Journal of Personality and Social Psychology, 42,* 239–247.

Borkan, G. A., et al. (1986). Body weight and coronary heart disease risk: Patterns of risk factor change associated with long-term weight change. The Normative Aging Study. *American Journal of Epidemiology, 124,* 410–419.

Bornstein, M. H., Kessen, W., & Weiskopf, S. (1976). The categories of hue in infancy. *Science, 191,* 201–202.

Bornstein, M. H., & Marks, L. E. (1982). Color revisionism. *Psychology Today, 16*(1), 64–73.

Boskind-White, M., & White, W. C. (1983). *Bulimarexia: The binge/purge cycle.* New York: W. W. Norton.

Boskind-White, M., & White, W. C. (1986). Bulimarexia: A historical-sociocultural perspective. In K. D. Brownell & J. P. Foreyt (Eds.), *Handbook of eating disorders.* New York: Basic Books.

Boston Women's Health Book Collective. (1984). *The new our bodies, ourselves.* New York: Simon and Schuster.

Bouchard, T. J., Jr., & McGue, M. (1981). Familial studies of intelligence: A review. *Science, 212,* 1055–1059.

Bower, G. H. (1981). Mood and memory. *American Psychologist, 36,* 129–148.

Bowerman, M. F. (1982). Starting to talk worse: Clues to language acquisition from children's late speech errors. In S. Strauss (Ed.), *U-shaped behavioral growth.* New York: Academic Press.

Bowlby, J. (1973). Separation. *Attachment and loss,* Vol. 2. New York: Basic Books.

Boyatzis, R. E. (1974). The effect of alcohol consumption on the aggressive behavior of men. *Quarterly Journal for the Study of Alcohol, 35,* 959–972.

Bradley, R. H., & Caldwell, B. M. (1976). The relation of infants' home environments to mental test performance at 54 months: A follow-up study. *Child Development, 47,* 1172–1174.

Bradley, R. H., & Caldwell, B. M. (1984). The relation of infants' home environments to achievement test performance in first grade: A follow-up study. *Child Development, 55,* 803–809.

Braitman, L. E., Adlin, E. V., & Stanton, J. L., Jr. (1985). Obesity and caloric intake. *Journal of Chronic Diseases, 38,* 727–732.

Bram, S. (1984). Voluntarily childless women: Traditional or nontraditional? *Sex Roles, 10,* 195–206.

Bransford, J. D., Nitsch, K. E., & Franks, J. J. (1977). Schooling and the facilitation of knowing. In R. C. Anderson, R. J. Spiro, & W. E. Montague (Eds.), *Schooling and the acquisition of knowledge.* Hillsdale, NJ: Erlbaum.

Brantley, P. J., McKnight, G. T., Jones, G. N., Dietz, L. S., & Tulley, R. (1988). Convergence between the daily stress inventory and endocrine measures of stress. *Journal of Consulting and Clinical Psychology, 56,* 549–551.

Braun, B. (1988). *The treatment of multiple personality disorder.* Washington, DC: American Psychiatric Press.

Bray, D. W. (1982). The assessment center and the study of lives. *American Psychologist, 37,* 180–189.

Bray, N. W., Hersh, R. E., & Turner, L. A. (1985). Selective remembering during adolescence. *Developmental Psychology, 21,* 290–294.

Bray, R. M., & Sugarman, R. (1980). Social facilitation among interaction groups: Evidence for the evaluation-apprehension hypothesis. *Personality and Social Psychology Bulletin, 6,* 137–142.

Breckler, S. J. (1984). Empirical validation of affect, behavior, and cognition as distinct components of attitude. *Journal of Personality and Social Psychology, 47,* 1191–1205.

Brent, E., & Granberg, D. (1982). Subjective agreement with the presidential candidates of 1976 and 1980. *Journal of Personality and Social Psychology, 42,* 393–403.

Brewer, W. F., & Pani, J. R. (1984). The structure of human memory. In G. H. Bower (Ed.), *The psychology of learning and motivation,* Vol. 17. New York: Academic Press.

Briddell, D. W., & Wilson, G. T. (1976). Effects of alcohol and expectancy set on male sexual arousal. *Journal of Abnormal Psychology, 85,* 225–234.

Bridges, K. (1932). Emotional development in early infancy. *Child Development, 3,* 324–341.

Bridgwater, C. A. (1982). What candor can do. *Psychology Today, 16*(5), 16.

Brigham, J. C. (1980). Limiting conditions of the "physical attractiveness stereotype": Attributions about divorce. *Journal of Research in Personality, 14,* 365–375.

Brigham, T. A., Hopper, C., Hill, B., DeArmas, A., & Newsom, P. (1985). A self-management program for disruptive adolescents in the school: A clinical replication analysis. *Behavior Therapy, 16,* 99–115.

Brim, O. G., & Kagan, J. (1980). *Continuity and change in human development.* Cambridge, MA: Harvard University Press.

Brody, J. E. (1988, May 5). Sifting fact from myth in the face of asthma's growing threat to American children. *The New York Times,* p. B19.

Broman, S. H., Nichols, P. L., & Kennedy, N. A. (1975). *Preschool IQ: Prenatal and early developmental correlates.* Hillsdale, NJ: Erlbaum.

Bronfenbrenner, U. (1960). Freudian theories of identification and their derivatives. *Child Development, 31,* 15–40.

Brook, J. S., Lukoff, J. F., & Whiteman, M. (1980). Initiation into marihuana use. *Journal of Genetic Psychology, 137,* 133–142.

Brooks, J. (1985). Polygraph testing: Thoughts of a skeptical legislator. *American Psychologist, 40,* 348–354.

Brooks, J., Ruble, D. N., & Clarke, A. E. (1977). College women's attitudes and expectations concerning menstrual-related changes. *Psychosomatic Medicine, 39,* 288.

Brooks, V. R. (1982). Sex differences in student dominance behavior in female and male professors' classrooms. *Sex Roles, 8,* 683–690.

Broverman, I. K., Vogel, S. R., Broverman, D. M., Clarkson, F. E., & Rosenkrantz, P. S. (1972). Sex role stereotypes: A current appraisal. *Journal of Social Issues, 28,* 59–78.

Brown, B. B., & Altman, J. (1981). Territoriality and residential crime. In P. A. Brantingham & P. L. Brantingham (Eds.), *Urban crime and environmental criminology.* Beverly Hills, CA: Sage Press.

Brown, E. L., & Deffenbacher, K. (1979). *Perception and the senses.* Oxford: Oxford University Press.

Brown, F. G. (1983). *Principles of educational and psychological testing.* New York: Holt, Rinehart and Winston.

Brown, M., Amoroso, D., & Ware, E. (1976). Behavioral aspects of viewing pornography. *Journal of Social Psychology, 98,* 235–245.

Brown, R. (1970). The first sentences of child and chimpanzee. In R. Brown (Ed.), *Psycholinguistics.* New York: Free Press.

Brown, R. (1973). *A first language: The early stages.* Cambridge, MA: Harvard University Press.

Brown, R., & Hanlon, C. (1970). Derivational complexity and order of acquisition in child speech. In J. R. Hayes (Ed.), *Cognition and the development of language.* New York: Wiley.

Brown, R., & Kulik, J. (1977). Flashbulb memories. *Cognition, 5,* 73–99.

Brown, R., & McNeill, D. (1966). The tip-of-the-tongue phenomenon. *Journal of Verbal Learning and Verbal Behavior, 5,* 325–337.

Brown, S. A. (1985). Expectancies versus background in the prediction of college drinking patterns. *Journal of Consulting and Clinical Psychology, 53,* 123–130.

Brown, S. A., Goldman, M. S., & Christiansen, B. A. (1985). Do alcohol expectancies mediate drinking patterns of adults? *Journal of Consulting and Clinical Psychology, 53,* 512–519.

Brown, S. A., Goldman, M. S., Inn, A., & Anderson, L. R. (1980). Expectations of reinforcement from alcohol. *Journal of Consulting and Clinical Psychology, 48,* 419–426.

Brown, W. A., Monti, P. M., & Corriveau, D. P. (1978). Serum testosterone and sexual activity and interest in men. *Archives of Sexual Behavior, 7,* 97–103.

Browne, M. A., & Mahoney, M. J. (1984). Sport psychology. *Annual Review of Psychology, 35,* 605–625.

Brownell, K. D. (1982). Obesity: Understanding and treating a serious, prevalent, and refractory disorder. *Journal of Consulting and Clinical Psychology, 50,* 820–840.

Brownell, K. D. (1986). In A. Toufexis, et al. (1986, January 20). Dieting: The losing game. *Time Magazine,* pp. 54–60.

Brownell, K. D. (1988). Yo-yo dieting. *Psychology Today, 22*(1), 20–23.

Brownell, K. D., & Wadden, T. A. (1986). Behavior therapy for obesity: Modern approaches and better results. In K. D. Brownell & J. P. Foreyt (Eds.), *Handbook of eating disorders: Physiology, psychology, and treatment of obesity, anorexia, and bulimia.* New York: Basic Books.

Brownlee-Duffeck, M., Peterson, L., Simonds, J. F., Goldstein, D., Kilo, C., & Hoette, S. (1987). The role of health beliefs in the regimen adherence and metabolic control of adolescents and adults with diabetes mellitus. *Journal of Consulting and Clinical Psychology, 55,* 139–144.

Bruner, J. S. (1960). *The process of education.* New York: Vintage Books.

Bruner, J. S. (1983). *Child's talk: Learning to use language.* New York: W. W. Norton.

Bruner, J. S., Goodnow, J. J., & Austin, G. A. (1956). *A study of thinking.* New York: Wiley.

Brunson, B. I., & Matthews, K. A. (1981). The Type-A coronary-prone behavior pattern and reactions to uncontrollable stress. *Journal of Personality and Social Psychology, 40,* 906–918.

Bry, B. H. (1983). Predicting drug abuse: Review and reformulation. *International Journal of the Addictions, 18,* 223–233.

Bryant, P. (1982). Piaget's questions. *British Journal of Psychology, 73,* 157–163.

Budzynski, T. H., & Stoyva, J. M. (1984). Biofeedback methods in the treatment of anxiety and stress. In R. L. Woolfolk & P. M. Lehrer (Eds.), *Principles and practice of stress management.* New York: Guilford Press.

Buffone, G. W. (1980). Exercise as therapy: A closer look. *Journal of Counseling and Psychotherapy, 3,* 101–115.

Buffone, G. W. (1984). Running and depression. In M. L. Sachs & G. W. Buffone (Eds.), *Running as therapy: An integrated approach.* Lincoln, NE: University of Nebraska Press.

Bulman, R. J., & Wortman, C. B. (1977). Attribution of blame and coping in the "real world": Severe accident victims react to their lot. *Journal of Personality and Social Psychology, 35,* 351–363.

Burns, G. L., & Farina, A. (1987). Physical attractiveness and self-perception of mental disorder. *Journal of Abnormal Psychology, 96,* 161–163.

Burnstein, E. (1983). Persuasion as argument processing. In M. Brandstatter, J. H. Davis, & G. Stocker-Kreichgauer (Eds.), *Group decision processes.* London: Academic Press.

Burros, M. (1988, January 6). What Americans really eat: Nutrition can wait. *The New York Times,* pp. C1, C6.

Burt, M. R. (1980). Cultural myths and supports for rape. *Journal of Personality and Social Psychology, 38,* 217–230.

Bushnell, E. W., Shaw, L., & Strauss, D. (1985). Relationship between visual and tactual exploration by 6-month-olds. *Developmental Psychology, 21,* 591–600.

Buss, A. H. (1983). Social rewards and personality. *Journal of Personality and Social Psychology, 44,* 553–563.

Buss, A. H. (1986). *Social behavior and personality.* Hillsdale, NJ: Erlbaum.

Buss, D. M. (1984). Toward a psychology of person–environment (PE) correlation: The role of spouse selection. *Journal of Personality and Social Psychology, 47,* 361–377.

Buss, D. M., & Barnes, M. (1986). Preferences in human mate selection. *Journal of Personality and Social Psychology, 50,* 559–570.

Buss, D. M., Gomes, M., Higgins, D. S., & Lauterbach, K. (1987). Tactics of manipulation. *Journal of Personality and Social Psychology, 52,* 1219–1229.

Bustillo, M., et al. (1984). Delivery of a healthy infant following nonsurgical ovum transfer. *Journal of the American Medical Association, 251,* 889.

Butcher, J. N., Braswell, L., & Raney, D. (1983). A cross-cultural comparison of American Indian, black, and white inpatients on the MMPI and presenting symptoms. *Journal of Consulting and Clinical Psychology, 51,* 587–594.

Butler, N. R., & Goldstein, H. (1973). Smoking in pregnancy and subsequent child development. *British Medical Journal, 4,* 573–575.

Byrne, D. (1971). *The attraction paradigm.* New York: Academic Press.

Byrne, D., Baskett, G. D., & Hodges, L. (1971). Behavioral indicators of interpersonal attraction. *Journal of Applied Social Psychology, 1,* 137–149.

Byrne, D., & Murnen, S. (1987). Maintaining love relationships. In R. J. Sternberg & M. L. Barnes (Eds.), *The anatomy of love.* New Haven: Yale University Press.

Cadoret, R. J. (1978). Psychopathology in adopted-away offspring of biologic parents with antisocial behavior. *Archives of General Psychiatry, 35,* 176–184.

Cadoret, R. J., Cain, C. A., & Grove, W. M. (1980). Development of alcoholism in adoptees raised apart from alcoholic biologic relatives. *Archives of General Psychiatry, 37,* 561–563.

Calder, B. J., Ross, M., & Inkso, C. A. (1973). Attitude change and attitude attribution: Effects of incentive, choice, and consequences. *Journal of Personality and Social Psychology, 25,* 84–99.

Caldwell, B. M., Wright, C. M., Honig, A. S., & Tannenbaum, J. (1970). Infant day care and attachment. *American Journal of Orthopsychiatry, 40,* 397–412.

Calhoun, J. B. (1962). Population density and social pathology. *Scientific American, 206,* 139–148.

Calne, D. B. (1977). Developments in the pharmacology and therapeutics of Parkinsonism. *Annals of Neurology, 1,* 111–119.

Campbell, F. L., Townes, B. D., & Beach, L. R. (1982). Motivational bases of childbearing decisions. In G. L. Fox (Ed.), *The childbearing decision.* Beverly Hills, CA: Sage.

Campos, J. J., Hiatt, S., Ramsey, D., Henderson, C., & Svejda, M. (1978). The emergence of fear on the visual cliff. In M. Lewis & L. Rosenblum (Eds.), *The origins of affect.* New York: Plenum Publishing Co.

Campos, J. J., Langer, A., & Krowitz, A. (1970). Cardiac responses on the visual cliff in prelocomotor infants. *Science, 170,* 196–197.

Cannon, D. S., & Baker, T. B. (1981). Emetic and electric shock alcohol aversion therapy. *Journal of Consulting and Clinical Psychology, 49,* 20–33.

Cannon, W. B. (1927). The James-Lange theory of emotions: A critical examination and an alternative theory. *American Journal of Psychology, 39,* 106–124.

Cannon, W. B. (1929). *Bodily changes in pain, hunger, fear, and rage.* New York: Appleton.

Cantor, P. C. (1976). Personality characteristics found among youthful female suicide attempters. *Journal of Abnormal Psychology, 85,* 324–329.

Cantrell, R. P., Stenner, A. J., & Katzenmeyer, W. G. (1977). Teacher knowledge, attitudes, and classroom teaching correlates of student achievement. *Journal of Educational Psychology, 69,* 180–190.

Cantwell, D. P. (1980). A clinician's guide to the use of stimulant medication for the psychiatric disorders of children. *Developmental and Behavioral Pediatrics, 1,* 133–140.

Caplan, L. (1984, July 2). The insanity defense. *The New Yorker,* pp. 45–78.

Caplan, P. J., MacPherson, G. M., & Tobin, P. (1985). Do sex-related differences in spatial abilities exist? A multilevel critique with new data. *American Psychologist, 40,* 786–799.

Carlson, N. R. (1988). *Foundations of physiological psychology.* Boston: Allyn & Bacon.

Carmichael, L. L., Hogan, H. P., & Walter, A. A. (1932). An experimental study of the effect of language on the reproduction of visually perceived form. *Journal of Experimental Psychology, 15,* 73–86.

Carmody, D. (1988, September 20). Blacks gain again in college admission tests. *The New York Times,* p. A30.

Carr, D. B., et al. (1981). Physical conditioning facilitates the exercise-induced secretion of beta-endorphins and beta-lipotropin in women. *New England Journal of Medicine, 305,* 560–563.

Carroll, D. (1985). *Living with dying.* New York: McGraw-Hill.

Carson, R. C., Butcher, J. N., & Coleman, J. C. (1988). *Abnormal psychology and modern life,* 8th ed. Glenview, IL: Scott, Foresman and Company.

Cartwright, R. D. (1978). *A primer on sleep and dreaming.* Reading, MA: Addison-Wesley.

Cartwright, R. D., Lloyd, S., Nelson, J. B., & Bass, S. (1983). The traditional-liberated woman dimension: Social stereotype and self-concept. *Journal of Personality and Social Psychology, 44,* 581–588.

Carver, C. S., & Ganellen, R. J. (1983). Depression and components of self-punitiveness: High standards, self-criticism, and overgeneralization. *Journal of Abnormal Psychology, 92,* 330–337.

Carver, C. S., Ganellen, R. J., & Behar-Mitrani, V. (1985). Depression and cognitive style: Comparisons between measures. *Journal of Personality and Social Psychology, 49,* 722–728.

Cash, T. F., & Kilcullen, R. N. (1985). The age of the beholder: Susceptibility to sexism and beautyism in the evaluation of managerial applicants. *Journal of Applied Social Psychology, 15,* 591–605.

Castelli, W. (1988). Cited in Kolata, G. (1988, August 3). Study backs heart benefit in light drinking. *The New York Times,* p. A24.

Cattell, R. B. (1949). *The culture-free intelligence test.* Champaign, IL: Institute for Personality and Ability Testing.

Cattell, R. B. (1965). *The scientific analysis of personality.* Baltimore: Penguin Books.

Cattell, R. B. (1973). Personality pinned down. *Psychology Today, 7,* 40–46.

Centers for Disease Control. (1988). 1988 STD treatment guidelines. *Morbidity and mortality report.*

Centers for Disease Control. (1985). Self-reported behavioral change among gay and bisexual men—San Francisco. *Morbidity and mortality weekly report, 34,* 613–615.

Cermak, L. (1978). *Improving your memory.* New York: McGraw-Hill.

Chaiken, S., & Eagly, A. H. (1983). Communication modality as a determinant of persuasion: The role of communicator salience. *Journal of Personality and Social Psychology, 45,* 241–256.

Charry, J. M., & Hawkinshire, F. B. W., Jr. (1981). Effects of atmospheric electricity on some substrates of disordered social behavior. *Journal of Personality and Social Psychology, 41,* 185–197.

Chasnoff, I. J., et al. (1985). Cocaine use in pregnancy. *New England Journal of Medicine, 313,* 666–669.

Chassin, L., Mann, L. M., & Sher, K. J. (1988). Self-awareness theory, family history of alcoholism, and adolescent alcohol involvement. *Journal of Abnormal Psychology, 97,* 206–217.

Chemers, M. M., Hays, R. B., Rhodewalt, F., & Wysocki, J. (1985). A personenvironment analysis of job stress: A contingency model explanation. *Journal of Personality and Social Psychology, 49,* 628–635.

Chesler, P. (1972). *Women and madness.* Garden City, NY: Doubleday.

Chesney, M. A., & Rosenman, R. H. (Eds.) (1985). *Anger and hostility in cardiovascular and behavioral disorders.* Washington, DC: Hemisphere.

Chesno, F. A., & Kilmann, P. R. (1975). Effects of stimulation intensity on sociopathic avoidance learning. *Journal of Abnormal Psychology, 84,* 144–151.

Chess, S., & Thomas, A. (1982). Infant bonding: Mystique and reality. *American Journal of Orthopsychiatry, 52,* 213–222.

Chomsky, N. (1965). *Aspects of the theory of syntax.* Cambridge, MA: MIT Press.

Chomsky, N. (1968). *Language and mind.* New York: Harcourt Brace Jovanovich.

Chomsky, N. (1980). Rules and representations. *Behavior and Brain Science, 3,* 1–15.

Chouinard, G., et al. (1983). New concepts on benzodiazepine therapy: Rebound anxiety and new indications for the more potent benzodiazepines. *Progress in Neuro-Psychopharmacology and Biological Psychiatry, 7,* 669–673.

Christiansen, B. A., Goldman, M. S., & Inn, A. (1982). Development of alcohol-related expectancies in adolescence. *Journal of Consulting and Clinical Psychology, 50,* 336–344.

Chwalisz, K., Diener, E., & Gallagher, D. (1988). Autonomic arousal feedback and emotional experience: Evidence from the spinal cord injured. *Journal of Personality and Social Psychology, 54,* 820–828.

Cipolli, C., & Salzarulo, P. (1978). Sleep and memory: Reproduction of syntactic structures previously evoked within REM-related reports. *Perceptual and Motor Skills, 46,* 111–114.

Clark, E. V. (1973). What's in a word? On the child's acquisition of semantics in his first language. In E. Moore (Ed.), *Cognitive development and the acquisition of language.* New York: Academic Press.

Clark, E. V. (1975). Knowledge, context, and strategy in the acquisition of meaning. In D. P. Dale (Ed.), *Georgetown University roundtable on language and linguistics.* Washington, DC: Georgetown University Press.

Clark, E. V. (1983). Meanings and concepts. In J. H. Flavell & E. M. Markman (Eds.), *Handbook of child psychology: Vol. 3. Cognitive development.* New York: Wiley.

Clark, H. H., & Clark, E. V. (1977). *Psychology and language: An introduction to psycholinguistics.* New York: Harcourt Brace Jovanovich.

Clark, M., et al. (1985, August 12). AIDS. *Newsweek,* pp. 19–27.

Cleckley, H. (1964). *The mask of sanity.* St. Louis: Mosby.

Cleek, M., & Pearson, T. (1985). Perceived causes of divorce: An analysis of interrelationships. *Journal of Marriage and the Family, 47,* 179–183.

Cline, V. B., Croft, R. C., & Courrier, S. (1973). The desensitization of children to television violence. *Journal of Personality and Social Psychology, 27,* 360–365.

Clore, G. L., Wiggins, N. H., & Itkin, S. (1975). Gain and loss in attraction: Attributions from nonverbal behavior. *Journal of Personality and Social Psychology, 31,* 706–712.

Cochran, S. D., & Hammen, C. L. (1985). Perceptions of stressful life events and depression: A test of attributional models. *Journal of Personality and Social Psychology, 48,* 1562–1571.

Coe, W. C., & Yaskinski, E. (1985). Volitional experiences associated with breaching posthypnotic amnesia. *Journal of Personality and Social Psychology, 48,* 716–722.

Cohen, S., Evans, G. W., Krantz, D. S., & Stokols, D. (1980). Physiological, motivational, and cognitive effects of aircraft noise on children. *American Psychologist, 35,* 231–243.

Cohen, S., Evans, G. W., Krantz, D. S., Stokols, D., & Kelly, S. (1981). Aircraft noise and children: Longitudinal and cross-sectional evidence on adaptation to noise and the effectiveness of noise abatement. *Journal of Personality and Social Psychology, 40,* 331–345.

Cohen, S., Evans, G. W., Stokols, D., & Krantz, D. S. (1986). *Behavior, health, and environmental stress.* New York: Plenum Publishing Co.

Cohen, S., Glass, D. C., & Singer, J. E. (1973). Apartment noise, auditory discrimination, and reading ability in children. *Journal of Experimental Social Psychology, 9,* 407–422.

Cohen, S., & Wills, T. A. (1985). Stress, social supports and the buffering hypothesis. *Psychological Bulletin, 98,* 310–357.

Cohn, B. (1988, August 1). A glimpse of the "flex" future. *Newsweek,* pp. 38–39.

Colby, A., Kohlberg, L., Gibbs, J., & Lieberman, M. (1983). A longitudinal study of moral judgment. *Monographs of the Society for Research in Child Development, 48* (Serial No. 200).

Colby, C. Z., Lanzetta, J. T., & Kleck, R. E. (1977). Effects of the expression of pain on autonomic and pain tolerance response to subject-controlled pain. *Psychophysiology, 14,* 537–540.

Cole, D. A. (1988). Hopelessness, social desirability, depression, and parasuicide in two college student samples. *Journal of Consulting and Clinical Psychology, 56,* 131–136.

Coleman, M., & Ganong, L. H. (1985). Love and sex role stereotypes: Do macho men and feminine women make better lovers? *Journal of Personality and Social Psychology, 49,* 170–176.

Colligan, M. J., & Murphy, L. R. (1982). A review of mass psychogenic illness in work settings. In M. J. Colligan, J. W. Pennebaker, & L. R. Murphy (Eds.), *Mass psychogenic illness.* Hillsdale, NJ: Erlbaum.

Collins, R. L., Parks, G. A., & Marlatt, G. A. (1985). Social determinants of alcohol consumption: The effects of social interaction and model status on the self-administration of alcohol. *Journal of Consulting and Clinical Psychology, 53,* 189–200.

Comarr, A. E. (1970). Sexual function among patients with spinal cord injury. *Urologia Internationalis, 25,* 134–168.

Conant, M., et al. (1986). Condoms prevent transmission of the AIDS-associated retrovirus. *Journal of the American Medical Association, 255,* 1706.

Condiotte, M. M., & Lichtenstein, E. (1981). Self-efficacy and relapse in smoking cessation programs. *Journal of Consulting and Clinical Psychology, 49,* 648–658.

Conger, J. J., & Petersen, A. (1984). *Adolescence and youth: Psychological development in a changing world.* New York: Harper and Row.

Conley, J. J. (1984). Longitudinal consistency of adult personality: Self-reported psychological characteristics across 45 years. *Journal of Personality and Social Psychology, 47,* 1325–1333.

Conley, J. J. (1985). Longitudinal stability of personality traits: A multitrait-multimethod-multioccasion analysis. *Journal of Personality and Social Psychology, 49,* 1266–1282.

Connor, J. (1972). Olfactory control of aggressive and sexual behavior in the mouse. *Psychonomic Science, 27,* 1–3.

Conover, M. R. (1982). Modernizing the scarecrow to protect crops from birds. *Frontiers of Plant Science, 35,* 7–8.

Conte, H. R., Plutchik, R., Wild, K. V., & Karasu, T. B. (1986). Combined psychotherapy and pharmacotherapy for depression: A systematic analysis of the evidence. *Archives of General Psychiatry, 43,* 471–479.

Conway, E., & Brackbill, Y. (1970). Delivery medication and infant outcome: An empirical study. *Monographs of the Society for Research in Child Development, 35*(4), 24–34.

Cook, A. S., West, J. S., & Hamner, T. J. (1982). Changes in attitude toward parenting among college women: 1972 and 1979 samples. *Family Relations, 31,* 109–113.

Cooney, J. L., & Zeichner, A. (1985). Selective attention to negative feedback in Type A and Type B individuals. *Journal of Abnormal Psychology, 94,* 110–112.

Cooper, A. J. (1978). Neonatal olfactory bulb lesions: Influences on subsequent behavior of male mice. *Bulletin of the Psychonomic Society, 11,* 53–56.

Cooper, H. M. (1979). Statistically combining independent studies: A meta-analysis of sex differences in conformity research. *Journal of Personality and Social Psychology, 37,* 131–146.

Cooper, J. (1980). Reducing fears and increasing assertiveness: The role of dissonance reduction. *Journal of Experimental Social Psychology, 16,* 199–213.

Cooper, K. H. (1982). *The aerobics program for total well-being.* New York: Evans.

Cooper, K. H. (1985). *Running without fear: How to reduce the risks of heart attack and sudden death during aerobic exercise.* New York: Evans.

Cooper, M. L., Russell, M., & George, W. H. (1988). Coping, expectancies, and alcohol abuse: A test of social learning formulations. *Journal of Abnormal Psychology, 97,* 218–230.

Cooper, R., & Zubek, J. (1958). Effects of enriched and restricted early environments on the learning ability of bright and dull rats. *Canadian Journal of Psychology, 12,* 159–164.

Cordes, C. (1984). The plight of the homeless mentally ill. *APA Monitor, 15*(2), 1, 13.

Cordes, C. (1985). Common threads found in suicide. *APA Monitor, 16*(10), 11.

Corkin, S. (1980). A prospective study of cingulotomy. In E. S. Valenstein (Ed.), *The psychosurgery debate.* San Francisco: W. H. Freeman.

Corkin, S., Cohen, N. J., Sullivan, E. V., Clegg, R. A., Rosen, T. J., & Ackerman, R. H. (1985). Analyses of global memory impairments of different etiologies. In D. S. Olton, E. Gamzu, & S. Corkin (Eds.), *Memory dysfunction.* New York: New York Academy of Sciences.

Costa, E. (1985). Benzodiazepine/GABA interactions: A model to investigate the neurobiology of anxiety. In A. H. Tuma & J. D. Maser (Eds.), *Anxiety and the anxiety disorders.* Hillsdale, NJ: Erlbaum.

Costa, P. T., Jr., & McCrae, R. R. (1984). Personality as a lifelong determinant of wellbeing. In C. Z. Malatesta & C. E. Izard (Eds.), *Emotion in adult development.* Beverly Hills: Sage Publications.

Costa, P. T., Jr., & McCrae, R. R. (1985). Hypochondriasis, neuroticism, and aging: When are somatic complaints unfounded? *American Psychologist, 40,* 19–28.

Costa, P. T., Jr., Zonderman, A. B., McCrae, R. R., & Williams, R. B., Jr. (1985). Content and comprehensiveness in the MMPI: An item factor analysis in a normal adult sample. *Journal of Personality and Social Psychology, 48,* 925–933.

Cousins, N. (1979). *Anatomy of an illness as perceived by the patient: Reflections on healing and regeneration.* New York: Norton.

Cousins, N. (1983). *The healing heart: Antidote to panic and helplessness.* New York: Norton.

Cowan, P. A. (1978). *Piaget with feeling.* New York: Holt, Rinehart and Winston.

Cowen, E. L. (1983). Primary prevention: Past, present, and future. In R. D. Felner et al. (Eds.), *Preventive psychology: Theory, research, and practice.* New York: Pergamon Press.

Cowley, G. (1988, April 11). Science and the cigarette. *Newsweek,* pp. 66–67.

Coyle, J. T., Price, D. L., & DeLong, M. R. (1983). Alzheimer's disease: A disorder of cortical cholinergic innervation. *Science, 219,* 1184–1190.

Coyne, J. C., Kessler, R. C., Tal, M., Turnbull, J., Wortman, C. B., & Greden, J. F. (1987). Living with a depressed person. *Journal of Consulting and Clinical Psychology, 55,* 347–352.

Cozby, P. C. (1973). Self-disclosure: A literature review. *Psychological Bulletin, 79,* 73–91.

Craik, F. I. M., & Lockhart, R. S. (1972). Levels of processing: A framework for memory research. *Journal of Verbal Learning and Verbal Behavior, 11,* 671–684.

Craik, F. I. M., & Watkins, M. J. (1973). The role of rehearsal in short-term memory. *Journal of Verbal Learning and Verbal Behavior, 12,* 599–607.

Crawford, C. (1979). George Washington, Abraham Lincoln, and Arthur Jensen: Are they compatible? *American Psychologist, 34,* 664–672.

Crawford, H. J. (1982). Hypnotizability, daydreaming styles, imagery vividness, and absorption: A multidimensional study. *Journal of Personality and Social Psychology, 42,* 915–926.

Creese, I., Burt, D. R., & Snyder, S. H. (1978). Biochemical actions of neuroleptic drugs. In L. L. Iverson, S. D. Iverson, & S. H. Snyder (Eds.), *Handbook of psychopharmacology,* Vol. 10. New York: Plenum Publishing Co.

Crews, D., & Moore, M. C. (1986). Evolution of mechanisms controlling mating behavior. *Science, 231,* 121– 125.

Crick, F., & Mitchison, G. (1983). The function of dream sleep. *Nature, 304,* 111–114.

Cronbach, L. J. (1975). Five decades of public controversy over mental testing. *American Psychologist, 30,* 1–14.

Crooks, R., & Baur, K. (1987). Our sexuality, 3d ed. Menlo Park, CA: Benjamin/Cummings.

Crowley, J. (1985). Cited in D. Zuckerman (1985). Retirement: R & R or risky? *Psychology Today, 19*(2), 80.

Croyle, R. T., & Cooper, J. (1983). Dissonance arousal: Physiological evidence. *Journal of Personality and Social Psychology, 45,* 782–791.

Crusco, A. H., & Wetzel, C. G. (1984). The midas touch: The effects of interpersonal touch on restaurant tipping. *Personality and Social Psychology Bulletin, 10,* 512–517.

Cummings, N. A. (1979). Turning bread into stones: Our modern antimiracle. *American Psychologist, 34,* 1119–1129.

Cunningham, M. R. (1979). Weather, mood, and helping behavior. *Journal of Personality and Social Psychology, 37,* 1947–1956.

Damon, W. (1977). *The social world of the child.* San Francisco: Jossey-Bass.

Daniel, W. F., & Crovitz, H. F. (1983a). Acute memory impairment following electroconvulsive therapy: 1. Effects of electrical stimulus and number of treatments. *Acta Psychiatrica Scandinavica, 67,* 1–7.

Daniel, W. F., & Crovitz, H. F. (1983b). Acute memory impairment following electroconvulsive therapy: 2. Effects of electrode placement. *Acta Psychiatrica Scandinavica, 67,* 57–68.

Daniels, D., & Plomin, R. (1985). Origins of individual differences in infant shyness. *Developmental Psychology, 21,* 118–121.

Darley, J. M., & Gross, P. H. (1983). A hypothesis-confirming bias in labeling effects. *Journal of Personality and Social Psychology, 44,* 20–33.

Darley, J. M., & Latané, B. (1968). Bystander intervention in emergencies: Diffusion of responsibility. *Journal of Personality and Social Psychology, 8,* 377–383.

Darlington, R. B., Royce, J. M., Snipper, A. S., Murray, H. W., & Lazar, I. (1980). Preschool programs and later school competence of children from low-income families. *Science, 208,* 202–204.

Darwin, C. A. (1872). *The expression of the emotions in man and animals.* London: J. Murray.

Dauber, R. B. (1984). Subliminal psychodynamic activation in depression: On the role of autonomy issues in depressed college women. *Journal of Abnormal Psychology, 93,* 9–18.

Davidson, J. M., et al. (1982). Hormonal replacement and sexuality in men. *Clinics in endocrinology and metabolism, 11,* 599–623.

Davis, J. H., Tindale, R. S., Nagao, D. H., Hinsz, V. B., & Robertson, B. (1984). Order effects in multiple decisions by groups: A demonstration with mock juries and trial procedures. *Journal of Personality and Social Psychology, 47,* 1003–1012.

Davis, K. E. (1985). Near and dear: Friendship and love compared. *Psychology Today, 19*(2), 22–30.

Davison, G. C., & Neale, J. M. (1986). *Abnormal psychology,* 4th ed. New York: Wiley.

Davitz, J. R. (1969). *The language of emotion.* New York: Academic Press.

Deaux, K. (1976). *The behavior of men and women.* Monterey, CA: Brooks/Cole.

Deaux, K. (1984). From individual differences to social categories: Analysis of a decade's research on gender. *American Psychologist, 39,* 105–116.

DeBacker, G. et al. (1983). Behavior, stress, and psychosocial traits as risk factors. *Preventative Medicine, 12,* 32–36.

DeCasper, A. J., & Fifer, W. P. (1980). Of human bonding: Newborns prefer their mothers' voices. *Science, 208,* 1174–1176.

DeFries, J. C., Plomin, R., & LaBuda, M. C. (1987). Genetic stability of cognitive development from childhood to adulthood. *Developmental Psychology, 23,* 4–12.

DeGree, C. E., & Snyder, C. R. (1985). Adler's psychology (of use) today: Personal history of traumatic life events as a self-handicapping strategy. *Journal of Personality and Social Psychology, 48,* 1512–1519.

Delanoy, R. L., Merrin, J. S., & Gold, P. E. (1982). Moderation of long-term potentiation (LTP) by adrenergic agonists. *Neuroscience Abstracts, 8,* 316.

Delgado, J. M. R. (1969). *Physical control of the mind.* New York: Harper & Row.

DeLongis, A., Coyne, J. C., Dakof, G., Folkman, S., & Lazarus, R. S. (1982). Relationship of daily hassles, uplifts, and major life events to health status. *Health Psychology, 1,* 119–136.

Dembroski, T. M., Lasater, T. M., & Ramirez, A. (1978). Communicator similarity, fear-arousing communications, and compliance with health care recommendations. *Journal of Applied Social Psychology, 8,* 254–269.

Dembroski, T. M., MacDougall, J. M., Williams, R. B., Haney, T. L., & Blumenthal, J. A. (1985). Components of Type A, hostility, and anger-in: Relationship to angroginphic findings. *Psychosomatic Medicine, 47,* 219–233.

Dement, W. (1972). Sleep and dreams. In A. M. Freedman & H. I. Kaplan (Eds.), *Human behavior: Biological, psychological, and sociological.* New York: Atheneum.

Denton, L. (1988). Memory: Not place, but process. *APA Monitor, 19*(11), 4.

DePaulo, B. M., Rosenthal, R., Eisenstat, R. A., Rogers, P. L., & Finkelstein, S. (1978). Decoding discrepant nonverbal cues. *Journal of Personality and Social Psychology, 38,* 313–323.

Depue, R. A., Slater, J. F., Wolfstetter-Kausch, H., Klein, D., Goplerud, E., & Farr, D. (1981). A behavioral paradigm for identifying persons at risk for bipolar depressive disorder. *Journal of Abnormal Psychology, 90,* 381–438.

Dermer, M., & Thiel, D. L. (1975). When beauty may fail. *Journal of Personality and Social Psychology, 31,* 1168–1176.

DeRubeis, R. J. (1983, December). The cognitive-pharmacotherapy project: Study design, outcome, and clinical follow-up. Paper presented to the Association for the Advancement of Behavior Therapy, Washington, DC.

Dethier, V. G. (1978). Other tastes, other worlds. *Science, 201,* 224–228.

DeValois, R. L., & Jacobs, G. H. (1984). Neural mechanisms of color vision. In I. Darian-Smith (Ed.), *Handbook of physiology, Vol. 3.* Bethesda, MD: American Physiological Society.

Diamond, E. L. (1982). The role of anger and hostility in essential hypertension and coronary heart disease. *Psychological Bulletin, 92,* 410–433.

Diamond, M. (1977). Human sexual development: Biological foundations for social development. In F. A. Beach (Ed.), *Human sexuality in four perspectives.* Baltimore: Johns Hopkins University Press.

Diamond, M. (1984). A love affair with the brain. *Psychology Today, 18*(11), 62–73.

Dickson, P. (1975). *The future of the workplace: The coming revolution in jobs.* New York: Weybright and Talley.

Diener, E. (1980). Deindividuation: The absence of self-awareness and self-regulation in group members. In P. Paulus (Ed.), *The psychology of group influence.* Hillsdale, NJ: Erlbaum.

Digman, J. M., & Inouye, J. (1986). Further specification of the five robust factors of personality. *Journal of Personality and Social Psychology, 50,* 116–123.

Dill, C. A., Gilden, E. R., Hill, P. C., & Hanselka, L. L. (1982). Federal human subjects regulations: A methodological artifact. *Personality and Social Psychology Bulletin, 8,* 417–425.

DiMatteo, M. R., & DiNicola, D. D. (1982). *Achieving patient compliance: The psychology of the medical practitioner's role.* New York: Pergamon Press.

Dimsdale, J. E., & Moss, J. (1980). Plasma catecholamines in stress and exercise. *Journal of the American Medical Association, 243,* 340–342.

DiNicola, D. D., & DiMatteo, M. R. (1984). Practitioners, patients, and compliance with medical regimens: A social psychological perspective. In A. Baum, S. E. Taylor, & J. E. Singer (Eds.), *Handbook of psychology and health: Vol. 4. Social psychological aspects of health.* Hillsdale, NJ: Erlbaum.

Dion, K. K., Berscheid, E., & Walster, E. (1972). What is beautiful is good. *Journal of Personality and Social Psychology, 24,* 285–290.

Dishman, R. K. (1982). Compliance/adherence in health-related exercise. *Health Psychology, 1,* 237–267.

Doctorow, M., Wittrock, M. C., & Marks, C. (1978). Generative processes in reading comprehension. *Journal of Educational Psychology, 70,* 109–118.

Dodge, K. A., & Frame, C. L. (1982). Social cognitive biases and deficits in aggressive boys. *Child Development, 53,* 620–635.

Dodge, L. J. T., Glasgow, R. E., & O'Neill, H. K. (1982). Bibliotherapy in the treatment of female orgasmic dysfunction. *Journal of Consulting and Clinical Psychology, 50,* 442–443.

Doherty, W. J., & Jacobson, N. S. (1982). Marriage and family. In B. B. Wolman (Ed.), *Handbook of developmental psychology.* Englewood Cliffs, NJ: Prentice-Hall.

Doherty, W. J., Schrott, H. G., Metcalf, L., & Iasiello-Vailas, L. (1983). Effects of spouse support and health beliefs on medication adherence. *Journal of Family Practice, 17,* 837–841.

Dohrenwend, B. P., & Shrout, P. E. (1985). "Hassles" in the conceptualization and measurement of life stress variables. *American Psychologist, 40,* 780–785.

Dohrenwend, B. S., Dohrenwend, B. P., Dodson, M., & Shrout, P. E. (1984). Symptoms, hassles, social supports and life events: The problem of confounded measures. *Journal of Abnormal Psychology, 93,* 222–230.

Dohrenwend, B. S., Krasnoff, L., Askenasy, A. R., & Dohrenwend, B. P. (1982). The psychiatric epidemiology research interview life events scale. In L. Goldberger & S. Breznitz (Eds.), *Handbook of stress: Theoretical and clinical aspects.* New York: Free Press.

Doll, R., & Peto, R. (1981). *The causes of cancer.* New York: Oxford University Press.

Dollard, J., Doob, L. W., Miller, N. E., Mowrer, O. H., & Sears, R. R. (1939). *Frustration and aggression.* New Haven, CT: Yale University Press.

Donahoe, C. P., Jr., Lin, D. H., Kirschenbaum, D. S., & Keesey, R. E. (1984). Metabolic consequences of dieting and exercise in the treatment of obesity. *Journal of Consulting and Clinical Psychology, 52,* 827–836.

Donnerstein, E. I. (1980). Aggressive erotica and violence against women. *Journal of Personality and Social Psychology, 39,* 269–277.

Donnerstein, E. I., & Linz, D. G. (1984). Sexual violence in the media: A warning. *Psychology Today, 18*(1), 14–15.

Donnerstein, E. I., & Linz, D. G. (1986). The question of pornography. *Psychology Today, 20*(12), 56–60.

Donnerstein, E. I., & Linz, D. G. (1987). *The question of pornography.* New York: The Free Press.

Donnerstein, E. I., & Wilson, D. W. (1976). Effects of noise and perceived control on ongoing and subsequent aggressive behavior. *Journal of Personality and Social Psychology, 34,* 774–781.

Doob, A. N., & Wood, L. (1972). Catharsis and aggression: The effects of annoyance and retaliation on aggressive behavior. *Journal of Personality and Social Psychology, 22,* 236–245.

Dovidio, J. H., Evans, N., & Tyler, R. B. (1986). Racial stereotypes: The contents of their cognitive representations. *Journal of Experimental Social Psychology, 22,* 22–37.

Dowd, M. (1984, March 12). Twenty years after the murder of Kitty Genovese, the question remains: Why? *The New York Times,* pp. B1, B4.

Doyle, W. (1986). Classroom organization and management. In M. Wittrock (Ed.), *Handbook of research on teaching,* 3d ed. New York: Macmillan.

Doyne, E. J., Chambless, D. L., & Bentler, L. E. (1983). Aerobic exercise as treatment for depression in women. *Behavior Therapy, 14,* 434–440.

Doyne, E. J., Ossip-Klein, D. J., Bowman, E. D., Osborn, K. M., McDougall-Wilson, I. B., & Neimeyer, R. A. (1987). Running versus weight lifting in the treatment of depression. *Journal of Consulting and Clinical Psychology, 55,* 748–754.

Driscoll, R., Davis, K. E., & Lipetz, M. E. (1972). Parental interference and romantic love. *Journal of Personality and Social Psychology, 24,* 1–10.

Duke, M. P., & Nowicki, S. (1972). A new measure and social learning model for interpersonal distance. *Journal of Experimental Research in Personality, 6,* 119–132.

Dunn, H. G., et al. (1977). Maternal cigarette smoking during pregnancy and the child's subsequent development: II. Neurological and intellectual maturation to the age of $6\frac{1}{2}$ years. *Canadian Journal of Public Health, 68,* 43–50.

Dutton, D. G., & Aron, A. P. (1974). Some evidence for heightened sexual attraction under conditions of high anxiety. *Journal of Personality and Social Psychology, 30,* 510–517.

Dyer, E. D. (1983). *Courtship, marriage, and family: American style.* Homewood, IL: Dorsey.

Dywan, J., & Bowers, K. S. (1983). The use of hypnosis to enhance recall. *Science, 222,* 184–185.

Eagly, A. H. (1974). Comprehensibility of persuasive arguments as a determinant of opinion change. *Journal of Personality and Social Psychology, 29,* 758–773.

Eagly, A. H. (1978). Sex differences in influenceability. *Psychological Bulletin, 85,* 86–116.

Eagly, A. H. (1983). Gender and social influence: A social psychological analysis. *American Psychologist, 38,* 971–981.

Eagly, A. H., & Carli, L. L. (1981). Sex of researchers and sex-typed communications as determinants of sex differences in influenceability: A meta-analysis of social influence studies. *Psychological Bulletin, 90,* 1–20.

Eagly, A. H., & Steffen, V. J. (1984). Gender stereotypes stem from the distribution of men and women into social roles. *Journal of Personality and Social Psychology, 46,* 735–754.

Eagly, A. H., Wood, W., & Chaiken, S. (1978). Causal inferences about communicators and their effect on opinion change. *Journal of Personality and Social Psychology, 36,* 424–435.

Eagly, A. H., Wood, W., & Fishbaugh, L. (1981). Sex differences in conformity: Surveillance by the group as a determinant of male conformity. *Journal of Personality and Social Psychology, 40,* 384–394.

Easterbrooks, M. A., & Goldberg, W. A. (1985). Effects of early maternal employment on toddlers, mothers, and fathers. *Developmental Psychology, 21,* 774–783.

Ebbeson, E. B., & Bowers, J. B. (1974). Proportion of risky to conservative arguments in a group discussion and choice shift. *Journal of Personality and Social Psychology, 29,* 316–327.

Ebbinghaus, H. (1885). *Memory: A contribution to experimental psychology.* (H. A. Roger & C. E. Bussenius, trans.). New York: Columbia University Press, 1913.

Eccles, J. S. (1985). Sex differences in achievement patterns. In T. Sonderegger (Ed.), *Nebraska symposium on motivation.* Lincoln: University of Nebraska Press.

Eccles, J. S., & Hoffman, L. W. (1984). Sex roles, socialization, and occupational behavior. In H. W. Stevenson & A. E. Siegel (Eds.), *Research in child development and social policy,* Vol. 1. Chicago: University of Chicago Press.

Eckenrode, J. (1984). Impact of chronic and acute stressors on daily reports of mood. *Journal of Personality and Social Psychology, 46,* 907–918.

Eckert, E. D., et al. (1986). Homosexuality in monozygotic twins reared apart. *British Journal of Psychiatry, 148,* 421–425.

Eckhardt, M. J., et al. (1981). Health hazards associated with alcohol consumption. *Journal of the American Medical Association, 246,* 648–666.

Eden, C., & Sims, D. (1981). Computerized vicarious experience: The future for management induction? *Personnel Review, 10,* 22–25.

Edwards, D. J. A. (1972). Approaching the unfamiliar: A study of human interaction differences. *Journal of Behavioral Sciences, 1,* 249–250.

Efran, M. G. (1974). The effect of physical appearance on the judgment of guilt, interpersonal attraction, and severity of recommended punishment in a simulated jury task. *Journal of Research in Personality, 8,* 45–54.

Egeland, J. A., et al. (1987). Bipolar affective disorder linked to DNA markers on chromosome 11. *Nature, 325,* 783–787.

Ehrhardt, A. A., & Baker, S. W. (1975). Hormonal aberrations and their implications for the understanding of normal sex differentiation. In P. H. Mussen, J. J. Conger, & J. Kagan (Eds.), *Basic and contemporary issues in developmental psychology.* New York: Harper & Row.

Eibl-Eibesfeldt, I. (1974). *Love and hate: The natural history of behavior patterns.* New York: Schocken Books.

Eiger, M. S., & Olds, S. W. (1986). *The complete book of breast-feeding,* 2d ed. New York: Bantam Books.

Eisdorfer, C. (1983). Conceptual models of aging: The challenge of a new frontier. *American Psychologist, 38,* 197–202.

Ekman, P. (1980). *The face of man.* Garland STPM Press.

Ekman, P. (1985). Cited in B. Bower (1985, July 6). The face of emotion. *Science News, 128,* 12–13.

Ekman, P., et al. (1987). Universals and cultural differences in the judgments of facial expressions of emotion. *Journal of Personality and Social Psychology, 53,* 712–717.

Ekman, P., Levenson, R. W., & Friesen, W. V. (1983). Autonomic nervous system activity distinguishes among emotions. *Science, 221,* 1208–1210.

Ekman, P., & Oster, H. (1979). Facial expressions of emotion. *Annual Review of Psychology, Vol. 30.* Palo Alto, CA: Annual Reviews.

Elardo, R., Bradley, R. H., & Caldwell, B. M. (1975). The relation of infants' home environments to mental test performance from 6 to 36 months: A longitudinal analysis. *Child Development, 46,* 71–76.

Elardo, R., Bradley, R. H., & Caldwell, B. M. (1977). A longitudinal study of the relation of infants' home environments to language development at age 3. *Child Development, 48,* 595–603.

Eliot, R. S., & Buell, J. C. (1983). The role of the central nervous system in sudden cardiac death. In T. M. Dembroski, T. Schmidt, & G. Blunchen (Eds.), *Biobehavioral bases of coronary-prone behavior.* New York: Karger.

Elkin, I., et al. (1985). NIMH treatment of depression collaborative research program. *Archives of General Psychiatry, 42,* 305–316

Elkins, R. L. (1980). Covert sensitization treatment of alcoholism. *Addictive Behaviors, 5,* 67–89.

Elliot, A. J. (1981). *Child language.* Cambridge: Cambridge University Press.

Ellis, A. (1977). The basic clinical theory or rational-emotive therapy. In A. Ellis & R. Grieger (Eds.), *Handbook of rational-emotive therapy.* New York: Springer.

Ellis, A. (1985). Cognition and affect in emotional disturbance. *American Psychologist, 40,* 471–472.

Ellis, A. (1987). The impossibility of achieving consistently good mental health. *American Psychologist, 42,* 364–375.

Ellis, L., & Ames, M. A. (1987). Neurohormonal functioning and sexual orientation: A theory of homosexuality–heterosexuality. *Psychological Bulletin, 101,* 233–258.

Ellison, G. D. (1977). Animal models of psychopathology: The low-norepinephrine and low-serotonin rat. *American Psychologist, 32,* 1036–1045.

Ellsworth, P. C., Carlsmith, J. M., & Henson, A. (1972). The stare as a stimulus to flight in human subjects. *Journal of Personality and Social Psychology, 21,* 302–311.

Ellsworth, P. C., & Langer, E. J. (1976). Staring and approach: An interpretation of the stare as a nonspecific activator. *Journal of Personality and Social Psychology, 33,* 117–122.

Emmer, E. T., Evertson, C. M., Sanford, J. P., Clements, B., & Worsham, M. (1984). *Classroom management for secondary teachers.* Englewood Cliffs, NJ: Prentice-Hall.

Epstein, L. H., & Perkins, K. A. (1988). Smoking, stress, and coronary heart disease. *Journal of Consulting and Clinical Psychology, 56,* 342–349.

Epstein, L. H., & Wing, R. R. (1980). Aerobic exercise and weight. *Addictive Behaviors, 5,* 371–388.

Epstein, L. H., Wing, R. R., Koeske, R., & Valoski, A. (1984a). Effects of diet plus exercise on weight change in parents and children. *Journal of Consulting and Clinical Psychology, 52,* 429–437.

Epstein, L. H., Wing, R. R., Woodall, K., Penner, B. C., Kress, M. J., & Koeske, R. (1985). Effects of family-based behavioral treatment on obese 5- to 8-year-old children. *Behavior Therapy, 16,* 205–212.

Epstein, L. H., Woodall, K., Goreczny, A. J., Wing, R. R., & Robertson, R. J. (1984b). The modification of activity patterns and energy expenditure in obese young girls. *Behavior Therapy, 15,* 101–108.

Erdman, H. P., Klein, M. H., & Greist, J. H. (1985). Direct patient computer interviewing. *Journal of Consulting and Clinical Psychology, 53,* 760–773.

Erikson, E. H. (1963). *Childhood and society.* New York: W. W. Norton.

Erikson, E. H. (1975). *Life history and the historical moment.* New York: W. W. Norton.

Erikson, E. H. (1983). Cited in E. Hall (1983). A conversation with Erik Erikson. *Psychology Today, 17*(6), 22–30.

Eriksson, K. (1972). Behavior and physiological differences among rat strains specially selected for their alcohol consumption. *Annals of the New York Academy of Science, 197,* 32–41.

Erlenmeyer-Kimling, L., & Jarvik, L. F. (1963). Genetics and intelligence: A review. *Science, 142,* 1477–1479.

Eron, L. D. (1982). Parent–child interaction, television violence, and aggression of children. *American Psychologist, 37,* 197–211.

Eron, L. D. (1987). The development of aggressive behavior from the perspective of a developing behaviorism. *American Psychologist, 42,* 435–442.

Erwin, J., Maple, T., Mitchell, G., & Willott, J. (1974). Follow-up study of isolation-reared rhesus monkeys paired with preadolescent cospecifics in late infancy: Cross-sex pairings. *Developmental Psychology, 6,* 808–814.

Estes, W. K. (1972). An associative basis for coding and organization in memory. In A. W. Melton & E. Martin (Eds.), *Coding processes in human memory.* Washington, DC: Winston.

Evans, H. J. (1981). Abnormalities and cigarette smoking. *Lancet, 1,* 627–634.

Evans, R. I., Rozelle, R. M., Lasater, T. M., Dembroski, T. M., & Allen, B. P. (1970). Fear arousal, persuasion, and actual versus implied behavioral change: New perspective utilizing a real-life dental hygiene program. *Journal of Personality and Social Psychology, 16,* 220–227.

Evertson, C. M., Emmer, E. T., Clements, B. S., Sanford, J. P., & Worsham, M. E. (1984). *Classroom management for elementary teachers.* Englewood Cliffs, NJ: Prentice-Hall.

Eysenck, H. J. (1952). The effects of psychotherapy: An evaluation. *Journal of Consulting Psychology, 16,* 319–324.

Eysenck, H. J., & Eysenck, M. W. (1985). *Personality and individual differences.* New York: Plenum Publishing Co.

Fabian, W. D., Jr., & Fishkin, S. M. (1981). A replicated study of self-reported changes in psychological absorption with marijuana intoxication. *Journal of Abnormal Psychology, 90,* 546–553.

Fabricius, W. V., & Wellman, H. M. (1983). Children's understanding of retrieval cue utilization. *Developmental Psychology, 19,* 15–21.

Fagot, B. I. (1974). Sex differences in toddlers' behavior and parental reaction. *Developmental Psychology, 10,* 554–558.

Fagot, B. I. (1978). The influence of sex of child on parental reactions to toddler children. *Child Development, 49,* 459–465.

Fagot, B. I. (1982). Adults as socializing agents. In T. M. Field (Ed.), *Review of human development.* New York: Wiley.

Fagot, B. I. (1985a). Beyond the reinforcement principle: Another step toward understanding sex role development. *Developmental Psychology, 21,* 1097–1104.

Fagot, B. I. (1985b). Changes in thinking about early sex role development. *Developmental Review, 5,* 83–98.

Fairbanks, L. A., McGuire, M. T., & Harris, C. J. (1982). Nonverbal interaction of patients and therapists during psychiatric interviews. *Journal of Abnormal Psychology, 91,* 109–119.

Fallon, A. E., & Rozin, P. (1985). Sex differences in perceptions of desirable body shape. *Journal of Abnormal Psychology, 94,* 102–105.

Fantz, R. L. (1961). The origin of form perception. *Scientific American, 204*(5), 66–72.

Farber, B. A. (Ed.). (1983). *Stress and burnout in the human service professions.* Elmsford, NY: Pergamon Press.

Farber, E., & Egeland, B. (1987). *The invulnerable child.* New York: Guilford Press.

Farina, A., Burns, G. L., Austad, C., Bugglin, C. S., & Fischer, E. H. (1986). The role of physical attractiveness in the readjustment of discharged psychiatric patients. *Journal of Abnormal Psychology, 95,* 139–143.

Farthing, G. W., Venturino, M., & Brown, S. W. (1984). Suggestion and distraction in the control of pain: Test of two hypotheses. *Journal of Abnormal Psychology, 93,* 266–276.

Fazio, R. H. (1986). How do attitudes guide behavior? In R. M. Sorrentino & E. T. Higgins (Eds.), *The handbook of motivation and cognition: Foundations of social behavior.* New York: Guilford Press.

Fazio, R. H., Chen, J., McDonel, E. C., & Sherman, S. J. (1982). Attitude accessibility, attitude-behavior consistency, and the strength of the object-evaluation association. *Journal of Experimental Social Psychology, 18,* 339–357.

Fazio, R. H., & Cooper, J. (1983). Arousal in the dissonance process. In J. T. Cacioppo & R. E. Petty (Eds.), *Social psychophysiology.* New York: Guilford Press.

Fazio, R. H., Sanbonmatsu, D. M., Powell, M. C., & Kardes, F. R. (1986). On the automatic activation of attitudes. *Journal of Personality and Social Psychology, 50,* 229–238.

Fazio, R. H., Sherman, S. J., & Herr, P. M. (1982). The feature-positive effect in the self-perception process: Does not doing matter as much as doing? *Journal of Personality and Social Psychology, 42,* 404–411.

Feder, H. H. (1984). Hormones and sexual behavior. *Annual Review of Psychology, 35,* 165–200.

Fein, G. G., Schwartz, P. M., Jacobson, S. W., & Jacobson, J. L. (1983). Environmental toxins and behavioral development: A new role for psychological research. *American Psychologist, 38,* 1188–1197.

Feist, J., & Brannon, L. (1988). *Health psychology.* Belmont, CA: Wadsworth Publishing Co.

Feldman, D. (1980). *Beyond universals in cognitive development.* Norwood, NJ: Ablex.

Feldman, J. (1966). *The dissemination of health information.* Chicago: Aldine.

Felsenthal, N. (1976). *Orientations to mass communications.* Chicago: Science Research.

Fenigstein, A. (1979). Does aggression cause a preference for viewing media violence? *Journal of Personality and Social Psychology, 37,* 2307–2317.

Fenigstein, A., Scheier, M. F., & Buss, A. H. (1975). Public and private self-consciousness: Assessment and theory. *Journal of Consulting and Clinical Psychology, 43,* 522–527.

Ferguson, C. A., & Farwell, C. (1975). Words and sounds in early language acquisition: English consonants in the first 50 words. *Language, 51,* 419–439.

Festinger, L. (1957). *A theory of cognitive dissonance.* Evanston, IL: Row, Peterson.

Festinger, L., & Carlsmith, J. M. (1959). Cognitive consequences of forced compliance. *Journal of Abnormal and Social Psychology, 58,* 203–210.

Findley, M. J., & Cooper, H. M. (1983). Locus of control and academic achievement: A literature review. *Journal of Personality and Social Psychology, 44,* 419–427.

Finnuchi, J., & Childs, B. (1981). Are there really

sex differences in dyslexia? In A. Ansara, N. Geschwind, A. Galaburda, M. Albert, & N. Gartrell (Eds.), *Sex differences in dyslexia.* Towson, MD: The Orton Dyslexia Society.

Fiore, J. (1980). *Global satisfaction scale.* Unpublished manuscript, University of Washington, Department of Psychiatry and Behavioral Sciences, Seattle.

Fischman, J. (1987a). Getting tough. *Psychology Today, 21*(12), 26–28.

Fischman, J. (1987b). Type A on trial. *Psychology Today, 21*(2), 42–50.

Fisher, J. D., Bell, P. A., & Baum, A. (1984). *Environmental psychology,* 2d ed. New York: Holt, Rinehart and Winston.

Fisher, K. (1982). Debate rages on 1973 Sobell study. *APA Monitor, 13*(11), 8–9.

Fisher, K. (1984). Family violence cycle questioned. *APA Monitor, 15*(12), 30.

Fisher, W. A., & Byrne, D. (1978). Sex differences in response to erotica? Love versus lust. *Journal of Personality and Social Psychology, 36,* 117–125.

Fishman, S. M., & Sheehan, D. V. (1985). Anxiety and panic: Their cause and treatment. *Psychology Today, 19*(4), 26–32.

Fiske, S. T., & Taylor, S. E. (1984). *Social cognition.* Reading, MA: Addison-Wesley.

Fitch, G. (1970). Effects of self-esteem, perceived performance, and choice of causal attribution. *Journal of Personality and Social Psychology, 16,* 311–315.

Flaherty, J. F., & Dusek, J. B. (1980). An investigation of the relationship between psychological androgyny and components of self-concept. *Journal of Personality and Social Psychology, 38,* 984–992.

Flavell, J. H. (1982). Structures, stages, and sequences in cognitive development. In W. A. Collins (Ed.), *The concept of development: The Minnesota symposia on child psychology,* Vol. 15. Hillsdale, NJ: Erlbaum.

Flavell, J. H. (1985). *Cognitive development.* Englewood Cliffs, NJ: Prentice-Hall.

Flavell, J. H., Speer, J. R., Green, F. L., & August, D. L. (1981). The development of comprehension monitoring and knowledge about communication. *Monographs of the Society for Research in Child Development, 46*(5, Serial No. 192).

Flaxman, J. (1978). Quitting smoking now or later: Gradual, abrupt, immediate, and delayed quitting. *Behavior Therapy, 9,* 260–270.

Fleming, M. Z., MacGowan, B. R., Robinson, L., Spitz, J., & Salt, P. (1982). The body image of the postoperative female-to-male transsexual. *Journal of Consulting and Clinical Psychology, 50,* 461–462.

Floderus-Myrhed, B., Pederson, N., & Rasmuson, I. (1980). Assessment of heritability for personality based on a short form of the Eysenck Personality Inventory: A study of 12,898 twin pairs. *Behavior Genetics, 10,* 153–162.

Fodor, E. M. (1984). The power motive and reactivity to power stresses. *Journal of Personality and Social Psychology, 47,* 853–859.

Fodor, E. M. (1985). The power motive, group conflict, and physiological arousal. *Journal of Personality and Social Psychology, 49,* 1408–1415.

Fodor, E. M., & Smith, T. (1982). The power motive as an influence on group decision making. *Journal of Personality and Social Psychology, 42,* 178–185.

Fodor, J. A., Bever, T. G., & Garrett, M. F. (1974). *The psychology of language.* New York: McGraw-Hill.

Fogel, M. L. (1980). Warning: Auto fumes may lower your kid's IQ. *Psychology Today, 14*(1), 108.

Folkins, C. H., & Sime, W. E. (1981). Physical fitness training and mental health. *American Psychologist, 36,* 373–389.

Folkman, S., & Lazarus, R. S. (1985). If it changes it must be a process: Study of emotion and coping during three stages of a college examination. *Journal of Personality and Social Psychology, 48,* 150–170.

Ford, C. S., & Beach, F. A. (1951). *Patterns of sexual behavior.* New York: Harper & Row.

Foreyt, J. P. (1986). Treating the diseases of the 1980s: Eating disorders. *Contemporary Psychology, 31,* 658–660.

Foulkes, D. (1971). Longitudinal studies of dreams in children. In J. Masserman (Ed.), *Science and psychoanalysis.* New York: Grune & Stratton.

Fouts, R. S., & Fouts, D. H. (1985). *Friends of Washoe, 4,* 3–8.

Fowler, R. D. (1985). Landmarks in computer-assisted psychological assessment. *Journal of Consulting and Clinical Psychology, 53,* 748–759.

Fox, S. (1984). *The mirror makers.* New York: Morrow.

Foy, D. W., Nunn, L. B., & Rychtarik, R. G. (1984). Broad-spectrum behavioral treatment for chronic alcoholics: Effects of training controlled drinking skills. *Journal of Consulting and Clinical Psychology, 52,* 218–230.

Francis, D. (1984). *Will you still need me, will you still feed me, when I'm 84?* Bloomington: Indiana University Press.

Franck, K. D., Unseld, C. T., & Wentworth, W. E. (1974). Adaptation of the newcomer: A process of construction. Unpublished manuscript, City University of New York.

Freedman, J. L., & Fraser, S. C. (1966). Compliance without pressure: The foot-in-the-door technique. *Journal of Personality and Social Psychology, 4,* 195–202.

Freedman, J. L., Wallington, S. A., & Bless, E. (1967). Compliance without pressure: The effect of guilt. *Journal of Personality and Social Psychology, 7,* 117–124.

Freedman, R. R., & Sattler, H. L. (1982). Physiological and psychological factors in sleep-onset insomnia. *Journal of Abnormal Psychology, 91,* 380–389.

French, G. M., & Harlow, H. F. (1962). Variability of delayed-reaction performance in normal and brain-damaged rhesus monkeys. *Journal of Neurophysiology, 25,* 585–599.

French-Belgian Collaborative Group (1982). Ischemic heart disease and psychological patterns: Prevalence and incidence in Belgium and France. *Advances in Cardiology, 29,* 25–31.

Freud, S. (1909). Analysis of a phobia in a 5-year-old boy. In *Collected papers,* Vol. 3, trans. A. & J. Strachey. New York: Basic Books, 1959.

Freud, S. (1927). A religious experience. In *Standard edition of the complete psychological works of Sigmund Freud,* Vol. 21. London: Hogarth Press, 1964.

Freud, S. (1930). *Civilization and its discontents,* trans. J. Strachey. New York: W. W. Norton, 1961.

Freud, S. (1933). New introductory lectures. In *Standard edition of the complete psychological works of Sigmund Freud,* Vol. 22. London: Hogarth Press, 1964.

Friedman, H. S., & Booth-Kewley, S. (1987). Personality, Type A behavior, and coronary heart disease: The role of emotional expression. *Journal of Personality and Social Psychology, 53,* 783–792.

Friedman, M., & Rosenman, R. H. (1974). *Type A behavior and your heart.* New York: Harper & Row.

Friedman, M., & Ulmer, D. (1984). *Treating Type A behavior and your heart.* New York: Fawcett Crest.

Friedman, M. I., & Stricker, E. M. (1976). The physiological psychology of hunger: A physiological perspective. *Psychological Review, 83,* 409–431.

Friman, P. C., & Christopherson, E. R. (1983). Behavior therapy and hyperactivity: A brief review of therapy for a big problem. *The Behavior Therapist, 6,* 175–176.

Frisch, H. L. (1977). Sex stereotypes in adult–infant play. *Child Development, 48,* 1671–1675.

Frodi, A. M. (1981). Contribution of infant characteristics to child abuse. *Journal of Mental Deficiency, 85,* 341–349.

Frodi, A. M., Macauley, J., & Thome, P. R. (1977). Are women always less aggressive than men? A review of the experimental literature. *Psychological Bulletin, 84,* 634–660.

Fromm, E. (1956). *The art of loving.* New York: Harper & Row.

Funkenstein, D. (1955, May). The physiology of fear and anger. *Scientific American.*

Fustero, S. (1984). Home on the street. *Psychology Today, 18*(2), 56–63.

Galanter, E. (1962). Contemporary psychophysics. In R. Brown et al. (Eds.), *New directions in psychology.* New York: Holt, Rinehart and Winston.

Galassi, J. P., Frierson, H. T., & Sharer, R. (1981). Behavior of high, moderate, and low test anxious students during an actual test situation. *Journal of Consulting and Clinical Psychology, 49,* 51–62.

Galizio, M., & Hendrick, C. (1972). Effect of musical accompaniment on attitude: The guitar as a prop for persuasion. *Journal of Applied Social Psychology, 2,* 350–359.

Gallup, G. G., & Suarez, S. D. (1985). Alternatives to the use of animals in psychological research. *American Psychologist, 40,* 1104–1111.

Ganellen, R. J., & Blaney, P. H. (1984). Hardiness and social support as moderators of the effects of life stress. *Journal of Personality and Social Psychology, 47,* 156–163.

Garcia, J. (1981). The logic and limits of mental aptitude testing. *American Psychologist, 36,* 1172–1180.

Garcia, J., & Koelling, R. A. (1966). Relation of cue to consequences in avoidance learning. *Psychonomic Science 4,* 123–124.

Gardner, B. T., & Gardner, R. A. (1980). Two comparative psychologists look at language acquisition. In K. E. Nelson (Ed.), *Children's language,* Vol. 2. New York: Gardner Press.

Gardner, H. (1983). *Frames of mind: The theory of multiple intelligences.* New York: Basic Books.

Garfield, S. L. (1981). Psychotherapy: A 40-year appraisal. *American Psychologist, 36,* 174–183.

Garfield, S. L. (1982). Eclecticism and integration in psychotherapy. *Behavior Therapy, 13,* 610–623.

Garwood, S. G., Cox, L., Kaplan, V., Wasserman, N., & Sulzer, J. L. (1980). Beauty is only "name deep": The effect of first name in ratings of physical attraction. *Journal of Applied Social Psychology, 10,* 431–435.

Gastorf, J. W., & Galanos, A. N. (1983). Patient compliance and physicians' attitude. *Family Practice Research Journal, 2,* 190–198.

Gatchel, R. J., & Proctor, J. D. (1976). Effectiveness of voluntary heart rate control in reducing speech anxiety. *Journal of Consulting and Clinical Psychology, 44,* 381–389.

Gazzaniga, M. S. (1972). One brain—two minds? *American Science, 60,* 311–317.

Gazzaniga, M. S. (1983). Right hemisphere language following brain bisection: A 20-year perspective. *American Psychologist, 38,* 525–537.

Gazzaniga, M. S. (1985). The social brain. *Psychology Today, 19*(11), 29–38.

Geen, R. G. (1981). Behavioral and physiological reactions to observed violence: Effects of prior exposure to aggressive stimuli. *Journal of Personality and Social Psychology, 40,* 868–875.

Geen, R. G., Stonner, D., & Shope, G. L. (1975). The facilitation of aggression by aggression. Evidence against the catharsis hypothesis. *Journal of Personality and Social Psychology, 31,* 721–726.

Geer, J. T., O'Donohue, W. T., & Schorman, R. H. (1986). Sexuality. In M. G. H. Coles et al. (Eds.), *Psychophysiology: Systems, processes, and applications.* New York: Guilford Press.

Gelman, D., et al. (1985, August 12). The social fallout from an epidemic. *Newsweek,* pp. 28–29.

Gerard, H. B., Wilhelmy, R. A., & Conolley, E. S. (1968). Conformity and group size. *Journal of Personality and Social Psychology, 8,* 79–82.

Gerbner, G., & Gross, L. (1976). The scary world of TV's heavy viewer. *Psychology Today, 9,* 41–45.

Gerrard, G. (1986). Are men and women really different? In K. Kelley (Ed.), *Females, males, and sexuality.* Albany, NY: State University of New York at Albany Press.

Getzels, J. W., & Jackson, P. W. (1962). *Creativity and intelligence: Explorations with gifted students.* New York: Wiley.

Gibson, J. L., Ivancevich, J. M., & Donnelly, J. H., Jr. (1985). *Organizations: Behavior, structure, processes.* Plano, TX: Business Publications, Inc.

Gilbert, S. J. (1981). Another look at the Milgram obedience studies: The role of the gradated series of shocks. *Personality and Social Psychology Bulletin, 7,* 690–695.

Gill, J. S., et al. (1986). Stroke and alcohol consumption. *New England Journal of Medicine, 315,* 1041–1046.

Gillen, B. (1981). Physical attractiveness: A determinant of two types of goodness. *Personality and Social Psychology Bulletin, 7,* 277–281.

Gilligan, C. (1982). *In a different voice.* Cambridge, MA: Harvard University Press.

Gillis, J. S., & Avis, W. E. (1980). The male-taller norm in mate selection. *Personality and Social Psychology Bulletin, 6,* 396–401.

Gilovich, T. (1983). Biased evaluation and persistence in gambling. *Journal of Personality and Social Psychology, 44,* 1110–1126.

Ginzberg, E. (1972). Toward a theory of occupational choice: A restatement. *Vocational Guidance Quarterly, 20,* 169–176.

Gladue, B. A., Green, R., & Hellman, R. E. (1984). Neuroendocrine response to estrogen and sexual orientation. *Science, 225,* 1496–1499.

Glasgow, R. E., Klesges, R. C., Godding, P. R., & Gegelman, R. (1983). Controlled smoking, with or without carbon monoxide feedback, as an alternative for chronic smokers. *Behavior Therapy, 14,* 396–397.

Glasgow, R. E., Klesges, R. C., Godding, P. R., Vasey, M. W., & O'Neill, H. K. (1984). Evaluation of a worksite-controlled smoking program. *Journal of Consulting and Clinical Psychology, 52,* 137–138.

Glasgow, R. E., Klesges, R. C., Klesges, L. M., Vasey, M. W., & Gunnarson, D. F. (1985). Long-term effects of a controlled smoking program: A two and one-half year follow-up. *Behavior Therapy, 16,* 303–307.

Glasgow, R. E., & Terborg, J. R. (1988). Occupational health promotion programs to reduce cardiovascular risk. *Journal of Consulting and Clinical Psychology, 56,* 365–373.

Glass, D. C. (1977). *Stress and coronary-prone behavior.* Hillsdale, NJ: Erlbaum.

Glass, D. C., & Singer, J. E. (1972). *Urban stress.* New York: Academic Press.

Gleitman, L. R., Newport, E. L., & Gleitman, H. (1984). The current status of the motherese hypothesis. *Journal of Child Language, 11,* 43–79.

Goddard, H. H. (1917). Mental tests and the immigrant. *The Journal of Delinquency, 2,* 243–277.

Godden, D. R., & Baddeley, A. D. (1975). Context-dependent memory in two natural environments: On land and underwater. *British Journal of Psychology, 66,* 325–331.

Goeders, N. E., & Smith, J. E. (1983). Cortical dopaminergic involvement in cocaine reinforcement. *Science, 221,* 773–775.

Goelet, P., et al. (1986). The long and the short of long-term memory—A molecular framework. *Nature, 322,* 419–422.

Gold, J. A., Ryckman, R. M., & Mosley, N. R. (1984). Romantic mood induction and attraction to a dissimilar other: Is love blind? *Personality and Social Psychology Bulletin, 10,* 358–368.

Gold, P. E., & King, R. A. (1974). Retrograde amnesia: Storage failure versus retrieval failure. *Psychological Review, 81,* 465–469.

Goldberg, L. W. (1978). Differential attribution of trait-descriptive terms to oneself as compared to well-liked, neutral, and disliked others. *Journal of Personality and Social Psychology, 36,* 1012–1028.

Goldberg, S. (1983). Parent–infant bonding: Another look. *Child Development, 54,* 1355–1382.

Goldberg, S., & Lewis, M. (1969). Play behavior in the year-old infant: Early sex differences. *Child Development, 40,* 21–31.

Goldfoot, D. A., Essock-Vitale, S. M., Asa, C. S., Thornton, J. E., & Leshner, A. I. (1978). Anosmia in male rhesus monkeys does not alter copulatory activity with cycling females. *Science, 199,* 1095–1096.

Goldfried, M. R., Linehan, M. M., & Smith, J. L. (1978). Reduction of test anxiety through cognitive restructuring. *Journal of Consulting and Clinical Psychology, 46,* 32–39.

Goldsmith, H. H. (1983). Genetic influences on personality from infancy to adulthood. *Child Development, 54,* 331–355.

Goldsmith, J. R. (1968). Effects of air pollution on human health. In A. C. Stearn (Ed.), *Air pollution.* New York: Academic Press.

Goldstein, I. L., & Buxton, V. M. (1982). Training and human performance. In M. D. Dunnette & E. A. Fleishman (Eds.), *Human Performance and Productivity, 1,* 135–177.

Goldstein, M., & Davis, E. E. (1972). Race and belief: A further analysis of the social determinants of behavioral intentions. *Journal of Personality and Social Psychology, 22,* 345–355.

Goldstein, T. (1988, February 12). Women in the law aren't yet equal partners. *The New York Times,* p. B7.

Goleman, D. J. (1982). Staying up. *Psychology Today, 16*(3), 24–35.

Goleman, D. J. (1985, January 15). Pressure mounts for analysts to prove theory is scientific. *The New York Times,* pp. C1, C9.

Golub, S. (1976). The effect of premenstrual anxiety and depression on cognitive function. *Journal of Personality and Social Psychology, 34,* 99–104.

Goodheart, D. E. (1985). Some psychological effects associated with positive and negative thinking about stressful event outcomes. *Journal of Personality and Social Psychology, 48,* 216–232.

Goodwin, D. W. (1979). Alcoholism and heredity. *Archives of General Psychiatry, 36,* 57–61.

Goodwin, D. W. (1985). Alcoholism and genetics. *Archives of General Psychiatry, 42,* 171–174.

Goodwin, D. W., et al. (1973). Alcohol problems in adoptees raised apart from alcoholic biological parents. *Archives of General Psychiatry, 30,* 239–243.

Gordon, E. W., & Terrell, M. D. (1981). The changed social context of testing. *American Psychologist, 36,* 1167–1171.

Gordon, T., & Doyle, J. T. (1987). Drinking and mortality: The Albany Study. *American Journal of Epidemiology, 125,* 263–270.

Gormally, J., Sipps, G., Raphael, R., Edwin, D., & Varvil-Weld, D. (1981). The relationship between maladaptive cognitions and social anxiety. *Journal of Consulting and Clinical Psychology, 49,* 300–301.

Gotlib, I. H. (1982). Self-reinforcement and depression in interpersonal interaction: The role of performance level. *Journal of Abnormal Psychology, 91,* 3–13.

Gotlib, I. H. (1984). Depression and general psychopathology in university students. *Journal of Abnormal Psychology, 93,* 19–30.

Gottman, J., Notarius, C., Gonso, J., & Markman, H. (1976). *A couple's guide to communication.* Champaign, IL: Research Press.

Gould, R. (1975). Adult life stages: Growth toward self-tolerance. *Psychology Today, 8,* 74–81.

Goy, R. W., & Goldfoot, D. A. (1976). Neuroendocrinology: Animal models and problems of human sexuality. In E. A. Rubenstein et al. (Eds.), *New directions in sex research.* New York: Plenum Publishing Co.

Goy, R. W., & McEwen, B. S. (1982). *Sexual differentiation of the brain.* Cambridge, MA: MIT Press.

Graesser, A. C., & Nakamura, G. V. (1982). The impact of a schema on comprehension and memory. In G. H. Bower (Ed.), *The psychology of learning and motivation,* Vol. 16. New York: Academic Press.

Graham, J. (1977). *The MMPI: A practical guide.* New York: Oxford University Press.

Granberg, D., & Brent, E. (1983). When prophecy bends: The preference–expectation link in U.S. presidential elections. *Journal of Personality and Social Psychology, 45,* 477–491.

Gray, V. R. (1984). The psychological response of the dying patient. In P. S. Chaney (Ed.), *Dealing with death and dying,* 2d ed. Springhouse, PA: International Communications.

Graziano, W., Brothen, T., & Berscheid, E. (1978). Height and attraction: Do men and women see eye-to-eye? *Journal of Personality, 46,* 128–145.

Green, J. A., Jones, L. E., & Gustafson, G. E. (1987). Perception of cries by parents and nonparents: Relation to cry acoustics. *Developmental Psychology, 23,* 370–382.

Green, R. (1987). *The "sissy boy syndrome" and the development of homosexuality.* New Haven: Yale University Press.

Green, S. K., Buchanan, D. R., & Heuer, S. K. (1984). Winners, losers, and choosers: A field investigation of dating initiation. *Personality and Social Psychology Bulletin, 10,* 502–511.

Greenbaum, P., & Rosenfeld, H. M. (1978). Patterns of avoidance in response to interpersonal staring and proximity: Effects of bystanders on drivers at a traffic intersection. *Journal of Personality and Social Psychology, 36,* 575–587.

Greenberg, R., Pearlman, C., Schwartz, W. R., & Grossman, H. Y. (1983). Memory, emotion, and REM sleep. *Journal of Abnormal Psychology, 92,* 378–381.

Greene, J. (1982). The gambling trap. *Psychology Today, 16*(9), 50–55.

Gregory, R. L. (1973). *Eye and brain,* 2d ed. New York: World Universities Library.

Greist, J. H. (1984). Exercise in the treatment of depression. *Coping with mental stress: The potential and limits of exercise intervention.* Washington, DC: National Institute of Mental Health.

Grinspoon, L. (1987, July 28). Cancer patients should get marijuana. *The New York Times,* p. A23.

Grossman, K., Thane, K., & Grossman, K. E. (1981). Maternal tactual contact of the newborn after various postpartum conditions of mother–infant contact. *Developmental Psychology, 17,* 158–169.

Groth, A. N., & Birnbaum, H. J. (1979). *Men who rape.* New York: Plenum Publishing Co.

Groth, A. N., & Burgess, A. W. (1980). Male rape: Offenders and victims. *American Journal of Psychiatry, 137,* 806–810.

Gronlund, N. E. (1985). *Measurement and evaluation in teaching,* 5th ed. New York: Macmillan.

Grünbaum, A. (1985). Cited in Goleman, D. J. (1985, January 15). Pressure mounts for analyst to prove theory is scientific. *The New York Times,* pp. C1, C9.

Grush, J. E. (1980). The impact of candidate expenditures, regionality, and prior outcomes on the 1976 Democratic presidential primaries. *Journal of Personality and Social Psychology, 38,* 337–347.

Guilford, J. P. (1959). Traits of creativity. In H. H. Anderson (Ed.), *Creativity and its cultivation.* New York: Harper & Row.

Guilford, J. P. (1967). *The nature of human intelligence.* New York: McGraw-Hill.

Guilford, J. P., & Hoepfner, R. (1971). *The analysis of intelligence.* New York: McGraw-Hill.

Haaf, R. A., Smith, P. H., & Smitley, S. (1983). Infant response to facelike patterns under fixed trial and infant-control procedures. *Child Development, 54,* 172–177.

Haber, R. N. (1969). Eidetic images. *Scientific American, 220,* 36–55.

Haber, R. N. (1980). Eidetic images are not just imaginary. *Psychology Today, 14*(11), 72–82.

Haber, R. N., & Hershenson, M. (1980). *The psychology of visual perception.* New York: Holt, Rinehart and Winston.

Hackett, T. P., & Cassem, N. H. (1970). Psychological reactions to life-threatening illness: Acute myocardial infarction. In H. S. Abram (Ed.), *Psychological aspects of stress.* Springfield, IL: Charles C. Thomas.

Haley, J. (1987). *Problem-solving therapy,* 2d ed. San Francisco: Jossey-Bass.

Hall, C. S. (1966). *The meaning of dreams.* New York: McGraw-Hill.

Hall, C. S. (1984). "A ubiquitous sex difference in dreams" revisited. *Journal of Personality and Social Psychology, 46,* 1109–1117.

Hall, E. T. (1968). Proxemics. *Current Anthropology, 9,* 83–107.

Hall, J. A., & Taylor, M. C. (1985). Psychological androgyny and the masculinity-femininity interaction. *Journal of Personality and Social Psychology, 49,* 429–435.

Hall, N. R. S. (1988). The virology of AIDS. *American Psychologist, 43,* 907–913.

Hall, R. G., Sachs, D. P. L., Hall, S. M., & Benowitz, N. L. (1984). Two-year efficacy and safety of rapid smoking therapy in patients with cardiac and pulmonary disease. *Journal of Consulting and Clinical Psychology, 52,* 574–581.

Hall, S. M., Rugg, D., Tunstall, C., & Jones, R. T. (1984). Preventing relapse to cigarette smoking by behavioral skill training. *Journal of Consulting and Clinical Psychology, 52,* 372–382.

Hall, S. M., Tunstall, C., Rugg, D., Jones, R. T., & Benowitz, N. (1985). Nicotine gum and behavioral treatment in smoking cessation. *Journal of Consulting and Clinical Psychology, 53,* 256–258.

Hall, V. C., & Kaye, D. B. (1980). Early patterns of cognitive development. *Monographs of the Society for Research in Child Development, 45*(2), Serial No. 184.

Halmi, K. A., Eckert, E., LaDu, T. J., & Cohen, J. (1986). Treatment efficacy of cyproheptadine and amitriptyline. *Archives of General Psychiatry, 43,* 177–181.

Halperin, K. M., & Snyder, C. R. (1979). Effects of enhanced psychological test feedback on treatment outcome: Therapeutic implications of the Barnum effect. *Journal of Consulting and Clinical Psychology, 47,* 140–146.

Hamilton, R. J. (1985). A framework for the evaluation of the effectiveness of adjunct questions and objectives. *Review of Educational Research, 55,* 47–86.

Hamm, N. M., Baum, M. R., & Nikels, K. W. (1975). Effects of race and exposure on judgments of interpersonal favorability. *Journal of Experimental Social Psychology, 11,* 14–24.

Hammen, C., Marks, T., Mayol, A., & deMayo, R. (1985). Depressive self-schemas, life stress, and vulnerability to depression. *Journal of Abnormal Psychology, 94,* 308–319.

Hammen, C., & Mayol, A. (1982). Depression and cognitive characteristics of stressful life-event types. *Journal of Abnormal Psychology, 91,* 165–174.

Hansel, C. E. M. (1980). *ESP and parapsychology: A critical evaluation.* Buffalo, NY: Prometheus Books.

Hansen, G. O. (1975). Meeting house challenges: Involvement—the elderly. In *Housing issues.* Lincoln, NE: University of Nebraska Press.

Hanson, J. W., Streissguth, A. P., & Smith, D. W. (1978). The effects of moderate alcohol consumption during pregnancy on growth and morphogenesis. *The Journal of Pediatrics, 92,* 457–460.

Harackiewicz, J. M., Sansone, C., Blair, L. W., Epstein, J. A., & Manderlink, G. (1987). Attributional processes in behavior change and maintenance: Smoking cessation and continued abstinence. *Journal of Consulting and Clinical Psychology, 55,* 372–378.

Harbeson, G. E. (1971). *Choice and challenge for the American woman,* revised ed. Cambridge, MA: Schenckman.

Harburg, E., Erfurt, J. C., Hauenstein, L. S., Chape, C., Schull, W. J., & Schork, M. A. (1973). Socioecological stress, suppressed hostility, skin color, and black-white male blood pressure: Detroit. *Psychosomatic Medicine, 35,* 276–296.

Harder, D. W., Gift, T. E., Strauss, J. S., Ritzler, B. A., & Kokes, R. F. (1981). Life events and two-year outcome in schizophrenia. *Journal of Consulting and Clinical Psychology, 49,* 619–626.

Hare-Mustin, R. (1983). An appraisal of the relationship between women and psychotherapy: 80 years after the case of Dora. *American Psychologist, 38,* 593–601.

Harlow, H. F. (1959). Love in infant monkeys. *Scientific American, 200,* 68–86.

Harlow, H. F. (1965). Sexual behavior in the rhesus monkey. In F. A. Beach (Ed.), *Sex and behavior.* New York: Wiley.

Harlow, H. F., & Harlow, M. K. (1966). Learning to love. *American Scientist, 54,* 244–272.

Harlow, H. F., Harlow, M. K., & Meyer, D. R. (1950). Learning motivated by a manipulation drive. *Journal of Experimental Psychology, 40,* 228–234.

Harlow, H. F., & Zimmermann, R. R. (1959). Affectional responses in the infant monkey. *Science, 130,* 421–432.

Harlow, M. K., & Harlow, H. F. (1966). Affection in primates. *Discovery, 27,* 11–17.

Harrell, T. W., & Harrell, M. S. (1945). Army General Classification Test scores for civilian occupations. *Educational and Psychological Measurement, 5,* 229–239.

Harris, D. K., & Cole, W. E. (1980). *Sociology of aging.* Boston: Houghton Mifflin.

Harris, G. W., & Levine, S. (1965). Sexual differentiation of the brain and its experimental control. *Journal of Physiology, 181,* 379–400.

Harris, L. (1988). *Inside America.* New York: Vintage.

Harris, T. A. (1967). *I'm OK—You're OK.* New York: Harper & Row.

Harrison, A. A., & Saeed, L. (1977). Let's make a deal: An analysis of revelations and stipulations in lonely hearts advertisements. *Journal of Personality and Social Psychology, 35,* 257–264.

Hartmann, E. L. (1973). *The functions of sleep.* New Haven, CT: Yale University Press.

Hartmann, E. L. (1981). The strangest sleep disorder. *Psychology Today, 15*(4), 14–18.

Hartmann, E. L., & Stern, W. C. (1972). Desynchronized sleep deprivation: Learning deficit and its reversal by increased catecholamines. *Physiology and Behavior, 8,* 585–587.

Hartz, A. J., et al. (1984). The association of girth measurements with disease in 32,856 women. *American Journal of Epidemiology, 119,* 71–80.

Harvey, J. H., Ickes, W. J., & Kidd, R. F. (Eds.) (1976). *New directions in attributional research,* Vol. 1. Hillsdale, NJ: Erlbaum.

Harvey, J. H., Ickes, W. J., & Kidd, R. F. (Eds.) (1978). *New directions in attributional research,* Vol. 2. Hillsdale, NJ: Erlbaum.

Hass, R. G., & Linder, D. E. (1972). Counterargument availability and the effects of message structure on persuasion. *Journal of Personality and Social Psychology, 23,* 219–233.

Hassett, J. (1978). Sex and smell. *Psychology Today, 12*(10), 40–42, 45.

Hatfield, E. (1983). What do women and men want from love and sex? In E. R. Allgeier & N. B. McCormick (Eds.), *Changing boundaries: Gender roles and sexual behavior.* Palo Alto, CA: Mayfield.

Hatfield, E., & Sprecher, S. (1986). *Mirror, mirror . . . The importance of looks in everyday life.* Albany, NY: State University of New York at Albany Press.

Hatfield, E., Sprecher, S., & Traupman, J. (1978). Men's and women's reactions to sexually explicit films: A serendipitous finding. *Archives of Sexual Behavior, 6,* 583–592.

Havighurst, R. J. (1972). *Developmental tasks and education,* 3d ed. New York: McKay.

Haynes, R. B. (1976). A critical review of the determinants of patient compliance with therapeutic regimens. In D. L. Sackett & R. B. Haynes (Eds.), *Compliance with therapeutic regimens.* Baltimore: Johns Hopkins University Press.

Haynes, R. B. (1979). Determinants of compliance: The disease and the mechanics of treatment. In R. B. Haynes, D. W. Taylor, & D. L. Sackett (Eds.), *Compliance in health care.* Baltimore: Johns Hopkins University Press.

Haynes, S. G., Feinleib, M., & Eaker, E. D. (1983). Type A behavior and the ten-year incidence of coronary heart disease in the Framingham heart study. In R. H. Rosenman (Ed.), *Psychosomatic risk factors and coronary heart disease.* Bern: Hans Huber.

Haynes, S. G., Feinlieb, M., & Kannel, W. B. (1980). The relationship of psychosocial factors to coronary heart disease in the Framingham study: III. Eight-year incidence of coronary heart disease. *American Journal of Epidemiology, 111,* 37–58.

Haynes, S. N., Adams, A., & Franzen, M. (1981). The effects of presleep stress on sleep-onset insomnia. *Journal of Abnormal Psychology, 90,* 601–606.

Haynes, S. N., Follingstad, D. R., & McGowan, W. T. (1974). Insomnia: Sleep patterns and anxiety level. *Journal of Psychosomatic Research, 18,* 69–74.

Haynes, S. N., Sides, H., & Lockwood, G. (1977). Relaxation instructions and frontalis electromyographic feedback intervention with sleep-onset insomnia. *Behavior Therapy, 8,* 644–652.

Haynes, S. N., Woodward, S., Moran, R., & Alexander, D. (1974). Relaxation treatment of insomnia. *Behavior Therapy, 5,* 555–558.

Hearst, P. (1988). Cited in Gross, J. (1988, September 10). A full circle: Patty Hearst's new life. *The New York Times,* pp. 29–30.

Heaton, R. K., & Victor, R. G. (1976). Personality characteristics associated with psychedelic flashbacks in natural and experimental settings. *Journal of Abnormal Psychology, 85,* 83–90.

Heiby, E., & Becker, J. D. (1980). Effect of filmed modeling on the self-reported frequency of masturbation. *Archives of Sexual Behavior, 9,* 115–122.

Heider, F. (1958). *The psychology of interpersonal relations.* New York: Wiley.

Heiman, J. R. (1975). The physiology of erotica: Women's sexual arousal. *Psychology Today, 9,* 90–94.

Heiman, J. R., & LoPiccolo, J. (1987). *Becoming orgasmic,* 2d ed. Englewood Cliffs, NJ: Prentice Hall Books.

Heingartner, A., & Hall, J. V. (1974). Affective consequences in adults and children of repeated exposure to auditory stimuli. *Journal of Personality and Social Psychology, 29,* 719–723.

Helmreich, R. L., Spence, J. T., & Holahan, C. J. (1979). Psychological androgyny and sex-role flexibility: A test of two hypotheses. *Journal of Personality and Social Psychology, 37,* 1631–1644.

Helson, R., & Moane, G. (1987). Personality change in women from college to midlife. *Journal of Personality and Social Psychology, 53,* 176–186.

Hemstone, M., & Jaspars, J. (1982). Explanations for racial discrimination: The effects of group decision on intergroup attributions. *European Journal of Social Psychology, 12,* 1–16.

Henderson, N. D. (1982). Human behavior genetics. In M. R. Rosenzweig & L. W. Porter (Eds.), *Annual Review of Psychology, 33.* Palo Alto, CA: Annual Reviews.

Hendrick, C., & Hendrick, S. (1986). A theory and method of love. *Journal of Personality and Social Psychology, 50,* 392–402.

Hendrick, C. D., Wells, K. S., & Faletti, M. V. (1982). Social and emotional effects of geographical relocation on elderly retirees. *Journal of Personality and Social Psychology, 42,* 951–962.

Hendrick, J., & Hendrick, C. D. (1977). *Aging in mass society: Myths and realities.* Cambridge, MA: Winthrop.

Hendrick, S., Hendrick, C., Slapion-Foote, M. J., & Foote, F. H. (1985). Gender differences in sexual attitudes. *Journal of Personality and Social Psychology, 48,* 1630–1642.

Hennigan, K. M., Cook, T. D., & Gruder, C. L. (1982). Cognitive tuning set, source credibility, and the temporal persistence of attitude change. *Journal of Personality and Social Psychology, 42,* 412–425.

Hennigan, K. M., DelRosario, M. L., Heath, L., Cook, T. D., Wharton, J. D., & Calder, B. J. (1982). Impact of the introduction of television on crime in the United States. *Journal of Personality and Social Psychology, 42,* 461–477.

Hensley, W. E. (1981). The effects of attire, location, and sex on aiding behavior: A similarity explanation. *Journal of Nonverbal Behavior, 6,* 3–11.

Hersen, M., Bellack, A. S., Himmelhoch, J. M., & Thase, M. E. (1984). Effect of social skill training, amitriptyline, and psychotherapy in unipolar depressed women. *Behavior Therapy, 15,* 21–40.

Heston, L. L. (1966). Psychiatric disorders in foster-home-reared children of schizophrenic mothers. *British Journal of Psychiatry, 112,* 819–825.

Hetherington, E. M. (1972). Effects of father absence on personality development in adolescent daughters. *Developmental Psychology, 7,* 313–326.

Heuch, I., et al. (1983). Use of alcohol, tobacco and coffee, and risk of pancreatic cancer. *British Journal of Cancer, 48,* 637–643.

Hilgard, E. R. (1977). *Divided consciousness: Multiple controls in human thought and action.* New York: Wiley-Interscience.

Hilgard, E. R. (1978). Hypnosis and pain. In R. A. Sternbach (Ed.), *The psychology of pain.* New York: Raven Press.

Hill, C. (1987). Affiliation motivation: People who need people . . . but in different ways. *Journal of Personality and Social Psychology, 52,* 1008–1018.

Hinds, M. D. (1988, January 16). Coping with self-help books. *The New York Times,* p. 33.

Hinds, M. D. (1988, July 23). Finding new ways to make smell sell. *The New York Times,* p. 52.

Hinds, M. W., et al. (1984). Dietary vitamin A, carotene, vitamin C and risk of lung cancer in Hawaii. *American Journal of Epidemiology, 119,* 227–237.

Hines, C. V., Cruickshank, D. R., & Kennedy, J. (1985). Teacher clarity and its relation to student achievement and satisfaction. *American Educational Research Journal, 22,* 87–99.

Hinshaw, S. P., Henker, B., & Whalen, C. K. (1984). Cognitive-behavioral and pharmacologic interventions for hyperactive boys: Comparative and combined effects. *Journal of Consulting and Clinical Psychology, 52,* 739–749.

Hirsch, J. (1975). Jensenism: The bankruptcy of "science" without scholarship. *Educational Theory, 25,* 3–28.

Hite, S. (1976). *The Hite report: A nationwide study on female sexuality.* New York: Macmillan.

Hite, S. (1981). *The Hite report on male sexuality.* New York: Knopf.

Hite, S. (1987). *Women and love, a cultural revolution in progress.* New York: Knopf.

Hittleman, J. N., O'Donohue, N., Zilkha, S., & Parekh, A. (1980). Mother–infant assessment of the LeBoyer "nonviolent" method of childbirth. Paper presented to the meeting of the American Psychological Association, Montreal.

Hobbs, N., & Robinson, S. (1982). Adolescent development and public policy. *American Psychologist, 37,* 212–223.

Hoberman, H. M., Lewinsohn, P. M., & Tilson, M. (1988). Group treatment of depression: Individual predictors of outcome. *Journal of Consulting and Clinical Psychology, 56,* 393–398.

Hobson, J. A., & McCarley, R. W. (1977). The brain as a dream state generator: An activation-synthesis hypothesis of the dream process. *American Journal of Psychiatry, 134,* 1335–1348.

Hoffman, L. W., & Manis, J. D. (1978). Influences of children on marital interaction and parental satisfaction and dissatisfaction. In R. M. Lerner & G. B. Spanier (Eds.), *Child influences on marital and family interaction.* New York: Academic Press.

Hoffman, M. L. (1981). Is altruism part of human nature? *Journal of Personality and Social Psychology, 40,* 121–137.

Hoffmann-Plotkin, D., & Twentyman, C. T. (1984). A multimodal assessment of behavioral and cognitive deficits in abused and neglected preschoolers. *Child Development, 55,* 794–802.

Holahan, C. J. (1986). Environmental psychology. In M. R. Rosensweig & L. W. Porter (Eds.), *Annual Review of Psychology, 37,* 381–407.

Holahan, C. J., & Moos, R. H. (1985). Life stress and health: Personality, coping, and family support in stress resistance. *Journal of Personality and Social Psychology, 49,* 739–747.

Holland, J. L. (1975). *Vocational preference inventory.* Palo Alto, CA: Consulting Psychologists Press.

Hollingshead, A. B., & Redlich, F. C. (1958). *Social class and mental illness: A community study.* New York: Wiley.

Hollon, S., & Beck, A. T. (1986). Research on cognitive therapies. In S. L. Garfield & A. E. Bergin (Eds.), *Handbook of psychotherapy and behavior change,* 3d ed. New York: Wiley.

Holmes, D. S. (1984). Meditation and somatic arousal reduction: A review of the experimental evidence. *American Psychologist, 39,* 1–10.

Holmes, D. S. (1985). To meditate or to simply rest, that is the question: A response to the comments of Shapiro. *American Psychologist, 40,* 722–725.

Holmes, D. S., McGilley, B. M., & Houston, B. K. (1984). Task-related arousal of Type A and Type B persons: Level of challenge and response specificity. *Journal of Personality and Social Psychology, 46,* 1322–1327.

Holmes, D. S., Solomon, S., Cappo, B. M., & Greenberg, J. L. (1983). Effects of transcendental meditation versus resting on physiological and subjective arousal. *Journal of Personality and Social Psychology, 44,* 1244–1252.

Holmes, D. S., & Will, M. J. (1985). Expression of interpersonal aggression by angered and nonangered persons with the Type A and Type B behavior patterns. *Journal of Personality and Social Psychology, 48,* 723–727.

Holmes, T. H., & Rahe, R. H. (1967). The social readjustment rating scale. *Journal of Psychosomatic Research, 11,* 213–218.

Holroyd, K. A., Westbrook, T., Wolf, M., & Badhorn, E. (1978). Performance, cognition, and physiological responding in test anxiety. *Journal of Abnormal Psychology, 87,* 442–451.

Holt, R. R. (1982). Occupational stress. In L. Goldberger & S. Brenitz (Eds.), *Handbook of stress.* New York: Free Press.

Honts, C., Hodes, R., & Raskin, D. (1985). *Journal of Applied Psychology, 70*(1).

Horn, J. M. (1983). The Texas adoption project: Adopted children and their intellectual resemblance to biological and adoptive parents. *Child Development, 54,* 268–275.

Horney, K. (1967). *Feminine psychology.* New York: W. W. Norton.

Horvath, T. (1981). Physical attractiveness: The influence of selected torso parameters. *Archives of Sexual Behavior, 10,* 21–24.

House, J. S. (1981). *Work stress and social support.* Reading, MA: Addison-Wesley.

House, J. S. (1984). Barriers to work stress: I. Social support. In W. D. Gentry, H. Benson, & C. deWolff (Eds.), *Behavioral medicine: Work, stress, and health.* The Hague: Nijhoff.

House, J. S., Robbins, C., & Metzner, H. L. (1982). The association of social relationships and activities with mortality: Prospective evidence from the Tecumseh Community Health Study. *American Journal of Epidemiology, 116,* 123–140.

Howard, D. V. (1983). *Cognitive psychology.* New York: Macmillan.

Howard, J. A., Blumstein, P., & Schwartz, P. (1987). Social or evolutionary theories: Some observations on preferences in mate selection. *Journal of Personality and Social Psychology, 53,* 194–200.

Howard, J. L., Liptzin, M. B., & Reifler, C. B. (1973). Is pornography a problem? *Journal of Social Issues, 29,* 133–145.

Howard, K. I., Kopta, S. M., Krause, M. S., & Orlinksy, D. E. (1986). The dose-effect relationship in psychotherapy. *American Psychologist, 41,* 159–164.

Howard, L., & Polich, J. (1985). P300 latency and memory span development. *Developmental Psychology, 21,* 283–289.

Howes, M. J., Hokanson, J. E., & Loewenstein, D. A. (1985). Induction to depressive affect after prolonged exposure to a mildly depressed individual. *Journal of Personality and Social Psychology, 49,* 1110–1113.

Hrncir, E. J., Speller, G. M., & West, M. (1985). What are we testing? *Developmental Psychology, 21,* 226–232.

Hsu, L. K. G. (1986). The treatment of anorexia nervosa. *American Journal of Psychiatry, 143,* 573–581.

Huesmann, L. R., Eron, L. D., Klein, R., Brice, P., & Fischer, P. (1983). Mitigating the imitation of aggressive behaviors by changing children's attitudes about media violence. *Journal of Personality and Social Psychology, 44,* 899–910.

Hugdahl, K., & Ohman, A. (1977). Effects of instruction on acquisition and extinction of electrodermal response to fear-relevant stimuli. *Journal of Experimental Psychology: Human Learning and Memory, 3,* 608–618.

Hughes, P. L., et al. (1986). Treating bulimia with desipramine. *Archives of General Psychiatry, 43,* 182–186.

Hull, J. G. (1981). A self-awareness model of the causes and effects of alcohol consumption. *Journal of Abnormal Psychology, 90,* 586–600.

Hull, J. G., Van Treuren, R. R., & Virnelli, S. (1987). Hardiness and health: A critique and alternative approach. *Journal of Personality and Social Psychology, 53,* 518–530.

Humphreys, L. G. (1981). The primary mental ability. In M. P. Friedman, J. P. Das, & N. O'Connor (Eds.), *Intelligence and learning.* New York: Plenum Publishing Co.

Hunt, M. (1974). *Sexual behavior in the 1970s.* Chicago: Playboy Press.

Hunter, J. E., & Schmidt, F. L. (1983). Quantifying the effects of psychological interventions on employee job performance and work-force productivity. *American Psychologist, 38,* 473–478.

Hurvich, L. M. (1981). *Color vision.* Sunderland, MA: Sinauer Associates.

Huston, A. C. (1983). Sex-typing. In P. H. Mussen (Ed.), *Handbook of child psychology, Vol. 4: Socialization, personality, and social development.* New York: Wiley.

Hutchings, B., & Mednick, S. A. (1974). Registered criminality in the adoptive and biological parents of registered male adoptees. In S. A. Mednick, F. Schulsinger, J. Higgins, & B. Bell (Eds.), *Genetics, environment, and psychopathology.* New York: Elsevier.

Huxley, A. (1939). *Brave new world.* New York: Harper & Row.

Hyde, J. S. (1981). How large are cognitive gender differences? *American Psychologist, 36,* 892–901.

Ilgen, D. (1988). Cited in D. Goleman, Why job criticism fails: Psychology's new findings. *The New York Times,* July 26, 1988, pp. C1, C15.

Insko, C. A. (1985). Balance theory, the Jordan paradigm, and the Wiest tetrahedron. In L. Berkowitz (Ed.), *Advances in experimental social psychology.* New York: Academic Press.

Insko, C. A., Smith, R. H., Alicke, M. D., Wade, J., & Taylor, S. (1985). Conformity and group size: The concern with being right and the concern with being liked. *Personality and Social Psychology Bulletin, 11,* 41–50.

Israel, A. C., Stolmaker, L., & Andrian, C. A. G. (1985). The effects of training parents in general child management skills on a behavioral weight loss program for children. *Behavior Therapy, 16,* 169–180.

Istvan, J., & Griffitt, W. (1978). Emotional arousal and sexual attraction. Unpublished manuscript, Kansas State University.

Ivancevich, J. M., & Matteson, M. T. (1980). *Stress and work: A managerial perspective.* Glenview, IL: Scott, Foresman.

Ivey, M. E., & Bardwick, J. M. (1968). Patterns of affective fluctuation in the menstrual cycle. *Psychosomatic Medicine, 30,* 336–345.

Izard, C. E. (1978). On the development of emotions and emotion-cognition relationships in infancy. In M. Lewis & L. Rosenblum (Eds.), *The development of affect.* New York: Plenum Publishing Co.

Izard, C. E. (Ed.) (1982). *Measuring emotions in infants and children.* New York: Cambridge University Press.

Izard, C. E. (1984). Emotion-cognition relationships and human development. In C. E. Izard, J. Kagan, & R. B. Zajonc (Eds.), *Emotions, cognition, and behavior.* New York: Cambridge University Press.

Jacklin, C. N., & Maccoby, E. E. (1983). Issues of gender differentiation. In M. D. Levine, et al. (Eds.), *Developmental-behavioral pediatrics.* Philadelphia: W. B. Saunders.

Jackson, J. M., & Harkins, S. G. (1985). Equity in effort: An explanation of the social loafing effect. *Journal of Personality and Social Psychology, 49,* 1199–1206.

Jacobs, T. J., & Charles, E. (1980). Life events and the occurrence of cancer in children. *Psychosomatic Medicine, 42,* 11–24.

Jacobson, E. (1938). *Progressive relaxation.* Chicago: University of Chicago Press.

Jaffe, H. W., et al. (1983). Acquired immune deficiency syndrome in the United States. *Journal of Infectious Diseases, 148,* 339–345.

James, W. (1890). *The principles of psychology.* New York: Henry Holt and Company.

James, W. (1904). Does "consciousness" exist? *Journal of Philosophy, Psychology, and Scientific Methods, 1,* 477–491.

Jamison, K. K., & Akiskal, H. S. (1983). Medication compliance in patients with bipolar disorder. *Psychiatric Clinics of North America, 6,* 175–192.

Janda, L. H., & O'Grady, E. E. (1980). Development of a sex anxiety inventory. *Journal of Consulting and Clinical Psychology, 48,* 169–175.

Janicak, P. G., et al. (1985). Efficacy of ECT: A meta-analysis. *American Journal of Psychiatry, 142,* 297–302.

Janis, I. L. (1982). *Groupthink: Psychological studies of policy decisions and fiascoes,* 2d ed. Boston: Houghton Mifflin.

Janis, I. L., Kaye, D., & Kirschner, P. (1965). Facilitating effects of "eating while reading" on responsiveness to persuasive communications. *Journal of Personality and Social Psychology, 1,* 181–186.

Janis, I. L., & Wheeler, D. (1978). Thinking clearly about career choices. *Psychology Today, 12*(12), 66–76, 121–122.

Jankowitz, A. D. (1987). Whatever became of George Kelly? Applications and implications. *American Psychologist, 42,* 481–487.

Jannoun, L., Oppenheimer, C., & Gelder, M. (1982). A self-help treatment program for anxiety state patients. *Behavior Therapy, 13,* 103–111.

Janowitz, H. D., & Grossman, M. I. (1949). Effects of variations in nutritive density on intake of food in dogs and cats. *American Journal of Physiology, 158,* 184–193.

Jeffery, R. W. (1988). Dietary risk factors and their modification in cardiovascular disease. *Journal of Consulting and Clinical Psychology, 56,* 350–357.

Jelliffe, D. B., & Jelliffe, E. F. P. (1983). Recent scientific knowledge concerning breastfeeding. *Rev. Epidem. et Sante. Publ., 31,* 367–373.

Jellison, J. M., & Green, J. (1981). A self-presentation approach to the fundamental attribution error: The norm of internality. *Journal of Personality and Social Psychology, 40,* 643–649.

Jellison, J. M., & Oliver, D. F. (1983). Attitude similarity and attraction: An impression management approach. *Personality and Social Psychology Bulletin, 9,* 111–115.

Jemmott, J. B., Borysenko, J. Z., Borysenko, M., McClelland, D. C., Chapman, R., Meyer, D., & Benson, H. (1983). Academic stress, power motivation, and decrease in secretion rate of salivary secretory immunoglobin A. *Lancet, 1,* 1400–1402.

Jenkins, C. D. (1988). Epidemiology of cardiovascular diseases. *Journal of Consulting and Clinical Psychology, 56,* 324–332.

Jiao, S., Ji, G., & Jing, Q. (1986). Comparative study of behavioral qualities of only children and sibling children. *Child Development, 57,* 357–361.

Johns, M. W., Masterson, J. P., & Bruce, D. W. (1971). Relationship between sleep habits, adrenocortical activity, and personality. *Psychosomatic Medicine, 33,* 499–507.

Johnson, J. H., Butcher, J. N., Null, C., & Johnson, K. N. (1984). Replicated item level factor analysis of the full MMPI. *Journal of Personality and Social Psychology, 48,* 105–114.

Johnson, J. T., Cain, L. M., Falke, T. L., Hayman, J., & Perillo, E. (1985). The "Barnum effect" revisited: Cognitive and motivational factors in the acceptance of personality descriptions. *Journal of Personality and Social Psychology, 49,* 1378–1391.

Johnson, J. T., & Judd, C. M. (1983). Overlooking the incongruent: Categorization biases in the identification of political statements. *Journal of Personality and Social Psychology, 45,* 978–996.

Johnson, P. B. (1981). Achievement motivation and success: Does the end justify the means? *Journal of Personality and Social Psychology, 40,* 374–375.

Johnson, S. M., & White, G. (1971). Self-observation as an agent of behavioral change. *Behavior Therapy, 2,* 488–497.

Johnston, J., & Ettema, J. S. (1982). *Positive images: Breaking stereotypes with children's television.* Beverly Hills, CA: Sage.

Johnston, L. D. (1988). Institute for Social Research, University of Michigan. Cited in Kerr, P. (1988).

Jones, E. (1961). *The life and work of Sigmund Freud.* New York: Basic Books.

Jones, E. (1979). The rocky road from acts to dispositions. *American Psychologist, 34,* 107–117.

Jones, K. L. (1975). The fetal alcohol syndrome. In R. D. Harbison (Ed.), *Perinatal addiction.* New York: Halsted.

Jones, M. (1975). Community care for chronic mental patients: The need for a reassessment. *Hospital and Community Psychiatry, 26,* 94–98.

Jones, M. C. (1924). Elimination of children's fears. *Journal of Experimental Psychology, 7,* 381–390.

Joos, S. K., Pollitt, E., Mueller, W. H., & Albright, D. L. (1983). The Bacon Chow study: Maternal nutritional supplementation and infant behavioral development. *Child Development, 54,* 669–676.

Julien, R. M. (1986). *A primer of drug action,* 2d ed. San Francisco: Freeman.

Judd, C. M., & Park, B. (1988). Out-group homogeneity: Judgments of variability at the individual and group levels. *Journal of Personality and Social Psychology, 54,* 778–788.

Jurkovic, G. J. (1980). The juvenile delinquent as a moral philosopher: A structural-developmental perspective. *Psychological Bulletin, 88,* 709–727.

Jus, A., et al. (1976). Epidemiology of tardive dyskinesia. *Diseases of the Nervous System, 37,* 210–214.

Justice, A. (1985). Review of the effects of stress on cancer in laboratory animals: Importance of time of stress application and type of tumor. *Psychological Bulletin, 98,* 108–138.

Justice, B., & Justice, R. (1976). *The abusing family.* New York: Human Sciences Press.

Kagan, J. (1964). Acquisition and significance of sex-typing and sex-role identity. In M. L. Hoffman & L. W. Hoffman (Eds.), *Review of child development research,* Vol. 1. New York: Russell Sage.

Kagan, J. (1972). The plasticity of early intellectual development. Paper presented at the meeting of the Association for the Advancement of Science, Washington, DC.

Kagan, J. (1984). *The nature of the child.* New York: Basic Books.

Kahn, E. (1985). Heinz Kohut and Carl Rogers: A timely comparison. *American Psychologist, 40,* 893–904.

Kail, R., & Nippold, M. A. (1984). Unrestrained retrieval from semantic memory. *Child Development, 55,* 944–951.

Kalish, R. A. (1985). *Death, grief, and caring relationships,* 2d ed. Monterey, CA: Brooks/Cole.

Kalish, R. A., & Reynolds, D. K. (1976). *Death and ethnicity: A psycho-cultural study.* Los Angeles: University of Southern California Press.

Kallmann, F. J. (1952). Comparative twin study on the genetic aspects of male homosexuality. *Journal of Nervous and Mental Disease, 115,* 283–298.

Kamens, L. (1980). Cognitive and attribution factors in sleep-onset insomnia. Unpublished doctoral dissertation, Southern Illinois University at Carbondale.

Kamin, L. J. (1969). Predictability, surprise, attention, and conditioning. In B. A. Campbell & R. M. Church (Eds.), *Classical conditioning: A symposium.* New York: Appleton-Century-Crofts.

Kamin, L. J. (1973, May). Heredity, intelligence, politics, and psychology. Paper presented at the meeting of the Eastern Psychological Association, Washington, DC.

Kamin, L. J. (1982). Mental testing and immigration. *American Psychologist, 37,* 97–98.

Kandel, D. B. (1980). Drug and drinking behavior among youth. *Annual Review of Sociology, 6,* 235–285.

Kandel, D. B., et al. (1986). The consequences in young adulthood of adolescent drug involvement. *Archives of General Psychiatry, 43,* 746–754.

Kandel, E. R., & Schwartz, J. H. (1982). Molecular biology of learning: Modulation of neurotransmitter release. *Science, 218,* 433–443.

Kanfer, F., & Goldfoot, D. (1966). Self-control and tolerance of noxious stimulation. *Psychological Reports, 18,* 79–85.

Kanin, E. J., & Parcell, S. R. (1977). Sexual aggression: A second look at the offended female. *Archives of Sexual Behavior, 6,* 67–76.

Kanin, G. (1978). *It takes a long time to become young.* Garden City, NY: Doubleday.

Kanner, A. D., Coyne, J. C., Schaefer, C., & Lazarus, R. S. (1981). Comparison of two modes of stress measurement: Daily hassles and uplifts versus major life events. *Journal of Behavioral Medicine, 4,* 1–39.

Kaplan, A. S., & Woodside, D. B. (1987). Biological aspects of anorexia nervosa and bulimia nervosa. *Journal of Consulting and Clinical Psychology, 55,* 645–653.

Kaplan, H. S. (1987). *The real truth about women and AIDS.* New York: Simon & Schuster/Fireside.

Kaplan, R. M., & Singer, R. D. (1976). Television violence and viewer aggression: A reexamination of the evidence. *Journal of Social Issues, 32,* 35–70.

Karacan, I. (1978). Advances in the psychophysiological evaluation of male erectile impotence. In J. LoPiccolo & L. LoPiccolo (Eds.), *Handbook of Sex Therapy.* New York: Plenum Publishing Co.

Karlin, R. A., McFarland, D., Aiello, J. R., & Epstein, Y. M. (1976). Normative mediation of reactions to crowding. *Environmental Psychology and Non-Verbal Behavior, 1,* 30–40.

Karp, L. (1980). The arguable propriety of preconceptual sex determination. *American Journal of Medical Genetics, 6,* 185–187.

Katchadourian, H. A. (1988). *Fundamentals of hu-*

man sexuality. New York: Holt, Rinehart and Winston.

Katzell, R. A., & Guzzo, R. A. (1983). Psychological approaches to productivity improvement. *American Psychologist, 38,* 468–472.

Kavale, K. (1982). The efficacy of stimulant drug treatment for hyperactivity: A meta-analysis. *Journal of Learning Disabilities, 15,* 280–289.

Kazdin, A. E., Moser, J., Colbus, D., & Bell, R. (1985). Depressive symptoms among physically abused and psychiatrically disturbed children. *Journal of Abnormal Psychology, 94,* 298–307.

Kazdin, A. E., & Wilcoxin, L. A. (1976). Systematic desensitization and nonspecific treatment effects: A methodological evaluation. *Psychological Bulletin, 83,* 729–758.

Keating, C. F., et al. (1985). Psychosocial enhancement of immunocompetence in a geriatric population. *Health Psychology, 4,* 25–41.

Keefe, F. J., et al. (1987). Pain coping strategies in osteoarthritis patients. *Journal of Consulting and Clinical Psychology, 55,* 208–212.

Keesey, R. E. (1980). A set-point analysis of the regulation of body weight. In A. J. Stunkard (Ed.), *Obesity.* Philadelphia: W. B. Saunders Co.

Keesey, R. E., & Powley, T. L. (1975). Hypothalamic regulation of body weight. *American Scientist, 63,* 558–565.

Keesey, R. E., & Powley, T. L. (1986). The regulation of body weight. *Annual Review of Psychology, 37,* 109–133.

Keinan, G. (1987). Decision making under stress: Scanning of alternatives under controllable and uncontrollable threats. *Journal of Personality and Social Psychology, 52,* 639–644.

Kelley, C. K., & King, G. D. (1979). Behavioral correlates of the 2–7–8 MMPI profile type in students at a university mental health center. *Journal of Consulting and Clinical Psychology, 47,* 679–685.

Kelley, H. H. (1973). The processes of causal attribution. *American Psychologist, 28,* 107–128.

Kelley, H. H. (1979). *Personal relationships: Their structure and processes.* Hillsdale, NJ: Erlbaum.

Kelley, H. H., & Michela, J. L. (1980). Attribution theory and research. *Annual Review of Psychology, 31,* 457–501.

Kelly, G. A. (1955). *The psychology of personal constructs,* Vols. 1 & 2. New York: W. W. Norton.

Kelly, G. A. (1958). Man's construction of his alternatives. In G. Lindzey (Ed.), *Assessment of human motives.* New York: Holt, Rinehart and Winston.

Kendall, P. C., & Norton-Ford, J. D. (1982). Therapy outcome research methods. In P. C. Kendall & J. N. Butcher (Eds.), *Handbook of research methods in clinical psychology.* New York: Wiley.

Kennell, J. H., et al. (1974). Maternal behavior one year after early and extended post-partum contact. *Developmental Medicine and Child Neurology, 16,* 172–179.

Kennell, J. H., & Klaus, M. H. (1984). Mother–infant bonding: Weighing the evidence. *Developmental Review, 4,* 275–282.

Kenrick, D. T., & MacFarlane, S. W. (1986). Ambient temperature and horn honking: A field study of the heat/aggression relationship. *Environment and Behavior, 18,* 179–191.

Kerpelman, J. P., & Himmelfarb, S. (1971). Partial reinforcement effects in attitude acquisition and counterconditioning. *Journal of Personality and Social Psychology, 19,* 301–305.

Kerr, N. L. (1983). Motivation losses in small groups: A social dilemma analysis. *Journal of Personality and Social Psychology, 45,* 819–828.

Kerr, N. L., & MacCoun, R. J. (1985). The effects of jury size and polling method on the process and product of jury deliberation. *Journal of Personality and Social Psychology, 48,* 349–363.

Kerr, P. (1988, July 10). The American drug problem takes on two faces. *The New York Times,* Section 4, p. 5.

Kershner, J. R., & Ledger, G. (1985). Effect of sex, intelligence, and style of thinking on creativity: A comparison of gifted and average IQ children. *Journal of Personality and Social Psychology, 48,* 1033–1040.

Kesey, K. (1962). *One flew over the cuckoo's nest.* New York: Viking.

Kessner, D. M. (1973). *Infant death: An analysis by maternal risk and health care.* Washington, DC: National Academy of Sciences.

Keverne, E. B. (1977). Pheromones and sexual behavior. In J. Money & H. Musaph (Eds.), *Handbook of sexology.* Amsterdam: Excerpta Medica.

Keye, W. R. (1983). Update: Premenstrual syndrome. *Endocrine and Fertility Forum, 6*(4), 1–3.

Keyes, D. (1982). *The minds of Billy Milligan.* New York: Bantam Books.

Kiecolt-Glaser, J. K., Speicher, C. E., Holliday, J. E., & Glaser, R. (1984). Stress and the transformation of lymphocytes in Epstein-Barr virus. *Journal of Behavioral Medicine, 7,* 1–12.

Kiesler, C. A. (1982). Mental hospitalization and alternative care. *American Psychologist, 37,* 349–360.

Kihlstrom, J. F. (1980). Posthypnotic amnesia for recently learned material: Interactions with "episodic" and "semantic" memory. *Cognitive Psychology, 12,* 227–251.

Kihlstrom, J. F., Brenneman, H. A., Pistole, D. D., & Shor, R. E. (1985). Hypnosis as a retrieval cue in posthypnotic amnesia. *Journal of Abnormal Psychology, 94,* 264–271.

Kilbride, J. E., Komin, S., Leahy, P., Thurman, B., & Wirsing, R. (1981). Culture and the perception of social dominance from facial expression. *Journal of Personality and Social Psychology, 40,* 615–626.

Kimble, D. P. (1988). *Biological psychology.* New York: Holt, Rinehart and Winston.

Kimble, D. P., BreMiller, R., & Stickrod, G. (1986). Fetal brain implants improve maze performance in hippocampal-lesioned rats. *Brain Research, 363,* 358–363.

Kimmel, D. C. (1974). *Adulthood and aging: An interdisciplinary developmental view.* New York: Wiley.

Kimura, D. (1988, November). Paper presented to the Society for Neuroscience, Toronto, Canada.

Kinsey, A. C., Pomeroy, W. B., & Martin, C. E. (1948). *Sexual behavior in the human male.* Philadelphia: W. B. Saunders Co.

Kinsey, A. C., Pomeroy, W. B., Martin, C. E., & Gebhard, P. H. (1953). *Sexual behavior in the human female.* Philadelphia: W. B. Saunders Co.

Klagsbrun, G. (1985). *Married people: Staying together in the age of divorce.* New York: Bantam Books.

Klass, P. (1988, April 10). Are women better doctors? *The New York Times Magazine,* pp. 32–35, 46–97.

Klatsky, A. L., Freidman, G. D., & Siegelaub, A. B. (1981). Alcohol and mortality: A ten-year Kaiser-Permanente experience. *Annals of Internal Medicine, 95,* 139–145.

Klatzky, R. L. (1980). *Human memory: Structures and processes,* 2d ed. San Francisco: W. H. Freeman.

Klatzky, R. L. (1983). The icon is dead: Long live the icon. *Behavioral and Brain Sciences, 6,* 27–28.

Klaus, M. H., & Kennell, J. H. (1976). *Maternal–infant bonding.* St. Louis: Mosby.

Klaus, M. H., & Kennell, J. H. (1978). In J. H. Stevens, Jr. & M Mathews (Eds.), *Mother/child, father/child relationships.* Washington, DC: National Association for the Education of Young Children.

Klein, D. F., & Rabkin, J. G. (1984). Specificity and strategy in psychotherapy research and practice. In R. L. Spitzer & J. R. W. Williams (Eds.), *Psychotherapy research: Where are we and where should we go?* New York: Guilford Press.

Klein, D. N., & Depue, R. A. (1985). Obsessional personality traits and risk for bipolar affective disorder: An offspring study. *Journal of Abnormal Psychology, 94,* 291–297.

Klein, D. N., Depue, R. A., & Slater, J. F. (1985). Cyclothymia in the adolescent offspring of parents with bipolar affective disorder. *Journal of Abnormal Psychology, 94,* 115–127.

Klein, M. H., et al. (1985). A comparative outcome study of group psychotherapy versus exercise treatments for depression. *International Journal of Mental Health, 13,* 148–175.

Klein, R. P. (1985). Caregiving arrangements by employed women with children under 1 year of age. *Developmental Psychology, 21,* 403–406.

Kleinginna, P. R., & Kleinginna, A. M. (1988). Current trends toward convergence of the behavioristic, functional, and cognitive perspectives in experimental psychology. *The Psychological Record, 38,* 369–392.

Kleinke, C. L. (1977). Compliance to requests made by gazing and touching experimenters in field settings. *Journal of Experimental Social Psychology, 13,* 218–223.

Kleinke, C. L., & Staneski, R. A. (1980). First impressions of female bust size. *Journal of Social Psychology, 110,* 123–134.

Kleinke, C. L., & Walton, J. H. (1982). Influence of reinforced smiling on affective responses in an interview. *Journal of Personality and Social Psychology, 42,* 557–565.

Kleinmuntz, B. (1982). *Personality and psychological assessment.* New York: St. Martin's Press.

Kleinmuntz, B., & Szucko, J. J. (1984). Lie detection in ancient and modern times: A call for contemporary scientific study. *American Psychologist, 39,* 766–776.

Knapp, M. L. (1978). *Nonverbal communication in human interaction.* New York: Holt, Rinehart and Winston.

Knaub, P. K., Eversoll, D. B., & Voss, J. H. (1983). Is parenthood a desirable adult role? An assessment of attitudes held by contemporary adult women. *Sex Roles, 9,* 355–362.

Knowlton, W. A., Jr., & Mitchell, T. R. (1980). Effects of causal attributions on a supervisor's evaluation of subordinate performance. *Journal of Applied Psychology, 65,* 459–466.

Kobasa, S. C. (1979). Stressful life events, personality, and health: An inquiry into hardiness. *Journal of Personality and Social Psychology, 37,* 1–11.

Kobasa, S. C. (1985). Personality and health: Specifying and strengthening the conceptual links. In P. Shaver (Ed.), *Self, situations, and social behavior.* Beverly Hills, CA: Sage Press.

Kobasa, S. C., Maddi, S. R., & Kahn, S. (1982). Hardiness and health: A prospective study. *Journal of Personality and Social Psychology, 42,* 168–177.

Kobasa, S. C., Maddi, S. R., & Zola, M. A. (1983). Type A and hardiness. *Journal of Behavioral Medicine, 6,* 41–51.

Kobasa, S. C., & Puccetti, M. C. (1983). Personality and social resources in stress resistance. *Journal of Personality and Social Psychology, 45,* 839–850.

Koffka, K. (1925). *The growth of the mind.* New York: Harcourt Brace Jovanovich.

Kogan, B. A. (1973). *Human sexual expression.* New York: Harcourt Brace Jovanovich.

Kohen, W., & Paul, G. L. (1976). Current trends and recommended changes in extended care placements of mental patients: The Illinois system as a case in point. *Schizophrenia Bulletin, 2,* 575–594.

Kohlberg, L. (1966). A cognitive-developmental analysis of children's sex-role concepts and attitudes. In E. E. Maccoby (Ed.), *The development of sex differences.* Stanford, CA: Stanford University Press.

Kohlberg, L. (1969). *Stages in the development of moral thought and action.* New York: Holt, Rinehart and Winston.

Kohlberg, L. (1981). *The philosophy of moral development: Moral stages and the idea of justice.* San Francisco: Harper & Row.

Köhler, W. (1925). *The mentality of apes.* New York: Harcourt Brace Jovanovich.

Kohn, P. M., Barnes, G. E., & Hoffman, F. M. (1979). Drug-use history and experience seeking among adult male correctional inmates. *Journal of Consulting and Clinical Psychology, 47,* 708–715.

Kolata, G. (1987, November 10). Alcoholism: Genetic links grow clearer. *The New York Times,* pp. C1, C2.

Kolata, G. (1988, February 16). Recent setbacks stirring doubts about search for AIDS vaccine. *The New York Times,* pp. 1, C13.

Kolata, G. (1988, August 30). Latest surgery for Parkinson's is disappointing. *The New York Times,* pp. C1, C3.

Kolko, D. J., & Rickard-Figueroa, J. L. (1985). Effects of video games on the adverse corollaries of chemotherapy in pediatric oncology patients: A single-case analysis. *Journal of Consulting and Clinical Psychology, 53,* 223–228.

Komacki, J., & Dore-Boyce, K. (1978). Self-recording: Its effects on individuals high and low in motivation. *Behavior Therapy, 9,* 65–72.

Konner, M. (1988, January 17). Caffeine high. *The New York Times Magazine,* pp. 47–48.

Koocher, G. P. (1977). Bathroom behavior and human dignity. *Journal of Personality and Social Psychology, 35,* 120–121.

Koop, C. E. (1987). Report of the surgeon general's workshop on pornography and public health. *American Psychologist, 42,* 944–945.

Koop, C. E. (1987). Cited in, Koop urges AIDS test before getting pregnant. *The New York Times,* March 25, 1987, p. B4.

Koop, C. E. (1988, May 17). Excerpts from Koop report on smoking. *The New York Times,* p. C4.

Koop, C. E. (1988). *Understanding AIDS.* HHS Publication No. (CDC) HHS-88-8404. U.S. Government Printing Office, Washington, DC.

Kornblum, W. (1988). *Sociology in a changing world.* New York: Holt, Rinehart and Winston.

Korner, A. F., et al. (1975). Effects of waterbed flotation on premature infants: A pilot study. *Pediatrics, 56,* 361–367.

Koss, M. P., Butcher, J. L., & Strupp, H. H. (1986). Brief psychotherapy methods in clinical research. *Journal of Consulting and Clinical Psychology, 54,* 60–67.

Koss, M. P., Gidycz, C. A., & Wisniewski, N. (1987). The scope of rape: Incidence and prevalence of sexual aggression and victimization in a national sample of higher education students. *Journal of Consulting and Clinical Psychology, 55,* 162–170.

Kramsch, D. M., et al. (1981). Reduction of coronary atherosclerosis by moderate conditioning exercise in monkeys on an atherogenic diet. *New England Journal of Medicine, 305,* 1483–1489.

Krantz, D. S., Contrada, R. J., Hill, D. R., & Friedler, E. (1988). Environmental stress and biobehavioral antecedents of coronary heart disease. *Journal of Consulting and Clinical Psychology, 56,* 333–341.

Krantz, D. S., Grunberg, N. E., & Baum, A. (1985). Health psychology. *Annual Review of Psychology, 36,* 349–383.

Krech, D., Crutchfield, R. S., & Ballachey, E. L. (1962). *Individual in society.* New York: McGraw-Hill.

Krieger, D. T. (1983). Brain peptides: What, where, and why? *Science, 222,* 975–985.

Kromhout, D., Bosschieter, E. B., & de Lezenne Coulander, C. (1985). The inverse relation between fish consumption and 20-year mortality from coronary heart disease. *New England Journal of Medicine, 312,* 1205–1209.

Kübler-Ross, E. (1969). *On death and dying.* New York: Macmillan.

Kübler-Ross, E., & Magno, J. B. (1983). *Hospice.* Santa Fe, NM: Bear.

Kuhn, D., Kohlberg, L., Langer, J., & Haan, N. (1977). The development of formal operations in logical and moral judgment. *Genetic Psychology Monographs.*

Kuntzleman, C. T. (1978). *Rating the exercises.* New York: Morrow.

Kurdek, A., Blisk, D., & Siesky, A. E. (1981). Correlates of children's long-term adjustment to their parents' divorce. *Developmental Psychology, 17,* 565–579.

LaBerge, S. P. (1986). *Lucid dreaming.* New York: Valentine Books.

LaBerge, S. P. (1988). In Blakeslee, S. (1988, August 11). New methods help researchers explore the dark world of dreams. *The New York Times,* p. B5.

LaBerge, S. P., Nagel, L. E., Dement, W. C., & Zarcone, V. P., Jr. (1981). Evidence for lucid dreaming during REM sleep. *Sleep Research, 10,* 148.

LaChance, C. C., Chestnut, R. W., & Lubitz, A. (1978). The "decorative" female model: Sexual stimuli and the recognition of advertisements. *Journal of Advertising, 6,* 11–14.

Ladas, A. K., Whipple, B., & Perry, J. D. (1982). *The G spot and other recent discoveries about human sexuality.* New York: Holt, Rinehart and Winston.

Lahey, B. B., & Drabman, R. S. (1981). Behavior modification in the classroom. In W. E. Craighead, A. E. Kazdin, & M. J. Mahoney (Eds.), *Behavior modification: Principles, issues and applications,* 2d ed. Boston: Houghton Mifflin.

Laird, J. D. (1974). Self-attribution of emotion: The effects of expressive behavior on the quality of emotional experience. *Journal of Personality and Social Psychology, 29,* 475–486.

Laird, J. D. (1984). The real role of facial response in the experience of emotion: A reply to Tourangeau and Ellsworth, and others. *Journal of Personality and Social Psychology, 47,* 909–917.

Lam, D. H., Brewin, C. R., Woods, R. T., & Bebbington, P. E. (1987). Cognition and social adversity in the depressed elderly. *Journal of Abnormal Psychology, 96,* 23–26.

Lamaze, F. (1981). *Painless childbirth.* New York: Simon & Schuster.

Lamb, M. E. (1981). The development of father–infant relationships. In M. E. Lamb (Ed.), *The role of the father in child development.* New York: Wiley.

Lamb, M. E. (1982). Early contact and maternal–infant bonding: One decade later. *Pediatrics, 70,* 763–768.

Lambert, B. (1987, December 13). New York City maps deadly pattern of AIDS. *The New York Times,* pp. 1, 58.

Lambert, M. J., Shapiro, D. A., & Bergin, A. E. (1986). The effectiveness of psychotherapy. In S. L. Garfield & A. E. Bergin (Eds.), *Handbook of psychotherapy and behavior change,* 3d ed. New York: Wiley.

Landesman-Dwyer, S., & Emanuel, I. (1979). Smoking during pregnancy. *Teratology, 19,* 119–126.

Landreth, C. (1967). *Early childhood.* New York: Knopf.

Landy, D., & Sigall, H. (1974). Beauty is talent: Task evaluation as a function of the performer's physical attractiveness. *Journal of Personality and Social Psychology, 30,* 299–304.

Landy, F. J. (1985). *Psychology of work behavior.* Homewood, IL: Dorsey Press.

Landy, F. J., & Farr, J. L. (1983). *The measurement of work performance: Methods, theory, and applications.* New York: Academic Press.

Lang, A. R., Goeckner, D. J., Adesso, V. J., & Marlatt, G. A. (1975). Effects of alcohol on aggression in male social drinkers. *Journal of Abnormal Psychology, 84,* 508–518.

Lang, P. J., & Melamed, B. B. (1969). Case report: Avoidance conditioning therapy of an infant with chronic ruminative vomiting. *Journal of Abnormal Psychology, 74,* 1–8.

Langer, E. J., Rodin, J., Beck, P., Weinan, C., & Spitzer, L. (1979). Environmental determinants of memory improvement in late adulthood. *Journal of Personality and Social Psychology, 37,* 2003–2013.

Langford, H. G., et al. (1985). Dietary therapy slows the return of hypertension after stopping prolonged medication. *Journal of the American Medical Association, 253,* 657–664.

Lanzetta, J. T., Cartwright-Smith, J., & Kleck, R. E. (1976). Effects of nonverbal dissimulation on emotional experience and autonomic arousal. *Journal of Personality and Social Psychology, 33,* 354–370.

Laroche, S., & Bloch, V. (1982). Conditioning of hippocampal cells and long-term potentiation: An approach to mechanisms of posttrial memory facilitation. In C. Ajmone Marsan & H. Matthies (Eds.), *Neuronal plasticity and memory formation.* New York: Raven Press.

Larsen, J. (1984). Cited in, Sad news for the happy hour. *Newsweek,* March 19, 1984, p. 67.

Larson, C. C. (1982). Taub conviction revives centuries-old debate. *APA Monitor, 13*(1), 1, 12–13.

Lashley, K. S. (1950). In search of the engram. In *Symposium of the Society for Experimental Biology,* Vol. 4. New York: Cambridge University Press.

Latané, B., & Dabbs, J. M. (1975). Sex, group size, and helping in three cities. *Sociometry, 38,* 180–194.

Latané, B., & Nida, S. (1981). Ten years of research on group size and helping. *Psychological Bulletin, 89,* 308–324.

Latané, B., Williams, K., & Harkins, S. (1979). Many hands make light the work: The causes and consequences of social loafing. *Journal of Personality and Social Psychology, 37,* 822–832.

Lau, R. R., & Hartman, K. A. (1983). Common sense representations of common illnesses. *Health Psychology, 2,* 167–185.

Lau, R. R., & Russell, D. (1980). Attributions in the sports pages. *Journal of Personality and Social Psychology, 39,* 29–38.

Laube, D. (1985). Premenstrual syndrome. *The Female Patient, 6,* 50–61.

Laudenslager, M. L., et al. (1983). Coping and immunosuppression: Inescapable but not escapable shock suppresses lymphocyte proliferation. *Science, 221,* 568–570.

Lavin, D. E. (1965). *The prediction of academic performance: A theoretical analysis and review of research.* New York: Russell Sage.

Lavrakas, P. J. (1975, May). Female preferences for male physiques. Paper presented at the Midwestern Psychological Association, Chicago.

Lawler, E. E., III. (1985, January/February). Quality circles after the fad. *Harvard Business Review,* pp. 65–71.

Layne, C. (1979). The Barnum effect: Rationality versus gullibility? *Journal of Consulting and Clinical Psychology, 47,* 219–221.

Lazar, I., & Darlington, R. (1982). Lasting effects of early education: A report from the Consortium of Longitudinal Studies. *Monographs of the Society for Research in Child Development, 47*(2–3), Serial No. 195.

Lazarus, R. S. (1984). Puzzles in the study of daily hassles. *Journal of Behavioral Medicine, 7,* 375–389.

Lazarus, R. S. (1984). The trivialization of distress. In B. L. Hammonds & C. J. Scheirer (Eds.), *Psychology and health: The master lecture series.* Washington, DC: American Psychological Association.

Lazarus, R. S., DeLongis, A., Folkman, S., & Gruen, R. (1985). Stress and adaptational outcomes: The problem of confounded measures. *American Psychologist, 40,* 770–779.

Lazarus, R. S., & Folkman, S. (1984). *Stress, appraisal, and coping.* New York: Springer.

Leak, G. K., & Christopher, S. B. (1982). Freudian psychoanalysis and sociobiology: A synthesis. *American Psychologist, 37,* 313–322.

Lear, M. (1987, December 20). The pain of loneliness. *The New York Times Magazine,* pp. 47–48.

Leary, W. E. (1988, July 14). Rare venereal diseases increase sharply. *The New York Times,* p. B6.

LeBon, G. (1895). *The crowd.* New York: Viking, 1960.

LeBow, M. D., Goldberg, P. S., & Collins, A. (1977). Eating behavior of overweight and nonoverweight persons in the natural environment. *Journal of Consulting and Clinical Psychology, 45,* 1204–1205.

Leboyer, F. (1975). *Birth without violence.* New York: Knopf.

Lee, T., & Seeman, P. (1977). Dopamine receptors in normal and schizophrenic human brains. *Proceedings of the Society of Neurosciences, 3,* 443.

Lefcourt, H. M., & Martin, R. A. (1986). *Humor and life stress: Antidote to adversity.* New York: Springer-Verlag.

Lefcourt, H. M., Miller, R. S., Ware, E. E., & Sherk, D. (1981). Locus of control as a modifier of the relationship between stressors and moods. *Journal of Personality and Social Psychology, 41,* 357–369.

Leiblum, S., & Ersner-Hershfield, R. (1977). Sexual enhancement groups for dysfunctional women: An evaluation. *Journal of Sex and Marital Therapy, 3,* 139–152.

Leibowitz, S. F. (1986). Brain monoamines and peptides: Role in the control of eating behavior. *Federation Proceedings, 45,* 599–615.

Leifer, A. D., Leiderman, P. H., Barnett, C. R., & Williams, J. A. (1972). Effects of mother–infant separation on maternal behavior. *Child Development, 43,* 1203–1218.

Leifer, M. (1980). *Psychological effects of motherhood: A study of first pregnancy.* New York: Praeger.

Leippe, M. R. (1985). The influence of eyewitness non-identifications on mock-jurors' judgments of a court case. *Journal of Applied Social Psychology, 15,* 656–672.

Lenneberg, E. H. (1967). *Biological foundations of language.* New York: Wiley.

Lenneberg, E. H. (1969). On explaining language. *Science, 164,* 635–643.

Leonard, C. V. (1974). Depression and suicidality. *Journal of Consulting and Clinical Psychology, 42,* 98–104.

Leonard, C. V. (1977). The MMPI as a suicide predictor. *Journal of Consulting and Clinical Psychology, 45,* 367–377.

Lerner, M. J., Miller, D. T., & Holmes, J. G. (1975). Deserving versus justice: A contemporary dilemma. In L. Berkowitz & E. Walster (Eds.), *Advances in experimental social psychology,* Vol. 12. New York: Academic Press.

Lerner, R. M., & Gellert, E. (1969). Body build identification, preference, and aversion in children. *Developmental Psychology, 1,* 456–462.

Lesnik-Oberstein, M., & Cohen, L. (1984). Cognitive style, sensation seeking, and assortive mating. *Journal of Personality and Social Psychology, 46,* 112–117.

Lester, B. M., Als, H., & Brazelton, T. B. (1982). Regional obstetric anesthesia and newborn behavior: A reanalysis toward synergistic effects. *Child Development, 53,* 687–692.

Leventhal, H. (1970). Findings and theory in the study of fear communication. In L. Berkowitz (Ed.), *Advances in experimental social psychology,* Vol. 5. New York: Academic Press.

Leventhal, H., Meyer, D., & Nerenz, D. R. (1980). The commonsense representation of illness danger. In S. Rachman (Ed.), *Medical psychology,* Vol. 2. New York: Pergamon Press.

Leventhal, H., Nerenz, D. R., & Steele, D. J. (1984). Illness representations and coping with health threats. In A. Baum, S. E. Taylor, & J. E. Singer (Eds.), *Handbook of psychology and health: Vol. 4. Social psychological aspects of health.* Hillsdale, NJ: Erlbaum.

Leventhal, H., Watts, J. C., & Paogano, F. (1967). Effects of fear and instructions on how to cope with danger. *Journal of Personality and Social Psychology, 6,* 313–321.

Levine, J. D., Gordon, N. C., & Fields, H. L. (1979). Naloxone dose dependently produces analgesia and hyperalgesia in post-operative pain. *Nature, 278,* 740–741.

Levinger, G. (1980). Toward the analysis of close relationships. *Journal of Experimental Social Psychology, 16,* 510–544.

Levinson, D. J., Darrow, C. N., Klein, E. B., Levinson, M. H., & McKee, B. (1978). *The seasons of a man's life.* New York: Knopf.

Levitt, M. J. (1980). Contingent feedback, familiarization, and infant affect: How a stranger becomes a friend. *Developmental Psychology, 16,* 425–432.

Levitt, R. A. (1981). *Physiological psychology.* New York: Holt, Rinehart and Winston.

Levy, J. (1985). Right brain, left brain: Fact and fiction. *Psychology Today, 19*(5), 38–44.

Levy, S. M. (1985). *Behavior and cancer: Life-style and psychosocial factors in the initiation and progression of cancer.* San Francisco: Jossey-Bass.

Levy, S. M., Herberman, R. B., Maluish, A. M., Schlien, B., & Lippman, M. (1985). Prognostic risk assessment in the primary breast cancer by behavioral and immunological parameters. *Health Psychology, 4,* 99–113.

Lewinsohn, P. M. (1975). The behavioral study and treatment of depression. In M. Hersen, R. M. Eisler, & P. M. Miller (Eds.), *Progress in behavior modification,* Vol. 1. New York: Academic Press.

Lewinsohn, P. M., & Amenson, C. S. (1978). Some relations between pleasant and unpleasant mood-related events and depression. *Journal of Abnormal Psychology, 87,* 644–654.

Lewinsohn, P. M., & Graf, M. (1973). Pleasant activities and depression. *Journal of Consulting and Clinical Psychology, 41,* 261–268.

Lewinsohn, P. M., & Libet, J. (1972). Pleasant events, activity schedules, and depression. *Journal of Abnormal Psychology, 79,* 291–295.

Lichtenstein, E. (1982). The smoking problem: A behavioral perspective. *Journal of Consulting and Clinical Psychology, 50,* 804–819.

Lichtenstein, E., & Glasgow, R. E. (1977). Rapid smoking: Side effects and safeguards. *Journal of Consulting and Clinical Psychology, 45,* 815–821.

Lick, J. R., & Heffler, D. (1977). Relaxation training and attention placebo in the treatment of severe insomnia. *Journal of Consulting and Clinical Psychology, 45,* 153–161.

Lieberman, M. A., Yalom, I. D., & Miles, M. (1973). *Encounter groups: First facts.* New York: Basic Books.

Ling, G. S. F., et al. (1984). Separation of morphine analgesia from physical dependence. *Science, 226,* 462–464.

Linn, S., et al. (1982). Coffee and pregnancy. *New England Journal of Medicine, 306,* 141–145.

Linz, D., Donnerstein, E., & Penrod, S. (1987). The findings and recommendations of the Attorney General's Commission on Pornography. *American Psychologist, 42,* 946–953.

Lipinski, D. P., Black, J. L., Nelson, R. O., & Ciminero, A. R. (1975). Influence of motivational variables on the reactivity and reliability of self-recording. *Journal of Consulting and Clinical Psychology, 43,* 637–646.

Lipsky, M., Kassinove, H., & Miller, N. (1980). Effects of rational-emotive therapy, rational role reversal, and rational-emotive imagery on the emotional adjustment of community-mental-health-center patients. *Journal of Consulting and Clinical Psychology, 48,* 366–374.

Lipton, D. N., McDonel, E. C., & McFall, R. M. (1987). Heterosocial perception in rapists. *Journal of Consulting and Clinical Psychology, 55,* 17–21.

Lloyd, C., Alexander, A. A., Rice, D. G., & Greenfield, N. S. (1980). Life events as predictors of academic performance. *Journal of Human Stress, 6,* 15–25.

Lochman, J. E. (1987). Self- and peer perceptions and attributional biases of aggressive and nonaggressive boys in dyadic interactions. *Journal of Consulting and Clinical Psychology, 55,* 404–410.

Loehlin, J. C., Willerman, L., & Horn, J. M. (1982). Personality resemblances between unwed mothers and their adopted-away offspring. *Journal of Personality and Social Psychology, 42,* 1089–1099.

Loftus, E. F. (1979). *Eyewitness testimony.* Cambridge, MA: Harvard University Press.

Loftus, E. F. (1983). Silence is not golden. *American Psychologist, 38,* 564–572.

Loftus, E. F., & Burns, T. E. (1982). Mental shock can produce retrograde amnesia. *Memory and Cognition, 10,* 318–323.

Loftus, E. F., & Loftus, G. R. (1980). On the permanence of stored information in the brain. *American Psychologist, 35,* 409–420.

Loftus, E. F., & Palmer, J. C. (1974). Reconstruction of automobile destruction: An example of interaction between language and memory. *Journal of Verbal Learning and Verbal Behavior, 13,* 585–589.

Loftus, G. R. (1983). The continuing persistence of the icon. *Behavioral and Brain Sciences, 6,* 28.

Loftus, G. R., & Loftus, E. F. (1976). *Human memory: The processing of information.* Hillsdale, NJ: Erlbaum.

Lohr, J. M., & Staats, A. (1973). Attitude conditioning in Sino-Tibetan languages. *Journal of Personality and Social Psychology, 26,* 196–200.

Long, B. C. (1984). Aerobic conditioning and stress inoculation: A comparison of stress-management interventions. *Cognitive Therapy and Research, 8,* 517–542.

Long, G. M., & Beaton, R. J. (1982). The case for peripheral persistence: Effects of target and background luminance on a partial-report task. *Journal of Experimental Psychology: Human Perception and Performance, 8,* 383–391.

Long, M. E. (1987, December). What Is This Thing Called Sleep? *National Geographic,* pp. 787–821.

Loomis, J. M., & Lederman, S. J. (1986). Tactual perception. In K. Boff, L. Kaufman, & J. Thomas (Eds.), *Handbook of perception and human performance,* Vol. 1. New York: Wiley.

LoPiccolo, J., Heiman, J. R., Hogan, D. R., & Roberts, C. W. (1985). Effectiveness of single therapists versus cotherapy teams in sex therapy. *Journal of Consulting and Clinical Psychology, 53,* 287–294.

LoPiccolo, J., & Stock, W. E. (1986). Treatment of sexual dysfunction. *Journal of Consulting and Clinical Psychology, 54,* 158–167.

Lorenz, K. Z. (1966). *On aggression.* New York: Harcourt Brace Jovanovich.

Lorenz, K. Z. (1981). *The foundations of ethology.* New York: Springer-Verlag.

Lott, B. (1981). A feminist critique of androgyny: Toward the elimination of gender attributions for learned behavior. In C. Mayo & N. M. Henley (Eds.), *Gender and nonverbal behavior.* New York: Springer.

Lott, B. (1985). The potential enhancement of social/personality psychology through feminist research and vice versa. *American Psychologist, 40,* 155–164.

Lourea, D., Rila, M., & Taylor, C. (1986). Sex in the age of AIDS. Paper presented to the Western Region Conference of the Society for the Scientific Study of Sex, Scottsdale, AZ.

Lowenthal, M. F., & Haven, C. (1981). Interaction and adaptation: Intimacy as a critical variable. In L. D. Steinberg (Ed.), *The life cycle.* New York: Columbia University Press.

Lubin, B., Larsen, R. M., Matarazzo, J. D., & Seever, M. (1985). Psychological test usage patterns in five professional settings. *American Psychologist, 40,* 857–861.

Lublin, J. S. (1984, March 8). Couples working different shifts take on new duties and pressures. *The Wall Street Journal,* p. 33.

Luborsky, L., & DeRubeis, R. J. (1984). The use of psychotherapy treatment manuals: A small revolution in psychotherapy research style. *Clinical Psychology Review, 4,* 5–15.

Luborsky, L., & Spence, D. P. (1971). Quantitative research on psychoanalytic therapy. In A. E. Bergin & S. L. Garfield (Eds.), *Handbook of psychotherapy and behavior change: An empirical analysis.* New York: Wiley.

Lucariello, J., & Nelson, K. (1985). Slot-filler categories as memory organizers for young children. *Developmental Psychology, 21,* 272–281.

Luchins, A. S. (1957). Primacy-recency in impression formation. In C. I. Hovland (Ed.), *The order of presentation in persuasion.* New Haven, CT: Yale University Press.

Luparello, T. J., et al. (1971). Psychologic factors and bronchial asthma. *New York State Journal of Medicine, 71,* 2161–2165.

Lutjen, P., et al. (1984). The establishment and maintenance of pregnancy using in vitro fertilization and embryo donation in a patient with primary ovarian failure. *Nature, 307,* 174–175.

Lykken, D. T. (1957). A study of anxiety in the sociopathic personality. *Journal of Abnormal and Social Psychology, 55,* 6–10.

Lykken, D. T. (1981). *A tremor in the blood: Uses and abuses of the lie detector.* New York: McGraw-Hill.

Lykken, D. T. (1982). Fearlessness: Its carefree charm and deadly risks. *Psychology Today, 16*(9), 20–28.

Lyons, J. S., Rosen, A. J., & Dysken, M. W. (1985). Behavioral effects of tricyclic drugs in depressed patients. *Journal of Consulting and Clinical Psychology, 53,* 17–24.

Maccoby, E. E. (1988). Gender as a social category. *Developmental Psychology, 24,* 755–765.

Maccoby, E. E., & Feldman, S. S. (1972). Mother-attachment and stranger reactions in the third year of life. *Monographs of the Society for Research in Child Development, 37* (No. 1).

Maccoby, E. E., & Jacklin, C. N. (1974). *The psychology of sex differences.* Stanford, CA: Stanford University Press.

Maccoby, E. E., & Jacklin, C. N. (1980). Sex differences in aggression: A rejoinder and reprise. *Child Development, 51,* 964–980.

Macfarlane, A. (1977). *The psychology of childbirth.* Cambridge, MA: Harvard University Press.

Mackay, A. V. P., et al. (1982). Increased brain dopamine and dopamine receptors in schizophrenia. *Archives of General Psychiatry, 39,* 991–997.

Mackett-Stout, J., & Dewar, R. (1981). Evaluation of public information signs. *Human Factors, 23*(2), 139–151.

Maddi, S. R. (1980). *Personality theories: A comparative analysis.* Homewood, IL: Dorsey Press.

Maddi, S. R., & Kobasa, S. C. (1984). *The hardy executive: Health under stress.* Homewood, IL: Dow Jones–Irwin.

Maddison, S., Wood, R. J., Rolls, E. T., Rolls, B. J., & Gibbs, J. (1980). Drinking in the rhesus monkey: Peripheral factors. *Journal of Comparative and Physiological Psychology, 94,* 365–374.

Madsen, C. H., Becker, W. C., & Thomas, D. R. (1968). Rules, praise, and ignoring: Elements of elementary classroom control. *Journal of Applied Behavior Analysis, 1,* 139–150.

Mahoney, M. J. (1980). *Abnormal psychology.* New York: Harper & Row.

Maier, N. R. F., & Schneirla, T. C. (1935). *Principles of animal psychology.* New York: McGraw-Hill.

Main, M., & George, C. (1985). Responses of abused and disadvantaged toddlers to distress in agemates: A study in the day care setting. *Developmental Psychology, 21,* 407–412.

Maital, S. (1982). The tax-evasion virus. *Psychology Today, 16*(3), 74–78.

Malamuth, N. M. (1981). Rape fantasies as a function of exposure to violent sexual stimuli. *Archives of Sexual Behavior, 10,* 33–48.

Malamuth, N. M., Heim, N., & Feshbach, S. (1980). Sexual responsiveness of college students to rape depictions: Inhibitory or disinhibitory effects. *Journal of Personality and Social Psychology, 38,* 399–408.

Malatesta, V. J., Sutker, P. B., & Treiber, F. A. (1981). Sensation seeking and chronic public drunkenness. *Journal of Consulting and Clinical Psychology, 49,* 282–294.

Mandler, G. (1984). *Mind and body: The psychology of emotion and stress.* New York: W. W. Norton.

Mankiewicz, F., & Swerdlow, J. (1977). *Remote control.* New York: Quadrangle.

Mann, L. (1981). The baiting crowd in episodes of threatened suicide. *Journal of Personality and Social Psychology, 41,* 703–709.

Mann, L., Newton, J. W., & Innes, J. M. (1982). A test between deindividuation and emergent norm theories of crowd aggression. *Journal of Personality and Social Psychology, 42,* 260–272.

Mann, L. M., Chassin, L., & Sher, K. J. (1987). Alcohol expectancies and risk for alcoholism. *Journal of Consulting and Clinical Psychology, 55,* 411–417.

Manning, M. M., & Wright, T. L. (1983). Self-efficacy expectancies, outcome expectancies, and the persistence of pain control in childbirth. *Journal of Personality and Social Psychology, 45,* 421–431.

Manucia, G. K., Baumann, D. J., & Cialdini, R. B. (1984). Mood influences on helping: Direct effects or side effects? *Journal of Personality and Social Psychology, 46,* 357–364.

Mansnerus, L. (1988, April 24). Smoking becomes "deviant behavior." *The New York Times,* Section 4, pp. 1, 6.

Marano, H. (1979). Breast-feeding. New evidence: It's far more than nutrition. *Medical World News, 20,* 62–78.

Maratsos, M. (1983). Some current issues in the study of the acquisition of grammar. In J. H. Flavell & E. M. Markman (Eds.), *Handbook of child psychology: Vol. 3. Cognitive development.* New York: Wiley.

Marcus, T. L., & Corsini, D. A. (1978). Parental expectations of preschool children as related to child gender and socioeconomic status. *Child Development, 49,* 243–246.

Marin, P. (1983). A revolution's broken promises. *Psychology Today, 17*(7), 50–57.

Markman, H. J. (1981). Prediction of marital distress: A five-year follow-up. *Journal of Consulting and Clinical Psychology, 49,* 760–762.

Marks, G., Miller, N., & Maruyama, G. (1981). Effect of targets' physical attractiveness on assumption of similarity. *Journal of Personality and Social Psychology, 41,* 198–206.

Marks, I. M. (1982). Toward an empirical clinical science: Behavioral psychotherapy in the 1980s. *Behavior Therapy, 13,* 63–81.

Marks, M. L. (1986). The question of quality circles. *Psychology Today, 20*(3), 36–38, 42, 44, 46.

Marks, P. A., & Monroe, L. J. (1976). Correlates of adolescent poor sleepers. *Journal of Abnormal Psychology, 85,* 243–246.

Markus, H. (1981). The drive for integration: Some comments. *Journal of Experimental Social Psychology, 17,* 257–261.

Marlatt, G. A. (1985). Controlled drinking: The controversy rages on. *American Psychologist, 40,* 374–375.

Marlatt, G. A., & Gordon, J. R. (1980). Determinants of relapse: Implications for the maintenance of behavior change. In P. O. Davidson & S. M. Davidson (Eds.), *Behavioral medicine: Changing health lifestyles.* New York: Brunner/Mazel.

Marlatt, G. A., & Rohsenow, D. J. (1981). The think-drink effect. *Psychology Today, 15*(12), 60–69.

Marston, A. R., London, P., Cohen, N., & Cooper, L. M. (1977). In vivo observation of the eating behavior of obese and nonobese subjects. *Journal of Consulting and Clinical Psychology, 45,* 335–336.

Martelli, M. F., Auerbach, S. M., Alexander, J., & Mercuri, L. G. (1987). Stress management in the health care setting: Matching interventions with patient coping styles. *Journal of Consulting and Clinical Psychology, 55,* 201–207.

Martin, C. L. (1987). A ratio measure of sex stereotyping. *Journal of Personality and Social Psychology, 52,* 489–499.

Martin, R. A., & Lefcourt, H. M. (1983). Sense of humor as a moderator of the relation between stressors and moods. *Journal of Personality and Social Psychology, 45,* 1313–1324.

Martin, R. L., et al. (1985). Mortality in a follow-up of 500 psychiatric outpatients: I. Total mortality. *Archives of General Psychiatry, 42,* 47–54.

Martinez, G. A., & Krieger, F. W. (1985). The 1984 milk-feeding patterns in the United States. *Pediatrics, 76,* 1004–1008.

Maruyama, G., Fraser, S. C., & Miller, N. (1982). Personal responsibility and altruism in children. *Journal of Personality and Social Psychology, 42,* 658–664.

Maruyama, G., & Miller, N. (1975). *Physical attractiveness and classroom acceptance.* Social Science Research Institute Report No. 75–2, University of Southern California.

Maslach, C. (1976, September). Burned out. *Human Behavior, 5,* pp. 16–22.

Maslach, C. (1978). Emotional consequences of arousal without reason. In C. E. Izard (Ed.), *Emotions and psychopathology.* New York: Plenum Publishing Co.

Maslow, A. H. (1963). The need to know and the fear of knowing. *Journal of General Psychology, 68,* 111–124.

Maslow, A. H. (1970). *Motivation and personality,* 2d ed. New York: Harper & Row.

Maslow, A. H. (1971). *The farther reaches of human nature.* New York: Viking.

Masters, W. H., & Johnson, V. E. (1966). *Human sexual response.* Boston: Little, Brown.

Masters, W. H., & Johnson, V. E. (1970). *Human sexual inadequacy.* Boston: Little, Brown.

Masters, W. H., & Johnson, V. E. (1979). *Homosexuality in perspective.* Boston: Little, Brown.

Masters, W. H., Johnson, V. E., & Kolodny, R. C. (1985). *Human sexuality,* 2d ed. Boston: Little, Brown.

Matefy, R. (1980). Role-playing theory of psychedelic flashbacks. *Journal of Consulting and Clinical Psychology, 48,* 551–553.

Mathes, E. W., Adams, H. E., & Davies, R. M. (1985). Jealousy: Loss of relationship rewards, loss of self-esteem, depression, anxiety, and anger. *Journal of Personality and Social Psychology, 48,* 1552–1561.

Matlin, M. (1983). *Cognition.* New York: Holt, Rinehart and Winston.

Matlin, M. (1987). *The psychology of women.* New York: Holt, Rinehart and Winston.

Matsumoto, D. (1987). The role of facial response in the experience of emotion: More methodological problems and a meta-analysis. *Journal of Personality and Social Psychology, 52,* 769–774.

Mattes, J. A., & Gittelman, R. (1983). Growth of hyperactive children on maintenance regimen of methylphenidate. *Archives of General Psychiatry, 40,* 317–321.

Matteson, M. T., & Ivancevich, J. M. (1987). *Controlling work stress.* San Francisco: Jossey-Bass.

Matthews, K. A., & Haynes, S. G. (1986). Type A behavior pattern and coronary disease risk: Update and critical evaluation. *American Journal of Epidemiology, 123,* 923–960.

Matthews, K. A., Krantz, D. S., Dembroski, T. M., & MacDougall, J. M. (1982). Unique and common variance in structured interview and Jenkins Activity Survey measures of the Type A behavior pattern. *Journal of Personality and Social Psychology, 42,* 303–313.

Maugh, T. H. (1982). Marijuana "justifies serious concern." *Science, 215,* 1488–1489.

May, J. L., & Hamilton, P. A. (1980). Effects of musically evoked affect on women's interpersonal attraction toward and perceptual judgments of physical attractiveness of men. *Motivation and Emotion, 4,* 217–228.

May, K. A., & Perrin, S. P. (1985). Prelude: Pregnancy and birth. In S. M. H. Hanson & F. W. Bozett (Eds.), *Dimensions of fatherhood.* Beverly Hills, CA: Sage.

May, P. R. (1975). A follow-up study of treatment of schizophrenia. In R. L. Spitzer & D. F. Klein (Eds.), *Evaluation of psychological therapies.* Baltimore: The Johns Hopkins University Press.

Mays, V. M., & Cochran, S. D. (1988). Issues in the perception of AIDS risk and risk reduction activities by Black and Hispanic/Latina women. *American Psychologist, 43,* 949–957.

McArthur, L. Z., & Resko, B. G. (1975). The portrayal of men and women in American film commercials. *Journal of Social Psychology, 97,* 209–220.

McBurney, D. H., & Collings, V. (1977). *Introduction to sensation/perception.* Englewood Cliffs, NJ: Prentice-Hall.

McBurney, D. H., Levine, J. M., & Cavanaugh, P. H. (1977). Psychophysical and social ratings of human body odor. *Personality and Social Psychology Bulletin, 3,* 135–138.

McCann, I. L., & Holmes, D. S. (1984). Influence of aerobic exercise on depression. *Journal of Personality and Social Psychology, 46,* 1142–1147.

McCanne, T. R., & Anderson, J. A. (1987). Emotional responding following manipulation of facial electromyographic activity. *Journal of Personality and Social Psychology, 52,* 759–768.

McCaul, K. D., & Haugvedt, C. (1982). Attention, distraction, and cold-pressor pain. *Journal of Personality and Social Psychology, 43,* 154–162.

McCaul, K. D., Holmes, D. S., & Solomon, S. (1982). Voluntary expressive changes and emotion. *Journal of Personality and Social Psychology, 42,* 145–152.

McCauley, C., Woods, K., Coolidge, C., & Kulick, W. (1983). More aggressive cartoons are funnier. *Journal of Personality and Social Psychology, 44,* 817–823.

McClearn, G. E., & DeFries, J. C. (1973). *Introduction to behavioral genetics.* San Francisco: Freeman.

McClelland, D. C. (1958). Methods of measuring human motivation. In J. W. Atkinson (Ed.), *Motives in fantasy, action, and society.* Princeton, NJ: Van Nostrand.

McClelland, D. C. (1965). Achievement and entrepreneurship: A longitudinal study. *Journal of Personality and Social Psychology, 1,* 389–392.

McClelland, D. C. (1979). Inhibited power motivation and high blood pressure in man. *Journal of Abnormal Psychology, 88,* 182–190.

McClelland, D. C. (1985). How motives, skills, and values determine what people do. *American Psychologist, 40,* 812–825.

McClelland, D. C., Alexander, C., & Marks, E. (1982). The need for power, stress, immune functions, and illness among male prisoners. *Journal of Abnormal Psychology, 91,* 61–70.

McClelland, D. C., Atkinson, J. W., Clark, R. A., & Lowell, E. L. (1953). *The achievement motive.* New York: Appleton.

McClelland, D. C., Davidson, R. J., Floor, E., & Saron, C. (1980). Stressed power motivation, sympathetic activation, immune function and illness. *Journal of Human Stress, 6*(2), 11–19.

McClelland, D. C., & Jemmott, J. B., III (1980). Power motivation, stress and physical illness. *Journal of Human Stress, 6*(4), 6–15.

McClelland, D. C., & Pilon, D. A. (1983). Sources of adult motives in patterns of parent behavior in early childhood. *Journal of Personality and Social Psychology, 44,* 564–574.

McClintock, M. K. (1971). Menstrual synchrony and suppression. *Nature, 229,* 244–245.

McClintock, M. K. (1979). Estrous synchrony and its mediation by airborne chemical communication. *Hormones and Behavior, 10,* 264.

McConaghy, M. J. (1979). Gender permanence and the genital basis of gender: Stages in the development of constancy of gender. *Child Development, 50,* 1223–1226.

McConaghy, N., & Blaszczynski, A. (1980). A pair of monozygotic twins discordant for homosexuality: Sex-dimorphic behavior and penile volume responses. *Archives of Sexual Behavior, 9,* 123–124.

McConnell, J. V., Jacobson, A. L., & Kimble, D. P. (1959). The effects of regeneration upon retention of a conditioned response in the planarian. *Journal of Comparative and Physiological Psychology, 52,* 1–5.

McConnell, J. V., Shigehisa, T., & Salive, H. (1970). Attempts to transfer approach and avoidance responses by RNA injections in rats. In K. H. Pribram & D. E. Broadbent (Eds.), *Biology of memory.* New York: Academic Press.

McCormick, E. J., & Ilgen, D. (1985). *Industrial and organizational psychology,* 8th ed. Englewood Cliffs, NJ: Prentice-Hall.

McCrady, B. S. (1985). Comments on the controlled drinking controversy. *American Psychologist, 40,* 370–371.

McDougall, W. (1904). The sensations excited by a single momentary stimulation of the eye. *British Journal of Psychology, 1,* 78–113.

McDougall, W. (1908). *An introduction to social psychology.* London: Methuen.

McFadden, D., & Wightman, F. L. (1983). Audition. *Annual Review of Psychology, 34,* 95–128.

McFalls, J. A. (1983). Where have all the children gone? The future of reproduction in the United States. In O. Pocs (Ed.), *Human sexuality, 83/84.* Guilford, CT: Dushkin.

McGaugh, J. L. (1983). Preserving the presence of the past: Hormonal influences on memory storage. *American Psychologist, 38,* 161–174.

McGaugh, J. L., Martinez, J. L., Jr., Jensen, R. A., Messing, R. B., & Vasquez, B. J. (1980). Central and peripheral catecholamine function in learning and memory processes. In *Neural mechanisms of goal-directed behavior and learning.* New York: Academic Press.

McGoldrick, M., & Carter, E. A. (1982). *The family life cycle in normal family processes.* London: Guilford Press.

McGowan, R. J., & Johnson, D. L. (1984). The mother–child relationship and other antecedents of childhood intelligence: A causal analysis. *Child Development, 55,* 810–820.

McGrath, J. J., & Cohen, D. B. (1978). REM sleep facilitation of adaptive waking behavior: A review of the literature. *Psychological Bulletin, 85,* 24–57.

McGregor, D. (1960). *The human side of enterprise.* New York: McGraw-Hill.

McGurk, H., Turnura, C., & Creighton, S. J. (1977). Auditory-visual coordination in neonates. *Child Development, 48,* 138–143.

McKay, M., Davis, M., & Fanning, P. (1983). *Messages: The communication book.* Oakland, CA: New Harbinger.

McKenna, J. F., Oritt, P. L., & Wolff, H. K. (1981). Occupational stress as a predictor in the turnover decision. *Journal of Human Stress,* 7(12), 12–17.

McMullen, S., & Rosen, R. C. (1979). Self-administered masturbation training in the treatment of primary orgasmic dysfunction. *Journal of Consulting and Clinical Psychology, 47,* 912–918.

McNeill, D. (1970). The development of language. In P. H. Mussen (Ed.), *Carmichael's manual of child psychology,* Vol. 1, 3d ed. New York: Wiley.

Mead, M. (1935). *Sex and temperament in three primitive societies.* New York: Morrow.

Mechanic, D. (1978). *Medical sociology.* New York: Free Press.

Mednick, S. A. (1962). The associative basis of the creative process. *Psychological Review, 69,* 220–232.

Mednick, S. A. (1985). Crime in the family tree. *Psychology Today, 19*(3), 58–61.

Meece, J. L., Parsons, J. E., Kaczala, C. M., Goff, S. B., & Futterman, R. (1982). Sex differences in math achievement: Toward a model of academic choice. *Psychological Bulletin, 91,* 324–348.

Meer, J. (1985). Turbulent teens: The stress factors. *Psychology Today, 19*(5), 15–16.

Mehrabian, A., & Weinstein, L. (1985). Temperament characteristics of suicide attempters. *Journal of Consulting and Clinical Psychology, 53,* 544–546.

Meichenbaum, D. (1976). Toward a cognitive theory of self-control. In G. Schwartz & D. Shapiro (Eds.), *Consciousness and self-regulation: Advances in research.* New York: Plenum Publishing Co.

Meichenbaum, D. (1977). *Cognitive behavior modification: An integrative approach.* New York: Plenum Publishing Co.

Meichenbaum, D., & Butler, L. (1980). Toward a conceptual model for the treatment of test anxiety: Implications for research and treatment. In I. G. Sarason (Ed.), *Test anxiety: Theory, research, and application.* Hillsdale, NJ: Erlbaum.

Meichenbaum, D., & Jaremko, M. E. (Eds.) (1983). *Stress reduction and prevention.* New York: Plenum Publishing Co.

Meikle, S., Peitchinis, J. A., & Pearce, K. (1985). *Teenage sexuality.* San Diego: College-Hill Press.

Mellstrom, M., Jr., Cicala, G. A., & Zuckerman, M. (1976). General versus specific trait anxiety measures in the prediction of fear of snakes, heights, and darkness. *Journal of Consulting and Clinical Psychology, 44,* 83–91.

Melzack, R. (1973). *The puzzle of pain.* New York: Basic Books.

Melzack, R. (1980). Psychological aspects of pain. In J. J. Bonica (Ed.), *Pain.* New York: Raven Press.

Melzack, R., & Scott, T. H. (1957). The effects of early experience on the response to pain. *Journal of Comparative and Physiological Psychology, 50,* 155–161.

Mendelson, J. H., Rossi, A. M., & Meyer, R. E. (Eds.) (1974). *The use of marihuana: A psychological and physiological inquiry.* New York: Plenum Publishing Co.

Mertz, G., et al. (1985). Frequency of acquisition of first-episode genital infection with herpes simplex virus from symptomatic and asymptomatic source contacts. *Sexually Transmitted Diseases, 12,* 33–39.

Mewborn, C. R., & Rogers, R. W. (1979). Effects of reassuring and threatening components of fear appraisals of physiological and verbal measures of emotion and attitudes. *Journal of Experimental Social Psychology, 15,* 242–253.

Meyer, D., Leventhal, H., & Gutman, M. (1985). Common-sense models of illness: The example of hypertension. *Health Psychology, 4,* 115–135.

Meyer, J. P., & Pepper, S. (1977). Need compatibility and marital adjustment in young married couples. *Journal of Personality and Social Psychology, 35,* 331–342.

Meyers, J. K., et al. (1984). Six-month prevalence of psychiatric disorders in three communities. *Archives of General Psychiatry, 41,* 959–967.

Michael, R. P., Keverne, E. B., & Bonsall, R. W. (1971). Pheromones: Isolation of male sex attractants from a female primate. *Science, 172,* 964–966.

Michelini, R. L., & Snodgrass, S. R. (1980). Defendant characteristics and juridic decisions. *Journal of Research in Personality, 14,* 340–350.

Mider, P. A. (1984). Failures in alcoholism and drug dependence prevention and learning from the past. *American Psychologist, 39,* 183.

Middlemist, R. D., Knowles, E. S., & Matter, C. F. (1976). Personal space invasions in the lavatory. *Journal of Personality and Social Psychology, 33,* 541–546.

Middlemist, R. D., Knowles, E. S., & Matter, C. F. (1977). What to do and what to report: A reply to Koocher. *Journal of Personality and Social Psychology, 35,* 122–124.

Milam, J. R., & Ketcham, K. (1981). *Under the influence: A guide to the myths and realities of alcoholism.* Seattle: Madrove Publishers.

Milgram, S. (1963). Behavioral study of obedience. *Journal of Abnormal and Social Psychology, 67,* 371–378.

Milgram, S. (1970). The experience of living in cities. *Science, 167,* 1461–1468.

Milgram, S. (1974). *Obedience to authority.* New York: Harper & Row.

Milgram, S. (1977). *The individual in a social world.* Reading, MA: Addison-Wesley.

Miller, A. G. (1986). *The obedience experiments: A case study of controversy in social science.* New York: Praeger.

Miller, C. A. (1985). Infant mortality in the United States. *Scientific American, 235,* 31–37.

Miller, G. A. (1956). The magical number seven, plus or minus two: Some limits on our capacity for processing information. *Psychological Review, 63,* 81–97.

Miller, I. W., Klee, S. H., & Norman, W. H. (1982). Depressed and nondepressed inpatients' cognitions of hypothetical events, experimental tasks, and stressful life events. *Journal of Abnormal Psychology, 91,* 78–81.

Miller, N. E. (1969). Learning of visceral and glandular responses. *Science, 163,* 434–445.

Miller, N. E. (1985). Rx: Biofeedback. *Psychology Today, 19*(2), 54–59.

Miller, N. E. (1985). The value of behavioral research on animals. *American Psychologist, 40,* 423–440.

Miller, N. E., & Dollard, J. (1941). *Social learning and imitation.* New Haven, CT: Yale University Press.

Miller, P. H., Heldmeyer, K. H., & Miller, S. A. (1975). Facilitation of conservation of number in young children. *Developmental Psychology, 11,* 253.

Miller, P. M., & Mastria, M. A. (1977). *Alternatives to alcohol abuse: A social learning model.* Champaign, IL: Research Press.

Miller, S. M. (1980). Why having control reduces stress: If I can stop the roller coaster I don't want to get off. In J. Garber & M. E. P. Seligman (Eds.), *Human helplessness: Theory and research.* New York: Academic Press.

Miller, S. M., Lack, E. R., & Asroff, S. (1985). Preference for control and the coronary-prone behavior pattern. *Journal of Personality and Social Psychology, 49,* 492–499.

Miller, W. R. (1982). Treating problem drinkers: What works? *The Behavior Therapist, 5*(1), 15–18.

Miller, W. R., & Hester, R. K. (1980). Treating the problem drinker. In W. R. Miller (Ed.), *The addictive behaviors.* New York: Pergamon Press.

Miller, W. R., & Muñoz, R. F. (1983). *How to control your drinking,* 2d ed. Albuquerque: University of New Mexico Press.

Millette, B., & Hawkins, J. (1983). *The passage through menopause.* Reston, VA: Reston Publishing.

Millon, T. (1983). The DSM–III: An insider's perspective. *American Psychologist, 38,* 804–814.

Mills, J., & Harvey, J. (1972). Opinion change as a function of when information about the communicator is received and whether he is attractive or expert. *Journal of Personality and Social Psychology, 21,* 52–55.

Milner, B. R. (1966). Amnesia following operation on temporal lobes. In C. W. M. Whitty & O. L. Zangwill (Eds.), *Amnesia.* London: Butterworth.

Milner, J. S., Gold, R. G., Ayoub, C., & Jacewitz, M. M. (1984). Predictive validity of the child abuse potential inventory. *Journal of Consulting and Clinical Psychology, 52,* 879–884.

Mirsky, A. F., & Orzack, M. H. (1980). Two retrospective studies of psychosurgery. In E. S. Valenstein (Ed.), *The psychosurgery debate.* San Francisco: W. H. Freeman.

Mirsky, I. A. (1958). Physiologic, psychologic, and social determinants in the etiology of duodenal ulcer. *American Journal of Digestive Diseases, 3,* 285–315.

Mischel, W. (1977). On the future of personality measurement. *American Psychologist, 32,* 246–254.

Mischel, W. (1986). *Introduction to personality,* 4th ed. New York: Holt, Rinehart and Winston.

Mishkin, M., & Appenzeller, T. (1987). The anatomy of memory. *Scientific American, 256,* 80–89.

Mitchell, J. E., & Eckert, E. D. (1987). Scope and significance of eating disorders. *Journal of Consulting and Clinical Psychology, 55,* 628–634.

Mittelmark, M. B., et al. (1987). Predicting experimentation with cigarettes: The Childhood Antecedents of Smoking Study. *American Journal of Public Health, 77,* 206–208.

Modahl, C., & Newton, N. (1979). Mood state differences between breast- and bottle-feeding mothers. In L. Carenza & L. Zichella (Eds.), *Emotion and reproduction.* New York: Academic Press.

Money, J. (1960). Phantom orgasm in the dreams of paraplegic men and women. *Archives of General Psychiatry, 3,* 373–382.

Money, J. (1974). Prenatal hormones and posthormonal socialization in gender identity differentiation. In J. K. Cole & R. Dienstbier (Eds.), *Nebraska Symposium on Motivation.* Lincoln, NE: University of Nebraska Press.

Money, J. (1977). Human hermaphroditism. In F. A. Beach (Ed.), *Human sexuality in four perspectives.* Baltimore, MD: The Johns Hopkins University Press.

Money, J. (1980). *Love and love sickness.* Baltimore, MD: The Johns Hopkins University Press.

Money, J. (1987). Sin, sickness, or status? Homosexual gender identity and psychoneuroendocrinology. *American Psychologist, 42,* 384–399.

Money, J., & Ehrhardt, A. (1972). *Man and woman, boy and girl.* Baltimore, MD: The Johns Hopkins University Press.

Monmaney, T., et al. (1988, January 18). Heredity and drinking: How strong is the link? *Newsweek,* pp. 66–67.

Monroe, L. J. (1967). Psychological and physiological differences between adolescent poor and good sleepers. *Journal of Abnormal Psychology, 72,* 255–264.

Monroe, L. J., & Marks, P. A. (1977). MMPI differences between adolescent poor and good sleepers. *Journal of Consulting and Clinical Psychology, 45,* 151–152.

Monroe, S. M. (1982). Life events and disorder: Event-symptom associations and the course of disorder. *Journal of Abnormal Psychology, 91,* 14–24.

Monroe, S. M. (1983). Major and minor life events as predictors of psychological distress: Further issues and findings. *Journal of Behavioral Medicine, 6,* 189–205.

Monte, C. F. (1980). *Beneath the mask: An introduction to theories of personality.* New York: Holt, Rinehart and Winston.

Montrose, M. (1978, May). New options in childbirth, Part 1: Family-centered maternity care. *American Baby,* pp. 52–54, 58ff.

Moolgavkar, S. H. (1983). A model for human carcinogenesis: Hereditary cancers and premalignant lesions. In R. G. Crispen (Ed.), *Cancer: Etiology and prevention.* New York: Elsevier Biomedical.

Moon, J. R., & Eisler, R. M. (1983). Anger control: An experimental comparison of three behavioral treatments. *Behavior Therapy, 14,* 493–505.

Moore, J. E., & Chaney, E. F. (1985). Outpatient group treatment of chronic pain: Effects of spouse involvement. *Journal of Consulting and Clinical Psychology, 53,* 325–334.

Moos, R. (1968). The development of the Menstrual Distress Questionnaire. *Psychosomatic Medicine, 30,* 853.

Moreland, R. L., & Zajonc, R. B. (1982). Exposure effects in person perception: Familiarity, similarity, and attraction. *Journal of Experimental Social Psychology, 18,* 395–415.

Morganthau, T., et al. (1986, January 6). Abandoned: The chronic mentally ill. *Newsweek,* pp. 14–19.

Moriarty, T. (1975). Crimes, commitment, and the responsive bystander: Two field experiments. *Journal of Personality and Social Psychology, 31,* 370–376.

Morin, C. M., & Azrin, N. H. (1987). Stimulus control and imagery training in treating sleep-maintenance insomnia. *Journal of Consulting and Clinical Psychology, 55,* 260–262.

Morokoff, P. J. (1985). Effects of sex guilt, repression, sexual "arousability," and sexual experience on female sexual arousal during erotica and fantasy. *Journal of Personality and Social Psychology, 49,* 177–187.

Morris, J. N., et al. (1953). Coronary heart disease and physical activity of work. *Lancet, 2,* 1053–1057, 1111–1120.

Morris, N. M., & Udry, J. R. (1978). Pheromonal influences on human sexual behavior: An experimental search. *Journal of Biosocial Science, 10,* 147–157.

Morris, W. N., Miller, R. S., & Spangenberg, S. (1977). The effects of dissenter position and task difficulty on conformity and response conflict. *Journal of Personality, 45,* 251–256.

Moscovici, S. (1985). Social influence and conformity. In G. Lindzey & E. Aronson (Eds.), *Handbook of social psychology,* Vol. 2. New York: Random House.

Motowidlo, S. T. (1982). Sex role orientation and behavior in a work setting. *Journal of Personality and Social Psychology, 42,* 935–945.

Mowrer, O. H. (1947). On the dual nature of learning—a reinterpretation of "conditioning" and "problem-solving." *Harvard Educational Review, 17,* 102–148.

Mueser, K. T., Grau, B. W., Sussman, S., & Rosen, A. J. (1984). You're only as pretty as you feel: Facial expression as a determinant of physical attractiveness. *Journal of Personality and Social Psychology, 46,* 469–478.

Mullen, B., et al. (1987). Newscasters' facial expressions and voting behavior of viewers: Can a smile elect a president? *Journal of Personality and Social Psychology, 53,* in press.

Murphy, G. E., et al. (1984). Cognitive therapy and pharmacotherapy: Singly and together in the treatment of depression. *Archives of General Psychiatry, 41,* 33–41.

Murray, A. D. (1985). Aversiveness is in the mind of the beholder. In B. M. Lester & C. F. Z. Boukydis (Eds.), *Infant crying.* New York: Plenum Publishing Co.

Murray, A. D., Dolby, R. M., Nation, R. L., & Thomas, D. B. (1981). Effects of epidural anesthesia on newborns and their mothers. *Child Development, 52,* 71–82.

Murray, E. A., & Mishkin, M. (1985). Amygdalectomy impairs cross-modal association in monkeys. *Science, 228,* 604–606.

Murray, H. A. (1938). *Explorations in personality.* New York: Oxford University Press.

Murstein, B. I. (1972). Physical attractiveness and marital choice. *Journal of Personality and Social Psychology, 22,* 8–12.

Murstein, B. I., & Christy, P. (1976). Physical attractiveness and marital adjustment in middle-aged couples. *Journal of Personality and Social Psychology, 34,* 537–542.

Musante, L., MacDougall, J. M., Dembroski, T. M., & Van Horn, A. E. (1983). Component analysis of the Type A coronary-prone behavior pattern in male and female college students. *Journal of Personality and Social Psychology, 45,* 1104–1117.

Myers, A. M., & Gonda, G. (1982). Utility of the masculinity–femininity construct: Comparison of traditional and androgyny approaches. *Journal of Personality and Social Psychology, 43,* 514–523.

Myers, B. J. (1984). Mother–infant bonding: The status of this critical period hypothesis. *Developmental Review, 4,* 283–288.

Myers, D. G. (1983). Polarizing effects of social interaction. In H. Brandstatter, J. H. Davis, & G. Stocker-Kreichgauer (Eds.), *Group decision processes.* London: Academic Press.

Myers, D. G., & Lamm, H. (1976). The group polarization phenomenon. *Psychological Bulletin, 85,* 602–627.

Myers, M. B., Templer, D. I., & Brown, R. (1984). Coping ability of women who become victims of rape. *Journal of Consulting and Clinical Psychology, 52,* 73–78.

Myers, M. B., Templer, D. I., & Brown, R. (1985). Reply to Wieder on rape victims: Vulnerability does not imply responsibility. *Journal of Consulting and Clinical Psychology, 53,* 431.

Naffziger, C. C., & Naffziger, K. (1974). Development of sex role stereotypes. *Family Coordinator, 23,* 251–258.

Nahemow, L., & Lawton, M. P. (1975). Similarity and propinquity in a friendship formation. *Journal of Personality and Social Psychology, 32,* 205–213.

Narayanan, V. K., & Nath, R. (1982). A field test of some attitudinal and behavioral consequences of flexitime. *Journal of Applied Psychology, 67,* 214–218.

Nathans, J., Thomas, D., & Hogness, D. S. (1986). Molecular genetics of human color vision: The genes encoding blue, green, and red pigments. *Science, 232,* 193–202.

National Academy of Sciences (1981). *The effect on human health from long-term exposure to noise.* (Report of Working Group 81). Washington, DC: National Academy Press.

National Center on Child Abuse and Neglect Report (1982, January–February). *Children Today,* pp. 27–28.

National Institute of Mental Health (1982). Television and behavior: Ten years of scientific progress and implications for the eighties. Washington, DC: National Institute of Mental Health.

National Institute of Mental Health (1985). *Electroconvulsive therapy: Consensus Development Conference statement.* Bethesda, MD: U.S. Department of Health and Human Services.

National Institutes of Health (1985). *National cancer program: 1983–1984 director's report and annual plan, FY 1986–1990.* (NIH Publication No. 85-2765). Washington, DC: U.S. Government Printing Office.

Neimark, E. D., Slotnik, N., & Ulrich, T. (1971). Development of memorization strategies. *Developmental Psychology, 5,* 427–432.

Nelson, N., et al. (1980). A randomized clinical trial of the Leboyer approach to childbirth. *New England Journal of Medicine, 302,* 655–660.

Neugarten, B. (1971). Grow old with me, the best is yet to be. *Psychology Today, 5*(5), 45–49.

Neugarten, B. (1982). Understanding psychological man. *Psychology Today, 16*(5), 54–55.

Neuringer, C. (1982). Affect configurations and changes in women who threaten suicide following a crisis. *Journal of Consulting and Clinical Psychology, 50,* 182–186.

Nevid, J. S. (1984). Sex differences in factors of romantic attraction. *Sex Roles, 11*(5/6), 401–411.

Nevid, J. S., & Rathus, S. A. (1978). Multivariate and normative data pertaining to the RAS with the college population. *Behavior Therapy, 9,* 675.

Newberne, P. M., & Suphakarn, V. (1983). Nutrition and cancer: A review, with emphasis on the role of vitamins C and E and selenium. *Nutrition and Cancer, 5,* 107–119.

Newcomb, M., & Bentler, P. (1980). Assessment of personality and demographic aspects of cohabitation and marital success. *Journal of Personality Development, 4,* 11–24.

Newcomb, T. M. (1971). Dyadic balance as a source of clues about interpersonal attraction. In B. I. Murstein (Ed.), *Theories of attraction and love.* New York: Springer.

Newcomb, T. M. (1981). Heiderian balance as a group phenomenon. *Journal of Personality and Social Psychology, 40,* 862–867.

Newcombe, N., & Bandura, M. M. (1983). The effect of age at puberty on spatial ability in girls: A question of mechanism. *Developmental Psychology, 19,* 215–224.

Newcombe, N., Bandura, M. M., & Taylor, D. G. (1983). Sex differences in spatial ability and spatial activity. *Sex Roles, 9,* 377–386.

Newman, J., & McCauley, C. (1977). Eye contact with strangers in city, suburb, and small town. *Environment and Behavior, 9,* 547–558.

Newmark, C. S., Frerking, R. A., Cook, L., & Newmark, L. (1973). Endorsement of Ellis's irrational beliefs as a function of psychopathology. *Journal of Clinical Psychology, 29,* 300–302.

Newport, E. (1976). Motherese: The speech of mothers to young children. In N. J. Castellan, D. B. Pisoni, & G. R. Potts (Eds.), *Cognitive theory,* Vol. 2. Hillsdale, NJ: Erlbaum.

Newton, N. (1971). Psychologic differences between breast and bottle feeding. *American Journal of Clinical Nutrition, 24,* 993–1004.

Newton, N. (1972). Battle between breast and bottle. *Psychology Today, 6,* 68–70, 88–89.

Newton, N. (1979). Key psychological issues in human lactation. In L. R. Waletzky (Ed.), *Symposium on human lactation.* Rockville, MD: DHEW Publication No. HSA 79-5107.

New York Times, The (1985, May 12). Poll finds many women seek marriage plus jobs. *The New York Times,* p. 19.

New York Times, The (1987, September 14). For now, Compaq isn't rushing to follow I.B.M. *The New York Times,* pp. D1, D8.

New York Times, The (1987, November 1). Smoking vs. life expectancy. *The New York Times.*

New York Times, The (1987, December 7). Divorce may be the price of living together first. *The New York Times,* p. A25.

New York Times, The (1988, February 20). AIDS risk articles criticized. *The New York Times,* p. 9.

Nezu, A. M., & Ronan, G. F. (1985). Life stress, current problems, problem solving, and depressive symptoms: An integrative model. *Journal of Consulting and Clinical Psychology, 53,* 693–697.

Nias, D. K. B. (1979). Marital choice: Matching or complementation? In M. Cook & G. Wilson (Eds.), *Love and attraction.* New York: Pergamon Press.

Niaura, R. S., et al. (1988). Relevance of cue reactivity to understanding alcohol and smoking relapse. *Journal of Abnormal Psychology, 97,* 133–152.

Nicassio, P., & Bootzin, R. (1974). A comparison of progressive relaxation and autogenic training as treatments for insomnia. *Journal of Abnormal Psychology, 83,* 253–260.

Nicholson, R. A., & Berman, J. S. (1983). Is follow-up necessary in evaluating psychotherapy? *Psychological Bulletin, 93,* 261–278.

Nickerson, R. A., & Adams, N. J. (1979). Long-term memory for a common object. *Cognitive Psychology, 11,* 287–307.

Nieberg, P., et al. (1985). The fetal tobacco syndrome. *Journal of the American Medical Association, 253,* 2998–2999.

NIMH. See National Institute of Mental Health.

Nisan, M. (1984). Distributive justice and social norms. *Child Development, 55,* 1020–1029.

Nisbett, R. E., & Ross, L. (1980). *Human inference: Strategies and shortcomings of social judgment.* Englewood Cliffs, NJ: Prentice-Hall.

Nogrady, H., McConkey, K. M., & Perry, C. (1985). Enhancing visual memory: Trying hypnosis, trying imagination, and trying again. *Journal of Abnormal Psychology, 94,* 195–204.

Nolan, J. D. (1968). Self-control procedures in the modification of smoking behavior. *Journal of Consulting and Clinical Psychology, 32,* 92–93.

Noles, S. W., Cash, T. F., & Winstead, B. A. (1985). Body image, physical attractiveness, and depression. *Journal of Consulting and Clinical Psychology, 53,* 88–94.

Noller, P., Law, H., & Comrey, A. L. (1987). Cattell, Comrey, & Eysenck personality factors compared: More evidence for the five robust factors? *Journal of Personality and Social Psychology, 53,* 775–782.

Norman, D. A. (1988). *The psychology of everyday things.* New York: Basic Books.

Norton, G. R., Harrison, B., Hauch, J., & Rhodes, L. (1985). Characteristics of people with infrequent panic attacks. *Journal of Abnormal Psychology, 94,* 216–221.

Notman, M. T., & Nadelson, C. C. (1982). Changing views of the relationship between femininity and reproduction. In C. C. Nadelson & M. T. Notman (Eds.), *The woman patient,* Vol. 2. New York: Plenum Publishing Co.

Novaco, R. (1974). A treatment program for the management of anger through cognitive and relaxation controls. Doctoral dissertation, Indiana University.

Novaco, R. (1977). A stress inoculation approach to anger management in the training of law enforcement officers. *American Journal of Community Psychology, 5,* 327–346.

Novin, D., et al. (1983). Is there a role for the liver in the control of food intake? *American Journal of Clinical Nutrition, 9,* 233–246.

Novin, D., Wyrwick, W., & Bray, G. A. (1976). *Hunger: Basic mechanisms and clinical implications.* New York: Raven Press.

Nowlis, G. H., & Kessen, W. (1976). Human newborns differentiate differing concentrations of sucrose and glucose. *Science, 191,* 865–866.

Nussbaum, M., et al. (1985). Follow-up investigation of patients with anorexia nervosa. *The Journal of Pediatrics, 106,* 835–840.

O'Grady, K. E. (1982). Sex, physical attractiveness, and perceived risk for mental illness. *Journal of Personality and Social Psychology, 43,* 1064–1071.

O'Hara, M. W., Neunaber, D. J., & Zekoski, E. M. (1984). Prospective study of postpartum depression: Prevalence, course, and predictive factors. *Journal of Abnormal Psychology, 93,* 158–171.

Ohman, A., Fredrikson, M., Hugdahl, K., & Rimmo, P. (1976). The premise of equipotentiality in human classical conditioning: Conditioned electrodermal responses to potentially phobic stimuli. *Journal of Experimental Psychology: General, 105,* 313–337.

Okun, B. F. (1984). *Working with adults: Individual, family, and career development.* Monterey, CA: Brooks/Cole.

O'Leary, K. D. (1980). Pills or skills for hyperactive children? *Journal of Applied Behavior Analysis, 13,* 191–204.

Olds, J. (1969). The central nervous system and the reinforcement of behavior. *American Psychologist, 24,* 114–132.

Olds, J., & Milner, P. (1954). Positive reinforcement produced by electrical stimulation of the septal area and other regions of the rat brain. *Journal of Comparative and Physiological Psychology, 47,* 419–427.

Olson, R. P., Ganley, R., Devine, D. T., & Dorsey, G. (1981). Long-term effects of behavior versus insight-oriented therapy with inpatient alcoholics. *Journal of Consulting and Clinical Psychology, 49,* 866–877.

O'Malley, M. N., & Becker, L. A. (1984). Removing the egocentric bias: The relevance of distress cues to evaluation of fairness. *Personality and Social Psychology Bulletin, 10,* 235–242.

O'Malley, S. S., et al. (1988). Therapist competence and patient outcome in interpersonal psychotherapy of depression. *Journal of Consulting and Clinical Psychology, 56,* 496–501.

Opstad, P. K., et al. (1978). Performance, mood and clinical symptoms in men exposed to prolonged, severe physical work and sleep deprivation. *Aviation, Space and Environmental Medicine, 49,* 1065–1073.

Orenberg, C. L. (1981). *DES: The complete story.* New York: St. Martin's Press.

Orme-Johnson, D. (1973). Autonomic stability and transcendental meditation. *Psychosomatic Medicine, 35,* 341–349.

Orne, M. T., Soskis, D. A., & Dinges, D. F. (1984). Hypnotically-induced testimony and the criminal justice system. In G. L. Wells & E. F. Loftus (Eds.), *Eyewitness testimony: Psychological perspectives.* New York: Cambridge University Press.

Ortega, D. F., & Pipal, J. E. (1984). Challenge seeking and the Type A coronary-prone behavior pattern. *Journal of Personality and Social Psychology, 46,* 1328–1334.

Osborn, D. K., & Endsley, R. C. (1971). Emotional reactions of young children to TV violence. *Child Development, 42,* 321–331.

O'Sullivan, M., Ekman, P., Friesen, W., & Scherer, K. (1985). What you say and how you say it: The contribution of speech quality and voice content to judgments of others. *Journal of Personality and Social Psychology, 48,* 54–62.

Ouchi, W. (1981). *Theory Z: How American business can meet the Japanese challenge.* Reading, MA: Addison-Wesley.

Owen, P. (1984). Prostaglandin synthetase inhibitors in the treatment of primary dysmenorrhea: Outcome trials reviewed. *American Journal of Obstetrics and Gynecology, 148,* 96–103.

Paffenbarger, R. S., Jr. (1972). Factors predisposing to fatal stroke in longshoremen. *Preventive Medicine, 1,* 522–527.

Paffenbarger, R. S., Jr., et al. (1978). Physical activity as an index of heart attack risk in college alumni. *American Journal of Epidemiology, 108,* 161–175.

Paffenbarger, R. S., Jr., et al. (1984). A natural history of athleticism and cardiovascular health. *Journal of the American Medical Association, 252,* 491–495.

Paffenbarger, R. S., Jr., et al. (1986). Physical activity, all-cause mortality, and longevity of college alumni. *New England Journal of Medicine, 314,* 605–613.

Page, R. A. (1977). Noise and helping behavior. *Environment and Behavior, 9,* 311–334.

Pagel, M., & Becker, J. (1987). Depressive thinking and depression: Relations with personality and social resources. *Journal of Personality and Social Psychology, 52,* 1043–1052.

Paige, K. E. (1971). Effects of oral contraceptives on affective fluctuations associated with the menstrual cycle. *Psychosomatic Medicine, 33,* 515–537.

Paige, K. E. (1973). Women learn to sing the menstrual blues. *Psychology Today, 7,* 41.

Palmer, D. L., & Kalin, R. (1985). Dogmatic responses to belief dissimilarity in the "bogus stranger" paradigm. *Journal of Personality and Social Psychology, 48,* 171–179.

Palmer, F. H. (1976). *The effects of minimal early intervention on subsequent IQ scores and reading achievement.* Report to the Education Commission of the States, contract 13–76–06846, State University of New York at Stony Brook.

Pantin, H. M., & Carver, C. S. (1982). Induced competence and the bystander effect. *Journal of Applied Social Psychology, 12,* 100–111.

Park, B., & Rothbart, M. (1982). Perception of out-group homogeneity and levels of social categorization: Memory for the subordinate attributes of in-group and out-group members. *Journal of Personality and Social Psychology, 42,*1051–1068.

Parkes, C. M., & Weiss, R. S. (1983). *Recovery from bereavement.* New York: Basic Books.

Parlee, M. B. (1979). The friendship bond: *Psychology Today's* survey report on friendship in America. *Psychology Today, 13*(4), 43–54, 113.

Parloff, M. B. (1986). Placebo controls in psychotherapy research: A sine qua non or a placebo for research problems? *Journal of Consulting and Clinical Psychology, 54,* 79–87.

Parloff, M. B., Waskow, I. E., & Wolfe, B. E. (1978). Research on therapist variables in relation to process and outcome. In S. L. Garfield & A. E. Bergin (Eds.), *Handbook of psychotherapy and behavior change,* 2d ed. New York: Wiley.

Parron, D. L., Solomon, F., & Jenkins, C. D. (Eds.) (1982). *Behavior, health risks, and social disadvantage.* Washington, DC: National Academy Press.

Parsons, T. (1978). *Action theory and the human condition.* New York: Free Press.

Patterson, F. G. (1980). Innovative uses of language by a gorilla: A case study. In K. E. Nelson (Ed.), *Children's language,* Vol. 2. New York: Gardner Press.

Patterson, F. G., Patterson, C. H., & Brentari, D. K. (1987). Language in child, chimp, and gorilla. *American Psychologist, 42,* 270–272.

Pattison, E. M. (1977). *The experience of dying.* Englewood Cliffs, NJ: Prentice-Hall.

Paul, G. L. (1969a). Outcome of systematic desensitization II: Controlled investigations of individual treatment, technique variations, and current status. In C. M. Franks (Ed.), *Behavior therapy: Appraisal and status.* New York: McGraw-Hill.

Paul, G. L. (1969b). Physiological effects of relaxation training and hypnotic suggestion. *Journal of Abnormal Psychology, 74,* 425–437.

Pavlov, I. (1927). *Conditioned reflexes.* London: Oxford University Press.

Pearl, D., Bouthilet, L., & Lazar, J. (Eds.) (1982). *Television and behavior: Ten years of scientific progress and implications for the eighties,* Vols. 1 & 2. Washington, DC: U.S. Government Printing Office.

Pearlman, C. A., and Greenberg, R. (1973). Posttrial REM sleep: A critical period for consolidation of shuttlebox avoidance. *Animal Learning and Behavior, 1,* 49–51.

Pearlman, K., Schmidt, F. L., & Hunter, J. E. (1980). Test of a new model of validity generalization: Results for job proficiency and training criteria in clerical occupations. *Journal of Applied Psychology, 65,* 373–406.

Peck, R. C. (1968). Psychological developments in the second half of life. In B. L. Neugarten (Ed.), *Middle age and aging.* Chicago: University of Chicago Press.

Peele, S. (1984). The cultural context of psychological approaches to alcoholism: Can we control the effects of alcohol? *American Psychologist, 39,* 1337–1351.

Pelham, W. E. (1983). The effects of psychostimulants on academic achievement in hyperactive and learning-disabled children. *Thalamus, 3,* 1–49.

Pempus, E., Sawaya, C., & Cooper, R. E. (1975). "Don't fence me in": Personal space depends on architectural enclosure. Paper presented to the American Psychological Association, Chicago.

Penfield, W. (1969). Consciousness, memory, and man's conditioned reflexes. In K. H. Pribram (Ed.), *On the biology of learning.* New York: Harcourt Brace Jovanovich.

Pennebaker, J. W., & Skelton, J. A. (1981). Selective monitoring of physical sensations. *Journal of Personality and Social Psychology, 41,* 213–223.

Peplau, L. A., & Perlman, D. (1982). Perspectives on loneliness. In L. A. Peplau & D. Perlman (Eds.), *Loneliness: A sourcebook of current theory, research, and therapy.* New York: Wiley.

Perkins, D. (1982). The assessment of stress using life events scales. In L. Goldberger & S. Brenitz (Eds.), *Handbook of stress: Theoretical and clinical aspects.* New York: Free Press.

Perlman, B., & Hartman, A. (1982). Burnout: Summary and future research. *Human Relations, 35,* 283–305.

Perlman, S. D., & Abramson, P. R. (1982). Sexual satisfaction among married and cohabiting individuals. *Journal of Consulting and Clinical Psychology, 50,* 458–460.

Perls, F. S. (1971). *Gestalt therapy verbatim.* New York: Bantam Books.

Perri, M. G., et al. (1988). Effects of four maintenance programs on the long-term management of obesity. *Journal of Consulting and Clinical Psychology, 56,* 529–534.

Perri, M. G., Richards, C. S., & Schultheis, K. R. (1977). Behavioral self-control and smoking reduction: A study of self-initiated attempts to reduce smoking. *Behavior Therapy, 8,* 360–365.

Perry, D. G., & Bussey, K. (1979). The social learning theory of sex differences: Imitation is alive and well. *Journal of Personality and Social Psychology, 37,* 1699–1712.

Persons, J. B., & Rao, P. A. (1985). Longitudinal study of cognitions, life events, and depression in psychiatric patients. *Journal of Abnormal Psychology, 94,* 51–63.

Petersen, S. E., et al. (1988). Positron emission tomograph studies of the cortical anatomy of single-word processing. *Nature, 331,* 585–589.

Peterson, C., Schwartz, S. M., & Seligman, M. E. P. (1981). Self-blame and depressive symptoms. *Journal of Personality and Social Psychology, 41,* 253–259.

Peterson, J. L., & Marin, G. (1988). Issues in the prevention of AIDS among Black and Hispanic men. *American Psychologist, 43,* 871–877.

Peterson, L. R., & Peterson, M. J. (1959). Short-term retention of individual verbal items. *Journal of Experimental Psychology, 58,* 193–198.

Peto, R., et al. (1981). Can dietary beta-carotene materially reduce human cancer rates? *Nature, 290,* 201–208.

Petrie, K., & Chamberlain, K. (1983). Hopelessness and social desirability as moderator variables in predicting suicidal behavior. *Journal of Consulting and Clinical Psychology, 51,* 485–487.

Pettingale, K. W., et al. (1985). Mental attitudes to cancer: An additional prognostic factor. *Lancet, 1,* 750.

Petty, R. E., & Cacioppo, J. T. (1986). The elaboration-likelihood model of persuasion. In L. Berkowitz (Ed.), *Advances in experimental social psychology,* Vol. 19. New York: Academic Press.

Peyser, H. (1982). Stress and alcohol. In L. Goldberger & S. Brenitz (Eds.), *Handbook of stress: Theoretical and clinical aspects.* New York: Free Press.

Phares, E. J. (1984). *Introduction to personality.* Columbus, OH: Charles E. Merrill.

Piaget, J. (1962). *The moral judgment of the child.* New York: Collier.

Piaget, J. (1963). *The origins of intelligence in children.* New York: W. W. Norton.

Piaget, J. (1971). *The construction of reality in the child.* New York: Ballantine Books.

Piaget, J. (1976). *The grasp of consciousness.* Cambridge, MA: Harvard University Press.

Pierrel, R., & Sherman, J. G. (1963, February). Train your pet the Barnabus way. *Brown University Alumni Quarterly,* pp. 8–14.

Pietropinto, A., & Simenauer, J. (1979). *Husbands and wives.* New York: Times Books.

Pine, C. J. (1985). Anxiety and eating behavior in obese and nonobese American Indians and White Americans. *Journal of Personality and Social Psychology, 49,* 774–780.

Pines, A., & Aronson, E. (1983). Antecedents, correlates, and consequences of sexual jealousy. *Journal of Personality, 51,* 108–136.

Pinto, R. P., & Hollandsworth, J. G., Jr. (1984). A measure of possessiveness in intimate relationships. *Journal of Social and Clinical Psychology, 2,* 273–279.

Pliner, P., Hart, H., Kohl, J., & Saari, D. (1974). Compliance without pressure: Some further data on the foot-in-the-door technique. *Journal of Experimental Social Psychology, 10,* 17–22.

Plomin, R. (1982). Quoted in M. Pines (1982, June 29). Behavior and heredity: Links for specific traits are growing stronger. *The New York Times,* pp. C1–C2.

Plomin, R., & DeFries, J. C. (1980). Genetics and intelligence: Recent data. *Intelligence, 4,* 15–24.

Plutchik, R. (1980). *Emotion: A psychoevolutionary synthesis.* New York: Harper & Row.

Podlesny, J. A., & Raskin, D. C. (1977). Physiological measures and the detection of deception. *Psychological Bulletin, 84,* 782–799.

Polivy, J., & Herman, C. P. (1985). Dieting and binging: A causal analysis. *American Psychologist, 40,* 193–201.

Polivy, J., & Herman, C. P. (1987). Diagnosis and treatment of normal eating. *Journal of Consulting and Clinical Psychology, 55,* 635–644.

Pollock, M. L., Wilmore, J. H., & Fox, S. M., III. (1978). *Health and fitness through physical activity.* New York: Wiley.

Pomazal, R. J., & Clore, G. L. (1973). Helping on the highway: The effects of dependency and sex. *Journal of Applied Social Psychology, 3,* 150–164.

Popham, R. E., Schmidt, W., & Israelstam, S. (1984). Heavy alcohol consumption and physical health problems: A review of the epidemiologic evidence. In R. G. Smart et al. (Eds.), *Research advances in alcohol and drug problems,* Vol. 8. New York: Plenum Publishing Co.

Popper, K. (1985). Cited in Goleman (1985).

Porter, N., Geis, F. L., Cooper, E., & Newman, E. (1985). Androgyny and leadership in mixed-sex groups. *Journal of Personality and Social Psychology, 49,* 808–823.

Postman, L. (1975). Verbal learning and memory. *Annual Review of Psychology, 26,* 291–335.

Powledge, T. M. (1981). Unnatural selection. In H. B. Holmes et al. (Eds.), *The custom-made child? Women-centered perspectives.* Clifton, NJ: Humana Press.

Premack, A. J., & Premack, D. (1975). Teaching language to an ape. In R. C. Atkinson (Ed.), *Psychology in Progress.* San Francisco: W. H. Freeman.

Prescott, P., & DeCasper, A. J. (1981). Do newborns prefer their fathers' voices? Apparently not. Paper presented to the Society for Research in Child Development, Boston.

Press, A., et al. (1985, March 18). The war against pornography. *Newsweek,* pp. 58–66.

Preti, G., et al. (1986). Human axillary secretions influence women's menstrual cycles: The role of donor extract from females. *Hormones and Behavior.*

Prewett, M. J., van Allen, P. K., & Milner, J. S. (1978). Multiple electroconvulsive shocks and feeding and drinking behavior in the rat. *Bulletin of the Psychonomic Society, 12,* 137–139.

Price, D. D., et al. (1984). A psychophysical analysis of acupuncture analgesia. *Pain, 19,* 27–42.

Pritchard, D., & Rosenblatt, A. (1980). Racial bias in the MMPI: A methodological review. *Journal of Consulting and Clinical Psychology, 48,* 129–142.

Probber, J. (1987, November 25). At Monell, it's all in the taste and smell. *The New York Times,* pp. C1, C8.

Purtillo, D. F., & Sullivan, J. L. (1979). Immunological basis for superior survival of females. *American Journal of Diseases of Children, 133,* 1251–1253.

Pyszczynski, T., Holt, K., & Greenberg, J. (1987). Depression, self-focused attention, and expectancies for positive and negative future life events for self and others. *Journal of Personality and Social Psychology, 52,* 994–1001.

Qualls, P. J., & Sheehan, P. W. (1981). Imagery encouragement, absorption capacity, and relaxation during electromyographic feedback. *Journal of Personality and Social Psychology, 41,* 370–379.

Quattrone, G. A. (1982). Overattribution and unit formation: When behavior engulfs the person. *Journal of Personality and Social Psychology, 42,* 593–607.

Quinn, S. (1987). *A mind of her own: The life of Karen Horney.* New York: Summit Books.

Quinsey, V. L., Chaplin, T. C., & Upfold, D. (1984). Sexual arousal to nonsexual violence and sadomasochistic themes among rapists and non-sex-offenders. *Journal of Consulting and Clinical Psychology,* 52, 651–657.

Rabkin, J. G. (1980). Stressful life events and schizophrenia: A review of the literature. *Psychological Bulletin, 87,* 408–425.

Rada, R. T., & Kellner, R. (1979). Drug treatment in alcoholism. In J. Davis & D. J. Greenblatt (Eds.), *Recent developments in psychopharmacology.* New York: Grune & Stratton.

Radin, N. (1982). Primary caregiving and role-sharing behaviors. In M. E. Lamb (Ed.), *Nontraditional families: Parenting and child development.* Hillsdale, NJ: Erlbaum.

Raether, H. C., & Slater, R. C. (1977). Immediate postdeath activities in the United States. In H. Feifel (Ed.), *New meanings of death.* New York: McGraw-Hill.

Ragland, D. R., & Brand, R. J. (1988). Type A behavior and mortality from coronary heart disease. *New England Journal of Medicine, 318,* 65–69.

Rapoport, K., & Burkhart, B. R. (1984). Personality and attitudinal characteristics of sexually coercive college males. *Journal of Abnormal Psychology, 93,* 216–221.

Rappaport, N. B., McAnulty, D. P., & Brantley, P. J. (1988). Exploration of the Type A behavior pattern in chronic headache sufferers. *Journal of Consulting and Clinical Psychology, 56,* 621–623.

Rapport, M. D. (1984). Hyperactivity and stimulant treatment: *Abusus non tollit usum. The Behavior Therapist, 7,* 133–134.

Raps, C. S., Peterson, C., Reinhard, K. E., Abramson, L. Y., & Seligman, M. E. P. (1982). Attributional style among depressed patients. *Journal of Abnormal Psychology, 91,* 102–108.

Rasmussen, T., & Milner, B. (1975). Clinical and surgical studies of the cerebral speech areas in man. In K. J. Zulch, O. Creutzfeldt, & G. C. Galbraith (Eds.), *Cerebral localization.* Berlin: Springer-Verlag.

Rassin, D. K., et al. (1984). Incidence of breast-feeding in a low socioeconomic group of mothers in the United States: Ethnic patterns. *Pediatrics, 73,* 132–137.

Rathus, S. A. (1973a). A 30-item schedule for assessing assertive behavior. *Behavior Therapy, 4,* 398–406.

Rathus, S. A. (1973b). Motoric, autonomic, and cognitive reciprocal inhibition of a case of hysterical bronchial asthma. *Adolescence, 8,* 29–32.

Rathus, S. A. (1975). Principles and practices of assertive training: An eclectic overview. *The Counseling Psychologist,* 5(4), 9–20.

Rathus, S. A. (1978). Assertiveness training: Rationales, procedures, and controversies. In J. M. Whiteley & J. V. Flowers (Eds.), *Approaches to assertion training.* Monterey, CA: Brooks/Cole.

Rathus, S. A. (1983). *Human sexuality.* New York: Holt, Rinehart and Winston.

Rathus, S. A. (1988). *Understanding child development.* New York: Holt, Rinehart and Winston.

Rathus, S. A., & Nevid, J. S. (1977). *Behavior therapy.* Garden City, NY: Doubleday.

Rathus, S. A., & Nevid, J. S. (1989). *Psychology and the challenges of life: Adjustment and growth.* New York: Holt, Rinehart and Winston.

Rebok, G. (1987). *Life-span cognitive development.* New York: Holt, Rinehart and Winston.

Redd, W. H., Jacobsen, P. B., Die-Trill, M., Dermatis, H., McEvoy, M., & Holland, J. C. (1987). Cognitive/attentional distraction in the control of conditioned nausea in pediatric cancer patients receiving chemotherapy. *Journal of Consulting and Clinical Psychology, 55,* 391–395.

Reeder, G. D. (1982). Let's give the fundamental attribution error another chance. *Journal of Personality and Social Psychology, 43,* 341–344.

Reeder, G. D., Henderson, D. J., & Sullivan, J. J. (1982). From dispositions to behaviors: The flip side of attribution. *Journal of Research in Personality, 16,* 355–375.

Reeder, G. D., & Spores, J. M. (1983). The attribution of morality. *Journal of Personality and Social Psychology, 44,* 736–745.

Regan, D. T., Williams, M., & Sparling, S. (1972). Voluntary expiation of guilt: A field experiment. *Journal of Personality and Social Psychology, 24,* 42–45.

Rehm, L. P. (1978). Mood, pleasant events, and unpleasant events. *Journal of Consulting and Clinical Psychology, 46,* 854–859.

Reich, J. W., & Zautra, A. (1981). Life events and personal causation: Some relationships with satisfaction and distress. *Journal of Personality and Social Psychology, 41,* 1002–1012.

Reinisch, J. M. (1988, August 14). Sexual behavior in the age of AIDS. Paper presented to the annual meeting of the American Psychological Association, Atlanta, GA.

Reinisch, J. M., Sanders, S. A., & Ziemba-Davis, M. (1988). The study of sexual behavior in relation to the transmission of human immunodeficiency virus: Caveats and recommendations. *American Psychologist, 43,* 921–927.

Reinke, B. J., Holmes, D. S., & Harris, R. L. (1985). The timing of psychosocial changes in women's lives. *Journal of Personality and Social Psychology, 48,* 1353–1364.

Reis, H. T., Senchak, M., & Solomon, B. (1985). Sex differences in the intimacy of social interaction. *Journal of Personality and Social Psychology, 48,* 1205–1217.

Rempel, J. K., Holmes, J. G., & Zanna, M. P. (1985). Trust in close relationships. *Journal of Personality and Social Psychology, 49,* 95–112.

Renninger, K. A., & Wozniak, R. H. (1985). Effect of interest on attentional shift, recognition, and recall in young children. *Developmental Psychology, 21,* 624–632.

Reschly, D. J. (1981). Psychological testing in educational testing and placement. *American Psychologist, 36,* 1094–1102.

Rescorla, R. A. (1967). Pavlovian conditioning and its proper control procedures. *Psychological Review, 74,* 71–80.

Rescorla, R. A. (1988). Pavlovian conditioning: It's not what you think it is. *American Psychologist, 43,* 151–160.

Rescorla, R. A., & Holland, P. C. (1982). Behavioral studies of associative learning in animals. *Annual Review of Psychology, 33,* 265–308.

Rescorla, R. A., & Solomon, R. L. (1967). Two-process learning theory: Relationships between Pavlovian conditioning and instrumental learning. *Psychological Review, 74,* 151–182.

Rest, J. R. (1983). Morality. In P. H. Mussen, J. Flavell, & E. Markman (Eds.), *Handbook of child psychology, Vol. 3: Cognitive development.* New York: Wiley.

Restak, R. (1975, August 9). José Delgado: Exploring inner space. *Saturday Review.*

Reuman, D. A., Alwin, D. F., & Veroff, J. (1984). Assessing the validity of the achievement motive in the presence of random measurement error. *Journal of Personality and Social Psychology, 47,* 1347–1362.

Rheingold, H. F., Gewirtz, J. L., & Ross, H. W. (1959). Social conditioning of vocalizations in the infant. *Journal of Comparative and Physiological Psychology, 51,* 68–73.

Rhine, J. B. (Ed.) (1971). *Progress in parapsychology.* Durham, NC: Parapsychology Press.

Rhoden, W. C. (1988, October 2). Varying standards on steroid use. *The New York Times,* Section 4, p. 9.

Rhodewalt, F., & Agustsdottir, S. (1984). On the relationship of hardiness to the Type A behavior pattern: Perception of life events versus coping with life events. *Journal of Research in Personality, 18,* 212–223.

Rice, B. (1979). Brave new world of intelligence testing. *Psychology Today, 13*(9), 27.

Rice, B. (1985). Why am I in this job? *Psychology Today, 19*(1), 54–59.

Richardson, D. C., Bernstein, S., & Taylor, S. P. (1979). The effect of situational contingencies on female retaliative behavior. *Journal of Personality and Social Psychology, 37,* 2044–2048.

Richardson, S. (1972). Ecology of malnutrition. In Pan American Health Organization Scientific Publication No. 251, *Nutrition, the nervous system and behavior.*

Richter, C. P. (1957). On the phenomenon of sudden death in animals and man. *Psychosomatic Medicine, 19,* 191–198.

Ridon, J., & Langer, E. J. (1977). Long-term effects of control-relevant intervention with the institutionalized aged. *Journal of Personality and Social Psychology, 35,* 897–902.

Rieser, J., Yonas, A., & Wilkner, K. (1976). Radial localization of odors by human newborns. *Child Development, 47,* 856–859.

Riggio, R. E., & Woll, S. B. (1984). The role of nonverbal cues and physical attractiveness in the selection of dating partners. *Journal of Social and Personal Relationships, 1,* 347–357.

Riley, V. (1981). Psychoneuroendocrine influences on immunocompetence and neoplasia. *Science, 212,* 1100–1109.

Ringler, N., et al. (1975). Mother-to-child speech at 2 years—Effects of early postnatal contact. *Journal of Pediatrics, 86*(1), 141–144.

Rinn, W. E. (1984). The neuropsychology of facial expression: A review of the neurological and psychological mechanisms for producing facial expressions. *Psychological Bulletin, 95,* 52–77.

Rizley, R. (1978). Depression and distortion in the attribution of causality. *Journal of Abnormal Psychology, 87,* 32–48.

Robertson, T. S., Zielinski, J., & Ward, S. (1984). *Consumer behavior.* Glenview, IL: Scott, Foresman.

Robinson, M. H., & Robinson, B. (1979). By dawn's early light: Matutinal mating and sex attractants in a neotropical mantid. *Science, 205,* 825–827.

Rock, I., & Victor, J. (1964). Vision and touch: An experimentally created conflict between the two senses. *Science, 143,* 594–596.

Rodhölm, M. (1981). Effects of father–infant postpartum contact on their interaction three months after birth. *Early Human Development, 5,* 79–86.

Rodin, J. (1976). Menstruation, reattribution, and competence. *Journal of Personality and Social Psychology, 33,* 345.

Rodin, J. (1980). Current status of the internal-external hypothesis of obesity: What went wrong? *American Psychologist, 36,* 361–372.

Rodin, J. (1986). Aging and health: Effects of the sense of control. *Science, 233,* 1271–1276.

Rogers, C. R. (1951). *Client-centered therapy.* Boston: Houghton Mifflin.

Rogers, C. R. (1959). A theory of therapy, personality and interpersonal relationships, as developed in the client-centered framework. In S. Koch (Ed.), *Psychology: A study of science,* Vol. 3. New York: McGraw-Hill.

Rogers, C. R. (1963). The actualizing tendency in relationship to "motives" and to consciousness. In M. R. Jones (Ed.), *Nebraska symposium on motivation.* Lincoln, NE: University of Nebraska Press.

Rogers, C. R. (1974). In retrospect: 46 years. *American Psychologist, 29,* 115–123.

Rogers, C. R. (1985). Cited in S. Cunningham (1985). Humanists celebrate gains, goals. *APA Monitor, 16*(5), 16, 18.

Rogers, C. R., & Dymond, R. F. (Eds.) (1954). *Psychotherapy and personality change.* Chicago: University of Chicago Press.

Rogers, M. F. (1985). AIDS in children: A review of the clinical, epidemiological and public health aspects. *Pediatric Infectious Disease, 4,* 230–236.

Rogers, R. (1987). APA's position on the insanity defense: Empiricism versus emotionalism. *American Psychologist, 42,* 840–848.

Rogers, R. W. (1983). Preventive health psychology: An interface of social and clinical psychology. *Journal of Social and Clinical Psychology, 1,* 120–127.

Rogers, R. W., & Deckner, C. W. (1975). Effects of fear appeals and physiological arousal upon emotions, attitudes, and cigarette smoking. *Journal of Personality and Social Psychology, 32,* 222–230.

Rogers, R. W., & Prentice-Dunn, S. (1981). Deindividuation and anger-mediated interracial aggression: Unmasking regressive racism. *Journal of Personality and Social Psychology, 41,* 63–73.

Rohsenow, D. J. (1983). Drinking habits and expectancies about alcohol's effects for self versus others. *Journal of Consulting and Clinical Psychology, 51,* 752–756.

Rollin, B. E. (1985). The moral status of research animals in psychology. *American Psychologist, 40,* 920–926.

Ronen, S. (1981). *Flexible working hours.* New York: McGraw-Hill.

Rook, K. S., & Dooley, D. (1985). Applying social support research: Theoretical problems and future directions. *Journal of Social Issues, 41,* 5–28.

Rook, K. S., & Peplau, L. A. (1982). Perspectives on helping the lonely. In L. A. Peplau & D. Perlman (Eds.), *Loneliness: A sourcebook of current theory, research, and therapy.* New York: Wiley.

Rorschach, H. (1921). *Psychodiagnostics.* Bern, Switzerland: Hans Huber.

Rosch, E. H. (1974). Linguistic relativity. In A. Silverstein (Ed.), *Human communication: Theoretical perspectives.* New York: Halsted Press.

Rosch, E. H. (1975). Cognitive representations of semantic categories. *Journal of Experimental Psychology: General, 104,* 192–233.

Rose, R. M. (1975). Testosterone, aggression, and homosexuality: A review of the literature and implications for future research. In E. J. Sachar (Ed.), *Topics in psychoendocrinology.* New York: Grune & Stratton.

Rose, S. A. (1983). Differential rates of visual information processing in full-term and preterm infants. *Child Development, 54,* 1189–1198.

Rosen, G. M., Glasgow, R. E., & Barrera, M., Jr. (1976). A controlled study to assess the efficacy of totally self-administered systematic desensitization. *Journal of Consulting and Clinical Psychology, 44,* 208–217.

Rosenbaum, M., & Hadari, D. (1985). Personal efficacy, external locus of control, and perceived contingency of parental reinforcement among depressed, paranoid, and normal subjects. *Journal of Personality and Social Psychology, 49,* 539–547.

Rosenberg, M. S. (1987). New directions for research on the psychological maltreatment of children. *American Psychologist, 42,* 166–171.

Rosenberg, M. S., & Repucci, N. D. (1985). Primary prevention of child abuse. *Journal of Consulting and Clinical Psychology, 53,* 576–585.

Rosenblum, L. A., & Paully, G. S. (1984). The effects of varying environmental demands on maternal and infant behavior. *Child Development, 55,* 305–314.

Rosenhan, D. L. (1973). On being sane in insane places. *Science, 179,* 250–258.

Rosenhan, D. L., Salovey, P., & Hargis, K. (1981). The joys of helping. *Journal of Personality and Social Psychology, 40,* 899–905.

Rosenstock, I. M., & Kirscht, J. P. (1979). Why people seek health care. In G. C. Stone, F. Cohen, & N. E. Adler (Eds.), *Health psychology: A handbook.* San Francisco: Jossey-Bass.

Rosenthal, D. M. (1980). The modularity and maturation of cognitive capacities. *Behavior and Brain Science, 3,* 32–34.

Rosenzweig, M. R. (1969). Effects of heredity and environment on brain chemistry, brain anatomy, and learning ability in the rat. In M. Manosovitz et al. (Eds.), *Behavioral genetics.* New York: Appleton.

Rosenzweig, M. R., Bennett, E. L., & Diamond, M. C. (1972). Brain changes in response to experience. *Scientific American, 226,* 22–29.

Rosenzweig, M. R., & Leiman, A. L. (1982). *Physiological psychology.* Lexington, MA: Heath.

Rosett, H. L., & Sander, L. W. (1979). Effects of maternal drinking on neonatal morphology and state regulation. In J. D. Osofsky (Ed.), *Handbook of infant development.* New York: Wiley-Interscience.

Roskies, E., et al. (1986). The Montreal Type A Intervention Project: Major findings. *Health Psychology, 5,* 45–69.

Ross, G. (1985). Use of Bayley scales to characterize abilities of premature infants. *Child Development, 56,* 835–842.

Ross, L. D. (1988). Situationist perspectives on the obedience experiments. *Contemporary Psychology, 33,* 101–104.

Rotter, J. B. (1966). Generalized expectancies for internal versus external locus of control of reinforcement. *Psychological Monographs, 80*(609).

Rotter, J. B. (1971). External control and internal control. *Psychology Today, 5,* 37–42, 58–59.

Rotter, J. B. (1972). Beliefs, social attitudes, and behavior: A social learning analysis. In J. B. Rotter, J. E. Chance, & E. J. Phares (Eds.), *Applications of a social learning theory of personality.* New York: Holt, Rinehart and Winston.

Rotter, J. B. (1975). Some problems and misconceptions related to the construct of internal versus external control of reinforcement. *Journal of Consulting and Clinical Psychology, 43,* 56–67.

Rotton, J., & Frey, J. (1985). Air pollution, weather, and violent crimes: Concomitant time-series analysis of archival data. *Journal of Personality and Social Psychology, 49,* 1207–1220.

Roueche, B. (1980). *The medical detectives.* New York: Truman Talley.

Rounsaville, B. J., et al. (1987). The relation between specific and general dimensions of the psychotherapy process in interpersonal psychotherapy of depression. *Journal of Consulting and Clinical Psychology, 55,* 379–384.

Rovet, J., & Netley, C. (1983). The triple X chromosome syndrome in childhood: Recent empirical findings. *Child Development, 54,* 831–845.

Rozensky, R. H., & Pasternak, J. F. (1985). Cited in J. C. Horn (1985), Fighting migraines with The Force. *Psychology Today, 19*(11), 74.

Rozin, P., & Fallon, A. (1988). Body image, attitudes to weight, and misperceptions of figure preferences of the opposite sex: A comparison of men and women in two generations. *Journal of Abnormal Psychology, 97,* 342–345.

Rubin, Z. (1970). Measurement of romantic love. *Journal of Personality and Social Psychology, 16,* 265–273.

Rubin, Z. (1973). *Liking and loving: An invitation to social psychology.* New York: Holt, Rinehart and Winston.

Rubin, Z. (1982). Children without friends. In L. A. Peplau & D. Perlman (Eds.), *Loneliness: A sourcebook of current theory, research, and therapy.* New York: Wiley.

Rubinstein, E. A. (1983). Television and behavior: Research conclusions of the 1982 NIMH report and their policy implications. *American Psychologist, 38,* 820–825.

Ruderman, A. J. (1985). Dysphoric mood and overeating: A test of restraint theory's disinhibition hypothesis. *Journal of Abnormal Psychology, 94,* 78–85.

Ruiz, P., & Ruiz, P. P. (1983). Treatment compliance among Hispanics. *Journal of Operational Psychiatry, 14,* 112–114.

Rundus, D. (1971). Analysis of rehearsal processes in free recall. *Journal of Experimental Psychology, 89,* 63–77.

Ruopp, R. (1979). *Children at the center.* Cambridge, MA: Abt Associates.

Ruppenthal, G. C., Arling, G. L., Harlow, H. F., Sackett, G. P., & Suomi, S. J. (1976). A ten-year perspective on motherless-mother monkey behavior. *Journal of Abnormal Psychology, 85,* 341–349.

Rush, A. J., Khatami, M., & Beck, A. T. (1975). Cognitive and behavior therapy in chronic depression. *Behavior Therapy, 6,* 398–404.

Rush, A. J., Beck, A. T., Kovacs, M., Weissenberger, J., & Hollon, S. D. (1982). Comparison of the effects of cognitive therapy and pharmacotherapy on hopelessness and self-concept. *American Journal of Psychiatry, 139,* 862–866.

Rush, D., et al. (1980). *Diet in pregnancy: A randomized controlled trial of nutritional supplements.* New York: Liss.

Russell, J. A., & Mehrabian, A. (1977). Evidence for a three-factor theory of emotions. *Journal of Research in Personality, 11,* 273–294.

Rüstemli, A. (1986). Male and female personal space needs and escape reactions under intrusion: A Turkish sample. *International Journal of Psychology.*

Rutkowski, G. K., Gruder, C. L., & Romer, D. (1983). Group cohesiveness, social norms, and bystander intervention. *Journal of Personality and Social Psychology, 44,* 545–552.

Rutter, M. (1979). Separation experiences: A new look at an old topic. *Pediatrics, 95*(1), 147–154.

Rutter, M. (1981). *Maternal deprivation reassessed.* Middlesex, England: Penguin Books.

Sackeim, H. A. (1985). The case for ECT. *Psychology Today, 19*(6), 36–40.

Sackeim, H. A., et al. (1985). Cognitive consequences of low dosage ECT. In S. Malitz & H. A. Sackeim (Eds.), *Electroconvulsive therapy: Clinical and basic research issues.* New York: Annals of the New York Academy of Science.

Sackett, D. L., & Snow, J. C. (1979). The magnitude of compliance and noncompliance. In R. B. Haynes, et al. (Eds.), *Compliance in health care.* Baltimore: Johns Hopkins University Press.

Sacks, C. H., & Bugental, D. B. (1987). Attributions as moderators of affective and behavioral responses to social failure. *Journal of Personality and Social Psychology, 53,* 939–947.

Sadalla, E. K., Kenrick, D. T., & Vershure, B. (1987). Dominance and heterosexual attraction. *Journal of Personality and Social Psychology, 52,* 730–738.

Saddler, J. (1987, February 12). Low pay, high turnover plague day-care industry. *Wall Street Journal,* p. 27.

Sadker, M., & Sadker, D. (1985). Sexism in the schoolroom of the 1980s. *Psychology Today, 19*(3), 54–57.

Saegert, S. C., & Hart, R. (1976). The development of sex differences in the environmental competence of children. In P. Burnett (Ed.), *Women in society.* Chicago: Maaroufa Press.

Saegert, S. C., & Jellison, J. M. (1970). Effects of initial level of response competition and frequency of exposure to liking and exploratory behavior. *Journal of Personality and Social Psychology, 16,* 553–558.

Safer, M. A. (1980). Attributing evil to the subject, not the situation: Student reactions to Milgram's film on obedience. *Personality and Social Psychology Bulletin, 6,* 205–209.

Sagar, H. A., & Schofield, J. W. (1980). Racial and behavioral cues in black and white children's perceptions of ambiguously aggressive acts. *Journal of Personality and Social Psychology, 39,* 590–598.

Saghir, M. T., & Robins, E. (1973). *Male and female homosexuality: A comprehensive investigation.* Baltimore: Williams & Wilkins.

Sanchez-Craig, M., Annis, H. M., Bornet, A. R., & MacDonald, K. R. (1984). Random assignment to abstinence or controlled drinking: Evaluation of a cognitive-behavioral program for problem drinkers. *Journal of Consulting and Clinical Psychology, 52,* 390–403.

Sanders, B., & Soares, M. P. (1986). Sexual maturation and spatial ability in college students. *Developmental Psychology, 22,* 199–203.

Sanders, B., Soares, M. P., & D'Aquila, J. M. (1982). The sex difference on one test of spatial visualization: A nontrivial difference. *Child Development, 53,* 1106–1110.

Sanders, G. S. (1984). Effects of context cues on eyewitness identification responses. *Journal of Applied Social Psychology, 14,* 386–397.

Santee, R. T., & Maslach, C. (1982). To agree or not to agree: Personal dissent amid social pressure to conform. *Journal of Personality and Social Psychology, 42,* 690–700.

Sarason, I. G. (1978). The test anxiety scale. In C. D. Spielberger & I. G. Sarason (Eds.), *Stress and anxiety,* Vol. 5. New York: Halsted-Wiley.

Sarbin, T. R., & Coe, W. C. (1972). *Hypnosis.* New York: Holt, Rinehart and Winston.

Sarrell, L. J., & Sarrell, P. M. (1984). *Sexual turning points.* New York: Macmillan.

Satir, V. (1967). *Conjoint family therapy.* Palo Alto, CA: Science and Behavior Books.

Satow, K. L. (1975). Social approval and helping. *Journal of Experimental Social Psychology, 11,* 501–509.

Saunders, C. (1984). St. Christopher's hospice. In E. S. Shneidman (Ed.), *Death: Current perspectives,* 3rd ed. Palo Alto, CA: Mayfield.

Savage-Rumbaugh, E. S., & Rumbaugh, D. M. (1980). Language analogue project I phase II: Theory and tactics. In K. E. Nelson (Ed.), *Children's language,* Vol. 2. New York: Gardner Press.

Savage-Rumbaugh, E. S., Rumbaugh, D. M., & Boysen, S. (1980). Do apes use language? *American Scientist, 68,* 49–61.

Savage-Rumbaugh, E. S., Rumbaugh, D. M., Smight, S. T., & Lawson, J. (1980). Reference: The linguistic essential. *Science, 210,* 922–924.

Sawrey, W. L., Conger, J. J., & Turrell, E. S. (1956). An experimental investigation of the role of psychological factors in the production of gastric ulcers in rats. *Journal of Comparative and Physiological Psychology, 49,* 457–461.

Sawrey, W. L., & Weisz, J. D. (1956). An experimental method of producing gastric ulcers. *Journal of Comparative and Physiological Psychology, 49,* 269–270.

Saxe, L., Dougherty, D., & Cross, T. (1985). The validity of polygraph testing: Scientific analysis and public controversy. *American Psychologist, 40,* 355–366.

Scarr, S. (1981a). Testing *for* children: Assessment and the many determinants of intellectual competence. *American Psychologist, 36,* 1159–1166.

Scarr, S. (1981b). *Race, social class, and individual differences in IQ.* Hillsdale, NJ: Erlbaum.

Scarr, S. (1985). An author's frame of mind. (Review of *Frames of mind,* by Howard Gardner.) *New Ideas in Psychology, 3,* 95–100.

Scarr, S., & Kidd, K. K. (1983). Developmental behavior genetics. In M. Haith & J. J. Campos (Eds.), *Handbook of child psychology.* New York: Wiley.

Scarr, S., Webber, P. L., Weinberg, R. A., & Wittig, M. A. (1981). Personality resemblance among adolescents and their parents in biologically related and adoptive families. *Journal of Personality and Social Psychology, 41,* 885–898.

Scarr, S., & Weinberg, R. A. (1976). IQ test performance of black children adopted by white families. *American Psychologist, 31,* 726–739.

Scarr, S., & Weinberg, R. A. (1977). Intellectual similarities within families of both adopted and biological children. *Intelligence, 1,* 170–191.

Scarr, S., & Weinberg, R. A. (1983). The Minnesota adoption studies: Genetic differences and malleability. *Child Development, 54,* 260–267.

Schachter, S. (1959). *The psychology of affiliation.* Stanford, CA: Stanford University Press.

Schachter, S. (1971a). *Emotion, obesity, and crime.* New York: Academic Press.

Schachter, S. (1971b). Some extraordinary facts about obese humans and rats. *American Psychologist, 26,* 129–144.

Schachter, S. (1977). Nicotine regulation in heavy and light smokers. *Journal of Experimental Psychology: General, 106,* 5–12.

Schachter, S. (1982). Recidivism and self-cure of smoking and obesity. *American Psychologist, 37,* 436–444.

Schachter, S., & Gross, L. P. (1968). Manipulated time and eating behavior. *Journal of Personality and Social Psychology, 10,* 98–106.

Schachter, S., Kozlowski, L. T., & Silverstein, B. (1977). Effects of urinary pH on cigarette smoking. *Journal of Experimental Psychology: General, 106,* 13–19.

Schachter, S., & Latané, B. (1964). Crime, cognition, and the autonomic nervous system. In D. Levine (Ed.), *Nebraska symposium on motivation.* Lincoln, NE: University of Nebraska Press.

Schachter, S., & Rodin, J. (1974). *Obese humans and rats.* Washington, DC: Erlbaum/Halsted.

Schachter, S., & Singer, J. E. (1962). Cognitive, social, and physiological determinants of emotional state. *Psychological Review, 69,* 379–399.

Schaeffer, J., Andrysiak, T., & Ungerleider, J. T. (1981). Cognition and long-term use of ganja (cannabis). *Science, 213,* 465–466.

Schechter, M., et al. (1984, June 9). Changes in sexual behavior and fear of AIDS. *Lancet,* p. 1293.

Scheier, M. F., Buss, A. H., & Buss, D. M. (1978). Self-consciousness, self-report of aggressiveness, and aggression. *Journal of Research in Personality, 12,* 133–140.

Schiavi, R. C., et al. (1977). Luteinizing hormone and testosterone during nocturnal sleep: Relation to penile tumescent cycles. *Archives of Sexual Behavior, 6,* 97–104.

Schiedel, D. G., & Marcia, J. E. (1985). Ego identity, intimacy, sex-role orientation, and gender. *Developmental Psychology, 21,* 149–160.

Schifter, D. E., & Ajzen, I. (1985). Intention, perceived control, and weight loss: An application of the theory of planned behavior. *Journal of Personality and Social Psychology, 49,* 843–851.

Schindler, B. A. (1985). Stress, affective disorders, and immune function. *Medical Clinics of North America, 69,* 585–597.

Schindler, G. L. (1979). *Testosterone concentration, personality patterns, and occupational choice in women.* Unpublished doctoral dissertation, University of Houston.

Schleidt, M., & Hold, B. (1981). Paper presented to the Conference on the Determination of Behavior by Chemical Stimuli, Hebrew University, Jerusalem.

Schmauk, F. J. (1970). Punishment, arousal, and avoidance learning in sociopaths. *Journal of Abnormal Psychology, 76,* 443–453.

Schmeck, H. M., Jr. (1987, December 29). New light on the chemistry of dreams. *The New York Times,* pp. C1, C12.

Schmeck, H. M., Jr. (1988, May 5). Expert panel affirms success of ear implants for the profoundly deaf. *The New York Times,* p. B19.

Schmidt, F. L., Hunter, J. E., & Pearlman, K. (1981). Task differences as moderators of aptitude test validity in selection: A red herring. *Journal of Applied Psychology, 66,* 161–185.

Schneider, B. H., & Byrne, B. M. (1987). Individualizing social skills training for behavior-disordered children. *Journal of Consulting and Clinical Psychology, 55,* 444–445.

Schneidman, B., & McGuire, L. (1976). Group therapy for nonorgasmic women: Two age levels. *Archives of Sexual Behavior, 5,* 239–247.

Schotte, D. E., & Clum, G. A. (1982). Suicide ideation in a college population: A test of a model. *Journal of Consulting and Clinical Psychology, 50,* 690–696.

Schotte, D. E., & Clum, G. A. (1987). Problem-solving skills in suicidal psychiatric patients. *Journal of Consulting and Clinical Psychology, 55,* 49–54.

Schuckit, M. A. (1987). Biological vulnerability to alcoholism. *Journal of Consulting and Clinical Psychology, 55,* 301–309.

Schulsinger, F. (1972). Psychopathy: Heredity and environment. *International Journal of Mental Health, 1,* 190–206.

Schulte, L. (1986). The new dating game. *New York, 19*(9), 92–94, 96, 98, 103–104, 106.

Schultz, D. P. (1978). *Psychology and industry today.* New York: Macmillan.

Schultz, N. R., Jr., & Moore, D. W. (1984). Loneliness: Correlates, attributions, and coping among older adults. *Personality and Social Psychology Bulletin, 10,* 67–77.

Schwartz, J. C., Strickland, R. G., & Krolick, G. (1974). Infant day care: Behavioral effects at preschool age. *Developmental Psychology, 10,* 502–506.

Schwartz, L. M., Foa, U. G., & Foa, E. B. (1983). Multichannel nonverbal communication: Evidence for combinatory rules. *Journal of Personality and Social Psychology, 45,* 274–281.

Schwartz, M. F., Saffran, E. M., & Marin, O. S. M. (1980). The word order problem in agrammatism: I: Comprehension. *Brain and Language, 10,* 249–262.

Schwartz, R. M. (1982). Cognitive behavior modification: A conceptual review. *Clinical Psychology Review, 2,* 267–293.

Schwartz, R. M., & Gottman, J. M. (1976). Toward a task analysis of assertive behavior. *Journal of Consulting and Clinical Psychology, 44,* 910–920.

Scott, J. P., & Fuller, J. L. (1965). *Genetics and the social behavior of the dog.* Chicago: University of Chicago Press.

Scott, W. J., & Morgan, C. S. (1983). An analysis of factors affecting traditional family expectations and perceptions of ideal fertility. *Sex Roles, 9,* 901–914.

Scovern, A. W., & Kilmann, P. R. (1980). Status of electroconvulsive therapy: A review of the outcome literature. *Psychological Bulletin, 87,* 260–303.

Searles, J. S. (1988). The role of genetics in the pathogenesis of alcoholism. *Journal of Abnormal Psychology, 97,* 153–167.

Sears, R. R., Maccoby, E. E., & Levin, H. (1957). *Patterns of child rearing.* New York: Harper & Row.

Seer, P. (1979). Psychological control of essential hypertension: Review of the literature and methodological critique. *Psychological Bulletin, 86,* 1015–1043.

Segal, M. W. (1974). Alphabet and attraction: An unobtrusive measure of the effect of propinquity in the field setting. *Journal of Personality and Social Psychology, 30,* 654–657.

Segovia-Riquelma, N., et al. (1971). Appetite for alcohol. In Y. Israel & J. Mardones (Eds.), *Biological basis of alcoholism.* New York: Wiley.

Seligman, M. E. P. (1973). Fall into helplessness. *Psychology Today, 7,* 43–48.

Seligman, M. E. P., Abramson, L. Y., Semmel, A., & von Baeyer, C. (1979). Depressive attributional style. *Journal of Abnormal Psychology, 88,* 242–247.

Seligman, M. E. P., et al. (1984). Attributional style and depressive symptoms among children. *Journal of Abnormal Psychology, 93,* 235–238.

Seligman, M. E. P., & Rosenhan, D. L. (1984). *Abnormal psychology.* New York: W. W. Norton.

Selye, H. (1976). *The stress of life,* rev. ed. New York: McGraw-Hill.

Selye, H. (1980). The stress concept today. In I. L. Kutash, et al. (Eds.), *Handbook on stress and anxiety.* San Francisco: Jossey-Bass.

Semans, J. (1956). Premature ejaculation: A new approach. *Southern Medical Journal, 49,* 353–358.

Serlin, E. (1980). Emptying the nest: Women in the launching stage. In D. G. McGuigan (Ed.), *Women's lives: New theory, research, and policy.* Ann Arbor: University of Michigan, Center for Continuing Education of Women.

Serrill, M. S. (1987, February 16). In the grip of the scourge. *Newsweek,* pp. 58–59.

Seta, J. J. (1982). The impact of comparison processes on coactors' task performance. *Journal of Personality and Social Psychology, 42,* 281–291.

Shadish, W. R., Hickman, D., & Arrick, M. C. (1981). Psychological problems of spinal injury patients: Emotional distress as a function of time and locus of control. *Journal of Consulting and Clinical Psychology, 49,* 297.

Shanteau, J., & Nagy, G. (1979). Probability of acceptance in dating choice. *Journal of Personality and Social Psychology, 37,* 522–533.

Shapiro, D. (1985). Clinical use of meditation as a self-regulation strategy: Comments on Holmes' conclusions and implications. *American Psychologist, 40,* 719–722.

Shapiro, D., & Goldstein, I. B. (1982). Behavioral perspectives on hypertension. *Journal of Consulting and Clinical Psychology, 50,* 841–859.

Shapiro, D. A., & Shapiro, D. (1982). Meta-analysis of comparative therapy outcome studies: A replication and refinement. *Psychological Bulletin, 92,* 581–594.

Shapley, R., & Enroth-Cugell, C. (1984). Visual adaptation and retinal gain controls. In N. Osborne & G. Chaders (Eds.), *Progress in retinal research,* Vol. 3. Oxford: Pergamon Press.

Shaw, E. D., Stokes, P. E., Mann, J. J., & Manevitz, A. Z. A. (1987). Effects of lithium carbonate on the memory and motor speed of bipolar patients. *Journal of Abnormal Psychology, 96,* 64–69.

Shaw, J. S. (1982). Psychological androgyny and stressful life events. *Journal of Personality and Social Psychology, 43,* 145–153.

Sheehy, G. (1976). *Passages: Predictable crises of adult life.* New York: Dutton.

Sheehy, G. (1981). *Pathfinders.* New York: Morrow.

Sheingold, K., & Tenney, Y. J. (1982). Memory for a salient childhood event. In U. Niesser (Ed.), *Memory observed: Remembering in natural contexts.* San Francisco: Freeman.

Shekelle, R. B., et al. (1983). Hostility, risk of coronary heart disease, and mortality. *Psychosomatic Medicine, 45,* 109–114.

Shekelle, R. B., et al. (1985). The MRFIT behavior pattern study: II. Type A behavior and incidence of coronary heart disease. *American Journal of Epidemiology, 122,* 559–570.

Sherif, M. (1966). *In common predicament: Social psychology of intergroup conflict and cooperation.* Boston: Houghton Mifflin.

Sherrington, R., Brynjolfsson, J., Petursson, H., Potter, M., Dudleston, K., Barraclough, B., Wasmuth, J., Dobbs, M., & Gurling, H. (1988). Localization of a susceptibility locus for schizophrenia on chromosome 5. *Nature, 336,* 164–167.

Shertzer, B. (1985). *Career planning,* 3rd ed. Boston: Houghton Mifflin.

Sherwin, B. B., Gelfand, M. M., & Brender, W. (1985). Androgen enhances sexual motivation in females: A prospective crossover study of sex steroid medication in the surgical menopause. *Psychosomatic Medicine, 47,* 339–351.

Sherwin, R., & Sherry, C. (1985). Campus sexual norms and lasting relationships: A trend analysis. *Journal of Sex Research, 21,* 258–274.

Shinn, M., Rosario, M., Morch, H., & Chestnut, D. E. (1984). Coping with job stress and burnout in the human services. *Journal of Personality and Social Psychology, 46,* 864–876.

Shipley, R. H. (1981). Maintenance of smoking cessation: Effect of follow-up letters, smoking motivation, muscle tension, and health locus of control. *Journal of Consulting and Clinical Psychology, 49,* 982–984.

Shipley, R. H., Butt, J. H., Horwitz, B., & Farbry, J. E. (1978). Preparation for a stressful medical procedure: Effect of amount of stimulus preexposure and coping style. *Journal of Consulting and Clinical Psychology, 46,* 499–507.

Shneidman, E. S. (Ed.) (1984). *Death: Current perspectives,* 3rd ed. Palo Alto, CA: Mayfield.

Shneidman, E. S. (1985). *Definition of suicide.* New York: Wiley.

Shneidman, E. S. (1987). A psychological approach to suicide. In G. R. VanderBos & B. K. Bryant (Eds.), *Cataclysms, cries, and catastrophes: Psychology in action* (Master Lecture Series, Vol. 6, pp. 151–183). Washington, DC: American Psychological Association.

Shneidman, E. S., Farberow, N. L., & Litman, R. E. (Eds). (1970). *The psychology of suicide.* New York: Science House.

Shotland, R. L., & Heinold, W. D. (1985). Bystander response to arterial bleeding: Helping skills, the decision-making process, and differentiating the helping response. *Journal of Personality and Social Psychology, 49,* 347–356.

Sieber, J. E. (1983). Deception in social research III: The nature and limits of debriefing. *IRB: A Review of Human Subjects Research, 5*(3), 1–4.

Siegler, R. S., & Liebert, R. M. (1972). Effects of presenting relevant rules and complete feedback on the conservation of liquid quantity task. *Developmental Psychology, 7,* 133–138.

Siegman, A. W., & Feldstein, S. (Eds.). (1977). *Nonverbal behavior and communication.* Hillsdale, NJ: Erlbaum.

Silverstein, B. (1982). Cigarette smoking, nicotine addiction, and relaxation. *Journal of Personality and Social Psychology, 42,* 946–950.

Silverstein, B., Koslowski, L. T., & Schachter, S. (1977). Social life, cigarette smoking, and urinary pH. *Journal of Experimental Psychology: General, 106,* 20–23.

Simone, C. B. (1983). *Cancer and nutrition.* New York: McGraw-Hill.

Simons, A. D., et al. (1985). Exercise as a treatment for depression: An update. *Clinical Psychology Review, 5,* 553–568.

Simons, A. D., et al. (1986). Cognitive therapy and pharmacotherapy for depression: Sustained improvement over one year. *Archives of General Psychiatry, 43,* 43–48.

Singer, D. G. (1983). A time to reexamine the role of television in our lives. *American Psychologist, 38,* 815–816.

Singer, J. L. (1975). *The inner world of daydreaming.* New York: Harper & Row.

Singer, J. L., & Singer, D. G. (1981). *Television, imagination, and aggression: A study of preschoolers.* Hillsdale, NJ: Erlbaum.

Singer, J. L., & Singer, D. G. (1983). Psychologists look at television: Cognitive, developmental, personality, and social policy implications. *American Psychologist, 38,* 826–834.

Sirota, A. D., Schwartz, G. E., & Shapiro, D. (1976). Voluntary control of human heart rate: Effect of reaction to aversive stimulation: A replication and extension. *Journal of Abnormal Psychology, 85,* 473–477.

Siscovick, D. S., et al. (1982). Physical activity and primary cardiac arrest. *Journal of the American Medical Association, 248,* 3113–3117.

Siscovick, D. S., et al. (1984). The incidence of primary cardiac arrest during vigorous exercise. *New England Journal of Medicine, 311,* 874–877.

Sistrunk, F., & McDavid, J. W. (1971). Sex variable in conforming behavior. *Journal of Personality and Social Psychology, 17,* 200–207.

Skalka, P. (1984). *The American Medical Association guide to health and well-being after fifty.* New York: Random House.

Skinner, B. F. (1938). *The behavior of organisms: An experimental analysis.* New York: Appleton.

Skinner, B. F. (1948). *Walden Two.* New York: Macmillan.

Skinner, B. F. (1957). *Verbal behavior.* New York: Appleton.

Skinner, B. F. (1960). Pigeons in a pelican. *American Psychologist, 15,* 28–37.

Skinner, B. F. (1972). *Beyond freedom and dignity.* New York: Knopf.

Skinner, B. F. (1979). *The shaping of a behaviorist.* New York: Knopf.

Skinner, B. F. (1983). Intellectual self-management in old age. *American Psychologist, 38,* 239–244.

Skinner, B. F. (1987). Whatever happened to psychology as the science of behavior? *American Psychologist, 42,* 780–786.

Slater, E., & Shields, J. (1969). Genetic aspects of anxiety. In M. H. Luder (Ed.), *Studies of anxiety.* Ashford, England: Headley Brothers.

Slater, J. F., & Depue, R. A. (1981). The contribution of environmental events and social support to serious suicide attempts in primary depressive disorder. *Journal of Abnormal Psychology, 90,* 275–285.

Sloane, B. (1983). Health care: Physical and mental. In D. S. Woodruff & J. E. Birren (Eds.), *Aging: Scientific perspectives and social issues.* Monterey, CA: Brooks/Cole.

Slobin, D. I. (1971). *Psycholinguistics.* Glenview, IL: Scott, Foresman.

Slobin, D. I. (1973). Cognitive prerequisites for the development of grammar. In C. A. Ferguson & D. I. Slobin (Eds.), *Studies of child development.* New York: Holt, Rinehart and Winston.

Smedley, J. W., & Bayton, J. A. (1978). Evaluative race-class stereotypes by race and perceived class of subjects. *Journal of Personality and Social Psychology, 36,* 530–535.

Smith, A., & Stansfeld, S. (1986). Aircraft noise exposure, noise sensitivity, and everyday errors. *Environment and Behavior, 18,* 214–226.

Smith, B. M. (1971). *The polygraph in contemporary psychology.* San Francisco: Freeman.

Smith, C. P., & Graham, J. R. (1981). Behavioral correlates for the MMPI *F* scale and for a modified *F* scale for black and white psychiatric patients. *Journal of Consulting and Clinical Psychology, 49,* 455–459.

Smith, D. (1982). Trends in counseling and psychotherapy. *American Psychologist, 37,* 802–809.

Smith, D., & Kraft, W. A. (1983). DSM-III: Do psychologists really want an alternative? *American Psychologist, 38,* 777–785.

Smith, D., King, M., & Hoebel, B. G. (1970). Lateral hypothalamic control of killing: Evidence for a cholinoceptive mechanism. *Science, 167,* 900–901.

Smith, G. F., & Dorfman, D. (1975). The effect of stimulus uncertainty on the relationship between frequency of exposure and liking. *Journal of Personality and Social Psychology, 31,* 150–155.

Smith, M. L., & Glass, G. V. (1977). Meta-analysis of psychotherapy outcome studies. *American Psychologist, 32,* 752–760.

Smith, M. L., Glass, G. V., & Miller, T. I. (1980). *The benefits of psychotherapy.* Baltimore, MD: The Johns Hopkins University Press.

Smith, R. E., & Winokur, G. (1983). Affective disorders. In R. E. Tarter (Ed.), *The child at psychiatric risk.* New York: Oxford University Press.

Smith, S. M., Glenberg, A. M., & Bjork, R. A. (1978). Environmental context and human memory. *Memory and Cognition, 6,* 342–355.

Smith, S. S., & Richardson, D. (1983). Amelioration of deception and harm in psychological research: The important role of debriefing. *Journal of Personality and Social Psychology, 44,* 1075–1082.

Smith, T. W. (1983). Change in irrational beliefs and the outcome of rational-emotive psychotherapy. *Journal of Consulting and Clinical Psychology, 51,* 156–157.

Smith, T. W., Snyder, C. R., & Handelsman, M. M. (1982). On the self-serving function of an academic wooden leg: Test anxiety as a self-handicapping strategy. *Journal of Personality and Social Psychology, 42,* 314–321.

Smith, T. W., Snyder, C. R., & Perkins, S. C. (1983). The self-serving function of hypochondriacal complaints: Physical symptoms as self-handicapping strategies. *Journal of Personality and Social Psychology, 44,* 787–797.

Smith, U. (1985, January). American Heart Association Science Writers Forum presentation. Monterey, CA.

Snarey, J. R. (1987). A question of morality. *Psychology Today, 21*(6), 6–8.

Snarey. J. R., Reimer, J., & Kohlberg, L. (1985). Development of social-moral reasoning among kibbutz adolescents: A longitudinal cross-cultural study. *Developmental Psychology, 21,* 3–17.

Snow, M. E., Jacklin, C. N., & Maccoby, E. E. (1983). Sex of child differences in father–child interaction at one year of age. *Child Development, 54,* 227–232.

Snyder, D. (1979). Multidimensional assessment of marital satisfaction. *Journal of Marriage and the Family, 41,* 813–823.

Snyder, D. K., Kline, R. B., & Podany, E. C. (1985). Comparison of external correlates of MMPI substance abuse scales across sex and race. *Journal of Consulting and Clinical Psychology, 53,* 520–525.

Snyder, M., & Cunningham, M. R. (1975). To comply or not to comply: Testing the self-perception explanation of the foot-in-the-door phenomenon. *Journal of Personality and Social Psychology, 31,* 64–67.

Snyder, M., & DeBono, G. (1985). Appeals to image and claims about quality: Understanding the psychology of advertising. *Journal of Personality and Social Psychology, 49,* 586–597.

Snyder, M., Grether, J., & Keller, K. (1974). Staring and compliance: A field experiment on hitchhiking. *Journal of Applied Social Psychology, 4,* 165–170.

Snyder, S. H. (1977). Opiate receptors and internal opiates. *Scientific American, 236,* 44–56.

Snyder, S. H. (1980). *Biological aspects of mental disorder.* New York: Oxford University Press.

Snyder, S. H. (1984). Drug and neurotransmitter receptors in the brain. *Science, 224,* 22–31.

Sommer, B. (1972). Menstrual cycle changes and intellectual performance. *Psychosomatic Medicine, 34,* 263–269.

Sommer, B. (1973). The effects of menstruation on cognitive and perceptual motor behavior: A review. *Psychosomatic Medicine, 35,* 515–534.

Sommers, S. (1981). Emotionality reconsidered: The role of cognition in emotional responsiveness. *Journal of Personality and Social Psychology, 41,* 553–561.

Sonstroem, R. J. (1984). Exercise and self-esteem. *Exercise and Sport Sciences Reviews, 12,* 123–155.

Sorce, J. F., Emde, R. N., Campos, J. J., & Klinnert, M. D. (1985). Maternal emotional signaling: Its effect on the visual-cliff behavior of 1-year-olds. *Developmental Psychology, 21,* 195–200.

Sorlie, P., Gordon, T., & Kannel, W. B. (1980). Body build and mortality—The Framingham Study. *Journal of the American Medical Association, 243,* 1828–1831.

Spanos, N. P., Jones, B., & Malfara, A. (1982). Hypnotic deafness: Now you hear it—now you still hear it. *Journal of Abnormal Psychology, 91,* 75–77.

Spanos, N. P., McNeil, C., Gwynn, M. I., & Stam, H. J. (1984). Effects of suggestion and distraction on reported pain in subjects high and low on hypnotic suggestibility. *Journal of Abnormal Psychology, 93,* 277–284.

Spanos, N. P., Radtke, H. L., & Dubreuil, D. L. (1982). Episodic and semantic memory in posthypnotic amnesia: A reevaluation. *Journal of Personality and Social Psychology, 43,* 565–573.

Spanos, N. P., & Radtke-Bodorik, H. L. (1980, April). Integrating hypnotic phenomena with cognitive psychology: An illustration using suggested amnesia. *Bulletin of the British Society for Experimental and Clinical Hypnosis,* pp. 4–7.

Spanos, N. P., Weekes, J. R., & Bertrand, L. D. (1985). Multiple personality: A social psychological perspective. *Journal of Abnormal Psychology, 94,* 362–376.

Spence, J. T., Helmreich, R., & Stapp, J. (1975). Ratings of self and peers on sex-role attributes and their relation to self-esteem and concepts of masculinity and femininity. *Journal of Personality and Social Psychology, 32,* 29–39.

Sperling, G. (1960). The information available in brief visual presentations. *Psychological Monographs, 74,* 1–29.

Sperry, R. W. (1974). Lateral specialization in the surgically separated hemispheres. In F. O. Schmitt & F. G. Worden (Eds.), *The neurosciences: Third study program.* Cambridge, MA: MIT Press.

Spielberger, C. D., et al. (1985). In M. A. Chesney & R. H. Rosenman (Eds.), *Anger and hostility in cardiovascular and behavioral disorders.* New York: Hemisphere/McGraw-Hill.

Spitzer, R. L. (1981, October). Nonmedical myths and the DSM–III. *APA Monitor.*

Spitzer, R. L., Forman, J. B. W., & Nee, J. (1979). DSM–III field trials: Initial interrater diagnostic reliability. *American Journal of Psychiatry, 136,* 815–817.

Squire, L. R. (1977). ECT and memory loss. *American Journal of Psychiatry, 134,* 997–1001.

Squire, L. R. (1986). Mechanisms of memory. *Science, 232,* 1612–1619.

Squire, L. R., Cohen, N. J., & Nadel, L. (1984). The medial temporal region and memory consolidations: A new hypothesis. In H. Weingartner & E. Parker (Eds.), *Memory consolidation.* Hillsdale, NJ: Erlbaum.

Squire, L. R., & Slater, P. C. (1978). Bilateral and unilateral ECT: Effects on verbal and nonverbal memory. *American Journal of Psychiatry, 135,* 1316–1320.

Staats, A. W., & Burns, G. L. (1981). Intelligence and child development: What intelligence is and how it is learned and functions. *Genetic Psychology Monographs, 104,* 237–301.

Stall, R. D., Coates, T. J., & Hoff, C. (1988). Behavioral risk reduction for HIV infection among gay and bisexual men: A review of results from the United States. *American Psychologist, 43,* 878–885.

Stalonas, P. M., & Kirschenbaum, D. S. (1985). Behavioral treatments for obesity: Eating habits revisited. *Behavior Therapy, 16,* 1–14.

Stamler, J., et al. (1986). Is the relationship between serum cholesterol and risk of premature death from coronary heart disease continuous and graded? Findings in 356,222 primary screenees of the Multiple Risk Factor Intervention Trial (MRFIT). *Journal of the American Medical Association, 256,* 2823–2828.

Stampfer, M., & Hennekens, C. (1988, August 4). *New England Journal of Medicine, 319.*

Stapp, J., Tucker, A. M., & VandenBos, G. R. (1985). Census of psychological personnel: 1983. *American Psychologist, 40,* 1317–1351.

Staub, E., Tursky, B., & Schwartz, G. (1971). Self-control and predictability: Their effects on reactions to aversive stimulation. *Journal of Personality and Social Psychology, 18,* 157–162.

Steck, L., Levitan, D., McLane, D., & Kelley, H. H. (1982). Care, need, and conceptions of love. *Journal of Personality and Social Psychology, 43,* 481–491.

Steele, B. F., & Pollock, C. B. (1974). A psychiatric study of parents who abuse infants and small children. In R. E. Helfer & C. H. Kempe (Eds.), *The battered child,* 2d ed. Chicago: University of Chicago Press.

Steele, C. M., & Josephs, R. A. (1988). Drinking your troubles away II: An attention-allocation model of alcohol's effect on psychological stress. *Journal of Abnormal Psychology, 97,* 196–205.

Stehr, P. A., et al. (1985). Dietary vitamin A deficiencies and stomach cancer. *American Journal of Epidemiology, 121,* 65–70.

Steinberg, L. D., Catalano, R., & Dooley, D. (1981). Economic antecedents of child abuse and neglect. Paper presented to the meeting of the Society for Research in Child Development, Boston.

Steiner, J. E. (1979). Facial expressions in response to taste and smell discrimination. In H. W. Reese & L. P. Lipsitt (Eds.), *Advances in child development and behavior,* Vol. 13. New York: Academic Press.

Steinmetz, J. L., Lewinsohn, P. M., & Antonuccio, D. O. (1983). Prediction of individual outcome in a group intervention for depression. *Journal of Consulting and Clinical Psychology, 51,* 331–337.

Stephan, C. W., & Langlois, J. H. (1984). Baby beautiful: Adult attributions of infant competence as a function of infant attractiveness. *Child Development, 55,* 576–585.

Stephan, W. G., & Rosenfield, D. (1978). Effects of desegregation on racial attitudes. *Journal of Personality and Social Psychology, 36,* 795–804.

Stericker, A., & LeVesconte, S. (1982). Effect of brief training on sex-related differences in visual-spatial skill. *Journal of Personality and Social Psychology, 43,* 1018–1029.

Sternberg, R. J. (1979). Stalking the IQ quark. *Psychology Today, 13*(9), 42–54.

Sternberg, R. J. (1982). Who's intelligent? *Psychology Today, 16*(4), 30–39.

Sternberg, R. J. (1985). *Beyond IQ: A triarchic theory of human intelligence.* New York: Cambridge University Press.

Sternberg, R. J., Conway, B. E., Ketron, J. L., & Bernstein, M. (1981). People's conception of intelligence. *Journal of Personality and Social Psychology, 41,* 37–55.

Sternberg, R. J., & Grajek, S. (1984). The nature of love. *Journal of Personality and Social Psychology, 47,* 312–329.

Stevenson, H. W., Lee, S. Y., & Stigler, J. W. (1986). Mathematics achievement of Chinese, Japanese, and American children. *Science, 231,* 693–699.

Stevenson, H. W., et al. (1985). Cognitive performance and academic achievement of Japanese, Chinese, and American children. *Child Development, 56,* 718–734.

Stewart, J. E., II. (1980). Defendant's attractiveness as a factor in the outcome of criminal trials: An observational study. *Journal of Applied Social Psychology, 10,* 348–361.

Stewart, V., & Stewart, A. (1982). *Business applications of repertory grid.* London: McGraw-Hill.

Stier, D. S., & Hall, J. A. (1984). Gender differences in touch: An empirical and theoretical review. *Journal of Personality and Social Psychology, 47,* 440–459.

Stillman, M. J. (1977). Women's health beliefs about cancer and breast self-examination. *Nursing Research, 26,* 121–127.

Stone, A. A., & Neale, J. M. (1984). Effects of severe daily events on mood. *Journal of Personality and Social Psychology, 46,* 137–144.

Stone, K., Grimes, D., & Magder, L. (1986). Primary prevention of sexually transmitted diseases: A primer for clinicians. *Journal of the American Medical Association, 255,* 1763–1766.

Storandt, M. (1983). Psychology's response to the graying of America. *American Psychologist, 38,* 323–326.

Storms, M. D. (1980). Theories of sexual orientation. *Journal of Personality and Social Psychology, 38,* 783–792.

Strack, F., Martin, L. L., & Stepper, S. (1988). Inhibiting and facilitating conditions of the human smile: A nonobtrusive test of the facial feedback hypothesis. *Journal of Personality and Social Psychology, 54,* 768–777.

Strahan, R. F. (1981). Time urgency, Type A behavior, and effect strength. *Journal of Consulting and Clinical Psychology, 49,* 134.

Stretch, R. H. (1986). Posttraumatic stress disorder among Vietnam and Vietnam-era veterans. In C. R. Figley (Ed.), *Trauma and its wake: Vol. 2. Traumatic stress theory, research, and intervention.* New York: Brunner/Mazel.

Stretch, R. H. (1987). Posttraumatic stress disorder among U.S. army reservists: Reply to Nezu and Carnevale. *Journal of Consulting and Clinical Psychology, 55,* 272–273.

Strober, M. (1986). Anorexia nervosa: History and psychological concepts. In K. D. Brownell & J. P. Foreyt (Eds.), *Handbook of eating disorders.* New York: Basic Books.

Strom, J. C., & Buck, R. W. (1979). Staring and participants' sex: Physiological and subjective reactions. *Personality and Social Psychology Bulletin, 5,* 114–117.

Strube, M. J., Berry, J. M., Goza, B. K., & Fennimore, D. (1985). Type A behavior, age, and psychological well being. *Journal of Personality and Social Psychology, 49,* 203–218.

Strube, M. J., & Werner, C. (1985). Relinquishment of control and the Type A behavior pattern. *Journal of Personality and Social Psychology, 48,* 688–701.

Stunkard, A. J. (1959). Obesity and the denial of hunger. *Psychosomatic Medicine, 1,* 281–289.

Stunkard, A. J., et al. (1986). An adoption study of human obesity. *New England Journal of Medicine, 314,* 193, 198.

Suinn, R. M. (1976). How to break the vicious cycle of stress. *Psychology Today, 10,* 59–60.

Suinn, R. A. (1982). Intervention with Type A behaviors. *Journal of Consulting and Clinical Psychology, 50,* 933–949.

Suler, J. R. (1985). Meditation and somatic arousal: A comment on Holmes's review. *American Psychologist, 40,* 717.

Sullivan, W. (1988, February 16). New studies link exercise to delays in menstruation—and less cancer. *The New York Times,* p. C3.

Sunday, S., & Lewin, M. (1985). Integrating nuclear issues into the psychology curriculum. Paper presented to the meeting of the Eastern Psychological Association.

Super, D. E., & Hall, D. T. (1978). Career development: Exploration and planning. In M. R. Rosenzweig & L. W. Porter (Eds.), *Annual Review of Psychology, 29.* Palo Alto, CA: Annual Reviews.

Svejda, M. J., Campos, J. J., & Emde, R. N. (1980). Mother–infant "bonding": Failure to generalize. *Child Development, 51,* 775–779.

Sweet, R. (1985). Chlamydia, group B streptococcus, and herpes in pregnancy. *Birth, 12,* 17–24.

Sweeney, P. D., & Gruber, K. L. (1984). Selective exposure: Voter information preferences and the Watergate affair. *Journal of Personality and Social Psychology, 46,* 1208–1221.

Swensen, C. H. (1983). A respectable old age. *American Psychologist, 38,* 327–334.

Symons, D. (1979). *The evolution of human sexuality.* New York: Oxford University Press.

Szasz, T. S. (1961). *The myth of mental illness.* New York: Harper & Row.

Szasz, T. S. (1984). *The therapeutic state: Psychiatry in the mirror of current events.* Buffalo: Prometheus.

Szmukler, G. I., & Russell, G. F. M. (1986). Outcome and prognosis of anorexia nervosa. In K. D. Brownell & J. P. Foreyt (Eds.), *Handbook of eating disorders.* New York: Basic Books.

Szucko, J. J., & Kleinmuntz, B. (1981). Statistical versus clinical lie detection. *American Psychologist, 36,* 488–496.

Talbott, E., et al. (1985). Occupational noise exposure, noise-induced hearing loss, and the epidemiology of high blood pressure. *American Journal of Epidemiology, 121,* 501–514.

Tavris, C., & Sadd, S. (1977). *The Redbook report on female sexuality.* New York: Delacorte.

Taylor, C. B., et al. (1977). Relaxation therapy and high blood pressure. *Archives of General Psychiatry, 34,* 339–343.

Taylor, S. E. (1983). Adjustment to threatening events: A theory of cognitive adaptation. *American Psychologist, 38,* 1161–1173.

Taylor, S. P., & Epstein, S. (1967). Aggression as a function of the interaction of the sex of the aggressor and the sex of the victim. *Journal of Personality, 35,* 474–486.

Taylor, W. N. (1985). Super athletes made to order. *Psychology Today, 19*(5), 62–66.

Teders, S. J., Blanchard, E. B., Andrasik, F., Jurish, S. E., Neff, D. F., & Arena, J. G. (1984). Relaxation training for tension headache: Comparative efficacy and cost-effectiveness of a minimal-therapist-contact versus a therapist-delivered procedure. *Behavior Therapy, 15,* 59–70.

Télégdy, G. (1977). Prenatal androgenization of primates and humans. In J. Money & H. Musaph (Eds.), *Handbook of sexology.* Amsterdam: Excerpta Medica.

Terkel, J., & Rosenblatt, J. S. (1972). Humoral factors underlying maternal behavior at parturition: Cross transfusion between freely moving rats. *Journal of Comparative and Physiological Psychology, 80,* 365–371.

Terrace, H. S. (1987a). *Nim,* 2d ed. New York: Knopf.

Terrace, H. S. (1987b). Reply to Bernstein and Kent. *American Psychologist, 42,* 273.

Terrace, H. S., et al. (1980). On the grammatical capacity of apes. In K. E. Nelson (Ed.), *Children's language,* Vol. 2. New York: Gardner Press.

Tetlock, P. E. (1983). Accountability and complexity of thought. *Journal of Personality and Social Psychology, 45,* 74–83.

Thigpen, C. H., & Cleckley, H. M. (1984). On the incidence of multiple personality disorder. *International Journal of Clinical and Experimental Hypnosis, 32,* 63–66.

Thoits, P. A. (1983). Dimensions of life events as influences upon the genesis of psychological distress and associated conditions: An evaluation and synthesis of the literature. In H. B. Kaplan (Ed.), *Psychosocial stress: Trends in theory and research.* New York: Academic Press.

Thomas, M. H., Horton, R. W., Lippincott, E. C., & Drabman, R. S. (1977). Desensitization to portrayals of real-life aggression as a function of exposure to television violence. *Journal of Personality and Social Psychology, 35,* 450–458.

Thompson, C. P., & Cowan, T. (1986). The neurobiology of learning and memory. *Science, 233,* 941–947.

Thompson, P. D. (1982). Cardiovascular hazards of physical activity. *Exercise and Sport Sciences Reviews, 10,* 208–235.

Thompson, R. F. (1986). The neurobiology of learning and memory. *Science, 233,* 941–947.

Thompson, S. (1988, August). An intervention to increase physician–patient communication. Paper presented to the American Psychological Association, Atlanta.

Thompson, T. (1988). *Benedictus* behavior analysis: B. F. Skinner's magnum opus at fifty. *Contemporary Psychology, 33,* 397–402.

Thompson, W. C., Cowan, C. L., & Rosenhan, D. L. (1980). Focus of attention mediates the impact of negative affect on altruism. *Journal of Personality and Social Psychology, 38,* 291–300.

Thomson, M. E., & Kramer, M. S. (1984). Methodologic standards for controlled clinical trials of early contact and maternal–infant behavior. *Pediatrics, 73,* 294–300.

Thornton, D., & Reid, R. L. (1982). Moral reasoning and type of criminal offense. *British Journal of Social Psychology, 21,* 231–238.

Thurstone, L. L. (1938). Primary mental abilities. *Psychometric Monographs, 1.*

Thurstone, L. L., & Thurstone, T. G. (1963). *SRA primary abilities.* Chicago: SRA.

Tobias, S. (1982). Sexist equations. *Psychology Today, 16*(1), 14–17.

Tolman, E. C., & Honzik, C. H. (1930). Introduction and removal of reward, and maze performance in rats. *University of California Publications in Psychology, 4,* 257–275.

Tolstedt, B., & Stokes, J. (1983). Relation of verbal, affective, and physical intimacy to marital satisfaction. *Journal of Counseling Psychology, 30,* 573–580.

Torgersen, S. (1983). Genetic factors in anxiety disorders. *Archives of General Psychiatry, 40,* 1085–1089.

Toufexis, A., Garcia, C., & Kalb, B. (1986, January 20). Dieting: The losing game. *Time magazine,* pp. 54–60.

Touhey, J. C. (1972). Comparison of two dimensions of attitude similarity on heterosexual attraction. *Journal of Personality and Social Psychology, 23,* 8–10.

Trost, C. (1987, February 12). Child-care center at Virginia firm boosts worker morale and loyalty. *Wall Street Journal,* p. 27.

Trussell, J., & Westoff, C. (1980). Contraceptive practice and trends in coital frequency. *Family Planning Perspectives, 12,* 246–249.

Tryon, R. C. (1940). Genetic differences in maze learning in rats. *Yearbook of the National Society for Studies in Education, 39,* 111–119.

Tulving, E. (1972). Episodic and semantic memory. In E. Tulving & W. Donaldson (Eds.), *Organization of memory.* New York: Academic Press.

Tulving, E. (1974). Cue-dependent forgetting. *American Scientist, 62,* 74–82.

Tulving, E. (1982). *Elements of episodic memory.* New York: Oxford University Press.

Tulving, E. (1985). How many memory systems are there? *American Psychologist, 40,* 385–398.

Turk, D. C., Meichenbaum, D., & Genest, M. (1983). *Pain and behavioral medicine: A cognitive behavioral perspective.* New York: Guilford Press.

Turkington, C. (1983). Drugs found to block dopamine receptors. *APA Monitor, 14,* 11.

Turkington, C. (1984). Hormones in rats found to control sexual behavior. *APA Monitor, 15*(11), 40–41.

Turkington, C. (1985). Taste inhibitors. *APA Monitor, 16*(10), 3.

Turkington, C. (1987). Alzheimer's and aluminum. *APA Monitor, 18*(1), 13–14.

Turnbull, C. M. (1961). Notes and discussion: Some observations regarding the experiences and behavior of the Bambute pygmies. *American Journal of Psychology, 7,* 304–308.

Turner, A. M., Greenough, W. T. (1985). Differential rearing effects on rat visual cortex synapses: I. Synaptic and neuronal density and synapses per neuron. *Brain Research, 329,* 195–203.

Turner, J. A., & Chapman, C. R. (1982a). Psychological interventions for chronic pain: A critical review: I. Relaxation training and biofeedback. *Pain, 12,* 1–21.

Turner, J. A., & Chapman, C. R. (1982b). Psychological interventions for chronic pain: A critical review: II. Operant conditioning, hypnosis, and cognitive-behavior therapy. *Pain, 12,* 23–46.

Turner, J. S., & Helms. D. B. (1987). *Lifespan development,* 3rd ed. New York: Holt, Rinehart and Winston.

Turner, R. H., & Killian, L. M. (1972). *Collective behavior.* Englewood Cliffs, NJ: Prentice-Hall.

Turner, S. M. (1987). Psychopathology in the offspring of anxiety disorders patients. *Journal of Consulting and Clinical Psychology, 55,* 229–235.

Tversky, A., & Kahneman, D. (1974). Judgment under uncertainty: Heuristics and biases. *Science, 185,* 1124–1131.

Tzuriel, D. (1984). Sex role typing and ego identity in Israeli, Oriental, and Western adolescents. *Journal of Personality and Social Psychology, 46,* 440–457.

Udry, J. R. (1971). *The social context of marriage.* Philadelphia: Lippincott.

Ugwuegbu, D. C. E. (1979). Racial and evidential factors in juror attribution of legal responsibility. *Journal of Experimental Social Psychology, 15,* 133–146.

Ullman, C. (1982). Cognitive and emotional antecedents of religious conversion. *Journal of Personality and Social Psychology, 43,* 183–192.

Umberson, D., & Hughes, M. (1984, August). The impact of physical attractiveness on achievement and psychological well-being. Paper presented at the meeting of the American Sociological Association, San Antonio.

Underwood, B., & Moore, B. S. (1981). Sources of behavioral consistency. *Journal of Personality and Social Psychology, 40,* 780–785.

Unger, R. K., Hilderbrand, M., & Madar, T. (1982). Physical attractiveness and assumptions about social deviance: Some sex-by-sex comparisons. *Personality and Social Psychology Bulletin, 8,* 293–301.

Ungerer, J. A., & Sigman, M. (1983). Developmental lags in preterm infants from one to three years. *Child Development, 54,* 1217–1228.

U.S. Bureau of the Census. (1985). *Statistical abstract of the United States,* 105th ed. Washington, DC: U.S. Government Printing Office.

U.S. Congress (1983, November). *Scientific validity of polygraph testing: A research review and evaluation* (OTA-TM-H-15). Washington, DC: Office of Technology Assessment.

U.S. Department of Health and Human Services (1984). *The 1984 report of the Joint National Committee on Detection, Evaluation, and Treatment of High Blood Pressure.* (DHHS Publication No. NIH: 84-1088). Washington, DC: U.S. Government Printing Office.

U.S. Riot Commission (1968). *Report of the National Advisory Commission on Civil Disorders.* New York: Bantam Books.

Vaillant, G. E. (1982). *The natural history of alcoholism.* Cambridge, MA: Harvard University Press.

Vaillant, G. E., & Milofsky, E. S. (1982). The etiology of alcoholism. *American Psychologist, 37,* 494–503.

Valenstein, E. S. (1978). Science-fiction fantasy and the brain. *Psychology Today, 12*(7), 28–39.

Valenstein, E. S. (1980). *The psychosurgery debate.* San Francisco: W. H. Freeman.

Valenstein, E. S. (1986). *Great and desperate cures: The rise and decline of psychosurgery and other radical treatments for mental illness.* New York: Basic Books.

Valins, S. (1966). Cognitive effects of false heart-rate feedback. *Journal of Personality and Social Psychology, 4,* 400–408.

Vallis, M., McCabe, S. B., & Shaw, B. F. (1986, June). The relationships between therapist skill in cognitive therapy and general therapy skill. Paper presented to the Society for Psychotherapy Research, Wellesley, MA.

Van der Pligt, J., & Eiser, J. R. (1983). Actors' and observers' attributions, self-serving bias, and positivity bias. *European Journal of Social Psychology, 13,* 95–104.

Van Dyke, C., & Byck, R. (1982). Cocaine. *Scientific American, 44*(3), 128–141.

Verbrugge, L. M. (1983). Multiple roles and physical health of women and men. *Journal of Health and Social Behavior, 24,* 16–30.

Vestre, N. D. (1984). Irrational beliefs and self-reported depressed mood. *Journal of Abnormal Psychology, 93,* 239–241.

Visintainer, M. A., Volpicelli, J. R., & Seligman, M. E. P. (1982). Tumor rejection in rats after inescapable or escapable shock. *Science, 216*(23), 437–439.

Von Békésy, G. (1957, August). The ear. *Scientific American,* 66–78.

Waber, D. P., Mann, M. B., Merola, J., & Moylan, P. M. (1985). Physical maturation rate and cognitive performance in early adolescence: A longitudinal examination. *Developmental Psychology, 21,* 666–681.

Wachtel, P. L. (1982). What can dynamic therapies contribute to behavior therapy? *Behavior Therapy, 13,* 594–609.

Wagner, R. K., & Sternberg, R. J. (1985). Practical intelligence in real-world pursuits: The role of tacit knowledge. *Journal of Personality and Social Psychology, 49,* 436–458.

Walker, A. M., Rablen, R. A., & Rogers, C. R. (1960). Development of a scale to measure process changes in psychotherapy. *Journal of Clinical Psychology, 16,* 79–85.

Walker, B. B. (1983). Treating stomach disorders: Can we reinstate regulatory processes? In W. E. Whitehead & R. Holzl (Eds.), *Psychophysiology of the gastrointestinal tract.* New York: Plenum Publishing Co.

Walker, W. B., & Franzini, L. R. (1985). Low-risk aversive group treatments, physiological feedback, and booster treatments for smoking cessation. *Behavior Therapy, 16,* 263–274.

Wallace, J. (1985). The alcoholism controversy. *American Psychologist, 40,* 372–373.

Wallington, S. A. (1973). Consequences of transgression: Self-punishment and depression. *Journal of Personality and Social Psychology, 29,* 1–7.

Wallston, B. S., & Wallston, K. A. (1984). Social psychological models of health behavior: An examination and integration. In A. Baum, S. E. Taylor, & J. E. Singer (Eds.), *Handbook of psychology and health: Vol. 4. Social psychological aspects of health.* Hillsdale, NJ: Erlbaum.

Walsh, B. T., et al. (1984). Treatment of bulimia with phenelzine: A double-blind, placebo-controlled study. *Archives of General Psychiatry, 41,* 1105–1109.

Walstedt, J. J., Geis, F. L., & Brown, V. (1980). Influence of television commercials on women's self-confidence and independent judgment. *Journal of Personality and Social Psychology, 38,* 203–210.

Walster, E., Aronson, E., & Abrahams, D. (1966a). On increasing the persuasiveness of a low prestige communicator. *Journal of Experimental Social Psychology, 2,* 325–342.

Walster, E., Aronson, E., Abrahams, D., & Rottman, L. (1966b). Importance of physical attractiveness in dating behavior. *Journal of Personality and Social Psychology, 4,* 508–516.

Walster, E., & Walster, G. W. (1978). *A new look at love.* Reading, MA: Addison-Wesley.

Walster, E., Walster, G. W., Piliavin, J., & Schmidt, L. (1973). "Playing hard to get": Understanding an illusive phenomenon. *Journal of Personality and Social Psychology, 26,* 113–121.

Walter, T., & Siebert, A. (1987). *Student success: How to succeed in college and still have time for your friends,* 4th ed. New York: Holt, Rinehart and Winston.

Walton, S. (1985). Girls and science: The gap remains. *Psychology Today, 19*(6), 14.

Watkins, M. J., Ho, E., & Tulving, E. (1976). Context effects on recognition memory for faces. *Journal of Verbal Learning and Verbal Behavior, 15,* 505–518.

Watson, J. B. (1913). Psychology as the behaviorist views it. *Psychological Review, 20,* 158–177.

Watson, J. B. (1924). *Behaviorism.* New York: Norton.

Watson, J. B., & Rayner, R. (1920). Conditioned emotional reactions. *Journal of Experimental Psychology, 3,* 1–14.

Watson, S. J., et al. (1978). Effects of naloxone on schizophrenia: Reduction in hallucinations in a subpopulation of subjects. *Science, 201,* 73–76.

Watt, N. F., Grubb, T. W., & Erlenmeyer-Kimling, L. (1982). Social, emotional, and intellectual behavior among children at high risk for schizophrenia. *Journal of Consulting and Clinical Psychology, 50,* 171–181.

Weber, R., & Crocker, J. (1983). Cognitive processes in the revision of stereotypic beliefs. *Journal of Personality and Social Psychology, 45,* 961–977.

Wechsler, D. (1975). Intelligence defined and undefined: A relativistic appraisal. *American Psychologist, 30,* 135–139.

Wegner, D. M. (1979). Hidden Brain Damage Scale. *American Psychologist, 34,* 192–193.

Weil, G., & Goldfried, M. R. (1973). Treatment of insomnia in an eleven-year-old child through self-relaxation. *Behavior Therapy, 4,* 282–294.

Weinberg, J., & Levine, S. (1980). Psychobiology of coping in animals: The effects of predictability. In S. Levine & H. Ursin (Eds.), *Coping and health.* New York: Plenum Publishing Co.

Weinberg, R. S., Yukelson, S., & Jackson, A. (1980). Effect of public and private efficacy expectations on competitive performance. *Journal of Sport Psychology, 2,* 340–349.

Weinberg, S. L., & Richardson, M. S. (1981). Dimensions of stress in early parenting. *Journal of Consulting and Clinical Psychology, 49,* 688–693.

Weiner, H., et al. (1957). Relation of specific psychological characteristics to rate of gastric secretion. *Psychosomatic Medicine, 17,* 1–10.

Weiner, M. J., & Wright, F. E. (1973). Effects of undergoing arbitrary discrimination upon subsequent attitudes toward a minority group. *Journal of Applied Social Psychology, 3,* 94–102.

Weinraub, M., & Wolf, B. M. (1983). Effects of stress and social supports on mother–child interactions in single- and two-parent families. *Child Development, 54,* 1297–1311.

Weinstein, N. D. (1980). Unrealistic optimism about future life events. *Journal of Personality and Social Psychology, 39,* 806–820.

Weinstein, N. D. (1984). Why it won't happen to me: Perceptions of risk factors and susceptibility. *Health Psychology, 3,* 431–457.

Weiss, J. M. (1972). Psychological factors in stress and disease. *Scientific American, 226*(6), 104–113.

Weiss, J. M. (1982, August). A model for the neurochemical study of depression. Paper presented to the American Psychological Association, Washington, DC.

Weiss, J. M., Glazer, H. I., & Pohorecky, L. A. (1976). Coping behavior and neurochemical changes: An alternative explanation for the original "learned helplessness" experiments. In G. Serban & A. Kling (Eds.), *Animal models of human psychobiology.* New York: Plenum Publishing Co.

Weiss, M., & Richter-Heinrich, E. (1985). Type A behavior in a population of Berlin, GDR: Its relation to personality and sociological variables, and association to coronary heart disease. *Activitas Nervosa Superior (Prague), 27,* 7–9.

Weissman, M., et al. (1981). Depressed outpatients. Results one year after treatment with drugs and/or interpersonal psychotherapy. *Archives of General Psychology, 18,* 51–55.

Wender, P. H., et al. (1974). Cross-fostering: A research strategy for clarifying the role of genetic and experiential factors in the etiology of schizophrenia. *Archives of General Psychiatry, 30,* 121–128.

Werner, C. M., Brown, B. B., & Damron, G. (1981). Territorial marking in a game arcade. *Journal of Personality and Social Psychology, 41,* 1094–1104.

West, M. A. (1985). Meditation and somatic arousal reduction. *American Psychologist, 40,* 717–719.

Wetzler, S. E., & Sweeney, J. A. (1986). Childhood amnesia. In D. C. Rubin (Ed.), *Autobiographical memory.* New York: Cambridge University Press.

Wexler, D. A., & Butler, J. M. (1976). Therapist modification of client expressiveness in client-centered therapy. *Journal of Consulting and Clinical Psychology, 44,* 261–265.

Whalen, C. K., Kenker, B., Swanson, J. M., Granger, D., Kliewer, W., & Spencer, J. (1987). Natural social behaviors in hyperactive children: Dose effects of methylphenidate. *Journal of Consulting and Clinical Psychology, 55,* 187–193.

Wheeler, L., Deci, L., Reis, H., & Zuckerman, M. (1978). *Interpersonal influence.* Boston: Allyn & Bacon.

White, G. L., Fishbein, S., & Rutstein, J. (1981). Passionate love and the misattribution of arousal. *Journal of Personality and Social Psychology, 41,* 56–62.

White, M. (1975). Interpersonal distance as affected by room size, status, and sex. *Journal of Social Psychology, 95,* 241–249.

Whitehead, W. E., & Bosmajian, L. S. (1982). Behavioral medicine approaches to gastrointestinal disorders. *Journal of Consulting and Clinical Psychology, 50,* 972–983.

Whitley, B. E., Jr. (1983). Sex role orientation and self-esteem: A critical meta-analysis. *Journal of Personality and Social Psychology, 44,* 765–788.

Whorf, B. (1956). *Language, thought, and reality.* New York: Wiley.

Whyte, W. W. (1956). *The organization man.* New York: Simon & Schuster.

Wiens, A. N., & Menustik, C. E. (1983). Treatment outcome and patient characteristics in an aversion therapy program for alcoholism. *American Psychologist, 38,* 1089–1096.

Wiggins, J. S., Wiggins, N., & Conger, J. C. (1968). Correlates of heterosexual somatic preference. *Journal of Personality and Social Psychology, 10,* 82–90.

Wilcox, B. L. (1981). Social support, life stress, and psychological adjustment. *American Journal of Community Psychology, 9*(4), 371–386.

Wilcoxon, L. A., Shrader, S. L., & Sherif, C. W. (1976). Daily self-reports on activities, life events, moods, and somatic changes during the menstrual cycle. *Psychosomatic Medicine, 38,* 399.

Wilder, D. A. (1977). Perception of groups, size of opposition, and social influence. *Journal of Experimental Social Psychology, 13,* 253–268.

Wilder, D. A., & Thompson, J. E. (1980). Intergroup contact with independent manipulations of in-group and out-group interaction. *Journal of Personality and Social Psychology, 38,* 589–603.

Willerman, L. (1977). *The psychology of individual and group differences.* San Francisco: Freeman.

Williams, J. G., & Solano, C. H. (1983). The social reality of feeling lonely: Friendship and reciprocation. *Personality and Social Psychology Bulletin, 9,* 237–242.

Williams, K. (1986, February 7). The role of appraisal salience in the performance evaluation process. Paper presented at a colloquium, State University of New York at Albany.

Williams, K., Harkins, S., & Latané, B. (1981). Identifiability as a deterrent to social loafing. *Journal of Personality and Social Psychology, 40,* 303–311.

Williams, R. L. (1974). Scientific racism and IQ: The silent mugging of the black community. *Psychology Today, 8*(5).

Williams, R. M., Goldman, M. S., & Williams, D. L. (1981). Expectancy and pharmacological effects of alcohol on human cognitive and motor performance: The compensation for alcohol effect. *Journal of Abnormal Psychology, 90,* 267–270.

Wills, T. A. (1986). Stress and coping in adolescence: Relationships to substance use in urban school samples. *Health Psychology, 5,* 503–530.

Wilson, G. T. (1982). Psychotherapy process and procedure: The behavioral mandate. *Behavior Therapy, 13,* 291–312.

Wilson, G. T. (1987). Cognitive studies in alcoholism. *Journal of Consulting and Clinical Psychology, 55,* 325–331.

Wilson, G. T., & Lawson, D. M. (1978). Expectancies, alcohol, and sexual arousal in women. *Journal of Abnormal Psychology, 87,* 609–616.

Wilson, G. T., Leaf, R. C., & Nathan, P. E. (1975). The aversive control of excessive alcohol consumption by chronic alcoholics in the laboratory setting. *Journal of Applied Behavior Analysis, 8,* 13–26.

Wilson, R. S. (1983). The Louisville twin study: Developmental synchronies in behavior. *Child Development, 54,* 298–316.

Wilson, T. D., & Linville, P. W. (1982). Improving the performance of college freshmen: Attribution therapy revisited. *Journal of Personality and Social Psychology, 42,* 367–376.

Wing, R. R., Epstein, L. H., & Shapira, B. (1982). The effect of increasing initial weight loss with the Scarsdale diet on subsequent weight loss in a behavioral treatment program. *Journal of Consulting and Clinical Psychology, 50,* 446–447.

Wingard, D. L., Berkman, L. F., & Brand, R. J. (1982). A multivariate analysis of health-related practices: A nine-year mortality follow-up of the Alameda County Study. *American Journal of Epidemiology, 116,* 765–775.

Winterbottom, M. (1958). The relation of need for achievement to learning experiences in independence and mastery. In J. Atkinson (Ed.), *Motives in fantasy, action, and society.* Princeton, NJ: Van Nostrand.

Witkin, H. A., et al. (1976). Criminality in XYY and XXY men. *Science, 193,* 547–555.

Wittig, M. A. (1985). Metatheoretical dilemmas in the psychology of gender. *American Psychologist, 40,* 800–811.

Wlodkowski, R. J. (1982). Making sense out of motivation. *Educational Psychologist, 16,* 101–110.

Wolfe, L. (1981). *The Cosmo report.* New York: Arbor House.

Wolinsky, J. (1982). Responsibility can delay aging. *APA Monitor, 13*(3), 14, 41.

Wolock, I., & Horowitz, B. (1984). Child maltreatment as a social problem: The neglect of neglect. *American Journal of Orthopsychiatry, 54,* 530–543.

Wolpe, J. (1958). *Psychotherapy by reciprocal inhibition.* Stanford, CA: Stanford University Press.

Wolpe, J. (1973). *The practice of behavior therapy.* New York: Pergamon Press.

Wolpe, J. (1985). Existential problems and behavior therapy. *The Behavior Therapist, 8*(7), 126–127.

Wolpe, J., & Lazarus, A. A. (1966). *Behavior therapy techniques.* New York: Pergamon Press.

Wolpe, J., & Rachman, S. (1960). Psychoanalytic "evidence": A critique based on Freud's case of Little Hans. *Journal of Nervous and Mental Disease, 131,* 135–147.

Wood, W. (1982). Retrieval of attitude-relevant information from memory: Effects on susceptibility to persuasion and on intrinsic motivation. *Journal of Personality and Social Psychology, 42,* 798–810.

Wood, W., & Eagly, A. H. (1981). Steps in the positive analysis of causal attributions and message comprehension. *Journal of Personality and Social Psychology, 40,* 246–259.

Woolfolk, A. E. (1987). *Educational psychology,* 3rd ed. Englewood Cliffs, NJ: Prentice-Hall.

Woolfolk, R. L., & McNulty, T. F. (1983). Relaxation treatment for insomnia: A component analysis. *Journal of Consulting and Clinical Psychology, 51,* 495–503.

Worchel, S., & Brown, E. H. (1984). The role of plausibility in influencing environmental attributions. *Journal of Experimental Social Psychology, 20,* 86–96.

Wright, J. C., & Huston, A. C. (1983). A matter of form: Potentials of television for young viewers. *American Psychologist, 38,* 835–843.

Wright, L. (1988). The Type A behavior pattern and coronary artery disease: Quest for the active ingredients and the elusive mechanism. *American Psychologist, 43,* 2–14.

Wu, C., & Shaffer, C. R. (1987). Susceptibility to persuasive appeals as a function of source credibility and prior experience with the attitude object. *Journal of Personality and Social Psychology, 52,* 677–688.

Yankelovich, D. (1981). New rules in American life: Searching for self-fulfillment in a world turned upside down. *Psychology Today, 15*(4), 35–91.

Yarnold, P. R., & Grimm, L. G. (1982). Time urgency among coronary-prone individuals. *Journal of Abnormal Psychology, 91,* 175–177.

Yarnold, P. R., Mueser, K. T., & Grimm, L. G. (1985). Interpersonal dominance of Type A's in group discussion. *Journal of Abnormal Psychology, 94,* 233–236.

Yates, A., et al. (1983). Running—An analogue of anorexia? *New England Journal of Medicine, 308,* 251–255.

Yogev, S., & Vierra, A. (1983). The state of motherhood among professional women. *Sex Roles, 9,* 391–397.

Yonas, A., Granrud, C. E., & Pettersen, L. (1985). Infants' sensitivity to relative size information for distance. *Developmental Psychology, 21,* 161–167.

Yost, W. A., & Nielson, D. W. (1985). *Fundamentals of hearing,* 2d ed. New York: Holt, Rinehart and Winston.

Youkilis, H. D., & Bootzin, R. R. (1981). A psychophysiological perspective on the etiology and treatment of insomnia. In S. N. Haynes & L. R. Gannon (Eds.), *Psychosomatic disorders.* New York: Praeger.

Young, J. E. (1982). Loneliness, depression, and cognitive therapy. In L. A. Peplau & D. Perlman (Eds.), *Loneliness: A sourcebook of current theory, research, and therapy.* New York: Wiley.

Yu, B., Zhang, W., Jing, Q., Peng, R., Zhang, G., & Simon, H. A. (1985). STM capacity for Chinese and English language materials. *Memory and Cognition, 13,* 202–207.

Zaiden, J. (1982). Psychodynamic therapy: Clinical applications. In A. J. Rush (Ed.), *Short-term psychotherapies for depression.* New York: Guilford Press.

Zajonc, R. B. (1965). Social facilitation. *Science, 149,* 269–274.

Zajonc, R. B. (1968). Attitudinal effects of mere exposure. *Journal of Personality and Social Psychology, Monograph Supplement 2, 9,* 1–27.

Zajonc, R. B. (1980). Compresence. In P. Paulus (Ed.), *The psychology of group influence.* Hillsdale, NJ: Erlbaum.

Zajonc, R. B. (1984). On the primacy of affect. *American Psychologist, 39,* 117–123.

Zajonc, R. B. (1985). Cited in B. Bower (1985). The face of emotion. *Science News, 128,* 12–13.

Zamansky, H. S., & Bartis, S. P. (1985). The dissociation of an experience. *Journal of Abnormal Psychology, 94,* 243–248.

Zarski, J. J. (1984). Hassles and health: A replication. *Health Psychology, 3,* 243–251.

Zatz, S., & Chassin, L. (1985). Cognitions of test-anxious children under naturalistic test-taking conditions. *Journal of Consulting and Clinical Psychology, 53,* 393–401.

Zigler, E., Abelson, W. D., Trickett, P. K., & Seitz, V. (1982). Is an intervention program necessary to improve economically disadvantaged children's IQ scores? *Child Development, 53,* 340–348.

Zigler, E., & Berman, W. (1983). Discerning the future of early childhood intervention. *American Psychologist, 38,* 894–906.

Zigler, E., & Butterfield, E. C. (1968). Motivational aspects of change in IQ test performance of culturally deprived nursery school children. *Child Development, 39,* 1–14.

Zigler, E., & Valentine, E. (Eds.) (1979). *Project Head Start: A legacy of the war on poverty.* New York: Free Press.

Zilbergeld, B., & Evans, M. (1980). The inadequacy of Masters and Johnson. *Psychology Today, 14*(8), 29–34, 47–53.

Zillmann, D., & Bryant, J. (1983). Effects of massive exposure to pornography. In N. M. Malamuth & E. Donnerstein (Eds.), *Pornography and sexual aggression.* New York: Academic Press.

Zimbardo, P. G. (1969). The human choice: Individuation, reason, and order versus deindividuation, impulse, and chaos. In W. J. Arnold & D. Levine (Eds.), *Nebraska symposium on motivation,* Vol. 17. Lincoln, NE: University of Nebraska Press.

Zimbardo, P. G., Ebbeson, E. B., & Maslach, C. (1977). *Influencing attitudes and changing behavior.* Reading, MA: Addison-Wesley.

Zimmer, D. (1983). Interaction patterns and communication skills in sexually distressed, maritally distressed, and normal couples: Two experimental studies. *Journal of Sex and Marital Therapy, 9,* 251–265.

Zubek, J. P. (1973). Review of effects of prolonged deprivation. In J. E. Rasmussen (Ed.), *Man in isolation and confinement.* Chicago: Aldine.

Zuckerman, M. (1974). The sensation-seeking motive. In B. Maher (Ed.), *Progress in experimental personality research, 7.* New York: Academic Press.

Zuckerman, M. (1980). Sensation seeking. In H. London & J. Exner (Eds.), *Dimensions of personality.* New York: Wiley.

Zuckerman, M. (1987). Cited in D. J. Goleman (1987, November 24). Teen-age risk-taking: Rise in deaths prompts new research effort. *The New York Times,* p. C17.

Zuckerman, M., Eysenck, S., & Eysenck, H. J. (1978). Sensation seeking in England and America: Cross-cultural, age, and sex comparisons. *Journal of Consulting and Clinical Psychology, 46,* 139–149.

Zuckerman, M., Klorman, R., Larrance, D. T., & Spiegel, N. H. (1981). Facial, autonomic, and subjective components of emotion. *Journal of Personality and Social Psychology, 41,* 929–944.

Zuckerman, M., Miserandino, M., & Bernieri, F. (1983). Civil inattention exists—in elevators. *Personality and Social Psychology Bulletin, 9,* 578–586.

Zuger, B. (1976). Monozygotic twins discordant for homosexuality: Report of a pair and significance of the phenomenon. *Comprehensive Psychiatry, 17,* 661–669.

Zuroff, D. C., & Mongrain, M. (1987). Dependency and self-criticism: Vulnerability factors for depressive affective states. *Journal of Abnormal Psychology, 96,* 14–22

Zyazema, N. Z. (1984). Toward better patient drug compliance and comprehension: A challenge to medical and pharmaceutical services in Zimbabwe. *Social Science and Medicine, 18,* 551–554.

PHOTO CREDITS

CHAPTER ONE Page xxxvi: 4X5 Inc. Page 2: Art Resource. Page 6: Roy Morsch/The Stock Market. Page 7: Ken Robert Buck/ The Picture Cube. Page 10: The National Library of Medicine. Page 11 top: Johns Hopkins University. Page 11B: The Bettmann Archive. Page 12 top left: Yale Joel/Life Picture Service. Page 12 top right: Animal Behavior Enterprises. Page 12 bottom: Ken Heyman. Page 13 bottom: The National Library of Medicine. Page 14: 3 Lions/Superstock. Page 19 top: Courtesy of Albert Bandura. Page 19B: Tom and Pat Leeson/Photo Researchers. Page 21: Bill Weems/Woodfin Camp & Associates. Page 23: Gary Sigman. Page 26: William Edward Smith. Page 29: Charles Adams/The New Yorker. Page 35: Jeff Albertson/Stock Boston. Page 39: Henley & Savage/The Stock Market.

CHAPTER TWO Page 42: Gabe Palmer/The Stock Market. Page 44: G-Jon Mili/Life Magazine. Page 45 top: David M. Phillips/ Visuals Unlimited. Page 45 bottom: John Cunningham/Visuals Unlimited. Page 47: Curtis, Jacobson, Marcus—*An Intro. to the Neurosciences* (filmstrip), Philadelphia: WB Saunders and Co. Page 52: Kathy Taranola/The Picture Cube. Page 58 top: Dan McCoy/Rainbow. Page 58 bottom: Bruce Berman/The Stock Market. Page 59: NIH/Science Source/Photo Researchers. Page 74: Shooting Star. Page 82: David Dempster/Offshoot. Page 88: David Dempster/Offshoot.

CHAPTER THREE Page 90: William Edward Smith/Offshoot. Page 96: David Dempster/Offshoot. Page 101: Scanning electron micrograph of neurons, rods and cones, by Frank Werblin and Edwin Lewis, University of CA, Berkeley. Page 104 bottom: Courtesy of Inmont Corporation. Page 106 top left: Georges Seurat, *Sunday Afternoon on the Island of La Grande Jatte,* 1884–86, oil on canvas, 207.6 × 308.0 cm., Helen Birch Bartlett Memorial Collection, 1926.224. Page 106 top right: Georges Seurat, *Sunday Afternoon on the Island of La Grande Jatte,* 1884–86, oil on canvas, 207.6 × 308.0 cm, Helen Birch Bartlett Memorial Collection, 1926.224; detail B: close-up of leaves on tree at far left. Page 109: MOMA. Page 110: Courtesy of the Escher Estate. Page 114: Courtesy of the New York Stock Exchange. Page 115 top: Tobey/The New Yorker. Page 115 bottom left: Courtesy of the Escher Estate. Page 115 bottom right: Hogarth/The Bettmann Archive. Page 117: David Dempster/Offshoot. Page 121: Courtesy of the Escher Estate. Page 132: David Dempster. Page 135 top: Larry Gordon/The Image Bank. Page 135 bottom: Courtesy of Dr. Bernard Brucker.

CHAPTER FOUR Page 142: 3 Lions/Superstock. Page 145: Fred Bodin/Offshoot. Page 150: Courtesy of Spencer Rathus. Page 151: 3 Lions/Superstock. Page 155: Louis Psihoyos/Matrix. Page 159 left: David Schaefer/The Picture Cube. Page 159 right: Tim Eagan/Woodfin Camp & Associates. Page 163: Jane Schreibman/Photo Researchers. Page 165: Roy Morsch/The Stock Market. Page 169: David Dempster. Page 173: David Parker/Photo Researchers.

CHAPTER FIVE Page 182: Russ Schleipman/Offshoot. Page 187: Copyright 1974, Thaves, NEA Inc. Page 190: Susan McElhimery/Archive Pictures. Page 197 top: Courtesy of Teachers College, Columbus, Ohio. Page 198: Courtesy of Pfizer Inc. Page 200 top: "BC" by permission of Johnny Hart and Field Enterprises. Page 200 bottom: Russ Schleipman/Offshoot. Page 201: King Picture Syndicate, 1974. Page 202: Opie/The New Yorker. Page 208: Erickson Photography. Page 213: David Dempster/ Offshoot. Page 218: David Dempster/Offshoot.

CHAPTER SIX Page 224: Carol Palmer/The Picture Cube. Page 225: Rick Friedman/The Picture Cube. Page 229: David Dempster/Offshoot. Page 238: Charles Steiner/Sygma. Page 242: Russ Kinne/Photo Researchers. Page 245: Sepp Seitz/Woodfin Camp & Associates. Page 248: David Dempster/Offshoot.

CHAPTER SEVEN Page 258: Rodin/Philadelphia Museum of Art. Page 264: Siteman Studios/The Picture Cube. Page 268: Charles Harbutt Photography. Page 281: NASA. Page 284: John S. Abbott/ Courtesy of Yale University. Page 288 top: Archives of the History of American Psychology. Page 288 bottom: David Dempster/ Offshoot.

CHAPTER EIGHT Page 300: Guy Savage/Photo Researchers. Page 302: Baron/Byrne—Paramont Pictures. Page 304: Focus on Sports. Page 305: Toni Angermayer/Photo Researchers. Page 308: David Dempster/Offshoot. Page 309: Courtesy of Dr. Neil Miller/Yale University. Page 310: David Dempster/Offshoot. Page 311: Vic Bader/Click Chicago. Page 313 bottom: Guy Savage/Photo Researchers. Page 316 left: Harry F. Harlow/University of Wisconsin Primate Lab. Page 316 right: Yerkes Regional Primate Research Center. Page 319: Miro Vintoniv/The Picture Cube. Page 323: David Dempster/Offshoot. Page 326: Courtesy of Dr. Paul Ekman. Page 331: J. Barry O'Rourke/The Stock Market.

CHAPTER NINE Page 342: Bonnier Fakta. Page 346: MacDonald Photography. Page 347: Archives of the History of American Psychology. Page 351: Bonnier Fakta. Page 352: Courtesy of Creative Playthings. Page 354: Enrico Ferorelli. Page 356: The Bettmann Archive. Page 358: Harry F. Harlow/University of Wisconsin Primate Lab. Page 359 left and right: Nina Leen/Life Magazine. Page 361: David Dampster/Offshoot. Page 362: AP/Wide World Photos. Page 365: George Zimbel/Monkmeyer Press Photo. Page 375: Richard Steedman/The Stock Market. Page 378 top: John Curtis/Offshoot. Page 378 bottom: Gabe Palmer/The Stock Market. Page 400: Ed Arno/The New Yorker. Page 376: Jerry Howard/Positive Images.

CHAPTER TEN Page 390: "Ruth Leserman"/David Hockney, 1982. Page 395 left and right: MOMA Film Stills Archives. Page 396: David Dempster/Offshoot. Page 398: Russ Schleipman/ Offshoot. Page 399: The National Library of Medicine. Page 400 top: The Bettmann Archive. Page 401 top: Courtesy of the Association for the Advancement of Psychoanalysis of the Karen Horney Psychoanalytic Institute and Center. Page 401 bottom: Harvard University Press Office. Page 404: Archives of the History of American Psychology. Page 405 top: Courtesy of Raymond Cattell. Page 405 bottom: Courtesy of the Institute of Psychiatry, University of London. Page 409: Courtesy of Julian B. Rotter. Page 410: Focus on Sports. Page 415: Richard Dunoff/The Stock Market. Page 423: Courtesy of Harvard University. Page 426: AS Feinberg/The Picture Cube.

CHAPTER ELEVEN Page 428: Lou Jones. Page 433 left: Susan McCartney/Photo Researchers. Page 433 right: Roy Morsch/The Stock Market. Page 441: Mark Godfrey/Archive Pictures. Page 443: Focus On Sports. Page 444: Sharp Shooters. Page 453: Roy Morsch/The Stock Market. Page 463: Gabe Palmer/The Stock Market. Page 467: David Dempster/Offshoot. Page 469 top: Russ Schleipman/Offshoot. Page 469 bottom: Hank Morgan/Rainbow.

CHAPTER TWELVE Page 475: Art Resource. Page 503: The University of Pennsylvania Museum. Page 485: Brent Jones. Page 487: Robert Ellison/Black Star. Page 491: MOMA Film Stills Archive. Page 494: David Dempster/Offshoot. Page 499: Jeff Jacobson/Archive Pictures. Page 503: Gene Spatz/Sygma. Page 508: Doug Bruce/Picture Group. Page 513: Chip Henderson/Woodfin Camp & Associates.

CHAPTER THIRTEEN Page 516: David Dempster/Offshoot. Page 520 top and bottom: The Bettmann Archive. Page 523: Courtesy of Edmund Engelman. Page 526: Yale University Archives. Page 527: Jim Wilson/Woodfin Camp & Associates. Page 528: Courtesy of Grove Press. Page 532 top: Courtesy of Albert Ellis. Page 532 bottom: Courtesy of the Center for Cognitive Therapy. Page 535 top: Courtesy of Joseph Wolpe. Page 535 bottom: Courtesy of Arnold Lazarus. Page 536: Rick Freidman/Black Star. Page 537: Courtesy of Dr. Albert Bandura. Page 538: Lester Sloan/Woodfin Camp & Associates. Page 539: Handelsman, 1978 The New Yorker. Page 543: Stacy Pick/Stock Boston. Page 550: Handelsman, The New Yorker. Page 552: Phillippe Gontier/The Image Works. Page 553: Wm. McIntyer/Photo Researchers. Page 558: David Dempster/Offshoot.

CHAPTER FOURTEEN Page 560: Fred Bodin/Offshoot. Page 562: Robert Huntzinger/The Stock Market. Page 565 left: Bob Krist. Page 565 right: MacDonald Photography/The Picture Cube. Page 573 left: Betsy Lee/Taurus. Page 573 right: David Strickler/Monkmeyer Photo Press. Page 579: Tom McHuge/Photo Researchers. Page 581: *Newsweek.* Page 589: David Dempster/Offshoot. Page 395: Susan Van Etten/The Picture Cube.

CHAPTER FIFTEEN Page 598: GA Rossi/The Image Bank. Page 602: David Dempster/Offshoot. Page 605: Robert V. Eckert Jr./EKM–Nepenthe. Page 609 top: Tom Korody/Sygma. Page 609 bottom: AP/Wide World. Page 611: Richard Hutchings/Photo Researchers. Page 616: Frank Cezus/Click Chicago. Page 617: R. Melloul/Sygma. Page 626: Courtesy of the Estate of Stanley Milgram. Page 627: Courtesy of the Estate of Stanley Milgram. Page 630: Courtesy of William Vandivert. Page 633: Michael Kevin Daly/The Stock Market. Page 635: Maslin 1985, The New Yorker. Page 639 top and bottom: David Dempster/Offshoot. Page 644: David Dempster/Offshoot.

CHAPTER SIXTEEN Page 646: Chris Sorensen. Page 651: Eric Roth/The Picture Cube. Page 653: Mark Antman/The Image Works. Page 658: Bob Krist. Page 659: Chris Sorensen. Page 662: Courtesy of Damage Jeanswear. Page 664: Thomas Braise/The Stock Market. Page 674 left: AP/Wide World. Page 674 right: Wm. Karel/Sygma. Page 676: Focus On Sports. Page 678: Ellis Herwig. Page 684: David Dempster/Offshoot.

LITERARY CREDITS

Table 3.1, page 94: Adapted from E. Galanter, "Contemporary psychophysics," in R. Brown et al. (eds.), *New Directions in Psychology.* New York: Holt, Rinehart and Winston, 1962. Page 261: The lines from "since feeling is first" are reprinted from IS 5 poems by E. E. Cummings, edited by George James Firmage, by permission of Liveright Publishing Corporation. Copyright © 1985 by E. E. Cummings Trust. Copyright 1926 by Horace Liveright. Copyright © 1954 by E. E. Cummings. Copyright © 1985 by George James Firmage.

Table 7.1, page 263: Adapted from E. H. Lenneberg, *Biological Foundations of Language,* page 128. Copyright © 1967 by John Wiley & Sons, Inc. Reprinted by permission.

Table 7.2, page 275: Adaptation reprinted by permission. From Luchins, Abraham S., and Luchins, Edith H., *Rigidity of Behavior* (Eugene: University of Oregon Books, 1959), page 109. Also in *Wertheimer's Seminars Revisited: Problem Solving and Thinking* (Albany, N.Y.: SUNY/Albany Faculty-Student Association, 1970), vol. iii, page 4.

Questionnaire, page 280: Items adapted from The Remote Associates Test, page 252, from *Cognition* by Margaret Matlin. Copyright © 1983 by Holt, Rinehart and Winston. Adapted by permission.

Table 8.2, page 330: From Schachter, S., and Singer, J. E. Cognitive, social and psychological determinants of emotional state, *Psychological Review, 69* (1962): 379–399. Copyright 1962 by the American Psychological Association. Reprinted by permission of the publisher and authors.

Table 9.3, page 364: Adapted from *Lifespan Development*, 2nd ed., by Jeffrey S. Turner and Donald B. Helms. Copyright © 1983 by Holt, Rinehart and Winston. Copyright © 1979 by W. B. Saunders Company. Also adapted from *Piaget with Feeling: Cognitive, Social, and Emotional Dimensions* by Philip A. Cowan. Copyright © 1978 by Holt, Rinehart and Winston. Adaptations by permission of Holt, Rinehart and Winston.

Table 9.4, page 370: Reprinted with permission from James R. Rest, The hierarchical nature of moral judgment: A study of patterns of comprehension and preference of moral stages, *Journal of Personality, 41* (March 1973): 92–93. Copyright 1973 by Duke University Press.

Table 10.2, page 402: Based on information from pages 247–269 in Erik H. Erikson, *Childhood and Society,* 2nd ed. by permission of W. W. Norton & Company, Inc. Copyright 1950, © 1963 by W. W. Norton & Company, Inc. Copyright renewed 1978 by Erik H. Erikson.

Questionnaire, pages 433–434: From Peggy Blake, Robert Fry, and Michael Pesjack, *Self-assessment and Behavior Change Manual* (New York: Random House, 1984), pages 43–47. Reprinted by permission of Random House, Inc.

Questionnaire, page 443: Reprinted with permission of Professors Stephen Nowicki and Bonnie Strickland, Emory University.

Questionnaire, page 540: From Spencer Rathus, A 30-item schedule for assessing assertive behavior, *Behavior Therapy, 4* (1973): 399.

Table 14.1, page 564: Adapted from I. K. Broverman et al., Sex-role stereotypes: A current appraisal, *Journal of Social Issues, 28* (2): 63. Used with permission.

Questionnaire, page 585: From Martha R. Burt, Cultural myths and supports for rape, *Journal of Personality and Social Psychology, 38*: 217–230. Copyright 1980 by the American Psychological Association. Reprinted by permission of the publisher and author.

Page 585: List from Boston Women's Health Book Collective, *The New Our Bodies, Ourselves* (New York: Simon & Schuster, 1984). Page 612: From "Getting to Know You," from *The King and I.* Copyright © 1951 by Richard Rodgers and Oscar Hammerstein II. Copyright renewed. Williamson Music Co., owner of publication and allied rights. Used by permission. All rights reserved.

Figures 16.2, 16.3, and 16.5, pages 660–661: Based on drawings on pages 355, 356, and 362 in E. J. McCormick and D. Ilgen, *Industrial and Organizational Psychology,* 8th ed. Englewood Cliffs, N.J.: Prentice-Hall, 1985.

NAME INDEX

SUBJECT INDEX

Terms in the running glossary are indicated by page numbers in boldface type.